# ESSENTIAL MATHEMATICS FOR ECONOMIC ANALYSIS

Pearson

At Pearson, we have a simple mission: to help people make more of their lives through learning.

We combine innovative learning technology with trusted content and educational expertise to provide engaging and effective learning experiences that serve people wherever and whenever they are learning.

From classroom to boardroom, our curriculum materials, digital learning tools and testing programmes help to educate millions of people worldwide – more than any other private enterprise.

Every day our work helps learning flourish, and wherever learning flourishes, so do people.

To learn more, please visit us at **www.pearson.com/uk**

ESSENTIAL MATHEMATICS FOR ECONOMIC ANALYSIS

SIXTH EDITION

Knut Sydsæter, Peter Hammond,
Arne Strøm and Andrés Carvajal

Pearson

Harlow, England • London • New York • Boston • San Francisco • Toronto • Sydney • Dubai • Singapore • Hong Kong
Tokyo • Seoul • Taipei • New Delhi • Cape Town • São Paulo • Mexico City • Madrid • Amsterdam • Munich • Paris • Milan

PEARSON EDUCATION LIMITED
KAO Two
KAO Park
Harlow CM17 9NA
United Kingdom
Tel: +44 (0)1279 623623
Web: www.pearson.com/uk

First published by Prentice Hall, Inc. 1995 (print)
Second edition published 2006 (print)
Third edition published 2008 (print)
Fourth edition published by Pearson Education Limited 2012 (print)
Fifth edition published 2016 (print and electronic)

© Prentice Hall, Inc. 1995 (print)
© Knut Sydsæter, Peter Hammond, Arne Strøm and Andrés Carvajal 2016 (print and electronic)
© Knut Sydsæter, Peter Hammond, Arne Strøm and Andrés Carvajal 2021 (print and electronic)

The rights of Knut Sydsæter, Peter Hammond, Arne Strøm and Andrés Carvajal to be identified as authors of this work has been asserted by them in accordance with the Copyright, Designs and Patents Act 1988.

The print publication is protected by copyright. Prior to any prohibited reproduction, storage in a retrieval system, distribution or transmission in any form or by any means, electronic, mechanical, recording or otherwise, permission should be obtained from the publisher or, where applicable, a licence permitting restricted copying in the United Kingdom should be obtained from the Copyright Licensing Agency Ltd, Barnard's Inn, 86 Fetter Lane, London EC4A 1EN.

The ePublication is protected by copyright and must not be copied, reproduced, transferred, distributed, leased, licensed or publicly performed or used in any way except as specifically permitted in writing by the publishers, as allowed under the terms and conditions under which it was purchased, or as strictly permitted by applicable copyright law. Any unauthorised distribution or use of this text may be a direct infringement of the authors' and the publisher's rights and those responsible may be liable in law accordingly.

Pearson Education is not responsible for the content of third-party internet sites.

ISBN: 978-1-292-35928-1 (print)
       978-1-292-35929-8 (PDF)
       978-1-292-35932-8 (ePub)

British Library Cataloguing-in-Publication Data
A catalogue record for the print edition is available from the British Library

Library of Congress Cataloging-in-Publication Data
Names: Sydsæter, Knut, author. | Hammond, Peter J., 1945- author.
Title: Essential mathematics for economic analysis / Knut Sydsæter, Peter Hammond, Arne Strøm and Andrés Carvajal.
Description: Sixth edition. | Hoboken, NJ: Pearson, 2021. | Includes bibliographical references and index. | Summary: "The subject matter that modern economics students are expected to master makes significant mathematical demands. This is true even of the less technical "applied" literature that students will be expected to read for courses in fields such as public finance, industrial organization, and labour economics, amongst several others. Indeed, the most relevant literature typically presumes familiarity with several important mathematical tools, especially calculus for functions of one and several variables, as well as a basic understanding of multivariable optimization problems with or without constraints. Linear algebra is also used to some extent in economic theory, and a great deal more in econometrics"– Provided by publisher.
Identifiers: LCCN 2021006079 (print) | LCCN 2021006080 (ebook) | ISBN 9781292359281 (paperback) | ISBN 9781292359298 (pdf) | ISBN 9781292359328 (epub)
Subjects: LCSH: Economics, Mathematical.
Classification: LCC HB135 .S886 2021 (print) | LCC HB135 (ebook) | DDC 330.01/51–dc23
LC record available at https://lccn.loc.gov/2021006079
LC ebook record available at https://lccn.loc.gov/2021006080

10 9 8 7 6 5 4 3 2 1
25 24 23 22 21

Cover design by Michelle Morgan, At the Pop Ltd.

Front cover image © yewkeo/iStock//Getty Images Plus

Print edition typeset in 10/13pt TimesLTPro by SPi Global
Printed and bound by L.E.G.O. S.p.A., Italy

NOTE THAT ANY PAGE CROSS REFERENCES REFER TO THE PRINT EDITION

To Knut Sydsæter (1937–2012), an inspiring mathematics teacher, as well as wonderful friend and colleague, whose vision, hard work, high professional standards, and sense of humour were all essential in creating this book.

—Arne, Peter and Andrés

To Else, my loving and patient wife.

—Arne

To the memory of my parents Elsie (1916–2007) and Fred (1916–2008), my first teachers of Mathematics, basic Economics, and many more important things.

—Peter

To Yeye and Tata, my best ever students of "matemáquinas", who wanted this book to start with "Once upon a time …". E para a Pipoca, com amor infinito à infinito.

—Andrés

CONTENTS

Preface — xiii

I PRELIMINARIES — 1

1 Essentials of Logic and Set Theory — 3
1.1 Essentials of Set Theory — 3
1.2 Essentials of Logic — 10
1.3 Mathematical Proofs — 16
1.4 Mathematical Induction — 18
Review Exercises — 20

2 Algebra — 23
2.1 The Real Numbers — 23
2.2 Integer Powers — 26
2.3 Rules of Algebra — 33
2.4 Fractions — 38
2.5 Fractional Powers — 43
2.6 Inequalities — 48
2.7 Intervals and Absolute Values — 52
2.8 Sign Diagrams — 56
2.9 Summation Notation — 59
2.10 Rules for Sums — 62
2.11 Newton's Binomial Formula — 66
2.12 Double Sums — 70
Review Exercises — 72

3 Solving Equations — 77
3.1 Solving Equations — 77
3.2 Equations and Their Parameters — 80
3.3 Quadratic Equations — 83
3.4 Some Nonlinear Equations — 89
3.5 Using Implication Arrows — 91
3.6 Two Linear Equations in Two Unknowns — 92
Review Exercises — 96

4 Functions of One Variable — 99
4.1 Introduction — 99
4.2 Definitions — 100
4.3 Graphs of Functions — 106
4.4 Linear Functions — 110
4.5 Linear Models — 116
4.6 Quadratic Functions — 120
4.7 Polynomials — 127
4.8 Power Functions — 135
4.9 Exponential Functions — 136
4.10 Logarithmic Functions — 141
Review Exercises — 147

5 Properties of Functions — 151
5.1 Shifting Graphs — 151
5.2 New Functions from Old — 156

viii CONTENTS

5.3	Inverse Functions	160
5.4	Graphs of Equations	166
5.5	Distance in the Plane	170
5.6	General Functions	174
	Review Exercises	177

II SINGLE VARIABLE CALCULUS 179

6 Differentiation 181

6.1	Slopes of Curves	181
6.2	Tangents and Derivatives	183
6.3	Increasing and Decreasing Functions	189
6.4	Economic Applications	192
6.5	A Brief Introduction to Limits	195
6.6	Simple Rules for Differentiation	201
6.7	Sums, Products, and Quotients	205
6.8	The Chain Rule	212
6.9	Higher-Order Derivatives	218
6.10	Exponential Functions	220
6.11	Logarithmic Functions	224
	Review Exercises	230

7 Derivatives in Use 233

7.1	Implicit Differentiation	233
7.2	Economic Examples	240
7.3	The Inverse Function Theorem	244
7.4	Linear Approximations	248
7.5	Polynomial Approximations	253
7.6	Taylor's Formula	256
7.7	Elasticities	259
7.8	Continuity	264
7.9	More on Limits	270
7.10	The Intermediate Value Theorem	279
7.11	Infinite Sequences	283
7.12	L'Hôpital's Rule	287
	Review Exercises	292

8 Concave and Convex Functions 295

8.1	Intuition	295
8.2	Definitions	297
8.3	General Properties	305
8.4	First-Derivative Tests	309
8.5	Second-Derivative Tests	312
8.6	Inflection Points	316
	Review Exercises	319

9 Optimization 321

9.1	Extreme Points	321
9.2	Simple Tests for Extreme Points	324
9.3	Economic Examples	328
9.4	The Extreme and Mean Value Theorems	334
9.5	Further Economic Examples	340
9.6	Local Extreme Points	345
	Review Exercises	352

10 Integration 355

10.1	Indefinite Integrals	355
10.2	Area and Definite Integrals	361
10.3	Properties of Definite Integrals	368
10.4	Economic Applications	373
10.5	Integration by Parts	380
10.6	Integration by Substitution	384
10.7	Improper Integrals	389
	Review Exercises	396

11 Topics in Finance and Dynamics 399

11.1	Interest Periods and Effective Rates	399
11.2	Continuous Compounding	403
11.3	Present Value	405
11.4	Geometric Series	408
11.5	Total Present Value	414
11.6	Mortgage Repayments	419
11.7	Internal Rate of Return	423
11.8	A Glimpse at Difference Equations	425
11.9	Essentials of Differential Equations	428
11.10	Separable and Linear Differential Equations	435
	Review Exercises	441

III MULTIVARIABLE ALGEBRA 445

12 Matrix Algebra 447

12.1	Matrices and Vectors	447

12.2	Systems of Linear Equations	450
12.3	Matrix Addition	453
12.4	Algebra of Vectors	455
12.5	Matrix Multiplication	458
12.6	Rules for Matrix Multiplication	463
12.7	The Transpose	470
12.8	Gaussian Elimination	473
12.9	Geometric Interpretation of Vectors	479
12.10	Lines and Planes	487
	Review Exercises	492

13 Determinants, Inverses, and Quadratic Forms 495

13.1	Determinants of Order 2	495
13.2	Determinants of Order 3	499
13.3	Determinants in General	504
13.4	Basic Rules for Determinants	508
13.5	Expansion by Cofactors	514
13.6	The Inverse of a Matrix	517
13.7	A General Formula for the Inverse	524
13.8	Cramer's Rule	527
13.9	The Leontief Model	531
13.10	Eigenvalues and Eigenvectors	536
13.11	Diagonalization	543
13.12	Quadratic Forms	547
	Review Exercises	556

IV MULTIVARIABLE CALCULUS 559

14 Functions of Many Variables 561

14.1	Functions of Two Variables	561
14.2	Partial Derivatives with Two Variables	565
14.3	Geometric Representation	571
14.4	Surfaces and Distance	578
14.5	Functions of n Variables	581
14.6	Partial Derivatives with Many Variables	586
14.7	Convex Sets	590
14.8	Concave and Convex Functions	595
14.9	Economic Applications	606
14.10	Partial Elasticities	608
	Review Exercises	610

15 Partial Derivatives in Use 613

15.1	A Simple Chain Rule	613
15.2	Chain Rules for Many Variables	619
15.3	Implicit Differentiation along a Level Curve	623
15.4	Level Surfaces	628
15.5	Elasticity of Substitution	632
15.6	Homogeneous Functions of Two Variables	634
15.7	Homogeneous and Homothetic Functions	639
15.8	Linear Approximations	645
15.9	Differentials	654
15.10	Systems of Equations	659
15.11	Differentiating Systems of Equations	663
	Review Exercises	669

16 Multiple Integrals 673

16.1	Double Integrals Over Finite Rectangles	673
16.2	Infinite Rectangles of Integration	680
16.3	Discontinuous Integrands and Other Extensions	682
16.4	Integration Over Many Variables	684

V MULTIVARIABLE OPTIMIZATION 687

17 Unconstrained Optimization 689

17.1	Two Choice Variables: Necessary Conditions	690
17.2	Two Choice Variables: Sufficient Conditions	694
17.3	Local Extreme Points	699
17.4	Linear Models with Quadratic Objectives	705
17.5	The Extreme Value Theorem	712
17.6	Functions of More Variables	717
17.7	Comparative Statics and the Envelope Theorem	722
	Review Exercises	728

18 Equality Constraints — 731

- 18.1 The Lagrange Multiplier Method — 731
- 18.2 Interpreting the Lagrange Multiplier — 739
- 18.3 Multiple Solution Candidates — 742
- 18.4 Why Does the Lagrange Multiplier Method Work? — 744
- 18.5 Sufficient Conditions — 749
- 18.6 Additional Variables and Constraints — 753
- 18.7 Comparative Statics — 759
- Review Exercises — 765

19 Linear Programming — 769

- 19.1 A Graphical Approach — 770
- 19.2 Introduction to Duality Theory — 776
- 19.3 The Duality Theorem — 781
- 19.4 A General Economic Interpretation — 786
- 19.5 Complementary Slackness — 788
- Review Exercises — 794

20 Nonlinear Programming — 797

- 20.1 Two Variables and One Constraint — 797
- 20.2 Many Variables and Inequality Constraints — 804
- 20.3 Nonnegativity Constraints — 812
- Review Exercises — 817

Appendix — 819

- Geometry — 819
- The Greek Alphabet — 822
- Bibliography — 822

Solutions to the Exercises — 823

Index — 943

Publisher's Acknowledgements — 953

Supporting resources

Visit **go.pearson.com/uk/he/resources** to find valuable online resources

For students

- A new Student's Manual provides more detailed solutions to the problems marked (SM) in the book

For instructors

- The fully updated Instructor's Manual provides instructors with a collection of problems that can be used for tutorials and exams

---

In MyLab Maths you will find:

- A study plan, which creates a personalised learning path through resources, based on diagnostic tests;
- A wealth of questions and activities, including algorithmic, graphing and multiple-choice questions and exercises;
- Pearson eText, an online version of your textbook which you can take with you anywhere and which allows you to add notes, highlights, bookmarks and easily search the text;
- If assigned by your lecturer, additional homework, quizzes and tests.

Lecturers additionally will find:

- A powerful gradebook, which tracks student performance and can highlight areas where the whole class needs more support;
- Additional questions and exercises, which can be assigned to students as homework, quizzes and tests, freeing up the time in class to take learning further;
- Lecturer resources, which support the delivery of the module;
- Communication tools, such as discussion boards, to drive student engagement.

PREFACE

Once upon a time there was a sensible straight line who was hopelessly in love with a dot. 'You're the beginning and the end, the hub, the core and the quintessence,' he told her tenderly, but the frivolous dot wasn't a bit interested, for she only had eyes for a wild and unkempt squiggle who never seemed to have anything on his mind at all. All of the line's romantic dreams were in vain, until he discovered . . . angles! Now, with newfound self-expression, he can be anything he wants to be—a square, a triangle, a parallelogram . . . And that's just the beginning!
—Norton Juster (*The Dot and the Line: A Romance in Lower Mathematics* 1963)

I came to the position that mathematical analysis is not one of many ways of doing economic theory: It is the only way. Economic theory is mathematical analysis. Everything else is just pictures and talk.
—R. E. Lucas, Jr. (2001)

Purpose

The subject matter that modern economics students are expected to master makes significant mathematical demands. This is true even of the less technical "applied" literature that students will be expected to read for courses in fields such as public finance, industrial organization, and labour economics, amongst several others. Indeed, the most relevant literature typically presumes familiarity with several important mathematical tools, especially calculus for functions of one and several variables, as well as a basic understanding of multivariable optimization problems with or without constraints. Linear algebra is also used to some extent in economic theory, and a great deal more in econometrics.

The purpose of *Essential Mathematics for Economic Analysis*, therefore, is to help economics students acquire enough mathematical skill to access the literature that is most relevant to their undergraduate study. This should include what some students will need to conduct successfully an undergraduate research project or honours thesis.

As the title suggests, this is a book on *mathematics*, whose material is arranged to allow progressive learning of mathematical topics. That said, we do frequently emphasize economic applications, many of which are listed on the inside front cover. These not only help motivate particular mathematical topics; we also want to help prospective economists acquire mutually reinforcing intuition in both mathematics and economics. Indeed, as the list of examples on the inside front cover suggests, a considerable number of economic concepts and ideas receive some attention.

We emphasize, however, that this is not a book about economics or even about mathematical economics. Students should learn economic theory systematically from other courses, which use other textbooks. We will have succeeded if they can concentrate on the economics in these courses, having already thoroughly mastered the relevant mathematical tools this book presents.

Special Features and Accompanying Material

Virtually all sections of the book conclude with exercises, often quite numerous. There are also many review exercises at the end of each chapter. Solutions to almost all these exercises are provided at the end of the book, sometimes with several steps of the answer laid out.

There are two main sources of supplementary material. The first, for both students and their instructors, is via MyLab. Students who have arranged access to this web site for our book will be able to generate a practically unlimited number of additional problems which test how well some of the key ideas presented in the text have been understood. More explanation of this system is offered after this preface. The same web page also has a "student resources" tab with access to a *Student's Manual* with more extensive answers (or, in the case of a few of the most theoretical or difficult problems in the book, the only answers) to problems marked with the special symbol SM.

The second source, for instructors who adopt the book for their course, is an *Instructor's Manual* that may be downloaded from the publisher's Instructor Resource Centre.

In addition, for courses with special needs, there is a brief online appendix on trigonometric functions and complex numbers. This is also available via MyLab.

Prerequisites

Experience suggests that it is quite difficult to start a book like this at a level that is really too elementary.[1] These days, in many parts of the world, students who enter college or university and specialize in economics have an enormous range of mathematical backgrounds and aptitudes. These range from, at the low end, a rather shaky command of elementary algebra, up to real facility in the calculus of functions of one variable. Furthermore, for many economics students, it may be some years since their last formal mathematics course. Accordingly, as mathematics becomes increasingly essential for specialist studies in economics, we feel obliged to provide as much quite elementary material as is reasonably possible. Our aim here is to give those with weaker mathematical backgrounds the chance to get started, and even to acquire a little confidence with some easy problems they can really solve on their own.

---

[1] In a recent test for 120 first-year students intending to take an elementary economics course, there were 35 different answers to the problem of expanding $(a + 2b)^2$.

To help instructors judge how much of the elementary material students really know before starting a course, the *Instructor's Manual* provides some diagnostic test material. Although each instructor will obviously want to adjust the starting point and pace of a course to match the students' abilities, it is perhaps even more important that each individual student appreciates his or her own strengths and weaknesses, and receives some help and guidance in overcoming any of the latter. This makes it quite likely that weaker students will benefit significantly from the opportunity to work through the early more elementary chapters, even if they may not be part of the course itself.

As for our economic discussions, students should find it easier to understand them if they already have a certain very rudimentary background in economics. Nevertheless, the text has often been used to teach mathematics for economics to students who are studying elementary economics at the same time. Nor do we see any reason why this material cannot be mastered by students interested in economics before they have begun studying the subject in a formal university course.

Topics Covered

After the introductory material in Chapters 1 to 3, a fairly leisurely treatment of standard single variable differential calculus is contained in Chapters 4 to 7. This is followed by Chapter 8 on concave and convex functions, by Chapter 9 on optimization, Chapter 10 on integration, and then by some basic financial models as well as difference and differential equations in Chapter 11. This may be as far as some elementary courses will go. Students who already have a thorough grounding in single variable calculus, however, may only need to go fairly quickly over some special topics in these chapters such as elasticity and conditions for global optimization that are often not thoroughly covered in standard calculus courses.

We have already suggested the importance for budding economists of the algebra of matrices and determinants (Chapters 12 and 13), of multivariable calculus (Chapters 14–16), and of optimization theory with and without constraints (Chapters 17–20). These last nine chapters in some sense represent the heart of the book, on which students with a thorough grounding in single variable calculus can probably afford to concentrate.

Satisfying Diverse Requirements

The less ambitious student can concentrate on learning the key concepts and techniques of each chapter. Often, these appear boxed and/or in colour, in order to emphasize their importance. Problems are essential to the learning process, and the easier ones should definitely be attempted. These basics should provide enough mathematical background for the student to be able to understand much of the economic theory that is embodied in applied work at the advanced undergraduate level.

Students who are more ambitious, or who are led on by more demanding teachers, can try the more difficult problems. They can also study the more technical material which is intended to encourage students to ask why a result is true, or why a problem should be tackled in a particular way. If more readers gain at least a little additional mathematical insight from working through these more challenging parts of our book, so much the better.

The most able students, especially those intending to undertake postgraduate study in economics or some related subject, will benefit from a fuller explanation of some topics than we have been able to provide here. On a few occasions, therefore, we take the liberty of referring to our more advanced companion volume, *Further Mathematics for Economic Analysis* (usually abbreviated to FMEA). This is written jointly with our colleague Atle Seierstad in Oslo. In particular, FMEA offers a proper treatment of topics like systems of difference and differential equations, as well as dynamic optimization, that we think go rather beyond what is really "essential" for all economics students.

Changes in the Fourth Edition

We have been gratified by the number of students and their instructors from many parts of the world who appear to have found the first three editions useful.[2] We have accordingly been encouraged to revise the text thoroughly once again. There are numerous minor changes and improvements, including the following in particular:

1. The main new feature is MyMathLab Global,[3] explained on the page after this preface, as well as on the back cover.
2. New exercises have been added for each chapter.
3. Some of the figures have been improved.

Changes in the Fifth Edition

The most significant change in this edition is that, tragically, we have lost the main author and instigator of this project. Our good friend and colleague Knut Sydsæter died suddenly on 29th September 2012, while on holiday in Spain with his wife Malinka Staneva, a few days before his 75th birthday. An obituary written by Jens Stoltenberg, at that time the Prime Minister of Norway, includes this tribute to Knut's skills as one of his teachers:

> With a small sheet of paper as his manuscript he introduced me and generations of other economics students to mathematics as a tool in the subject of economics. With professional weight, commitment, and humour, he was both a demanding and an inspiring lecturer. He opened the door into the world of mathematics. He showed that mathematics is a language that makes it possible to explain complicated relationships in a simple manner.

At a web page that hosts a copy of this obituary one can also find other tributes to Knut, including some recollections of how previous editions of this book came to be written.[4]

Despite losing Knut as its main author, it was clear that this book needed to be kept alive, following desires that Knut himself had often expressed while he was still with us.

---

[2] Different English versions of this book have been translated into Albanian, French, German, Hungarian, Italian, Portuguese, Spanish, and Turkish.
[3] Superseded by MyLab for this sixth edition.
[4] See https://web.stanford.edu/~hammond/sydsaeter.html

Fortunately, it had already been agreed that the team of co-authors should be joined by Andrés Carvajal, a former colleague of Peter's at Warwick who, at the time of preparing the Fifth Edition, had just joined the University of California at Davis. Andrés had already produced a new Spanish version of the previous edition of this book; he has now become a co-author of this latest English version. It is largely on his initiative that we have taken the important step of extensively rearranging the material in the first three chapters in a more logical order, with set theory now coming first.

The other main change is one that we hope is invisible to the reader. Previous editions had been produced using the "plain TEX" typesetting system that dates back to the 1980s, along with some ingenious macros that Arne had devised in collaboration with Arve Michaelsen of the Norwegian typesetting firm Matematisk Sats. For technical reasons we decided that the new edition had to be produced using the enrichment of plain TEX called LATEX that has by now become the accepted international standard for typesetting mathematical material. We have therefore attempted to adapt and extend some standard LATEX packages in order to preserve as many good features as possible of our previous editions.

Changes in the Sixth Edition

For this sixth edition, the surviving authors decided to rearrange the chapters considerably. Recent previous editions included a chapter on linear programming, which was deferred until after the two chapters on matrix algebra. Yet the key idea of complementary slackness had arisen previously in an earlier chapter on nonlinear programming. So we have moved matrix algebra much further forward, so that it precedes multivariate calculus. This allows new tools to be used in our treatment of multivariate calculus, and subsequently in the last four chapters that are now devoted exclusively to optimization.

Not only have the existing chapters been rearranged, however. We have increased their number from 17 to 20. This is partly because the chapter on constrained optimization has been split into two. The first part dealing with equality constraints now comes in Chapter 18, before Chapter 19 on linear programming, including its discussion of complementary slackness. The last part of the earlier chapter on inequality constraints is now the separate Chapter 20.

The other two extra chapters are new. Chapter 8 considers concave and convex functions of one variable, including results on supergradients of concave functions and subgradients of convex functions that play a key role in the theory of optimization. Later chapters extend some of these results to functions of 2 and then n variables. There is also a brief chapter (16) on multiple integrals.

Finally, we mention significant additions to Chapter 13 that consider eigenvalues and quadratic forms. These additions allow a more extensive treatment, based on the Hessian matrix, of second-order conditions for, in Chapter 15, a function of several variables to be concave, and in Chapter 17, for a critical point to be a maximum or minimum. As a result, we can provide a somewhat better discussion in Chapter 20 of how, for the case of concave programming problems, the Karush–Kuhn–Tucker conditions provide sufficient conditions for an optimal point.

Other Acknowledgements

Over the years we have received help from so many colleagues, lecturers at other institutions, and students, that it is impractical to mention them all.

Andrés Carvajal is indebted to: Yiqian Zhao and Xinhui Yang, for all their great work in the revision of the material for this edition; Professor Janine Wilson for encouraging him in the idea that the more economic applications the book contains, the better is the mathematical explanation; Professor Jim Wiseman, for his feedback on the previous edition and for sharing his views on how it could be improved; and to the following UC Davis students who patiently went over different chapters, fishing for mistakes and making sure that all was well: Xinghe Bai, Veronica Contreras, Nathan Gee, Anjali Khalasi, Yannan Li, Daniel Scates, Kelly Stangl, and Yiping Su.

As in previous editions of this book, we are very happy to acknowledge with gratitude the encouragement and assistance of our contacts at Pearson. For this sixth edition, these include Catherine Yates (Product Manager) and Melanie Carter (Senior Content Producer). We were also glad to be able to work successfully with Vivek Khandelwal of SPi Global, who was in charge of the typesetting, and Lou Attwood of SpacedEns Editorial Services, who assisted us with proof-reading. All were very helpful and attentive in answering our frequent e-mails in a friendly and encouraging way, while making sure that this new edition really is getting into print in a timely manner.

On the more academic side, very special thanks go to Prof. Dr Fred Böker at the University of Göttingen. He is not only responsible for translating several previous editions of this book into German, but has also shown exceptional diligence in paying close attention to the mathematical details of what he was translating. We appreciate the resulting large number of valuable suggestions for improvements and corrections that he has continued to provide, sometimes at the instigation of Dr Egle Tafenau, who was also using the German version of our textbook in her teaching.

We are also grateful to Kenneth Judd of the Hoover Institution at Stanford for taking the trouble to persuade us that we should follow what has become the standard practice of attaching the name of William Karush, along with those of Harold Kuhn and Albert Tucker, to the key "KKT conditions" presented in Chapter 20 for solving a nonlinear programming problem with inequality constraints.

Thanks too, to Dr Mauro Bambi at Durham University for creating and curating question content for MyLab Maths, and to Professor Carsten Berthram Haahr Andersen at Aarhus University, Denmark for his feedback on the MyLab.

To these and all the many unnamed persons and institutions who have helped us make this text possible, including some whose anonymous comments on earlier editions were forwarded to us by the publisher, we would like to express our deep appreciation and gratitude. We hope that all those who have assisted us may find the resulting product of benefit to their students. This, we can surely agree, is all that really matters in the end.

Andrés Carvajal, Peter Hammond, and Arne Strøm
Davis, Coventry, and Oslo, January 2021

I PRELIMINARIES

1 ESSENTIALS OF LOGIC AND SET THEORY

It is clear that economics, if it is to be a science at all, must be a mathematical science.
—William Stanley Jevons[1]

Arguments in mathematics require tight logical reasoning, and arguments in modern economic analysis are no exception to this rule. It is useful for us, then, to present some basic concepts from logic, as well as a brief section on mathematical proofs.

We precede this with a short introduction to set theory. This is useful not just for its importance in mathematics, but also because of a key role that sets play in economics: in most economic models, it is assumed that economic agents pursue some specific goal like profit, and make an optimal choice from a specified feasible set of alternatives.

The chapter winds up with a discussion of mathematical induction. Occasionally, this method is used directly in economic arguments; more often, it is needed to understand mathematical results which economists use.

1.1 Essentials of Set Theory

In daily life, we constantly group together objects of the same kind. For instance, the faculty of a university signifies all the members of its academic staff. A garden refers to all the plants that are growing in it. An economist may talk about all Scottish firms with over 300 employees, or all taxpayers in Germany who earned between €50 000 and €100 000 in 2019. Or suppose a student who is planning what combination of laptop and smartphone to buy for use in college. The student may consider all combinations whose total price does not exceed what she can afford. In all these cases, we have a collection of objects that we may want to view as a whole. In mathematics, such a collection is called a *set*, and the objects that belong to the set are called its *elements*, or its *members*.

---

[1] *The Theory of Political Economy* (1871)

The simplest way to specify a set is to list its members, in any order, between the opening brace { and the closing brace }. An example is the set whose members are the first three letters in the English alphabet, $S = \{a, b, c\}$. Or it might be a set consisting of three members represented by the letters a, b, and c. For example, if $a = 0, b = 1$, and $c = 2$, then $S = \{0, 1, 2\}$. Also, $S = \{a, b, c\}$ denotes the set of roots of the cubic equation $(x - a)(x - b)(x - c) = 0$ in the unknown x, where a, b, and c are any three real numbers. Verbally, the braces are read as "the set consisting of".

Since a set is fully specified by listing all its members, two sets A and B are considered *equal* if they contain exactly the same elements: each element of A is an element of B; conversely, each element of B is an element of A. In this case, we write $A = B$. Consequently, $\{1, 2, 3\} = \{3, 2, 1\}$, because the order in which the elements are listed has no significance; and $\{1, 1, 2, 3\} = \{1, 2, 3\}$, because a set is not changed if some elements are listed more than once.

The symbol "∅" denotes the set that has no elements. It is called the *empty set*. Note that it is *the*, and not *an*, empty set. This is so, following the principle that a set is completely defined by listing all its members: there can only be one set that contains no elements. The empty set is the same, whether it is being studied by a child in elementary school who thinks about cows that can jump over the moon, or by a physicist at CERN who thinks about subatomic particles that move faster than the speed of light—or, indeed, by an economics student reading this book!

Specifying a Property

Not every set can be defined by listing all its members, however. For one thing, some sets are infinite—that is, they contain infinitely many members. Such infinite sets are rather common in economics. Take, for instance, the budget set that arises in consumer theory. Suppose there are two goods with quantities denoted by x and y. Suppose these two goods can be bought at prices per unit that equal p and q, respectively. A consumption bundle is a pair of quantities of the two goods, (x, y). Its value at prices p and q is $px + qy$. Suppose that a consumer has an amount m to spend on the two goods. Then the *budget constraint* is $px + qy \leq m$, assuming that the consumer is free to underspend. If one also accepts that the quantity consumed of each good must be nonnegative, then the *budget set*, which will be denoted by B, consists of all those consumption bundles (x, y) satisfying the three inequalities $px + qy \leq m$, $x \geq 0$, and $y \geq 0$. This set is illustrated in Fig. 4.4.12. Standard notation for it is

$$B = \{(x, y) : px + qy \leq m, \ x \geq 0, \ y \geq 0\} \tag{1.1.1}$$

The two braces { and } are still used to denote "the set consisting of". However, instead of listing all the members, which is impossible for the infinite set of points in the triangular budget set B, it is specified in two parts. First, before the colon, (x, y) is used to denote the typical member of B, here a consumption bundle that is specified by listing the respective quantities of the two goods. The colon is read as "such that".[2] Second, after the colon, the three properties that these typical members must satisfy are all listed.

---

[2] Alternative notation for "such that" is |.

This completes the specification of B. Indeed, Eq. (1.1.1) is an example of the general specification:

$$S = \{\text{typical member} : \text{defining properties}\}$$

Note that it is not just infinite sets that can be specified by properties like this—finite sets can too. Indeed, some finite sets almost *have* to be specified in this way, such as the set of all human beings currently alive.

Set Membership

As we stated earlier, sets contain members or elements. Some convenient standard notation is used to express the relation between a set and its members. First,

$$x \in S$$

indicates that *x is an element of S*. Note the special "belongs to" symbol $\in$ (which is a variant of the Greek letter ε, or "epsilon").

To express the fact that x is *not* a member of S, we write $x \notin S$. For example, $d \notin \{a, b, c\}$ says that d is not an element of the set $\{a, b, c\}$.

To see how set membership notation can be applied, consider again the example of a first-year college student who *must* buy both a laptop and a smartphone. Suppose that there are two types of each device, "cheap" and "expensive". Suppose too that the student cannot afford to combine the expensive smartphone with the expensive laptop. Then the set of three combinations that the student can afford is {cheap laptop and cheap smartphone, expensive laptop and cheap smartphone, cheap laptop and expensive smartphone}. Thus, the student is restricted to choosing one of the three combinations in this set. If we denote the choice by s and the affordable set by B, we can say that the student's choice is constrained by the requirement that $s \in B$. If we denote by t the unaffordable combination of an expensive laptop and an expensive smartphone, we can express this unaffordability by writing $t \notin B$.

Let A and B be any two sets. Set A is a *subset* of B if it is true that every member of A is also a member of B. When that is the case, we write $A \subseteq B$. In particular, $A \subseteq A$ and $\varnothing \subseteq A$. Recall that two sets are *equal* if they contain the same elements. From the definitions, we see that $A = B$ when, and only when, both $A \subseteq B$ and $B \subseteq A$.

To continue the previous example, suppose that the student can make do with a cheap smartphone, so she chooses not to buy an expensive one. Having made this choice, she only needs to decide which laptop to buy in addition to the cheap smartphone. Let A denote the set {cheap laptop and cheap smartphone, expensive laptop and cheap smartphone} of options the student has not ruled out. Then we have $A \subseteq B$.

Set Operations

Sets can be combined in many different ways. Especially important are three operations: the *union*, *intersection*, and the *difference* of any two sets A and B, as shown in Table 1.1.1.

Table 1.1.1 Elementary set operations

Notation	Name	The set that consists of:
$A \cup B$	A union B	all elements belonging to at least one of the sets A and B
$A \cap B$	A intersection B	all elements belonging to both A and B
$A \setminus B$	A minus B	all elements belonging to set A, but not to B

In symbols:

$$A \cup B = \{x : x \in A \text{ or } x \in B\}$$

$$A \cap B = \{x : x \in A \text{ and } x \in B\}$$

$$A \setminus B = \{x : x \in A \text{ and } x \notin B\}$$

It is important to notice that the word "or" in mathematics is *inclusive*, in the sense that the statement "$x \in A$ or $x \in B$" allows for the possibility that $x \in A$ and $x \in B$ are *both* true.

EXAMPLE 1.1.1 Let $A = \{1, 2, 3, 4, 5\}$ and $B = \{3, 6\}$. Find $A \cup B$, $A \cap B$, $A \setminus B$, and $B \setminus A$.[3]

Solution: $A \cup B = \{1, 2, 3, 4, 5, 6\}$, $A \cap B = \{3\}$, $A \setminus B = \{1, 2, 4, 5\}$, $B \setminus A = \{6\}$.

As an economic example, considering everybody who worked in California during the year 2019. Let A denote the set of all those workers who have an income of at least $35 000 for the year; let B denote the set of all who have a net worth of at least $200 000. Then $A \cup B$ would be those workers who earned at least $35 000 or who had a net worth of at least $200 000, whereas $A \cap B$ are those workers who earned at least $35 000 and who also had a net worth of at least $200 000. Finally, $A \setminus B$ would be those who earned at least $35 000 but whose net worth was less than $200 000.

If two sets A and B have no elements in common, they are said to be *disjoint*. Thus, the sets A and B are disjoint if $A \cap B = \emptyset$.

A collection of sets is often referred to as a *family* of sets. When considering a certain family of sets, it is often natural to think of each set in the family as a subset of one particular fixed set $\mathcal{U}$, hereafter called the *universal set*. In the previous example, the set of all residents of California in 2019 would be an obvious choice for a universal set.

If A is a subset of the universal set $\mathcal{U}$, then according to the definition of difference, $\mathcal{U} \setminus A$ is the set of elements of $\mathcal{U}$ that are not in A. This set is called the *complement* of A in $\mathcal{U}$ and is denoted by A^c.[4] When finding the complement of a set, it is *very* important to be clear about which universal set is being used.

EXAMPLE 1.1.2 Let the universal set $\mathcal{U}$ be the set of all students at a particular university. Among these, let F denote the set of female students, M the set of all mathematics students, C the set of students in the university choir, B the set of all biology students, and T the set of all tennis

---
[3] Here and throughout the book, we often write the examples in the form of exercises. We strongly suggest that you first attempt to solve the problem, while covering the solution, and then gradually reveal the proposed solution to see if you are right.

[4] Other ways of denoting the complement of A include $\complement A$ and $\tilde{A}$.

players. Describe the members of the following sets: $\mathcal{U} \setminus M$, $M \cup C$, $F \cap T$, $M \setminus (B \cap T)$, and $(M \setminus B) \cup (M \setminus T)$.

Solution: $\mathcal{U} \setminus M$ consists of those students who are not studying mathematics, $M \cup C$ of those students who study mathematics and/or are in the choir. The set $F \cap T$ consists of those female students who play tennis. The set $M \setminus (B \cap T)$ has those mathematics students who do not both study biology and play tennis. Finally, the last set $(M \setminus B) \cup (M \setminus T)$ has those students who either are mathematics students not studying biology or mathematics students who do not play tennis. Can you see that the last two sets must be equal?[5]

Venn Diagrams

When considering how different sets may be related, it is often both instructive and extremely helpful to represent each set by a region in a plane. Diagrams constructed in this manner are called *Venn diagrams*.[6]

For pairs of sets, the definitions discussed in the previous section can be illustrated as in Fig. 1.1.1. By using the definitions directly, or by illustrating sets with Venn diagrams, one can derive formulas that are universally valid regardless of which sets are being considered. For example, the formula $A \cap B = B \cap A$ follows immediately from the definition of the intersection between two sets.

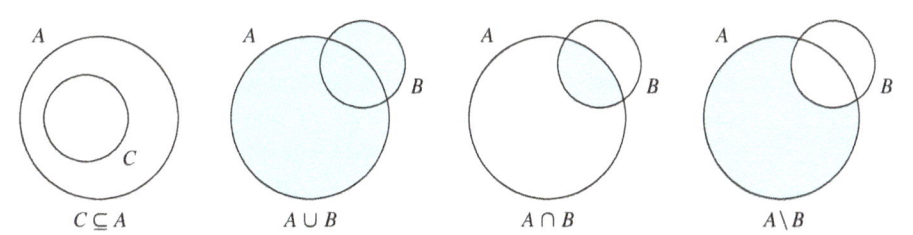

Figure 1.1.1 Four Venn diagrams

When dealing with three general sets A, B, and C, it is important to draw the Venn diagram so that all possible relations between an element and each of the three sets are represented. In other words, as in Fig. 1.1.3, the following eight different regions should all be nonempty:[7]

1. $(A \cap B) \setminus C$
2. $(B \cap C) \setminus A$
3. $(C \cap A) \setminus B$
4. $A \setminus (B \cup C)$
5. $B \setminus (C \cup A)$
6. $C \setminus (A \cup B)$
7. $(A \cap B) \cap C$
8. $((A \cup B) \cup C)^c$

---

[5] For arbitrary sets M, B, and T, it is true that $(M \setminus B) \cup (M \setminus T) = M \setminus (B \cap T)$. It should become easier to verify this equality after you have studied the following discussion of Venn diagrams.

[6] Named after the English mathematician John Venn (1834–1923), who was the first to use them extensively.

[7] That is, all should be nonempty unless something more is known about the relation between the three sets. For example, one might have specified that the sets must be disjoint, meaning that $A \cap B \cap C = \emptyset$. In this case region (7) in Fig. 1.1.3 disappears.

Figure 1.1.2 Venn diagram for $A \cap (B \cup C)$

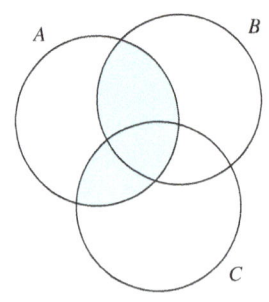

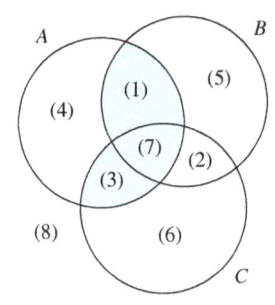

Figure 1.1.3 Venn diagram for three sets

Venn diagrams are particularly useful when limited to no more than three sets. For instance, consider the following possible relationship between the three sets A, B, and C:

$$A \cap (B \cup C) = (A \cap B) \cup (A \cap C) \tag{1.1.2}$$

Using only the definitions in Table 1.1.1, it is somewhat difficult to verify that Eq. (1.1.2) holds for all sets A, B, C. Using a Venn diagram, however, it is easily seen that the two sets on the left- and right-hand sides of (1.1.2) are both represented by the region made up of the three regions that are shaded in both Fig. 1.1.2 and Fig. 1.1.3. This confirms Eq. (1.1.2). Similar reasoning allows one to prove that

$$A \cup (B \cap C) = (A \cup B) \cap (A \cup C) \tag{1.1.3}$$

Using either the definition of intersection and union or appropriate Venn diagrams, one can see that $A \cup (B \cup C) = (A \cup B) \cup C$ and that $A \cap (B \cap C) = (A \cap B) \cap C$. Consequently, in such cases it does not matter where the parentheses are placed, so they can be dropped and the expressions written as $A \cup B \cup C$ and $A \cap B \cap C$. That said, note that the parentheses cannot generally be removed in the two expressions on the left-hand sides of Eqs (1.1.2) and (1.1.3). This is because $A \cap (B \cup C)$ is generally not equal to $(A \cap B) \cup C$, and $A \cup (B \cap C)$ is generally not equal to $(A \cup B) \cap C$.[8]

Notice, however, that this way of representing sets in the plane becomes unmanageable if four or more sets are involved. This is because a Venn diagram with, for example, four sets would have to contain $2^4 = 16$ regions.[9]

Georg Cantor

The founder of set theory is Georg Cantor (1845–1918), who was born in Saint Petersburg but moved to Germany at the age of eleven. He is regarded as one of history's great mathematicians. This is not because of his contributions to the development of the useful, but relatively trivial, aspects of set theory outlined above. Rather, Cantor is remembered for his profound study of infinite sets. Below we try to give just a hint of his theory's implications.

---

[8] For practice, demonstrate this fact by considering the case where $A = \{1, 2, 3\}$, $B = \{2, 3\}$, and $C = \{4, 5\}$, or by using a Venn diagram.

[9] One can show that a Venn diagram with n sets would have to contain 2^n regions.

A collection of individuals are gathering in a room that has a certain number of chairs. How can we find out if there are exactly as many individuals as chairs? One method would be to count the chairs and count the individuals, and then see if they total the same number. Alternatively, we could ask all the individuals to sit down. If they all have a seat to themselves and there are no chairs unoccupied, then there are exactly as many individuals as chairs. In that case each chair corresponds to an individual and each individual corresponds to a chair—i.e., there is a "one-to-one correspondence" between individuals and chairs.

Generally mathematicians say that two sets of elements have the same *cardinality*, if there is a one-to-one correspondence between the sets. This definition is also valid for sets with an infinite number of elements. Cantor struggled for three years to prove a surprising implication of this definition—that there are as many points in a square as there are points on one of its edges of the square, in the sense that the two sets have the same cardinality.[10]

EXERCISES FOR SECTION 1.1

1. Let $A = \{2, 3, 4\}$, $B = \{2, 5, 6\}$, $C = \{5, 6, 2\}$, and $D = \{6\}$.

   (a) Determine which of the following six statements are true: $4 \in C$; $5 \in C$; $A \subseteq B$; $D \subseteq C$; $B = C$; and $A = B$.

   (b) List all members of each of the following eight sets: $A \cap B$; $A \cup B$; $A \setminus B$; $B \setminus A$; $(A \cup B) \setminus (A \cap B)$; $A \cup B \cup C \cup D$; $A \cap B \cap C$; and $A \cap B \cap C \cap D$.

2. Let F, M, C, B, and T be the sets in Example 1.1.2.

   (a) Describe the following sets: $F \cap B \cap C$, $M \cap F$, and $((M \cap B) \setminus C) \setminus T$.

   (b) Write the following statements in set terminology:

      (i) All biology students are mathematics students.

      (ii) There are female biology students in the university choir.

      (iii) No tennis player studies biology.

      (iv) Those female students who neither play tennis nor belong to the university choir all study biology.

3. A survey revealed that 50 people liked coffee and 40 liked tea. Both these figures include 35 who liked both coffee and tea. Finally, ten did not like either coffee or tea. How many people in all responded to the survey?

4. Make a complete list of all the different subsets of the set $\{a, b, c\}$. How many are there if the empty set and the set itself are included? Do the same for the set $\{a, b, c, d\}$.

5. Determine which of the following formulas are true. If any formula is false, find a counter example to demonstrate this, using a Venn diagram if you find it helpful.

---

[10] In 1877, in a letter to German mathematician Richard Dedekind (1831–1916), Cantor wrote of this result: "I see it, but I do not believe it."

(a) $A \setminus B = B \setminus A$
(b) $A \cap (B \cup C) \subseteq (A \cap B) \cup C$
(c) $A \cup (B \cap C) \subseteq (A \cup B) \cap C$
(d) $A \setminus (B \setminus C) = (A \setminus B) \setminus C$

6. Use Venn diagrams to prove that: (a) $(A \cup B)^c = A^c \cap B^c$; and (b) $(A \cap B)^c = A^c \cup B^c$

7. If A is a set with a finite number of distinct elements, let $n(A)$ denote its *cardinality*, defined as the number of elements in A. If A and B are arbitrary finite sets, prove the following:

(a) $n(A \cup B) = n(A) + n(B) - n(A \cap B)$
(b) $n(A \setminus B) = n(A) - n(A \cap B)$

8. A thousand people took part in a survey to reveal which newspaper, A, B, or C, they had read on a certain day. The responses showed that 420 had read A, 316 had read B, and 160 had read C. These figures include 116 who had read both A and B, 100 who had read A and C, and 30 who had read B and C. Finally, all these figures include 16 who had read all three papers.

(a) How many had read A, but not B?

(b) How many had read C, but neither A nor B?

(c) How many had read neither A, B, nor C?

(d) Denote the complete set of all people in the survey by $\mathcal{U}$. Applying the notation in Exercise 7, we have $n(A) = 420$ and $n(A \cap B \cap C) = 16$, for example. Describe the numbers given in the previous answers using the same notation. Why is

$$n(\mathcal{U} \setminus (A \cup B \cup C)) = n(\mathcal{U}) - n(A \cup B \cup C)?$$

(SM) 9. [HARDER] The equalities proved in Exercise 6 are particular cases of the *De Morgan's laws*. State and prove these two laws:

(a) The complement of the union of any family of sets equals the intersection of all the sets' complements.

(b) The complement of the intersection of any family of sets equals the union of all the sets' complements.

1.2 Essentials of Logic

Mathematical models play a critical role in the empirical sciences, including modern economics. This has been a useful development, but demands that practitioners exercise great care. Otherwise errors in mathematical reasoning, which are all too easy to make, can easily lead to nonsensical conclusions.

Here is a typical example of how faulty logic can lead to an incorrect answer. The example involves square roots, which are briefly discussed after the example.

EXAMPLE 1.2.1   Suppose that we want to find *all* the values of x for which the following equality is true: $x + 2 = \sqrt{4 - x}$.

Squaring each side of the equation gives $(x+2)^2 = (\sqrt{4-x})^2$. Expanding the left-hand side while using the definition of square root yields $x^2 + 4x + 4 = 4 - x$. Rearranging this last equation gives $x^2 + 5x = 0$. Cancelling x results in $x + 5 = 0$, and therefore $x = -5$.

According to this reasoning, the answer should be $x = -5$. Let us check this. For $x = -5$, we have $x + 2 = -3$. Yet $\sqrt{4-x} = \sqrt{9} = 3$, so this answer is incorrect.[11]

This example highlights the dangers of routine calculation without adequate thought. It may be easier to avoid similar mistakes after studying the structure of logical reasoning, which we discuss in the rest of this subsection.

A Reminder about Square Roots

The square root $\sqrt{a}$ of a nonnegative number a is the (unique) nonnegative number x such that $x^2 = a$. Thus, in particular, $\sqrt{9} = 3$, because 3 is the only nonnegative number whose square is 9.

Some older mathematical writing may claim that a positive number has two square roots, one positive and the other negative. For instance, $\sqrt{64}$ could be either 8 or -8. Allowing two values like this has now become obsolete, as it easily leads to confusion. For example, $\sqrt{49} + \sqrt{25}$ could mean any of the four numbers $7 + 5$, $7 - 5$, $-7 + 5$, and $-7 - 5$. To avoid such confusion, instead of $\sqrt{a}$ we use the more explicit notation $\pm\sqrt{a}$ to denote the set $\{\sqrt{a}, -\sqrt{a}\}$ consisting, in case $a > 0$, of the two distinct solutions to $x^2 = a$.

So remember that $\sqrt{a}$ always denotes the unique *nonnegative* solution of the equation $x^2 = a$. Of course, if a is negative, then it has no square root at all (as long as we insist that the square root must be a real number).

Propositions

Assertions that are either true or false are called statements, or *propositions*. Most of the propositions in this book are mathematical ones, but other kinds may arise in daily life. "All individuals who breathe are alive" is an example of a true proposition, whereas the assertion "all individuals who breathe are healthy" is a false proposition. Note that if the words used to express such an assertion lack precise meaning, it will often be difficult to tell whether it is true or false. For example, the assertion "67 is a large number" is neither true nor false without a precise definition of "large number".

The assertion "$x^2 - 1 = 0$" includes the variable x. For an assertion like this, by substituting various real numbers for the variable x, we can generate many different propositions, some true and some false. For this reason we say that the assertion is an "open proposition". In fact, the particular proposition $x^2 - 1 = 0$ happens to be true if $x = 1$ or -1, but not otherwise. Thus, an open proposition is not simply true or false. Instead, it is neither true nor false until we choose a particular value for the variable. Or for several variables in case of assertions like $x^2 + y^2 = 1$.

---

[11] Note the wisdom of checking your answer whenever you think you have solved an equation. In Example 1.2.4, below, we explain how the error arose.

Implications

In order to keep track of each step in a chain of logical reasoning, it often helps to use *implication arrows*. Suppose P and Q are two propositions such that whenever P is true, then Q is necessarily true. In this case, we usually write

$$P \implies Q$$

This can be read as "P implies Q", but it can also be read as "if P, then Q"; or "Q is a consequence of P"; or "Q if P". Furthermore, since in this case Q cannot be false while P is true, the implication can also be read as "P only if Q". The symbol $\implies$ is an *implication arrow*, which points in the direction of the logical implication. Thus $P \implies Q$ can also be written as $Q \impliedby P$.

EXAMPLE 1.2.2 Here are some examples of correct implications:[12]

(a) $x > 2 \implies x^2 > 4$
(b) $xy = 0 \implies$ (either $x = 0$ or $y = 0$)
(c) S is a square $\implies$ S is a rectangle
(d) She lives in Paris $\implies$ She lives in France

In certain cases where the implication $P \implies Q$ is valid, it may also be possible to draw a logical conclusion in the other direction: $Q \implies P$ (or $P \impliedby Q$). In such cases, we can write both implications together in a single *logical equivalence*:

$$P \iff Q$$

We then say that "P is equivalent to Q". Because both "P if Q" and "P only if Q" are true, we also say that "P if and only if Q", which is often written as "P iff Q" for short. Unsurprisingly, the symbol $\iff$ is called an *equivalence arrow*.

In Example 1.2.2, we see that the implication arrow in (b) could be replaced with the equivalence arrow, because it is also true that $x = 0$ or $y = 0$ implies $xy = 0$. Note, however, that no other implication in Example 1.2.2 can be replaced by the equivalence arrow, because:

(a) even if x^2 is larger than 4, it is not necessarily true that x is larger than 2 (for instance, x might be -3);

(c) a rectangle is not necessarily a square;

(d) there are millions of people who live in France but not in Paris.

EXAMPLE 1.2.3 Here are three examples of correct equivalences:

(a) $(x < -2 \text{ or } x > 2) \iff x^2 > 4$
(b) $xy = 0 \iff (x = 0 \text{ or } y = 0)$
(c) $A \subseteq B \iff (B^c \subseteq A^c)$

---

[12] Of course, in part (d) we are talking about Paris, France, rather than Paris, Texas, or Paris, Ontario.

The Contrapositive Principle

Suppose P and Q are propositions such that the implication $P \Rightarrow Q$ is valid. This means that *if* P is true, then Q must also be true. From this it follows that if Q is false, then P is also false. Therefore we have the implication (not $Q \Rightarrow$ not P).

We have just shown that $P \Rightarrow Q$ implies that (not $Q \Rightarrow$ not P). Suppose we replace P by not Q and Q by not P in this implication. The new implication that results is (not $Q \Rightarrow$ not P) implies (not not $P \Rightarrow$ not not Q). But (not not P) is true if and only if (not P) is false, in other words if and only if P is true. In the same way we can see that (not not Q) is the same as Q.

Thus we have shown that $P \Rightarrow Q$ implies (not $Q \Rightarrow$ not P), and that (not $Q \Rightarrow$ not P) implies $P \Rightarrow Q$. We formalize this result as follows:

THE CONTRAPOSITIVE PRINCIPLE

The statement $P \Rightarrow Q$ is logically equivalent to the statement

$$\text{not } Q \Rightarrow \text{not } P$$

This principle is often useful when proving mathematical results.

Necessity and Sufficiency

There are other commonly used ways of expressing the statement that proposition P implies proposition Q, or the alternative statement that P is equivalent to Q. Thus, if proposition P implies proposition Q, we say that P is a "sufficient condition" for Q; after all, for Q to be true, it is sufficient that P be true. Accordingly, we know that if P is satisfied, then it is certain that Q is also satisfied. In this case, because Q must necessarily be true if P is true, we say that Q is a "necessary condition" for P. Hence:

NECESSARY AND SUFFICIENT CONDITIONS

(a) $P \Rightarrow Q$ means both that P is a *sufficient condition* for Q and, equivalently, that Q is a *necessary condition* for P.

(b) The corresponding verbal expression for $P \Leftrightarrow Q$ is that P is a *necessary and sufficient condition* for Q.

It is worth noting how important it is to distinguish between the three propositions "P is a necessary condition for Q", "P is a sufficient condition for Q", and "P is a necessary and sufficient condition for Q". To emphasize this point, consider the propositions:

Living in France is a necessary condition for a person to live in Paris.

and

Living in Paris is a necessary condition for a person to live in France.

The first proposition is clearly true. But the second is false,[13] because it is possible to live in France, but outside Paris. What is true, though, is that

Living in Paris is a sufficient condition for a person to live in France.

In the following pages, we shall repeatedly refer to necessary conditions, to sufficient conditions, as well as to necessary and sufficient conditions—i.e., conditions that are both necessary and sufficient. Understanding these three, and the differences between them, is a necessary condition for understanding much of economic analysis. It is not a sufficient condition, alas!

EXAMPLE 1.2.4 In solving Example 1.2.1, why did we need to check that the values we found were actually solutions? To answer this, we must analyse the logical structure of our analysis. Using implication arrows marked by letters, we can express the "solution" proposed there as follows:

$$x + 2 = \sqrt{4 - x} \stackrel{(a)}{\Longrightarrow} (x+2)^2 = 4 - x$$
$$\stackrel{(b)}{\Longrightarrow} x^2 + 4x + 4 = 4 - x$$
$$\stackrel{(c)}{\Longrightarrow} x^2 + 5x = 0$$
$$\stackrel{(d)}{\Longrightarrow} x(x+5) = 0$$
$$\stackrel{(e)}{\Longrightarrow} [x = 0 \text{ or } x = -5]$$

Implication (a) is true, because $a = b \Rightarrow a^2 = b^2$ and $(\sqrt{a})^2 = a$. It is important to note, however, that the implication cannot be replaced by an equivalence: if $a^2 = b^2$, then either $a = b$ or $a = -b$; it need not be true that $a = b$. Implications (b), (c), (d), and (e) are also all true; moreover, all could have been written as equivalences, though this is not necessary in order to find the solution. In the end, therefore, we have obtained a chain of implications that leads from the equation $x + 2 = \sqrt{4 - x}$ to the proposition "$x = 0$ or $x = -5$".

Because the implication (a) cannot be reversed, there is no corresponding chain of implications going in the opposite direction. All we have done is verify that if the number x satisfies $x + 2 = \sqrt{4 - x}$, then x must be either 0 or -5; no other value can satisfy the given equation. However, we have not yet shown that either 0 or -5 really satisfies the equation. Only after we try inserting 0 and -5 into the equation do we see that $x = 0$ is the only solution.

Looking back at Example 1.2.4, we can now see that two errors were committed. First, the implication $x^2 + 5x = 0 \Rightarrow x + 5 = 0$ is wrong, because $x = 0$ is also a solution of $x^2 + 5x = 0$. Second, it is logically necessary to check if 0 or -5 really satisfies the equation.

---

[13] As is the proposition *Living in France is equivalent to living in Paris.*

EXERCISES FOR SECTION 1.2

1. There are many other ways to express implications and equivalences, apart from those already mentioned. Use appropriate implication or equivalence arrows to represent the following propositions:

    (a) The equation $2x - 4 = 2$ is fulfilled only when $x = 3$.

    (b) If $x = 3$, then $2x - 4 = 2$.

    (c) The equation $x^2 - 2x + 1 = 0$ is satisfied if $x = 1$.

    (d) If $x^2 > 4$, then $|x| > 2$, and conversely.

2. Determine which of the following formulas are true. If any formula is false, find a counter example to demonstrate this, using a Venn diagram if you find it helpful.

    (a) $A \subseteq B \Leftrightarrow A \cup B = B$

    (b) $A \subseteq B \Leftrightarrow A \cap B = A$

    (c) $A \cap B = A \cap C \Rightarrow B = C$

    (d) $A \cup B = A \cup C \Rightarrow B = C$

    (e) $A = B \Leftrightarrow (x \in A \Leftrightarrow x \in B)$

3. In each of the following implications, where x, y, and z are numbers, decide: (i) if the implication is true; and (ii) if the converse implication is true.

    (a) $x = \sqrt{4} \Rightarrow x = 2$

    (b) $(x = 2 \text{ and } y = 5) \Rightarrow x + y = 7$

    (c) $(x-1)(x-2)(x-3) = 0 \Rightarrow x = 1$

    (d) $x^2 + y^2 = 0 \Rightarrow x = 0 \text{ or } y = 0$

    (e) $(x = 0 \text{ and } y = 0) \Rightarrow x^2 + y^2 = 0$

    (f) $xy = xz \Rightarrow y = z$

4. Consider the proposition $2x + 5 \geq 13$.

    (a) Is the condition $x \geq 0$ necessary, or sufficient, or both necessary and sufficient for the inequality to be satisfied?

    (b) Answer the same question when $x \geq 0$ is replaced by $x \geq 50$.

    (c) Answer the same question when $x \geq 0$ is replaced by $x \geq 4$.

SM 5. [HARDER] If P is a statement, its *negation* is that statement which is true when P is false, and false when P is true. For example, the negation of the statement $2x + 3y \leq 8$ is $2x + 3y > 8$. For each of the following six propositions, state the negation as simply as possible.

    (a) $x \geq 0$ and $y \geq 0$.

    (b) All x satisfy $x \geq a$.

    (c) Neither x nor y is less than 5.

    (d) For each $\varepsilon > 0$, there exists a $\delta > 0$ such that B is satisfied.

    (e) No one can help liking cats.

    (f) Everyone loves somebody some of the time.

1.3 Mathematical Proofs

In mathematics, the most important results are called *theorems*. Constructing logically valid proofs for these results often can be very complicated.[14] In this book, we often omit formal proofs of theorems. Instead, the emphasis is on providing a good intuitive grasp of what the theorems tell us. That said, it is still useful to understand something about the different types of proof that are used in mathematics.

Every mathematical theorem can be formulated as one or more implications of the form

$$P \implies Q \qquad (*)$$

where P represents a proposition, or a series of propositions, called *premises* ("what we already know"), and Q represents a proposition or a series of propositions that are called the *conclusions* ("what we want to know").

Usually, it is most natural to prove a result of the type $(*)$ by starting with the premises P and successively working forward to the conclusions Q; we call this a *direct proof*. Sometimes, however, it is more convenient to prove the implication $P \Rightarrow Q$ by a *contrapositive* or *indirect proof*. In this case, we begin by supposing that Q is not true, and on that basis demonstrate that P cannot be true either. This is completely legitimate, because of the contrapositive principle set out in Section 1.2.

The method of indirect proof is closely related to an alternative one known as *proof by contradiction* or *reductio ad absurdum*. According to this method, in order to prove that $P \Rightarrow Q$, one assumes that P is true and Q is not, and develops an argument that leads to something that *cannot* be true. So, since P and the negation of Q lead to something absurd, it must be that whenever P holds, so does Q.

EXAMPLE 1.3.1   Show that $-x^2 + 5x - 4 > 0 \Rightarrow x > 0$.

Solution: We can use any of the three methods of proof:

(a) *Direct proof*: Suppose $-x^2 + 5x - 4 > 0$. Adding $x^2 + 4$ to each side of the inequality gives $5x > x^2 + 4$. Because $x^2 + 4 \geq 4$, for all x, we have $5x > 4$, and so $x > 4/5$. In particular, $x > 0$.

(b) *Contrapositive proof*: Suppose $x \leq 0$. Then $5x \leq 0$ and so $-x^2 + 5x - 4$, as a sum of three nonpositive terms, is itself nonpositive.

(c) *Proof by contradiction*: Assume that $-x^2 + 5x - 4 > 0$ and $x \leq 0$ are true simultaneously. Then, as in the first step of the direct proof, we have $5x > x^2 + 4$. But since $5x \leq 0$, as in the first step of the contrapositive proof, we are forced to conclude that $0 >$

---

[14] For example, the "four-colour theorem" considers any map that divides a plane into several regions, and the problem of colouring these regions in order that no two adjacent regions have the same colour. As its name suggests, the theorem states that at most four colours are needed. The result was conjectured in the mid 19th century. Yet proving this involved checking hundreds of thousands of different cases. Not until the 1980s did a sophisticated computer program make possible a proof that mathematicians now generally accept as correct.

$x^2 + 4$. Since the latter cannot possibly be true, we have proved that $-x^2 + 5x - 4 > 0$ and $x \leq 0$ cannot be both true, so that $-x^2 + 5x - 4 > 0 \Rightarrow x > 0$, as desired.

Deductive and Inductive Reasoning

The methods of proof just outlined are all examples of *deductive reasoning*—that is, reasoning based on consistent rules of logic. In contrast, many branches of science use *inductive reasoning*. This process draws general conclusions based only on a few (or even many) observations. For example, the statement that "the price level has increased every year for the last n years; therefore, it will surely increase next year too" demonstrates inductive reasoning. This inductive approach is of fundamental importance in the experimental and empirical sciences, despite the fact that conclusions based upon it never can be absolutely certain. Indeed, in economics, such examples of inductive reasoning (or the implied predictions) often turn out to be false, with hindsight.

In mathematics, inductive reasoning is not recognized as a form of proof. Suppose, for instance, that students in a geometry course are asked to show that the sum of the angles of a triangle is always 180 degrees. Suppose they painstakingly measure as accurately as possible, say, one thousand different triangles, and demonstrate that in every case the sum of the angles is 180 degrees. This would not prove the assertion. At best, it would represent a very good indication that the proposition is true, yet it is not a mathematical proof. Similarly, in business economics, the fact that a particular company's profits have risen for each of the past 20 years is no guarantee that they will rise once again this year.

EXERCISES FOR SECTION 1.3

1. Which of the following statements are equivalent to the (dubious) statement: "If inflation increases, then unemployment decreases"?

   (a) For unemployment to decrease, inflation must increase.

   (b) A sufficient condition for unemployment to decrease is that inflation increases.

   (c) Unemployment can only decrease if inflation increases.

   (d) If unemployment does not decrease, then inflation does not increase.

   (e) A necessary condition for inflation to increase is that unemployment decreases.

2. Analyse the following epitaph, using logic:

   Those who knew him, loved him. Those who loved him not, knew him not.

   Might this be a case where poetry is better than logic?

3. Use the contrapositive principle to show that if x and y are integers and xy is an odd number, then x and y are both odd.

1.4 Mathematical Induction

Unlike inductive reasoning, mathematical induction is a form of argument that relies entirely on logic. It sees widespread use in proving formulas and even theorems that involve natural numbers. Consider, for example, the sum of the first n odd numbers. A little calculation shows that for $n = 1, 2, 3, 4, 5$ one has

$$1 = 1 = 1^2$$
$$1 + 3 = 4 = 2^2$$
$$1 + 3 + 5 = 9 = 3^2$$
$$1 + 3 + 5 + 7 = 16 = 4^2$$
$$1 + 3 + 5 + 7 + 9 = 25 = 5^2$$

This suggests a general pattern, with the sum of the first n odd numbers equal to n^2:

$$P(n): \quad 1 + 3 + 5 + \cdots + (2n - 1) = n^2 \quad (*)$$

We call Eq. (∗) the *induction hypothesis*, a proposition that we denote by $P(n)$. To prove that $P(n)$ really is valid for general n, we can proceed as follows. First, start with the *base case*, denoted by $P(1)$, which states that the formula (∗) is correct when n equals 1.

Next, the key *induction step* involves showing that, for any $k \geq 1$, if $P(k)$ is true, then it follows that $P(k + 1)$ is true. In other words, one proves that $P(k) \Rightarrow P(k + 1)$. To do this, simply add the $(k + 1)$th odd number, which is $2k + 1$, to each side of (∗). This gives

$$1 + 3 + 5 + \cdots + (2k - 1) + (2k + 1) = k^2 + (2k + 1) = (k + 1)^2$$

But this is precisely $P(k + 1)$ in which: (i) the left-hand side of formula (∗) ends, not with the kth odd number $2k - 1$, but with the $(k + 1)$th odd number $2k + 1$; (ii) the right-hand side of (∗) has been "stepped up" from k^2 to $(k + 1)^2$. This completes the proof of the "induction step" showing that, if $P(k)$ holds because the sum of the first k odd numbers really is k^2, then $P(k + 1)$ holds because the sum of the first $k + 1$ odd numbers equals $(k + 1)^2$.

Given the base case stating that formula (∗) is valid for $n = 1$, this "induction step" *implies* that (∗) is valid for general n. This is because, if (∗) holds for $n = 1$, the induction step we have just shown implies that it holds also for $n = 2$; that if it holds for $n = 2$, then it also holds for $n = 3$; ...; that if it holds for n, then it holds also for $n + 1$; and so on.

A proof of this type is called a *proof by induction*.[15] It requires showing: (i) first that the formula is indeed valid in the base case when $n = 1$; (ii) second that, *if* the formula is valid when $n = k$, then it is also valid when $n = k + 1$, which is the induction step. It follows by induction that the formula is valid for all natural numbers n.

---

[15] Arguments by induction can be traced as far back as ancient Greek philosophers and mathematicians, including Plato and Euclid.

EXAMPLE 1.4.1 Prove by induction that, for all positive integers n,

$$3 + 3^2 + 3^3 + 3^4 + \cdots + 3^n = \tfrac{1}{2}(3^{n+1} - 3) \qquad (**)$$

Solution: In the base case when $n = 1$, both sides are 3. For the induction step, suppose that $(**)$ is true for $n = k$. Then adding the next term 3^{k+1} to each side of $(**)$ gives

$$3 + 3^2 + 3^3 + 3^4 + \cdots + 3^k + 3^{k+1} = \tfrac{1}{2}(3^{k+1} - 3) + 3^{k+1} = \tfrac{1}{2}(3^{k+2} - 3)$$

But this is precisely $(**)$ restated for $n = k + 1$ instead of k. So, by induction, $(**)$ is true for all n.

Following these examples, the general structure of an induction proof can be explained as follows. The aim is to prove that a logical statement, for instance a mathematical formula $P(n)$ that depends on n, is true for all natural numbers n. In the two previous examples, the respective statements $P(n)$ were

$$P(n): \quad 1 + 3 + 5 + \cdots + (2n - 1) = n^2$$

and

$$P(n): \quad 3 + 3^2 + 3^3 + 3^4 + \cdots + 3^n = \tfrac{1}{2}(3^{n+1} - 3)$$

The steps required in each proof are as follows. First, as the base case, verify that $P(1)$ is valid, which means that the formula is correct for $n = 1$. Second, prove that for each natural number k, *if* $P(k)$ is true, *then* it follows that $P(k + 1)$ must be true. Here, the fact that $P(k)$ is true is called *the induction hypothesis*, and the move from $P(k)$ to $P(k + 1)$ is called *the induction step* of the proof. When $P(1)$ is true and the induction step has been proved for an arbitrary natural number k, we can conclude, by induction, that statement $P(n)$ is true for all n.

The general principle can be formulated as follows:

THE PRINCIPLE OF MATHEMATICAL INDUCTION

For each natural number n, let $P(n)$ denote a statement that depends on n. Suppose that:

(a) $P(1)$ is true; and

(b) for each natural number k, *if* $P(k)$ is true *then* $P(k + 1)$ is true.

It follows that $P(n)$ is true for all natural numbers n.

The principle of mathematical induction seems intuitively obvious. If the truth of $P(k)$ for each k implies the truth of $P(k + 1)$, then because $P(1)$ is true, it follows that $P(2)$ must be true, which, in turn, means that $P(3)$ is true, and so on indefinitely.[16] That is, we have established the infinite chain of implications

$$P(1) \Rightarrow P(2) \Rightarrow P(3) \Rightarrow \cdots \Rightarrow P(k) \Rightarrow P(k+1) \Rightarrow \cdots$$

The principle of mathematical induction can easily be extended to the case when a statement $P(n)$ is true for each integer greater than or equal to an arbitrary integer n_0. Indeed, suppose we can prove that $P(n_0)$ is valid and moreover that, for each $k \geq n_0$, if $P(k)$ is true, then $P(k+1)$ is true. It follows that $P(n)$ is true for all $n \geq n_0$.

EXERCISES FOR SECTION 1.4

1. Prove by induction that for all natural numbers n,

$$1 + 2 + 3 + \cdots + n = \frac{1}{2}n(n+1) \qquad (*)$$

2. Prove by induction that

$$\frac{1}{1 \cdot 2} + \frac{1}{2 \cdot 3} + \frac{1}{3 \cdot 4} + \cdots + \frac{1}{n(n+1)} = \frac{n}{n+1} \qquad (**)$$

3. After noting that the sum $1^3 + 2^3 + 3^3 = 36$ is divisible by 9, prove by induction that the sum $n^3 + (n+1)^3 + (n+2)^3$ of three consecutive cubes is always divisible by 9.

4. Let $P(n)$ be the statement:

   Any collection of n people in one room all have the same income.

   Find what is wrong with the following "induction argument":

   $P(1)$ is obviously true. Suppose $P(n)$ is true for some natural number n. We will then prove that $P(n + 1)$ is true. So take any collection of $n + 1$ people in one room and send one of them outside. The remaining n people all have the same income by the induction hypothesis. Bring the person back inside and send another outside instead. Again the remaining people will have the same income. But then all the $n + 1$ people will have the same income. By induction, this proves that all n people have the same income.

REVIEW EXERCISES

1. Let $A = \{1, 3, 4\}$, $B = \{1, 4, 6\}$, $C = \{2, 4, 3\}$, and $D = \{1, 5\}$. Find $A \cap B$; $A \cup B$; $A \setminus B$; $B \setminus A$; $(A \cup B) \setminus (A \cap B)$; $A \cup B \cup C \cup D$; $A \cap B \cap C$; and $A \cap B \cap C \cap D$.

---

[16] Here is an analogy: Consider climbing a ladder with an infinite number of steps. Suppose you can climb the first step and suppose, moreover, that after each step, you can always climb the next. Then you are able to climb up to any step. Literally, induction arguments prove general statements *step by step!*

2. Let the universal set be $\Omega = \{1, 2, 3, 4, \ldots, 11\}$, and define $A = \{1, 4, 6\}$ and $B = \{2, 11\}$. Find $A \cap B$; $A \cup B$; $\Omega \setminus B$; A^c.

3. A liberal arts college has one thousand students. The numbers studying various languages are: English 780; French 220; and Spanish 52. These figures include 110 who study English and French, 32 who study English and Spanish, 15 who study French and Spanish. Finally, all these figures include ten students taking all three languages.

   (a) How many study English and French, but not Spanish?

   (b) How many study English, but not French?

   (c) How many study no languages?

4. Let x and y be real numbers. Consider the following implications and decide in each case: (i) if the implication is true; and (ii) if the converse implication is true.

   (a) $x = 5$ and $y = -3 \Rightarrow x + y = 2$
   (b) $x^2 = 16 \Rightarrow x = 4$
   (c) $(x - 3)^2(y + 2)$ is a positive number $\Rightarrow y$ is greater than -2
   (d) $x^3 = 8 \Rightarrow x = 2$

5. [HARDER] (If you are not yet familiar with inequalities and with nth powers, see Sections 2.2 and 2.6 in Chapter 2.) Prove the following result, known as *Bernoulli's inequality*:[17] for every real number $x \geq -1$ and every natural number n, one has $(1 + x)^n \geq 1 + nx$.

---

[17] Named after Jacob Bernoulli (1654–1705), one of a large extended family of prominent mathematicians and other scholars.

2

ALGEBRA

God made the integers, all else is the work of Man.
—Leopold Kronecker[1]

The main topic covered in this chapter is elementary algebra. Nevertheless, we also briefly consider a few other topics that you might find the need to review. Indeed, tests reveal that even students with a good background in mathematics often benefit from a brief review of what they had learned in the past. These students should browse through the material in this chapter, and do some of the less simple exercises. Students with a weaker background in mathematics, however, or those who have been away from mathematics for a long time, should read the text carefully and then do most of the exercises. Finally, those students who have considerable difficulties with this chapter should turn to a more elementary book on algebra.

2.1 The Real Numbers

We start by reviewing some important facts and concepts concerning numbers. The basic numbers are the *natural numbers*:

$$1, 2, 3, 4, \ldots$$

also called *positive integers*. Of these, the multiples of 2 are the *even numbers* 2, 4, 6, 8, …, whereas 1, 3, 5, 7, … are the *odd numbers*. Though familiar, such numbers are in reality rather abstract and advanced concepts. Civilization crossed a significant threshold when it grasped the idea that a flock of four sheep and a collection of four stones have something in common, namely "fourness". This idea came to be represented by symbols such as the primitive ∷ (still used on dominoes, dice, and playing cards), the Roman numeral IV, and eventually the modern 4. Most children grasp this key notion

---
[1] Attributed; circa 1886.

even while quite young, and then continually refine it as they develop their mathematical skills.

The positive integers, together with 0 and the *negative integers* $-1, -2, -3, -4, \ldots,$ make up the integers, which are

$$0, \pm 1, \pm 2, \pm 3, \pm 4, \ldots$$

They can be represented on a *number line* like the one shown in Fig. 2.1.1, where the arrow gives the direction in which the numbers increase.

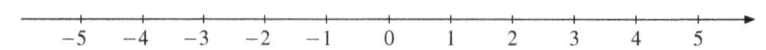

Figure 2.1.1 The number line

The *rational numbers* are those like 3/5 that can be written in the form a/b, where a and b are both integers and $b \neq 0$. Any integer n is also a rational number, because $n = n/1$. Other examples of rational numbers are

$$\frac{1}{2}, \quad \frac{11}{70}, \quad \frac{125}{7}, \quad -\frac{10}{11}, \quad 0 = \frac{0}{1}, \quad -19, \quad -1.26 = -\frac{126}{100}$$

The rational numbers can also be represented on the number line. Suppose that we first mark 1/2 and all the multiples of 1/2. Next we mark 1/3 and all the multiples of 1/3, then all the multiples of 1/4, and so forth. You can be excused for thinking that "finally" there will be no gaps left in which one can find other points on the line. But in fact this is quite wrong. The ancient Greeks already understood that "holes" would remain in the number line even after all the rational numbers had been marked off. For instance, there are no integers p and q such that $\sqrt{2} = p/q$. Hence, $\sqrt{2}$ is not a rational number.[2]

The rational numbers are therefore insufficient for measuring all possible lengths, let alone areas and volumes. This deficiency can be remedied by extending the concept of numbers to allow for the so-called *irrational numbers*. As explained below, this extension can be carried out rather naturally by using decimal notation.

The way most people write numbers today is called the *decimal*, or *base 10 system*. It is a positional system with 10 as the base number. Every natural number can be written using only the symbols, $0, 1, 2, \ldots, 9$, which are called (decimal) *digits*.[3] The positional decimal system uses a list of decimal digits to represent a sum of powers of 10. For example,

$$1984 = 1 \cdot 10^3 + 9 \cdot 10^2 + 8 \cdot 10^1 + 4 \cdot 10^0$$

Each natural number can be uniquely expressed in this manner. With the use of the signs + and −, all integers, positive or negative, can be written in the same way. Decimal points also enable us to express rational numbers that are not natural numbers. For example,

$$3.1415 = 3 + \frac{1}{10^1} + \frac{4}{10^2} + \frac{1}{10^3} + \frac{5}{10^4}$$

---

[2] The first full proof that has survived appeared in Euclid's *Elements*, dating from around the year 300 BCE.

[3] You may recall that a digit is either a finger or a thumb, and that most humans and indeed other primates have ten digits.

Rational numbers that can be written exactly using only a finite number of decimal places are called *finite decimal fractions*.

Each finite decimal fraction is a rational number, but not every rational number can be written as a finite decimal fraction. We must also allow *infinite decimal fractions* such as
$$\frac{100}{3} = 33.333\ldots$$
where the three dots at the end indicate that the digit 3 is repeated indefinitely.

If the decimal fraction is a rational number, then it will always be *periodic* or *recurring* —that is, after a certain place in the decimal expansion, it either stops or continues by repeating indefinitely a finite sequence of digits. For example,
$$\frac{11}{70} = 0.1\,\underbrace{571428}\,\underbrace{571428}\ldots$$
using notation which indicates that the sequence 571428 of six successive digits is repeated infinitely often.

Our definition of a real number follows from the previous discussion. We define a *real number* as an arbitrary infinite decimal fraction. Hence, a real number is of the form $x = \pm m.\alpha_1\alpha_2\alpha_3\ldots$, where m is a nonnegative integer, and for each natural number n, the symbol α_n indicates a *decimal digit* that belongs to the set $\{0, 1, 2, 3, 4, 5, 6, 7, 8, 9\}$.[4]

We have already identified the periodic decimal fractions with the rational numbers. In addition, there are infinitely many new numbers given by nonperiodic decimal fractions. These new numbers are called *irrational numbers*. Examples include the numbers $\sqrt{2}, -\sqrt{5}, \pi, 2^{\sqrt{2}}$, and $0.12112111211112\ldots$.[5]

We mentioned earlier that each rational number can be represented by a unique point on the number line. Even after all the rational numbers have been positioned on this line, there are still some "holes" which can be "filled up" with irrational numbers. Thus, an unbroken and endless straight line with an origin and a positive unit of length constitutes a satisfactory model for the real numbers. We frequently state that there is a *one-to-one correspondence* between the real numbers and the points on a number line. For this reason, one often speaks of the "real line" rather than the "number line".

Both the set of rational numbers as well as the complementary set of irrational numbers are said to be "dense" in the number line. This means that between any two different real numbers, no matter how close they are to each other, we can always find both a rational and an irrational number—in fact, we can always find infinitely many of each.

When applied to the real numbers, each of the four basic arithmetic operations of addition, subtraction, multiplication and division always results in a unique real number. The only exception is that we cannot divide by 0: in words usually attributed to the

---

[4] It is worth noting that any finite decimal fraction (except 0) can also be written as an infinite decimal fraction with a tail entirely of repeated 9s. For instance, $5.347 = 5.346999\ldots$.

[5] In general, mathematicians find it very difficult to show that a number which seems evidently irrational really is. For example, whereas it has been known since the year 1776 that π is irrational, it took until 1927 to determine that $2^{\sqrt{2}}$ is irrational. For many other numbers the challenge of proving their irrationality remains.

American stand-up comedian Steven Wright, "Black holes are where God divided by zero."

> **DIVISION BY ZERO**
>
> The ratio $a/0$ is *not* defined for any real number a.

This exception is very important; it should not be confused with the fact that $0/b = 0$ for all $b \neq 0$. Notice especially that $0/0$ is not defined as any real number. For example, if a car requires 60 litres of fuel to go 600 kilometres, then its fuel consumption is $60/600 = 10$ litres per 100 kilometres. However, if told that a car uses 0 litres of fuel to go 0 kilometres, we know nothing about its fuel consumption; $0/0$ is completely undefined.

EXERCISES FOR SECTION 2.1

1. Which of the following statements are true?

   (a) 1984 is a natural number.
   (b) -5 is to the right of -3 on the number line.
   (c) -13 is a natural number.
   (d) There is no natural number that is not rational.
   (e) 3.1415 is not rational.
   (f) The sum of two irrational numbers is irrational.
   (g) $-3/4$ is rational.
   (h) All rational numbers are real.

2. Explain why the infinite decimal expansion

   $$1.010010001000010000001\ldots$$

   is not a rational number.

2.2 Integer Powers

You should recall that we often write 3^4 instead of the fourfold product $3 \cdot 3 \cdot 3 \cdot 3$. Furthermore, the number $\frac{1}{2} \cdot \frac{1}{2} \cdot \frac{1}{2} \cdot \frac{1}{2} \cdot \frac{1}{2}$ can be written as $\left(\frac{1}{2}\right)^5$, and $(-10)^3$ is the triple product $(-10)(-10)(-10) = -1000$. Indeed, if a is any real number and n is any natural number, then a^n is defined by

$$a^n = \underbrace{a \cdot a \cdot \ldots \cdot a}_{n \text{ factors}}$$

The expression a^n is called the *nth power* of a; here a is the *base*, and n is the *exponent*. For example, we have $a^2 = a \cdot a$, and $x^4 = x \cdot x \cdot x \cdot x$. When $a = p/q$ and $n = 5$ we have

$$\left(\frac{p}{q}\right)^5 = \frac{p}{q} \cdot \frac{p}{q} \cdot \frac{p}{q} \cdot \frac{p}{q} \cdot \frac{p}{q}$$

By convention, the first power $a^1 = a$ is a "product" with only one factor.

We usually drop the multiplication sign if this is unlikely to create misunderstanding. For example, we write abc instead of $a \cdot b \cdot c$, but it is safest to keep the multiplication sign in expressions with decimal points like $1.05^3 = 1.05 \cdot 1.05 \cdot 1.05$.

For any real number $a \neq 0$, we also define its "zeroth" power $a^0 = 1$. Thus, $5^0 = 1$; $(-16.2)^0 = 1$; and $(x \cdot y)^0 = 1$, if $x \cdot y \neq 0$. But in case $a = 0$, we do *not* assign a numerical value to a^0: the expression 0^0 is *undefined*.

We also need to define powers with negative exponents. What do we mean by 3^{-2}? It turns out that the sensible definition is to set 3^{-2} equal to $1/3^2 = 1/9$. In general,

$$a^{-n} = \frac{1}{a^n}$$

whenever n is a natural number and $a \neq 0$. In particular, $a^{-1} = 1/a$. In this way we have defined a^x for all integers x, regardless of whether x is positive, negative, or zero.

Properties of Powers

There are some rules for powers that you really must not only know by heart, but also understand why they are true. The two most important are:

PROPERTIES OF POWERS

For any real number a, and any integer numbers r and s:

$$a^r \cdot a^s = a^{r+s}$$

while

$$(a^r)^s = a^{rs}$$

Note carefully what these rules say. According to the first rule, powers with the same base are multiplied by *adding* the exponents. For example,

$$a^3 \cdot a^5 = \underbrace{a \cdot a \cdot a}_{3 \text{ factors}} \cdot \underbrace{a \cdot a \cdot a \cdot a \cdot a}_{5 \text{ factors}} = \underbrace{a \cdot a \cdot a \cdot a \cdot a \cdot a \cdot a \cdot a}_{3+5 = 8 \text{ factors}} = a^8 = a^{3+5}$$

Here is an example of the second rule:

$$(a^2)^4 = \underbrace{\underbrace{a \cdot a}_{2 \text{ factors}} \cdot \underbrace{a \cdot a}_{2 \text{ factors}} \cdot \underbrace{a \cdot a}_{2 \text{ factors}} \cdot \underbrace{a \cdot a}_{2 \text{ factors}}}_{4 \text{ factors}} = \underbrace{a \cdot a \cdot a \cdot a \cdot a \cdot a \cdot a \cdot a}_{4 \cdot 2 = 8 \text{ factors}} = a^8 = a^{2 \cdot 4}$$

Division of two powers with the same nonzero base goes like this:

$$a^r \div a^s = \frac{a^r}{a^s} = a^r \frac{1}{a^s} = a^r \cdot a^{-s} = a^{r-s}$$

Thus we divide two powers with the same base by *subtracting* the exponent in the denominator from that in the numerator.[6] For example, $a^3 \div a^5 = a^{3-5} = a^{-2}$.

Finally, note that

$$(ab)^r = \underbrace{ab \cdot ab \cdot \ldots \cdot ab}_{r \text{ factors}} = \underbrace{a \cdot a \cdot \ldots \cdot a}_{r \text{ factors}} \cdot \underbrace{b \cdot b \cdot \ldots \cdot b}_{r \text{ factors}} = a^r b^r$$

and

$$\left(\frac{a}{b}\right)^r = \underbrace{\frac{a}{b} \cdot \frac{a}{b} \cdot \ldots \cdot \frac{a}{b}}_{r \text{ factors}} = \frac{\overbrace{a \cdot a \cdot \ldots \cdot a}^{r \text{ factors}}}{\underbrace{b \cdot b \cdot \ldots \cdot b}_{r \text{ factors}}} = \frac{a^r}{b^r} = a^r b^{-r}$$

These rules can be extended to cases where there are several factors. For instance,

$$(abcde)^r = a^r b^r c^r d^r e^r$$

We saw that $(ab)^r = a^r b^r$. What about $(a+b)^r$? One of the most common errors committed in elementary algebra is to equate this to $a^r + b^r$. For example, $(2+3)^3 = 5^3 = 125$, but $2^3 + 3^3 = 8 + 27 = 35$. Thus, in general, $(a+b)^r \neq a^r + b^r$.

EXAMPLE 2.2.1 Simplify the expressions:

(a) $x^p x^{2p}$, where p is an integer

(b) $t^s \div t^{s-1}$, where $t \neq 0$ and s is an integer

(c) $a^2 b^3 a^{-1} b^5$, where $a \neq 0$

(d) $\dfrac{t^p t^{q-1}}{t^r t^{s-1}}$, where $t \neq 0$ and p, q, r, s are integers

Solution:

(a) $x^p x^{2p} = x^{p+2p} = x^{3p}$

(b) $t^s \div t^{s-1} = t^{s-(s-1)} = t^{s-s+1} = t^1 = t$

(c) $a^2 b^3 a^{-1} b^5 = a^2 a^{-1} b^3 b^5 = a^{2-1} b^{3+5} = a^1 b^8 = a b^8$

(d) Finally,

$$\frac{t^p \cdot t^{q-1}}{t^r \cdot t^{s-1}} = \frac{t^{p+q-1}}{t^{r+s-1}} = t^{p+q-1-(r+s-1)} = t^{p+q-1-r-s+1} = t^{p+q-r-s}$$

EXAMPLE 2.2.2 If $x^{-2} y^3 = 5$, compute $x^{-4} y^6$, $x^6 y^{-9}$, and $x^2 y^{-3} + 2 x^{-10} y^{15}$.

Solution: First, note that $x^{-2} y^3 = 5$ is only possible if $x \neq 0$ and $y \neq 0$. Now, in computing $x^{-4} y^6$, how can we make use of the assumption that $x^{-2} y^3 = 5$? A moment's reflection might lead you to see that $(x^{-2} y^3)^2 = x^{-4} y^6$, and hence $x^{-4} y^6 = 5^2 = 25$. Similarly,

$$x^6 y^{-9} = (x^{-2} y^3)^{-3} = 5^{-3} = 1/125$$

---

[6] An important motivation for introducing the definitions $a^0 = 1$ and $a^{-n} = 1/a^n$ is that we want the properties of powers to be valid for negative and zero exponents as well as for positive ones. For example, we want $a^r \cdot a^s = a^{r+s}$ to be valid when $r = 5$ and $s = 0$. This requires that $a^5 \cdot a^0 = a^{5+0} = a^5$, so we must choose $a^0 = 1$. If $a^n \cdot a^m = a^{n+m}$ is to be valid when $m = -n$, we must have $a^n \cdot a^{-n} = a^{n+(-n)} = a^0 = 1$. Because $a^n \cdot (1/a^n) = 1$, we *must* define a^{-n} to be $1/a^n$.

and
$$x^2y^{-3} + 2x^{-10}y^{15} = (x^{-2}y^3)^{-1} + 2(x^{-2}y^3)^5 = 5^{-1} + 2 \cdot 5^5 = 6250.2$$

EXAMPLE 2.2.3 It is easy to make mistakes when dealing with powers. The following examples highlight some common sources of confusion.

(a) There is an important difference between $(-10)^2 = (-10)(-10) = 100$, and $-10^2 = -(10 \cdot 10) = -100$. The square of minus 10 is not equal to minus the square of 10.

(b) Note that $(2x)^{-1} = 1/(2x)$. Here the product $2x$ is raised to the power of -1. On the other hand, in $2x^{-1}$ only x is raised to the power -1, so $2x^{-1} = 2 \cdot (1/x) = 2/x$.

(c) The volume of a ball with radius r is $\frac{4}{3}\pi r^3$. What will the volume be if the radius is doubled? The new volume is

$$\frac{4}{3}\pi(2r)^3 = \frac{4}{3}\pi(2r)(2r)(2r) = \frac{4}{3}\pi 8r^3 = 8\left(\frac{4}{3}\pi r^3\right)$$

so the volume is 8 times the initial one. If we made the mistake of "simplifying" $(2r)^3$ to $2r^3$, the result would imply only a doubling of the volume; this should be contrary to common sense.

Percentages and Compound Interest

Powers are used in practically every branch of applied mathematics, including economics. To illustrate their use, recall how they are needed to calculate compound interest.

First, recall that the percentage 1% means one in a hundred, or 0.01. So 23%, for example, is $23 \cdot 0.01 = 0.23$. Then we can calculate 23% of 4000 as either $4000 \cdot 23/100 = 920$ or, equivalently, as $4000 \cdot 0.23 = 920$. It may be also be worth pointing out a subtlety of percentages that is often overlooked by those who know rather little mathematics. This is that, for example, it takes an increase of 100% to reverse an earlier decrease of 50%, and a decrease of 50% to offset an earlier increase of 100%.[7]

Now suppose you deposit $1 000 in a bank account paying 8% interest at the end of each year. After one year you will have earned $1 000 \cdot 0.08 = \$80$ in interest, so the total amount in your bank account will be $1 080. This can be rewritten as

$$1000 + \frac{1000 \cdot 8}{100} = 1000\left(1 + \frac{8}{100}\right) = 1000 \cdot 1.08$$

Suppose this new amount of $1 080 is left in the bank for another year at an interest rate of 8%. After a second year, the extra interest will be $1 000 \cdot 1.08 \cdot 0.08$. So the total amount will have grown to

$$1000 \cdot 1.08 + (1000 \cdot 1.08) \cdot 0.08 = 1000 \cdot 1.08(1 + 0.08) = 1000 \cdot (1.08)^2$$

---

[7] Compare review exercise 20 at the end of the chapter.

Extending this argument in an obvious way, we see that each year the amount will increase by the factor 1.08, and that at the end of t years it will have grown to $1\,000 \cdot (1.08)^t$.

If the original amount is $\$K$ and the interest rate is $p\%$ per year, by the end of the first year, the amount will be $K + K \cdot p/100 = K(1 + p/100)$ dollars. The growth factor per year is thus $1 + p/100$. In general, after t (whole) years, the original investment of $\$K$ will have grown to an amount

$$K\left(1 + \frac{p}{100}\right)^t$$

when the interest rate is $p\%$ per year and interest is added to the capital every year—that is, there is compound interest.

This example illustrates a general principle:

EXPONENTIAL GROWTH

A quantity K which increases by $p\%$ per year will have increased after t years to

$$K\left(1 + \frac{p}{100}\right)^t$$

Here $1 + p/100$ is called the *growth factor* for a growth of $p\%$.

If you see an expression like $(1.08)^t$ you should immediately be able to recognize it as the amount to which $\$1$ has grown after t years when the interest rate is 8% per year. How should you interpret $(1.08)^0$? Suppose you deposit $\$1$ at 8% per year, and leave the amount in the account for 0 years. Then you still have only $\$1$, because there has been no time to accumulate any interest. This explains why $(1.08)^0$ must necessarily equal 1.[8]

EXAMPLE 2.2.4 A new car has been bought for $\$30\,000$ and is assumed to decrease in value (depreciate) by 15% per year over a six-year period. What is its value after six years?

Solution: After one year its value is down to

$$30\,000 - \frac{30\,000 \cdot 15}{100} = 30\,000 \cdot \left(1 - \frac{15}{100}\right) = 30\,000 \cdot 0.85 = 25\,500$$

After two years its value is $\$30\,000 \cdot (0.85)^2 = \$21\,675$, and so on. After six years we realize that its value must be $\$30\,000 \cdot (0.85)^6 \approx \$11\,314$.

---

[8] Note that $1000 \cdot (1.08)^5$ is the amount you will have in your account after five years if you invest $\$1\,000$ at 8% interest per year. Using a calculator shows that you will have approximately $\$1\,469.33$. A rather common mistake is to put $1000 \cdot (1.08)^5 = (1000 \cdot 1.08)^5 = (1080)^5$. This is one trillion ($10^{12}$) times the right answer!

This example illustrates a general principle:

EXPONENTIAL DECLINE

A quantity K which decreases by $p\%$ per year will have shrunk after t years to

$$K\left(1 - \frac{p}{100}\right)^t$$

Here $1 - p/100$ is the growth factor that results from a decline of $p\%$ per year. (Note that a growth factor that is less than 1 indicates shrinkage.)

Do We Really Need Negative Exponents?

How much money should you have deposited in a bank five years ago in order to have $1 000 today, given that the interest rate has been 8% per year over this period? If we call this amount x, the requirement is that $x \cdot (1.08)^5$ must equal $1 000, or that $x \cdot (1.08)^5 = 1000$. Dividing by 1.08^5 on both sides yields

$$x = \frac{1000}{(1.08)^5} = 1000 \cdot (1.08)^{-5}$$

which is approximately $681. Thus, $(1.08)^{-5}$ is what you should have deposited five years ago in order to have $1 today, given the constant interest rate of 8%.

In general, $P(1 + p/100)^{-t}$ is what you should have deposited t years ago in order to have $P today, if the interest rate has been $p\%$ every year.

EXERCISES FOR SECTION 2.2

1. Compute the following numbers: (a) 10^3; (b) $(-0.3)^2$; (c) 4^{-2}; and (d) $(0.1)^{-1}$.

2. Write as powers of 2 the following numbers: (a) 4; (b) 1; (c) 64; and (d) 1/16.

3. Write as powers the following numbers:

(a) $15 \cdot 15 \cdot 15$ (b) $\left(-\frac{1}{3}\right)\left(-\frac{1}{3}\right)\left(-\frac{1}{3}\right)$ (c) $\frac{1}{10}$ (d) 0.0000001

(e) $tttttt$ (f) $(a-b)(a-b)(a-b)$ (g) $aabbbb$ (h) $(-a)(-a)(-a)$

4. Expand and simplify the following expressions:

(a) $2^5 \cdot 2^5$ (b) $3^8 \cdot 3^{-2} \cdot 3^{-3}$ (c) $(2x)^3$ (d) $(-3xy^2)^3$

(e) $\dfrac{p^{24} p^3}{p^4 p}$ (f) $\dfrac{a^4 b^{-3}}{(a^2 b^{-3})^2}$ (g) $\dfrac{3^4 (3^2)^6}{(-3)^{15} 3^7}$ (h) $\dfrac{p^\gamma (pq)^\sigma}{p^{2\gamma + \sigma} q^{\sigma - 2}}$

5. Expand and simplify the following expressions:

   (a) $2^0 \cdot 2^1 \cdot 2^2 \cdot 2^3$
   (b) $\left(\dfrac{4}{3}\right)^3$
   (c) $\dfrac{4^2 \cdot 6^2}{3^3 \cdot 2^3}$
   (d) $x^5 x^4$
   (e) $y^5 y^4 y^3$
   (f) $(2xy)^3$
   (g) $\dfrac{10^2 \cdot 10^{-4} \cdot 10^3}{10^0 \cdot 10^{-2} \cdot 10^5}$
   (h) $\dfrac{(k^2)^3 k^4}{(k^3)^2}$
   (i) $\dfrac{(x+1)^3 (x+1)^{-2}}{(x+1)^2 (x+1)^{-3}}$

6. The formula for the surface area of a sphere with radius r is $4\pi r^2$.

   (a) By what factor will the surface area increase if the radius is tripled?

   (b) If the radius increases by 16%, by how many % will the surface area increase?

7. Suppose that a and b are positive, while m and n are integers. Which of the following equalities are true and which are false?

   (a) $a^0 = 0$
   (b) $(a+b)^{-n} = 1/(a+b)^n$
   (c) $a^m \cdot a^m = a^{2m}$
   (d) $a^m \cdot b^m = (ab)^{2m}$
   (e) $(a+b)^m = a^m + b^m$
   (f) $a^n \cdot b^m = (ab)^{n+m}$

8. Complete the following implications:

   (a) $xy = 3 \implies x^3 y^3 = \ldots$
   (b) $ab = -2 \implies (ab)^4 = \ldots$
   (c) $a^2 = 4 \implies (a^8)^0 = \ldots$
   (d) n integer implies $(-1)^{2n} = \ldots$

9. Compute the following: (a) 13% of 150; (b) 6% of 2400; and (c) 5.5% of 200.

10. Give economic interpretations to each of the following expressions and then use a calculator to find the approximate values: (a) $\$50 \cdot (1.11)^8$; (b) €$10\,000 \cdot (1.12)^{20}$; and (c) £$5\,000 \cdot (1.07)^{-10}$.

11. A box containing five balls costs €8.50. If the balls are bought individually, they cost €2.00 each. How much cheaper is it, in percentage terms, to buy the box as opposed to buying five individual balls?

12. (a) £12 000 is deposited in an account earning 4% interest per year. What is the amount after 15 years?

    (b) If the interest rate is 6% each year, how much money should you have deposited in a bank five years ago in order to have £50 000 today?

13. A quantity increases by 25% each year for three years. How much is the combined percentage growth p over the three-year period?

14. A firm's annual profit increased by 20% between the years 2010 and 2011, but then it decreased by 17% between the years 2011 and 2012.

    (a) Which of the two years 2010 and 2012 had the higher annual profit?

    (b) What percentage decrease in profits from 2011 to 2012 would imply that annual profits were equal in the two years 2010 and 2012?

2.3 Rules of Algebra

You are no doubt already familiar with the most common rules of algebra. We have already used some in this chapter. Nevertheless, it may be useful to recall those that are most important.

RULES OF ALGEBRA

If a, b, and c are arbitrary numbers, then:

(a) $a + b = b + a$

(b) $(a + b) + c = a + (b + c)$

(c) $a + 0 = a$

(d) $a + (-a) = 0$

(e) $ab = ba$

(f) $(ab)c = a(bc)$

(g) $1 \cdot a = a$

(h) $aa^{-1} = 1$ for $a \neq 0$

(i) $(-a)b = a(-b) = -ab$

(j) $(-a)(-b) = ab$

(k) $a(b + c) = ab + ac$

(l) $(a + b)c = ac + bc$

EXAMPLE 2.3.1 These rules are used in the following equalities:

(a) $5 + x^2 = x^2 + 5$

(b) $(a + 2b) + 3b = a + (2b + 3b) = a + 5b$

(c) $x \cdot \frac{1}{3} = \frac{1}{3} \cdot x = \frac{1}{3}x$

(d) $(xy)y^{-1} = x(yy^{-1}) = x$

(e) $(-3)5 = 3(-5) = -(3 \cdot 5) = -15$

(f) $(-6)(-20) = 120$

(g) $3x(y + 2z) = 3xy + 6xz$

(h) $(t^2 + 2t)4t^3 = t^2 4t^3 + 2t 4t^3 = 4t^5 + 8t^4$

The rules of algebra specified in the previous box can be combined in several ways to give, for example:

$$a(b - c) = a[b + (-c)] = ab + a(-c) = ab - ac$$

which implies, when $b = c$, that $a \cdot 0 = a(b - b) = ab - ab = 0$

$$x(a + b - c + d) = xa + xb - xc + xd$$

$$(a + b)(c + d) = ac + ad + bc + bd$$

Figure 2.3.1 provides a geometric argument for the last of these algebraic rules for the case in which the numbers a, b, c, and d are all positive. The rule says that the area $(a + b)(c + d)$ of the large rectangle is the sum of the areas of the four small rectangles.

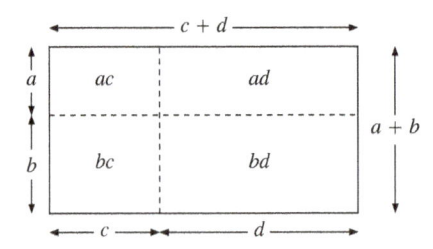

Figure 2.3.1 $(a+b)(c+d) = ac + ad + bc + bd$

The following three rules are so often used that you should definitely memorize them.

QUADRATIC IDENTITIES

$$(a+b)^2 = a^2 + 2ab + b^2$$
$$(a-b)^2 = a^2 - 2ab + b^2$$
$$a^2 - b^2 = (a+b)(a-b)$$

The last of these is called the *difference-of-squares formula*. The proofs are very easy. For example, $(a+b)^2$ means $(a+b)(a+b)$, which equals $aa + ab + ba + bb = a^2 + 2ab + b^2$.

EXAMPLE 2.3.2 Expand the following expressions:

(a) $(3x+2y)^2$ (b) $(1-2z)^2$ (c) $(4p+5q)(4p-5q)$

Solution:

(a) $(3x+2y)^2 = (3x)^2 + 2(3x)(2y) + (2y)^2 = 9x^2 + 12xy + 4y^2$
(b) $(1-2z)^2 = 1 - 2 \cdot 1 \cdot 2 \cdot z + (2z)^2 = 1 - 4z + 4z^2$
(c) $(4p+5q)(4p-5q) = (4p)^2 - (5q)^2 = 16p^2 - 25q^2$

We often encounter parentheses with a minus sign in front. Because $(-1)x = -x$, we have

$$-(a+b-c+d) = -a - b + c - d$$

In words: *When removing a pair of parentheses with a minus in front, change the signs of all the terms within the parentheses—do not leave any out.*

We saw how to multiply two factors such as $(a+b)$ and $(c+d)$. How do we compute products like this when there are several factors? Here is an example:

$$(a+b)(c+d)(e+f) = [(a+b)(c+d)](e+f)$$
$$= (ac + ad + bc + bd)(e+f)$$
$$= (ac + ad + bc + bd)e + (ac + ad + bc + bd)f$$
$$= ace + ade + bce + bde + acf + adf + bcf + bdf$$

EXAMPLE 2.3.3 Expand the expression $(r+1)^3$. Use the solution to compute by how much the volume of a ball with radius r metres expands if the radius increases by one metre.

Solution:

$$(r+1)^3 = [(r+1)(r+1)](r+1) = (r^2 + 2r + 1)(r+1) = r^3 + 3r^2 + 3r + 1$$

A ball with radius r metres has a volume of $\frac{4}{3}\pi r^3$ cubic metres. If the radius increases by one metre, its volume expands by

$$\tfrac{4}{3}\pi(r+1)^3 - \tfrac{4}{3}\pi r^3 = \tfrac{4}{3}\pi(r^3 + 3r^2 + 3r + 1) - \tfrac{4}{3}\pi r^3 = \tfrac{4}{3}\pi(3r^2 + 3r + 1)$$

Algebraic Expressions

Expressions involving letters such as $3xy - 5x^2y^3 + 2xy + 6y^3x^2 - 3x + 5yx + 8$ are called *algebraic expressions*. We call $3xy$, $-5x^2y^3$, $2xy$, $6y^3x^2$, $-3x$, $5yx$, and 8 the *terms* in the expression that is formed by adding all the terms together. The numbers 3, -5, 2, 6, -3, and 5 are the *numerical coefficients* of the first six terms. Two terms where only the numerical coefficients are different, such as $-5x^2y^3$ and $6y^3x^2$, are called *terms of the same type*. In order to simplify expressions, we collect terms of the same type. Then within each term, we put any numerical coefficients at the front, succeeded by the letters in alphabetical order. Thus,

$$3xy - 5x^2y^3 + 2xy + 6y^3x^2 - 3x + 5yx + 8 = x^2y^3 + 10xy - 3x + 8$$

EXAMPLE 2.3.4 Expand and simplify the expression:

$$(2pq - 3p^2)(p + 2q) - (q^2 - 2pq)(2p - q)$$

Solution: The expression equals

$$2pqp + 2pq2q - 3p^3 - 6p^2q - (q^22p - q^3 - 4pqp + 2pq^2)$$
$$= 2p^2q + 4pq^2 - 3p^3 - 6p^2q - 2pq^2 + q^3 + 4p^2q - 2pq^2$$
$$= -3p^3 + q^3$$

Factoring

When we write $49 = 7 \cdot 7$ and $672 = 2 \cdot 2 \cdot 2 \cdot 2 \cdot 3 \cdot 7$, we have factored the two numbers 49 and 672 respectively. Algebraic expressions can often be factored in a similar way: to *factor an expression* means to express it as a product of simpler factors. For example, $6x^2y = 2 \cdot 3 \cdot x \cdot x \cdot y$ and $5x^2y^3 - 15xy^2 = 5 \cdot x \cdot y \cdot y(xy - 3)$.[9]

---

[9] Note that $9x^2 - 25y^2 = 3 \cdot 3 \cdot x \cdot x - 5 \cdot 5 \cdot y \cdot y$ does *not* factor $9x^2 - 25y^2$. A correct factoring is $9x^2 - 25y^2 = (3x - 5y)(3x + 5y)$.

EXAMPLE 2.3.5 Factor each of the following expressions:

(a) $5x^2 + 15x$

(b) $-18b^2 + 9ab$

(c) $K(1+r) + K(1+r)r$

(d) $\delta L^{-3} + (1-\delta)L^{-2}$

Solution:

(a) $5x^2 + 15x = 5x(x+3)$
(b) $-18b^2 + 9ab = 9ab - 18b^2 = 3 \cdot 3b(a - 2b)$
(c) $K(1+r) + K(1+r)r = K(1+r)(1+r) = K(1+r)^2$
(d) $\delta L^{-3} + (1-\delta)L^{-2} = L^{-3}[\delta + (1-\delta)L]$

The quadratic identities can often be used in reverse for factoring. They sometimes enable us to factor expressions that otherwise appear to have no factors.

EXAMPLE 2.3.6 Factor each of the following expressions:

(a) $16a^2 - 1$

(b) $x^2y^2 - 25z^2$

(c) $4u^2 + 8u + 4$

(d) $x^2 - x + \frac{1}{4}$

Solution:

(a) $16a^2 - 1 = (4a+1)(4a-1)$
(b) $x^2y^2 - 25z^2 = (xy + 5z)(xy - 5z)$
(c) $4u^2 + 8u + 4 = 4(u^2 + 2u + 1) = 4(u+1)^2$
(d) $x^2 - x + \frac{1}{4} = (x - \frac{1}{2})^2$

Sometimes finding a factoring requires a little inventiveness, as in this example:

$$\begin{aligned}4x^2 - y^2 + 6x^2 + 3xy &= (4x^2 - y^2) + 3x(2x+y)\\ &= (2x+y)(2x-y) + 3x(2x+y)\\ &= (2x+y)(2x - y + 3x)\\ &= (2x+y)(5x - y)\end{aligned}$$

Although it might be difficult, perhaps even impossible, to factor a given algebraic expression, it is very easy to verify a suggested factoring: simply multiply the factors. For example, one can simply expand $(x-a)(x-b)$ to check that

$$x^2 - (a+b)x + ab = (x-a)(x-b)$$

Most algebraic expressions *cannot* be factored. For example, there is no way to write $x^2 + 10x + 50$ as a product of simpler factors.[10]

---

[10] Unless we introduce "complex" numbers, that is.

EXERCISES FOR SECTION 2.3

1. Expand and simplify the following expressions:

   (a) $-3 + (-4) - (-8)$
   (b) $(-3)(2-4)$
   (c) $(-3)(-12)(-\frac{1}{2})$
   (d) $-3[4-(-2)]$
   (e) $-3(-x-4)$
   (f) $(5x-3y)9$
   (g) $2x\left(\dfrac{3}{2x}\right)$
   (h) $0 \cdot (1-x)$
   (i) $-7x\dfrac{2}{14x}$

2. Expand and simplify the following expressions:

   (a) $5a^2 - 3b - (-a^2 - b) - 3(a^2 + b)$
   (b) $-x(2x-y) + y(1-x) + 3(x+y)$
   (c) $12t^2 - 3t + 16 - 2(6t^2 - 2t + 8)$
   (d) $r^3 - 3r^2s + s^3 - (-s^3 - r^3 + 3r^2s)$

3. Expand and simplify the following expressions:

   (a) $-3(n^2 - 2n + 3)$
   (b) $x^2(1 + x^3)$
   (c) $(4n-3)(n-2)$
   (d) $6a^2b(5ab - 3ab^2)$
   (e) $(a^2b - ab^2)(a+b)$
   (f) $(x-y)(x-2y)(x-3y)$
   (g) $(ax+b)(cx+d)$
   (h) $(2-t^2)(2+t^2)$
   (i) $(u-v)^2(u+v)^2$

(SM) 4. Expand and simplify the following expressions:

   (a) $(2t-1)(t^2 - 2t + 1)$
   (b) $(a+1)^2 + (a-1)^2 - 2(a+1)(a-1)$
   (c) $(x+y+z)^2$
   (d) $(x+y+z)^2 - (x-y-z)^2$

5. Expand the following expressions:

   (a) $(x+2y)^2$
   (b) $\left(\dfrac{1}{x} - x\right)^2$
   (c) $(3u - 5v)^2$
   (d) $(2z - 5w)(2z + 5w)$

6. Complete the following expressions:

   (a) $201^2 - 199^2 =$
   (b) If $u^2 - 4u + 4 = 1$, then $u =$
   (c) $\dfrac{(a+1)^2 - (a-1)^2}{(b+1)^2 - (b-1)^2} =$

7. Compute $1000^2/(252^2 - 248^2)$ without using a calculator.

8. Verify the following cubic identities, which are occasionally useful:

   (a) $(a+b)^3 = a^3 + 3a^2b + 3ab^2 + b^3$
   (b) $(a-b)^3 = a^3 - 3a^2b + 3ab^2 - b^3$
   (c) $a^3 - b^3 = (a-b)(a^2 + ab + b^2)$
   (d) $a^3 + b^3 = (a+b)(a^2 - ab + b^2)$

9. Factor the following expressions:

   (a) $21x^2y^3$
   (b) $3x - 9y + 27z$
   (c) $a^3 - a^2b$
   (d) $8x^2y^2 - 16xy$
   (e) $28a^2b^3$
   (f) $4x + 8y - 24z$
   (g) $2x^2 - 6xy$
   (h) $4a^2b^3 + 6a^3b^2$
   (i) $7x^2 - 49xy$
   (j) $5xy^2 - 45x^3y^2$
   (k) $16 - b^2$
   (l) $3x^2 - 12$

10. Factor the following expressions:

(a) $a^2 + 4ab + 4b^2$ (b) $K^2L - L^2K$ (c) $K^{-4} - LK^{-5}$

(d) $9z^2 - 16w^2$ (e) $-\frac{1}{5}x^2 + 2xy - 5y^2$ (f) $a^4 - b^4$

11. Factor the following expressions:

(a) $x^2 - 4x + 4$ (b) $4t^2s - 8ts^2$ (c) $16a^2 + 16ab + 4b^2$

(d) $5x^3 - 10xy^2$ (e) $5x + 5y + ax + ay$ (f) $u^2 - v^2 + 3v + 3u$

(g) $P^3 + Q^3 + Q^2P + P^2Q$ (h) $K^3 - K^2L$ (i) $KL^3 + KL$

(j) $L^2 - K^2$ (k) $K^2 - 2KL + L^2$ (l) $K^3L - 4K^2L^2 + 4KL^3$

2.4 Fractions

Recall that

$$a \div b = \frac{a}{b} \quad \begin{matrix} \leftarrow \text{numerator} \\ \leftarrow \text{denominator} \end{matrix}$$

For example, $5 \div 8 = \frac{5}{8}$. For typographical reasons we often write 5/8 instead of $\frac{5}{8}$. Of course, we can write $5 \div 8 = 0.625$ to express the fraction as a decimal number. The fraction 5/8 is called a *proper fraction* because 5 is less than 8. The fraction 19/8 is an *improper fraction* because the numerator is larger than (or equal to) the denominator. An improper fraction can be written as a *mixed number*:[11]

$$\frac{19}{8} = 2 + \frac{3}{8} = 2\frac{3}{8}$$

The most important properties of fractions are listed below, followed by simple numerical examples. It is absolutely essential for you to master these rules, so you should carefully check that you both know and understand each of them.

PROPERTIES OF FRACTIONS

Let a, b, and c be any numbers, with the proviso that b, c, and d are $\neq 0$ whenever they appear in a denominator. Then,

(a) $\dfrac{a \cdot \cancel{c}}{b \cdot \cancel{c}} = \dfrac{a}{b}$

(b) $\dfrac{-a}{-b} = \dfrac{(-a) \cdot (-1)}{(-b) \cdot (-1)} = \dfrac{a}{b}$

(c) $-\dfrac{a}{b} = (-1)\dfrac{a}{b} = \dfrac{(-1)a}{b} = \dfrac{-a}{b}$

(d) $\dfrac{a}{c} + \dfrac{b}{c} = \dfrac{a+b}{c}$

(e) $\dfrac{a}{b} + \dfrac{c}{d} = \dfrac{a \cdot d + b \cdot c}{b \cdot d}$

(f) $a + \dfrac{b}{c} = \dfrac{a \cdot c + b}{c}$

(g) $a \cdot \dfrac{b}{c} = \dfrac{a \cdot b}{c}$

(h) $\dfrac{a}{b} \cdot \dfrac{c}{d} = \dfrac{a \cdot c}{b \cdot d}$

(i) $\dfrac{a}{b} \div \dfrac{c}{d} = \dfrac{a}{b} \cdot \dfrac{d}{c} = \dfrac{a \cdot d}{b \cdot c}$

---

[11] Here $2\frac{3}{8}$ means 2 plus $\frac{3}{8}$. On the other hand, $2 \cdot \frac{3}{8} = \frac{2 \cdot 3}{8} = \frac{3}{4}$ (by the rules reviewed in what follows). Note, however, that $2\frac{x}{8}$ also means $2 \cdot \frac{x}{8}$; the notation $\frac{2x}{8}$ or $2x/8$ is obviously preferable in this case. Indeed, $\frac{19}{8}$ or 19/8 is probably better than $2\frac{3}{8}$ because it also helps avoid ambiguity.

SECTION 2.4 / FRACTIONS 39

EXAMPLE 2.4.1 The following expressions illustrate the nine properties of fractions, one by one:

(a) $\dfrac{21}{15} = \dfrac{7 \cdot 3}{5 \cdot 3} = \dfrac{7}{5}$ (b) $\dfrac{-5}{-6} = \dfrac{5}{6}$

(c) $-\dfrac{13}{15} = (-1)\dfrac{13}{15} = \dfrac{(-1)13}{15} = \dfrac{-13}{15}$ (d) $\dfrac{5}{3} + \dfrac{13}{3} = \dfrac{18}{3} = 6$

(e) $\dfrac{3}{5} + \dfrac{1}{6} = \dfrac{3 \cdot 6 + 5 \cdot 1}{5 \cdot 6} = \dfrac{23}{30}$ (f) $5 + \dfrac{3}{5} = \dfrac{5 \cdot 5 + 3}{5} = \dfrac{28}{5}$

(g) $7 \cdot \dfrac{3}{5} = \dfrac{21}{5}$ (h) $\dfrac{4}{7} \cdot \dfrac{5}{8} = \dfrac{4 \cdot 5}{7 \cdot 8} = \dfrac{4 \cdot 5}{7 \cdot 2 \cdot 4} = \dfrac{5}{14}$

(i) $\dfrac{3}{8} \div \dfrac{6}{14} = \dfrac{3}{8} \cdot \dfrac{14}{6} = \dfrac{3 \cdot 2 \cdot 7}{2 \cdot 2 \cdot 2 \cdot 3} = \dfrac{7}{8}$

Of the nine properties in the box above, property (a) is especially important. It is the rule used to reduce fractions by factoring the numerator and the denominator, then cancelling *common factors*—that is, dividing both the numerator and denominator by the same nonzero quantity.[12]

EXAMPLE 2.4.2 Simplify the expressions:

(a) $\dfrac{5x^2yz^3}{25xy^2z}$ (b) $\dfrac{x^2 + xy}{x^2 - y^2}$ (c) $\dfrac{4 - 4a + a^2}{a^2 - 4}$

Solution: For (a), note that

$$\dfrac{5x^2yz^3}{25xy^2z} = \dfrac{5 \cdot x \cdot x \cdot y \cdot z \cdot z \cdot z}{5 \cdot 5 \cdot x \cdot y \cdot y \cdot z} = \dfrac{xz^2}{5y}$$

For (b),

$$\dfrac{x^2 + xy}{x^2 - y^2} = \dfrac{x(x+y)}{(x-y)(x+y)} = \dfrac{x}{x-y}$$

and for (c)

$$\dfrac{4 - 4a + a^2}{a^2 - 4} = \dfrac{(a-2)(a-2)}{(a-2)(a+2)} = \dfrac{a-2}{a+2}$$

EXAMPLE 2.4.3 When we simplify fractions, only *common* factors can be removed. A frequently occurring error is illustrated in the following expression:

Wrong! → $\dfrac{2x + 3y}{xy} = \dfrac{2 + 3y}{y} = \dfrac{2 + 3}{1} = 5$

In fact, the numerator and the denominator in the fraction $(2x + 3y)/xy$ do not have any common factors. But a correct simplification is this: $(2x + 3y)/xy = 2/y + 3/x$.

Another common error is:

Wrong! → $\dfrac{x}{x^2 + 2x} = \dfrac{x}{x^2} + \dfrac{x}{2x} = \dfrac{1}{x} + \dfrac{1}{2}$

A correct way of simplifying the fraction is to cancel the common factor x, which yields the fraction $1/(x+2)$.

---

[12] When we use property (a) in reverse, we are *expanding* the fraction. For example, $5/8 = 5 \cdot 125/8 \cdot 125 = 625/1000 = 0.625$.

Properties (d), (e), and (f) in the previous box are those used to add fractions. Note that we can derive (e) from (a) and (d). Indeed:

$$\frac{a}{b} + \frac{c}{d} = \frac{a \cdot d}{b \cdot d} + \frac{c \cdot b}{d \cdot b} = \frac{a \cdot d + b \cdot c}{b \cdot d}$$

An easy extension shows that, for example,

$$\frac{a}{b} - \frac{c}{d} + \frac{e}{f} = \frac{adf}{bdf} - \frac{cbf}{bdf} + \frac{ebd}{bdf} = \frac{adf - cbf + ebd}{bdf} \quad (*)$$

If the numbers b, d, and f have common factors, the computation carried out in $(*)$ involves unnecessarily large numbers. We can simplify the process by first finding the *least* or *lowest common denominator*, or LCD, of the fractions. To do so, factor each denominator completely; the LCD is the product of all the distinct factors that appear in any denominator, each raised to the highest power to which it gets raised in any denominator. The use of the LCD is demonstrated in the following example.

EXAMPLE 2.4.4   Simplify the following expressions:

(a) $\dfrac{1}{2} - \dfrac{1}{3} + \dfrac{1}{6}$ (b) $\dfrac{2+a}{a^2 b} + \dfrac{1-b}{ab^2} - \dfrac{2b}{a^2 b^2}$ (c) $\dfrac{x-y}{x+y} - \dfrac{x}{x-y} + \dfrac{3xy}{x^2 - y^2}$

Solution:

(a) Because $6 = 2 \cdot 3$, the LCD is 6, and so

$$\frac{1}{2} - \frac{1}{3} + \frac{1}{6} = \frac{1 \cdot 3}{2 \cdot 3} - \frac{1 \cdot 2}{2 \cdot 3} + \frac{1}{2 \cdot 3} = \frac{3 - 2 + 1}{6} = \frac{2}{6} = \frac{1}{3}$$

(b) Here the LCD is $a^2 b^2$, and so

$$\frac{2+a}{a^2 b} + \frac{1-b}{ab^2} - \frac{2b}{a^2 b^2} = \frac{(2+a)b}{a^2 b^2} + \frac{(1-b)a}{a^2 b^2} - \frac{2b}{a^2 b^2} = \frac{2b + ab + a - ba - 2b}{a^2 b^2}$$

$$= \frac{a}{a^2 b^2} = \frac{1}{ab^2}$$

(c) Because $x^2 - y^2 = (x+y)(x-y)$, the LCD is $(x+y)(x-y)$, and so

$$\frac{x-y}{x+y} - \frac{x}{x-y} + \frac{3xy}{x^2 - y^2} = \frac{(x-y)(x-y)}{(x-y)(x+y)} - \frac{(x+y)x}{(x+y)(x-y)} + \frac{3xy}{(x-y)(x+y)}$$

$$= \frac{x^2 - 2xy + y^2 - x^2 - xy + 3xy}{(x-y)(x+y)}$$

$$= \frac{y^2}{x^2 - y^2}$$

The expression $1 - \frac{5-3}{2}$ means that from the number 1, we subtract the number $\frac{5-3}{2} = \frac{2}{2} = 1$, so $1 - \frac{5-3}{2} = 0$. Alternatively,

$$1 - \frac{5-3}{2} = \frac{2}{2} - \frac{(5-3)}{2} = \frac{2 - (5-3)}{2} = \frac{2 - 5 + 3}{2} = \frac{0}{2} = 0$$

In the same way,

$$\frac{2+b}{ab^2} - \frac{a-2}{a^2b}$$

means that we subtract $(a-2)/a^2b$ from $(2+b)/ab^2$:

$$\frac{2+b}{ab^2} - \frac{a-2}{a^2b} = \frac{(2+b)a}{a^2b^2} - \frac{(a-2)b}{a^2b^2} = \frac{(2+b)a - (a-2)b}{a^2b^2} = \frac{2(a+b)}{a^2b^2}$$

It is a good idea first to enclose in parentheses the numerators of the fractions, as in the next example.

EXAMPLE 2.4.5 Simplify the expression:

$$\frac{x-1}{x+1} - \frac{1-x}{x-1} - \frac{-1+4x}{2(x+1)}$$

Solution:

$$\frac{x-1}{x+1} - \frac{1-x}{x-1} - \frac{-1+4x}{2(x+1)} = \frac{(x-1)}{x+1} - \frac{(1-x)}{x-1} - \frac{(-1+4x)}{2(x+1)}$$

$$= \frac{2(x-1)^2 - 2(1-x)(x+1) - (-1+4x)(x-1)}{2(x+1)(x-1)}$$

$$= \frac{2(x^2-2x+1) - 2(1-x^2) - (4x^2-5x+1)}{2(x+1)(x-1)}$$

$$= \frac{x-1}{2(x+1)(x-1)} = \frac{1}{2(x+1)}$$

Next, we prove property (i) in the previous box by writing $(a/b) \div (c/d)$ as a ratio of fractions:

$$\frac{a}{b} \div \frac{c}{d} = \frac{\frac{a}{b}}{\frac{c}{d}} = \frac{b \cdot d \cdot \frac{a}{b}}{b \cdot d \cdot \frac{c}{d}} = \frac{\cancel{b} \cdot d \cdot a}{b \cdot \cancel{d} \cdot c} = \frac{d \cdot a}{b \cdot c} = \frac{a \cdot d}{b \cdot c}$$

When we deal with fractions of fractions, we should be sure to emphasize which is the fraction line of the dominant fraction. For example,

$$\frac{a}{\frac{b}{c}} = a \div \frac{b}{c} = \frac{ac}{b} \qquad (*)$$

whereas

$$\frac{\frac{a}{b}}{c} = \frac{a}{b} \div c = \frac{a}{bc} \qquad (**)$$

Of course, it is safer to write $\frac{a}{b/c}$ or $a/(b/c)$ in the first case, and $\frac{a/b}{c}$ or $(a/b)/c$ in the second case.[13]

---

[13] As a numerical example of (∗) and (∗∗), note that $\frac{1}{\frac{3}{5}} = \frac{5}{3}$, whereas $\frac{\frac{1}{3}}{5} = \frac{1}{15}$.

EXERCISES FOR SECTION 2.4

1. Simplify the following expressions:

(a) $\dfrac{3}{7} + \dfrac{4}{7} - \dfrac{5}{7}$ (b) $\dfrac{3}{4} + \dfrac{4}{3} - 1$ (c) $\dfrac{3}{12} - \dfrac{1}{24}$ (d) $\dfrac{1}{5} - \dfrac{2}{25} - \dfrac{3}{75}$

(e) $3\dfrac{3}{5} - 1\dfrac{4}{5}$ (f) $\dfrac{3}{5} \cdot \dfrac{5}{6}$ (g) $\left(\dfrac{3}{5} \div \dfrac{2}{15}\right) \cdot \dfrac{1}{9}$ (h) $\left(\dfrac{2}{3} + \dfrac{1}{4}\right) \div \left(\dfrac{3}{4} + \dfrac{3}{2}\right)$

2. Simplify the following expressions:

(a) $\dfrac{x}{10} - \dfrac{3x}{10} + \dfrac{17x}{10}$ (b) $\dfrac{9a}{10} - \dfrac{a}{2} + \dfrac{a}{5}$ (c) $\dfrac{b+2}{10} - \dfrac{3b}{15} + \dfrac{b}{10}$

(d) $\dfrac{x+2}{3} + \dfrac{1-3x}{4}$ (e) $\dfrac{3}{2b} - \dfrac{5}{3b}$ (f) $\dfrac{3a-2}{3a} - \dfrac{2b-1}{2b} + \dfrac{4b+3a}{6ab}$

3. Cancel common factors in the following expressions:

(a) $\dfrac{325}{625}$ (b) $\dfrac{8a^2b^3c}{64abc^3}$ (c) $\dfrac{2a^2 - 2b^2}{3a + 3b}$ (d) $\dfrac{P^3 - PQ^2}{(P+Q)^2}$

4. If $x = 3/7$ and $y = 1/14$, find the simplest forms of the following fractions:

(a) $x + y$ (b) $\dfrac{x}{y}$ (c) $\dfrac{x-y}{x+y}$ (d) $13\dfrac{2x - 3y}{2x + 1}$

(SM) 5. Simplify the following expressions:

(a) $\dfrac{1}{x-2} - \dfrac{1}{x+2}$ (b) $\dfrac{6x+25}{4x+2} - \dfrac{6x^2+x-2}{4x^2-1}$ (c) $\dfrac{18b^2}{a^2-9b^2} - \dfrac{a}{a+3b} + 2$

(d) $\dfrac{1}{8ab} - \dfrac{1}{8b(a+2)}$ (e) $\dfrac{2t-t^2}{t+2} \cdot \left(\dfrac{5t}{t-2} - \dfrac{2t}{t-2}\right)$ (f) $2 - \dfrac{a\left(1 - \frac{1}{2a}\right)}{0.25}$

(SM) 6. Simplify the following expressions:

(a) $\dfrac{2}{x} + \dfrac{1}{x+1} - 3$ (b) $\dfrac{t}{2t+1} - \dfrac{t}{2t-1}$ (c) $\dfrac{3x}{x+2} - \dfrac{4x}{2-x} - \dfrac{2x-1}{x^2-4}$

(d) $\dfrac{1/x + 1/y}{1/xy}$ (e) $\dfrac{1/x^2 - 1/y^2}{1/x^2 + 1/y^2}$ (f) $\dfrac{a/x - a/y}{a/x + a/y}$

7. Verify that $x^2 + 2xy - 3y^2 = (x+3y)(x-y)$, and then simplify the expression:

$$\dfrac{x-y}{x^2 + 2xy - 3y^2} - \dfrac{2}{x-y} - \dfrac{7}{x+3y}$$

(SM) 8. Simplify the following expressions:

(a) $\left(\dfrac{1}{4} - \dfrac{1}{5}\right)^{-2}$ (b) $n - \dfrac{n}{1 - \frac{1}{n}}$ (c) $\dfrac{1}{1+x^{p-q}} + \dfrac{1}{1+x^{q-p}}$

(d) $\dfrac{\dfrac{1}{x-1} + \dfrac{1}{x^2-1}}{x - \dfrac{2}{x+1}}$ (e) $\dfrac{\dfrac{1}{(x+h)^2} - \dfrac{1}{x^2}}{h}$ (f) $\dfrac{\dfrac{10x^2}{x^2-1}}{\dfrac{5x}{x+1}}$

2.5 Fractional Powers

Textbooks and research articles in economics frequently include mathematical expressions involving powers with fractional exponents such as $K^{1/4}L^{3/4}$ and $Ar^{2.08}p^{-1.5}$. How do we define a^x when x is a rational number? Of course, we would like the usual rules for powers still to apply.

You probably know the meaning of a^x if $x = 1/2$. In fact, if a is nonnegative and $x = 1/2$, then we define $a^x = a^{1/2}$ as equal to $\sqrt{a}$, the *square root* of a. Thus, $a^{1/2} = \sqrt{a}$ is defined as the nonnegative number that when multiplied by itself gives a. This definition makes sense because $a^{1/2} \cdot a^{1/2} = a^{1/2+1/2} = a^1 = a$. Note that any real number r multiplied by itself must always be nonnegative, whether r is positive, negative, or zero. Hence, if $a \geq 0$,

$$a^{1/2} = \sqrt{a}$$

For example, $\sqrt{16} = 16^{1/2} = 4$ because $4^2 = 16$, whereas $\sqrt{1/25} = 1/5$ because $(1/5)^2 = (1/5) \cdot (1/5) = 1/25$.

PROPERTIES OF SQUARE ROOTS

(i) If a and b are nonnegative numbers, then $\sqrt{ab} = \sqrt{a}\sqrt{b}$.

(ii) If a is nonnegative and b is positive, then $\sqrt{\dfrac{a}{b}} = \dfrac{\sqrt{a}}{\sqrt{b}}$.

Of course, these two rules can also be written as $(ab)^{1/2} = a^{1/2}b^{1/2}$ and $(a/b)^{1/2} = a^{1/2}/b^{1/2}$. For example, $\sqrt{16 \cdot 25} = \sqrt{16} \cdot \sqrt{25} = 4 \cdot 5 = 20$, and $\sqrt{9/4} = \sqrt{9}/\sqrt{4} = 3/2$.

Note that formulas (i) and (ii) are not valid if a or b or both are negative. For example, $\sqrt{(-1)(-1)} = \sqrt{1} = 1$, whereas $\sqrt{-1} \cdot \sqrt{-1}$ is not defined (unless one uses complex numbers).

It is important to recall that, in general, $(a+b)^r \neq a^r + b^r$. For $r = 1/2$, this implies that we generally have[14]

$$\sqrt{a+b} \neq \sqrt{a} + \sqrt{b}$$

Note also that $(-2)^2 = 4$ and $2^2 = 4$, so both $x = -2$ and $x = 2$ are solutions of the equation $x^2 = 4$. Therefore we have $x^2 = 4$ if and only if $x = \pm\sqrt{4} = \pm 2$. Note, however, that the symbol $\sqrt{4}$ means *only* 2, not -2.

We can use a calculator to find that $\sqrt{2} \div \sqrt{3} \approx 1.414 \div 1.732 \approx 0.816$. Yet doing the calculation this way is unnecessarily tedious because it involves two different approximate square roots, at least one of which needs to be stored somewhere part way through. A simpler alternative finds that $\sqrt{2} \div \sqrt{3} = \sqrt{2 \div 3} \approx \sqrt{0.667} \approx 0.817$. Suppose, however, that we "rationalize the denominator" by multiplying both numerator and denominator by

---

[14] The following observation illustrates just how frequently this fact is overlooked: During an examination in a basic course in mathematics for economists, 22% of students simplified $\sqrt{1/16 + 1/25}$ incorrectly and claimed that it was equal to $1/4 + 1/5 = 9/20 = 0.45$. It is actually equal to $\sqrt{(25/400) + (16/400)} = \sqrt{41/400} = \sqrt{41}/20 \approx 0.32$.

the same term ($\sqrt{3}$) in order to remove all square roots from the denominator. The process is then easier because it involves only one square root:

$$\frac{\sqrt{2}}{\sqrt{3}} = \frac{\sqrt{2} \cdot \sqrt{3}}{\sqrt{3} \cdot \sqrt{3}} = \frac{\sqrt{2 \cdot 3}}{3} = \frac{\sqrt{6}}{3} \approx \frac{2.449}{3} \approx 0.816$$

Sometimes the difference-of-squares formula of Section 2.3 can be used to eliminate square roots from the denominator of a fraction. Here is an example:

$$\frac{1}{\sqrt{5}+\sqrt{3}} = \frac{\sqrt{5}-\sqrt{3}}{\left(\sqrt{5}+\sqrt{3}\right)\left(\sqrt{5}-\sqrt{3}\right)} = \frac{\sqrt{5}-\sqrt{3}}{5-3} = \frac{1}{2}\left(\sqrt{5}-\sqrt{3}\right)$$

The nth Root

What do we mean by $a^{1/n}$, where n is a natural number, and a is positive? For example, what does $5^{1/3}$ mean? Suppose we insist that the second property $(a^r)^s = a^{rs}$ of powers that we introduced in Section 2.2 should still apply here. Then we must have $(5^{1/3})^3 = 5^1 = 5$, which implies that $x = 5^{1/3}$ must solve the equation $x^3 = 5$. It can be shown that this kind of equation has a unique positive solution which we denote by $\sqrt[3]{5}$, the *cube root* of 5. Therefore, we must define $5^{1/3}$ as $\sqrt[3]{5}$.

In general, one has $(a^{1/n})^n = a^1 = a$. Thus, we should define the fractional power $x = a^{1/n}$ so that it solves $x^n = a$. Again, this equation can be shown to have a unique positive solution.[15] This solution we denote by $\sqrt[n]{a}$, the *nth root* of a, implying that:

$$\sqrt[n]{a} = a^{1/n}$$

THE nTH ROOT

If a is positive and n is a natural number, then $\sqrt[n]{a}$ is the unique positive number that, raised to the nth power, gives a—that is,

$$\left(\sqrt[n]{a}\right)^n = a$$

EXAMPLE 2.5.1 Compute the following fractional powers:

(a) $\sqrt[3]{27}$ (b) $(1/32)^{1/5}$ (c) $(0.0001)^{0.25} = (0.0001)^{1/4}$

Solution:

(a) $\sqrt[3]{27} = 3$, because $3^3 = 27$
(b) $(1/32)^{1/5} = 1/2$ because $(1/2)^5 = 1/32$
(c) $(0.0001)^{1/4} = 0.1$ because $(0.1)^4 = 0.0001$

---

[15] Following Example 7.10.3, one way to prove this uses the intermediate value theorem, a result which appears later as Theorem 7.10.1. Examples 2.6.4 and 2.10.3 later in this chapter suggest alternative proofs, first of uniqueness, then of existence.

EXAMPLE 2.5.2
An amount $5\,000$ in an account has increased to $10\,000$ in 15 years. What constant yearly interest rate p has been used?

Solution: After 15 years the amount of $5\,000$ has grown to $5000(1+p/100)^{15}$, so we have the equation

$$5000\left(1+\frac{p}{100}\right)^{15} = 10\,000$$

or, equivalently,

$$\left(1+\frac{p}{100}\right)^{15} = 2$$

In general, $(a^t)^{1/t} = a^1 = a$ for $t \neq 0$. Raising each side to the power of 1/15 yields

$$1+\frac{p}{100} = 2^{1/15}$$

or $p = 100(2^{1/15} - 1)$. With a calculator we find $p \approx 4.73$.

We proceed to define $a^{p/q}$ whenever p is an integer, q is a natural number, and a is positive. Consider first $5^{2/3}$. We have already defined $5^{1/3}$. We now define $5^{2/3}$ in order to satisfy once again the second property of powers set out in Section 2.2, namely that $(a^r)^s = a^{rs}$. In the case considered here, this requires that $5^{2/3} = (5^{1/3})^2$. So we must define $5^{2/3}$ as $\left(\sqrt[3]{5}\right)^2$.

In general, for any positive number a, whenever p is an integer and q is a natural number, we define

$$a^{p/q} = \left(a^{1/q}\right)^p = \left(\sqrt[q]{a}\right)^p$$

Using the second property of powers yet again, this definition implies that

$$a^{p/q} = \left(a^{1/q}\right)^p = \left(a^p\right)^{1/q} = \sqrt[q]{a^p}$$

Thus, to compute $a^{p/q}$, we could: either first take the qth root of a and then raise the result to the power p; or first raise a to the power p and then take the qth root of the result. We obtain the same answer either way.[16] For example,

$$4^{7/2} = (4^7)^{1/2} = 16384^{1/2} = 128 = 2^7 = (4^{1/2})^7$$

EXAMPLE 2.5.3
Compute the numbers:

(a) $16^{3/2}$ (b) $16^{-1.25}$ (c) $\left(\frac{1}{27}\right)^{-2/3}$

Solution:

(a) $16^{3/2} = (16^{1/2})^3 = 4^3 = 64$

(b) $16^{-1.25} = 16^{-5/4} = \frac{1}{16^{5/4}} = \frac{1}{\left(\sqrt[4]{16}\right)^5} = \frac{1}{2^5} = \frac{1}{32}$

(c) $(1/27)^{-2/3} = 27^{2/3} = \left(\sqrt[3]{27}\right)^2 = 3^2 = 9$

---

[16] Tests reveal that many students, while they are able to handle quadratic identities, nevertheless make mistakes when dealing with more complicated powers. Here are examples taken from tests: (a) $(1+r)^{20}$ is *not* equal to $1^{20} + r^{20}$. (b) If $u = 9 + x^{1/2}$, it does *not* follow that $u^2 = 81 + x$; instead $u^2 = 81 + 18x^{1/2} + x$. (c) $(e^x - e^{-x})^p$ is *not* equal to $e^{xp} - e^{-xp}$, unless $p = 1$.

EXAMPLE 2.5.4 Here are two practical illustrations of why we need powers with rational exponents:

(a) The formula $S \approx 4.84 V^{2/3}$ gives the approximate surface area S of a ball as a function of its volume V—see Exercise 11.

(b) Let Y be the net national product, K be capital stock, L be labour, and t be time. A formula like $Y = 2.262 K^{0.203} L^{0.763} (1.02)^t$ often appears in studies of national economic growth. Thus, powers with fractional exponents do often arise in economics.

EXAMPLE 2.5.5 Simplify the following expressions so that the answers contain only positive exponents:

(a) $\dfrac{a^{3/8}}{a^{1/8}}$ (b) $(x^{1/2} x^{3/2} x^{-2/3})^{3/4}$ (c) $\left(\dfrac{10 p^{-1} q^{2/3}}{80 p^2 q^{-7/3}}\right)^{-2/3}$

Solution:

(a) $\dfrac{a^{3/8}}{a^{1/8}} = a^{3/8 - 1/8} = a^{2/8} = a^{1/4} = \sqrt[4]{a}$

(b) $(x^{1/2} x^{3/2} x^{-2/3})^{3/4} = (x^{1/2 + 3/2 - 2/3})^{3/4} = (x^{4/3})^{3/4} = x$

(c) $\left(\dfrac{10 p^{-1} q^{2/3}}{80 p^2 q^{-7/3}}\right)^{-2/3} = (8^{-1} p^{-1-2} q^{2/3 - (-7/3)})^{-2/3} = 8^{2/3} p^2 q^{-2} = 4 \dfrac{p^2}{q^2}$

If q is an odd number and p is an integer, then $a^{p/q}$ can be defined even when a is negative. For example, to define $(-8)^{1/3}$ we note that $(-2)^3 = -8$ and so take $(-8)^{1/3} = \sqrt[3]{-8} = -2$. However, in defining $a^{p/q}$ when a is negative, the denominator q must be odd. Otherwise, allowing q to be even could lead to logical contradictions such as "$-2 = (-8)^{1/3} = (-8)^{2/6} = \sqrt[6]{(-8)^2} = \sqrt[6]{64} = 2$".

We already saw that when a is positive, it is often easier to compute $a^{n/m}$ by finding $\sqrt[m]{a}$ first and then raising the result to the nth power. When a is negative and m is odd, the same applies: for example, $(-64)^{5/3} = (\sqrt[3]{-64})^5 = (-4)^5 = -1024$.

EXAMPLE 2.5.6 Let p and q be natural numbers with q odd, and a any negative real number. Find the sign of: (a) $a^{1/q}$; (b) $a^{p/q}$; (c) $a^{-p/q}$.

Solution:

(a) Because $(a^{1/q})^q = a$ which is negative, it follows that $a^{1/q}$ is also negative.

(b) Note that $a^{p/q} = (a^{1/q})^p = (-1)^p (-a^{1/q})^p$. Because $a^{1/q}$ is negative and so $(-a^{1/q})^p$ is positive, it follows that $a^{p/q}$ has the sign of $(-1)^p$. This is positive iff p is even, and negative iff p is odd.

(c) Because $a^{p/q} \cdot a^{-p/q} = 1$, the sign of $a^{-p/q}$ must be the same as the sign of $a^{p/q}$.

EXERCISES FOR SECTION 2.5

1. Compute the following numbers:

   (a) $\sqrt{9}$ (b) $\sqrt{1600}$ (c) $(100)^{1/2}$ (d) $\sqrt{9 + 16}$

   (e) $(36)^{-1/2}$ (f) $(0.49)^{1/2}$ (g) $\sqrt{0.01}$ (h) $\sqrt{1/25}$

SECTION 2.5 / FRACTIONAL POWERS

2. Let a and b be positive numbers. Decide whether each "?" should be replaced by $=$ or $\neq$. Justify your answer.

(a) $\sqrt{25 \cdot 16}$? $\sqrt{25} \cdot \sqrt{16}$ (b) $\sqrt{25 + 16}$? $\sqrt{25} + \sqrt{16}$

(c) $(a+b)^{1/2}$? $a^{1/2} + b^{1/2}$ (d) $(a+b)^{-1/2}$? $(\sqrt{a+b})^{-1}$

3. Solve for x the following equalities:

(a) $\sqrt{x} = 9$ (b) $\sqrt{x} \cdot \sqrt{4} = 4$ (c) $\sqrt{x+2} = 25$

(d) $\sqrt{3} \cdot \sqrt{5} = \sqrt{x}$ (e) $2^{2-x} = 8$ (f) $2^x - 2^{x-1} = 4$

4. Rationalize the denominator and simplify the following expressions:

(a) $\dfrac{6}{\sqrt{7}}$ (b) $\dfrac{\sqrt{32}}{\sqrt{2}}$ (c) $\dfrac{\sqrt{3}}{4\sqrt{2}}$

(d) $\dfrac{\sqrt{54} - \sqrt{24}}{\sqrt{6}}$ (e) $\dfrac{2}{\sqrt{3}\sqrt{8}}$ (f) $\dfrac{4}{\sqrt{2y}}$

(g) $\dfrac{x}{\sqrt{2x}}$ (h) $\dfrac{x(\sqrt{x}+1)}{\sqrt{x}}$

(SM) 5. Simplify the following expressions by making the denominators rational:

(a) $\dfrac{1}{\sqrt{7}+\sqrt{5}}$ (b) $\dfrac{\sqrt{5}-\sqrt{3}}{\sqrt{5}+\sqrt{3}}$ (c) $\dfrac{x}{\sqrt{3}-2}$

(d) $\dfrac{x\sqrt{y}-y\sqrt{x}}{x\sqrt{y}+y\sqrt{x}}$ (e) $\dfrac{h}{\sqrt{x+h}-\sqrt{x}}$ (f) $\dfrac{1-\sqrt{x+1}}{1+\sqrt{x+1}}$

6. Compute, without using a calculator, the following numbers:

(a) $\sqrt[3]{125}$ (b) $(243)^{1/5}$ (c) $(-8)^{1/3}$

(d) $\sqrt[3]{0.008}$ (e) $81^{1/2}$ (f) $64^{-1/3}$

(g) $16^{-2.25}$ (h) $\left(\dfrac{1}{3^{-2}}\right)^{-2}$

7. Using a calculator, find approximations to:

(a) $\sqrt[3]{55}$ (b) $(160)^{1/4}$ (c) $(2.71828)^{1/5}$ (d) $(1+0.0001)^{10\,000}$

8. The population of a nation increased from 40 million to 60 million in 12 years. What is the yearly percentage rate of growth p?

9. Simplify the following expressions:

(a) $\left(27x^{3p}y^{6q}z^{12r}\right)^{1/3}$ (b) $\dfrac{(x+15)^{4/3}}{(x+15)^{5/6}}$ (c) $\dfrac{8\sqrt[3]{x^2}\sqrt[4]{y}\sqrt{1/z}}{-2\sqrt[3]{x}\sqrt{y^5}\sqrt{z}}$

10. Simplify the following expressions, so that each contains only a single exponent:

(a) $\{[(a^{1/2})^{2/3}]^{3/4}\}^{4/5}$ (b) $a^{1/2} \cdot a^{2/3} \cdot a^{3/4} \cdot a^{4/5}$

(c) $\{[(3a)^{-1}]^{-2}(2a^{-2})^{-1}\}/a^{-3}$ (d) $\dfrac{\sqrt[3]{a} \cdot a^{1/12} \cdot \sqrt[4]{a^3}}{a^{5/12} \cdot \sqrt{a}}$

48 CHAPTER 2 / ALGEBRA

11. The formulas for the surface area S and the volume V of a ball with radius r are $S = 4\pi r^2$ and $V = (4/3)\pi r^3$. Express S as a power function of V.

SM 12. Which of the following equations are valid for all real x and y?

(a) $(2^x)^2 = 2^{x^2}$

(b) $3^{x-3y} = \dfrac{3^x}{3^{3y}}$

(c) $3^{-1/x} = \dfrac{1}{3^{1/x}}$, with $x \neq 0$

(d) $5^{1/x} = \dfrac{1}{5^x}$, with $x \neq 0$

(e) $a^{x+y} = a^x + a^y$, with a positive

(f) $2^{\sqrt{x}} \cdot 2^{\sqrt{y}} = 2^{\sqrt{xy}}$ with x and y positive

13. If a firm uses x units of input in process A, where x is nonnegative, then it produces $32x^{3/2}$ units of output. In the alternative process B, the same input quantity produces $4x^3$ units of output. For what levels of input does process A produce more than process B?

2.6 Inequalities

The real numbers consist of the positive numbers, as well as 0 and the negative numbers. If a is a positive number, we write $a > 0$ (or equivalently $0 < a$), and we say that a is greater than zero. If the number c is negative, we write $c < 0$ (or equivalently $0 > c$).

A fundamental property of the positive numbers is that:

$$(a > 0 \text{ and } b > 0) \implies (a + b > 0 \text{ and } a \cdot b > 0) \tag{2.6.1}$$

In general, we say that *the number a is greater than the number b*, and we write $a > b$ (or say that *b is smaller than a* and write $b < a$), if $a - b$ is positive. Thus, $4.11 > 3.12$ because $4.11 - 3.12 = 0.99 > 0$, and $-3 > -5$ because $-3 - (-5) = 2 > 0$. On the number line shown in Fig. 2.1.1, the inequality $a > b$ holds if and only if a lies to the right of b.

When $a > b$, we often say that *a is strictly greater than b* in order to emphasize that $a = b$ is ruled out. If $a > b$ or $a = b$, then we write $a \geq b$ (or $b \leq a$) and say that a is greater than or equal to b, or sometimes that a is *no less than* b. Thus, $a \geq b$ means that $a - b \geq 0$. For example, $4 \geq 4$ and $4 \geq 2$.[17]

We call $>$ and $<$ *strict* inequalities, whereas $\geq$ and $\leq$ are *weak* inequalities. The difference between weak and strict inequalities is often very important in economic analysis.

One can prove a number of important properties of the inequalities $>$ and $\geq$. For example, for any real numbers a, b, and c, one has;

$$a > b \iff a + c > b + c \tag{2.6.2}$$

Figure 2.6.1 $a > b \implies a + c > b + c$

The proof is simple: one has $(a + c) - (b + c) = a + c - b - c = a - b$ for all numbers a, b, and c. Hence $a - b > 0$ holds if and only if $(a + c) - (b + c) > 0$, so the conclusion

---
[17] Note in particular that it *is* correct to write $4 \geq 2$, because $4 - 2$ *is* positive or 0.

follows. On the number line shown in Fig. 2.6.1 this implication is self-evident (here c is chosen to be negative).

Dealing with more complicated inequalities involves using the following properties:

PROPERTIES OF INEQUALITIES

Let a, b, c, and d all be real numbers. Then

$$(a > b \text{ and } b > c) \implies a > c \tag{2.6.3}$$

$$(a > b \text{ and } c > 0) \implies ac > bc \tag{2.6.4}$$

$$(a > b \text{ and } c < 0) \implies ac < bc \tag{2.6.5}$$

$$(a > b \text{ and } c > d) \implies a + c > b + d \tag{2.6.6}$$

All four properties remain valid when each $>$ is replaced by $\geq$, as well as when each $<$ is replaced by $\leq$. The properties all follow easily from (2.6.1). For example, property (2.6.5) can be proved as follows: Suppose $a > b$ and $c < 0$. Then $a - b > 0$ and $-c > 0$, so, according to (2.6.1), $(a-b)(-c) > 0$. Hence $-ac + bc > 0$, implying that $ac < bc$.

According to (2.6.4) and (2.6.5), if the two sides of an inequality are multiplied:

(a) by a positive number, the direction of the inequality is preserved.

(b) by a negative number, the direction of the inequality is reversed.

It is important that you understand these rules, and realize that they correspond to everyday experience. For instance, (2.6.4) can be interpreted this way: given two rectangles with the same base, the one with the larger height has the larger area.

EXAMPLE 2.6.1   Find what values of x satisfy $3x - 5 > x - 3$.

Solution: Because of (2.6.2), we can add 5 to both sides of the inequality. This yields $3x - 5 + 5 > x - 3 + 5$, or $3x > x + 2$. Using (2.6.2) again to add $(-x)$ to both sides yields $3x - x > x - x + 2$, which reduces to $2x > 2$. Finally, (2.6.4) allow us to multiply both sides by the positive number $\frac{1}{2}$, so we get $x > 1$. The argument can obviously be reversed, so the solution is $x > 1$.

Double Inequalities

Two inequalities that are valid simultaneously are often written as a *double inequality*. For example, if $a \leq z$ and moreover $z < b$, it is natural to write $a \leq z < b$.[18]

---

[18] On the other hand, if $a \leq z$ and $z > b$, but we do not know which is the larger of a and b, then we cannot write $a \leq b < z$ or $b \leq a \leq z$. Moreover, we try to avoid writing $a \leq z > b$.

50   CHAPTER 2 / ALGEBRA

EXAMPLE 2.6.2   One day, the lowest temperature in Buenos Aires was 50°F, and the highest was 77°F. What is the corresponding temperature variation in degrees Celsius?[19]

Solution: The temperature C in degrees Celsius must satisfy

$$50 \leq \frac{9}{5}C + 32 \leq 77$$

Now (2.6.1) allows us to subtract 32 from each of the three terms. The result is

$$50 - 32 \leq \frac{9}{5}C \leq 77 - 32, \quad \text{which reduces to} \quad 18 \leq \frac{9}{5}C \leq 45$$

Finally, (2.6.4) tells us that multiplying all three terms by the positive number 5/9 preserves both inequalities. Hence $10 \leq C \leq 25$. So the variation is between 10°C and 25°C.

The following example demonstrates an important property of power functions. This is that, given any real number $x > 0$, as the natural number n increases, so x^n: (i) increases if and only if $x > 1$; (ii) decreases if and only if $0 < x < 1$.

EXAMPLE 2.6.3   Prove by induction on n that, for every natural number n:

(a) if $x > 1$, then $x^{n+1} > x^n > 1$;

(b) if $0 < x < 1$, then $0 < x^{n+1} < x^n < 1$.

Solution: (a) In case $x > 1$, applying rule (2.6.4) for inequalities gives $x \cdot x > x \cdot 1$ and so $x^2 > x^1 > 1$. For the induction step, suppose that $x^{k+1} > x^k > 1$ for some $k \geq 1$. Applying rule (2.6.4) once again gives $x \cdot x^{k+1} > x \cdot x^k$ and so $x^{k+2} > x^{k+1} > 1$, which completes the induction step.

(b) In case $1 > x > 0$, applying rule (2.6.4) for inequalities again gives $x \cdot 1 > x \cdot x$ and so $1 > x > x^2$. For the induction step, suppose that $1 > x^k > x^{k+1}$ for some $k \geq 1$. Applying rule (2.6.4) once again gives $x \cdot x^k > x \cdot x^{k+1}$ and so $1 > x^{k+1} > x^{k+2}$, which completes the induction step.

Our last example concerns solutions of the equation $x^n = a$, where $a > 0$ is a real number and n is a natural number. In Section 2.5 we claimed that this equation would have a unique positive solution, which we used to define the fractional power or nth root $a^{1/n} = \sqrt[n]{a}$. The following example offers a proof that any positive solution to $x^n = a$ is unique. Later in Example 2.10.3 we shall offer a constructive proof that a positive solution exists.

EXAMPLE 2.6.4   Given any natural number n, show that:

(a) if $0 < y < x$, then $y^n < x^n$;   (b) the equation $x^n = a$ has a unique positive solution.

---

[19] Recall that if F denotes a temperature in degrees Fahrenheit and C denotes the same temperature in degrees Celsius, then $F = \frac{9}{5}C + 32$.

Solution: (a) This is obviously true if $n = 1$. If $n > 1$, then

$$x^n - y^n = (x - y)(x^{n-1} + x^{n-2}y + \cdots + xy^{n-2} + y^{n-1}) \qquad (*)$$

The easiest way to verify this is simply to multiply out the product on the right. Most of the terms will cancel each other pairwise and we are left with $x^n - y^n$. Now the expression in parentheses in $(*)$ is a sum of n terms of the form $x^{n-k}y^{k-1}$ ($k = 1, \ldots, n$). Each term is a product of positive numbers, so positive by Exercise 7, which also implies that the sum of the n positive terms is positive. Then, because $x - y$ is positive, the product on the right-hand side of $(*)$ is positive, so $x^n - y^n > 0$.

(b) By part (a), if $x^n = y^n = a$ for any positive x and y, then $x = y$.

EXERCISES FOR SECTION 2.6

1. Decide which of the following inequalities are true:

   (a) $-6.15 > -7.16$ (b) $6 \geq 6$ (c) $(-5)^2 \leq 0$ (d) $-\frac{1}{2}\pi < -\frac{1}{3}\pi$

   (e) $\frac{4}{5} > \frac{6}{7}$ (f) $2^3 < 3^2$ (g) $2^{-3} < 3^{-2}$ (h) $\frac{1}{2} - \frac{2}{3} < \frac{1}{4} - \frac{1}{3}$

2. Find what values of x satisfy the following inequalities:

   (a) $-x - 3 \leq 5$ (b) $3x + 5 < x - 13$ (c) $3x - (x - 1) \geq x - (1 - x)$

   (d) $\dfrac{2x - 4}{3} \leq 7$ (e) $\dfrac{1}{3}(1 - x) \geq 2(x - 3)$ (f) $\dfrac{x}{24} - (x + 1) + \dfrac{3x}{8} < \dfrac{5}{12}(x + 1)$

3. Solve the following inequalities:

   (a) $1 \leq \dfrac{1}{3}(2x - 1) + \dfrac{8}{3}(1 - x) < 16$ (b) $-5 < \dfrac{1}{x} < 0$

SM 4. Fill in each blank with "$\Rightarrow$", "$\Leftarrow$", or "$\Leftrightarrow$" in order to complete a true statement:

   (a) $x(x + 3) < 0$ _____ $x > -3$ (b) $x^2 < 9$ _____ $x < 3$

   (c) $x^2 > 0$ _____ $x > 0$ (d) $x > y^2$ _____ $x > 0$

5. Decide whether the following inequalities are valid for all x and y:

   (a) $x + 1 > x$ (b) $x^2 > x$ (c) $x + x > x$ (d) $x^2 + y^2 \geq 2xy$

6. Recall from Example 2.6.2 the formula $F = \frac{9}{5}C + 32$ for converting degrees Celsius (C) to degrees Fahrenheit (F).

   (a) The temperature for storing potatoes should be between 4°C and 6°C. What are the corresponding temperatures in degrees Fahrenheit?

   (b) The freshness of a bottle of milk is guaranteed for seven days if it is kept at a temperature between 36°F and 40°F. Find the corresponding temperature variation in degrees Celsius.

7. Suppose that the n numbers $a_1, a_2, \ldots, a_n$ are all positive. Use (2.6.1) to prove by induction that both the sum $a_1 + a_2 + \cdots + a_n$ and the product $a_1 \cdot a_2 \cdot \ldots \cdot a_n$ of all n numbers are positive.

SM 8. If a and b are two positive numbers, define their *arithmetic*, *geometric*, and *harmonic means*, respectively, by $m_A = \frac{1}{2}(a+b)$, $m_G = \sqrt{ab}$ and

$$m_H = 2\left(\frac{1}{a} + \frac{1}{b}\right)^{-1}$$

Prove that $m_A \geq m_G \geq m_H$, with strict inequalities unless $a = b$.[20]

2.7 Intervals and Absolute Values

Let a and b be any two numbers on the real line. Then we call the set of all numbers that lie between a and b an *interval*. In many situations, it is important to distinguish between the intervals that include their end points and the intervals that do not. When $a < b$, there are four different intervals that all have a and b as end points, as shown in Table 2.7.1.

Table 2.7.1 Intervals on the real line

Notation	Name	Consists of all x satisfying:
(a, b)	The *open* interval from a to b	$a < x < b$
$[a, b]$	The *closed* interval from a to b	$a \leq x \leq b$
$(a, b]$	A *half-open* interval from a to b	$a < x \leq b$
$[a, b)$	A *half-open* interval from a to b	$a \leq x < b$

Note that an open interval includes neither of its end points, but a closed interval includes both of its end points. There are two half-open intervals in Table 2.7.1: each contains one of its end points, but not both. All four intervals in Table 2.7.1, however, have the same length, $b - a$.

We usually illustrate intervals on the number line as in Fig. 2.7.1, with included end points represented by solid dots, and excluded end points at the tips of arrows.

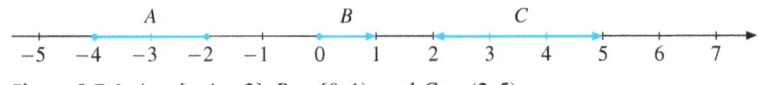

Figure 2.7.1 $A = [-4, -2]$, $B = [0, 1)$, and $C = (2, 5)$

The intervals mentioned so far are all *bounded*. We also use the word "interval" to signify certain unbounded sets of numbers. For example, using set notation, the interval $[a, \infty) = \{x : x \geq a\}$ consists of all numbers $x \geq a$; and the interval $(-\infty, b) = \{x : x < b\}$ contains all numbers with $x < b$.

Here, "∞" is the common symbol for infinity. This symbol is not a number at all, and therefore the usual rules of arithmetic do not apply to it. In the notation $[a, \infty)$, the symbol

---

[20] You should first test these inequalities by choosing some specific numbers, using a calculator if you wish. To show that $m_A \geq m_G$, start with the obvious inequality $(\sqrt{a} - \sqrt{b})^2 \geq 0$, and then expand. To show that $m_G \geq m_H$, start by applying the inequality $m_A \geq m_G$ to the pair x, y to show that $\sqrt{xy} \leq \frac{1}{2}(x + y)$. Then let $x = 1/a$, $y = 1/b$.

∞ is only intended to indicate that we are considering the collection of *all* numbers larger than or equal to a, without any upper bound on the size of the number. Similarly, $(-\infty, b)$ has no lower bound.

From the preceding, it should be apparent what we mean by (a, ∞) and $(-\infty, b]$. According to the convention we are using, the collection of all real numbers is an open interval that can be denoted by the symbol $(-\infty, \infty)$.

The Interior of an Interval

From time to time we shall need to speak of the *interior points* of an interval I, which are the points in I that are not end points. Then the collection of all interior points of I constitutes the *interior* of I.

These definitions imply that, when $a < b$, the four different intervals $[a, b]$, $[a, b)$, $(a, b]$, and (a, b) all have the same interior, which is the open interval (a, b). Moreover, the interiors of $(-\infty, b]$ and of $(-\infty, b)$ are both equal to the same interval $(-\infty, b)$, and similarly for $[a, \infty)$ and (a, ∞). Finally, the entire real line $(-\infty, \infty)$ is its own interior.

The important thing about an interior point c of an interval I is that offers a little "wiggle room" allowing us to shift point c a little way either to the left or to the right without forcing it outside the interval. In other words, all points that are sufficiently close to c also belong to I. Just draw a picture and you will see what this means.

Absolute Value

Let a be a real number and imagine its position on the real line. The distance between a and 0 is called the *absolute value* of a. If a is positive or 0, then the absolute value is the number a itself; if a is negative, then because distance must be positive, the absolute value is equal to the positive number $-a$. That is:

ABSOLUTE VALUE

The *absolute value* of the number a is the number $|a|$ defined by

$$|a| = \begin{cases} a & \text{if } a \geq 0 \\ -a & \text{if } a < 0 \end{cases} \qquad (2.7.1)$$

For example, $|13| = 13$, $|-5| = -(-5) = 5$, $|-1/2| = 1/2$, and $|0| = 0$. Note in particular that $|-a| = |a|$.[21]

---

[21] It is a common fallacy to assume that a must denote a positive number, even if this is not explicitly stated. Similarly, on seeing $-a$, many students are led to believe that this expression is always negative. Observe, however, that the number $-a$ is positive when a itself is negative. For example, if $a = -5$, then $-a = -(-5) = 5$. Nevertheless, it is often a useful convention in economics to define variables so that, as far as possible, their values are positive rather than negative.

EXAMPLE 2.7.1 Compute $|x - 2|$ for $x = -3$, $x = 0$, and $x = 4$. Then use the definition of absolute value to rewrite $|x - 2|$ as an expression like (2.7.1).

Solution: Using definition (2.7.1) for $x = -3$ gives $|x - 2| = |-3 - 2| = |-5| = 5$, For $x = 0$, it gives $|x - 2| = |0 - 2| = |-2| = 2$. Similarly, for $x = 4$ one has $|x - 2| = |4 - 2| = |2| = 2$.

Replacing a by $x - 2$ in (2.7.1) gives $|x - 2| = x - 2$ if $x - 2 > 0$, that is, if $x \geq 2$. However, suppose $x - 2 < 0$, that is, $x < 2$. In this case $|x - 2| = -(x - 2) = 2 - x$. Summarizing,

$$|x - 2| = \begin{cases} x - 2, & \text{if } x \geq 2 \\ 2 - x, & \text{if } x < 2 \end{cases}$$

An alternative definition of absolute value would be $|a| = \sqrt{a^2}$. This works because of the following more general result, which follows from the discussion in Section 2.5.

EXAMPLE 2.7.2 For any natural number n and any real $x \neq 0$, prove that

$$\sqrt[n]{x^n} = \begin{cases} x & \text{if } n \text{ is odd;} \\ |x| & \text{if } n \text{ is even.} \end{cases}$$

Solution: If n is odd, then regardless of the sign of x, which equals the sign of x^n, the real number $y = \sqrt[n]{x^n}$ is the unique solution of $y^n = x^n$. This implies that $y = x$.

But if n is even and $x \neq 0$, then x^n is positive regardless of the sign of x. Now the real number $y = \sqrt[n]{x^n}$ is the unique positive solution of $y^n = x^n$. This implies that $y = x$ if x is positive, but $y = -x$ if x is negative. That is, $y = |x|$.

Let x_1 and x_2 be two arbitrary numbers. The distance between x_1 and x_2 on the number line is $x_1 - x_2$ if $x_1 \geq x_2$, and $-(x_1 - x_2)$ if $x_1 < x_2$. Therefore, we have:

DISTANCE BETWEEN NUMBERS

The *distance* between x_1 and x_2 on the number line is

$$|x_1 - x_2| = |x_2 - x_1| \tag{2.7.2}$$

In Fig. 2.7.2 we have used long double-headed arrows to indicate geometrically that the distance between 7 and 2 is 5, whereas that between -3 and -5 is equal to 2. The latter is correct because $|-3 - (-5)| = |-3 + 5| = |2| = 2$.

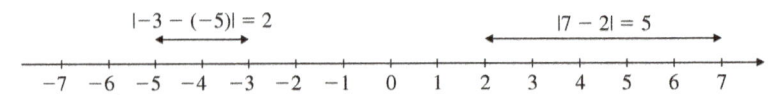

Figure 2.7.2 The distances between 7 and 2 and between -3 and -5.

Suppose $|x| = 5$. What values can x have? There are only two possibilities: either $x = 5$ or $x = -5$, because no other numbers have absolute value equal to 5. Generally, if a is greater than or equal to 0, then $|x| = a$ implies that $x = a$ or $x = -a$. Because definition (2.7.1) implies that $|x| \geq 0$ for all x, the equation $|x| = a$ has no solution when $a < 0$.

If a is a positive number and $|x| < a$, then the distance from x to 0 is less than a. Furthermore, when a is nonnegative, and $|x| \leq a$, the distance from x to 0 is less than or equal to a. In symbols:

$$|x| < a \iff -a < x < a \tag{2.7.3}$$

$$|x| \leq a \iff -a \leq x \leq a \tag{2.7.4}$$

EXAMPLE 2.7.3 Check first to see if the inequality $|3x - 2| \leq 5$ holds for $x = -3$, $x = 0$, $x = 7/3$, and $x = 10$. Then find all the x such that the inequality holds.

Solution: For $x = -3$ one has $|3x - 2| = |-9 - 2| = 11$; for $x = 0$ one has $|3x - 2| = |-2| = 2$; for $x = 7/3$ one has $|3x - 2| = |7 - 2| = 5$; and for $x = 10$ one has $|3x - 2| = |30 - 2| = 28$. Hence, the given inequality is satisfied for $x = 0$ and $x = 7/3$, but not for $x = -3$ or $x = 10$.

For general x, it follows from (2.7.4) that the inequality $|3x - 2| \leq 5$ holds if and only if $-5 \leq 3x - 2 \leq 5$. Adding 2 to all three expressions gives

$$-5 + 2 \leq 3x - 2 + 2 \leq 5 + 2$$

This simplifies to $-3 \leq 3x \leq 7$. Dividing throughout by 3 gives $-1 \leq x \leq 7/3$.

EXERCISES FOR SECTION 2.7

1. (a) Calculate $|2x - 3|$ for $x = 0$, $1/2$, and $7/2$.

   (b) Solve the equation $|2x - 3| = 0$.

   (c) Rewrite $|2x - 3|$ by using the definition of absolute value.

2. (a) Calculate $|5 - 3x|$ for $x = -1$, $x = 2$, and $x = 4$.

   (b) Solve the equation $|5 - 3x| = 5$.

   (c) Rewrite $|5 - 3x|$ by using the definition of absolute value.

3. Determine x such that the following expressions hold true:

   (a) $|3 - 2x| = 5$ (b) $|x| \leq 2$ (c) $|x - 2| \leq 1$

   (d) $|3 - 8x| \leq 5$ (e) $|x| > \sqrt{2}$ (f) $|x^2 - 2| \leq 1$

4. A customer orders an iron bar whose advertised length is 5 metres, but with a tolerance of 1 mm. That is, the bar's length may not deviate by more than 1 mm from what is stipulated. Write a specification for the bar's acceptable length x in metres: (a) by using a double inequality; (b) with the aid of an absolute-value sign.

2.8 Sign Diagrams

Sign diagrams can be a useful tool for solving an inequality, in the sense of finding the intervals on which the inequality is valid. We begin with a simple example that illustrates their construction and use.

EXAMPLE 2.8.1 Check whether the inequality $(x-1)(3-x) > 0$ is satisfied for $x = -3$, $x = 2$, and $x = 5$. Then find the solution set of all values of x that satisfy the same inequality.

Solution: For $x = -3$, we have $(x-1)(3-x) = (-4) \cdot 6 = -24 < 0$. Next, for $x = 2$, we have $(x-1)(3-x) = 1 \cdot 1 = 1 > 0$. Finally, for $x = 5$, we have $(x-1)(3-x) = 4 \cdot (-2) = -8 < 0$. Hence, the inequality is satisfied for $x = 2$, but not for $x = -3$ or $x = 5$.

To find the entire solution set, we use a *sign diagram*. First, we determine the sign variation for each factor in the product. For example, the factor $x - 1$ is negative when $x < 1$; it is 0 when $x = 1$; and it is positive when $x > 1$.

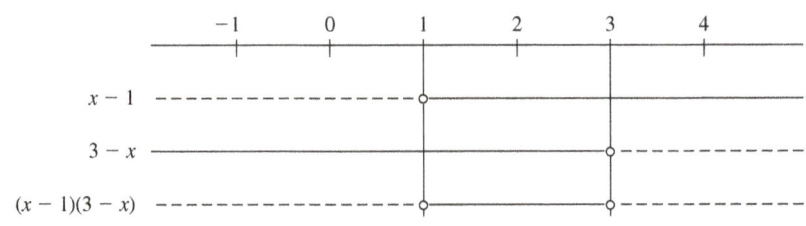

Figure 2.8.1 Sign diagram for $(x-1)(3-x)$

The sign variation of the two factors, as well as of their product, is represented in Fig. 2.8.1. In this diagram, consider first the horizontal line labelled $x - 1$. The dashed part of this line to the left of the vertical line $x = 1$ indicates that $x - 1 < 0$ if $x < 1$; the small circle indicates that $x - 1 = 0$ when $x = 1$; and the solid line to the right of $x = 1$ indicates that $x - 1 > 0$ if $x > 1$. In a similar way, the horizontal line labelled $3 - x$ represents the sign variation for $3 - x$.

The sign variation of the product $(x-1)(3-x)$ is obtained as follows. If $x < 1$, then $x - 1$ is negative and $3 - x$ is positive, so the product is negative. If $1 < x < 3$, then both factors are positive, so the product is positive. If $x > 3$, then $x - 1$ is positive and $3 - x$ is negative, so the product is negative.

To conclude: the solution set consists of those x that are greater than 1, but less than 3. That is $(x-1)(3-x) > 0 \Leftrightarrow 1 < x < 3$.

EXAMPLE 2.8.2 Find all values of p that satisfy the inequality:

$$\frac{2p-3}{p-1} > 3 - p$$

Solution: It is tempting to begin by multiplying each side of the inequality by $p - 1$. Then, however, Eq. (2.6.5) implies that we must reverse the inequality sign in case $p - 1 < 0$. So we would have to distinguish between the two cases $p - 1 > 0$ and $p - 1 < 0$.

Fortunately there is an alternative method that avoids the need to distinguish between two different cases. We begin by adding $p - 3$ to both sides. This yields

$$\frac{2p - 3}{p - 1} + p - 3 > 0$$

Making $p - 1$ the common denominator gives

$$\frac{2p - 3 + (p - 3)(p - 1)}{p - 1} > 0$$

Note that the numerator of this fraction simplifies to

$$2p - 3 + (p - 3)(p - 1) = 2p - 3 + p^2 - 4p + 3 = p^2 - 2p = p(p - 2)$$

This allows the inequality to be reduced to

$$\frac{p(p - 2)}{p - 1} > 0$$

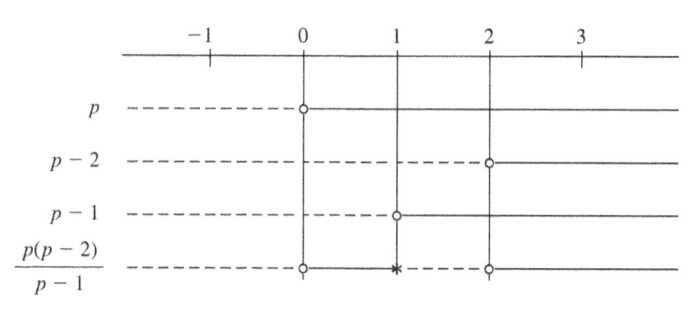

Figure 2.8.2 Sign diagram for $\dfrac{p(p - 2)}{p - 1}$

To find the solution set, we use the sign diagram shown in Fig. 2.8.2 in order to determine the sign variation of $p(p - 2)/(p - 1)$ based on that of p, $p - 2$, and $p - 1$. For example, in case $0 < p < 1$, then p is positive and $(p - 2)$ is negative, so $p(p - 2)$ is negative. But $p - 1$ is also negative on this interval, so $p(p - 2)/(p - 1)$ is positive. Arguing in this way for all four relevant intervals leads to the sign diagram shown.[22] So the original inequality is satisfied if and only if $0 < p < 1$ or $p > 2$.

Two notes of warning are in order. First, note the most common error committed in solving inequalities, which is precisely that indicated in Example 2.8.2: if we multiply by $p - 1$, the inequality is preserved *only* if $p - 1$ is positive—that is, if $p > 1$. Second, it is vital that you really understand the method of sign diagrams. Another common error is illustrated by the following example.

---

[22] The original inequality has no meaning when $p = 1$. This is indicated by a small $*$ where $p = 1$ on the lowest horizontal line of the diagram.

EXAMPLE 2.8.3

Find all values of x that satisfy the inequality:
$$\frac{(x-2) + 3(x+1)}{x+3} \leq 0$$

"Solution": Suppose we construct the inappropriate sign diagram shown in Fig. 2.8.3.

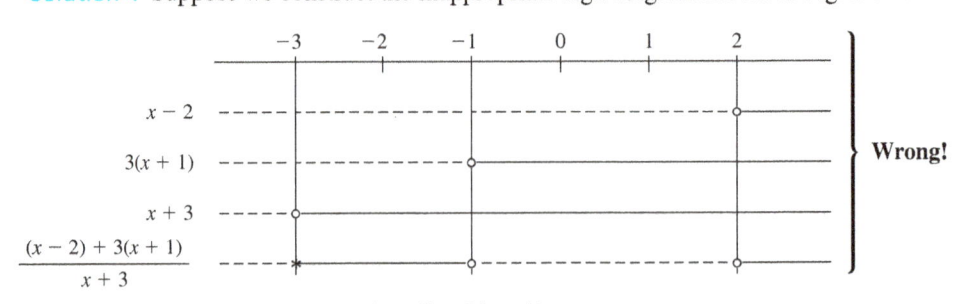

Figure 2.8.3 Wrong sign diagram for $\dfrac{(x-2) + 3(x+1)}{x+3}$

According to the sign diagram in Fig. 2.8.3, the inequality should be satisfied for $x < -3$ and for $-1 \leq x \leq 2$. However, for $x = -4$ (which is < -3), the fraction reduces to 15, which is positive. What went wrong? Suppose $x < -3$. Then $x - 2 < 0$ and $3(x+1) < 0$, so the numerator $(x-2) + 3(x+1)$ is negative. Because the denominator $x + 3$ is also negative for $x < -3$, the fraction is positive. The sign variation indicated in Fig. 2.8.3 for the fraction is, therefore, completely wrong. The product of two negative numbers is positive, but their sum is negative, and not positive as the wrong sign diagram suggests.

To obtain a correct solution to the problem, first collect all the terms in the numerator so that the inequality becomes $(4x+1)/(x+3) \leq 0$. Now construct your own sign diagram for this inequality in order to reveal the correct answer, which is $-3 < x \leq -1/4$.

EXERCISES FOR SECTION 2.8

(SM) 1. Solve the following inequalities:

(a) $2 < \dfrac{3x+1}{2x+4}$
(b) $\dfrac{120}{n} + 1.1 \leq 1.85$
(c) $g^2 - 2g \leq 0$
(d) $\dfrac{1}{p-2} + \dfrac{3}{p^2 - 4p + 4} \geq 0$
(e) $\dfrac{-n-2}{n+4} > 2$
(f) $x^4 < x^2$

2. Solve the following inequalities:

(a) $\dfrac{x+2}{x-1} < 0$
(b) $\dfrac{2x+1}{x-3} > 1$
(c) $5a^2 \leq 125$
(d) $(x-1)(x+4) > 0$
(e) $(x-1)^2(x+4) > 0$
(f) $(x-1)^3(x-2) \leq 0$
(g) $(5x-1)^{10}(x-1) < 0$
(h) $(5x-1)^{11}(x-1) < 0$
(i) $\dfrac{3x-1}{x} > x+3$
(j) $\dfrac{x-3}{x+3} < 2x-1$
(k) $x^2 - 4x + 4 > 0$
(l) $x^3 + 2x^2 + x \leq 0$

3. Solve the inequality $\left(\dfrac{1}{x} - 1\right) \div \left(\dfrac{1}{x} + 1\right) \geq 1$.

2.9 Summation Notation

Economists often make use of census data. Suppose, for instance, that a country is divided into six regions. Let N_i denote the population in region i. Then the total population is given by

$$N_1 + N_2 + N_3 + N_4 + N_5 + N_6$$

It is convenient to have an abbreviated notation for such lengthy expressions. The capital Greek letter sigma, written as Σ, is conventionally used as a *summation symbol*. Its use allows the sum to be written more concisely as

$$\sum_{i=1}^{6} N_i$$

This should be read as "the sum, from $i = 1$ to $i = 6$, of N_i".

With n rather than six regions, one expression denoting total population is

$$N_1 + N_2 + \cdots + N_n \tag{$*$}$$

Here the dots $\cdots$ between the last two plus signs indicate that the obvious previous pattern continues, but ends with the last term N_n. In summation notation, we write

$$\sum_{i=1}^{n} N_i$$

This summation notation tells us to form the sum of all the terms that result when we substitute successive integers for i, starting with its lower limit $i = 1$ and ending with the upper limit $i = n$. The symbol i is called the *index of summation*. It is a "dummy variable" that can be replaced by any other letter (which has not already been used for something else). Thus, both $\sum_{j=1}^{n} N_j$ and $\sum_{k=1}^{n} N_k$ represent the same sum as ($*$).

As well as the upper limit of summation, the lower limit can also vary. Consider, for example, the sum

$$\sum_{i=30}^{35} N_i = N_{30} + N_{31} + N_{32} + N_{33} + N_{34} + N_{35}$$

This is the total population in the six regions numbered from 30 to 35.

More generally, suppose the lower and upper limits are the integers p and q with $q \geq p$. Then the sum of the numbers a_i as the integer i varies over successive integers in the range from $i = p$ to $i = q$ can be written as

$$\sum_{i=p}^{q} a_i = a_p + a_{p+1} + \cdots + a_q$$

If the upper and lower limits of summation are equal, then the "sum" collapses to the one term $a_p = a_q$. But if the upper limit is less than the lower limit, then there are no terms at all. In this case the usual convention is that the "sum" of the zero terms reduces to zero.

EXAMPLE 2.9.1 Compute the following sums:

(a) $\sum_{i=1}^{5} i^2$ (b) $\sum_{k=3}^{6}(5k-3)$ (c) $\sum_{j=0}^{2}\dfrac{(-1)^j}{(j+1)(j+3)}$

Solution:

(a) $\sum_{i=1}^{5} i^2 = 1^2 + 2^2 + 3^2 + 4^2 + 5^2 = 1 + 4 + 9 + 16 + 25 = 55$

(b) $\sum_{k=3}^{6}(5k-3) = (5\cdot 3 - 3) + (5\cdot 4 - 3) + (5\cdot 5 - 3) + (5\cdot 6 - 3) = 78$

(c) $\sum_{j=0}^{2}\dfrac{(-1)^j}{(j+1)(j+3)} = \dfrac{1}{1\cdot 3} + \dfrac{-1}{2\cdot 4} + \dfrac{1}{3\cdot 5} = \dfrac{40 - 15 + 8}{120} = \dfrac{33}{120} = \dfrac{11}{40}$

Economists often use summation notation, so it is important to know how to interpret it. Often, as well as the summation index, there can be several other variables or parameters.

EXAMPLE 2.9.2 Expand the following expressions:[23]

(a) $\sum_{i=1}^{n} p_t^{(i)} q^{(i)}$ (b) $\sum_{j=-3}^{1} x^{5-j} y^j$ (c) $\sum_{i=1}^{N}(x_{ij} - \bar{x}_j)^2$

Solution:

(a) $\sum_{i=1}^{n} p_t^{(i)} q^{(i)} = p_t^{(1)} q^{(1)} + p_t^{(2)} q^{(2)} + \cdots + p_t^{(n)} q^{(n)}$

(b) $\sum_{j=-3}^{1} x^{5-j} y^j = x^8 y^{-3} + x^7 y^{-2} + x^6 y^{-1} + x^5 + x^4 y$

(c) $\sum_{i=1}^{N}(x_{ij} - \bar{x}_j)^2 = (x_{1j} - \bar{x}_j)^2 + (x_{2j} - \bar{x}_j)^2 + \cdots + (x_{Nj} - \bar{x}_j)^2$

EXAMPLE 2.9.3 Write the following sums using summation notation:

(a) $1 + 3 + 3^2 + 3^3 + \cdots + 3^{81}$

(b) $a_i^6 + a_i^5 b_j + a_i^4 b_j^2 + a_i^3 b_j^3 + a_i^2 b_j^4 + a_i b_j^5 + b_j^6$

Solution:

(a) This is easy if we note that $1 = 3^0$ and $3 = 3^1$, so that the sum can be written as $3^0 + 3^1 + 3^2 + 3^3 + \cdots + 3^{81}$. The general term is 3^i, and we have

$$1 + 3 + 3^2 + 3^3 + \cdots + 3^{81} = \sum_{i=0}^{81} 3^i$$

(b) This is more difficult. Note, however, that the indices i and j never change. Also, the exponent for a_i decreases step by step from 6 to 0, whereas that for b_j increases from 0 to 6. The general term has the form $a_i^{6-k} b_j^k$, where k varies from 0 to 6. Thus,

$$a_i^6 + a_i^5 b_j + a_i^4 b_j^2 + a_i^3 b_j^3 + a_i^2 b_j^4 + a_i b_j^5 + b_j^6 = \sum_{k=0}^{6} a_i^{6-k} b_j^k$$

---

[23] Note that t is *not* an index of summation in (a), and that j is *not* one in (c).

SECTION 2.9 / SUMMATION NOTATION   61

EXAMPLE 2.9.4   (**Price indices**). Suppose there are changes to the prices of several different goods within a country. In order to summarize the overall effect of price changes, a number of alternative *price indices* have been suggested. Consider a "basket" of n commodities which consists, for each $i = 1, \ldots, n$, of q^i units of good i. Let p_0^i denote the price per unit of good i in year 0; let p_t^i denote the price per unit of good i in year t. Then the total cost of the basket in year 0 is

$$\sum_{i=1}^{n} p_0^i q^i = p_0^1 q^1 + p_0^2 q^2 + \cdots + p_0^n q^n$$

whereas the total cost of the basket in year t is

$$\sum_{i=1}^{n} p_t^i q^i = p_t^1 q^1 + p_t^2 q^2 + \cdots + p_t^n q^n$$

Using year 0 as the base year in which, by definition, the price index is 100, we can calculate a price index for year t as 100 times the ratio of the costs of the fixed basket in years 0 and t respectively. That is, the index in year t is

$$\left(\frac{\sum_{i=1}^{n} p_t^i q^i}{\sum_{i=1}^{n} p_0^i q^i} \right) \cdot 100 \qquad \text{(price index)}$$

For example, if the cost of the basket is 1032 in year 0 and the cost of the same basket in year t is 1548, then the price index is $(1548/1032) \cdot 100 = 150$.

In the case where the quantities q^i are levels of consumption in the base year 0, this is called the *Laspeyres price index*. But if the quantities q^i are levels of consumption in the year t, this is called the *Paasche price index*.

EXERCISES FOR SECTION 2.9

1. Evaluate the following sums:

    (a) $\sum_{i=1}^{10} i$
    (b) $\sum_{k=2}^{6} (5 \cdot 3^{k-2} - k)$
    (c) $\sum_{m=0}^{5} (2m + 1)$
    (d) $\sum_{l=0}^{2} 2^{2^l}$
    (e) $\sum_{i=1}^{10} 2$
    (f) $\sum_{j=1}^{4} \frac{j+1}{j}$

2. Expand the following sums:

    (a) $\sum_{k=-2}^{2} 2\sqrt{k+2}$ (b) $\sum_{i=0}^{3} (x + 2i)^2$ (c) $\sum_{k=1}^{n} a_{ki} b^{k+1}$ (d) $\sum_{j=0}^{m} f(x_j) \Delta x_j$

3. Express the following sums in summation notation:

    (a) $4 + 8 + 12 + 16 + \cdots + 4n$
    (b) $1^3 + 2^3 + 3^3 + 4^3 + \cdots + n^3$
    (c) $1 - \frac{1}{3} + \frac{1}{5} - \frac{1}{7} + \cdots + (-1)^n \frac{1}{2n+1}$
    (d) $a_{i1} b_{1j} + a_{i2} b_{2j} + \cdots + a_{in} b_{nj}$
    (e) $3x + 9x^2 + 27x^3 + 81x^4 + 243x^5$
    (f) $a_i^3 b_{i+3} + a_i^4 b_{i+4} + \cdots + a_i^p b_{i+p}$
    (g) $a_i^3 b_{i+3} + a_{i+1}^4 b_{i+4} + \cdots + a_{i+p}^{p+3} b_{i+p+3}$
    (h) $81\,297 + 81\,495 + 81\,693 + 81\,891$

4. Compute the price index in Example 2.9.4, for $n = 3$, when:

    $$p_0^1 = 1, \; p_0^2 = 2, \; p_0^3 = 3, \; p_t^1 = 2, \; p_t^2 = 3, \; p_t^3 = 4, \; q^1 = 3, \; q^2 = 5, \text{ and } q^3 = 7$$

5. Insert the appropriate limits of summation in the right-hand side of the following sums:

   (a) $\sum_{k=1}^{10}(k-2)t^k = \sum_{m=} \quad mt^{m+2}$

   (b) $\sum_{n=0}^{N} 2^{n+5} = \sum_{j=} \quad 32 \cdot 2^{j-1}$

6. Since early 2020, the European Economic Area consists of 30 nations, who have agreed in principle to the free mobility of persons throughout the area. For the year 2025, let c_{ij} denote an estimate of the number of persons who will move from nation i to nation j, for each $i \neq j$. If, say, $i = 25$ and $j = 10$, then we write $c_{25,10}$ for c_{ij}. Explain the meaning of the two sums: (a) $\sum_{j=1}^{30} c_{ij}$, and (b) $\sum_{i=1}^{30} c_{ij}$.

SM 7. Decide which of the following equalities are generally valid.

   (a) $\sum_{k=1}^{n} ck^2 = c \sum_{k=1}^{n} k^2$

   (b) $\left(\sum_{i=1}^{n} a_i\right)^2 = \sum_{i=1}^{n} a_i^2$

   (c) $\sum_{j=1}^{n} b_j + \sum_{j=n+1}^{N} b_j = \sum_{j=1}^{N} b_j$

   (d) $\sum_{k=3}^{7} 5^{k-2} = \sum_{k=0}^{4} 5^{k+1}$

   (e) $\sum_{i=0}^{n-1} a_{i,j}^2 = \sum_{k=1}^{n} a_{k-1,j}^2$

   (f) $\sum_{k=1}^{n} a_k/k = \frac{1}{k} \sum_{k=1}^{n} a_k$

2.10 Rules for Sums

The following properties are helpful when manipulating sums:

$$\sum_{i=1}^{n} (a_i + b_i) = \sum_{i=1}^{n} a_i + \sum_{i=1}^{n} b_i \qquad (2.10.1)$$

and

$$\sum_{i=1}^{n} ca_i = c \sum_{i=1}^{n} a_i \qquad (2.10.2)$$

These properties are known, respectively, as *additivity* and *homogeneity*. Their proofs are straightforward. For example, (2.10.2) is proved by noting that

$$\sum_{i=1}^{n} ca_i = ca_1 + ca_2 + \cdots + ca_n = c(a_1 + a_2 + \cdots + a_n) = c \sum_{i=1}^{n} a_i$$

The homogeneity property states that a constant factor can be moved outside the summation sign. In particular, if $a_i = 1$ for all i, then

$$\sum_{i=1}^{n} c = nc \qquad (2.10.3)$$

This just states that a constant c summed n times is equal to n times c.

The summation rules can be applied in combination to give formulas like

$$\sum_{i=1}^{n} (a_i + b_i - c_i + d) = \sum_{i=1}^{n} a_i + \sum_{i=1}^{n} b_i - \sum_{i=1}^{n} c_i + nd$$

SECTION 2.10 / RULES FOR SUMS

EXAMPLE 2.10.1 Evaluate the sum

$$\sum_{m=2}^{n} \frac{1}{(m-1)m} = \frac{1}{1 \cdot 2} + \frac{1}{2 \cdot 3} + \cdots + \frac{1}{(n-1)n}$$

by using the equality

$$\frac{1}{(m-1)m} = \frac{1}{m-1} - \frac{1}{m}$$

Solution:

$$\sum_{m=2}^{n} \frac{1}{m(m-1)} = \sum_{m=2}^{n} \left(\frac{1}{m-1} - \frac{1}{m} \right)$$

$$= \sum_{m=2}^{n} \frac{1}{m-1} - \sum_{m=2}^{n} \frac{1}{m}$$

$$= \left(\frac{1}{1} + \frac{1}{2} + \frac{1}{3} + \cdots + \frac{1}{n-1} \right) - \left(\frac{1}{2} + \frac{1}{3} + \cdots + \frac{1}{n-1} + \frac{1}{n} \right)$$

$$= 1 - \frac{1}{n}$$

To derive the last equality, note that the terms $\frac{1}{2}, \frac{1}{3}, \ldots, \frac{1}{n-1}$ all cancel pairwise. The only terms left after this cancellation are the first term within the first parentheses, which is 1, and the last term within the last parentheses, which is $-\frac{1}{n}$.

This powerful cancellation trick is commonly used to calculate some special sums of this kind. See Exercise 4 below for some other examples.

EXAMPLE 2.10.2 The *arithmetic mean* or *mean*, μ_x, of T numbers $x_1, x_2, \ldots, x_T$ is defined as the sum of all the numbers divided by the number of terms, T. That is,

$$\mu_x = \frac{1}{T} \sum_{t=1}^{T} x_t$$

Prove that $\sum_{t=1}^{T} (x_t - \mu_x) = 0$ and $\sum_{t=1}^{T} (x_t - \mu_x)^2 = \sum_{t=1}^{T} x_t^2 - T\mu_x^2$.

Solution: The difference $x_t - \mu_x$ between x_t and the mean is called the *deviation*. We first use the above definition of μ_x to prove that the sum of these deviations is 0:

$$\sum_{t=1}^{T} (x_t - \mu_x) = \sum_{t=1}^{T} x_t - \sum_{t=1}^{T} \mu_x = \sum_{t=1}^{T} x_t - T\mu_x = T\mu_x - T\mu_x = 0$$

Furthermore, the sum of the squares of the deviations is

$$\sum_{t=1}^{T} (x_t - \mu_x)^2 = \sum_{t=1}^{T} (x_t^2 - 2\mu_x x_t + \mu_x^2) = \sum_{t=1}^{T} x_t^2 - 2\mu_x \sum_{t=1}^{T} x_t + \sum_{t=1}^{T} \mu_x^2$$

$$= \sum_{t=1}^{T} x_t^2 - 2\mu_x T\mu_x + T\mu_x^2 = \sum_{t=1}^{T} x_t^2 - T\mu_x^2$$

Dividing by T, the *mean square deviation* $\frac{1}{T}\sum_{t=1}^{T}(x_t - \mu_x)^2$ is therefore equal to the mean square $\frac{1}{T}\sum_{t=1}^{T}x_t^2$ minus the square μ_x^2 of the mean.

Useful Formulas

A (very) demanding teacher once asked his students to calculate the sum[24]

$$81\,297 + 81\,495 + 81\,693 + \cdots + 100\,899$$

It turns out that there are one hundred terms and that the difference between any two successive terms is a constant equal to 198. Carl Gauss (1777–1855), later one of the world's leading mathematicians, was in the class, and (at age nine!) is reputed to have given the right answer in only a few minutes. You already took a key step toward finding the solution to this question in Exercise 1.4.1, using mathematical induction. Applied to that easier problem of finding the sum $x = 1 + 2 + \cdots + n$, Gauss's argument was probably different, as follows: First, write the sum x in two ways

$$x = 1 + 2 + \cdots + (n-1) + n$$
$$x = n + (n-1) + \cdots + 2 + 1$$

Summing these two equations term by term while grouping terms vertically gives

$$2x = (1+n) + [2+(n-1)] + \cdots + [(n-1)+2] + (n+1)$$
$$= (1+n) + (1+n) + \cdots + (1+n) + (1+n)$$
$$= n(1+n)$$

Thus, solving for x gives the result:

$$\sum_{i=1}^{n} i = 1 + 2 + \cdots + n = \frac{1}{2}n(n+1) \tag{2.10.4}$$

The following two summation formulas are occasionally useful in economics.[25] Exercise 1 below asks you to provide their proofs.

$$\sum_{i=1}^{n} i^2 = 1^2 + 2^2 + 3^2 + \cdots + n^2 = \frac{1}{6}n(n+1)(2n+1) \tag{2.10.5}$$

$$\sum_{i=1}^{n} i^3 = 1^3 + 2^3 + 3^3 + \cdots + n^3 = \left(\frac{1}{2}n(n+1)\right)^2 = \left(\sum_{i=1}^{n} i\right)^2 \tag{2.10.6}$$

---

[24] This version of the story seems to have originated in Eric Temple Bell's book *Men of Mathematics*, first published in 1937.
[25] Check to see if they are true for $n = 1, 2, 3$.

Decimal Notation

The discussion in Section 2.1 showed how decimal notation could represent any positive real number as $x = m.\alpha_1\alpha_2\alpha_3\ldots$. Here m is a nonnegative integer. Then, after the decimal point, for each natural number n the symbol α_n indicates the nth *decimal digit* that belongs to the set $\{0, 1, 2, \ldots, 9\}$. In case the decimal terminates after p decimal places, it is $x = m.\alpha_1\alpha_2\alpha_3\ldots\alpha_p$, which corresponds uniquely to the finite sum $x = m + \sum_{k=1}^{p} \alpha_k \cdot 10^{-k}$ of increasing negative powers of 10.

In case the decimal never terminates, however, it takes the form $x = m.\alpha_1\alpha_2\ldots\alpha_k\ldots$. This corresponds uniquely to the sum of infinitely many terms, which we write as the infinite sum $x = m + \sum_{k=1}^{\infty} \alpha_k \cdot 10^{-k}$. Note that m is the largest nonnegative integer such that $m \leq x$. Next, the nonnegative integer $10[m + \alpha_1 \cdot 10^{-1}] = 10m + \alpha_1$ is the largest which is no greater than $x \cdot 10$, and so on. Indeed, for each natural number p, the sum to p decimal places, which we denote by S_p, is defined by $S_p = m + \sum_{k=1}^{p} \alpha_k \cdot 10^{-k}$. It has the property that $S_p \cdot 10^p$ is the largest integer which does not exceed $x \cdot 10^p$.

In Example 2.6.4 we demonstrated that any positive solution to the equation $x^n = a$ must be unique. Now we outline a method for constructing the solution.

EXAMPLE 2.10.3 Describe how to construct the decimal number $x = m + \sum_{k=1}^{p} \alpha_k \cdot 10^{-k}$ which is the unique positive solution to the equation $x^n = a$, where a is positive.

Solution: First, choose m as the largest nonnegative integer such that $m^n \leq a$.

Second, given m constructed at the first stage, choose α_1 as the largest nonnegative integer such that $(m + \alpha_1 \cdot 10^{-1})^n \leq a$. By definition of m, one has $(m+1)^n > a \geq m^n$, implying that $0 \leq \alpha_1 \leq 9$.

In general, for $p = 1, 2, \ldots$, let S_{p-1} denote the expansion $m + \sum_{k=1}^{p-1} \alpha_k \cdot 10^{-k}$ to $p - 1$ decimal places that was constructed at the pth stage. As the induction hypothesis, suppose that $(S_{p-1})^n \leq a < (S_{p-1} + 10^{2-p})^n$, as is true when $p = 1$ or 2.

Next, let us construct α_p in the pth decimal place as the largest nonnegative integer such that the expansion $S_{p-1} + \alpha_p \cdot 10^{-p}$ to p decimal places, which we denote by S_p, satisfies $(S_p)^n \leq a$. The induction hypothesis implies that $0 \leq \alpha_p \leq 9$. In particular, one has $(S_p)^n \leq a < (S_p + 10^{1-p})^n$, which proves the induction step. So there exists an infinite sequence S_p ($p = 1, 2, \ldots,$) of decimal expansions with this property.

If you were able to repeat this construction indefinitely, the result would be a unique decimal number $x = m + \sum_{k=1}^{\infty} \alpha_k \cdot 10^{-k}$. By construction, this is the largest possible decimal number satisfying $x^n \leq a$. Intuitively, it must therefore satisfy $x^n = a$.

EXERCISES FOR SECTION 2.10

1. Prove formulas (2.10.5) and (2.10.6), using the principle of mathematical induction seen in Section 1.4.

2. Use results (2.10.1) to (2.10.5) to find $\sum_{k=1}^{n}(k^2 + 3k + 2)$.

66 CHAPTER 2 / ALGEBRA

3. Use results (2.10.1) to (2.10.4) to prove the summation formula for an *arithmetic series*:

$$\sum_{i=0}^{n-1}(a + d \cdot i) = na + \frac{n(n-1)d}{2}$$

Apply the formula to find the sum Gauss is supposed to have calculated at age 9.

4. (a) Prove that $\sum_{k=1}^{n}(a_{k+1} - a_k) = a_{n+1} - a_1$ by using the cancellation trick set out in the solution to Example 2.10.1.

   (b) Use the result in (a) to compute the following:

   (i) $\sum_{k=1}^{50}\left(\frac{1}{k} - \frac{1}{k+1}\right)$ (ii) $\sum_{k=1}^{12}(3^{k+1} - 3^k)$ (iii) $\sum_{k=1}^{n}(ar^{k+1} - ar^k)$

2.11 Newton's Binomial Formula

It is obvious that $(a+b)^1 = a+b$. By now you should know that $(a+b)^2 = a^2 + 2ab + b^2$. After all, it is the first of the three quadratic identities that you were asked to memorize in Section 2.3. To get the next two powers we recognize that $(a+b)^3 = (a+b)(a+b)^2$ and $(a+b)^4 = (a+b)(a+b)^3$. So first we multiply each side of $(a+b)^2 = a^2 + 2ab + b^2$ by $a+b$, then do the same again to the resulting expression for $(a+b)^3$. Here are the results:

$$(a+b)^1 = a+b$$
$$(a+b)^2 = a^2 + 2ab + b^2$$
$$(a+b)^3 = a^3 + 3a^2b + 3ab^2 + b^3$$
$$(a+b)^4 = a^4 + 4a^3b + 6a^2b^2 + 4ab^3 + b^4$$

(2.11.1)

Here is the corresponding formula for $(a+b)^m$, where m is any natural number:

NEWTON'S BINOMIAL FORMULA

$$(a+b)^m = a^m + \binom{m}{1}a^{m-1}b + \cdots + \binom{m}{m-1}ab^{m-1} + \binom{m}{m}b^m \quad (2.11.2)$$

Formula (2.11.2) involves, for $k = 1, 2, \ldots, m$, the m binomial coefficients $\binom{m}{k}$. For $m = 0, 1, 2, \ldots, 9$, these coefficients are all shown in Table 2.11.1.[26] They form the corresponding ten rows (numbered from 0) of the triangular pattern. For instance, the numbers in row 6 are

---

[26] Though the triangle is named after the French mathematician Blaise Pascal (1623–1662), it was actually known centuries earlier in several different parts of the world, including India and China.

SECTION 2.11 / NEWTON'S BINOMIAL FORMULA

$$\binom{6}{0}, \quad \binom{6}{1}, \quad \binom{6}{2}, \quad \binom{6}{3}, \quad \binom{6}{4}, \quad \binom{6}{5}, \quad \binom{6}{6}$$

Table 2.11.1 Pascal's triangle

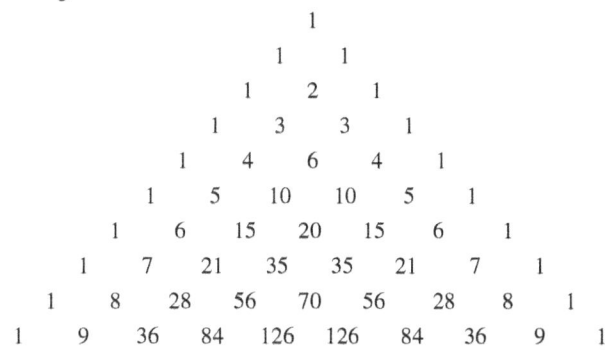

```
                              1
                           1     1
                        1     2     1
                     1     3     3     1
                  1     4     6     4     1
               1     5    10    10     5     1
            1     6    15    20    15     6     1
         1     7    21    35    35    21     7     1
      1     8    28    56    70    56    28     8     1
   1     9    36    84   126   126    84    36     9     1
```

In principle, Table 2.11.1 can be continued indefinitely in order to include arbitrarily large values of the exponent m.

Each binomial coefficient $\binom{m}{k}$ can be read as "m choose k". To help explain this, consider the case when $m = 3$. Then for Eqs (2.11.1) and (2.11.2) to be consistent, we require that $\binom{3}{1} = \binom{3}{2} = 3$. Now consider the following expansion of $(a + b)^3$ in $2^3 = 8$ terms:

$$(a+b)^3 = aaa + aab + aba + abb + baa + bab + bba + bbb$$

In Eq. (2.11.1) the coefficients of a^2b and ab^2 are both 3 because there are $\binom{3}{1} = 3$ ways of choosing one factor b to accompany two factors a, and $\binom{3}{2} = 3$ ways of choosing two factors b to accompany one factor a. For general m and $k \leq m$, the number $\binom{m}{k}$ will count how many ways there are of choosing k factors b to accompany $m - k$ factors a in forming the coefficient of the term $a^{m-k}b^k$.

Before trying to define the binomial coefficients $\binom{m}{k}$, it is convenient first to introduce the standard notation $k!$, read as "k factorial", for the product $1 \cdot 2 \cdot 3 \cdots (k-1) \cdot k$ of the first k natural numbers. That is

$$k! = 1 \cdot 2 \cdot 3 \cdots (k-1) \cdot k \tag{2.11.3}$$

We also introduce the convention that $0! = 1$ since, like the zeroth power $x^0 = 1$ of any real number x, the factorial $0!$ should be the product of zero numbers. Evidently, the definition (2.11.3) implies that

$$k! = k \cdot [1 \cdot 2 \cdot 3 \cdots (k-1)] = k(k-1)! \quad \text{for} \quad k = 1, 2, \ldots$$

Applying this formula repeatedly to find the first five factorials gives

$$0! = 1, \quad 1! = 1 \cdot 0! = 1, \quad 2! = 2 \cdot 1! = 2, \quad 3! = 3 \cdot 2! = 6, \quad 4! = 4 \cdot 3! = 24$$

Following this pattern, the next four are $5! = 120$, $6! = 720$, $7! = 5040$, $8! = 10\,320$. Factorial numbers grow remarkably quickly! Since we shall use it very shortly, we also note how definition (2.11.3) implies that, whenever k and m are natural numbers with $k \leq m$, one must have

$$m! = [m(m-1)\cdots(m-k+1)](m-k)! \tag{2.11.4}$$

Now that we have explained factorial notation, we can move on to define, for each $m = 1, 2, \ldots$ and then for each $k = 0, 1, 2, \ldots, m$, the binomial coefficient as

$$\binom{m}{k} = \frac{m!}{k!(m-k)!} \tag{2.11.5}$$

This formula implies in particular that

$$\binom{m}{0} = \frac{m!}{0!m!} = 1, \quad \binom{m}{1} = \frac{m!}{1!(m-1)!} = m, \quad \text{and} \quad \binom{m}{m} = \frac{m!}{m!0!} = 1$$

Because of Eq. (2.11.4), definition (2.11.5) is equivalent to

$$\binom{m}{k} = \frac{m(m-1)\cdots(m-k+1)}{k!}$$

Then when $m = 5$, for example, we have

$$\binom{5}{2} = \frac{5 \cdot 4}{1 \cdot 2} = 10, \quad \binom{5}{3} = \frac{5 \cdot 4 \cdot 3}{1 \cdot 2 \cdot 3} = 10, \quad \binom{5}{4} = \frac{5 \cdot 4 \cdot 3 \cdot 2}{1 \cdot 2 \cdot 3 \cdot 4} = 5$$

So (2.11.2) implies that $(a+b)^5 = a^5 + 5a^4b + 10a^3b^2 + 10a^2b^3 + 5ab^4 + b^5$.

Next we note two general properties of the numbers in Table 2.11.1. Of these, the first is that the numbers are obviously symmetric about a vertical line drawn down the middle. This symmetry can be expressed as

$$\binom{m}{k} = \binom{m}{m-k} \tag{2.11.6}$$

For example, $\binom{6}{2} = 15 = \binom{6}{4}$. Generally, this symmetry is an obvious implication of the fact that interchanging k and $m-k$ makes no difference to the definition in Eq. (2.11.5).

The second property is more subtle. Apart from the 1 at both ends of each row, each number in Table 2.11.1 happens to equal the sum of the two adjacent numbers in the row above. For instance, the element 56 in row 8 is equal to the sum of the two adjacent elements 21 and 35 just above it in row 7. In symbols,

$$\binom{m+1}{k} = \binom{m}{k-1} + \binom{m}{k} \tag{2.11.7}$$

In Exercise 2 you are asked to prove the two properties in Eqs (2.11.6) and (2.11.7).

Finally, we offer a proof of Newton's binomial formula. Before doing so, we use summation notation to express it as

$$(a+b)^m = a^m + \sum_{k=1}^{m-1} \binom{m}{k} a^{m-k} b^k + b^m \qquad (2.11.8)$$

EXAMPLE 2.11.1 Use induction on m to prove Eq. (2.11.8) for $m = 1, 2, \ldots$.

Solution: When $m = 1$, the summation part of the right-hand side of (2.11.8) disappears completely, and the equation is trivially true.

For the induction step, suppose that (2.11.8) holds for any particular natural number m. Multiplying each side of (2.11.8) by $a + b$ gives

$$(a+b)^{m+1} = a^{m+1} + a^m b + \sum_{k=1}^{m-1} \binom{m}{k} (a^{m-k+1} b^k + a^{m-k} b^{k+1}) + ab^m + b^{m+1} \qquad (*)$$

In this expression, the coefficient of $a^m b$ is $1 + \binom{m}{1} = \binom{m}{0} + \binom{m}{1}$, where the second term comes from the first part of the sum in $(*)$ when $k = 1$. On the other hand, the coefficient of ab^m is $\binom{m}{m-1} + 1 = \binom{m}{m-1} + \binom{m}{m}$, where the first term comes from the second part of the sum in $(*)$ when $k = m - 1$. Then, for each $k = 2, 3, \ldots, m - 1$, the coefficient of $a^{m+1-k} b^k$ is $\binom{m}{k-1} + \binom{m}{k}$, where the first term comes from the second part of the sum in $(*)$ with k reduced by 1, whereas the second term comes directly from the first part of the sum in $(*)$.

It follows that for each $k = 1, 2, 3, \ldots, m - 1, m$, the coefficient of $a^{m+1-k} b^k$ is the sum $\binom{m}{k-1} + \binom{m}{k}$. But applying Eq. (2.11.7) reduces this to $\binom{m+1}{k}$. So we have proved that

$$(a+b)^{m+1} = a^{m+1} + \sum_{k=1}^{m} \binom{m+1}{k} a^{m-k+1} b^k + b^{m+1}$$

But this is precisely Eq. (2.11.8) with m replaced by $m + 1$. This completes the proof of the induction step, and so the proof by induction on m.

EXERCISES FOR SECTION 2.11

1. Use Newton's binomial formula to find $(a+b)^6$.

2. (a) Verify by direct computation that

$$\binom{8}{3} = \binom{8}{8-3} \quad \text{and} \quad \binom{8+1}{4} = \binom{8}{4} + \binom{8}{4-1}$$

   (b) Use definition (2.11.5) to verify (2.11.6) and (2.11.7).

3. Use the binomial formula with $a = b = 1$ to evaluate the sum $\sum_{k=0}^{m} \binom{m}{k}$.

2.12 Double Sums

Often one has to combine two or even more summation signs. Consider, for instance, the following rectangular array of numbers:

$$\begin{matrix} a_{11} & a_{12} & \cdots & a_{1n} \\ a_{21} & a_{22} & \cdots & a_{2n} \\ \vdots & \vdots & & \vdots \\ a_{m1} & a_{m2} & \cdots & a_{mn} \end{matrix} \qquad (2.12.1)$$

The array can be regarded as a *spreadsheet*, as it would be in an economic example where each a_{ij} indicates the total revenue of a firm from its sales in region i in month j.

A typical entry in the array takes the form a_{ij}, where i indicates the row, and j the column, with $1 \leq i \leq m$ and $1 \leq j \leq n$. So there are $n \cdot m$ numbers in all. Suppose we are asked to find the sum of all the $n \cdot m$ numbers in the array.

One way to do this would be to find first the sum of the n numbers in each of the m rows, followed by adding all these row sums. The m different row sums can be written in the form $\sum_{j=1}^{n} a_{1j}, \sum_{j=1}^{n} a_{2j}, \ldots, \sum_{j=1}^{n} a_{mj}$. The sum of these m row sums is equal to $\sum_{j=1}^{n} a_{1j} + \sum_{j=1}^{n} a_{2j} + \cdots + \sum_{j=1}^{n} a_{mj}$. A key idea is to realize that using summation notation twice allows this expression to be written as the double sum $\sum_{i=1}^{m} \left(\sum_{j=1}^{n} a_{ij} \right)$.

Alternatively we can first add the numbers in each of the n columns, and then add these column sums. This gives

$$\sum_{i=1}^{m} a_{i1} + \sum_{i=1}^{m} a_{i2} + \cdots + \sum_{i=1}^{m} a_{in} = \sum_{j=1}^{n} \left(\sum_{i=1}^{m} a_{ij} \right)$$

Either way, we have calculated the sum of all the numbers in the array. For this reason, we must have

$$\sum_{i=1}^{m} \sum_{j=1}^{n} a_{ij} = \sum_{j=1}^{n} \sum_{i=1}^{m} a_{ij}$$

where, according to usual practice, we have deleted the parentheses. This formula says that *in a (finite) double sum, the order of summation is immaterial*. It is important to note that, for this to hold, the summation limits for i and j must be independent of each other.[27] In our economic example, both these double sums equal the total revenues over all m regions summed over all the n months.

---

[27] Otherwise, changing the order in a double sum like $\sum_{j=1}^{n} \sum_{i=1}^{j} a_{ij}$ to obtain $\sum_{i=1}^{j} \sum_{j=1}^{n} a_{ij}$ results in an expression that makes little sense.

SECTION 2.12 / DOUBLE SUMS

EXAMPLE 2.12.1 Compute $\sum_{i=1}^{3} \sum_{j=1}^{4} (i + 2j)$.

Solution:

$$\sum_{i=1}^{3} \sum_{j=1}^{4} (i + 2j) = \sum_{i=1}^{3} [(i+2) + (i+4) + (i+6) + (i+8)]$$

$$= \sum_{i=1}^{3} (4i + 20) = 24 + 28 + 32 = 84$$

You should check that the result is the same if one sums over i first instead.

EXERCISES FOR SECTION 2.12

SM 1. Expand and compute the following double sums:

(a) $\sum_{i=1}^{3} \sum_{j=1}^{4} i \cdot 3^{j}$

(b) $\sum_{s=0}^{2} \sum_{r=2}^{4} \left(\frac{rs}{r+s} \right)^{2}$

(c) $\sum_{i=1}^{m} \sum_{j=1}^{n} (i + j^{2})$

(d) $\sum_{i=1}^{m} \sum_{j=1}^{2} i^{j}$

2. Consider a group of individuals each having a certain number of units of m different goods. Let a_{ij} denote the number of units of good i owned by person j, for $i = 1, \ldots, m$ and for $j = 1, \ldots, n$. Explain in words the meaning of the following sums:

(a) $\sum_{j=1}^{n} a_{ij}$

(b) $\sum_{i=1}^{m} a_{ij}$

(c) $\sum_{j=1}^{n} \sum_{i=1}^{m} a_{ij}$

3. Prove that the sum of all the numbers in the triangular array

$$\begin{array}{cccc}
a_{11} & & & \\
a_{21} & a_{22} & & \\
a_{31} & a_{32} & a_{33} & \\
\vdots & \vdots & \vdots & \ddots \\
a_{m1} & a_{m2} & a_{m3} & \cdots & a_{mm}
\end{array}$$

can be written as $\sum_{i=1}^{m} \left(\sum_{j=1}^{i} a_{ij} \right)$ and also as $\sum_{j=1}^{m} \left(\sum_{i=j}^{m} a_{ij} \right)$.

SM 4. [HARDER] Consider the $m \cdot n$ numbers a_{ij} in the rectangular array (2.12.1). Denote the arithmetic mean of them all by $\bar{a}$, and the mean of the numbers in the jth column by $\bar{a}_j$, so

$$\bar{a} = \frac{1}{mn} \sum_{r=1}^{m} \sum_{s=1}^{n} a_{rs} \quad \text{and} \quad \bar{a}_j = \frac{1}{m} \sum_{r=1}^{m} a_{rj}.$$

Prove that $\bar{a}$ is the mean of the column means $\bar{a}_j$ ($j = 1, \ldots, n$) and that

$$\sum_{r=1}^{m} \sum_{s=1}^{m} (a_{rj} - \bar{a})(a_{sj} - \bar{a}) = m^{2} (\bar{a}_j - \bar{a})^{2} \quad (*)$$

REVIEW EXERCISES

1. (a) Suppose that the price of a phone, denoted by a, includes VAT (value added tax) at the rate 20%. What is its price before VAT is included?

   (b) A person buys x_1, x_2, and x_3 units of three goods whose prices per unit are respectively p_1, p_2, and p_3. What is the total expenditure?

   (c) A rental car costs F dollars per day in fixed charges, plus b dollars per kilometre. What does the rental car company charge for driving the car x kilometres in one day?

   (d) A company has fixed costs of F dollars per year and variable costs of c dollars per unit produced. Find an expression for the total cost per unit (total average cost) incurred by the company if it produces x units in one year.

   (e) An employee starts with an annual salary of $\$L$, subsequently raised by $p\%$, followed by a second increase of $q\%$. What is the employee's salary after these two raises?

2. Express as single real numbers, in decimal notation:

   (a) 5^3 (b) 10^{-3} (c) $\dfrac{1}{3^{-3}}$ (d) $\dfrac{-1}{10^{-3}}$

   (e) $3^{-2}3^3$ (f) $(3^{-2})^{-3}$ (g) $-\left(\dfrac{5}{3}\right)^0$ (h) $\left(-\dfrac{1}{2}\right)^{-3}$

3. Which of the following expressions are defined, and what are their values if they are?

   (a) $(0+2)^0$ (b) 0^{-2} (c) $\dfrac{(10)^0}{(0+1)^0}$ (d) $\dfrac{(0+1)^0}{(0+2)^0}$

4. Simplify the following expressions:

   (a) $(2^3 2^{-5})^3$ (b) $\left(\dfrac{2}{3}\right)^{-1} - \left(\dfrac{4}{3}\right)^{-1}$ (c) $(3^{-2} - 5^{-1})^{-1}$ (d) $(1.12)^{-3}(1.12)^3$

SM 5. Simplify the following expressions:

   (a) $(2x)^4$ (b) $(2^{-1} - 4^{-1})^{-1}$ (c) $\dfrac{24x^3 y^2 z^3}{4x^2 yz^2}$

   (d) $[-(-ab^3)^{-3}(a^6 b^6)^2]^3$ (e) $\dfrac{a^5 \cdot a^3 \cdot a^{-2}}{a^{-3} \cdot a^6}$ (f) $\left[\left(\dfrac{x}{2}\right)^3 \cdot \dfrac{8}{x^{-2}}\right]^{-3}$

6. Complete the following statements:

   (a) $x^{-1} y^{-1} = 3 \implies x^3 y^3 = \cdots$ (b) $x^7 = 2 \implies (x^{-3})^6 (x^2)^2 = \cdots$

   (c) $\left(\dfrac{xy}{z}\right)^{-2} = 3 \implies \left(\dfrac{z}{xy}\right)^6 = \cdots$ (d) $a^{-1} b^{-1} c^{-1} = \tfrac{1}{4} \implies (abc)^4 = \cdots$

7. Give economic interpretations to each of the following expressions and then find their approximate values:

   (a) €$100 \cdot (1.01)^8$ (b) £$50\,000 \cdot (1.15)^{10}$ (c) $\$6\,000 \cdot (1.03)^{-8}$

8. (a) $\$100\,000$ is deposited into an account earning 8% interest per year. If there are no subsequent deposits or withdrawals, how much is in the account ten years later?

   (b) If the interest rate is 8% each year, how much money should you have deposited in a bank six years ago to have $\$25\,000$ today?

CHAPTER 2 / REVIEW EXERCISES

SM 9. Expand and simplify the following expressions:

(a) $a(a-1)$ (b) $(x-3)(x+7)$ (c) $-\sqrt{3}\left(\sqrt{3}-\sqrt{6}\right)$

(d) $\left(1-\sqrt{2}\right)^2$ (e) $(x-1)^3$ (f) $(1-b^2)(1+b^2)$

(g) $(1+x+x^2+x^3)(1-x)$ (h) $(1+x)^4$

10. Factor the following expressions:

(a) $25x-5$ (b) $3x^2-x^3y$ (c) $50-x^2$ (d) $a^3-4a^2b+4ab^2$

SM 11. Factor the following expressions:

(a) $5(x+2y)+a(x+2y)$ (b) $(a+b)c-d(a+b)$ (c) $ax+ay+2x+2y$

(d) $2x^2-5yz+10xz-xy$ (e) p^2-q^2+p-q (f) $u^3+v^3-u^2v-v^2u$

12. Compute the following numbers, without using a calculator:

(a) $16^{1/4}$ (b) $243^{-1/5}$ (c) $5^{1/7}\cdot 5^{6/7}$ (d) $(4^8)^{-3/16}$

(e) $64^{1/3}+\sqrt[3]{125}$ (f) $(-8/27)^{2/3}$ (g) $(-1/8)^{-2/3}+(1/27)^{-2/3}$ (h) $\dfrac{1000^{-2/3}}{\sqrt[3]{5^{-3}}}$

13. Solve the following equations for x:

(a) $2^{2x}=8$ (b) $3^{3x+1}=1/81$ (c) $10^{x^2-2x+2}=100$

14. Find the unknown x in each of the following equations:

(a) $25^5\cdot 25^x=25^3$ (b) $3^x-3^{x-2}=24$ (c) $3^x\cdot 3^{x-1}=81$

(d) $3^5+3^5+3^5=3^x$ (e) $4^{-6}+4^{-6}+4^{-6}+4^{-6}=4^x$ (f) $\dfrac{2^{26}-2^{23}}{2^{26}+2^{23}}=\dfrac{x}{9}$

SM 15. Simplify the following expressions:

(a) $\dfrac{s}{2s-1}-\dfrac{s}{2s+1}$ (b) $\dfrac{x}{3-x}-\dfrac{1-x}{x+3}-\dfrac{24}{x^2-9}$ (c) $\left(\dfrac{1}{x^2y}-\dfrac{1}{xy^2}\right)\div\left(\dfrac{1}{x^2}-\dfrac{1}{y^2}\right)$

SM 16. Reduce the following fractions:

(a) $\dfrac{25a^3b^2}{125ab}$ (b) $\dfrac{x^2-y^2}{x+y}$ (c) $\dfrac{4a^2-12ab+9b^2}{4a^2-9b^2}$ (d) $\dfrac{4x-x^3}{4-4x+x^2}$

17. Solve the following inequalities:

(a) $2(x-4)<5$ (b) $\frac{1}{3}(y-3)+4\geq 2$ (c) $8-0.2x\leq\dfrac{4-0.1x}{0.5}$

(d) $\dfrac{x-1}{-3}>\dfrac{-3x+8}{-5}$ (e) $|5-3x|\leq 8$ (f) $|x^2-4|\leq 2$

18. Using a mobile phone costs $30 per month, and an additional $0.16 per minute of use.

(a) What is the cost for one month if the phone is used for a total of x minutes?

(b) What are the smallest and largest numbers of *hours* you can use the phone in a month if the monthly telephone bill is to be between $102 and $126?

19. If a rope could be wrapped around the Earth's surface at the equator, it would be approximately circular and about 40 million metres long. Suppose we wanted to extend the rope to make it 1 metre above the equator at every point. How many more metres of rope would be needed? (Recall that the circumference of a circle with radius r is $2\pi r$.)

20. (a) Prove that $a + \dfrac{a \cdot p}{100} - \dfrac{(a + \frac{a \cdot p}{100}) \cdot p}{100} = a\left[1 - \left(\dfrac{p}{100}\right)^2\right]$.

(b) An item initially costs $2\,000$ and then its price is increased by 5%. Afterwards the price is lowered by 5%. What is the final price?

(c) An item initially costs a dollars and then its price is increased by $p\%$. Afterwards the (new) price is lowered by $p\%$. What is the final price of the item? (After considering this exercise, look at the expression in part (a).)

(d) What is the result if one first *lowers* a price by $p\%$ and then *increases* it by $p\%$?

21. (a) If $a > b$, is it necessarily true that $a^2 > b^2$?

(b) Show that if $a + b > 0$, then $a > b$ implies $a^2 > b^2$.

22. (a) If $a > b$, use numerical examples to check whether $1/a > 1/b$, or $1/a < 1/b$.

(b) Prove that if $a > b$ and $ab > 0$, then $1/b > 1/a$.

23. Prove that, for all real numbers a and b, one has:

(a) $|ab| = |a| \cdot |b|$ (b) $|a + b| \leq |a| + |b|$

The inequality in (b) is called the *triangle inequality*.

(SM) 24. Consider a fixed equilateral triangle, and let P be an arbitrary point within the triangle. Let h_1, h_2, and h_3 be the shortest distances from P to each of the three sides. Show that the sum $h_1 + h_2 + h_3$ is independent of where point P is placed in the triangle. (*Hint*: Compute the area of the triangle as the sum of three triangles.)

25. Evaluate the following sums:

(a) $\displaystyle\sum_{i=1}^{4} \dfrac{1}{i(i+2)}$ (b) $\displaystyle\sum_{j=5}^{9} (2j - 8)^2$ (c) $\displaystyle\sum_{k=1}^{5} \left(\dfrac{k-1}{k+1}\right)$

(d) $\displaystyle\sum_{n=2}^{5} (n-1)^2(n+2)$ (e) $\displaystyle\sum_{k=1}^{5} \left(\dfrac{1}{k} - \dfrac{1}{k+1}\right)$ (f) $\displaystyle\sum_{i=-2}^{3} (i+3)^i$

26. Express the following sums in summation notation:

(a) $3 + 5 + 7 + \cdots + 199 + 201$ (b) $\dfrac{2}{1} + \dfrac{3}{2} + \dfrac{4}{3} + \cdots + \dfrac{97}{96}$

(c) $4 \cdot 6 + 5 \cdot 7 + 6 \cdot 8 + \cdots + 38 \cdot 40$ (d) $\dfrac{1}{x} + \dfrac{1}{x^2} + \cdots + \dfrac{1}{x^n}$

(e) $1 + \dfrac{x^2}{3} + \dfrac{x^4}{5} + \dfrac{x^6}{7} + \cdots + \dfrac{x^{32}}{33}$ (f) $1 - \dfrac{1}{2} + \dfrac{1}{3} - \dfrac{1}{4} + \cdots - \dfrac{1}{80} + \dfrac{1}{81}$

27. Which of these equalities are always right and which of them are sometimes wrong?

(a) $\sum_{i=1}^{n} a_i = \sum_{j=3}^{n+2} a_{j-2}$

(b) $\sum_{i=1}^{n} (a_i + b_i)^2 = \sum_{i=1}^{n} a_i^2 + \sum_{i=1}^{n} b_i^2$

(c) $\sum_{k=0}^{n} 5a_{k+1,j} = 5 \sum_{k=1}^{n+1} a_{k,j}$

(d) $\sum_{i=1}^{3} \frac{a_i}{b_i} = \frac{\sum_{i=1}^{3} a_i}{\sum_{i=1}^{3} b_i}$

SM 28. Find the following two sums:

(a) $3 + 5 + 7 + \cdots + 197 + 199 + 201$

(b) $1001 + 2002 + 3003 + \cdots + 8008 + 9009 + 10\,010$

3 SOLVING EQUATIONS

The true mathematician is not a juggler of numbers, but of concepts.
—From Ian Stewart *Concepts of Modern Mathematics* (1975)

Virtually all applications of mathematics involve equations that have to be solved. Economics is no exception, so this chapter considers some types of equation that appear frequently in economic models.

Many students are used to dealing with algebraic expressions and equations involving *only one* variable, usually denoted by *x*. Often they have difficulties, at first, in dealing with expressions involving several variables with a wide variety of names, and denoted by different letters. For economists, however, it is very important to be able to handle with ease such algebraic expressions and equations.

3.1 Solving Equations

To *solve* an equation means to find all values of the variables for which the equation is satisfied. Consider the following simple example

$$3x + 10 = x + 4$$

which contains the *variable x*. In order to isolate x on one side of the equation, we add $-x$ to both sides. This gives $2x + 10 = 4$. Adding -10 to both sides of this equation yields $2x = 4 - 10 = -6$. Dividing by 2 we get the solution $x = -3$.

This procedure was probably already familiar to you. The method is summed up next, noting that two equations that have exactly the same solutions are called *equivalent*.

EQUIVALENT EQUATIONS

To get an equivalent equation, do either of the following on both sides of the equality sign:

(i) add (or subtract) the same number;

(ii) multiply (or divide) by the same number different from 0.

It is important to note that not only is division by 0 excluded; so is multiplication by 0. For example, if one multiplies each side of the equation $x = 1$ by 0, the result is the trivial equation $0 = 0$. Now, it is not very interesting but harmless to assert that $x = 1 \Rightarrow 0 = 0$. But $0 = 0$ definitely does not imply that $x = 1$, so the two equations are definitely not equivalent.

When faced with more complicated equations involving parentheses and fractions, we usually begin by multiplying out the parentheses, and then we multiply both sides of the equation by the lowest common denominator for all the fractions.

EXAMPLE 3.1.1 Solve the equation

$$6p - \frac{1}{2}(2p - 3) = 3(1 - p) - \frac{7}{6}(p + 2)$$

Solution: First multiply out the parentheses: $6p - p + \frac{3}{2} = 3 - 3p - \frac{7}{6}p - \frac{7}{3}$. Second, multiply both sides by the lowest common denominator: $36p - 6p + 9 = 18 - 18p - 7p - 14$. Third, gather terms: $55p = -5$. Thus $p = -5/55 = -1/11$.

If a value of a variable makes an expression in an equation undefined, that value is not allowed. For instance, the variable z is not allowed to have the value 5 in any equation that involves the expression

$$\frac{z}{z - 5}$$

because 5/0 is undefined. As the next example shows, a restriction such as $z \neq 5$ can imply that a particular equation has no solutions at all.

EXAMPLE 3.1.2 Find what values of z solve the equation

$$\frac{z}{z - 5} + \frac{1}{3} = \frac{-5}{5 - z}$$

Solution: We now know that z cannot be 5. Remembering this restriction, we clear fractions by multiplying both sides by $3(z - 5)$, which is their lowest common denominator. The result is $3z + z - 5 = 15$, which has the unique solution $z = 5$. Because we had to assume $z \neq 5$, we must conclude that the original equation has no solution.

SECTION 3.1 / SOLVING EQUATIONS

The next example shows, again, that sometimes a surprising degree of care is needed to find the right solutions.

EXAMPLE 3.1.3 Solve the equation

$$\frac{x+2}{x-2} - \frac{8}{x^2 - 2x} = \frac{2}{x}$$

Solution: Since $x^2 - 2x = x(x-2)$, the lowest common denominator is $x(x-2)$. We see that $x = 2$ and $x = 0$ both make the equation absurd, because then at least one of the denominators becomes 0. Provided that $x \neq 0$ and $x \neq 2$, we can multiply both sides of the equation by the common denominator $x(x-2)$ to obtain

$$\frac{x+2}{x-2} \cdot x(x-2) - \frac{8}{x(x-2)} \cdot x(x-2) = \frac{2}{x} \cdot x(x-2)$$

Cancelling common factors, this reduces to $(x+2)x - 8 = 2(x-2)$ or $x^2 + 2x - 8 = 2x - 4$, and so $x^2 = 4$. Equations of the form $x^2 = a$, where $a > 0$, have two solutions $x = \sqrt{a}$ and $x = -\sqrt{a}$. In our case, $x^2 = 4$ has solutions $x = 2$ and $x = -2$. But $x = 2$ makes the original equation absurd, so *only* $x = -2$ is a solution.

Often, solving a problem in economic analysis requires formulating an appropriate *algebraic* equation.

EXAMPLE 3.1.4 A firm manufactures a commodity that costs $20 per unit to produce. In addition, the firm has fixed costs of $2 000. Each unit sells for $75. How many units must the firm sell if it is to meet a profit target of $14 500?

Solution: Let Q denote the number of units produced and sold. Then the revenue of the firm is $75Q$ and the total cost of production is $20Q + 2000$. Because profit is the difference between total revenue and total cost, it can be written as $75Q - (20Q + 2000)$. To meet the profit target of $14 500, therefore, requires satisfying the equation

$$75Q - (20Q + 2000) = 14\,500$$

It is now easy to find the solution: $Q = 16\,500/55 = 300$ units.

EXERCISES FOR SECTION 3.1

1. Solve each of the following equations:

   (a) $2x - (5 + x) = 16 - (3x + 9)$
   (b) $-5(3x - 2) = 16(1 - x)$
   (c) $4x + 2(x - 4) - 3 = 2(3x - 5) - 1$
   (d) $(8x - 7)5 - 3(6x - 4) + 5x^2 = x(5x - 1)$
   (e) $x^2 + 10x + 25 = 0$
   (f) $(3x - 1)^2 + (4x + 1)^2 = (5x - 1)(5x + 1) + 1$

2. Solve each of the following equations:

   (a) $3x = \frac{1}{4}x - 7$
   (b) $\frac{x-3}{4} + 2 = 3x$
   (c) $\frac{1}{2x+1} = \frac{1}{x+2}$
   (d) $\sqrt{2x + 14} = 16$

3. Solve each of the following equations:

(a) $\dfrac{x-3}{x+3} = \dfrac{x-4}{x+4}$ (b) $\dfrac{3}{x-3} - \dfrac{2}{x+3} = \dfrac{9}{x^2-9}$ (c) $\dfrac{6x}{5} - \dfrac{5}{x} = \dfrac{2x-3}{3} + \dfrac{8x}{15}$

4. Solve the following problems, by first formulating an equation in each case:

(a) The sum of three successive natural numbers is 10 more than twice the smallest of them. Find the numbers.

(b) Jane receives double pay for every hour she works over and above 38 hours per week. Last week, she worked 48 hours and earned a total of $812. What is Jane's regular hourly wage?

(c) James has invested £15 000 at an annual interest rate of 10%. How much additional money should he invest at the interest rate of 12%, if he wants the total interest earned by the end of the year to equal £2 100?

(d) When Mr Barnes passed away, 2/3 of his estate was left to his wife, 1/4 was shared by his children, and the remainder, $100 000, was donated to a charity. How big was Mr Barnes's estate?

5. Solve the following equations:

(a) $\dfrac{3y-1}{4} - \dfrac{1-y}{3} + 2 = 3y$ (b) $\dfrac{4}{x} + \dfrac{3}{x+2} = \dfrac{2x+2}{x^2+2x} + \dfrac{7}{2x+4}$

(c) $\dfrac{2 - z/(1-z)}{1+z} = \dfrac{6}{2z+1}$ (d) $\dfrac{1}{2}\left(\dfrac{p}{2} - \dfrac{3}{4}\right) - \dfrac{1}{4}\left(1 - \dfrac{p}{3}\right) - \dfrac{1}{3}(1-p) = -\dfrac{1}{3}$

6. Ms Preston has y euros to spend on apples, bananas, and cherries. She decides to spend the same amount of money on each kind of fruit. The prices per kilo are 3 for apples, 2 for bananas, and 6 for cherries. What is the total weight of fruit she buys, and how much does she pay per kilo of fruit?[1]

3.2 Equations and Their Parameters

Economists use mathematical models to describe how different economic variables affect each other, or what we call their "interdependence". Macroeconomic models, for instance, are designed to explain the broad outlines of a country's economy; in these models, the variables that economists use most often include the total output of the economy (or its gross domestic product), as well as its total consumption and its total investment.

The simplest kind of relationship between two variables occurs when the response of one variable to a change of one unit in the other one is always the same. In this case, the relationship can be described by a *linear equation*, such as

$$y = 10x, \quad \text{or } y = 3x + 4, \quad \text{or } y = -\dfrac{8}{3}x - \dfrac{7}{2} \tag{3.2.1}$$

In these three cases, the response of variable y to an increase of one unit in variable x is, respectively, 10, 3, and $-\tfrac{8}{3}$.

---

[1] This is an example of "dollar cost" averaging, which we will encounter again in Exercise 14.5.4

The three equations (3.2.1) share a common structure. This makes it possible to write down a general linear equation covering all the special cases where x and y are the only two variables:

$$y = ax + b \qquad (3.2.2)$$

Here a and b are real numbers. For example, letting $a = 3$ and $b = 4$ yields the particular case where $y = 3x + 4$. Note that when $a = 0$, the value of y is constant and the graph of the equation is a horizontal straight line. Graphs which are vertical straight lines are also possible. They occur when x is a constant, denoted by c, but y varies. In order to accommodate this case, we interchange the values of x and y, and write $x = c$.

The numbers a and b are called *parameters*, as they take on different, but "fixed" values.[2] In economics, parameters often have interesting interpretations.

EXAMPLE 3.2.1 Consider the basic macroeconomic model

$$Y = C + \bar{I} \qquad (3.2.3)$$

and

$$C = a + bY \qquad (3.2.4)$$

where Y is the gross domestic product (GDP), C is consumption, and $\bar{I}$ is total investment, which is treated as fixed. Equation (3.2.3) says that GDP is, by definition, the sum of consumption and total investment. Equation (3.2.4) says that consumption is a linear function of GDP. Here, a and b are positive parameters of the model, with $b < 1$.[3] Solve the model for Y in terms of $\bar{I}$ and the parameters.

Solution: Substituting (3.2.4) into (3.2.3) gives

$$Y = a + bY + \bar{I}$$

Now, we rearrange this equation so that all the terms containing Y are on the left-hand side. This can be done by adding $-bY$ to both sides, thus cancelling the bY term on the right-hand side. The result is

$$Y - bY = a + \bar{I}$$

Notice that the left-hand side is equal to $(1 - b)Y$, so $(1 - b)Y = a + \bar{I}$. Next, divide both sides by $1 - b$, to make the coefficient of Y equal to 1. This gives the answer:

$$Y = \frac{a}{1-b} + \frac{1}{1-b}\bar{I} \qquad (3.2.5)$$

---

[2] Linear equations are studied in more detail in Section 4.4.
[3] Parameter a is often referred to as *autonomous consumption*, as it represents the part of consumption that is *not* proportional to the economy's income. The increase of consumption caused by an increase of one unit in income is measured by b; accordingly, this parameter is generally known as *marginal propensity to consume*. Special cases of the model are obtained by choosing particular numerical values for the parameters, such as $\bar{I} = 100$, $a = 500$, $b = 0.8$, or $\bar{I} = 150$, $a = 600$, $b = 0.9$. Inserting these particular parameter values gives, respectively, $Y = C + 100$ and $C = 500 + 0.8Y$; or $Y = C + 150$ and $C = 600 + 0.9Y$.

This solution is a linear equation expressing Y in terms of $\bar{I}$ and the parameters a and b.

Note the power of the approach used here: the model is solved only once, and then numerical answers are found simply by substituting appropriate numerical values for the parameters of the model. For instance, if $\bar{I} = 100$, $a = 500$, $b = 0.8$, then $Y = 3000$.

Economists usually call Eqs (3.2.3) and (3.2.4) the *structural form* of the model, whereas Eq. (3.2.5) is called its *reduced form*. In the reduced form, the number $1/(1-b)$ is itself a parameter. This is known as the *investment multiplier*, because it measures the response in income to an "exogenous" increase in investment.

Of course, we often need to solve more complicated *nonlinear equations*. These often involve "strange" letters denoting their parameters and variables.

EXAMPLE 3.2.2   Suppose that the total demand for money in an economy is given by

$$M = \alpha Y + \beta (r - \gamma)^{-\delta} \quad (*)$$

Here M is the quantity of money in circulation, Y is national income and r is the interest rate. Also α, β, γ, and δ are all positive parameters, with δ a rational number.

(a) Solve the model for r in terms of the other variables.

(b) For the USA during the period 1929–1952, the four parameters have been estimated as $\alpha = 0.14$, $\beta = 76.03$, $\gamma = 2$, and $\delta = 0.84$. Show that r is then given by

$$r = 2 + \left(\frac{76.03}{M - 0.14Y} \right)^{25/21}$$

Solution:

(a) It follows easily from the equation $(*)$ that $(r - \gamma)^{-\delta} = (M - \alpha Y)/\beta$. Now, raise each side to the power $-1/\delta$ (which is also rational) to obtain

$$r - \gamma = [(M - \alpha Y)/\beta]^{-1/\delta}$$

Next, add γ to both sides and use the equality $(a/b)^{-p} = (b/a)^p$. This yields the solution

$$r = \gamma + \left(\frac{\beta}{M - \alpha Y} \right)^{1/\delta} \quad (**)$$

(b) The specified values of the four parameters imply that $1/\delta = 1/0.84 = 100/84 = 25/21$. The required formula then follows immediately from Eq. $(**)$.

EXERCISES FOR SECTION 3.2

1. Find the value of Y for the case when $Y = C + 150$ and $C = 600 + 0.9Y$ in the model of Example 3.2.1. Verify that Eq. (3.2.5) gives the same result.

SM 2. Solve the following equations for x:

(a) $\dfrac{1}{ax} + \dfrac{1}{bx} = 2$

(b) $\dfrac{ax+b}{cx+d} = A$

(c) $\tfrac{1}{2}px^{-1/2} - w = 0$

(d) $\sqrt{1+x} + \dfrac{ax}{\sqrt{1+x}} = 0$

(e) $a^2x^2 - b^2 = 0$

(f) $(3+a^2)^x = 1$

3. Solve the following equations for the indicated variables:

(a) The demand function, $q = 0.15p + 0.14$, for the price p;

(b) The supply function, $S = \alpha + \beta P$, for the price P;

(c) The area of a triangle, $A = \tfrac{1}{2}bh$, for its base b;

(d) The volume of a ball, $V = \tfrac{4}{3}\pi r^3$, for its radius r;

(e) The production function $AK^\alpha L^\beta = Y_0$, for its labour input L.

SM 4. Solve the following equations for the indicated variables:

(a) $\alpha x - a = \beta x - b$ for x

(b) $\sqrt{pq} - 3q = 5$ for p

(c) $Y = 94 + 0.2(Y - (20 + 0.5Y))$ for Y

(d) $K^{1/2}\left(\tfrac{1}{2}\tfrac{r}{w}K\right)^{1/4} = Q$ for K

(e) $\dfrac{\tfrac{1}{2}K^{-1/2}L^{1/4}}{\tfrac{1}{4}L^{-3/4}K^{1/2}} = \dfrac{r}{w}$ for L

(f) $\tfrac{1}{2}pK^{-1/4}\left(\tfrac{1}{2}\tfrac{r}{w}\right)^{1/4} = r$ for K

5. Solve the following equations for the indicated variables:

(a) $1/s + 1/T = 1/t$ for s

(b) $\sqrt{KLM} - \alpha L = B$ for M

(c) $\dfrac{x - 2y + xz}{x - z} = 4y$ for z

(d) $V = C\left(1 - \dfrac{T}{N}\right)$ for T

3.3 Quadratic Equations

The general quadratic equation in the unknown variable x has the form

$$ax^2 + bx + c = 0 \qquad (3.3.1)$$

where the constants a, b, and c are given real numbers. Note that if $a = 0$ the equation reduces to $bx + c = 0$, which is linear rather than quadratic. So we assume that $a \neq 0$. This allows us to divide each term by a to get the equivalent equation $x^2 + (b/a)x + c/a = 0$. Now define $p = b/a$ and $q = c/a$, so the equation reduces to

$$x^2 + px + q = 0 \qquad (3.3.2)$$

Two special cases are easy to handle. If $q = 0$, so that there is no "constant term", the equation reduces to $x^2 + px = 0$. This is equivalent to $x(x + p) = 0$. Then, since the product of two numbers can be 0 only if at least one of them is 0, we conclude that $x = 0$ or $x = -p$. In short,

$$x^2 + px = 0 \iff x = 0 \text{ or } x = -p$$

Now, if $p \neq 0$, then the equation $x^2 + px = 0$ has the two solutions $x = 0$ and $x = -p$, but no others. Alternatively, if $p = 0$ we have the trivial equation $x^2 = 0$, whose only solution is $x = 0$.

The second special case is when $q \neq 0$ but $p = 0$, so that there is no term involving x. Here Eq. (3.3.2) reduces to $x^2 + q = 0$. Then $x^2 = -q$, and there are two cases to consider. If $q > 0$, the equation has no solution because squaring any number never gives a negative result. In the alternative case when $q \leq 0$, both $x = \sqrt{-q}$ and $x = -\sqrt{-q}$ solve the equation. As discussed in Section 2.5, let us use the notation $x = \pm\sqrt{-q}$ to indicate the two values $\sqrt{-q}$ and $-\sqrt{-q}$ which solve $x^2 + q = 0$. So, assuming that $q \leq 0$, we can write in short

$$x^2 + q = 0 \iff x = \pm\sqrt{-q}$$

These results can be applied to solve any instance of the two simple cases.

EXAMPLE 3.3.1   Solve the following equations:

(a) $5x^2 - 8x = 0$ (b) $x^2 - 4 = 0$ (c) $x^2 + 3 = 0$

Solution:

(a) Dividing each term by 5 yields $x^2 - (8/5)x = x(x - 8/5) = 0$, so $x = 0$ or $x = 8/5$.
(b) The equation yields $x^2 = 4$, so $x = \pm\sqrt{4} = \pm 2$. Alternatively, one has $x^2 - 4 = (x+2)(x-2)$ so the equation is equivalent to $(x+2)(x-2) = 0$. Either way, one concludes that x is either 2 or -2.
(c) Because x^2 is never less than 0, the left-hand side of the equation $x^2 + 3 = 0$ is always strictly positive. Hence, the equation has no solution.

More Difficult Cases

If both coefficients p and q in Eq. (3.3.2) differ from 0, solving it becomes harder. Consider, for example, the equation

$$x^2 - (4/3)x - 1/4 = 0$$

We could, of course, try to find the values of x that satisfy the equation by trial and error. However, it is not easy that way to find the only two solutions, which are $x = 3/2$ and $x = -1/6$. Here are two attempts to solve the equation that fail:

(a) A first attempt rearranges $x^2 - (4/3)x - 1/4 = 0$ to give $x^2 - (4/3)x = 1/4$, and so $x(x - 4/3) = 1/4$. Thus, the product of x and $x - 4/3$ must be 1/4. But there are infinitely many pairs of numbers whose product is 1/4, so this is of very little help in finding x.
(b) A second attempt is to divide each term by x to get $x - 4/3 = 1/4x$. Because the equation involves terms in both x and $1/x$, as well as a constant term, we have made no progress whatsoever.

Evidently, we need a completely new idea in order to find the solution of (3.3.2). The following example illustrates a general method enabling us to solve this harder equation.

EXAMPLE 3.3.2 Solve the equation $x^2 + 8x - 9 = 0$.

Solution: It is natural to begin by moving 9 to the right-hand side:

$$x^2 + 8x = 9 \qquad (*)$$

Because x occurs in two terms, however, it is not obvious how to proceed. A method called *completing the square*, one of the oldest tricks in mathematics, turns out to work.

Let us begin by recalling the quadratic identities in Section 2.3, of which the first implies that $(x+b)^2 = x^2 + 2bx + b^2$. Putting $b = 4$ in this identity gives $(x+4)^2 = x^2 + 8x + 16$, of which the first two terms match the left-hand side of $(*)$. To get the third term 16 as well, we add 16 to each side of the equation $(*)$, which yields

$$x^2 + 8x + 16 = 9 + 16 \qquad (**)$$

whose left-hand side is the complete square $x^2 + 8x + 16 = (x+4)^2$. Thus, Eq. $(**)$ is equivalent to

$$(x+4)^2 = 25 \qquad (***)$$

Now, the equation $z^2 = 25$ has two solutions, which are $z = \pm\sqrt{25} = \pm 5$. Thus, $(***)$ implies that either $x + 4 = 5$ or $x + 4 = -5$. The required solutions are, therefore, $x = 1$ and $x = -9$.

Alternatively, Eq. $(***)$ can be written as $(x+4)^2 - 5^2 = 0$. Using the difference-of-squares formula set out in Section 2.3, we can write this as $(x+4-5)(x+4+5) = 0$. This reduces to $(x-1)(x+9) = 0$. So we have the following *factorization*

$$x^2 + 8x - 9 = (x-1)(x+9)$$

Note that $(x-1)(x+9)$ is 0 precisely when $x = 1$ or $x = -9$.

The General Case

We now apply the method of completing the squares to the quadratic equation (3.3.2). This equation obviously has the same solutions as $x^2 + px = -q$. One half of the coefficient of x is $p/2$. Adding the square of this number to each side of the equation yields

$$x^2 + px + \left(\frac{p}{2}\right)^2 = \left(\frac{p}{2}\right)^2 - q$$

The left-hand side is now a complete square, so

$$\left(x + \frac{p}{2}\right)^2 = \frac{p^2}{4} - q \qquad (3.3.3)$$

Note that if $p^2/4 - q < 0$, then the right-hand side is negative. Because $(x + p/2)^2$ is non-negative for all choices of x, we conclude that Eq. (3.3.3) has no solution in this case. On the other hand, if $p^2/4 - q > 0$, Eq. (3.3.3) yields two possibilities:

$$x + p/2 = \sqrt{p^2/4 - q} \quad \text{and} \quad x + p/2 = -\sqrt{p^2/4 - q}$$

The values of x are then easily found. These formulas are correct even if $p^2/4 - q = 0$, though then they give just the one solution $x = -p/2$. In conclusion:

SIMPLE QUADRATIC FORMULA

Provided that $\frac{1}{4}p^2 \geq q$ one has

$$x^2 + px + q = 0 \text{ if and only if } x = -\frac{1}{2}p \pm \sqrt{\frac{1}{4}p^2 - q} \qquad (3.3.4)$$

Faced with an equation of the type (3.3.1) where $a \neq 0$, we can always find its solutions by first dividing the equation by a and then using (3.3.4). Sometimes, however, it is convenient to have the formula for the solution expressed in terms of the original coefficients a, b, and c of (3.3.1). Recall that dividing Eq. (3.3.1) by a yields the equivalent equation Eq. (3.3.2), with $p = b/a$ and $q = c/a$. Substituting these particular values in (3.3.4) gives the solutions $x = -b/2a \pm \sqrt{b^2/4a^2 - c/a}$. Because $\sqrt{b^2/4a^2 - c/a} = \sqrt{b^2 - 4ac}/2a$, this implies:

GENERAL QUADRATIC FORMULA

Provided that $b^2 - 4ac \geq 0$ and $a \neq 0$, one has

$$ax^2 + bx + c = 0 \text{ if and only if } x = \frac{-b \pm \sqrt{b^2 - 4ac}}{2a} \qquad (3.3.5)$$

It is probably a good idea to spend a few minutes of your life thoroughly memorizing this formula, or the equivalent (3.3.4). Once you have done so, you can immediately write down the solutions of any quadratic equation. Only if $b^2 - 4ac \geq 0$ are the solutions real numbers. If we use the formula when $b^2 - 4ac < 0$, the square root of a negative number appears and no real solution exists. The solutions are often called the *roots* of the equation.[4]

EXAMPLE 3.3.3 Use the quadratic formula to find the solutions of the equation

$$2x^2 - 2x - 40 = 0$$

Solution: Write the equation as $2x^2 + (-2)x + (-40) = 0$. This equation matches the pattern $ax^2 + bx + c = 0$ just in case $a = 2$, $b = -2$, and $c = -40$. So applying the quadratic formula (3.3.5) yields

$$x = \frac{-(-2) \pm \sqrt{(-2)^2 - 4 \cdot 2 \cdot (-40)}}{2 \cdot 2} = \frac{2 \pm \sqrt{4 + 320}}{4} = \frac{2 \pm 18}{4} = \frac{1}{2} \pm \frac{9}{2}$$

The solutions are, therefore, $x = 1/2 + 9/2 = 5$ and $x = 1/2 - 9/2 = -4$.

---

[4] The quadratic formula is very useful, but you should not become an unthinking "quadratic formula fanatic" who uses it always. For example, when $b = 0$ or $c = 0$, we explained at the beginning of this section how to solve the equation very easily. As another example, while answering an exam question that required the equation $(x - 4)^2 = 0$ to be solved, one candidate displayed extreme fanaticism by expanding the parentheses to obtain $x^2 - 8x + 16 = 0$, then eventually using the quadratic formula to get the (correct) answer, $x = 4$. What would you have done?

To use formula (3.3.4) instead, divide each term by 2 to get $x^2 - x - 20 = 0$. Then the solutions are

$$x = 1/2 \pm \sqrt{1/4 + 20} = 1/2 \pm \sqrt{81/4} = 1/2 \pm 9/2$$

which are exactly the same as before.

Suppose $p^2/4 - q \geq 0$ and let x_1 and x_2 be the solutions of Eq. (3.3.2). By using the difference-of-squares formula as we did to obtain the factorization in Example 3.3.2, we see that Eq. (3.3.3) is equivalent to $(x - x_1)(x - x_2) = 0$. It follows also that:

QUADRATIC FACTORIZATION

If x_1 and x_2 are the solutions of $ax^2 + bx + c = 0$, then

$$ax^2 + bx + c = a(x - x_1)(x - x_2) \tag{3.3.6}$$

This is a very important result, because it shows how to factor a general quadratic function. If $b^2 - 4ac < 0$, there is no factorization of $ax^2 + bx + c$. If $b^2 - 4ac = 0$, then $x_1 = x_2 = -b/2a$ and $ax^2 + bx + c = a(x - x_1)^2 = a(x - x_2)^2$.

EXAMPLE 3.3.4 Factor, if possible, the following quadratic polynomials:

(a) $\frac{1}{3}x^2 + \frac{2}{3}x - \frac{14}{3}$ (b) $-2x^2 + 40x - 600$

Solution:

(a) $\frac{1}{3}x^2 + \frac{2}{3}x - \frac{14}{3} = 0$ has the same solutions as $x^2 + 2x - 14 = 0$. By formula (3.3.2), its solutions are $x = -1 \pm \sqrt{1 + 14} = -1 \pm \sqrt{15}$, which also solve the given equation. Then applying Eq. (3.3.6) with $a = \frac{1}{3}$, $x_1 = -1 + \sqrt{15}$ and $x_2 = -1 - \sqrt{15}$ gives the factorization:

$$\frac{1}{3}x^2 + \frac{2}{3}x - \frac{14}{3} = \frac{1}{3}\left[x - \left(-1 + \sqrt{15}\right)\right]\left[x - \left(-1 - \sqrt{15}\right)\right]$$

$$= \frac{1}{3}\left(x + 1 - \sqrt{15}\right)\left(x + 1 + \sqrt{15}\right)$$

(b) We apply (3.3.5) with $a = -2$, $b = 40$, and $c = -600$, and get $b^2 - 4ac = 1600 - 4800 = -3200 < 0$. Therefore, no factoring exists in this case.

Expanding the right-hand side of the identity $x^2 + px + q = (x - x_1)(x - x_2)$ yields $x^2 + px + q = x^2 - (x_1 + x_2)x + x_1x_2$. Equating like powers of x gives $x_1 + x_2 = -p$ and $x_1x_2 = q$. Thus:

RULES FOR QUADRATIC FUNCTIONS

If x_1 and x_2 are the roots of $x^2 + px + q = 0$, then

$$x_1 + x_2 = -p \quad \text{and} \quad x_1 x_2 = q \qquad (3.3.7)$$

In words, the sum of the two roots is minus the coefficient of the first-order term, whereas the product of the roots is the constant term. The formulas (3.3.7) can also obtained by adding and multiplying the two solutions found in (3.3.4).

EXERCISES FOR SECTION 3.3

1. Solve the following quadratic equations, if they have solutions:
   (a) $15x - x^2 = 0$
   (b) $p^2 - 16 = 0$
   (c) $(q - 3)(q + 4) = 0$
   (d) $2x^2 + 9 = 0$
   (e) $x(x + 1) = 2x(x - 1)$
   (f) $x^2 - 4x + 4 = 0$

2. Solve the following quadratic equations by using the method of completing the square, and factor, if possible, the left-hand side:
   (a) $x^2 - 5x + 6 = 0$
   (b) $y^2 - y - 12 = 0$
   (c) $2x^2 + 60x + 800 = 0$
   (d) $-\frac{1}{4}x^2 + \frac{1}{2}x + \frac{1}{2} = 0$
   (e) $m(m - 5) - 3 = 0$
   (f) $0.1p^2 + p - 2.4 = 0$

SM 3. Use the quadratic formula to solve the following equations:
   (a) $r^2 + 11r - 26 = 0$
   (b) $3p^2 + 45p = 48$
   (c) $20\,000 = 300K - K^2$
   (d) $r^2 + (\sqrt{3} - \sqrt{2})r = \sqrt{6}$
   (e) $0.3x^2 - 0.09x = 0.12$
   (f) $\frac{1}{24} = p^2 - \frac{1}{12}p$

4. Solve the following equations, by using the quadratic formula:
   (a) $x^2 - 3x + 2 = 0$
   (b) $5t^2 - t = 3$
   (c) $6x = 4x^2 - 1$
   (d) $9x^2 + 42x + 44 = 0$
   (e) $30\,000 = x(x + 200)$
   (f) $3x^2 = 5x - 1$

SM 5. Solve the following problems:
   (a) Find the lengths of the sides of a rectangle whose perimeter is 40 cm and whose area is 75 cm².
   (b) Find two successive natural numbers whose sum of squares is 13.
   (c) In a right-angled triangle, the hypotenuse is 34 cm. One of the short sides is 14 cm longer than the other. Find the lengths of the two short sides.
   (d) A motorist drove 80 km. In order to save 16 minutes, he had to drive 10 km/h faster than usual. What was his usual driving speed?

6. [HARDER] Solve the following equations:
   (a) $x^3 - 4x = 0$
   (b) $x^4 - 5x^2 + 4 = 0$
   (c) $z^{-2} - 2z^{-1} - 15 = 0$

3.4 Some Nonlinear Equations

We now study a more general form of equation, in which the product of several factors must be zero. The form encompasses linear equations, as well as quadratic equations when they have a solution. Such equations are ubiquitous in economics, so we must be able to handle them in order to obtain as much information about their solution as possible.

EXAMPLE 3.4.1 Solve each of the following three separate equations:

(a) $x^3\sqrt{x+2} = 0$ (b) $x(y+3)(z^2+1)\sqrt{w-3} = 0$ (c) $x^2 - 3x^3 = 0$

Solution:

(a) If $x^3\sqrt{x+2} = 0$, then either $x^3 = 0$ or $\sqrt{x+2} = 0$. The equation $x^3 = 0$ has only the solution $x = 0$, while $\sqrt{x+2} = 0$ gives $x = -2$. The solutions of the equation are therefore $x = 0$ and $x = -2$.

(b) There are four factors in the product on the left-hand side. The factor $z^2 + 1$ is never 0. Hence, the solutions are: $x = 0$ or $y = -3$ or $w = 3$.

(c) First factor $x^2 - 3x^3$ to obtain the equation $x^2(1 - 3x) = 0$. The product $x^2(1 - 3x)$ is 0 if and only if $x^2 = 0$ or $1 - 3x = 0$. Hence, the solutions are $x = 0$ and $x = 1/3$.[5]

In solving these equations, we have repeatedly used the fact that a product of two or more factors is 0 if and only if at least one of the factors is 0. In particular,

$$ab = ac \quad \text{is equivalent to} \quad a = 0 \quad \text{or} \quad b = c \qquad (3.4.1)$$

This is because the equation $ab = ac$ is equivalent to $ab - ac = 0$, or $a(b - c) = 0$. Of course, if $ab = ac$ and $a \neq 0$, we conclude from Eq. (3.4.1) that $b = c$.

EXAMPLE 3.4.2 What conclusions about the variables can we draw if

(a) $x(x + a) = x(2x + b)$ (b) $\lambda y = \lambda z^2$ (c) $xy^2(1 - y) - 2\lambda(y - 1) = 0$

Solution:

(a) The equation can be expressed as $x(x + a - 2x - b) = 0$, which simplifies to $x(-x + a - b) = 0$. Its solutions are therefore $x = 0$ and $x = a - b$.

(b) Here one has $\lambda(y - z^2) = 0$, so $\lambda = 0$ or $y = z^2$. It is easy to forget the first possibility.

(c) The equation is equivalent to

$$xy^2(1 - y) + 2\lambda(1 - y) = 0$$

---

[5] When trying to solve an equation, an easy way to make a serious mistake is to cancel a factor which might be zero. For instance, suppose one cancels the common factor x^2 in the equation $x^2 - 3x^3 = 0$. The result is $1 - 3x = 0$, implying that $x = 1/3$. Yet one part of the solution is $x = 0$, which has been lost. Thus, it is important always to check that the factor being cancelled really is not zero.

which can be written as
$$(1 - y)(xy^2 + 2\lambda) = 0$$

We conclude from the last equation that $1 - y = 0$ or $xy^2 + 2\lambda = 0$, that is $y = 1$ or $\lambda = -\frac{1}{2}xy^2$.

Finally, we consider some equations involving fractions. Recall that the fraction a/b is not defined if $b = 0$. If $b \neq 0$, then $a/b = 0$ is equivalent to $a = 0$.

EXAMPLE 3.4.3 Solve the following equations:

(a) $\dfrac{1 - K^2}{\sqrt{1 + K^2}} = 0$ (b) $\dfrac{45 + 6r - 3r^2}{(r^4 + 2)^{3/2}} = 0$ (c) $\dfrac{x^2 - 5x}{\sqrt{x^2 - 25}} = 0$

Solution:

(a) The denominator is never 0, so the fraction is 0 when $1 - K^2 = 0$, that is when $K = \pm 1$.

(b) Again the denominator is never 0. The fraction is 0 when $45 + 6r - 3r^2 = 0$, that is $3r^2 - 6r - 45 = 0$. Solving this quadratic equation, we find that $r = -3$ or $r = 5$.

(c) The numerator is equal to $x(x - 5)$, which is 0 if $x = 0$ or $x = 5$. At $x = 0$ the denominator is $\sqrt{-25}$, which is not defined, and at $x = 5$ the denominator is 0. We conclude that the equation has no solutions.

EXERCISES FOR SECTION 3.4

1. Solve the following equations:

   (a) $x(x + 3) = 0$ (b) $x^3(1 + x^2)(1 - 2x) = 0$ (c) $x(x - 3) = x - 3$

   (d) $\sqrt{2x + 5} = 0$ (e) $\dfrac{x^2 + 1}{x(x + 1)} = 0$ (f) $\dfrac{x(x + 1)}{x^2 + 1} = 0$

SM 2. Solve the following equations:

   (a) $\dfrac{5 + x^2}{(x - 1)(x + 2)} = 0$ (b) $1 + \dfrac{2x}{x^2 + 1} = 0$

   (c) $\dfrac{(x + 1)^{1/3} - \frac{1}{3}x(x + 1)^{-2/3}}{(x + 1)^{2/3}} = 0$ (d) $\dfrac{x}{x - 1} + 2x = 0$

SM 3. Examine what conclusions can be drawn about the variables if:

   (a) $z^2(z - a) = z^3(a + b)$, $a \neq 0$ (b) $(1 + \lambda)\mu x = (1 + \lambda)y\mu$

   (c) $\dfrac{\lambda}{1 + \mu} = \dfrac{-\lambda}{1 - \mu^2}$ (d) $ab - 2b - \lambda b(2 - a) = 0$

3.5 Using Implication Arrows

Implication and equivalence arrows are very useful in helping to avoid mistakes when solving equations. Consider first the following example.

EXAMPLE 3.5.1 Solve the equation $(2x-1)^2 - 3x^2 = 2\left(\frac{1}{2} - 4x\right)$.

Solution: By expanding $(2x-1)^2$ and also multiplying out the right-hand side, we obtain a new equation that obviously has the same solutions as the original one:

$$(2x-1)^2 - 3x^2 = 2(\tfrac{1}{2} - 4x) \iff 4x^2 - 4x + 1 - 3x^2 = 1 - 8x$$

Adding $8x - 1$ to each side of the second equation and then gathering terms gives another equivalent equation:

$$4x^2 - 4x + 1 - 3x^2 = 1 - 8x \iff x^2 + 4x = 0$$

Now $x^2 + 4x = x(x+4)$, and the latter product is 0 if and only if $x = 0$ or $x = -4$. That is,

$$x^2 + 4x = 0 \iff x(x+4) = 0 \iff [x = 0 \text{ or } x = -4]$$

where we have used brackets, for the sake of clarity, in the last expression. Putting everything together, we have derived a chain of equivalence arrows showing that the given equation is satisfied for the two values $x = 0$ and $x = -4$, and for no other values of x.

EXAMPLE 3.5.2 Solve the equation $x + 2 = \sqrt{4-x}$ for x.[6]

Solution: Squaring both sides of the given equation yields

$$(x+2)^2 = \left(\sqrt{4-x}\right)^2$$

Consequently $x^2 + 4x + 4 = 4 - x$ that is, $x^2 + 5x = 0$. From the latter equation, it follows that $x(x+5) = 0$ which yields $x = 0$ or $x = -5$. Thus, a necessary condition for x to solve $x + 2 = \sqrt{4-x}$ is that $x = 0$ or $x = -5$. Yet when $x = -5$, the left-hand side of the original equation is negative, whereas the right-hand side is a square root, which we have defined to be nonnegative. This leaves $x = 0$ as unique solution to the equation.

The method used in solving Example 3.5.2 is the most common. It involves setting up a chain of implications that starts from the given equation and ends with the set of all possible solutions. By testing each of these trial solutions in turn, we find which of them really do satisfy the equation. Even if the chain of implications is also a chain of equivalences, such a test is always a useful check of both logic and calculations.

---

[6] Recall Example 1.2.1.

EXERCISES FOR SECTION 3.5

1. Using implication arrows, solve the equation

$$\frac{(x+1)^2}{x(x-1)} + \frac{(x-1)^2}{x(x+1)} - 2\frac{3x+1}{x^2-1} = 0$$

2. Using implication arrows, solve the following equations:

   (a) $x + 2 = \sqrt{4x + 13}$ (b) $|x+2| = \sqrt{4-x}$ (c) $x^2 - 2|x| - 3 = 0$

(SM) 3. Using implication arrows, solve the following equations:

   (a) $\sqrt{x-4} = \sqrt{x+5} - 9$ (b) $\sqrt{x-4} = 9 - \sqrt{x+5}$

4. Consider the following attempt to solve the equation $x + \sqrt{x+4} = 2$:

   "From the given equation, it follows that $\sqrt{x+4} = 2 - x$. Squaring both sides gives $x + 4 = 4 - 4x + x^2$. Rearranging terms shows that this equation implies $x^2 - 5x = 0$. Cancelling x, we obtain $x - 5 = 0$, which is satisfied when $x = 5$."

   (a) Mark with arrows the implications or equivalences expressed in the text. Which ones are correct?

   (b) Solve the equation correctly.

3.6 Two Linear Equations in Two Unknowns

Example 3.2.1 features a macroeconomic model that involves two equations. There we focused on the solution for the value of GDP, but economists are often interested in the solution for *all* the endogenous variables in their models. In that example, total consumption should also be included in the solution.

For the case of two variables that are related through two linear equations, a general method is easy to develop. The following example allows us to develop the main ideas before we address the general case.

EXAMPLE 3.6.1   Find the values of x and y that satisfy both of the equations

$$2x + 3y = 18$$
$$3x - 4y = -7$$

Solution: There are two general ways of solving a system like this.

   Method 1: A first possibility is to deal with one of the variables first, as we did in Section 3.2, and then use that variable's solution to solve for the other. That is, follow a two-step procedure: (i) solve one of the equations for one of the variables in terms of the other; (ii) substitute the result into the other equation. This leaves only one equation in one unknown, which is easily solved.[7]

To apply this method to our system, we first solve the first equation for y in terms of x. Indeed the first equation $2x + 3y = 18$ implies that $3y = 18 - 2x$ and so

$$y = 6 - (2/3)x \qquad (*)$$

Substituting this expression for y into the second equation gives

$$3x - 4\left(6 - \frac{2}{3}x\right) = -7, \text{ which reduces to } 3x - 24 + \frac{8}{3}x = -7$$

Multiplying each side of this equation by 3 gives $9x - 72 + 8x = -21$, or $17x = 51$. Hence $x = 3$. To find y we use $(*)$ once again with $x = 3$ to obtain $y = 6 - (2/3) \cdot 3 = 4$. The solution of the system is, therefore, $x = 3$ and $y = 4$.[8]

Method 2: This method is based on eliminating one of the variables by adding or subtracting a multiple of one equation from the other. Suppose we want to eliminate y. To do this, we can multiply the first equation in the system by 4 and the second by 3. The resulting coefficients of y in both equations will be the same except for the sign. If we then add the transformed equations, the term in y disappears and we obtain

$$8x + 12y = 72$$
$$9x - 12y = -21$$
$$\overline{}$$
$$17x \quad = 51$$

Hence, $x = 3$. To find the value for y, substitute 3 for x in either of the original equations and solve for y. This gives $y = 4$, which agrees with the earlier result.

Analysis of 2 × 2 Linear Systems

Systems of two equations in two unknowns are usually known as 2×2 systems. The general 2×2 linear system is

$$ax + by = c \qquad (3.6.1)$$
$$dx + ey = f \qquad (3.6.2)$$

---

[7] The solution to Example 3.2.1 we gave went through the first of these two steps. The second step would be to substitute (3.2.5) into (3.2.4), to find the solution for C, which is

$$C = \frac{a + b\bar{I}}{1 - b}$$

In combination with Eq. (3.2.5) for Y, this equation completes the reduced form of the model.

[8] A useful check is to verify such a solution by direct substitution. Indeed, substituting $x = 3$ and $y = 4$ in the original system of two equations gives $2 \cdot 3 + 3 \cdot 4 = 18$ and $3 \cdot 3 - 4 \cdot 4 = -7$.

Here a, b, c, d, e, and f are arbitrary given numbers, whereas x and y are the variables, or "unknowns". Note that when $a = 2$, $b = 3$, $c = 18$, $d = 3$, $e = -4$, and $f = -7$, this system reduces to the one in Example 3.6.1.

Before plunging recklessly into an algebraic analysis of what solutions there may be, we do two things first: (i) eliminate a trivial case; (ii) analyse the equations geometrically.

The **trivial case** occurs when at least one of the four coefficients a, b, d, and e is zero. Suppose for example that $e = 0$. Then (3.6.2) reduces to the simple equation $dx = f$. This has a solution $x = f/d$ in case $d \neq 0$, no solution at all if $d = 0$ and $f \neq 0$, and leaves x arbitrary in case $d = f = 0$. When x does solve $dx = f$, the solution to the two equations together is the pair (x, y) where y can be determined from the equation $by = c - ax$ provided that either $b \neq 0$ or $b = 0$ and $ax = c$.

In case $e \neq 0$ but at least one of a, b, and d is zero, at least one of the two equations reduces to a single equation in one unknown, which can be solved immediately. Then, just as in the case when $e = 0$, the other unknown can be find by using simple substitution to leave just one equation in a single unknown.

Now for the **geometric analysis**. Having excluded the trivial case, none of the four coefficients a, b, d, and e is zero. So we can divide (3.6.1) by b and (3.6.2) by d, then rearrange, to get the equivalent pair of equations

$$y = (c - ax)/b \quad \text{and} \quad y = (f - dx)/e \qquad (3.6.3)$$

As discussed subsequently in Section 4.4, these are the equations of two straight lines in the (x, y)-plane, whose respective slopes are the coefficients $-a/b$ and $-d/e$ of x. Now there are three different cases we need to consider.

1. First we have the *intersecting case* when the slopes of the two lines differ. That is, one has $-a/b \neq -d/e$. Multiplying each side of this inequality by the nonzero number $-be$ gives the equivalent inequality $ae \neq bd$ or $ae - bd \neq 0$. In this case the two lines do intersect, and the point of intersection is the unique solution. This point could be found using either Method 1 or Method 2 for solving Example 3.6.1.

   Alternatively, note that the two equations (3.6.3) have a solution (x, y) iff their right-hand sides are equal. That is, one must have $(c - ax)/b = (f - dx)/e$. Multiplying each side by be gives $e(c - ax) = b(f - dx)$, which can be reduced to $ce - bf = (ae - bd)x$. Because $ae - bd \neq 0$ in this intersecting case, the last equation implies that $x = (ce - bf)/(ae - bd)$. To find y, we can substitute this value of x back in either equation of (3.6.3).

   Either way finds the same unique solution for both x and y, which is

   $$x = \frac{ce - bf}{ae - bd} \quad \text{and} \quad y = \frac{af - cd}{ae - bd} \qquad (3.6.4)$$

2. In the second *parallel case*, equations (3.6.1) and (3.6.2) have no solution because the two lines (3.6.3) are parallel and distinct. Obviously these two lines are parallel iff their

Table 3.6.1 2×2 linear equation systems

Consider the 2×2 system of linear equations in (x, y):

$$ax + by = c \text{ and } dx + ey = f$$

1. In the **intersecting case** when $ae \neq bd$, there is a unique solution given by

$$x = \frac{ce - bf}{ae - bd} \text{ and } y = \frac{af - cd}{ae - bd}$$

2. In the **parallel case** when $ae = bd$ and $bf \neq ce$, the system has no solution.
3. In the **coincident case** when $ae = bd$ and $bf = ce$, there are infinitely many solutions along each of the two coincident lines $ax + by = c$ and $dx + ey = f$.

---

slopes are equal, which occurs iff $-a/b = -d/e$. Multiplying each side of this equality by the nonzero number $-be$ gives the equivalent equality $ae - bd = 0$. This equality holds, of course, iff (3.6.4) fails to define a solution. Finally, in this case the two parallel lines given by (3.6.3) are distinct iff they cross the vertical axis $x = 0$ at different points, which is true iff $c/b \neq f/e$ or $bf \neq ce$.

3. In the third *coincident case*, the two lines (3.6.3) are not only parallel, but coincide. This happens iff the two equations (3.6.1) and (3.6.2) define one and the same straight line. This is the case when $ae - bd = bf - ce = 0$. Then the two equations have infinitely many solutions which lie along either of these two coincident straight lines.

Table 3.6.1 specifies for the three different cases the set of possible solutions to the 2×2 linear equation system given by (3.6.1) and (3.6.2). Though we started with the assumption that all the coefficients a, b, d, and e are nonzero, the results of Table 3.6.1 remain valid even if one or more of them are zero.

In Section 12.2 we will study possible solutions for this kind of linear system, but with arbitrarily many equations and unknowns.

EXERCISES FOR SECTION 3.6

1. Solve the following systems of equations:

    (a) $x - y = 5$ and $x + y = 11$
    (b) $4x - 3y = 1$ and $2x + 9y = 4$
    (c) $3x + 4y = 2.1$ and $5x - 6y = 7.3$

2. Solve the following systems of equations:

    (a) $5x + 2y = 3$ and $2x + 3y = -1$
    (b) $x - 3y = -25$ and $4x + 5y = 19$
    (c) $2x + 3y = 3$ and $6x + 6y = -1$

96 CHAPTER 3 / SOLVING EQUATIONS

3. Solve the following systems of equations:
   (a) $23p + 45q = 181$ and $10p + 15q = 65$
   (b) $0.01r + 0.21s = 0.042$ and $-0.25r + 0.55s = -0.47$

4. (a) Find two numbers whose sum is 52 and whose difference is 26.

   (b) Five tables and 20 chairs cost $1 800, whereas two tables and three chairs cost $420. What is the price of each table and each chair?

   (c) A firm produces headphones in two qualities, Basic (B) and Premium (P). For the coming year, the estimated output of B is 50% higher than that of P. The profit per unit sold is $300 for P and $200 for B. If the profit target is $180 000 over the next year, how much of each of the two qualities must be produced?

   (d) At the beginning of the year a person had a total of $10 000 in two accounts. The interest rates were 5% and 7.2% per year, respectively. If the person has made no transfers during the year, and has earned a total of $676 interest, what was the initial balance in each of the two accounts?

REVIEW EXERCISES

1. Solve each of the following equations:
   (a) $3x - 20 = 16$
   (b) $-5x + 8 + 2x = -(4-x)$
   (c) $-6(x - 5) = 6(2 - 3x)$
   (d) $\dfrac{4 - 2x}{3} = -5 - x$
   (e) $\dfrac{5}{2x - 1} = \dfrac{1}{2 - x}$
   (f) $\sqrt{x - 3} = 6$

(SM) 2. Solve each of the following equations:
   (a) $\dfrac{x - 3}{x - 4} = \dfrac{x + 3}{x + 4}$
   (b) $\dfrac{3(x + 3)}{x - 3} - 2 = 9\dfrac{x}{x^2 - 9} + \dfrac{27}{(x + 3)(x - 3)}$
   (c) $\dfrac{2x}{3} = \dfrac{2x - 3}{3} + \dfrac{5}{x}$
   (d) $\dfrac{x - 5}{x + 5} - 1 = \dfrac{1}{x} - \dfrac{11x + 20}{x^2 - 5x}$

3. Solve the following equations for the variables specified:
   (a) $x = \tfrac{2}{3}(y - 3) + y$, for y
   (b) $ax - b = cx + d$, for x
   (c) $AK\sqrt{L} = Y_0$, for L
   (d) $px + qy = m$, for y
   (e) $\dfrac{1/(1+r) - a}{1/(1+r) + b} = c$, for r
   (f) $Px(Px + Q)^{-1/3} + (Px + Q)^{2/3} = 0$, for x

(SM) 4. Solve the following equations for the variables indicated:
   (a) $3K^{-1/2}L^{1/3} = \tfrac{1}{5}$, for K
   (b) $(1 + r/100)^t = 2$, for r
   (c) $p - abx_0^{b-1} = 0$, for x_0
   (d) $\left[(1 - \lambda)a^{-\rho} + \lambda b^{-\rho}\right]^{-1/\rho} = c$, for b

5. Solve the following quadratic equations:
   (a) $z^2 = 8z$
   (b) $x^2 + 2x - 35 = 0$
   (c) $p^2 + 5p - 14 = 0$
   (d) $12p^2 - 7p + 1 = 0$
   (e) $y^2 - 15 = 8y$
   (f) $42 = x^2 + x$

6. Solve the following equations:

   (a) $(x^2 - 4)\sqrt{5-x} = 0$ (b) $(x^4 + 1)(4+x) = 0$ (c) $(1-\lambda)x = (1-\lambda)y$

7. Johnson invested $1 500, part of it at 15% interest and the remainder at 20%. His total yearly income from the two investments was $275. How much did he invest at each rate?

8. Consider the macroeconomic model described by the three equations

$$Y = C + \bar{I} + G, \qquad C = b(Y - T), \qquad T = tY$$

   Here b denotes the marginal propensity to consume, and t the tax rate. Both these parameters are positive and less than 1. The variable Y denotes the gross domestic product (GDP), whereas C is consumption expenditure, $\bar{I}$ is total investment, T denotes tax revenue, and G is government expenditure.

   (a) Express Y and C in terms of $\bar{I}$, G, and the parameters.

   (b) What happens to Y and C as t increases?

9. If $5^{3x} = 25^{y+2}$ and $x - 2y = 8$, what is $x - y$?

10. [HARDER] Solve the following systems of equations:

    (a) $\dfrac{2}{x} + \dfrac{3}{y} = 4$ and $\dfrac{3}{x} - \dfrac{2}{y} = 19$ (b) $3\sqrt{x} + 2\sqrt{y} = 2$ and $2\sqrt{x} - 3\sqrt{y} = \frac{1}{4}$

    (c) $x^2 + y^2 = 13$ and $4x^2 - 3y^2 = 24$

4　FUNCTIONS OF ONE VARIABLE

... —mathematics is not so much a subject as a way of studying any subject, not so much a science as a way of life.
—George F.J. Temple (1981)

Functions are important in practically every area of pure and applied mathematics, including mathematics applied to economics. The language of economic analysis is full of terms like demand and supply functions, cost functions, production functions, consumption functions, etc. Though teachers of elementary economics may prefer terms like demand and supply *curves*, these are merely graphical representations of underlying functions. In this chapter we present a discussion of functions of one real variable, illustrated by some very important economic examples.

4.1 Introduction

One variable is a function of another if the first variable *depends* upon the second. For instance, the area of a circle is a function of its radius. If the radius r is given, then the area A is determined: $A = \pi r^2$, where π is the numerical constant $3.14159\ldots$.

One does not need a mathematical formula to convey the idea that one variable is a function of another. A table can also show the relationship. For instance, Table 4.1.1 shows the growth of total final consumption expenditure, measured in current euros, without allowing for inflation, in the European Union.[1] The table runs from the first quarter of 2013, which we write as 13Q1, to the last quarter of 2014, which we write as 14Q4. It defines consumption expenditure, denoted by C, as a function of the calendar quarter, denoted by Q.

Table 4.1.1　Final consumption expenditure in the EU, 2013Q1–2014Q4 (billions of euros)

Q	13Q1	13Q2	13Q3	13Q4	14Q1	14Q2	14Q3	14Q4
C	1 917.5	1 924.9	1 934.3	1 946.0	1 958.6	1 973.4	1 995.1	2 008.2

---

[1] The EU expanded from 27 to 28 member states when Croatia joined on 1st July 2013.

In ordinary conversation we sometimes use the word "function" in a similar way. For example, we might say that the infant mortality rate of a country is a function of the quality of its health care, or that a country's national product is a function of the level of investment.

The dependence between two real variables can also be illustrated by means of a graph. In Fig. 4.1.1 we have drawn a curve that allegedly played an important role some years ago in the discussion of "supply side economics". It shows the presumed relationship between a country's income tax rate and its total income tax revenue. Obviously, if the tax rate is 0%, then tax revenue is 0. However, if the tax rate is 100%, then tax revenue will also be (about) 0, since nobody is willing to work if their entire income is going to be confiscated. This curve, which has generated considerable controversy, is supposed to have been drawn in 1974 on the back of a restaurant napkin by an American economist, Arthur Laffer, who later popularized its message with the public.[2]

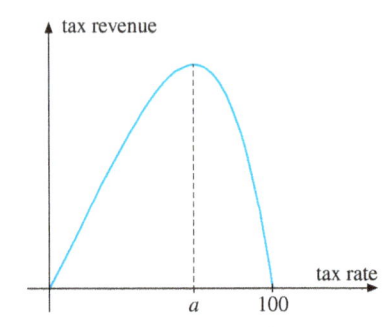

Figure 4.1.1 The "Laffer curve", which relates tax revenue to tax rates

In some instances a graph is preferable to a formula. A case in point is an electrocardiogram (ECG) showing the heartbeat pattern of a patient. Here the doctor studies the pattern of repetitions directly from the graphs; the patient might die before the doctor could understand a formula approximating the ECG picture.

All of the relationships discussed above have one characteristic in common: a definite rule relates each value of one variable to a definite value of another variable. In the ECG example the function is the rule showing electrical activity as a function of time.

In all of our examples it is implicitly assumed that the variables are subject to certain constraints. For instance, in Table 4.1.1 only the eight quarters in the two years of 2013 and 2014 are treated as relevant.

4.2 Definitions

The examples in the preceding section lead to the following general definition, with D a set of real numbers:

---

[2] Actually, many economists previously had essentially the same idea. See, for instance, part (b) in Example 7.2.2.

FUNCTION

A (real-valued) *function* of a real variable x with *domain* D is a rule $x \mapsto f(x)$ that assigns a unique real number $f(x)$ to each real number x in D. As x varies over the whole domain, the set of all possible resulting values $f(x)$ is called the *range* of f.

The word "rule" is used in a very broad sense. *Every* rule with the properties described can be called a function, whether that rule is given by a formula, described in words, specified by a table, illustrated by a curve, or expressed by any other means.

Many functions are given letter names, such as f, g, F, or φ. If f is a function and x is a number in its domain D, then $f(x)$ denotes the number that the function f assigns to x. The symbol $f(x)$ is pronounced "f of x". It is important to note the difference between f, which is a symbol for the function (the rule), and $f(x)$, which denotes the value of f at the particular point x of the domain.

If f is a function, we sometimes let y denote the value of f at x, so $y = f(x)$. Then, we call x the *independent variable*, or the *argument* of f, whereas y is called the *dependent variable*, because the value y (in general) depends on the value of x. The domain of the function f is then the set of all possible values of the independent variable, whereas the range is the set of corresponding values of the dependent variable. In economics, x is often called the *exogenous* variable, which is supposed to be fixed *outside* the economic model, whereas for each given x the equation $y = f(x)$ serves to determine the *endogenous* variable y *inside* the economic model.

A function is often defined by a formula, such as $y = 8x^2 + 3x + 2$. The function is then the rule $x \mapsto 8x^2 + 3x + 2$ that assigns the number $8x^2 + 3x + 2$ to each value of x.

Functional Notation

To become familiar with the relevant notation, it helps to look at some examples of functions that are defined by formulas.

EXAMPLE 4.2.1   Suppose that a function is defined for all real numbers by the following rule:

Assign to any number its third power.

This function will assign $0^3 = 0$ to 0, $3^3 = 27$ to 3, $(-2)^3 = (-2)(-2)(-2) = -8$ to -2, and $(1/4)^3 = 1/64$ to $1/4$. In general, it assigns the number x^3 to the number x. If we denote this third power function by f, then $f(x) = x^3$. So we have $f(0) = 0^3 = 0, f(3) = 3^3 = 27$, $f(-2) = (-2)^3 = -8$, and $f(1/4) = (1/4)^3 = 1/64$. In general, substituting a for x in the formula for f gives $f(a) = a^3$, whereas

$$f(a+1) = (a+1)^3 = (a+1)(a+1)(a+1) = a^3 + 3a^2 + 3a + 1$$

A common error is to presume that $f(a) = a^3$ implies $f(a+1) = a^3 + 1$. The error can be illustrated by considering a simple interpretation of f. If a is the edge of a cube measured in metres, then $f(a) = a^3$ is the volume of the cube measured in cubic metres, or m³. Suppose that each edge of the cube expands by 1 m. Then the volume of the new cube is $f(a+1) = (a+1)^3$ m³, as shown in Fig. 4.2.1. On the other hand, the number $a^3 + 1$ can be interpreted as the total volume obtained when a cube with edge a has a cube with edge 1 added to it, as shown in Fig. 4.2.2. The two figures make it clear that the first volume $(a+1)^3$ is quite a bit more than the second volume $a^3 + 1$. Indeed, we can use the binomial formula (2.11.2) to calculate the precise difference, which is

$$(a+1)^3 - (a^3 + 1) = 3a^2 + 3a = 3a(a+1)$$

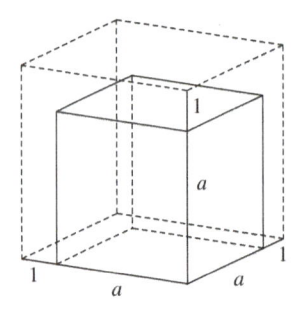

Figure 4.2.1 Volume $f(a+1) = (a+1)^3$

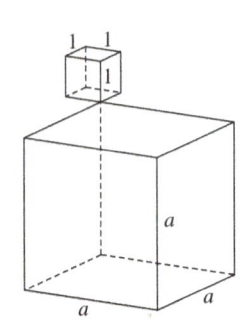

Figure 4.2.2 Volume $a^3 + 1$

EXAMPLE 4.2.2   Suppose that, for each nonnegative integer x, the total dollar cost of producing x units of a product is given by

$$C(x) = 100x\sqrt{x} + 500$$

(a) Find the cost of producing 16 units.

(b) Assuming that the firm is already producing a units, find the *increase* in the cost due to producing one additional unit.

Solution:

(a) The cost of producing 16 units is found by substituting 16 for x in the formula for $C(x)$:

$$C(16) = 100 \cdot 16\sqrt{16} + 500 = 100 \cdot 16 \cdot 4 + 500 = 6900$$

(b) The cost of producing a units is $C(a) = 100a\sqrt{a} + 500$, and the cost of producing $a+1$ units is $C(a+1)$. Thus the increase in cost is

$$C(a+1) - C(a) = 100(a+1)\sqrt{a+1} + 500 - 100a\sqrt{a} - 500$$
$$= 100\left[(a+1)\sqrt{a+1} - a\sqrt{a}\right]$$

In economic theory, we often study functions that depend on a number of parameters, as well as the independent variable. An obvious generalization of Example 4.2.2 follows.

EXAMPLE 4.2.3 Suppose that the cost of producing x units of a commodity is

$$C(x) = Ax\sqrt{x} + B$$

where A and B are constants. Find the cost of producing 0, 10, and $x + h$ units.

Solution: The cost of producing 0 units is $C(0) = A \cdot 0 \cdot \sqrt{0} + B = 0 + B = B$.[3] Similarly, $C(10) = A10\sqrt{10} + B$. Finally,

$$C(x+h) = A(x+h)\sqrt{x+h} + B$$

which comes from substituting $x + h$ for x in the given formula.

So far we have used x to denote the independent variable, but we could just as well have used almost any other symbol. For example, the following formulas define exactly the same function (and hence we can say $f = g = \varphi$):

$$f(x) = x^4, \qquad g(t) = t^4, \qquad \varphi(\xi) = \xi^4$$

For that matter, we could also express this function as $x \mapsto x^4$, or alternatively as $f(\cdot) = (\cdot)^4$. Here it is understood that the dot between the parentheses can be replaced by an arbitrary number, or an arbitrary letter, or even another function (like $1/y$). Thus,

$$1 \mapsto 1^4 = 1, \quad k \mapsto k^4, \quad \text{and} \quad 1/y \mapsto (1/y)^4$$

or alternatively

$$f(1) = 1^4 = 1, \quad f(k) = k^4, \quad \text{and} \quad f(1/y) = (1/y)^4$$

Specifying the Domain and the Range

Unless the domain of a function is already obvious, its definition remains incomplete until its domain has been specified explicitly. The natural domain of the function f defined by $f(x) = x^3$ is the set of all real numbers. In Example 4.2.2, where $C(x) = 100x\sqrt{x} + 500$ denotes the cost of producing x units of a product, the domain was specified as the set of nonnegative integers. Actually, a more natural domain is the set of numbers $0, 1, 2, \ldots, x_0$, where x_0 is the maximum number of items the firm can produce. For a producer like an iron mine, however, where output x can be regarded as a continuous variable such as tonnes of iron ore, the natural domain is the closed interval $[0, x_0]$.

We shall adopt the convention that *if a function is defined using an algebraic formula, the domain consists of all values of the independent variable for which the formula gives a unique value, unless another domain is explicitly mentioned.*

EXAMPLE 4.2.4 Find the domains of

(a) $f(x) = \dfrac{1}{x+3}$ (b) $g(x) = \sqrt{2x+4}$ (c) $h(x) = \dfrac{3}{\sqrt{x+1} - 3}$

---

[3] Parameter B simply represents fixed costs. These are the costs that must be paid whether or not anything is actually produced, such as a taxi driver's annual licence fee.

Solution:

(a) For $x = -3$, the formula reduces to the meaningless expression "1/0". For all other values of x, the formula makes $f(x)$ a well-defined number. Thus, the domain consists of all numbers $x \neq -3$.

(b) The expression $\sqrt{2x+4}$ is uniquely defined for all x such that $2x + 4$ is nonnegative. Solving the inequality $2x + 4 \geq 0$ for x gives $x \geq -2$. The domain of g is therefore the interval $[-2, \infty)$.

(c) As in (a), we need to avoid the expression "1/0". This requires that $\sqrt{x+1} - 3 \neq 0$, which means that we cannot allow $x = 8$. As in (b), on the other hand, the expression $\sqrt{x+1}$ requires that $x + 1 \geq 0$, which in turn requires that $x \geq -1$. The domain of h is the set of all x that satisfy both of these conditions, namely the union of the two intervals $[-1, 8)$ and $(8, \infty)$.

Let f be a function with domain D. The set of all values $f(x)$ that the function assumes is called the *range* of f. Often, we denote the domain of f by D_f, and its range by R_f. These concepts are illustrated in Fig. 4.2.3, using the idea of the graph of a function which we formally discuss in Section 4.3.

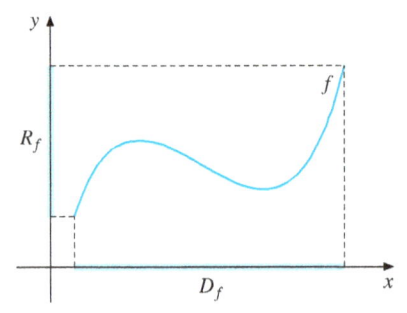

Figure 4.2.3 The domain D_f and range R_f of f

Alternatively, we can think of any function f as an engine $x \mapsto f(x)$ operating so that if x in the domain is an input, the output is $f(x)$. The range of f is then the set of all the numbers we get as output using all numbers in the domain as input. If we try to use as an input a number not in the domain, the engine does not work, so there is no output.

EXAMPLE 4.2.5 Consider the function $g(x) = \sqrt{2x+4}$.

(a) Show that the number 4 belongs to its range.
(b) Find the entire range of g.

Solution:

(a) To show that 4 is in the range of g, we must find a number x such that $g(x) = 4$. That is, we must solve the equation $\sqrt{2x+4} = 4$ for x. By squaring both sides of the equation, we get $2x + 4 = 4^2 = 16$, that is, $x = 6$. Because $g(6) = 4$, the number 4 does belong to the range R_g.

(b) In order to determine the whole range of g, we must answer the question: As x runs through the whole of the interval $[-2, \infty)$, what are all the possible values of $\sqrt{2x+4}$? For $x = -2$, one has $\sqrt{2x+4} = 0$, and $\sqrt{2x+4}$ can never be negative. We claim that whatever number $y_0 \geq 0$ is chosen, there exists a number x_0 such that $\sqrt{2x_0+4} = y_0$. Indeed, squaring each side of this last equation gives $2x_0 + 4 = y_0^2$. Hence, $2x_0 = y_0^2 - 4$, which implies that $x_0 = \frac{1}{2}(y_0^2 - 4)$. Because $y_0^2 \geq 0$, we have $x_0 = \frac{1}{2}(y_0^2 - 4) \geq \frac{1}{2}(-4) = -2$. Hence, for every number $y_0 \geq 0$, we have found a number $x_0 \geq -2$ such that $g(x_0) = y_0$. The range of g is, therefore, $[0, \infty)$.

Even if a function is completely specified by a formula, including a specific domain, it is not always easy to find the range of the function. For example, without using the methods of differential calculus that we have yet to introduce, it is hard to find R_f exactly for a function such as $f(x) = 3x^3 - 2x^2 - 12x - 3$ defined on the domain $D_f = [-2, 3]$.

A function f is called *(weakly) increasing* or *nondecreasing* if $x_1 < x_2$ implies $f(x_1) \leq f(x_2)$, and *strictly increasing* if $x_1 < x_2$ implies $f(x_1) < f(x_2)$. *Decreasing* and *strictly decreasing* functions are defined in the obvious way. (See Section 6.3.) The function g in Example 4.2.5 is strictly increasing on its domain $[-2, \infty)$.

EXERCISES FOR SECTION 4.2

(SM) 1. Let $f(x) = x^2 + 1$.

(a) Compute $f(0), f(-1), f(1/2)$, and $f(\sqrt{2})$.

(b) For what values of x is it true that:

(i) $f(x) = f(-x)$? (ii) $f(x+1) = f(x) + f(1)$? (iii) $f(2x) = 2f(x)$?

2. Suppose $F(x) = 10$, for all x. Find $F(0)$, $F(-3)$, and $F(a+h) - F(a)$.

3. Let $f(t) = a^2 - (t-a)^2$, where a is a constant.

(a) Compute $f(0), f(a), f(-a)$, and $f(2a)$. (b) Compute $3f(a) + f(-2a)$.

4. Let $f(x) = x/(1+x^2)$.

(a) Compute $f(-1/10), f(0), f(1/\sqrt{2}), f(\sqrt{\pi})$, and $f(2)$.

(b) Show that $f(-x) = -f(x)$ for all x, and that $f(1/x) = f(x)$ for $x \neq 0$.

5. Let $F(t) = \sqrt{t^2 - 2t + 4}$. Compute $F(0)$, $F(-3)$, and $F(t+1)$.

6. The cost of producing x units of a commodity is given by $C(x) = 1000 + 300x + x^2$.

(a) Compute $C(0), C(100)$, and $C(101) - C(100)$.

(b) Compute $C(x+1) - C(x)$, and explain in words the meaning of this difference.

7. As a function of its price P, the demand for cotton in the US during the period 1915–1919 has been estimated as $Q = D(P) = 6.4 - 0.3P$, with appropriate units for the price P and the quantity Q.

(a) Find the demand quantity in each case if the price is 8, 10, and 10.22.

(b) If the demand quantity is 3.13, what is the price?

8. (a) If $f(x) = 100x^2$, show that $f(tx) = t^2 f(x)$ for all t.

(b) If $P(x) = x^{1/2}$, show that $P(tx) = t^{1/2} P(x)$ for all $t \geq 0$.

9. The cost of removing $p\%$ of the impurities in a lake is given by $b(p) = 10p/(105 - p)$.

(a) Find $b(0)$, $b(50)$, and $b(100)$.

(b) What does $b(50 + h) - b(50)$ mean (where $h \geq 0$)?

10. Only for very special "additive" functions is it true that $f(a + b) = f(a) + f(b)$ for all a and b. Determine whether $f(2 + 1) = f(2) + f(1)$ for each of the following functions:

(a) $f(x) = 2x^2$ (b) $f(x) = -3x$ (c) $f(x) = \sqrt{x}$

11. (a) If $f(x) = Ax$, show that $f(a + b) = f(a) + f(b)$ for all numbers a and b.

(b) If $f(x) = 10^x$, show that $f(a + b) = f(a) \cdot f(b)$ for all natural numbers a and b.

12. A friend of yours claims that $(x + 1)^2 = x^2 + 1$. Can you use a geometric argument to show that this is wrong?

(SM) 13. Find the domains of the functions defined by the following formulas:

(a) $y = \sqrt{5 - x}$ (b) $y = \dfrac{2x - 1}{x^2 - x}$ (c) $y = \sqrt{\dfrac{x - 1}{(x - 2)(x + 3)}}$

14. Let $f(x) = (3x + 6)/(x - 2)$.

(a) Find the domain of the function.

(b) Show that 5 is in the range of f, by finding an x such that $(3x + 6)/(x - 2) = 5$.

(c) Show that 3 is not in the range of f.

15. Find the domain and the range of $g(x) = 1 - \sqrt{x + 2}$.

4.3 Graphs of Functions

You may recall from an elementary mathematics course that a *Cartesian* (or *rectangular*) coordinate system is obtained by first drawing two perpendicular lines, called coordinate axes. The two axes are respectively the *x-axis* (or *horizontal axis*) and the *y-axis* (or *vertical axis*). The point O where the two axes intersect is called the *origin*. We measure the real numbers along each of these lines, as shown in Fig. 4.3.1. The unit distance on the *x*-axis is not necessarily the same as on the *y*-axis, although it is in Fig. 4.3.1.

The Cartesian coordinate system in Fig. 4.3.1 is also called the *xy-plane*. The coordinate axes separate the plane into four quadrants, which traditionally are numbered as in

SECTION 4.3 / GRAPHS OF FUNCTIONS

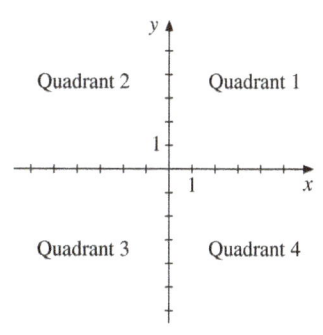

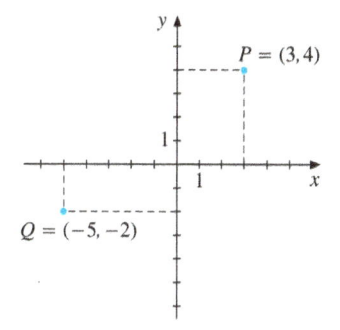

Figure 4.3.1 A coordinate system

Figure 4.3.2 Points $(3, 4)$ and $(-5, -2)$

Fig. 4.3.1. Any point P in the plane can be represented by a unique pair (x, y) of real numbers. These numbers can be found by drawing two dashed lines, like those in Fig. 4.3.2, that are perpendicular to the two axes. The particular point represented by the ordered pair (a, b) occurs where $x = a$ and $y = b$; it lies where the vertical straight line $x = a$ intersects the horizontal straight line $y = b$.

Conversely, any pair of real numbers represents a unique point in the plane. For example, in Fig. 4.3.2, if the ordered pair $(3, 4)$ is given, the corresponding point P lies at the intersection of $x = 3$ with $y = 4$. Thus, point P lies 3 units to the right of the y-axis and 4 units above the x-axis. We call $(3, 4)$ the *coordinates* of P. Similarly, point Q lies 5 units to the left of the y-axis and 2 units below the x-axis, so the coordinates of Q are $(-5, -2)$.

Note that we call (a, b) an *ordered pair*. This is because the order of the two numbers in the pair is important. For instance, $(3, 4)$ and $(4, 3)$ represent two different points. Indeed, the two points (a, b) and (b, a) coincide iff $a = b$.

As you will surely recall, each function of one variable can be represented by a graph in such a rectangular coordinate system. Because the shape of the graph reflects the properties of the function, this helps us visualize it.

GRAPH

The *graph* of a function f is the set of all ordered pairs $(x, f(x))$, where x belongs to the domain of f.

EXAMPLE 4.3.1 Consider the function $f(x) = x^2 - 4x + 3$. The values of $f(x)$ for some special choices of x are given in Table 4.3.1. Suppose we plot in an xy-plane the five points $(0, 3)$, $(1, 0)$, $(2, -1)$, $(3, 0)$, and $(4, 3)$ obtained from this table, and then draw a smooth curve through these points. The result is the graph of the function, as shown in Fig. 4.3.3.[4]

---
[4] This graph is called a *parabola*, as you will see in Section 4.6.

CHAPTER 4 / FUNCTIONS OF ONE VARIABLE

Table 4.3.1 Values of $f(x) = x^2 - 4x + 3$

x	0	1	2	3	4
$f(x) = x^2 - 4x + 3$	3	0	−1	0	3

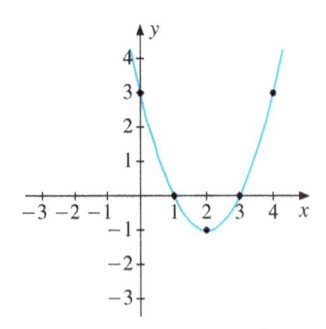

Figure 4.3.3 Graph of $f(x) = x^2 - 4x + 3$

Figure 4.3.4 Graph of $g(x) = 2x - 1$

EXAMPLE 4.3.2 Find some of the points on the graph of $g(x) = 2x - 1$, and sketch it.

Solution: Here $g(-1) = 2 \cdot (-1) - 1 = -3$, $g(0) = 2 \cdot 0 - 1 = -1$, and $g(1) = 2 \cdot 1 - 1 = 1$. Moreover, $g(2) = 3$. There are infinitely many points on the graph, so we cannot write them all down. In Fig. 4.3.4 the four points $(-1, -3)$, $(0, -1)$, $(1, 1)$, and $(2, 3)$ are marked with dots, which all lie on one straight line. That line is the graph.

Some Important Graphs

Figures 4.3.5–4.3.10 show graphs of six special functions. These occur so often that you should learn to recognize them. For each function you should confirm the shape of the corresponding graph by making a table of function values like Table 4.3.1.

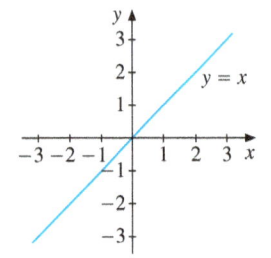

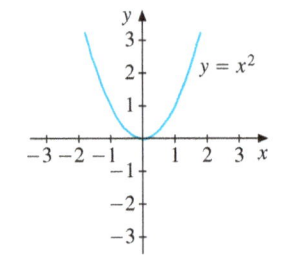

Figure 4.3.5 $y = x$

Figure 4.3.6 $y = x^2$

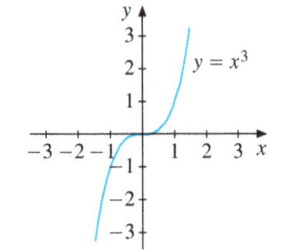

Figure 4.3.7 $y = x^3$

Note that when plotting the graph of a function, we must try to include enough points. Otherwise we might omit some important features of the graph. Actually, by merely plotting a finite set of points, we can never be entirely sure that no wiggles or bumps have been missed. For more complicated functions we have to use techniques of differential calculus that we introduce later in order to decide how many bumps and wiggles there really are.

SECTION 4.3 / GRAPHS OF FUNCTIONS 109

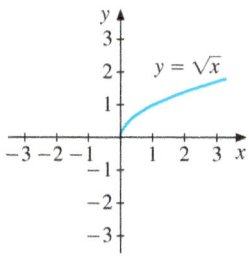

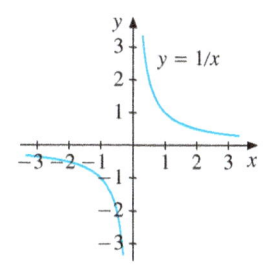

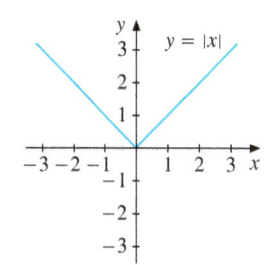

Figure 4.3.8 $y = \sqrt{x}$

Figure 4.3.9 $y = 1/x$

Figure 4.3.10 $y = |x|$

EXERCISES FOR SECTION 4.3

1. Plot all the five points $(2, 3)$, $(-3, 2)$, $(-3/2, -2)$, $(4, 0)$, and $(0, 4)$ in one coordinate system.

2. The graph of function f is given in Fig. 4.3.11.

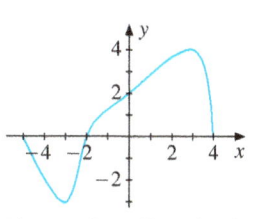

   Figure 4.3.11 Exercise 2

   (a) Find $f(-5), f(-3), f(-2), f(0), f(3)$, and $f(4)$ by examining the graph.
   (b) Determine the domain and the range of f.

3. Fill in the tables and draw the graphs of the following functions:

   (a)
x	0	1	2	3	4
$g(x) = -2x + 5$					

   (b)
x	-2	-1	0	1	2	3	4
$h(x) = x^2 - 2x - 3$							

   (c)
x	-2	-1	0	1	2
$F(x) = 3^x$					

   (d)
x	-2	-1	0	1	2	3
$G(x) = 1 - 2^{-x}$						

4.4 Linear Functions

Linear equations occur very often in economics. Recall from Eq. (3.2.2) that the typical linear equation is

$$y = ax + b$$

where a and b are constants. As we saw in Example 4.3.2, the graph of this equation is a straight line. If we let f denote the function that assigns y to x, then $f(x) = ax + b$. In this case f is called a *linear* function.

Take an arbitrary value of x. Then

$$f(x + 1) - f(x) = a(x + 1) + b - ax - b = a$$

This shows that a measures the change in the value of the function when x increases by 1 unit. For this reason, the number a is called the *slope* of the line (or function). If the slope a is positive, then the line slants upward to the right. Furthermore, the larger is the value of a, the steeper is the line. On the other hand, if a is negative, then the line slants downward to the right. Then the absolute value of a measures the steepness of the line. For example, when $a = -3$, the steepness is 3. In the special case when $a = 0$, the steepness is zero, because the line is horizontal: the line $y = ax + b$ becomes $y = b$ for all x.

The three different cases are illustrated in Figs 4.4.1 to 4.4.3. When $x = 0$ the function value is $y = ax + b = b$. This number b is called the *y-intercept*, or often just the intercept.

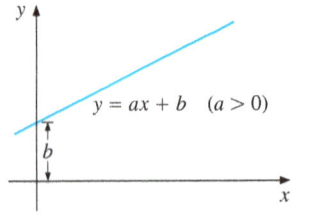

Figure 4.4.1 Increasing 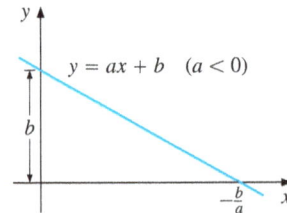 **Figure 4.4.2** Decreasing 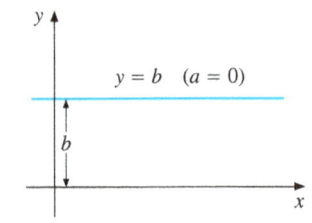 **Figure 4.4.3** Constant

EXAMPLE 4.4.1

Find and interpret the slopes of the following straight lines.

(a) The cost function for the US Steel Corp. during the period 1917–1938 was estimated to be $C = 55.73x + 182\,100\,000$, where C is the total cost in dollars per year, and x is the production of steel in tons per year.

(b) The demand function for monthly ride-sharing trips in some large city is estimated to be approximately $q = -4.5p + 150$, where $10 \leq p \leq 20$ is price per mile (in units of some currency), and q is millions of trips.

Solution:

(a) The slope is 55.73, which means that if production increases by one ton, then the cost *increases* by $55.73.

(b) The slope is −4.5, which tells us that if the price increases by one unit, then the number of ride-sharing trips *decreases* by 4.5 million.

Computing the slope of a straight line in the plane is easy. Pick two different points on the line $P = (x_1, y_1)$ and $Q = (x_2, y_2)$, as shown in Fig. 4.4.4. The slope of the line is the ratio $(y_2 - y_1)/(x_2 - x_1)$.

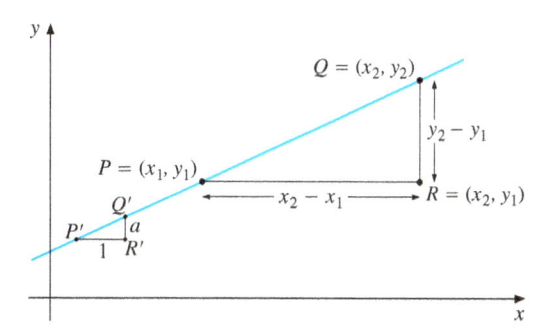

Figure 4.4.4 Slope $a = (y_2 - y_1)/(x_2 - x_1)$.

If we denote the slope by a, then:

SLOPE OF A STRAIGHT LINE

The *slope* of the straight, non-vertical line ℓ is

$$a = \frac{y_2 - y_1}{x_2 - x_1} \qquad (4.4.1)$$

where (x_1, y_1) and (x_2, y_2) are any two distinct points on ℓ. (If ℓ contains two distinct points (x_1, y_1) and (x_2, y_2) with $x_1 = x_2$, then it is vertical.)

Multiplying both the numerator and the denominator of $(y_2 - y_1)/(x_2 - x_1)$ by -1 gives $(y_1 - y_2)/(x_1 - x_2)$, which does not change the ratio. This shows that it does not make any difference which point is P and which is Q. Moreover, suppose that instead of P and Q, we used the points P' and Q' in Fig. 4.4.4 to measure the slope. Then we would get the same answer because the properties of similar triangles imply that the ratios $Q'R'/P'R'$ and QR/PR in the small and large triangles of Fig. 4.4.4 must be equal. For this reason, the number $a = (y_2 - y_1)/(x_2 - x_1)$ is always equal to the change in the value of y when x increases by 1 unit; this change is constant and equat to the slope of the straight line.

EXAMPLE 4.4.2 Determine the slopes of the three straight lines ℓ, m, and n whose graphs are shown in Figs 4.4.5 to 4.4.7 respectively.

Solution: The lines ℓ, m, and n all pass through the common point $P = (2, 2)$. In Fig. 4.4.5, the point Q is $(4, 3)$, whereas in Fig. 4.4.6 it is $(1, -2)$, and in Fig. 4.4.7 it is $(5, -1)$. By Eq. (4.4.1), therefore, the respective slopes of the three straight lines ℓ, m, and n are

$$a_\ell = \frac{3-2}{4-2} = \frac{1}{2}, \qquad a_m = \frac{-2-2}{1-2} = 4, \qquad a_n = \frac{-1-2}{5-2} = -1$$

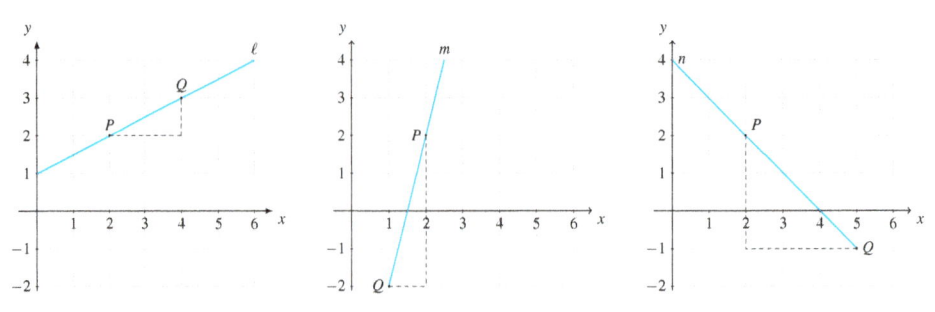

Figure 4.4.5 Line ℓ

Figure 4.4.6 Line m

Figure 4.4.7 Line n

The Point–Slope and Point–Point Formulas

Let us find the equation of a straight line ℓ passing through the point $P = (x_1, y_1)$ whose slope is a. If (x, y) is any other point on the line, applying Eq. (4.4.1) with x and y replacing x_2 and y_2 respectively implies that the slope a must satisfy the formula:

$$\frac{y - y_1}{x - x_1} = a$$

When the slope a is given, multiplying each side by $x - x_1$ gives $y - y_1 = a(x - x_1)$. Hence,

---
POINT–SLOPE FORMULA OF A STRAIGHT LINE

The equation of the straight line passing through (x_1, y_1) with slope a is

$$y - y_1 = a(x - x_1)$$

Note that when using this formula, x_1 and y_1 are fixed numbers giving the coordinates of the given point P. On the other hand, x and y are variables denoting the coordinates of an arbitrary point on the line.

EXAMPLE 4.4.3 Find the equation of the line through the point $(-2, 3)$ with slope -4. Then find the y-intercept as well as the point where this line intersects the x-axis.

Solution: Applying the point–slope formula with $(x_1, y_1) = (-2, 3)$ and $a = -4$ gives the equation $y - 3 = (-4)[x - (-2)]$, or $y - 3 = -4(x + 2)$. This implies that $4x + y = -5$. The y-intercept has $x = 0$, so $y = -5$. The line intersects the x-axis at a point where $y = 0$, and so where $4x = -5$ or $x = -5/4$. The point of intersection with the x-axis is therefore $(-5/4, 0)$.[5]

Often we need to find the equation of the straight line that passes through two given distinct points. To do so we can combine the slope formula with the point–slope formula.

---

[5] It is a good exercise for you to draw a graph and verify this solution.

POINT–POINT FORMULA OF A STRAIGHT LINE

The equation of the straight line passing through (x_1, y_1) and (x_2, y_2), where $x_1 \neq x_2$, is obtained as follows:

1. Compute the slope of the line, which is

$$a = \frac{y_2 - y_1}{x_2 - x_1}$$

2. Substitute the expression for a into the point–slope formula. The result is

$$y - y_1 = \frac{y_2 - y_1}{x_2 - x_1}(x - x_1) \tag{4.4.2}$$

EXAMPLE 4.4.4 Find the equation of the line passing through $(-1, 3)$ and $(5, -2)$.

Solution: Let $(x_1, y_1) = (-1, 3)$ and $(x_2, y_2) = (5, -2)$. Then the point–point formula (4.4.2) gives

$$y - 3 = \frac{-2 - 3}{5 - (-1)}[x - (-1)] = -\frac{5}{6}(x + 1), \quad \text{which simplifies to } 5x + 6y = 13.$$

Graphical Solutions of Linear Equations

Section 3.6 dealt with algebraic methods for solving a system of two linear equations in two unknowns. Each equation is linear, so its graph is a straight line. The coordinates of any point on a line satisfy the equation of that line. Thus, the two lines intersect at a point in the plane if and only if its coordinates satisfy both equations.

EXAMPLE 4.4.5 Solve each of the following three pairs of equations graphically:

(a) $x + y = 5$ and $x - y = -1$;   (b) $3x + y = -7$ and $x - 4y = 2$;

(c) $3x + 4y = 2$ and $6x + 8y = 24$.

Solution:

(a) Figure 4.4.8 shows the graphs of the straight lines $x + y = 5$ and $x - y = -1$. There is only one point of intersection, which is $(2, 3)$. The solution of the system is, therefore, $x = 2, y = 3$.

(b) Figure 4.4.9 shows the graphs of the straight lines $3x + y = -7$ and $x - 4y = 2$. There is only one point of intersection, which is $(-2, -1)$. The solution of the system is, therefore, $x = -2, y = -1$.

(c) Figure 4.4.10 shows the graphs of the straight lines $3x + 4y = 2$ and $6x + 8y = 24$. These lines are parallel and so have no point of intersection. The system has no solution.

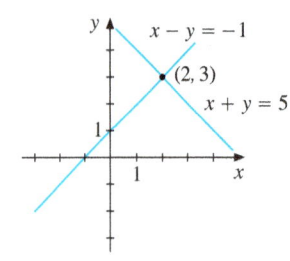

Figure 4.4.8 $x + y = 5$ and $x - y = -1$

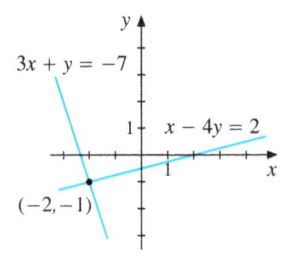

Figure 4.4.9 $3x + y = -7$ and $x - 4y = 2$

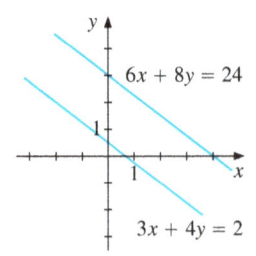

Figure 4.4.10 $3x + 4y = 2$ and $6x + 8y = 24$

Linear Inequalities

This section concludes by discussing how to represent linear inequalities geometrically. We present two examples.

EXAMPLE 4.4.6   Sketch in the xy-plane the set $\{(x, y) : 2x + y \leq 4\}$ of all ordered pairs (x, y) that satisfy the inequality $2x + y \leq 4$.

Solution: The inequality can be written as $y \leq -2x + 4$. The set of points (x, y) that satisfy the equation $y = -2x + 4$ is a straight line. Therefore, the set of points (x, y) that satisfy the inequality $y \leq -2x + 4$ must have y-values below those of points on the line $y = -2x + 4$. So it must consist of all points that lie on or below this line. See Fig. 4.4.11.

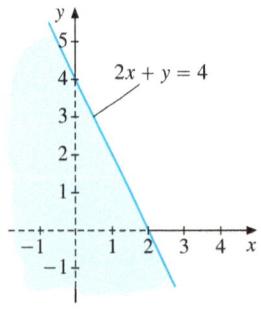

Figure 4.4.11 $\{(x, y) : 2x + y \leq 4\}$

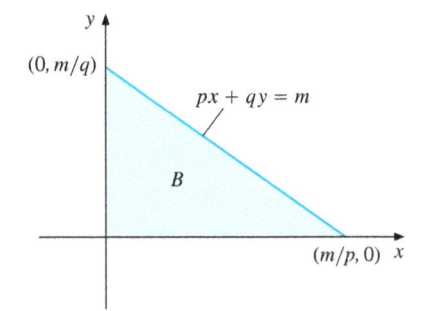

Figure 4.4.12 Budget set: $px + qy \leq m$, $x \geq 0$, and $y \geq 0$

EXAMPLE 4.4.7   A person has a budget of $\$m$ to spend on purchasing two commodities. The prices of the two commodities are $\$p$ and $\$q$ per unit, both positive. Suppose the person buys x units

SECTION 4.4 / LINEAR FUNCTIONS 115

of the first commodity and y units of the second commodity. Assuming that negative purchases of either commodity are impossible, one must have both $x \geq 0$ and $y \geq 0$. Assuming too that not all the budget need be spent, it follows that the person is restricted to the *budget set* given by

$$B = \{(x, y) : px + qy \leq m, \ x \geq 0, \ y \geq 0\}$$

as in Eq. (1.1.1). Sketch the budget set B in the xy-plane. Find the slope of the budget line $px + qy = m$, as well as its x- and y-intercepts.

Solution: The set of points (x, y) that satisfy $x \geq 0$ and $y \geq 0$ is the first (nonnegative) quadrant. If we impose the additional requirement that $px + qy \leq m$, we obtain the triangular domain B shown in Fig. 4.4.12.

If $px + qy = m$, then $qy = -px + m$ and so $y = (-p/q)x + m/q$. This shows that the slope is $-p/q$. The budget line intersects the x-axis when $y = 0$. Then $px = m$, so $x = m/p$. The budget line intersects the y-axis when $x = 0$. Then $qy = m$, so $y = m/q$. So the two points of intersection are $(m/p, 0)$ and $(0, m/q)$, as shown in Fig. 4.4.12.

A budget line like the one in Example 4.4.7 features so often in economics courses that all the details of Fig. 4.4.12 are well worth committing to memory.

EXERCISES FOR SECTION 4.4

1. Find the slopes of the lines passing through the following pairs of points:

   (a) $(2, 3)$ and $(5, 8)$ (b) $(-1, -3)$ and $(2, -5)$ (c) $\left(\frac{1}{2}, \frac{3}{2}\right)$ and $\left(\frac{1}{3}, -\frac{1}{5}\right)$

2. Draw graphs for the following straight lines:

   (a) $3x + 4y = 12$ (b) $\dfrac{x}{10} - \dfrac{y}{5} = 1$ (c) $x = 3$

3. Suppose demand D for a good is a linear function of its price per unit, P. When price is \$10, demand is 200 units, and when price is \$15, demand is 150 units. Find the demand function.

4. Decide which of the following relationships between two variables are linear:

   (a) $5y + 2x = 2$ (b) $P = 10(1 - 0.3t)$

   (c) $C = (0.5x + 2)(x - 3)$ (d) $p_1 x_1 + p_2 x_2 = R$, where p_1, p_2, and R are constants.

5. A printing company quotes the price of \$1 400 for producing 100 copies of a report, and \$3 000 for 500 copies. Assuming a linear relation, what would be the price of printing 300 copies?

6. Find the slopes of the five lines ℓ_1 to ℓ_5 shown in Fig. 4.4.13, and for each, give an equation that it represents graphically.

7. Determine the equations for the following straight lines:

   (a) ℓ_1 passes through $(1, 3)$ and has a slope of 2.

   (b) ℓ_2 passes through $(-2, 2)$ and $(3, 3)$.

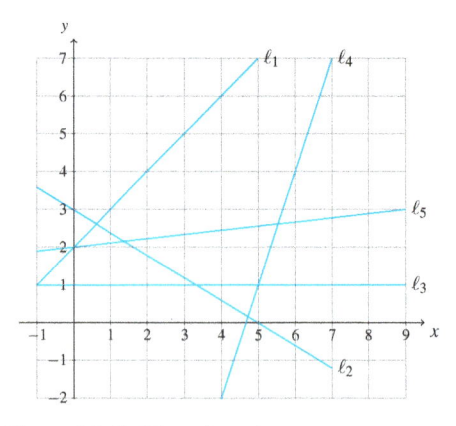

Figure 4.4.13 Lines ℓ_1 to ℓ_5

(c) ℓ_3 passes through the origin and has a slope of $-1/2$.

(d) ℓ_4 passes through $(a, 0)$ and $(0, b)$, with $a \neq 0$.

8. Solve each of the following systems of equations graphically, where possible:

   (a) $x - y = 5$ and $x + y = 1$

   (b) $x + y = 2$, $x - 2y = 2$, and $x - y = 2$

   (c) $3x + 4y = 1$ and $6x + 8y = 6$

9. Sketch in the xy-plane the set of all pairs of numbers (x, y) that satisfy the following inequalities:

   (a) $2x + 4y \geq 5$

   (b) $x - 3y + 2 \leq 0$

   (c) $100x + 200y \leq 300$

(SM) 10. Sketch in the xy-plane the set of all pairs of numbers (x, y) that satisfy all the following three inequalities: $3x + 4y \leq 12$, $x - y \leq 1$, and $3x + y \geq 3$.

4.5 Linear Models

Linear relations occur frequently in mathematical models. One illustration is Example 2.6.2, where we used the linear equation $F = \frac{9}{5}C + 32$ to convert a temperature measured in degrees Celsius to the same temperature measured in degrees Fahrenheit. Most of the linear models in economics are approximations to more complicated models. Two illustrations are those shown in Example 4.4.1. Statistical methods have been devised to construct linear relations that approximate the actual data as closely as possible. Let us consider one very naïve attempt to construct a linear model based on some population data.

EXAMPLE 4.5.1   A United Nations report estimated that the European population was 606 million in 1960, and would become 657 million in 1970. Use these estimates to construct a linear function of time t that approximates the population in Europe. Then use the function to estimate the population in 1930, 2000, and 2015.

Solution: Let t denote the number of years from 1960, so that $t = 0$ is 1960, $t = 1$ is 1961, and so on. Let P denote the European population in millions. We represent its growth using a linear equation of the form $P = at + b$. The data tell us that the graph of this function must be the straight line that passes through the two points $(t_1, P_1) = (0, 606)$ and $(t_2, P_2) = (10, 657)$. So we use the point–point formula (4.4.2), replacing x and y with t and P, respectively. This gives

$$P - 606 = \frac{657 - 606}{10 - 0}(t - 0) = \frac{51}{10}t$$

or

$$P = 5.1t + 606 \qquad (*)$$

In Table 4.5.1, we have compared our estimates with those of the UN. Note that because $t = 0$ corresponds to 1960, $t = -30$ will correspond to 1930.

Table 4.5.1 Population estimates for Europe (in millions)

Year	1930	2000	2015
t	-30	40	55
UN estimates	549	726	738
Formula $(*)$ gives	555	810	887

Note that the slope of line $(*)$ is 5.1. This means that if the European population had developed according to equation $(*)$, then the annual increase in the population would have been constant and equal to 5.1 million.[6]

EXAMPLE 4.5.2 **(The Consumption Function).** "Keynesian macroeconomic theory" is the term used by most economists to describe a collection of models named after the influential British economist John Maynard Keynes (1883–1946). A key feature of these models is the claim that, at least in the short run, the level of economic activity, as measured by the national income Y, is determined by the aggregate demand of the economy. Moreover, the total consumption expenditure on goods and services, denoted by C, is assumed to be a function of national income Y, with $C = f(Y)$, where $f(Y)$ is the *consumption function*. Following the work of Keynes's associate Richard F. Kahn (1905–1989) in Cambridge, in many models the consumption function is assumed to be linear, so that $C = a + bY$. The slope b of this line is called the *marginal propensity to consume*. For example, if C and Y are measured in billions of dollars, the number b tells us by how many billions of dollars consumption would increase if national income were to increase by 1 billion dollars. Following Kahn's insight, the number b is usually thought to lie between 0 and 1.

---

[6] Actually, Europe's population grew unusually fast during the 1960s. Of course, it grew unusually slowly when millions died during the war years 1939–1945. We see that formula $(*)$ does not give very good results compared to the UN estimates. For a better way to model population growth see Example 4.9.1.

In a study of the US economy for the period 1929–1941, Norwegian economist Trygve Haavelmo[7] estimated the consumption function as $C = 95.05 + 0.712\,Y$. Here, the marginal propensity to consume is equal to 0.712.

EXAMPLE 4.5.3 (**Supply and Demand**). Over a fixed period of time such as a week, the quantity of a specific good that consumers demand (that is, are willing to buy) will depend on the price of that good. Usually, as the price increases the demand will decrease.[8] Also, the number of units that the producers are willing to supply to the market during a certain period depends on the price they are able to obtain. Usually, the supply will increase as the price increases. So typical demand and supply curves are as indicated in Fig. 4.5.1.

In Fig. 4.5.1 the point E at which the demand and supply curves cross represents an *equilibrium*. The price P^e at which this occurs is the *equilibrium price*; the corresponding quantity Q^e is the *equilibrium quantity*. Thus, the equilibrium price P^e is defined so that consumers desire to buy the same amount of the good at price P^e as producers wish to sell.

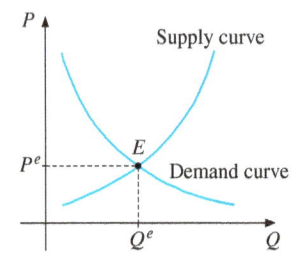

Figure 4.5.1 Demand and supply curves

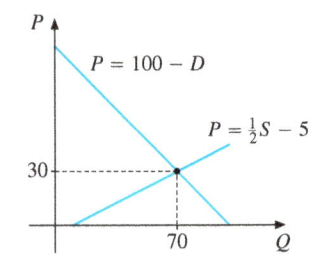

Figure 4.5.2 $D = 100 - P$ and $S = 10 + 2P$

As a very simple example, consider the linear demand function $D = 100 - P$ and supply function $S = 10 + 2P$. The inverse functions are $P = 100 - D$ and $P = \frac{1}{2}S - 5$, whose graphs are shown in Fig. 4.5.2.[9] The quantity demanded D equals the quantity supplied S provided $100 - P = 10 + 2P$, implying that $3P = 90$. So the equilibrium price is $P^e = 30$, with equilibrium quantity $Q^e = 70$.

---

[7] 1911–1999. He was awarded the Nobel prize in 1989.

[8] For certain luxury goods like perfume, which are often given as presents, demand might increase as the price increases. For absolutely essential goods, like insulin for diabetics, demand might be almost independent of the price. Occasionally dietary staples could also be "Giffen goods" for which demand rises as price rises. The explanation offered is that these foodstuffs are so essential to a very poor household's survival that a rise in price lowers real income substantially, and so makes alternative sources of nourishment even less affordable.

[9] When specifying a linear supply function, the sign of the constant term can be problematic. In the case we just introduced, a negative constant has the unintuitive implication that supply is positive even when the price is zero – in our case, it is 10 units. One possibility for something like this to occur would be when the producer owns a stock of the product and this is highly perishable. But having the supply be positive and increasing at very low prices can be inconsistent with the producer's behaviour. The difficulty is that a positive constant brings about a problem too: that at some low prices, the producer's supply is negative. We will overlook these issues here, but they serve as a warning that overly simplified models can sometimes display undesirable features.

A peculiarity of Figs 4.5.1 and 4.5.2 is that, although the quantities demanded and supplied are usually regarded as functions of price, economists usually measure price on the vertical axis and quantity on the horizontal axis. This has been standard practice in elementary price theory since the fundamental ideas of the French mathematician and economist Antoine-Augustin Cournot (1801–1877) and several other European contemporaries. The English economist Alfred Marshall (1842–1924) did much to popularize the practice late in the late 19th century.

EXAMPLE 4.5.4 **(Linear Supply and Demand Functions).** Consider the following general linear demand and supply schedules: $D = a - bP$ and $S = \alpha + \beta P$, where a and b are positive parameters of the demand function D, while α and β are positive parameters of the supply function.[10]

The equilibrium price P^e occurs where demand equals supply. But $D = S$ at $P = P^e$, implying that $a - bP^e = \alpha + \beta P^e$, or $a - \alpha = (\beta + b)P^e$. The corresponding equilibrium quantity is $Q^e = a - bP^e$. So equilibrium occurs at

$$P^e = \frac{a - \alpha}{\beta + b} \quad \text{and} \quad Q^e = a - b\frac{a - \alpha}{\beta + b} = \frac{a\beta + \alpha b}{\beta + b}$$

EXERCISES FOR SECTION 4.5

1. The consumption function $C = 4141 + 0.78Y$ was estimated for the UK during the period 1949–1975. What is the marginal propensity to consume?

2. Find the equilibrium price for each of the following linear models of supply and demand:

   (a) $D = 75 - 3P$ and $S = 2P$

   (b) $D = 100 - 0.5P$ and $S = -20 + 0.5P$

3. The total cost C of producing x units of some commodity is a linear function of x. Records show that on one occasion, 100 units were made at a total cost of $200, and on another occasion, 150 units were made at a total cost of $275. Express the linear equation for total cost C in terms of the number of units x produced.

4. The expenditure of a household on consumer goods, C, is related to the household's income, y, in the following way: When the household's income is $1 000, the expenditure on consumer goods is $900, and whenever income increases by $100, the expenditure on consumer goods increases by $80. Express the expenditure on consumer goods as a function of income, assuming a linear relationship.

5. For most assets such as cars, electronic equipment, and furniture, the value decreases, or *depreciates*, each year. If the value of an asset is assumed to decrease by a fixed percentage of the original value each year, it is referred to as *straight line depreciation*.

   (a) Suppose the value of a car which initially costs $20 000 depreciates by 10% of its original value each year. Find a formula for its value $P(t)$ after t years.

---

[10] Such linear supply and demand functions play an important role in economics. It is often the case that the market for a particular commodity, such as copper, can be represented approximately by suitably estimated linear demand and supply functions.

(b) If a $500 washing machine is completely depreciated after ten years (straight line depreciation), find a formula for its value $W(t)$ after t years.

4.6 Quadratic Functions

Economists often find that linear functions are too simple for modelling economic phenomena with acceptable accuracy. Indeed, many economic models involve functions that either decrease down to some minimum value and then increase, or else increase up to some maximum value and then decrease. Some simple functions with this property are the *quadratic* functions that we first saw in Section 3.3. Their general form is

$$f(x) = ax^2 + bx + c \tag{4.6.1}$$

where a, b, and c are constants with $a \neq 0$ (otherwise the function would be linear).

In general, the graph of $f(x) = ax^2 + bx + c$ is called a *parabola*. The shape of this parabola roughly resembles ∩ when $a < 0$ and ∪ when $a > 0$. Three typical cases are illustrated in Figs 4.6.1 to 4.6.3.

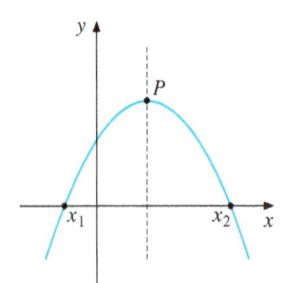

Figure 4.6.1 $a < 0, b^2 > 4ac$ 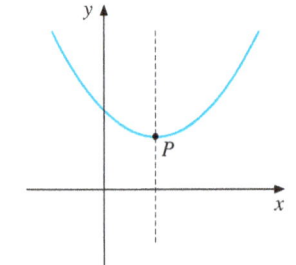 **Figure 4.6.2** $a > 0, b^2 < 4ac$ **Figure 4.6.3** $a > 0, b^2 = 4ac$

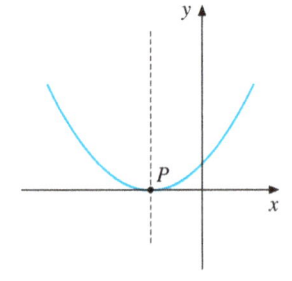

To learn more about the function $f(x) = ax^2 + bx + c$, we address these two questions:

(a) For which values of x (if any) is $ax^2 + bx + c = 0$?

(b) What are the coordinates of the extremum (maximum or minimum) point P, also called the *vertex* of the parabola?

The answer to question (a) was given by the quadratic formula (3.3.5) and the subsequent discussion of that formula.

The easiest way to handle question (b) is to use derivatives, which is the topic of Chapter 6, especially Exercise 6.2.7. However, let us briefly consider how the "method of completing the squares" from Section 3.3 can answer question (b). In fact, this method yields

$$f(x) = ax^2 + bx + c = a\left(x + \frac{b}{2a}\right)^2 - \frac{b^2 - 4ac}{4a} \tag{4.6.2}$$

as is easily verified by expanding the right-hand side and gathering terms. Now, when x varies, only the value of $a(x+b/2a)^2$ changes. This squared term equals 0 only when $x = -b/2a$. Provided $a > 0$, it is never less than 0. So when $a > 0$, the function $f(x)$ attains its minimum when $x = -b/2a$, and the minimum value is given by

$$f(-b/2a) = -(b^2 - 4ac)/4a = c - b^2/4a$$

On the other hand, if $a < 0$ then $a(x+b/2a)^2 \leq 0$ for all x, and the squared term equals 0 only when $x = -b/2a$. Hence, $f(x)$ attains its maximum when $x = -b/2a$ in this case.

To summarize, we have shown the following:

EXTREMA OF QUADRATIC FUNCTIONS

If $a < 0$, then $f(x) = ax^2 + bx + c$ has its *maximum* at $x = -b/2a$ (4.6.3)

If $a > 0$, then $f(x) = ax^2 + bx + c$ has its *minimum* at $x = -b/2a$ (4.6.4)

The *axis of symmetry* for a parabola is the vertical line about which its graph is symmetric. In Figs 4.6.1–4.6.3 this axis is shown as a dashed line that passes through the *vertex* of the parabola, which is marked as the point P in each case. To justify this, in Section 5.2 a general function f will be defined as *symmetric about* $x = x_0$ just in case $f(x_0 + t) = f(x_0 - t)$ for all t. Now, for any number t, putting $x = -\frac{b}{2a} \pm t$ in formula (4.6.2) implies that

$$f\left(-\frac{b}{2a} + t\right) = at^2 - \frac{b^2 - 4ac}{4a} = f\left(-\frac{b}{2a} - t\right)$$

This confirms that the quadratic function $f(x) = ax^2 + bx + c$ is indeed symmetric about the vertical line $x = -b/2a$ which passes through the extremum P.

Quadratic Optimization Problems in Economics

Much of economic analysis is concerned with optimization problems. Economics, after all, is the science of choice, and optimization problems are the form in which economists usually model choice mathematically. A general discussion of such problems must be postponed until we have developed the necessary tools from calculus. Here we show how the simple results from this section on maximizing quadratic functions can be used to illustrate some basic economic ideas.

EXAMPLE 4.6.1   (**Expectation**). Suppose that there is an urn containing T balls, each of them with a number written on it. One of the balls will be drawn at random, and you are asked to guess what number will come out on that ball. Let us denote by y_t the number written on ball t, for $t = 1, 2, \ldots, T$. Your job is to give a guess, say $\hat{y}$, which is close to y_t.

Obviously, the mistake in your guess $\hat{y}$ if ball t is drawn is $|y_t - \hat{y}|$. Here, we use the absolute value of the difference between the guess and the actual number, because underestimating the truth seems just as bad as overestimating it by the same amount. An alternative way to obtain such a symmetric measure of the error is to use the square of the difference, $(y_t - \hat{y})^2$. For reasons that will become clear later, this so-called *squared error* is widely used in statistics. Indeed, statisticians commonly assume that a person's guess in this situation should minimize the (arithmetic) *mean squared error*, as defined in Example 2.10.2. That is, a person's guess should be chosen so as to minimize the *loss function*

$$L(\hat{y}) = \frac{1}{T}\sum_{t=1}^{T}(y_t - \hat{y})^2$$

Using the rules (2.10.1) to (2.10.3) for summation, we get

$$L(\hat{y}) = \frac{1}{T}\sum_{t=1}^{T}y_t^2 - \frac{1}{T}\sum_{t=1}^{T}2y_t\hat{y} + \frac{1}{T}\sum_{t=1}^{T}\hat{y}^2 = \frac{1}{T}\sum_{t=1}^{T}y_t^2 - \left(\frac{2}{T}\sum_{t=1}^{T}y_t\right)\hat{y} + \hat{y}^2$$

Using μ_y to denote the mean of the numbers $y_1, y_2, \ldots, y_T$ allows us to rewrite this as

$$L(\hat{y}) = \frac{1}{T}\sum_{t=1}^{T}y_t^2 - 2\mu_y\hat{y} + \hat{y}^2 \qquad (*)$$

This is a quadratic function in $\hat{y}$, like Eq. (4.6.1), with $a = 1$ and $b = -2\mu_y$. It follows from Eq. (4.6.3) that the guess that minimizes the loss function is

$$\hat{y} = -\frac{b}{2a} = -\frac{2\mu_y}{2} = \mu_y$$

That is, the guess that minimizes the mean squared error is precisely the mean of the *random variable y*. This is why the mean of y is often referred to as its *expectation* or *expected value*.

EXAMPLE 4.6.2 Suppose that when a firm produces and sells Q units of output, it receives a price P per unit given by $P = 102 - 2Q$. Suppose too that the firm's cost of producing and selling Q units is $C = 2Q + \frac{1}{2}Q^2$. Then the firm's profit is[11]

$$\pi(Q) = PQ - C = (102 - 2Q)Q - \left(2Q + \frac{1}{2}Q^2\right) = 100Q - \frac{5}{2}Q^2$$

Find the value of Q which maximizes profits, and the corresponding maximal profit.

Solution: Using formula (4.6.4), we find that profit is maximized at

$$Q = Q^* = -\frac{100}{2\cdot(-5/2)} = 20$$

The resulting profit is

$$\pi^* = \pi(Q^*) = 100 \cdot 20 - \frac{5}{2}\cdot 400 = 1000$$

This example is a special case of the monopoly problem studied in the next example.

---

[11] In mathematics the Greek letter π is used to denote the constant ratio $3.1415\ldots$ between the circumference of a circle and its diameter. In economics, this constant is not used very often. Also, p and P usually denote a price, so π has come to denote profit.

EXAMPLE 4.6.3 (**A monopoly problem**). Consider a firm that is the only seller of the commodity it produces, possibly a patented medicine, so it enjoys a monopoly. The monopolist's total costs are assumed to be given by the quadratic function

$$C = \alpha Q + \beta Q^2$$

of its output level $Q \geq 0$, where α and β are positive constants. For each Q, assume that the price P per unit at which it sells its output is determined by the linear "inverse" demand function

$$P = a - bQ$$

where a and b are constants with $a > 0$ and $b \geq 0$. So for any nonnegative Q, the monopolist's total revenue R is given by the quadratic function $R = PQ = (a - bQ)Q$, and its profit by the quadratic function

$$\pi(Q) = R - C = (a - bQ)Q - \alpha Q - \beta Q^2 = (a - \alpha)Q - (b + \beta)Q^2$$

Assuming that the monopolist's objective is to maximize the profit function $\pi = \pi(Q)$, find its optimal output level Q^M and corresponding optimal profit π^M.

Solution: By using (4.6.4), we see that π reaches its maximum when

$$Q^M = \frac{a - \alpha}{2(b + \beta)} \qquad (4.6.5)$$

with

$$\pi^M = \frac{(a-\alpha)^2}{2(b+\beta)} - (b+\beta)\frac{(a-\alpha)^2}{4(b+\beta)^2} = \frac{(a-\alpha)^2}{4(b+\beta)}$$

This result is valid if $a > \alpha$; if $a \leq \alpha$, the firm will not produce anything, but will have $Q^M = 0$ and $\pi^M = 0$. The two cases are illustrated in Figs 4.6.4 and 4.6.5. In each figure the part of the parabola to the left of $Q = 0$ is dashed, because it is not really relevant given the natural requirement that $Q \geq 0$. The price and cost associated with Q^M in (4.6.5) can be found by routine algebra.

If we put $b = 0$ in the price function $P = a - bQ$, then $P = a$ for all Q. In this case, the firm's choice of quantity does not influence the price at all and so the firm is said to be

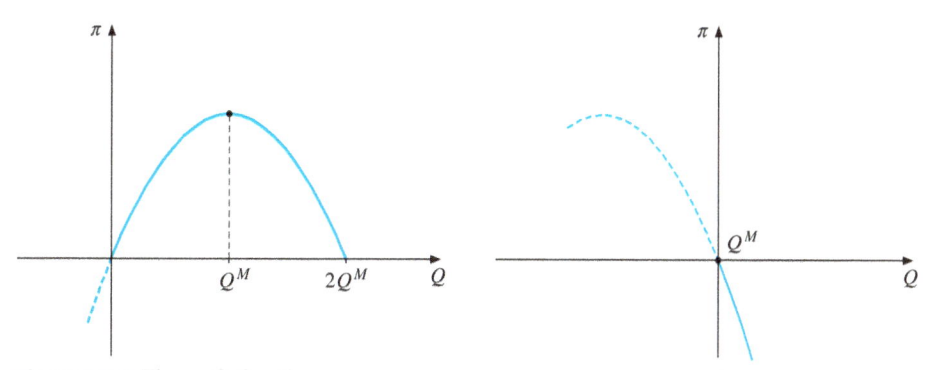

Figure 4.6.4 The profit function, $a > \alpha$

Figure 4.6.5 The profit function, $a \leq \alpha$

perfectly competitive. In this case, by replacing a by P in our previous expressions, we see that profit is maximized at the output level

$$Q^* = \frac{P - \alpha}{2\beta} \tag{4.6.6}$$

The resulting maximum profit is

$$\pi^* = \frac{(P - \alpha)^2}{4\beta}$$

provided that $P > \alpha$. If $P \leq \alpha$, then $Q^* = 0$ and $\pi^* = 0$.

Solving (4.6.6) for P yields $P = \alpha + 2\beta Q^*$. Thus, the equation

$$P = \alpha + 2\beta Q \tag{4.6.7}$$

represents the *supply curve* of this perfectly competitive firm for $P > \alpha$. For $P \leq \alpha$, the profit-maximizing output Q^* is 0. The supply curve relating the price on the market to the firm's choice of output quantity is shown in Fig. 4.6.6; it includes all the points of the line segment between the origin and $(0, \alpha)$, where the price is too low for the firm to earn any profit by producing a positive output.

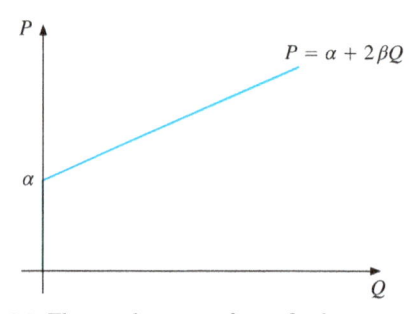

Figure 4.6.6 The supply curve of a perfectly competitive firm

Let us return to the monopoly firm (which has no supply curve). If it could somehow be made to act like a competitive firm, taking price as given, it would be on the supply curve (4.6.7). Given the demand curve $P = a - bQ$, equilibrium between supply and demand occurs when (4.6.7) is also satisfied, and so $P = a - bQ = \alpha + 2\beta Q$. Solving the second equation for Q, and then substituting for P and π in turn, we see that the respective equilibrium levels of output, price, and profit would be

$$Q^e = \frac{a - \alpha}{b + 2\beta}, \quad P^e = \frac{2a\beta + \alpha b}{b + 2\beta}, \quad \pi^e = \frac{\beta(a - \alpha)^2}{(b + 2\beta)^2}$$

In order to have the monopolist mimic a competitive firm by choosing to be at (Q^e, P^e), it may be necessary to tax (or subsidize) the output of the monopolist. Suppose that the monopolist is required to pay a specific tax of τ per unit of output. Because the tax payment, $\tau \cdot Q$, is added to the firm's costs, the new total cost function is

$$C = \alpha Q + \beta Q^2 + \tau Q = (\alpha + \tau)Q + \beta Q^2$$

Carrying out the same calculations as before, but with α replaced by $\alpha + \tau$, gives the monopolist's choice of output as

$$Q_\tau^M = \begin{cases} \dfrac{a - \alpha - \tau}{2(b + \beta)}, & \text{if } a \geq \alpha + \tau; \\ 0, & \text{otherwise} \end{cases}$$

So $Q_\tau^M = Q^e$ when

$$\frac{a - \alpha - \tau}{2(b + \beta)} = \frac{a - \alpha}{b + 2\beta}$$

Solving this equation for τ yields

$$\tau = -\frac{(a - \alpha)b}{b + 2\beta}$$

Note that τ is actually negative, indicating the desirability of *subsidizing* the output of the monopolist in order to encourage additional production.[12]

EXERCISES FOR SECTION 4.6

1. Let $f(x) = x^2 - 4x$.

   (a) Complete the following table and use it to sketch the graph of f:

x	-1	0	1	2	3	4	5
$f(x)$							

   (b) Use Eq. (4.6.3) to determine the minimum point of f.

   (c) Solve the equation $f(x) = 0$.

2. Let $f(x) = -\frac{1}{2}x^2 - x + \frac{3}{2}$.

   (a) Complete the following table and sketch the graph of f

x	-4	-3	-2	-1	0	1	2
$f(x)$							

   (b) Use Eq. (4.6.4) to determine the maximum point of f.

   (c) Solve the equation $f(x) = 0$.

   (d) Show that $f(x) = -\frac{1}{2}(x - 1)(x + 3)$, and use this to study how the sign of $f(x)$ varies with x. Compare the result with your graph.

---

[12] Of course, subsidizing monopolists is usually felt to be unjust, and many additional complications need to be considered carefully before formulating an appropriate policy for regulating a monopolist. Still the previous analysis suggests that if it is thought to be ethically desirable to lower a monopolist's price or its profit, it might be much better to do this directly rather than by taxing its output.

3. Determine the maximum/minimum points of the following functions, by using Eq. (4.6.3) or (4.6.4), as appropriate:

   (a) $x^2 + 4x$
   (b) $x^2 + 6x + 18$
   (c) $-3x^2 + 30x - 30$
   (d) $9x^2 - 6x - 44$
   (e) $-x^2 - 200x + 30\,000$
   (f) $x^2 + 100x - 20\,000$

4. Find all the zeros of each quadratic function in Exercise 3, and where possible write each function in the form $a(x - x_1)(x - x_2)$.

5. Find solutions to the following equations, where a and b are parameters.

   (a) $x^2 - 3ax + 2a^2 = 0$
   (b) $x^2 - (a+b)x + ab = 0$
   (c) $2x^2 + (4b - a)x = 2ab$

6. A model in the theory of efficient loan markets involves the function
$$U(x) = 72 - (4+x)^2 - (4-rx)^2$$
where r is a constant. Find the value of x for which $U(x)$ attains its largest value.

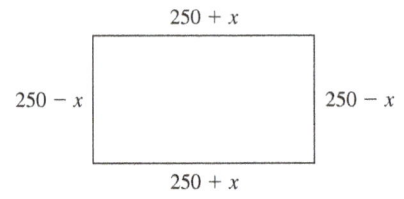

Figure 4.6.7 A plot of land

7. A farmer has one thousand metres of fence wire with which to make a rectangular enclosure, as illustrated in Fig. 4.6.7. Let the base have length $250 + x$. Then the height is $250 - x$, as in Fig. 4.6.7.

   (a) Find the values of x and the areas for the three rectangles whose bases are 100, 250, and 350 metres.

   (b) What choice of x gives the maximum area?[13]

SM 8. If a cocoa shipping firm sells Q tons of cocoa in the UK, the price it receives is given by $P_U = \alpha_1 - \frac{1}{3}Q$. On the other hand, if it buys Q tons of cocoa from its only source in Ghana, the price it has to pay is given by $P_G = \alpha_2 + \frac{1}{6}Q$. In addition, it costs γ per ton to ship cocoa from its supplier in Ghana to its customers in the UK (its only market). The numbers α_1, α_2, and γ are all positive.

   (a) Express the cocoa shipper's profit as a function of Q, the number of tons shipped.

   (b) Assuming that $\alpha_1 - \alpha_2 - \gamma > 0$, find the profit-maximizing shipment of cocoa. What happens if $\alpha_1 - \alpha_2 - \gamma \leq 0$?

   (c) Suppose the government of Ghana imposes an export tax on cocoa of τ per ton. Find the new expression for the shipper's profits and the new profit-maximizing quantity shipped.

   (d) Calculate the Ghanaian government's export tax revenue as a function of τ, and compare the graph of this function with the Laffer curve presented in Fig. 4.1.1.

---

[13] In antiquity, when selling rectangular pieces of land to farmers, certain surveyors would write contracts in which only the perimeter was specified. As a result, the lots they sold were long narrow rectangles.

(e) Advise the Ghanaian government on how to obtain as much tax revenue as possible.

9. [HARDER] Let $a_1, a_2, \ldots, a_n$ and $b_1, b_2, \ldots, b_n$ be arbitrary real numbers. The inequality

$$(a_1b_1 + a_2b_2 + \cdots + a_nb_n)^2 \leq (a_1^2 + a_2^2 + \cdots + a_n^2)(b_1^2 + b_2^2 + \cdots + b_n^2) \quad (4.6.8)$$

is called the *Cauchy–Schwarz inequality*.

(a) Check the inequality for $n = 2$, when $a_1 = -3$, $a_2 = 2$, $b_1 = 5$, and $b_2 = -2$.

(b) Prove (4.6.8) by means of the following trick: first, define f for all x by

$$f(x) = (a_1x + b_1)^2 + \cdots + (a_nx + b_n)^2$$

It should be obvious that $f(x) \geq 0$ for all x. Write $f(x)$ as $Ax^2 + Bx + C$, where the expressions for the coefficients A, B, and C are related to the terms in (4.6.8). Because $Ax^2 + Bx + C \geq 0$ for all x, we must have $B^2 - 4AC \leq 0$. Why?

(c) Show that (4.6.8) then follows.

4.7 Polynomials

Cubic Functions

After considering linear and quadratic functions, the logical next step is to examine *cubic functions* of the form

$$f(x) = ax^3 + bx^2 + cx + d \quad (4.7.1)$$

where a, b, c, and d are constants and $a \neq 0$. It is relatively easy to examine the behaviour of linear and quadratic functions. Cubic functions are considerably more complicated, because the shape of their graphs changes drastically as the coefficients a, b, c, and d vary. Two examples are given in Figs 4.7.1 and 4.7.2. Cubic functions do occasionally appear in economic models.

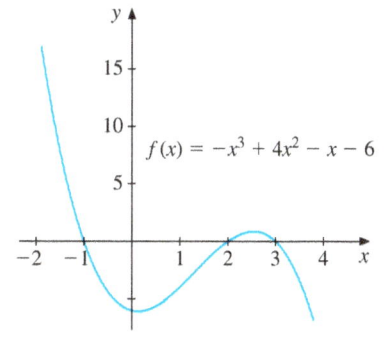

Figure 4.7.1 A cubic function

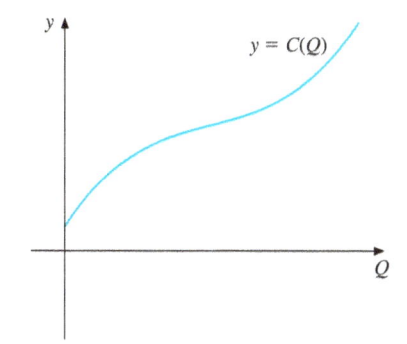

Figure 4.7.2 A cubic cost function

EXAMPLE 4.7.1 Consider a firm producing a single commodity. The total cost of producing Q units of the commodity is $C(Q)$. Cost functions often have the following properties: First, $C(0)$ is positive, because an initial fixed expenditure is involved. When production increases, costs also increase. In the beginning, costs increase rapidly, but the rate of increase slows down as production equipment is used for a higher proportion of each working week. However, at high levels of production, costs again increase at a fast rate, because of technical bottlenecks and overtime payments to workers, for example. The cubic cost function $C(Q) = aQ^3 + bQ^2 + cQ + d$ exhibits this type of behaviour provided that $a > 0, b < 0, c > 0, d > 0$, and $3ac > b^2$. Such a function is sketched in Fig. 4.7.2.

Cubic cost functions whose coefficients have a different sign pattern have also been studied. For instance, a study of a particular electric power generating plant revealed that over a certain period, the cost of fuel as a function of output Q was given by

$$C(Q) = -Q^3 + 214.2Q^2 - 7900Q + 320\,700$$

Note, however, that this cost function cannot be valid for all Q, because it suggests that fuel costs would be negative for large enough Q.

Studying cubic functions in detail is made easier by using differential calculus, as will be seen later.

General Polynomials

Linear, quadratic, and cubic functions are all examples of *polynomials*.

GENERAL POLYNOMIAL

Consider the function P, defined for all x, by

$$P(x) = a_n x^n + a_{n-1} x^{n-1} + \cdots + a_1 x + a_0 \tag{4.7.2}$$

where $a_0, a_1, \ldots, a_n$ are constants. In case $a_n \neq 0$, this is called the *general polynomial of degree n*, with *coefficients* $a_n, a_{n-1}, \ldots, a_0$.

For instance, when $n = 4$, we obtain $P(x) = a_4 x^4 + a_3 x^3 + a_2 x^2 + a_1 x + a_0$, which is the general *quartic function*, or *polynomial of degree 4*. Of course, there are many functions like $5 + x^{-2}$ or $1/(x^3 - x + 2)$ that are not polynomials.

Definition (4.7.2) writes the polynomial as the sum of decreasing powers of x. When $|x| > 1$ so that $|x|^n$ increases with n, this puts the most significant terms first. But especially when $|x| < 1$, there are advantages to using the reverse order, in which one can also use summation notation to write $P(x) = \sum_{k=0}^{n} a_k x^k$.

Factoring Polynomials

Like all algebraic expressions, polynomials can be added, subtracted and multiplied. One polynomial can also be divided by another to yield a function that is defined at all points where the denominator is nonzero. Sometimes the result of this division will be a new polynomial. But sometimes, as when one divides one integer by another, there will be a remainder. Here is a useful result:

REMAINDER THEOREM

Let $P(x)$ be a polynomial of degree m, and $Q(x)$ a polynomial of degree n, where $m > n$. Then there exists a unique pair of polynomials $q(x)$ of degree $m - n$ and $r(x)$ of degree less than n such that

$$P(x) = q(x)Q(x) + r(x) \tag{4.7.3}$$

Evidently Eq. (4.7.3) can be written in the form

$$\frac{P(x)}{Q(x)} = q(x) + \frac{r(x)}{Q(x)} \quad \text{for all } x \text{ such that } Q(x) \neq 0$$

In this sense, the polynomial $r(x)$ is what gets left over after trying to divide $P(x)$ by $Q(x)$, which is why we call it the *remainder*.

If (4.7.3) holds with $r(x) = 0$ for all x, then we say that $Q(x)$ *is a factor of* $P(x)$, and that $P(x)$ *is divisible by* $Q(x)$. Then $P(x) = q(x)Q(x)$ or $P(x)/Q(x) = q(x)$.

An important special case is when $Q(x) = x - a$. Then $Q(x)$ is of degree 1, so the remainder $r(x)$ must have degree 0, and is therefore a constant. In this special case

$$P(x) = q(x)(x - a) + r \quad \text{for all } x$$

For $x = a$ in particular, we get $P(a) = r$. It follows that $x - a$ divides $P(x)$ if and only if $P(a) = 0$. This important observation can be formulated as follows:

POLYNOMIAL FACTORING

The polynomial $P(x)$ has the factor $x - a$ if and only if $P(a) = 0$ \hfill (4.7.4)

EXAMPLE 4.7.2   Prove that $x - 5$ is a factor of the polynomial $P(x) = x^3 - 3x^2 - 50$.

Solution: $P(5) = 125 - 75 - 50 = 0$, so according to (4.7.4), $x - 5$ divides $P(x)$. In fact, note that $P(x) = (x - 5)(x^2 + 2x + 10)$.

Numerous problems in mathematics and its applications involve polynomials. Often, one is particularly interested in finding the number and location of the *zeros* of $P(x)$, defined as the values of x such that $P(x) = 0$.

The *general equation of degree n* takes the form

$$a_n x^n + a_{n-1} x^{n-1} + \cdots + a_1 x + a_0 = 0 \tag{4.7.5}$$

It will soon be shown that this equation has *at most n* (real) solutions, also called *roots*, but it need not have any. The corresponding *n*th-degree polynomial has a graph with at most $n-1$ *turning points* at which the function switches from being strictly increasing to strictly decreasing, or vice versa. But there may be fewer turning points. For example, the 100th-degree equation $x^{100} + 1 = 0$ has no solutions because $x^{100} + 1$ is always greater than or equal to 1, and its graph has only one turning point at $x = 0$.

According to the *fundamental theorem of algebra*, every polynomial of the form (4.7.2) can be written as a product of polynomials of degree 1 or 2. It follows from (4.7.4) that each zero $x = a$ of a polynomial $P(x)$ gives rise to a different factor of the form $x - a$. So if $P(x)$ is of degree n, it can have *at most n* different zeros.

Integer Roots

Note that each integer m that satisfies the cubic equation

$$-x^3 + 4x^2 - x - 6 = 0 \qquad (*)$$

must satisfy the equation $m(-m^2 + 4m - 1) = 6$. Evidently $-m^2 + 4m - 1$ is also an integer, so m must be a factor of the constant term 6. Since ± 1, ± 2, ± 3, and ± 6 are the factors of 6, they are the only possible integer solutions. Direct substitution into the left-hand side of equation $(*)$ reveals that of these eight possibilities, the roots of the equation are -1, 2, and 3. A third-degree equation has at most three roots, so we have found them all. In fact,

$$-x^3 + 4x^2 - x - 6 = -(x+1)(x-2)(x-3)$$

In general, Eq. (4.7.5) can be rewritten as

$$x(a_n x^{n-1} + a_{n-1} x^{n-2} + \cdots + a_1) = -a_0 \qquad (4.7.6)$$

So if the coefficients $a_n, a_{n-1}, \ldots, a_1, a_0$ are all integers, and if x is an integer root of (4.7.5), then the expression in parentheses on the left-hand side of (4.7.6) is also an integer, implying that x must be a factor of a_0. To summarize:

INTEGER ROOTS

Consider the equation

$$a_n x^n + a_{n-1} x^{n-1} + \cdots + a_1 x + a_0 = 0 \qquad (4.7.7)$$

where the coefficients $a_n, a_{n-1}, \ldots, a_1, a_0$ are all integers. Then all possible integer roots must be factors of the constant term a_0.

EXAMPLE 4.7.3 Find all possible integer roots of the equation

$$\tfrac{1}{2}x^3 - x^2 + \tfrac{1}{2}x - 1 = 0$$

Solution: We multiply both sides of the equation by 2 to obtain the equivalent equation $x^3 - 2x^2 + x - 2 = 0$ whose coefficients are all integers. Now, all integer roots must be factors of 2, so the only possibilities are ± 1 and ± 2. Checking these four shows only $x = 2$ is a root. In fact, because $x^3 - 2x^2 + x - 2 = (x - 2)(x^2 + 1)$, this is the only real root.

EXAMPLE 4.7.4 Find possible quadratic and cubic functions which have the graphs in Figs 4.7.3 and 4.7.4, respectively.

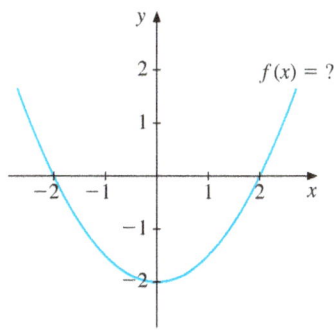

Figure 4.7.3 A quadratic function

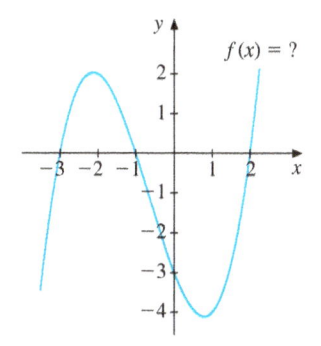

Figure 4.7.4 A cubic function

Solution: For Fig 4.7.3, since the graph intersects the x-axis at the two points $x = -2$ and $x = 2$, we try the quadratic function $f(x) = a(x - 2)(x + 2)$. Then $f(0) = -4a$. According to the graph, $f(0) = -2$, so $a = 1/2$, and hence

$$f(x) = \frac{1}{2}(x - 2)(x + 2) = \frac{1}{2}x^2 - 2$$

For Fig. 4.7.4, because the equation $f(x) = 0$ has roots $x = -3, -1, 2$, we try the cubic function $f(x) = b(x + 3)(x + 1)(x - 2)$. Then $f(0) = -6b$. According to the graph, $f(0) = -3$. So $b = 1/2$, and hence

$$f(x) = \frac{1}{2}(x + 3)(x + 1)(x - 2)$$

Polynomial Division

One can divide polynomials in much the same way as one uses long division to divide numbers. To remind ourselves how long division works, consider a simple numerical example:

$$
\begin{array}{r}
2735 \div \quad 5 = 500 + 40 + 7 \\
\underline{2500} \leftarrow 500 \times 5 \\
235 \\
\underline{200} \leftarrow 40 \times 5 \\
35 \\
\underline{35} \leftarrow 7 \times 5 \\
0 \qquad\qquad \leftarrow \text{the remainder}
\end{array}
$$

Note that each arrow indicates that the product on its right, which is formed from multiplying a decimal digit of the answer by the quotient, should be included on the left.

Thereupon, each horizontal line instructs you to subtract the number immediately above the line from the number above that.[14] In the end, we find the answer $2735 \div 5 = 547$.

Next we show how to apply a similar method to this example
$$(-x^3 + 4x^2 - x - 6) \div (x - 2)$$
of polynomial division. Here are the steps:

$$
\begin{array}{rl}
-x^3 + 4x^2 - x - 6 \div \quad x - 2 & = -x^2 + 2x + 3 \\
\underline{-x^3 + 2x^2} \quad\quad\quad \leftarrow \quad -x^2(x - 2) & \\
+ 2x^2 - x - 6 & \\
\underline{+ 2x^2 - 4x} \quad\quad \leftarrow \quad 2x(x - 2) & \\
+ 3x - 6 & \\
\underline{+ 3x - 6} \leftarrow \quad 3(x - 2) & \\
0 \quad\quad\quad \leftarrow \text{ the remainder} &
\end{array}
$$

We conclude that $(-x^3 + 4x^2 - x - 6) \div (x - 2) = -x^2 + 2x + 3$. However, it is easy to check that $-x^2 + 2x + 3 = -(x + 1)(x - 3)$. So
$$-x^3 + 4x^2 - x - 6 = -(x + 1)(x - 3)(x - 2)$$

EXAMPLE 4.7.5 Prove that the polynomial $P(x) = -2x^3 + 2x^2 + 10x + 6$ has a zero at $x = 3$, then factor the polynomial.

Solution: Inserting $x = 3$ yields $P(3) = 0$, so this is a zero. By (4.7.4), the polynomial $P(x)$ has $x - 3$ as a factor. Performing the division $(-2x^3 + 2x^2 + 10x + 6) \div (x - 3)$ yields the quotient $-2x^2 - 4x - 2 = -2(x + 1)^2$. Hence $P(x) = -2(x - 3)(x + 1)^2$.

Polynomial Division with a Remainder

The division $2734 \div 5$ gives 546 and leaves the remainder 4. So $2734/5 = 546 + 4/5$. We consider a similar form of division for polynomials.

EXAMPLE 4.7.6 Perform the division: $(x^4 + 3x^2 - 4) \div (x^2 + 2x)$.

Solution: Proceeding as before,[15]

$$
\begin{array}{rl}
x^4 \quad\quad + 3x^2 \quad\quad - 4 \div \quad x^2 + 2x & = x^2 - 2x + 7 \\
\underline{x^4 + 2x^3} \quad\quad\quad\quad \leftarrow \quad x^2(x^2 + 2x) & \\
- 2x^3 + 3x^2 \quad\quad - 4 & \\
\underline{- 2x^3 - 4x^2} \quad\quad \leftarrow \quad -2x(x^2 + 2x) & \\
7x^2 \quad - 4 & \\
\underline{7x^2 + 14x} \leftarrow \quad 7(x^2 + 2x) & \\
- 14x - 4 \quad\quad \leftarrow \text{ the remainder} &
\end{array}
$$

---

[14] You may be more accustomed to a different way of arranging the numbers, but the idea is always the same.

[15] The polynomial $x^4 + 3x^2 - 4$ has no terms in x^3 and x, so we inserted some extra space between the powers of x to make room for the terms in x^3 and x that arise in the course of the calculations.

It follows that $x^4 + 3x^2 - 4 = (x^2 - 2x + 7)(x^2 + 2x) + (-14x - 4)$ and so

$$\frac{x^4 + 3x^2 - 4}{x^2 + 2x} = x^2 - 2x + 7 - \frac{14x + 4}{x^2 + 2x}$$

The remainder theorem results from the claim that when dividing any polynomial $P(x)$ by another polynomial $Q(x)$ of lower degree, this division procedure always works and produces a unique result satisfying (4.7.3).

Rational Functions

A *rational function* is any function $R(x) = P(x)/Q(x)$ that can be expressed as the ratio of two polynomials $P(x)$ and $Q(x)$. This function is defined for all x where $Q(x) \neq 0$.

The rational function $R(x)$ is called *proper* if the degree of $P(x)$ is less than the degree of $Q(x)$. When the degree of $P(x)$ is no less than that of $Q(x)$, the function $R(x)$ is called an *improper* rational function. By using polynomial division as in Example 4.7.6, any improper rational function can be expressed as a polynomial plus a proper rational function.

EXAMPLE 4.7.7 One of the simplest types of rational function is

$$R(x) = \frac{ax + b}{cx + d}$$

We assume that $c \neq 0$. Otherwise, if $c = 0$, then $R(x)$ is either a linear function in case $d \neq 0$, or else is undefined if $d = 0$ as well.

The graph of R is a *hyperbola*. See Fig. 5.1.7 for a typical example where $R(x) = (3x - 5)/(x - 2)$.[16] A very simple case is $R(x) = a/x$, where $a > 0$. Figure 4.7.5 shows the graph of this function in the first quadrant. Note that the shaded area $A = x_0(a/x_0)$ is always equal to a, independent of which point P we choose on the curve.

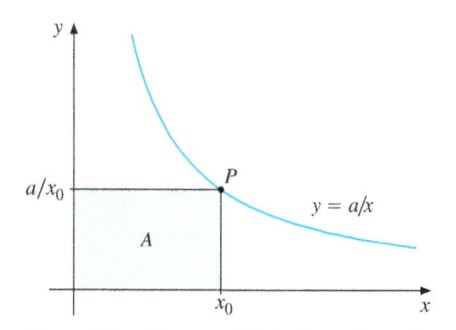

Figure 4.7.5 The area A is independent of P

Studying the behaviour of more complicated rational functions becomes easier once we have developed the proper tools from calculus.[17]

---

[16] See also the end of Section 5.5.
[17] See, for instance, Exercise 7.9.9.

EXERCISES FOR SECTION 4.7

1. Find all integer roots of the following equations:

   (a) $x^4 - x^3 - 7x^2 + x + 6 = 0$

   (b) $2x^3 + 11x^2 - 7x - 6 = 0$

   (c) $x^4 + x^3 + 2x^2 + x + 1 = 0$

   (d) $\frac{1}{4}x^3 - \frac{1}{4}x^2 - x + 1 = 0$

2. Find all integer roots of the following equations:

   (a) $x^2 + x - 2 = 0$

   (b) $x^3 - x^2 - 25x + 25 = 0$

   (c) $x^5 - 4x^3 - 3 = 0$

SM 3. Perform the following divisions:

   (a) $(2x^3 + 2x - 1) \div (x - 1)$

   (b) $(x^4 + x^3 + x^2 + x) \div (x^2 + x)$

   (c) $(x^5 - 3x^4 + 1) \div (x^2 + x + 1)$

   (d) $(3x^8 + x^2 + 1) \div (x^3 - 2x + 1)$

SM 4. Find a possible formula for each of the three polynomials with graphs shown in Figs 4.7.6 to 4.7.8.

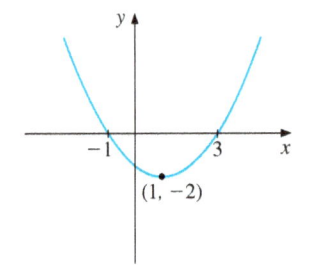

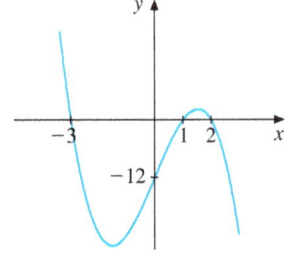

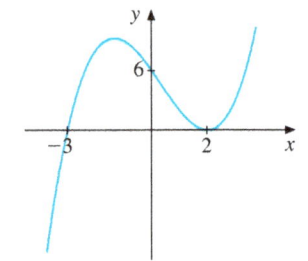

Figure 4.7.6 Exercise 4(a)

Figure 4.7.7 Exercise 4(b)

Figure 4.7.8 Exercise 4(c)

5. Perform the following divisions:

   (a) $(x^2 - x - 20) \div (x - 5)$

   (b) $(x^3 - 1) \div (x - 1)$

   (c) $(-3x^3 + 48x) \div (x - 4)$

6. Show that the division $(x^4 + 3x^2 + 5) \div (x - c)$ leaves a remainder for all values of c.

7. Prove that, provided both $c \neq 0$ and $cx + d \neq 0$, one has

$$\frac{ax+b}{cx+d} = \frac{a}{c} + \frac{bc-ad}{c(cx+d)}$$

SM 8. A function which has been used in demand theory is

$$E = \alpha \frac{x^2 - \gamma x}{x + \beta}$$

with α, β, and γ being constants. Perform the division $(x^2 - \gamma x) \div (x + \beta)$, and use the result to express E as a sum of a linear function and a proper fraction.

4.8 Power Functions

We saw in Section 2.5 how the number x^r can be defined for all positive real numbers x and for all rational numbers r. In order for x^r to be defined for all real numbers r, we also need to consider x^r when r is irrational. How do we define an expression like 5 raised to the irrational power π? Because π is close to 3.1, we should expect that 5^π is approximately

$$5^{3.1} = 5^{31/10} = \sqrt[10]{5^{31}}$$

which *is* defined. An even better approximation is

$$5^\pi \approx 5^{3.14} = 5^{314/100} = 5^{157/50} = \sqrt[50]{5^{157}}$$

We can continue adding ever more decimal places to the approximation $\pi = 3.141\,592\,653\,5\ldots$. The result will get closer to 5^π with every additional decimal digit. Then the meaning of 5^π should be reasonably clear. For the moment, however, let us be content with just using a calculator to find that $5^\pi \approx 156.993$. Later, Section 7.11 provides a more complete discussion of how to define x^r as a limit when r is irrational.

POWER FUNCTION

The general *power function* is defined for $x > 0$ by the formula

$$f(x) = Ax^r \qquad (4.8.1)$$

where r and A are constants.

When we consider the power function, we always assume that $x > 0$. This is because for many values of r such as $r = 1/2$, the symbol x^r is not defined for negative values of x. And we exclude $x = 0$ because 0^r is undefined if $r \leq 0$.

Graphs of Power Functions

Consider the power function $f(x) = x^r$ on the domain of $x > 0$. It is defined for all real numbers r. For every real r we always have $f(1) = 1^r = 1$, so the graph of the function passes through the point $(1, 1)$ in the xy-plane. The shape of the graph depends crucially on the value of r, as Figs 4.8.1 to 4.8.3 indicate.

If $0 < r < 1$, the graph is like that in Fig. 4.8.1, which resembles the graph of $f(x) = x^{0.5}$ shown in Fig. 4.3.8. For $r > 1$ the graph is like that shown in Fig. 4.8.2; for instance, if $r = 2$ the graph is the right-hand half of the parabola $y = x^2$ shown in Fig. 4.3.6. Finally, for $r < 0$, the graph is shown in Fig. 4.8.3, which, if $r = -1$, is half of the hyperbola $y = 1/x$ shown in Fig. 4.3.9. Figure 4.8.4 further illustrates how the graph of $y = x^r$ changes with changing positive values of the exponent r.

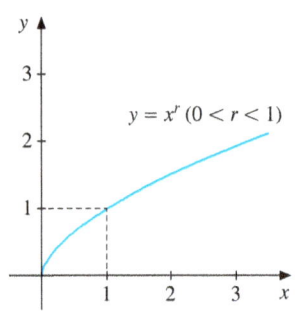

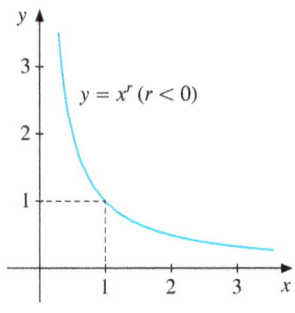

Figure 4.8.1 $0 < r < 1$

Figure 4.8.2 $r > 1$

Figure 4.8.3 $r < 0$

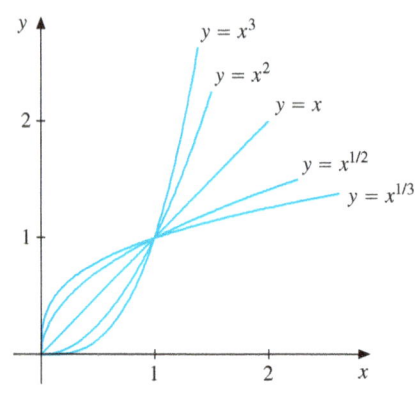

Figure 4.8.4 $y = x^r$

EXERCISES FOR SECTION 4.8

1. Sketch the graphs of $y = x^{-3}$, $y = x^{-1}$, $y = x^{-1/2}$, and $y = x^{-1/3}$, defined for $x > 0$.

2. Use a calculator to find approximate values for $\sqrt{2}^{\sqrt{2}}$ and π^π.

3. Solve the following equations for x:

   (a) $2^{2x} = 8$ (b) $3^{3x+1} = 1/81$ (c) $10^{x^2-2x+2} = 100$

4. Find t when: (a) $3^{5t}9^t = 27$; and (b) $9^t = (27)^{1/5}/3$.

4.9 Exponential Functions

A quantity that increases (or decreases) by a fixed factor per unit of time is said to *increase* (or *decrease*) *exponentially*. If the fixed factor is a, this leads to the exponential function:

$$f(t) = Aa^t \tag{4.9.1}$$

where $a > 0$ and A are constants. In what follows, we shall consider the case where A is positive. But if A is negative, we can consider $-f(t) = (-A)a^t$ instead, then change sign.

Note that if $f(t) = Aa^t$, then $f(t+1) = Aa^{t+1} = Aa^t \cdot a^1 = af(t)$, so the value of f at time $t+1$ is a times the value of f at time t. If $a > 1$, then f is increasing; if $0 < a < 1$, then f is decreasing—see Figs 4.9.1 and 4.9.2. Because $f(0) = Aa^0 = A$, we can always write $f(t) = f(0)a^t$.

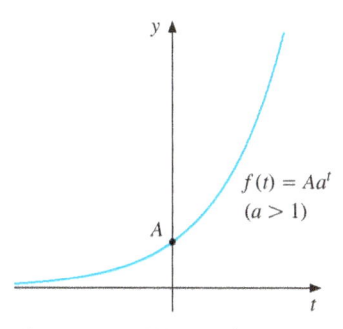

Figure 4.9.1 $f(t) = Aa^t, a > 1$

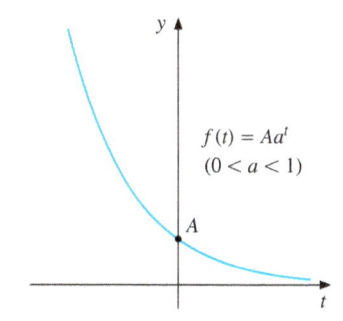

Figure 4.9.2 $f(t) = Aa^t, 0 < a < 1$

It is important to recognize the fundamental difference between the exponential function $f(x) = a^x$ and the typical power function $g(x) = x^a$ that was discussed in Section 4.8. Indeed, for the exponential function a^x, it is the exponent x that varies, while the base a is constant; for the power function x^a, on the other hand, the exponent a is constant, while the base x varies.

Exponential functions appear in many important economic, social, and physical models. For instance, economic growth, population growth, continuously accumulated interest, radioactive decay, and decreasing illiteracy have all been described by exponential functions. In addition, the exponential function is one of the most important functions in statistics. Here is one application:

EXAMPLE 4.9.1 (**Population growth**). Consider a growing population like that of Europe during the 20th century. In Example 4.5.1, we constructed a linear function $P = 5.1t + 606$, where P denotes the population in millions, $t = 0$ corresponds to the year 1960 when the population was 606 million, and $t = 10$ corresponds to the year 1970 when the population estimate was 657 million. This linear formula says that there was a constant increase 5.1 million in population each year, which is very unreasonable. After all, it implies that for years before 1841, when $t \leq -119$, the population of Europe was negative!

In fact, according to UN estimates, the European population grew at a proportional rate of about 0.45% per year during the period 1960 to 2000. If the growth rate had been constant then, starting from a population of 606 million in 1960, in 1961 the population would have been $606 \cdot 1.0045$ (see Section 2.2), or about 609 million. Next year, in 1962, it would have grown to $606 \cdot 1.0045^2$, or about 611 million. In fact, the population would have grown by the factor 1.0045 each year. The population t years after 1960 would have been

$$P(t) = 606 \cdot 1.0045^t$$

This makes $P(t)$ an exponential function of the form (4.9.1). For the year 2015, corresponding to $t = 55$, the formula yields the estimate $P(55) \approx 776$ million.[18]

Many countries, particularly in Africa, have recently had far faster population growth than Europe. For instance, during the 1970s and 1980s, the annual growth rate of Zimbabwe's population was close to 3.5%. Let $t = 0$ correspond to the census year 1969 when the population was 5.1 million. At this growth rate, the population t years after 1969 is $P(t) = 5.1 \cdot 1.035^t$. If we calculate $P(20)$, $P(40)$, and $P(60)$ using this formula, we get roughly 10, 20, and 40. Thus, the population of Zimbabwe roughly doubles after 20 years; during the next 20 years, it doubles again, and so on. Of course, this kind of extrapolation is quite dubious, because exponential population growth cannot go on forever: if population were to continue growing at 3.5% annually with no emigration, then Exercise 4.10.10 asks you to show that by the year 2296 the average Zimbabwean would have only one square metre of land to live on.

EXAMPLE 4.9.2 (**Compound interest**). As seen in Section 2.2, a savings account of K that increases by $p\%$ interest each year will have grown after t years to $K(1 + p/100)^t$. According to this formula with $K = 1$, a deposit of \$1 earning interest at 8% per year (so $p = 8$) will have increased after t years to $(1 + 8/100)^t = 1.08^t$ dollars.

Table 4.9.1 shows how fast the savings account grows. After 30 years, \$1 of savings will have increased to more than \$10, and after 200 years, to more than \$4.8 million!

Table 4.9.1 How \$1 of savings increases with time at 8% annual interest

t	1	2	5	10	20	30	50	100	200
$(1.08)^t$	1.08	1.17	1.47	2.16	4.66	10.06	46.9	2199.8	4 838 949.6

Observe that the expression 1.08^t defines an exponential function of the type (4.9.1), with $a = 1.08$. Even if a is only slightly larger than 1, eventually the power a^t will increase very quickly as t becomes large.

EXAMPLE 4.9.3 (**Continuous depreciation**). Each year the value of most assets such as cars, electronic equipment, or furniture decreases, or *depreciates*. If the value of an asset is assumed to decrease by a fixed percentage each year, then the depreciation is called *continuous*.[19]

Suppose that a car whose value at time $t = 0$ was P_0 subsequently depreciates at the rate of 20% each year over a five-year period. What is its value $A(t)$ at time t, for $t = 1, 2, 3, 4, 5$?

Solution: After one year, its value is $P_0 - (20 P_0/100) = P_0(1 - 20/100) = P_0(0.8)^1$. Thereafter, it depreciates each subsequent year by the factor 0.8. Thus, after t years, its value is $A(t) = P_0(0.8)^t$. In particular, $A(5) = P_0(0.8)^5 \approx 0.32 P_0$, so after five years its value has decreased to about 32% of its original value.

---

[18] The actual figure was about 738 million, which shows the limitations of such naïve projections.
[19] Recall the case of linear depreciation discussed in Exercise 4.5.5.

Here are the definition and a key property of the exponential function:

EXPONENTIAL FUNCTION

The *general exponential function* with base $a > 0$ is

$$f(x) = Aa^x$$

where a is the factor by which $f(x)$ changes when x increases by 1.
For each unit increase in x:

1. if $a = 1 + p/100$ where $p > 0$, then $f(x)$ will increase by $p\%$;
2. if $a = 1 - p/100$ where $0 < p < 100$, then $f(x)$ will decrease by $p\%$.

The Natural Exponential Function

Each base a of $f(x) = Aa^x$ gives a different exponential function. In mathematics, one particular value of a gives an exponential function that is far more important than all others. One might guess that $a = 2$ or $a = 10$ would be this special base. Certainly, powers to the base of 2 are important in computing, and powers to the base 10 occur in our usual decimal number system. Nevertheless, once we have studied some calculus, it will turn out that the most important base for an exponential function is an irrational number a little larger than 2.7. In fact, it is so distinguished that it is denoted by the single letter e, possibly because it is the first letter of the word "exponential".[20] Its value to 15 decimal places is

$$e = 2.718\,281\,828\,459\,045\ldots \tag{4.9.2}$$

Many formulas in calculus become much simpler when e is used as the base for exponential functions. Given this base e, the corresponding exponential function

$$f(x) = e^x \tag{4.9.3}$$

is called the *natural exponential function*. In Examples 7.5.4 and 7.6.2 we shall give an explicit way of approximating e^x to an arbitrary degree of accuracy. The graphs of $f(x) = e^x$ and $f(x) = e^{-x}$ are given in Fig. 4.9.3. Of course, all the usual rules for powers apply also to the natural exponential function. In particular,

(a) $e^s e^t = e^{s+t}$ (b) $e^s/e^t = e^{s-t}$ (c) $(e^s)^t = e^{st}$

Powers with e as their base, even e^1, are difficult to compute by hand. A calculator with an $\boxed{e^x}$ function key can do this immediately, however. For instance, one finds that $e^{1.0} \approx 2.7183$, $e^{0.5} \approx 1.6487$, and $e^{-\pi} \approx 0.0432$.

---

[20] Though this number had been defined implicitly over 100 years earlier, the Swiss scientist and mathematician Leonhard Euler (1707–1783) was the first to denote it by the letter e. He subsequently proved that it was irrational and calculated an approximation that is accurate to 23 decimal places.

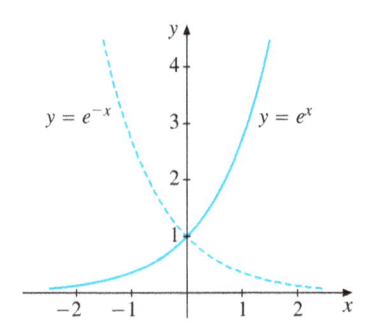

Figure 4.9.3 The graphs of $y = e^x$ and $y = e^{-x}$

Sometimes the notation $\exp(u)$, or even $\exp u$, is used in place of e^u. If u is a complicated expression like $x^3 + x\sqrt{x - 1/x} + 5$, it is certainly much easier to read and write $\exp(x^3 + x\sqrt{x - 1/x} + 5)$ instead of $e^{x^3 + x\sqrt{x - 1/x} + 5}$.

EXERCISES FOR SECTION 4.9

1. A savings account with an initial deposit of $100 earns 12% interest per year. What is the amount of savings after t years? Make a table similar to Table 4.9.1, stopping at 50 years.

2. Fill in the following table and sketch the graphs of $y = 2^x$ and $y = 2^{-x}$.

x	-3	-2	-1	0	1	2	3
2^x							
2^{-x}							

3. The *normal density function*
$$\varphi(x) = \frac{1}{\sqrt{2\pi}} e^{-\frac{1}{2}x^2}$$
is one of the most important functions in statistics. Its graph is often called the "bell curve" because of its shape. Use your calculator to fill in the following table:

x	-2	-1	0	1	2
$y = \varphi(x)$					

4. Which of the following equations do *not* define exponential functions of x?

   (a) $y = 3^x$
   (b) $y = x^{\sqrt{2}}$
   (c) $y = (\sqrt{2})^x$
   (d) $y = x^x$
   (e) $y = (2.7)^x$
   (f) $y = 1/2^x$

5. Suppose that all prices rise at the same proportional (inflation) rate of 19% per year. For an item that currently costs P_0, use the implied formula for the price after t years in order to predict the prices of:

(a) A 20 kg bag of corn, presently costing $16, after five years.

(b) A $4.40 can of coffee after ten years.

(c) A $250 000 house after four years.

6. Find possible exponential functions whose graphs are A to C as shown in Figs 4.9.4 to 4.9.6.

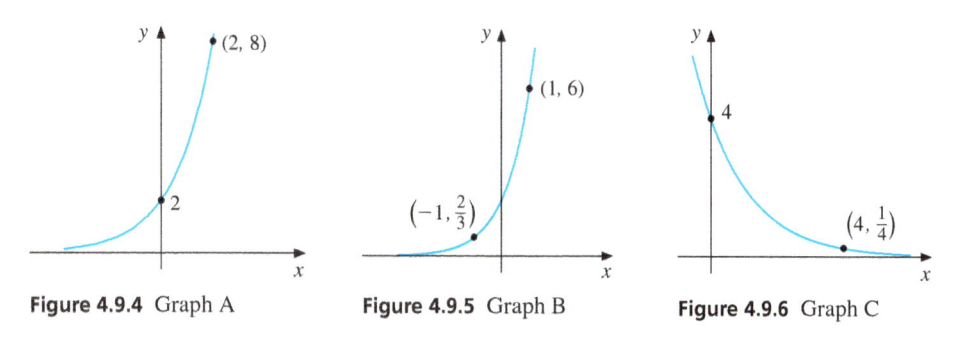

Figure 4.9.4 Graph A

Figure 4.9.5 Graph B

Figure 4.9.6 Graph C

4.10 Logarithmic Functions

Economists are often concerned with questions like these:

(a) At the present rate of inflation, how long will it take the price level to triple?

(b) If the world's population grows at 2% per year, how long does it take to double its size?

(c) If $1000 is invested in a savings account bearing interest at the annual rate of 8%, how long does it take for the account to reach $10 000?

All these questions involve solving equations of the form $a^x = b$ for x. For instance, problem (c) reduces to the finding which x solves the equation $1000(1.08)^x = 10\,000$.

We begin with equations in which the base of the exponential is e, which was, as you recall, the irrational number $2.718\ldots$. Here are three examples: $e^x = 4$; $5e^{-3x} = 16$; and $A\alpha e^{-\alpha x} = k$. In all these equations, the unknown x occurs as an exponent. We therefore introduce the following useful definition. If $e^u = a$, we call u the *natural logarithm* of a, and we write $u = \ln a$. Hence, we have the following definition of the symbol $\ln a$:

NATURAL LOGARITHM

For any positive number a, its natural logarithm $\ln a$ is the unique solution of the equation

$$e^{\ln a} = a \qquad (4.10.1)$$

Thus, $\ln a$ is the power of e you need to get a.

Because e^u is a strictly increasing function of u, it follows that $\ln a$ *is* uniquely determined by the definition (4.10.1). You should memorize this definition. It is the foundation for everything in this section, and for a good part of what comes later. The following example illustrates how to use this definition.

EXAMPLE 4.10.1   Find the following numbers:

(a) $\ln 1$ (b) $\ln e$ (c) $\ln(1/e)$ (d) $\ln 4$ (e) $\ln(-6)$

Solution:

(a) $\ln 1 = 0$, because $e^0 = 1$ and so 0 is the power of e that you need to get 1.
(b) $\ln e = 1$, because $e^1 = e$ and so 1 is the power of e that you need to get e.
(c) $\ln(1/e) = \ln e^{-1} = -1$, because -1 is the power of e that you need to get $1/e$.
(d) $\ln 4$ is the power of e you need to get 4. Because $e^1 \approx 2.7$ and $e^2 = e^1 \cdot e^1 \approx 7.3$, the number $\ln 4$ must lie between 1 and 2. By using a calculator, you should be able to find a good approximation to $\ln 4$ by trial and error. Of course, it is easier to press 4 and then the $\ln x$ key, when you find at once that $\ln 4 \approx 1.386$. Thus, $e^{1.386} \approx 4$.
(e) $\ln(-6)$ would be the power of e you need to get -6. Because e^x is positive for all x, obviously $\ln(-6)$ must be undefined. (The same is true for $\ln x$ whenever $x \leq 0$.)

The box below displays some basic properties for convenient reference.

BASIC PROPERTIES OF NATURAL LOGARITHMS

$\ln 1 = 0$, $\ln e = 1$, and generally

$$\ln e^x = x \text{ for all real } x; \quad x = e^{\ln x} \text{ for all real } x > 0 \qquad (4.10.2)$$

Of course, the first two equalities were proved in parts (a) and (b) of Example 4.10.1. To prove (4.10.2), note first that $x = e^{\ln x}$ is just definition (4.10.1) with a replaced by x. But then, if $x = \ln y$, it follows that $y = e^x$ and so $\ln e^x = \ln y = x$.

The following box collects some other important rules for natural logarithms.

RULES FOR THE NATURAL LOGARITHM FUNCTION ln x

Let x and y denote any positive real numbers.

(a) The logarithm of the *product* xy is the *sum* of the logarithms of x and y: that is, $\ln(xy) = \ln x + \ln y$.
(b) The logarithm of the *quotient* x/y is the *difference* between the logarithms of its numerator and denominator: that is, $\ln \dfrac{x}{y} = \ln x - \ln y$.
(c) The logarithm of the *power* x^p is the exponent p multiplied by the logarithm of the base x: that is, $\ln x^p = p \ln x$.

First, to prove rule (a), start by observing that the definition of natural logarithm implies that $e^{\ln x} = x$, $e^{\ln y} = y$, and $e^{\ln(xy)} = xy$. It follows that

$$e^{\ln(xy)} = xy = e^{\ln x}e^{\ln y} = e^{\ln x + \ln y} \qquad (*)$$

where the last step uses the rule $e^s e^t = e^{s+t}$. In general, $e^u = e^v$ implies $u = v$, so we conclude from (*) that $\ln(xy) = \ln x + \ln y$.

The proofs of rules (b) and (c) are based on the rules $e^s/e^t = e^{s-t}$ and $(e^s)^t = e^{st}$, respectively, and are left to the reader.

It is *tempting* to replace $\ln(x+y)$ by $\ln x + \ln y$, but this is entirely *wrong*. In fact $\ln x + \ln y$ is equal to $\ln(xy)$, not to $\ln(x+y)$.

LOG OF A SUM

There are *no* simple formulas for $\ln(x+y)$ and $\ln(x-y)$.

Here are some examples that apply the previous rules.

EXAMPLE 4.10.2 Express the following as multiples of $\ln 2$:

(a) $\ln 4$ (b) $\ln \sqrt[3]{2^5}$ (c) $\ln(1/16)$.

Solution:

(a) $\ln 4 = \ln(2 \cdot 2) = \ln 2 + \ln 2 = 2\ln 2$, or, alternatively $\ln 4 = \ln 2^2 = 2\ln 2$.

(b) We have $\sqrt[3]{2^5} = 2^{5/3}$. Therefore, $\ln \sqrt[3]{2^5} = \ln 2^{5/3} = (5/3)\ln 2$.

(c) $\ln(1/16) = \ln 1 - \ln 16 = 0 - \ln 2^4 = -4\ln 2$. Or, $\ln(1/16) = \ln 2^{-4} = -4\ln 2$.

EXAMPLE 4.10.3 Solve the following equations for x:

(a) $5e^{-3x} = 16$ (b) $A\alpha e^{-\alpha x} = k$ (c) $(1.08)^x = 10$ (d) $e^x + 4e^{-x} = 4$

Solution:

(a) Take ln of each side of the equation to obtain $\ln(5e^{-3x}) = \ln 16$. The product rule gives $\ln(5e^{-3x}) = \ln 5 + \ln e^{-3x}$. By rule (d) $\ln e^{-3x} = -3x$. The equation becomes $\ln 5 - 3x = \ln 16$, whose only solution is

$$x = \frac{1}{3}(\ln 5 - \ln 16) = \frac{1}{3}\ln\frac{5}{16}$$

(b) We argue as in (a) to obtain $\ln(A\alpha e^{-\alpha x}) = \ln k$, or $\ln(A\alpha) + \ln e^{-\alpha x} = \ln k$ It follows that $\ln(A\alpha) - \alpha x = \ln k$. Finally, therefore,

$$x = \frac{1}{\alpha}[\ln(A\alpha) - \ln k] = \frac{1}{\alpha}\ln\frac{A\alpha}{k}$$

(c) Again we take the ln of each side of the equation and obtain $x \ln 1.08 = \ln 10$. So the solution is $x = \ln 10 / \ln 1.08$, which is ≈ 29.9. Thus, it takes just short of 30 years for $1 to increase to $10 when the interest rate is 8%. (See Table 4.9.1, in Example 4.9.2.)

(d) It is very tempting to begin with $\ln(e^x + 4e^{-x}) = \ln 4$, but this leads nowhere, because $\ln(e^x + 4e^{-x})$ cannot be further evaluated. Instead, we put $u = e^x$ in the equation. Because then $e^{-x} = 1/e^x = 1/u$, the equation becomes $u + 4/u = 4$. But $u \neq 0$, so we can multiply each side by u to obtain the quadratic equation $u^2 + 4 = 4u$, which reduces to $(u - 2)^2 = 0$. So $u = 2$ is the only solution. Because $u = e^x = 2$, one has $x = \ln 2$.

The Function $g(x) = \ln x$

For each positive number x, the number $\ln x$ is defined by $e^{\ln x} = x$. In other words, $u = \ln x$ is the solution of the equation $e^u = x$. This definition is illustrated in Fig. 4.10.1. The *natural logarithm* of x, defined for all $x > 0$, is then the function g defined by

$$g(x) = \ln x \tag{4.10.3}$$

Think of x as a point moving upwards on the vertical axis from the origin. As x increases from values less than 1 to values greater than 1, so $g(x)$ increases from negative to positive values. Because e^u tends to 0 as u becomes large and negative, so $g(x)$ becomes large and negative as x tends to 0. Repeating the definition of $\ln x$, then inserting $y = \ln x$ and taking the ln of each side, one obtains Eq. (4.10.2): that is $e^{\ln x} = x$ for all $x > 0$; and $\ln e^y = y$ for all y.

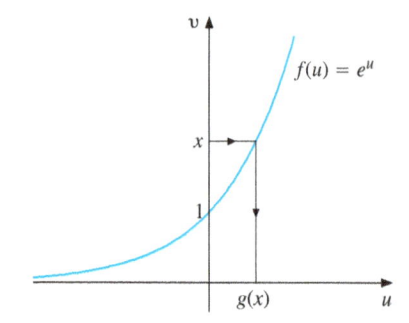

Figure 4.10.1 Construction of $g(x) = \ln x$

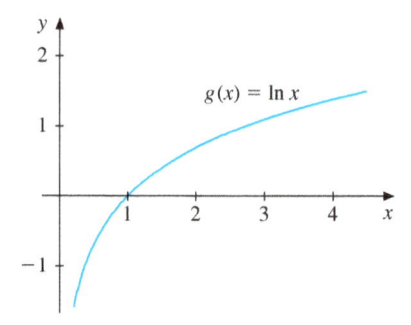

Figure 4.10.2 $g(x) = \ln x$

Figure 4.10.2 shows the graph of $g(x) = \ln x$, whose shape ought to be remembered. It can be obtained by reflecting the graph of Fig. 4.10.1 about the 45° line, so that the u- and v-axes are interchanged and become respectively the y- and x-axes of Fig. 4.10.2. According to Example 4.10.1, we have $g(1/e) = -1$, $g(1) = 0$, and $g(e) = 1$. Observe that these values correspond well with the graph.

Logarithms with Bases other than e

Recall that we defined $\ln x$ as the exponent to which we must raise the base e in order to obtain x. From time to time, it is useful to have logarithms whose base is a number other than e. For many years, until the use of mechanical and then electronic calculators became widespread, tables of logarithms to the base 10 were frequently used to simplify complicated calculations involving multiplication, division, square roots, and so on.[21]

Suppose that a is a fixed positive number (usually chosen larger than 1). If $a^u = x$, then we call u the *logarithm of x to base a* and write $u = \log_a x$. The symbol $\log_a x$ is then defined for every positive number x by the following:

LOGARITHM OF x TO BASE a

$$a^{\log_a x} = x \qquad (4.10.4)$$

For instance, $\log_2 32 = 5$ because $2^5 = 32$, whereas $\log_{10}(1/100) = -2$ because $10^{-2} = 1/100$. Note that $\ln x$ is $\log_e x$.

By taking the ln on each side of (4.10.4) and then applying rule (c) for ln, we obtain $\log_a x \cdot \ln a = \ln x$. Provided that $a > 1$ and so $\ln a \neq 0$, it follows that

$$\log_a x = \frac{1}{\ln a} \ln x \qquad (4.10.5)$$

This reveals that the logarithm of x in the system with base a is proportional to $\ln x$, with a proportionality factor $1/\ln a$. It follows immediately that $\log_a 1 = 0$ and $\log_a a = 1$, as well as that $\log_a$ obeys the same rules (a)–(c) as ln, namely:

(a) $\log_a(xy) = \log_a x + \log_a y$; (b) $\log_a(x/y) = \log_a x - \log_a y$; (c) $\log_a x^p = p \log_a x$.

Rule (a), for example, follows directly from the corresponding rule for ln, because

$$\log_a(xy) = \frac{1}{\ln a} \ln(xy) = \frac{1}{\ln a}(\ln x + \ln y) = \frac{1}{\ln a} \ln x + \frac{1}{\ln a} \ln y = \log_a x + \log_a y$$

Doubling Times

Provided that $a > 1$ and $A > 0$, the exponential function $f(t) = Aa^t$ is an increasing function of time t. Its *doubling time* is defined as the time it takes for $f(t)$ to become twice as large. That is, starting from $f(0) = A$ at time $t = 0$, the doubling time t^* is given by the equation $f(t^*) = Aa^{t^*} = 2A$, or after cancelling A, by

$$a^{t^*} = 2 \qquad (4.10.6)$$

So the doubling time of the exponential function $f(t) = Aa^t$ is the power to which a must be raised in order to get 2. Exercise 11 asks you to show that the doubling time is independent of which year you take as the base.

Taking the natural logarithm of each side of (4.10.6) implies that $\ln(a^{t^*}) = t^* \ln a = \ln 2$, and so $t^* = \ln 2 / \ln a$. Then Eq. (4.10.5) implies that $t^* = 1/\log_2 a$. Finally, taking the

---

[21] One of the authors remembers being the proud owner of a book with some 200 pages devoted to a very long table of logarithms to base 10, all to 7 decimal places.

logarithm to base a of each side of (4.10.6) implies that $\log_a(a^{t^*}) = t^* \log_a a = t^* = \log_a 2$. To summarize:

DOUBLING TIME

Given $a > 1$ and $A > 0$, the exponential function $f(t) = Aa^t$ has a unique *doubling time* t^* which solves $a^{t^*} = 2$. It satisfies

$$t^* = \frac{\ln 2}{\ln a} = \log_a 2 = \frac{1}{\log_2 a} \qquad (4.10.7)$$

EXAMPLE 4.10.4   Use your calculator to find the doubling time of:

(a) a population, like that of Zimbabwe, increasing at 3.5% annually (thus confirming the earlier calculations).

(b) the population of Kenya in the 1980s, whose annual growth rate of population in that decade was 4.2%, the highest of any country in the world.

Solution:

(a) The doubling time t^* is given by the equation $1.035^{t^*} = 2$. Using a calculator shows that $1.035^{15} \approx 1.68$, whereas $1.035^{25} \approx 2.36$. Thus, t^* must lie between 15 and 25. Because $1.035^{20} \approx 1.99$, t^* is close to 20. In fact, $t^* = \ln 2 / \ln 1.035 \approx 20.15$.

(b) The doubling time t^* is given by the equation $1.042^{t^*} = 2$, whose unique solution is $t^* = \ln 2 / \ln 1.042$. Using a calculator, we find that $t^* \approx 16.85$. Thus, if the growth rate of 4.2% were sustained, Kenya's population would double in less than 17 years.

EXERCISES FOR SECTION 4.10

1. Express the following as multiples of $\ln 3$:

   (a) $\ln 9$ (b) $\ln \sqrt{3}$ (c) $\ln \sqrt[5]{3^2}$ (d) $\ln(1/81)$

2. Solve the following equations for x:

   (a) $3^x = 8$ (b) $\ln x = 3$ (c) $\ln(x^2 - 4x + 5) = 0$

   (d) $\ln[x(x-2)] = 0$ (e) $\dfrac{x \ln(x+3)}{x^2+1} = 0$ (f) $\ln(\sqrt{x} - 5) = 0$

SM 3. Solve the following equations for x:

   (a) $3^x 4^{x+2} = 8$ (b) $3 \ln x + 2 \ln x^2 = 6$ (c) $4^x - 4^{x-1} = 3^{x+1} - 3^x$

   (d) $\log_2 x = 2$ (e) $\log_x e^2 = 2$ (f) $\log_3 x = -3$

SM 4. Suppose that $f(t) = Ae^{rt}$ and $g(t) = Be^{st}$, where $A > 0$, $B > 0$, and $r \neq s$. Solve the equation $f(t) = g(t)$ for t.

SM 5. For 1990 an estimate of the GDP of China was $1.2 \cdot 10^{12}$ US dollars, whereas for the USA in the same year it was $5.6 \cdot 10^{12}$ US dollars. The two countries' annual rates of growth were estimated to be 9% and 2% respectively, implying that t years after 1990, their GDP should be Ae^{rt} and Be^{st} respectively, where $r = 0.09$, $s = 0.02$, and A, B are suitable constants. Assuming that these rates of growth were maintained, use the answer to Exercise 4 to determine the date when the two nations' GDP would have become the same.

6. Assume that all the variables in the formulas below are positive. Which of these formulas are always true, and which are sometimes false?

(a) $(\ln A)^4 = 4 \ln A$

(b) $\ln B = 2 \ln \sqrt{B}$

(c) $\ln A^{10} - \ln A^4 = 3 \ln A^2$

(d) $\ln \dfrac{A+B}{C} = \ln A + \ln B - \ln C$

(e) $\ln \dfrac{A+B}{C} = \ln(A+B) - \ln C$

(f) $\ln \dfrac{A}{B} + \ln \dfrac{B}{A} = 0$

(g) $p \ln(\ln A) = \ln(\ln A^p)$

(h) $p \ln(\ln A) = \ln(\ln A)^p$

(i) $\dfrac{\ln A}{\ln B + \ln C} = \ln A (BC)^{-1}$

7. Simplify the following expressions:

(a) $\exp[\ln(x)] - \ln[\exp(x)]$

(b) $\ln[x^4 \exp(-x)]$

(c) $\exp[\ln(x^2) - 2 \ln y]$

8. If the population of Europe were to grow at the constant proportional rate of 0.72% annually, what would be its doubling time?

9. The population of Botswana was estimated to be 1.22 million in 1989, and to be growing at the rate of 3.4% annually. If $t = 0$ denotes 1989, find a formula for the population $P(t)$ at date t. What is the doubling time?

10. The area of Zimbabwe is approximately $3.91 \cdot 10^{11}$ m². Referring to Example 4.9.1 and using a calculator, solve the equation $5.1 \cdot 10^6 \cdot 1.035^t = 3.91 \cdot 10^{11}$ for t, and interpret the solution.

11. With $f(t) = Aa^t$, if $f(t + t^*) = 2f(t)$, prove that $a^{t^*} = 2$. This shows that the doubling time t^* of the general exponential function is independent of the initial time t.

REVIEW EXERCISES

1. Let $f(x) = 3 - 27x^3$.

(a) Compute $f(0), f(-1), f(1/3)$, and $f(\sqrt[3]{2})$.

(b) Show that $f(x) + f(-x) = 6$ for all x.

2. Let $F(x) = 1 + \dfrac{4x}{x^2 + 4}$.

(a) Compute $F(0), F(-2), F(2)$, and $F(3)$.

(b) What happens to $F(x)$ when x becomes large and positive, or large and negative?

(c) Give a rough sketch of the graph of F.

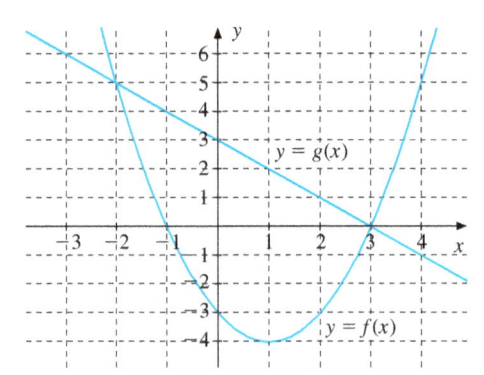

Figure 4.R.1 Two functions

3. Consider Fig 4.R.1, which combines the graphs of a quadratic function f and a linear function g. Use the two graphs to find those x where: (a) $f(x) \leq g(x)$; (b) $f(x) \leq 0$; and (c) $g(x) \geq 0$.

4. Find the domains of the following functions:

   (a) $f(x) = \sqrt{x^2 - 1}$ (b) $g(x) = \dfrac{1}{\sqrt{x-4}}$ (c) $h(x) = \sqrt{(x-3)(5-x)}$

5. The cost of producing x units of a commodity is given by $C(x) = 100 + 40x + 2x^2$.

   (a) Find $C(0)$, $C(100)$, and $C(101) - C(100)$.

   (b) Find $C(x+1) - C(x)$, and explain in words the meaning of the difference.

6. Find the slopes of the following straight lines:

   (a) $y = -4x + 8$;   (b) $3x + 4y = 12$;   (c) $\dfrac{x}{a} + \dfrac{y}{b} = 1$.

7. Find equations for the following straight lines:

   (a) ℓ_1 passes through $(-2, 3)$ and has a slope of -3.

   (b) ℓ_2 passes through $(-3, 5)$ and $(2, 7)$.

   (c) ℓ_3 passes through (a, b) and $(2a, 3b)$, where $a \neq 0$.

8. If $f(x) = ax + b$, $f(2) = 3$, and $f(-1) = -3$, then $f(-3) = $?

9. Fill in the following table, then make a rough sketch of the graph of $y = x^2 e^x$.

x	-5	-4	-3	-2	-1	0	1
$y = x^2 e^x$							

10. Find the equation for the parabola $y = ax^2 + bx + c$ that passes through the three points $(1, -3)$, $(0, -6)$, and $(3, 15)$—that is, determine a, b, and c.

11. If a firm sells Q tons of a product, the price P received per ton is $P = 1000 - \frac{1}{3}Q$. The price it has to pay per ton is $P = 800 + \frac{1}{5}Q$. In addition, it has transportation costs of 100 per ton.

(a) Express the firm's profit π as a function of Q, the number of tons sold, and find the profit-maximizing quantity.

(b) Suppose the government imposes a tax on the firm's product of 10 per ton. Find the new expression for the firm's profits $\hat{\pi}$ and the new profit-maximizing quantity shipped.

12. In Example 4.6.2, suppose a tax of τ per unit produced is imposed. If $\tau < 100$, what production level now maximizes profits?

13. A firm produces a commodity and receives $100 for each unit sold. The cost of producing and selling x units is $20x + 0.25x^2$ dollars.

(a) Find the production level that maximizes profits.

(b) If a tax of $10 per unit is imposed, what is the new optimal production level?

(c) Answer the question in (b) if the sales price per unit is p, the total cost of producing and selling x units is $\alpha x + \beta x^2$, and the tax per unit is τ where $\tau \leq p - \alpha$.

SM 14. Write the following polynomials as products of linear factors:

(a) $p(x) = x^3 + x^2 - 12x$ (b) $q(x) = 2x^3 + 3x^2 - 18x + 8$

15. Which of the following divisions leave no remainder?

(a) $\dfrac{x^3 - x - 1}{x - 1}$ (b) $\dfrac{2x^3 - x - 1}{x - 1}$

(c) $\dfrac{x^3 - ax^2 + bx - ab}{x - a}$ (a and b are constants)   (d) $\dfrac{x^{2n} - 1}{x + 1}$ (n is a natural number)

16. Find the values of k that make the polynomial $q(x)$ divide the polynomial $p(x)$ when:

(a) $p(x) = x^2 - kx + 4, \ q(x) = x - 2$ (b) $p(x) = k^2 x^2 - kx - 6, \ q(x) = x + 2$

(c) $p(x) = x^3 - 4x^2 + x + k, \ q(x) = x + 2$ (d) $p(x) = k^2 x^4 - 3kx^2 - 4, \ q(x) = x - 1$

SM 17. The cubic function $p(x) = \frac{1}{4}x^3 - x^2 - \frac{11}{4}x + \frac{15}{2}$ has three real zeros. Verify that $x = 2$ is one of them, and find the other two.

18. In 1964 a five-year plan was introduced in Tanzania. One objective was to double the real income per capita over the next 15 years. What is the average annual rate of growth of real income per capita required to achieve this objective?

19. Recall that: (i) the relationship between the Celsius (C) and Fahrenheit (F) temperature scales is linear; (ii) water freezes at 0°C and 32°F; and (iii) water boils at 100°C and 212°F.

(a) Determine the equation that converts C to F;

(b) Which temperature is represented by the same number in both scales?

20. Solve the following equations for t:

(a) $x = e^{at+b}$ (b) $e^{-at} = \frac{1}{2}$ (c) $\dfrac{1}{\sqrt{2\pi}} e^{-\frac{1}{2}t^2} = \frac{1}{8}$

SM 21. Figure 4.R.2 shows the graph of the function $y = f(x) = (ax + b)/(x + c)$. Check which of the constants a, b, and c are positive, zero, or negative.

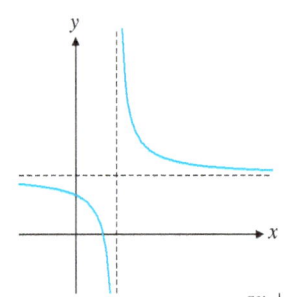

Figure 4.R.2 Graph of $y = \dfrac{ax+b}{x+c}$

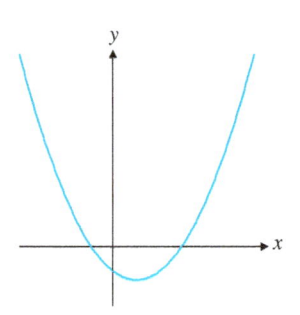

Figure 4.R.3 Graph of $y = px^2 + qx + r$

22. Figure 4.R.3 shows the graph of the function $y = g(x) = px^2 + qx + r$. Check which of the constants p, q, and r are positive, zero, or negative.

23. For each of the functions (a)–(e) in the following table, find one of six graphs A–F in Figs 4.R.4 to 4.R.9 that matches it. Then specify a suitable function in (f) that matches the sixth graph.

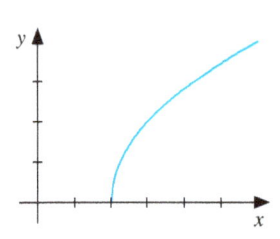

Figure 4.R.4 Graph A

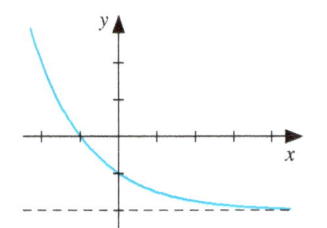

Figure 4.R.5 Graph B

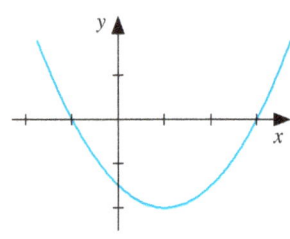

Figure 4.R.6 Graph C

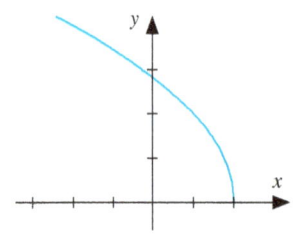

Figure 4.R.7 Graph D

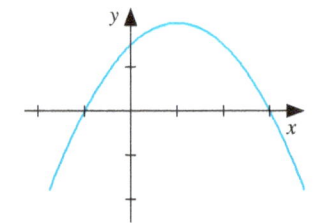

Figure 4.R.8 Graph E

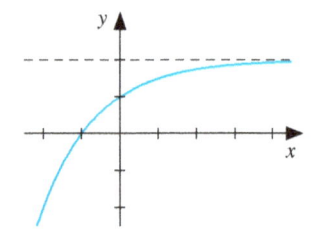

Figure 4.R.9 Graph F

(a) $y = \frac{1}{2}x^2 - x - \frac{3}{2}$ has graph _____
(b) $y = 2\sqrt{2-x}$ has graph _____
(c) $y = -\frac{1}{2}x^2 + x + \frac{3}{2}$ has graph _____
(d) $y = \left(\frac{1}{2}\right)^x - 2$ has graph _____
(e) $y = 2\sqrt{x-2}$ has graph _____
(f) $y =$ _____ has graph _____

SM 24. Prove the following equalities, with appropriate restrictions on the variables:

(a) $\ln x - 2 = \ln \dfrac{x}{e^2}$

(b) $\ln x - \ln y + \ln z = \ln \dfrac{xz}{y}$

(c) $3 + 2\ln x = \ln(e^3 x^2)$

(d) $\dfrac{1}{2}\ln x - \dfrac{3}{2}\ln \dfrac{1}{x} - \ln(x+1) = \ln \dfrac{x^2}{x+1}$

5
PROPERTIES OF FUNCTIONS

The paradox is now fully established that the utmost abstractions are the true weapons with which to control our thought of concrete facts.
—Alfred North Whitehead (1925)

This chapter begins by examining more closely functions of one variable and their graphs. In particular, we shall consider how changes in a function relate to shifts in its graph, and how to construct new functions from old ones. Next we discuss when a function has an inverse, and explain how an inverse function reverses the effect of the original function.

Any equation in two variables can be represented by a curve (or a set of points) in the *xy*-plane. Some examples illustrate this. The chapter ends with a discussion of the general concept of a function, which is one of the most fundamental in mathematics, of great importance also in economics.

5.1 Shifting Graphs

Bringing a significant new oil field into production will affect the supply curve for oil, with consequences for its equilibrium price. Adopting an improved technology in the production of a commodity will imply an upward shift in its production function, and a downward shift in its cost function.

This section studies in general how the graph of a function $f(x)$ relates to the graphs of the associated functions $f(x) + c$, $f(x + c)$, $cf(x)$, and $f(-x)$, where c is a constant. Before formulating any general rules, consider the following example.

EXAMPLE 5.1.1 The graph of $y = \sqrt{x}$ is drawn in Fig. 4.3.8. Sketch the graphs of $y = f(x)$ for the eight functions $\sqrt{x} + 2$, $\sqrt{x} - 2$, $\sqrt{x+2}$, $\sqrt{x-2}$, $2\sqrt{x}$, $\sqrt{x/2}$, $-\sqrt{x}$, and $\sqrt{-x}$.

Solution: All the Figs 5.1.1–5.1.5 show the graph of $y = \sqrt{x}$ as the same dashed curve.

The graphs of $y = \sqrt{x} + 2$ and $y = \sqrt{x} - 2$, shown as solid curves in Fig. 5.1.1, are obviously obtained by moving the graph of $y = \sqrt{x}$ up and then down by two units.

152   CHAPTER 5 / PROPERTIES OF FUNCTIONS

The function $y = \sqrt{x+2}$ is defined for $x + 2 \geq 0$, that is, for $x \geq -2$. Its graph, which is shown in Fig. 5.1.2, is obtained by moving the graph of $y = \sqrt{x}$ two units to the left. In the same way the graph of $y = \sqrt{x-2}$ is obtained by moving the graph of $y = \sqrt{x}$ two units to the right, as shown in Fig. 5.1.2.

The graph of $y = 2\sqrt{x}$ is obtained by stretching the graph of f vertically upwards by a factor of two, as shown in Fig. 5.1.3. That same figure shows how the graph $y = \sqrt{x/2}$ is obtained by shrinking that of f vertically downwards by a factor of $\sqrt{1/2} = \frac{1}{2}\sqrt{2}$.

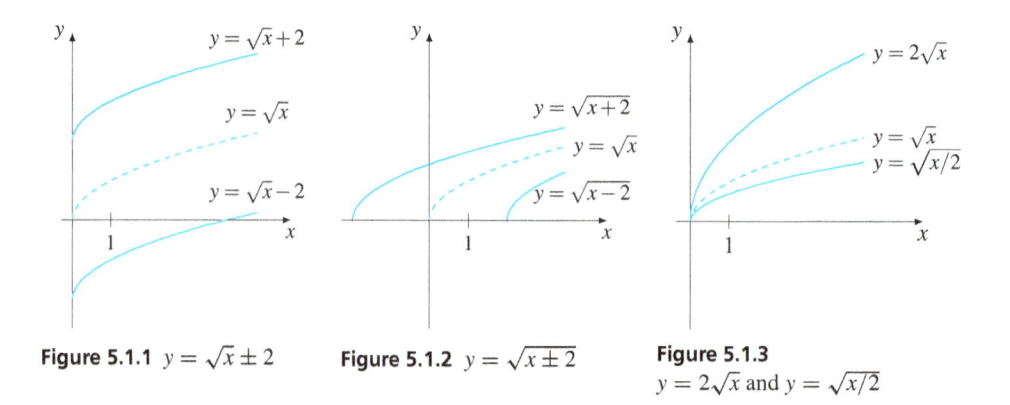

Figure 5.1.1 $y = \sqrt{x} \pm 2$

Figure 5.1.2 $y = \sqrt{x \pm 2}$

Figure 5.1.3 $y = 2\sqrt{x}$ and $y = \sqrt{x/2}$

The graph of $y = -\sqrt{x}$ is obtained by reflecting the graph of $y = \sqrt{x}$ about the x-axis, as shown in Fig. 5.1.4.

Finally, consider the function $y = \sqrt{-x}$. It is defined for $-x \geq 0$, that is, for $x \leq 0$. Its graph in Fig. 5.1.5 is obtained by reflecting that of $y = \sqrt{x}$ about the y-axis.

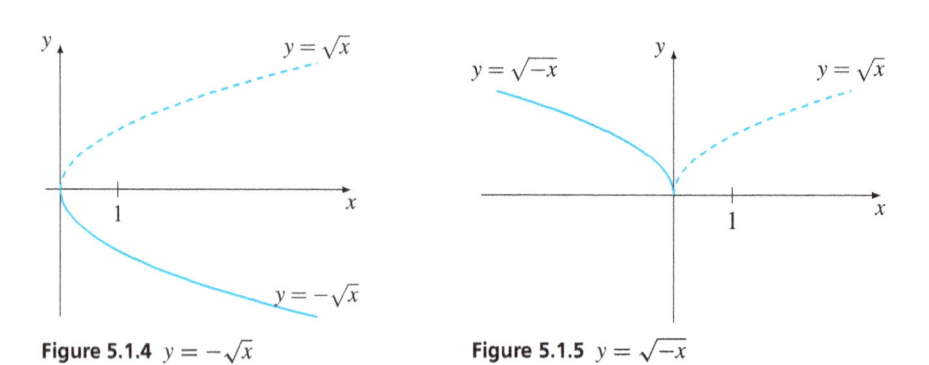

Figure 5.1.4 $y = -\sqrt{x}$

Figure 5.1.5 $y = \sqrt{-x}$

Table 5.1.1 provides some general rules for shifting the graph of a function.

In case the independent variable is y and $x = g(y)$, then in the first two rules you should interchange the words "upwards" with "to the right", and "downwards" with "to the left". In the third rule, the word "vertically" would become "horizontally", and in this and the last rule the term "y-axis" would become "x-axis".

Table 5.1.1 General rules for shifting the graph of $y = f(x)$

If $y = f(x)$ is replaced by:
(i) $y = f(x) + c$, the graph is moved upwards by c units if $c > 0$; it is moved downwards if $c < 0$.
(ii) $y = f(x + c)$, the graph is moved c units to the left if $c > 0$; it is moved to the right if $c < 0$.
(iii) $y = cf(x)$, the graph is stretched vertically if $c > 1$ or shrunk vertically if $0 < c < 1$; it is stretched or shrunk vertically and then reflected about the x-axis if $c < 0$.
(iv) $y = f(-x)$, the graph is reflected about the y-axis.

Applying these rules to the graphs shown in Figs 4.3.5–4.3.10 allows many useful new graphs to be sketched with ease, as the following example illustrates.

EXAMPLE 5.1.2 Sketch the graphs of

(a) $y = 2 - (x + 2)^2$
(b) $y = \dfrac{1}{x - 2} + 3$

Solution:

(a) First, reflect the graph of $y = x^2$ about the x-axis to obtain that of $y = -x^2$. Then move this new graph 2 units to the left, resulting in the graph of $y = -(x + 2)^2$. Finally, raise this new graph by 2 units, resulting in the graph shown in Fig. 5.1.6.

(b) Start with the graph of $y = 1/x$ in Fig. 4.3.9. Moving this graph 2 units to the right results in the graph of $y = 1/(x - 2)$ (not shown). Finally, moving this 3 units up results in the graph of $y = 1/(x - 2) + 3$ shown in Fig. 5.1.7.

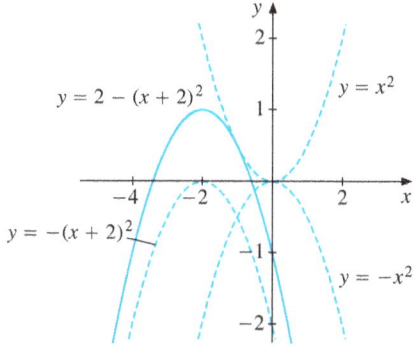

Figure 5.1.6 $y = 2 - (x + 2)^2$

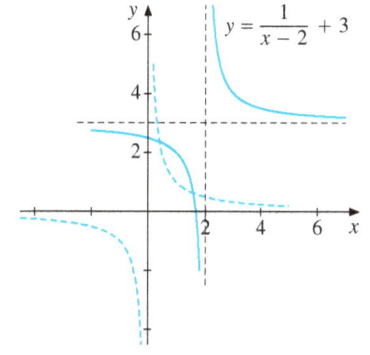

Figure 5.1.7 $y = 1/(x - 2) + 3$

EXAMPLE 5.1.3

In Example 4.5.3 we studied the simple demand and supply functions $D = 100 - P$ and $S = 10 + 2P$, which gave the equilibrium price $P^e = 30$ with corresponding quantity $Q^e = 70$. Suppose that there is a shift to the right in the supply curve, so that the new supply at price P is $\tilde{S} = 16 + 2P$. Then the new equilibrium price $\tilde{P}^e$ is determined by the equation $100 - \tilde{P}^e = 16 + 2\tilde{P}^e$. As shown in Fig. 5.1.8, this gives $\tilde{P}^e = 28$, with corresponding quantity $\tilde{Q}^e = 100 - 28 = 72$. Hence the new equilibrium price is lower than the old one, while the quantity is higher. The outward shift in the supply curve from S to $\tilde{S}$ implies that the equilibrium point moves down to the right along the unchanged demand curve.

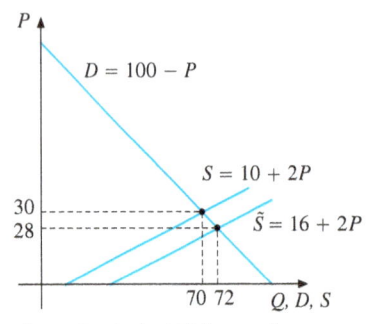

Figure 5.1.8 A shift in supply

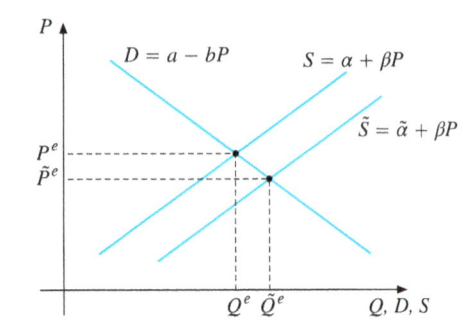

Figure 5.1.9 A shift in supply

In Example 4.5.4 we studied the general linear demand and supply functions $D = a - bP$, and $S = \alpha + \beta P$, where a, b, α, and β are all positive parameters. The equilibrium price P^e and corresponding equilibrium quantity Q^e were determined to be

$$P^e = \frac{a - \alpha}{\beta + b} \quad \text{and} \quad Q^e = \frac{a\beta + \alpha b}{\beta + b}$$

Suppose that there is a shift in the supply curve, as shown in Fig. 5.1.9, so that the new supply at each price P is $\tilde{S} = \tilde{\alpha} + \beta P$, where $\tilde{\alpha} > \alpha$. Then the new equilibrium price $\tilde{P}^e$ is determined by the equation $a - b\tilde{P}^e = \tilde{\alpha} + \beta \tilde{P}^e$, implying that

$$\tilde{P}^e = \frac{a - \tilde{\alpha}}{\beta + b}, \quad \text{with} \quad \tilde{Q}^e = a - b\tilde{P}^e = \frac{a\beta + \tilde{\alpha} b}{\beta + b}$$

The differences between the new and the old equilibrium prices and quantities are

$$\tilde{P}^e - P^e = \frac{\alpha - \tilde{\alpha}}{\beta + b} \quad \text{and} \quad \tilde{Q}^e - Q^e = \frac{(\tilde{\alpha} - \alpha)b}{\beta + b} = -b(\tilde{P}^e - P^e)$$

From Fig. 5.1.9 we see that $\tilde{P}^e$ is less than P^e (because $\tilde{\alpha} > \alpha$), while $\tilde{Q}^e$ is larger than Q^e. The rightward shift in the supply curve from S to $\tilde{S}$ implies that the equilibrium point moves down and to the right along the unchanged demand curve. Upward shifts in the supply curve resulting from, for example, taxation or increased cost, can be analysed in the same way, as can shifts in the demand curve.

EXAMPLE 5.1.4 Suppose a person earning y dollars in a given year pays $f(y)$ dollars that year in income tax. The government decides to reduce income tax.

One proposal is to allow every individual to deduct d dollars from their taxable income before the tax is calculated.

An alternative proposal is to calculate each person's income tax on the full amount of their taxable income, then allow a "tax credit" that deducts c dollars from the total tax due.

Illustrate graphically the two proposals for a "normal" tax function f. Then mark off the income y^* where the two proposals yield the same tax revenue.

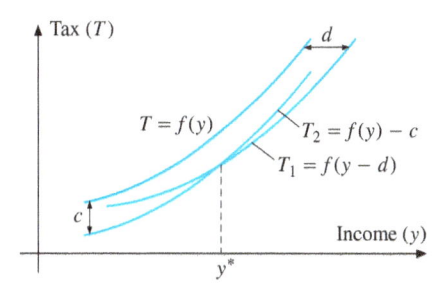

Figure 5.1.10 The graphs of $T_1 = f(y-d)$ and $T_2 = f(y) - c$

Solution: The function $T = f(y)$ whose graph is shown in Figure 5.1.10 is a so-called "progressive" tax schedule in which, by definition, the average tax rate $T/y = f(y)/y$ is an increasing function of y.[1] If taxable income is y and the deduction is d, then $y - d$ is the reduced taxable income, and so the tax liability is $f(y-d)$. To obtain the graph of $T_1 = f(y-d)$, shift the graph of $T = f(y)$ by d units to the right.

The graph of $T_2 = f(y) - c$ is obtained by lowering the graph of $T = f(y)$ by c units. The income y^* which gives the same tax under the two different schemes is given by the equation

$$f(y^* - d) = f(y^*) - c$$

Note that $T_1 > T_2$ when $y < y^*$, but that $T_1 < T_2$ when $y > y^*$. Thus, the tax credit is worth more to those with low incomes, whereas the deduction is worth more to those with high incomes (as one might expect).

EXERCISES FOR SECTION 5.1

1. Use the graph of $y = x^2$ in Fig. 4.3.6 and the rules for shifting graphs in order to sketch the graphs of the following functions:

   (a) $y = x^2 + 1$ (b) $y = (x+3)^2$ (c) $y = 3 - (x+1)^2$

2. Suppose that $y = f(x)$ has the graph drawn in Fig. 5.1.11. Sketch the graphs of:

   (a) $y = f(x-2)$ (b) $y = f(x) - 2$ (c) $y = f(-x)$

3. Suppose that in the first model of Example 5.1.3 there is a positive shift in demand, so that the new demand at price P is $\tilde{D} = 106 - P$. Find the new equilibrium point and illustrate it in a graph.

---

[1] Example 5.4.4 considers the US Federal Income Tax, which has this property.

156 CHAPTER 5 / PROPERTIES OF FUNCTIONS

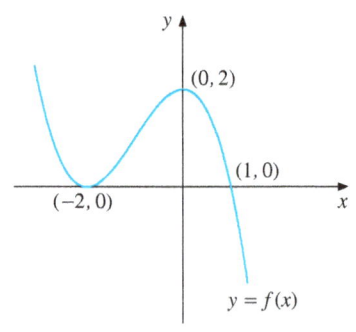

Figure 5.1.11 The function f for Exercise 2

4. Use Fig. 4.3.10 and the rules for shifting graphs to sketch the graph of $y = 2 - |x + 2|$.

5. Starting with the graph of $f(x) = 1/x^2$, sketch the graph of $g(x) = 2 - (x + 2)^{-2}$.

6. Suppose in Example 5.1.4 that $f(y) = Ay + By^2$ where A and B are positive parameters. Find y^* in this case.

5.2 New Functions from Old

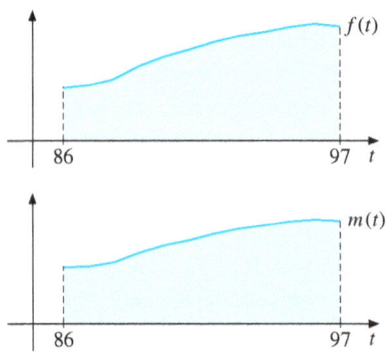

Figure 5.2.1 Male and female students

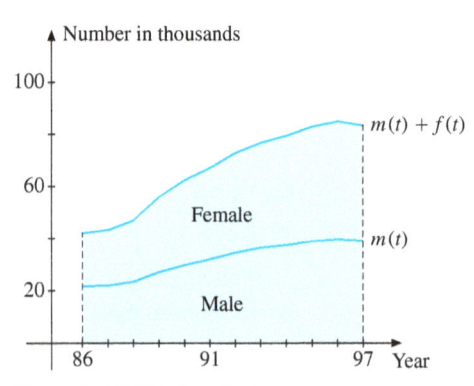

Figure 5.2.2 Total students

Figure 5.2.1 gives graphs of the number of male and female students who were registered at a certain university during the years 1986–1997. Let $f(t)$ and $m(t)$ denote the number of female and male students in year t, and let $n(t)$ denote the total number of students. Of course, $n(t) = f(t) + m(t)$. The graph of the total number of students $n(t)$ is obtained by piling the graph of $f(t)$ on top of the graph of $m(t)$, as shown in Fig. 5.2.2.

Suppose in general that f and g are two functions that are both defined on a set A of real numbers. The function h defined by the formula $h(x) = f(x) + g(x)$ is called the *sum* of f and g, and we write $h = f + g$. The function ℓ defined by $\ell(x) = f(x) - g(x)$ is called the *difference* between f and g, and we write $\ell = f - g$. For the example in the previous paragraph, the difference between the numbers of female and male students in year t is $f(t) - m(t)$. The graph of this function can be obtained by piling the graph of $f(t)$ on top of the graph of $-m(t)$.

Sums and differences of functions are often seen in economic models. Consider the following typical examples.

EXAMPLE 5.2.1   The cost of producing $Q > 0$ units of a commodity is $C(Q)$. The cost per unit of output, $A(Q) = C(Q)/Q$, is called the *average cost*. Suppose in particular that the cost function given by
$$C(Q) = aQ^3 + bQ^2 + cQ + d$$
is of the type whose graph is shown in Fig. 4.7.2. Then the average cost is
$$A(Q) = aQ^2 + bQ + c + \frac{d}{Q}$$
Thus $A(Q)$ is a sum of a quadratic function $y = aQ^2 + bQ + c$ and the hyperbola $y = d/Q$. To obtain the graph of the average cost function $A(Q)$, one must pile the hyperbola $y = d/Q$ shown in Fig. 5.2.4 on top of the parabola $y = aQ^2 + bQ + c$ shown in Fig. 5.2.3. Figure 5.2.5 shows the result.

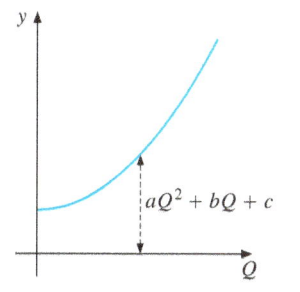

Figure 5.2.3 Graph of $aQ^2 + bQ + c$

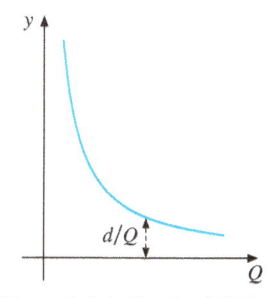

Figure 5.2.4 Graph of d/Q

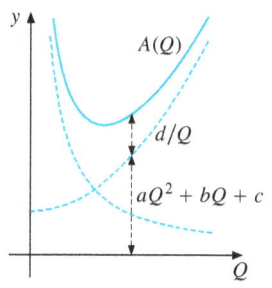

Figure 5.2.5 Graph of $A(Q)$

Note that for small values of Q the graph of $A(Q)$ is close to the graph of $y = d/Q$, since d/Q is large when Q is small. For large values of Q, on the other hand, the graph is close to the parabola, since d/Q is small when Q is large.

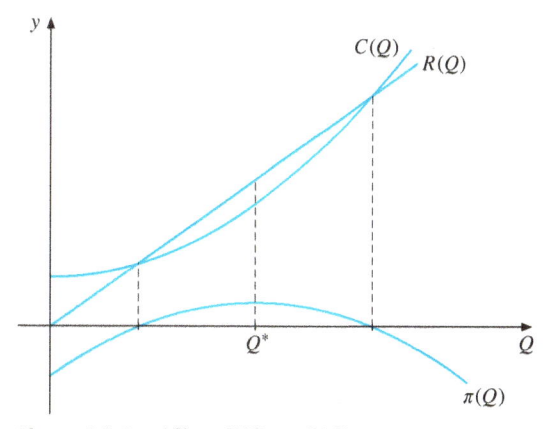

Figure 5.2.6 $\pi(Q) = R(Q) - C(Q)$

Next, let $R(Q)$ denote the *revenue* obtained by selling Q units. Then, the *profit* $\pi(Q)$ is given by $\pi(Q) = R(Q) - C(Q)$. Figure 5.2.6 illustrates how to construct the graph of the profit function $\pi(Q)$. In this case the firm gets a fixed price p per unit, so that the graph of $R(Q)$ is a straight line of slope p through the origin. Then the graph of $-C(Q)$ must be added to that of $R(Q)$.

Finally, the production level that maximizes profit is Q^*, where the height of the line $y = R(Q) = pQ$ is as far as possible above the curve $y = R(Q) = pQ$.

Products and Quotients

Suppose that the two functions f and g are defined on the same domain A. Then the function h defined on A by $h(x) = f(x) \cdot g(x)$ is called the *product* of f and g, and we write $h = f \cdot g$ (or simply fg). The function ℓ defined at points of A where $g(x) \neq 0$ by $\ell(x) = f(x)/g(x)$ is called the *quotient* of f and g, and we write $\ell = f/g$. We have already seen examples of these operations. Unlike $f + g$ and $f - g$, it is difficult to infer useful rules about the graphs of fg and f/g based on the graphs of f and g.

Composite Functions

Suppose the demand for a commodity is a function of its price. Suppose that price is not constant, but depends on time. Then it is natural to regard the demand of the commodity as a function of time. In general, if y is a function of x, and z is a function of y, then z can be regarded as a function of x. We call z a *composite function* of x. Suppse we denote the two functions involved by f and g, with $y = f(x)$ and $z = g(y)$. Then we can replace y by $f(x)$ in the latter equation, and so write z in the form $z = g(f(x))$.

Note that when computing z, we first apply f to x to obtain $y = f(x)$, and then we apply g to y. Here $f(x)$ is called the *interior function*, while g is called the *exterior function*. The function that maps x to $z = g(f(x))$ is called the *composition* of g with f. This is often denoted by $g \circ f$ and is read as "g of f". Formally,

COMPOSITION OF g WITH f

Let f and g be functions whose domains are D_f and D_g, and whose ranges R_f and R_g respectively. Provided that $R_f \subseteq D_g$, the *composition* of g with f is the function $h = g \circ f$, with domain $D_h = D_f$ and range $R_h \subseteq R_g$, which is defined by

$$h(x) = g(f(x)) \tag{5.2.1}$$

If the assumption that $R_f \subseteq D_g$ is violated, there are values of x for which $f(x)$ is defined but $h(x)$ is not. In general, there may be values of z in the range R_g of g which are not in the range R_h of h.

It is easy to confuse $g \circ f$ with $g \cdot f$ typographically. But these two functions are defined in entirely different ways. When we evaluate $g \circ f$ at x, we first compute $f(x)$ and then evaluate g at $f(x)$. On the other hand, the product $g \cdot f$ of g and f is the function whose value at a particular number x is simply the product of $g(x)$ and $f(x)$, so $(g \cdot f)(x) = g(x) \cdot f(x)$.

Whereas $g \circ f$ denotes the function that maps x to $g(f(x))$, the reversed notation $f \circ g$ denotes the function that maps x to $f(g(x))$. Thus, we have

$$(f \circ g)(x) = f(g(x)) \quad \text{and} \quad (g \circ f)(x) = g(f(x))$$

Usually, $f \circ g$ and $g \circ f$ are quite different functions. For instance, if $g(v) = 2 - v^2$ and $f(u) = u^3$, then $(f \circ g)(x) = (2 - x^2)^3$, whereas $(g \circ f)(x) = 2 - (x^3)^2 = 2 - x^6$; the two resulting polynomials are not the same.

EXAMPLE 5.2.2 Write the following as composite functions:

(a) $z = (x^3 + x^2)^{50}$ 　　(b) $z = e^{-(x-\mu)^2}$, where μ is a constant.

Solution:

(a) Given a value of x, you first compute $x^3 + x^2$, which gives the interior function, $f(x) = x^3 + x^2$. Then take the 50th power of the result, so the exterior function is $g(y) = y^{50}$. Hence, $g(f(x)) = g(x^3 + x^2) = (x^3 + x^2)^{50}$.

(b) We can choose the interior function as $f(x) = -(x - \mu)^2$ and the exterior function as $g(y) = e^y$. Then $g(f(x)) = g(-(x - \mu)^2) = e^{-(x-\mu)^2}$. Alternatively, we could choose $f(x) = (x - \mu)^2$ and $g(y) = e^{-y}$.

Symmetry

The function $f(x) = x^2$ satisfies $f(-x) = f(x)$, as indeed does any even power x^{2n}, where n is any integer, positive or negative. Inspired by this example, if the function f satisfies $f(-x) = f(x)$ for all x in its domain, then f is called an *even* function. This condition implies that the graph of f is *symmetric about the y-axis*, as shown in Fig. 5.2.7.

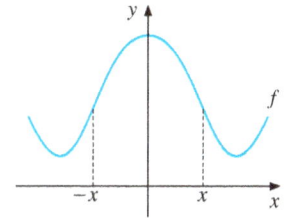

Figure 5.2.7 Even function 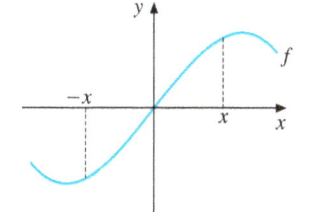　　**Figure 5.2.8** Odd function 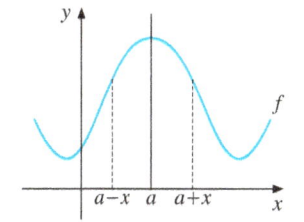　　**Figure 5.2.9** Symmetry about $x = a$

On the other hand, any odd power x^{2n+1} such as $f(x) = x^3$ satisfies $f(-x) = -f(x)$. So if $f(-x) = -f(x)$ for all x in the domain of f, then f is called an *odd* function. In this case, as shown in Fig. 5.2.8, the graph of f has the "odd" (!) symmetry property of being unchanged if it is rotated through 180° about the origin either clockwise or anti-clockwise.

Finally, the function f is *symmetric about a* if $f(a+x) = f(a-x)$ for all x. Then the graph of f is *symmetric about the line* $x = a$, as shown in Fig. 5.2.9. One example arose in Section 4.6, where we showed that the quadratic function $f(x) = ax^2 + bx + c$ with $a \neq 0$ is symmetric about $x = -b/2a$. A second example is the composite function $z = e^{-(x-\mu)^2}$ in part (b) of Example 5.2.2, which is symmetric about $x = \mu$.

EXERCISES FOR SECTION 5.2

1. Assuming $x > 0$, draw three graphs like those in Figs 5.2.1 and 5.2.2 which show how the graph of $y = \frac{1}{4}x^2 + 1/x$ results from adding the graph of $1/x$ on top of the graph of $y = \frac{1}{4}x^2$.

2. Sketch the graphs of the following functions:

   (a) $y = \sqrt{x} - x$ (b) $y = e^x + e^{-x}$ (c) $y = e^{-x^2} + x$

3. If $f(x) = 3x - x^3$ and $g(x) = x^3$, compute the six expressions $(f+g)(x)$, $(f-g)(x)$, $(fg)(x)$, $(f/g)(x)$, $f(g(1))$, and $g(f(1))$.

4. Let $f(x) = 3x + 7$. Compute $f(f(x))$, and find the value x^* at which $f(f(x^*)) = 100$.

5. Compute $\ln(\ln e)$ and $(\ln e)^2$. What do you notice?[2]

5.3 Inverse Functions

Suppose that the demand quantity D for a commodity depends on the price per unit P according to $D = 30/P^{1/3}$. This formula tells us the demand D corresponding to a given price P. If, for example, $P = 27$, then $D = 30/27^{1/3} = 10$. So D is a function of P. That is, $D = f(P)$ with $f(P) = 30/P^{1/3}$. Note that demand decreases as the price increases.

From a producer's point of view, however, it may be more natural to treat output as something it can choose, and then consider the resulting price. Thus, the producer wants to know the *inverse* demand function, in which price depends on the quantity sold instead of the other way round. In our example this functional relationship is obtained by solving $D = 30/P^{1/3}$ for P. First we obtain $P^{1/3} = 30/D$ and then $(P^{1/3})^3 = (30/D)^3$, so that $P = 27\,000/D^3$. This equation gives us the price P corresponding to a given output D. For example, if $D = 10$, then $P = 27\,000/10^3 = 27$. In this case, P is a function $g(D)$ of D, with $g(D) = 27\,000/D^3$.

The two variables D and P in this example are related in a way that allows each to be regarded as a function of the other. In fact, the two functions

$$f(P) = 30P^{-1/3} \quad \text{and} \quad g(D) = 27\,000D^{-3} \qquad (5.3.1)$$

---

[2] This illustrates how, if we define the function f^2 by $f^2(x) = (f(x))^2$, then, in general, $f^2(x) \neq f(f(x))$.

are *inverses* of each other. We say that f is the inverse of g, and that g is the inverse of f.

Note that the two functions f and g convey exactly the same information. For example, the fact that demand is 10 at price 27 can be expressed using either f or g: the two statements $f(27) = 10$ and $g(10) = 27$ are entirely equivalent. In Example 4.5.3 we considered an even simpler demand function $D = 100 - P$. Solving for P we get $P = 100 - D$, which was referred to as the inverse demand function.

Suppose in general that f is a function with domain $D_f = A$. This means that to each x in A there corresponds a unique number $f(x)$. Recall that if f has domain A, then the range of f is the set $B = R_f = \{f(x) : x \in A\}$, which is also denoted by $f(A)$. That is, the range B consists of all numbers $f(x)$ obtained by letting x vary in A. Now, the function f is said to be *one-to-one* in A if f never has the same value at any two different points in A. In other words, for each one y in B, there is exactly one x in A such that $y = f(x)$. Equivalently, f is one-to-one in A provided that, whenever x_1 and x_2 both lie in A with $x_1 \neq x_2$, then $f(x_1) \neq f(x_2)$.

It is evident that if a function is either strictly increasing in all of A, or strictly decreasing in all of A, then it is one-to-one. A particular one-to-one function f is illustrated in Fig. 5.3.1. The function g shown in Fig. 5.3.2 is not one-to-one because, for example, the two x-values x_1 and x_2 are both associated with the same y-value y_1.

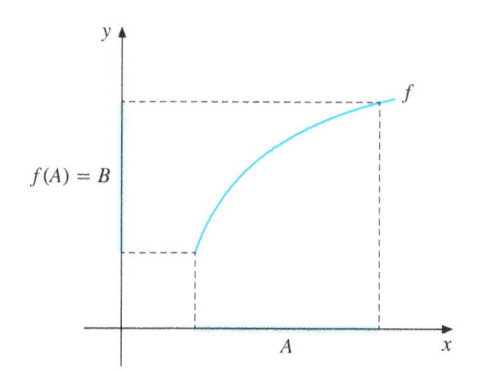

Figure 5.3.1 f is one-to-one with domain A and range B. f has an inverse

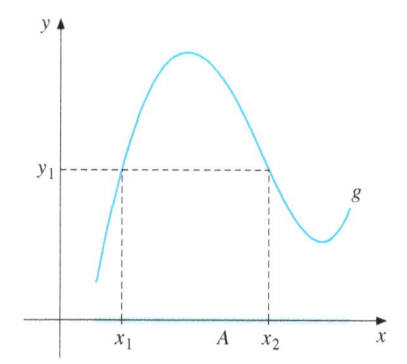

Figure 5.3.2 g is *not* one-to-one and hence has no inverse over A.

INVERSE FUNCTION

Let f be a function with domain A and range B. If and only if f is one-to-one, it has an *inverse function* g with domain B and range A. The function g is given by the following rule: For each y in B, the value $g(y)$ is the unique number x in A such that $f(x) = y$. Then

$$g(y) = x \iff y = f(x) \qquad \text{(for all } x \in A \text{ and } y \in B\text{)} \qquad (5.3.2)$$

A direct implication of (5.3.2) is that

$$g(f(x)) = x \text{ for all } x \text{ in } A \quad \text{and} \quad f(g(y)) = y \text{ for all } y \text{ in } B \tag{5.3.3}$$

The equation $g(f(x)) = x$ shows what happens if we first apply f to x and then apply g to $f(x)$: we get x back because g undoes what f did to x. Note that if g is the inverse of a function f, then f is also the inverse of g. If g is the inverse of f, it is standard to use the notation f^{-1} for g.[3]

In the introductory example, in order to derive the functions f and g that appear in Eq. (5.3.1), we solved the equation $D = 30/P^{1/3}$ to express P in terms of D. In simple cases we can often use the same method to find the inverse of a given function (and hence automatically verify that the inverse exists). Here are some more examples.

EXAMPLE 5.3.1   Solve the following equations for x and find the corresponding inverse functions:

(a) $y = 4x - 3$ (b) $y = \sqrt[5]{x+1}$ (c) $y = \dfrac{3x-1}{x+4}$

Solution:

(a) Solving the equation for x yields, for all x and y, the following equivalences:

$$y = 4x - 3 \Leftrightarrow 4x = y + 3 \Leftrightarrow x = \frac{1}{4}y + \frac{3}{4}$$

We conclude that $f(x) = 4x - 3$ and $g(y) = \frac{1}{4}y + \frac{3}{4}$ are inverses of each other.

(b) Raising each side to the fifth power yields the equivalences

$$y = \sqrt[5]{x+1} \Leftrightarrow y^5 = x + 1 \Leftrightarrow x = y^5 - 1$$

These are valid for all x and all y. Hence, we have shown that $f(x) = \sqrt[5]{x+1}$ and $g(y) = y^5 - 1$ are inverses of each other.

(c) Multiplying both sides of the equation by $x+4$ implies $y(x+4) = 3x - 1$. This equation yields $yx + 4y = 3x - 1$ or $x(3-y) = 4y + 1$. Solving for x in terms of y gives

$$x = \frac{4y+1}{3-y}$$

We conclude that $f(x) = (3x-1)/(x+4)$ and $g(y) = (4y+1)/(3-y)$ are inverses of each other. Observe that f is only defined for $x \neq -4$, and g is only defined for $y \neq 3$. So the equivalence in (5.3.2) is valid only with these restrictions.

A Geometric Characterization of Inverse Functions

In our introductory example, Eq. (5.3.1) states that $f(P) = 30p^{-1/3}$ and $g(D) = 27\,000\,D^{-3}$ are inverse functions. The specific interpretation of the symbols P and D made it natural to

---

[3] This sometimes leads to confusion. If a is a number such that $a \neq 0$, then a^{-1} means $1/a$. But $f^{-1}(x)$ does *not* mean $1/f(x)$, which equals $f(x)^{-1}$ instead. For example, the two functions defined by $y = 1/(x^2 + 2x + 3)$ and $y = x^2 + 2x + 3$ are *not* inverses of each other, but reciprocals.

describe these functions as we did. In other circumstances, it may be convenient to use the same variable as argument in both f and g. In Example 5.3.1(a), we saw that $f(x) = 4x - 3$ and $g(y) = \frac{1}{4}y + \frac{3}{4}$ were inverses of each other. If also we use x instead of y as the variable of the function g, we find that

$$f(x) = 4x - 3 \text{ and } g(x) = \tfrac{1}{4}x + \tfrac{3}{4} \text{ are inverses of each other} \qquad (*)$$

In the same way, on the basis of part (b) of the same example, we can say that

$$f(x) = (x+1)^{1/5} \text{ and } g(x) = x^5 - 1 \text{ are inverses of each other} \qquad (**)$$

The two graphs of any pair of inverse functions f and g like those in $(*)$ and $(**)$ have an interesting geometric property. In fact they must be mirror images of each other when reflected in the line $y = x$, as shown in Figs 5.3.3 and 5.3.4.

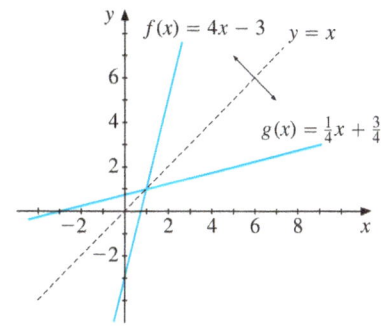

Figure 5.3.3 f and g are inverses

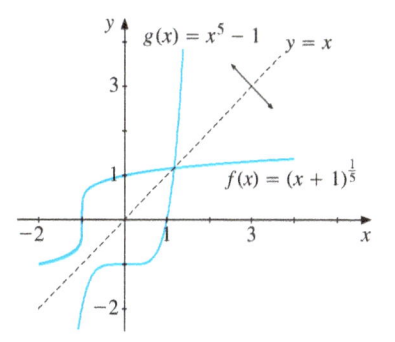

Figure 5.3.4 f and g are inverses

Suppose in general that f and g are inverses of each other. The fact that (a, b) lies on the graph f means that $b = f(a)$. According to (5.3.2), this implies that $g(b) = a$, so that (b, a) lies on the graph of g. Now, Exercise 8 asks you to show that (a, b) and (b, a) lie symmetrically about the line $y = x$. This leads to the following conclusion:

SYMMETRY OF INVERSE FUNCTIONS

Suppose the two functions f and g are inverses of each other. Provided that the scales of the coordinate axes are the same, the graphs of $y = f(x)$ and $y = g(x)$ are symmetric about the line $y = x$.

When the functions f and g are inverses of each other, then by definition (5.3.2), the equations $y = f(x)$ and $x = g(y)$ are equivalent. The two functions actually have exactly the same graph, though in the second case we should think of x depending on y, instead of the other way around. On the other hand, the graphs of $y = f(x)$ and $y = g(x)$ are symmetric about the line $y = x$.

For instance, Examples 4.5.3 and 5.1.3 discuss demand and supply curves. These can be thought of as the graphs of a function where quantity Q depends on price P, or equivalently as the graphs of the inverse function where price P depends on quantity Q.

In all the examples examined so far, the inverse could be expressed in terms of known formulas. It turns out that even if a function has an inverse, it may be impossible to express it in terms of a function we know. *Inverse functions are actually an important source of new functions.* A typical case is based on the exponential function. In Section 4.9 we showed that $y = e^x$ is strictly increasing, as well as that it tends to 0 as x tends to $-\infty$, and to ∞ as x tends to ∞. Hence, for each positive y there exists a uniquely determined x such that $e^x = y$. In Section 4.10 we called the new function the natural logarithm function, denoted by ln. By definition, we have the equivalence $y = e^x \Leftrightarrow x = \ln y$. This equivalence demonstrates that the *functions $f(x) = e^x$ and $g(y) = \ln y$ are inverses of each other.* Because the ln function appears in so many connections, it has been extensively tabulated. Moreover, on many calculators it is represented by its own special key.[4]

If f and g are inverses of each other, the domain of f is equal to the range of g, and vice versa. Consider the following examples.

EXAMPLE 5.3.2 The function $f(x) = \sqrt{3x+9}$, defined on the interval $[-3, \infty)$, *is* strictly increasing and hence has an inverse. Find a formula for the inverse. Use x as the free variable for both functions.

Solution: As x increases from -3 to ∞, the function value $f(x)$ increases from 0 to ∞, so the range of f is $[0, \infty)$. Hence f has an inverse g defined on $[0, \infty)$. To find a formula for the inverse, we solve the equation $y = \sqrt{3x+9}$ for x. Squaring gives $y^2 = 3x + 9$, with solution $x = \frac{1}{3}y^2 - 3$. Interchanging x and y in this expression to make x the free variable gives the inverse function of f, which is $y = g(x) = \frac{1}{3}x^2 - 3$, defined on $[0, \infty)$. See Fig. 5.3.5.

EXAMPLE 5.3.3 Consider the function f defined by the formula $f(x) = 4\ln(\sqrt{x+4} - 2)$.

(a) For which values of x is $f(x)$ defined? Determine the range of f.

(b) Find a formula for its inverse. Use x as the free variable.

---

[4] If a calculator has a certain function f represented by one key, then it will usually have another which represents the inverse function f^{-1}. For example, if it has an $\boxed{e^x}$-key, it will also have an $\boxed{\ln x}$-key. Now the definition of inverse implies that $f^{-1}(f(x)) = x$. So if we enter any number x, then press the $\boxed{f}$-key followed by the $\boxed{f^{-1}}$-key, then we should get x back again. If you have access to the right sort of calculator, you can experiment by entering 5, then using the $\boxed{e^x}$-key followed by the $\boxed{\ln x}$-key. This should take you back close to 5; rounding errors may prevent you getting back to 5 exactly.

SECTION 5.3 / INVERSE FUNCTIONS

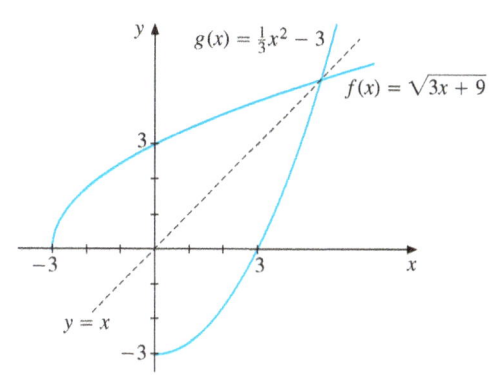

Figure 5.3.5 $f(x) = \sqrt{3x+9}$ and $g(x) = \frac{1}{3}x^2 - 3$

Solution:

(a) For $\sqrt{x+4}$ to be defined, we must have $x \geq -4$. But for $\ln(\sqrt{x+4} - 2)$ to be defined, we must also ensure that $\sqrt{x+4} - 2 > 0$. But $\sqrt{x+4} - 2 > 0$ implies that $\sqrt{x+4} > 2$, or $x + 4 > 4$, and so $x > 0$. The domain of f is therefore $(0, \infty)$. As x varies from near 0 to ∞, so $f(x)$ increases from $-\infty$ to ∞. The range of f is therefore $(-\infty, \infty)$.

(b) If $y = 4\ln(\sqrt{x+4} - 2)$, then $\ln(\sqrt{x+4} - 2) = y/4$, implying that $\sqrt{x+4} - 2 = e^{y/4}$ and so $\sqrt{x+4} = 2 + e^{y/4}$. Squaring each side gives $x + 4 = (2 + e^{y/4})^2 = 4 + 4e^{y/4} + e^{y/2}$, so $x = 4e^{y/4} + e^{y/2}$. The inverse function, with x replacing y as the free variable, is therefore $y = e^{x/2} + 4e^{x/4}$. This is defined on $(-\infty, \infty)$, with range $(0, \infty)$.

EXERCISES FOR SECTION 5.3

1. Demand D as a function of price P is given by $D = \frac{32}{5} - \frac{3}{10}P$. Solve the equation for P and find the inverse function.

2. The demand D for sugar in the US in the period 1915–1929, as a function of the price P, was estimated to be $D = f(P) = 157.8/P^{0.3}$. Solve the equation for P and so find the inverse of f.

3. Find the domains, ranges, and inverses of the functions given by the following formulas:
   (a) $y = -3x$ (b) $y = 1/x$ (c) $y = x^3$ (d) $y = \sqrt{\sqrt{x} - 2}$

4. The function f is defined by the following table:

x	-4	-3	-2	-1	0	1	2
$f(x)$	-4	-2	0	2	4	6	8

   (a) Denote the inverse of f by f^{-1}. What is its domain? What is the value of $f^{-1}(2)$?

   (b) Find a formula for a function $f(x)$, defined for all real x, which agrees with this table. What is the formula for its inverse?

5. Why does $f(x) = x^2$, for x in $(-\infty, \infty)$, have no inverse function? Show that f restricted to $[0, \infty)$ has an inverse, and find that inverse.

6. Formalize the following statements:

   (a) Halving and doubling are inverse operations.

   (b) The operation of multiplying a number by 3 and then subtracting 2 is the inverse of the operation of adding 2 to the number and then dividing by 3.

   (c) The operation of subtracting 32 from a number and then multiplying the result by 5/9 is the inverse of the operation of multiplying a number by 9/5 and then adding 32. "Fahrenheit to Celsius, and Celsius to Fahrenheit".[5]

7. Suppose that $Q = f(C)$ is the function that tells you how many kilograms of carrots Q you can buy for a specified amount of money C. What does the inverse function f^{-1} tell you?

8. On a coordinate system in the plane:

   (a) Show that points $(3, 1)$ and $(1, 3)$ are symmetric about the line $y = x$, and the same for $(5, 3)$ and $(3, 5)$.

   (b) Use properties of congruent triangles to prove that points (a, b) and (b, a) in the plane are symmetric about the line $y = x$. What is the point half-way between them?

SM 9. Find inverses of the following functions, with x as the independent variable:

   (a) $f(x) = (x^3 - 1)^{1/3}$ (b) $f(x) = \dfrac{x + 1}{x - 2}$ (c) $f(x) = (1 - x^3)^{1/5} + 2$

SM 10. The functions defined by the following formulas are strictly increasing in their domains. Find the domain of each inverse function, and a formula for the corresponding inverse.

   (a) $y = e^{x+4}$ (b) $y = \ln x - 4$, $x > 0$ (c) $y = \ln\left(2 + e^{x-3}\right)$

11. [HARDER] Find the inverse of $f(x) = \frac{1}{2}(e^x - e^{-x})$. (*Hint*: Solve a quadratic equation in $z = e^x$.)

5.4 Graphs of Equations

The three equations $x\sqrt{y} = 2$, $x^2 + y^2 = 16$, and $y^3 + 3x^2 y = 13$ are each an example of one equation in two variables x and y. A *solution* of such an equation is an ordered pair (a, b) such that the equation is satisfied when we replace x by a and y by b. The *solution set* of the equation is the set of all such solutions. Representing all pairs in the solution set in a Cartesian coordinate system gives a set called the *graph* of the equation.

EXAMPLE 5.4.1   Find some solutions of each of the equations $x\sqrt{y} = 2$ and $x^2 + y^2 = 16$, and try to sketch their graphs.

Solution: From $x\sqrt{y} = 2$ we obtain $y = 4/x^2$. Hence it is easy to find corresponding values for x and y as given in Table 5.4.1. The graph is drawn in Fig. 5.4.1, along with the four points in the table.

---
[5] Recall Example 2.6.2 and Review Exercise 4.19.

SECTION 5.4 / GRAPHS OF EQUATIONS   167

Table 5.4.1 Solutions of $x\sqrt{y} = 2$

x	1	2	4	6
y	4	1	1/4	1/9

Table 5.4.2 Solutions of $x^2 + y^2 = 16$

x	-4	-3	-1	0	1	3	4
y	0	$\pm\sqrt{7}$	$\pm\sqrt{15}$	± 4	$\pm\sqrt{15}$	$\pm\sqrt{7}$	0

For $x^2 + y^2 = 16$, if $y = 0$, then $x^2 = 16$, so $x = \pm 4$. Two solutions are $(4, 0)$ and $(-4, 0)$. Table 5.4.2 adds some other solutions. In Fig. 5.4.2 the 12 points specified in the table are plotted. The graph in Fig. 5.4.2 seems to be a circle, as we will confirm in Section 5.5.

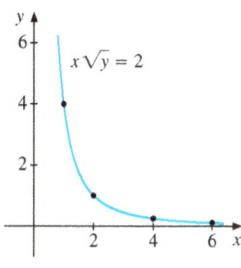

Figure 5.4.1
Graph of $x\sqrt{y} = 2$

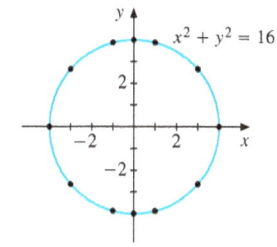

Figure 5.4.2
Graph of $x^2 + y^2 = 16$

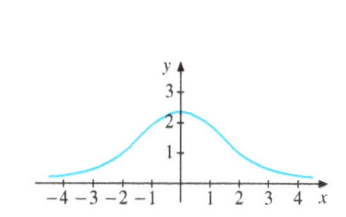

Figure 5.4.3
Graph of $y^3 + 3x^2 y = 13$

EXAMPLE 5.4.2   What can you say about the graph of the equation $y^3 + 3x^2 y = 13$?

Solution: If $x = 0$, then $y^3 = 13$, so that $y = \sqrt[3]{13} \approx 2.35$. Hence $(0, \sqrt[3]{13})$ lies on the graph. Because x is squared, note that if (x_0, y_0) lies on the graph, then so does $(-x_0, y_0)$. So the graph is symmetric about the y-axis. Note that $(2, 1)$, and hence $(-2, 1)$, are both solutions.

Suppose we write the equation in the form

$$y = \frac{13}{y^2 + 3x^2} \tag{5.4.1}$$

Then we see that no point (x, y) on the graph can have $y \leq 0$, so all the graph lies above the x-axis. From (5.4.1) it also follows that if $|x|$ is large, then y must be small.

Figure 5.4.3 displays the graph, which accords with these findings. Solving Eq. (5.4.1) for x shows that it consists of all points (x, y) satisfying $x = \pm\sqrt{(13 - y^3)/3y}$.

Vertical-Line Test

Graphs of different functions can have innumerable different shapes. However, not all curves in the plane are graphs of functions. By definition, a function assigns to each point x in the domain only one y-value. *The graph of a function therefore has the property that a vertical* line through any point on the x-axis has at most one point of intersection with the graph. This simple *vertical-line test* is illustrated in Figs 5.4.4 and 5.4.5.

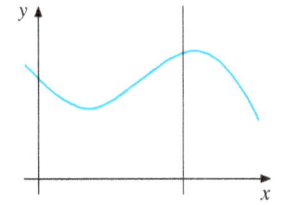

Figure 5.4.4 A function

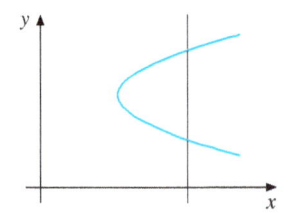

Figure 5.4.5 *Not* a function

The graph of the circle $x^2 + y^2 = 16$, shown in Fig. 5.4.2, is a typical example of a graph that does *not* represent a function, since it does not pass the vertical-line test. A vertical line $x = a$ for any a with $-4 < a < 4$ intersects the circle at *two* points. Solving the equation $x^2 + y^2 = 16$ for y, we obtain $y = \pm\sqrt{16 - x^2}$. Note that the upper semicircle alone is the graph of the function $y = \sqrt{16 - x^2}$, and the lower semicircle is the graph of the function $y = -\sqrt{16 - x^2}$. Both these functions are defined on the interval $[-4, 4]$.

Choosing Units

A function of one variable is a rule assigning numbers in its range to numbers in its domain. When we describe an empirical relationship by means of a function, we must first choose the units of measurement. For instance we might measure time in years, days, or weeks. We might measure money in dollars, yen, or euros. The choice we make will influence the visual impression conveyed by the graph of the function.

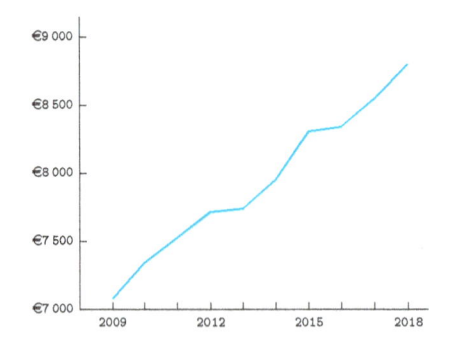

Figure 5.4.6 An optimistic view

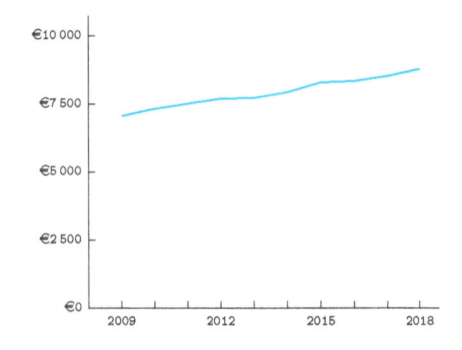

Figure 5.4.7 A pessimistic view

Figures 5.4.6 and 5.4.7 both display the time series of total consumption expenditure during the period 2009–2018 for the 28 countries that belonged to EU in 2018. The data are in *current* euros, meaning that there has been no correction to allow for the effect of inflation. These graphs illustrate a standard trick which is often used to influence people's impressions of empirical relationships. In both diagrams time is measured in years and consumption in billions of euros. They both graph the same function. But if you were trying to impress an audience with the performance of the European economy, which one would you choose?

Piecewise Functions

Sometimes a function is defined in several pieces, by giving a separate formula for each of a number of disjoint parts of the domain. One example that should already be familiar is the absolute value function $y = |x|$ defined by Eq. (2.7.1).[6] Two more examples of such *piecewise functions* are presented next.

EXAMPLE 5.4.3   Draw the graph of the function f defined by

$$f(x) = \begin{cases} -x & \text{for } x \leq 0 \\ x^2 & \text{for } 0 < x \leq 1 \\ 1.5 & \text{for } x > 1 \end{cases}$$

Solution: The graph is drawn in Fig. 5.4.8. The arrow at $(1, 1.5)$ indicates that this point is not part of the graph of the function. As we shall explain in Section 7.8, the function has a *discontinuity* at $x = 1$.

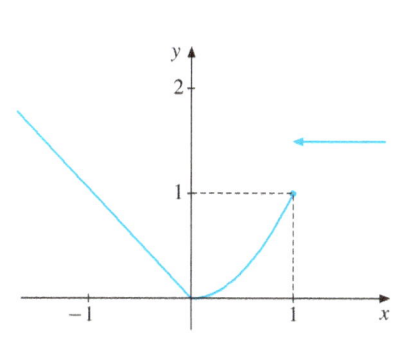

Figure 5.4.8 The function in Example 3

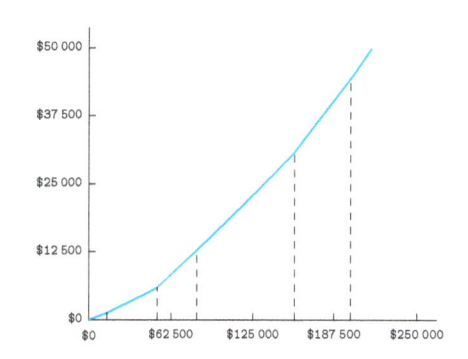

Figure 5.4.9 US Federal Income Tax in 2018

EXAMPLE 5.4.4   **(US Federal Income Tax, 2018).**   Figure 5.4.9 has part of the graph of the function showing how much income tax a head of household had to pay, as a function of net income.[7]

---

[6] As pointed out in Example 2.7.2, the alternative definition $y = \sqrt{x^2}$ of the absolute value would avoid having a separate formula for different parts of the real line. Still, the usual definition of $y = |x|$ does distinguish between the cases when $x > 0$ and $x < 0$.

[7] Of course, Fig. 5.4.9 is an idealization. The true income tax function is defined only for an integer number of dollars. More precisely, its graph is that of a discontinuous "step function" which jumps up slightly whenever income rises by one dollar. We also note that taxable net income excludes any personal allowance, any allowance for children or other dependants, as well as various "itemized deductions" for approved expenses such as mortgage interest for an owner-occupied house.

For net income below $13 600, the tax rate was 10%, so a person with income x paid $y = 0.1x$ in taxes. For incomes in the bracket between $13 601 and $51 800, the tax was $1 360 plus 12% of the income above $13 600: a person with income x in this bracket paid $y = 1360 + 0.12(x - 13\,600)$ in taxes. The coefficient of $0.12 = 12\%$ is known as *marginal rate* for incomes in this bracket. The marginal tax rates for higher income brackets are higher, which explains why the graph becomes steeper as we move to the right. For instance, for incomes between $82 501 and $157 500, the marginal rate was 24%; it reaches 37% for incomes above $500 001. In public finance, tax functions whose marginal rate increases with the taxpayer's income are often known as *progressive*.

EXERCISES FOR SECTION 5.4

SM 1. Find some particular solutions of the following two equations, then sketch their graphs:

(a) $x^2 + 2y^2 = 6$ (b) $y^2 - x^2 = 1$

2. Try to sketch the graph of $\sqrt{x} + \sqrt{y} = 5$ by finding some particular solutions.

3. The function F is defined for all $r \geq 0$ by the following formula:

$$F(r) = \begin{cases} 0 & \text{for } r \leq 7500 \\ 0.044(r - 7500) & \text{for } r > 7500 \end{cases}$$

Compute $F(100\,000)$, and sketch the graph of F.

5.5 Distance in the Plane

Let $P_1 = (x_1, y_1)$ and $P_2 = (x_2, y_2)$ be two points in the xy-plane, as shown in Fig. 5.5.1. By Pythagoras's theorem, stated in the appendix, the distance d between P_1 and P_2 satisfies the equation $d^2 = (x_2 - x_1)^2 + (y_2 - y_1)^2$. This gives the following important formula:

DISTANCE FORMULA

The distance between the two points (x_1, y_1) and (x_2, y_2) is

$$d = \sqrt{(x_2 - x_1)^2 + (y_2 - y_1)^2} \tag{5.5.1}$$

We considered two points in the first quadrant to prove the distance formula. It turns out that the same formula is valid wherever the two points P_1 and P_2 may lie. Note also that since $(x_1 - x_2)^2 = (x_2 - x_1)^2$ and $(y_1 - y_2)^2 = (y_2 - y_1)^2$, it makes no difference which point is P_1 and which is P_2.

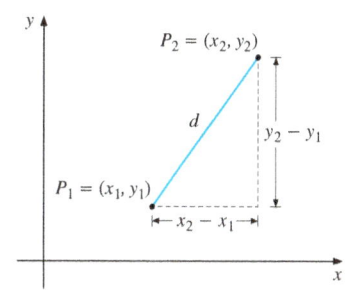

Figure 5.5.1 Distance between two general points P_1 and P_2

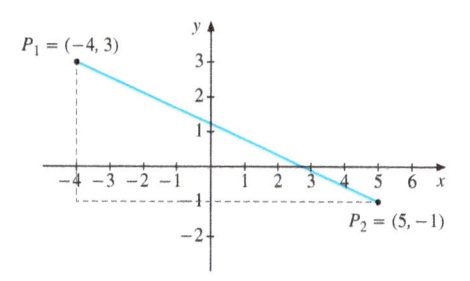

Figure 5.5.2 Distance between the two points $(-4, 3)$ and $(5, -1)$

Some find formula (5.5.1) hard to grasp. It may help to express it entirely in words. It tells us that we can find the distance between two points in the plane as follows: *First, take the difference between the two x-coordinates and square what you get. Second, do the same with the y-coordinates. Then add the two results. Finally, take the square root.*

EXAMPLE 5.5.1 Find the distance d between $P_1 = (-4, 3)$ and $P_2 = (5, -1)$.

Solution: See Fig. 5.5.2 for an illustration. Using (5.5.1) with $x_1 = -4$, $y_1 = 3$ and $x_2 = 5$, $y_2 = -1$, we have

$$d = \sqrt{(5-(-4))^2 + (-1-3)^2} = \sqrt{9^2 + (-4)^2} = \sqrt{81 + 16} = \sqrt{97} \approx 9.85$$

Circles

Let (a, b) be a point in the plane. *The circle with radius r and centre at (a, b) is the set of all points (x, y) whose distance from (a, b) is equal to r.* Applying the distance formula to the typical point (x, y) on the circle shown in Fig. 5.5.3 gives the equation

$$\sqrt{(x-a)^2 + (y-b)^2} = r$$

Squaring each side yields:

EQUATION OF A CIRCLE

The equation of a circle with centre at (a, b) and radius r is

$$(x-a)^2 + (y-b)^2 = r^2 \tag{5.5.2}$$

A graph of Eq. (5.5.2) is shown in Fig. 5.5.3. Note that if we let $a = b = 0$ and $r = 4$, then (5.5.2) reduces to $x^2 + y^2 = 16$. This is the equation of a circle with centre at $(0, 0)$ and radius 4, as shown in Fig. 5.4.2.

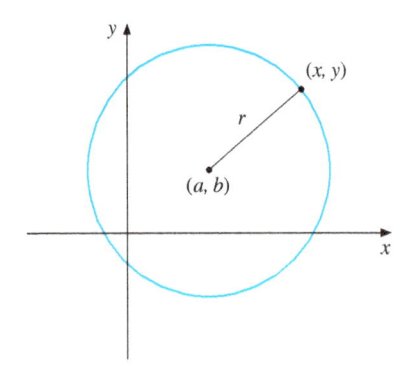

Figure 5.5.3 Circle with centre at (a, b) and radius r

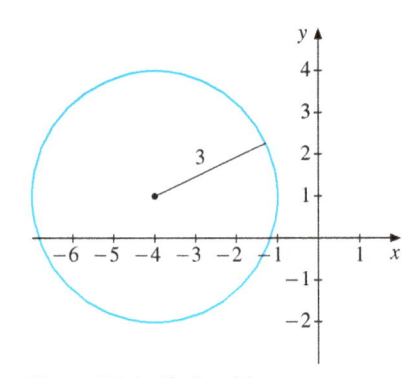

Figure 5.5.4 Circle with centre at $(-4, 1)$ and radius 3

EXAMPLE 5.5.2   Find the equation of the circle with centre at $(-4, 1)$ and radius 3.

Solution: See Fig. 5.5.4. Here $a = -4$, $b = 1$, and $r = 3$. So according to (5.5.2), the equation for the circle is

$$(x + 4)^2 + (y - 1)^2 = 9 \qquad (*)$$

Expanding the squares gives $x^2 + 8x + 16 + y^2 - 2y + 1 = 9$. Collecting terms then gives

$$x^2 + y^2 + 8x - 2y + 8 = 0 \qquad (**)$$

Equation $(**)$ has the disadvantage that we cannot immediately read off the centre and radius of the circle. If we do start with equation $(**)$, however, the method of "completing the squares" allows us to deduce $(*)$, as shown in Exercise 5.

Ellipses and Hyperbolas

All the planets, including the Earth, move around the Sun in orbits that are approximately elliptical. This makes ellipses a very important type of curve in physics and astronomy. Occasionally, ellipses also appear in economics and statistics.

The simplest type of ellipse has the equation

$$\frac{(x - x_0)^2}{a^2} + \frac{(y - y_0)^2}{b^2} = 1 \qquad (5.5.3)$$

This ellipse has centre at (x_0, y_0). Its graph is shown in Fig. 5.5.5. Note that when $a = b$, the ellipse degenerates into a circle whose radius is $r = a = b$.

Changing the plus sign in Eq. (5.5.3) to a minus gives a different kind of curve, called a *hyperbola*. Figures 5.5.6 and 5.5.7 show the respective graphs of the two hyperbolas

$$\frac{(x - x_0)^2}{a^2} - \frac{(y - y_0)^2}{b^2} = +1 \quad \text{and} \quad \frac{(x - x_0)^2}{a^2} - \frac{(y - y_0)^2}{b^2} = -1 \qquad (5.5.4)$$

Each of these two figures also contains two dashed lines through the centre (a, b). These lines are the *asymptotes* which, by definition, result from rotating them about the centre until they get as close as possible to the hyperbola without ever quite meeting it. These asymptotes are the same pair of lines in each figure. Their equations are $y - y_0 = \pm (b/a)(x - x_0)$.

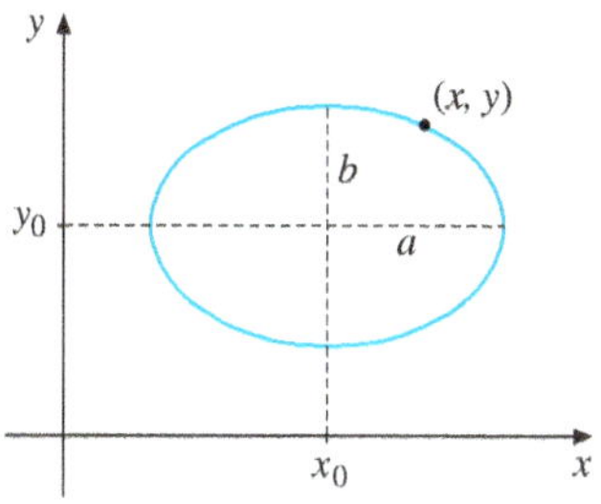

Figure 5.5.5 Ellipse 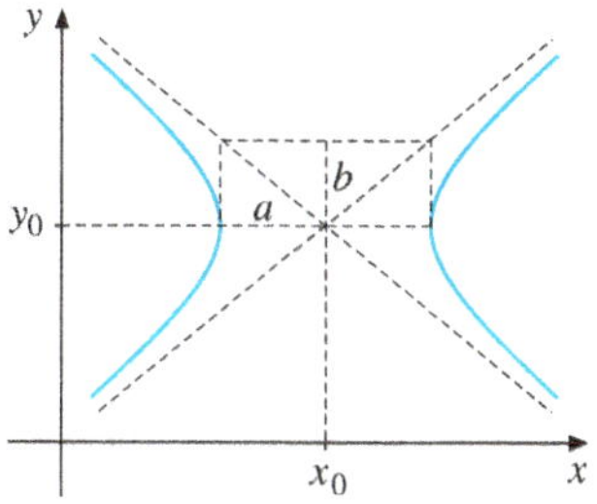   **Figure 5.5.6** Hyperbola 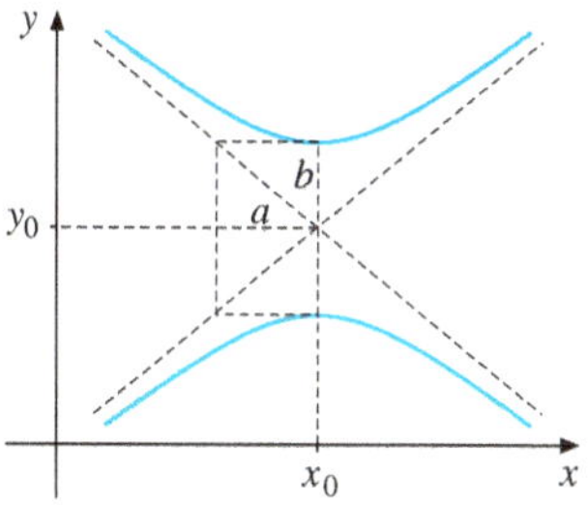   **Figure 5.5.7** Hyperbola

We end this section by considering the general quadratic equation

$$Ax^2 + Bxy + Cy^2 + Dx + Ey + F = 0 \qquad (5.5.5)$$

where A, B, and C are not all 0. We note that its graph has one of the following three shapes:

(i) If $4AC > B^2$, either an ellipse (possibly a circle), or a single point, or empty.

(ii) If $4AC = B^2$, either a parabola, or one line or two parallel lines, or empty.

(iii) If $4AC < B^2$, either a hyperbola, or two intersecting lines.

EXERCISES FOR SECTION 5.5

1. Determine the distances between the following pairs of points:

    (a) $(1, 3)$ and $(2, 4)$
    (b) $(-1, 2)$ and $(-3, 3)$
    (c) $(3/2, -2)$ and $(-5, 1)$
    (d) (x, y) and $(2x, y+3)$
    (e) (a, b) and $(-a, b)$
    (f) $(a, 3)$ and $(2+a, 5)$

2. The distance between $(2, 4)$ and $(5, y)$ is $\sqrt{13}$. Find y, and explain geometrically why there must be two values of y.

3. Find the distances between each pair of points:

    (a) $(3.998, 2.114)$ and $(1.130, -2.416)$;
    (b) $(\pi, 2\pi)$ and $(-\pi, 1)$.

4. Find the equations of: (a) The circle with centre at $(2, 3)$ and radius 4. (b) The circle with centre at $(2, 5)$ and one point at $(-1, 3)$.

5. To show that the graph of $x^2 + y^2 - 10x + 14y + 58 = 0$ is a circle, we can argue like this: First rearrange the equation to read $(x^2 - 10x) + (y^2 + 14y) = -58$. Completing the two squares gives: $(x^2 - 10x + 5^2) + (y^2 + 14y + 7^2) = -58 + 5^2 + 7^2 = 16$. Thus the equation becomes

$$(x-5)^2 + (y+7)^2 = 16$$

whose graph is a circle with centre $(5, -7)$ and radius $\sqrt{16} = 4$. Use this method to find the centre and the radius of the two circles with equations:

(a) $x^2 + y^2 + 10x - 6y + 30 = 0$
(b) $3x^2 + 3y^2 + 18x - 24y = -39$

6. Prove that if the distance from a point (x, y) to the point $(-2, 0)$ is twice the distance from (x, y) to $(4, 0)$, then (x, y) must lie on the circle with centre $(6, 0)$ and radius 4.

7. In Example 4.7.7 we considered the function $y = (ax + b)/(cx + d)$, and we claimed that for $c \neq 0$ the graph was a hyperbola. See how this accords with the classification (i) to (iii) given after Eq. (5.5.5).

SM 8. [HARDER] Consider the equation $x^2 + y^2 + Ax + By + C = 0$, where A, B, and C are constants. Show that its graph is a circle if $A^2 + B^2 > 4C$. Use the method of Exercise 5 to find its centre and radius. What happens if $A^2 + B^2 \leq 4C$?

SM 9. [HARDER] Consider Eq. (5.5.5) in the case when $A > 0$ and $D = E = 0$. Use the method of completing the square in order to investigate the possible shapes of its graph.

5.6 General Functions

So far we have studied functions of one variable. These are functions whose domain is a set of real numbers, and whose range is also a set of real numbers. Yet a realistic description of many economic phenomena requires considering a large number of variables simultaneously. For example, the demand for a good like butter is a function of several variables such as the price of the good, and the prices of complements like bread, as well as substitutes like olive oil or margarine. It can also depend on consumers' incomes, their doctors' advice, how many are vegan, and so on.

Actually, you have probably already seen many special functions of several variables. Consider, for instance, the formula $V = \pi r^2 h$ for the volume V of a circular cylinder with base radius r and height h.[8] This formula defines a function of two variables. We can change either one of these two variables without affecting the value of the other. Indeed, for each pair of positive numbers (r, h), there is a definite value for the volume V. To emphasize that V depends on the values of both r and h, we write

$$V(r, h) = \pi r^2 h$$

For $r = 2$ and $h = 3$, we obtain $V(2, 3) = 12\pi$, whereas $r = 3$ and $h = 2$ give $V(3, 2) = 18\pi$. Also, $r = 1$ and $h = 1/\pi$ give $V(1, 1/\pi) = 1$. Note in particular that $V(2, 3) \neq V(3, 2)$.

In some abstract economic models, it may be enough to know that there is some functional relationship between variables, without specifying the dependence more closely. For instance, suppose a market sells three commodities whose prices per unit are respectively p, q, and r. Then economists generally assume that the demand for one of the commodities by an individual with income m is given by a function $f(p, q, r, m)$ of four variables, without necessarily specifying the precise form of that function.

---

[8] Of course, in this case π denotes the mathematical constant $\pi \approx 3.14159$.

An extensive discussion of functions of several variables begins in Chapter 14. This section introduces an even more general type of function. This concept of function is fundamentally important in practically every area of pure and applied mathematics, including mathematics applied to economics. Here is the general definition:

FUNCTION

A *function from A to B* is a rule which specifies, for each element in the set A, one and only one element in the set B.

The following example illustrates how very wide this concept of a function can be.

EXAMPLE 5.6.1

(a) The function that specifies the area of each triangle in a plane.

(b) The function that determines the social security number, or other identification number, of each taxpayer.

(c) The function that for each point P in a horizontal plane determines the point lying 3 units above P.

(d) Let A be the set of possible actions that a person can choose in a certain situation. Suppose that every action a in A produces a certain result (such as profit) $\varphi(a)$. In this way, we have defined a function φ with domain A.

If we denote the function by f, the set A on which it is defined is called its *domain*. The other set B that contains the function value is called its *target set* or its *codomain*. This generalizes the definitions given in Section 4.2: the two sets A and B need not consist of numbers, but can be sets of arbitrary elements. In the end, the definition of a function requires three objects to be specified: (i) a domain, A; (ii) a target set, B; and (iii) a rule that assigns a *unique* element in B to *each* element in A.[9]

An important requirement in the definition of a function is that to each element in the domain A, there corresponds a *unique* element in the target B. For example, it is meaningful to talk about the function that, for each child, assigns the mother who gave birth to that child. On the other hand, the rule that assigns the aunt to each child does not, in general, define a function, because many children have more than one aunt.

To test your understanding of these ideas, explain why the following rule, as opposed to the one in Example 5.6.1(c), does not define a function: "to any point P in the plane, assign a point that lies 3 units away from P".

If f is a function with domain A and target B, we often say that f is a *function from A to B*, and write $f : A \to B$. The functional relationship is often represented as in Fig. 5.6.1.

---

[9] Nevertheless, in many cases, we refrain from specifying the sets A and/or B explicitly when the context makes it obvious what these two sets are.

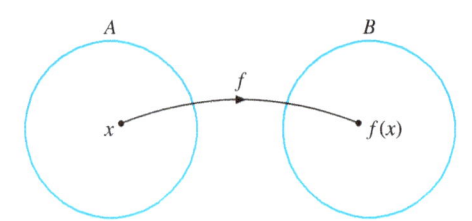

Figure 5.6.1 A function from A to B

Other words that are sometimes used instead of "function" include *transformation* and *map* or *mapping*. Sometimes the notation $x \mapsto f(x)$ is used to indicate a function that maps each point x of the domain A to a unique point $f(x)$ of the target B.[10]

The particular value $f(x)$ is often called the *image* of the element x by the function f. The set of all elements in B that are the image of at least one element in A is called the *range* of the function. Thus, the range is a subset of the target. If we denote the range of f by R_f, then $R_f = \{f(x) : x \in A\}$. This is also written as $f(A)$. The range of the function in Example 5.6.1(a) is the set of all positive numbers. In Example 5.6.1 (c), the range is the (whole) horizontal plane that results from shifting up the original plane by 3 units.

The definition of a function requires that only *one* element in B be assigned to each element in A. However, different elements in A might be mapped to the same element in B. In Example 5.6.1(a), for instance, many different triangles have the same area. If each element of B is the image of at most one element in A, the function f is called *one-to-one*. Otherwise, if one or more elements of B are the images of more than one element in A, the function f is many-to-one.[11]

The social security function in Example 5.6.1(b) is one-to-one, because two different taxpayers should always have different social security numbers. Can you explain why the function defined in Example 5.6.1(c) is also one-to-one, whereas the function that assigns to each child his or her mother is not?

Inverse Functions

The definition of inverse function in Section 5.3 can easily be extended to general functions. Suppose f is a one-to-one function from a set A to a set B, and assume that the range of f is all of B. We can then define a function g from B to A by the following obvious rule: Assign to each element v of B the one and only element $u = g(v)$ of A that f maps to v—that is, the u satisfying $v = f(u)$. Because f is one-to-one, there can be only one u in A such that $v = f(u)$. So g is a function whose domain is B, whereas its target and range are both equal to A. The function g is called the *inverse function* of f. For instance, the inverse of the social security function mentioned in Example 5.6.1(b) is the function that, to each social security number in its range, assigns the unique person who carries that number.

---

[10] The even fuller notation $A \ni x \mapsto f(x) \in B$ also makes explicit both the domain and codomain of f.

[11] If a relation is one-to-many, it is not even a function.

EXERCISES FOR SECTION 5.6

(SM) 1. Which of the following rules define functions?

(a) The rule that assigns to each person in a classroom his or her height.

(b) The rule that assigns to each mother her youngest surviving child.

(c) The rule that assigns the perimeter of a rectangle to its area.

(d) The rule that assigns the surface area of a spherical ball to its volume.

(e) The rule that assigns the pair of numbers $(x + 3, y)$ to the pair of numbers (x, y).

2. Determine which of the functions defined in Exercise 1 are one-to-one, and which then have an inverse. Determine each inverse when it exists.

REVIEW EXERCISES

1. Use Figs 4.3.5 to 4.3.10 and the rules for shifting graphs to sketch a graph for each of the following functions:

(a) $y = |x| + 1$
(b) $y = |x + 3|$
(c) $y = 3 - |x + 1|$

2. If $f(x) = x^3 - 2$ and $g(x) = (1 - x)x^2$, evaluate the following expressions:

(a) $(f + g)(x)$
(b) $(f - g)(x)$
(c) $(fg)(x)$
(d) $(f/g)(x)$
(e) $f(g(1))$
(f) $g(f(1))$

3. Consider the demand and supply curves $D = 150 - \frac{1}{2}P$ and $S = 20 + 2P$, where the price P is measured in dollars.

(a) Find the equilibrium price P^* and the corresponding equilibrium quantity Q^*.

(b) Suppose a tax of $2 per unit is imposed on the producer's output. How will this influence the equilibrium price?

(c) Compute the total revenue obtained by the producer before the tax is imposed (R^*) and after ($\widehat{R}$).

4. Demand D as a function of price P is given by $D = \frac{32}{5} - \frac{3}{10}P$. Solve the equation for P and find the inverse demand function.[12]

5. The demand D for a product as a function of the price P is given by $D = 120 - 5P$. Solve the equation for P and so find the inverse demand function.

6. Find the inverses of the functions given by the formulas:

(a) $y = 100 - 2x$
(b) $y = 2x^5$
(c) $y = 5e^{3x-2}$

---

[12] See Exercise 4.2.7 for an economic interpretation.

178 CHAPTER 5 / PROPERTIES OF FUNCTIONS

SM **7.** The following two functions are both strictly increasing in their domains. Find for each the domain of its inverse, as well as a formula for its inverse that uses x as the free variable.

(a) $f(x) = 3 + \ln(e^x - 2)$, defined on the domain $x \in (\ln 2, \infty)$;

(b) $f(x) = \dfrac{a}{e^{-\lambda x} + a}$, where a and λ are positive, defined on the domain $x \in (-\infty, \infty)$.

8. Determine the distances between the following pairs of points:

(a) $(2, 3)$ and $(5, 5)$; (b) $(-4, 4)$ and $(-3, 8)$; (c) $(2a, 3b)$ and $(2 - a, 3b)$.

9. Find the equations of the circles with:

(a) centre at $(2, -3)$ and radius 5; (b) centre at $(-2, 2)$ and passing through $(-10, 1)$.

10. A point P moves in the plane so that it is always equidistant between the two points $A = (3, 2)$ and $B = (5, -4)$. Find a simple equation that the coordinates (x, y) of P must satisfy. (*Hint:* Compute the square of the distance from P to the points A and B, respectively.)

11. Each person in a team is known to have red blood cells that belong to one and only one of four blood groups denoted A, B, AB, and O. Consider the function that assigns each person in the team to his or her blood group. Can this function be one-to-one if the team consists of five people?

II

SINGLE VARIABLE CALCULUS

6 DIFFERENTIATION

To think of [differential calculus] merely as a more advanced technique is to miss its real content. In it, mathematics becomes a dynamic mode of thought, and that is a major mental step in the ascent of man.
—Jacob Bronowski (1973)

An important topic in many scientific disciplines, including economics, is the study of how quickly quantities change over time. In order to compute the future position of a planet, or predict the population growth of a biological species, or estimate the future demand for a commodity, scientists need information about rates of change.

The fundamental and central concept that mathematicians use to describe the rate of change of a function is the derivative. This chapter defines the derivative of a function and presents some of the important rules for calculating it.

Isaac Newton (England, 1642–1727) and Gottfried Wilhelm Leibniz (Germany, 1646–1716) discovered most of these general rules independently of each other. Their discoveries initiated differential calculus, which has been an essential foundation for modern science. Differential calculus has also been vitally important in developing much of modern economic science.

6.1 Slopes of Curves

When studying the graph of a function, we would like to have a precise measure of its steepness at any of its points. We know that for the function $y = px + q$, its graph is a straight line with constant slope p. If p is large and positive, then the line rises steeply from left to right; if p is large and negative,[1] the line falls steeply. But when the graph of an arbitrary function f is not linear, how steep is it?

Given any point P on the graph of a function, or on any other curve in the xy-plane, a tangent to the curve at P is a straight line which just touches the curve at P. So a natural answer is to define the steepness or *slope* of a curve at a point P as the slope of its tangent at P.

---

[1] Note: By a large negative number, we mean a negative number whose absolute value is large. That is the number is somehow "close" to $-\infty$.

Consider the curve labelled $y = f(x)$ in Fig. 6.1.1, and the point P with coordinates $(a, f(a))$. The straight line labelled L is the tangent at P. Because this line has slope $\frac{1}{2}$, the steepness of the curve at point P is seen to be $\frac{1}{2}$.

The slope of the tangent to the graph at P is called the *derivative* of $f(x)$ at $x = a$. The usual notation for this number is $f'(a)$, pronounced as "*f prime a*". In Fig. 6.1.1, we have $f'(a) = \frac{1}{2}$. To summarize:

DERIVATIVE

$f'(a)$ is the slope of the tangent to the curve $y = f(x)$ at the point $(a, f(a))$.

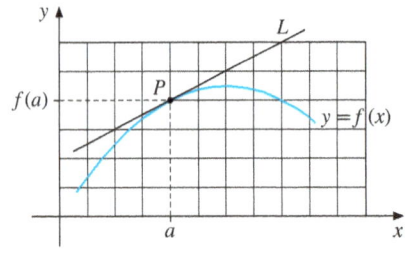

Figure 6.1.1 $f'(a) = \frac{1}{2}$

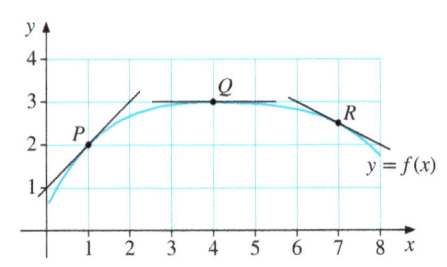

Figure 6.1.2 Example 6.1.1

An important note of caution is that when defining the derivative of a function at a particular point, we refer to *the* tangent line. Implicitly, we are assuming that there is *only one* tangent to the curve at that point. If the curve has a "kink" at point $(a, f(a))$, there are multiple lines that touch the curve only at that point and can thus serve as alternative tangent lines. When this happens, we *do not* define the derivative of the function at $x = a$; instead we say that $f'(a)$ does not exist.

EXAMPLE 6.1.1 Find $f'(1), f'(4),$ and $f'(7)$ for the function whose graph is shown in Fig. 6.1.2.

Solution: At the point $P = (1, 2)$, the tangent goes through the point $(0, 1)$, so it has slope 1. At the point $Q = (4, 2\frac{1}{2})$ the tangent is horizontal, and so has slope 0. At the point $R = (7, 3\frac{1}{2})$, the tangent goes through $(8, 3)$, and so has slope $-1/2$. It follows that $f'(1) = 1$, $f'(4) = 0$, and $f'(7) = -1/2$.

EXERCISES FOR SECTION 6.1

1. Figure 6.1.3 shows the graph of a function f. Find the values of $f(3)$ and $f'(3)$.

2. Figure 6.1.4 shows the graph of a function g. Find the values of $g(5)$ and $g'(5)$.

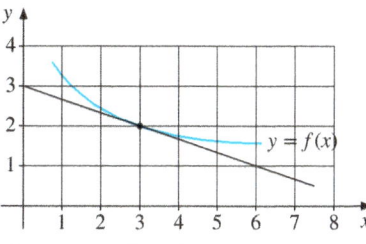

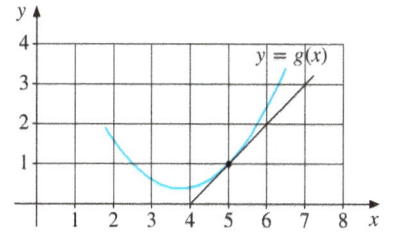

Figure 6.1.3 Exercise 1

Figure 6.1.4 Exercise 2

6.2 Tangents and Derivatives

The previous section gave a rather vague geometric definition of the tangent to a curve at a point. All we said is that it is a straight line which just touches the curve at that point. In future we will need a more precise and formal definition of the same concept, which we now provide.

The idea behind the geometric definition is easy to understand. Consider Fig. 6.2.1, in which P is a point on a curve in the xy-plane. Furthermore PT indicates the straight line that forms the tangent to the curve at P. In case the curve is the graph of a function, in order to determine the derivative at P, we need to find the slope of the tangent PT.

To find this slope, start by taking any other point Q on the curve. The entire straight line through P and Q is called a *secant* because it intersects the curve in at least two points, so the line can be used to cut off all the curve that does not lie between those two points. Now suppose we keep P fixed, but let the other point Q move along the curve toward P. Then the secant line PQ will rotate around P, as indicated in Fig. 6.2.2. As the line rotates, the difference between the slopes of the two lines PQ and PT in the figure shrinks steadily to zero. When the difference in slopes does reach zero, the secant line PQ will have reached the *tangent line PT*. The slope of this tangent line must therefore be the limiting value of the slope of PQ.

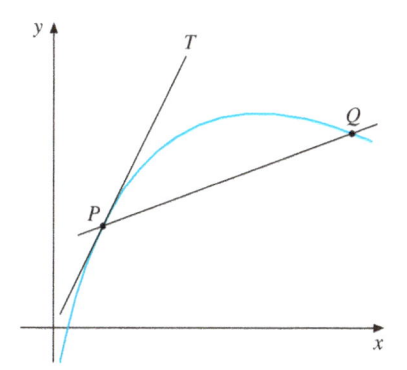

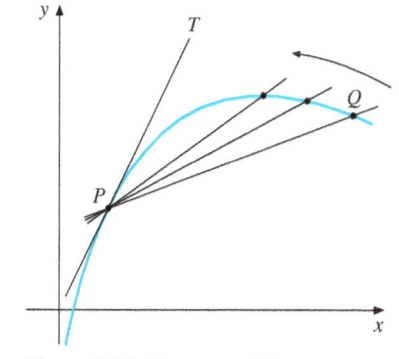

Figure 6.2.1 A secant

Figure 6.2.2 Secants and the tangent

Now suppose that the curve in Fig. 6.2.1 is the graph of a function f. Figure 6.2.3 starts by reproducing the curve, the points P and Q, and the tangent PT in Fig. 6.2.1. Point P

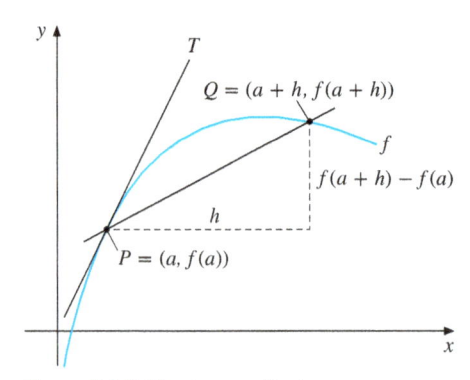

Figure 6.2.3 Newton quotient

in Fig. 6.2.3 has coordinates $(a, f(a))$. Point Q is also on the graph of f. Suppose that the x-coordinate of Q is $a + h$, where $h \neq 0$. Because Q lies on the graph of f, its y-coordinate is $f(a + h)$. Hence, the point Q has coordinates $(a + h, f(a + h))$. Using Eq. (4.4.1), the slope of the secant PQ is, therefore,

$$\frac{f(a+h) - f(a)}{h} \tag{6.2.1}$$

The fraction (6.2.1) is called the *Newton quotient* of f (at a).

We are interested in what happens to this Newton quotient as h gets close to 0, and so as Q moves close to P. Note that we cannot simply put $h = 0$ in formula (6.2.1), because h is the denominator of the quotient, which is therefore undefined. In fact both numerator and denominator are 0, so the quotient is " 0/0 ", which is not any real number.

After this false start, we focus instead on the fact that the Newton quotient is the slope of the secant line PQ. Moreover, this slope approaches that of the tangent PT as Q approaches P, which happens as h approaches 0. Expressed in mathematical language, we consider the limit of (6.2.1) as h tends to 0, and so as Q tends to P. In fact, we *define* the slope of the tangent at P as the limit of the slope of the secant PQ as h tends to 0. Now, mathematicians use the abbreviated notation $\lim_{h \to 0}$ to indicate "the limit as h tends to zero" of any following expression involving h. This leads us to the following definition:

DEFINITION OF DERIVATIVE

The derivative of function f at point a, denoted by $f'(a)$, is

$$f'(a) = \lim_{h \to 0} \frac{f(a+h) - f(a)}{h} \tag{6.2.2}$$

The number $f'(a)$ gives the slope of the tangent to the curve $y = f(x)$ at the point $(a, f(a))$. By the point–slope formula, the equation for a straight line passing through (x_1, y_1) and having slope b is given by $y = y_1 + b(x - x_1)$. So we obtain:

TANGENT

Provided that the derivative $f'(a)$ given by (6.2.2) exists, there is a unique tangent to the graph of $y = f(x)$ at the point $(a, f(a))$ whose equation is

$$y = f(a) + f'(a)(x - a) \qquad (6.2.3)$$

So far the concept of a limit in the definition of $f'(a)$ is somewhat imprecise. Section 6.5 will discuss this concept in more detail. Because it is relatively complicated, we rely on intuition for the time being. Consider the following simple example.

EXAMPLE 6.2.1 Let $f(x) = x^2$.

(a) Use (6.2.2) to compute $f'(a)$.

(b) Find in particular $f'(1/2)$ and $f'(-1)$.

(c) Give graphical illustrations, and find the equation for the tangent at each of the two points $(1/2, 1/4)$ and $(-1, 1)$.

Solution:

(a) For $f(x) = x^2$, we have $f(a+h) = (a+h)^2 = a^2 + 2ah + h^2$, and so

$$f(a+h) - f(a) = (a^2 + 2ah + h^2) - a^2 = 2ah + h^2$$

Hence, for all $h \neq 0$, we obtain

$$\frac{f(a+h) - f(a)}{h} = \frac{2ah + h^2}{h} = \frac{h(2a+h)}{h} = 2a + h \qquad (*)$$

where the last equality holds because we can cancel h whenever $h \neq 0$. But as h tends to 0, so $2a + h$ obviously tends to $2a$. Thus, we can write

$$f'(a) = \lim_{h \to 0} \frac{f(a+h) - f(a)}{h} = \lim_{h \to 0} (2a + h) = 2a$$

This shows that for the function $f(x) = x^2$, one has $f'(a) = 2a$.

(b) For $a = 1/2$, we obtain $f'(1/2) = 2 \cdot 1/2 = 1$. Similarly, $f'(-1) = 2 \cdot (-1) = -2$.

(c) Figure 6.2.4 provides a graphical illustration of (*). In Fig. 6.2.5, we have drawn the tangents to the curve $y = x^2$ corresponding to $a = 1/2$ and $a = -1$. At $a = 1/2$, we have $f(a) = (1/2)^2 = 1/4$ and $f'(1/2) = 1$. According to (2), the equation of the tangent is $y - 1/4 = 1 \cdot (x - 1/2)$ or $y = x - 1/4$.[2] Note that the formula $f'(a) = 2a$ shows that $f'(a) < 0$ when $a < 0$, and $f'(a) > 0$ when $a > 0$. Does this agree with the graph?

If f is a relatively simple function, we can find $f'(a)$ by using the recipe set out below.

---

[2] Can you show that the other tangent drawn in Fig. 6.2.5 has the equation $y = -2x - 1$?

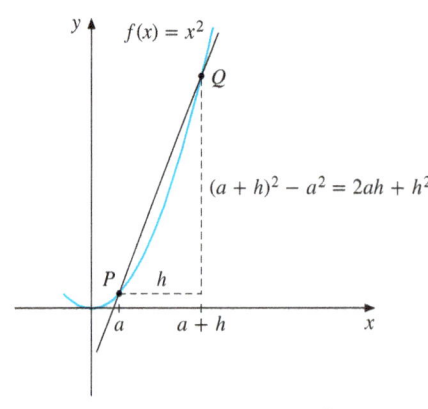

Figure 6.2.4 A secant of $f(x) = x^2$

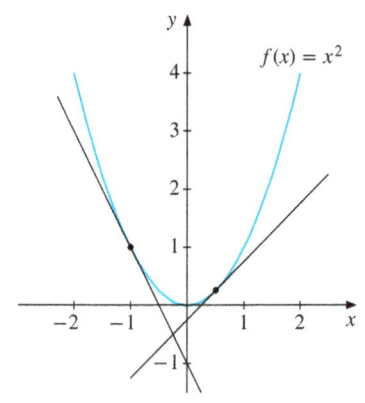

Figure 6.2.5 Tangents of $f(x) = x^2$

COMPUTING THE DERIVATIVE

In order to compute the derivative $f'(a)$ of f at a:

(i) Add h to a and compute $f(a+h)$.

(ii) Compute the corresponding change in the function value: $f(a+h) - f(a)$.

(iii) For $h \neq 0$, form the Newton quotient (6.2.1).

(iv) Simplify the fraction in step (iii) as much as possible; then, wherever possible, cancel h from both numerator and denominator to simplify the Newton quotient.

(v) Then $f'(a)$ is the limit, as h tends to 0, of the simplified Newton quotient.

Let us apply this recipe to another example.

EXAMPLE 6.2.2   Compute $f'(a)$ when $f(x) = x^3$.

Solution: We follow the recipe step by step:

(i) $f(a+h) = (a+h)^3 = a^3 + 3a^2h + 3ah^2 + h^3$

(ii) $f(a+h) - f(a) = (a^3 + 3a^2h + 3ah^2 + h^3) - a^3 = 3a^2h + 3ah^2 + h^3$

(iii)–(iv) $\dfrac{f(a+h) - f(a)}{h} = \dfrac{3a^2h + 3ah^2 + h^3}{h} = 3a^2 + 3ah + h^2$

(v) As h tends to 0, so $3ah + h^2$ also tends to 0; hence, the entire expression $3a^2 + 3ah + h^2$ tends to $3a^2$. Therefore, $f'(a) = 3a^2$.

We have thus shown that the graph of the function $f(x) = x^3$ at the point $x = a$ has a tangent with slope $3a^2$. Note that $f'(a) = 3a^2 > 0$ when $a \neq 0$, and $f'(0) = 0$. The tangent points upwards to the right for all $a \neq 0$, and is horizontal at the origin. You should look at the graph of $f(x) = x^3$ in Fig. 4.3.7 to confirm this behaviour.

The recipe works well for simple functions like those in Examples 6.2.1 and 6.2.2. But for more complicated functions such as $f(x) = \sqrt{3x^2 + x + 1}$ it is unnecessarily cumbersome. The powerful rules we will explain in Section 6.6 allow the derivatives of even quite complicated functions to be found quite easily. Understanding these rules, however, relies on the more precise concept of limit that we will provide in Section 6.5.

On Notation

We showed in Example 6.2.1 that if $f(x) = x^2$, then for every a we have $f'(a) = 2a$. We frequently use x as the symbol for a quantity that can take any value, so we write $f'(x) = 2x$. Using this notation, our results from Examples 6.2.1 and 6.2.2 can be expressed as follows:

$$f(x) = x^2 \Rightarrow f'(x) = 2x \tag{6.2.4}$$

$$f(x) = x^3 \Rightarrow f'(x) = 3x^2 \tag{6.2.5}$$

The result in (6.2.4) is a special case of the following rule, which you are asked to show in Exercise 7: given constants a, b, and c,

$$f(x) = ax^2 + bx + c \Rightarrow f'(x) = 2ax + b \tag{6.2.6}$$

Here are some applications of (6.2.6):

$$f(x) = 3x^2 + 2x + 5 \Rightarrow f'(x) = 2 \cdot 3x + 2 = 6x + 2$$

$$f(x) = -16 + \tfrac{1}{2}x - \tfrac{1}{16}x^2 \Rightarrow f'(x) = \tfrac{1}{2} - \tfrac{1}{8}x$$

$$f(x) = (x - p)^2 = x^2 - 2px + p^2 \Rightarrow f'(x) = 2x - 2p$$

where p is any constant. If we use y to denote the typical value of the function $y = f(x)$, we often denote the derivative simply by y'. We can then write

$$y = x^3 \Rightarrow y' = 3x^2$$

Several other forms of notation for the derivative are often used in mathematics and its applications. One of them, originally due to Leibniz, is called the *differential notation*. If $y = f(x)$, then in place of $f'(x)$, we write

$$\frac{dy}{dx}, \quad \frac{df(x)}{dx}, \quad \text{or} \quad \frac{d}{dx}f(x)$$

For instance, if $y = x^2$, then

$$\frac{dy}{dx} = 2x \quad \text{or} \quad \frac{d}{dx}(x^2) = 2x$$

We can think of the symbol "d/dx" as an instruction to differentiate the expression that follows, taken as a function of x.[3] In mathematical jargon, the instruction "d/dx" indicates

---

[3] At this point, we will only think of the symbol "dy/dx" as meaning $f'(x)$. We will not consider how it might relate to the quotient $dy \div dx$. Section 7.4 will introduce the concept of *differential* of a function, which will further clarify the notation.

"differentiate with respect to x". It occurs so often in mathematics that it has become standard to use *w.r.t.* as an abbreviation for *with respect to*.

When we use letters other than f, x, and y, the notation for the derivative changes accordingly. For example:

$$P(t) = t^2 \Rightarrow P'(t) = 2t, \quad Y = K^3 \Rightarrow Y' = 3K^2, \quad \text{and} \quad A = \pi r^2 \Rightarrow \frac{dA}{dr} = 2\pi r$$

EXERCISES FOR SECTION 6.2

1. Let $f(x) = 4x^2$. Show that $\dfrac{f(5+h) - f(5)}{h} = 40 + 4h$ for $h \neq 0$. Use this result to find $f'(5)$. Compare the answer with Eq. (6.2.6).

2. Let $f(x) = 3x^2 + 2x - 1$.
   (a) Show that $\dfrac{f(x+h) - f(x)}{h} = 6x + 2 + 3h$ for $h \neq 0$, and use this result to find $f'(x)$.
   (b) Find in particular $f'(0), f'(-2)$, and $f'(3)$. Find also the equation of the tangent to the graph at the point $(0, -1)$.

3. The demand function for a commodity with price P is given by the formula $D(P) = a - bP$. Use rule (6.2.6) to find $dD(P)/dP$.

4. The cost of producing x units of a commodity is given by the formula $C(x) = p + qx^2$. Use rule (6.2.6) to find $C'(x)$.[4]

5. For $f(x) = 1/x$, show that
$$\frac{f(x+h) - f(x)}{h} = -\frac{1}{x(x+h)}$$
and use this to show that $f(x) = x^{-1} \Rightarrow f'(x) = -x^{-2}$.

6. In each case below, find the slope of the tangent to the graph of f at the specified point:
   (a) $f(x) = 3x + 2$, at $(0, 2)$ (b) $f(x) = x^2 - 1$, at $(1, 0)$ (c) $f(x) = 2 + \dfrac{3}{x}$, at $(3, 3)$
   (d) $f(x) = x^3 - 2x$, at $(0, 0)$ (e) $f(x) = x + \dfrac{1}{x}$, at $(-1, -2)$ (f) $f(x) = x^4$, at $(1, 1)$

7. Let $f(x) = ax^2 + bx + c$.
   (a) Show that $[f(x+h) - f(x)]/h = 2ax + b + ah$. Use this to show that $f'(x) = 2ax + b$.
   (b) For what value of x is $f'(x) = 0$? Explain this result in the light of (4.6.3) and (4.6.4).

8. Figure 6.2.6 shows the graph of a function f. Determine the sign of the derivative $f'(x)$ for each of the four values a, b, c, and d of x.

---

[4] In Section 6.4, this derivative is interpreted as the *marginal cost*.

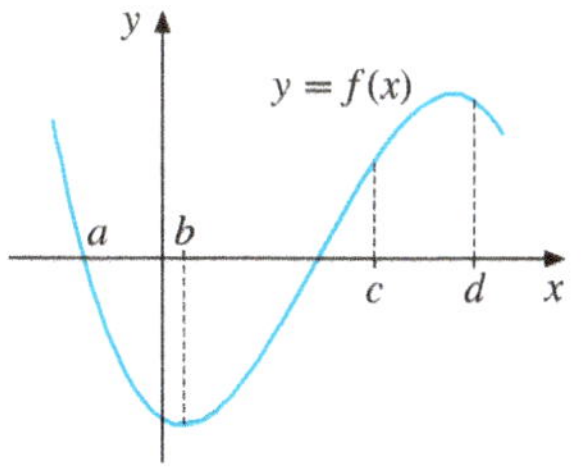

Figure 6.2.6 Exercise 8

⑨ **9.** Let $f(x) = \sqrt{x} = x^{1/2}$.

(a) Show that $(\sqrt{x+h} - \sqrt{x})(\sqrt{x+h} + \sqrt{x}) = h$.

(b) Use the result in part (a) to show that the Newton quotient of $f(x)$ is $1/(\sqrt{x+h} + \sqrt{x})$.

(c) Use the result in part (b) to show that for $x > 0$ one has $f'(x) = \dfrac{1}{2\sqrt{x}} = \dfrac{1}{2}x^{-1/2}$.

10. Let $f(x) = ax^3 + bx^2 + cx + d$.

(a) Show that the Newton quotient is $3ax^2 + 2bx + c + 3axh + ah^2 + bh$ for $h \neq 0$, and find $f'(x)$.

(b) Show that the result in part (a) generalizes Example 6.2.2 and Exercise 7.

11. [HARDER] Apply the results of Exercise 2.3.8 to prove first that

$$\left[(x+h)^{1/3} - x^{1/3}\right]\left[(x+h)^{2/3} + (x+h)^{1/3}x^{1/3} + x^{2/3}\right] = h$$

Then follow the argument used to solve Exercise 9 to show that $f(x) = x^{1/3} \Rightarrow f'(x) = \tfrac{1}{3}x^{-2/3}$.

6.3 Increasing and Decreasing Functions

The terms *increasing* and *decreasing* have been used previously to describe the behaviour of a function as we travel from *left to right* along its graph. In order to establish a definite terminology, we introduce the following definitions. We assume in every case that f is defined in an interval I and that x_1 and x_2 are numbers from that interval.

INCREASING AND DECREASING FUNCTIONS

(i) If $f(x_2) \geq f(x_1)$ whenever $x_2 > x_1$, then f is *increasing* in I.

(ii) If $f(x_2) > f(x_1)$ whenever $x_2 > x_1$, then f is *strictly increasing* in I.

(iii) If $f(x_2) \leq f(x_1)$ whenever $x_2 > x_1$, then f is *decreasing* in I.

(iv) If $f(x_2) < f(x_1)$ whenever $x_2 > x_1$, then f is *strictly decreasing* in I

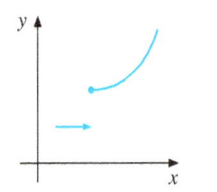

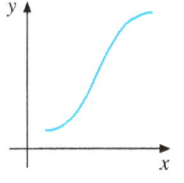

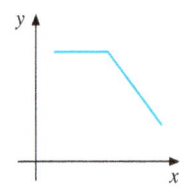

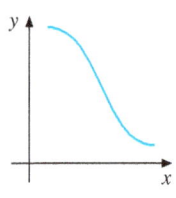

Figure 6.3.1 Increasing **Figure 6.3.2** Strictly increasing **Figure 6.3.3** Decreasing **Figure 6.3.4** Strictly decreasing

Figures 6.3.1–6.3.4 respectively illustrate these definitions. Note that we allow an increasing, or decreasing, function to have sections where the graph is horizontal. This does not quite agree with common language: few people would say that their salary increases when it stays constant! For this reason, sometimes an increasing function is called nondecreasing, and a decreasing function is called nonincreasing.

To find out where a function is (strictly) increasing or (strictly) decreasing using these definitions, we need to consider the sign of $f(x_2) - f(x_1)$ whenever $x_2 > x_1$. This is usually quite difficult to do directly by checking the values of $f(x)$ at different points x. Fortunately the sign of the derivative of a function provides a good test of whether it is increasing or decreasing:

$$f'(x) \geq 0 \text{ for all } x \text{ in the interval } I \iff f \text{ is increasing in } I \qquad (6.3.1)$$

$$f'(x) \leq 0 \text{ for all } x \text{ in the interval } I \iff f \text{ is decreasing in } I \qquad (6.3.2)$$

The fact that the derivative of a function equals the slope of the tangent to its graph makes the equivalences in (6.3.1) and (6.3.2) almost obvious. Here is another equally correct observation:

$$f'(x) = 0 \text{ for all } x \text{ in the interval } I \iff f \text{ is constant in } I \qquad (6.3.3)$$

Precise proofs of (6.3.1)–(6.3.3) rely on the mean value theorem, the subject of Section 9.4.

EXAMPLE 6.3.1   Use the result of Eq. (6.2.6) to find the derivative of $f(x) = \tfrac{1}{2}x^2 - 2$. Then examine where f is increasing/decreasing.

Solution: We find that $f'(x) = x$, which is nonnegative for $x \geq 0$, and nonpositive if $x \leq 0$. We conclude that f is increasing in $[0, \infty)$ and decreasing in $(-\infty, 0]$. See Fig. 6.3.5 to confirm this.

EXAMPLE 6.3.2   Examine where $f(x) = -\tfrac{1}{3}x^3 + 2x^2 - 3x + 1$ is increasing/decreasing. Use the result in Exercise 6.2.10 to find its derivative.

Solution: The formula in the exercise can be used with $a = -1/3$, $b = 2$, $c = -3$, and $d = 1$. Thus $f'(x) = -x^2 + 4x - 3$. Solving the equation $f'(x) = -x^2 + 4x - 3 = 0$ yields $x = 1$ and $x = 3$, and thus $f'(x) = -(x - 1)(x - 3) = (x - 1)(3 - x)$. A sign diagram for $(x - 1)(3 - x)$ reveals that $f'(x) = (x - 1)(3 - x)$ is nonnegative in the interval $[1, 3]$, but nonpositive in both $(-\infty, 1]$ and $[3, \infty)$.[5] We conclude that $f(x)$ is increasing in $[1, 3]$, but decreasing in both $(-\infty, 1]$ and $[3, \infty)$. See Fig. 6.3.6.

---

[5] See Example 2.8.1.

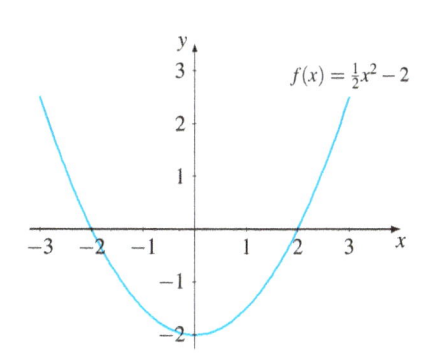

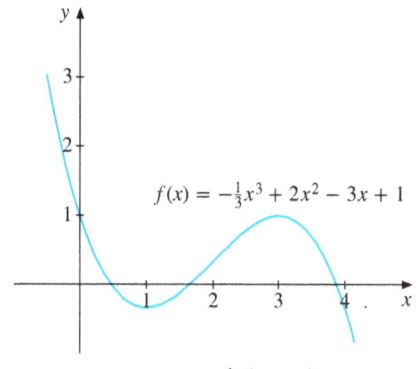

Figure 6.3.5 $f(x) = \frac{1}{2}x^2 - 2$

Figure 6.3.6 $f(x) = -\frac{1}{3}x^3 + 2x^2 - 3x + 1$

If $f'(x)$ is strictly positive in an interval, we would expect the function to be strictly increasing. Indeed,

$$f'(x) > 0 \text{ for all } x \text{ in the interval } I \implies f \text{ is strictly increasing in } I \quad (6.3.4)$$

$$f'(x) < 0 \text{ for all } x \text{ in the interval } I \implies f \text{ is strictly decreasing in } I \quad (6.3.5)$$

The implications in (6.3.4) and (6.3.5) only give *sufficient* conditions for f to be strictly increasing or decreasing. They cannot be reversed to give necessary conditions, yet the following statement is often seen: "Suppose that f is strictly increasing—that is, $f'(x) > 0$." The example $f(x) = x^3$ shows that the statement is wrong, since $f'(0) = 0$ although f is strictly increasing – see Exercise 3. A function, then, can be strictly increasing even though the derivative is 0 at certain points.[6]

EXERCISES FOR SECTION 6.3

1. Use Eqs (6.2.6), (6.3.1), and (6.3.2) to find the values of x at which $f(x) = x^2 - 4x + 3$ is increasing/decreasing. Compare with Fig. 4.3.3.

2. Use the result in Exercise 6.2.10 to examine where $f(x) = -x^3 + 4x^2 - x - 6$ is increasing/decreasing. Compare with Fig. 4.7.1

3. Show algebraically that $f(x) = x^3$ is strictly increasing by studying the sign of

$$x_2^3 - x_1^3 = (x_2 - x_1)(x_1^2 + x_1 x_2 + x_2^2) = (x_2 - x_1)\left[\left(x_1 + \tfrac{1}{2}x_2\right)^2 + \tfrac{3}{4}x_2^2\right]$$

---

[6] On the other hand, suppose that $f'(x) \geq 0$ for all x in I and $f'(x) = 0$ at only a finite number of points in I. Then $f'(x) > 0$ in each subinterval between any two adjacent zeros of $f'(x)$, and so f is strictly increasing on each such subinterval. It follows that f is strictly increasing on the whole interval.

6.4 Economic Applications

The derivative of a function at a particular point was defined as the slope of the tangent to its graph at that point. Economists interpret the derivative in many important ways, starting with the rate of change of an economic variable.

Suppose that a quantity y is related to a quantity x by $y = f(x)$. If x has the value a, then the value of the function is $f(a)$. Suppose that a is changed to $a + h$. The new value of y is $f(a + h)$, and the change in the value of the function when x is changed from a to $a + h$ is $f(a + h) - f(a)$. The change in y per unit change in x has a particular name; it is called the *average rate of change of f over the interval from a to $a + h$*. It is equal to

$$\frac{f(a+h) - f(a)}{h}$$

Note that this fraction is precisely the Newton quotient of f at a. Taking the limit as h tends to 0 gives the derivative of f at a, which we interpret as follows:

RATE OF CHANGE

The *rate of change of f at a* is $f'(a)$.

This very important concept appears whenever we study quantities that change. When time t is the independent variable, we often use the "dot notation" $\dot{x}$ to indicate the time derivative dx/dt of x w.r.t. t. For example, if $x(t) = t^2$, then $\dot{x}(t) = 2t$. We often refer to a time derivative like this as the *instantaneous* rate of change.

EXAMPLE 6.4.1 Let $N(t)$ be the number of individuals in the population of a species of animal at time t. If t increases to $t + s$, then the change in population is equal to $N(t + s) - N(t)$ individuals. Hence,

$$\frac{N(t+s) - N(t)}{s}$$

is *the average rate of change*. Taking the limit as s tends to 0 gives $\dot{N}(t) = dN/dt$ for *the instantaneous rate of change of population at time t*.

In Example 4.5.1, the formula $P = 5.1t + 606$ was used as an (inaccurate) estimate of Europe's population, in millions, at a date which comes t years after 1960. In this case, the rate of change is $dP/dt = 5.1$ million per year, the same for all t.

EXAMPLE 6.4.2 Let $K(t)$ be the capital stock in an economy at time t. The rate of change $\dot{K}(t)$ of $K(t)$ is called the *net rate of investment* at time t,[7] and is usually denoted by $I(t)$:

$$\dot{K}(t) = I(t) \tag{6.4.1}$$

---
[7] This differs from gross investment because some investment is needed to replace depreciated capital.

Sometimes we are interested in studying the proportion $f'(a)/f(a)$. This proportion can be interpreted as follows:

RELATIVE RATE OF CHANGE

The *relative rate of change* of f at a is $\dfrac{f'(a)}{f(a)}$.

EXAMPLE 6.4.3 As in Example 6.4.1, let $N(t)$ be the number of animals at time t. If t increases to $t + s$, then *the average relative rate of change* in this number equals

$$\frac{1}{N(t)} \frac{N(t+s) - N(t)}{s}$$

Taking the limit as $s \to 0$ gives $\dfrac{1}{N} \dot{N}(t) = \dfrac{1}{N} \dfrac{dN}{dt}$ for *the instantaneous relative rate of change* of the animal population at time t.

In economics, such relative rates of change are often seen. Sometimes they are called *proportional rates of change*. They are usually quoted in percentages per unit of time — for example, percentages per year.[8] Often we will describe a variable as increasing at, say, 3% a year if there is a relative rate of change of $3/100 = 0.03$ each year.

For the next example, note that it is common to denote a (small) change in a variable x, say, by Δx, where Δ is the upper-case Greek letter delta. Here Δx should be regarded as one symbol, not as the product of Δ and x.

EXAMPLE 6.4.4 Consider a firm producing some commodity in a given period, and let $C(x)$ denote its cost of producing x units. The derivative $C'(x)$ at x is called the *marginal cost* at x. According to the definition, it is equal to

$$C'(x) = \lim_{\Delta x \to 0} \frac{C(x + \Delta x) - C(x)}{\Delta x} \tag{6.4.2}$$

When Δx is small in absolute value, we obtain the approximation

$$C'(x) \approx \frac{C(x + \Delta x) - C(x)}{\Delta x} \tag{6.4.3}$$

The difference $\Delta C(x) = C(x + \Delta x) - C(x)$ is called the *incremental cost* of producing Δx units of extra output. For Δx small, a linear approximation to this incremental cost is $C'(x)\Delta x$, the product of the marginal cost and the change in output. This is true even when $\Delta x < 0$, signifying a decrease in output and, provided that $C'(x) > 0$, a lower cost.

Note that putting $\Delta x = 1$ in (6.4.3) makes marginal cost *approximately* equal to

$$C'(x) \approx C(x + 1) - C(x) \tag{6.4.4}$$

---

[8] Or per annum, for those who think Latin is still a useful language.

Marginal cost is then approximately equal to the *incremental cost* $C(x+1) - C(x)$, that is, the *additional cost of producing one more unit than x*. In elementary economics books marginal cost is often defined as the difference $C(x+1) - C(x)$ because more appropriate concepts from differential calculus are not available.

In this book, we will sometimes offer comparable economic interpretations that consider the change in a function when a variable x is increased by one unit; it would be more accurate to consider the change in the function per unit increase, for small increases. Here is an example.

EXAMPLE 6.4.5   Let $C(x)$ denote the cost in millions of dollars for removing $x\%$ of the pollution in a lake. Give an economic interpretation of the equality $C'(50) = 3$.

Solution: Because of the linear approximation $C(50 + \Delta x) - C(50) \approx C'(50)\Delta x$, the precise interpretation of $C'(50) = 3$ is that, for small changes in pollution that start at 50%, for each extra 1% of pollution that is removed, the extra cost is about 3 million dollars. Much less precisely, $C'(50) = 3$ means that it costs about 3 million dollars extra to remove 51% instead of 50% of the pollution.

Following these examples, economists often use the word "marginal" to indicate a derivative. To mention just two of many examples we shall encounter, the *marginal propensity to consume* is the derivative of the consumption function with respect to income; similarly, the *marginal product*, or *productivity*, of labour is the derivative of the production function with respect to labour input.

The concept is so important that it underlies most of our understanding of economics. For example, Adam Smith, seen by many as the founder of the science, struggled to understand why a non-essential commodity such as a diamond could be worth so much more than an essential one, such as water. Using marginal analysis, Carl Menger (1840–1921), Léon Walras (1834–1910), and Stanley Jevons (1835–1882) explained this seeming paradox: if offered a choice between *only* water or *only* diamonds, people would surely choose water, as it is essential; but, given the water and the diamonds a person already owns, they may value one *extra* glass of water very much less than one *extra* diamond. This fundamental understanding of optimal decisions led to the three economists to be considered founders of the "Marginalist" school of economic thought.

EXERCISES FOR SECTION 6.4

1. Let $C(x) = x^2 + 3x + 100$ be the cost function of a firm. Show that when x is changed from 100 to $100 + \Delta x$, where $\Delta x \neq 0$, the average rate of change per unit of output is

$$\frac{C(100 + \Delta x) - C(100)}{\Delta x} = 203 + \Delta x$$

What is the marginal cost $C'(100)$? Then use (6.2.6) to find $C'(x)$ and, in particular, $C'(100)$.

2. If the cost function of a firm is $C(x) = \bar{C} + cx$, give economic interpretations of the parameters c and $\bar{C}$.

3. If the total saving of a country is a function $S(Y)$ of the national product Y, then $S'(Y)$ is called the *marginal propensity to save*, or MPS. Find the MPS for the following functions:

   (a) $S(Y) = \bar{S} + sY$

   (b) $S(Y) = 100 + 0.1Y + 0.0002Y^2$

4. Let $T(y)$ denote the income tax a person is liable to pay, as a function of personal income y. Then $T'(y)$ is called the *marginal tax rate*. Consider the case when $T(y) = t(y - a) - b$, where t is a constant number in the interval $(0, 1)$, while a and b are nonnegative constants. Characterize this tax function by determining its marginal rate.

5. Let $x(t)$ denote the number of barrels of oil left in a well at time t, where time is measured in minutes. What is the interpretation of the equation $x'(0) = -3$?

6. The total cost of producing $x \geq 0$ units of a commodity is $C(x) = x^3 - 90x^2 + 7500x$.

   (a) Use the result in Exercise 6.2.10, to compute the marginal cost function $C'(x)$.

   (b) For what value of x is the marginal cost the least?

7. (a) A firm's profit function is $\pi(Q) = 24Q - Q^2 - 5$. Find the marginal profit, and the value Q^* of Q which maximizes profits.

   (b) A firm's revenue function is $R(Q) = 500Q - \frac{1}{3}Q^3$. Find the marginal revenue.

   (c) For the particular cost function $C(Q) = -Q^3 + 214.2Q^2 - 7900Q + 320\,700$ which was considered in Example 4.7.1, find the marginal cost.

8. Referring to the definitions given in Example 6.4.4, compute the marginal cost in the following cases:

   (a) $C(x) = a_1 x^2 + b_1 x + c_1$

   (b) $C(x) = a_1 x^3 + b_1$

6.5 A Brief Introduction to Limits

In Section 6.2, we defined the derivative of a function based on the concept of a limit. The same concept has many other uses in mathematics, as well as in economic analysis, so now we should take a closer look. Here we give a preliminary definition and formulate some important rules for limits. In Section 7.9, we will discuss the limit concept more closely.

EXAMPLE 6.5.1 Consider the function F defined by the formula

$$F(x) = \frac{e^x - 1}{x}$$

where the number $e \approx 2.718$ is the base for the natural exponential function that was introduced in Section 4.9. Note that if $x = 0$, then $e^0 = 1$, and the fraction collapses to the absurd expression "$0/0$". Thus, the function F is not defined for $x = 0$. Yet one can still ask what happens to $F(x)$ when x is close to 0. Using a calculator, we find the values shown in Table 6.5.1, as well as " 0/0 " at $h = 0$ where $F(0)$ is undefined.

Table 6.5.1 Values of $F(x) = (e^x - 1)/x$ when x is close to 0

x	-0.1	-0.001	-0.0001	0	0.0001	0.001	0.1
$F(x)$	0.9516	0.9995	1.0000	" 0/0 "	1.0001	1.0005	1.0517

From the table, it appears that as x gets closer and closer to 0, so the fraction $F(x)$ gets closer and closer to 1. It therefore seems reasonable to assume that $F(x)$ tends to 1 in the limit as x tends to 0. Indeed, as we argue later, our definition of e is motivated by the requirement that this limit equal 1. So we write:

$$\lim_{x \to 0} \frac{e^x - 1}{x} = 1 \quad \text{or} \quad \frac{e^x - 1}{x} \to 1 \text{ as } x \to 0$$

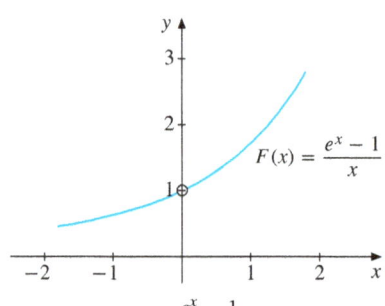

Figure 6.5.1 $y = \dfrac{e^x - 1}{x}$

Figure 6.5.1 shows a portion of the graph of F. The function F is defined for all x, except at $x = 0$, and $\lim_{x \to 0} F(x) = 1$. A small circle is used to indicate that the corresponding point $(0, 1)$ is not in the graph of F.

Suppose, in general, that a function f is defined for all x near a, but not necessarily at $x = a$. Then we say that *the number A is the limit of $f(x)$ as x tends to a* if $f(x)$ tends to A as x tends to (but is not equal to) a. We write:

$$\lim_{x \to a} f(x) = A, \quad \text{or} \quad f(x) \to A \text{ as } x \to a$$

It is possible, however, that the value of $f(x)$ does not tend to any fixed number as x tends to a. Then we say that $\lim_{x \to a} f(x)$ *does not exist*, or that $f(x)$ *does not have a limit as x tends to a*.

EXAMPLE 6.5.2 Using a calculator, examine the limit $\lim_{h \to 0} \dfrac{\sqrt{h+1} - 1}{h}$.

Solution: By choosing numbers h close to 0, we find the values in Table 6.5.2.

Table 6.5.2 Values of $F(h) = (\sqrt{h+1} - 1)/h$ when h is close to 0

h	-0.5	-0.2	-0.1	-0.01	0	0.01	0.1	0.2	0.5
$F(h)$	0.586	0.528	0.513	0.501	"0/0"	0.499	0.488	0.477	0.449

These numbers suggest that the desired limit is 0.5.

The limits that we claimed to have found in Examples 6.5.1 and 6.5.2 are both based on a rather shaky numerical procedure. For instance, in Example 6.5.2, how can we be certain that our guess is correct? If we chose h values even closer to 0, could the fraction tend to a limit other than 0.5? Could it even have no limit at all? Further numerical computations will support our belief that the initial guess is correct, but we can never make a table that has *all* the values of h close to 0. Thus, no matter how many numerical computations we make, on their own they can never establish with certainty what the true limit is.

This illustrates the need to have a rigorous procedure for finding limits, based on a precise mathematical definition of limit. This precise definition is given in Section 7.9; here we merely give a preliminary definition which will convey the right idea.

LIMIT

The expression
$$\lim_{x \to a} f(x) = A \tag{6.5.1}$$
means that we can make $f(x)$ as close to A as we want by making sure that x is sufficiently close to, but not equal to, a.

We emphasize:

(a) The number $\lim_{x \to a} f(x)$ depends on how $f(x)$ behaves for values of x close to a, but not on what happens to f at the precise value $x = a$. Indeed, when finding $\lim_{x \to a} f(x)$, we are simply not interested in the value $f(a)$, or even in whether f is defined at a.

(b) When computing $\lim_{x \to a} f(x)$, we must consider values of x on both sides of a.

Rules for Limits

Since limits cannot really be determined merely by numerical computations, we use simple rules instead. Their validity can be shown later once we have a precise definition of limit as a mathematical concept. These rules are very straightforward; we have even used a few of them already in the previous section.

Suppose that f and g are defined as functions of x in a neighbourhood of a (even if not necessarily at a). Then we have the following rules, written down in a way that makes them easy to refer to later:[9]

---

[9] Because of the identities $f(x) - g(x) = f(x) + (-1)g(x)$, and $f(x)/g(x) = f(x)(g(x))^{-1}$, it is clear that some of these rules follow from others.

RULES FOR LIMITS

If $\lim_{x \to a} f(x) = A$ and $\lim_{x \to a} g(x) = B$, then

$$\lim_{x \to a} [f(x) \pm g(x)] = A \pm B \qquad (6.5.2)$$

$$\lim_{x \to a} [f(x) \cdot g(x)] = A \cdot B \qquad (6.5.3)$$

$$\lim_{x \to a} \frac{f(x)}{g(x)} = \frac{A}{B}, \quad \text{if } B \neq 0 \qquad (6.5.4)$$

$$\lim_{x \to a} [f(x)]^r = A^r, \quad \text{if } A^r \text{ is defined and } r \text{ is a real number} \qquad (6.5.5)$$

It is easy to give intuitive explanations for these rules. Suppose that $\lim_{x \to a} f(x) = A$ and that $\lim_{x \to a} g(x) = B$. These equations imply that, when x is close to a, then $f(x)$ is close to A and $g(x)$ is close to B. So intuitively the sum $f(x) + g(x)$ is close to $A + B$, the difference $f(x) - g(x)$ is close to $A - B$, the product $f(x)g(x)$ is close to $A \cdot B$, and so on.

Rules (6.5.2) and (6.5.3) can be used repeatedly to obtain the new extended rules

$$\lim_{x \to a} \left[f_1(x) + f_2(x) + \cdots + f_n(x) \right] = \lim_{x \to a} f_1(x) + \lim_{x \to a} f_2(x) + \cdots + \lim_{x \to a} f_n(x)$$

$$\lim_{x \to a} \left[f_1(x) \cdot f_2(x) \cdot \ldots \cdot f_n(x) \right] = \lim_{x \to a} f_1(x) \cdot \lim_{x \to a} f_2(x) \cdot \ldots \cdot \lim_{x \to a} f_n(x)$$

In words: *the limit of a sum is the sum of the limits, and the limit of a product is equal to the product of the limits.*

There are two special cases when the limit is obvious. First, suppose the function $f(x)$ is equal to the same constant value c for every x. Then, at every point a, one has $\lim_{x \to a} c = c$. Second, it is also evident that if $f(x) = x$, then, again at every point a, one has $\lim_{x \to a} f(x) = \lim_{x \to a} x = a$. Combining these two simple limits with the general rules allows easy computation of the limits for certain combinations of functions.

EXAMPLE 6.5.3   Use the rules labelled (6.5.2) to (6.5.5) to compute the following limits:

(a) $\lim_{x \to -2} (x^2 + 5x)$ (b) $\lim_{x \to 4} \frac{2x^{3/2} - \sqrt{x}}{x^2 - 15}$ (c) $\lim_{x \to a} Ax^n$

Solution:

(a) By rule (6.5.2), $\lim_{x \to -2} (x^2 + 5x)$ equals $\lim_{x \to -2} (x \cdot x) + \lim_{x \to -2} (5 \cdot x)$. Using rule (6.5.3) twice, the latter can be computed as

$$\lim_{x \to -2} x \cdot \lim_{x \to -2} x + \lim_{x \to -2} 5 \cdot \lim_{x \to -2} x$$

It follows that

$$\lim_{x \to -2} (x^2 + 5x) = (-2)(-2) + 5 \cdot (-2) = -6$$

(b) $\lim_{x \to 4} \dfrac{2x^{3/2} - \sqrt{x}}{x^2 - 15} = \dfrac{2\lim_{x \to 4} x^{3/2} - \lim_{x \to 4} \sqrt{x}}{\lim_{x \to 4} x^2 - 15} = \dfrac{2 \cdot 4^{3/2} - \sqrt{4}}{4^2 - 15} = \dfrac{2 \cdot 8 - 2}{16 - 15} = 14$

(c) $\lim_{x \to a} Ax^n = \lim_{x \to a} A \cdot \lim_{x \to a} x^n = A \cdot \left(\lim_{x \to a} x \right)^n = Aa^n$

This last example was straightforward. Examples 6.5.1 and 6.5.2 were more difficult, as they involved a fraction whose numerator and denominator both tended to 0. A simple observation can sometimes help us find such limits, provided that they exist. Because $\lim_{x \to a} f(x)$ can only depend on the values of f when x is close to, but not equal to a, we have the following:

EQUALITY OF LIMITS

If the functions f and g are equal for all x close to a, but not necessarily at $x = a$, then

$$\lim_{x \to a} f(x) = \lim_{x \to a} g(x) \qquad (6.5.6)$$

whenever either limit exists.

Here are some examples of how this rule works.

EXAMPLE 6.5.4 Compute the limit

$$\lim_{x \to 2} \dfrac{3x^2 + 3x - 18}{x - 2}$$

Solution: We see that both numerator and denominator tend to 0 as x tends to 2. Because the numerator $3x^2 + 3x - 18$ is equal to 0 for $x = 2$, it has $x - 2$ as a factor. In fact, $3x^2 + 3x - 18 = 3(x - 2)(x + 3)$. Hence,

$$f(x) = \dfrac{3x^2 + 3x - 18}{x - 2} = \dfrac{3(x - 2)(x + 3)}{x - 2}$$

For $x \neq 2$, we can cancel $x - 2$ from both numerator and denominator to obtain $3(x + 3)$. So the functions $f(x)$ and $g(x) = 3(x + 3)$ are equal for all $x \neq 2$. By (6.5.6), it follows that

$$\lim_{x \to 2} \dfrac{3x^2 + 3x - 18}{x - 2} = \lim_{x \to 2} 3(x + 3) = 3(2 + 3) = 15$$

EXAMPLE 6.5.5 Compute the limits:

(a) $\lim_{h \to 0} \dfrac{\sqrt{h + 1} - 1}{h}$

(b) $\lim_{x \to 4} \dfrac{x^2 - 16}{4\sqrt{x} - 8}$

Solution:

(a) The numerator and the denominator both tend to 0 as h tends to 0, so rule (6.5.4) cannot be applied. But a little trick saves the day. This trick is to multiply both numerator and denominator by $\sqrt{h + 1} + 1$ to get

$$\dfrac{\sqrt{h + 1} - 1}{h} = \dfrac{\left(\sqrt{h + 1} - 1\right)\left(\sqrt{h + 1} + 1\right)}{h\left(\sqrt{h + 1} + 1\right)} = \dfrac{h + 1 - 1}{h\left(\sqrt{h + 1} + 1\right)} = \dfrac{1}{\sqrt{h + 1} + 1}$$

where at the last step the common factor h has been cancelled. For all $h \neq 0$ (and $h \geq -1$), the given function is equal to $1/(\sqrt{h+1}+1)$, which tends to $1/2$ as $h \to 0$. We conclude that the limit equals $1/2$, which confirms the result in Example 6.5.2.

(b) Because $x = 4$ gives "0/0", again we use a trick to factorize the fraction as follows:

$$\frac{x^2-16}{4\sqrt{x}-8} = \frac{(x+4)(x-4)}{4(\sqrt{x}-2)} = \frac{(x+4)(\sqrt{x}+2)(\sqrt{x}-2)}{4(\sqrt{x}-2)} \qquad (*)$$

The last step uses the factorization $x - 4 = (\sqrt{x}+2)(\sqrt{x}-2)$, which is correct for all $x \geq 0$. In the last fraction of $(*)$, we can cancel $\sqrt{x}-2$ whenever $\sqrt{x}-2 \neq 0$—that is, whenever $x \neq 4$. Using (6.5.6) again allows us to take limits of each side of $(*)$, so

$$\lim_{x \to 4} \frac{x^2-16}{4\sqrt{x}-8} = \lim_{x \to 4} \frac{1}{4}(x+4)(\sqrt{x}+2) = \frac{1}{4}(4+4)(\sqrt{4}+2) = 8$$

EXERCISES FOR SECTION 6.5

1. Determine the following by using the rules for limits:

(a) $\lim\limits_{x \to 0} (3 + 2x^2)$

(b) $\lim\limits_{x \to -1} \dfrac{3+2x}{x-1}$

(c) $\lim\limits_{x \to 2} (2x^2+5)^3$

(d) $\lim\limits_{t \to 8} \left(5t + t^2 - \frac{1}{8}t^3\right)$

(e) $\lim\limits_{y \to 0} \dfrac{(y+1)^5 - y^5}{y+1}$

(f) $\lim\limits_{z \to -2} \dfrac{1/z + 2}{z}$

2. Examine the following limits numerically by using a calculator:

(a) $\lim\limits_{h \to 0} \dfrac{1}{h}(2^h - 1)$

(b) $\lim\limits_{h \to 0} \dfrac{1}{h}(3^h - 1)$

(c) $\lim\limits_{\lambda \to 0} \dfrac{1}{\lambda}(3^\lambda - 2^\lambda)$

3. Consider the limit $\lim\limits_{x \to 1} \dfrac{x^2+7x-8}{x-1}$.

(a) Examine the limit numerically by making a table of values of the fraction when x is close to 1.

(b) Find the limit precisely by using the method in Example 6.5.4.

4. Compute the following limits, where $h \neq 0$ in (f):

(a) $\lim\limits_{x \to 2} (x^2 + 3x - 5)$

(b) $\lim\limits_{y \to -3} \dfrac{1}{y+8}$

(c) $\lim\limits_{x \to 0} \dfrac{x^3-2x-1}{x^5-x^2-1}$

(d) $\lim\limits_{x \to 0} \dfrac{x^3+3x^2-2x}{x}$

(e) $\lim\limits_{h \to 0} \dfrac{(x+h)^3-x^3}{h}$

(f) $\lim\limits_{x \to 0} \dfrac{(x+h)^3-x^3}{h}$

SM 5. Compute the following limits:

(a) $\lim\limits_{h \to 2} \dfrac{\frac{1}{3}-\frac{2}{3h}}{h-2}$

(b) $\lim\limits_{x \to 0} \dfrac{x^2-1}{x^2}$

(c) $\lim\limits_{t \to 3} \dfrac{\sqrt[3]{32t-96}}{t^2-2t-3}$

(d) $\lim\limits_{h \to 0} \dfrac{\sqrt{h+3}-\sqrt{3}}{h}$

(e) $\lim\limits_{t \to -2} \dfrac{t^2-4}{t^2+10t+16}$

(f) $\lim\limits_{x \to 4} \dfrac{2-\sqrt{x}}{4-x}$

6. If $f(x) = x^2 + 2x$, compute the following limits:

(a) $\lim_{x \to 1} \dfrac{f(x) - f(1)}{x - 1}$

(b) $\lim_{x \to 2} \dfrac{f(x) - f(1)}{x - 1}$

(c) $\lim_{h \to 0} \dfrac{f(2 + h) - f(2)}{h}$

(d) $\lim_{x \to a} \dfrac{f(x) - f(a)}{x - a}$

(e) $\lim_{h \to 0} \dfrac{f(a + h) - f(a)}{h}$

(f) $\lim_{h \to 0} \dfrac{f(a + h) - f(a - h)}{h}$

7. [HARDER] Compute the following limits, where in part (c) n denotes any natural number:

(a) $\lim_{x \to 2} \dfrac{x^2 - 2x}{x^3 - 8}$

(b) $\lim_{h \to 0} \dfrac{\sqrt[3]{27 + h} - 3}{h}$ (*Hint*: Put $u = \sqrt[3]{27 + h}$.)

(c) $\lim_{x \to 1} \dfrac{x^n - 1}{x - 1}$

6.6 Simple Rules for Differentiation

Recall that Eq. (6.2.2) defined the derivative of a function f by the formula

$$f'(x) = \lim_{h \to 0} \dfrac{f(x + h) - f(x)}{h} \qquad (*)$$

If this limit exists, we say that f is *differentiable* at x. The process of finding the derivative of a function is called *differentiation*. It is useful to think of this as an operation that transforms one function f into a new function f', which is defined for the values of x where the limit in $(*)$ exists. If $y = f(x)$, we can use the symbols y' and dy/dx as alternatives to $f'(x)$.

In Section 6.2 we used formula $(*)$ to differentiate some simple functions. However, it is difficult and time consuming to apply formula $(*)$ directly in each separate case. We now embark on a systematic programme to find general rules which ultimately will give mechanical and efficient procedures for differentiating very many differentiable functions specified by a formula, even one that is complicated. We start with some simple rules.

DERIVATIVE OF A CONSTANT

If f is a constant function, then its derivative is 0:

$$f(x) = A \quad \Longrightarrow \quad f'(x) = 0 \qquad (6.6.1)$$

The result is easy to see geometrically. The graph of $f(x) = A$ is a straight line parallel to the x-axis. The tangent to the graph is the line itself, which has slope 0 at each point, as shown in Fig. 6.6.1. You should now use the definition of $f'(x)$ to get the same answer.

The next two rules are also very useful.

SIMPLE RULES

When taking derivatives, additive constants disappear while multiplicative constants are preserved. In symbols:

$$y = A + f(x) \implies y' = f'(x) \qquad (6.6.2)$$

$$y = Af(x) \implies y' = Af'(x) \qquad (6.6.3)$$

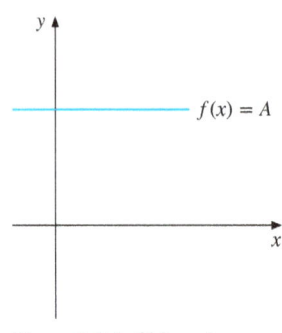

Figure 6.6.1 $f(x) = A$

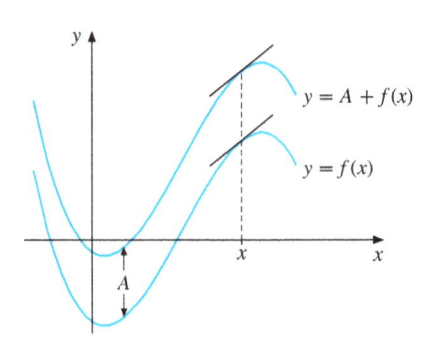

Figure 6.6.2 $f(x)$ and $A + f(x)$

Rule (6.6.2) is illustrated in Fig. 6.6.2, in the case when A is positive. Recall from Section 5.1 that the graph of $A + f(x)$ is that of $f(x)$ shifted upwards by A units in the direction of the y-axis. So the tangents to the two curves $y = f(x)$ and $y = f(x) + A$ at the same value of x must be parallel. In particular, they must have the same slope. Again you should try to use the definition of $f'(x)$ to give a formal proof of this assertion.

Let us prove rule (6.6.3) by using the definition of a derivative. If $g(x) = Af(x)$, then

$$g(x+h) - g(x) = Af(x+h) - Af(x) = A[f(x+h) - f(x)]$$

and so

$$g'(x) = \lim_{h \to 0} \frac{g(x+h) - g(x)}{h} = A \lim_{h \to 0} \frac{f(x+h) - f(x)}{h} = Af'(x)$$

For an economic illustration of rule (6.6.3), suppose that $R(t)$ denotes firm A's sales revenue at time t. Suppose too that firm B's revenue $S(t)$ at each time is three times as large as A's. Then the absolute growth rate of B's revenue is three times as large as A's. In mathematical notation: $S(t) = 3R(t) \implies S'(t) = 3R'(t)$. Nevertheless, the firms' *relative* growth rates $R'(t)/R(t)$ and $S'(t)/S(t)$ are equal.

Using Leibniz's notation, the three results (6.6.1)–(6.6.3) can be written as follows:

$$\frac{d}{dx}A = 0, \quad \frac{d}{dx}[A + f(x)] = \frac{d}{dx}f(x), \quad \frac{d}{dx}[Af(x)] = A\frac{d}{dx}f(x)$$

EXAMPLE 6.6.1   Suppose we know $f'(x)$. Find the derivatives of:

(a) $5 + f(x)$ (b) $f(x) - \frac{1}{2}$ (c) $4f(x)$

(d) $-\dfrac{f(x)}{5}$ (e) $\dfrac{Af(x) + B}{C}$, where $C \neq 0$

Solution: Applying rules (6.6.2) and (6.6.3), we obtain:

(a) $\dfrac{d}{dx}[5 + f(x)] = f'(x)$

(b) $\dfrac{d}{dx}\left[f(x) - \dfrac{1}{2}\right] = \dfrac{d}{dx}\left[-\dfrac{1}{2} + f(x)\right] = f'(x)$

(c) $\dfrac{d}{dx}[4f(x)] = 4f'(x)$

(d) $\dfrac{d}{dx}\left[-\dfrac{f(x)}{5}\right] = \dfrac{d}{dx}\left[-\dfrac{1}{5}f(x)\right] = -\dfrac{1}{5}f'(x)$

(e) $\dfrac{d}{dx}\left[\dfrac{Af(x) + B}{C}\right] = \dfrac{d}{dx}\left[\dfrac{A}{C}f(x) + \dfrac{B}{C}\right] = \dfrac{A}{C}f'(x)$

The Power Rule

Few rules of differentiation are more useful than the following:

THE POWER RULE

Given any constant a, suppose that: either (i) a is a natural number; or else (ii) $x > 0$. Then one has

$$f(x) = x^a \implies f'(x) = ax^{a-1} \tag{6.6.4}$$

For $a = 2$ and $a = 3$ rule (6.6.4) was confirmed in Eqs (6.2.4) and (6.2.5). When a is a natural number $n > 3$, the rule is most easily confirmed by using rule (6.7.3) for differentiating products, as shown in Example 6.7.5. When a is a negative integer $-n$, we apply to $1/x^n$ the rule for differentiating quotients, as shown in Example 6.7.8. Ultimately, provided that $x > 0$, in Section 6.11 we will use the equalities $\ln(x^a) = a \ln x$ and so $x^a = \exp(a \ln x)$ in order to derive (6.11.7), which states that rule (6.6.4) is valid for all real powers a.

EXAMPLE 6.6.2   Use rule (6.6.4) to compute the derivatives of:

(a) $y = x^5$ (b) $y = 3x^8$ (c) $y = \dfrac{x^{100}}{100}$

Solution:

(a) $y = x^5 \Rightarrow y' = 5x^{5-1} = 5x^4$

(b) $y = 3x^8 \Rightarrow y' = 3 \cdot 8x^{8-1} = 24x^7$

(c) $y = \dfrac{x^{100}}{100} = \dfrac{1}{100}x^{100} \Rightarrow y' = \dfrac{1}{100} \cdot 100x^{100-1} = x^{99}$

EXAMPLE 6.6.3   Assuming each relevant variable is positive, use rule (6.6.4) to compute:

(a) $\dfrac{d}{dx}\left(x^{-0.33}\right)$ (b) $\dfrac{d}{dr}(-5r^{-3})$ (c) $\dfrac{d}{dp}(Ap^\alpha + B)$ (d) $\dfrac{d}{dx}\left(\dfrac{A}{\sqrt{x}}\right)$

Solution:

(a) $\dfrac{d}{dx}\left(x^{-0.33}\right) = -0.33x^{-0.33-1} = -0.33x^{-1.33}$

(b) $\dfrac{d}{dr}(-5r^{-3}) = (-5)(-3)r^{-3-1} = 15r^{-4}$

(c) $\dfrac{d}{dp}(Ap^\alpha + B) = A\alpha p^{\alpha-1}$

(d) $\dfrac{d}{dx}\left(\dfrac{A}{\sqrt{x}}\right) = \dfrac{d}{dx}(Ax^{-1/2}) = A\left(-\dfrac{1}{2}\right)x^{-1/2-1} = -\dfrac{1}{2}Ax^{-3/2} = \dfrac{-A}{2x\sqrt{x}}$

EXAMPLE 6.6.4   Let $r > 0$ denote a household's income measured in, say, dollars per year. The *Pareto income distribution* is described by the formula

$$f(r) = \dfrac{B}{r^\beta} = Br^{-\beta} \qquad (6.6.5)$$

where B and β are positive constants. As explained more fully in Section 10.4, $f(r)\Delta r$ is approximately the proportion of the population whose income is between r and $r + \Delta r$. The distribution function (6.6.5) gives a good approximation for incomes above a certain threshold. For these, empirical estimates of β have usually been in the range $2.4 < \beta < 2.6$.

Using (6.6.4), we find that $f'(r) = -\beta Br^{-\beta-1} = -\beta B/r^{\beta+1}$. It follows that $f'(r) < 0$, so $f(r)$ is strictly decreasing.

EXERCISES FOR SECTION 6.6

1. Compute the derivatives of the following functions:

   (a) $y = 5$ (b) $y = x^4$ (c) $y = 9x^{10}$ (d) $y = \pi^7$

2. Suppose we know $g'(x)$. Find expressions for the derivatives of the following:

   (a) $2g(x) + 3$ (b) $-\dfrac{1}{6}g(x) + 8$ (c) $\dfrac{g(x) - 5}{3}$

3. Find the derivatives of the following:

   (a) x^6 (b) $3x^{11}$ (c) x^{50} (d) $-4x^{-7}$

   (e) $\dfrac{x^{12}}{12}$ (f) $\dfrac{-2}{x^2}$ (g) $\dfrac{3}{\sqrt[3]{x}}$ (h) $\dfrac{-2}{x\sqrt{x}}$

4. Compute the following:

   (a) $\dfrac{d}{dr}(4\pi r^2)$
   (b) $\dfrac{d}{dy}(Ay^{b+1})$
   (c) $\dfrac{d}{dA}\left(\dfrac{1}{A^2\sqrt{A}}\right)$

5. Explain why $f'(a) = \lim_{x\to a}\dfrac{f(x)-f(a)}{x-a}$. Then use this formula to find $f'(a)$ when $f(x) = x^2$.

6. For each of the following functions, find a function $F(x)$ having $f(x)$ as its derivative—that is, find a function that satisfies $F'(x) = f(x)$.[10]

   (a) $f(x) = x^2$
   (b) $f(x) = 2x + 3$
   (c) $f(x) = x^a$, for $a \neq -1$

7. [HARDER] The following limits all take the form $\lim_{h\to 0}[f(a+h)-f(a)]/h$. Use your knowledge of derivatives to find the limits.

   (a) $\lim_{h\to 0}\dfrac{(5+h)^2-5^2}{h}$
   (b) $\lim_{s\to 0}\dfrac{(s+1)^5-1}{s}$
   (c) $\lim_{h\to 0}\dfrac{5(x+h)^2+10-5x^2-10}{h}$

6.7 Sums, Products, and Quotients

If we know $f'(x)$ and $g'(x)$, then what are the derivatives of $f(x)+g(x)$, $f(x)-g(x)$, $f(x)\cdot g(x)$, and $f(x)/g(x)$? You will probably guess the first two correctly, but are less likely to be right about the last two, unless you have already learned the answers.

Sums and Differences

Suppose f and g are both defined on a set A of real numbers.

DERIVATIVES OF SUMS AND DIFFERENCES

If both f and g are differentiable at x, then the sum $f+g$ and the difference $f-g$ are both differentiable at x, with

$$F(x) = f(x) \pm g(x) \implies F'(x) = f'(x) \pm g'(x) \qquad (6.7.1)$$

In Leibniz's notation:

$$\frac{d}{dx}(f(x) \pm g(x)) = \frac{d}{dx}f(x) \pm \frac{d}{dx}g(x)$$

We can give a formal proof of (6.7.1).

---

[10] Note that you are not asked to find $f'(x)$.

Proof: Consider the case when $F(x) = f(x) + g(x)$, The Newton quotient of F is

$$\frac{F(x+h) - F(x)}{h} = \frac{(f(x+h) + g(x+h)) - (f(x) + g(x))}{h}$$

$$= \frac{f(x+h) - f(x)}{h} + \frac{g(x+h) - g(x)}{h}$$

When $h \to 0$, the last two fractions tend to $f'(x)$ and $g'(x)$, respectively, and thus the sum of the fractions tends to $f'(x) + g'(x)$. Hence,

$$F'(x) = \lim_{h \to 0} \frac{F(x+h) - F(x)}{h} = f'(x) + g'(x)$$

This proves (6.7.1) for the sum. The proof of the result for the difference is similar—only some of the signs change in an obvious way.

EXAMPLE 6.7.1 Compute $\frac{d}{dx}\left(3x^8 + \frac{x^{100}}{100}\right)$.

Solution: Using (6.7.1) and the results from Example 6.6.2 gives

$$\frac{d}{dx}\left(3x^8 + \frac{x^{100}}{100}\right) = \frac{d}{dx}(3x^8) + \frac{d}{dx}\left(\frac{x^{100}}{100}\right) = 24x^7 + x^{99}$$

EXAMPLE 6.7.2 Example 6.4.4 used $C(x)$ to denote the cost of producing x units of some commodity in a given period. If $R(x)$ is the revenue from selling those x units, then the profit function $\pi(x) = R(x) - C(x)$ is the difference between the revenue and cost. According to (6.7.1), $\pi'(x) = R'(x) - C'(x)$. In particular, $\pi'(x) = 0$ when $R'(x) = C'(x)$. In words: *Marginal profit is 0 when marginal revenue is equal to marginal cost.*

Rule (6.7.1) can be extended to sums of an arbitrary number of terms. For example,

$$\frac{d}{dx}[f(x) - g(x) + h(x)] = f'(x) - g'(x) + h'(x) \quad (6.7.2)$$

This we can see by writing $f(x) - g(x) + h(x)$ as $[f(x) - g(x)] + h(x)$, then using (6.7.1) twice. Repeatedly using the rules above, including the power rule (6.6.4), makes it routine to differentiate any polynomial.

Products

Suppose $f(x) = x$ and $g(x) = x^2$, then $(f \cdot g)(x) = x^3$. Here $f'(x) = 1$, $g'(x) = 2x$, and $(f \cdot g)'(x) = 3x^2$. Hence, the derivative of $(f \cdot g)(x)$ is *not* equal to $f'(x) \cdot g'(x) = 2x$. The correct rule for differentiating a product is a little more complicated.

DERIVATIVE OF A PRODUCT

If the two functions f and g are both differentiable at the point x, then so is the product $F = f \cdot g$, and

$$F(x) = f(x) \cdot g(x) \quad \Longrightarrow \quad F'(x) = f'(x) \cdot g(x) + f(x) \cdot g'(x) \quad (6.7.3)$$

Formulated in words: *The derivative of the product of two functions is equal to the derivative of the first times the second, plus the first times the derivative of the second.* The formula, however, is much easier to digest than these words.

In Leibniz's notation, the product rule is expressed as:

$$\frac{d}{dx}[f(x) \cdot g(x)] = \left[\frac{d}{dx}f(x)\right] \cdot g(x) + f(x) \cdot \left[\frac{d}{dx}g(x)\right]$$

Before demonstrating why (6.7.3) is valid, here are two examples.

EXAMPLE 6.7.3 Find $h'(x)$ when $h(x) = (x^3 - x) \cdot (5x^4 + x^2)$. Confirm the answer by expanding $h(x)$ as a single polynomial, then differentiating the result.

Solution: We see that $h(x) = f(x) \cdot g(x)$ with $f(x) = x^3 - x$ and $g(x) = 5x^4 + x^2$. Here $f'(x) = 3x^2 - 1$ and $g'(x) = 20x^3 + 2x$. Thus, from (6.7.3),

$$h'(x) = f'(x) \cdot g(x) + f(x) \cdot g'(x) = (3x^2 - 1) \cdot (5x^4 + x^2) + (x^3 - x) \cdot (20x^3 + 2x)$$

Usually we simplify the answer by expanding to obtain just one polynomial. Routine computations give $h'(x) = 35x^6 - 20x^4 - 3x^2$.

Alternatively, expanding $h(x)$ as a single polynomial gives $h(x) = 5x^7 - 4x^5 - x^3$. From rules (6.6.4) and (6.7.1), its derivative is $h'(x) = 35x^6 - 20x^4 - 3x^2$.

EXAMPLE 6.7.4 Let $D(P)$ denote the demand function for a product. By selling $D(P)$ units at price P per unit, the producer earns revenue $R(P)$ given by $R(P) = PD(P)$. Usually $D'(P)$ is negative because demand goes down when the price increases. According to the product rule for differentiation,

$$R'(P) = D(P) + PD'(P) \qquad (*)$$

For an economic interpretation, suppose P increases by one dollar. The revenue $R(P)$ changes for two reasons. First, $R(P)$ increases by $1 \cdot D(P)$, because each of the $D(P)$ units brings in one dollar more. But a one dollar increase in the price per unit causes demand to change by $D(P + 1) - D(P)$ units, which is approximately $D'(P)$. The (positive) loss due to a one dollar increase in the price per unit is then $-PD'(P)$, which must be subtracted from $D(P)$ to obtain $R'(P)$, as in equation (*). The resulting expression merely expresses the simple fact that $R'(P)$, the total rate of change of $R(P)$, is what you gain minus what you lose.

Now we offer a proof of the rule for differentiating a product:

Proof of (6.7.3): Suppose both f and g are differentiable at x. Then as h tends to 0 the two Newton quotients

$$\frac{f(x+h) - f(x)}{h} \quad \text{and} \quad \frac{g(x+h) - g(x)}{h}$$

tend to the limits $f'(x)$ and $g'(x)$, respectively. We must show that the Newton quotient of F also tends to a limit, which is precisely $f'(x)g(x) + f(x)g'(x)$. The Newton quotient of F is

$$\frac{F(x+h) - F(x)}{h} = \frac{f(x+h)g(x+h) - f(x)g(x)}{h} \qquad (**)$$

To proceed further we must somehow transform the right-hand side (RHS) to involve the Newton quotients of f and g. We use a trick: The numerator of the RHS is unchanged if we both subtract and add the number $f(x)g(x+h)$. Hence, with a suitable regrouping of terms, we have

$$\frac{F(x+h)-F(x)}{h} = \frac{f(x+h)g(x+h)-f(x)g(x+h)+f(x)g(x+h)-f(x)g(x)}{h}$$

$$= \frac{f(x+h)-f(x)}{h}g(x+h)+f(x)\frac{g(x+h)-g(x)}{h}$$

Now, as h tends to 0, the two Newton quotients tend to $f'(x)$ and $g'(x)$, respectively. Moreover, we can write $g(x+h)$ for $h \neq 0$ as

$$g(x+h) = \left[\frac{g(x+h)-g(x)}{h}\right]h + g(x)$$

The product rule for limits and the definition of $g'(x)$ together imply that $g(x+h)$ tends to $g'(x) \cdot 0 + g(x) = g(x)$ as h tends to 0. It follows that the Newton quotient of F, which is given by (∗∗), indeed tends to $f'(x)g(x)+f(x)g'(x)$ as h tends to 0. ∎

To conclude, now that we have seen how to differentiate products of two functions, let us consider products of more than two functions. For example, suppose that $y=f(x)g(x)h(x)$. What is y'? We adapt the technique used to show (6.7.2) and put $y=[f(x)g(x)]h(x)$. A double application of rule (6.7.3) for differentiating the product gives

$$y' = [f(x)g(x)]'\,h(x) + [f(x)g(x)]\,h'(x)$$
$$= \left[f'(x)g(x)+f(x)g'(x)\right]h(x)+f(x)g(x)h'(x)$$
$$= f'(x)g(x)h(x)+f(x)g'(x)h(x)+f(x)g(x)h'(x)$$

If none of the three functions is equal to 0, we can write the result as follows:[11]

$$\frac{(fgh)'}{fgh} = \frac{f'}{f} + \frac{g'}{g} + \frac{h'}{h}$$

By analogy, it is easy to write down the corresponding result for a product of n functions. In words, the relative rate of growth of an n-fold product is the sum of the n relative rates at which each factor is changing.

The next example uses the rule for differentiating products in order to confirm the power rule for the case when the power is any natural number.

EXAMPLE 6.7.5   **(Power rule for x^n).** Use mathematical induction to confirm that, for all real x, the power rule

$$f(x) = x^n \implies f'(x) = nx^{n-1} \tag{6.7.4}$$

holds in the case when n is any natural number.

---

[11] If all the functions are positive, this result is easier to show using logarithmic differentiation. See Section 6.11.

Solution: As discussed in connection with (6.6.4), the result (6.7.4) holds for $n = 1, 2, 3$. Suppose it holds when $n = m$, for any natural number m. Then the rule for differentiating the product $x^{m+1} = x \cdot x^m$ implies that

$$\frac{d}{dx}x^{m+1} = \left(\frac{d}{dx}x\right)x^m + x\left(\frac{d}{dx}x^m\right) = 1 \cdot x^m + x \cdot mx^{m-1} = (m+1)x^m$$

This confirms (6.7.4) for $n = m + 1$, which is the induction step. The proof is complete. ∎

Quotients

Bearing in mind the complications in the formula (6.7.3) for differentiating a product, one might be somewhat reluctant to try guessing quickly the corresponding formula for differentiating a quotient.

Suppose that $F(x) = f(x)/g(x)$, where f and g are differentiable in x with $g(x) \neq 0$. In fact, it is quite easy to find the formula for $F'(x)$ provided we *assume* that $F(x)$ is differentiable. Indeed $F(x) = f(x)/g(x)$ implies that $f(x) = F(x)g(x)$. Then the product rule gives $f'(x) = F'(x) \cdot g(x) + F(x) \cdot g'(x)$. Because we assumed that $g(x) \neq 0$, we can solve this last equation for $F'(x)$ to obtain

$$F'(x) = \frac{f'(x) - F(x)g'(x)}{g(x)} = \frac{f'(x) - [f(x)/g(x)]\,g'(x)}{g(x)}$$

Multiplying both numerator and denominator of the last fraction by $g(x)$ gives the following important formula.

DERIVATIVE OF A QUOTIENT

If f and g are differentiable at x and $g(x) \neq 0$, then $F = f/g$ is differentiable at x, and

$$F(x) = \frac{f(x)}{g(x)} \quad \Longrightarrow \quad F'(x) = \frac{f'(x) \cdot g(x) - f(x) \cdot g'(x)}{[g(x)]^2} \tag{6.7.5}$$

In words: *The derivative of a quotient is equal to the derivative of the numerator times the denominator minus the numerator times the derivative of the denominator, this difference then being divided by the square of the denominator.* In simpler notation, we have $(f/g)' = (f'g - fg')/g^2$.

Note that in the product rule formula, the two functions appear symmetrically, so that it is easy to remember. In the formula for the derivative of a quotient, the two expressions in the numerator must be in the right order. Here is one way to check that you have the order right. Write down the formula you believe is correct. Put $g \equiv 1$. Then $g' \equiv 0$, and your formula ought to reduce to f'. If you get $-f'$, then your signs are wrong.

Formula (6.7.5) was derived *under the assumption* that f/g is differentiable. In Exercise 6.8.13 you are asked to prove that this quotient really is differentiable.

EXAMPLE 6.7.6 Compute $F'(x)$ and $F'(4)$ when

$$F(x) = \frac{3x - 5}{x - 2}$$

Solution: We apply formula (6.7.5) with $f(x) = 3x - 5$ and $g(x) = x - 2$. Then $f'(x) = 3$ and $g'(x) = 1$. For $x \neq 2$, we obtain:

$$F'(x) = \frac{3 \cdot (x - 2) - (3x - 5) \cdot 1}{(x - 2)^2} = \frac{3x - 6 - 3x + 5}{(x - 2)^2} = \frac{-1}{(x - 2)^2}$$

To find $F'(4)$, we put $x = 4$ in the formula for $F'(x)$ to get $F'(4) = -1/(4 - 2)^2 = -1/4$. Note that $F'(x) < 0$ for all $x \neq 2$. Hence F is strictly decreasing both for $x < 2$ and for $x > 2$. Note also that $F(x) = 3 + 1/(x - 2)$. Its graph is shown in Fig. 5.1.7.

EXAMPLE 6.7.7 Let $C(x)$ be the total cost of producing x units of a commodity. Then $C(x)/x$ is the *average cost* of producing x units. Find an expression for $\frac{d}{dx}\left[\frac{C(x)}{x}\right]$.

Solution:

$$\frac{d}{dx}\left[\frac{C(x)}{x}\right] = \frac{C'(x)x - C(x)}{x^2} = \frac{1}{x}\left[C'(x) - \frac{C(x)}{x}\right] \tag{6.7.6}$$

This shows that average cost increases as output increases if and only if the marginal cost $C'(x)$ exceeds the average cost $C(x)/x$.[12]

The formula for the derivative of a quotient becomes more symmetric if we consider relative rates of change. By using (6.7.5), simple computation shows that

$$F(x) = \frac{f(x)}{g(x)} \implies \frac{F'(x)}{F(x)} = \frac{f'(x)}{f(x)} - \frac{g'(x)}{g(x)} \tag{6.7.7}$$

That is, *the relative rate of change of a quotient is equal to the relative rate of change of the numerator minus the relative rate of change of the denominator.*

Compare (6.7.7) with the formula

$$\frac{[f(x)g(x)]'}{f(x)g(x)} = \frac{f'(x)}{f(x)} + \frac{g'(x)}{g(x)}$$

for the relative rate of change of a product.

Let $W(t)$ be the nominal wage rate and $P(t)$ the price index at time t. Then $w(t) = W(t)/P(t)$ is called the *real wage rate*. According to (6.7.7),

$$\frac{\dot{w}(t)}{w(t)} = \frac{\dot{W}(t)}{W(t)} - \frac{\dot{P}(t)}{P(t)}$$

---

[12] Similarly, if a basketball team recruits a new player, then the team's average height increases if and only if the new player's height exceeds the team's old average height.

That is, the relative rate of change of the real wage rate is equal to the difference between the relative rates of change of the nominal wage rate and the price index. Thus, if nominal wages increase at the rate of 5% per year but prices rise by 6% per year, then real wages fall by 1%. Also, if inflation leads to wages and prices increasing at the same relative rate, then the real wage rate is constant.

Finally, here is one more version of the power rule (6.6.4):

EXAMPLE 6.7.8 [Power rule for x^{-n}] Suppose that n is any natural number. Prove that the function $f(x) = x^{-n}$ is differentiable for all $x \neq 0$, with $f'(x) = -nx^{-n-1}$.

Solution: We apply the quotient rule to $1/x^n$. It implies that x^{-n} is differentiable for all $x \neq 0$, with derivative

$$\frac{d}{dx} x^{-n} = \frac{d}{dx}\left(\frac{1}{x^n}\right) = \frac{0 \cdot x^n - 1 \cdot nx^{n-1}}{(x^n)^2} = -nx^{-n-1}$$

EXERCISES FOR SECTION 6.7

1. Differentiate the following functions w.r.t. x:

   (a) $x + 1$
   (b) $x + x^2$
   (c) $3x^5 + 2x^4 + 5$
   (d) $8x^4 + 2\sqrt{x}$
   (e) $\frac{1}{2}x - \frac{3}{2}x^2 + 5x^3$
   (f) $1 - 3x^7$

2. Differentiate the following functions w.r.t. x:

   (a) $\frac{3}{5}x^2 - 2x^7 + \frac{1}{8} - \sqrt{x}$
   (b) $(2x^2 - 1)(x^4 - 1)$
   (c) $\left(x^5 + \frac{1}{x}\right)(x^5 + 1)$

SM 3. Differentiate the following functions w.r.t. x:

   (a) $\frac{1}{x^6}$
   (b) $x^{-1}(x^2 + 1)\sqrt{x}$
   (c) $\frac{1}{\sqrt{x^3}}$
   (d) $\frac{x+1}{x-1}$
   (e) $\frac{x+1}{x^5}$
   (f) $\frac{3x-5}{2x+8}$
   (g) $3x^{-11}$
   (h) $\frac{3x-1}{x^2+x+1}$

4. Differentiate the following functions w.r.t. x:

   (a) $\frac{\sqrt{x}-2}{\sqrt{x}+1}$
   (b) $\frac{x^2-1}{x^2+1}$
   (c) $\frac{x^2+x+1}{x^2-x+1}$

5. Let $x = f(L)$ be the output when L units of labour are used as input. Assume that $f(0) = 0$ and that $f'(L) > 0, f''(L) < 0$ for all $L > 0$. Average productivity is defined by the formula $g(L) = f(L)/L$.

   (a) Let $L^* > 0$. Indicate on a figure the values of $f'(L^*)$ and $g(L^*)$. Which is larger?

   (b) How does the average productivity change when labour input increases?

SM 6. For each of the following functions, determine the intervals where it is increasing.

   (a) $y = 3x^2 - 12x + 13$
   (b) $y = \frac{1}{4}(x^4 - 6x^2)$
   (c) $y = \frac{2x}{x^2+2}$
   (d) $y = \frac{x^2-x^3}{2(x+1)}$

7. Find the equations for the tangents to the graphs of the following functions at the specified points:

(a) $y = 3 - x - x^2$ at $x = 1$

(b) $y = \dfrac{x^2 - 1}{x^2 + 1}$ at $x = 1$

(c) $y = \left(\dfrac{1}{x^2} + 1\right)(x^2 - 1)$ at $x = 2$

(d) $y = \dfrac{x^4 + 1}{(x^2 + 1)(x + 3)}$ at $x = 0$

8.
Consider an oil well where $x(t)$ denotes the rate of extraction in barrels per day and $p(t)$ denotes the price in dollars per barrel, both at time t. Then $R(t) = p(t)x(t)$ is the revenue in dollars per day. Find an expression for $\dot{R}(t)$, and give it an economic interpretation in the case when $p(t)$ and $x(t)$ are both increasing. (*Hint*: $R(t)$ increases for two reasons.)

9. Differentiate the following functions w.r.t. t:

(a) $\dfrac{at + b}{ct + d}$

(b) $t^n \left(a\sqrt{t} + b\right)$

(c) $\dfrac{1}{at^2 + bt + c}$

10.
If $f(x) = \sqrt{x}$, then $f(x) \cdot f(x) = x$. Differentiate this equation using the product rule in order to find a formula for $f'(x)$. Compare this with the result in Exercise 6.2.9.

11.
Suppose that $a = -n$ where n is any natural number. By using the relation $x^{-n} = 1/x^n$ and the quotient rule (6.7.5) when $x \neq 0$, prove the power rule stating that $y = x^a \Rightarrow y' = ax^{a-1}$.

6.8 The Chain Rule

Suppose that y is a function of x, and that z is a function of y. Recall from Section 5.2 that in this case z is a composite function of x. Now suppose that x changes. This gives rise to a two-stage "chain reaction": first, y reacts directly to the change in x; second, z reacts to this induced change in y. Suppose too that we know the rates of change dy/dx and dz/dy. Then what is the rate of change dz/dx? It turns out that we can use a very simple rule.

THE CHAIN RULE

If z is a differentiable function of y, and y is a differentiable function of x, then z is a differentiable function of x, and

$$\frac{dz}{dx} = \frac{dz}{dy} \cdot \frac{dy}{dx} \qquad (6.8.1)$$

The use of Leibniz's notation in (6.8.1) should make it easier to remember the chain rule. The reason is that the left-hand side of 6.8.1 is exactly what results if we "cancel" the two symbols dy on the right-hand side. Of course this is just a mnemonic because dz/dy and dy/dx are not fractions, but merely symbols for two different derivatives. Also, because dy is not a number, cancelling it is *not* defined![13] So in our subsequent discussion we must be more careful.

---

[13] It has been suggested that "proving" (6.8.1) by cancelling dy is not much better than "proving" that $64/16 = 4$ by cancelling the two sixes: $\cancel{6}4/1\cancel{6} = 4$.

An important special case is when z is a power function.

THE GENERALIZED POWER RULE

If $z = y^a$ and y is a differentiable function of x, then

$$z' = ay^{a-1}y' \qquad (6.8.2)$$

The chain rule is very powerful. Facility in applying it comes from a lot of practice.

EXAMPLE 6.8.1   Find dz/dx when:

(a) $z = y^5$ and $y = 1 - x^3$ \qquad (b) $z = \dfrac{10}{(x^2 + 4x + 5)^7}$

Solution:

(a) Here we can use (6.8.1) directly. Since $dz/dy = 5y^4$ and $dy/dx = -3x^2$, we have

$$\frac{dz}{dx} = \frac{dz}{dy} \cdot \frac{dy}{dx} = 5y^4(-3x^2) = -15x^2 y^4 = -15x^2(1-x^3)^4$$

Note the last step, where we have used the definition of y to reduce the answer to a function of x.

(b) Here we write $y = x^2 + 4x + 5$, implying that z is the power function $10y^{-7}$. Applying the generalized power rule (6.8.2) gives

$$\frac{dz}{dx} = 10(-7)y^{-8}y' = -70y^{-8}(2x+4) = \frac{-140(x+2)}{(x^2+4x+5)^8}$$

After a little training, the intermediate steps become unnecessary. For example, to differentiate the composite function

$$z = (\underbrace{1 - x^3}_{y})^5$$

suggested by part (a) of Example 6.8.1, we can *think* of z as $z = y^5$, where $y = 1 - x^3$. We can then differentiate both y^5 and $1 - x^3$ in our heads, and write down $z' = 5(1 - x^3)^4(-3x^2)$ immediately.

Note that if you differentiate $y = x^5/5$ using the quotient rule, you obtain the right answer, but commit a small "mathematical crime". This is because it is much easier to write y as $y = (1/5)x^5$ to get $y' = (1/5)5x^4 = x^4$. In the same way, it is unnecessarily cumbersome to apply the quotient rule to the function given in part (b) of Example 6.8.1. The generalized power rule is much more effective.

EXAMPLE 6.8.2 Differentiate the functions:

(a) $z = (x^3 + x^2)^{50}$ (b) $z = \left(\dfrac{x-1}{x+3}\right)^{1/3}$ (c) $z = \sqrt{x^2 + 1}$

Solution:

(a) Introduce the variable $y = x^3 + x^2$ so that $z = (x^3 + x^2)^{50} = y^{50}$. Then $y' = 3x^2 + 2x$ so (6.8.2) gives
$$z' = 50y^{50-1} \cdot y' = 50(x^3 + x^2)^{49}(3x^2 + 2x)$$

(b) Again, we use (6.8.2), this time with $y = (x-1)/(x+3)$, which implies that
$$z = \left(\dfrac{x-1}{x+3}\right)^{1/3} = y^{1/3}$$

First, using the quotient rule gives
$$y' = \dfrac{1 \cdot (x+3) - (x-1) \cdot 1}{(x+3)^2} = \dfrac{4}{(x+3)^2}$$

So finally
$$z' = \dfrac{1}{3}y^{(1/3)-1} \cdot y' = \dfrac{1}{3}\left(\dfrac{x-1}{x+3}\right)^{-2/3} \cdot \dfrac{4}{(x+3)^2} = \dfrac{4}{3}(x-1)^{-2/3}(x+3)^{-4/3}$$

(c) Note first that $z = \sqrt{x^2 + 1} = (x^2 + 1)^{1/2}$, so $z = y^{1/2}$ where $y = x^2 + 1$. Hence,
$$z' = \dfrac{1}{2}y^{(1/2)-1} \cdot y' = \dfrac{1}{2}(x^2 + 1)^{-1/2} \cdot 2x = \dfrac{x}{\sqrt{x^2 + 1}}$$

The formulation of the chain rule may appear abstract and difficult. However, when we interpret the derivatives involved in (6.8.1) as rates of change, the chain rule becomes rather intuitive, as the next example from economics will indicate.

EXAMPLE 6.8.3 The demand x for a commodity depends on price p, which we suppose depends on time t. Then x is a composite function of t. Applying the chain rule yields
$$\dfrac{dx}{dt} = \dfrac{dx}{dp} \cdot \dfrac{dp}{dt}$$

Suppose, for instance, that the demand for butter decreases by 5 000 pounds if the price goes up by one dollar per pound. So $dx/dp \approx -5\,000$. Suppose further that the price per pound increases by five cents per month, so $dp/dt \approx 0.05$. What is the decrease in demand in pounds per month?

Solution: Because the price per pound increases by $0.05 per month, and the demand decreases by 5000 pounds for every dollar increase in the price, the demand *decreases* by approximately $5000 \cdot 0.05 = 250$ pounds per month. This means that $dx/dt \approx -250$, measured in pounds per month.

The next example uses the chain rule several times.

EXAMPLE 6.8.4 Find $x'(t)$ when $x(t) = 5(1 + \sqrt{t^3 + 1})^{25}$.

Solution: The initial step is to let $x(t) = 5u^{25}$, where $u = 1 + \sqrt{t^3 + 1}$. Then

$$x'(t) = 5 \cdot 25u^{24}\frac{du}{dt} = 125u^{24}\frac{du}{dt} \qquad (*)$$

The new feature in this example is that we cannot write down du/dt at once: we must use the chain rule a second time. Let $u = 1 + \sqrt{v} = 1 + v^{1/2}$, where $v = t^3 + 1$. Then

$$\frac{du}{dt} = \tfrac{1}{2}v^{(1/2)-1} \cdot \frac{dv}{dt} = \tfrac{1}{2}v^{-1/2} \cdot 3t^2 = \tfrac{1}{2}(t^3 + 1)^{-1/2} \cdot 3t^2 \qquad (**)$$

Finally, substituting $(**)$ in $(*)$ gives

$$x'(t) = 125\left(1 + \sqrt{t^3 + 1}\right)^{24} \cdot \tfrac{1}{2}(t^3 + 1)^{-1/2} \cdot 3t^2$$

Suppose, as in the last example, that x is a function of u, u is a function of v, and v is in turn a function of t. Then x is a composite function of t, and the chain rule can be used twice to obtain

$$\frac{dx}{dt} = \frac{dx}{du} \cdot \frac{du}{dv} \cdot \frac{dv}{dt}$$

This is precisely the formula used in the Example 6.8.4. Again the notation is suggestive because the it is exactly what results if we "cancel" both du and dv on the right-hand side.

An Alternative Formulation of the Chain Rule

Although Leibniz's notation makes it very easy to remember the chain rule, it suffers from the defect of not specifying where each derivative is evaluated. We remedy this by introducing names for the functions involved. So let $y = f(x)$ and $z = g(y)$. Then z can be written as

$$z = (g \circ f)(x) = g(f(x))$$

Here z is a *composite function* of x, as considered in Section 5.2, with g as the *exterior function* and f as the *inner function*.

THE CHAIN RULE

Suppose that f is differentiable at x_0, and g is differentiable at $y_0 = f(x_0)$. Then the composite function $F = g \circ f$ is differentiable at x_0, and

$$F'(x_0) = g'(y_0)f'(x_0) = g'(f(x_0))f'(x_0) \qquad (6.8.3)$$

In words: *to differentiate a composite function, first differentiate the exterior function w.r.t. the inner function, and then multiply by the derivative of the inner function.*

216   CHAPTER 6 / DIFFERENTIATION

EXAMPLE 6.8.5   Find the derivative of the compound function $F(x) = g(f(x))$ at $x_0 = -3$ in case $g(y) = y^3$ and $f(x) = 2 - x^2$.

Solution: In this case one has $g'(y) = 3y^2$ and $f'(x) = -2x$. So according to (6.8.3), one has $F'(-3) = g'(f(-3))f'(-3)$. Now $f(-3) = 2 - (-3)^2 = 2 - 9 = -7$; $f'(-3) = 6$; and $g'(f(-3)) = g'(-7) = 3(-7)^2 = 3 \cdot 49 = 147$. So $F'(-3) = g'(f(-3))f'(-3) = 147 \cdot 6 = 882$.

Finally, we prove that the Chain Rule is correct. Using this alternative formulation, it is tempting to argue as follows:

Faulty "proof" of (6.8.3): We use simplified notation as above, with $z = F(x) = g(y)$ and $y = f(x)$. Now define $\Delta z = F(x) - F(x_0)$, as well as $\Delta y = y - y_0 = f(x) - f(x_0)$, and $\Delta x = x - x_0$. Since the function f is continuous, one has $\Delta y \to 0$ as $x \to x_0$, and so

$$F'(x_0) = \lim_{x \to x_0} \frac{F(x) - f(x_0)}{x - x_0} = \lim_{\Delta x \to 0} \frac{\Delta z}{\Delta x} = \lim_{\Delta x \to 0} \left(\frac{\Delta z}{\Delta y} \cdot \frac{\Delta y}{\Delta x} \right)$$

$$= \lim_{\Delta y \to 0} \frac{\Delta z}{\Delta y} \cdot \lim_{\Delta x \to 0} \frac{\Delta y}{\Delta x} = \frac{dz}{dy} \cdot \frac{dy}{dx} = g'(y_0) f'(x_0)$$

There is a catch, however, because Δy may be equal to 0 for values of x arbitrarily close to x_0, and then $\Delta z / \Delta y$ will be undefined. A correct argument goes as follows:

Correct proof of (6.8.3): Define auxiliary functions φ and γ as:

$$\varphi(x) = \begin{cases} \frac{f(x) - f(x_0)}{x - x_0} & \text{if } x \neq x_0 \\ f'(x_0) & \text{if } x = x_0 \end{cases} \quad \text{and} \quad \gamma(y) = \begin{cases} \frac{g(y) - g(y_0)}{y - y_0} & \text{if } y \neq y_0 \\ g'(y_0) & \text{if } y = y_0 \end{cases}$$

Then the hypotheses used in (6.8.3) imply that $\lim_{x \to x_0} \varphi(x) = \varphi(x_0)$ and $\lim_{y \to y_0} \gamma(y) = \gamma(y_0)$. Moreover, for all x in an interval around x_0 and all y in an interval around y_0, one has

$$f(x) - f(x_0) = \varphi(x)(x - x_0) \quad \text{and} \quad g(y) - g(y_0) = \gamma(y)(y - y_0)$$

For all h close to 0, therefore, one has

$$F(x_0 + h) - F(x_0) = g(f(x_0 + h)) - g(f(x_0))$$
$$= \gamma(f(x_0 + h)) \cdot [f(x_0 + h) - f(x_0)]$$
$$= \gamma(f(x_0 + h)) \cdot \varphi(x_0 + h) \cdot h$$

It follows that

$$F'(x_0) = \lim_{h \to 0} \frac{F(x_0 + h) - F(x_0)}{h} = \gamma(f(x_0)) \cdot \varphi(x_0) = g'(f(x_0)) f'(x_0)$$

EXERCISES FOR SECTION 6.8

1. Use the chain rule (6.8.1) to find dz/dx for the following:

   (a) $z = 5y^4$, where $y = 1 + x^2$

   (b) $z = y - y^6$, where $y = 1 + \frac{1}{x}x$

2. Compute the following:

   (a) dY/dt when $Y = -3(V + 1)^5$ and $V = \frac{1}{3}t^3$.

   (b) dK/dt when $K = AL^a$ and $L = bt + c$, where A, a, b, and c are positive constants.

SM 3. Find the derivatives of the following functions, where a, p, q, and b are constants:

   (a) $y = \dfrac{1}{(x^2 + x + 1)^5}$

   (b) $y = \sqrt{x + \sqrt{x + \sqrt{x}}}$

   (c) $y = x^a(px + q)^b$

4. If Y is a function of K, and K is a function of t, find the formula for the derivative of Y with respect to t at $t = t_0$.

5. If $Y = F(K)$ and $K = h(t)$, find the formula for dY/dt.

6. Consider the demand function $x = b - \sqrt{ap - c}$, where a, b, and c are positive constants, x is the quantity demanded, and the price p satisfies $p > c/a$. Compute dx/dp.

7. Find a formula for $h'(x)$ when:

   (a) $h(x) = f(x^2)$

   (b) $h(x) = g(x^n f(x))$

8. Let $s(t)$ be the distance in kilometres a car goes in t hours. Let $B(s)$ be the number of litres of fuel the car uses to go s kilometres. Provide an interpretation of the function $b(t) = B(s(t))$, and find a formula for $b'(t)$.

9. Suppose that $C = 20q - 4q\left(25 - \frac{1}{2}x\right)^{1/2}$, where q is a constant and $x < 50$. Find dC/dx.

10. Differentiate each of the following in two different ways:

    (a) $y = (x^4)^5 = x^{20}$

    (b) $y = (1 - x)^3 = 1 - 3x + 3x^2 - x^3$

11. Suppose you invest €1 000 at $p\%$ interest per year. Let $g(p)$ denote how many euros you will have after 10 years.

    (a) Give economic interpretations of $g(5) \approx 1629$ and $g'(5) \approx 155$.

    (b) To check the numbers in (a), find a formula for $g(p)$, then compute $g(5)$ and $g'(5)$.

12. If f is differentiable at x, find expressions for the derivatives of the following functions:

    (a) $x + f(x)$
    (b) $[f(x)]^2 - x$
    (c) $[f(x)]^4$
    (d) $x^2 f(x) + [f(x)]^3$

    (e) $xf(x)$
    (f) $\sqrt{f(x)}$
    (g) $\dfrac{x^2}{f(x)}$
    (h) $\dfrac{[f(x)]^2}{x^3}$

SM 13. (a) Use a direct argument to show that the function $\varphi(x) = 1/x$ is differentiable for all $x \neq 0$.

(b) Assuming that the functions f and g are both differentiable at x with $g(x) \neq 0$, use (a) to prove that the functions $1/g(x)$ and $f(x)/g(x)$ are both differentiable at x.

6.9 Higher-Order Derivatives

Let $f(x)$ be a differentiable function of x. The derivative $f'(x)$ is again a function of x, called the *first derivative* of f. If $f'(x)$ is also differentiable with respect to x, then we can differentiate f' in turn. The result $(f')'$ is called the *second derivative*, written more concisely as f''. We use $f''(x)$ to denote the second derivative of f evaluated at the particular point x.

EXAMPLE 6.9.1   Find $f'(x)$ and $f''(x)$ when $f(x) = 2x^5 - 3x^3 + 2x$.

Solution: The rules for differentiating polynomials imply that $f'(x) = 10x^4 - 9x^2 + 2$. Then we differentiate each side of this equality to get $f''(x) = 40x^3 - 18x$.

The different forms of notation for the second derivative are analogous to those for the first derivative. For example, we write $y'' = f''(x)$ in order to denote the second derivative of $y = f(x)$. The Leibniz notation for the second derivative is also used. In the notation dy/dx or $df(x)/dx$ for the first derivative, we interpreted the symbol d/dx as an operator indicating that what follows is to be differentiated with respect to x. The second derivative is obtained by using the operator d/dx twice: $f''(x) = (d/dx)(d/dx)f(x)$. We usually think of this as $f''(x) = (d/dx)^2 f(x)$, and so write

$$f''(x) = \frac{d^2 f(x)}{dx^2} \quad \text{or} \quad y'' = \frac{d^2 y}{dx^2}$$

Pay special attention to where the superscripts are placed! Of course, the notation y'' for the second derivative must change if the variable involved has a name other than y.

EXAMPLE 6.9.2   Find:

(a) Y'' when $Y = AK^a$ is a function of $K > 0$, with A and a as constants.

(b) $d^2 L/dt^2$ when $L = \frac{t}{t+1}$, and $t \geq 0$.

Solution:

(a) Differentiating $Y = AK^a$ once with respect to K gives $Y' = AaK^{a-1}$. Differentiating a second time with respect to K yields $Y'' = Aa(a-1)K^{a-2}$.

(b) First, use the quotient rule to find that

$$\frac{dL}{dt} = \frac{d}{dt}\left(\frac{t}{t+1}\right) = \frac{1 \cdot (t+1) - t \cdot 1}{(t+1)^2} = (t+1)^{-2}$$

Then,

$$\frac{d^2 L}{dt^2} = \frac{d}{dt}(t+1)^{-2} = -2(t+1)^{-3} = \frac{-2}{(t+1)^3}$$

Third and Higher Derivatives

If $y = f(x)$, the derivative of $y'' = f''(x)$ w.r.t x is called the *third derivative*, customarily denoted by $y''' = f'''(x)$. It is notationally cumbersome to continue using more and more primes to indicate repeated differentiation, so the *fourth derivative* is usually denoted by $y^{(4)} = f^{(4)}(x)$.[14] The same derivative can be expressed as d^4y/dx^4. In general, let

$$y^{(n)} = f^{(n)}(x) \quad \text{or} \quad \frac{d^n y}{dx^n}$$

denote the *n*th *derivative* of f at x. The natural number n is called the *order* of the derivative. For example, $f^{(6)}(x_0)$ denotes the sixth derivative of f calculated at x_0, found by differentiating six times.

EXAMPLE 6.9.3 Compute all the derivatives up to and including order 4 of

$$f(x) = 3x^{-1} + 6x^3 - x^2$$

where $x \neq 0$.

Solution: Repeated differentiation gives

$$f'(x) = -3x^{-2} + 18x^2 - 2x, \qquad f''(x) = 6x^{-3} + 36x - 2$$

$$f'''(x) = -18x^{-4} + 36, \qquad f^{(4)}(x) = 72x^{-5}$$

EXERCISES FOR SECTION 6.9

1. Compute the second derivatives of:

   (a) $y = x^5 - 3x^4 + 2$ (b) $y = \sqrt{x}$ (c) $y = (1 + x^2)^{10}$

2. Find d^2y/dx^2 when $y = \sqrt{1 + x^2} = (1 + x^2)^{1/2}$.

3. Compute:

   (a) y'' for $y = 3x^3 + 2x - 1$ (b) Y''' for $Y = 1 - 2x^2 + 6x^3$
   (c) d^3z/dt^3 for $z = 120t - (1/3)t^3$ (d) $f^{(4)}(1)$ for $f(z) = 100z^{-4}$

4. Find $g''(2)$ when $g(t) = \dfrac{t^2}{t - 1}$.

5. Find formulas for y'' and y''' when $y = f(x)g(x)$.

6. Find d^2L/dt^2 when $L = 1/\sqrt{2t - 1}$.

---

[14] We put the number 4 in parentheses in order to avoid confusion with y^4, the fourth power of y.

7. If $u(y)$ denotes an individual's utility of having income y, then $R = -yu''(y)/u'(y)$ is the coefficient of *relative risk aversion*.[15] Compute R for the following utility functions, where A_1, A_2, and ρ are positive constants with $\rho \neq 1$, and we assume that $y > 0$:

   (a) $u(y) = A_1 y$ (b) $u(y) = \sqrt{y}$ (c) $u(y) = A_1 - A_2 y^{-2}$ (d) $u(y) = A_1 + A_2 \dfrac{y^{1-\rho}}{1-\rho}$

8. The US Secretary of Defense claimed in 1985 that Congress had reduced the defence budget. Representative Gray pointed out that the budget had not been reduced: instead, Congress had only reduced the rate of increase. If P denotes the size of the defence budget, translate these two statements into equivalent statements about the signs of P' and P''.

9. Sentence in a newspaper: "The rate of increase of bank loans is increasing at an increasing rate." If $L(t)$ denotes total bank loans at time t, represent the sentence by a mathematical statement about the sign of an appropriate derivative of L.

6.10 Exponential Functions

Exponential functions were introduced in Section 4.9. They were shown to be well suited to describing certain economic phenomena such as growth and compound interest. In particular we introduced the *natural* exponential function $f(x) = e^x$, where $e \approx 2.71828$, as well as the alternative notation $\exp x$.

Now we explain why this particular exponential function deserves to be called "natural". Consider the Newton quotient of $f(x) = e^x$, which is

$$\frac{f(x+h) - f(x)}{h} = \frac{e^{x+h} - e^x}{h} \qquad (*)$$

Now, if we can establish that this Newton quotient tends to a limit as h tends to 0, it will follow that $f(x) = e^x$ is differentiable and that $f'(x)$ is precisely equal to this limit.

To simplify the right-hand side of $(*)$, we make use of the rule $e^{x+h} = e^x \cdot e^h$ to write $e^{x+h} - e^x$ as $e^x(e^h - 1)$. So $(*)$ can be rewritten as

$$\frac{f(x+h) - f(x)}{h} = e^x \cdot \frac{e^h - 1}{h} \qquad (**)$$

We now evaluate the limit of the right-hand side as $h \to 0$. Note that e^x is a constant when we vary only h. As for $(e^h - 1)/h$, in Example 6.5.1 we saw that this fraction seems to tend to 1 as h tends to 0, although in that example the variable was x and not h. For now, let us simply accept that $\lim_{h \to 0} \frac{1}{h}(e^h - 1) = 1$. Then taking the limit of $(**)$ as $h \to 0$ gives:

DERIVATIVE OF THE NATURAL EXPONENTIAL FUNCTION

$$f(x) = e^x \implies f'(x) = e^x \qquad (6.10.1)$$

---

[15] By contrast, $R_A = -u''(y)/u'(y)$ is the degree of *absolute risk aversion*.

Thus the *natural exponential function* $f(x) = e^x$ has the remarkable property that its derivative is equal to the function itself. This is the main reason why this function appears so often in mathematics and its applications. An implication of (6.10.1) is that differentiating its right-hand side again repeatedly yields $f''(x) = e^x$ first, and then $f^{(n)}(x) = e^x$ for all natural numbers n.

Because $e^x > 0$ for all x, both $f'(x)$ and $f''(x)$ are positive. Hence, both f and f' are strictly increasing. This confirms the convex shape indicated in Fig. 4.9.3, where the graph curves with its hollow side upwards. (See Chapter 8 for more about convex functions.)

Combining (6.10.1) with the other rules of differentiation, we can differentiate many expressions involving the exponential function e^x.

EXAMPLE 6.10.1   Find the first and second derivatives of:

(a) $y = x^3 + e^x$ 　　　　(b) $y = x^5 e^x$ 　　　　(c) $y = e^x/x$

Solution:

(a) We find that $y' = 3x^2 + e^x$ and $y'' = 6x + e^x$.

(b) First, using the product rule gives $y' = 5x^4 e^x + x^5 e^x = x^4 e^x (5 + x)$. To find y'', we differentiate $y' = 5x^4 e^x + x^5 e^x$ once more to obtain

$$y'' = 20x^3 e^x + 5x^4 e^x + 5x^4 e^x + x^5 e^x = x^3 e^x (x^2 + 10x + 20)$$

(c) Applying the quotient rule to $y = \dfrac{e^x}{x}$ yields $y' = \dfrac{e^x x - e^x \cdot 1}{x^2} = \dfrac{e^x(x-1)}{x^2}$. Differentiating $y' = \dfrac{e^x x - e^x}{x^2}$ once more w.r.t. x gives

$$y'' = \frac{(e^x x + e^x - e^x)x^2 - (e^x x - e^x)2x}{(x^2)^2} = \frac{e^x(x^2 - 2x + 2)}{x^3}$$

Next we explore some of the rather complicated possibilities that emerge when (6.10.1) is used in combination with the chain rule (6.8.1). First, note that $y = e^{g(x)}$ can be re-written as $y = e^u$, where $u = g(x)$. Then $y' = e^u \cdot u'$ and $u' = g'(x)$, so that:

$$y = e^{g(x)} \implies y' = e^{g(x)} g'(x) \qquad (6.10.2)$$

EXAMPLE 6.10.2   Differentiate the functions:

(a) $y = e^{-x}$ 　　(b) $y = x^p e^{ax}$, where p and a are constants 　　(c) $y = \sqrt{e^{2x} + x}$

Solution:

(a) Direct use of rule (6.10.2) gives $y = e^{-x} \implies y' = e^{-x} \cdot (-1) = -e^{-x}$. This derivative is always negative, so the function is strictly decreasing. Furthermore, one has $y'' = e^{-x} > 0$, so the negative slope increases toward 0. This agrees with the graph shown in Fig. 4.9.3.

(b) The derivative of e^{ax} is ae^{ax}. Hence, using the product rule gives:
$$y' = px^{p-1}e^{ax} + x^p ae^{ax} = x^{p-1}e^{ax}(p + ax)$$

(c) Let $y = \sqrt{e^{2x} + x} = \sqrt{u}$, with $u = e^{2x} + x$. Then $u' = 2e^{2x} + 1$, where we used the chain rule. Using the chain rule again, we obtain
$$y = \sqrt{e^{2x} + x} = \sqrt{u} \implies y' = \frac{1}{2\sqrt{u}} \cdot u' = \frac{2e^{2x} + 1}{2\sqrt{e^{2x} + x}}$$

EXAMPLE 6.10.3 For each of the following functions, find the intervals where they are increasing:

(a) $y = e^x/x$ (b) $y = x^4 e^{-2x}$ (c) $y = xe^{-\sqrt{x}}$

Solution:

(a) According to Example 6.10.1(c), $y' = e^x(x-1)/x^2$, so $y' \geq 0$ when $x \geq 1$. Thus y is increasing in $[1, \infty)$.

(b) From Example 6.10.2(b), with $p = 4$ and $a = -2$, we have $y' = x^3 e^{-2x}(4 - 2x)$. A sign diagram reveals that y is increasing in $[0, 2]$.

(c) The function is only defined for $x \geq 0$. Using the chain rule, for $x > 0$ the derivative of $e^{-\sqrt{x}}$ is $-e^{-\sqrt{x}}/2\sqrt{x}$, so by the product rule, the derivative of $y = xe^{-\sqrt{x}}$ is
$$y' = 1 \cdot e^{-\sqrt{x}} - \frac{xe^{-\sqrt{x}}}{2\sqrt{x}} = e^{-\sqrt{x}}\left(1 - \frac{1}{2}\sqrt{x}\right)$$
where the second equality results from the fact that $x/\sqrt{x} = \sqrt{x}$. It follows that y is increasing when $x > 0$ and $1 - \frac{1}{2}\sqrt{x} \geq 0$. Because $y = 0$ when $x = 0$ and $y > 0$ when $x > 0$, it follows that y is increasing in $[0, 4]$.

A common error when differentiating exponential functions is to believe that the derivative of e^x w.r.t. x is "xe^{x-1}". Actually, this is the derivative of e^x w.r.t. e. The exponential function e^x of x has been confused with the power function e^x of e!

PROPERTIES OF THE NATURAL EXPONENTIAL FUNCTION

The natural exponential function
$$f(x) = \exp(x) = e^x$$
is differentiable and strictly increasing. In fact, $f'(x) = f(x) = e^x$. The following properties hold for all exponents s and t:
$$e^s e^t = e^{s+t}, \quad e^s/e^t = e^{s-t}, \quad \text{and} \quad (e^s)^t = e^{st}$$

Moreover,
$$\lim_{x \to -\infty} e^x = 0 \quad \text{and} \quad \lim_{x \to \infty} e^x = \infty \tag{6.10.3}$$

To justify the statements in (6.10.3), we extend the concept of limit introduced in Section 6.5 to allow limits as $x \to \pm\infty$, and so as $|x|$ becomes indefinitely large. The first claim in (6.10.3) holds because if $0 < h < 1$, then no matter how small h may be, one will have $0 < e^x < h$ for all $x < \ln h < 0$. Similarly, the second claim in (6.10.3) holds because no matter how large y may be, one will have $e^x > y$ for all $x > \ln y$.

Differentiating other Exponential Functions

So far we have considered only the derivative of e^x, where $e = 2.71828\ldots$. How can we differentiate $y = a^x$, where a is any other positive constant? According to definition (4.10.1), we have $a = e^{\ln a}$. So, using the general property $(e^r)^s = e^{rs}$, we have the formula

$$a^x = (e^{\ln a})^x = e^{(\ln a)x}$$

This shows that in functions involving the expression a^x, we can just as easily work with the special exponential function e^{bx}, where b is a constant equal to $\ln a$. In particular, we can differentiate a^x by differentiating $e^{x \ln a}$. According to (6.10.2), with $g(x) = (\ln a)x$, we have

$$y = a^x \implies y' = a^x \ln a \qquad (6.10.4)$$

EXAMPLE 6.10.4 Find the derivatives of: (a) $f(x) = 10^{-x}$; and (b) $g(x) = x2^{3x}$.

Solution:

(a) Rewrite $f(x) = 10^{-x} = 10^u$, where $u = -x$. Using (6.10.4) and the chain rule gives $f'(x) = -10^{-x} \ln 10$.

(b) Rewrite $y = 2^{3x} = 2^u$, where $u = 3x$. By the chain rule,

$$y' = (2^u \ln 2)u' = (2^{3x} \ln 2) \cdot 3 = 3 \cdot 2^{3x} \ln 2$$

Applying the product rule to $g(x) = x2^{3x} = xy$, we obtain

$$g'(x) = 1 \cdot 2^{3x} + x \cdot 3 \cdot 2^{3x} \ln 2 = 2^{3x}(1 + 3x \ln 2)$$

EXERCISES FOR SECTION 6.10

1. Find the first-order derivatives w.r.t. x of:

   (a) $y = e^x + x^2$ (b) $y = 5e^x - 3x^3 + 8$ (c) $y = \dfrac{x}{e^x}$ (d) $y = \dfrac{x+x^2}{e^x+1}$

   (e) $y = -x-5-e^x$ (f) $y = x^3 e^x$ (g) $y = e^x x^{-2}$ (h) $y = (x+e^x)^2$

2. Find the first derivatives w.r.t. t of the following functions, where a, b, c, p, and q are constants:

   (a) $x = (a + bt + ct^2)e^t$ (b) $x = \dfrac{p + qt^3}{te^t}$ (c) $x = \dfrac{(at + bt^2)^2}{e^t}$

3. Find the first and second derivatives of:

   (a) $y = e^{-3x}$ (b) $y = 2e^{x^3}$ (c) $y = e^{1/x}$ (d) $y = 5e^{2x^2 - 3x + 1}$

4. Find the intervals where the following functions are increasing:

(a) $y = x^3 + e^{2x}$ (b) $y = 5x^2 e^{-4x}$ (c) $y = x^2 e^{-x^2}$

5. Find the intervals where the following functions are increasing:

(a) $y = x^2/e^{2x}$ (b) $y = e^x - e^{3x}$ (c) $y = \dfrac{e^{2x}}{x+2}$

6. Find:

(a) $\dfrac{d}{dx}\left(e^{(e^x)}\right)$ (b) $\dfrac{d}{dt}\left(e^{t/2} + e^{-t/2}\right)$ (c) $\dfrac{d}{dt}\left(\dfrac{1}{e^t + e^{-t}}\right)$ (d) $\dfrac{d}{dz}\left(e^{z^3} - 1\right)^{1/3}$

7. Differentiate:

(a) $y = 5^x$ (b) $y = x2^x$ (c) $y = x^2 2^{x^2}$ (d) $y = e^x 10^x$.

6.11 Logarithmic Functions

In Section 4.10 we introduced the natural logarithmic function, $g(x) = \ln x$. It is defined for all $x > 0$ and has the graph shown in Fig. 4.10.2.

According to Section 5.3, this function has $f(x) = e^x$ as its *inverse*. If we *assume* that $g(x) = \ln x$ has a derivative for all $x > 0$, we can easily find that derivative. To do so, consider the equation defining $g(x) = \ln x$, which is

$$e^{g(x)} = x \qquad (*)$$

Using (6.10.2), we differentiate each side of $(*)$ w.r.t. x, which gives $e^{g(x)} g'(x) = 1$. Since $e^{g(x)} = x$, this implies that $xg'(x) = 1$, and so $g'(x) = 1/x$. This gives us:

DERIVATIVE OF THE NATURAL LOGARITHMIC FUNCTION

$$g(x) = \ln x \implies g'(x) = \frac{1}{x} \qquad (6.11.1)$$

For all $x > 0$, this gives $g'(x) > 0$, implying that $g(x)$ is *strictly* increasing. Note moreover that $g''(x) = -1/x^2$, which is less than 0 for all $x > 0$, so that $g(x)$ is concave—that is, it curves with its hollow side downwards. (See Chapter 8 for more about concave functions.) This confirms the shape of the graph in Fig. 4.10.2. In fact, the function $\ln x$ grows quite slowly: for example, $\ln x$ does not pass the value 10 until $x > 22026$, because $\ln x = 10$ gives $x = e^{10} \approx 22026.5$.

EXAMPLE 6.11.1 Compute y' and y'' when:

(a) $y = x^3 + \ln x$ (b) $y = x^2 \ln x$ (c) $y = \dfrac{\ln x}{x}$

Solution:

(a) We find easily that $y' = 3x^2 + 1/x$. Furthermore, $y'' = 6x - 1/x^2$.

(b) The product rule gives $y' = 2x \ln x + x^2(1/x) = 2x \ln x + x$. Differentiating the last expression w.r.t. x gives $y'' = 2 \ln x + 2x(1/x) + 1 = 2 \ln x + 3$.

(c) Here we use the quotient rule:
$$y' = \frac{(1/x)x - (\ln x) \cdot 1}{x^2} = \frac{1 - \ln x}{x^2}$$

Differentiating again yields
$$y'' = \frac{-(1/x)x^2 - (1 - \ln x)2x}{(x^2)^2} = \frac{2 \ln x - 3}{x^3}$$

We often need to consider composite functions involving natural logarithms. Because $\ln u$ is defined only when $u > 0$, a composite function of the form $y = \ln h(x)$ will only be defined for values of x satisfying $h(x) > 0$.

Combining the rule for differentiating $\ln x$ with the chain rule allows us to differentiate many different types of function. Suppose, for instance, that $y = \ln h(x)$, where $h(x)$ is differentiable and positive. By the chain rule, $y = \ln u$ with $u = h(x)$ implies that $y' = (1/u)u' = (1/h(x)) h'(x)$, so:

DERIVATIVE OF THE NATURAL LOGARITHM OF A FUNCTION

If $h(x) > 0$ for all x, then

$$y = \ln h(x) \implies y' = \frac{h'(x)}{h(x)} \qquad (6.11.2)$$

Note that if $N(t)$ is a function of t satisfying $N(t) > 0$ for all t, then the derivative of its natural logarithm is
$$\frac{d}{dt} \ln N(t) = \frac{1}{N(t)} \frac{dN(t)}{dt} = \frac{\dot{N}(t)}{N(t)}$$

This is the relative rate of growth of $N(t)$.

EXAMPLE 6.11.2 Find the domains of the following functions and then compute their derivatives:

(a) $y = \ln(1 - x)$ (b) $y = \ln(4 - x^2)$ (c) $y = \ln\left(\frac{x-1}{x+1}\right) - \frac{x}{4}$

Solution:

(a) $\ln(1 - x)$ is defined if $1 - x > 0$, that is if $x < 1$. To find its derivative, we use (6.11.2), with $h(x) = 1 - x$. Then $h'(x) = -1$, and
$$y' = \frac{-1}{1-x} = \frac{1}{x-1}$$

(b) $\ln(4 - x^2)$ is defined if $4 - x^2 > 0$, which is satisfied if and only if $-2 < x < 2$. On the interval $(-2, 2)$, formula (6.11.2) gives

$$y' = \frac{-2x}{4 - x^2} = \frac{2x}{x^2 - 4}$$

(c) We can write $y = \ln u - \frac{1}{4}x$, where $u = (x - 1)/(x + 1)$. For the function to be defined, we require that $u > 0$. A sign diagram shows that this is satisfied if $x < -1$ or $x > 1$, or iff $|x| > 1$. Using (6.11.2), we obtain

$$y' = \frac{u'}{u} - \frac{1}{4}$$

where

$$u' = \frac{1 \cdot (x + 1) - 1 \cdot (x - 1)}{(x + 1)^2} = \frac{2}{(x + 1)^2}$$

We conclude that

$$y' = \frac{2(x + 1)}{(x + 1)^2 (x - 1)} - \frac{1}{4} = \frac{9 - x^2}{4(x^2 - 1)} = \frac{(3 - x)(3 + x)}{4(x - 1)(x + 1)}$$

EXAMPLE 6.11.3   Find the intervals where the following functions are increasing:

(a) $y = x^2 \ln x$ (b) $y = 4x - 5\ln(x^2 + 1)$ (c) $y = 3\ln(1 + x) + x - \frac{1}{2}x^2$

Solution:

(a) The function is defined for $x > 0$, and

$$y' = 2x \ln x + x^2(1/x) = x(2 \ln x + 1)$$

Hence, $y' \geq 0$ when $\ln x \geq -1/2$, that is, when $x \geq e^{-1/2}$. That is, y is increasing in the interval $[e^{-1/2}, \infty)$.

(b) We find that

$$y' = 4 - \frac{10x}{x^2 + 1} = \frac{4(x - 2)\left(x - \frac{1}{2}\right)}{x^2 + 1}$$

A sign diagram reveals that y is increasing in each of the intervals $(-\infty, \frac{1}{2}]$ and $[2, \infty)$.

(c) The function is defined for $x > -1$, and

$$y' = \frac{3}{1 + x} + 1 - x = \frac{(2 - x)(2 + x)}{x + 1}$$

A sign diagram reveals that y is increasing in $(-1, 2]$.

PROPERTIES OF THE NATURAL LOGARITHMIC FUNCTION

The natural logarithmic function

$$g(x) = \ln x$$

is differentiable and strictly increasing in $(0, \infty)$. In fact,

$$g'(x) = 1/x, \quad g''(x) = -1/x^2$$

By definition, $e^{\ln x} = x$ for all $x > 0$, and $\ln e^x = x$ for all x. The following properties hold for all $x > 0$ and all $y > 0$:

$$\ln(xy) = \ln x + \ln y, \ \ln(x/y) = \ln x - \ln y, \ \text{and} \ \ln x^p = p \ln x$$

Moreover,

$$\ln x \to -\infty \text{ as } x \to 0 \text{ from the right} \qquad (6.11.3)$$

and

$$\lim_{x \to \infty} \ln x = \infty \qquad (6.11.4)$$

The limits in (6.11.3) and (6.11.4) can be established by adapting the arguments we used to justify (6.10.3). Indeed, given any $y < 0$, no matter how large $|y|$ may be, one has $\ln x < y$ whenever $0 < x < e^y$. This justifies (6.11.3). Also, given any $z > 0$, no matter how large, one has $\ln x > z$ for all $x > e^z$, which justifies (6.11.4).

Logarithmic Differentiation

When differentiating an expression containing products, quotients, roots, powers, and combinations of these, it is often an advantage to use *logarithmic differentiation*. The method is illustrated by two examples:

EXAMPLE 6.11.4 Find the derivative of $y = x^x$ defined for all $x > 0$.

Solution: Recall that the power rule of differentiation, which is $y = x^a \Rightarrow y' = ax^{a-1}$, requires the exponent a to be a constant. On the other hand the rule $y = a^x \Rightarrow y' = a^x \ln a$ requires that the base a is constant. In the expression x^x both the exponent and the base vary with x, so neither of these two rules can be used.

Instead we begin by taking the natural logarithm of each side, which gives $\ln y = x \ln x$. Differentiating each side w.r.t. x gives $y'/y = 1 \cdot \ln x + x(1/x) = \ln x + 1$. Multiplying by $y = x^x$ gives us the final result:

$$y = x^x \quad \Longrightarrow \quad y' = x^x(\ln x + 1)$$

EXAMPLE 6.11.5 Find the derivative of $y = [A(x)]^\alpha [B(x)]^\beta [C(x)]^\gamma$, where α, β, and γ are constants, whereas A, B, and C are functions with positive values for all $x > 0$.

Solution: First, take the natural logarithm of each side to obtain

$$\ln y = \alpha \ln(A(x)) + \beta \ln(B(x)) + \gamma \ln(C(x))$$

Next, differentiate w.r.t. x to obtain

$$\frac{y'}{y} = \alpha \frac{A'(x)}{A(x)} + \beta \frac{B'(x)}{B(x)} + \gamma \frac{C'(x)}{C(x)}$$

Multiplying by y, we have

$$y' = \left[\alpha \frac{A'(x)}{A(x)} + \beta \frac{B'(x)}{B(x)} + \gamma \frac{C'(x)}{C(x)} \right] [A(x)]^\alpha [B(x)]^\beta [C(x)]^\gamma$$

In Eq. (4.10.5), we showed that the logarithm of x in the system with base a, denoted by $\log_a x$, satisfies $\log_a x = (1/\ln a) \ln x$. Differentiating each side of this equality w.r.t. x, it follows immediately that:

$$y = \log_a x \Rightarrow y' = \frac{1}{\ln a} \frac{1}{x} \qquad (6.11.5)$$

Approximating the Number e

If $g(x) = \ln x$, then $g'(x) = 1/x$, and in particular $g'(1) = 1$. To derive the next equality, we use in turn: (i) the definition of $g'(1)$; (ii) the fact that $\ln 1 = 0$; (iii) the rule $\ln x^p = p \ln x$. The result is

$$1 = g'(1) = \lim_{h \to 0} \frac{\ln(1+h) - \ln 1}{h} = \lim_{h \to 0} \frac{1}{h} \ln(1+h) = \lim_{h \to 0} \ln(1+h)^{1/h}$$

Because $\ln(1+h)^{1/h}$ tends to 1 as h tends to 0 and the exponential mapping is continuous, it follows that $(1+h)^{1/h} = \exp\left[\ln(1+h)^{1/h}\right]$ itself must tend to $\exp 1 = e$. That is,

EULER'S NUMBER e

$$e = \lim_{h \to 0} (1+h)^{1/h} \qquad (6.11.6)$$

To illustrate this limit, Table 6.11.1 gives some function values that were computed using a calculator. These numbers seem to confirm that the decimal expansion $2.718281828\ldots$ that Eq. (4.9.2) gave for e starts out correctly. Of course, this by no means proves that the limit exists. But it does suggest that closer and closer approximations to e can be obtained by choosing h smaller and smaller.[16]

Table 6.11.1 Values of $(1+h)^{1/h}$ as $h > 0$ gets smaller and smaller

h	1	1/2	1/10	1/1000	10^{-6}	10^{-10}
$(1+h)^{1/h}$	2	2.25	2.5937…	2.7169…	2.7182805…	2.7182818283…

---

[16] Example 7.5.4 provides a much better way to approximate e^x, for general real x.

Power Functions

In Section 6.6 we claimed that, for all real numbers a and all $x > 0$ one has

$$f(x) = x^a \implies f'(x) = ax^{a-1} \tag{6.11.7}$$

So far this important rule, stated earlier as (6.6.4), has only been properly established when the power a is an integer, in which case it holds for all real x when $a > 0$, and for all $x \neq 0$ when $a \leq 0$.

More generally, suppose that x and a are both real numbers, with $x > 0$. Then, because $x = \exp(\ln x)$, we have $x^a = [\exp(\ln x)]^a = \exp(a \ln x)$. Using the chain rule with $y = a \ln x$ to differentiate, we get

$$\frac{d}{dx}(x^a) = \frac{d}{dx}\exp(a \ln x) = \frac{d(\exp(y))}{dy} \cdot \frac{dy}{dx} = \exp(y) \cdot \frac{a}{x} = x^a \frac{a}{x} = ax^{a-1}$$

So, even when the a is not an integer but $x > 0$, this justifies using the power rule to differentiate x^a w.r.t. x.

EXERCISES FOR SECTION 6.11

1. Compute the first and second derivatives of:

(a) $y = \ln x + 3x - 2$ (b) $y = x^2 - 2\ln x$ (c) $y = x^3 \ln x$ (d) $y = \dfrac{\ln x}{x}$

2. Find the derivatives of:

(a) $y = x^3(\ln x)^2$ (b) $y = \dfrac{x^2}{\ln x}$ (c) $y = (\ln x)^{10}$ (d) $y = (\ln x + 3x)^2$

SM 3. Find the derivatives of:

(a) $\ln(\ln x)$ (b) $\ln \sqrt{1 - x^2}$ (c) $e^x \ln x$ (d) $e^{x^3} \ln x^2$

(e) $\ln(e^x + 1)$ (f) $\ln(x^2 + 3x - 1)$ (g) $2(e^x - 1)^{-1}$ (h) $e^{2x^2 - x}$

4. Determine the domains of the functions defined by:

(a) $y = \ln(x + 1)$ (b) $y = \ln\left(\dfrac{3x - 1}{1 - x}\right)$ (c) $y = \ln |x|$

SM 5. Determine the domains of the functions defined by:

(a) $y = \ln(x^2 - 1)$ (b) $y = \ln(\ln x)$ (c) $y = \dfrac{1}{\ln(\ln x) - 1}$

SM 6. Find the intervals where the following functions are increasing:

(a) $y = \ln(4 - x^2)$ (b) $y = x^3 \ln x$ (c) $y = \dfrac{(1 - \ln x)^2}{2x}$

7. Find the equations for the tangents to the graph of

(a) $y = \ln x$ at the three points with x-coordinates: 1, $\frac{1}{2}$, and e.

(b) $y = xe^x$ at the three points with x-coordinates: 0, 1, and -2.

8. Use logarithmic differentiation to find $f'(x)/f(x)$ when:

   (a) $f(x) = x^{2x}$ (b) $f(x) = \sqrt{x-2}\,(x^2+1)(x^4+6)$ (c) $f(x) = \left(\dfrac{x+1}{x-1}\right)^{1/3}$

SM 9. Differentiate the following functions using logarithmic differentiation:

   (a) $y = (2x)^x$ (b) $y = x^{\sqrt{x}}$ (c) $y = (\sqrt{x})^x$

10. Prove that if u and v are differentiable functions of x, and $u > 0$, then
$$y = u^v \Rightarrow y' = u^v \left(v' \ln u + \dfrac{vu'}{u}\right)$$

SM 11. [HARDER] If $f(x) = e^x - 1 - x$, then $f'(x) = e^x - 1 > 0$ for all $x > 0$. The function $f(x)$ is therefore strictly increasing in the interval $[0, \infty)$. Since $f(0) = 0$, it follows that $f(x) > 0$ for all $x > 0$, and so $e^x > 1 + x$ for all $x > 0$. Use the same method to prove the following inequalities:

   (a) $e^x > 1 + x + x^2/2$ for $x > 0$ (b) $\tfrac{1}{2}x < \ln(1+x) < x$ for $0 < x < 1$

   (c) $\ln x < 2(\sqrt{x} - 1)$ for $x > 1$

REVIEW EXERCISES

1. Let $f(x) = x^2 - x + 2$. Show that the Newton quotient is $2x - 1 + h$ and use this to find $f'(x)$.

2. Let $f(x) = -2x^3 + x^2$. Compute the Newton quotient and find $f'(x)$.

3. Compute the first- and second-order derivatives of the following functions:

   (a) $y = 2x - 5$ (b) $y = \tfrac{1}{3}x^9$ (c) $y = 1 - \tfrac{1}{10}x^{10}$ (d) $y = 3x^7 + 8$

   (e) $y = \tfrac{1}{10}(x - 5)$ (f) $y = x^5 - x^{-5}$ (g) $y = \tfrac{1}{4}x^4 + \tfrac{1}{3}x^3 + \tfrac{1}{2}5^2$ (h) $y = x^{-1} + x^{-2}$

4. Let $C(Q)$ denote the cost of producing Q units per month of a commodity. What is the interpretation of $C'(1000) = 25$? Suppose the price obtained per unit is fixed at 30 and that the current output per month is 1000. Is it profitable to increase production?

5. For each of the following functions, find the equation for the tangent to the graph at the specified point:

   (a) $y = -3x^2$ at $x = 1$ (b) $y = \sqrt{x} - x^2$ at $x = 4$ (c) $y = \dfrac{x^2 - x^3}{x + 3}$ at $x = 1$

6. Let $A(x)$ denote the dollar cost of building a house with a floor area of x square metres. What is the interpretation of $A'(100) = 250$?

7. Differentiate the following functions:

   (a) $f(x) = x(x^2 + 1)$ (b) $g(w) = w^{-5}$ (c) $h(y) = y(y-1)(y+1)$

   (d) $G(t) = \dfrac{2t+1}{t^2+3}$ (e) $\varphi(\xi) = \dfrac{2\xi}{\xi^2+2}$ (f) $F(s) = \dfrac{s}{s^2+s-2}$

8. Find the derivatives:

   (a) $\dfrac{d}{da}(a^2 t - t^2)$ (b) $\dfrac{d}{dt}(a^2 t - t^2)$ (c) $\dfrac{d}{d\varphi}(x\varphi^2 - \sqrt{\varphi})$

9. Use the chain rule to find dy/dx for the following:

   (a) $y = 10u^2$, where $u = 5 - x^2$ (b) $y = \sqrt{u}$, where $u = \dfrac{1}{x} - 1$

10. Compute the following:

    (a) dZ/dt when $Z = (u^2 - 1)^3$ and $u = t^3$.   (b) dK/dt when $K = \sqrt{L}$ and $L = 1 + 1/t$.

11. If $a(t)$ and $b(t)$ are positive valued differentiable functions of t, and if A, α, and β are constants, find expressions for $\dot{x}/x$ where:

    (a) $x = a(t)^2 \cdot b(t)$ (b) $x = A \cdot a(t)^\alpha \cdot b(t)^\beta$ (c) $x = A \cdot [a(t)^\alpha + b(t)^\beta]^{\alpha+\beta}$

12. If $R = S^\alpha$, $S = 1 + \beta K^\gamma$, and $K = At^p + B$, find an expression for dR/dt.

13. Find the derivatives of the following functions, where a, b, p, and q are constants:

    (a) $h(L) = (L^a + b)^p$ (b) $C(Q) = aQ + bQ^2$ (c) $P(x) = (ax^{1/q} + b)^q$

14. Find the first derivatives of:

    (a) $y = -7e^x$ (b) $y = e^{-3x^2}$ (c) $y = \dfrac{x^2}{e^x}$ (d) $y = e^x \ln(x^2 + 2)$

    (e) $y = e^{5x^3}$ (f) $y = 2 - x^4 e^{-x}$ (g) $y = (e^x + x^2)^{10}$ (h) $y = \ln(\sqrt{x} + 1)$

(SM) 15. Find the intervals where the following functions are increasing:

    (a) $y = (\ln x)^2 - 4$ (b) $y = \ln(e^x + e^{-x})$ (c) $y = x - \tfrac{3}{2}\ln(x^2 + 2)$

16. (a) Suppose $\pi(Q) = QP(Q) - cQ$, where P is a differentiable function and c is a constant. Find an expression for $d\pi/dQ$.

    (b) Suppose $\pi(L) = PF(L) - wL$, where F is a differentiable function and P and w are constants. Find an expression for $d\pi/dL$.

7 DERIVATIVES IN USE

Although this may seem a paradox, all science is dominated by the idea of approximation.
—Bertrand Russell

Many economic models involve functions that are defined implicitly by one or more equations. We begin this chapter by showing how to compute derivatives of such functions, including how to differentiate the inverse. It is very important for economists to master the technique of implicit differentiation.

Next we consider linear approximations and differentials, followed by a discussion of quadratic and higher-order polynomial approximations. Section 7.6 studies Taylor's formula, which makes it possible to analyse the resulting error when a function is approximated by a polynomial. A discussion of the important economic concept of elasticity follows in Section 7.7.

The word *continuous* is common even in everyday language. We use it, in particular, to characterize changes that are gradual rather than sudden. This usage is closely related to the idea of a continuous function. In Section 7.8 we discuss this concept and explain its close relationship with the concept of limit. Limits and continuity are key ideas in mathematics, and also very important in the application of mathematics to economics. The practical example based on property taxes that we present toward the end of Section 7.8 helps make this point.

Our next topic is limits, for which the preliminary discussion in Section 6.5 was necessarily very sketchy. In Section 7.9 we take a closer look at this concept and extend it in several directions. Next we present the intermediate value theorem, which makes precise the idea that a continuous function has a "connected" graph. This makes it possible to prove that certain equations have solutions. A brief discussion of Newton's method for finding approximate solutions to equations is given. A short section on infinite sequences follows. Finally, Section 7.12 presents l'Hôpital's rule for indeterminate forms, which is sometimes a useful tool for evaluating limits.

7.1 Implicit Differentiation

The previous chapter was devoted to exploring ways in which one can differentiate a function given by an explicit formula of the form $y = f(x)$. Now we consider how to differentiate functions defined implicitly by an equation such as $g(x, y) = c$, where c is a constant. We begin with a very simple example.

EXAMPLE 7.1.1   Consider the following equation involving the two real variables x and y:

$$xy = 5 \tag{7.1.1}$$

If $x = 1$, then $y = 5$. Also, $x = 3$ gives $y = 5/3$. And $x = 5$ gives $y = 1$. In general, for each number $x \neq 0$, there is a unique number y such that the pair (x, y) satisfies Eq. (7.1.1). We say that equation (∗) *defines y implicitly as a function of x.* The graph of Eq. (7.1.1) for $x > 0$ is shown in Fig. 7.1.1.

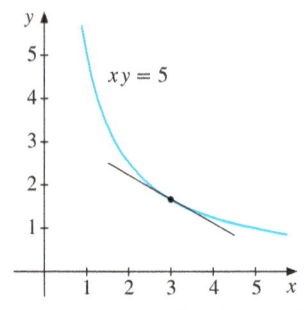

Figure 7.1.1 $xy = 5$, with $x > 0$

Economists often need to know the slope of the tangent at an arbitrary point on such a graph. That is, they need to know the derivative of y as a function of x. The answer can be found by *implicit differentiation* of Eq. (7.1.1), which defines y as a function of x. If we denote this function by f, then replace y by $f(x)$ in Eq. (7.1.1), the new equation is

$$xf(x) = 5 \text{ for all } x > 0 \tag{7.1.2}$$

Equation (7.1.2) involves only the single variable x. Because its left- and right-hand sides are equal for all $x > 0$, the derivatives of its left- and right-hand sides w.r.t. x must be equal. But the derivative of the constant 5 is 0. To differentiate $xf(x)$, we must use the product rule. So equating the derivatives of the two sides of Eq. (7.1.2) w.r.t. x yields

$$1 \cdot f(x) + xf'(x) = 0$$

It follows that for all $x > 0$ one has

$$f'(x) = -\frac{f(x)}{x}$$

If $x = 3$, then $f(3) = 5/3$, and so $f'(3) = -(5/3)/3 = -5/9$. These numerical values evidently agree with Fig. 7.1.1.

Usually, we do not introduce an explicit name like f for y as a function of x. Instead, we simply differentiate each side of Eq. (7.1.1) w.r.t. x, while recalling that y is a differentiable function of x. Using the product rule again, this leads to $y + xy' = 0$. Solving for y' gives

$$y' = -\frac{y}{x} \tag{7.1.3}$$

For this particular example, there is another way to find the answer. Solving Eq. (7.1.2) for y gives $y = 5/x = 5x^{-1}$. Differentiating each side of this equation directly gives $y' = 5(-1)x^{-2} = -5/x^2$. Note that substituting $5/x$ for y in (7.1.3) yields $y' = -5/x^2$ once again.

EXAMPLE 7.1.2 In Example 5.4.2, we studied the graph shown in Fig. 7.1.2 of the equation

$$y^3 + 3x^2 y = 13 \qquad (*)$$

It passes through the point $(2, 1)$. Find the slope of the graph at that point.

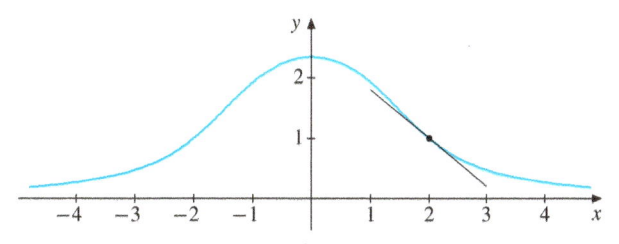

Figure 7.1.2 Graph of $y^3 + 3x^2 y = 13$

Solution: In this case expressing y as an explicit function of x would involve solving a cubic equation. So we use implicit differentiation instead. Wherever y occurs, we think of it as an unspecified differentiable function of x. In this way the expression $y^3 + 3x^2 y$ becomes a differentiable function of x, and equation $(*)$ requires it to equal the constant 13 for all x. Differentiating each side of $(*)$, we see that it requires that the derivative of $y^3 + 3x^2 y$ w.r.t. x to equal zero for all x.

According to the chain rule, the derivative of y^3 w.r.t. x is equal to $3y^2 y'$. Using the product rule, the derivative of $3x^2 y$ is equal to $6xy + 3x^2 y'$. Hence, differentiating $(*)$ gives

$$3y^2 y' + 6xy + 3x^2 y' = 0 \qquad (7.1.4)$$

Finally, solving this equation for y' yields

$$y' = \frac{-6xy}{3x^2 + 3y^2} = \frac{-2xy}{x^2 + y^2} \qquad (7.1.5)$$

For $x = 2$, $y = 1$ we find $y' = -4/5$, which agrees with Fig. 7.1.2.[1]

Examples 7.1.1 and 7.1.2 illustrate the following general method.

IMPLICIT DIFFERENTIATION

To find y' when an equation relates two variables x and y:

---

[1] Recall Fig. 5.4.3.

(i) Differentiate each side of the equation w.r.t. x, considering y as a function of x.

(ii) Solve the resulting equation for y'.

We note that step (i) will usually require the chain rule.

Section 7.2 offers several economic examples of this procedure. A particularly important application of this method occurs in Chapter 9, where we consider, for optimization problems whose parameters change, how these changes affect the solution.

EXAMPLE 7.1.3 The equation $x^2y^3 + (y+1)e^{-x} = x + 2$ defines y as a differentiable function of x in a neighbourhood of $(x, y) = (0, 1)$. Compute y' at this point.

Solution: Implicit differentiation w.r.t. x gives

$$2xy^3 + x^2 3y^2 y' + y' e^{-x} + (y+1)(-e^{-x}) = 1$$

Inserting $x = 0$ and $y = 1$ yields $y' + 2(-1) = 1$, implying that $y' = 3$.

EXAMPLE 7.1.4 Suppose y is defined implicitly as a function of x by the equation

$$g(xy^2) = xy + 1 \qquad (*)$$

where g is a given differentiable function of one variable. Find an expression for y'.

Solution: We differentiate each side of the equation w.r.t. x, considering y as a function of x. The derivative of $g(xy^2)$ w.r.t. x is $g'(xy^2)(y^2 + x2yy')$. So differentiating $(*)$ yields $g'(xy^2)(y^2 + x2yy') = y + xy'$. Solving for y' gives us

$$y' = \frac{y\left[yg'(xy^2) - 1\right]}{x\left[1 - 2yg'(xy^2)\right]}$$

EXAMPLE 7.1.5 Suppose that a person has to decide how much of her current income she will save for future consumption.[2] In economics it is common to assume that a function $u(c)$, defined over the positive real numbers, measures the value to the consumer of consuming c in a given period. If she consumes c_t in year t, her "instantaneous utility" is $u(c_t)$. Economists typically assume that the individual is impatient, in the sense that she values present consumption more than future consumption. We assume for simplicity that the individual lives for only two periods, which we call "present" and "future". Then we model her "intertemporal utility" as

$$u(c_1) + \beta u(c_2) \qquad (7.1.6)$$

Here β is a constant parameter satisfying $0 \leq \beta \leq 1$. Its difference from 1 measures the individual's impatience. Economists call the number β the individual's "discount factor".

---

[2] Example 9.5.4 will study this problem further.

Obviously saving more will reduce present consumption, denoted by c_1. By how much will the individual's future consumption c_2 have to change, if her intertemporal utility given by (7.1.6) is to remain constant? Suppose that without any change in saving, her intertemporal utility level would be $\bar{U}$. In order to keep our previous notation, let us put $x = c_1$ and $y = c_2$. It follows that y is implicitly defined as a function of x by

$$u(x) + \beta u(y) = \bar{U} \qquad (7.1.7)$$

The question we have asked is by how much must y change when x changes. Assuming the change Δx in x is small, the approximate change in y is given by $y' \cdot \Delta x$. To find y', we differentiate each side of (7.1.7) implicitly w.r.t. x, which gives

$$u'(x) + \beta u'(y) y' = 0$$

This implies that

$$y' = -\frac{u'(x)}{\beta u'(y)} \qquad (7.1.8)$$

It is normal to assume that $u'(c) > 0$ for all c, so that the individual prefers to consume more. Under that assumption, $y' < 0$, which is as it should be: if the individual's present consumption *decreases*, her future consumption *must increase* if she is to remain indifferent. The ratio $u'(x)/\beta u'(y)$ is an example of what economists call the "marginal rate of substitution" between, in this example, present and future consumption. In case $x = y$ or $c_1 = c_2$, this marginal rate of substitution is $1/\beta$. So in case $0 < \beta < 1$ and so $1/\beta > 1$, this marginal rate of substitution measures how much more value at the margin is attached to present consumption over future consumption at any point where consumption is the same in both time periods. The concept is explored further in Section 15.3.

The Second Derivative of Functions Defined Implicitly

The following examples suggest how to compute the second derivative of a function that is defined implicitly by an equation like (7.1.1).

EXAMPLE 7.1.6   Compute y'' when y is given implicitly as a function of x by $xy = 5$.

Solution: In Example 7.1.1 we used implicit differentiation to find that $y + xy' = 0$, and so $y' = -y/x$ for all $x \neq 0$. Differentiating the equation $y + xy' = 0$ implicitly w.r.t. x, while recognizing that both y and y' depend on x, gives us $y' + y' + xy'' = 0$ and so $y'' = -2y'/x$. Substituting $y' = -y/x$ gives $y'' = 2y/x^2$.

We see that if $y > 0$, then $y'' > 0$, which accords with Fig. 7.1.1 since the graph bends upwards. Because $y = 5/x$, we also get $y'' = 10/x^3$.

In order to find y'' we can also start with the formula $y' = -y/x$ that appeared as (7.1.3) in Example 7.1.1. Using the quotient rule to differentiate this fraction w.r.t. x, again taking into account that y depends on x, we obtain[3]

$$y'' = \frac{d}{dx}\left(\frac{-y}{x}\right) = -\frac{y'x - y}{x^2} = -\frac{(-y/x)x - y}{x^2} = \frac{2y}{x^2}$$

---
[3] In this simple case we can check the answer directly. Since $y = 5x^{-1}$ and $y' = -5x^{-2}$, we have $y'' = 10x^{-3}$.

EXAMPLE 7.1.7 For the function in Example 7.1.2 that was implicitly defined by the equation $y^3 + 3x^2y = 13$, find y'' at the point $(x, y) = (2, 1)$.

Solution: The easiest approach is to differentiate each side of (7.1.4) w.r.t. x. The derivative of $3y^2y'$ w.r.t. x is $(6yy')y' + 3y^2y'' = 6y(y')^2 + 3y^2y''$. The two other terms are differentiated in a similar way. Ultimately we obtain

$$6y(y')^2 + 3y^2y'' + 6y + 6xy' + 6xy' + 3x^2y'' = 0$$

Now insert $x = 2$, $y = 1$, and the value $y' = -4/5$ found in Example 7.1.2. Solving the resulting equation gives $y'' = 78/125$.

An obvious alternative approach is to differentiate w.r.t. x the fraction on the right-hand side of (7.1.5).

EXAMPLE 7.1.8 Recall the intertemporal utility problem studied in Example 7.1.5. The pairs (x, y) that satisfy Eq. (7.1.7) are the combinations of present and future consumption that leave the individual's intertemporal utility constant. The graph of all such pairs is known as the consumer's *indifference curve*, which is shown in Fig. 7.1.3.

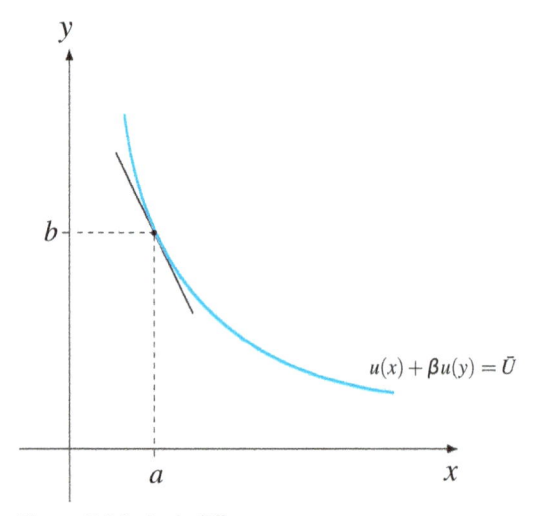

Figure 7.1.3 An indifference curve

Repeating Eq. (7.1.8), one has $y' = -u'(x)/u'(y)$, so $y' < 0$. This tells us that the indifference curve is downward sloping. Moreover, as discussed in Example 7.1.5, the absolute value of its slope at any point (a, b), given by $|y'| = u'(a)/\beta u'(b)$, is the marginal rate of substitution at that point.

We can now determine the sign of y'', which tells us more about the shape of the indifference curve. Indeed, differentiating the equation $y' = -u'(x)/u'(y)$ w.r.t. x gives

$$y'' = -\frac{u'(y)u''(x) - u'(x)u''(y)y'}{\beta[u'(y)]^2} = -\frac{1}{\beta[u'(y)]^2}\left[u'(y)u''(x) + \frac{[u'(x)]^2}{\beta u'(y)}u''(y)\right] \quad (*)$$

where we have used $y' = -u'(x)/u'(y)$ a second time in order to substitute for y'.

Economists normally assume that the first derivative of u, while positive, is decreasing. The idea is that each additional unit of consumption gives the individual a smaller increase in utility than the previous one. The assumption can be stated as $u''(c) < 0$ for all $c > 0$. This implies that in (∗) one has both $u''(x) < 0$ and $u''(y) < 0$, so $y'' > 0$.

Figure 7.1.3 includes a typical indifference curve, as well as the tangent to that curve at the point (a, b). The slope of the tangent is y', given by Eq. (7.1.8). The absolute value of that slope is the marginal rate of substitution. In the context of the example, it is called the "intertemporal" marginal rate of substitution between present and future consumption.

Equation (∗) tells us that $y'' > 0$, so y' increases with x. Because $y' < 0$, it follows that the absolute value of y' decreases as x increases. This corresponds to the fact that the indifference curve becomes flatter as one moves down and to the right. The economic interpretation is that the increase in future consumption required to compensate any fixed sacrifice of present consumption becomes lower as the person's present consumption becomes higher.

EXERCISES FOR SECTION 7.1

1. For the equation $3x^2 + 2y = 5$, find y' by implicit differentiation. Check by solving the equation for y and then differentiating.

2. For the equation $x^2y = 1$, find dy/dx and d^2y/dx^2 by implicit differentiation. Check by solving the equation for y and then differentiating.

(SM) 3. Find dy/dx and d^2y/dx^2 by implicit differentiation when: (a) $x - y + 3xy = 2$; and (b) $y^5 = x^6$.

4. A curve in the uv-plane is given by $u^2 + uv - v^3 = 0$. Compute dv/du by implicit differentiation. Find the point (u, v) on the curve where $dv/du = 0$ and $u \neq 0$.

5. Suppose that y is a differentiable function of x that satisfies the equation $2x^2 + 6xy + y^2 = 18$. Find y' and y'' at the point $(x, y) = (1, 2)$.

6. For each of the following equations, answer the question: If $y = f(x)$ is a differentiable function that satisfies the equation, what is y'? Here, a is a positive constant.

   (a) $x^2 + y^2 = a^2$ (b) $\sqrt{x} + \sqrt{y} = \sqrt{a}$ (c) $x^4 - y^4 = x^2y^3$ (d) $e^{xy} - x^2y = 1$

7. Consider the curve $2xy - 3y^2 = 9$.

   (a) Find the slope of the tangent line to the curve at $(x, y) = (6, 1)$.

   (b) Compute also the second derivative at the point.

(SM) 8. In each of the following equations, suppose g is a given differentiable function of one variable. Suppose the equation defines y implicitly as a function of x. Find an expression for y' in each case.

   (a) $xy = g(x) + y^3$ (b) $g(x + y) = x^2 + y^2$ (c) $(xy + 1)^2 = g(x^2y)$

9. Suppose F is a differentiable function of one variable, with $F(0) = 0$ and $F'(0) \neq -1$. Suppose too that y is defined implicitly as a differentiable function of x by the equation

$$x^3 F(xy) + e^{xy} = x$$

Find an expression for y' at the point $(x, y) = (1, 0)$.

(SM) 10. The elegant curve shown in Fig. 7.1.4 is known as a *lemniscate*. In the late 1600s, the Swiss mathematician Johann Bernoulli (1667–1748) discovered that it is the graph of the equation

$$(x^2 + y^2)^2 = a^2(x^2 - y^2)$$

where a is a positive constant.

(a) Find the slope of the tangent to this curve at any point (x, y) where $y \neq 0$.

(b) Determine those points on the curve where the tangent is parallel to the x-axis.

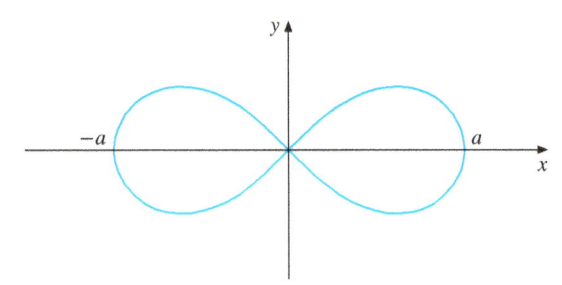

Figure 7.1.4 A lemniscate

7.2 Economic Examples

Few mathematical techniques are more important in economics than implicit differentiation. This is because so many functions in economic models are defined implicitly by an equation or by a system of equations. Often the variables have names other than x and y, so one needs to practise differentiating equations with other names for the variables.

EXAMPLE 7.2.1　　Example 3.2.1 presented a standard macroeconomic model for determining national income. The somewhat generalized version set out in Example 4.5.2 involves the two equations: (i) $Y = C + \bar{I}$; and (ii) $C = f(Y)$. Here, Eq. (i) states that GDP, denoted by Y, is divided up between consumption C and investment $\bar{I}$. The latter is assumed to be an exogenous constant. On the other hand, Eq. (ii) is the generalized consumption function presented in Example 4.5.2. We assume that $f'(Y)$, the *marginal propensity to consume*, lies between 0 and 1.

(a) Consider first the special case when $C = f(Y) = 95.05 + 0.712Y$, as in Haavelmo's estimate of the consumption function discussed in Example 4.5.2. Use equations (i) and (ii) to find Y in terms of $\bar{I}$ in this case.

(b) Reverting to the case of a general function $f(Y)$, inserting the expression for C from (ii) into (i) gives $Y = f(Y) + \bar{I}$. Suppose that this equation defines Y as a differentiable function of $\bar{I}$. Find an expression for $dY/d\bar{I}$.

(c) Assuming that $f''(Y)$ exists, find $Y'' = d^2Y/d\bar{I}^2$.

Solution:

(a) In this special case, one has $Y = 95.05 + 0.712Y + \bar{I}$. Solving for Y yields

$$Y = (95.05 + \bar{I})/(1 - 0.712) \approx 3.47\bar{I} + 330.03$$

In particular, $dY/d\bar{I} \approx 3.47$. This indicates that an increase of $\bar{I}$ by $1 billion leads to an increase in GDP of approximately $3.47 billion.

(b) Differentiating $Y = f(Y) + \bar{I}$ w.r.t. $\bar{I}$, then using the chain rule, we have

$$\frac{dY}{d\bar{I}} = f'(Y)\frac{dY}{d\bar{I}} + 1 \quad \text{or, equivalently,} \quad \frac{dY}{d\bar{I}}[1 - f'(Y)] = 1 \quad (7.2.1)$$

Solving for $dy/d\bar{I}$ yields

$$\frac{dY}{d\bar{I}} = \frac{1}{1 - f'(Y)} \quad (7.2.2)$$

For example, if $f'(Y) = 1/2$, then $dY/d\bar{I} = 2$. If $f'(Y) = 0.712$ as in part (a), then $dY/d\bar{I} \approx 3.47$. In general, the assumption that $f'(Y)$ lies between 0 and 1 implies that $1 - f'(Y)$ also lies between 0 and 1. Hence $1/[1 - f'(Y)]$ is always greater than 1. In this model, therefore, a $1 billion increase in investment will always lead to a more than $1 billion increase in GDP. Also, the greater is $f'(Y)$, the marginal propensity to consume, the smaller is $1 - f'(Y)$, and so the greater is $dY/d\bar{I}$.

(c) To find Y'' we differentiate the first equation in (7.2.1) implicitly w.r.t. $\bar{I}$. The derivative of $f'(Y)$ w.r.t. $\bar{I}$ is $f''(Y)(dY/d\bar{I})$. Now, differentiating the product $f'(Y)(dY/d\bar{I})$ w.r.t. $\bar{I}$ gives

$$\frac{d}{d\bar{I}}\left[f'(Y)\frac{dY}{d\bar{I}}\right] = f''(Y)\frac{dY}{d\bar{I}}\frac{dY}{d\bar{I}} + f'(Y)\frac{d^2Y}{d\bar{I}^2}$$

Hence, the derivative we want satisfies

$$\frac{d^2Y}{d\bar{I}^2} = f''(Y)\left(\frac{dY}{d\bar{I}}\right)^2 + f'(Y)\frac{d^2Y}{d\bar{I}^2} \quad (7.2.3)$$

It follows from (7.2.3) and then (7.2.2) that

$$\frac{d^2Y}{d\bar{I}^2} = \frac{f''(Y)}{[1 - f'(Y)]}\left(\frac{dY}{d\bar{I}}\right)^2 = \frac{f''(Y)}{[1 - f'(Y)]^3}$$

EXAMPLE 7.2.2 In the linear supply and demand model of Example 4.5.4, suppose that consumers are required to pay a tax of τ per unit, thus raising the price per unit that they face from P to $P + \tau$. Then
$$D = a - b(P + \tau), \quad S = \alpha + \beta P \qquad (7.2.4)$$

Here a, b, α, and β are positive constants. The equilibrium price is determined by equating supply and demand, so that
$$a - b(P + \tau) = \alpha + \beta P \qquad (7.2.5)$$

(a) Equation (7.2.5) implicitly defines the price P as a function of the unit tax τ. Compute $dP/d\tau$ by implicit differentiation. What is its sign? What is the sign of $(d/d\tau)(P + \tau)$? Check the result by first solving Eq. (7.2.5) for P and then finding $dP/d\tau$ explicitly.

(b) Compute tax revenue T as a function of τ. For what value of τ does the quadratic function T reach its maximum?

(c) Generalize the model by assuming that $D = f(P + \tau)$ and $S = g(P)$, where f and g are differentiable functions with $f' < 0$ and $g' > 0$. The equilibrium condition $f(P + \tau) = g(P)$ defines P implicitly as a differentiable function of τ. Find an expression for $dP/d\tau$ by implicit differentiation. Illustrate geometrically.

Solution:

(a) Differentiating (7.2.5) w.r.t. τ yields
$$-b\left(\frac{dP}{d\tau} + 1\right) = \beta \frac{dP}{d\tau}$$

Solving this equality gives
$$\frac{dP}{d\tau} = \frac{-b}{b + \beta}$$

We see that $dP/d\tau$ is negative. Because P is the price received by the producer, this price will go down if the tax rate τ increases. But $P + \tau$ is the price paid by the consumer. Also
$$\frac{d}{d\tau}(P + \tau) = \frac{dP}{d\tau} + 1 = \frac{-b}{b+\beta} + 1 = \frac{-b+b+\beta}{b+\beta} = \frac{\beta}{b+\beta}$$

It follows that $0 < d(P+t)/d\tau < 1$. Thus, the consumer price $P + \tau$ increases, but by less than the increase in the tax.

If we solve (7.2.5) for P, we obtain
$$P = \frac{a - \alpha - b\tau}{b + \beta} = \frac{a - \alpha}{b + \beta} - \frac{b}{b + \beta}\tau$$

This equation shows that the equilibrium producer price P is a linear function of τ, the tax per unit, with slope $-b/(b + \beta)$.

(b) The total tax revenue is $T = S\tau = (\alpha + \beta P)\tau$, where P is the equilibrium price. Thus,
$$T = \left[\alpha + \beta\left(\frac{a-\alpha}{b+\beta} - \frac{b}{b+\beta}\tau\right)\right]\tau = \frac{-b\beta}{b+\beta}\tau^2 + \frac{\alpha b + \beta a}{b+\beta}\tau$$

Following the analysis in Section 4.6, this quadratic function has its maximum at $\tau = (\alpha b + \beta a)/2b\beta$.

(c) Differentiating the equation $f(P + \tau) = g(P)$ w.r.t. τ yields

$$f'(P + \tau)\left(\frac{dP}{d\tau} + 1\right) = g'(P)\frac{dP}{d\tau} \qquad (7.2.6)$$

Solving for $dP/d\tau$ gives

$$\frac{dP}{d\tau} = \frac{f'(P + \tau)}{g'(P) - f'(P + \tau)}$$

Again, because $f' < 0$ and $g' > 0$, we see that $dP/d\tau$ is negative in this case as well. Moreover,

$$\frac{d}{d\tau}(P + \tau) = \frac{dP}{d\tau} + 1 = \frac{f'(P + \tau)}{g'(P) - f'(P + \tau)} + 1 = \frac{g'(P)}{g'(P) - f'(P + \tau)}$$

which implies that $0 < d(P + \tau)/d\tau < 1$.

Figure 7.2.1 has a graph which illustrates this answer. As usual in economics, we measure quantity on the horizontal axis, and price on the vertical axis. The demand curve with the tax included in the price is represented by the curve $Q = f(P + \tau)$. Its graph is obtained by shifting down by τ units the graph of $Q = f(P)$, which is also the graph of the inverse demand curve $P = f^{-1}(Q)$. The shifted graph is that of $P = f^{-1}(Q) - \tau$, which is also the graph of $Q = f(P + \tau)$.

The figure confirms that, when the tax τ increases, the new equilibrium is at E', where the new quantity is lower than at E, and so is the price received by the suppliers. Nevertheless, the price $P + \tau$ paid by buyers increases because the decrease in P is smaller than the increase in τ.

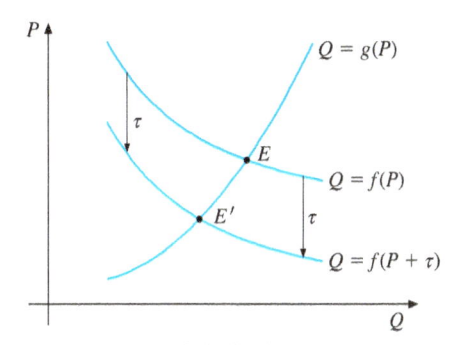

Figure 7.2.1 Shift in the demand curve

EXERCISES FOR SECTION 7.2

1. According to a study, the demand Q for butter in Stockholm during the period 1925–1937 was related to the price P by the equation $Q \cdot P^{1/2} = 38$. Find dQ/dP by implicit differentiation. Check the answer by using a different method to compute the derivative.

2. Consider a profit-maximizing firm producing a single commodity. If the firm gets a fixed price P per unit sold, its profit from selling Q units is $\pi(Q) = PQ - C(Q)$, where $C(Q)$ is the cost function. Assume that $C'(Q) > 0$ and $C''(Q) > 0$. In Example 8.5.1, it will be shown that $Q = Q^* > 0$ maximizes profits w.r.t. Q provided that

$$P = C'(Q^*) \qquad (*)$$

Thus, at the optimum, marginal cost must equal the price per unit.

(a) By implicitly differentiating $(*)$ w.r.t. P, find an expression for dQ^*/dP.

(b) Comment on the sign of dQ^*/dP.

3. Consider the equation $AP^{-\alpha} r^{-\beta} = S$ where A, α, β, and S are positive constants. The left-hand side of the equation expresses the demand for a commodity as a decreasing function of both its price P and the interest rate r. In equilibrium, this demand must equal a fixed supply quantity S.

(a) Take natural logarithms of both sides and find dP/dr by implicit differentiation.

(b) How does the equilibrium price react to an increase in the interest rate?

(SM) 4. Extending the standard macroeconomic model of Example 7.2.1 for an economy open to international trade gives: (i) $Y = C + \bar{I} + \bar{X} - M$; (ii) $C = f(Y)$; and (iii) $M = g(Y)$. Here $\bar{X}$ is an exogenous constant that denotes exports, whereas M denotes the volume of imports. The consumption function f in (ii) satisfies that $0 < f'(Y) < 1$. The function g in (iii) is called an *import function* and is assumed to satisfy $0 < g'(Y) < f'(Y)$.

(a) By inserting (ii) and (iii) into (i), obtain an equation that defines Y as a function of exogenous investment $\bar{I}$.

(b) Find an expression for $dY/d\bar{I}$ by implicit differentiation. Discuss the sign of $dY/d\bar{I}$.

(c) Find an expression for $d^2 Y/d\bar{I}^2$.

5. In part (c) of Example 7.2.2, find an expression for $d^2 P/d\tau^2$ by differentiating (7.2.6) w.r.t. τ.

6. In Example 7.2.2 we studied a model of supply and demand where a tax is imposed on the consumers. Instead, suppose that the producers have to pay a tax per unit sold that is equal to a fraction τ of the sales price P they receive, where $0 < \tau < 1$. This implies that the equilibrium condition with the tax is

$$f(P) = g(P - \tau P) \qquad (*)$$

We assume that $f' < 0$ and $g' > 0$.

(a) Differentiate $(*)$ w.r.t. τ and find an expression for $dP/d\tau$.

(b) Find the sign of $dP/d\tau$ and give an economic interpretation.

7.3 The Inverse Function Theorem

Section 5.3 offered an introduction to inverse functions. As explained there, if f is a one-to-one function defined on an interval I, it has an inverse function g defined on the range $f(I)$ of f. What is the relationship between the derivatives of f and g? Here is a simple example.

EXAMPLE 7.3.1 Provided that $a \neq 0$, the two linear functions $f(x) = ax + b$ and $g(x) = (x - b)/a$ are inverses of each other, as you can verify. The graphs are straight lines which are symmetric about the line $y = x$. The slopes are respectively a and $1/a$. Look back at Fig. 5.3.3, and notice that this result is confirmed, since the slope of f is 4 and the slope of g is 1/4.

More generally, recall that if f and g are inverses of each other, then by definition for all x in I one has

$$g(f(x)) = x \tag{7.3.1}$$

By implicit differentiation, *provided that* both f and g are differentiable, it is easy to find the relationship between the derivatives of f and g. Indeed, differentiating (7.3.1) w.r.t. x gives $g'(f(x))f'(x) = 1$. Hence, at any x where $f'(x) \neq 0$, one has $g'(f(x)) = 1/f'(x)$.

The most important facts about inverse functions are summed up in the following theorem. Recall that a point of an interval is said to be *interior* if and only if it is *not* one of the interval's end points.

THEOREM 7.3.1 (INVERSE FUNCTION THEOREM)

If f is differentiable and strictly increasing (strictly decreasing) in an interval I, then it has an inverse function g, which is strictly increasing (strictly decreasing) in the interval $f(I)$.

If, in addition, a is an interior point of I, and $f'(a) \neq 0$, then g is differentiable at $b = f(a)$, and

$$g'(b) = \frac{1}{f'(a)} \tag{7.3.2}$$

Formula (7.3.2) is used as follows to find the derivative of g at a point b. First find, if possible, the point a in I at which $f(a) = b$. Thereafter, compute $f'(x)$, and then find $f'(a)$. If $f'(a) \neq 0$, then g has a derivative at b given by $g'(b) = 1/f'(a)$. An implication of (7.3.2) is that f' and g' must have the same sign. So if f is strictly increasing (decreasing), then g is strictly increasing (decreasing), and vice versa.

The geometric interpretation of formula (7.3.2) is shown in Fig. 7.3.1, where f and g are inverses of each other. The coordinates of P are (a, b), while Q is the point (b, a). Let $y' = f'(a)$ be the slope of the tangent at P. Then the slope of the tangent at Q is $g'(b) = 1/y'$.

EXAMPLE 7.3.2 Suppose that the function f is defined for all real x by the formula $f(x) = x^5 + 3x^3 + 6x - 3$. Show that f has an inverse function g. Then, given that $f(1) = 7$, use Eq. (7.3.2) to find $g'(7)$.

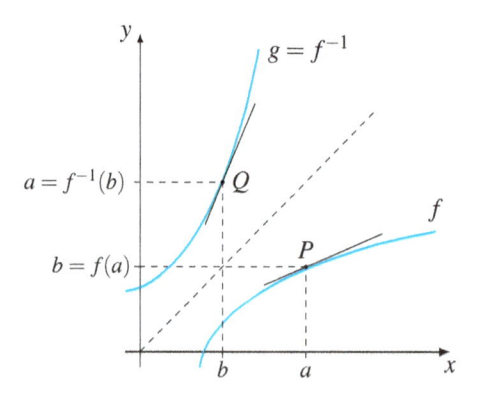

Figure 7.3.1 The slope at P is y', and the slope at Q is $1/y'$.

Solution: Differentiating $f(x)$ yields $f'(x) = 5x^4 + 9x^2 + 6$. Clearly, $f'(x) > 0$ for all x, so f is strictly increasing and consequently it is one-to-one. It therefore has an inverse function g. To find $g'(7)$, we use formula (7.3.2) with $a = 1$ and $b = 7$. Since $f'(1) = 20$, we obtain $g'(7) = 1/f'(1) = 1/20$. Note that we have found $g'(7)$ exactly even though it is impossible to find any algebraic formula for the inverse function g.

EXAMPLE 7.3.3   Suppose that f and g are both twice differentiable functions which are inverses of each other. By differentiating $g'(f(x)) = 1/f'(x)$ w.r.t. x at any point where $f'(x) \neq 0$, find an expression for $g''(f(x))$. Do f'' and g'' have the same, or opposite signs?

Solution: Differentiating each side of the equation $g'(f(x)) = 1/f'(x)$ w.r.t. x yields

$$g''(f(x))f'(x) = (-1)(f'(x))^{-2} f''(x)$$

It follows that if $f'(x) \neq 0$, then

$$g''(f(x)) = -\frac{f''(x)}{(f'(x))^3} \qquad (7.3.3)$$

So if $f' > 0$, then $f''(x)$ and $g''(f(x))$ have opposite signs, but they have the same sign if $f' < 0$. In particular, if f is strictly increasing and $f''(x) < 0$ for all x, then the inverse g is strictly increasing and $g''(x) > 0$ for all x, as shown in Fig. 7.3.1.

It is common to present the formula in (7.3.2) in the deceptively simple way:

$$\frac{dx}{dy} = \frac{1}{dy/dx} \qquad (7.3.4)$$

as if dx and dy could be manipulated like ordinary numbers. Formula (7.3.3) shows that similar use of the differential notation for second derivatives fails drastically. The formula "$d^2x/dy^2 = 1/(dy^2/d^2x)$", for instance, makes no sense at all.

EXAMPLE 7.3.4

Suppose that, instead of the linear demand function of Example 4.5.4, one has the function $\ln Q = a - b \ln P$. This function is linear in the logarithms of the price and the quantity, so is known as *log-linear*.[4]

(a) Express Q as a function of P, and show that $dQ/dP = -bQ/P$.

(b) Express P as a function of Q, and find dP/dQ.

(c) Check that your answer satisfies that $dP/dQ = 1/(dQ/dP)$, as implied by Eq. (7.3.4).

Solution:

(a) Taking exponentials gives

$$Q = e^{a-b\ln P} = e^a (e^{\ln P})^{-b} = e^a P^{-b}$$

from which it follows that $dQ/dP = -be^a P^{-b-1} = -bQ/P$.

(b) Solving $Q = e^a P^{-b}$ for P gives $P = e^{a/b} Q^{-1/b}$, so $dP/dQ = (-1/b) e^{a/b} Q^{-1-1/b}$.

(c) Using part (b) and then part (a), one has $dP/dQ = (-1/b) P/Q = 1/(dQ/dP)$.

EXERCISES FOR SECTION 7.3

1. The function defined for all x by $f(x) = e^{2x-2}$ has an inverse g. Find x such that $f(x) = 1$. Then, use (7.3.2) to find $g'(1)$. Check your result by finding a formula for g.

2. The function f is defined, for $-2 \le x \le 2$, by the formula $f(x) = \frac{1}{3} x^3 \sqrt{4 - x^2}$.

   (a) Find the intervals where f increases, and the intervals where f decreases, then sketch its graph.

   (b) Explain why f has an inverse g on $[0, \sqrt{3}]$, and find $g'(\frac{1}{3}\sqrt{3})$. (*Hint:* $f(1) = \frac{1}{3}\sqrt{3}$.)

3. Let f be defined by $f(x) = \ln(2 + e^{x-3})$, for all x.

   (a) Show that f is strictly increasing and find the range of f.

   (b) Find an expression for the inverse function, g, of f. Where is g defined?

   (c) Verify that $f'(3) = 1/g'(f(3))$.

4. According to Exercise 5.3.2, during the period 1915–1929 the demand for sugar in the USA, as a function of the price P, was given by $D = 157.8/P^{0.3}$. Use (7.3.4) to find dP/dD.

(SM) 5. Use (7.3.4) to find dx/dy when:

   (a) $y = e^{-x-5}$
   (b) $y = \ln(e^{-x} + 3)$
   (c) $xy^3 - x^3 y = 2x$

---

[4] Note that the inverse demand function can be expressed as $\ln P = \frac{1}{b}(a - \ln Q)$, which is also log-linear.

7.4 Linear Approximations

Much of modern economic analysis relies on numerical calculations, nearly always only approximate. Often, therefore, rather than work with a complicated function, we approximate it by one that is simpler. Since linear functions are especially simple, it seems natural to try using a "linear approximation" first.

Consider a function $f(x)$ that is differentiable at $x = a$. Suppose we approximate the graph of f by its tangent line at the particular point $(a, f(a))$, as shown in Fig. 7.4.1. By formula (6.2.3), this line is the graph of the function $y = p(x) = f(a) + f'(a)(x - a)$.

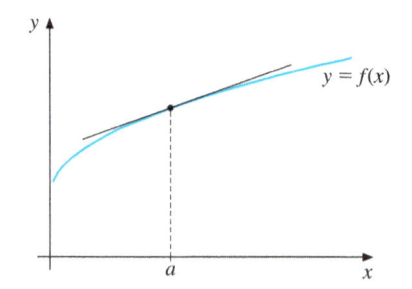

Figure 7.4.1 Approximation to a function by its tangent

LINEAR APPROXIMATION TO A DIFFERENTIABLE f ABOUT x = a

For x close to a,
$$f(x) \approx f(a) + f'(a)(x - a) \tag{7.4.1}$$

Note that both $f(x)$ and its linear approximation $p(x) = f(a) + f'(a)(x - a)$ have the same value and the same derivative at $x = a$.[5]

EXAMPLE 7.4.1 Find the linear approximation to $f(x) = \sqrt[3]{x}$ about $x = 1$.

Solution: We have $f(x) = \sqrt[3]{x} = x^{1/3}$, so $f(1) = 1$, and $f'(x) = \frac{1}{3}x^{-2/3}$, implying that $f'(1) = \frac{1}{3}$. Inserting these values into (7.4.1), when $a = 1$, yields

$$\sqrt[3]{x} \approx f(1) + f'(1)(x - 1) = 1 + \tfrac{1}{3}(x - 1) \quad \text{(for all } x \text{ close to 1)}$$

For example, $\sqrt[3]{1.03} \approx 1 + \tfrac{1}{3}(1.03 - 1) = 1.01$. The correct value to 4 decimal places is 1.0099.

EXAMPLE 7.4.2 Use (7.4.1) to show that $\ln(1 + x) \approx x$ for x close to 0.

Solution: With $f(x) = \ln(1 + x)$, we get $f(0) = 0$ and $f'(x) = 1/(1 + x)$, implying that $f'(0) = 1$. Then (7.4.1) yields $\ln(1 + x) \approx x$.

---

[5] One can prove that if f is differentiable, then $f(x) - f(a) = f'(a)(x - a) + \varepsilon \cdot (x - a)$ where $\varepsilon \to 0$ as $x \to a$. So if $x - a$ is very small, then ε is very small, and $\varepsilon \cdot (x - a)$ is "very very small".

EXAMPLE 7.4.3 **(Rule of 70).** Suppose that an amount K accrues interest at the rate of $p\%$ a year. Then the doubling time of the amount in the account, using formula (4.10.7) in Section 4.10, is $t^* = \ln 2 / \ln(1 + p/100)$. Combining the approximation $\ln(1+x) \approx x$ from Example 7.4.2 with $\ln 2 \approx 0.7$, we have

$$t^* = \frac{\ln 2}{\ln(1 + p/100)} \approx \frac{0.7}{p/100} = \frac{70}{p}$$

This yields the "rule of 70" according to which, if the interest rate is $p\%$ per year, then the doubling time is approximately 70 divided by p. For instance, if $p = 3.5$, then t^* is 20, which is close to the exact value $t^* = \ln 2 / \ln 1.035 \approx 20.1$.[6]

EXAMPLE 7.4.4 Use (7.4.1) to find an approximate value for $(1.001)^{50}$.

Solution: We put $f(x) = x^{50}$. Then $f(1) = 1$ and $f'(x) = 50x^{49}$, implying that $f'(1) = 50 \cdot 1^{49} = 50$. Applying formula (7.4.1) with $x = 1.001$ and $a = 1$ gives

$$(1.001)^{50} \approx 1 + 50 \cdot 0.001 = 1.05$$

(Using a calculator gives us the closer approximation $(1.001)^{50} \approx 1.0512$.)

The Differential of a Function

Consider a differentiable function $f(x)$, and let dx denote an arbitrary small change in the variable x. In this notation, "dx" is not a product of d (or d) and x. Rather, the one symbol dx represents a small change in the value of x. The expression $f'(x)\,\mathrm{d}x$ is called the *differential* of $y = f(x)$. This differential is denoted by dy (or d$f(x)$), so that

$$\mathrm{d}y = \mathrm{d}f(x) = f'(x)\,\mathrm{d}x \tag{7.4.2}$$

Note that dy is proportional to dx, with the derivative $f'(x)$ as the factor of proportionality.

Now, if x changes by dx, then the corresponding change in $y = f(x)$ is

$$\Delta y = f(x + \mathrm{d}x) - f(x) \tag{7.4.3}$$

In the linear approximation (7.4.1), suppose we replace x by $x + \mathrm{d}x$ and a by x. The result is $f(x + \mathrm{d}x) \approx f(x) + f'(x)\,\mathrm{d}x$. Using the definitions of dy and Δy in (7.4.2) and (7.4.3) respectively, we get the approximation $\Delta y \approx \mathrm{d}y$.

The differential dy is not the actual increment in y as x is changed to $x + \mathrm{d}x$. Rather it is the change in y that would occur if y were to continue changing at the fixed rate $f'(x)$ as x changes to $x + \mathrm{d}x$. In Fig. 7.4.2 the error resulting from using the approximation dy rather than the exact change Δy is represented graphically as the distance $|\Delta y - \mathrm{d}y|$ between the two points R and Q.

---

[6] Luca Pacioli, considered by many as the father of modern accounting, proposed in Venice in 1494 an equivalent "rule of 72" whereby $t^* = 72/p$. This is more convenient because 72 is divisible by more integers than 70. A more accurate approximation is the "rule of 69.3", because $\ln 2 \approx 0.693$ to three decimal places.

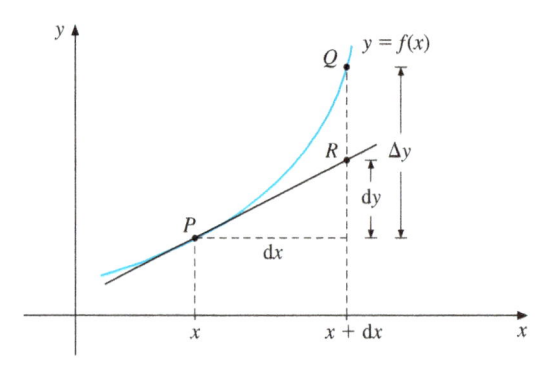

Figure 7.4.2 The differential dy and $\Delta y = f(x + dx) - f(x)$

To explore this error further, consider first the movement from P to Q along the graph: as x moves to $x + dx$ and so changes by dx, the actual change in the vertical height of the point is $f(x + dx) - f(x) = \Delta y$. Suppose instead that we can only move along the tangent to the graph at P. Going from P to R along the tangent, which changes x by the amount dx, induces a corresponding change in height of dy. As Fig. 7.4.2 suggests, the approximation $\Delta y \approx dy$ is usually closer if dx is smaller in absolute value. This is because the length $|RQ| = |\Delta y - dy|$ of the line segment RQ tends to 0 as dx tends to 0. In fact, this length $|RQ|$ becomes small so fast that the ratio $|RQ|/dx$ tends to 0 as $dx \to 0$. See Exercise 12.

Rules for Differentials

The notation $(d/dx)(\cdot)$ calls for the expression represented by the $\cdot$ inside the parentheses to be differentiated with respect to x. For example, $(d/dx)(x^3) = 3x^2$. Similarly, we let $d(\cdot)$ denote the differential of whatever is inside the parentheses. For example, $d(x^3) = 3x^2 dx$.

EXAMPLE 7.4.5 Compute the following differentials:

(a) $d(Ax^a + B)$, where A, B, and a are constants.

(b) $d(f(K))$, where f is a differentiable function of K.

Solution:

(a) Putting $f(x) = Ax^a + B$, we get $f'(x) = Aax^{a-1}$, so $d(Ax^a + B) = Aax^{a-1}dx$.

(b) $d(f(K)) = f'(K)dK$.

RULES FOR DIFFERENTIALS

Let f and g be differentiable functions of x, and let a and b be constants. Then the following rules hold:

$$d(af + bg) = a\, df + b\, dg \qquad (7.4.4)$$

$$d(fg) = g\,df + f\,dg \tag{7.4.5}$$

and, provided that $g \neq 0$,

$$d\left(\frac{f}{g}\right) = \frac{g\,df - f\,dg}{g^2} \tag{7.4.6}$$

Here is a proof of rule (7.4.5):

$$d(fg) = (fg)'\,dx = (f'g + fg')\,dx = gf'\,dx + fg'\,dx = g\,df + f\,dg$$

The two other rules can be proved in a similar way.

Suppose that $y = f(x)$ and that $x = g(t)$ is a function of t. Then $y = h(t) = f(g(t))$ is a function of t. The differential of $y = h(t)$ is $dy = h'(t)\,dt$. According to the chain rule, one has $h'(t) = f'(g(t))g'(t)$, implying that $dy = f'(g(t))g'(t)\,dt$. Because $x = g(t)$, however, the differential of x is equal to $dx = g'(t)\,dt$. It follows that $dy = f'(x)\,dx$. This shows that *if $y = f(x)$, then the differential of y is equal to $dy = f'(x)\,dx$, whether x depends on another variable or not.*

Economists often use differentials in their models. A typical example follows.

EXAMPLE 7.4.6 Consider again the macroeconomic model presented in Example 7.2.1. Find the differential dY, expressed in terms of $d\bar{I}$. If employment N is also a function $g(Y)$ of national income, find the differential dN expressed in terms of $d\bar{I}$.

Solution: Taking the differential of equation (i) in Example 7.2.1 yields $dY = dC + d\bar{I}$. Doing the same for equation (ii) gives $dC = f'(Y)\,dY$. Substituting dC from the latter into the former, then solving for dY, we obtain

$$dY = \frac{1}{1 - f'(Y)}\,d\bar{I}$$

This accords with formula (7.2.2). Also $N = g(Y)$ implies that $dN = g'(Y)dY$, so

$$dN = \frac{g'(Y)}{1 - f'(Y)}\,d\bar{I}$$

Economists usually claim that employment increases as GDP increases (so $g'(Y) > 0$), and that $f'(Y)$, the marginal propensity to consume, is between 0 and 1. Our formula for dN shows that these claims imply that if investment $\bar{I}$ increases, then so does employment.

EXERCISES FOR SECTION 7.4

1. Prove that $\sqrt{1+x} \approx 1 + \frac{1}{2}x$ for x close to 0, and illustrate this approximation by drawing the two graphs of $y = 1 + \frac{1}{2}x$ and $y = \sqrt{1+x}$ in the same coordinate system.

2. Use (7.4.1) to find the linear approximation to $f(x) = (5x + 3)^{-2}$ about $x = 0$.

3. Find the linear approximations to the following functions about $x = 0$:

   (a) $f(x) = (1+x)^{-1}$ (b) $f(x) = (1+x)^5$ (c) $f(x) = (1-x)^{1/4}$

4. Find the linear approximation to $F(K) = AK^\alpha$ about $K = 1$.

5. Let p, q, and r be constants. Find the following differentials:

   (a) $d(10x^3)$ (b) $d(5x^3 - 5x^2 + 5x + 5)$ (c) $d(1/x^3)$ (d) $d(\ln x)$

   (e) $d(x^p + x^q)$ (f) $d(x^p x^q)$ (g) $d(px+q)^r$ (h) $d(e^{px} + e^{qx})$

6. (a) Prove that $(1+x)^m \approx 1 + mx$ for x close to 0.

   (b) Use this to find approximations to the following numbers:

   (i) $\sqrt[3]{1.1} = \left(1 + \tfrac{1}{10}\right)^{1/3}$ (ii) $\sqrt[5]{33} = 2\left(1 + \tfrac{1}{32}\right)^{1/5}$ (iii) $\sqrt[3]{9} = \sqrt[3]{8+1}$ (iv) $(0.98)^{25}$

7. Compute $\Delta y = f(x+dx) - f(x)$ and the differential $dy = f'(x)\,dx$ for the following cases:

   (a) $f(x) = x^2 + 2x - 3$ when $x = 2$ and: (i) $dx = 1/10$; or (ii) $dx = 1/100$;

   (b) $f(x) = 1/x$ when $x = 3$ and: (i) $dx = -1/10$; or (ii) $dx = -1/100$;

   (c) $f(x) = \sqrt{x}$ when $x = 4$ and: (i) $dx = 1/20$; or (ii) $dx = 1/100$.

8. The equation $3xe^{xy^2} - 2y = 3x^2 + y^2$ defines y as a differentiable function of x about the point $(x, y) = (1, 0)$.

   (a) Find the slope of the graph at this point by implicit differentiation.

   (b) What is the linear approximation to y about $x = 1$?

9. A circle with radius r has area $A(r) = \pi r^2$. Then $A'(r) = 2\pi r$, the circumference of the circle.

   (a) Explain geometrically the approximation $A(r + dr) - A(r) \approx 2\pi r\,dr$.

   (b) Explain geometrically the approximation $V(r+dr) - V(r) \approx 4\pi r^2\,dr$, where $V(r) = \tfrac{4}{3}\pi r^3$ is the volume of a ball with radius r, and $V'(r) = 4\pi r^2$ is the surface area of a sphere with radius r.

10. Suppose an amount K is charged to a credit card on which the interest rate is $p\%$ per year. Then unless some payments are made beforehand, after t years the outstanding balance will have grown to $K_t = K(1 + p/100)^t$ (even without any penalty charges for failing to make minimum payments). Using the approximation $\ln(1 + p/100) \approx p/100$ derived in Example 7.4.2, prove that $\ln K_t \approx \ln K + pt/100$. Find the corresponding approximate percentage interest rate p, as well as the exact interest rate p^*, at which the balance doubles after t^* years.

11. Consider the function $g(\mu) = A(1 + \mu)^{a/(1+b)} - 1$ where A, a, and b are positive constants. Find the linear approximation to the function about the point $\mu = 0$.

12. Suppose the function f is differentiable at a. Show that as $h \to 0$, the error in the linear approximation $f(a+h) \approx f(a) + f'(a)h$ tends to 0 faster than h does. In other words,

$$\lim_{h \to 0} \frac{f(a+h) - (f(a) + f'(a)h)}{h} = 0$$

7.5 Polynomial Approximations

The previous section discussed approximations of functions of one variable by linear functions. In particular, Example 7.4.1 established the approximation

$$\sqrt[3]{x} \approx 1 + \tfrac{1}{3}(x-1)$$

for x close to 1. In this case, at $x = 1$, the two functions $y = \sqrt[3]{x}$ and $y = 1 + \tfrac{1}{3}(x-1)$ both have the same value 1, and the same derivative $1/3$. Approximation by linear functions, however, may well be insufficiently accurate. So it is natural to try quadratic approximations, or approximations by polynomials of a higher order.

Quadratic Approximations

We begin by showing how a twice differentiable function $y = f(x)$ can be approximated near $x = a$ by a quadratic polynomial

$$p(x) = A + B(x-a) + C(x-a)^2 \tag{7.5.1}$$

With a fixed, there are three coefficients A, B, and C to determine. We use three conditions to do so. Specifically, at $x = a$, we arrange that $f(x)$ and $p(x)$ given by (7.5.1) should have: (i) the same value; (ii) the same derivative; and (iii) the same second derivative. In symbols, we require $f(a) = p(a)$, $f'(a) = p'(a)$, and $f''(a) = p''(a)$. Now $p'(x) = B + 2C(x-a)$ and $p''(x) = 2C$. So, after inserting $x = a$ into these expressions, we need to have

$$A = p(a) = f(a), \quad B = p'(a) = f'(a), \quad \text{and} \quad C = \tfrac{1}{2}p''(a) = \tfrac{1}{2}f''(a)$$

This justifies the following:

QUADRATIC APPROXIMATION TO f(x) ABOUT x = a

For x close to a,

$$f(x) \approx f(a) + f'(a)(x-a) + \tfrac{1}{2}f''(a)(x-a)^2 \tag{7.5.2}$$

Note that, compared with (7.4.1), we have simply added the extra term in $(x-a)^2$. For $a = 0$ in particular, we obtain the following approximation for x close to 0:

$$f(x) \approx f(0) + f'(0)x + \tfrac{1}{2}f''(0)x^2 \tag{7.5.3}$$

EXAMPLE 7.5.1 Find the quadratic approximation to $f(x) = \sqrt[3]{x}$ about $x = 1$.

Solution: Here $f'(x) = \tfrac{1}{3}x^{-2/3}$ and $f''(x) = \tfrac{1}{3}\left(-\tfrac{2}{3}\right)x^{-5/3}$. It follows that $f'(1) = 1/3$ and $f''(1) = -2/9$. Because $f(1) = 1$, using (7.5.2) yields

$$\sqrt[3]{x} \approx 1 + \tfrac{1}{3}(x-1) - \tfrac{1}{9}(x-1)^2 \quad \text{(for all } x \text{ close to 1)}$$

For example, $\sqrt[3]{1.03} \approx 1 + \frac{1}{3} \cdot 0.03 - \frac{1}{9}(0.03)^2 = 1 + 0.01 - 0.0001 = 1.0099$. This is correct to four decimal places, which is better than the linear approximation derived in Example 7.4.1.

EXAMPLE 7.5.2 Find the quadratic approximation to $y = y(x)$ about $x = 0$ when y is defined implicitly as a function of x near $(x, y) = (0, 1)$ by $xy^3 + 1 = y$.

Solution: Implicit differentiation w.r.t. x yields

$$y^3 + 3xy^2 y' = y' \qquad (*)$$

Substituting $x = 0$ and $y = 1$ into $(*)$ gives $y' = 1$. Differentiating $(*)$ w.r.t. x now yields

$$3y^2 y' + (3y^2 + 6xyy')y' + 3xy^2 y'' = y''$$

Substituting $x = 0$, $y = 1$, and $y' = 1$, we obtain $y'' = 6$. Hence, according to (7.5.3),

$$y(x) \approx y(0) + y'(0)x + \tfrac{1}{2} y''(0) x^2 = 1 + x + 3x^2$$

Higher-Order Approximations

So far, we have considered linear and quadratic approximations. For functions with third- and higher-order derivatives, we can find even better approximations near one point by using polynomials of a higher degree. Suppose we want to approximate a function $f(x)$ over an interval that contains $x = a$ with an nth-degree polynomial of the form

$$p(x) = A_0 + A_1(x - a) + A_2(x - a)^2 + A_3(x - a)^3 + \cdots + A_n(x - a)^n \qquad (7.5.4)$$

Because $p(x)$ has $n + 1$ coefficients, we can impose the following $n + 1$ conditions on this polynomial:

$$f(a) = p(a), \quad f'(a) = p'(a), \quad \ldots, \quad f^{(n)}(a) = p^{(n)}(a)$$

These conditions require that $p(x)$ and its first n derivatives agree with the value of $f(x)$ and its first n derivatives at $x = a$.

Let us see what these conditions become when $n = 3$. In this case,

$$p(x) = A_0 + A_1(x - a) + A_2(x - a)^2 + A_3(x - a)^3$$

Repeated differentiation gives the three equalities

$$p'(x) = A_1 + 2A_2(x - a) + 3A_3(x - a)^2, \quad p''(x) = 2A_2 + 2 \cdot 3A_3(x - a), \quad p'''(x) = 2 \cdot 3A_3.$$

Putting $x = a$ gives $p(a) = A_0$, $p'(a) = 1! A_1$, $p''(a) = 2! A_2$, and $p'''(a) = 3! A_3$. This suggests that we should use the approximation:

$$f(x) \approx f(a) + \frac{1}{1!} f'(a)(x - a) + \frac{1}{2!} f''(a)(x - a)^2 + \frac{1}{3!} f'''(a)(x - a)^3$$

Thus, we have added an extra term to the quadratic approximation (7.5.2).

The general case when $n > 3$ follows the same pattern. We obtain the following approximation to $f(x)$ by an nth-degree polynomial:

TAYLOR APPROXIMATION TO $f(x)$ ABOUT $x = a$

For x close to a,

$$f(x) \approx f(a) + \frac{f'(a)}{1!}(x-a) + \frac{f''(a)}{2!}(x-a)^2 + \cdots + \frac{f^{(n)}(a)}{n!}(x-a)^n \qquad (7.5.5)$$

The right-hand side of (7.5.5) is called the nth-order *Taylor polynomial*, or *Taylor approximation* for f about $x = a$. The function f and its nth-order Taylor polynomial have such a high degree of contact at $x = a$ that it is reasonable to expect the approximation in (7.5.5) to be good over some (possibly small) interval centred about $x = a$.

The next section analyses the error that results from using such polynomial approximations. In the case when f is itself a polynomial whose degree does not exceed n, the formula becomes exact, without any approximation error at any point.

EXAMPLE 7.5.3 Find the third-order Taylor approximation to $f(x) = \sqrt{1+x}$ about $x = 0$.

Solution: We write $f(x) = \sqrt{1+x} = (1+x)^{1/2}$. Its first three derivatives are

$$f'(x) = \tfrac{1}{2}(1+x)^{-1/2}, \ f''(x) = \tfrac{1}{2}\left(-\tfrac{1}{2}\right)(1+x)^{-3/2}, \ \text{and} \ f'''(x) = \tfrac{1}{2}\left(-\tfrac{1}{2}\right)\left(-\tfrac{3}{2}\right)(1+x)^{-5/2}$$

Putting $x = 0$ gives $f(0) = 1$, $f'(0) = 1/2$, $f''(0) = (1/2)(-1/2) = -1/4$, and finally $f'''(0) = (1/2)(-1/2)(-3/2) = 3/8$. Applying (7.5.5) for the case $n = 3$ gives

$$f(x) \approx 1 + \frac{1}{1!}\frac{1}{2}x + \frac{1}{2!}\left(-\frac{1}{4}\right)x^2 + \frac{1}{3!}\frac{3}{8}x^3 = 1 + \frac{1}{2}x - \frac{1}{8}x^2 + \frac{1}{16}x^3$$

EXAMPLE 7.5.4 For any natural number n, write down the nth-order Taylor approximation to $f(x) = e^x$ about $x = 0$.

Solution: This case is particularly simple, because all the derivatives of f are equal to e^x. So $f^{(k)}(0) = 1$ for all $k = 1, 2, \ldots, n$. Hence, formula (7.5.5) yields

$$e^x \approx 1 + \frac{x}{1!} + \frac{x^2}{2!} + \cdots + \frac{x^n}{n!} \qquad (7.5.6)$$

This is an important result that deserves to be remembered.

EXERCISES FOR SECTION 7.5

1. Find quadratic approximations to the following functions about the specified points:

   (a) $f(x) = (1+x)^5$ about $x = 0$
   (b) $F(K) = AK^\alpha$ about $K = 1$
   (c) $f(\varepsilon) = \left(1 + \tfrac{3}{2}\varepsilon + \tfrac{1}{2}\varepsilon^2\right)^{1/2}$ about $\varepsilon = 0$
   (d) $H(x) = (1-x)^{-1}$ about $x = 0$

256 CHAPTER 7 / DERIVATIVES IN USE

⒮ **2.** Find the fifth-order Taylor approximation to $f(x) = \ln(1+x)$ about $x = 0$.

⒮ **3.** Find the second-order Taylor approximation to $f(x) = 5\left(\ln(1+x) - \sqrt{1+x}\right)$ about $x = 0$.

4. A study of attitudes to risk is based on the following approximation
$$U(y+m) \approx U(y) + U'(y)\, m + \tfrac{1}{2} U''(y)\, m^2$$
to a consumer's utility function, where y represents the consumer's initial income, and m is a random prize she may receive. Explain how to derive this approximation.

5. Suppose that y is defined implicitly, as a function of x, by the equation $1 + x^3 y + x = y^{1/2}$. Find the quadratic approximation for y about $(x, y) = (0, 1)$.

6. Let the function $x(t)$ be given by the conditions $x(0) = 1$ and $\dot{x}(t) = tx(t) + 2[x(t)]^2$. Determine the second-order Taylor polynomial for $x(t)$ about $t = 0$.

7. Establish the approximation $e^{\sigma\sqrt{t/n}} \approx 1 + \sigma\sqrt{t/n} + \sigma^2 t/2n$.

8. Establish the approximation
$$\left(1 + \frac{p}{100}\right)^n \approx 1 + n\frac{p}{100} + \frac{n(n-1)}{2}\left(\frac{p}{100}\right)^2$$

9. Suppose that the function h is defined, for all $x > 0$, by $h(x) = (x^p - x^q)/(x^p + x^q)$, where $p > q > 0$. Find its first-order Taylor approximation about $x = 1$.

7.6 Taylor's Formula

Any approximation like (7.5.5) is of limited use unless something is known about the error it implies. Taylor's formula remedies this deficiency. This formula is often used by economists, and is regarded as one of the main results in mathematical analysis. Consider the following nth order Taylor approximation about $x = 0$, found by putting $a = 0$ in (7.5.5):

$$f(x) \approx f(0) + \frac{1}{1!}f'(0)x + \frac{1}{2!}f''(0)x^2 + \cdots + \frac{1}{n!}f^{(n)}(0)x^n \qquad (*)$$

Except at $x = 0$, function $f(x)$ and the Taylor polynomial on the right-hand side of (*) are usually different. The difference between the two will depend on x as well as on n. It is called the *remainder* after n terms, which we denote by $R_{n+1}(x)$. Hence,

$$f(x) = f(0) + \frac{1}{1!}f'(0)x + \cdots + \frac{1}{n!}f^{(n)}(0)x^n + R_{n+1}(x) \qquad (7.6.1)$$

The following theorem gives an important explicit formula for the remainder.[7] Its proof is deferred to Section 9.4.

---

[7] English mathematician Brook Taylor (1685–1731) had already found polynomial approximations of the general form (*) in 1715. Italian–French mathematician Joseph-Louis Lagrange (1736–1813) (born Giuseppe Luigi Lagrangia) proved (7.6.2) approximately 50 years later.

LAGRANGE'S FORM OF THE REMAINDER

Suppose f is differentiable $n+1$ times throughout an interval that includes 0 and $x \neq 0$. Then the remainder $R_{n+1}(x)$ given in (7.6.1) can be written as

$$R_{n+1}(x) = \frac{1}{(n+1)!}f^{(n+1)}(z)x^{n+1} \tag{7.6.2}$$

for some number z strictly between 0 and x.

Using this formula for $R_{n+1}(x)$ in (7.6.1), we obtain

TAYLOR'S FORMULA

Suppose f is differentiable $n+1$ times throughout an interval that includes 0 and $x \neq 0$. Then

$$f(x) = f(0) + \frac{1}{1!}f'(0)x + \cdots + \frac{1}{n!}f^{(n)}(0)x^n + \frac{1}{(n+1)!}f^{(n+1)}(z)x^{n+1} \tag{7.6.3}$$

for some number z strictly between 0 and x.

Note that the remainder resembles the preceding terms in the sum. The only difference is that in the formula for the remainder, the $(n+1)$th derivative $f^{(n+1)}$ is evaluated at a point z, where z is some unspecified number between 0 and x. This is in contrast to all the other terms, where the derivative is evaluated at 0. The number z is not fixed because it depends, in general, on x as well as on n.

If we put $n = 1$ in formula (7.6.3), we obtain that, for some z strictly between 0 and x,

$$f(x) = f(0) + f'(0)x + \tfrac{1}{2}f''(z)x^2 \tag{7.6.4}$$

This formula tells us that $\tfrac{1}{2}f''(z)x^2$ is the error that results if we replace $f(x)$ by its linear approximation about $x = 0$.

How do we use the remainder formula? It suggests an upper limit for the error that results if we replace f with its nth-order Taylor polynomial approximation. Suppose, for instance, that for all x in an interval I, the absolute value of $f^{(n+1)}(x)$ is at most M. Then formula (7.6.3) tells us that in this interval

$$\left|R_{n+1}(x)\right| \leq \frac{M}{(n+1)!}|x|^{n+1} \tag{7.6.5}$$

Note that if n is a large number and if x is close to 0, then $|R_{n+1}(x)|$ is small for two reasons: first, if n is large, the number $(n+1)!$ in the denominator in (7.6.5) is large; second, if $|x|$ is less than 1, then $|x|^{n+1}$ is also small when n is large.

EXAMPLE 7.6.1 Use formula (7.6.4) to approximate the function

$$f(x) = \sqrt{25+x} = (25+x)^{1/2}$$

Use the result to estimate $\sqrt{25.01}$, with a bound on the absolute value of the remainder.

Solution: To apply (7.6.4), we differentiate to obtain

$$f'(x) = \tfrac{1}{2}(25+x)^{-1/2}, \text{ and } f''(x) = \tfrac{1}{2}\left(-\tfrac{1}{2}\right)(25+x)^{-3/2}$$

Then $f(0) = 5$, whereas $f'(0) = 1/2 \cdot 1/5 = 1/10$ and $f''(z) = -(1/4)(25+z)^{-3/2}$. So by (7.6.4), for all $x \neq 0$ there exists z strictly between 0 and x such that

$$\sqrt{25+x} = 5 + \tfrac{1}{10}x + \tfrac{1}{2}\left(-\tfrac{1}{4}\right)(25+z)^{-3/2}x^2 = 5 + \tfrac{1}{10}x - \tfrac{1}{8}(25+z)^{-3/2}x^2 \quad (*)$$

In order to estimate $\sqrt{25.01}$, we write $25.01 = 25 + 0.01$ and use (*). If $x = 0.01$, then z lies between 0 and 0.01, so $25 + z > 25$. Then $(25+z)^{-3/2} < (25)^{-3/2} = 1/125$. So the absolute value of the remainder term in (*) satisfies

$$|R_2(0.01)| = \left|-\tfrac{1}{8}(25+z)^{-3/2}\left(\tfrac{1}{100}\right)^2\right| < \frac{1}{80\,000} \cdot \frac{1}{125} = 10^{-7}$$

We conclude that $\sqrt{25.01} \approx 5 + 1/10 \cdot 1/100 = 5.001$, with an error less than 10^{-7}.

EXAMPLE 7.6.2 Find Taylor's formula for $f(x) = e^x$, and estimate the error for $n = 3$ and $x = 0.1$.

Solution: From Example 7.5.4, it follows that there exists a number z between 0 and x such that

$$e^x = 1 + \frac{x}{1!} + \frac{x^2}{2!} + \cdots + \frac{x^n}{n!} + \frac{x^{n+1}}{(n+1)!}e^z \qquad (7.6.6)$$

Because z lies strictly between 0 and x, it follows that $|z| < |x|$ and so for each fixed $x \neq 0$, the remainder term $R_{n+1}(x) = \frac{x^{n+1}}{(n+1)!}e^z$ in (7.6.6) satisfies $|R_{n+1}(x)| < \frac{|x|^{n+1}e^{|x|}}{(n+1)!}$. Now choose m so that $m \geq 2|x|$ and so $|x|/m \leq \tfrac{1}{2}$. Then, for any $n > m$, this choice of m ensures that $|x|/k < \tfrac{1}{2}$ for $k = m+2, m+3, \ldots, n+1$, and so

$$|R_{n+1}(x)| < \frac{|x|^{n+1}e^{|x|}}{(n+1)!} = \frac{|x|^{m+1}e^{|x|}}{(m+1)!}|x|^{n-m}\frac{(m+1)!}{(n+1)!} < \frac{|x|^{m+1}e^{|x|}}{(m+1)!}2^{-(n-m)}$$

Now, as $n \to \infty$ one has $2^{-(n-m)} \to 0$ and so evidently $|R_{n+1}(x)| \to 0$ as well. For any x one could therefore use (7.6.6) to find the value of e^x to an arbitrary degree of accuracy. Nevertheless, the absolute value of the ratio of any two successive terms before the remainder in (7.6.6) is $(|x^n|/n!) \div (|x^{n-1}|/(n-1)!) = |x|/n$. Thus, in case $|x| > 1$, at least $|x|$ terms are needed before successive terms stop increasing, and this ratio falls below 1, which allows terms to start approaching 0. So if $|x|$ is large, a large number of terms are needed for an accurate approximation.

For $n = 3$ and $x = 0.1$, Eq. (7.6.6) implies that, for some z in the interval $(0, 0.1)$, one has

$$e^{0.1} = 1 + \frac{1}{10} + \frac{1}{200} + \frac{1}{6000} + \frac{(0.1)^4}{24}e^z \qquad (*)$$

For $z < 0.1$ we have $e^z < e^{0.1}$. We claim that $e^{0.1} < 1.2$. To prove this note that $(1.2)^{10} \approx 6.2 > e$, so $e < (1.2)^{10}$. It follows that $e^z < e^{0.1} < [(1.2)^{10}]^{0.1} = 1.2$, implying that

$$\left|R_4\left(\tfrac{1}{10}\right)\right| = \frac{(0.1)^4}{24}e^z < \frac{1}{240\,000}1.2 = 0.000\,005 = 5 \cdot 10^{-6}$$

So the error that results from dropping the remainder in (∗) is less than $5 \cdot 10^{-6}$.

Suppose we consider the Taylor formula on an interval about $x = a$ instead of $x = 0$. The first $n + 1$ terms on the right-hand side of Eq. (7.6.3) become replaced by those of Eq. (7.5.5), and for all $x \neq a$ the new remainder is

$$R_{n+1}(x) = \frac{1}{(n+1)!} f^{(n+1)}(z)(x-a)^{n+1} \qquad (7.6.7)$$

for some z strictly between x and a. One easily shows that (7.6.7) follows from Eqs (7.6.2) and (7.6.3) by considering the function g defined by $g(t) = f(a+t)$ when t is close to 0.

EXERCISES FOR SECTION 7.6

1. Write Taylor's formula (7.6.3) with $n = 2$ for $f(x) = \ln(1+x)$.

2. (a) Use the approximation
$$(1+x)^m \approx 1 + mx + \tfrac{1}{2}m(m-1)x^2$$
and the fact that $\sqrt[3]{25} = 3(1 - 2/27)^{1/3}$ in order to find an approximate value of $\sqrt[3]{25}$.

   (b) Use a similar starting point to find an approximation to $\sqrt[5]{33}$. Then check these approximations by using a calculator.

3. Show that $\sqrt[3]{9} = 2(1 + 1/8)^{1/3}$. Use formula (7.6.3), with $n = 2$, to compute $\sqrt[3]{9}$ to three decimal places.

4. Let $g(x) = \sqrt[3]{1+x}$.

   (a) Find the Taylor polynomial of $g(x)$ of order 2 about the origin.

   (b) For $x \geq 0$ show that $|R_3(x)| \leq 5x^3/81$.

   (c) Find $\sqrt[3]{1003}$ to 7 decimal places.

7.7 Elasticities

Economists often study how the demand for a commodity such as coffee reacts to a change in its price. We can ask by how much the quantity demanded, measured in units such as kilograms, will change per unit increase in price, measured in units such as euros. The answer is a concrete number. But this is rather unsatisfactory because the number depends crucially on those units: is it measured in kilos per euro, or in pounds per dollar? For example, in order to know whether coffee demand is more sensitive to price changes in the Eurozone or in the USA, we need to adjust for the different units of both quantity and price. Another problem arises because a $1 increase in the price of a pound of coffee may be considerable, whereas a $1 increase in the price of a car is insignificant.

Such difficulties are largely eliminated if we consider relative price and quantity changes instead. Specifically, we can ask by what *percentage* the quantity of coffee demanded changes when its price increases by 1%. The resulting number does not depend at all on the units in which both quantities and prices are measured. This numerical ratio is called the *price elasticity of the demand*. Like the derivative of a function, this elasticity depends on the price at which it is measured.

Suppose we read that, in 1960, the price elasticity of butter in a certain country was estimated to be -1. This means that, if all other factors that influence demand remain constant, an increase of 1% in the price would lead to a decrease of 1% in the demand. Suppose we also read that the price elasticity for potatoes was estimated to be -0.2. How should this number be interpreted? Why do you think the absolute value of this elasticity is so much less than that for butter?

Assume that the demand for a commodity can be described by the function $x = D(p)$ of the price p. When the price changes from p to $p + \Delta p$, the quantity demanded, denoted by x, also changes. The absolute change in x is $\Delta x = D(p + \Delta p) - D(p)$, whereas the *relative*, or *proportional*, change is

$$\frac{\Delta x}{x} = \frac{D(p + \Delta p) - D(p)}{D(p)}$$

The ratio between the relative changes in the quantity demanded and in the price is therefore

$$\frac{\Delta x}{x} \div \frac{\Delta p}{p} = \frac{p}{x} \frac{\Delta x}{\Delta p} = \frac{p}{D(p)} \frac{D(p + \Delta p) - D(p)}{\Delta p} \qquad (7.7.1)$$

When $\Delta p = p/100$ so that p increases by 1%, then (7.7.1) becomes $(\Delta x/x) \cdot 100$, which is the percentage change in the quantity demanded. We call the proportion in (7.7.1) the *average elasticity of x in the interval* $[p, p + \Delta p]$. Observe that the number defined in (7.7.1) depends on both the price change Δp and on the price p. But it is unit free in the sense that it makes no difference whether the quantity change is measured in tons, kilograms, or pounds, or whether the price change is measured in dollars, pounds, or euros.

We would like to define the elasticity of D at p so that it also does not depend on the size of the increase in p. We can do this if D is a differentiable function of p. For then it is natural to define the elasticity of D w.r.t. p as the limit of the ratio in (7.7.1) as Δp tends to 0. But differentiability implies that the Newton quotient $[D(p + \Delta p) - D(p)]/\Delta p$ tends to the derivative $D'(p)$ as Δp tends to 0. So we obtain:

PRICE ELASTICITY OF DEMAND

The elasticity of the demand function $D(p)$ with respect to the price p is

$$\frac{p}{D(p)} \frac{dD(p)}{dp} \qquad (7.7.2)$$

Often we can get a good approximation to the elasticity by letting $\Delta p/p = 1/100 = 1\%$ and computing $p\Delta x/(x\Delta p)$.

The General Definition of Elasticity

The above definition of elasticity concerned a function determining quantity demanded as a function of price. Economists, however, also consider income elasticities of demand, when demand is regarded as a function of income. They also consider elasticities of supply, elasticities of substitution, and several other kinds of elasticity. It is therefore helpful to see how elasticity can be defined for a general differentiable function. At the same time, we also introduce the notation $\mathrm{El}_x f(x)$ for the elasticity of the function $f(x)$ w.r.t. x.

ELASTICITY

If f is differentiable at x and $f(x) \neq 0$, the *elasticity of f w.r.t. x* is

$$\mathrm{El}_x f(x) = \frac{x}{f(x)} f'(x) \qquad (7.7.3)$$

EXAMPLE 7.7.1 Find the elasticity of $f(x) = Ax^b$, where A and b are constants, with $A \neq 0$.

Solution: In this case, one has $f'(x) = Abx^{b-1}$. Hence, $\mathrm{El}_x(Ax^b) = (x/Ax^b)Abx^{b-1} = b$, so

$$f(x) = Ax^b \;\Rightarrow\; \mathrm{El}_x f(x) = b \qquad (7.7.4)$$

The elasticity of the power function Ax^b w.r.t. x is simply the exponent b. So this function has constant elasticity. In fact, it is the only type of function which has constant elasticity, as Exercise 11.10.6 asks you to show.

EXAMPLE 7.7.2 Assume that the quantity demanded of a commodity, as a function of its price p, is given by $D(p) = 8000p^{-1.5}$. Compute the elasticity of $D(p)$. Also, find the exact percentage change in quantity demanded when the price increases by 1% from $p = 4$.

Solution: Using (7.7.4), we find that $\mathrm{El}_p D(p) = -1.5$. That is, an increase in the price of 1% causes the quantity demanded to decrease by about 1.5%.

In this case, we can also compute the decrease in demand exactly. When the price is 4, the quantity demanded is $D(4) = 8000 \cdot 4^{-1.5} = 1000$. If the price $p = 4$ increases by 1%, then the new price will be $4 \cdot 1.01 = 4.04$. So the change in demand is

$$\Delta D = D(4.04) - D(4) = 8000 \cdot 4.04^{-1.5} - 1000 = -14.81$$

Then the percentage change in demand from $D(4)$ is $-(14.81/1000) \cdot 100 = -1.481\%$.

EXAMPLE 7.7.3 Let $D(P)$ denote the demand function for a product. By selling $D(P)$ units at price P, the producer earns revenue $R(P) = P \cdot D(P)$. The elasticity of $R(P)$ w.r.t. P is

$$\mathrm{El}_P R(P) = \frac{P}{R(P)} \frac{d}{dP}[P \cdot D(P)] = \frac{1}{D(P)}[D(P) + P \cdot D'(P)] = 1 + \mathrm{El}_P D(P)$$

Observe that if $\text{El}_P D(P) = -1$, then $\text{El}_P R(P) = 0$. Thus, when the price elasticity of the demand at a point is equal to -1, a small price change will have (almost) no influence on the revenue. More generally, the marginal revenue dR/dP generated by a price change is positive if the price elasticity of demand is greater than -1, and negative if the elasticity is less than -1.

Economists sometimes use the following terminology:

1. If $|\text{El}_x f(x)| > 1$, then f is elastic at x.
2. If $|\text{El}_x f(x)| = 1$, then f is unit elastic at x.
3. If $|\text{El}_x f(x)| < 1$, then f is inelastic at x.
4. If $|\text{El}_x f(x)| = 0$, then f is perfectly inelastic at x.
5. If $|\text{El}_x f(x)| = \infty$, then f is perfectly elastic at x.

Suppose the function $y = f(x)$ has an inverse $x = g(y)$. Then Theorem 7.3.1 implies that

$$\text{El}_y(g(y)) = \frac{y}{g(y)} g'(y) = \frac{f(x)}{x} \frac{1}{f'(x)} = \frac{1}{\text{El}_x f(x)} \tag{7.7.5}$$

A formulation that corresponds nicely to (7.3.2) follows:

$$\text{El}_y x = \frac{1}{\text{El}_x y} \tag{7.7.6}$$

There are rules for elasticities of sums, products, quotients, and composite functions that are occasionally useful. You might like to derive these rules by solving Exercise 9.

Elasticities as Logarithmic Derivatives

Suppose that, as in Example 7.7.1, the two variables x and y are related by the equation $y = Ax^b$, where x, y, and the parameter A are all positive. Taking the natural logarithm of each side of the equation, then applying the rules for logarithms set out in Section 4.10, we have

$$\ln y = \ln A + b \ln x \tag{7.7.7}$$

So $\ln y$ is a linear function of $\ln x$. This leads us to say that (7.7.7) is a *log-linear* relation between x and y.

For the function $y = Ax^b$, we know from Example 7.7.1 that $\text{El}_x y = b$. So from (7.7.7) we see that $\text{El}_x y$ is equal to the (double) logarithmic derivative $d(\ln y)/d(\ln x)$, which is the constant slope of this log-linear relationship. This example illustrates the general rule that elasticities are equal to such logarithmic derivatives. In fact, whenever x and y are both positive variables, with y a differentiable function of x, a proof based on repeatedly applying the chain rule shows that

$$\text{El}_x y = \frac{x}{y} \frac{dy}{dx} = \frac{d(\ln y)}{d(\ln x)} \tag{7.7.8}$$

The transformation from the original equation $y = Ax^b$ to Eq. (7.7.7) is often seen in economic models, sometimes using logarithms to a base other than e.

EXERCISES FOR SECTION 7.7

1. Find the elasticities of the functions given by the following formulas:

   (a) $3x^{-3}$ (b) $-100x^{100}$ (c) $\sqrt{x}$ (d) $A/x\sqrt{x}$, where A is a constant

2. A study of transport economics uses the relation $T = 0.4K^{1.06}$, where K is expenditure on road construction, and T is a measure of traffic volume. Find the elasticity of T w.r.t. K. In this model, if expenditure increases by 1%, by what percentage (approximately) does traffic volume increase?

3. A study of Norway's State Railways revealed that, for rides up to 60 km, the price elasticity of the volume of traffic was approximately -0.4.

   (a) According to this study, what is the consequence of a 10% increase in fares?

   (b) The corresponding elasticity for journeys over 300 km was calculated to be approximately -0.9. Can you think of a reason why this elasticity is larger in absolute value than the previous one?

4. Use definition (7.7.3) to find $\text{El}_x y$ for the following functions, where a and p are constants:

   (a) $y = e^{ax}$ (b) $y = \ln x$ (c) $y = x^p e^{ax}$ (d) $y = x^p \ln x$

5. Prove that $\text{El}_x(f(x)^p) = p \, \text{El}_x f(x)$, where p is a constant.

6. The demand D for apples in the US during the period 1927 to 1941, as a function of income r, was estimated as $D = Ar^{1.23}$, where A is a constant. Find and interpret the income elasticity of demand, or *Engel elasticity*, defined as the elasticity of D w.r.t. r.

7. A study of the transit systems in 37 American cities estimated for each city the average travel time to work, m (in minutes), as a function of population, N. They found that $m = e^{-0.02} N^{0.19}$. Write the relation in log-linear form. What is the value of m when $N = 480\,000$?

8. Show that, when finding elasticities:

   (a) Multiplicative constants disappear: $\text{El}_x (Af(x)) = \text{El}_x f(x)$.

   (b) Additive constants do *not* disappear:
   $$\text{El}_x (A + f(x)) = \frac{f(x) \, \text{El}_x f(x)}{A + f(x)}$$

SM 9. [HARDER] Prove that if f and g are positive-valued differentiable functions of x and A is a constant, then the following rules hold. Here we write, for instance, $\text{El}_x f$ instead of $\text{El}_x f(x)$.

   (a) $\text{El}_x A = 0$

   (b) $\text{El}_x (fg) = \text{El}_x f + \text{El}_x g$

   (c) $\text{El}_x (f/g) = \text{El}_x f - \text{El}_x g$

   (d) $\text{El}_x (f + g) = \dfrac{f \, \text{El}_x f + g \, \text{El}_x g}{f + g}$

   (e) $\text{El}_x (f - g) = \dfrac{f \, \text{El}_x f - g \, \text{El}_x g}{f - g}$

   (f) $\text{El}_x f(g(x)) = \text{El}_u f(u) \, \text{El}_x g$ $(u = g(x))$

10. [HARDER] Use the rules of Exercise 9 to evaluate the following:

(a) $\text{El}_x(-10x^{-5})$

(b) $\text{El}_x(x + x^2)$

(c) $\text{El}_x(x^3 + 1)^{10}$

(d) $\text{El}_x(\text{El}_x 5x^2)$

(e) $\text{El}_x(1 + x^2)$

(f) $\text{El}_x\left(\dfrac{x-1}{x^5+1}\right)$

7.8 Continuity

Roughly speaking, a function $y = f(x)$ is continuous if small changes in the independent variable x lead to small changes in the function value y. Geometrically, *a function is continuous on an interval if its graph is connected, in the sense that it has no breaks*. An example is presented in Fig. 7.8.1.

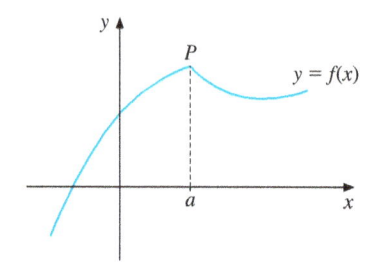

Figure 7.8.1 A continuous function

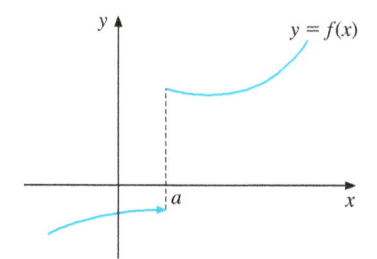

Figure 7.8.2 A discontinuous function

It is often said that a function is continuous if its graph can be drawn without lifting one's pencil off the paper. On the other hand, if the graph includes one or more jumps, we say that f is *discontinuous*. Thus, the function whose graph is shown in Fig. 7.8.2 is discontinuous at $x = a$, but continuous at all other points of its domain. The graph indicates that $f(x) < 0$ for all $x < a$, but $f(x) > 0$ for all $x \geq a$, so there is a jump at $x = a$.

Why are we interested in distinguishing between continuous and discontinuous functions? One important reason is that we must usually work with numerical approximations. For instance, if a function f is given by some formula and we wish to compute $f(\sqrt{2})$, we usually take it for granted that we can compute $f(1.4142)$ and obtain a good approximation to $f(\sqrt{2})$. In fact, this implicitly assumes that f is continuous. If it is, then because 1.4142 is close to $\sqrt{2}$, the function value $f(1.4142)$ must be close to $f(\sqrt{2})$.

In applications of mathematics to natural sciences and economics, a function will often represent how some phenomenon changes over time. Continuity of the function will then reflect continuity of the phenomenon, in the sense of gradual rather than sudden changes. For example, a person's body temperature is a function of time which changes from one value to another only after passing through all the intermediate values.

On the other hand, the market price of Brent crude oil, when examined closely enough, is actually a discontinuous function of time. One reason is that the price, generally quoted in dollars per barrel, must always have a rather small number of decimal places. A second, more interesting, reason for occasional large jumps in the price is the sudden arrival of news or a rumour that significantly affects either the demand or supply. One example might be a sudden unpredicted change in the government of a major oil-exporting country. Another example would be if several oil exporting countries with government controlled operations agree to limit their supply.

Economic analysis needs a definition of continuity that is not based solely on geometric intuition. Providing a more precise definition based on limits is our next topic.

Continuity in Terms of Limits

As discussed above, a function $y = f(x)$ is continuous at $x = a$ if small changes in x lead to small changes in $f(x)$. Stated differently, if x is close to a, then $f(x)$ must be close to $f(a)$. This motivates the following definition:

CONTINUITY

$$\text{The function } f \text{ is continuous at } x = a \text{ if } \lim_{x \to a} f(x) = f(a) \tag{7.8.1}$$

This definition implies that, in order for f to be continuous at $x = a$, the following three conditions must all be fulfilled: (i) the function f must be defined at $x = a$; (ii) the limit of $f(x)$ as x tends to a must exist; and (iii) this limit must be equal to $f(a)$. Unless all three of these conditions are satisfied, we say that f is *discontinuous* at a.

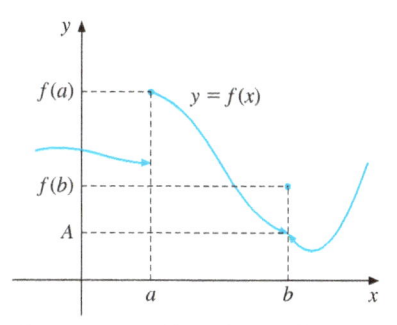

Figure 7.8.3 A discontinuous function

Figure 7.8.3 distinguishes between two important different types of discontinuity that can occur. At $x = a$, the function is discontinuous because $f(x)$ clearly has no limit as x tends to a. Hence, condition (ii) is not satisfied. This kind of discontinuity is called "irremovable" because it cannot be removed by appropriately redefining f at $x = a$.

On the other hand, the limit of $f(x)$ as x tends to b exists and is equal to A. Because $A \neq f(b)$, however, condition (iii) is not satisfied, so f is discontinuous at b. This is a "removable" discontinuity that would disappear if the function were redefined at $x = b$ to make $f(b)$ equal to A.

Properties of Continuous Functions

Mathematicians have discovered many important results that hold only for continuous functions. This makes it important to know how to determine whether or not a given function is continuous. In fact, for many types of function, the rules for limits set out in Section 6.5 make it easy to establish their continuity.

First, note that because $\lim_{x \to a} c = c$ and $\lim_{x \to a} x = a$ at each point a,

the two functions $f(x) = c$ and $f(x) = x$ are continuous everywhere (7.8.2)

This is as it should be, because the graphs of these functions are straight lines.

Next, definition (7.8.1) and the limit rules (6.5.2)–(6.5.5) evidently imply the following:

PROPERTIES OF CONTINUOUS FUNCTIONS

If f and g are continuous at a, then:

(a) the sum $f + g$ and difference $f - g$ are continuous at a;

(b) the product fg and, in case $g(a) \neq 0$, the quotient f/g are continuous at a;

(c) given any real number r, the power $[f(x)]^r$ is continuous at any point a where $[f(a)]^r$ is defined;

(d) if f has an inverse on the interval I, then its inverse f^{-1} is continuous on $f(I)$.

For instance, to prove the first statement in (b), suppose that both f and g are continuous at a. Then $f(x) \to f(a)$ and $g(x) \to g(a)$ as $x \to a$. Now, according to the rules for limits, $f(x)g(x) \to f(a)g(a)$ as $x \to a$, which means precisely that fg is continuous at $x = a$. The result in (d) is a little trickier to prove, but it is easy to believe once one realizes that the graphs of f and its inverse f^{-1} are symmetric about the line $y = x$, as we saw in Section 5.3.

By combining these properties and (7.8.2), it follows that functions like $h(x) = x + 8$ and $k(x) = 3x^3 + x + 8$ are continuous. In general, because a polynomial is a sum of continuous functions, it is continuous everywhere. Moreover, consider any rational function

$$R(x) = \frac{P(x)}{Q(x)}, \quad \text{where } P(x) \text{ and } Q(x) \text{ are polynomials}$$

Then property (b) implies that $R(x)$ is continuous at all x where $Q(x) \neq 0$.

Next, consider any composite function $g(f(x))$ where f and g are both continuous. If x is close to a, then continuity of f at a implies that $f(x)$ is close to $f(a)$. In turn $g(f(x))$ is close to $g(f(a))$ because g is continuous at $f(a)$, so $g \circ f$ is continuous at a. In short, *composites of continuous functions are continuous*.

To summarize, we have the following powerful general result:

PRESERVATION OF CONTINUITY

A function is continuous at all points where it is defined provided that it can be constructed from other continuous functions by combining one or more operations of addition, subtraction, multiplication, division (except by zero), and composition.

By using the results just discussed, a mere glance at the formula defining a function will often suffice to determine the points at which it is continuous.

EXAMPLE 7.8.1 Determine for which values of x the functions f and g are continuous:

(a) $f(x) = \dfrac{x^4 + 3x^2 - 1}{(x-1)(x+2)}$ (b) $g(x) = (x^2 + 2)\left(x^3 + \dfrac{1}{x}\right)^4 + \dfrac{1}{\sqrt{x+1}}$

Solution:

(a) This is a rational function that is continuous for all x where the denominator $(x-1)(x+2) \neq 0$. So f is continuous for all x other than 1 and -2.

(b) This function is defined when $x \neq 0$ and $x + 1 > 0$. By properties (a), (b), and (c), it follows that g is continuous in the domain $(-1, 0) \cup (0, \infty)$.

Knowing where a function is continuous simplifies the computation of many limits. If the function f is continuous at $x = a$, then the limit of $f(x)$ as x tends to a is found simply by evaluating $f(a)$. For instance, since the function $f(x) = x^2 + 5x$ studied in Example 6.5.3 is a continuous function of x, one has

$$\lim_{x \to -2} (x^2 + 5x) = f(-2) = (-2)^2 + 5(-2) = 4 - 10 = -6$$

Of course, simply evaluating $f(-2)$ like this is much easier than using the rules for limits.

Functions such as those in Examples 5.4.3 and 5.4.4 are defined "piecewise" by different formulas which apply to disjoint intervals. Such piecewise functions are frequently discontinuous at the junction points. As another example, the amount of postage you pay for a letter is a discontinuous function of its weight. (As long as we use preprinted postage stamps, it would be extremely inconvenient to have the "postage function" be even approximately continuous.) On the other hand, given any tax schedule that looks like the one in Example 5.4.4, the tax you pay is (essentially) a continuous function of your net income.

EXAMPLE 7.8.2 An economically significant example of a discontinuous function emerges from the system for taxing house purchases in the UK that existed prior to the reform of 3 December 2014. Any house buyer had to pay a tax that was called "stamp duty", known officially as the "Stamp Duty Land Tax", usually abbreviated to SDLT. Prior to 3 December 2014,

SDLT was levied at increasing average rates under a "slab system". From 24 March 2012 to 3 December 2014, these rates were as shown in Table 7.8.1.[8]

Table 7.8.1 Rates of stamp duty on English house purchases, prior to 3 December 2014

Purchase price of property	Rate of SDLT
Up to $125 000	Zero
$125 000 to $250 000	2%
$250 000 to $925 000	5%
$925 000 to $1.5 million	10%
Over $1.5 million	12%

An important implication of this slab system was that the amount of tax to be paid underwent a discontinuous jump whenever the rate increased. Specifically, the tax on a house bought for $125 000 was zero. But if the house were bought for $125 001 instead, the tax payable would rise to 2% of the purchase price, which is $2 500.02. Similarly, the tax on a house bought for $250 000 was 2% of the purchase price, which is $5 000. But if the house were bought for $250 001 instead, the tax payable would rise to 5% of the purchase price, which is $12 500.05.

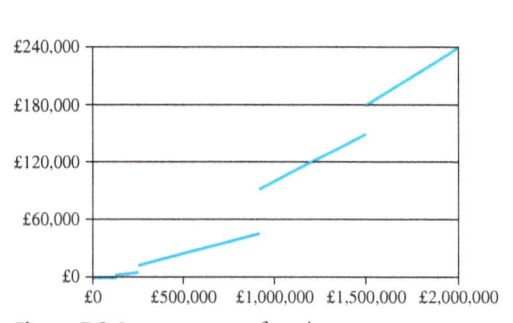

Figure 7.8.4 SDLT revenue function

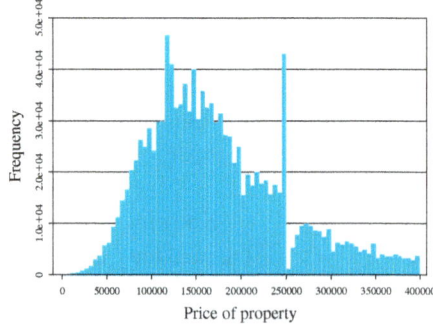

Figure 7.8.5 Frequency distribution of house purchases

Figure 7.8.4 has a graph of this old SDLT revenue function, with discontinuous jumps at each of the four prices where there is an increase in the rate. Figure 7.8.5 is a bar chart showing the frequency distribution of house purchases at different prices for the year 2006.[9] Not surprisingly, there are huge troughs in the distribution at a price just above one where the rate increases. In particular, notice the huge increase in frequency in the bar just to the left of $250 000, and the huge drop almost to zero in the bar just to the right of $250 000.

---

[8] The official source is http://www.hmrc.gov.uk/sdlt/rates-tables.htm#3

[9] This bar chart is adapted, with the authors' kind permission, from the paper by Teemu Lyytikäinen and Christian Hilber entitled "Housing transfer taxes and household mobility: Distortion on the housing or labour market?" available at https://econpapers.repec.org/paper/ferwpaper/47.htm

An economist finds this easy to explain. After all, if both buyer and seller agree that a house is really worth $251 000, on which the tax payable is $12 550, they could instead agree to record the purchase price at $249 000, on which the tax payable is only $4 950. This saves the purchaser $7 600 in tax, some of which could be used to pay the seller at least $2 000 extra for "fixtures and fittings" like carpets and curtains which, in the UK, are often not included in the price of the house itself.[10]

Eventually, the UK Treasury recognized that this was a serious defect in the tax system.[11] So on 3 December 2014, it was announced that the SDLT tax schedule would be reformed immediately. It became more like the US Federal income tax system described in Example 5.4.4, with several bands. Between these bands, the marginal rate would increase, but the average tax rate and total tax payable are both continuous functions of the price. It remains to be seen whether this move to continuity leads to a more regular frequency distribution of prices paid for English houses, and for the land on which they are built.[12]

By the way, *The Economist*, in its discussion of this tax reform in the issue dated 6 December 2014, described the new revenue function as "less kinky". This is mathematical nonsense. Kinks are corners where the slope of the tangent to the graph changes discontinuously.[13] So kinks are different from jumps. The old schedule had jumps but otherwise no kinks. The new schedule has kinks but, because it is continuous, it has no jumps.

EXERCISES FOR SECTION 7.8

1. Which of the following functions are likely to be continuous functions of time?

   (a) The price of an ounce of gold in the Zurich gold market.

   (b) The height of a growing child.

   (c) The height of an aeroplane above sea level.

   (d) The distance travelled by a car.

2. Let f and g be defined for all x by

$$f(x) = \begin{cases} x^2 - 1, & \text{for } x \leq 0 \\ -x^2, & \text{for } x > 0 \end{cases} \quad \text{and} \quad g(x) = \begin{cases} 3x - 2, & \text{for } x \leq 2 \\ -x + 6, & \text{for } x > 2 \end{cases}$$

   Draw a graph of each function. Is f continuous at $x = 0$? Is g continuous at $x = 2$?

---

[10] Lyytikäinen and Hilber point out that when SDLT replaced an older system in 2003, it "was designed to crack down on tax evasion. In the old system it was possible to evade taxes by selling 'fixtures and fittings' separately at excessive prices. In the current system [in 2006], the sale of fixtures and fittings is declared together with the property and the Land Registry compares purchase prices with typical prices paid in the area to detect evasion." The anomalies in the frequency distribution of house prices suggest that such evasion was imperfectly deterred, to say the least.

[11] Actually, these taxes applied only in England and Wales, not in Scotland and Northern Ireland.

[12] A subsequent reform dated 22 November 2017 actually reintroduced the discontinuous slab system, but only for first-time buyers of residential property intended as a main residence that is valued between $300 000 and $500 000. See https://assets.publishing.service.gov.uk/government/uploads/system/uploads/attachment_data/file/759714/Stamp_Duty_Land_Tax_relief_for_first_time_buyers_-_guidance_note.pdf

[13] As discussed in (7.9.4) below.

3. For what values of x is each function defined by the following formulas continuous?

(a) $x^5 + 4x$
(b) $\dfrac{x}{1-x}$
(c) $\dfrac{1}{\sqrt{2-x}}$
(d) $\dfrac{x}{x^2+1}$
(e) $\dfrac{x^8 - 3x^2 + 1}{x^2 + 2x - 2}$
(f) $\dfrac{1}{\sqrt{x}} + \dfrac{x^7}{(x+2)^{3/2}}$

4. Figure 7.8.6 indicates for each x the height y of an aeroplane above the point on the ground vertically below. Draw the graph of y as a function of x. Is y a continuous function of x?

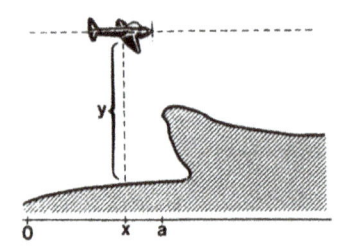

Figure 7.8.6 Exercise 4

5. For what value of a is the following function continuous for all x?

$$f(x) = \begin{cases} ax - 1 & \text{for } x \leq 1 \\ 3x^2 + 1 & \text{for } x > 1 \end{cases}$$

6. Sketch the graph of a function f that is one-to-one on an interval, but is neither strictly increasing nor strictly decreasing. (*Hint*: f cannot be continuous.)

7.9 More on Limits

Section 6.5 gave a preliminary discussion of limits. We now supplement this with some additional concepts and results, still keeping the discussion at an intuitive level. The reason for this gradual approach is that it is important and quite easy to acquire a working knowledge of limits. Experience suggests, however, that the kind of precise definition we are leading up to presents more of a challenge, as do proofs based on such a definition.

Suppose f is defined for all x close to a, but not necessarily at a. According to Definition (6.5.1), as x tends to a, the function $f(x)$ has A as its limit provided that the number $f(x)$ can be made as close to A as one pleases by making x sufficiently close, but not equal, to a. Then we say that the limit exists. Now consider a case in which the limit does not exist.

EXAMPLE 7.9.1 Try to determine $\lim\limits_{x \to -2} \dfrac{1}{(x+2)^2}$ by using a calculator.

Solution: Choosing x-values that approach -2 yields the function values in Table 7.9.1.

SECTION 7.9 / MORE ON LIMITS

Table 7.9.1 Values of $1/(x+2)^2$ when x is close to -2

x	-1.8	-1.9	-1.99	-1.999	-2.0	-2.001	-2.01	-2.1	-2.2
$1/(x+2)^2$	25	100	10 000	1 000 000	"0/0"	1 000 000	10 000	100	25

As x gets closer and closer to -2, we see that the value of the fraction becomes larger and larger. By extending the values in the table, we see, for example, that for $x = -2.0001$ and $x = -1.9999$, the value of the fraction is 100 million. Figure 7.9.1 shows the graph of $f(x) = 1/(x+2)^2$. The line $x = -2$ is called a *vertical asymptote* for the graph of f.

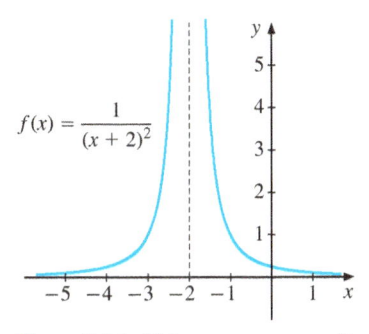

Figure 7.9.1 $f(x) \to \infty$ as $x \to -2$

Figure 7.9.2 $\lim_{x \to a} f(x)$ does not exist

In fact we can obviously make the fraction $1/(x+2)^2$ as large as we like by choosing x sufficiently close to -2, so it does not tend to any limit as x tends to -2. Instead, we say that it "tends to infinity", and even write

$$\frac{1}{(x+2)^2} \to \infty \quad \text{as} \quad x \to -2$$

Note that ∞ is *not* a number, so ∞ is *not* a limit.

One-Sided Limits

The function whose graph is shown in Fig. 7.9.2 evidently fails to have a limit as x tends to a. However, the figure does indicate that if x tends to a through values less than a, then $f(x)$ tends to the number B. We say, therefore, that the *limit of $f(x)$ as x tends to a from below is B*, and write

$$\lim_{x \to a^-} f(x) = B \quad \text{or} \quad f(x) \to B \text{ as } x \to a^-$$

Analogously, Fig. 7.9.2 also indicates that if x tends to a through values greater than a, then $f(x)$ tends to the number A. Accordingly, we say that the *limit of $f(x)$ as x tends to a from above is A*, and write

$$\lim_{x \to a^+} f(x) = A \quad \text{or} \quad f(x) \to A \text{ as } x \to a^+$$

We call these *one-sided limits*, the first *from below* and the second *from above*. They can also be called the *left limit* and *right limit*, respectively.

A necessary and sufficient condition for the (ordinary) limit to exist is that the two one-sided limits of f at a exist and are equal:

$$\lim_{x \to a} f(x) = A \iff \left[\lim_{x \to a^-} f(x) = A \text{ and } \lim_{x \to a^+} f(x) = A \right] \qquad (7.9.1)$$

It should now also be clear what is meant by

$$f(x) \to \pm\infty \text{ as } x \to a^- \quad \text{and} \quad f(x) \to \pm\infty \text{ as } x \to a^+$$

The example $\lim_{x \to 0^+} \ln x = -\infty$ has already been explained while justifying Eq. (6.11.3).

EXAMPLE 7.9.2 Figure 7.9.3 shows the graph of a function f defined on the interval $[0, 9]$. Use the figure to check that the following limiting statements seem correct:

$$\lim_{x \to 2} f(x) = 3, \quad \lim_{x \to 4^-} f(x) = 1/2, \quad \lim_{x \to 4^+} f(x) = 3, \quad \text{and} \quad \lim_{x \to 6^-} f(x) = \lim_{x \to 6^+} f(x) = -\infty$$

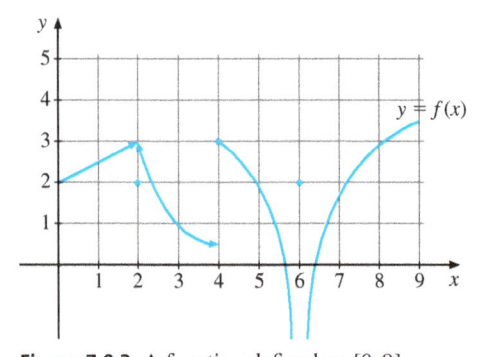

Figure 7.9.3 A function defined on $[0, 9]$

Following Eq. (7.9.1), here we allow ourselves to write simply $\lim_{x \to 6} f(x) = -\infty$ even though neither the lower nor the upper limit really exists.

EXAMPLE 7.9.3 Explain the following limits:

$$\frac{1}{\sqrt{2-x}} \to \infty \text{ as } x \to 2^- \quad \text{and} \quad \frac{-1}{\sqrt{x-2}} \to -\infty \text{ as } x \to 2^+$$

Solution: If x is slightly smaller than 2, then $2 - x$ is small and positive. Hence, $\sqrt{2-x}$ is close to 0, and $1/\sqrt{2-x}$ is a large positive number. For example, $1/\sqrt{2 - 1.9999} = 1/\sqrt{0.0001} = 100$. As x tends to 2^-, so $1/\sqrt{2-x}$ tends to ∞.

The other limit is similar, because if x is slightly larger than 2, then $\sqrt{x-2}$ is positive and close to 0, and $-1/\sqrt{x-2}$ is a large negative number.

One-Sided Continuity

The introduction of one-sided limits allows us to define one-sided continuity. Suppose f is defined on the half-open interval $(c, a]$. If $f(x)$ tends to $f(a)$ as x tends to a^-, we say that f

is *left continuous* at a. Similarly, if f is defined on $[a, d)$, we say that f is *right continuous* at a if $f(x)$ tends to $f(a)$ as x tends to a^+. Because of (7.9.1), we see that a function f is continuous at a if and only if f is both left and right continuous at a.

EXAMPLE 7.9.4   Consider again the function f whose graph is shown in Fig. 7.9.3. Because $\lim_{x \to 4^+} f(x)$ exists and is equal to $f(4) = 3$, it follows that f is right continuous at $x = 4$. But at $x = 2$ one has $\lim_{x \to 2^-} f(x) = \lim_{x \to 2^+} f(x) = 3$, yet a dot in the graph indicates that $f(2) = 2$. It follows that f is neither right nor left continuous at $x = 2$.

Consider a function f which is defined on a closed bounded interval $[a, b]$. We usually say that f is continuous in $[a, b]$ if it is not only continuous at each point of the open interval (a, b), but also both right continuous at a and left continuous at b. It should be obvious how to define continuity on half-open intervals. The continuity of a function at all points of an interval (including one-sided continuity at the end points) is often a minimum requirement we impose when speaking about "well-behaved" functions.

Limits at Infinity

We can also use the language of limits to describe the behaviour of a function as its argument becomes infinitely large through positive or negative values. Let f be defined for arbitrarily large positive numbers x. We say that $f(x)$ *has the limit A as x tends to infinity* if $f(x)$ can be made arbitrarily close to A by making x sufficiently large. We write

$$\lim_{x \to \infty} f(x) = A \quad \text{or} \quad f(x) \to A \text{ as } x \to \infty$$

In the same way,

$$\lim_{x \to -\infty} f(x) = B \quad \text{or} \quad f(x) \to B \text{ as } x \to -\infty$$

indicates that $f(x)$ can be made arbitrarily close to B by making x a sufficiently large negative number. The two limits are illustrated in Fig. 7.9.4. The horizontal line $y = A$ is a *horizontal asymptote* for the graph of f as x tends to ∞, whereas $y = B$ is a horizontal asymptote for the graph as x tends to $-\infty$.

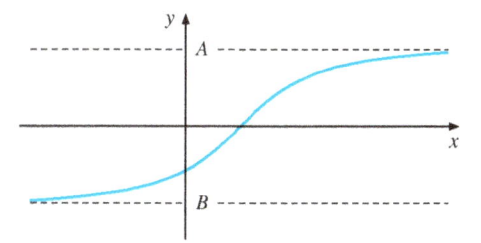

Figure 7.9.4 $y = A$ and $y = B$ are horizontal asymptotes

We remark that the limit $\lim_{x \to -\infty} e^x = 0$ has already been discussed when justifying one of the two limits appearing in Eq. (6.10.3). We also note that $\lim_{x \to +\infty} e^x = +\infty$ is an infinite limit that appeared in Eq. (6.10.3), whereas $\lim_{x \to +\infty} \ln x = +\infty$ appeared in Eq. (6.11.4).

EXAMPLE 7.9.5   Examine the following functions as $x \to \infty$ and as $x \to -\infty$:

(a) $f(x) = \dfrac{3x^2 + x - 1}{x^2 + 1}$

(b) $g(x) = \dfrac{1 - x^5}{x^4 + x + 1}$

Solution:

(a) Away from $x = 0$ we can divide each term in the numerator and the denominator by the highest power of x, which is x^2, to obtain

$$f(x) = \frac{3x^2 + x - 1}{x^2 + 1} = \frac{3 + (1/x) - (1/x^2)}{1 + (1/x^2)}$$

If x is large in absolute value, then both $1/x$ and $1/x^2$ are close to 0. So $f(x)$ is arbitrarily close to 3 if $|x|$ is sufficiently large. It follows that $f(x) \to 3$ both as $x \to -\infty$ and $x \to \infty$.

(b) Note that

$$g(x) = \frac{1 - x^5}{x^4 + x + 1} = \frac{(1/x^4) - x}{1 + (1/x^3) + (1/x^4)}$$

Now you should be able to finish the argument yourself, along the lines given in part (a). One has $g(x) \to +\infty$ as $x \to -\infty$, but $g(x) \to -\infty$ as $x \to +\infty$.

Warnings

We have extended the original definition of a limit in several different directions. For these extended limit concepts, the previous limit rules set out in Section 6.5 still apply. For example, all the usual limit rules are valid if we consider left-hand limits or right-hand limits. Also, if we replace $x \to a$ by $x \to \infty$ or $x \to -\infty$, then again the corresponding limit properties hold. Provided at least one of the two limits A and B is nonzero, the four rules in (6.5.2)–(6.5.5) remain valid if at most one of A and B is infinite.

When $f(x)$ and $g(x)$ both tend to ∞ as x tends to a, however, much more care is needed. Because $f(x)$ and $g(x)$ can each be made arbitrarily large if x is sufficiently close to a, both $f(x) + g(x)$ and $f(x)g(x)$ can also be made arbitrarily large. But, in general, we cannot say what are the limits of $f(x) - g(x)$ and $f(x)/g(x)$. The limits of these expressions will depend on how "fast" $f(x)$ and $g(x)$, respectively, tend to ∞ as x tends to a. Briefly formulated:

PROPERTIES OF INFINITE LIMITS

If $f(x) \to \infty$ and $g(x) \to \infty$ as $x \to a$, then

$$f(x) + g(x) \to \infty \quad \text{and} \quad f(x)g(x) \to \infty \quad \text{as} \quad x \to a \qquad (7.9.2)$$

However, there is no rule for the limits of $f(x) - g(x)$ and $f(x)/g(x)$ as $x \to a$.

Thus, it is important to note that the limits of $f(x) - g(x)$ and $f(x)/g(x)$ cannot be determined without more information about f and g. We do not even know whether or not either of these limits exists. The following example illustrates some of the possibilities.

EXAMPLE 7.9.6 Let $f(x) = 1/x^2$ and $g(x) = 1/x^4$. As $x \to 0$, so $f(x) \to \infty$ and $g(x) \to \infty$. Examine the limit as $x \to 0$ for each of the following four expressions:

$$f(x) - g(x), \quad g(x) - f(x), \quad \frac{f(x)}{g(x)}, \quad \text{and} \quad \frac{g(x)}{f(x)}$$

Solution: $f(x) - g(x) = (x^2 - 1)/x^4$. As $x \to 0$, the numerator tends to -1 and the denominator is positive and tends to 0, so the fraction tends to $-\infty$. For the other three limits as $x \to 0$, we have:

$$g(x) - f(x) = \frac{1-x^2}{x^4} \to \infty, \quad \frac{f(x)}{g(x)} = x^2 \to 0, \quad \text{and} \quad \frac{g(x)}{f(x)} = \frac{1}{x^2} \to \infty$$

The above four examples serve to illustrate that infinite limits require extreme care. Other tricky examples involve the product $f(x)g(x)$ of two functions, where $g(x)$ tends to 0 as x tends to a. Will the product $f(x)g(x)$ also tend to 0? Not necessarily. If $f(x)$ tends to a finite limit A, then we know that $f(x)g(x)$ tends to $A \cdot 0 = 0$. But if $f(x)$ tends to $\pm\infty$, then it is easy to construct examples in which the product $f(x)g(x)$ does not tend to 0 at all. You should try to construct some examples of your own before turning to Exercise 4.

Continuity and Differentiability

Consider the function f whose graph appears in Fig. 7.9.5. At the point $(a, f(a))$ the graph does not have a unique tangent. Thus f has no derivative at $x = a$, even though f is continuous at $x = a$. So a function can be continuous at a point without being differentiable at that point. A standard example is the absolute value function whose graph is shown in Fig. 4.3.10: that function is continuous everywhere, but not differentiable at the origin.

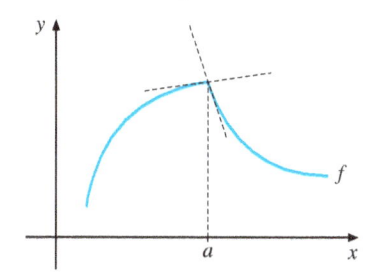

Figure 7.9.5 f is continuous, but not differentiable at $x = a$

On the other hand, differentiability implies continuity:

CONTINUITY AND DIFFERENTIABILITY

If a function f is differentiable at $x = a$, then it is continuous at $x = a$. (7.9.3)

The proof of this result is, in fact, not difficult:

Proof: The function f is continuous at $x = a$ provided $f(a + h) - f(a)$ tends to 0 as $h \to 0$. Now, for all $h \neq 0$, it is trivial that

$$f(a + h) - f(a) = \frac{f(a + h) - f(a)}{h} \cdot h \qquad (*)$$

If f is differentiable at $x = a$, then by definition the Newton quotient $[f(a + h) - f(a)]/h$ tends to the number $f'(a)$ as $h \to 0$. So the right-hand side of $(*)$ tends to $f'(a) \cdot 0 = 0$ as $h \to 0$. This proves that f is continuous at $x = a$. ∎

Suppose that f is some function whose Newton quotient tends to a limit as h tends to 0 through positive values. Then the limit is called the *right derivative* of f at a. The *left derivative* of f at a is defined similarly. So when the relevant one-sided limits of the Newton quotient exist, we denote them by

$$f'(a^+) = \lim_{h \to 0^+} \frac{f(a + h) - f(a)}{h} \quad \text{and} \quad f'(a^-) = \lim_{h \to 0^-} \frac{f(a + h) - f(a)}{h} \qquad (7.9.4)$$

Suppose that the function f is continuous at a and has left and right derivatives that satisfy $f'(a^+) \neq f'(a^-)$. In this case when the two derivatives differ, the graph of f is said to have a *kink* at $(a, f(a))$.

EXAMPLE 7.9.7 **(US Federal Income Tax, 2018).** Let $\tau(x)$ denotes the tax liability of somebody whose income during 2018 was x, both amounts measured in US dollars. This income tax function τ was discussed in Example 5.4.4, and its graph illustrated in Fig. 5.4.9. This graph has kinks at, for instance, both $x = 13\,600$ and $x = 51\,800$. Indeed, the tax rate on incomes below $13\,600 was 10\%, whereas a taxpayer with an income between $13\,600 and $51\,800 paid 10\% of the "first" $13\,600 plus 12\% of any income above $13\,600. Thus, there is a kink at $13\,600 with $\tau'(13\,600^-) = 0.1$ and $\tau'(13\,600^+) = 0.12$. Similarly, another kink occurs at $51\,800 where $\tau'(51\,800^-) = 0.12$ and $\tau'(51\,800^+) = 0.22$. The highest kink was at $500\,000 where the highest marginal rate of tax kicks in. Because this is 37\%, one has $\tau'(500\,000^+) = 0.37$. ∎

A Rigorous Definition of Limits

In our preliminary definition (6.5.1) of the limit concept, we interpreted $\lim_{x \to a} f(x) = A$ to mean that we can make $f(x)$ as close to A as we want by choosing x sufficiently close (but not equal) to a. Now we make the notion of closeness more precise, following Eq. (2.7.2): two numbers y and z are close if the distance $|y - z|$ between them is small. This allows our preliminary definition to be reformulated as follows:

LIMIT

$\lim_{x \to a} f(x) = A$ means that we can make $|f(x) - A|$ as small as we want for all $x \neq a$ with $|x - a|$ sufficiently small.

SECTION 7.9 / MORE ON LIMITS

Towards the end of the 19th century some of the world's best mathematicians gradually realized that this definition can be made precise in the following way:[14]

THE $\varepsilon - \delta$ DEFINITION OF LIMIT

We say that $f(x)$ has limit A as x tends to a if, for each number $\varepsilon > 0$, there exists an associated number $\delta > 0$ such that $|f(x) - A| < \varepsilon$ for every x with $0 < |x - a| < \delta$. When this holds, we say that $f(x)$ tends to A as x tends to a, and write
$$\lim_{x \to a} f(x) = A$$

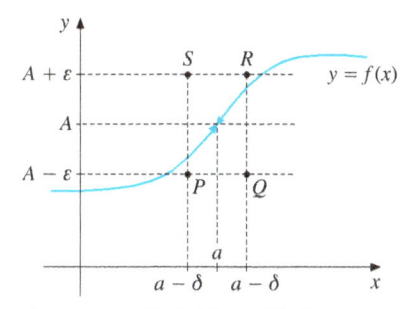

Figure 7.9.6 Definition of limit

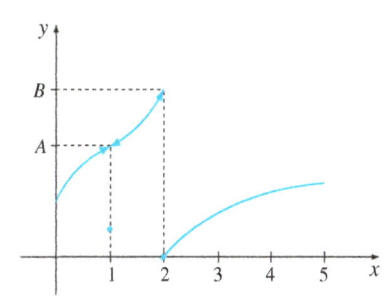

Figure 7.9.7 Exercise 1

This definition forms the basis of all mathematically rigorous work on limits. Figure 7.9.6 illustrates the definition. In the figure it implies that, for every $\varepsilon > 0$ and every associated δ, the graph of f must remain within the rectangular box $PQRS$, for all $x \neq a$ in $(a - \delta, a + \delta)$. In particular, the graph cannot pass from the interior of the box to its exterior by crossing either of the horizontal line segments PQ and SR; instead, it must cross the vertical line segments PS and QR.

Seeing this formal ε–δ definition of a limit should be regarded as a part of anybody's general mathematical education. In this book, however, we rely only on an intuitive understanding of limits.

EXERCISES FOR SECTION 7.9

1. Function f, defined for $0 < x < 5$, has the graph that appears in Fig. 7.9.7. Determine the following limits:

   (a) $\lim_{x \to 1^-} f(x)$ (b) $\lim_{x \to 1^+} f(x)$ (c) $\lim_{x \to 2^-} f(x)$ (d) $\lim_{x \to 2^+} f(x)$

---

[14] This specific idea is often attributed to the two German mathematicians Eduard Heine (1821–1881) and Karl Weierstrass (1815–1897), although really there is no consensus about this.

CHAPTER 7 / DERIVATIVES IN USE

SM 2. Evaluate the following limits:

(a) $\lim_{x \to 0^+} (x^2 + 3x - 4)$

(b) $\lim_{x \to 0^-} \dfrac{x + |x|}{x}$

(c) $\lim_{x \to 0^+} \dfrac{x + |x|}{x}$

(d) $\lim_{x \to 0^+} \dfrac{-1}{\sqrt{x}}$

(e) $\lim_{x \to 3^+} \dfrac{x}{x - 3}$

(f) $\lim_{x \to 3^-} \dfrac{x}{x - 3}$

3. Evaluate

(a) $\lim_{x \to \infty} \dfrac{x - 3}{x^2 + 1}$

(b) $\lim_{x \to -\infty} \sqrt{\dfrac{2 + 3x}{x - 1}}$

(c) $\lim_{x \to \infty} \dfrac{(ax - b)^2}{(a - x)(b - x)}$

4. Let $f_1(x) = x$, $f_2(x) = x$, $f_3(x) = x^2$, and $f_4(x) = 1/x$. Determine $\lim_{x \to \infty} f_i(x)$ for $i = 1, 2, 3, 4$. Then examine whether the rules for limits in Section 6.5 apply to the following limits as $x \to \infty$.

(a) $f_1(x) + f_2(x)$

(b) $f_1(x) - f_2(x)$

(c) $f_1(x) - f_3(x)$

(d) $f_1(x)/f_2(x)$

(e) $f_1(x)/f_3(x)$

(f) $f_1(x)f_2(x)$

(g) $f_1(x)f_4(x)$

(h) $f_3(x)f_4(x)$

SM 5. The line $y = ax + b$ is said to be an *asymptote* as $x \to \infty$ (or $x \to -\infty$) to the curve $y = f(x)$ if

$$f(x) - (ax + b) \to 0 \text{ as } x \to \infty \quad (\text{or } x \to -\infty)$$

This condition means that the vertical distance between any point $(x, f(x))$ on the curve and the corresponding point $(x, ax + b)$ on the line tends to 0 as $x \to \pm\infty$, as shown in Fig. 7.9.8.

Suppose that $f(x) = P(x)/Q(x)$ is a rational function where the degree of the polynomial $P(x)$ is exactly one greater than that of the polynomial $Q(x)$. In this case $f(x)$ will have an asymptote. Indeed, to find this one begins by performing the polynomial division $P(x) \div Q(x)$ with remainder that was explained in Section 4.7. The result will be a polynomial of degree 1, plus a remainder term that tends to 0 as $x \to \pm\infty$. Use this method to find asymptotes for the graph of each of the following functions of x:

(a) $\dfrac{x^2}{x + 1}$

(b) $\dfrac{2x^3 - 3x^2 + 3x - 6}{x^2 + 1}$

(c) $\dfrac{3x^2 + 2x}{x - 1}$

(d) $\dfrac{5x^4 - 3x^2 + 1}{x^3 - 1}$

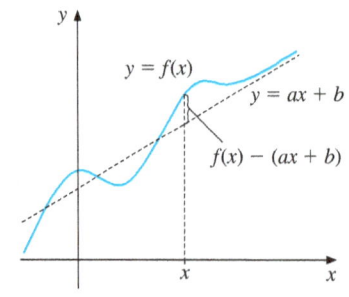

Figure 7.9.8 Exercise 5

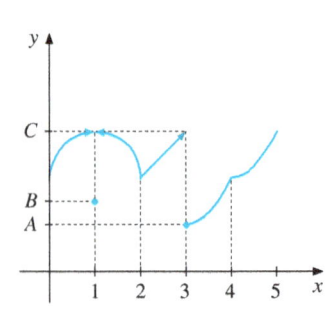

Figure 7.9.9 Exercise 7

6. Consider the cost function defined for all $x \geq 0$ by

$$C(x) = A \dfrac{x(x + b)}{x + c} + d$$

where A, b, c, and d are positive constants. Find its asymptotes.

7. Let f be the function which is defined for all x satisfying $0 < x < 5$, and whose graph appears in Fig. 7.9.9. Study the continuity and differentiability of the function at each of the points: (a) $x = 1$; (b) $x = 2$; (c) $x = 3$; and (d) $x = 4$.

8. Graph the function f defined by $f(x) = 0$ for $x \leq 0$, and $f(x) = x$ for $x > 0$. Compute $f'(0^+)$ and $f'(0^-)$.

(SM) 9. Consider the function f defined by the formula
$$f(x) = \frac{3x}{-x^2 + 4x - 1}$$
Compute $f'(x)$ and then use a sign diagram to determine where the function increases. (The function is not defined when $-x^2 + 4x - 1 = 0$, which occurs for $x = 2 \pm \sqrt{3}$.)

7.10 The Intermediate Value Theorem

An important reason for introducing the concept of a continuous function was to make precise the idea of a function whose graph is connected, in the sense of lacking any breaks. The following result, which can be proved by using the ε-δ definition of limit, expresses this property in mathematical language.

THEOREM 7.10.1 (THE INTERMEDIATE VALUE THEOREM)

Let f be a function which is continuous in the interval $[a, b]$.

(i) If $f(a)$ and $f(b)$ have different signs, then there is at least one c in (a, b) such that $f(c) = 0$.

(ii) If $f(a) \neq f(b)$, then for every *intermediate value* y in the open interval between $f(a)$ and $f(b)$, there is at least one c in (a, b) such that $f(c) = y$.

The conclusion in part (ii) follows from applying part (i) to the function $g(x) = f(x) - y$. You should draw a figure to help convince yourself that a function for which there is no such c must have at least one discontinuity.

Given an equation that cannot be solved explicitly, Theorem 7.10.1 is important in ensuring that a solution exists. We defer its proof until Section 7.11.

EXAMPLE 7.10.1 Prove that the equation $x^6 + 3x^2 - 2x - 1 = 0$ has at least one solution c between 0 and 1.

Solution: The polynomial $f(x) = x^6 + 3x^2 - 2x - 1$ is continuous for all x and, in particular, for all x in $[0, 1]$. Moreover, $f(0) = -1$ and $f(1) = 1$. So Theorem 7.10.1 implies that there exists at least one number c in $(0, 1)$ such that $f(c) = 0$.

Sometimes it is important to prove that a particular equation has a unique solution. Consider the following example.

EXAMPLE 7.10.2   Prove that the equation $2x - 5e^{-x}(1 + x^2) = 0$ has a unique solution, and that it lies in the interval $(0, 2)$.

Solution: Define $g(x) = 2x - 5e^{-x}(1 + x^2)$. Then $g(0) = -5$ and $g(2) = 4 - 25/e^2$. In fact $g(2) > 0$ because $e > 5/2$. According to the intermediate value theorem, therefore, the continuous function g must have at least one zero in $(0, 2)$. Moreover, note that

$$g'(x) = 2 + 5e^{-x}(1 + x^2) - 10xe^{-x} = 2 + 5e^{-x}(1 - 2x + x^2) = 2 + 5e^{-x}(x - 1)^2$$

Now $g'(x) > 0$ for all x, so g is strictly increasing. Hence g can have only one zero.

The following example confirms the assertion in Section 2.5 that, for any $a > 0$, the nth root $\sqrt[n]{a}$ is well defined as the unique solution of $x^n = a$.

EXAMPLE 7.10.3   Suppose n is any natural number with $n \geq 2$, whereas a is any positive real number. Show that the equation $x^n = a$ has a unique solution x^* between 1 and a.

Solution: First, note that the function $f(x) = x^n$, as the n-fold product of the function $g(x) = x$, is continuous for all x. Now we consider two cases:

1. $0 < a < 1$: Here Example 2.6.3 implies that $a^n < a$, so $f(a) < a < f(1)$.
2. $a > 1$: Here Example 2.6.3 implies that $a^n > a$, so $f(a) > a > f(1)$.

In both cases, therefore, the intermediate value theorem implies that there exists x^* between 1 and a such that $f(x^*) = a$. Moreover, the function f is differentiable for all $x > 0$ with $f'(x) = nx^{n-1} > 0$ for all x. This ensures that the solution x^* to $f(x) = a$ is unique.

Newton's Method

The intermediate value theorem can often be used to show that an equation $f(x) = 0$ has a solution in a given interval. But it says nothing more about where to find this zero. This subsection presents an effective method for finding a good approximate solution. The method was first suggested by Isaac Newton. It has an easy geometric explanation.

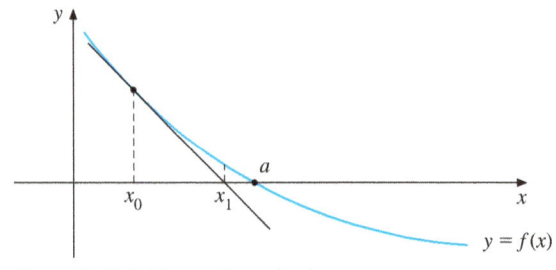

Figure 7.10.1 Newton's method

Consider the graph of the function $y = f(x)$ shown in Fig. 7.10.1. It has a zero at $x = a$, but this zero is not known. In order to look for it, start with x_0 as an initial estimate of a. It is usually better to start with x_0 not too far from a, if possible.

In order to improve the estimate x_0, first we construct the tangent line to the graph at the point $(x_0, f(x_0))$. The next approximation is the point x_1 at which the tangent crosses the x-axis, as shown in Fig. 7.10.1.

Often x_1 is a significantly better estimate of a than x_0 was. Indeed, if f happens to be linear, then the constructed tangent line will be the graph of the function, implying that $f(x_1) = 0$ and so $x_1 = a$. Actually, this might happen by very lucky coincidence even if f is not linear.

Otherwise, if the estimate x_1 satisfies $f(x_1) \neq 0$, we repeat the procedure by constructing the tangent line to the curve at the point $(x_1, f(x_1))$. Let x_2 denote the point where this new tangent line crosses the x-axis. Repeating this procedure, we obtain a sequence $x_1, x_2, \ldots$ of points which may well converge very quickly to a.

It is easy to find formulas for $x_1, x_2, \ldots$. The slope of the tangent at x_0 is $f'(x_0)$. According to the point–slope formula, the equation for the tangent line through the point $(x_0, f(x_0))$ with slope $f'(x_0)$ is given by

$$y - f(x_0) = f'(x_0)(x - x_0)$$

At the point where this tangent line crosses the x-axis, we have $y = 0$ and $x = x_1$. Hence $-f(x_0) = f'(x_0)(x_1 - x_0)$. Solving this equation for x_1 gives the first new approximation

$$x_1 = x_0 - \frac{f(x_0)}{f'(x_0)} \qquad (*)$$

The next step starts at the x_1 we have just found, and uses the same procedure to find the second new approximation x_2. To derive the relevant formula, on the left-hand side of $(*)$ we must replace the end point x_1 by x_2, and then on the right-hand side we must replace the starting point x_0 by x_1. The result is

$$x_2 = x_1 - \frac{f(x_1)}{f'(x_1)}.$$

In general, we derive the nth approximation x_n by following the same procedure n times. The nth step starts at x_{n-1} and moves to x_n. So to modify $(*)$ suitably we must replace x_1 by x_n and x_0 by x_{n-1}. This gives the following formula:

NEWTON'S METHOD

As long as $f'(x_{n-1}) \neq 0$, Newton's method generates the sequence of points given by the formula

$$x_n = x_{n-1} - \frac{f(x_{n-1})}{f'(x_{n-1})}, \qquad n = 1, 2, \ldots \qquad (7.10.1)$$

Often, the infinite sequence $x_1, x_2, \ldots$ converges quickly to a zero of f.

EXAMPLE 7.10.4 In Example 7.10.1, we considered the function

$$f(x) = x^6 + 3x^2 - 2x - 1$$

Use Newton's method once to find an approximate value for the zero of f in the interval $[0, 1]$.

Solution: Choose $x_0 = 1$. Then $f(x_0) = f(1) = 1$. Because $f'(x) = 6x^5 + 6x - 2$, we have $f'(1) = 10$. Hence, equation (1) for $n = 0$ yields

$$x_1 = 1 - \frac{f(1)}{f'(1)} = 1 - \frac{1}{10} = \frac{9}{10} = 0.9$$

EXAMPLE 7.10.5 Use Newton's method twice to find an approximate value for $\sqrt[15]{2}$.

Solution: We need an equation of the form $f(x) = 0$ which has $x = \sqrt[15]{2} = 2^{1/15}$ as a root. The equation $x^{15} = 2$ has this root, so we let $f(x) = x^{15} - 2$. Choose $x_0 = 1$. Then $f(x_0) = f(1) = -1$, and because $f'(x) = 15x^{14}$, we have $f'(1) = 15$. Thus, for $n = 0$, (1) gives

$$x_1 = 1 - \frac{f(1)}{f'(1)} = 1 - \frac{-1}{15} = \frac{16}{15} \approx 1.0667$$

Moreover,

$$x_2 = x_1 - \frac{f(x_1)}{f'(x_1)} = \frac{16}{15} - \frac{f(16/15)}{f'(16/15)} = \frac{16}{15} - \frac{(16/15)^{15} - 2}{15(16/15)^{14}} \approx 1.047\,294\,12$$

Using a suitable calculator shows that this is actually correct to 8 decimal places.

How Fast Does Newton's Method Converge?

A frequently used rule of thumb says that, to obtain an approximation that is correct to k decimal places, repeat Newton's method for just enough steps to ensure that the first k decimal places of the approximation x_n are the same as those of x_{n-1}. This, however, may be more steps than necessary, because of the following result.

THEOREM 7.10.2 (CONVERGENCE OF NEWTON'S METHOD)

Suppose that:
1. the function f is twice differentiable, with $f(x^*) = 0$ and $f'(x^*) \neq 0$;
2. there exist numbers $K > 0$ and $\delta > 0$, with $K\delta < 1$, such that for all x in the open interval $I = (x^* - \delta, x^* + \delta)$ one has $\dfrac{|f(x)f''(x)|}{f'(x)^2} \leq K|x - x^*|$.

Then, provided that the infinite sequence $x_1, x_2, \ldots$ in Eq. (7.10.1) starts at an x_0 in I, it will converge to x^*, with an error $|x_n - x^*|$ that, for all n, satisfies

$$|x_n - x^*| \leq \frac{(\delta K)^{2^n}}{K}.$$

In most cases Newton's method is very efficient. Nevertheless, it can happen sometimes that the infinite sequence $x_1, x_2, \ldots$ defined by (7.10.1) fails to converge. Figure 7.10.2 shows an example where x_1 is a much worse approximation to a than x_0 was. Usually, Newton's method fails only if the absolute value of $f'(x_n)$ becomes too small, for some n. Of course, formula (7.10.1) breaks down entirely if $f'(x_n) = 0$.

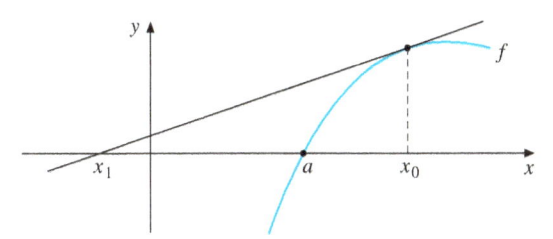

Figure 7.10.2 Newton's method

EXERCISES FOR SECTION 7.10

1. Show that each of the following equations has at least one root in the given interval.
   (a) $x^7 - 5x^5 + x^3 - 1 = 0$, in $(-1, 1)$
   (b) $x^3 + 3x - 8 = 0$, in $(1, 3)$
   (c) $\sqrt{x^2 + 1} = 3x$, in $(0, 1)$
   (d) $e^{x-1} = 2x$, in $(0, 1)$

2. Explain why anybody who is taller than 1 metre today was once exactly 1 metre tall.

3. Find a better approximation to $\sqrt[3]{17} \approx 2.5$ by using Newton's method once.

SM 4. The equation $x^4 + 3x^3 - 3x^2 - 8x + 3 = 0$ has an integer root. Find it. The three additional roots are close to -1.9, 0.4, and 1.5. Find better approximations by using Newton's method once for each root that is not an integer.

5. The equation $(2x)^x = 15$ has a solution which is approximately an integer. Find a better approximation by using Newton's method once.

6. In Fig. 7.10.1, $f(x_0) > 0$ and $f'(x_0) < 0$. Moreover, x_1 is to the right of x_0. Verify that this agrees with the formula (7.10.1) for $n = 0$. Check the other combinations of signs for $f(x_0)$ and $f'(x_0)$ to see both geometrically and analytically on which side of x_0 the point x_1 lies.

7.11 Infinite Sequences

We often encounter functions like those in Newton's method which associate a number $s(n)$ to each natural number n. Such a function is called an *infinite sequence*, or just a sequence. Its terms $s(1), s(2), s(3), \ldots, s(n), \ldots$ are usually denoted by using subscripts: thus, they become $s_1, s_2, s_3, \ldots, s_n, \ldots$. We often use the more concise notation $(s_n)_{n=1}^{\infty}$, or simply

(s_n), for an arbitrary infinite sequence.[15] For example, if $s_n = 1/n$ for $n = 1, 2, 3, \ldots$, then the terms of the sequence are

$$1, \frac{1}{2}, \frac{1}{3}, \frac{1}{4}, \ldots, \frac{1}{n}, \ldots$$

If we choose n large enough, the terms of this sequence can be made as small as we like. We say that the sequence *converges* to 0. In general, we introduce the following definition: A sequence (s_n) is said to **converge** to a number s if s_n can be made arbitrarily close to s by choosing n sufficiently large. When this happens, we write

$$\lim_{n \to \infty} s_n = s \quad \text{or} \quad s_n \to s \text{ as } n \to \infty$$

This definition is just an adaptation of the previous definition that $f(x) \to A$ as $x \to \infty$. All the ordinary limit rules in Section 6.5 apply to limits of sequences.

A sequence that does not converge to any real number is said to *diverge*. Consider the following two sequences

$$(2^n)_{n=0}^{\infty} \quad \text{and} \quad ((-1)^n)_{n=1}^{\infty}$$

Explain why they both diverge.[16]

EXAMPLE 7.11.1   For $n \geq 3$, let A_n be the area of a regular polygon with n equal sides and n equal angles, sometimes called an *n-gon*, which is inscribed in a circle with radius 1. For $n = 1$ or $n = 2$, the polygon collapses to a single point or a line interval, respectively, Both have zero area, so we take $A_1 = A_2 = 0$.

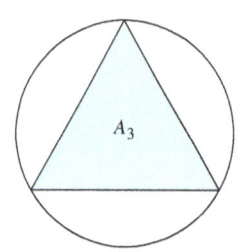

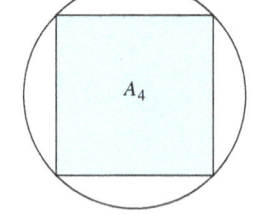

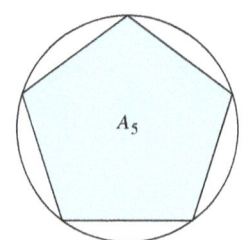

Figure 7.11.1 Three *n*-gons

Thereafter, for $n = 3$, the area A_3 is that of a triangle; for $n = 4$, the area A_4 is that of a square; for $n = 5$, the area A_5 is that of a pentagon; and so on. See Fig. 7.11.1.

The area A_n evidently increases with n. But it is always less than the number π, which can be defined as the area of a circle of radius 1. It seems intuitively obvious that we can make the difference between the areas A_n and π as small as we wish by choosing n sufficiently large, This justifies the claim that $A_n \to \pi$ as $n \to \infty$.

---

[15] The alternative notation $\{s_n\}_{n=1}^{\infty}$, or simply $\{s_n\}$, is sometimes used. A reason to avoid it is that it suggests an unordered set, whereas a sequence is an ordered set.

[16] Occasionally, as in the first of these sequences, the starting index is not 1, but another integer, which is 0 in this case.

EXAMPLE 7.11.2 Equation (6.11.6) states that $\lim_{h \to 0}(1+h)^{1/h}$ is $e = 2.718\ldots$. If we put $h = 1/n$, then $h \to 0$ as the natural number $n \to \infty$. This yields the following important limit:

$$e = \lim_{n \to \infty} (1 + 1/n)^n \qquad (7.11.1)$$

Proof of The Intermediate Value Theorem

Suppose that the two sequences $(a_n)_{n=1}^{\infty}$ and $(b_n)_{n=1}^{\infty}$ together satisfy the condition:

$$a_n \leq a_{n+1} \leq b_{n+1} \leq b_n \quad \text{for all } n = 1, 2, \ldots \qquad (7.11.2)$$

Suppose too that

$$\lim_{n \to \infty} |b_n - a_n| = 0 \qquad (7.11.3)$$

Then a fundamental property of the real line states that the two sequences have a common limit c^* such that $\lim_{n \to \infty} a_n = \lim_{n \to \infty} b_n = c^*$.

This property allows us to prove the intermediate value theorem as follows:

Proof of Theorem 7.10.1 Consider the following construction of a shrinking sequence of intervals $[a_n, b_n]$. Start with $a_0 = a$ and $b_0 = b$. Then $f(a_0)$ and $f(b_0)$ have opposite signs, by hypothesis. Let c_0 be the mid-point $\frac{1}{2}(a_0 + b_0)$ of the interval $[a_0, b_0]$. If it happens that $f(c_0) = 0$, then we can take $c = c_0$, and the construction is complete.

Otherwise, if $f(c_0) \neq 0$, then either $f(c_0)$ and $f(a_0)$ have opposite signs, or else $f(c_0)$ and $f(b_0)$ have opposite signs. In the first case, choose $a_1 = a_0$ and $b_1 = c_0$; in the second case, choose $a_1 = c_0$ and $b_1 = b_0$. In this way we have constructed a new interval $[a_1, b_1]$ such that $f(a_1)$ and $f(b_1)$ have opposite signs. Moreover, our construction implies that either $|b_1 - a_1| = |c_0 - a_0| = \frac{1}{2}|b_0 - a_0|$ or $|b_1 - a_1| = |b_0 - c_0| = \frac{1}{2}|b_0 - a_0|$. In either case, the new interval is half as long as the old. Finally, note that $a_0 \leq a_1 \leq b_1 \leq b_0$.

This construction can be repeated as often as necessary to yield a sequence of intervals $[a_n, b_n]$ with $|b_{n+1} - a_{n+1}| = \frac{1}{2}|b_n - a_n|$ such that the function values $f(a_n)$ and $f(b_n)$ have opposite signs at these end points. The construction will stop after n steps if we ever happen to reach a point c_n at which $f(c_n) = 0$. Otherwise, we get an infinite sequence of intervals $[a_n, b_n]$ whose lengths satisfy $|b_n - a_n| = 2^{-n}|b_0 - a_0|$, and so converge to zero. Also, the sequence a_n of lower bounds is nondecreasing, whereas the sequence b_n of upper bounds is nonincreasing.

By construction, the two sequences $(a_n)_{n=1}^{\infty}$ and $(b_n)_{n=1}^{\infty}$ satisfy (7.11.2) and (7.11.3). So there exists a real number c^* which is a common limit for which a_n converges to c^* from below, whereas b_n converges to c^* from above. But we have assumed that the function f is continuous on the interval $[a, b]$. So definition (7.8.1) implies that both $f(a_n) \to f(c^*)$ and $f(b_n) \to f(c^*)$ as $n \to \infty$.

Now, note that because $f(a_n)$ and $f(b_n)$ always have opposite signs, we have $f(a_n)f(b_n) \leq 0$ for all $n = 0, 1, 2, \ldots$. So the above limit properties imply that

$$[f(c^*)]^2 = \lim_{n \to \infty} f(a_n)f(b_n) \leq 0$$

But this is only possible if $f(c^*) = 0$, so we can take $c = c^*$.

We note that the fundamental properties (7.11.2) and (7.11.3) of the real line used in this proof do not hold if we restrict ourselves to the set of rational numbers. Indeed, consider the function $f(x) = x^2 - 2$ on the interval $[1, 2]$. All the other conditions of the intermediate value theorem hold. One can even construct an infinite sequence of intervals $[a_n, b_n]$ with all the above properties, except that there is no limit point among the rational numbers. Indeed, there is no rational number such that $f(x) = 0$ because $\sqrt{2}$ is irrational.

Irrational Numbers as Limits of Sequences

In Example 7.11.1, we considered the sequence (A_n) of areas of regular n-gons, and claimed that this sequence converges to the irrational number $\pi = 3.14159265\ldots$. But at the end of Section 2.10 we considered successive decimal expansions. In the case of π, these expansions generate the sequence $s_1 = 3.1$, $s_2 = 3.14$, $s_3 = 3.141$, $s_4 = 3.1415$, etc. Here each s_n is the expansion of π to n decimal places. By construction one has $s_n \leq \pi \leq s_n + 10^{-n}$ because s_n must be the largest fraction to n decimal places that does not exceed π. In fact the pair of sequences $\{s_n\}$ and $\{s_n + 10^{-n}\}$ satisfy (7.11.2) and (7.11.3), implying that they have a common limit as $n \to \infty$ which must be π.

Let a be any fixed positive real number. Section 2.5 defined the power a^x when x is rational. Subsequently, by considering the special case of 5^π, Section 4.8 suggested how to define a^x when x is irrational. Now, let r be an arbitrary irrational number. Then, just as for π, there exists a sequence (r_n) of rational numbers such that $r_n \to r$ as $n \to \infty$. The power a^{r_n} is well defined for all n. Since r_n converges to r, it is reasonable to define a^r as the limit of a^{r_n} as n approaches infinity:

$$a^r = \lim_{n \to \infty} a^{r_n} \qquad (*)$$

Actually, there are infinitely many sequences (r_n) of rational numbers that converge to any given irrational number r. Nevertheless, one can show that the limit in $(*)$ exists and is independent of which sequence we choose.

EXERCISES FOR SECTION 7.11

1. Let $\alpha_n = \dfrac{3-n}{2n-1}$ and $\beta_n = \dfrac{n^2 + 2n - 1}{3n^2 - 2}$, for $n = 1, 2, \ldots$. Find the following limits:

    (a) $\lim\limits_{n \to \infty} \alpha_n$ (b) $\lim\limits_{n \to \infty} \beta_n$ (c) $\lim\limits_{n \to \infty} (3\alpha_n + 4\beta_n)$

    (d) $\lim\limits_{n \to \infty} \alpha_n \beta_n$ (e) $\lim\limits_{n \to \infty} \dfrac{\alpha_n}{\beta_n}$ (f) $\lim\limits_{n \to \infty} \sqrt{\beta_n - \alpha_n}$

2. Examine the convergence of the sequences whose general terms are as follows:

    (a) $s_n = 5 - \dfrac{2}{n}$ (b) $s_n = \dfrac{n^2 - 1}{n}$ (c) $s_n = \dfrac{3n}{\sqrt{2n^2 - 1}}$

3. Prove that $e^x = \lim\limits_{n \to \infty} \left(1 + \dfrac{x}{n}\right)^n$ for $x > 0$.[17]

---

[17] The same limit is valid also for $x < 0$.

7.12 L'Hôpital's Rule

We often need to consider the limit as x tends to a of a quotient in which both numerator and denominator tend to 0. Then we write

$$\lim_{x \to a} \frac{f(x)}{g(x)} = \text{``0/0''}$$

We call such a limit an *indeterminate form of type* 0/0. Here a may be replaced by a^+, a^-, ∞, or $-\infty$. The words "indeterminate form" indicate that the limit—or one-sided limit—cannot be found without further examination.

We start with the simple case where f and g are differentiable at $x = a$, with $f(a) = g(a) = 0$. When $x \neq a$ and $g(x) \neq g(a)$, then some routine algebra allows us to write

$$\frac{f(x)}{g(x)} = \frac{[f(x) - f(a)]/(x-a)}{[g(x) - g(a)]/(x-a)}$$

The right-hand side is the ratio of two Newton quotients. Taking the limit as $x \to a$, we see that provided $g'(a) \neq 0$, this ratio tends to $f'(a)/g'(a)$. This gives the following result:

L'HÔPITAL'S RULE

Suppose that the functions f and g are both differentiable at $x = a$, with $f(a) = g(a) = 0$ and $g'(a) \neq 0$. Then

$$\lim_{x \to a} \frac{f(x)}{g(x)} = \frac{f'(a)}{g'(a)} \tag{7.12.1}$$

According to (7.12.1), provided that $g'(a) \neq 0$, we can find the limit of an indeterminate form of type "0/0" by differentiating both numerator and denominator separately.

EXAMPLE 7.12.1 Use L'Hôpital's rule to confirm the result in Example 6.5.1—namely,

$$\lim_{x \to 0} \frac{e^x - 1}{x} = 1$$

Solution: Put $f(x) = e^x - 1$ and $g(x) = x$ in Eq. (7.12.1). Note that $f(0) = e^0 - 1 = 0$ and $g(0) = 0$. Also, $f'(x) = e^x$ and $g'(x) = 1$, so $f'(0) = g'(0) = 1$. Thus (7.12.1) implies that

$$\lim_{x \to 0} \frac{e^x - 1}{x} = \frac{f'(0)}{g'(0)} = \frac{1}{1} = 1$$

EXAMPLE 7.12.2 Assuming that $x > 0$ and $y > 0$, compute

$$\lim_{\lambda \to 0} \frac{x^\lambda - y^\lambda}{\lambda}$$

Solution: In this limit x and y are kept fixed. Define $f(\lambda) = x^\lambda - y^\lambda$ and $g(\lambda) = \lambda$. Then $f(0) = g(0) = 0$. Using the rule $(d/dx)a^x = a^x \ln a$, we obtain $f'(\lambda) = x^\lambda \ln x - y^\lambda \ln y$, so that $f'(0) = \ln x - \ln y$. Moreover, $g'(\lambda) = 1$, so $g'(0) = 1$. Using l'Hôpital's rule gives

$$\lim_{\lambda \to 0} \frac{x^\lambda - y^\lambda}{\lambda} = \frac{\ln x - \ln y}{1} = \ln \frac{x}{y}$$

In particular, if $y = 1$, then

$$\lim_{\lambda \to 0} \frac{x^\lambda - 1}{\lambda} = \ln x \qquad (7.12.2)$$

which is a useful result.

Suppose we have a "0/0" form as in (7.12.1), but that $f'(a)/g'(a)$ is also of the type "0/0". Because $g'(a) = 0$, the argument for (7.12.1) breaks down. What to do then? Well, we differentiate both numerator and denominator separately once again. If we still get "0/0", we go on differentiating numerator and denominator repeatedly until the limit is determined, if possible. Here is an example from statistics.

EXAMPLE 7.12.3   Find

$$\lim_{x \to 0} \frac{e^{xt} - 1 - xt}{x^2}$$

Solution: The numerator and denominator are both 0 at $x = 0$. Applying l'Hôpital's rule twice, we have

$$\lim_{x \to 0} \frac{e^{xt} - 1 - xt}{x^2} = \text{``0/0''} = \lim_{x \to 0} \frac{te^{xt} - t}{2x} = \text{``0/0''} = \lim_{x \to 0} \frac{t^2 e^{xt}}{2} = \frac{1}{2}t^2$$

Here are two important warnings concerning the most common errors in attempting to apply l'Hôpital's rule:

1. Check that you really do have an indeterminate form; otherwise, as Exercise 5 shows, the method usually gives an erroneous result.
2. Compute the limit as $x \to a$ of the ratio f'/g'; do *not* differentiate f/g as a fraction.

The method explained here and used to solve Example 7.12.3 is built on Theorem 7.12.1 below. Note that the requirements on f and g are weaker than one in the examples presented so far. For instance, f and g need not even be differentiable at $x = a$. Thus the theorem actually gives a more general version of l'Hôpital's rule.

THEOREM 7.12.1 (L'HÔPITAL'S RULE FOR "0/0" FORMS)

Suppose that:

(i) The functions f and g are differentiable in an interval (α, β) that contains a, except possibly at a;

(ii) $f(x)$ and $g(x)$ both tend to 0 as x tends to a;

(iii) $g'(x) \neq 0$ for all $x \neq a$ in (α, β);

(iv) $f'(x)/g'(x) \to L$ as $x \to a$, where L can be finite, ∞, or $-\infty$.

Then
$$\lim_{x \to a} \frac{f(x)}{g(x)} = \lim_{x \to a} \frac{f'(x)}{g'(x)} = L$$

Extensions of L'Hôpital's Rule

L'Hôpital's rule can be extended to some other cases. For instance, a can be an end point of the interval (α, β). Thus, $x \to a$ can be replaced by $x \to a^+$ or $x \to a^-$. Also it is easy to see that a may be replaced by ∞ or $-\infty$, as Exercises 4 and 8 show.

The rule also applies to other indeterminate forms such as "$\pm \infty / \pm \infty$". Exercise 9 suggests one way to provide a proof, while leaving the reader to complete the details. Here is an example of how the rule can be applied:

$$\lim_{x \to \infty} \frac{\ln x}{x} = \text{"}\infty/\infty\text{"} = \lim_{x \to \infty} \frac{1/x}{1} = 0 \tag{7.12.3}$$

Indeed, there are various other indeterminate forms which algebraic manipulations or substitutions may be able to transform into expressions like those already mentioned.

EXAMPLE 7.12.4 Find $L = \lim_{x \to \infty} \left(\sqrt[5]{x^5 - x^4} - x \right)$.

Solution: First note that this is an "$\infty - \infty$" case. We use some algebraic manipulation to reduce it to a "0/0" case. Indeed, for $x \neq 0$, one has

$$\sqrt[5]{x^5 - x^4} - x = \left[x^5 \left(1 - \frac{1}{x} \right) \right]^{1/5} - x = x \left(1 - \frac{1}{x} \right)^{1/5} - x$$

Rewriting the RHS leads to

$$\lim_{x \to \infty} \left(\sqrt[5]{x^5 - x^4} - x \right) = \lim_{x \to \infty} \frac{(1 - 1/x)^{1/5} - 1}{1/x} = \text{"0/0"}$$

Using l'Hôpital's rule, we have

$$L = \lim_{x \to \infty} \frac{(1/5)(1 - 1/x)^{-4/5}(1/x^2)}{-1/x^2} = \lim_{x \to \infty} \left[-\frac{1}{5} \left(1 - \frac{1}{x} \right)^{-4/5} \right] = -\frac{1}{5}$$

EXAMPLE 7.12.5 Suppose that if a firm uses as inputs $K > 0$ units of capital and $L > 0$ units of labour, the amount Y of output it obtains is given by

$$Y = A \left[aK^{-\rho} + (1-a)L^{-\rho} \right]^{-1/\rho} \tag{$*$}$$

where $A > 0$, $a \in (0, 1)$, and $\rho \neq 0$ are constants. Keeping A, K, L, and a fixed, apply l'Hôpital's rule to $z = \ln[Y/A]$ as $\rho \to 0$ in order to show that[18]

$$\lim_{\rho \to 0} \left\{ A \left[aK^{-\rho} + (1-a)L^{-\rho} \right]^{-1/\rho} \right\} = AK^a L^{1-a} \qquad (**)$$

Solution: We get

$$\ln \left(aK^{-\rho} + (1-a)L^{-\rho} \right)^{-1/\rho} = -\ln \left(aK^{-\rho} + (1-a)L^{-\rho} \right) / \rho \to \text{``0/0''} \text{ as } \rho \to 0$$

Because $(d/d\rho)K^{-\rho} = -K^{-\rho} \ln K$ and $(d/d\rho)L^{-\rho} = -L^{-\rho} \ln L$, applying l'Hôpital's rule gives

$$\lim_{\rho \to 0} z = \lim_{\rho \to 0} \left[\frac{aK^{-\rho} \ln K + (1-a)L^{-\rho} \ln L}{aK^{-\rho} + (1-a)L^{-\rho}} \right] \div 1$$

$$= a \ln K + (1-a) \ln L$$

$$= \ln K^a L^{1-a}$$

Hence $e^z \to K^a L^{1-a}$. By definition of z, it follows that $F(K, L) \to AK^a L^{1-a}$ as $\rho \to 0$. ∎

An Important Limit

If a is an arbitrary number greater than 1, then one has $a^x \to \infty$ as $x \to \infty$. For example, $(1.0001)^x \to \infty$ as $x \to \infty$. Furthermore, if p is an arbitrary positive number, then $x^p \to \infty$ as $x \to \infty$. If we compare $(1.0001)^x$ and x^{1000}, it is clear that the former increases quite slowly at first, whereas the latter increases very quickly. Nevertheless, $(1.0001)^x$ eventually "overwhelms" x^{1000}. In general, given $a > 1$, for any fixed positive number p, one has

$$\lim_{x \to \infty} \frac{x^p}{a^x} = 0 \qquad (7.12.4)$$

For example, both x^2/e^x and $x^{10}/(1.1)^x$ tend to 0 as x tends to ∞. This result is actually quite remarkable. It can be expressed briefly by saying that, for an arbitrary base $a > 1$, *the exponential function a^x increases faster than any power x^p of x*. Even more succinctly, one may say that *"Exponentials overwhelm powers"*. (If $p \leq 0$, the limit is obviously 0.)

To prove (7.12.4), take the logarithm of the function on the left-hand side, which is

$$\ln \frac{x^p}{a^x} = p \ln x - x \ln a = x \left(p \frac{\ln x}{x} - \ln a \right) \qquad (*)$$

Now, as $x \to \infty$, we have $\ln x / x \to 0$ because of (7.12.3). So the term in parentheses in $(*)$ converges to $-\ln a$, which is negative because $a > 1$. It follows from $(*)$ that $\ln(x^p/a^x) \to -\infty$, and so $x^p/a^x = \exp[\ln(x^p/a^x)] \to 0$ because $e^z \to 0$ as $z \to -\infty$.

---

[18] The expression on the RHS of Eq. $(*)$ is known in economics as the "constant elasticity of substitution", or CES, function. The one on the RHS of Eq. $(**)$ is the Cobb–Douglas production function. Functions of two variables, like these, are not studied systematically until Chapter 14. Nevertheless, this example shows how applying l'Hôpital's rule to a function of two variables yields an economically significant result.

EXERCISES FOR SECTION 7.12

1. Use l'Hôpital's rule to find:

   (a) $\lim_{x \to 3} \dfrac{3x^2 - 27}{x - 3}$
   (b) $\lim_{x \to 0} \dfrac{e^x - 1 - x - \frac{1}{2}x^2}{3x^3}$
   (c) $\lim_{x \to 0} \dfrac{e^{-3x} - e^{-2x} + x}{x^2}$

2. Find the limits:

   (a) $\lim_{x \to a} \dfrac{x^2 - a^2}{x - a}$
   (b) $\lim_{x \to 0} \dfrac{2\sqrt{1+x} - 2 - x}{2\sqrt{1+x+x^2} - 2 - x}$

(SM) 3. Use l'Hôpital's rule to find the following limits:

   (a) $\lim_{x \to 1} \dfrac{x - 1}{x^2 - 1}$
   (b) $\lim_{x \to -2} \dfrac{x^3 + 3x^2 - 4}{x^3 + 5x^2 + 8x + 4}$
   (c) $\lim_{x \to 2} \dfrac{x^4 - 4x^3 + 6x^2 - 8x + 8}{x^3 - 3x^2 + 4}$
   (d) $\lim_{x \to 1} \dfrac{\ln x - x + 1}{(x - 1)^2}$
   (e) $\lim_{x \to 1} \dfrac{1}{x - 1} \ln\left(\dfrac{7x + 1}{4x + 4}\right)$
   (f) $\lim_{x \to 1} \dfrac{x^x - x}{1 - x + \ln x}$

4. Find the following limits:

   (a) $\lim_{x \to \infty} \dfrac{\ln x}{\sqrt{x}}$
   (b) $\lim_{x \to 0^+} x \ln x$
   (c) $\lim_{x \to 0^+} (xe^{1/x} - x)$

5. Find the error in the following line of reasoning:

   $$\lim_{x \to 1} \dfrac{x^2 + 3x - 4}{2x^2 - 2x} = \lim_{x \to 1} \dfrac{2x + 3}{4x - 2} = \lim_{x \to 1} \dfrac{2}{4} = \dfrac{1}{2}$$

   What is the correct value of the first limit?

6. With $\beta > 0$ and $\gamma > 0$, find $\lim_{v \to 0^+} \dfrac{1 - (1 + v^\beta)^{-\gamma}}{v}$. (*Hint:* Consider first the case $\beta = 1$.)

7. In the context of Examples 7.1.5 and 7.1.8, the family of CES utility functions is given by

   $$u(c) = \begin{cases} \dfrac{c^{1-\rho} - 1}{1 - \rho}, & \text{if } \rho \neq 1, \\ \ln c, & \text{if } \rho = 1. \end{cases}$$

   for all $c > 0$.[19] Use l'Hôpital's rule to show that $\lim_{\rho \to 1} \dfrac{c^{1-\rho} - 1}{1 - \rho} = \ln c$. In this sense, the family is "continuous in ρ".

8. [HARDER] Suppose that f and g are both differentiable for all large x and that $f(x)$ and $g(x)$ both tend to 0 as $x \to \infty$. If in addition $\lim_{x \to \infty} g'(x) \neq 0$, show that

   $$\lim_{x \to \infty} \dfrac{f(x)}{g(x)} = \text{``0/0''} = \lim_{x \to \infty} \dfrac{f'(x)}{g'(x)}$$

   by introducing $x = 1/t$ in the first fraction and then using l'Hôpital's rule as $t \to 0^+$.

---

[19] See Example 7.12.5. These are also known as constant relative risk aversion, or CRRA, utility functions.

SM 9. [HARDER] Suppose that $\lim_{x \to a} f(x)/g(x) = \pm\text{"}\infty/\infty\text{"} = L \neq 0$ where f and g are differentiable functions whose derivatives $f'(x)$ and $g'(x)$ converge to nonzero limits as x tends to a. By applying l'Hôpital's rule to the equivalent limit $\lim_{x \to a} [1/g(x)] / [1/f(x)] = \text{"}0/0\text{"}$, show that one has $L = \lim_{x \to a} [f'(x)/g'(x)]$ provided this limit exists.

REVIEW EXERCISES

1. Use implicit differentiation to find dy/dx and d^2y/dx^2 for each of the following equations:

   (a) $5x + y = 10$ (b) $xy^3 = 125$ (c) $e^{2y} = x^3$

   Check by solving each equation for y as a function of x, then differentiating.

2. Compute y' when y is defined implicitly by the equation $y^5 - xy^2 = 24$. Is y' ever 0?

3. The graph of the equation $x^3 + y^3 = 3xy$ passes through the point $(3/2, 3/2)$. Find the slope of the tangent line to the curve at this point. This equation has a nice graph, called *Descartes's folium*, which appears in Fig. 7.R.1.

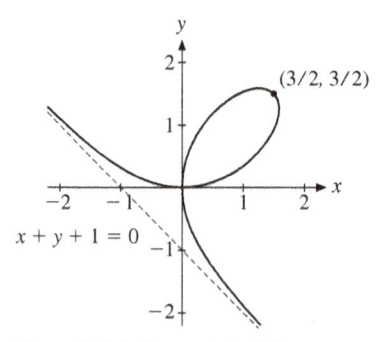

Figure 7.R.1 Descartes's folium

4. (a) Find the slope of the tangent to the curve $x^2y + 3y^3 = 7$ at $(x, y) = (2, 1)$.

   (b) Prove that $y'' = -210/13^3$ at $(2, 1)$.

5. If $K^{1/3}L^{1/3} = 24$, compute dL/dK by implicit differentiation.

6. The equation
   $$\ln y + y = 1 - 2\ln x - 0.2(\ln x)^2$$
   defines y as a function of x for $x > 0$, $y > 0$. Compute y' and show that $y' = 0$ for $x = e^{-5}$.

7. Consider the following macroeconomic model

   (i) $Y = C + I$ (ii) $C = f(Y - T)$ (iii) $T = \alpha + \beta Y$

   where Y is GDP, C is consumption, T denotes taxes, and the parameters α and β are constant. Assume that $f' \in (0, 1)$ and $\beta \in (0, 1)$.

   (a) From equations (i)–(iii) derive the equation $Y = f((1 - \beta)Y - \alpha) + I$.

(b) Differentiate the equation in (a) implicitly w.r.t. I and find an expression for dy/dI.

(c) Examine the sign of dy/dI.

8. (a) Find y' when y is given implicitly by the equation $x^2 - xy + 2y^2 = 7$.

(b) Find the points on the graph of the equation at which the tangent is horizontal, and those at which the tangent is vertical. Do your results accord with the graph shown in Fig. 7.R.2?

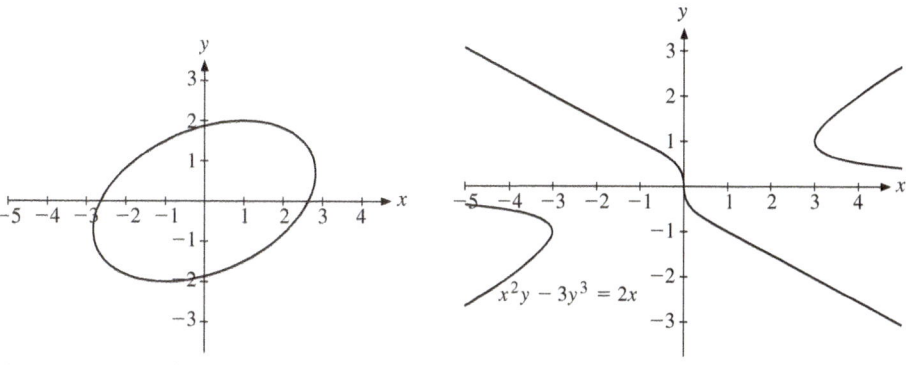

Figure 7.R.2 Exercise 8

Figure 7.R.3 Exercise 9

9. The graph of the equation $x^2y - 3y^3 = 2x$ passes through the point $(x, y) = (-1, 1)$.

(a) Find the slope of the graph at this point.

(b) Find the points at which the graph has a vertical tangent. Show that no point on the graph has a horizontal tangent. Do your results accord with the graph shown in Fig. 7.R.3?

SM 10. Let function f be defined by the formula $f(x) = \dfrac{1}{2} \ln \dfrac{1+x}{1-x}$.

(a) Determine the domain and range of f.

(b) Prove that f has an inverse g, and find a formula for the inverse. Note that $f\left(\tfrac{1}{2}\right) = \tfrac{1}{2} \ln 3$. Find $g'\left(\tfrac{1}{2} \ln 3\right)$ in two different ways.

11. Let $f(x)$ be defined for all $x > 0$ by $f(x) = (\ln x)^3 - 2(\ln x)^2 + \ln x$.

(a) Compute $f(e^2)$ and find the zeros of $f(x)$.

(b) Prove that $f(x)$ defined on $[e, \infty)$ has an inverse function h, then determine $h'(2)$.

SM 12. Find the quadratic approximations about $x = 0$ to the following functions:

(a) $f(x) = \ln(2x + 4)$ (b) $g(x) = (1 + x)^{-1/2}$ (c) $h(x) = xe^{2x}$

13. Find the differentials:

(a) $d(\sqrt{1 + x^2})$ (b) $d(4\pi r^2)$ (c) $d(100K^4 + 200)$ (d) $d[\ln(1 - x^3)]$

14. Compute the differential of $f(x) = \sqrt{1 + x^3}$. What is the approximate change in $f(x)$ when x changes from $x = 2$ to $x = 2 + dx$, where $dx = 0.2$?

15. Use formula (7.6.6) with $n = 5$ to find an approximate value of $\sqrt{e}$. Show that the answer is correct to three decimal places. (*Hint*: For $0 < z < 1/2$, note that $e^z < e^{1/2} < 2$.)

16. Find the quadratic approximation to $y = y(x)$ about $(x, y) = (0, 1)$ when y is defined implicitly as a function of x by the equation $y + \ln y = 1 + x$.

17. Determine the values of x at which each of the functions defined by the following formulas is continuous:

    (a) $e^x + e^{1/x}$ (b) $\dfrac{\sqrt{x} + 1/x}{x^2 + 2x + 2}$ (c) $\dfrac{1}{\sqrt{x+2}} + \dfrac{1}{\sqrt{2-x}}$

18. Let f be a given differentiable function of one variable. Suppose that each of the following equations defines y implicitly as a function of x. Find an expression for y' in each case.

    (a) $x = f(y^2)$ (b) $xy^2 = f(x) - y^3$ (c) $f(2x + y) = x + y^2$

19. The demands for margarine (marg) and for meals away from home (mah) in the UK during the period 1920–1937, as functions of personal income r, were estimated to be $D_{\text{marg}} = Ar^{-0.165}$ and $D_{\text{mah}} = Br^{2.39}$, respectively, for suitable constants A and B. Find and interpret the (Engel) elasticities of D_{marg} and D_{mah} w.r.t. r.

20. Find the elasticities of the functions given by the following formulas:

    (a) $50x^5$ (b) $\sqrt[3]{x}$ (c) $x^3 + x^5$ (d) $\dfrac{x-1}{x+1}$

21. The equation $x^3 - x - 5 = 0$ has a root close to 2. Find an approximation to this root by using Newton's method once, with $x_0 = 2$.

22. Prove that $f(x) = e^{\sqrt{x}} - 3$ has a unique zero in the interval $(1, 4)$. Find an approximate value for this zero by using Newton's method once, with $x_0 = 1$.

23. Evaluate the limits:

    (a) $\lim\limits_{x \to 3^-} (x^2 - 3x + 2)$ (b) $\lim\limits_{x \to -2^+} \dfrac{x^2 - 3x + 14}{x + 2}$ (c) $\lim\limits_{x \to -1} \dfrac{3 - \sqrt{x + 17}}{x + 1}$

    (d) $\lim\limits_{x \to 0} \dfrac{(2-x)e^x - x - 2}{x^3}$ (e) $\lim\limits_{x \to 3} \left(\dfrac{1}{x-3} - \dfrac{5}{x^2 - x - 6} \right)$ (f) $\lim\limits_{x \to 4} \dfrac{x - 4}{2x^2 - 32}$

    (g) $\lim\limits_{x \to 2} \dfrac{x^2 - 3x + 2}{x - 2}$ (h) $\lim\limits_{x \to -1} \dfrac{4 - \sqrt{x + 17}}{2x + 2}$ (i) $\lim\limits_{x \to \infty} \dfrac{(\ln x)^2}{3x^2}$

24. Examine the following limit for different values of the constants a, b, c, and d, assuming that b and d are positive:
$$\lim_{x \to 0} \dfrac{\sqrt{ax + b} - \sqrt{cx + d}}{x}$$

25. Evaluate $\lim\limits_{x \to 0} \dfrac{a^x - b^x}{e^{ax} - e^{bx}}$, where $a \ne b$, with a and b both positive.

26. The equation $x^{21} - 11x + 10 = 0$ has a root at $x = 1$, and another root in the interval $(0, 1)$. Starting from $x_0 = 0.9$, use Newton's method as many times as necessary to find the latter root to 3 decimal places.

8
CONCAVE AND CONVEX FUNCTIONS

We can only see a short distance ahead, but we can see plenty there that needs to be done.
—Alan Turing (1950)

Whether a function is concave or convex is crucial to many results in economic analysis, especially the multitude that involve maximization or minimization. According to the general definitions that we introduce, a function can be concave or convex whether or not it is differentiable.

We start in Section 8.1 by introducing some geometric intuition before turning to the key definitions in Section 8.2. While the definitions themselves are easy to understand, it can be unnecessarily difficult to determine whether a specified function satisfies them. So we follow them in Section 8.3 by considering the properties of sums, compositions, and inverses of concave functions. Next, Section 8.4 introduces the notions of supergradients and subgradients, and explores their links to functions that are respectively concave and convex. Thereafter Section 8.5 considers the characterizations based on the second derivative that economists use most often to determine whether a function is concave or convex. The final Section 8.6 considers briefly inflection points, which occur on the boundary between one interval on which a function is concave and an adjacent interval on which a function is convex.

8.1 Intuition

Imagine a person living in a cave who needs to hang a clothesline from its roof, which is shaped like the curve shown in Fig. 8.1.1. That shape makes it possible: if supports are put up in the roof at points A and B, a clothesline hanging between the two serves the purpose.

Now suppose that one of the same person's most frequented routes in and out of the cave goes across a significant ditch. Rather than scrambling down to the bottom of the ditch each time and then clambering back up out on the other side, the person would like to use a tightrope to cross it. Provided that the ditch is shaped like the graph in Fig. 8.1.2, this is also possible. One can fix supports at points C and D, and hang a tightrope between the two.[1]

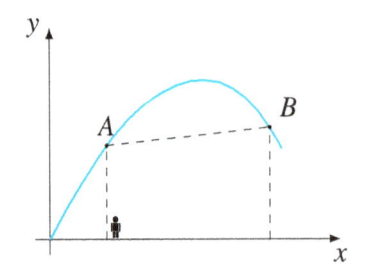

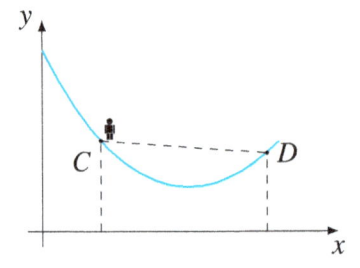

Figure 8.1.1 Clothesline hanging from a cave roof

Figure 8.1.2 Tightrope over a ditch

In both cases, the way the graph curves is critical. In Fig. 8.1.1, the straight line segment connecting points A and B is completely below the cave roof. In Fig. 8.1.2, the segment between C and D is completely above the ditch.

These two properties are so important that mathematicians have given them special names. The first one is called *concavity*, deriving from the Latin root *cav*, which means "hollow". The name of the second property, *convexity*, is less mnemonic. It comes from the Latin *vexus*, which means "bulk".[2]

Of course, there are graphs in which neither a clothesline below it nor a tightrope above it are possible. One such occurs in the graph of Fig. 8.1.3. Consider any straight line segment between points E and F that is supported at each end. The segment cannot be a clothesline that hangs free of a cave roof, nor can it be a tightrope that hangs entirely off the ground. So this graph violates both the concavity and convexity properties.

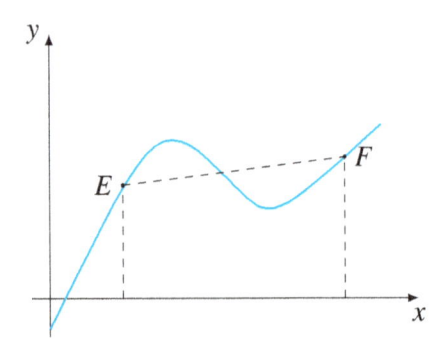

Figure 8.1.3 Neither a cave nor a ditch

---

[1] Figures 8.1.1 and 8.1.2 display the clothesline and tightrope as hanging in a completely straight line between the two supports at either end. This is an idealization because in trying to make the line or rope perfectly straight, then unless it is weightless, one must apply more and more tension until eventually either a support fails or the rope itself snaps.

[2] A person under the graph of Fig. 8.1.2 could explain that it was impossible for a straight clothesline to hang below the roof from nails at C and D because, unlike a more typical cave roof, this one has a bulky obstacle.

8.2 Definitions

Let I be an interval on the real line.

CONCAVE FUNCTION

A function f defined on I is said to be *concave* over I if

$$f(\lambda a + (1-\lambda)b) \geq \lambda f(a) + (1-\lambda)f(b). \tag{8.2.1}$$

for all a and b in I and all numbers λ in $[0, 1]$.

This property captures the intuition of trying to hang a clothesline between the two points $A = (a, f(a))$ and $B = (b, f(b))$ shown in Fig. 8.2.1. To show this, consider first the value $\lambda a + (1-\lambda)b$ of x that occurs on the left-hand side of the inequality (8.2.1). One has $x = b$ when $\lambda = 0$, and $x = a$ when $\lambda = 1$. As λ ranges from 0 to 1, we obtain *every* value $x = \lambda a + (1-\lambda)b$ between a and b.

Next, recall the point–point formula from Section 4.4. It tells us that the straight line through $A = (a, f(a))$ and $B = (b, f(b))$ has the equation

$$y - f(a) = \frac{f(b) - f(a)}{b - a}(x - a)$$

When $x = \lambda a + (1-\lambda)b$, one has $x - a = (1-\lambda)(b-a)$ and so $(x-a)/(b-a) = 1 - \lambda$. But then the corresponding y-value on the straight line through points A and B satisfies $y - f(a) = (1-\lambda)[f(b) - f(a)]$, or $y = \lambda f(a) + (1-\lambda)f(b)$. This shows that the line segment joining A to B consists of the set of points

$$\{(\lambda a + (1-\lambda)b,\ \lambda f(a) + (1-\lambda)f(b)) : 0 \leq \lambda \leq 1\}$$

On the other hand, the part of the graph of $y = f(x)$ that extends from A to B consists of the set of points

$$\{(\lambda a + (1-\lambda)b,\ f(\lambda a + (1-\lambda)b)) : 0 \leq \lambda \leq 1\}$$

So the inequality (8.2.1) says each point on this part of the graph of f is no lower than the corresponding point of the line segment from A to B. In other words, the function f is concave if and only if the graph of f never descends below the line segment connecting any two points on the graph.

Now, a concave function is one whose graph has its hollow side underneath. If the graph has its hollow side up above, the function is called *convex*.

CONVEX FUNCTION

A function f defined on I is said to be *convex* over I if

$$f(\lambda c + (1-\lambda)d) \leq \lambda f(c) + (1-\lambda)f(d). \tag{8.2.2}$$

for all c and d in I and all numbers λ in $[0, 1]$.

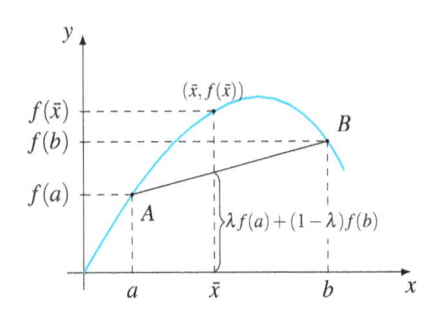

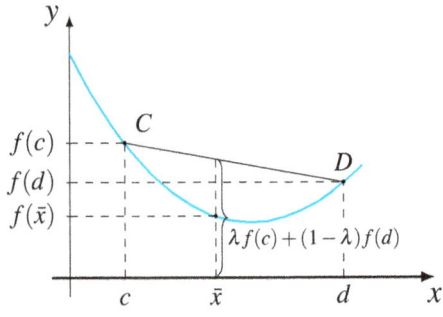

Figure 8.2.1 A concave function

Figure 8.2.2 A convex function

This property is represented in Fig. 8.2.2. Again, *any* x between c and d can be written as $x = \lambda c + (1 - \lambda)d$ for some $0 \leq \lambda \leq 1$. Thus, the inequality (8.2.2) states that the graph of f never ascends above the line segment connecting C and D.

It is important to understand that whether a function is concave or convex is independent of whether it is increasing or decreasing. Four possibilities are shown in Figs 8.2.3–8.2.6, which should be studied carefully. We also note that often I is the whole real line, in which case the interval is not mentioned explicitly.

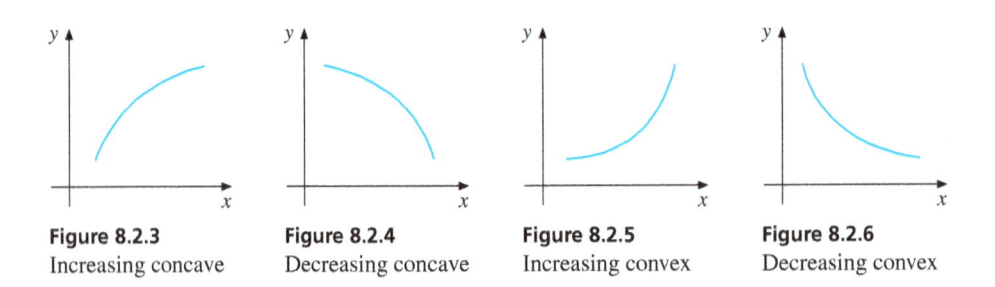

Figure 8.2.3 Increasing concave

Figure 8.2.4 Decreasing concave

Figure 8.2.5 Increasing convex

Figure 8.2.6 Decreasing convex

EXAMPLE 8.2.1

(a) The graph in Fig. 8.2.7 shows the crop of wheat $Y(N)$ when N pounds of fertilizer per acre are used. The curve is based on fertilizer experiments in Iowa during 1952. The function is concave: if we compute the weighted average of the output produced with 50 and with 250 pounds of fertilizer per acre, the result will be lower than if we first take a weighted average of 50 and 250 pounds, using the same weights, and then compute the output from using that amount of fertilizer per acre.

(b) Figure 8.2.8 shows a rough graph of the function $P(t)$ that measures the world population (in billions) for each year t between the dates 1500 and 2000. The figure suggests that $P(t)$ is not only increasing but also convex: for example, a simple average of the population in 1600 and the population in 2000 clearly exceeds the population in 1800.

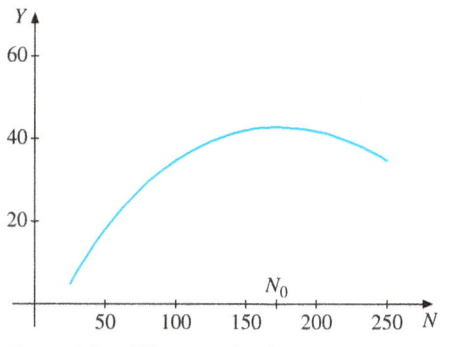

Figure 8.2.7 Wheat production

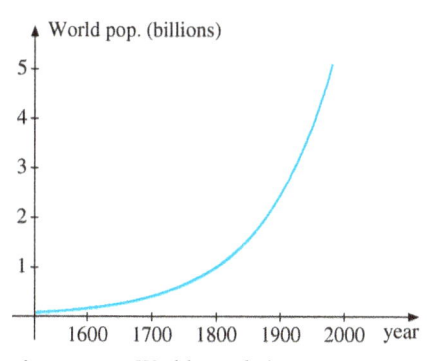

Figure 8.2.8 World population

EXAMPLE 8.2.2 Consider again the intertemporal decision problem of Example 7.1.5. For simplicity, assume that the discount factor β equals 1. Suppose too that the instantaneous utility function $u(c)$ is concave.

Now imagine that the agent is offered the choice between three alternative consumption plans. The first is (C, c) where $C \geq c$, meaning that she consumes no less in the first period than in the second. The second plan gives her (c, C), so that consumption is no lower in the second period. The third alternative allows her to consume in each period the same average amount

$$\bar{c} = \tfrac{1}{2}(C + c)$$

Even without knowing the exact function u, the assumption that it is concave allows economists to conclude that for this individual the third alternative with equal consumption in both periods is *at least as good* as either of the first two. Indeed we can apply (8.2.1) with $\lambda = \tfrac{1}{2}$ to show that concavity implies

$$u(\bar{c}) + u(\bar{c}) = 2u\left(\tfrac{1}{2}(C+c)\right) \geq 2\left[\tfrac{1}{2}u(C) + \tfrac{1}{2}u(c)\right] = u(C) + u(c) \quad (8.2.3)$$

EXAMPLE 8.2.3 Using a result from Exercise 2.6.8, show that: (i) the function $f(x) = \sqrt{x}$ is concave over the interval $[0, \infty)$; (ii) the function $g(x) = x^2$ is convex over the real line $(-\infty, \infty)$; (iii) the linear function $h(x) = ax + b$ is both concave and convex over $(-\infty, \infty)$.

Solution: (i) Exercise 2.6.8 tells us that, for any pair of positive numbers a and b, one has

$$\sqrt{ab} \leq \tfrac{1}{2}(a + b) \quad (*)$$

Obviously, this inequality also holds if one or both a and b equals 0. For any λ in $[0, 1]$ we have $\lambda(1 - \lambda) \geq 0$. So $(*)$ implies that, for all nonnegative numbers a and b, one has

$$2\lambda(1-\lambda)\sqrt{ab} \leq \lambda(1-\lambda)(a+b)$$
$$= \lambda(1-\lambda)a + \lambda(1-\lambda)b$$
$$= \lambda(1-\lambda)a + [1 - (1-\lambda)](1-\lambda)b$$
$$= \lambda a - \lambda^2 a + (1-\lambda)b - (1-\lambda)^2 b$$

Rearranging terms, this is equivalent to

$$\lambda^2 a + 2\lambda(1-\lambda)\sqrt{ab} + (1-\lambda)^2 b \leq \lambda a + (1-\lambda)b$$

This can be rewritten as

$$(\lambda\sqrt{a} + (1-\lambda)\sqrt{b})^2 \leq \lambda a + (1-\lambda)b$$

As the square root function $f(x) = \sqrt{x}$ is increasing in x, we get

$$\lambda\sqrt{a} + (1-\lambda)\sqrt{b} \leq \sqrt{\lambda a + (1-\lambda)b}$$

For arbitrary a, b, and λ, this reduces to the inequality (8.2.1) which determines that the function $f(x) = \sqrt{x}$ is concave.

(ii) To show that g is convex, given any a, b, and λ in $[0, 1]$, consider the difference between the two sides of inequality (8.2.2). For the function $g(x) = x^2$, this is

$$\begin{aligned}
g(\lambda a + (1-\lambda)b) &- (\lambda g(a) + (1-\lambda)g(b)) \\
&= (\lambda a + (1-\lambda)b)^2 - \lambda a^2 - (1-\lambda)b^2 \\
&= \lambda^2 a^2 + 2\lambda(1-\lambda)ab + (1-\lambda)^2 b^2 - \lambda a^2 - (1-\lambda)b^2 \\
&= \lambda(\lambda - 1)a^2 + 2\lambda(1-\lambda)ab + (1-\lambda)(1-\lambda-1)b^2 \\
&= \lambda(\lambda - 1)(a^2 - 2ab + b^2) = \lambda(\lambda - 1)(a-b)^2 \quad (**)
\end{aligned}$$

For all λ in $[0, 1]$ we have $\lambda(\lambda - 1) \leq 0$, so the final expression in $(**)$ is ≤ 0. By (8.2.2), this proves that g is convex.

(iii) To see that h is both concave and convex, simply notice that

$$\lambda h(x) + (1-\lambda)h(y) = \lambda(ax + b) + (1-\lambda)(ay + b) = h(\lambda x + (1-\lambda)y)$$

This equality implies that $h(x)$ satisfies both the inequality (8.2.1), as required by the definition of concavity, and the inequality (8.2.2), as required by the definition of convexity.

This example required quite a lot of work to verify the concavity or convexity of the first two relatively simple functions. Indeed, a quick glance at their graphs, which appeared in Figs 4.3.6 and 4.3.8, makes the result rather obvious. Fortunately, we shall see below that, rather than using the direct definitions (8.2.1) and (8.2.2), there are simpler ways based on derivatives to determine the concavity and/or convexity of a function. There is also the method shown in Example 8.2.5.

For the moment, it is important to note that the *only* functions that are *both* concave *and* convex are the linear functions introduced in Section 4.4. Now we introduce stronger versions of concavity and convexity, which no function can satisfy simultaneously.

In inequalities (8.2.1) and (8.2.2), suppose we restrict attention to the non-trivial case when $a \neq b$ and $0 < \lambda < 1$, which holds if and only if $\lambda a + (1-\lambda)b \notin \{a, b\}$. Then a function f is:

1. *strictly concave* if Eq. (8.2.1) is always satisfied with strict inequality;
2. *strictly convex* if Eq. (8.2.2) is always satisfied with strict inequality.

EXAMPLE 8.2.4   In the case of Example 8.2.2, assume that $C > c$ and that the function u is strictly concave. Then, we can strengthen our conclusion and say that the individual *strictly prefers* the consumption plan $(\bar{c}, \bar{c})$ that gives her the same consumption in the present as in the future. This is because the weak inequality (8.2.3) becomes the strict inequality

$$u(\bar{c}) + u(\bar{c}) = 2u\left(\tfrac{1}{2}(C+c)\right) > 2\left[\tfrac{1}{2}u(C) + \tfrac{1}{2}u(c)\right] = u(C) + u(c) \tag{8.2.4}$$

This result is important in macroeconomics, where it is known as *consumption smoothing*. It is a fundamental implication of the strict concavity of the instantaneous utility function. It is important to note that it does not require our simplifying assumption that $\beta = 1$. Indeed, given any consumption plan (c_1, c_2) with $c_1 \neq c_2$, suppose we define the particular weighted average

$$\bar{c} = \frac{1}{1+\beta}c_1 + \frac{\beta}{1+\beta}c_2$$

Then strict concavity of u implies that

$$u(\bar{c}) + \beta u(\bar{c}) = (1+\beta)u(\bar{c}) > (1+\beta)\left[\frac{1}{1+\beta}u(c_1) + \frac{\beta}{1+\beta}u(c_2)\right] = u(c_1) + \beta u(c_2)$$

Characterization by slopes

Let us recapitulate:

CONCAVE AND CONVEX FUNCTIONS

A function f defined on an interval I is:

(i) *concave* if for all a and b in I, and for all λ in $[0, 1]$, one has

$$f(\lambda a + (1-\lambda)b) \geq \lambda f(a) + (1-\lambda)f(b) \tag{8.2.1}$$

If the inequality is strict whenever $a \neq b$ and $0 < \lambda < 1$, then f is *strictly concave*.

(ii) *convex* if for all a and b in I, and for all λ in $[0, 1]$, one has

$$f(\lambda a + (1-\lambda)b) \leq \lambda f(a) + (1-\lambda)f(b)) \tag{8.2.2}$$

If the inequality is strict whenever $a \neq b$ and $0 < \lambda < 1$, then f is *strictly convex*.

In Section 6.2, especially Figs 6.2.1 and 6.2.2, we introduced the notion of the secant as a straight line that passes through two distinct points on the graph of a function. In (6.2.1) we defined the Newton quotient as the slope of such a secant. Such slopes can be used to provide an alternative characterization of concave and convex functions. Given a function f defined on an interval I, as well as any two distinct points $(a, f(a))$ and $(b, f(b))$ on its graph with $a \neq b$, let $s(a, b)$ denote the *slope* of the secant joining those two points, defined by

$$s(a, b) = \frac{f(a) - f(b)}{a - b} \tag{8.2.5}$$

Note that this definition evidently implies that $s(a, b) = s(b, a)$, so it does not matter which point of the pair $\{a, b\}$ is less than the other.

Now consider the concave function whose graph, as shown in Fig. 8.2.1, curves downwards as one moves to the right. Evidently, there is a secant joining each distinct pair of points in the set $\{(a, f(a)), (\bar{x}, f(\bar{x})), (b, f(b))\}$. Because the graph curves down, the three slopes (positive or negative) evidently satisfy

$$s(a, \bar{x}) > s(a, b) > s(\bar{x}, b) \tag{8.2.6}$$

On the other hand, for the convex function whose graph is shown in Fig. 8.2.2, which curves upwards as one moves to the right, the corresponding three slopes satisfy

$$s(c, \bar{x}) < s(c, d) < s(\bar{x}, d) \tag{8.2.7}$$

Inequalities like these provide a characterization of concave or convex functions.

THEOREM 8.2.1 (SLOPE CHARACTERIZATION)

A function $f(x)$ defined on an interval I is:

(i) concave if and only if, for every fixed a in I, the slope $s(a, x)$ is decreasing in x;

(ii) strictly concave if and only if, for every fixed a in I, the slope $s(a, x)$ is strictly decreasing in x;

(iii) convex if and only if, for every fixed a in I, the slope $s(a, x)$ is increasing in x;

(iv) strictly convex if and only if, for every fixed a in I, the slope $s(a, x)$ is strictly increasing in x.

Proof: Consider any three points a, x, y of the interval I that satisfy either $a < y < x$ or $a > y > x$. Now define $\lambda = (y - a)/(x - a)$. Then $\lambda \in (0, 1)$ and $y = \lambda x + (1 - \lambda)a$. By definition of s, one has

$$s(a, y) - s(a, x) = \frac{f(y) - f(a)}{y - a} - \frac{f(x) - f(a)}{x - a} = \frac{f(y) - f(a)}{\lambda(x - a)} - \frac{\lambda[f(x) - f(a)]}{\lambda(x - a)}$$

and so
$$s(a, y) - s(a, x) = \frac{f(y) - [\lambda f(x) + (1 - \lambda)f(a)]}{\lambda(x - a)} \qquad (*)$$

In case $x > a$, because $\lambda > 0$, Eq. (*) implies that the expression $f(y) - [\lambda f(x) + (1 - \lambda)f(a)]$ has the same sign as $s(a, y) - s(a, x)$, whereas in case $x < a$, it has the opposite sign.

To prove (i), consider any triple a, x, y of points with $a < y < x$ and $y = \lambda x + (1 - \lambda)a$ where $\lambda \in (0, 1)$. Then, if $s(a, x)$ is decreasing in x, one has $s(a, y) - s(a, x) \geq 0$, so by (*) it follows that $f(y) - [\lambda f(x) + (1 - \lambda)]f(a) \geq 0$, implying that f is concave.

Conversely, if f is concave, one has $f(y) - [\lambda f(x) + (1 - \lambda)]f(a) \geq 0$ and so by (*), in case $a < y < x$ one has $s(a, y) - s(a, x) \geq 0$. Alternatively, in case $a > y > x$, the same argument shows that $s(a, y) - s(a, x) \leq 0$. Either way, the slope $s(a, x)$ is decreasing in x.

To prove (ii), just replace each weak inequality ≥ 0 or ≤ 0 in the proof of (i) just above with the corresponding strict inequality.

To prove (iii) and (iv), just replace f by $-f$ and use part (i) or (ii), as appropriate.

Theorem 8.2.1 allows the results in Example 8.2.3 to be derived much more simply.

EXAMPLE 8.2.5 Using Theorem 8.2.1, show that: (i) the function $f(x) = \sqrt{x}$ is strictly concave over the interval $[0, \infty)$; (ii) the function $g(x) = x^2$ is strictly convex over the real line $(-\infty, \infty)$; (iii) the linear function $h(x) = ax + b$ is both concave and convex over $(-\infty, \infty)$.

Solution: (i) For every fixed $a \geq 0$ and every $x \neq a$ with $x \geq 0$, the slope satisfies
$$s(a, x) = \frac{\sqrt{x} - \sqrt{a}}{x - a} = \frac{1}{\sqrt{x} + \sqrt{a}}$$

This is evidently strictly decreasing in x, so f is strictly concave.

(ii) Here, for every fixed a and every $x \neq a$, the slope satisfies
$$s(a, x) = \frac{x^2 - a^2}{x - a} = x + a$$

This is evidently strictly increasing in x, so g is strictly convex.

(iii) In this case, for every fixed y and every $x \neq y$, the slope satisfies
$$s(y, x) = \frac{(ax + b) - (ay + b)}{x - y} = a$$

Because the slope is constant, it is both increasing and decreasing in x, so h is both concave and convex.

EXERCISES FOR SECTION 8.2

1. Consider the function whose graph appears in Fig. 8.2.9. Is the function concave, strictly concave, convex, or strictly convex?

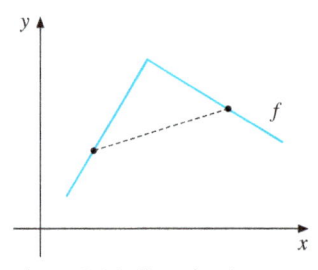

Figure 8.2.9 Exercise 1

2. Show that:

   (a) A strictly concave function is concave.

   (b) A function can be both concave and convex.

   (c) A function can be concave and not strictly concave.

   (d) A strictly concave function cannot be convex.

3. Determine whether each of the two functions whose graphs are shown in Figs 8.2.7 and 8.2.8 is concave, strictly concave, convex, or strictly convex.

4. Suppose that a firm like that in Example 5.2.1 faces a cost of producing $Q \geq 0$ units of its product given by the strictly convex function $c(Q)$, where $c(0) = 0$. Suppose also that the firm is given the possibility of opening a second plant with the same cost function, and then reallocating some of its production to that plant. Should it do so?

5. Use Theorem 8.2.1 to show that the US Federal Income Tax function introduced in Example 5.4.4 is convex but not strictly convex.

6. [HARDER] Prove that if the function f is increasing and strictly concave on the interval I, then it must be strictly increasing on I. (*Hint:* If f is increasing but not strictly increasing, then there must be an interval on which it is constant.)

7. [HARDER] For each $n = 2, 3, \ldots$, consider the power function which is defined for all real x by $f(x) = x^n$. Use Theorem 8.2.1 to prove that:

   (a) when $n = 2$, the function x^2 is strictly convex over $(-\infty, \infty)$;

   (b) for each $n = 2, 3, \ldots$, the function x^n is strictly convex over $[0, \infty)$;

   (c) when n is even, the function x^n is strictly convex over $(-\infty, 0]$;[3]

   (d) when n is odd, the function x^n is strictly concave over $(-\infty, 0]$.

   (*Hint:* For parts (c) and (d), consider the relation between the slopes $s(-a, -x)$ and $s(a, x)$.)

---

[3] Exercise 8.3.6 asks you to show that is strictly convex over the whole real line.

8. [HARDER] Let f be a function defined on an interval I which meets the definition of continuity set out in Section 7.8. Then a sufficient condition for f to be concave is that it is *midpoint concave*,[4] which requires that for all points a and b of I, one has

$$f\left(\tfrac{1}{2}a + \tfrac{1}{2}b\right) \geq \tfrac{1}{2}f(a) + \tfrac{1}{2}f(b)$$

Similarly, f is *midpoint convex* if the reverse inequality holds. Use the rules of the exponential and logarithmic functions to show that $f(x) = \ln x$ is midpoint concave and $g(x) = e^x$ is midpoint convex, which implies that $\ln x$ is concave whereas e^x is convex.

9. [HARDER] Let f be a concave function on an interval I. Show that for every natural number n, all collections $x_1, x_2, \ldots, x_n$ of n points in I, and all collections $\lambda_1, \lambda_2, \ldots, \lambda_n$ of n positive numbers whose sum satisfies $\sum_{i=1}^{n} \lambda_i = 1$, it is true that

$$f\left(\sum_{i=1}^{n} \lambda_i x_i\right) \geq \sum_{i=1}^{n} \lambda_i f(x_i)$$

(*Hint:* Remember the principle of mathematical induction.)

8.3 General Properties

This section presents some interesting properties of concave and convex functions. Our first result on multiples of concave and convex functions is almost immediate.

Note: If f is (strictly) concave and a is a constant, then af is (strictly) concave if $a > 0$, and (strictly) convex if $a < 0$. Similarly, for a (strictly) convex function g, the function ag is (strictly) convex if $a > 0$, and (strictly) concave if $a < 0$.

Sums of concave functions

Suppose that f and g are concave functions over an interval I, and that $h(x) = f(x) + g(x)$. Then for any pair of points a and b in I, and any number λ in $[0, 1]$, one has

$$h(\lambda a + (1-\lambda)b) = f(\lambda a + (1-\lambda)b) + g(\lambda a + (1-\lambda)b)$$

Since both f and g are concave, it follows that

$$f(\lambda a + (1-\lambda)b) \geq \lambda f(a) + (1-\lambda)f(b) \ \text{ and } \ g(\lambda a + (1-\lambda)b) \geq \lambda g(a) + (1-\lambda)g(b)$$

This implies that

$$\begin{aligned} h(\lambda a + (1-\lambda)b) &\geq \lambda f(a) + (1-\lambda)f(b) + \lambda g(a) + (1-\lambda)g(b) \\ &= \lambda[f(a) + g(a)] + (1-\lambda)[f(b) + g(b)] \\ &= \lambda h(a) + (1-\lambda)h(b) \end{aligned}$$

---

[4] The condition owes its name to the fact that $\tfrac{1}{2}a + \tfrac{1}{2}b$ is the midpoint of the line interval whose end points are a and b, and $(\tfrac{1}{2}a + \tfrac{1}{2}b, \tfrac{1}{2}f(a) + \tfrac{1}{2}f(b))$ is the midpoint of the line segment joining the two points $(a, f(a))$ and $(b, f(b))$ on the graph of the function f.

showing that h is concave too. Note immediately that if, in addition, at least one of f and g is strictly concave, then so is h. An analogous argument shows that the sum of two convex functions is always convex, and strictly convex if at least one of the two is strictly convex.

EXAMPLE 8.3.1 Check the convexity/concavity of the function $f(x) = x^2 - 2x + 2$

Proof: In Example 8.2.3 we established that x^2 and $-2x + 2$ are both convex functions. As the sum of two convex functions, f is convex.

Minima of concave functions

Suppose once again that f and g are concave functions over an interval I. Consider the function h defined on I by $h(x) = \min\{f(x), g(x)\}$. That is, for any x in I, the value $h(x)$ is the smaller or minimum of the two numbers $f(x)$ and $g(x)$. Now, given any pair of points a and b in I and any number λ in $[0, 1]$, the definition of h and the concavity of f and g together imply that

$$f(\lambda a + (1 - \lambda)b) \geq \lambda f(a) + (1 - \lambda)f(b) \geq \lambda h(a) + (1 - \lambda)h(b) \qquad (*)$$

and $\quad g(\lambda a + (1 - \lambda)b) \geq \lambda g(a) + (1 - \lambda)g(b) \geq \lambda h(a) + (1 - \lambda)h(b) \qquad (**)$

Evidently, if any three numbers u, v, w satisfy both $u \geq w$ and $v \geq w$, then their minimum satisfies $\min\{u, v\} \geq w$. So the two inequalities $(*)$ and $(**)$ together imply that

$$h(\lambda a + (1 - \lambda)b) = \min\{f(\lambda a + (1 - \lambda)b), g(\lambda a + (1 - \lambda)b)\} \geq \lambda h(a) + (1 - \lambda)h(b)$$

This proves that h is concave on the interval I.

On the other hand, if $h(x) = \max\{f(x), g(x)\}$ where f and g are convex functions, then $-h(x) = \min\{-f(x), -g(x)\}$ is the minimum of two concave functions, so concave. It follows that h, which is the maximum of two convex functions, is convex.

Exercise 4 asks you to extend these results to show that the minimum of any finite collection of concave functions is concave. It follows, of course, that the maximum of any finite collection of convex functions is convex.

EXAMPLE 8.3.2 Show that the absolute value function $f(x) = |x|$ is convex.

Proof: Note that $|x| = \max\{x, -x\}$. This is convex, as the maximum of the two convex functions x and $-x$.

Compositions of concave functions

We continue to assume that the function f is concave over an interval I. Let g be an increasing and concave function defined over the range of f. As in Section 6.8, define the composite function $h(x) = g(f(x))$. To see whether h is concave, fix any two distinct points a and b in the interval I, as well as any number λ satisfying $0 < \lambda < 1$. Now:

1. Because f is concave, one has $f(\lambda a + (1-\lambda)b) \geq \lambda f(a) + (1-\lambda)f(b)$.
2. Because g is increasing, one has $g(f(\lambda a + (1-\lambda)b)) \geq g(\lambda f(a) + (1-\lambda)f(b))$.
3. Because g is concave, one has $g(\lambda f(a) + (1-\lambda)f(b)) \geq \lambda g(f(a)) + (1-\lambda)g(f(b))$.
4. By definition of h, one has $h(\lambda a + (1-\lambda)b) = g(f(\lambda a + (1-\lambda)b))$, as well as both $g(f(a)) = h(a)$ and $g(f(b)) = h(b)$. Finally, therefore, the function h is also concave because the inequalities in steps 2 and 3 above jointly imply that

$$h(\lambda a + (1-\lambda)b) \geq \lambda h(a) + (1-\lambda)h(b)$$

Note that the argument requires the external function g to be not only concave, but also increasing. In case f is strictly concave and g is both strictly increasing and concave, one can replace the two weak inequalities in steps 1 and 2 of the above argument by strict inequalities. Then, even though the inequality in step 3 may be weak, one still has a strict inequality in the final step 4. This modified argument proves that the composite function h is also strictly concave.

The analogous result holds for convex functions: if f is (strictly) convex and g is (strictly) increasing and convex, then h is (strictly) convex.

EXAMPLE 8.3.3 Check the convexity/concavity of the function $f(x) = ax^2 + bx + c$.

Solution: Whether this function is concave or convex depends on the sign of the number a. If $a = 0$, we know from Example 8.2.3 that f is both concave and convex.

Consider next the case when $a > 0$. By Example 8.2.3, we know that x^2 is convex, and so it follows from the Note at the beginning of Section 8.3 that ax^2 is convex. Since $bx + c$ is convex too, it follows that $f(x) = g(x^2) + bx + c$ is convex.

Finally, suppose that $a < 0$. Then ax^2 is concave, and since $bx + c$ is concave too, it follows that so is $f(x)$.

Inverses of concave functions

For the final general property of concave or convex functions, we consider the inverse $g = f^{-1}$ of a function f that is *increasing and concave*. Because f is concave and $g = f^{-1}$, for any points a and b and any number λ in $[0, 1]$, one has

$$f(\lambda g(a) + (1-\lambda)g(b)) \geq \lambda f(g(a)) + (1-\lambda)f(g(b)) = \lambda a + (1-\lambda)b \qquad (*)$$

Since f is increasing, so is g, as in Section 7.3. Hence

$$g(f(\lambda g(a) + (1-\lambda)g(b))) \geq g(\lambda a + (1-\lambda)b) \qquad (**)$$

Because $g = f^{-1}$, it follows that

$$\lambda g(a) + (1-\lambda)g(b) \geq g(\lambda a + (1-\lambda)b)$$

So g is *convex*. This is illustrated in Fig. 7.3.1. At the risk of being repetitive: *the inverse of an increasing and concave function is increasing but convex*.

EXAMPLE 8.3.4 In Exercise 8.2.8 you were asked to show that the logarithmic function $\ln x$ is concave and the exponential function e^x is convex. Note that only one of the two arguments was really necessary: since they are inverses of each other and both are increasing, concavity of $\ln x$ implies convexity of e^x, and vice versa.

Suppose, on the other hand, that f is *decreasing and concave*, with inverse $g = f^{-1}$. Again concavity of f implies (∗). Because f is decreasing, so is g, which reverses the inequality in (∗∗). Hence

$$g(f(\lambda g(a) + (1-\lambda)g(b))) \leq g(\lambda a + (1-\lambda)b)$$

Because $g = f^{-1}$, it follows that

$$\lambda g(a) + (1-\lambda)g(b) \leq g(\lambda a + (1-\lambda)b)$$

Hence, g is *concave* too. That is: *the inverse of a decreasing and concave function is decreasing and concave as well.*

For convex functions, as before, similar results hold. If the function is increasing and convex, its inverse is also increasing but concave; if it is decreasing and convex, however, the inverse is both decreasing and convex.

EXERCISES FOR SECTION 8.3

1. Show that if f is strictly concave and g is concave, then $f + g$ is strictly concave.

2. Using the fact that $\sqrt{x}$ is concave, prove that for $x \geq 0$ and $a \geq 0$, the function $f(x) = ax^2 + b$ is convex.

3. In Section 8.3 we argued that the composite function $g \circ f$ is concave provided that f and g are both concave, with g increasing. We also argued that $g \circ f$ would be strictly concave provided that f is strictly concave and g is strictly increasing. Show that both these properties must hold strictly: specifically, give two examples where each holds only weakly and yet, although the other property holds strictly, the composite function $g \circ f$ is only (weakly) concave.

4. Let I be any interval of the real line. For each $i = 1, 2, \ldots, n$, suppose that the function $f_i(x)$ defined on I is concave. Prove by induction on n that the function $f^*(x)$ defined on I by $f^*(x) = \min\{f_i(x) : 1, 2, \ldots, n\}$ is concave.

5. Consider the two functions $f(x) = -|x - 1|$ and $g(x) = |x + 1|$, both defined on $(-\infty, \infty)$.

   (a) Show that f is concave and that g is convex on $(-\infty, \infty)$.

   (b) For what values of a and b is the function $f + g$ defined on the interval (a, b): (i) concave; (ii) convex; (iii) both concave and convex; (iv) neither concave nor convex? (Case (iv) shows that when f is concave and g is convex, the function $f + g$ need be neither concave nor convex.)

6. Once again, consider for each $n = 2, 3, \ldots$ the power function defined for all x by $f(x) = x^n$. Use the results of Exercise 8.2.7 and those for the composition of convex functions to prove that if n is even with $n = 2m \geq 4$, then $x^n = (x^2)^m$ is strictly convex over the whole of $(-\infty, \infty)$.

8.4 First-Derivative Tests

Figure 8.4.1 reproduces Fig. 7.4.1, which illustrates the graph of the linear approximation $y = f(a) + f'(a)(x - a)$ to the differentiable function f about the point a. This graph, of course, is the tangent line at a to the graph of the function f. Because the function f happens to be concave, this tangent lies completely on top of the graph of the function. For this reason, its slope, which equals the gradient $f'(a)$ at a, is known as a *supergradient*.

If a function is convex rather than concave, the tangent at any point will lie completely below the graph. In this case, the gradient $f'(a)$ at a is known as a *subgradient*.

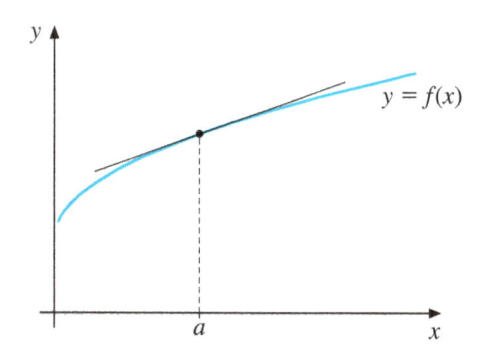

Figure 8.4.1 Supergradient of a concave function

This motivates the following definitions:

SUPERGRADIENTS AND SUBGRADIENTS

Let $f(x)$ be any function defined on an interval I, and a any point of I. The real number p is:

(i) a *supergradient* of f at $x = a$ if $f(x) \leq f(a) + p(x - a)$ for all x in I (8.4.1)

(ii) a *subgradient* of f at $x = a$ if $f(x) \geq f(a) + p(x - a)$ for all x in I (8.4.2)

THEOREM 8.4.1 (NECESSARY CONDITIONS FOR CONCAVITY AND CONVEXITY)

Suppose the function f is defined on an interval I, and is differentiable at an interior point a of I. Now:

(i) if f is concave, then $f'(a)$ is a supergradient at a;

(ii) if f is convex, then $f'(a)$ is a subgradient at a.

Proof: In case $x > a$, consider any $h > 0$ such that $a + h < x$. By Theorem 8.2.1, because f is concave, the slope $s(a, x) = [f(x) - f(a)]/(x - a)$ is decreasing in x. It follows that $s(a, a + h) \geq s(a, x)$, and so

$$\frac{f(a+h) - f(a)}{h} \geq \frac{f(x) - f(a)}{x - a}$$

Taking limits as $h \to 0^+$, the definition of derivative implies that

$$f'(a) = \lim_{h \to 0^+} \frac{f(a+h) - f(a)}{h} \geq \frac{f(x) - f(a)}{x - a}$$

Because $x - a > 0$, it follows that $f(x) - f(a) \leq f'(a)(x - a)$.

In case $x < a$, consider any $h < 0$ such that $a + h > x$. By a similar argument to the case when $x > a$, one has $s(a, a + h) \leq s(a, x)$, and so

$$f'(a) = \lim_{h \to 0^-} \frac{f(a+h) - f(a)}{h} \leq \frac{f(x) - f(a)}{x - a}$$

Because $x - a < 0$, it follows that $f(x) - f(a) \leq f'(a)(x - a)$ in this case also.

This completes the proof for the concave case. The convex case can be proved in the same way. But it is much simpler and faster to see that the subgradient property for the function f is equivalent to the supergradient property (8.4.3) for the function $-f$. ∎

Recall the definitions of left and right derivatives in Eq. (7.9.4). One can extend the above proof to show that if f is a concave function defined on the interval I, and if a is an interior point of I, then:

1. both the left derivative $f'(a^-)$ and the right derivative $f'(a^+)$ exist, even if $f'(a)$ does not;
2. one has $f'(a^-) \geq f'(a^+)$, and any p in the interval $[f'(a^+), f'(a^-)]$ is a supergradient.

As a corollary, note that a concave function defined on an interval has at least one supergradient at every interior point of that interval.

As ever, given these results if f is concave, there are obvious corresponding results if f is convex.

Supergradients and subgradients also provide important sufficient conditions for a function to be concave or convex.

THEOREM 8.4.2 (SUFFICIENT CONDITIONS FOR CONCAVITY AND CONVEXITY)

Suppose that the function f is defined on an interval I. Then f will be:

(i) concave if it is has a supergradient at every point of I;

(ii) convex if it is has a subgradient at every point of I.

Here is a straightforward proof of case (i); the proof of case (ii) is similar.

Proof: Fix a and b in I and λ in $[0, 1]$, then let $c = \lambda a + (1 - \lambda)b$. Suppose f has a supergradient at c, which we denote by p. Now (8.4.1) implies that both

$$f(a) \leq f(c) + p(a - c) \qquad (*)$$
$$f(b) \leq f(c) + p(b - c) \qquad (**)$$

Next, multiply both sides of $(*)$ by λ and then both sides of $(**)$ by $1 - \lambda$. Both inequalities are preserved because both multipliers are nonnegative. Adding the resulting two inequalities, then rearranging, we obtain

$$\lambda f(a) + (1 - \lambda)f(b) \leq [\lambda + (1 - \lambda)]f(c) + p[\lambda(a - c) + (1 - \lambda)(b - c)] = f(c)$$

The last equality holds because the two coefficients in square brackets evidently reduce to 1 and 0 respectively. This holds for all a, b, c with $c = \lambda a + (1 - \lambda)b$, so f is concave. ∎

Combining the results of Theorems 8.4.1 and 8.4.2 gives us the following:

CHARACTERIZATION OF CONCAVE AND CONVEX FUNCTIONS

Suppose that the function f is differentiable over an open interval I. Then,

(i) f is concave if and only if, for all a and x in I, one has

$$f(x) \leq f(a) + f'(a)(x - a) \qquad (8.4.3)$$

(ii) f is convex if and only if, for all a and x in I, one has

$$f(x) \geq f(a) + f'(a)(x - a) \qquad (8.4.4)$$

Notice that we have referred to the supergradient and subgradient inequalities (8.4.3) and (8.4.4) as *characterizations*. This is a way to emphasize that, for a differentiable function, the properties are logically equivalent to concavity or convexity: that is, they are both necessary and sufficient. The following examples show how this characterization by supergradients or subgradients can be used to test directly for concavity or convexity.

EXAMPLE 8.4.1 In Example 8.2.3 we concluded that $f(x) = \sqrt{x}$ is concave, that $g(x) = x^2$ is convex, and that $h(x) = ax + b$ is both concave and convex. Based on the fact that these functions are differentiable (except f when $x \leq 0$), use appropriate supergradient or subgradient properties to confirm these conclusions.

Solution: First, for $x > 0$ and $a > 0$, the linear approximation to $f(x)$ about $x = a$ is

$$f(a) + f'(a)(x - a) = \sqrt{a} + \frac{1}{2\sqrt{a}}(x - a) = \tfrac{1}{2}\left(\sqrt{a} + \sqrt{x^2/a}\right) \qquad (*)$$

Using the inequality $m_A \geq m_G$ of Exercise 2.6.8 for the numbers $\sqrt{a}$ and $\sqrt{x^2/a}$, we obtain

$$\tfrac{1}{2}\left(\sqrt{a} + \sqrt{x^2/a}\right) \geq \sqrt{\sqrt{a} \cdot \sqrt{x^2/a}} = \sqrt{x} = f(x) \qquad (**)$$

Together (∗) and (∗∗) confirm (8.4.3), which is the inequality for $f'(a)$ to be a supergradient of f at a. Since this holds for all $a > 0$, it follows that f is concave.

For the function g, note that the linear approximation about $x = a$ is

$$g(a) + g'(a)(x - a) = a^2 + 2a(x - a) = 2ax - a^2$$

The inequality $(a - x)^2 \geq 0$ tells us that $a^2 + x^2 \geq 2ax$, so

$$g(x) = x^2 \geq 2ax - a^2 = g(a) + g'(a)(x - a)$$

This confirms the subgradient inequality in (8.4.4), which implies that g is convex.

Finally, the function h is identical to its linear approximation about any point. So both weak inequalities (8.4.3) and (8.4.4) are immediately satisfied with equality. ∎

EXAMPLE 8.4.2   Use the subgradient inequality in (8.4.4) to verify that the function $f(x) = x^2 - 2x + 2$ is convex.

Solution: The linear approximation about a is

$$f(a) + f'(a)(x - a) = a^2 - 2a + 2 + (2a - 2)(x - a) = -a^2 + 2ax - 2x + 2$$

after some manipulation. Once again $a^2 + x^2 \geq 2ax$, so we have the subgradient inequality

$$f(a) + f'(a)(x - a) \leq x^2 - 2x + 2 = f(x)$$ ∎

8.5 Second-Derivative Tests

Recall from Section 6.3 how the sign of the first derivative determines whether a function is increasing or decreasing on an interval I. Indeed, if $f'(x) \geq 0$ (or $f'(x) \leq 0$) on I, then f is increasing (or decreasing) on I, and conversely. The second derivative $f''(x)$ is the derivative of $f'(x)$. Hence:

$$f''(x) \geq 0 \text{ on } I \iff f' \text{ is increasing on } I \qquad (8.5.1)$$

$$f''(x) \leq 0 \text{ on } I \iff f' \text{ is decreasing on } I \qquad (8.5.2)$$

The equivalence in (8.5.1) is illustrated in Fig. 8.5.1. The slope $f'(x)$ of the tangent at x is increasing as x increases. On the other hand, the slope of the tangent to the graph in Fig. 8.5.2 is decreasing as x increases.

To help visualize this, imagine sliding a ruler along the curve and keeping it aligned with the tangent to the curve at each point. As the ruler moves along the curve from left to right, the tangent rotates anticlockwise in Fig. 8.5.1, but clockwise in Fig. 8.5.2. This gives us the following characterization. It involves the interior of an interval which, you should recall, is the *open* interval with the same end points.

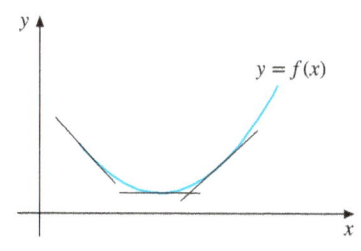

Figure 8.5.1 The slope of the tangent line increases as x increases.

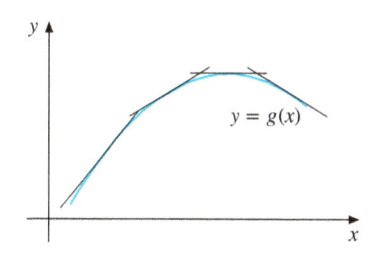

Figure 8.5.2 The slope of the tangent line decreases as x increases.

CONCAVE AND CONVEX FUNCTIONS

Suppose that f is continuous in the interval I and twice differentiable in the interior of I. Then,

$$f \text{ is concave on } I \iff f''(x) \leq 0 \text{ for all } x \text{ in the interior of } I \quad (8.5.3)$$

$$f \text{ is convex on } I \iff f''(x) \geq 0 \text{ for all } x \text{ in the interior of } I \quad (8.5.4)$$

EXAMPLE 8.5.1   Verify the convexity/concavity of the following functions:

(a) $f(x) = x^2 - 2x + 2$ (b) $f(x) = ax^2 + bx + c$

Solution:

(a) Here $f'(x) = 2x - 2$, so $f''(x) = 2$. Because $f''(x) > 0$ for all x, the function f is convex, which confirms what we showed in Example 8.4.2.

(b) Here $f'(x) = 2ax + b$, so $f''(x) = 2a$. If $a = 0$, then f is linear. In this case, the function f satisfies both Eq. (8.5.3) and (8.5.4), so it is both concave and convex. If $a > 0$, then $f''(x) > 0$, so f is convex. If $a < 0$, then $f''(x) < 0$, so f is concave. These conclusions are the same as those we obtained in Example 8.3.3.

EXAMPLE 8.5.2   Examine the concavity/convexity of the production function $Y = AK^a$, defined for all $K \geq 0$, where $A > 0$ and $a > 0$.

Solution: From Example 6.9.2, one has $Y'' = Aa(a-1)K^{a-2}$. Now there are three cases:

(i) If $a \in (0, 1)$, then the coefficient $Aa(a-1) < 0$, so that $Y'' < 0$ for all $K > 0$. Hence, the function is concave. The graph of $Y = AK^a$ for $0 < a < 1$, is shown in Fig. 8.5.3.

(ii) On the other hand, if $a > 1$, then $Y'' > 0$ and Y is a convex function of K, as shown in Fig. 8.5.4.

(iii) Finally, if $a = 1$, then Y is linear, so it is both concave and convex.

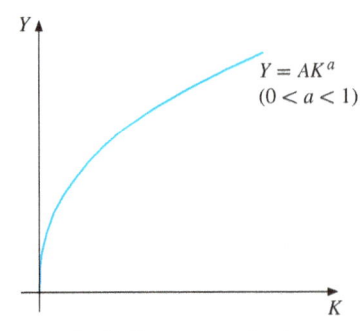

Figure 8.5.3 Concave production function

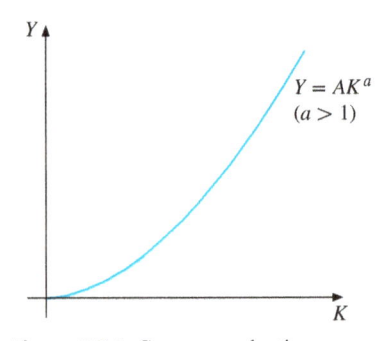

Figure 8.5.4 Convex production function

EXAMPLE 8.5.3 Suppose that the two functions f and g are both twice differentiable. Use the second-derivative test (8.5.3) to show that if both are concave, then so is their sum.

Solution: Let $h(x) = f(x) + g(x)$. Using Eq. (6.7.1) twice gives $h''(x) = f''(x) + g''(x)$. Since both f and g are concave, we have $f''(x) \leq 0$ and $g'(x) \leq 0$ at all x. This implies that $h''(x) \leq 0$, so h is concave as well.

EXAMPLE 8.5.4 Suppose that the functions U and g are both increasing and concave, with $U' \geq 0$, $U'' \leq 0$, $g' \geq 0$, and $g'' \leq 0$. Use Eqs (6.3.1) and (8.5.3) to confirm that the composite function $f(x) = g(U(x))$ is also increasing and concave.

Solution: Using the chain rule yields

$$f'(x) = g'(U(x)) \cdot U'(x) \qquad (*)$$

Because g' and U' are both ≥ 0, so $f'(x) \geq 0$. Hence, the function f is increasing. In words: *an increasing transformation of an increasing function is increasing.*

To find $f''(x)$, we must differentiate w.r.t. x the product on the RHS of $(*)$. According to the chain rule, the derivative of $g'(U(x))$ is equal to $g''(U(x)) \cdot U'(x)$. Hence,

$$f''(x) = g''(U(x)) \cdot [U'(x)]^2 + g'(U(x)) \cdot U''(x) \qquad (**)$$

Because $g'' \leq 0$, $g' \geq 0$, and $U'' \leq 0$, it follows that $f''(x) \leq 0$. Again, in words: *an increasing concave transformation of a concave function is concave.*

The second-derivative tests in (8.5.3) and (8.5.4) are particularly handy. For the concave case, we now prove (8.5.3). For the convex case (8.5.4), consider the concave function $-f$.

Proof of (8.5.3): First we prove that the hypothesis that $f''(x) \leq 0$ for all x in the interior of the interval I is sufficient for f to be concave. Indeed, fix any point a in I and note that, as shown in Section 7.6, Taylor's formula with remainder in the case $n = 1$ implies that for every x in I one can find a point z in the interior of I such that

$$f(x) = f(a) + f'(a)(x - a) + \tfrac{1}{2}f''(z)(x - a)^2$$

So the hypothesis that $f''(z) \leq 0$ for all z in the interior of I implies the supergradient property $f(x) \leq f(a) + f'(a)(x-a)$ for all x in I. By (8.4.3), this is sufficient for f to be concave.

Conversely, fix any point a in the domain I, as well as any number $h \neq 0$. If f is concave, then the supergradient property in Eq. (8.4.3) implies that

$$f(a+h) \leq f(a) + f'(a)h \quad \text{and} \quad f(a) \leq f(a+h) + f'(a+h)(-h)$$

Adding these two inequalities, then cancelling the common terms $f(a+h) + f(a)$, we obtain

$$0 \leq f'(a)h + f'(a+h)(-h)$$

Dividing this inequality by the negative number $-h^2$ yields

$$\frac{f'(a+h) - f'(a)}{h} \leq 0$$

But the expression on the LHS is the Newton quotient of the function f' at a. Letting $h \to 0$ preserves the weak inequality. Because f is twice differentiable at a, it yields $f''(a) \leq 0$. This completes the proof.

Finally, we state a corresponding second-derivative test for strict concavity or convexity. It is important to note, however, that it is only partly valid. Specifically, the condition is sufficient. But it is not necessary. Exercise 4 asks you to provide an example of this.

STRICTLY CONCAVE AND CONVEX FUNCTIONS

Suppose that f is continuous in the interval I and twice differentiable in the interior of I. Then,

$$f''(x) < 0 \text{ for all } x \text{ in the interior of } I \implies f \text{ is strictly concave on } I \quad (8.5.5)$$

$$f''(x) > 0 \text{ for all } x \text{ in the interior of } I \implies f \text{ is strictly concave on } I \quad (8.5.6)$$

EXERCISES FOR SECTION 8.5

1. Verify the results in Exercise 8.2.8 concerning the concavity/convexity of the two functions $\ln x$ (defined for $x > 0$) and e^x (defined for all real x).

2. Consider the sum of the two functions $f(x) = -x^2$, which is strictly concave on $[0, \infty)$, and $g(x) = x^3$, which is strictly convex on $[0, \infty)$. For what intervals (a, b) with $0 \leq a < b$ is it true that $f + g$ is: (a) concave; (b) convex; (c) neither concave nor convex? (This shows that the sum of a concave and a convex function may be concave, convex, or neither.)

3. Suppose that the functions $f(x)$ and $g(x)$ are both twice differentiable and concave. Prove that if g is increasing, then the composite function $h(x) = g(f(x))$ is also concave.

4. Give an example showing that $f''(x) < 0$ for all x in (a, b) is not a necessary condition for the function f to be strictly concave on (a, b).

5. Suppose that on the interval I the function f is twice differentiable and concave with $f' \neq 0$.

(a) Use Theorem 7.3.1 to show that the inverse function $g(y) = f^{-1}(y)$ is well defined and twice differentiable on the range $f(I)$.

(b) Use Eq. (7.3.3) to show that, for any x in I, the signs of $f''(x)$ and $g''(f(x))$ are the same or opposite according as f is decreasing is increasing.

(c) [HARDER] In case $f'' \neq 0$ throughout I, discuss how the results for inverses in Section 8.3 can be strengthened for functions that are strictly concave or strictly convex.

8.6 Inflection Points

Points at which a function changes from being convex to being concave, or *vice versa*, are called *inflection points*. For twice differentiable functions, here is a definition:

INFLECTION POINTS

If the function f is twice differentiable, a point c is called an *inflection point* for f if there exists an interval (a, b) about c such that:

(a) $f''(x) \geq 0$ in (a, c) and $f''(x) \leq 0$ in (c, b); *or*

(b) $f''(x) \leq 0$ in (a, c) and $f''(x) \geq 0$ in (c, b).

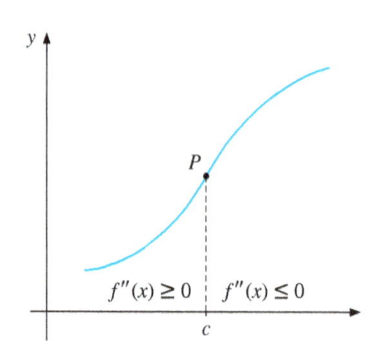

Figure 8.6.1 Point P is an inflection point on the graph; $x = c$ is an inflection point for the function

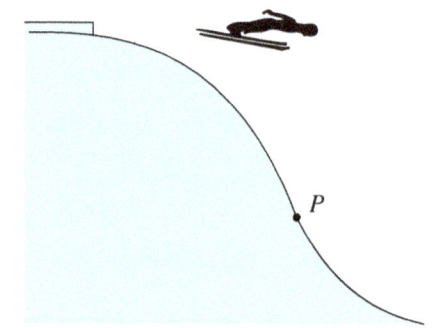

Figure 8.6.2 The point P, where the slope is steepest, is an inflection point

Briefly, $x = c$ is an inflection point if $f''(x)$ *changes sign* at $x = c$.[5] We also refer to the point $(c, f(c))$ as an inflection point on the graph. Figure 8.6.1 gives an example from mathematics, while Fig. 8.6.2 gives one from winter sports: it shows a (not quite realistic)

---

[5] We note that what a mathematician would call a turning point of a function f, which is a point at which the sign of $f'(x)$ changes, is often called an inflection point in popular parlance. Perhaps it is too much to expect popular parlance to take account of changes in the sign of the second derivative!

sketch of the profile of a ski jump. The point P, where the slope is steepest, is an inflection point.

When looking for possible inflection points of a function, we usually use part (ii) of the following theorem:

THEOREM 8.6.1 (TEST FOR INFLECTION POINTS)

Let f be a function with a continuous second derivative in an interval I, and let c be an interior point of I.

(i) If c is an inflection point for f, then $f''(c) = 0$.

(ii) If $f''(c) = 0$ and f'' changes sign at c, then c is an inflection point for f.

The proof of this theorem is rather simple:

Proof:

(i) Because $f''(x) \leq 0$ on one side of c and $f''(x) \geq 0$ on the other, and because f'' is continuous, it must be true that $f''(c) = 0$.

(ii) If f'' changes sign at c, then c is an inflection point for f, by definition.

This theorem implies that $f''(c) = 0$ is a *necessary* condition for c to be an inflection point. It is not a sufficient condition, however, because $f''(c) = 0$ does not imply that f'' changes sign at $x = c$. A typical case is given in the next example.

EXAMPLE 8.6.1   Show that $f(x) = x^4$ does not have an inflection point at $x = 0$, even though $f''(0) = 0$.

Solution: Here $f'(x) = 4x^3$ and $f''(x) = 12x^2$, so that $f''(0) = 0$. But $f''(x) > 0$ for all $x \neq 0$, and so f'' does not change sign at $x = 0$. Hence, $x = 0$ is not an inflection point. This is confirmed by the graph of f, which is shown in Fig. 8.6.3.

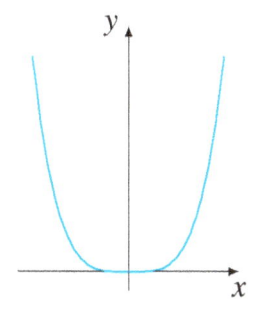

Figure 8.6.3 $y = x^4$

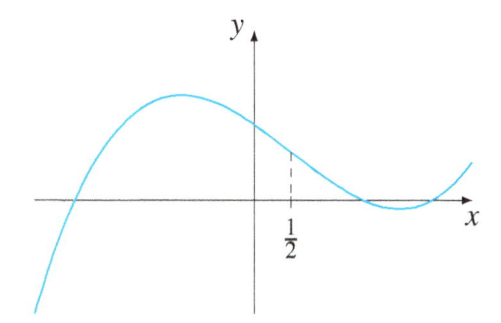

Figure 8.6.4 $y = \frac{1}{9}x^3 - \frac{1}{6}x^2 - \frac{2}{3}x + 1$

EXAMPLE 8.6.2

Find possible inflection points for $f(x) = \frac{1}{9}x^3 - \frac{1}{6}x^2 - \frac{2}{3}x + 1$.

Solution: We have $f'(x) = \frac{1}{3}(x+1)(x-2)$ and $f''(x) = \frac{2}{3}x - \frac{1}{3} = \frac{2}{3}\left(x - \frac{1}{2}\right)$. So $f''(x) \leq 0$ for $x \leq 1/2$, whereas $f''(1/2) = 0$ and $f''(x) \geq 0$ for $x > 1/2$. According to part (ii) in Theorem 8.6.1, $x = 1/2$ is an inflection point for f. This is confirmed by Fig. 8.6.4.

EXAMPLE 8.6.3

Find possible inflection points for $f(x) = x^6 - 10x^4$.

Solution: In this case $f'(x) = 6x^5 - 40x^3$ and

$$f''(x) = 30x^4 - 120x^2 = 30x^2(x^2 - 4) = 30x^2(x-2)(x+2)$$

A sign diagram for f'' is as follows:

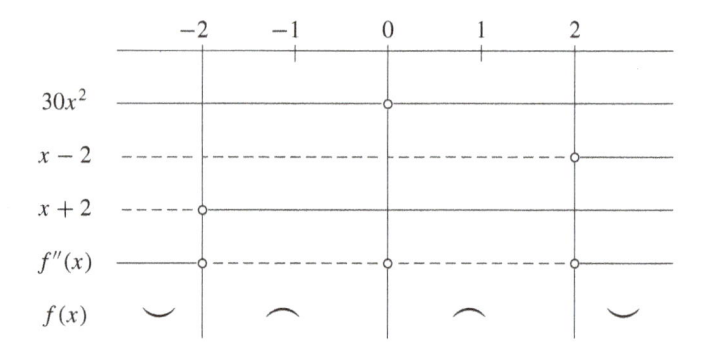

The sign diagram shows that f'' changes sign at $x = -2$ and $x = 2$, so these are inflection points. Since f'' does not change sign at $x = 0$, it is not an inflection point, even though $f''(0) = 0$.

Economic models often involve functions having inflection points. The cost function in Fig. 4.7.2 is a typical example. Here is another.

EXAMPLE 8.6.4

A firm produces a commodity using only one input. For $x \geq 0$, let $y = f(x)$ be the output obtained from x units of input. Then f is called a *production function*. Its first derivative measures the increase in output per unit of extra input when the extra input is infinitesimal; this derivative is called the firm's *marginal product*. It is often assumed that the graph of a production function is "S-shaped". That is, the marginal product $f'(x)$ is increasing up to a certain input level c, then decreasing. Figure 8.6.1 shows such a production function. If f is twice differentiable, then $f''(x) \geq 0$ in $[0, c]$, but $f''(x) \leq 0$ in $[c, \infty)$. So f is first convex and then concave, with c as an inflection point. Note that $x = c$ is where the marginal product achieves a maximum.

EXERCISES FOR SECTION 8.6

1. Let f be defined for all x by $f(x) = x^3 + \frac{3}{2}x^2 - 6x + 10$.

   (a) Find the points c where $f'(c) = 0$ and determine the intervals where f increases.

   (b) Find the inflection point for f.

2. Decide where the following functions are convex and determine possible inflection points:

   (a) $f(x) = \dfrac{x}{1+x^2}$ (b) $g(x) = \dfrac{1-x}{1+x}$ (c) $h(x) = xe^x$

SM 3. For each of the six functions defined by the following formulas, find the inflection points and determine the intervals where the functions are convex/concave.

   (a) $y = (x+2)e^{-x}$ (b) $y = \ln x + 1/x$ (c) $y = x^3 e^{-x}$
   (d) $y = \dfrac{\ln x}{x^2}$ (e) $y = e^{2x} - 2e^x$ (f) $y = (x^2 + 2x)e^{-x}$

4. Find the inflection points of the function f whose graph is shown in Fig. 8.6.5

5. Find numbers a and b such that the graph of $f(x) = ax^3 + bx^2$ passes through $(-1, 1)$ and has an inflection point at $x = 1/2$.

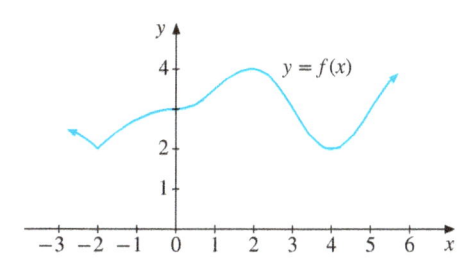

Figure 8.6.5 Exercise 8.6.4

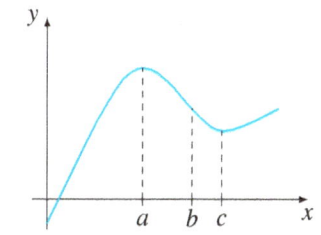

Figure 8.6.6 Review exercise 3

REVIEW EXERCISES

1. Let $f(x) = \sqrt{x}$ and $g(y) = y^3$. Determine the concavity/convexity of the composite function $g(f(x))$. Does this contradict any of the results for composite functions that were set out in Section 8.3?

2. Let $g(x) = 3x^3 - \frac{1}{5}x^5$.

   (a) Find $g'(x)$ and $g''(x)$.

   (b) Where is g increasing and where is it concave?

   (c) Sketch the graph of g.

3. Suppose that $f(x)$ is the twice differentiable function whose graph is depicted in Fig. 8.6.6. Which of the following four combinations of four statements is correct?

(a) $f'(a) = 0$, $f''(b) > 0$, $f'(c) = 0$, $f''(c) > 0$

(b) $f'(a) = 0$, $f'(b) < 0$, $f''(b) = 0$, $f''(c) > 0$

(c) $f''(a) < 0$, $f''(b) = 0$, $f'(c) = 0$, $f''(c) = 0$

(d) $f''(a) > 0$, $f''(b) = 0$, $f'(c) = 0$, $f''(c) > 0$

4. Find the intervals of concavity/convexity for each of the following functions:

   (a) $f(x) = 2x^3 - 12x^2 + 5$
   (b) $f(x) = x + 4/x$
   (c) $f(x) = \dfrac{x}{x^2 + 16}$

5. For $x \neq 0$, let $f(x) = e^{1/x}$. Compute $f'(x)$ and $f''(x)$, then examine where f is concave/convex.

6. Consider the cubic cost function that is defined for $x \geq 0$ by $C(x) = ax^3 + bx^2 + cx + d$, where the parameters are $a > 0, b < 0, c > 0$, and $d > 0$. Find the intervals where the function is convex and where it is concave. Find also the unique inflection point.

7. Use a single coordinate system to draw the graphs of two concave functions f and g, both defined for all x. Let the function h be defined by $h(x) = \min\{f(x), g(x)\}$. That is, for each x, the number $h(x)$ is the smaller of $f(x)$ and $g(x)$. Draw the graph of h and explain why this function is also concave.

9 OPTIMIZATION

If you want literal realism, look at the world around you; if you want understanding, look at theories.
—Robert Dorfman (1964)

Finding the best way to do a specific task involves what is called an *optimization problem*. Examples abound in almost all areas of human activity. A manager seeks those combinations of inputs, such as capital and labour, that maximize profit or minimize cost. A farmer might want to know what amount of fertilizer per hectare will maximize crop yield. An oil company may wish to find the optimal rate of extraction from its wells.

In general, no mathematical methods are more important in economics than those designed to solve optimization problems. Though in economics these problems usually involve several variables, the examples of quadratic optimization in Section 4.6 indicate how useful economic insights can be gained even from simple one-variable optimization.

9.1 Extreme Points

Those points in the domain of a function where it reaches its largest and smallest values are usually referred to as *maximum points* and *minimum points*, respectively. Thus, we define:

MAXIMUM AND MINIMUM POINTS

If $f(x)$ has domain D, then

(i) $a \in D$ is a *maximum point* for f, and $f(a)$ is the *maximum value*, if

$$f(x) \leq f(a) \quad \text{for all } x \text{ in } D \tag{9.1.1}$$

(ii) $b \in D$ is a *minimum point* for f, and $f(b)$ is the *minimum value*, if

$$f(x) \geq f(b) \quad \text{for all } x \text{ in } D \tag{9.1.2}$$

If we do not need to distinguish between maxima and minima, we use the collective names *extreme points*, or *extrema*, where the function reaches an *extreme value*. Other authors might refer to them as optimal points, where the function reaches an *optimal value*. Some authors prefer different terminology, referring to an extreme value as a maximum or minimum, and to a point where this value is reached as a *maximizer* or *minimizer*.

If the value of f at the point c is strictly larger than at any other point in D, then c is a *strict maximum* point. Similarly, d is a *strict minimum* point if $f(x) > f(d)$ for all $x \in D$ with $x \neq d$. Evidently a point x^* is a strict maximum point of f in D if and only if x^* is the unique point in D that maximizes f, and similarly for minimum points.

If f is any function with domain D, then the function $-f$ is defined for all x in D by $(-f)(x) = -f(x)$. Note that $f(x) \leq f(c)$ for all x in D if and only if $-f(x) \geq -f(c)$ for all x in D. Thus, the point c maximizes f in D if and only if it minimizes $-f$ in D. This simple observation, which is illustrated in Fig. 9.1.1, can be used to convert any maximization problem into a corresponding minimization problem, and vice versa.

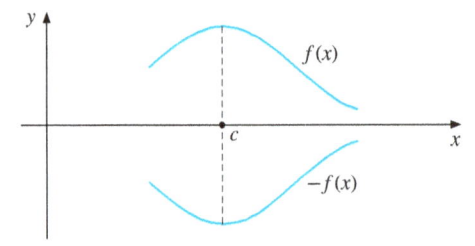

Figure 9.1.1 Point c is a maximum point for $f(x)$, and a minimum point for $-f(x)$

Sometimes, as with the quadratic optimization problems in Section 4.6, we can find the maximum and minimum points of a function simply by studying the formula that defines it. Here are two further examples:

EXAMPLE 9.1.1 Find possible maximum and minimum points for:

(a) $f(x) = 3 - (x - 2)^2$ (b) $g(x) = \sqrt{x - 5} - 100$, for $x \geq 5$

Solution:

(a) Because $(x - 2)^2 \geq 0$ for all x, it follows that $f(x) \leq 3$ for all x. But $f(x) = 3$ when $(x - 2)^2 = 0$, which occurs at $x = 2$. Therefore, $x = 2$ is a maximum point for f. Because $f(x) \to -\infty$ as $x \to \infty$, it follows that f has no minimum.

(b) Since $\sqrt{x - 5} \geq 0$ for all $x \geq 5$, it follows that $g(x) \geq -100$ for all $x \geq 5$. Since $g(5) = -100$, we conclude that $x = 5$ is a minimum point. Since $g(x) \to \infty$ as $x \to \infty$, it follows that g has no maximum.

Rarely can we find extreme points as simply as in Example 9.1.1. For more typical problems, an essential observation arises when f is a differentiable function that has a maximum or minimum at an interior point c of its domain. In this important case, the tangent line to its graph must be horizontal (parallel to the x-axis) at that point. That is, one must have $f'(c) = 0$. A point c at which f is differentiable and $f'(c) = 0$ is called a *critical*, or *stationary*, *point* for f. Here is a precisely formulated theorem:

THEOREM 9.1.1 (NECESSARY FIRST-ORDER CONDITION)

Suppose that the function f is differentiable in an interval I and that c is an interior point of I. If c is a maximum or minimum point for f in I, then it must be a critical point for f, that is,

$$f'(c) = 0 \qquad (9.1.3)$$

Proof: Suppose that f has a maximum at c. If the absolute value of d is sufficiently small, then $c + d \in I$ because c is an interior point of I. Because c is a maximum point, $f(c + d) - f(c) \leq 0$. So if d is sufficiently small and positive, then the Newton quotient satisfies $[f(c + d) - f(c)]/d \leq 0$. The limit of this quotient as $d \to 0^+$ is therefore less than or equal to 0 as well. But because $f'(c)$ exists, this limit is equal to $f'(c)$, so $f'(c) \leq 0$. For small negative values of d, on the other hand, we get $[f(c + d) - f(c)]/d \geq 0$. The limit of this expression as $d \to 0^-$ is therefore greater than or equal to 0. So $f'(c) \geq 0$. We have now proved both that $f'(c) \leq 0$ and that $f'(c) \geq 0$, so $f'(c) = 0$.

The proof in the case when c is a minimum point is similar.

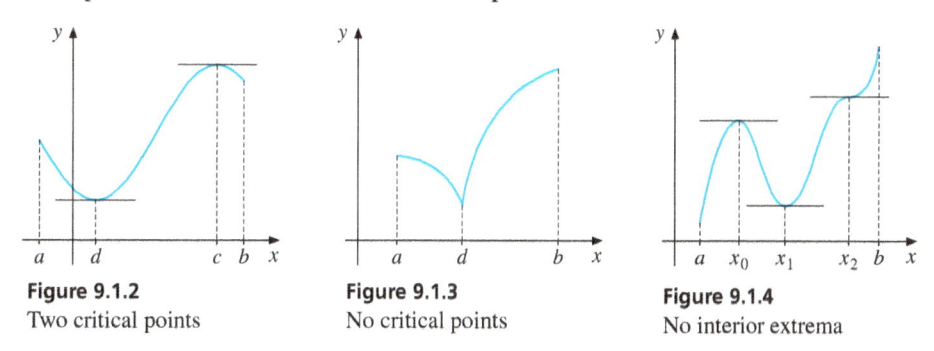

Figure 9.1.2
Two critical points

Figure 9.1.3
No critical points

Figure 9.1.4
No interior extrema

Before starting to explore systematically other properties of maxima and minima, we provide three geometric examples to illustrate the role that critical points play in the theory of optimization. Figure 9.1.2 shows the graph of a function f defined on a closed interval $[a, b]$ and having two critical points, c and d. At c, there is a maximum; at d, there is a minimum.

Figure 9.1.3 shows the graph of a function with no critical points. There is a maximum at the end point b and a minimum at the interior point d. At d, the function is not differentiable, so Theorem 9.1.1 does not apply. At b, the left-hand derivative is not 0.

Condition (9.1.3) is known as a first-order condition, or FOC, as it refers to the function's first derivative. Theorem 9.1.1 implies that (9.1.3) is a *necessary* condition for a differentiable function to have a maximum or minimum at an interior point in its domain. The condition is far from sufficient. This is illustrated in Fig. 9.1.4, where f has three critical points x_0, x_1, and x_2, but none is an extremum. Indeed, at the end point a there is a minimum, whereas at end point b there is a maximum.[1] At the critical point x_0 the function f has a

---
[1] Or, it could be that b is not in the domain of the function, and that $f(x)$ tends ∞ as x tends to b.

"local maximum", in the sense that its value at that point is higher than at all neighbouring points. Similarly, at x_1 it has a local "minimum", whereas x_2 is a critical point that is neither a local minimum nor a local maximum. In fact, it happens to be an inflection point of the kind we studied in Section 8.6.

Figure 9.1.2 illustrates what happens in most economic applications, where maximum and minimum points usually will usually occur at critical interior points. But Figs 9.1.3 and 9.1.4 illustrate situations that *can* occur, even in economic problems. Actually, the three figures represent important different aspects of single variable optimization problems. Because such problems are so important in economics, we must go beyond vague geometric insights. Instead, we need a firmer analytical framework solidly based on precisely formulated mathematical results.

EXERCISES FOR SECTION 9.1

1. Use arguments similar to those in Example 9.1.1 to find the maximum or minimum points for the following functions:

   (a) $f(x) = \dfrac{8}{3x^2 + 4}$
   (b) $g(x) = 5(x+2)^4 - 3$
   (c) $h(x) = \dfrac{1}{1 + x^4}$ for $x \in [-1, 1]$

   (d) $F(x) = \dfrac{-2}{2 + x^2}$
   (e) $G(x) = 2 - \sqrt{1-x}$
   (f) $H(x) = 100 - e^{-x^2}$

9.2 Simple Tests for Extreme Points

In many cases we can find maximum or minimum values for a function just by studying the sign of its first derivative. Suppose $f(x)$ is differentiable in an interval I and that it has only one critical point at $x = c$. Suppose further that $f'(x) \geq 0$ for all x in I such that $x \leq c$, whereas $f'(x) \leq 0$ for all x in I such that $x \geq c$. Then $f(x)$ is increasing to the left of c and decreasing to the right of c. This shows that $f(x) \leq f(c)$ for all $x \leq c$, and $f(x) \leq f(c)$ for all $x \geq c$. It follows that $x = c$ is a maximum point for f in I, as illustrated in Fig. 9.2.1.

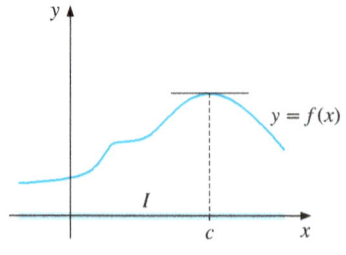

Figure 9.2.1 c is a maximum point

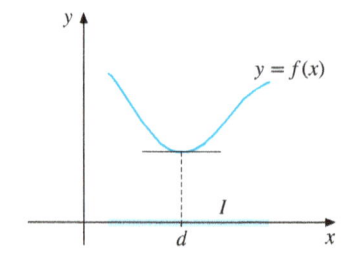

Figure 9.2.2 d is a minimum point

In case the inequalities are strict, there is a stronger result. Indeed, suppose $f'(x) > 0$ for all x in I such that $x < c$, whereas $f'(x) < 0$ for all x in I such that $x > c$. Then $f(x)$ is strictly increasing to the left of c and strictly decreasing to the right of c. It follows that $x = c$ is a strict maximum point for f in I, as in Fig. 9.2.1. With obvious modifications, a similar result holds for strict minimum points, as illustrated by point d in Fig. 9.2.2.

To summarize:[2]

THEOREM 9.2.1 (FIRST-DERIVATIVE TEST FOR EXTREMA)

Suppose the function $f(x)$ is differentiable in an interval I around the critical point c.

(i) If $f'(x) \geq 0$ for $x < c$ and $f'(x) \leq 0$ for $x > c$, then c is a maximum point for f over I. Moreover, if both weak inequalities are strict for all $x \neq c$ in I, then c is a strict maximum point.

(ii) If $f'(x) \leq 0$ for $x < c$ and $f'(x) \geq 0$ for $x > c$, then c is a minimum point for f over I. Moreover, if both weak inequalities are strict for all $x \neq c$ in I, then c is a strict minimum point.

EXAMPLE 9.2.1 Consider the function f, defined for all x by

$$f(x) = e^{2x} - 5e^x + 4 = (e^x - 1)(e^x - 4)$$

1. Find the zeros of $f(x)$ and compute $f'(x)$.
2. Find the intervals where f increases and decreases, and determine its possible extreme points and values.
3. Examine $\lim_{x \to -\infty} f(x)$, and sketch the graph of f.

Solution:

(a) $f(x) = (e^x - 1)(e^x - 4) = 0$ when $e^x = 1$ and when $e^x = 4$. Hence $f(x) = 0$ for $x = 0$ and for $x = \ln 4$. Differentiating $f(x)$ yields $f'(x) = 2e^{2x} - 5e^x$.

(b) $f'(x) = 2e^{2x} - 5e^x = e^x(2e^x - 5)$. Thus $f'(x) = 0$ for $e^x = 5/2 = 2.5$; that is, $x = \ln 2.5$. Furthermore, $f'(x) < 0$ for $x < \ln 2.5$, and $f'(x) > 0$ for $x > \ln 2.5$. So $f(x)$ is strictly decreasing in the interval $(-\infty, \ln 2.5)$, and strictly increasing in $(\ln 2.5, \infty)$. Hence $f(x)$ has a strict minimum at $x = \ln 2.5$, with $f(\ln 2.5) = (2.5 - 1)(2.5 - 4) = -2.25$. Since $f(x) \to \infty$ as $x \to \infty$, there is no maximum.

(c) As $x \to -\infty$, so e^x tends to 0, and $f(x)$ tends to 4. The graph is drawn in Fig. 9.2.3. Note that the dashed line $y = 4$ is a horizontal asymptote for the graph as $x \to -\infty$.

EXAMPLE 9.2.2 Measured in milligrams per litre, the concentration of a drug in the bloodstream, t hours after injection, is given by the formula $c(t) = t/(t^2 + 4)$, for $t \geq 0$. Find the time and amount of maximum concentration.

---

[2] Many books in mathematics for economists instruct students always to check second-order conditions like those we present in Theorem 9.6.2, even when this first-derivative test is much easier to use.

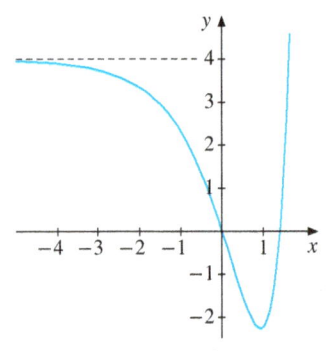

Figure 9.2.3 $f(x) = e^{2x} - 5e^x + 4$

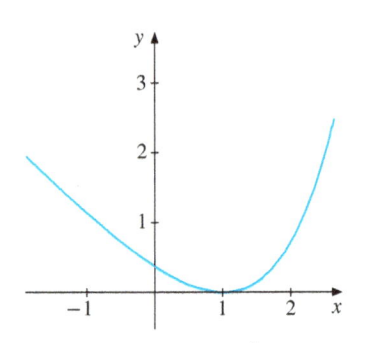

Figure 9.2.4 $f(x) = e^{x-1} - x$

Solution: Differentiating the formula with respect to t yields

$$c'(t) = \frac{1 \cdot (t^2 + 4) - t \cdot 2t}{(t^2 + 4)^2} = \frac{4 - t^2}{(t^2 + 4)^2} = \frac{(2 + t)(2 - t)}{(t^2 + 4)^2}$$

For $t \geq 0$, because the other terms are positive, the term $2 - t$ alone determines the sign of the fraction. Indeed, if $t < 2$, then $c'(t) > 0$; whereas if $t > 2$, then $c'(t) < 0$. We conclude that $t = 2$ is a strict maximum point. Thus, the concentration of the drug is highest two hours after injection. Because $c(2) = 1/4$, the (strict) maximum concentration is 0.25 milligrams per litre.

Extreme Points for Concave and Convex Functions

Let f be a concave function defined on an interval I. Recall part (i) of Theorem 8.4.1, stating that if f is differentiable at a point a in its domain, then its derivative $f'(a)$ at a is a supergradient. So in case c is a critical point in the interior of I, the zero derivative $f'(c)$ is a supergradient. Then the supergradient inequality implies that for all x in I one has

$$f(x) - f(c) \leq f'(c)(x - c) = 0 \cdot (x - c) = 0$$

It follows that c is a maximum point of f. Of course, part (ii) of Theorem 8.4.1 implies a similar result for convex functions, showing that any interior critical point must be a minimum point. To summarize:

THEOREM 9.2.2 (EXTREMA OF CONCAVE AND CONVEX FUNCTIONS)

Suppose that f is a function defined in an interval I and that c is a critical point for f in the interior of I.

(i) If f is concave, then c is a maximum point for f in I.

(ii) If f is convex, then c is a minimum point for f in I.

We emphasize that these results hold even when f is not differentiable at points of I other than the critical point.

EXAMPLE 9.2.3 Consider the function f defined for all x by $f(x) = e^{x-1} - x$. Show that f is convex and find its minimum point. Sketch the graph.

Solution: Here $f'(x) = e^{x-1} - 1$ and $f''(x) = e^{x-1} > 0$, so f is convex. Looking for critical points, note that $f'(x) = e^{x-1} - 1 = 0$ if and only if $x = 1$. From Theorem 9.2.2, it follows that $x = 1$ minimizes f. See Fig. 9.2.4 for the graph of f, which confirms the result.

The following uniqueness result is an important property of extreme points for a function which is either strictly concave or strictly convex.

THEOREM 9.2.3 (EXTREMA OF STRICTLY CONCAVE AND STRICTLY CONVEX FUNCTIONS)

Suppose that f is a function defined in an interval I.

(i) If f is strictly concave, then any maximum point for f in I is unique.

(ii) If f is strictly convex, then any minimum point for f in I is unique.

Proof: Let x^* be any maximum point for f in I, and let x be any other point in I. If f is strictly concave, then

$$f(x^*) \geq f(\tfrac{1}{2}x + \tfrac{1}{2}x^*) > \tfrac{1}{2}f(x) + \tfrac{1}{2}f(x^*)$$

It follows that $f(x^*) > f(x)$, so x cannot be a maximum point. When f is strictly convex and x^* is a minimum point, simply reverse the inequalities.

EXERCISES FOR SECTION 9.2

1. Let y denote the weekly average quantity of pork produced in Chicago during 1948, in millions of pounds, and let x be the total weekly work effort, in thousands of hours. A study estimated the relation $y = -2.05 + 1.06x - 0.04x^2$. Determine the value of x that maximizes y by studying the sign variation of y'.

2. (SM) Find the derivative of the function h, defined for all x by the formula $h(x) = 8x/(3x^2 + 4)$. Note that $h(x) \to 0$ as $x \to \pm\infty$. Use the sign variation of $h'(x)$ to find the extreme points of $h(x)$.

3. The height of a flowering plant after t months is given by $h(t) = \sqrt{t} - \tfrac{1}{2}t$, for t in $[0, 3]$. At what time is the plant at its tallest?

4. Show that

$$f(x) = \frac{2x^2}{x^4 + 1} \Rightarrow f'(x) = \frac{4x(1 + x^2)(1 + x)(1 - x)}{(x^4 + 1)^2}$$

and find the maximum value of f on $[0, \infty)$.

5. Find possible extreme points for $g(x) = x^3 \ln x$, for $x \in (0, \infty)$.

6. Find possible extreme points for $f(x) = e^{3x} - 6e^x$, for $x \in (-\infty, \infty)$.

7. Find the maximum of $y = x^2 e^{-x}$ on $[0, 4]$.

(SM) 8. Use Theorem 9.2.2 to find the values of x that maximize/minimize the functions given by the following formulas:

   (a) $y = e^x + e^{-2x}$ (b) $y = 9 - (x-a)^2 - 2(x-b)^2$ (c) $y = \ln x - 5x$, for $x > 0$

9. Consider n numbers $a_1, a_2, \ldots, a_n$. Find the number $\bar{x}$ which gives the best approximation to these numbers, in the sense of minimizing
$$d(x) = (x - a_1)^2 + (x - a_2)^2 + \cdots + (x - a_n)^2$$

(SM) 10. [HARDER] After the North Sea flood catastrophe in 1953, the Dutch government initiated a project to determine the optimal height of the dykes. One of the models involved finding the value of x minimizing $f(x) = I_0 + kx + Ae^{-\alpha x}$, for $x \geq 0$. Here x denotes the extra height in metres by which the dykes should be raised, whereas $I_0 + kx$ is the construction cost, and $Ae^{-\alpha x}$ is an estimate of the expected loss due to a potential flood. The parameters I_0, k, A, and α are all positive constants.

   (a) Suppose that $A\alpha > k$ and find $x_0 > 0$ that minimizes $f(x)$.

   (b) The constant A is defined as $A = p_0 V (1 + 100/\delta)$, where p_0 is the probability that the dykes will be flooded if they are not rebuilt, V is an estimate of the cost of flood damage, and δ is an interest rate. Show that
$$x_0 = \frac{1}{\alpha} \ln \left[\frac{\alpha p_0 V}{k} \left(1 + \frac{100}{\delta} \right) \right]$$

   Examine what happens to x_0 when any one of the variables p_0, V, δ, or k increases. Comment on the reasonableness of the results.[3]

9.3 Economic Examples

This section presents some other interesting examples of economic optimization problems.

EXAMPLE 9.3.1   **(Econometrics: Linear Regression I).** Empirical economics is concerned with analysing data in order to try to discern some pattern that helps in understanding the past, and possibly in predicting the future. For example, price and quantity data for a particular commodity such as natural gas may be used in order to try to estimate a demand function. This might then be used to predict how demand will respond to future price changes. The most commonly used technique for estimating such a function is *linear regression*.

Suppose it is thought that variable y depends upon variable x. Suppose that we have observations (x_t, y_t) of both variables at times $t = 1, 2, \ldots, T$. For the sake of simplicity,

---

[3] This problem is discussed in D. van Dantzig, "Economic Decision Problems for Flood Prevention". *Econometrica*, 24 (1956): 276–287.

assume that both variables have zero arithmetical mean.[4] In symbols, this means that

$$\mu_x = \frac{1}{T}\sum_{t=1}^{T} x_t = 0 \quad \text{and} \quad \mu_y = \frac{1}{T}\sum_{t=1}^{T} y_t = 0$$

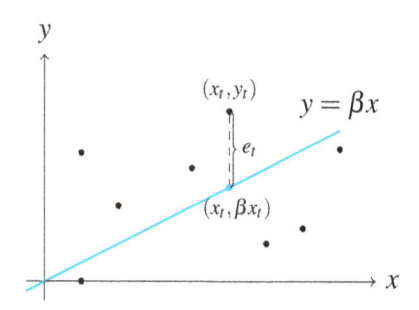

Figure 9.3.1 Linear regression

Then the technique of linear regression seeks to fit a linear function $y = \beta x$ to the data, as indicated in Fig. 9.3.1. Of course, an exact fit is possible only if there exista a number β for which $y_t = \beta x_t$ for $t = 1, 2, \ldots, T$. This is rarely the case. Generally, however β may be chosen, one has instead

$$y_t = \beta x_t + e_t, \quad t = 1, 2, \ldots, T$$

where e_t is an *error* or *disturbance* term. Obviously, one hopes that the errors will be small, on average. So the parameter β is chosen to make the errors as "small as possible", somehow. One idea would be to make the sum $\sum_{t=1}^{T}(y_t - \beta x_t)$ equal to zero. However, in this case, large positive discrepancies would cancel large negative discrepancies. Indeed, the sum of errors could be zero even though the line is very far from giving a good fit. We must somehow prevent large positive errors from cancelling large negative errors. Usually, this is done by minimizing the quadratic "loss" function

$$L(\beta) = \frac{1}{T}\sum_{t=1}^{T} e_t^2 = \frac{1}{T}\sum_{t=1}^{T}(y_t - \beta x_t)^2 \qquad (*)$$

which equals the mean (or average) square error. Expanding the square gives

$$L(\beta) = \frac{1}{T}\sum_{t=1}^{T}(y_t^2 - 2\beta x_t y_t + \beta^2 x_t^2) \qquad (**)$$

This is a quadratic function of β.

---

[4] This assumption is restrictive if we think of x and y as primitive, raw data. On the other hand, an analyst may think that deviations of, say, the interest rate from its historical average can cause analogous deviations in the unemployment rate. In that case, the means of the raw data are subtracted from each observation. Then it follows from Example 2.10.2 that the resulting *demeaned* data satisfy the assumption.

We shall show how to derive the *ordinary least-squares* estimates of β. To do so it helps to introduce some standard notation. Write

$$\sigma_{xx} = \frac{1}{T}\sum_{t=1}^{T} x_t^2, \quad \sigma_{yy} = \frac{1}{T}\sum_{t=1}^{T} y_t^2, \quad \text{and} \quad \sigma_{xy} = \frac{1}{T}\sum_{t=1}^{T} x_t y_t$$

Then σ_{xx} and σ_{yy} denote the *statistical variances* of the corresponding two variables x and y, whereas σ_{xy} denotes their *covariance*. In what follows, we shall assume that the x_t are not all equal, so that $\sigma_{xx} > 0$. Then expression (**) for $L(\beta)$ becomes

$$L(\beta) = \beta^2 \sigma_{xx} - 2\beta \sigma_{xy} + \sigma_{yy}$$

The first-order condition (9.1.3) for a minimum of $L(\beta)$ takes the form

$$L'(\beta) = 2\beta \sigma_{xx} - 2\sigma_{xy} = 0$$

So the unique critical point of $L(\beta)$ is $\hat{\beta} = \sigma_{xy}/\sigma_{xx}$. Furthermore, $L''(\beta) = 2\sigma_{xx} > 0$, so Eq. (8.5.4) tells us that L is convex. It follows from Theorem 9.2.2 that the critical point $\hat{\beta}$ minimizes $L(\beta)$. The problem is then solved: *The straight line through the origin that best fits the observations* $(x_1, y_1), (x_2, y_2), \ldots, (x_T, y_T)$, *in the sense of minimizing the mean square error given by* (*), *is* $y = \hat{\beta} x$ *where* $\hat{\beta} = \sigma_{xy}/\sigma_{xx}$.

EXAMPLE 9.3.2   Suppose $Y(N)$ bushels of wheat are harvested per acre of land when N pounds of fertilizer per acre are used. If p is the dollar price per bushel of wheat and q is the dollar price per pound of fertilizer, then for each $N \geq 0$ profit in dollars per acre is

$$\pi(N) = pY(N) - qN$$

Suppose there exists N^* such that $\pi'(N) \geq 0$ for $N \leq N^*$, whereas $\pi'(N) \leq 0$ for $N \geq N^*$. Then N^* maximizes profits, and $\pi'(N^*) = 0$. That is, $pY'(N^*) - q = 0$, so

$$pY'(N^*) = q \qquad (*)$$

Let us give an economic interpretation of this condition. Suppose N^* units of fertilizer are used and we contemplate increasing N^* by one unit. What do we gain? If N^* increases by one unit, then $Y(N^* + 1) - Y(N^*)$ more bushels are produced. Now $Y(N^* + 1) - Y(N^*) \approx Y'(N^*)$. For each of these bushels, we get p dollars, so *by increasing N^* by one unit, we gain approximately $pY'(N^*)$ dollars*. On the other hand, *by increasing N^* by one unit, we lose q dollars*, because this is the cost of one unit of fertilizer. Hence, we can interpret (*) as follows: In order to maximize profits, you should increase the amount of fertilizer to the level N^* at which an additional pound of fertilizer equates the changes in your gains and losses from the extra pound.

(a) In an (unrealistic) example, suppose that $Y(N) = \sqrt{N}$, $p = 10$, and $q = 0.5$. Find the amount of fertilizer which maximizes profits in this case.

(b) An agricultural study in Iowa estimated the yield function $Y(N)$ for the year 1952 as

$$Y(N) = -13.62 + 0.984N - 0.05N^{1.5}$$

Suppose that the price of wheat is $1.40 per bushel, and that the price of fertilizer is $0.18 per pound. Find the amount of fertilizer that maximizes profits.

SECTION 9.3 / ECONOMIC EXAMPLES

Solution:

(a) The profit function is

$$\pi(N) = PY(N) - qN = 10N^{1/2} - 0.5N$$

for $N \geq 0$. Then $\pi'(N) = 5N^{-1/2} - 0.5$. We see that $\pi'(N^*) = 0$ when $(N^*)^{-1/2} = 0.1$, hence $N^* = 100$. Moreover, it follows that $\pi'(N) \geq 0$ when $N \leq 100$ and $\pi'(N) \leq 0$ when $N \geq 100$. We conclude that $N^* = 100$ maximizes profits. See Fig. 9.3.2.

(b) In this case, the profit function and its derivative are

$$\pi(N) = 1.4(-13.62 + 0.984N - 0.05N^{1.5}) - 0.18N$$
$$= -19.068 + 1.1976N - 0.07N^{1.5}$$
$$\pi'(N) = 1.1976 - 0.07 \cdot 1.5N^{0.5} = 1.1976 - 0.105\sqrt{N}$$

Hence $\pi'(N^*) = 0$ when $0.105\sqrt{N^*} = 1.1976$. So $\sqrt{N^*} = 1.1976 \div 0.105 \approx 11.4$, which implies that $N^* \approx (11.4)^2 \approx 130$. By studying the expression for $\pi'(N)$, we see that $\pi'(N)$ is positive to the left of N^* and negative to the right of N^*. Hence, $N^* \approx 130$ maximizes profits. The graph of $\pi(N)$ is shown in Fig. 9.3.3.

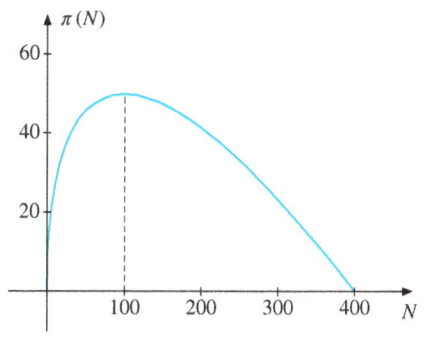

Figure 9.3.2 Example 9.3.2(a)

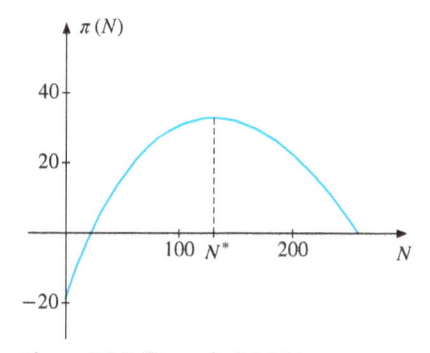

Figure 9.3.3 Example 9.3.2(b)

EXAMPLE 9.3.3

Suppose that the total cost of producing $Q > 0$ units of a commodity is $C(Q) = aQ^2 + bQ + c$, where a, b, and c are positive constants.

(a) Find the value of Q that minimizes the average cost defined by $A(Q) = C(Q)/Q$ in the special case when $C(Q) = 2Q^2 + 10Q + 32$.

(b) Show that in the general case, the average cost function has a minimum at $Q^* = \sqrt{c/a}$. In the same coordinate system, draw the graphs of the average cost, the marginal cost, and the straight line $P = aQ + b$.

Solution:

(a) Note that $A'(Q) = 2 - 32/Q^2$ and $A''(Q) = 64/Q^3$. The only critical point where $A'(Q) = 0$ occurs when $Q = 4$. Since $A''(Q) > 0$ for all $Q > 0$, the function $A(Q)$ is convex. It follows that $Q = 4$ is a minimum point.

(b) Here $A'(Q) = a - c/Q^2$ and $A''(Q) = 2c/Q^3$. Since $A''(Q) > 0$ for all $Q > 0$, the function $A(Q)$ is convex. Because $A'(Q) = 0$ for $Q^* = \sqrt{c/a}$, this is a minimum point. The three graphs are drawn in Fig. 9.3.4. Note that at the minimum point Q^*, marginal cost is equal to average cost. This is no coincidence, because it is true in general that $A'(Q) = 0$ if and only if $C'(Q) = A(Q)$.[5]

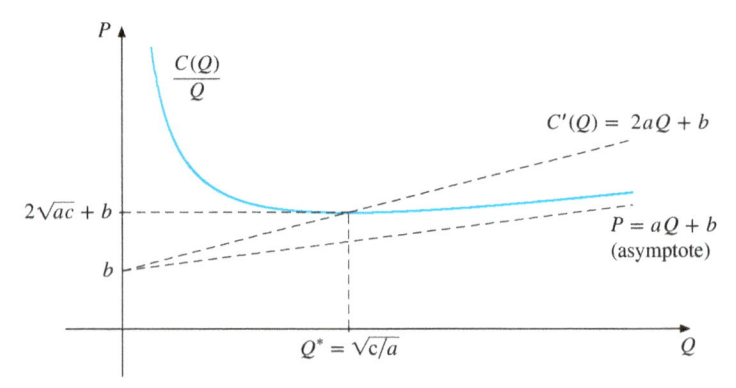

Figure 9.3.4 Average cost function in Example 9.3.3

The following example is typical of how economists use implicit differentiation to show how a change in a parameter affects the solution to an optimization problem.

EXAMPLE 9.3.4 A monopolist is faced with the inverse demand function $P(Q)$ denoting the price per unit that buyers pay when output is Q. The monopolist has a constant average cost k per unit produced.

(a) Find the profit function $\pi(Q)$. Then verify that the first-order condition for maximal profit at $Q = Q^*(k) > 0$ is

$$P'(Q^*(k))Q^*(k) + P(Q^*(k)) = k \qquad (*)$$

(b) By implicit differentiation of $(*)$, find a formula for the derivative of the monopolist's optimal output $Q^*(k)$ w.r.t. k.

(c) Express the monopolist's maximal profit as a function $\pi^*(k)$ of k. How does the optimal profit react to a change in k?

Solution:

(a) The profit function is $\pi(Q) = P(Q)Q - kQ$, so $\pi'(Q) = P'(Q)Q + P(Q) - k$. In order that $Q = Q^*(k) > 0$ should maximize $\pi(Q)$, one must have the first-order condition $\pi'(Q^*(k)) = 0$. This is equivalent to $(*)$.

(b) Assuming that equation $(*)$ defines $Q^*(k)$ as a differentiable function of k, and after dropping the argument k from $Q^*(k)$ wherever it is convenient, we obtain

---

[5] See Example 6.7.7. The minimum average cost is $A(Q^*) = a\sqrt{c/a} + b + c/\sqrt{c/a} = \sqrt{ac} + b + \sqrt{ac} = 2\sqrt{ac} + b$.

$$P''(Q^*)\frac{dQ^*}{dk}Q^* + P'(Q^*)\frac{dQ^*}{dk} + P'(Q^*)\frac{dQ^*}{dk} = 1$$

Solving for dQ^*/dk gives

$$\frac{dQ^*}{dk} = \frac{1}{P''(Q^*)Q^* + 2P'(Q^*)}$$

(c) Optimal profit $\pi^*(k)$ occurs where $Q = Q^*(k)$, and so $\pi^*(k) = P(Q^*(k))Q^*(k) - kQ^*(k)$. Differentiating each side of this equation w.r.t. k gives

$$\frac{d\pi^*}{dk} = P'(Q^*)\frac{dQ^*}{dk}Q^* + P(Q^*)\frac{dQ^*}{dk} - Q^* - k\frac{dQ^*}{dk}$$

Here the three terms containing dQ^*/dk all cancel because of the first-order condition ($*$). So $d\pi^*/dk = -Q^*$. Thus, if the cost increases by one unit, the optimal profit will decrease by approximately Q^*, the optimal output level.

EXERCISES FOR SECTION 9.3

1. (a) A firm produces $Q = 2\sqrt{L}$ units of a commodity when it employs L units of labour, its only input. Suppose that the price obtained per unit of output is €160, and the price per unit of labour is €40. What value of L maximizes its profit $\pi(L)$?

   (b) A firm produces $Q = f(L)$ units of a commodity when it employs L units of labour, its only input. Assume that $f'(L) > 0$ and $f''(L) < 0$. Suppose the price obtained per unit of output is 1 and the price per unit of labour is w. What is the first-order condition for maximizing profits at $L = L^*$?

   (c) By implicitly differentiating the first-order condition in (b) w.r.t. w, find how L^* changes when w changes.

SM 2. In Example 9.3.4, suppose that $P(Q) = a - Q$, and assume that $0 < k < a$.

   (a) Find the profit maximizing output Q^* and the associated monopoly profit $\pi(Q^*)$.

   (b) How does the monopoly profit react to changes in k? Find $d\pi(Q^*)/dk$.

   (c) The government argues that the monopoly produces too little. It wants to induce the monopolist to produce $\hat{Q} = a - k$ units by granting a subsidy of s per unit of output. Calculate the subsidy s required to reach the target.

3. A square tin plate whose edges are 18 cm long is to be made into an open square box x cm deep. This is to be done by cutting out equally sized squares of width x in each corner, then folding over the edges. Draw a figure, and show that the volume of the box, for $x \in [0, 9]$, is:

$$V(x) = x(18 - 2x)^2 = 4x^3 - 72x^2 + 324x$$

   Also find the maximum point of V in $[0, 9]$.

4. In one economic model the proportion of families whose income is no more than x, and who have a home computer, is given by $p(x) = a + k(1 - e^{-cx})$, where a, k, and c are positive constants. Determine $p'(x)$ and $p''(x)$. Does $p(x)$ have a maximum? Sketch the graph of p.

5. Suppose that the tax T a person pays on income w is given by $T = a(bw + c)^p + kw$, where a, b, c, and k are positive constants, and $p > 1$. Then the average tax rate is

$$\bar{T}(w) = \frac{T}{w} = a\frac{(bw + c)^p}{w} + k$$

At what level of income does a taxpayer face the minimum average tax rate?

9.4 The Extreme and Mean Value Theorems

The main result used so far in this chapter to locate extreme points is the first-order condition specified in Theorem 9.2.1. This requires the function to be steadily increasing on one side of the extreme point and steadily decreasing on the other. Yet many functions whose derivative violates these conditions may still have a maximum or minimum. This section shows how to locate possible extreme points for an important class of such functions.

Example 9.2.3 shows that it is relatively easy to find functions that have no extreme points. But an even simpler case is the function $f(x) = x$, defined over the whole real line. The following theorem gives important sufficient conditions for extreme points to exist.

THEOREM 9.4.1 (THE EXTREME VALUE THEOREM)

Suppose that f is a continuous function defined over a closed and bounded interval $[a, b]$. Then there exists a point d in $[a, b]$ where f has a minimum, and a point c in $[a, b]$ where it has a maximum—that is, where

$$f(d) \leq f(x) \leq f(c) \quad \text{for all } x \text{ in } [a, b]$$

One of the most common misunderstandings of the extreme value theorem is illustrated by the following statement from a student's exam paper: "The function is continuous, but since it is not defined on a closed, bounded interval, the extreme value theorem shows that there is no maximum." The misunderstanding here is that, although the conditions of the theorem are sufficient, they certainly are not *necessary* for the existence of an extreme point. In Exercise 9, you will study a function defined in an interval that is neither closed nor bounded, and moreover the function is not even continuous. Even so, it has both a maximum and a minimum.

In general, however, existence of extreme points cannot be guaranteed unless the assumptions of the theorem are satisfied. Indeed, Figures 9.4.1–9.4.3 display graphs of three functions that satisfy two of the three assumptions of Theorem 9.4.1, but not the third. In each case, the function has no maximum, even though it does have a minimum.

Figure 9.4.1
The domain is not closed

Figure 9.4.2
The domain is unbounded

Figure 9.4.3
A discontinuous function

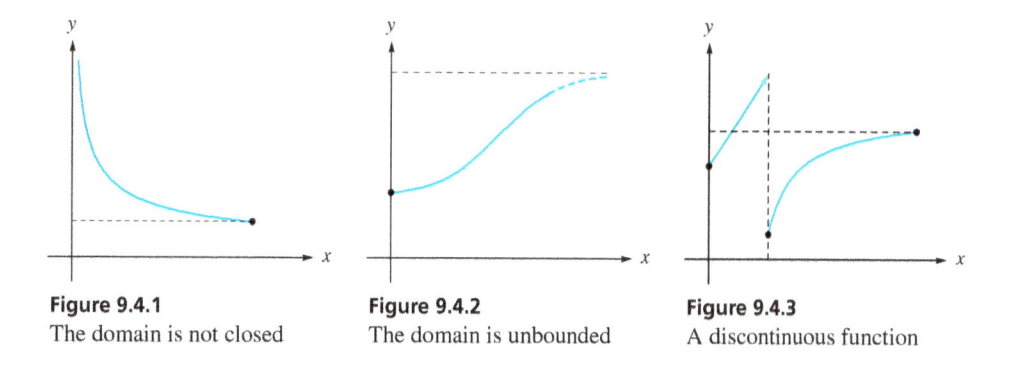

The proof of the extreme value theorem is somewhat involved.[6] Yet the result is not hard to believe. Imagine, for example, a mountainous stage of a cycle race like the Tour de France. Since roads avoid going over cliffs, the height of the road above sea level is a continuous function of the distance travelled, as illustrated in Fig. 9.4.4. As the figure also shows, the stage must take the cyclist over some highest point P, as well as through a lowest point Q. Of course, these points could also be at the start or finish of the ride.

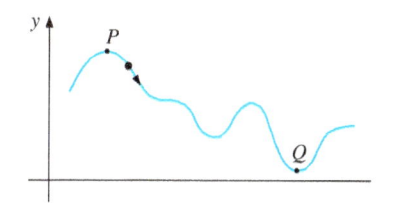

Figure 9.4.4 Altitude as a function of distance

How to Search for Maxima and Minima

Suppose we know that a function f has a maximum and/or a minimum in some bounded interval I. The optimum must occur either at an interior point of I, or else at an end point. If it occurs at an interior point of I at which f is differentiable, then the derivative f' is zero at that point. An additional possibility is that the optimum occurs at a point where f is not differentiable. To summarize, every extreme point must belong to one of the following three pairwise disjoint sets:

(a) interior points x in I where $f'(x) = 0$;
(b) end points of I, if they belong to I;
(c) interior points x in I where $f'(x)$ does not exist.

Points satisfying any one of these three conditions will be called *candidate extreme points*. Whether they are actual extreme points must be decided by carefully comparing

---

[6] The original proof was given by German mathematician Karl Weierstrass (1815–1897). Essentially, the argument is that if a continuous function is defined on a closed and bounded interval, its range is also a closed and bounded interval. The end points of the range are precisely the extreme values of the function.

FINDING THE EXTREMA OF FUNCTIONS

Let f be a differentiable function defined on a closed, bounded interval $[a, b]$. In order to find its maximum and minimum values:

(i) Find all critical points of f in (a, b), which, by definition, are the points x in (a, b) that satisfy the FOC $f'(x) = 0$.

(ii) Evaluate f at the end points a and b of the interval, and also at all critical points.

(iii) The largest function value found in (ii) is the maximum value, and the smallest function value is the minimum value of f in $[a, b]$.

A differentiable function is continuous, so the extreme value theorem assures us that maximum and minimum points do exist, provided that its domain is closed and bounded. Following the procedure just given, we can, in principle, find these extreme points.

EXAMPLE 9.4.1 Find the maximum and minimum values, for x in $[0, 3]$, of

$$f(x) = 3x^2 - 6x + 5$$

Solution: The function is differentiable everywhere, and $f'(x) = 6x - 6 = 6(x - 1)$. Hence $x = 1$ is the only critical point. The candidate extreme points are $x = 1$ as well as the end points 0 and 3. We calculate the value of f at these three points. The results are $f(1) = 2$, $f(0) = 5$, and $f(3) = 14$. We conclude that the maximum value is 14, obtained at the end point $x = 3$, and the minimum value is 2, obtained at the interior point $x = 1$.

EXAMPLE 9.4.2 Find the maximum and minimum values, for x in $[-1, 3]$, of

$$f(x) = \tfrac{1}{4}x^4 - \tfrac{5}{6}x^3 + \tfrac{1}{2}x^2 - 1$$

Solution: The function is differentiable everywhere, and

$$f'(x) = x^3 - \tfrac{5}{2}x^2 + x = x\left(x^2 - \tfrac{5}{2}x + 1\right)$$

Solving the quadratic equation $x^2 - \tfrac{5}{2}x + 1 = 0$ gives us the two roots $x = \tfrac{1}{2}$ and $x = 2$. Thus $f'(x) = 0$ for $x = 0$, $x = \tfrac{1}{2}$, and $x = 2$. These three points, together with the ends of the interval at $x = -1$ and $x = 3$, constitute the five candidate extreme points. We calculate

$$f(-1) = 7/12,\ f(0) = -1,\ f(\tfrac{1}{2}) = -185/192,\ f(2) = -5/3,\ \text{and}\ f(3) = 5/4$$

Thus, the maximum value of f is $5/4$ at $x = 3$, and the minimum value is $-5/3$ at $x = 2$.

Note that we found the maximum and minimum values without any need either to study the sign variation of $f'(x)$, or use other tests such as second-order conditions.

In Examples 9.4.1 and 9.4.2 one could easily find all the solutions to the equation $f'(x) = 0$. In many case, however, finding all those solutions might constitute a problem that is formidable, even insuperable. Consider, for instance, the function defined for all $x \in [-1, 5]$ by

$$f(x) = x^{26} - 32x^{23} - 11x^5 - 2x^3 - x + 28$$

As a polynomial, the function is continuous. So it does have a maximum and a minimum in $[-1, 5]$. Yet it is impossible to find any exact solution to the equation $f'(x) = 0$, which involves a polynomial of degree 25.

Difficulties like this often arise in practical optimization problems. In fact, only in very special cases can the equation $f'(x) = 0$ be solved exactly. Fortunately, there are standard numerical computer algorithms that in most cases will find points arbitrarily close to the actual solutions of such equations. Some are based on Newton's method discussed in Section 7.10. Even better, some algorithms are specifically designed to find the extreme points of a function.

The Mean Value Theorem

This subsection deals with the mean value theorem, which is a principal tool that allows results in calculus to be demonstrated precisely. The subsection is a bit more advanced than the rest of the book, so may be considered optional.

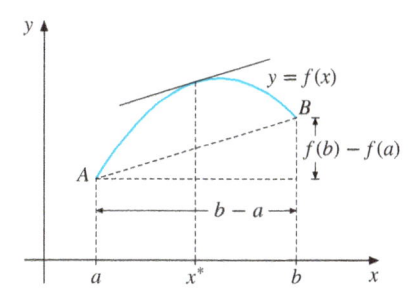

Figure 9.4.5 The mean value theorem

Consider a function f which is defined and continuous on a closed interval $[a, b]$, as well as differentiable in the open interval (a, b). As illustrated in Fig. 9.4.5, the graph of f joins the end points A and B by a connected curve having a tangent at each point of (a, b). It seems geometrically plausible that there is at least one value x^* of x between a and b at which the tangent to the graph should be parallel to the line AB, as shown in Fig. 9.4.5. The line AB has slope $[f(b) - f(a)]/(b - a)$. So the condition for the tangent line at $(x^*, f(x^*))$ to be parallel to the line AB is that $f'(x^*) = [f(b) - f(a)]/(b - a)$. In fact, x^* can be chosen so that the vertical distance between the graph of f and AB is as large as possible. The proof that follows is based on this fact.

THEOREM 9.4.2 (THE MEAN VALUE THEOREM)

Suppose that f is continuous in the closed and bounded interval $[a, b]$, as well as differentiable in the open interval (a, b). Then there exists at least one point x^* in (a, b) such that

$$f'(x^*) = \frac{f(b) - f(a)}{b - a} \qquad (9.4.1)$$

Proof: The point–point formula for the straight line joining A to B in Fig. 9.4.5 has the equation

$$y - f(a) = \frac{f(b) - f(a)}{b - a}(x - a)$$

The vertical distance between the graph of f and the line AB is therefore given by the function

$$g(x) = f(x) - f(a) - \frac{f(b) - f(a)}{b - a}(x - a)$$

Obviously, $g(a) = g(b) = 0$. Note that

$$g'(x) = f'(x) - \frac{f(b) - f(a)}{b - a} \qquad (*)$$

The function $g(x)$ obviously inherits from f the properties of being continuous in $[a, b]$ and differentiable in (a, b). By the extreme value theorem, $g(x)$ has a maximum and a minimum over $[a, b]$. Because $g(a) = g(b)$, at least one of these extreme points x^* must lie in (a, b). (If $g(x) \equiv 0$ throughout $[a, b]$, then all points in $[a, b]$ are extreme points for g.) Theorem 9.1.1 tells us that $g'(x^*) = 0$, so the conclusion follows from $(*)$.

EXAMPLE 9.4.3 Test the mean value theorem on the function $f(x) = x^3 - x$, defined over the interval $[0, 2]$.

Solution: We find that $[f(2) - f(0)]/(2 - 0) = 3$ and $f'(x) = 3x^2 - 1$. The equation $f'(x) = 3$ is equivalent to $3x^2 = 4$, which has the two solutions $x = \pm 2\sqrt{3}/3$. The positive root $x^* = 2\sqrt{3}/3$ belongs to $(0, 2)$. At this x^* one has

$$f'(x^*) = \frac{f(2) - f(0)}{2 - 0}$$

This confirms the mean value theorem in this case.

Two Implications of the Mean Value Theorem

This subsection contains formal proofs, and can be regarded as optional.

The mean value theorem can be used to provide the promised proofs of Eqs (6.3.1), (6.3.2), and (6.3.3). Indeed, recall from Section 6.3 that a function f is *increasing* in I if $f(x_2) \geq f(x_1)$ whenever $x_2 > x_1$ with x_1 and x_2 in I.

First, the definition of derivative makes it evident that if $f(x)$ is increasing and differentiable, then $f'(x) \geq 0$. To prove the converse, suppose that the function f is continuous in the interval I and that, for all x in the interior of I, the derivative $f'(x)$ exists and satisfies $f'(x) \geq 0$. Let x_1 and x_2 be two arbitrary numbers in I satisfying $x_2 > x_1$. According to the mean value theorem, there exists a number x^* in (x_1, x_2) such that

$$f(x_2) - f(x_1) = f'(x^*)(x_2 - x_1) \tag{9.4.2}$$

Because $x_2 > x_1$ and $f'(x^*) \geq 0$, it follows that $f(x_2) \geq f(x_1)$, so $f(x)$ is increasing. This proves statement (6.3.1). The equivalence in (6.3.2) can be proved by considering the condition for $-f$ to be increasing. Finally, (6.3.3) involves both f and $-f$ being increasing.[7]

We can also use the mean value theorem to prove Lagrange's remainder formula:

Proof of (7.6.2): We start by proving that the formula is correct for $n = 1$, in which case it reduces to Eq. (7.6.4). For $x \neq 0$, define the function $S(x)$ implicitly by the equation

$$f(x) = f(0) + f'(0)x + \tfrac{1}{2} S(x) x^2 \tag{$*$}$$

To establish Eq. (7.6.4), we prove that there is a c strictly between 0 and x such that $S(x) = f''(c)$. Indeed, keep x fixed and define the function g, for all t between 0 and x, by

$$g(t) = f(x) - [f(t) + f'(t)(x - t) + \tfrac{1}{2} S(x)(x - t)^2] \tag{$**$}$$

Then definitions ($*$) and ($**$) imply that

$$g(0) = f(x) - [f(0) + f'(0)x + \tfrac{1}{2} S(x) x^2] = 0 \text{ and } g(x) = 0$$

So, by the mean value theorem, there exists a number c strictly between 0 and x such that $g'(c) = 0$. Differentiating ($**$) with respect to t while keeping x fixed, we get

$$g'(t) = -f'(t) + f'(t) - f''(t)(x - t) + S(x)(x - t)$$

Putting $t = c$ gives $g'(c) = -f''(c)(x - c) + S(x)(x - c)$. Because $g'(c) = 0$ and $c \neq x$, it follows that $S(x) = f''(c)$. Hence, we have proved (7.6.4).

The proof for $n > 1$ is based on the same idea, generalizing ($*$) and ($**$) in the obvious way.

EXERCISES FOR SECTION 9.4

1. Given the function defined by $f(x) = 4x^2 - 40x + 80$ for $x \in [0, 8]$, find its maximum and minimum points, and draw its graph.

SM 2. Find the maximum and minimum points of each function over the indicated interval:

(a) $f(x) = -2x - 1$ over $[0, 3]$

(b) $f(x) = x^3 - 3x + 8$ over $[-1, 2]$

(c) $f(x) = \dfrac{x^2 + 1}{x}$ over $[\tfrac{1}{2}, 2]$

(d) $f(x) = x^5 - 5x^3$ over $[-1, \sqrt{5}]$

(e) $f(x) = x^3 - 4500 x^2 + 6 \cdot 10^6 x$ over $[0, 3000]$

---

[7] Alternatively it follows easily by using Eq. (9.4.2).

3. Suppose the function g is defined for all x in $[-1, 2]$ by $g(x) = \frac{1}{5}(e^{x^2} + e^{2-x^2})$. Calculate $g'(x)$ and find the extreme points of g.

4. A sports club plans to charter a plane, and to charge members who buy seats a commission of 10% of the price they pay. That price is arranged by the charter company. The standard fare for each passenger is $800. For each additional person above 60, all travellers (including the first 60) get a discount of $10. The plane can take at most 80 passengers.

    (a) What commission does the club earn when there are 61, 70, 80, and $60 + x$ passengers?

    (b) What number of passengers maximizes the sports club's total commission for this trip?

5. Let the function f be defined for x in $[1, e^3]$ by $f(x) = (\ln x)^3 - 2(\ln x)^2 + \ln x$.

    (a) Compute $f(e^{1/3}), f(e^2),$ and $f(e^3)$. Find the zeros of $f(x)$.

    (b) Find the extreme points of f.

    (c) Show that f defined over $[e, e^3]$ has an inverse function g and determine $g'(2)$.

SM 6. [HARDER] For each of the following functions, if we denote the specified interval by $[a, b]$, determine all numbers x^* in $[a, b]$ such that $f'(x^*) = [f(b) - f(a)]/(b - a)$:

    (a) $f(x) = x^2$, in $[1, 2]$
    (b) $f(x) = \sqrt{1 - x^2}$, in $[0, 1]$
    (c) $f(x) = 2/x$, in $[2, 6]$
    (d) $f(x) = \sqrt{9 + x^2}$, in $[0, 4]$

7. [HARDER] You are supposed to sail from point A in a lake to point B. What does the mean value theorem have to say about your trip?

8. [HARDER] Consider the function f defined for all x in $[-1, 1]$ by

$$f(x) = \begin{cases} x, & \text{if } x \in (-1, 1) \\ 0, & \text{if } x = -1 \text{ or } x = 1 \end{cases}$$

Is this function continuous? Does it attain a maximum or minimum?

9. [HARDER] Let f be defined for all x in $(0, \infty)$ by

$$f(x) = \begin{cases} x + 1, & \text{if } x \in (0, 1] \\ 1, & \text{if } x \in (1, \infty) \end{cases}$$

Prove that f attains maximum and minimum values. Verify that, nevertheless, *none* of the conditions in the extreme value theorem is satisfied.

9.5 Further Economic Examples

EXAMPLE 9.5.1   A firm that produces a single commodity wants to maximize its profit. Let $R(Q)$ denote the total revenue generated in a certain period by producing and selling Q units. Let

$C(Q)$ denote the associated total dollar production cost. Then the profit obtained as a result of producing and selling Q units is

$$\pi(Q) = R(Q) - C(Q)$$

Because of technical limitations, suppose there is a maximum quantity $\bar{Q}$ that can be produced by the firm in a given period. Assume too that the functions R and C are continuous in the interval $[0, \bar{Q}]$, and differentiable in $(0, \bar{Q})$. Then the profit function π is also continuous on $[0, \bar{Q}]$, so does have a maximum value. In special cases, that maximum might occur at $Q = 0$ or at $Q = \bar{Q}$. If not, it has an "interior maximum" where the production level Q^* satisfies $\pi'(Q^*) = 0$, and so

$$R'(Q^*) = C'(Q^*) \tag{9.5.1}$$

Hence, *production should be adjusted to a point where the marginal revenue is equal to the marginal cost.*

Consider the "competitive" case when the market determines the firm's price p per unit sold, over which it has no control. Then $R(Q) = pQ$, and (9.5.1) takes the form

$$p = C'(Q^*) \tag{9.5.2}$$

Thus, in this case, assuming an interior maximum, *production should be adjusted to a level at which the marginal cost is equal to the price per unit of the commodity.*

It is quite possible that the firm has functions $R(Q)$ and $C(Q)$ for which Eq. (9.5.1) has several solutions. If so, the maximum profit occurs at that point Q^* among the solutions of (9.5.1) which gives the highest value of $\pi(Q^*)$.

Equation (9.5.1) has an economic interpretation rather like that for the corresponding optimality condition in Example 9.3.2. Indeed, suppose we contemplate increasing production from the level Q^* by one unit. This would increase revenue by the amount $R(Q^* + 1) - R(Q^*) \approx R'(Q^*)$. It would increase cost by the amount $C(Q^* + 1) - C(Q^*) \approx C'(Q^*)$. Equation (9.5.1) equates $R'(Q^*)$ and $C'(Q^*)$, so that the approximate extra revenue earned by selling one extra unit is offset by the approximate extra cost of producing that unit.

EXAMPLE 9.5.2 Suppose that the firm in the preceding example obtains a fixed price $p = 121$ per unit, and that the cost function is $C(Q) = 0.02Q^3 - 3Q^2 + 175Q + 500$. The firm can produce at most $\bar{Q} = 110$ units.

(a) Make a table of the values of the three functions $R(Q) = 121Q$, $C(Q)$, and $\pi(Q) = R(Q) - C(Q)$, as Q takes the values 0, 10, 30, 50, 70, 90, and 110. Draw the graphs of $R(Q)$ and $C(Q)$ in the same coordinate system.

(b) Use the graphs in (a) to find approximate answer to the following questions:

  (i) How many units must be produced in order for the firm to make a profit?

  (ii) How many units must be produced for the profit to be $2 000?

  (iii) Which production level maximizes profits?

(c) Compute an exact answer to question (iii) in part (b).

(d) Suppose the firm produces at its full capacity of 110 units. What is the smallest price per unit the firm must charge in order not to lose money?

Solution:

(a) We form the following table:

Q	0	10	30	50	70	90	110
$R(Q) = 121Q$	0	1 210	3 630	6 050	8 470	10 890	13 310
$C(Q)$	500	1 970	3 590	4 250	4 910	6 530	10 070
$\pi(Q) = R(Q) - C(Q)$	−500	−760	40	1 800	3 560	4 360	3 240

The graphs of $R(Q)$ and $C(Q)$ are shown in Fig. 9.5.1.

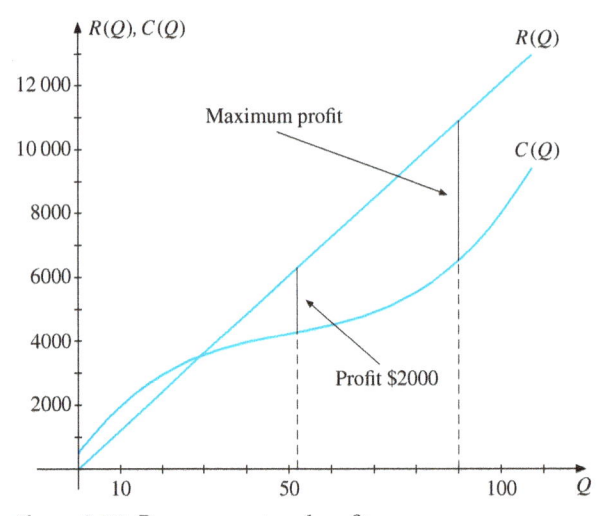

Figure 9.5.1 Revenue, cost, and profit

(b) (i) The firm earns a profit if $\pi(Q) > 0$, that is when $R(Q) > C(Q)$. The figure suggests that $R(Q) > C(Q)$ when Q is larger than about 30.

(ii) We must find where the "gap" between $R(Q)$ and $C(Q)$ is $2\,000. This seems to occur when $Q \approx 52$.

(iii) The profit is largest when the gap between $R(Q)$ and $C(Q)$ is largest. This seems to occur when $Q \approx 90$.

(c) We insert the formula for $C'(Q)$ into Eq. (9.5.2) with $P = 121$. The result is $121 = 0.06Q^2 - 6Q + 175$. Solving this quadratic equation yields $Q = 10$ and $Q = 90$. We know that $\pi(Q)$ must have a maximum point in $[0, 110]$. Including the two end points, the four candidate maximum points are $Q = 0$, $Q = 10$, $Q = 90$, and $Q = 110$. Using the table from part (a), we see that the associated profits from these quantities are:

$$\pi(0) = -500, \ \pi(10) = -760, \ \pi(90) = 4360, \ \pi(110) = 3240$$

The firm therefore attains maximum profit by producing 90 units.

(d) If the price per unit is p, the profit from producing 110 units is

$$\pi(110) = p \cdot 110 - C(110) = 110p - 10\,070$$

The smallest price p which ensures that, when producing 110 units, the firm does not lose money must satisfy $110p - 10\,070 = 0$, with solution $p \approx 91.55$. This price equals the average cost of producing 110 units. The price must be at least 91.55 if revenue is going to be enough to cover the cost of producing at full capacity.

EXAMPLE 9.5.3 In the model of the previous example, the firm took the price as given. Consider an example at the other extreme, where the firm has a monopoly in the sale of the commodity. Assume that the price $P(Q)$ per unit varies with Q according to the formula $P(Q) = 100 - \frac{1}{3}Q$ for $Q \in [0, 300]$. Suppose now the cost function is

$$C(Q) = \frac{1}{600}Q^3 - \frac{1}{3}Q^2 + 50Q + \frac{1000}{3}$$

Then the profit is

$$\pi(Q) = QP(Q) - C(Q) = -\frac{1}{600}Q^3 + 50Q - \frac{1000}{3}$$

Find the production level that maximizes profit, and compute the maximum profit.

Solution: The derivative of $\pi(Q)$ is $\pi'(Q) = -(Q^2/200) + 50$. Hence, $\pi'(Q) = 0$ for $Q^2 = 10\,000$. Because $Q < 0$ is not permissible, the only critical point is at $Q = 100$.

The values of $\pi(Q)$ at the two end points of $[0, 300]$ are $\pi(0) = -1000/3$ and $\pi(300) = -91\,000/3$. Since $\pi(100) = 3\,000$, we conclude that $Q = 100$ maximizes profit, and the maximum profit is $3\,000$.

EXAMPLE 9.5.4 (Either a borrower or a lender be.)[8] Recall Example 7.1.5, and suppose that a student has current income y_1 and expects future income y_2. Let δ denote her discount rate.[9] She plans her current consumption $c_1 > 0$ and future consumption $c_2 > 0$ in order to maximize the utility function

$$U = \ln c_1 + \frac{1}{1+\delta} \ln c_2 \qquad (*)$$

In case she chooses $c_1 > y_1$, she needs to borrow the amount $c_1 - y_1$. Then her future consumption, after repaying the loan with interest charged at rate r, will be

$$c_2 = y_2 - (1+r)(c_1 - y_1)$$

Alternatively, in case she chooses $c_1 < y_1$, she saves the amount $y_1 - c_1$ now. Then her future consumption, including the interest at rate r received on her saving, will be

$$c_2 = y_2 + (1+r)(y_1 - c_1)$$

Find the optimal plan of borrowing or saving.

Solution: Whether she borrows or saves, in both cases her second period consumption is

$$c_2 = y_2 - (1+r)(c_1 - y_1)$$

---

[8] According to Shakespeare, Polonius's advice to Hamlet was: "Neither a borrower nor a lender be".
[9] In the notation of Example 7.1.5, this implies that the discount factor β satisfies $\beta = 1/(1+\delta)$.

After substituting this value of c_2 in (∗), we see that the student will want to choose c_1 in order to maximize

$$U = \ln c_1 + \frac{1}{1+\delta} \ln[y_2 - (1+r)(c_1 - y_1)] \qquad (**)$$

We can obviously restrict attention to the interval $0 < c_1 < y_1 + (1+r)^{-1}y_2$, where both c_1 and c_2 are positive. Differentiating (∗∗) w.r.t. the choice variable c_1 gives

$$\frac{dU}{dc_1} = \frac{1}{c_1} - \frac{1+r}{1+\delta} \cdot \frac{1}{y_2 - (1+r)(c_1 - y_1)}$$

Rewriting the fractions so that they have a common denominator yields

$$\frac{dU}{dc_1} = \frac{(1+\delta)[y_2 - (1+r)(c_1 - y_1)] - (1+r)c_1}{c_1(1+\delta)[y_2 - (1+r)(c_1 - y_1)]}$$

Rearranging the numerator and equating the derivative to 0, we have

$$\frac{dU}{dc_1} = \frac{(1+\delta)[(1+r)y_1 + y_2] - (2+\delta)(1+r)c_1}{c_1(1+\delta)[y_2 - (1+r)(c_1 - y_1)]} = 0 \qquad (***)$$

Because we assume that $y_2 - (1+r)(c_1 - y_1) > 0$, the unique solution of this equation is

$$c_1^* = \frac{(1+\delta)[(1+r)y_1 + y_2]}{(2+\delta)(1+r)} = y_1 + \frac{(1+\delta)y_2 - (1+r)y_1}{(2+\delta)(1+r)}$$

From (∗∗∗) it follows that for $c_1 < c_1^*$ one has $dU/dc_1 > 0$, whereas for $c_1 > c_1^*$ one has $dU/dc_1 < 0$. We conclude from the first-derivative test in Theorem 9.2.1 that c_1^* indeed maximizes U. Moreover, the student lends if and only if $(1+\delta)y_2 < (1+r)y_1$. In the more likely case when $(1+\delta)y_2 > (1+r)y_1$ because future income is considerably higher than present income, she will borrow. Only if by some chance $(1+\delta)y_2$ is exactly equal to $(1+r)y_1$ will she "neither a borrower nor a lender be".

This discussion, however, has neglected the difference between borrowing and lending rates of interest that one always observes in reality (even in Shakespeare's time).

EXERCISES FOR SECTION 9.5

1. With reference to Example 9.5.1, suppose that $R(Q) = 10Q - Q^2/1000$ for all $Q \in [0, 10\,000]$, and that $C(Q) = 5000 + 2Q$ for all $Q \geq 0$. Find the value of Q that maximizes profits.

2. With reference to Example 9.5.1, let $R(Q) = 80Q$ and $C(Q) = Q^2 + 10Q + 900$. The firm can produce at most 50 units.

   (a) Draw the graphs of R and C in the same coordinate system.

   (b) Answer the following questions both graphically and by computation: (i) How many units must be produced for the firm to make a profit? (ii) How many units must be produced for the firm to maximize profits?

3. A pharmaceutical firm produces penicillin. The sales price per unit is 200, while the cost of producing x units is given by $C(x) = 500\,000 + 80x + 0.003x^2$. The firm can produce at most 30 000 units. What value of x maximizes profits?

SM 4. Consider Example 9.5.1 and find the production level which maximizes profits when

(a) $R(Q) = 1840Q$ and $C(Q) = 2Q^2 + 40Q + 5000$

(b) $R(Q) = 2240Q$ and $C(Q) = 2Q^2 + 40Q + 5000$

(c) $R(Q) = 1840Q$ and $C(Q) = 2Q^2 + 1940Q + 5000$

5. The price a firm obtains for a commodity varies with demand Q according to the formula $P(Q) = 18 - 0.006Q$. Total cost is $C(Q) = 0.004Q^2 + 4Q + 4500$.

(a) Find the firm's profit $\pi(Q)$ and the value of Q which maximizes profit.

(b) Find a formula for the elasticity of $P(Q)$ w.r.t. Q, and find the particular value Q^* of Q at which the elasticity is equal to -1.

(c) Show that the marginal revenue is 0 at Q^*.

6. With reference to Example 9.5.1, let $R(Q) = pQ$ and $C(Q) = aQ^b + c$, where p, a, b, and c are positive constants, with $b > 1$. Find the value of Q which maximizes the profit $\pi(Q)$, making use of Theorem 9.2.2.

9.6 Local Extreme Points

So far this chapter has discussed what are often referred to as *global* optimization problems. The reason for this terminology is that we have been seeking the largest or smallest values of a function when we compare the function values at *all* points in the domain, without exception. In applied optimization problems, especially those arising in economics, it is usually these global extrema that are of interest. Sometimes, however, one is interested in the local maxima and minima of a function. In this case, we compare the function value at the point in question only with alternative function values at nearby points.

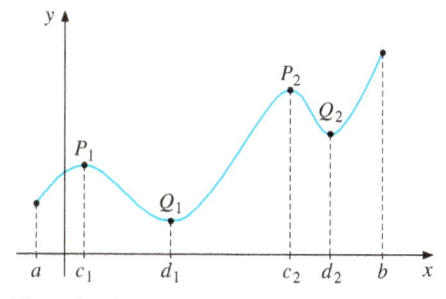

Figure 9.6.1 c_1, c_2, and b are local maximum points; a, d_1, and d_2 are local minimum points

Consider Fig. 9.6.1 and think of the graph as representing the profile of a landscape. Then the mountain tops P_1 and P_2 represent local maxima, whereas the valley bottoms Q_1 and Q_2 represent local minima. The precise definitions we need are as follows:

LOCAL EXTREMA

The function f has:

(i) a *local maximum* at c if there exists an interval (α, β) about c such that

$$f(x) \leq f(c) \quad \text{for all } x \text{ in } (\alpha, \beta) \text{ that belong to the domain of } f \qquad (9.6.1)$$

(ii) a *local minimum* at c if there exists an interval (α, β) about c such that

$$f(x) \geq f(c) \quad \text{for all } x \text{ in } (\alpha, \beta) \text{ that belong to the domain of } f \qquad (9.6.2)$$

A local extreme point is *strict* if $f(x) \neq f(c)$ for all $x \neq c$ in (α, β) that belong to the domain of f.

In Fig. 9.6.1, note that definition (9.6.2) of a local minimum applies to the end point a because, provided that $\alpha < a$, only the half-open subinterval $[a, \beta)$ of (α, β) can be in the domain of f. Similarly, definition (9.6.1) applies to the other end point b because, provided that $\beta > b$, only the half-open subinterval $(\alpha, b]$ of (α, β) can be in the domain of f.[10] So definition (9.6.2) implies that points a, d_1, and d_2 in Fig. 9.6.1 are all strict local minimum points, with d_1 as a global minimum point. Similarly, definition (9.6.1) implies that points b, c_1, and c_2 are strict local maximum points, with b as a global maximum point.

Function values corresponding to local maximum (minimum) points are called *local maximum (minimum) values*. As collective names we use the terms *local extreme points* and *local extreme values*.

A local maximum point c is a *strict local maximum* if (9.6.1) is modified to become $f(x) < f(c)$ for all x in (α, β) with $x \neq c$ that belong to the domain of f. A similar modification of (9.6.2) is used to define a *strict local minimum*.

In searching for (global) maximum and minimum points, Theorem 9.1.1 was very useful. Actually, the same result is valid for local extreme points:

At a local extreme point in the interior of the domain of a differentiable function, the derivative must be zero.

This is clear if we recall that when proving Theorem 9.1.1 we needed to consider the behaviour of the function in only a small interval about the optimal point. Once again, therefore, in order to find possible local maxima and minima of a function f defined in an interval I, we need only search among the following types of point: (i) interior points x in

---

[10] Some authors restrict the definition of local maximum/minimum points only to *interior* points of the domain of the function. According to this definition, a global maximum point that is not an interior point of the domain is not a local maximum point. To us it seems desirable that a global maximum/minimum point should always be a local maximum/minimum point as well, so we shall stick to definitions (9.6.1) and (9.6.2).

I where $f'(x) = 0$; (ii) end points of I, if included in I; and (iii) interior points x in I where $f'(x)$ does not exist.

So we have established *necessary* conditions for a function f defined in an interval I to have a local extreme point. But how do we decide whether a point satisfying the necessary conditions is a local maximum, a local minimum, or neither? In contrast to global extreme points, it does not help to calculate the function value at the different points satisfying these necessary conditions. To see why, consider again the function whose graph is given in Fig. 9.6.1. Point P_1 is a strict local maximum and Q_2 is a strict local minimum, but the function value at P_1 is *smaller* than the function value at Q_2.

The First-Derivative Test

There are two main ways of determining whether a given critical point is a local maximum, a local minimum, or neither. One of them is based on studying the sign of the first derivative about the critical point. It is an easy modification of Theorem 9.2.1.

THEOREM 9.6.1 (FIRST-DERIVATIVE TEST FOR LOCAL EXTREMA)

Consider the function $y = f(x)$, and suppose that c is a critical point of f.

(i) If $f'(x) \geq 0$ throughout some interval (a, c) to the left of c and $f'(x) \leq 0$ throughout some interval (c, b) to the right of c, then $x = c$ is a local maximum point.

(ii) If $f'(x) \leq 0$ throughout some interval (a, c) to the left of c and $f'(x) \geq 0$ throughout some interval (c, b) to the right of c, then $x = c$ is a local minimum point.

(iii) But if $f'(x) > 0$ both throughout some interval (a, c) to the left of c and throughout some interval (c, b) to the right of c, then $x = c$ is not a local extreme point for f. The same conclusion holds if $f'(x) < 0$ on both sides of c.

Only case (iii) is not already covered by Theorem 9.2.1. In fact, if $f'(x) > 0$ in (a, c) and also in (c, b), then $f(x)$ is strictly increasing in $(a, c]$ as well as in $[c, b)$. So $x = c$ cannot be a local extreme point.

EXAMPLE 9.6.1 Classify the critical points of $f(x) = \frac{1}{9}x^3 - \frac{1}{6}x^2 - \frac{2}{3}x + 1$.

Solution: As in Example 8.6.2, we have $f'(x) = \frac{1}{3}x^2 - \frac{1}{3}x - \frac{2}{3} = \frac{1}{3}(x+1)(x-2)$. Hence $x = -1$ and $x = 2$ are the critical points. The sign diagram for $f'(x)$ is shown in Fig. 9.6.2. It shows that $x = -1$ is a local maximum point whereas $x = 2$ is a local minimum point.

348   CHAPTER 9 / OPTIMIZATION

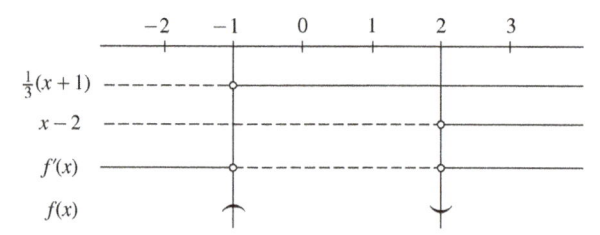

Figure 9.6.2 Sign diagram for $f'(x)$ in Example 9.6.1

EXAMPLE 9.6.2   Classify the critical points of $f(x) = x^2 e^x$.

Solution: Differentiating, we get $f'(x) = 2xe^x + x^2 e^x = xe^x(2+x)$. Then $f'(x) = 0$ for $x = 0$ and for $x = -2$. A sign diagram shows that f has a local maximum point at $x = -2$ and a local, as well as global, minimum point at $x = 0$. The graph of f is given in Fig. 9.6.3.

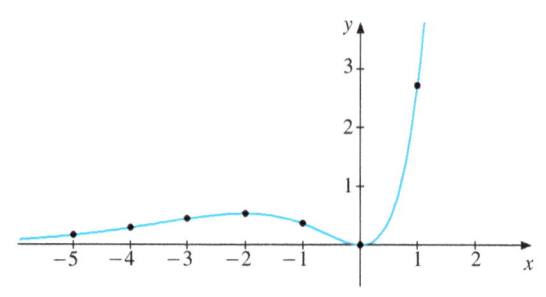

Figure 9.6.3 $f(x) = x^2 e^x$

The Second-Derivative Test

Most practical problems in economics involve a function defined by an explicit formula. Then the first-derivative test of Theorem 9.6.1 on its own will determine whether a critical point is a local maximum, a local minimum, or neither. The test requires knowing the sign of $f'(x)$ at points both to the left and to the right of the given critical point. The next test requires knowing the first two derivatives of the function, but only at the critical point itself.

THEOREM 9.6.2 (SECOND-DERIVATIVE TEST FOR LOCAL EXTREMA)

Let f be a twice differentiable function in an interval I, and let c be an interior point of I.

(i) If $f'(c) = 0$ and $f''(c) < 0$, then $x = c$ is a strict local maximum point.
(ii) If $f'(c) = 0$ and $f''(c) > 0$, then $x = c$ is a strict local minimum point.
(iii) If $f'(c) = 0$ and $f''(c) = 0$, then x could be a local maximum, a local minimum, or neither.

Proof of part (i): By definition of $f''(c)$ as the derivative of $f'(x)$ at c, one has

$$f''(c) = \lim_{h \to 0} \frac{f'(c+h) - f'(c)}{h} = \lim_{h \to 0} \frac{f'(c+h)}{h}$$

Because $f''(c) < 0$, it follows that $f'(c+h)/h < 0$ if $|h|$ is sufficiently small. In particular, if h is a small positive number, then $f'(c+h) < 0$, so f' is negative in an interval to the right of c. In the same way, we see that f' is positive in some interval to the left of c. But then c is a strict local maximum point for f.

Part (ii) can be proved in the same way.

In the inconclusive case (iii), where $f'(c) = f''(c) = 0$, "anything" can happen. Consider the three functions $f(x) = x^4$, $f(x) = -x^4$, and $f(x) = x^3$, whose graphs are shown in Figs 9.6.4 to 9.6.6. All satisfy $f'(0) = f''(0) = 0$. At $x = 0$, they have, respectively, a strict minimum, a strict maximum, and a point of inflection (recall Section 8.6). Usually, as with these three functions, the first-derivative test can be used to classify critical points at which $f'(c) = f''(c) = 0$.

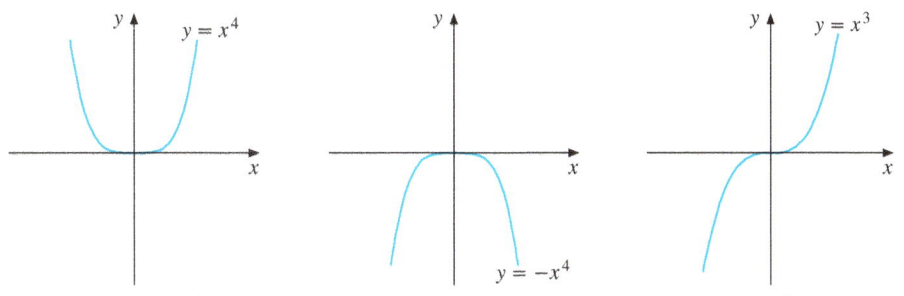

Figure 9.6.4 Strict minimum   **Figure 9.6.5** Strict maximum   **Figure 9.6.6** Inflection point

EXAMPLE 9.6.3 Use the second-derivative test to classify the critical points of $f(x) = \frac{1}{9}x^3 - \frac{1}{6}x^2 - \frac{2}{3}x + 1$.

Solution: We saw in Example 9.6.1 that

$$f'(x) = \tfrac{1}{3}x^2 - \tfrac{1}{3}x - \tfrac{2}{3} = \tfrac{1}{3}(x+1)(x-2)$$

with two critical points $x = -1$ and $x = 2$. Furthermore, $f''(x) = \frac{2}{3}x - \frac{1}{3}$, so that $f''(-1) = -1$ and $f''(2) = 1$. From Theorem 9.6.2 it follows that $x = -1$ is a local maximum point and $x = 2$ is a local minimum point. This confirms the results in Example 9.6.1.

EXAMPLE 9.6.4 Classify the critical points of $f(x) = x^2 e^x$, using the second-derivative test.

Solution: From Example 9.6.2, one has $f'(x) = 2xe^x + x^2 e^x$, with $x = 0$ and $x = -2$ as the two critical points. The second derivative of f is

$$f''(x) = 2e^x + 2xe^x + 2xe^x + x^2 e^x = e^x(2 + 4x + x^2)$$

At the two critical points we have $f''(0) = 2 > 0$ and $f''(-2) = -2e^{-2} < 0$. From Theorem 9.6.2 it follows that $x = 0$ is a strict local minimum point and $x = -2$ is a strict local maximum point. This confirms the results in Example 9.6.2.

Theorem 9.6.2 can be used to obtain a useful necessary condition for local extrema. Suppose that f is twice differentiable in the interval I and that c is an interior point of I where there is a local maximum. Then $f'(c) = 0$. Moreover, $f''(c) > 0$ is impossible, because by part (ii) in Theorem 9.6.2, this inequality would imply that c is a strict local minimum. Hence, $f''(c)$ has to be ≤ 0. In the same way, we see that $f''(c) \geq 0$ is a necessary condition for local minimum. Briefly formulated, we obtain the following second-order conditions, or SOC:

NECESSARY SECOND-ORDER CONDITIONS

If the function f is twice differentiable, then

$$\text{point } c \text{ is a local maximum point for } f \implies f''(c) \leq 0 \qquad (9.6.3)$$

$$\text{point } c \text{ is a local minimum point for } f \implies f''(c) \geq 0 \qquad (9.6.4)$$

Many results in economic analysis rely on postulating an appropriate sign for the second derivative rather than suitable variations in the sign of the first derivative.

EXAMPLE 9.6.5 Suppose that the firm in Example 9.5.1 faces a sales tax of τ dollars per unit. Then the firm's profit from producing and selling Q units is given by $\pi(Q) = R(Q) - C(Q) - \tau Q$. In order to maximize profits at some quantity Q^* satisfying $0 < Q^* < \bar{Q}$, one must have $\pi'(Q^*) = 0$. Hence,

$$R'(Q^*) - C'(Q^*) - \tau = 0 \qquad (*)$$

Suppose $R''(Q^*) < 0$ and $C''(Q^*) > 0$. Equation $(*)$ implicitly defines Q^* as a differentiable function of τ. Find an expression for $dQ^*/d\tau$ and discuss its sign. Also compute the derivative w.r.t. τ of the optimal value $\pi(Q^*)$ of the profit function, and show that $d\pi(Q^*)/d\tau = -Q^*$.

Solution: Differentiating $(*)$ with respect to τ yields

$$R''(Q^*)\frac{dQ^*}{d\tau} - C''(Q^*)\frac{dQ^*}{d\tau} - 1 = 0$$

Solving for $dQ^*/d\tau$ gives

$$\frac{dQ^*}{d\tau} = \frac{1}{R''(Q^*) - C''(Q^*)} \qquad (**)$$

The sign assumptions on R'' and C'' imply that $dQ^*/d\tau < 0$. Thus, the optimal number of units produced will decline if the tax rate τ increases.

The optimal value of the profit function is $\pi(Q^*) = R(Q^*) - C(Q^*) - \tau Q^*$. Taking into account the dependence of Q^* on τ, we get

$$\frac{d\pi(Q^*)}{d\tau} = R'(Q^*)\frac{dQ^*}{d\tau} - C'(Q^*)\frac{dQ^*}{d\tau} - Q^* - \tau\frac{dQ^*}{d\tau}$$

$$= \left[R'(Q^*) - C'(Q^*) - \tau\right]\frac{dQ^*}{d\tau} - Q^*$$

$$= -Q^* \quad \text{because of the FOC } (*)$$

SECTION 9.6 / LOCAL EXTREME POINTS 351

This is an instance of the "envelope theorem", which will be discussed in Section 18.7. For each 1¢ increase in the sales tax, profit decreases by approximately Q^* cents, where Q^* is the number of units produced at the optimum.

EXERCISES FOR SECTION 9.6

1. Consider the function f defined for all x by $f(x) = x^3 - 12x$. Find the critical points of f, and classify them by using both the first- and second-derivative tests.

SM 2. Determine possible local extreme points and values for the following functions:

(a) $f(x) = -2x - 1$ (b) $f(x) = x^3 - 3x + 8$ (c) $f(x) = x + \dfrac{1}{x}$

(d) $f(x) = x^5 - 5x^3$ (e) $f(x) = \frac{1}{2}x^2 - 3x + 5$ (f) $f(x) = x^3 + 3x^2 - 2$

SM 3. Let function f be given by the formula $f(x) = (1 + 2/x)\sqrt{x+6}$.

(a) Find the domain of f and the intervals where $f(x)$ is positive.

(b) Find possible local extreme points.

(c) Examine $f(x)$ as $x \to 0^-$, $x \to 0^+$, and $x \to \infty$. Also determine the limit of $f'(x)$ as $x \to \infty$. Does f have a maximum or a minimum in the domain?

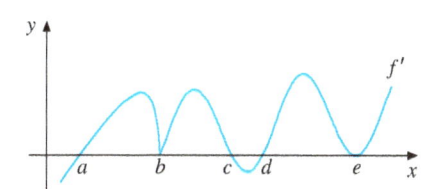

Figure 9.6.7 Exercise 4

4. Figure 9.6.7 graphs the *derivative* $y = f'(x)$ of a function f. Which of the points a, b, c, d, and e are: (i) strict local maximum points for f; (ii) strict local minimum points for f; (iii) neither?

5. Let $f(x) = x^3 + ax^2 + bx + c$. What requirements must be imposed on the constants a, b, and c in order that f will have:

(a) a local minimum at $x = 0$?   (b) critical points at $x = 1$ and $x = 3$?

6. Find the local extreme points of the functions:

(a) $f(x) = x^3 e^x$ (b) $g(x) = x^2 2^x$

SM 7. [HARDER] Find the local extreme points of $f(x) = x^3 + ax + b$. Use the answer to show that the equation $f(x) = 0$ has three different real roots if and only if $4a^3 + 27b^2 < 0$.

REVIEW EXERCISES

1. Let $f(x) = \dfrac{x^2}{x^2 + 2}$.

   (a) Compute $f'(x)$ and determine where $f(x)$ is increasing/decreasing.

   (b) Find possible inflection points.

   (c) Determine the limit of $f(x)$ as $x \to \pm\infty$, and sketch the graph of $f(x)$.

2. A firm's production function is $Q(L) = 12L^2 - \frac{1}{20}L^3$, where L denotes the number of workers, with $L \in [0, 200]$.

   (a) What size of the work force maximizes output $Q(L)$?

   (b) Let L^* denote the size of the work force that maximizes output per worker, $Q(L)/L$. Find L^* and note that $Q'(L^*) = Q(L^*)/L^*$. Is this a coincidence?

3. A farmer has one thousand metres of fence wire with which to make a rectangular enclosure, as in Exercise 4.6.7. But one side of this farmer's enclosure will border a straight canal bank, where no fencing is needed. What dimensions maximize the area of this farmer's enclosure?

4. By producing and selling Q units of some commodity, a firm earns a total revenue of $R(Q) = -0.0016Q^2 + 44Q$ and incurs a cost of $C(Q) = 0.0004Q^2 + 8Q + 64\,000$.

   (a) What production level maximizes profits?

   (b) Show that $\text{El}_Q\, C(Q) \approx 0.12$ for $Q = 1000$. Interpret this result.

5. The unit price P obtained by a firm in producing and selling $Q \geq 0$ units is $P(Q) = a - bQ^2$. The cost of producing and selling Q units is $C(Q) = \alpha + \beta Q$. The constants a, b, α, and β are all positive. Find the level of production that maximizes profits.

6. A competitive firm receives a price p for each unit of its output, and pays a price w for each unit of its only variable input. It also incurs set up costs of F. Its output from using x units of variable input is $f(x) = \sqrt{x}$.

   (a) Determine the firm's revenue, cost, and profit as functions of x.

   (b) Write out the first-order condition for profit maximization, and give it an economic interpretation. Check whether profit really is maximized at a point satisfying the first-order condition.

7. Let $g(x) = x - 2\ln(x + 1)$.

   (a) Where is the function g defined?

   (b) Find $g'(x)$ and $g''(x)$.

   (c) Find possible extreme points and inflection points of g, then sketch its graph.

8. Let $f(x) = \ln(x + 1) - x + \frac{1}{2}x^2 - \frac{1}{6}x^3$.

   (a) Find the domain of the function f and prove that $f'(x) = \dfrac{x^2 - x^3}{2(x + 1)}$ for all x in the domain.

   (b) Find possible extreme points and inflection points.

   (c) Check that $f(x)$ as $x \to (-1)^+$, then sketch the graph of f on the interval $(-1, 2]$.

SM 9. Consider the function defined, for all x, by $h(x) = e^x/(2 + e^{2x})$.

(a) Where is h increasing/decreasing? Find possible maximum and minimum points for h.

(b) If one restricts the domain of h to $(-\infty, 0]$, it has an inverse. Why? Find an expression for such inverse function.

10. Let $f(x) = (e^{2x} + 4e^{-x})^2$.

(a) Find $f'(x)$ and $f''(x)$.

(b) Determine where f is increasing/decreasing, and show that f is convex.

(c) Find possible global extreme points for f.

SM 11. [HARDER] Suppose that $a > 0$, and consider the function $f(x) = \dfrac{x}{\sqrt[3]{x^2 - a}}$.

(a) Find the domain D_f of f and the intervals where $f(x)$ is positive. Show that the graph of f is symmetric about the origin.

(b) Where is f increasing and where is it decreasing? Find possible local extreme points.

(c) Find possible inflection points for f.

SM 12. [HARDER] Classify the critical points of $f(x) = \dfrac{6x^3}{x^4 + x^2 + 2}$ by using the first-derivative test. Sketch the graph of f.

10 INTEGRATION

Is it right I ask; is it even prudence; to bore thyself and bore the students?
—Mephistopheles to Faust[1]

The main topic of Chapters 6 and 7 was differentiation, which can be directly applied to many interesting economic problems. Economists, however, especially when doing statistics, often face the mathematical problem of finding a function from information about its derivative. Reconstructing a function from its derivative can be regarded as the "inverse" of differentiation. Mathematicians call this process *integration*.

There are simple formulas that have been known since ancient times for calculating the area of any triangle, and so of any polygon that, by definition, is entirely bounded by straight lines and so can be split up into triangles that intersect only at their edges. Some 4000 years ago, however, the Babylonians became concerned with accurately measuring the area of plane surfaces, like circles, that are not bounded by straight lines. Finding this kind of area is intimately related to calculating an integral.

Apart from providing an introduction to integration, this chapter will also discuss some important applications of integrals that economists are expected to know. Their application to differential equations is discussed in the latter part of the next chapter, which is devoted to some simple dynamic models.

10.1 Indefinite Integrals

Suppose we do not know the function F, but we do know that its derivative is x^2, so that $F'(x) = x^2$. What is F? Since the derivative of x^3 is $3x^2$, we see that $\frac{1}{3}x^3$ has x^2 as its derivative. But so does $\frac{1}{3}x^3 + C$ where C is an arbitrary constant, since additive constants disappear with differentiation.

In fact, let $G(x)$ denote an arbitrary function having x^2 as its derivative. Then the derivative of $G(x) - \frac{1}{3}x^3$ is equal to 0 for all x. By (6.3.3), however, a function that has derivative

---

[1] In Johann Wolfgang von Goethe's *Faust*.

equal to 0 for all x must be constant. This shows that

$$F'(x) = x^2 \iff F(x) = \tfrac{1}{3}x^3 + C, \quad \text{where } C \text{ is an arbitrary constant}$$

EXAMPLE 10.1.1 Assume that the marginal cost function of a firm is $C'(Q) = 2Q^2 + 2Q + 5$, and that the fixed costs are 100. Find the cost function $C(Q)$.

Solution: Consider separately each of the three terms in the expression for $C'(Q)$. We realize that the cost function must have the form $C(Q) = \tfrac{2}{3}Q^3 + Q^2 + 5Q + c$, because differentiating this function gives us precisely $2Q^2 + 2Q + 5$. But the fixed costs are 100, which means that $C(0) = 100$. Inserting $Q = 0$ into the proposed formula for $C(Q)$ yields $c = 100$. Hence, the required cost function must be $C(Q) = \tfrac{2}{3}Q^3 + Q^2 + 5x + 100$.

Suppose $f(x)$ and $F(x)$ are two functions of x having the property that $f(x) = F'(x)$ for all x in some interval I. We pass from F to f by taking the derivative, so the reverse process of passing from f to F could appropriately be called taking the *antiderivative*. But following usual mathematical practice, we call F an *indefinite integral* of f over the interval I, and denote it by $\int f(x)\,dx$. If two functions have the same derivative throughout an interval, the derivative of their difference is zero, so this difference must be a constant. Hence:

THE INDEFINITE INTEGRAL

If $F'(x) = f(x)$, then

$$\int f(x)\,dx = F(x) + C \quad \text{where } C \text{ is an arbitrary constant} \qquad (10.1.1)$$

For instance, the solution to Example 10.1.1 implies that

$$\int (2x^2 + 2x + 5)\,dx = \tfrac{2}{3}x^3 + x^2 + 5x + C$$

The symbol $\int$ is the *integral sign*, and the function $f(x)$ appearing in (10.1.1) is the *integrand*. We use the notation dx to indicate that x is the *variable of integration*. Finally, C is a *constant of integration*. We read (10.1.1) this way: The indefinite integral of $f(x)$ w.r.t. x is $F(x)$ plus a constant. We call it an *indefinite* integral because $F(x) + C$ is not to be regarded as one definite function, but as a whole class of functions, all having the same derivative f.

Differentiating each side of (10.1.1) shows directly that

$$\frac{d}{dx}\int f(x)\,dx = f(x) \qquad (10.1.2)$$

That is, the derivative of an indefinite integral equals the integrand. Also, (10.1.1) can obviously be rewritten as

$$\int F'(x)\,dx = F(x) + C \qquad (10.1.3)$$

In this sense *integration and differentiation cancel each other out*.

Some Important Integrals

There are some important integration formulas which follow immediately from the corresponding rules for differentiation. Let a be a fixed number, different from -1. Because the derivative of $x^{a+1}/(a+1)$ is x^a, one has

---
INTEGRAL OF A POWER FUNCTION

If $a \neq -1$, then
$$\int x^a \, dx = \frac{1}{a+1} x^{a+1} + C \qquad (10.1.4)$$

This very important result states that the indefinite integral of any power of x, except x^{-1}, is obtained by increasing the exponent of x by 1, then dividing by the new exponent, before finally adding a constant of integration. Here are three prominent examples.

EXAMPLE 10.1.2 Applying Eq. (10.1.4) directly,

(a) $\int x \, dx = \int x^1 \, dx = \frac{1}{1+1} x^{1+1} + C = \frac{1}{2} x^2 + C$

(b) $\int \frac{1}{x^3} \, dx = \int x^{-3} \, dx = \frac{1}{-3+1} x^{-3+1} + C = -\frac{1}{2x^2} + C$

(c) $\int \sqrt{x} \, dx = \int x^{1/2} \, dx = \frac{1}{\frac{1}{2}+1} x^{\frac{1}{2}+1} + C = \frac{2}{3} x^{3/2} + C$

In case $a = -1$ formula in (10.1.4) is not valid because its right-hand side involves division by zero, which is meaningless. In this case the integrand is $1/x$, so the problem is to find a function which has $1/x$ as its derivative. Now $F(x) = \ln x$ has this property, but it is only defined for $x > 0$. Note, however, that $\ln(-x)$ is defined for $x < 0$. Moreover, according to the chain rule, its derivative is $[1/(-x)](-1) = 1/x$. Recall too that $|x| = x$ when $x \geq 0$ and $|x| = -x$ when $x < 0$. Thus, whether $x > 0$ or $x < 0$, we have:

INTEGRAL OF 1/X

$$\int \frac{1}{x} \, dx = \ln |x| + C \qquad (10.1.5)$$

Consider next the exponential function. The derivative of e^x is e^x. Thus $\int e^x \, dx = e^x + C$. More generally, since the derivative of $(1/a)e^{ax}$ is e^{ax}, we have:

INTEGRAL OF THE EXPONENTIAL FUNCTION

If $a \neq 0$, then

$$\int e^{ax}\,dx = \frac{1}{a}e^{ax} + C \tag{10.1.6}$$

For $a > 0$ we can write $a^x = e^{(\ln a)x}$. So, provided that $\ln a \neq 0$ because $a \neq 1$, we can replace a in (10.1.6) by $\ln a$ to obtain:

INTEGRAL OF AN ARBITRARY EXPONENTIAL

When $a > 0$ and $a \neq 1$,

$$\int a^x\,dx = \frac{1}{\ln a}a^x + C \tag{10.1.7}$$

Formulas (10.1.4)–(10.1.7) are examples of how knowing the derivative of a function given by a formula automatically gives us a corresponding indefinite integral. Indeed, suppose it were possible to construct a complete table with every function that we knew how to differentiate in the first column, and the corresponding derivative in the second column. For example, next to the entry $y = x^2 e^x$ in the first column would be $y' = 2xe^x + x^2 e^x$ in the second column. Because integration is the reverse of differentiation, we infer the corresponding integral $\int (2xe^x + x^2 e^x)\,dx = x^2 e^x + C$ for a constant C.

Even after this superhuman effort, you would look in vain for e^{-x^2} in the second column of this table. The reason is that there is no "elementary" function that has e^{-x^2} as its derivative. Indeed, the integral of e^{-x^2} is used in the definition of a new very special "error function" that plays a prominent role in statistics because of its relationship to the "normal distribution" discussed in Exercises 4.9.3 and 10.7.12. There are innumerable such "impossible integrals". A list of only very few is given in (10.3.9).

Using the proper rules systematically allows us to *differentiate* very complicated functions. On the other hand, finding the indefinite integral of even quite simple functions can be very difficult, or even impossible. Where it is possible, mathematicians have developed a number of *integration methods* to help in the task. Some of these methods will be explained in the rest of this chapter.

It is usually quite easy, however, to check whether a proposed indefinite integral is correct. We simply differentiate it to see if its derivative really is equal to the integrand.

EXAMPLE 10.1.3   Verify that, for $x > 0$, one has $\int \ln x\,dx = x \ln x - x + C$.

Solution: We put $F(x) = x \ln x - x + C$. Differentiating gives

$$F'(x) = 1 \cdot \ln x + x \cdot \frac{1}{x} - 1 = \ln x + 1 - 1 = \ln x$$

This shows that the integral formula is correct.

Some General Rules

The two differentiation rules (6.6.3) and (6.7.3) immediately imply that $(aF(x))' = aF'(x)$ and that $(F(x) + G(x))' = F'(x) + G'(x)$. These equalities give us the following:

BASIC INTEGRATION RULES

$$\int af(x)\,dx = a \int f(x)\,dx \quad \text{whenever } a \text{ is a constant} \tag{10.1.8}$$

$$\int [f(x) + g(x)]\,dx = \int f(x)\,dx + \int g(x)\,dx \tag{10.1.9}$$

Rule (10.1.8) says that a constant factor can be moved outside the integral, while rule (10.1.9) shows that the integral of a sum is the sum of the integrals. Repeated use of these two rules yields:

$$\int [a_1 f_1(x) + \cdots + a_n f_n(x)]\,dx = a_1 \int f_1(x)\,dx + \cdots + a_n \int f_n(x)\,dx \tag{10.1.10}$$

EXAMPLE 10.1.4 Use (10.1.10) to evaluate:

(a) $\int (3x^4 + 5x^2 + 2)\,dx$ \qquad (b) $\int \left(\dfrac{3}{x} - 8e^{-4x}\right) dx$

Solution:

(a) As well as (10.1.10), we invoke (10.1.4) to obtain

$$\int (3x^4 + 5x^2 + 2)\,dx = 3 \int x^4\,dx + 5 \int x^2\,dx + 2 \int 1\,dx$$

$$= 3\left(\frac{1}{5}x^5 + C_1\right) + 5\left(\frac{1}{3}x^3 + C_2\right) + 2(x + C_3)$$

$$= \frac{3}{5}x^5 + \frac{5}{3}x^3 + 2x + 3C_1 + 5C_2 + 2C_3$$

$$= \frac{3}{5}x^5 + \frac{5}{3}x^3 + 2x + C$$

Because C_1, C_2, and C_3 are arbitrary constants, $3C_1 + 5C_2 + 2C_3$ is also an arbitrary constant. So in the last line we have replaced it by just one constant C. In future examples of this kind, we will usually drop the middle two of the four equalities.

(b) $\int \left(3/x - 8e^{-4x}\right) dx = 3 \int (1/x)\,dx + (-8) \int e^{-4x}\,dx = 3\ln|x| + 2e^{-4x} + C$

So far, we have always used x as the variable of integration. In applications, the variables often have other labels, but this makes no difference to the rules of integration.

EXAMPLE 10.1.5 Evaluate (where in (d) n is any natural number):

(a) $\int (B/r^{2.5})\,dr$ (b) $\int (a + bs + cs^2)\,ds$ (c) $\int (1+t)^3\,dt$ (d) $\int (1+t)^n\,dt$

Solution:

(a) Write $B/r^{2.5}$ as $Br^{-2.5}$. By formula (10.1.4) with $n = -2.5$ and r replacing x, one has

$$\int \frac{B}{r^{2.5}}\,dr = B\int r^{-2.5}\,dr = B\frac{1}{-2.5+1}r^{-2.5+1} + C = -\frac{B}{1.5r^{1.5}} + C$$

(b) $\int (a + bs + cs^2)\,ds = as + \frac{1}{2}bs^2 + \frac{1}{3}cs^3 + C$

(c) $\int (1+t)^3\,dt = \int (1 + 3t + 3t^2 + t^3)\,dt = t + \frac{3}{2}t^2 + t^3 + \frac{1}{4}t^4 + C$. Note here that, because $(1+t)^4 = 1 + 4t + 6t^2 + 4t^3 + t^4$, this answer can be written as $\frac{1}{4}(1+t)^4 + C'$ for a different constant C'.

(d) Inspired by the answer to (c), and the fact that $\int y^n\,dy = y^{n+1}/(n+1) + C$, one might guess that $\int (1+t)^n\,dt = (1+t)^{n+1}/(n+1) + C$. This is easily confirmed by direct differentiation. Alternatively, integrate by substitution, as Section 10.6 explains.

EXERCISES FOR SECTION 10.1

1. Find the following integrals by using formula (10.1.4):

(a) $\int x^{13}\,dx$ (b) $\int x\sqrt{x}\,dx$ (c) $\int \frac{1}{\sqrt{x}}\,dx$ (d) $\int \sqrt{x\sqrt{x\sqrt{x}}}\,dx$

(e) $\int e^{-x}\,dx$ (f) $\int e^{x/4}\,dx$ (g) $\int 3e^{-2x}\,dx$ (h) $\int 2^x\,dx$

2. In the manufacture of a product, the marginal cost of producing x units is $C'(x)$ and fixed costs are $C(0)$. Find the total cost function $C(x)$ when:

(a) $C'(x) = 3x + 4$ and $C(0) = 40$ (b) $C'(x) = ax + b$ and $C(0) = C_0$

SM 3. Find the following integrals:

(a) $\int (x^3 + 2x - 3)\,dx$ (b) $\int (x-1)^2\,dx$ (c) $\int (x-1)(x+2)\,dx$

(d) $\int (x+2)^3\,dx$ (e) $\int (e^{3x} - e^{2x} + e^x)\,dx$ (f) $\int \frac{x^3 - 3x + 4}{x}\,dx$

SM 4. Find the following integrals:

(a) $\int \frac{(y-2)^2}{\sqrt{y}}\,dy$ (b) $\int \frac{x^3}{x+1}\,dx$ (c) $\int x(1+x^2)^{15}\,dx$

(*Hints*: In part (a), first expand $(y-2)^2$, and then divide each term by $\sqrt{y}$. In part (b), use polynomial division as in Section 4.7. In part (c), what is the derivative of $(1+x^2)^{16}$?)

5. Show that

(a) $\int x^2 \ln x\,dx = \frac{1}{3}x^3 \ln x - \frac{1}{9}x^3 + C$

(b) $\int \sqrt{x^2+1}\,dx = \frac{1}{2}x\sqrt{x^2+1} + \frac{1}{2}\ln\left(x + \sqrt{x^2+1}\right) + C$

6. Suppose that the *derivative* $f'(x)$ of f has the graph given in Fig. 10.1.1.

   (a) Suggest a quadratic formula for $f'(x)$.

   (b) Find an explicit function $f(x)$ satisfying $f(0) = 2$ which has this derivative.

   (c) Sketch the graph of $f(x)$.

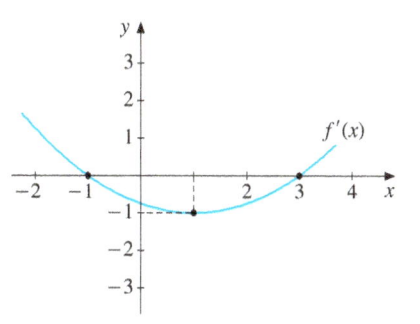

Figure 10.1.1 Exercise 6

Figure 10.1.2 Exercise 7

7. Suppose that $f(0) = 0$ and that the *derivative* $f'(x)$ of f has the graph shown in Fig. 10.1.2. Sketch the graph of $f(x)$ and find an explicit function $f(x)$ which has this graph.

8. Prove that $\displaystyle\int 2x \ln(x^2 + a^2)\, dx = (x^2 + a^2) \ln(x^2 + a^2) - x^2 + C$.

9. Provided $a \neq 0$ and $p \neq -1$, show that $\displaystyle\int (ax + b)^p\, dx = \frac{1}{a(p+1)}(ax + b)^{p+1} + C$.

10. Use the answer to Exercise 9 to evaluate the following integrals:

    (a) $\displaystyle\int (2x + 1)^4\, dx$ (b) $\displaystyle\int \sqrt{x + 2}\, dx$ (c) $\displaystyle\int \frac{1}{\sqrt{4 - x}}\, dx$

11. Find $F(x)$ if:

    (a) $F'(x) = \frac{1}{2}e^x - 2x$ and $F(0) = \frac{1}{2}$ (b) $F'(x) = x(1 - x^2)$ and $F(1) = \frac{5}{12}$

12. Find the general form of a function f whose second derivative is x^2. If we require in addition that $f(0) = 1$ and $f'(0) = -1$, what is $f(x)$?

SM 13. Suppose that $f''(x) = x^{-2} + x^3 + 2$ for $x > 0$, and $f(1) = 0$, $f'(1) = 1/4$. Find $f(x)$.

10.2 Area and Definite Integrals

This section will show how the concept of the integral can be used to calculate the area of many plane regions. This problem has been important for over 4000 years. Like all major rivers, the Tigris and Euphrates in ancient Mesopotamia and the Nile in Egypt would occasionally change course as a result of severe floods. Some farmers would gain new land from the river, while others would lose land. Since taxes were often assessed on land area, it became necessary to re-calculate the area of a parcel of land whose boundary might be an irregularly shaped river bank.

Around the year 360 BCE, the Greek mathematician Eudoxos developed a general *method of exhaustion* for determining the areas of irregularly shaped plane regions. The idea was to exhaust the area by inscribing within it an expanding sequence of polygonal regions, each of which has an area that can be calculated exactly by summing the areas of a finite collection of triangles. Provided that in the limit this sequence does indeed "exhaust" the area by including every point, we can define the *area* of the region as the limit of the increasing sequence of areas of the inscribed polygons. Moreover, one can bound the error of any finite approximation by circumscribing the region within a decreasing sequence of polygonal regions, whose intersection is the region itself.

Eudoxos and Archimedes, amongst others, used the method of exhaustion in order to determine quite accurate approximations to the areas of a number of specific plane regions, especially for a circular disk, as considered in Example 7.11.1. The method was able to provide exact answers, however, only for a limited number of special cases, largely because of the algebraic problems encountered. Nearly 1900 years passed after Eudoxos before an exact method could be devised, combining what we now call integration with the new differential calculus due to Newton and Leibniz. Besides allowing areas to be measured with complete accuracy, their ideas have many other applications. Demonstrating the precise logical relationship between differentiation and integration is one of the main achievements of mathematical analysis. It has even been argued that this discovery is the single most important in all of science.

The problem to be considered and solved in this section is illustrated in Fig. 10.2.1: *How do we compute the area A under the graph of a continuous and nonnegative function f over the interval [a, b]?*

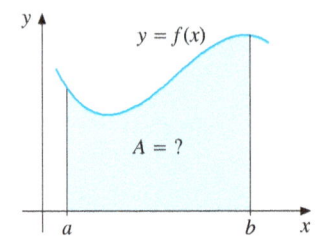

Figure 10.2.1 Area under the graph

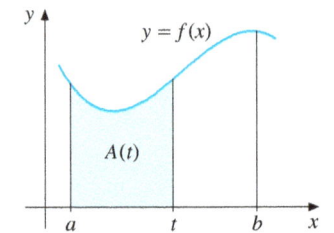

Figure 10.2.2 Area over $[a, t]$

Let t be an arbitrary point in $[a, b]$, and let $A(t)$ denote the area under the curve $y = f(x)$ over the interval $[a, t]$, as shown in Fig. 10.2.2. Clearly $A(a) = 0$ because the area collapses to zero when $t = a$. On the other hand, the area in Fig. 10.2.1 is $A = A(b)$. It is obvious from Fig. 10.2.2 that, because f is always positive, $A(t)$ increases as t increases. Suppose we increase t by a positive amount Δt. Then $A(t + \Delta t)$ is the area under the curve $y = f(x)$ over the interval $[a, t + \Delta t]$. Hence, the difference $A(t + \Delta t) - A(t)$ is the area ΔA under the curve over the interval $[t, t + \Delta t]$, as shown in Fig. 10.2.3.

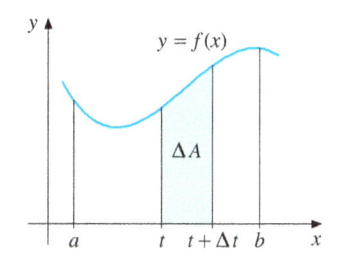

Figure 10.2.3 Change in area, ΔA

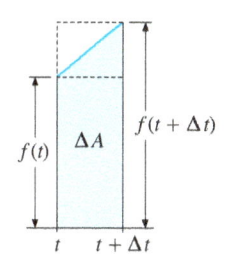

Figure 10.2.4 Approximating ΔA

In Fig. 10.2.4, the area ΔA has been magnified. It cannot be larger than the area of the rectangle with base Δt and height $f(t + \Delta t)$, nor smaller than the area of the rectangle with base Δt and height $f(t)$. Hence, for all $\Delta t > 0$, one has

$$f(t)\Delta t \leq A(t + \Delta t) - A(t) \leq f(t + \Delta t)\Delta t \qquad (*)$$

Because $\Delta t > 0$, this implies that

$$f(t) \leq \frac{A(t + \Delta t) - A(t)}{\Delta t} \leq f(t + \Delta t) \qquad (**)$$

Let us consider what happens to $(**)$ as $\Delta t \to 0$. The interval $[t, t + \Delta t]$ shrinks to the single point t. Because we are assuming that f is continuous, the function value $f(t + \Delta t)$ approaches $f(t)$. So the quotient $[A(t + \Delta t) - A(t)]/\Delta t$ is squeezed between $f(t)$ and a quantity $f(t + \Delta t)$ that tends to $f(t)$. This quotient must therefore tend to $f(t)$ in the limit as $\Delta t \to 0$.

Now notice that $[A(t + \Delta t) - A(t)]/\Delta t$ is the Newton quotient of the function $A(t)$, which measures the area under the graph of f over the interval $[a, t]$. This leads us to the remarkable conclusion that the function $A(t)$ is differentiable, with derivative given by

$$A'(t) = f(t), \text{ for all } t \text{ in } (a, b) \qquad (***)$$

This proves that:

The derivative of the area function $A(t)$ is the curve's "height function" $f(t)$, so the area function is one of the indefinite integrals of $f(t)$.[2]

Let us now use x as the free variable, and suppose that $F(x)$ is an arbitrary indefinite integral of $f(x)$. Then $F'(x) = f(x)$, and so $A'(x) - F'(x) = 0$ for x in (a, b). The equivalence

---

[2] The function f in Figs 10.2.3 and 10.2.4 happens to be increasing in the interval $[t, t + \Delta t]$. It is easy to see that the same conclusion is obtained whenever the function f is continuous on the closed interval $[t, t + \Delta t]$. On the left-hand side of $(*)$, just replace $f(t)$ by $f(c)$, where c is a minimum point of the continuous function f in the interval; and on the right-hand side, replace $f(t + \Delta t)$ by $f(d)$, where d is a maximum point of f in $[t, t + \Delta t]$. By continuity, both $f(c)$ and $f(d)$ must tend to $f(t)$ as $\Delta t \to 0$. So $(***)$ holds also for general continuous functions f.

(6.3.3) in Chapter 6 then shows that $A(x) = F(x) + C$ for some constant C. Recall that $A(a) = 0$. Hence, $0 = A(a) = F(a) + C$, so $C = -F(a)$. Therefore,

$$A(x) = F(x) - F(a), \quad \text{where} \quad F(x) = \int f(x)\,dx \qquad (10.2.1)$$

Note that this argument works for any arbitrary indefinite integral F of f. So if we have any other indefinite integral G of f, then $A(x)$ also equals $G(x) - G(a)$.

EXAMPLE 10.2.1   Calculate the area under the parabola $f(x) = x^2$ over the interval $[0, 1]$.

Solution: The area in question is the shaded region in Fig. 10.2.5. The area is equal to $A = F(1) - F(0)$ where $F(x)$ is any indefinite integral of x^2. But $\int x^2\,dx = \frac{1}{3}x^3 + C$, so we can choose $F(x) = \frac{1}{3}x^3$. So the required area is

$$A = F(1) - F(0) = \tfrac{1}{3} \cdot 1^3 - \tfrac{1}{3} \cdot 0^3 = \tfrac{1}{3}$$

Figure 10.2.5 suggests that this answer is reasonable, because the shaded region appears to have roughly 1/3 the area of the indicated square, whose sides all have length 1.

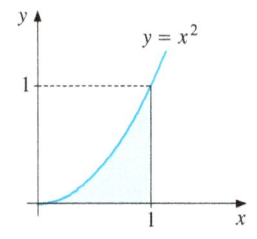

Figure 10.2.5 $y = x^2$

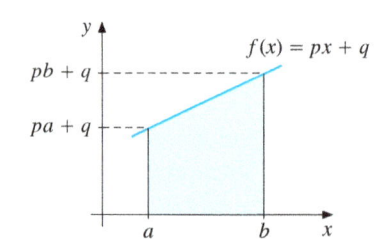

Figure 10.2.6 $y = px + q$

The argument leading to (10.2.1) is based on rather intuitive considerations. Formally, mathematicians choose to *define* the area under the graph of a continuous and nonnegative function f over the interval $[a, b]$ as the number $F(b) - F(a)$, where $F'(x) = f(x)$. The concept of area that emerges agrees with the usual concept for regions bounded by straight lines. The next example verifies this in a special case.

EXAMPLE 10.2.2   Find the area A under the straight line $f(x) = px + q$ over the interval $[a, b]$, where a, b, p, and q are all positive, with $b > a$.

Solution: The area is shown shaded in Fig. 10.2.6. It is equal to $F(b) - F(a)$ where $F(x)$ is any indefinite integral of $px + q$. But $\int (px + q)\,dx = \frac{1}{2}px^2 + qx + C$. The simplest choice of indefinite integral is $F(x) = \frac{1}{2}px^2 + qx$, which gives

$$A = F(b) - F(a) = \left(\tfrac{1}{2}pb^2 + qb\right) - \left(\tfrac{1}{2}pa^2 + qa\right) = \tfrac{1}{2}p(b^2 - a^2) + q(b - a) \qquad (*)$$

As Fig. 10.2.6 suggests, the area A is the sum of two areas. The first is that of a rectangle whose base is $b - a$ and whose height is $pa + q$. The second is that of a triangle whose base is $b - a$ and whose height is $p(b - a)$. The total area is $(b - a)(pa + q) + \tfrac{1}{2}p(b - a)^2$. This equals the answer in (*), as you should check.

The Definite Integral

Let f be a continuous function defined in the interval $[a, b]$. Suppose that the function F is continuous in $[a, b]$ and has a derivative with $F'(x) = f(x)$ for every x in (a, b). Then the difference $F(b) - F(a)$ is called the *definite integral* of f over $[a, b]$. We observed above that this difference does not depend on which of the indefinite integrals of f we choose as F. The definite integral of f over $[a, b]$ is therefore a *number* that depends only on the function f and the numbers a and b. We denote this number by

$$\int_a^b f(x)\, dx \tag{10.2.2}$$

This notation makes explicit both the integrand $f(x)$ (the function we integrate) and the interval of integration $[a, b]$. The two end points a and b are called, respectively, the *lower limit* and *upper limit* of integration.

The variable x in Eq. (10.2.2) is a *dummy variable* in the sense that it could be replaced by any other variable that does not occur elsewhere in the expression. For instance,

$$\int_a^b f(x)\, dx = \int_a^b f(y)\, dy = \int_a^b f(\xi)\, d\xi$$

are all equal to $F(b) - F(a)$. But you should never write anything like $\int_a^y f(y)\, dy$, with the same variable as both the upper limit and the dummy variable of integration. That would make it impossible to interpret y, so it would be meaningless.

The difference $F(b) - F(a)$ between the values of the indefinite integral $F(x)$ at the upper and lower limit of integration is denoted by $\Big|_a^b F(x)$, or alternatively by $[F(x)]_a^b$. Thus:

THE DEFINITE INTEGRAL

$$\int_a^b f(x)\, dx = \Big|_a^b F(x) = F(b) - F(a) \tag{10.2.3}$$

where F is any indefinite integral of f over an interval containing both a and b.

EXAMPLE 10.2.3 Evaluate the definite integrals:

(a) $\int_2^5 e^{2x}\, dx$

(b) $\int_{-2}^2 (x - x^3 - x^5)\, dx$

Solution:

(a) Since $\int e^{2x}\, dx = \frac{1}{2} e^{2x} + C$,

$$\int_2^5 e^{2x}\, dx = \Big|_2^5 \tfrac{1}{2} e^{2x} = \tfrac{1}{2} e^{10} - \tfrac{1}{2} e^4 = \tfrac{1}{2} e^4 (e^6 - 1)$$

(b) Here,

$$\int_{-2}^{2} (x - x^3 - x^5)\, dx = \Big|_{-2}^{2} \left(\tfrac{1}{2}x^2 - \tfrac{1}{4}x^4 - \tfrac{1}{6}x^6\right) = \left(2 - 4 - \tfrac{64}{6}\right) - \left(2 - 4 - \tfrac{64}{6}\right) = 0$$

In the next subsection we explain why $f(x) = x - x^3 - x^5$ has a graph that is symmetric about the origin, and why the answer to part (b) must therefore be 0.

Definition (10.2.3) does not necessarily require $a < b$. However, if $a > b$ and $f(x)$ is positive throughout the interval $[b, a]$, then $\int_a^b f(x)\, dx$ is a negative number. Note also that (10.2.3) makes sense without necessarily interpreting the definite integral geometrically as the area under a curve. In fact, depending on the context, it can have different interpretations. For instance, if $f(r)$ is an income density function, as in Section 10.4 below, then $\int_a^b f(r)\, dr$ is the proportion of people with income between a and b.

Although the notation for definite and indefinite integrals is similar, the two integrals are entirely different. In fact, $\int_a^b f(x)\, dx$ denotes a single number, whereas $\int f(x)\, dx$ represents any one of the infinite set of related functions that all have $f(x)$ as their derivative.

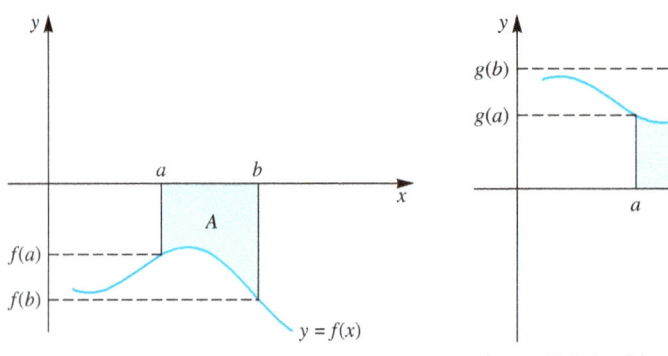

Figure 10.2.7 $f(x) \leq 0$

Figure 10.2.8 $g(x) = -f(x) \geq 0$

The Area when f(x) is Negative

If f is defined in $[a, b]$ and $f(x) \geq 0$ over $[a, b]$, then $\int_a^b f(x)\, dx$ is the area below the graph of f over $[a, b]$. But if $f(x) \leq 0$ for all x in $[a, b]$, then the graph of f, the x-axis, and the two lines $x = a$ and $x = b$ still enclose an area somewhat like that marked as area A in Fig. 10.2.7. Indeed, if we define $g(x) = -f(x)$ in $[a, b]$, then $g(x) \geq 0$, implying that $\int_a^b g(x)\, dx$ measures the area below the graph of g over $[a, b]$. By construction, however, this area equals the area A depicted in Fig. 10.2.8. It follows that the area over the graph of f and under $[a, b]$ is $\int_a^b (-f)(x)\, dx$. We have put a minus sign before the integrand because the area of a region must be nonnegative, whereas the definite integral of f is negative. Shortly, we will see from rule (10.3.3) how it is equivalent to putting the minus sign in front of the integral.

EXAMPLE 10.2.4 Figure 10.2.9 shows the graph of $f(x) = e^{x/3} - 3$. Evaluate the shaded area A between the x-axis and this graph over the interval $[0, b]$, where $b = 3\ln 3$ is chosen to satisfy $f(b) = 0$.

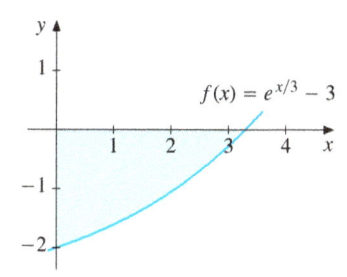

Figure 10.2.9 $e^{x/3} - 3$

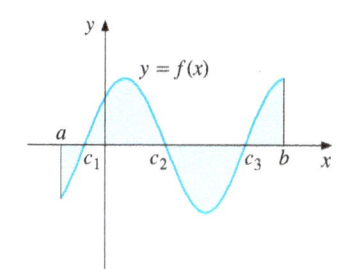

Figure 10.2.10 A function that takes positive and negative values

Solution: Because $f(x) \leq 0$ in the interval $[0, 3\ln 3]$, we obtain

$$A = -\int_0^{3\ln 3} \left(e^{x/3} - 3\right) dx = -\Big|_0^{3\ln 3} (3e^{x/3} - 3x) = -(3e^{\ln 3} - 3 \cdot 3\ln 3) + 3e^0$$
$$= -9 + 9\ln 3 + 3 = 9\ln 3 - 6 \approx 3.89$$

Is the answer reasonable? Yes, because the shaded set in Fig. 10.2.9 seems to have an area a little less than that of the triangle enclosed by the points $(0, 0)$, $(0, -2)$, and $(4, 0)$, whose area is 4. Also, its area is somewhat more than that of the inscribed triangle with vertices $(0, 0)$, $(0, -2)$, and $(3\ln 3, 0)$, whose area is $3\ln 3 \approx 3.30$.

Suppose that the function f is defined and continuous in $[a, b]$. Suppose too that, as shown in Fig. 10.2.10, it is positive in some subintervals, but negative in others because its graph crosses the x-axis at the three points c_1, c_2 and c_3. Then the definite integral $\int_a^b f(x)\, dx$ is the sum of the two shaded areas above the x-axis, minus the sum of the two shaded areas below the x-axis. On the other hand, consider the total area bounded by the graph of f, the x-axis, and the lines $x = a$ and $x = b$. To calculate this, first we must follow the previous definitions to compute in turn the positive area in each subinterval $[a, c_1]$, $[c_1, c_2]$, $[c_2, c_3]$, and $[c_3, b]$. Finally, we must add these four areas to arrive at the answer

$$-\int_a^{c_1} f(x)\, dx + \int_{c_1}^{c_2} f(x)\, dx - \int_{c_2}^{c_3} f(x)\, dx + \int_{c_3}^b f(x)\, dx$$

In fact, this illustrates a general result: the area between the graph of a function f and the x-axis is given by the definite integral $\int_a^b |f(x)|\, dx$ of the absolute value of the integrand $f(x)$, which equals the area under the graph of the nonnegative-valued function $|f(x)|$.

EXERCISES FOR SECTION 10.2

1. Compute the areas under the graphs, over $[0, 1]$, of:

(a) $f(x) = x^3$;

(b) $f(x) = x^{10}$.

2. Compute the area bounded by the graph of each of the following functions over the indicated interval. In (c), sketch the graph and indicate by shading the area in question.

   (a) $f(x) = 3x^2$, in $[0, 2]$ \hspace{2em} (b) $f(x) = x^6$, in $[0, 1]$

   (c) $f(x) = e^x$, in $[-1, 1]$ \hspace{2em} (d) $f(x) = 1/x^2$, in $[1, 10]$

3. Compute the area bounded by the graph of $f(x) = 1/x^3$, the x-axis, and the two lines $x = -2$ and $x = -1$. Make a drawing. (Hint: $f(x) < 0$ in $[-2, -1]$.)

4. Compute the area bounded by the graph of $f(x) = \frac{1}{2}(e^x + e^{-x})$, the x-axis, and the lines $x = -1$ and $x = 1$.

(SM) 5. Evaluate the following integrals:

   (a) $\int_0^1 x \, dx$ \hspace{2em} (b) $\int_1^2 (2x + x^2) \, dx$ \hspace{2em} (c) $\int_{-2}^{3} \left(\frac{1}{2}x^2 - \frac{1}{3}x^3 \right) dx$

   (d) $\int_0^2 (t^3 - t^4) \, dt$ \hspace{2em} (e) $\int_1^2 \left(2t^5 - \frac{1}{t^2} \right) dt$ \hspace{2em} (f) $\int_2^3 \left(\frac{1}{t-1} + t \right) dt$

(SM) 6. Let $f(x) = x(x-1)(x-2)$.

   (a) Calculate $f'(x)$. Where is $f(x)$ increasing?

   (b) Sketch the graph of f and calculate $\int_0^1 f(x) \, dx$.

7. The profit of a firm as a function of its output $x > 0$ is given by $f(x) = 4000 - x - \dfrac{3\,000\,000}{x}$.

   (a) Find the level of output that maximizes profit. Sketch the graph of f.

   (b) The actual output varies between 1 000 and 3 000 units. Compute the average profit

   $$I = \frac{1}{2000} \int_{1000}^{3000} f(x) \, dx$$

8. Evaluate the integrals:

   (a) $\int_1^3 \frac{3x}{10} \, dx$ \hspace{1em} (b) $\int_{-3}^{-1} \xi^2 \, d\xi$ \hspace{1em} (c) $\int_0^1 \alpha e^{\beta \tau} \, d\tau$, with $\beta \neq 0$ \hspace{1em} (d) $\int_{-2}^{-1} \frac{1}{y} \, dy$

10.3 Properties of Definite Integrals

The definition of the definite integral allows the following four properties to be derived.

PROPERTIES OF DEFINITE INTEGRALS

If f is a continuous function in an interval that contains the points a, b, and c, then:

$$\int_a^b f(x)\,dx = -\int_b^a f(x)\,dx \tag{10.3.1}$$

$$\int_a^a f(x)\,dx = 0 \tag{10.3.2}$$

$$\int_a^b \alpha f(x)\,dx = \alpha \int_a^b f(x)\,dx, \quad \text{where } \alpha \text{ is an arbitrary number} \tag{10.3.3}$$

$$\int_a^b f(x)\,dx = \int_a^c f(x)\,dx + \int_c^b f(x)\,dx \tag{10.3.4}$$

When the definite integral is interpreted as an area, (10.3.4) is the additivity property of areas, as illustrated in Fig. 10.3.1. Of course, rule (10.3.4) easily generalizes to the case when we partition the interval $[a, b]$ into an arbitrary finite number of subintervals.

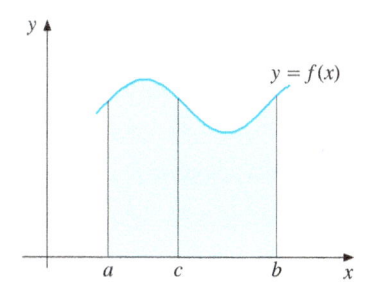

Figure 10.3.1 $\int_a^b f(x)\,dx = \int_a^c f(x)\,dx + \int_c^b f(x)\,dx$

Equations (10.3.3) and (10.3.4) are counterparts for definite integrals of, respectively, the constant multiple property (10.1.8) and the summation property (10.1.9) for indefinite integrals. In fact, if f and g are continuous in $[a, b]$, and if α and β are real numbers, then it is easy to prove that

$$\int_a^b [\alpha f(x) + \beta g(x)]\,dx = \alpha \int_a^b f(x)\,dx + \beta \int_a^b g(x)\,dx \tag{10.3.5}$$

Again, this rule can obviously be extended to more than two functions.

Differentiation with Respect to the Limits of Integration

Suppose that $F'(x) = f(x)$ for all x in an open interval (a, b). Suppose too that $a < t < b$. It follows that $\int_a^t f(x)\,dx = \big|_a^t F(x) = F(t) - F(a)$. So differentiating w.r.t. t gives

$$\frac{d}{dt} \int_a^t f(x)\,dx = F'(t) = f(t) \tag{10.3.6}$$

In words: *The derivative of the definite integral with respect to the upper limit of integration is equal to the integrand evaluated at that limit.*

Correspondingly, $\int_t^b f(x)\,dx = \big|_t^b F(x) = F(b) - F(t)$, so that

$$\frac{d}{dt} \int_t^b f(x)\,dx = -F'(t) = -f(t) \tag{10.3.7}$$

In words: *The derivative of the definite integral with respect to the lower limit of integration is equal to minus the integrand evaluated at that limit.*

These results are not surprising: Suppose that $f(x) \geq 0$ and $t < b$. We can interpret $\int_t^b f(x)\,dx$ as the area below the graph of f over the interval $[t, b]$. Then the interval shrinks as t increases, and the area will decrease at a rate given by the value of the integrand at the lower limit.

The results in (10.3.6) and (10.3.7) can be generalized. In fact, if $a(t)$ and $b(t)$ are differentiable and $f(x)$ is continuous, then

$$\frac{d}{dt} \int_{a(t)}^{b(t)} f(x)\,dx = f(b(t))b'(t) - f(a(t))a'(t) \tag{10.3.8}$$

To prove this formula, suppose F is an indefinite integral of f, so that $F'(x) = f(x)$. Then $\int_u^v f(x)\,dx = F(v) - F(u)$, so in particular,

$$\int_{a(t)}^{b(t)} f(x)\,dx = F(b(t)) - F(a(t))$$

Using the chain rule to differentiate the right-hand side of this equation w.r.t. t, we obtain $F'(b(t))b'(t) - F'(a(t))a'(t)$. But $F'(b(t)) = f(b(t))$ and $F'(a(t)) = f(a(t))$, so (10.3.8) results.[3]

Continuous Functions are Integrable

Suppose $f(x)$ is a continuous function in $[a, b]$. So far we have defined $\int_a^b f(x)\,dx$ as the number $F(b) - F(a)$, where $F(x)$ is any antiderivative function whose derivative is $f(x)$. In some cases, we are able to find an explicit expression for $F(x)$. But this is not always the case. Consider, for example, the standard normal density function in statistics. It is the

---

[3] Formula (10.3.8) is an important special case of Leibniz's formula discussed in Section 4.2 of FMEA.

positive valued function $f(x) = (1/\sqrt{2\pi})e^{-x^2/2}$, whose graph is shown in the answer to Exercise 4.9.3. It is impossible to find an explicit standard function of x whose derivative is $f(x)$. Yet $f(x)$ is continuous on any interval $[a, b]$ of the real line, so the area under the graph of f over this interval definitely exists and is equal to $\int_a^b f(x)\,dx$.

In fact, one can prove that any continuous function has an antiderivative. Here are some integrals that really are impossible to "solve", except by introducing special new functions:

$$\int e^{x^2}\,dx, \quad \int e^{-x^2}\,dx, \quad \int \frac{e^x}{x}\,dx, \quad \int \frac{1}{\ln x}\,dx, \quad \text{and} \quad \int \frac{1}{\sqrt{x^4+1}}\,dx \qquad (10.3.9)$$

The Riemann Integral

The kind of integral discussed so far, based on the antiderivative, is called the *Newton–Leibniz*, or *N–L*, *integral*. It is just one among many kinds of integral mathematicians have considered. For continuous functions, all give the same result as the N–L integral. We briefly describe the *Riemann integral* as one prominent example.[4] Its definition is closely related to the method of exhaustion that was described in Section 10.2.

Let f be a function which is defined and *bounded* in the interval $[a, b]$. For any fixed natural number n, we subdivide $[a, b]$ into n parts by choosing points $a = x_0 < x_1 < x_2 < \cdots < x_{n-1} < x_n = b$. We also choose an arbitrary number ξ_i in each interval $[x_i, x_{i+1}]$. Let Δx_i denote $x_{i+1} - x_i$, for $i = 0, 1, \ldots, n-1$. Then the sum

$$f(\xi_0)\,\Delta x_0 + f(\xi_1)\,\Delta x_1 + \cdots + f(\xi_{n-1})\,\Delta x_{n-1} \qquad (10.3.10)$$

of n terms is called a *Riemann sum* associated with the function f. You should draw a figure to help understand this construction.

The sum (10.3.10) obviously depends on f. But it also depends on the subdivision and on the choice of the different points ξ_i. Suppose however that, as n approaches infinity and simultaneously the largest of the numbers $\Delta x_0, \Delta x_1, \ldots, \Delta x_{n-1}$ approaches 0, the limit of the Riemann sum (10.3.10) always exists. Then f is called *Riemann integrable* (or *R integrable*) in the interval $[a, b]$. Furthermore, we define the *Riemann integral* (or *R integral*) of f over $[a, b]$ as the limit of these Riemann sums. Thus

$$\int_a^b f(x)\,dx = \lim \sum_{i=0}^{n-1} f(\xi_i)\,\Delta x_i$$

Textbooks on mathematical analysis show that this limit is independent of how the ξ_i are chosen, so the value of the R integral is well defined. They also show that every continuous function is R integrable, and that its R integral satisfies (10.2.3). The N–L and R integrals therefore coincide for continuous functions. But the R integral is defined for some (discontinuous) functions whose N–L integral does not exist.

---

[4] Introduced by German mathematician Bernhard Riemann (1826–1866).

EXERCISES FOR SECTION 10.3

1. Evaluate the following integrals:

   (a) $\int_0^5 (x + x^2)\, dx$
   (b) $\int_{-2}^2 (e^x - e^{-x})\, dx$
   (c) $\int_2^{10} \frac{1}{x-1}\, dx$
   (d) $\int_0^1 2xe^{x^2}\, dx$

   (e) $\int_{-4}^4 (x-1)^3\, dx$
   (f) $\int_1^2 (x^5 + x^{-5})\, dx$
   (g) $\int_0^4 \frac{1}{2}\sqrt{x}\, dx$
   (h) $\int_1^2 \frac{1+x^3}{x^2}\, dx$

2. If $\int_a^b f(x)\, dx = 8$ and $\int_a^c f(x)\, dx = 4$, what is $\int_c^b f(x)\, dx$?

3. If $\int_0^1 (f(x) - 2g(x))\, dx = 6$ and $\int_0^1 (2f(x) + 2g(x))\, dx = 9$, find $I = \int_0^1 (f(x) - g(x))\, dx$.

(SM) 4. Let p, q, and r be positive constants. Evaluate the integral $\int_0^1 x^p(x^q + x^r)\, dx$.

(SM) 5. Find the function $f(x)$ if $f'(x) = ax^2 + bx$, $f'(1) = 6$, $f''(1) = 18$ and $\int_0^2 f(x)\, dx = 18$.

(SM) 6. Evaluate the following integrals, assuming that all the constants in (d) are positive:

   (a) $\int_0^3 \left(\frac{1}{3}e^{3x-2} + (x+2)^{-1}\right) dx$
   (b) $\int_0^1 (x^2 + 2)^2\, dx$

   (c) $\int_0^1 \frac{x^2 + x + \sqrt{x+1}}{x+1}\, dx$
   (d) $\int_1^b \left(A\frac{x+b}{x+c} + \frac{d}{x}\right) dx$

7. Let $F(x) = \int_0^x (t^2 + 2)\, dt$ and $G(x) = \int_0^{x^2} (t^2 + 2)\, dt$. Find $F'(x)$ and $G'(x)$.

8. Define $H(t) = \int_0^{t^2} K(\tau) e^{-\rho \tau}\, d\tau$, where $K(\tau)$ is a given continuous function and ρ is a constant. Find $H'(t)$.

9. Find:

   (a) $\frac{d}{dt}\int_0^t x^2\, dx$
   (b) $\frac{d}{dt}\int_t^3 e^{-x^2}\, dx$
   (c) $\frac{d}{dt}\int_{-t}^t \frac{1}{\sqrt{x^4+1}}\, dx$
   (d) $\frac{d}{d\lambda}\int_{-\lambda}^2 (f(t) - g(t))\, dt$

10. Find the area between the two parabolas defined by the equations $y + 1 = (x-1)^2$ and $3x = y^2$. (Hint: The points of intersection have integer coordinates.)

(SM) 11. [HARDER] A theory of investment has used a function W defined for all $T > 0$ by

$$W(T) = \frac{K}{T}\int_0^T e^{-\rho t}\, dt$$

where K and ρ are positive constants. Evaluate the integral, then prove that $W(T)$ takes values in the interval $(0, K)$ and is strictly decreasing. (Hint: See Exercise 6.11.11.)

SM 12. [HARDER] Consider the function f defined, for all $x > 0$, by $f(x) = 4\ln(\sqrt{x+4} - 2)$.

(a) Show that f has an inverse function g, and find a formula for g.

(b) Draw the graphs of f and g in the same coordinate system.

(c) Give a geometric interpretation of $A = \int_5^{10} 4\ln(\sqrt{x+4} - 2)\,dx$, and explain why

$$A = 10a - \int_0^a (e^{x/2} + 4e^{x/4})\,dx$$

where $a = f(10)$. Use this equality to express A in terms of a.

10.4 Economic Applications

We motivated the definite integral as a way to find the area under a curve. Definite integrals, however, arise in many other mathematical and economic contexts. In statistics and econometrics, for example, many probability distributions such as the normal distribution are defined as the integral of a particular continuous probability density function. This section presents some other examples showing why integrals are important in economics.

Extraction from an Oil Well

Assume that at time $t = 0$ an oil producer starts extracting oil from a well that contains K barrels at that time. Let $x(t)$ denote the remaining stock of oil in the well at time t, measured as a number of barrels. In particular, $x(0) = K$. Assuming it is impractical to put oil back into the well, the function $x(t)$ is decreasing in t. Consider any time interval $[t, t+\delta]$, where $\delta > 0$. The amount of oil that is extracted during this interval is $x(t) - x(t+\delta)$, the reduction in the stock. The amount extracted per unit of time, therefore, is

$$\frac{x(t) - x(t+\delta)}{\delta} = -\frac{x(t+\delta) - x(t)}{\delta} \qquad (*)$$

If we assume that $x(t)$ is differentiable, then as $\delta \to 0$ the fraction $(*)$ tends to $-\dot{x}(t)$. If we let $u(t)$ denote the *rate of extraction* at time t, we have $\dot{x}(t) = -u(t)$, with $x(0) = K$. The solution to this equation is

$$x(t) = K - \int_0^t u(s)\,ds \qquad (**)$$

Indeed, we check $(**)$ as follows. First, setting $t = 0$ gives $x(0) = K$. Moreover, differentiating $(**)$ w.r.t. t according to rule (10.3.6) yields $\dot{x}(t) = -u(t)$.

The result $(**)$ may be interpreted as follows: The amount of oil left at time t is equal to the initial amount K, minus the total amount that has been extracted during the time interval $[0, t]$, which is $\int_0^t u(\tau)\,d\tau$.

If the rate of extraction is constant, with $u(t) = \bar{u}$, then (∗∗) yields

$$x(t) = K - \int_0^t \bar{u}\, ds = K - \Big|_0^t \bar{u} s = K - \bar{u} t$$

In particular, the well will be empty when $x(t) = 0$, or when $K - \bar{u}t = 0$, that is when $t = K/\bar{u}$. (Of course, this particular answer could have been found more directly, without recourse to integration.)

The example illustrates two concepts that it is important to distinguish in many economic arguments. The quantity $x(t)$ is a *stock*, measured in barrels. On the other hand, $u(t)$ is a *flow*, measured in barrels *per unit of time*.

Income Distribution

In many countries, data collected by income tax authorities can be used to reveal some facts regarding the income distribution within a given year, as well as how the distribution changes from year to year. Suppose we measure annual income in dollars. Let $F(r)$ denote the proportion of individuals that receive no more than r dollars in a particular year. Thus, if there are n individuals in the population, $nF(r)$ is the number of individuals with income no greater than r. If r_0 is the lowest and r_1 is the highest (registered) income in the group, we are interested in the function F defined on the interval $[r_0, r_1]$. Because r has to be a multiple of \$0.01 and $F(r)$ has to be a multiple of $1/n$, the definition of F makes it discontinuous and so not differentiable in $[r_0, r_1]$. If the population consists of a large number of individuals, however, then it is usually possible to find a "smooth" function that gives a good approximation to the true income distribution. Assume, therefore, that F is a function with a continuous derivative denoted by f, so that $f(r) = F'(r)$ for all r in (r_0, r_1). According to the definition of the derivative, for all small δ we have

$$f(r)\delta \approx F(r + \delta) - F(r)$$

Thus, $f(r)\delta$ is approximately equal to the proportion of individuals who have incomes between r and $r + \delta$. The function f is called an *income density function*, and F is the associated *cumulative distribution function*.[5]

Suppose that f is a continuous income distribution for a certain population with incomes in the interval $[r_0, r_1]$. If $r_0 \leq a \leq b \leq r_1$, then the previous discussion and the definition of the definite integral imply that $\int_a^b f(r)\,dr$ is the proportion of individuals with incomes in $[a, b]$. Thus, the *number of individuals* with incomes in $[a, b]$ is

$$N = n \int_a^b f(r)\, dr \qquad (10.4.1)$$

We will now find an expression for the combined income of all those who earn between a and b dollars. Let $M(r)$ denote the total income of those who earn no more than r dollars

---

[5] Readers who know some statistics may see the analogy with probability density functions and with cumulative (probability) distribution functions.

during the year, and consider the income interval $[r, r + \delta]$. There are approximately $nf(r)\delta$ individuals with incomes in this interval. Each of them has an income approximately equal to r, so that the total income $M(r + \delta) - M(r)$ of these individuals is approximately equal to $nrf(r)\delta$. So we have

$$\frac{M(r + \delta) - M(r)}{\delta} \approx nrf(r)$$

The approximation improves (in general) as δ decreases. By taking the limit as $\delta \to 0$, we obtain $M'(r) = nrf(r)$. Integrating over the interval from a to b gives $M(b) - M(a) = n \int_a^b rf(r)dr$. Hence, the *total income* of individuals with income in $[a, b]$ is

$$M = n \int_a^b rf(r)\,dr \tag{10.4.2}$$

The argument that leads to (10.4.2) can be made more exact: $M(r + \delta) - M(r)$ is the total income of those who have income in the interval $[r, r + \delta]$, when $\delta > 0$. In this income interval, there are $n[F(r + \delta) - F(r)]$ individuals each of whom earns at least r and at most $r + \delta$. Thus,

$$nr[F(r + \delta) - F(r)] \leq M(r + \delta) - M(r) \leq n(r + \delta)[F(r + \delta) - F(r)] \tag{$*$}$$

If $\delta > 0$, dividing by δ yields

$$nr\frac{F(r + \delta) - F(r)}{\delta} \leq \frac{M(r + \delta) - M(r)}{\delta} \leq n(r + \delta)\frac{F(r + \delta) - F(r)}{\delta} \tag{$**$}$$

On the other hand, if $\delta < 0$, then the inequalities in $(*)$ are left unchanged, whereas those in $(**)$ are reversed. Either way, letting $\delta \to 0$ gives $nrF'(r) \leq M'(r) \leq nrF'(r)$, so that $M'(r) = nrF'(r) = nrf(r)$.

Consider the group of all individuals whose incomes belonging to a specific interval $[a, b]$. The number of individuals N in this group is given by Eq. (10.4.1), and their total income M is given by Eq. (10.4.2). The income per head of this group, otherwise known as their "mean income", is the ratio M/N. Formally, then, the *mean income* of individuals with incomes in the interval $[a, b]$ is:

$$m = \frac{M}{N} = \frac{n \int_a^b rf(r)\,dr}{n \int_a^b f(r)\,dr} = \frac{\int_a^b rf(r)\,dr}{\int_a^b f(r)\,dr} \tag{10.4.3}$$

A function that approximates actual income distributions quite well, particularly for large incomes, is the *Pareto distribution* that was briefly discussed in Example 6.6.4, especially Eq. (6.6.5). For this distribution, the proportion of individuals who earn at most r dollars is given by

$$f(r) = \frac{B}{r^\beta} \tag{10.4.4}$$

Here B and β are positive constants. Empirical estimates of β are usually in the range $2.4 < \beta < 2.6$. For values of r close to 0, the formula is of no use. In fact, the integral $\int_0^a f(r)\,dr$ diverges to ∞, as will be seen using the arguments of Section 10.7.

EXAMPLE 10.4.1 Consider a population of n individuals in which the income density function for those with incomes between a and b is given by $f(r) = B/r^{2.5}$. Here $b > a > 0$, and B is positive. Determine the mean income of this group.

Solution: According to (10.4.1), the total number of individuals in this group is

$$N = n\int_a^b Br^{-2.5}\,dr = nB\left(-\tfrac{2}{3}r^{-1.5}\right)\Big|_a^b = \tfrac{2}{3}nB\left(a^{-1.5} - b^{-1.5}\right)$$

According to (10.4.2), the total income of these individuals is

$$M = n\int_a^b rBr^{-2.5}\,dr = nB\int_a^b r^{-1.5}\,dr = -2nB\,r^{-0.5}\Big|_a^b = 2nB\left(a^{-0.5} - b^{-0.5}\right)$$

So by (10.4.3), the mean income of the group is

$$m = \frac{M}{N} = \frac{2nB\left(a^{-0.5} - b^{-0.5}\right)}{\tfrac{2}{3}nB\left(a^{-1.5} - b^{-1.5}\right)} = 3\frac{a^{-0.5} - b^{-0.5}}{a^{-1.5} - b^{-1.5}}$$

Suppose that b is very large. Then $b^{-0.5}$ and $b^{-1.5}$ are both close to 0, so $m \approx 3a$. The mean income of those who earn at least a is therefore approximately $3a$.

The Influence of Income Distribution on Demand

Obviously each consumer's demand for a particular commodity depends on its price p. In addition, economists soon learn that it depends on the consumer's income r as well. Here, we consider the total demand quantity for a group of consumers whose individual demands are given by the same continuous function $D(p, r)$ of the single price p, as well as of individual income r whose distribution is given by a continuous density function $f(r)$ on the interval $[a, b]$.

Given a particular price p, let $T(r)$ denote the total demand for the commodity by all individuals whose income does not exceed r. Consider the income interval $[r, r + \delta]$, where $\delta > 0$. There are approximately $nf(r)\delta$ individuals with incomes in this interval. Because each of them demands approximately $D(p, r)$ units of the commodity, the total demand of all these individuals will be approximately $nD(p, r)f(r)\delta$. However, the actual total demand of individuals with incomes in the interval $[r, r + \delta]$ is $T(r + \delta) - T(r)$, by definition. So we must have $T(r + \delta) - T(r) \approx nD(p, r)f(r)\delta$, which implies that

$$\frac{T(r+\delta) - T(r)}{\delta} \approx nD(p, r)f(r)$$

In general, this approximation improves as δ decreases. Taking the limit as $\delta \to 0$, we obtain $T'(r) = nD(p, r)f(r)$. By definition of the definite integral, therefore, we must have

$$T(b) - T(a) = n\int_a^b D(p, r)f(r)\,dr$$

But $T(b) - T(a)$ is the total demand for the commodity by all the individuals with incomes in the interval $[a, b]$. In fact, this total demand will depend on the price p. So we denote it by $x(p)$. This implies that, as a function of p, total demand of these individuals is

$$x(p) = \int_a^b nD(p, r) f(r) \, dr \tag{10.4.5}$$

EXAMPLE 10.4.2 Suppose that the income distribution function for all individuals with incomes between a and b is as specified in Example 10.4.1. Suppose that the demand function of an individual with income r is $D(p, r) = Ap^{-1.5} r^{2.08}$. Compute the total demand function.

Solution: Using (10.4.5) gives

$$x(p) = \int_a^b nAp^{-1.5} r^{2.08} Br^{-2.5} \, dr = nABp^{-1.5} \int_a^b r^{-0.42} \, dr$$

Hence,

$$x(p) = nABp^{-1.5} \times \left. \frac{1}{0.58} r^{0.58} \right|_a^b = \frac{nAB}{0.58} p^{-1.5} (b^{0.58} - a^{0.58})$$

Consumer and Producer Surplus

Economists are interested in studying how much consumers and producers as a whole benefit (or lose) when market conditions change. A common (but conceptually questionable) measure of these benefits used by many applied economists is the total amount of consumer and producer surplus, which we are about to define.[6] The equilibrium point E in Fig. 10.4.1 occurs where the demand and supply curves cross, so demand is equal to supply. The corresponding equilibrium price P^* is the one which induces consumers to purchase (demand) precisely the same aggregate amount that producers are willing to offer (supply) at that price, as in Example 4.5.3. According to the demand curve in Fig. 10.4.1, there are consumers who are willing to pay more than P^* per unit. In fact, even if the price is almost as high as P_1, some consumers still wish to buy some units at that price. The total amount "saved" by all such consumers is called the *consumer surplus*, denoted by CS.

Consider the thin rectangle indicated in Fig. 10.4.2 whose left edge lies along the vertical line through the point labelled Q, with coordinates $(Q, 0)$. It has base ΔQ and height $f(Q)$, so its area is $f(Q) \cdot \Delta Q$. This area approximately represents the maximum additional amount that consumers as a whole are willing to pay for an extra ΔQ units, after they have already bought Q units at price $f(Q)$. For all those consumers who are willing to buy the commodity at price P^* or higher, the total amount they are willing to pay is the total area below the inverse demand curve $P = f(Q)$ over the interval $[0, Q^*]$, which is $\int_0^{Q^*} f(Q) \, dQ$. This area

---

[6] See, for example, H. Varian: *Intermediate Microeconomics: A Modern Approach*, 8th ed., Norton, 2009 for a more detailed treatment.

378 CHAPTER 10 / INTEGRATION

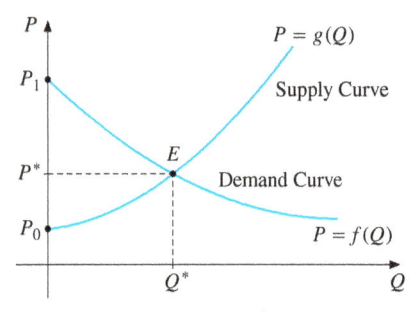

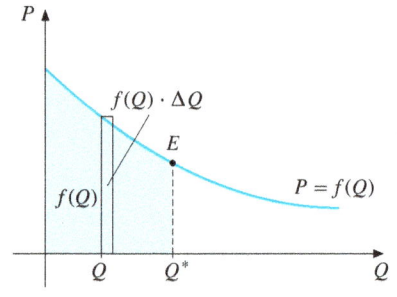

Figure 10.4.1 Market equilibrium

Figure 10.4.2 Consumer surplus, CS

is shaded in Fig. 10.4.2. If all consumers together buy Q^* units of the commodity, the total cost is P^*Q^*. This represents the area of the rectangle with base Q^* and height P^*. It can therefore be expressed as the integral $\int_0^{Q^*} P^* \, dQ$. The consumer surplus is defined as the total amount that consumers are willing to pay for the quantity Q^*, minus what they actually pay for Q^*. This difference equals the integral

$$\text{CS} = \int_0^{Q^*} [f(Q) - P^*] \, dQ \tag{10.4.6}$$

In Fig. 10.4.3, $\int_0^{Q^*} f(Q) \, dQ$ is the area OP_1EQ^*, whereas P^*Q^* is the area OP^*EQ^*. So the consumer surplus CS is equal to the area P^*P_1E between the inverse demand curve and the horizontal line $P = P^*$. In Fig. 10.4.3, this is the lighter-shaded area to the left of the curve $P = f(Q)$, which lies between the P-axis and the part P_1E of the curve $P = f(Q)$ above the price P^*.

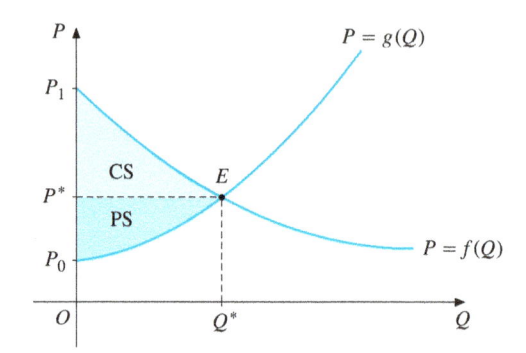

Figure 10.4.3 Consumer and producer surplus, CS and PS

Many producers also derive positive benefit or "surplus" from selling at the equilibrium price P^* because they would be willing to supply the commodity for less than P^*. In Fig. 10.4.3, even if the price is almost as low as P_0, some producers are still willing to supply the commodity. Consider the total surplus of all the producers who receive more than the price at which they are willing to sell. It is equal to the total revenue P^*Q^* that producers actually receive, minus the revenue that would make them willing to supply Q^*. We call this difference the *producer surplus*, denoted by PS.

Geometrically it is represented by the darker-shaded area in Fig. 10.4.3. Analytically, it is defined by

$$\text{PS} = \int_0^{Q^*} [P^* - g(Q)] \, dQ \tag{10.4.7}$$

In Fig. 10.4.3, the revenue P^*Q^* is again the area OP^*EQ^*, whereas $\int_0^{Q^*} g(Q) \, dQ$ is the area OP_0EQ^*. So PS is equal to the area P^*P_0E between the inverse supply curve $P = g(Q)$ and the line $P = P^*$. In Fig. 10.4.3, this is the darker-shaded area to the left of the supply curve—that is, between the P-axis and the part of the supply curve below the price P^*.

EXAMPLE 10.4.3 Suppose that the inverse demand curve for a commodity is $P = f(Q) = 50 - 0.1Q$ and the inverse supply curve is $P = g(Q) = 0.2Q + 20$. Find the equilibrium price. Then compute the consumer and producer surplus.

Solution: The equilibrium quantity is determined by the equation $50 - 0.1Q^* = 0.2Q^* + 20$, which gives $Q^* = 100$. Then $P^* = 0.2Q^* + 20 = 40 = 50 - 0.1Q^*$. Hence,

$$\text{CS} = \int_0^{100} [50 - 0.1Q - 40] \, dQ = \int_0^{100} [10 - 0.1Q] \, dQ = \Big|_0^{100} (10Q - 0.05Q^2) = 500$$

and

$$\text{PS} = \int_0^{100} [40 - (0.2Q + 20)] \, dQ = \int_0^{100} [20 - 0.2Q] \, dQ = \Big|_0^{100} (20Q - 0.1Q^2) = 1000$$

EXERCISES FOR SECTION 10.4

1. Assume that the rate of extraction $u(t)$ from an oil well decreases exponentially over time, with $u(t) = \bar{u}e^{-at}$, where $\bar{u}$ and a are positive constants. Given the initial stock $x(0) = K$, find an expression $x(t)$ for the remaining amount of oil at time t. Under what condition will the well never be exhausted?

(SM) 2. Following the pattern in Examples 10.4.1 and 10.4.2:

   (a) Find the mean income m over the interval $[b, 2b]$ when $f(r) = Br^{-2}$, assuming that there are n individuals in the population.

   (b) Assume that the individuals' demand function is $D(p, r) = Ap^\gamma r^\delta$ with $A > 0$, $\gamma < 0$, $\delta > 0$, $\delta \neq 1$. Compute the total demand $x(p)$ by using formula (10.4.5).

3. Solve the equation $S = \int_0^T e^{rt} \, dt$ for T.

4. Let $K(t)$ denote the capital stock of an economy at time t. Then *net investment* at time t, denoted by $I(t)$, is given by the rate of increase $\dot{K}(t)$ of $K(t)$.

   (a) If $I(t) = 3t^2 + 2t + 5$ for $t \geq 0$, what is the total increase in the capital stock during the interval from $t = 0$ to $t = 5$?

(b) If $K(t_0) = K_0$, find an expression for the total increase in the capital stock from time $t = t_0$ to $t = T$ when the investment function $I(t)$ is as in part (a).

5. An oil company is planning to extract oil from one of its fields, starting today at $t = 0$, where t is time measured in years. It has a choice between two different extraction profiles f and g giving the rates of output flow, measured in barrels of oil per year. Both extraction profiles last for 10 years, with $f(t) = 10t^2 - t^3$ and $g(t) = t^3 - 20t^2 + 100t$ for t in $[0, 10]$.

(a) Sketch the two profiles in the same coordinate system.

(b) Show that $\int_0^t g(\tau)\,d\tau \geq \int_0^t f(\tau)\,d\tau$ for all t in $[0, 10]$.

(c) The company sells its oil at a price per unit given by $p(t) = 1 + 1/(t+1)$. Total revenues from the two profiles are then given by $\int_0^{10} p(t)f(t)\,dt$ and $\int_0^{10} p(t)g(t)\,dt$ respectively. Compute these integrals. Which of the two extraction profiles earns the higher revenue?

6. Suppose that the inverse demand and supply curves are, respectively, $P = f(Q) = 200 - 0.2Q$ and $P = g(Q) = 20 + 0.1Q$. Find the equilibrium price and quantity, then compute the consumer and producer surplus.

7. Suppose the inverse demand and supply curves for a particular commodity are, respectively, $P = f(Q) = 6000/(Q+50)$ and $P = g(Q) = Q + 10$. Find the equilibrium price and quantity, then compute the consumer and producer surplus.

10.5 Integration by Parts

Mathematicians, statisticians, and economists often need to evaluate integrals like $\int x^3 e^{2x}\,dx$, whose integrand is a product of two functions. We know that $\frac{1}{4}x^4$ has x^3 as its derivative and that $\frac{1}{2}e^{2x}$ has e^{2x} as its derivative. Yet the product $\frac{1}{8}x^4 e^{2x}$ of $\frac{1}{4}x^4$ and $\frac{1}{2}e^{2x}$ certainly does not have $x^3 e^{2x}$ as its derivative. In general, because the derivative of a product is *not* the product of the derivatives, the integral of a product is not the product of the integrals.

The correct rule for differentiating a product allows us to derive an important and useful rule for integrating products. The product rule for differentiation in Eq. (6.7.3) states that

$$(f(x)g(x))' = f'(x)g(x) + f(x)g'(x) \qquad (*)$$

Now take the indefinite integral of each side in (∗), then use rule (10.1.9) stating that the integral of a sum is the sum of integrals. The result is

$$f(x)g(x) = \int f'(x)g(x)\,dx + \int f(x)g'(x)\,dx$$

where the constants of integration in both indefinite integrals have been left implicit. Rearranging this last equation yields the following formula:

INTEGRATION BY PARTS

$$\int f(x)g'(x)\,dx = f(x)g(x) - \int f'(x)g(x)\,dx \qquad (10.5.1)$$

At first sight, this formula does not look at all helpful. Yet the examples that follow show how this impression is quite wrong, once one has learned to use the formula properly.

Indeed, suppose we are asked to integrate a function $H(x)$ that can be written in the form $f(x)g'(x)$. By using (10.5.1), the problem can be transformed into that of integrating $f'(x)g(x)$. Usually, a function $H(x)$ can be written as $f(x)g'(x)$ in several different ways. The point is, therefore, to choose f and g so that it is easier to find $\int f'(x)g(x)\,dx$ than it is to find $\int f(x)g'(x)\,dx$.

EXAMPLE 10.5.1 Use integration by parts to evaluate $\int xe^x\,dx$.

Solution: In order to use (10.5.1), we must write the integrand in the form $f(x)g'(x)$. Let $f(x) = x$ and $g'(x) = e^x$, implying that $g(x) = e^x$. Then $f(x)g'(x) = xe^x$, and (10.5.1) gives

$$\int \underbrace{x \cdot e^x}_{f(x)g'(x)}\,dx = \underbrace{x \cdot e^x}_{f(x)g(x)} - \int \underbrace{1 \cdot e^x}_{f'(x)g(x)}\,dx = xe^x - \int e^x\,dx = xe^x - e^x + C$$

The derivative of $xe^x - e^x + C$ is indeed $e^x + xe^x - e^x = xe^x$, so the integration by parts formula (10.5.1) has given the correct answer.

An appropriate choice of f and g enabled us to evaluate the integral. Let us see what happens if we interchange the roles of f and g, and try $f(x) = e^x$ and $g'(x) = x$ instead. Then $g(x) = \frac{1}{2}x^2$. Again $f(x)g'(x) = e^x x = xe^x$, so, by (10.5.1),

$$\int \underbrace{e^x \cdot x}_{f(x)g'(x)}\,dx = \underbrace{e^x \cdot \tfrac{1}{2}x^2}_{f(x)g(x)} - \int \underbrace{e^x \cdot \tfrac{1}{2}x^2}_{f'(x)g(x)}\,dx$$

In this case, the integral on the right-hand side is more complicated than the one we started with. We conclude that this alternative choice of f and g fails to simplify the integral.

Example 10.5.1 illustrates why we must be careful about how we split the integrand. Insights into making a good choice, if there is one, come only with practice.

Sometimes integration by parts works not by producing a simpler integral, but one that is similar, as in part (a) of the next example.

EXAMPLE 10.5.2 Evaluate the following: (a) $I = \int (1/x) \ln x\,dx$; and (b) $J = \int x^3 e^{2x}\,dx$.

Solution:

(a) Choosing $f(x) = 1/x$ and $g'(x) = \ln x$ leads nowhere. Choosing $f(x) = \ln x$ and $g'(x) = 1/x$ instead gives

$$I = \int \frac{1}{x} \ln x\,dx = \int \underbrace{\ln x \cdot \frac{1}{x}}_{f(x)g'(x)}\,dx = \underbrace{\ln x \cdot \ln x}_{f(x)g(x)} - \int \underbrace{\frac{1}{x} \cdot \ln x}_{f'(x)g(x)}\,dx$$

This works better because the last integral is exactly the one we started with, namely I itself. So it must be true that $I = (\ln x)^2 - I + C_1$ for some constant C_1. Solving for I yields $I = \frac{1}{2}(\ln x)^2 + \frac{1}{2}C_1$. Putting $C = \frac{1}{2}C_1$, we conclude that

$$\int \frac{1}{x} \ln x \, dx = \frac{1}{2}(\ln x)^2 + C$$

As always, one should check the answer by differentiating $\frac{1}{2}(\ln x)^2$ w.r.t. x.

(b) We begin by arguing rather loosely as follows. Differentiation makes x^3 simpler by reducing the power in the derivative $3x^2$ from 3 to 2. On the other hand, e^{2x} becomes about equally simple whether we differentiate or integrate it. Therefore, we choose $f(x) = x^3$ and $g'(x) = e^{2x}$, so that integration by parts tells us to differentiate f and integrate g'. This yields $f'(x) = 3x^2$ and we can choose $g(x) = \frac{1}{2}e^{2x}$. Therefore,

$$J = \int x^3 e^{2x} \, dx = x^3(\tfrac{1}{2}e^{2x}) - \int (3x^2)(\tfrac{1}{2}e^{2x}) \, dx = \tfrac{1}{2}x^3 e^{2x} - \tfrac{3}{2}\int x^2 e^{2x} \, dx \quad (*)$$

The last integral *is* somewhat simpler than the one we started with, because the power of x has been reduced. Integrating by parts once more yields

$$\int x^2 e^{2x} \, dx = x^2(\tfrac{1}{2}e^{2x}) - \int (2x)(\tfrac{1}{2}e^{2x}) \, dx = \tfrac{1}{2}x^2 e^{2x} - \int x e^{2x} \, dx \quad (**)$$

Using integration by parts a third and final time gives

$$\int x e^{2x} \, dx = x(\tfrac{1}{2}e^{2x}) - \int \tfrac{1}{2}e^{2x} \, dx = \tfrac{1}{2}x e^{2x} - \tfrac{1}{4}e^{2x} + C_1 \quad (***)$$

Successively inserting the results of (***) and (**) into (*) yields:

$$J = \tfrac{1}{2}x^3 e^{2x} - \tfrac{3}{4}x^2 e^{2x} + \tfrac{3}{4}x e^{2x} - \tfrac{3}{8}e^{2x} + C$$

where $C = 3C_1/2$. A good idea is to double-check by verifying that $dJ/dx = x^3 e^{2x}$.

There is a corresponding result for definite integrals. From the definition of the definite integral and the product rule for differentiation, we have

$$\int_a^b \left[f'(x)g(x) + f(x)g'(x) \right] dx = \int_a^b \frac{d}{dx}[f(x)g(x)] \, dx = \Big|_a^b f(x)g(x)$$

Evidently, this implies that

$$\int_a^b f(x)g'(x) \, dx = \Big|_a^b f(x)g(x) - \int_a^b f'(x)g(x) \, dx \qquad (10.5.2)$$

EXAMPLE 10.5.3

Evaluate $\int_0^{10}(1+0.4t)e^{-0.05t}\,dt$.

Solution: Put $f(t) = 1 + 0.4t$ and $g'(t) = e^{-0.05t}$. Then we can choose $g(t) = -20e^{-0.05t}$, so that (10.5.2) yields

$$\int_0^{10}(1+0.4t)e^{-0.05t}\,dt = \Big|_0^{10}(1+0.4t)(-20)e^{-0.05t} - \int_0^{10}(0.4)(-20)e^{-0.05t}\,dt$$

$$= -100e^{-0.5} + 20 + 8\int_0^{10} e^{-0.05t}\,dt$$

$$= -100e^{-0.5} + 20 + 8\Big|_0^{10}(-20)e^{-0.05t}$$

$$= -100e^{-0.5} + 20 - 160(e^{-0.5} - 1)$$

$$= 180 - 260e^{-0.5} \approx 22.3$$

EXERCISES FOR SECTION 10.5

SM 1. Use integration by parts to evaluate the following:

(a) $\int xe^{-x}\,dx$ (b) $\int 3xe^{4x}\,dx$ (c) $\int (1+x^2)e^{-x}\,dx$ (d) $\int x\ln x\,dx$

SM 2. Use integration by parts to evaluate the following:

(a) $\int_{-1}^{1} x\ln(x+2)\,dx$ (b) $\int_0^2 x2^x\,dx$ (c) $\int_0^1 x^2 e^x\,dx$ (d) $\int_0^3 x\sqrt{1+x}\,dx$

In part (d) you should graph the integrand and decide if your answer is reasonable.

3. Use integration by parts to evaluate the following:

(a) $\int_1^4 \sqrt{t}\ln t\,dt$ (b) $\int_0^2 (x-2)e^{-x/2}\,dx$ (c) $\int_0^3 (3-x)3^x\,dx$

4. Of course, $f(x) = 1 \cdot f(x)$ for any function $f(x)$. Use this fact and integration by parts to prove that $\int f(x)\,dx = xf(x) - \int xf'(x)\,dx$. Apply this formula to $f(x) = \ln x$. Compare with Example 10.1.3.

5. Given $\rho \neq -1$, show that $\int x^\rho \ln x\,dx = \dfrac{x^{\rho+1}}{\rho+1}\ln x - \dfrac{x^{\rho+1}}{(\rho+1)^2} + C$.

SM 6. Evaluate the following integrals, for $r \neq 0$:

(a) $\int_0^T bte^{-rt}\,dt$ (b) $\int_0^T (a+bt)e^{-rt}\,dt$ (c) $\int_0^T (a - bt + ct^2)e^{-rt}\,dt$

10.6 Integration by Substitution

In this section we shall see how the chain rule for differentiation leads to an important method for evaluating many complicated integrals. We start with a two-part example that combines one indefinite integral with one definite integral.

EXAMPLE 10.6.1 Evaluate the integrals:

(a) $\int (x^2 + 10)^{50}\, 2x\, dx$

(b) $\int_0^a xe^{-cx^2}\, dx$, where $c \neq 0$

Solution:

(a) Attempts to use integration by parts fail. Expanding $(x^2 + 10)^{50}$ to get a polynomial of 51 terms, and then integrating term by term, would work in principle, but would be extremely cumbersome. Instead, let us introduce $u = x^2 + 10$ as a new variable. Using differential notation, we see that $du = 2x\, dx$. Inserting these into the integral $\int (x^2 + 10)^{50}\, 2x\, dx$ yields $\int u^{50}\, du$. This integral is easy; in fact we have $\int u^{50}\, du = \frac{1}{51} u^{51} + C$. Because $u = x^2 + 10$, it appears that

$$\int (x^2 + 10)^{50}\, 2x\, dx = \frac{1}{51}(x^2 + 10)^{51} + C \qquad (*)$$

To confirm this, we use the chain rule to differentiate the right-hand side of $(*)$. The derivative is precisely the integrand $(x^2 + 10)^{50}\, 2x$, so $(*)$ *is* correct.

(b) First, we consider the indefinite integral $\int xe^{-cx^2}\, dx$ and substitute $u = -cx^2$. Then $du = -2cx\, dx$, and thus $x\, dx = -du/2c$. Therefore

$$\int xe^{-cx^2}\, dx = \int -\frac{1}{2c} e^u\, du = -\frac{1}{2c} e^u + C = -\frac{1}{2c} e^{-cx^2} + C$$

The definite integral is

$$\int_0^a xe^{-cx^2}\, dx = -\frac{1}{2c} \Big|_0^a e^{-cx^2} = \frac{1}{2c}(1 - e^{-ca^2})$$

In both parts of Example 10.6.1, the integrand could be written in the form $f(u)u'$, where $u = g(x)$. In part (a) we put $f(u) = u^{50}$ with $u = g(x) = x^2 + 10$. In part (b) we put $f(u) = e^u$ with $u = g(x) = -cx^2$. Then the integrand xe^{-cx^2} is $f(g(x))g'(x)$ multiplied by the constant $-1/(2c)$.

Let us try the same method on the more general integral

$$\int f(g(x))g'(x)\, dx$$

If we put $u = g(x)$, then $du = g'(x)\, dx$, and so the integral reduces to $\int f(u)\, du$. Suppose we could find an antiderivative function $F(u)$ such that $F'(u) = f(u)$. Then, we would have $\int f(u)\, du = F(u) + C$, which implies that $\int f(g(x))g'(x)\, dx = F(g(x)) + C$.

Does this purely formal method always give the right result? To convince you that it does, we use the chain rule to differentiate $F(g(x)) + C$ w.r.t. x. The derivative is $F'(g(x))g'(x)$, which is precisely equal to $f(g(x))g'(x)$. This confirms the following rule:

CHANGE OF VARIABLE

Suppose that g is differentiable, and that f has an indefinite integral (or antiderivative) over the relevant range of g. Then putting $u = g(x)$ gives

$$\int f(g(x))g'(x)\, dx = \int f(u)\, du \tag{10.6.1}$$

EXAMPLE 10.6.2 Evaluate the integral $\int 8x^2(3x^3 - 1)^{16}\, dx$.

Solution: Here we substitute $u = 3x^3 - 1$. Then $du = 9x^2\, dx$, so $8x^2\, dx = \frac{8}{9}\, du$. Hence

$$\int 8x^2(3x^3 - 1)^{16}\, dx = \frac{8}{9}\int u^{16}\, du = \frac{8}{9}\cdot\frac{1}{17}u^{17} + C = \frac{8}{153}(3x^3 - 1)^{17} + C$$

The definite integral in part (b) of Example 10.6.1 can be evaluated more simply by "carrying over" the limits of integration. We used the substitution $u = -cx^2$. As x varies from 0 to a, so u varies from 0 to $-ca^2$. This allows us to write:

$$\int_0^a xe^{-cx^2}\, dx = \int_0^{-ca^2} -\frac{1}{2c}e^u\, du = -\frac{1}{2c}\times\left.e^u\right|_0^{-ca^2} = \frac{1}{2c}(1 - e^{-ca^2})$$

This method of carrying over the limits of integration works in general. In fact, corresponding to the change of variable formula (10.6.1) for an indefinite integral, for the definite integral the substitution $u = g(x)$ leads to

$$\int_a^b f(g(x))g'(x)\, dx = \int_{g(a)}^{g(b)} f(u)\, du \tag{10.6.2}$$

The argument is simple: Provided that $F'(u) = f(u)$, we obtain

$$\int_a^b f(g(x))g'(x)\, dx = \left.F(g(x))\right|_a^b = F(g(b)) - F(g(a)) = \int_{g(a)}^{g(b)} f(u)\, du$$

EXAMPLE 10.6.3 Evaluate the integral $\int_1^e \frac{1 + \ln x}{x}\, dx$.

Solution: We try the substitution $u = 1 + \ln x$. Then $du = (1/x)\, dx$. Also, when $x = 1$, then $u = 1$; and when $x = e$, then $u = 2$. So, we have

$$\int_1^e \frac{1 + \ln x}{x}\, dx = \int_1^2 u\, du = \left.\frac{1}{2}u^2\right|_1^2 = \frac{1}{2}(4 - 1) = \frac{3}{2}$$

More Complicated Cases

The examples of integration by substitution considered so far were relatively simple. Now we move on to some more challenging applications of this important method.

EXAMPLE 10.6.4 Assuming that $x > 0$, find a substitution that allows evaluation of

$$\int \frac{x - \sqrt{x}}{x + \sqrt{x}}\, dx$$

Solution: Because $\sqrt{x}$ occurs in both the numerator and the denominator, we try to simplify the integral by substituting $u = \sqrt{x}$. Then $x = u^2$ and $dx = 2u\, du$, so we get

$$\int \frac{x - \sqrt{x}}{x + \sqrt{x}}\, dx = \int \frac{u^2 - u}{u^2 + u} 2u\, du = 2\int \frac{u^2 - u}{u + 1}\, du$$

To evaluate this last integral, we use the technique introduced in Section 4.7 to perform the polynomial division $(u^2 - u) \div (u + 1)$ with a remainder. We obtain

$$\int \frac{x - \sqrt{x}}{x + \sqrt{x}}\, dx = 2\int \left(u - 2 + \frac{2}{u+1}\right) du = u^2 - 4u + 4\ln|u+1| + C$$

To obtain the final answer, we replace u by $\sqrt{x}$ in the last expression, while noting that $\sqrt{x} + 1 > 0$ for all x. This yields

$$\int \frac{x - \sqrt{x}}{x + \sqrt{x}}\, dx = x - 4\sqrt{x} + 4\ln\left(\sqrt{x} + 1\right) + C$$

The last example shows the method that is used most frequently. We can summarize it as follows:

A GENERAL METHOD

In order to find $\int G(x)\, dx$:

1. Pick out a "part" of $G(x)$ and introduce this "part" as a new variable, $u = g(x)$.
2. Compute $du = g'(x)\, dx$.
3. Use the substitution $u = g(x)$, implying that $du = g'(x)\, dx$, in order to simplify, if possible, the integral $\int G(x)\, dx$ to an integral of the form $\int f(u)\, du$.
4. Use ordinary integration, if possible, to find $\int f(u)\, du = F(u) + C$.
5. Replace u by $g(x)$.

Then the final answer is $\int G(x)\, dx = F(g(x)) + C$.

At step 3 of this general method, it is crucial that the substitution $u = g(x)$ results in an integrand $f(u)$ that only contains u (and du), without any remaining dependence on x.

Probably the most common error when integrating by substitution is to replace dx by du, rather than use the correct formula $du = g'(x)\,dx$.

Note that if one particular substitution does not work, one can always try another. But as explained in Section 10.3, there is the possibility that, no matter how hard one looks, in the end no substitution at all will work.

EXAMPLE 10.6.5 Evaluate the integrals:

(a) $\int x^3 \sqrt{1+x^2}\,dx$ (b) $\int_0^1 x^3 \sqrt{1+x^2}\,dx$

Solution:

(a) We follow steps 1 to 5:
 1. We pick a "part" of $x^3 \sqrt{1+x^2}$ as a new variable. Let us try $u = \sqrt{1+x^2}$.
 2. When $u = \sqrt{1+x^2}$, then $u^2 = 1 + x^2$ and so $2u\,du = 2x\,dx$, implying that $u\,du = x\,dx$. Note that this is easier than differentiating u directly.
 3. $\int x^3 \sqrt{1+x^2}\,dx = \int x^2 \sqrt{1+x^2}\, x\,dx = \int (u^2 - 1) u u\,du = \int (u^4 - u^2)\,du$
 4. $\int (u^4 - u^2)\,du = \frac{1}{5}u^5 - \frac{1}{3}u^3 + C$
 5. $\int x^3 \sqrt{1+x^2}\,dx = \frac{1}{5}(\sqrt{1+x^2})^5 - \frac{1}{3}(\sqrt{1+x^2})^3 + C$

(b) To evaluate the definite integral, we combine the results in steps 3 and 4 of part (a), while noting that $u = 1$ when $x = 0$ and that $u = \sqrt{2}$ when $x = 1$. The result is

$$\int_0^1 x^3 \sqrt{1+x^2}\,dx = \Big|_1^{\sqrt{2}} \left(\frac{1}{5}u^5 - \frac{1}{3}u^3 \right) = \frac{4\sqrt{2}}{5} - \frac{2\sqrt{2}}{3} - \frac{1}{5} + \frac{1}{3} = \frac{2}{15}(\sqrt{2}+1)$$

In this example the substitution $u = 1 + x^2$ also works.

Integrating Rational Functions and Partial Fractions

In Section 4.7 we defined a rational function as the ratio $P(x)/Q(x)$ of two polynomials. Just occasionally economists need to integrate such functions. So we will merely give two examples that illustrate a procedure one can use more generally. One example has already appeared in Example 10.6.4, where a substitution transformed the integrand to the rational function $(u^2 - u)/(u + 1)$. As explained in that example, the method of polynomial division with a remainder that we introduced in Section 4.7 allowed this function to be simplified so that it could be integrated directly.

That example was particularly simple because the denominator was a polynomial of degree 1 in x. When the degree of the denominator exceeds 1, however, it is generally necessary to combine polynomial division with a *partial fraction expansion* of the remainder. Here is an example:

EXAMPLE 10.6.6 Evaluate the integral

$$\int \frac{x^4 + 3x^2 - 4}{x^2 + 2x}\,dx$$

Solution: We apply polynomial division to the integrand, which yields

$$\frac{x^4 + 3x^2 - 4}{x^2 + 2x} = x^2 - 2x + 7 - \frac{14x + 4}{x^2 + 2x}$$

Integrating the first part of the right-hand side yields $\int (x^2 - 2x + 7)\,dx = \frac{1}{3}x^3 - x^2 + 7x + C_0$. The last term, however, is a fraction with a denominator of degree 2. It is, however, the product of the factors x and $x + 2$. To obtain an expression we can integrate, we expand this term as the following sum of two partial fractions

$$\frac{14x + 4}{x(x + 2)} = \frac{A}{x} + \frac{B}{x + 2} \quad (*)$$

where A and B are constants to be determined. Note that the fraction is undefined for $x = 0$ and $x = -2$. For all other x, multiplying each side of the equation by the common denominator $x(x + 2)$ gives $14x + 4 = A(x + 2) + Bx$, or $(14 - A - B)x + 4 - 2A = 0$. To make this true for all $x \neq 0$ and all $x \neq -2$, where the fraction is defined, we require that both the coefficient $14 - A - B$ of x and the constant $4 - 2A$ are 0. Solving these two simultaneous equations gives $A = 2$ and $B = 12$. Finally, therefore, we can integrate the fourth remainder term of the integrand to obtain

$$\int \frac{14x + 4}{x^2 + 2x}\,dx = \int \frac{2}{x}\,dx + \int \frac{12}{x + 2}\,dx = 2\ln|x| + 12\ln|x + 2| + C$$

Hence, the overall answer is

$$\int \frac{x^4 + 3x^2 - 4}{x^2 + 2x}\,dx = \frac{1}{3}x^3 - x^2 + 7x + 2\ln|x| + 12\ln|x + 2| + C$$

This answer, of course, should be verified by direct differentiation.

EXERCISES FOR SECTION 10.6

1. Use (10.6.1) to find each of the following integrals:

(a) $\int (x^2 + 1)^8 2x\,dx$
(b) $\int (x + 2)^{10}\,dx$
(c) $\int \frac{2x - 1}{x^2 - x + 8}\,dx$

SM 2. Use an appropriate substitution to find each of the following integrals:

(a) $\int x(2x^2 + 3)^5\,dx$
(b) $\int x^2 e^{x^3 + 2}\,dx$
(c) $\int \frac{\ln(x + 2)}{2x + 4}\,dx$
(d) $\int x\sqrt{1 + x}\,dx$
(e) $\int \frac{x^3}{(1 + x^2)^3}\,dx$
(f) $\int x^5\sqrt{4 - x^3}\,dx$

3. Find the following integrals:

(a) $\int_0^1 x\sqrt{1 + x^2}\,dx$
(b) $\int_1^e \frac{\ln x}{x}\,dx$
(c) $\int_1^3 \frac{1}{x^2}e^{2/x}\,dx$
(d) $\int_5^8 \frac{x}{x - 4}\,dx$

Hint: In (d), as alternative methods to find the integral, use both: (i) integration by substitution; (ii) expansion in partial fractions, as in Example 10.6.6.

4. For $x > 2$, solve the equation $\displaystyle\int_3^x \frac{2t-2}{t^2-2t}\,dt = \ln\left(\frac{2}{3}x-1\right)$.

5. Show that $\displaystyle\int_{t_0}^{t_1} S'(x(t))\dot{x}(t)\,dt = S(x(t_1)) - S(x(t_0))$.

SM 6. [HARDER] Calculate the following integrals:

(a) $\displaystyle\int_0^1 (x^4 - x^9)(x^5 - 1)^{12}\,dx$ (b) $\displaystyle\int \frac{\ln x}{\sqrt{x}}\,dx$ (c) $\displaystyle\int_0^4 \frac{1}{\sqrt{1+\sqrt{x}}}\,dx$

SM 7. [HARDER] Calculate the following integrals:

(a) $\displaystyle\int_1^4 \frac{e^{\sqrt{x}}}{\sqrt{x}(1+e^{\sqrt{x}})}\,dx$ (b) $\displaystyle\int_0^{1/3} \frac{1}{e^x+1}\,dx$ (c) $\displaystyle\int_{8.5}^{41} \frac{1}{\sqrt{2x-1} - \sqrt[4]{2x-1}}\,dx$

Hints: For (b), substitute $t = e^{-x}$. For (c), substitute $z^4 = 2x - 1$.

8. [HARDER] Use one substitution that eliminates both fractional exponents in $x^{1/2}$ and $x^{1/3}$ in order to find the integral
$$I = \int \frac{x^{1/2}}{1 - x^{1/3}}\,dx$$

9. [HARDER] Use the method of partial fractions suggested in Example 10.6.6 to write
$$f(x) = \frac{cx+d}{(x-a)(x-b)}$$

as a sum of two fractions. Then use the result to integrate:

(a) $\displaystyle\int \frac{x}{(x+1)(x+2)}\,dx$;   (b) $\displaystyle\int \frac{1-2x}{x^2-2x-15}\,dx$.

10.7 Improper Integrals

Infinite Intervals of Integration

In part (b) of Example 10.6.1, we proved that if $c \neq 0$, then
$$\int_0^a xe^{-cx^2}\,dx = \frac{1}{2c}(1 - e^{-ca^2})$$

Now let a tend to infinity. Provided that $c > 0$, the right-hand expression tends to $1/(2c)$. This makes it seem natural to write
$$\int_0^\infty xe^{-cx^2}\,dx = \frac{1}{2c}$$

390   CHAPTER 10 / INTEGRATION

In statistics and economics such integrals over an infinite interval appear quite often. In general, suppose f is a function that is continuous for all $x \geq a$. Then $\int_a^b f(x)\,dx$ is defined for each $b \geq a$. We can then let b tend to infinity, and consider the associated *improper integral* $\int_a^\infty f(x)\,dx$. In case $\int_a^b f(x)\,dx$ tends to a finite limit as $b \to \infty$, we say that it *converges*, and that f is *integrable over* $[a, \infty)$. Moreover, in this case one has

$$\int_a^\infty f(x)\,dx = \lim_{b \to \infty} \int_a^b f(x)\,dx \tag{10.7.1}$$

If there is *no finite limit*, however, the improper integral is said to *diverge*.

Analogously, in case f is continuous for all $x \leq b$, we define

$$\int_{-\infty}^b f(x)\,dx = \lim_{a \to -\infty} \int_a^b f(x)\,dx \tag{10.7.2}$$

If this limit exists, the improper integral is said to converge. Otherwise, it diverges.

In case $f(x) \geq 0$ in $[a, \infty)$, we interpret the integral (10.7.1) as the *area* below the graph of f over the infinite interval $[a, \infty)$. Here is an example:

EXAMPLE 10.7.1   The *exponential distribution* in statistics is defined for all $x \geq 0$ by the density function $f(x) = \lambda e^{-\lambda x}$, where λ denotes a positive constant. The area below the graph of f over $[0, \infty)$ is illustrated in Fig. 10.7.1. Show that this area is equal to 1.

Solution: For $b > 0$, the area below the graph of f over $[0, b]$ is equal to

$$\int_0^b \lambda e^{-\lambda x}\,dx = \Big|_0^b \left(-e^{-\lambda x}\right) = -e^{-\lambda b} + 1$$

As $b \to \infty$, so $-e^{-\lambda b} + 1$ approaches 1. Therefore,

$$\int_0^\infty \lambda e^{-\lambda x}\,dx = \lim_{b \to \infty} \int_0^b \lambda e^{-\lambda x}\,dx = \lim_{b \to \infty} \left(-e^{-\lambda b} + 1\right) = 1$$

EXAMPLE 10.7.2   For $a > 1$, show that

$$\int_1^\infty \frac{1}{x^a}\,dx = \frac{1}{a-1} \tag{*}$$

Then study the improper integral in case $a = 1$ and in case $a < 1$.

Solution: For all $a \neq 1$ and $b > 1$, one has

$$\int_1^b \frac{1}{x^a}\,dx = \int_1^b x^{-a}\,dx = \Big|_1^b \frac{1}{1-a} x^{1-a} = \frac{1}{1-a}(b^{1-a} - 1) \tag{**}$$

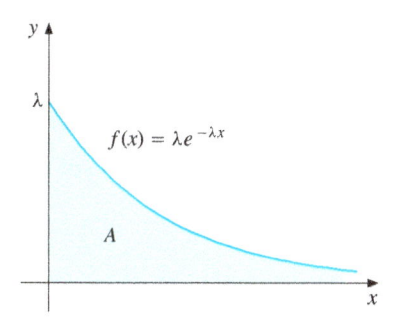

Figure 10.7.1 Area A has an unbounded base, but the height decreases to 0 so rapidly that the total area is 1.

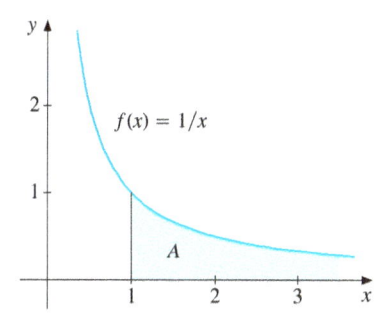

Figure 10.7.2 "$A = \int_1^\infty (1/x)\,dx = \infty$." The function $1/x$ does not approach 0 sufficiently fast, so the improper integral diverges.

In case $a > 1$, one has $b^{1-a} = 1/b^{a-1} \to 0$ as $b \to \infty$. So (∗) follows from (∗∗) by letting $b \to \infty$.

In case $a = 1$, the right-hand side of (∗∗) is undefined. Nevertheless, $\int_1^b (1/x)\,dx = \ln b - \ln 1 = \ln b$, which tends to ∞ as b tends to ∞. So $\int_1^\infty (1/x)\,dx$ diverges to $+\infty$, as suggested by Fig. 10.7.2.

In case $a < 1$, the last expression in (∗∗) tends to ∞ as b tends to ∞. So the integral diverges in this case also.

If both limits of integration are infinite, the improper integral of a continuous function f on $(-\infty, \infty)$ is defined by

$$\int_{-\infty}^{\infty} f(x)\,dx = \int_{-\infty}^{0} f(x)\,dx + \int_{0}^{\infty} f(x)\,dx \tag{10.7.3}$$

If *both* integrals on the right-hand side converge, the improper integral $\int_{-\infty}^{\infty} f(x)\,dx$ is said to *converge*; otherwise, it *diverges*. Instead of using 0 as the point of subdivision, one could use an arbitrary fixed real number c. The value assigned to the integral will always be the same, provided that the integral does converge.

It is important to note that definition (10.7.3) requires both integrals on the right-hand side to converge. Note in particular that

$$\lim_{b \to \infty} \int_{-b}^{b} f(x)\,dx \tag{10.7.4}$$

is *not* the definition of $\int_{-\infty}^{+\infty} f(x)\,dx$. Exercise 4 provides an example in which the integral (10.7.3) coverges, yet the integral in (10.7.4) diverges because $\int_{-b}^{0} f(x)\,dx \to -\infty$ as $b \to \infty$, and $\int_{0}^{b} f(x)\,dx \to \infty$ as $b \to \infty$. It follows that (10.7.4) is an unacceptable definition of $\int_{-\infty}^{\infty} f(x)\,dx$, whereas (10.7.3) is acceptable.

The following result is very important in statistics. It is also related to Exercise 12.

EXAMPLE 10.7.3 For $c > 0$, prove that the following integral converges, and find its value:

$$\int_{-\infty}^{+\infty} xe^{-cx^2}\,dx$$

Solution: In the introduction to this section, we recalled part (b) of Example 10.6.1 showing that $\int_0^\infty xe^{-cx^2}\,dx = 1/2c$. In the same way we see that

$$\int_{-\infty}^0 xe^{-cx^2}\,dx = \lim_{a \to -\infty} \int_a^0 xe^{-cx^2}\,dx = \lim_{a \to -\infty} \Big|_a^0 -\frac{1}{2c}e^{-cx^2} = -\frac{1}{2c}$$

It follows that

$$\int_{-\infty}^\infty xe^{-cx^2}\,dx = -\frac{1}{2c} + \frac{1}{2c} = 0 \tag{10.7.5}$$

Another way to show this is to note that the function $f(x) = xe^{-cx^2}$ satisfies $f(-x) = -f(x)$ for all x, and so its graph is symmetric about the origin. So for all $a \leq 0$ one has $\int_a^0 xe^{-cx^2}\,dx = -\int_0^{-a} xe^{-cx^2}\,dx$. Therefore the integral $\int_{-\infty}^0 xe^{-cx^2}\,dx$ must also converge to the limit $-1/2c$.

Integrals of Unbounded Functions

We turn next to improper integrals where the *integrand* is not bounded. Consider first the function $f(x) = 1/\sqrt{x}$ defined for $x \in (0, 2]$, with graph shown in Fig. 10.7.3. Note that $f(x) \to \infty$ as $x \to 0^+$. The function f is continuous in the interval $[h, 2]$ for any fixed number h in $(0, 2)$. So the definite integral of f over the interval $[h, 2]$ exists, and in fact

$$\int_h^2 \frac{1}{\sqrt{x}}\,dx = \Big|_h^2 2\sqrt{x} = 2\sqrt{2} - 2\sqrt{h}$$

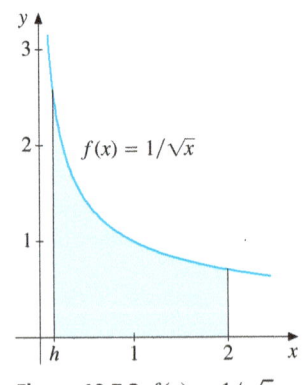

Figure 10.7.3 $f(x) = 1/\sqrt{x}$

The limit of this expression as $h \to 0^+$ is $2\sqrt{2}$. Then, by definition,

$$\int_0^2 \frac{1}{\sqrt{x}}\,dx = 2\sqrt{2}$$

The improper integral is said to converge in this case, and the area below the graph of f over the interval $(0, 2]$ is $2\sqrt{2}$. The area over the interval $(h, 2]$ is also shown in Fig. 10.7.3. As $h \to 0$ the shaded area becomes unbounded, but the graph of f approaches the y-axis so quickly that the total area is finite.

More generally, suppose that f is a continuous function in the interval $(a, b]$, but $f(x)$ is not defined at $x = a$. Then we can define

$$\int_a^b f(x)\,dx = \lim_{h \to 0^+} \int_{a+h}^b f(x)\,dx \tag{10.7.6}$$

provided the limit exists, in which case the improper integral of f is said to *converge*. If $f(x) \geq 0$ in $(a, b]$, we can identify the integral as the *area under the graph* of f over the interval $(a, b]$.

In the same way, if f is not defined at b, we can define

$$\int_a^b f(x)\,dx = \lim_{h \to 0^+} \int_a^{b-h} f(x)\,dx \tag{10.7.7}$$

provided the limit exists, in which case the improper integral of f is said to *converge*.

Next, suppose that f is continuous in (a, b), but f may not even be defined at a or b. For instance, suppose that $f(x) \to -\infty$ as $x \to a^+$ and that $f(x) \to +\infty$ as $x \to b^-$. In this case, let c be an arbitrary fixed number in (a, b). Then, provided that the two integrals $\int_a^c f(x)\,dx$ and $\int_c^b f(x)\,dx$ both converge, we say that f is *integrable* in (a, b), and define

$$\int_a^b f(x)\,dx = \int_a^c f(x)\,dx + \int_c^b f(x)\,dx \tag{10.7.8}$$

Here, neither the convergence of the integral nor its value depends on the choice of c from (a, b). On the other hand, if either of the integrals on the right-hand side of (10.7.8) does not converge, the left-hand side is not well defined.

A Test for Convergence

The following convergence test for integrals is occasionally useful because it does not require that the integral be evaluated.

THEOREM 10.7.1 (A COMPARISON TEST FOR CONVERGENCE)

Suppose that for all $x \geq a$, the two functions f and g are continuous, with $|f(x)| \leq g(x)$. If $\int_a^\infty g(x)\,dx$ converges, then $\int_a^\infty f(x)\,dx$ also converges, and

$$\left| \int_a^\infty f(x)\,dx \right| \leq \int_a^\infty g(x)\,dx$$

Considering the case in which $f(x) \geq 0$, Theorem 10.7.1 can be interpreted as follows: If the area below the graph of g is finite, then the area below the graph of f is finite as well, because at no point in $[a, \infty)$ does the graph of f lie above the graph of g. This result seems quite plausible, especially after drawing a suitable figure, so we shall not give an analytical proof. A corresponding theorem holds for the case where the lower limit of integration is $-\infty$. Also, similar comparison tests can be proved for unbounded functions defined on bounded intervals.

EXAMPLE 10.7.4 Integrals of the form

$$\int_{t_0}^\infty U(c(t)) e^{-\alpha t}\,dt \qquad (*)$$

often appear in economic growth theory. Here, $c(t)$ denotes consumption at time t, whereas U is an instantaneous utility function, and α is a positive discount rate. Suppose that there exist numbers M and β, with $\beta < \alpha$, such that

$$|U(c(t))| \leq M e^{\beta t} \qquad (**)$$

for all $t \geq t_0$ and for each possible consumption level $c(t)$ at time t. Thus, the absolute value of the utility of consumption is growing at a rate less than the discount rate α. Prove that in this case the utility integral $(*)$ converges.

Solution: From $(**)$, we have $\left| U(c(t)) e^{-\alpha t} \right| \leq M e^{-(\alpha-\beta)t}$ for all $t \geq t_0$. Moreover,

$$\int_{t_0}^T M e^{-(\alpha-\beta)t}\,dt = \left| -\frac{M}{\alpha - \beta} e^{-(\alpha-\beta)t} \right|_{t_0}^T = \frac{M}{\alpha - \beta}\left[e^{-(\alpha-\beta)t_0} - e^{-(\alpha-\beta)T} \right]$$

Because $\alpha - \beta > 0$, the last expression tends to $[M/(\alpha - \beta)] e^{-(\alpha-\beta)t_0}$ as $T \to \infty$. From Theorem 10.7.1 it follows that $(*)$ converges.

EXAMPLE 10.7.5 The function $f(x) = e^{-x^2}$ is extremely important in statistics. When multiplied by the particular constant $1/\sqrt{\pi}$, it is the density function associated with a *Gaussian*, or *normal*, distribution. We want to show convergence of the improper integral

$$\int_{-\infty}^{+\infty} e^{-x^2}\,dx \qquad (*)$$

Recall from Section 10.1 that the indefinite integral of $f(x) = e^{-x^2}$ cannot be expressed in terms of "elementary" functions. Yet, because $f(x) = e^{-x^2}$ is symmetric about the y-axis, it follows that $\int_{-\infty}^{\infty} e^{-x^2}\,dx = 2\int_0^{\infty} e^{-x^2}\,dx$. So it suffices to prove that $\int_0^{\infty} e^{-x^2}\,dx$ converges. To show this, subdivide the interval of integration so that

$$\int_0^{\infty} e^{-x^2}\,dx = \int_0^1 e^{-x^2}\,dx + \int_1^{\infty} e^{-x^2}\,dx \qquad (**)$$

Of course, $\int_0^1 e^{-x^2}\,dx$ presents no problem because it is the integral of a continuous function over a bounded interval. On the other hand, for $x \geq 1$, one has $x^2 \geq x$ and so $0 \leq e^{-x^2} \leq e^{-x}$. Now $\int_1^{\infty} e^{-x}\,dx$ converges (to $1/e$), so according to Theorem 10.7.1, the integral $\int_1^{\infty} e^{-x^2}\,dx$ must also converge. From $(**)$, it follows that $\int_0^{\infty} e^{-x^2}\,dx$ converges. Thus, the integral $(*)$ does converge, but we have not found its value. In fact, more advanced techniques of integration are used in FMEA to show that

$$\int_{-\infty}^{+\infty} e^{-x^2}\,dx = \sqrt{\pi} \qquad (10.7.9)$$

EXERCISES FOR SECTION 10.7

1. Determine the following integrals, if they converge. Indicate those that diverge.

   (a) $\int_1^{\infty} \frac{1}{x^3}\,dx$ (b) $\int_1^{\infty} \frac{1}{\sqrt{x}}\,dx$ (c) $\int_{-\infty}^0 e^x\,dx$ (d) $\int_0^a \frac{x}{\sqrt{a^2 - x^2}}\,dx$, where $a > 0$

2. In statistics, the *uniform*, or *rectangular*, *distribution* on the interval $[a, b]$ is described by the density function f defined for all x by $f(x) = 1/(b - a)$ for $x \in [a, b]$, and $f(x) = 0$ for $x \notin [a, b]$. Find the following:

   (a) $\int_{-\infty}^{+\infty} f(x)\,dx$ (b) $\int_{-\infty}^{+\infty} xf(x)\,dx$ (c) $\int_{-\infty}^{+\infty} x^2 f(x)\,dx$

SM 3. In connection with the exponential distribution defined in Example 10.7.1, find the following:

   (a) $\int_0^{\infty} x\lambda e^{-\lambda x}\,dx$ (b) $\int_0^{\infty} \left(x - \frac{1}{\lambda}\right)^2 \lambda e^{-\lambda x}\,dx$ (c) $\int_0^{\infty} \left(x - \frac{1}{\lambda}\right)^3 \lambda e^{-\lambda x}\,dx$

   The three numbers you obtain are called respectively the *expectation*, the *variance*, and the *third central moment* of the exponential distribution.

4. Prove that $\int_{-\infty}^{+\infty} x/(1 + x^2)\,dx$ diverges, but that $\lim_{b \to \infty} \int_{-b}^b x/(1 + x^2)\,dx$ converges.

SM 5. The function f is defined for all $x > 0$ by $f(x) = (\ln x)/x^3$.

   (a) Find the maximum and minimum points of f, if there are any.
   (b) Examine the convergence of $\int_0^1 f(x)\,dx$ and $\int_1^{\infty} f(x)\,dx$.

6. Use Theorem 10.7.1 to prove the convergence of $\int_1^\infty \dfrac{1}{1+x^2}\,dx$.

(SM) 7. Show that $\int_{-2}^{3}\left(\dfrac{1}{\sqrt{x+2}} + \dfrac{1}{\sqrt{3-x}}\right) dx = 4\sqrt{5}$.

8. The integral $z = \int_0^\infty e^{-rs} D(s)\,ds$ represents the present discounted value, at a constant interest rate r, of the time-dependent stream of depreciation allowances $D(s)$, defined for all $s \geq 0$. Find z as a function of τ in the following two cases:

   (a) constant depreciation with $D(s) = 1/\tau$ for $0 \leq s \leq \tau$, and $D(s) = 0$ for $s > \tau$;

   (b) straight-line depreciation $D(s) = 2(\tau - s)/\tau^2$ for $0 \leq s \leq \tau$, and $D(s) = 0$ for $s > \tau$.

9. Suppose you evaluate $\int_{-1}^{+1}(1/x^2)\,dx$ by using the definition of the definite integral without thinking carefully. Show that you get a negative answer even though the integrand is never negative. What has gone wrong?

10. Prove that the integral $\int_0^1 (\ln x/\sqrt{x})\,dx$ converges and find its value. (*Hint*: See part (b) of Exercise 10.6.6.)

11. Find the integral $I_k = \int_1^\infty \left(\dfrac{k}{x} - \dfrac{k^2}{1+kx}\right) dx$, where k is a positive constant. Then find the limit of I_k as $k \to \infty$, if it exists.

(SM) 12. [HARDER] In statistics, the normal or Gaussian density function with mean μ and variance σ^2 is defined by $f(x) = \dfrac{1}{\sigma\sqrt{2\pi}}\exp\left[-\dfrac{(x-\mu)^2}{2\sigma^2}\right]$ for all real x.[7] Prove that:

   (a) $\int_{-\infty}^{+\infty} f(x)\,dx = 1$ (b) $\int_{-\infty}^{+\infty} xf(x)\,dx = \mu$ (c) $\int_{-\infty}^{+\infty} (x-\mu)^2 f(x)\,dx = \sigma^2$

   (*Hint*: Use the substitution $u = (x-\mu)/\sqrt{2}\sigma$, together with Eqs (10.7.9) and (10.7.5).)

REVIEW EXERCISES

1. Find the following integrals:

   (a) $\int (-16)\,dx$ (b) $\int 5^5\,dx$ (c) $\int (3-y)\,dy$ (d) $\int (r - 4r^{1/4})\,dr$

   (e) $\int x^8\,dx$ (f) $\int x^2\sqrt{x}\,dx$ (g) $\int \dfrac{1}{p^5}\,dp$ (h) $\int (x^3 + x)\,dx$

2. Find the following integrals:

   (a) $\int 2e^{2x}\,dx$ (b) $\int (x - 5e^{\frac{2}{5}x})\,dx$ (c) $\int (e^{-3x} + e^{3x})\,dx$ (d) $\int \dfrac{2}{x+5}\,dx$

---

[7] The formula for this function, along with its bell-shaped graph and a portrait of its inventor Carl Friedrich Gauss (1777–1855), all appeared on the German 10 Deutsche mark banknote that was used between 1991 and 2001, in the decade before the euro currency started to circulate instead.

CHAPTER 10 / REVIEW EXERCISES

3. Evaluate the following integrals:

(a) $\int_0^{12} 50\,dx$
(b) $\int_0^2 (x - \frac{1}{2}x^2)\,dx$
(c) $\int_{-3}^3 (u+1)^2\,du$

(d) $\int_1^5 \frac{2}{z}\,dz$
(e) $\int_2^{12} \frac{3}{t+4}\,dt$
(f) $\int_0^4 v\sqrt{v^2+9}\,dv$

SM 4. Find the following integrals:

(a) $\int_1^\infty \frac{5}{x^5}\,dx$
(b) $\int_0^1 x^3(1+x^4)^4\,dx$
(c) $\int_0^\infty \frac{-5t}{e^t}\,dt$
(d) $\int_1^e (\ln x)^2\,dx$

(e) $\int_0^2 x^2\sqrt{x^3+1}\,dx$
(f) $\int_{-\infty}^0 \frac{e^{3z}}{e^{3z}+5}\,dz$
(g) $\int_{1/2}^{e/2} x^3 \ln(2x)\,dx$
(h) $\int_1^\infty \frac{e^{-\sqrt{x}}}{\sqrt{x}}\,dx$

SM 5. Find the following integrals:

(a) $\int_0^{25} \frac{1}{9+\sqrt{x}}\,dx$
(b) $\int_2^7 t\sqrt{t+2}\,dt$
(c) $\int_0^1 57x^2 \sqrt[3]{19x^3+8}\,dx$

6. Find $F'(x)$ if:

(a) $F(x) = \int_4^x \left(\sqrt{u} + \frac{x}{\sqrt{u}}\right)du$
(b) $F(x) = \int_{\sqrt{x}}^x \ln u\,du$.

7. Let $C(Y)$ be a consumption function for which the marginal propensity to consume satisfies $C'(Y) = 0.69$ for all Y. Given that $C(0) = 1000$, find $C(Y)$.

8. In manufacturing a product, the marginal cost of producing x units is $C'(x) = \alpha e^{\beta x} + \gamma$, with $\beta \neq 0$, whereas fixed costs are C_0. Find the total cost function $C(x)$.

9. Suppose that f and g are two continuous functions defined on $[-1, 3]$ for which one has

$$\int_{-1}^3 [f(x) + g(x)]\,dx = 6 \quad \text{and} \quad \int_{-1}^3 [3f(x) + 4g(x)]\,dx = 9$$

Find $\int_{-1}^3 [f(x) + 2g(x)]\,dx$.

SM 10. In the following two cases, the inverse demand curve is $f(Q)$ and the inverse supply curve is $g(Q)$. In each case, find the equilibrium price and quantity, then calculate the consumer and producer surplus.

(a) $f(Q) = 100 - 0.05Q$ and $g(Q) = 10 + 0.1Q$.

(b) $f(Q) = \dfrac{50}{Q+5}$ and $g(Q) = 4.5 + 0.1Q$.

SM 11. Suppose that f is defined for $t > 0$ by $f(t) = 4(\ln t)^2/t$.

(a) Find $f'(t)$ and $f''(t)$.

(b) Find possible local extreme points, and sketch the graph of f.

(c) Calculate the area below the graph of f over the interval $[1, e^2]$.

12. As discussed in Section 10.4, assume that a population of n individuals has an income density function $f(r) = (1/m)e^{-r/m}$ for r in $[0, \infty)$, where m is a positive constant.

   (a) Show that m is the mean income.

   (b) Suppose the demand function is $D(p, r) = ar - bp$. Compute the total demand $x(p)$ when $f(r)$ is the income density function.

11 TOPICS IN FINANCE AND DYNAMICS

I can calculate the motions of heavenly bodies, but not the madness of people.
—Isaac Newton[1]

This chapter begins by treating some basic topics in the mathematics of finance. The main concern is how the values of investments and loans at different times are affected by interest rates. Sections 2.2 and 4.9 have already discussed some elementary calculations of interest compounded at different constant rates. This chapter goes a step further and considers topics like alterations in the frequency at which interest accrues. It also discusses in turn effective rates of interest, continuously compounded interest, present values of future claims, annuities, mortgages, and the internal rate of return on investment projects. Some key calculations involve the summation formula for geometric series, which we therefore derive.

In the last three sections of the chapter we give a brief introduction to some simple dynamic models. In Section 11.8 we consider difference equations. They are followed by differential equations in Sections 11.9 and 11.10.

11.1 Interest Periods and Effective Rates

In advertisements that offer bank loans or savings accounts, interest is usually quoted as an *annual rate*, also called a *nominal rate*, even if interest actually interest accrues more frequently than once per year. The *interest period* is the time that elapses between successive dates when interest is added to the account. For some bank accounts the interest period is one year, but it has become increasingly common for financial institutions to offer other interest schemes. For instance, some bank accounts add interest daily, some others at least monthly. If a bank offers 1.5% annual rate of interest with interest payments each month, then $\frac{1}{12} \times 1.5\% = 0.125\%$ of the capital accrues at the end of each month. This illustrates

---

[1] Attributed. It is claimed that he said this in 1720 soon after losing a significant part of his financial wealth during the bursting of what was later known as the South Sea bubble.

how the annual rate must be divided by the number of interest periods to get the *periodic rate*—that is, the rate of interest per period.

Suppose a principal (or capital) of S_0 yields interest at the rate $p\%$ per period, for example one year. As explained in Section 2.2, after t periods it will have increased to the amount $S(t) = S_0(1+r)^t$, where $r = p/100$, which is $p\%$. Each period the principal increases by the factor $1 + r$.

The formula assumes that the interest is added to the principal at the end of each period. Suppose that the annual interest rate is $p\%$, but that interest is paid biannually (that is, twice a year) at the rate $\frac{1}{2}p/\%$. Then after half a year the principal will have increased to

$$S_0 + S_0 \frac{p/2}{100} = S_0\left(1 + \frac{r}{2}\right)$$

This illustrates how *the principal increases by the factor $1 + r/2$ each half year*. After two periods, namely one year, it will have increased to $S_0(1 + r/2)^2$, and after t whole years, to

$$S_0\left(1 + \frac{r}{2}\right)^{2t}$$

Note that a biannual interest payment at the rate $\frac{1}{2}r$ is better for a lender than an annual interest payment at the rate r. This is because $(1 + \frac{1}{2}r)^2 = 1 + r + \frac{1}{4}r^2 > 1 + r$.

More generally, suppose that interest at the rate $p/n\%$ is added to the principal at n different times distributed evenly throughout the year. For example, $n = 4$ if interest is added quarterly, $n = 12$ if it is added monthly, etc. Then, the *principal will be multiplied by a factor $(1 + r/n)^n$ each year*. After t years, the principal will have increased to

$$S_0\left(1 + \frac{r}{n}\right)^{nt} \tag{11.1.1}$$

Example 11.2.3 shows that a greater n leads to interest accruing faster to the lender.

EXAMPLE 11.1.1 A deposit of £5 000 is put into an account earning interest at the annual rate of 9%, with interest paid quarterly. How much will there be in the account after eight years?

Solution: The periodic rate r/n is $0.09/4 = 0.0225$ per quarter. The number of quarters in eight years is $4 \cdot 8 = 32$. So formula (11.1.1) gives:

$$5000(1 + 0.0225)^{32} \approx 10\,190.52$$

EXAMPLE 11.1.2 How long will it take for the deposit of £5 000 in Example 11.1.1 to increase to £15 000?

Solution: After t quarterly payments the account will grow to $5000(1 + 0.0225)^t$ pounds. This reaches £15 000 when $1.0225^t = 3$. Taking the natural logarithm of each side gives the equation $t \ln 1.0225 = \ln 3$, so

$$t = \frac{\ln 3}{\ln 1.0225} \approx 49.37$$

So it takes approximately 49.37 quarterly periods, or approximately 12 years and four months, for the account to increase to £15 000.

Effective Rate of Interest

A consumer who needs a loan may receive different offers from several competing financial institutions. It is therefore important to know how to compare various offers. The concept of *effective interest rate* is often used in making such comparisons.

Consider a loan which implies an annual interest rate of 9% with interest at the rate $9/12 = 0.75\%$ added 12 times a year. If no interest is paid in the meantime, after one year an initial principal of S_0 will have grown to a debt of $S_0(1 + 0.09/12)^{12} \approx S_0 \cdot 1.094$. In fact, as long as no interest is paid, the debt will grow at a constant proportional rate that is (approximately) 9.4% per year. For this reason, we call 9.4% the effective yearly rate. More generally:

EFFECTIVE YEARLY RATE

When interest is added n times during the year at the rate r/n per period, then the effective yearly rate, R, is defined as

$$R = \left(1 + \frac{r}{n}\right)^n - 1 \tag{11.1.2}$$

The effective yearly rate is independent of the amount S_0. For a given value of $r > 0$, it is increasing in n, as shown in Example 11.2.3.

EXAMPLE 11.1.3 What is the effective yearly rate R corresponding to an annual interest rate of 9% with interest compounded: (a) each quarter; (b) each month?

Solution:

(a) Applying formula (11.1.2) with $r = 0.09$ and $n = 4$, the effective rate is

$$R = \left(1 + \frac{0.09}{4}\right)^4 - 1 = (1 + 0.0225)^4 - 1 \approx 0.0931 \text{ or } 9.31\%$$

(b) In this case $r = 0.09$ and $n = 12$, so the effective rate is

$$R = \left(1 + \frac{0.09}{12}\right)^{12} - 1 = (1 + 0.0075)^{12} - 1 \approx 0.0938 \text{ or } 9.38\%$$

A typical case in which we can use the effective rate of interest to compare different financial offers is the following.

EXAMPLE 11.1.4 When investing in a savings account, which of the following offers are better: (i) 5.9% with interest paid quarterly; or (ii) 6% with interest paid twice a year?

Solution: Using formula (11.1.2), the effective rates for the two offers are, respectively:

$$R = (1 + 0.059/4)^4 - 1 \approx 0.0603 \text{ and } R = (1 + 0.06/2)^2 - 1 = 0.0609$$

The second offer is, therefore, better for the saver.

In many countries there is an official legal definition of effective interest rate which takes into account different forms of fixed or "closing" costs incurred when initiating a loan. The *effective rate of interest* is then defined as the rate which implies that the combined present value of all the costs is equal to the size of the loan. This is the internal rate of return, as defined in Section 11.7; present values are discussed in Section 11.3.

EXERCISES FOR SECTION 11.1

1. (a) What will be the size of an account after five years, if $8 000 is invested at an annual interest rate of 5% compounded: (i) monthly; or (ii) daily (with 365 days in a year)?

   (b) How long does it take for the investment to double with monthly compounding?

2. An investment of $5 000 earns interest at 3% per year.

   (a) What will this amount have grown to after ten years?

   (b) How long does it take for the investment to triple?

3. What annual percentage rate of growth is needed for a country's GDP to become 100 times as large after 100 years? (Use the approximation $\sqrt[100]{100} \approx 1.047$).

4. An amount of €2 000 is invested at 7% per year.

   (a) What is the balance in the account after (i) two years; and (ii) ten years?

   (b) How long does it take, approximately, for the balance to reach €6 000?

5. Calculate the effective yearly interest if the nominal rate is 17% and interest is added: (a) biannually; (b) quarterly; or (c) monthly.

6. Which terms are preferable for a borrower: (a) an annual interest rate of 21.5%, with interest paid yearly; or (b) an annual interest rate of 20%, with interest paid quarterly?

7. A sum of $12 000 is invested at 4% annual interest.

   (a) What will this amount have grown to after 15 years?

   (b) How much should you have deposited in a bank account five years ago in order to have $50 000 today, given that the interest rate has been 5% per year over the period?

8. A credit card is offered with interest on the outstanding balance charged at 2% per month. What is the effective annual rate of interest?

9. What is the nominal yearly interest rate if the effective yearly rate is 28% and interest is compounded quarterly?

11.2 Continuous Compounding

We saw in the previous section that if interest at the rate r/n is added to the principal S_0 at n different times during the year, the principal will be multiplied by a factor $(1 + r/n)^n$ each year. After t years, the principal will have increased to $S_0(1 + r/n)^{nt}$. In practice, there is a limit to how frequently interest can be added to an account. However, let us examine what happens to the expression as the annual frequency n tends to infinity. We put $r/n = 1/m$. Then $n = mr$ and so

$$S_0\left(1 + \frac{r}{n}\right)^{nt} = S_0\left(1 + \frac{1}{m}\right)^{mrt} = S_0\left[\left(1 + \frac{1}{m}\right)^m\right]^{rt} \qquad (11.2.1)$$

As $n \to \infty$ with r fixed, so $m = n/r \to \infty$. Then, according to Example 7.11.2, we have $(1 + 1/m)^m \to e$. Hence, the expression in (11.2.1) approaches $S_0 e^{rt}$ as n tends to infinity, implying that interest is compounded more and more frequently. In the limit, we talk about *continuous compounding* of interest:

CONTINUOUS COMPOUNDING OF INTEREST

If the annual interest is r and there is continuous compounding of interest, then after t years an initial principal of S_0 will have increased to

$$S(t) = S_0 e^{rt} \qquad (11.2.2)$$

EXAMPLE 11.2.1 Suppose the sum of £5 000 is invested in an account earning interest at an annual rate of 9%. What is the balance after eight years, if interest is compounded continuously?

Solution: Using formula (11.2.2) with $r = 9/100 = 0.09$, we see that the balance is

$$5000 e^{0.09 \cdot 8} = 5000 e^{0.72} \approx 10\,272.17$$

This is more than in the case of quarterly compounding studied in Example 11.1.1.

If $S(t) = S_0 e^{rt}$ as in (11.2.2), then applying formula (6.10.2) gives $S'(t) = S_0 r e^{rt} = rS(t)$. It follows that $S'(t)/S(t) = r$. Using the terminology introduced in Section 6.4:

With continuous compounding of interest at the rate r, the principal increases at the constant relative rate r, meaning that $S'(t)/S(t) = r$.

From Eq. (11.2.2), we infer that $S(1) = S_0 e^r$, so that the principal increases by the factor e^r during the first year. In general, $S(t+1) = S_0 e^{r(t+1)} = S_0 e^{rt} e^r = S(t) e^r$. Hence:

With continuous compounding of interest at the rate r, the principal increases each year by a fixed factor e^r.

Comparing Different Interest Periods

Given any fixed interest rate of $p\% = 100r$ per year, Example 11.2.3 shows that continuous compounding of interest is best for the lender. For comparatively low interest rates, however, and when the number of years of compounding is not too large, the difference between annual and continuous compounding of interest is quite small.

EXAMPLE 11.2.2   Let K denote the amount to which one dollar increases in the course of a year when the interest rate is 8% per year. Find K when interest is added: (a) yearly; (b) biannually; or (c) continuously.

Solution: In this case $r = 8/100 = 0.08$, and we obtain:

(a) $K = 1.08$
(b) $K = (1 + 0.08/2)^2 = 1.04^2 = 1.0816$
(c) $K = e^{0.08} \approx 1.08329$

If we increase either the interest rate or the number of years over which interest accumulates, then the difference between yearly and continuous compounding of interest increases.

In the previous section the effective yearly interest was defined by the formula $(1 + r/n)^n - 1$, when interest is compounded n times a year with rate r/n per period. Letting n approach infinity in this formula, we see that the expression approaches

$$e^r - 1 \qquad (11.2.3)$$

This is called the *effective interest* rate with continuous compounding at the annual rate r.

Part (d) of the following Example 11.2.3 shows, in particular, that *continuous compounding at interest rate r is more profitable for the lender than interest payments n times a year at interest rate r/n.*

EXAMPLE 11.2.3

(a) Define the function $h(u) = \ln(1+u) - u/(1+u)$ for all $u \geq 0$. Show that, for all $u > 0$, one has: (i) $h'(u) > 0$; (ii) $h(u) > 0$.

(b) Given any $r > 0$, consider the function defined by $g(x) = (1 + r/x)^x$ for all $x > 0$. Use logarithmic differentiation to show that

$$g'(x) = g(x)\left[\ln(1 + r/x) - \frac{r/x}{1 + r/x}\right] > 0$$

(c) Prove that $(1 + r/n)^n$ increases strictly with the natural number n.
(d) Prove that $(1 + r/n)^n < e^r$ for $n = 1, 2, \ldots$.

Solution:

(a) (i) We have $h'(u) = \dfrac{1}{1+u} - \dfrac{(1+u) - u}{(1+u)^2} = \dfrac{(1+u) - 1}{(1+u)^2} = \dfrac{u}{(1+u)^2} > 0.$

(ii) Also $h(0) = h'(0) = 0$, so $h(u) > 0$ for all $u > 0$.

(b) $\ln g(x) = x \ln(1 + r/x)$, so

$$\frac{d}{dx}[\ln g(x)] = \ln(1 + r/x) - \frac{x(r/x^2)}{1 + r/x} = \ln(1 + r/x) - \frac{r/x}{1 + r/x} = h(r/x) > 0$$

(c) Because $(1 + r/n)^n = g(n) > 0$ and $\ln g(x)$ is strictly increasing in x for $x > 0$, it follows that $(1 + r/n)^n$ is strictly increasing in n.

(d) The argument we used to justify Eq. (11.2.2) shows, in particular, that $(1 + r/n)^n \to e^r$ as $n \to \infty$. It follows from part (c) that $(1 + r/n)^n < e^r$ for $n = 1, 2, \ldots$.

EXERCISES FOR SECTION 11.2

1. (a) How much does $8 000 grow to after five years if the annual interest rate is 5%, with continuous compounding?

   (b) How long does it take before the initial amount has doubled?

2. An amount $1 000 earns interest at 5% per year. What will this amount have grown to after: (a) ten years, and (b) 50 years, when interest is compounded: (i) monthly, or (ii) continuously?

3. (a) Find the effective rate corresponding to an annual rate of 10% compounded continuously.

   (b) What is the maximum amount of compound interest that can be earned at an annual rate of 10%?

4. The value v_0 of a new car depreciates continuously at the annual rate of 10%, implying that its value after t years is $v(t) = v_0 e^{-\delta t}$ where $\delta = 0.1$. How many years does it take for the car to lose 90% of its original value?

5. The value of a machine depreciates continuously at the annual rate of 6%. How many years will it take for the value of the machine to halve?

11.3 Present Value

The sum of $1 000 in your hand today is worth more than $1 000 to be received at some date in the future. One important reason is that you can invest the $1 000 and hope to earn some interest or other positive return. Another reason is that if prices are expected to increase due to inflation, then $1 000 at some future date will buy less then than $1 000 does today.

If the interest rate is 11% per year, then after one year the original $1 000 will have grown to the amount $1000(1 + 11/100) = 1110$, and after six years, it will have grown to $1000(1 + 11/100)^6 = 1000 \cdot (1.11)^6 \approx 1870$. This shows that, at the interest rate 11% per year, $1 000 now has the same value as $1 110 next year, or $1 870 in six years, time. Accordingly, if the amount $1 110 is due for payment 1 year from now and the interest rate is 11% per year, then the *present value* of this amount is $1 000. Because $1 000 is less than $1 110, we often speak of $1 000 as the *present discounted value* (or PDV) of $1 110 next year. The ratio $1000/1110 = 1/(1 + 11/100) \approx 0.9009$ is called the (annual) *discount factor*, whose reciprocal 1.11 equals one plus the *discount rate*. This definition makes the discount rate equal to the interest rate of 11%. Similarly, if the interest rate is 11% per year, then the PDV of $1 870 due six years from now is $1 000. Again, the ratio $1000/1870 \approx 0.53$ is called the *discount factor*, this time for money due in six years, time.

Suppose that an amount K is due for payment t years after the present date. What is the *present value* when the interest rate is $p\%$ per year? Equivalently, how much must be deposited today earning $p\%$ annual interest in order to have the amount K after t years? If interest is paid annually, an amount A will have increased to $A(1 + p/100)^t$ after t years, so that we need $A(1 + p/100)^t = K$. Thus, $A = K(1 + p/100)^{-t} = K(1 + r)^{-t}$, where $r = p/100$. Here the annual discount factor is $(1 + r)^{-1}$, and $(1 + r)^{-t}$ is the discount factor appropriate for t years. But if interest is compounded continuously, then the amount A will have increased to Ae^{rt} after t years. Hence, $Ae^{rt} = K$, or $A = Ke^{-rt}$. Here e^{-rt} is the discount factor. To summarize:

PRESENT DISCOUNTED VALUE

Suppose that the interest or discount rate is $p\%$ per year. Let r denote $p/100$. Then the *present discounted value*, or PDV, of an amount K that is payable in t years is:

$$K(1 + r)^{-t} \text{ with annual interest payments} \tag{11.3.1}$$

$$Ke^{-rt} \text{ with continuous compounding of interest} \tag{11.3.2}$$

EXAMPLE 11.3.1 Find the present value of $100 000 which is due for payment after 15 years, if the interest rate is 6% per year, compounded: (a) annually; or (b) continuously.

Solution:

(a) Using Eq. (11.3.1), the present value is $100\,000(1 + 0.06)^{-15} \approx 41\,726.51$.

(b) Using Eq. (11.3.2), the dollar PDV is $100\,000 e^{-0.06 \cdot 15} = 100\,000 e^{-0.9} \approx 40\,656.97$.

As expected, the present value with continuous compounding is smaller because capital increases fastest with continuous compounding of interest.

EXAMPLE 11.3.2 **(When to Harvest a Tree?).** Consider a tree that is planted at time $t = 0$. Let $P(t)$ denote its current market value at time t, where $P(t)$ is differentiable with $P(t) > 0$ for all $t \geq 0$. Assume that the interest rate is $100r\%$ per year, compounded continuously.

(a) At what time t^* should this tree be cut down in order to maximize its present value?

(b) The optimal cutting time t^* depends on the interest rate r. Find dt^*/dr.

Solution:

(a) The present value is $f(t) = P(t)e^{-rt}$, whose derivative is

$$f'(t) = P'(t)e^{-rt} + P(t)(-r)e^{-rt} = e^{-rt}\left[P'(t) - rP(t)\right] \qquad (*)$$

A necessary condition for $t^* > 0$ to maximize $f(t)$ is that $f'(t^*) = 0$. This occurs when

$$P'(t^*) = rP(t^*) \qquad (**)$$

The tree, therefore, should be cut down at a time t^* when the relative rate of increase in the value of the tree is precisely equal to the interest rate. Of course, some conditions have to be placed on f in order for t^* to be a maximum point. It suffices to have $P'(t) \geq rP(t)$ for $t < t^*$ and $P'(t) \leq rP(t)$ for $t > t^*$.

(b) Differentiating $(**)$ w.r.t. r yields

$$P''(t^*)\frac{dt^*}{dr} = P(t^*) + rP'(t^*)\frac{dt^*}{dr}$$

Solving for dt^*/dr,

$$\frac{dt^*}{dr} = \frac{P(t^*)}{P''(t^*) - rP'(t^*)} \qquad (***)$$

Differentiating $(*)$ w.r.t. t yields

$$f''(t) = P''(t)e^{-rt} - rP'(t)e^{-rt} - P'(t)re^{-rt} + r^2P(t)e^{-rt}$$

Consider the second-order condition $f''(t^*) < 0$. By $(**)$, this is satisfied if and only if

$$e^{-rt}[P''(t^*) - 2rP'(t^*) + r^2P(t^*)] = e^{-rt}[P''(t^*) - rP'(t^*)] < 0$$

In this case $dt^*/dr < 0$. Thus, the optimal growing time shortens as r increases, which makes the foresters more impatient. In particular, given any $r > 0$, the optimal t^* is less than the time that maximizes current market value $P(t)$, which is optimal only if $r = 0$.

We did not consider how, after harvesting, the land that the tree grows on may have a further use, such as planting a new tree. This extension is the subject of Exercise 11.4.8.

EXERCISES FOR SECTION 11.3

1. Find the present value of £350 000 which is due after ten years if the interest rate is 8% per year: (a) compounded annually, or (b) compounded continuously.

2. Find the present value of €50 000 which is due after five years when the interest rate is 5.75% per year, paid: (a) annually, or (b) continuously.

3. With reference to Example 11.3.2, consider the case where, for all $t \geq 0$, $f(t) = (t+5)^2 e^{-0.05t}$.

    (a) Find the value of t that maximizes $f(t)$, and study the sign variation of $f'(t)$.

    (b) Find $\lim_{t \to \infty} f(t)$ and draw the graph of f.

11.4 Geometric Series

Geometric series have many applications in economics and finance. Here we shall use them to calculate annuities and mortgage payments.

EXAMPLE 11.4.1 This year a firm has an annual revenue of $100 million that it expects to increase throughout the next decade by 16% per year. How large is its expected revenue in the tenth year, and what is the total revenue expected over the whole period?

Solution: The expected revenue in the second year is $100(1 + 16/100) = 100 \cdot 1.16$, in millions of dollars, and in the third year it is $100 \cdot (1.16)^2$. In the tenth year, the expected revenue is $100 \cdot (1.16)^9$. The total revenue expected during the whole decade is, therefore,

$$100 + 100 \cdot 1.16 + 100 \cdot (1.16)^2 + \cdots + 100 \cdot (1.16)^9$$

If we use a calculator to add these ten different numbers, we obtain a sum that is approximately $2 132 million.

Finding the sum in Example 11.4.1 by adding ten different numbers on a calculator was very tedious. When there are infinitely many terms, it is obviously impossible. There is an easier method, as we now explain.

Consider the n numbers $a, ak, ak^2, \ldots, ak^{n-1}$. Each term is obtained by multiplying its predecessor by a constant k. We wish to find the sum

$$s_n = a + ak + ak^2 + \cdots + ak^{n-2} + ak^{n-1} \qquad (11.4.1)$$

of these numbers. We call this sum a finite *geometric series with quotient k*. The sum in Example 11.4.1 occurs in the case when $a = 100$, $k = 1.16$, and $n = 10$.

To find the sum s_n of the series, we use a trick. First multiply both sides of Eq. (11.4.1) by k, to obtain

$$ks_n = ak + ak^2 + ak^3 + \cdots + ak^{n-1} + ak^n$$

Subtracting (11.4.1) from this equation yields

$$ks_n - s_n = ak^n - a \qquad (11.4.2)$$

We reach this answer because all the other $n - 1$ terms cancel. That is the precisely the point of the trick!

In case $k = 1$, all the terms in (11.4.1) are equal to a, so we see immediately that the sum is $s_n = an$. For $k \neq 1$, however, Eq. (11.4.2) implies that

$$s_n = a \frac{k^n - 1}{k - 1}$$

In conclusion:

FINITE GEOMETRIC SERIES

Provided that $k \neq 1$, one has

$$a + ak + ak^2 + \cdots + ak^{n-1} = a \cdot \frac{k^n - 1}{k - 1} \tag{11.4.3}$$

EXAMPLE 11.4.2 For the sum in Example 11.4.1, we have $a = 100$, $k = 1.16$, and $n = 10$. Hence, Eq. (11.4.3) yields

$$100 + 100 \cdot 1.16 + \cdots + 100 \cdot (1.16)^9 = 100 \frac{(1.16)^{10} - 1}{1.16 - 1}$$

Now it takes many fewer operations on the calculator than in Example 11.4.1 to show that this sum is about 2132.

Infinite Geometric Series

Consider the infinite sequence of numbers

$$1, \frac{1}{2}, \frac{1}{4}, \frac{1}{8}, \frac{1}{16}, \frac{1}{32}, \ldots$$

Each term in the sequence is formed by halving its predecessor. This implies that the nth term is $1/2^{n-1}$. The sum of the n first terms is a finite geometric series with quotient $k = 1/2$ whose first term is $a = 1$. Hence, formula (11.4.3) gives

$$1 + \frac{1}{2} + \frac{1}{2^2} + \cdots + \frac{1}{2^{n-1}} = \frac{1 - (\frac{1}{2})^n}{1 - \frac{1}{2}} = 2(1 - 2^{-n}) = 2 - \frac{1}{2^{n-1}} \tag{$*$}$$

We now ask what is meant by the "infinite sum"

$$1 + \frac{1}{2} + \frac{1}{2^2} + \frac{1}{2^3} + \cdots + \frac{1}{2^{n-1}} + \cdots \tag{$**$}$$

Because all the terms are positive, and there are infinitely many of them, you might be inclined to think that the sum must be infinitely large. According to formula ($*$), however, the sum of the n first terms is equal to $2 - 1/2^{n-1}$. This number is never larger than 2, no matter how large is our choice of n. As n increases, the term $1/2^{n-1}$ comes closer and closer to 0, and the sum in ($*$) tends to 2 in the limit. This makes it natural to *define* the infinite sum in ($**$) as the number 2.

In general, we ask what meaning can be given to the "infinite sum"

$$a + ak + ak^2 + \cdots + ak^{n-1} + \cdots \tag{11.4.4}$$

We use the same idea as in (∗∗), and consider the sum s_n of the n first terms in (11.4.4). According to Eq. (11.4.3), when $k \neq 1$, we have

$$s_n = a \frac{1 - k^n}{1 - k}$$

What happens to this expression as n tends to infinity? The answer evidently depends on k^n, because only this term depends on n. In fact, k^n tends to 0 if $-1 < k < 1$, whereas k^n does not tend to any limit if either $k > 1$ or else $k \leq -1$.[2] It follows that if $|k| < 1$, then the sum s_n of the n first terms in (11.4.4) will tend to the limit $a/(1 - k)$, as n tends to infinity. In this case, we let the limit of (11.4.4) *define* the infinite sum, and we say that the infinite series in (11.4.4) *converges*. To summarize:

INFINITE GEOMETRIC SERIES

If $|k| < 1$, then

$$a + ak + ak^2 + \cdots + ak^{n-1} + \cdots = \frac{a}{1 - k} \tag{11.4.5}$$

Suppose now we extend to infinite sums the summation notation that was introduced in Section 2.9. In case $|k| < 1$, this allows us to write Eq. (11.4.5) as

$$\sum_{n=1}^{\infty} ak^{n-1} = \frac{a}{1 - k}$$

In case $|k| \geq 1$, however, we say that the infinite series (11.4.4) *diverges*. A divergent series has no finite sum. Divergence is obvious if $|k| > 1$. When $k = 1$, then $s_n = na$, which tends to $+\infty$ if $a > 0$ or to $-\infty$ if $a < 0$. When $k = -1$, then s_n is a when n is odd, but 0 when n is even; again there is no limit as $n \to \infty$ (except in the trivial case when $a = 0$).

EXAMPLE 11.4.3   Find the sum of the infinite series

$$1 + 0.25 + (0.25)^2 + (0.25)^3 + (0.25)^4 + \cdots$$

Solution: Inserting $a = 1$ and $k = 0.25$ in formula (11.4.5) gives

$$1 + 0.25 + (0.25)^2 + (0.25)^3 + (0.25)^4 + \cdots = \frac{1}{1 - 0.25} = \frac{1}{0.75} = \frac{4}{3}$$

---

[2] If you are not yet convinced by this claim, study the cases $k = -2$, $k = -1$, $k = -1/2$, $k = 1/2$, and $k = 2$.

EXAMPLE 11.4.4   A rough estimate at the beginning of 1999 of the total oil and gas reserves under the Norwegian continental shelf was $13 \cdot 10^9 = 13$ billion tons of oil equivalent. Output that year was approximately $250 \cdot 10^6 = 250$ million tons.

(a) When will the reserves be exhausted if output is kept at the same constant level?

(b) Suppose that, beginning in 1999, output each year falls by 2% per year. How long will the reserves last in this case?

Solution:

(a) With $13 \cdot 10^9$ tons of reserves being depleted at the rate of $250 \cdot 10^6$ tons per year, reserves will last for t years, where t satisfies $250 \cdot 10^6 \, t = 13 \cdot 10^9$. Hence $t = 13 \cdot 10^9 \div 250 \cdot 10^6 = 52$. So the reserves will be exhausted 52 years after the beginning of 1999, which is at the end of the year 2050.

(b) In 1999, output was $a = 250 \cdot 10^6$. In 2000, it would be $a - 2a/100 = a \cdot 0.98$. In 2001, it becomes $a \cdot 0.98^2$, and so on. If this rate of decline continues forever, the total amount extracted will be

$$a + a \cdot 0.98 + a \cdot (0.98)^2 + \cdots + a \cdot (0.98)^{n-1} + \cdots$$

This geometric series has quotient $k = 0.98$. By formula (11.4.5), the infinite sum is

$$s = \frac{a}{1 - 0.98} = 50a$$

Since $a = 250 \cdot 10^6$, the sum $s = 50 \cdot 250 \cdot 10^6 = 12.5 \cdot 10^9$, which is a little below $13 \cdot 10^9$. The reserves will last for ever, therefore, leaving $0.5 \cdot 10^9 = 500$ million tons as "stranded assets" which will never be extracted.

General Series[3]

We briefly consider general infinite series, not necessarily geometric, denoted by

$$a_1 + a_2 + a_3 + \cdots + a_n + \cdots \tag{11.4.6}$$

What does it mean to say that this infinite series converges? By analogy with our derivation of formula (11.4.5) for geometric series, we form the "partial" sum s_n of the n first terms:

$$s_n = a_1 + a_2 + \cdots + a_n \tag{11.4.7}$$

In particular, $s_1 = a_1$, $s_2 = a_1 + a_2$, $s_3 = a_1 + a_2 + a_3$, and so on. As n increases, these partial sums include more and more terms of the series. Hence, if s_n tends toward a limit s as n tends to ∞, it is reasonable to consider s as the sum of *all* the terms in the series. Then we say that the infinite series is *convergent* with sum s. But if s_n does not tend to a finite limit as n tends to infinity, we say that the series is *divergent*, and that it has no sum.[4]

---

[3] This subsection can be regarded as optional.
[4] As with limits of functions, if $s_n \to \pm\infty$ as $n \to \infty$, this is not regarded as a limit.

For a geometric series, the simple expression we found for s_n made it easy to determine when convergence occurs. For most series, however, there is no such simple formula for the sum of the first n terms, making it difficult to determine whether or not converge occurs. Nevertheless, several so-called *convergence* and *divergence criteria* do give the answer in many cases. These criteria are seldom used directly in economics.

Let us make one general observation: If the series (11.4.6) converges, then the nth term must tend to 0 as n tends to infinity. The argument is simple: If the series is convergent, then s_n in Eq. (11.4.7) will tend to a limit s as n tends to infinity. Now $a_n = s_n - s_{n-1}$, and by definition of convergence, s_{n-1} will also tend to s as n tends to infinity. It follows that $a_n = s_n - s_{n-1}$ must tend to $s - s = 0$ as n tends to infinity. Expressed briefly,

$$a_1 + a_2 + \cdots + a_n + \cdots \text{ converges} \implies \lim_{n \to \infty} a_n = 0 \tag{11.4.8}$$

Hence, convergence of a_n to 0 is necessary for convergence of the series, but not sufficient. That is, a series may satisfy the condition $\lim_{n \to \infty} a_n = 0$ and yet diverge. This is shown by the following standard example:

EXAMPLE 11.4.5 Consider the *harmonic series*

$$1 + \frac{1}{2} + \frac{1}{3} + \frac{1}{4} + \cdots + \frac{1}{n} + \cdots \tag{11.4.9}$$

Its nth term is $1/n$, which tends to 0. But the series is still divergent. To see this, we group the terms together in the following way:

$$1 + \frac{1}{2} + \left(\frac{1}{3} + \frac{1}{4}\right) + \left(\frac{1}{5} + \cdots + \frac{1}{8}\right) + \left(\frac{1}{9} + \cdots + \frac{1}{16}\right) + \left(\frac{1}{17} + \cdots + \frac{1}{32}\right) + \cdots \tag{$*$}$$

Between the first pair of parentheses are the two terms $1/3$ and $1/4$ whose sum exceeds $2/4 = 1/2$. Between the second pair of parentheses are four terms, three greater than $1/8$ and the last equal to $1/8$, so their sum exceeds $4/8 = 1/2$. Between the third pair of parentheses are eight terms, seven greater than $1/16$ and the last equal to $1/16$, so their sum exceeds $8/16 = 1/2$. This pattern repeats itself infinitely often: between the nth pair of parentheses are 2^n terms, of which $2^n - 1$ are greater than 2^{-n-1}, whereas the last is equal to 2^{-n-1}. So their sum exceeds $2^n \cdot 2^{-n-1} = 1/2$. Thus, no matter how large n may be, if m is large enough (in fact, if $m \geq 2^n$), then the sum of the first m terms in $(*)$ exceeds the sum $\frac{1}{2}n$ of n terms all equal to $\frac{1}{2}$. So the series in $(*)$ must diverge.[5]

In general, as you are asked to prove in Exercise 11:

$$\sum_{n=1}^{\infty} \frac{1}{n^p} \text{ is convergent} \iff p > 1 \tag{11.4.10}$$

---

[5] According to H.H. Goldstine (1977), quoting Joseph Hofmann's biography of Leibniz: "The determination of $\sum 1/n$ occupied Leibniz all his life but the solution never came within his grasp."

EXERCISES FOR SECTION 11.4

1. (a) Find s_n, the sum of the finite geometric series
$$1 + \frac{1}{3} + \frac{1}{3^2} + \cdots + \frac{1}{3^{n-1}}.$$
   (b) What is the limit of s_n when n approaches infinity?
   (c) Find the sum $\sum_{n=1}^{\infty}(1/3^{n-1})$.

2. Find the sums of the following geometric series:
   (a) $\frac{1}{5} + \left(\frac{1}{5}\right)^2 + \left(\frac{1}{5}\right)^3 + \left(\frac{1}{5}\right)^4 + \cdots$
   (b) $0.1 + (0.1)^2 + (0.1)^3 + (0.1)^4 + \cdots$
   (c) $517 + 517(1.1)^{-1} + 517(1.1)^{-2} + 517(1.1)^{-3} + \cdots$
   (d) $a + a(1+a)^{-1} + a(1+a)^{-2} + a(1+a)^{-3} + a(1+a)^{-4} + \cdots$, for $a > 0$
   (e) $5 + \frac{5 \cdot 3}{7} + \frac{5 \cdot 3^2}{7^2} + \cdots + \frac{5 \cdot 3^{n-1}}{7^{n-1}} + \cdots$

3. Determine whether the following series are geometric, and find the sums of those geometric series that do converge.
   (a) $8 + 1 + 1/8 + 1/64 + \cdots$
   (b) $-2 + 6 - 18 + 54 - \cdots$
   (c) $2^{1/3} + 1 + 2^{-1/3} + 2^{-2/3} + \cdots$
   (d) $1 - 1/2 + 1/3 - 1/4 + \cdots$

4. Examine the convergence of the following geometric series, and find their sums when they exist:
   (a) $\frac{1}{p} + \frac{1}{p^2} + \frac{1}{p^3} + \cdots$
   (b) $x + \sqrt{x} + 1 + \frac{1}{\sqrt{x}} + \cdots$
   (c) $\sum_{n=1}^{\infty} x^{2n}$

5. Find the sum $\sum_{k=0}^{\infty} b\left(1 + \frac{p}{100}\right)^{-k}$, for $p > 0$.

(SM) 6. Total world consumption of iron was approximately $794 \cdot 10^6$ tons in 1971. If consumption had increased by 5% each year and the resources available for mining in 1971 were $249 \cdot 10^9$ tons, how much longer would the world's iron resources have lasted?

7. The world's total consumption of natural gas was 1 824 million tons oil equivalent (MTOE) in 1994. The reserves at the end of that year were estimated to be 128 300 MTOE. If consumption had increased by 2% in each of the coming years, and no new sources were ever discovered, how much longer would these reserves have lasted?

(SM) 8. Consider Example 11.3.2. Assume that immediately after one tree is felled, a new tree of the same type is planted. If we assume that a new tree is planted at times t, $2t$, $3t$, etc., then the present value of all the trees will be $f(t) = P(t)e^{-rt} + P(t)e^{-2rt} + \cdots$.
   (a) Find the sum of this infinite geometric series.
   (b) Prove that if $f(t)$ has a maximum for some $t^* > 0$, then $P'(t^*)/P(t^*) = r/(1 - e^{-rt^*})$.
   (c) Examine the limit of $P'(t^*)/P(t^*)$ as $r \to 0$.

9. Show that the following series diverge:

(a) $\sum_{n=1}^{\infty} \frac{n}{1+n}$ (b) $\sum_{n=1}^{\infty} (101/100)^n$ (c) $\sum_{n=1}^{\infty} \frac{1}{(1+1/n)^n}$

10. Examine the convergence or divergence of the following series:

(a) $\sum_{n=1}^{\infty} \left(\frac{100}{101}\right)^n$ (b) $\sum_{n=1}^{\infty} \frac{1}{\sqrt{n}}$ (c) $\sum_{n=1}^{\infty} \frac{1}{n^{1.00000001}}$

(d) $\sum_{n=1}^{\infty} \frac{1+n}{4n-3}$ (e) $\sum_{n=1}^{\infty} \left(-\frac{1}{2}\right)^n$ (f) $\sum_{n=1}^{\infty} \left(\sqrt{3}\right)^{1-n}$

(SM) 11. Use the results in Example 10.7.2 to prove the equivalence in (11.4.10). (*Hint*: For $p > 0$, draw the graph of the function $f(x) = x^{-p}$ in $[1, \infty)$. Then interpret each of the two sums $\sum_{n=1}^{\infty} n^{-p}$ and $\sum_{n=2}^{\infty} n^{-p}$ geometrically as the sum of an infinite number of rectangular areas.)

11.5 Total Present Value

Suppose that three successive annual payments are to be made, with the amount $1 000 falling due after one year, then $1 500 after two years, and $2 000 after three years. How much must be deposited in an account today in order to have enough savings to cover these three payments, given that the interest rate is 11% per year? We call this amount the *present value* of the three payments.

In order to have $1 000 after one year, the amount x_1 we must deposit today must satisfy $x_1(1 + 0.11) = 1000$. That is,

$$x_1 = \frac{1000}{1+0.11} = \frac{1000}{1.11}$$

In order to have $1 500 after two years, the amount x_2 we must deposit today must satisfy $x_2(1 + 0.11)^2 = 1500$, so

$$x_2 = \frac{1500}{(1+0.11)^2} = \frac{1500}{(1.11)^2}$$

Finally, to have $2 000 after three years, the amount x_3 we must deposit today must satisfy $x_3(1 + 0.11)^3 = 2000$, so

$$x_3 = \frac{2000}{(1+0.11)^3} = \frac{2000}{(1.11)^3}$$

Hence, the total amount A that must be deposited today in order to cover all three payments, which is the total present value of the three payments, is given by

$$A = \frac{1000}{1.11} + \frac{1500}{(1.11)^2} + \frac{2000}{(1.11)^3}$$

The total is approximately $A \approx 900.90 + 1217.43 + 1462.38 = 3580.71$.

In general, suppose that n successive annual payments $a_1, \ldots, a_n$ will be made, with a_1 being paid after one year, a_2 after two years, and so on. Given that the annual interest is r, how much must be deposited today in order to have enough savings to cover all these future payments? In other words, what is the *present value* of these n payments?

In order to have a_1 after one year, we must deposit $a_1/(1+r)$ today; to have a_2 after two years we must deposit $a_2/(1+r)^2$ today; and so on. The total amount P_n that must be deposited today in order to cover all n payments is, therefore,

$$P_n = \frac{a_1}{1+r} + \frac{a_2}{(1+r)^2} + \cdots + \frac{a_n}{(1+r)^n} \tag{11.5.1}$$

Here, P_n is the *present value* of the n instalments.

An *annuity* is a sequence of equal payments over some time span made at fixed periods of time, typically one year. If $a_1 = a_2 = \cdots = a_n = a$ in Eq. (11.5.1), the equation represents the present value of an annuity. In this case the sum in (11.5.1) is a finite geometric series with n terms. The first term is $a/(1+r)$ and the quotient is $1/(1+r)$. According to the summation formula (11.4.3) for a geometric series, with $k = (1+r)^{-1}$, the sum is

$$P_n = \frac{a}{(1+r)} \frac{1-(1+r)^{-n}}{1-(1+r)^{-1}} = \frac{a}{r}\left[1 - \frac{1}{(1+r)^n}\right]$$

Here the second equality holds because the denominator of the middle expression reduces to r. To summarize:

PRESENT VALUE OF AN ANNUITY

Consider an annuity of a per payment period for n periods, at the rate of interest r per period, where each payment is at the end of the period. Its present value is given by

$$P_n = \frac{a}{1+r} + \cdots + \frac{a}{(1+r)^n} = \frac{a}{r}\left[1 - \frac{1}{(1+r)^n}\right] \tag{11.5.2}$$

This sum is illustrated in Fig. 11.5.1.

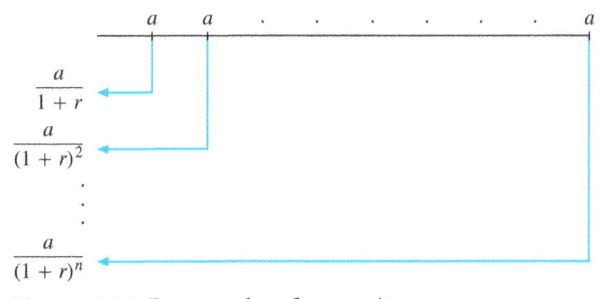

Figure 11.5.1 Present value of an annuity

Formula (11.5.2) gives the present value of n future claims, each of a dollars. Suppose instead we want to find how much has accumulated in the account after n periods, immediately after the last deposit. This is the *future value* F_n of the annuity, given by:

$$F_n = a + a(1+r) + a(1+r)^2 + \cdots + a(1+r)^{n-1} \qquad (*)$$

This different sum is illustrated in Fig. 11.5.2.

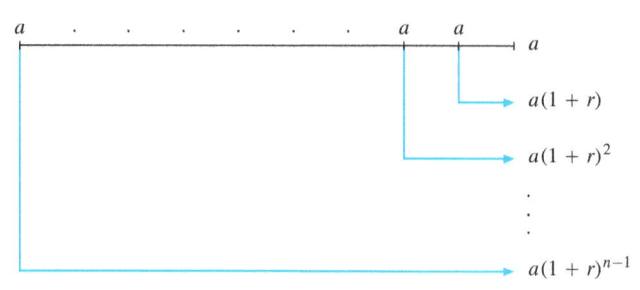

Figure 11.5.2 Future value of an annuity

The summation formula for a geometric series yields:

$$F_n = \frac{a[1-(1+r)^n]}{1-(1+r)} = \frac{a}{r}[(1+r)^n - 1]$$

We can also find the (undiscounted) future value by noticing that in the special case when $a_i = a$ for all i, the terms on the right-hand side of $(*)$ repeat those of the right-hand side of Eq. (11.5.1), when $a_1 = a_2 = \cdots = a_n = a$, but taken in the reverse order and multiplied by the interest factor $(1+r)^n$. This shows that $F_n = P_n(1+r)^n$, and so:

FUTURE VALUE OF AN ANNUITY

Suppose that an amount a is deposited in an account each period for n periods, earning interest at r per period. Then the future value of the account, immediately after the last deposit, is

$$F_n = \frac{a}{r}[(1+r)^n - 1] \qquad (11.5.3)$$

EXAMPLE 11.5.1 Compute the present and the future values of a deposit of $1\,000 in each of the coming eight years if the annual interest rate is 6%.

Solution: To find the present value, we apply formula (11.5.2) with $a = 1000$, $n = 8$ and $r = 6/100 = 0.06$. This gives

$$P_8 = \frac{1000}{0.06}\left(1 - \frac{1}{(1.06)^8}\right) \approx 6209.79$$

The future value is found by applying formula (11.5.3), which gives

$$F_8 = \frac{1000}{0.06}\left[(1.06)^8 - 1\right] \approx 9897.47$$

Alternatively, $F_8 = P_8(1.06)^8 \approx 6209.79 \cdot (1.06)^8 \approx 9897.47$.

Consider next an investment that pays a per period in perpetuity when the interest rate is $r > 0$. To find its present value, we modify formula (11.5.2) by letting n tend to infinity. Then $(1+r)^n$ tends to infinity and so P_n tends to a/r. In the limit, therefore, one has

$$\frac{a}{1+r} + \frac{a}{(1+r)^2} + \cdots = \frac{a}{r} \tag{11.5.4}$$

EXAMPLE 11.5.2   Compute the present value of a series of deposits of \$1 000 at the end of each year in perpetuity, when the annual interest rate is 14%.

Solution: According to formula (11.5.4), we obtain

$$\frac{1000}{1+0.14} + \frac{1000}{(1+0.14)^2} + \cdots = \frac{1000}{0.14} \approx 7142.86$$

The Value of a Continuous Income Stream

So far we have discussed the present and future values of a series of future payments which are made at specific discrete moments in time. Yet it may be useful to consider assets as accruing continuously, like the timber yield from a growing commercial forest. So we consider an income stream where:

1. income is received continuously from time $t = 0$ to time $t = T$ at the variable rate of $f(t)$ dollars per year at each time t;
2. interest is compounded continuously at the fixed rate r per year.

Let $P(t)$ denote the present discounted value (PDV) of all payments made over the time interval $[0, t]$. This means that $P(T)$ represents the amount of money you would have to deposit at time $t = 0$ in order to match what results from (continuously) depositing the income stream $f(t)$ at each time t during the time interval $[0, T]$. Given any $\Delta t > 0$, the present value of all the income received during the interval $[t, t + \Delta t]$ is $P(t + \Delta t) - P(t)$. If Δt is small, the total amount of income received during this time interval is approximately $f(t)\,\Delta t$, whose PDV is approximately $f(t)\,e^{-rt}\,\Delta t$. It follows that $P(t + \Delta t) - P(t) \approx f(t)\,e^{-rt}\,\Delta t$, so

$$[P(t + \Delta t) - P(t)]/\Delta t \approx f(t)\,e^{-rt} \tag{11.5.5}$$

This approximation improves as Δt gets smaller. In fact, the left-hand side of (11.5.5) is the Newton quotient at t of the function $P(t)$, whose limit as $\Delta t \to 0$ is the derivative $P'(t)$. So (11.5.5) implies that $P'(t) = f(t)\,e^{-rt}$. Because $P(0) = 0$, the definition of the definite integral implies that $P(T) = \int_0^T f(t)\,e^{-rt}dt$. So the *present discounted value* at time 0 of this continuous income stream is

$$\text{PDV} = \int_0^T f(t) e^{-rt} dt \qquad (11.5.6)$$

Formula (11.5.6) gives the value at time 0 of the income stream $f(t)$. The *future discounted value* (FDV) at time T of this income stream is $e^{rT} \int_0^T f(t) e^{-rt} dt$. Because e^{rT} is a constant, we can rewrite the integral as

$$\text{FDV} = \int_0^T f(t) e^{r(T-t)} dt \qquad (11.5.7)$$

An easy modification of the argument leading to formula (11.5.6) gives us the *discounted value* (DV) at any time s in $[0, T]$ of the part of the income stream received after time s. In fact, the DV at time s of the income $f(t)$ received in the small time interval $[t, t + dt]$ is $f(t) e^{-r(t-s)} dt$. Integrating over the time interval $[s, T]$ gives

$$\text{DV} = \int_s^T f(t) e^{-r(t-s)} dt \qquad (11.5.8)$$

In case $s = 0$, formula (11.5.8) reduces to (11.5.6), as one would expect.

EXAMPLE 11.5.3 Assume an interest rate of 8% annually, compounded continuously. Find the PDV and the FDV of a constant income stream of $1 000 per year over the next ten years.

Solution: We apply formulas (11.5.6) and (11.5.7) with $r = 0.08$ and $f(t) = 1000$ for t in the interval $[0, 10]$. The answers are

$$\text{PDV} = \int_0^{10} 1000 e^{-0.08t} dt = \Big|_0^{10} 1000 \left(-\frac{e^{-0.08t}}{0.08} \right) = \frac{1000}{0.08}(1 - e^{-0.8}) \approx 6883.39$$

and

$$\text{FDV} = e^{0.08 \cdot 10} \times \text{PDV} \approx e^{0.8} \cdot 6883.39 \approx 15\,319.27$$

EXERCISES FOR SECTION 11.5

1. What is the present value of 15 annual deposits of $3 500 if the first deposit is made after one year and the annual interest rate is 12%?

2. An account has been dormant for many years earning interest at the constant rate of 4% per year. Now the amount is $100 000. How much was in the account ten years ago?

3. At the end of each year for four years you deposit $10 000 into an account earning interest at a rate of 6% per year. How much is in the account at the end of the fourth year?

4. Suppose you are given a choice between the following two alternatives: (i) $13 000 paid after ten years; (ii) $1 000 paid each year for ten years, first payment today. The annual interest rate is 6% per year for the whole period. Which alternative would you choose?

5. An author is to be paid royalties for publishing a book. Two alternative offers are made:

   (i) The author can be paid $21 000 immediately,

   (ii) There can be five equal annual payments of $4 600, the first being paid at once.

   Which of these offers will be more valuable if the interest rate is 6% per annum?

6. Compute the present value of a series of deposits of $1 500 at the end of each year in perpetuity when the interest rate is 8% per year.

7. A trust fund is being set up with a single payment of K. This amount is to be invested at a fixed annual interest rate of r. The fund pays out a fixed annual amount. The first payment is to be made one year after the trust fund was set up. What is the largest amount that can be paid out each year if the fund is to last for ever?

8. The present discounted value of a payment D growing at a constant rate g when the discount rate is r is given by

$$\frac{D}{1+r} + \frac{D(1+g)}{(1+r)^2} + \frac{D(1+g)^2}{(1+r)^3} + \cdots$$

where r and g are positive. What is the condition for convergence? Show that if the series converges, its sum P_0 satisfies $P_0 = D/(r-g)$.

9. Find the PDV and FDV of a constant income stream of $500 per year over the next 15 years, assuming an interest rate of 6% annually, compounded continuously.

11.6 Mortgage Repayments

Suppose a family takes out a home mortgage at a fixed interest rate. This means that, like an annuity, equal payments are due each period (say, at the end of each month). Regular payments continue until the loan is paid off after, say, 20 years. Each payment goes partly to pay interest on the outstanding principal, and partly to repay principal (that is, to reduce the outstanding balance). The interest part is largest for the first period, when interest has to be paid on the whole loan. But it is smallest in the last period, because by then the outstanding balance is small. For the principal repayment, which is the difference between the fixed monthly payment and the interest, it is the other way around.

EXAMPLE 11.6.1 A person borrows $50 000 at the beginning of a year and is supposed to pay it off in five equal instalments at the end of each year, with interest at 15% compounding annually. Find the annual payment.

Solution: Suppose that the five repayments are each of amount $a. Then, according to formula (11.5.2), the present value of these payments in dollars is

$$\frac{a}{1.15} + \frac{a}{(1.15)^2} + \frac{a}{(1.15)^3} + \frac{a}{(1.15)^4} + \frac{a}{(1.15)^5} = \frac{a}{0.15}\left[1 - \frac{1}{(1.15)^5}\right]$$

Each payment should be chosen to make this sum equal to $50\,000$, implying that

$$\frac{a}{0.15}\left[1 - \frac{1}{(1.15)^5}\right] = 50\,000 \qquad (*)$$

This has the solution $a \approx 14\,915.78$. Alternatively, we can calculate the sum of the future values of all repayments and then equate it to the future value of the original loan. This yields the equation

$$a + a(1.15) + a(1.15)^2 + a(1.15)^3 + a(1.15)^4 = 50\,000(1.15)^5$$

This is equivalent to $(*)$.

To illustrate how the interest part and the principal repayment part of each yearly payment of $14\,915.78 vary from year to year, we construct the following table:

Year	Payment	Interest	Principal repayment	Outstanding balance
1	14 915.78	7 500.00	7 415.78	42 584.22
2	14 915.78	6 387.63	8 528.15	34 056.07
3	14 915.78	5 108.41	9 807.37	24 248.70
4	14 915.78	3 637.31	11 278.47	12 970.23
5	14 915.78	1 945.55	12 970.23	0

Note that the interest payment each year is 15% of the outstanding balance from the previous year. The rest of each annual payment of $14\,915.78 is the principal repayment that year. This is subtracted from the outstanding balance from the previous year. Figure 11.6.1 is a chart showing the amount of each year's interest and principal repayment.

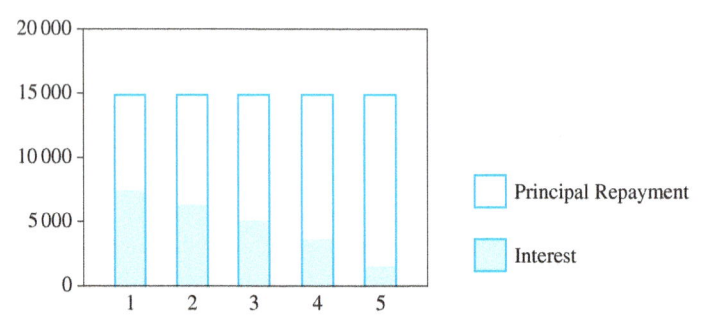

Figure 11.6.1 Interest and principal repayment in Example 11.6.1

Suppose a loan of K dollars is repaid in n equal instalments of a dollars each period, where the interest rate is $p\%$ per period. In effect, this is an annuity with an interest rate $r = p/100$. According to Eq. (11.5.2), the payment a each period must satisfy

$$K = \frac{a}{r}\left[1 - \frac{1}{(1+r)^n}\right] = \frac{a}{r}[1 - (1+r)^{-n}] \qquad (11.6.1)$$

Solving for a yields

$$a = \frac{rK}{1 - (1+r)^{-n}} \qquad (11.6.2)$$

EXAMPLE 11.6.2 Suppose that the loan in Example 11.6.1 is being repaid by equal monthly payments at the end of each month with interest at the nominal rate 15% per year, compounding monthly. Use formula (11.6.2) to find the monthly payment.

Solution: The interest period is one month and the monthly rate is $15/12 = 1.25\%$, so that $r = 1.25/100 = 0.0125$. Also, $n = 5 \cdot 12 = 60$, so with $K = 5000$ formula (11.6.2) gives:

$$a = \frac{0.0125 \cdot 5000}{1 - 1.0125^{-60}} \approx 1189.50$$

The annuities considered so far are *ordinary* annuities where each payment is made at the *end* of the payment period. If the payment each period is made at the beginning of the period, the annuity is called an *annuity due*. This kind of annuity can be handled easily by regarding it as an ordinary annuity, except that there is an immediate initial payment.

EXAMPLE 11.6.3 A person assumes responsibility for a loan of $335 000 which is due to be repaid in 15 equal repayments of $a each year, the first one immediately, and the following at the beginning of each subsequent year. Find a if the annual interest rate is 14%.

Solution: The present value of the first payment is obviously a. The present value of the subsequent 14 repayments is found by applying formula (11.6.1) with $r = 0.14$ and $n = 14$. The sum of the present values must be equal to $335 000$:

$$a + \frac{a}{0.14}\left[1 - \frac{1}{(1+0.14)^{14}}\right] = 335\,000$$

This reduces to $a + 6.0020715a = 335\,000$. Solving for a gives $a \approx \$47\,843$.

Some lenders prefer to specify a fixed payment each period, and let the loan run for however many periods it takes to pay off the debt. This way of paying off the loan functions essentially as an annuity. The difference is that there will have to be a final adjustment in the last payment in order to make the present value of all the payments equal the borrowed amount. In this case it is convenient to solve Eq. (11.6.1) for n. Notice that

$$K = \frac{a}{r}[1 - (1+r)^{-n}] \Leftrightarrow \frac{1}{(1+r)^n} = 1 - \frac{rK}{a} = \frac{a - rK}{a} \Leftrightarrow (1+r)^n = \frac{a}{a - rK}$$

Taking the natural logarithm of each side yields $n \ln(1 + r) = \ln[a/(a - rK)]$, so:

MORTGAGE REPAYMENT PERIOD

The number of periods needed to pay off a loan of amount K at the rate a per period, when the interest rate is r per period, is given by the smallest integer n such that

$$n \geq \frac{\ln a - \ln(a - rK)}{\ln(1 + r)} \tag{11.6.3}$$

Unless this happens to be an equality, the last payment will need to be less than a.

EXAMPLE 11.6.4 A loan of $50 000 at the annual interest rate of 15% is to be repaid with a payment of $20 000, covering both interest and the principal repayment, at the end of each succeeding year. When is the loan paid off? What is the final payment?

Solution: We begin by computing the number n of annual payments of $20 000 which are needed to pay off $50 000. According to Eq. (11.6.3), with $r = 0.15$, $a = 20\,000$, and $K = 50\,000$, we obtain n as the smallest integer greater than or equal to

$$\frac{\ln(20\,000) - \ln(20\,000 - 0.15 \cdot 50\,000)}{\ln(1 + 0.15)} = \frac{\ln 1.6}{\ln 1.15} \approx 3.3629$$

Thus, four payments are needed. The first three are $20 000, followed by an additional final payment in the fourth year. To find this final payment, we calculate the future value of the three payments of $20 000, three years after the loan was taken out. This value is:

$$20\,000 \cdot (1.15)^2 + 20\,000 \cdot 1.15 + 20\,000 = \frac{20\,000}{0.15}\left[(1.15)^3 - 1\right] \approx 69\,450$$

The future value of the $50 000 loan after the same three years is $50\,000 \cdot (1.15)^3 = \$76\,043.75$. Thus the remaining debt after the third payment is $\$76\,043.75 - \$69\,450 = \$6593.75$. If the remaining debt and the accumulated interest are paid one year later, the amount due is $\$6593.75 \cdot 1.15 = \$7582.81$.

Deposits within an Interest Period

Many bank accounts have an interest period of one year, or at least one month. If you deposit an amount *within* an interest period, the bank will often use simple interest, not compound interest. In this case, if you make a deposit within an interest period, then at the end of the period the amount you deposited will be multiplied by the factor $1 + rt$, where t is the remaining fraction of the interest period.

EXAMPLE 11.6.5 At the end of each quarter, beginning on 31 March, 2009, a person deposits $100 in an account on which interest is paid annually at the rate 10% per year. How much is there in the account on 31 December, 2011?

Solution: The deposits during 2009 are illustrated here:

```
31/3         30/6         30/9         31/12
 |------------|------------|------------|
100          100          100          100
```

These four deposits are made at the end of each quarter within the year 1999. In order to find the balance at the end of 1999 (the interest period), we use simple (not compound) interest. This gives

$$100\left(1 + 0.10 \cdot \frac{3}{4}\right) + 100\left(1 + 0.10 \cdot \frac{2}{4}\right) + 100\left(1 + 0.10 \cdot \frac{1}{4}\right) + 100 = 415$$

Doing the same for the years 2010 and 2011 as well, we replace the 12 original deposits by the amount $415 at the end of each of the years 2009, 2010, and 2011, as shown here:

```
  31/12/1999           31/12/2000           31/12/2001
  |--------------------|--------------------|
       415                  415                  415
```

The balance at the end of the three years is $415 \cdot (1.10)^2 + 415 \cdot 1.10 + 415 = 1373.65$. So on 31 December, 2011, the person has \$1 373.65.

EXERCISES FOR SECTION 11.6

1. A person borrows \$80 000 at the beginning of one year.

   (a) Suppose that the loan is to be repaid in ten equal instalments at the end of each year, with interest at 7% compounding annually. Find the annual payment.

   (b) Suppose that the loan is to be repaid in 120 equal instalments at the end of each month, with interest at the annual rate of 7%, compounded monthly. Find the monthly payment.

2. Suppose that each year for six years, you deposit \$8 000 in an account that earns interest at the annual rate 7%. How much do you have immediately after the last deposit? How much do you have four years after the last deposit?

3. Ronald invests money in a project which triples his money in 20 years. Assuming annual compounding of interest, what is the rate of interest? What if you assume continuous compounding?

4. [HARDER] A construction firm wants to buy a building site and has the choice between three different payment schedules:

   (i) Pay \$670 000 in cash.

   (ii) Pay \$120 000 per year for eight years, where the first instalment is to be paid at once.

   (iii) Pay \$220 000 in cash and thereafter \$70 000 per year for 12 years, where the first instalment is to be paid after one year.

   Determine which schedule is least expensive if the interest rate is 11.5% and the firm has at least \$670 000 available to spend in cash. What happens if the interest rate is 12.5%?

11.7 Internal Rate of Return

Suppose the numbers $a_0, a_1, \ldots, a_n$ represent the returns earned by an investment project in $n+1$ successive years. Negative numbers represent losses, whereas positive numbers represent profits, so each a_i is actually the *net return*. Also, for $i = 1, 2, \ldots n$ we think of a_i as associated with year i, whereas a_0 is associated with the present period. In most investment projects, a_0 is a big negative number, because a large initial expense precedes any positive returns. Consider an interest rate of $p\%$ per year, and let $r = p/100$. Then the net present value of the profits accruing from the project is given by

$$A = a_0 + \frac{a_1}{1+r} + \frac{a_2}{(1+r)^2} + \cdots + \frac{a_n}{(1+r)^n}$$

Several different criteria are used to compare alternative investment projects. One is simply to choose the project whose profit stream has the largest present value. The interest rate to use could be an accepted rate for capital investments. A different criterion is based on the *internal rate of return*, which is defined as an interest rate that makes the present value of all payments equal to 0.

As a simple example, suppose you invest an amount a which pays back b one year later. Then the rate of return is the interest rate r that makes the present value of the investment project equal to zero. That is, r must satisfy $-a + (1+r)^{-1}b = 0$, so $r = (b/a) - 1$. For example, when $a = 1000$ and $b = 1200$, the rate of return is $r = (1200/1000) - 1 = 0.2$, or 20% per year.

For a general investment project yielding returns $a_0, a_1, \ldots, a_n$, the internal rate of return is a number r such that

$$a_0 + \frac{a_1}{1+r} + \frac{a_2}{(1+r)^2} + \cdots + \frac{a_n}{(1+r)^n} = 0 \tag{11.7.1}$$

If two investment projects both have a unique internal rate of return, then a criterion for choosing between them is to prefer the project that has the higher internal rate of return. Note that Eq. (11.7.1) is a polynomial equation of degree n in the discount factor $(1+r)^{-1}$. In general, this equation does not have a unique positive solution r.

EXAMPLE 11.7.1 An investment project has an initial outlay of $50 000, and at the end of the next two years its returns are $30 000 and $40 000, respectively. Find the associated internal rate of return.

Solution: In this case, Eq. (11.7.1) takes the form

$$-50\,000 + \frac{30\,000}{1+r} + \frac{40\,000}{(1+r)^2} = 0$$

Put $s = (1+r)^{-1}$. Then the equation becomes

$$40\,000 s^2 + 30\,000 s - 50\,000 = 0$$

This can be reduced to the quadratic equation $4s^2 + 3s - 5 = 0$. Its only positive solution is $s = \tfrac{1}{8}(\sqrt{89} - 3) \approx 0.804$. Then $r = 1/s - 1 \approx 0.243 = 24.3\%$.

Suppose that $a_0 < 0$ and $a_1, \ldots, a_n$ are all > 0. In this case Eq. (11.7.1) has a unique solution r^* satisfying $1 + r^* > 0$. So there is a unique internal rate of return $r^* > -1$. Also, the internal rate of return is positive if $\sum_{i=0}^{n} a_i > 0$. Exercise 3 asks you to prove these results.

EXERCISES FOR SECTION 11.7

1. An investment project has an initial outlay of $50 000 and at the end of each of the next two years has returns of $30 000. Find the associated internal rate of return r.

2. Suppose that in Eq. (11.7.1) we have $a_0 < 0$ and $a_i = a > 0$ for $i = 1, 2, \ldots$. Find an expression for the internal rate of return in the limit as $n \to \infty$.

3. Consider an investment project with an initial loss, so that $a_0 < 0$, and thereafter no losses. Suppose also that the sum of the later profits is larger than the initial loss. Prove that there is a unique internal rate of return, $r^* > -1$, and that $r^* > 0$ if $\sum_{i=0}^{n} a_i > 0$. (*Hint*: Define $f(r)$ as the expression on the left side of (11.7.1). Then study the signs of $f(r)$ and $f'(r)$ on the interval $(0, \infty)$.)

4. An investment in a certain machine is expected to earn a profit of $400 000 each year. What is the maximum price that should be paid for the machine if it has a lifetime of seven years, the interest rate is 17.5%, and the annual profit is earned at the end of each year?

SM 5. [HARDER] An investment project has an initial outlay of $100 000, and at the end of each of the next 20 years has a return of $10 000. Show that there is a unique positive internal rate of return, and find its approximate value. (*Hint*: Use $s = (1+r)^{-1}$ as a new variable. Prove that the equation you obtain for s has a unique positive solution. Verify that $s = 0.928$ is an approximate root.)

6. [HARDER] Alice is obliged to pay Bob $1 000 yearly for five years, starting at the end of the first year. Bob sells this claim to Cathy for $4 340 in cash. Find an equation that determines the rate of return p that Cathy obtains from this investment. Prove that it is a little less than 5%.

11.8 A Glimpse at Difference Equations

Many of the quantities economists study, such as income, consumption, and savings, are recorded at fixed time intervals such as each day, week, quarter, or year. Equations that relate such quantities at different discrete moments of time are called *difference equations*. In fact difference equations can be viewed as the discrete time counterparts of the differential equations in continuous time that will be studied in Sections 11.9 and 11.10.

Let $t = 0, 1, 2, \ldots$ denote different discrete time periods or moments of time. We usually call $t = 0$ the *initial period*. If $x(t)$ is a function defined for $t = 0, 1, 2, \ldots$, we often use $x_0, x_1, x_2, \ldots$ to denote $x(0), x(1), x(2), \ldots$. Thus, in general, we write x_t for $x(t)$.

A simple example of a first-order difference equation is

$$x_{t+1} = ax_t \qquad (11.8.1)$$

for $t = 0, 1, \ldots$, where a is a constant. This is a first-order equation because it relates the value of a function in period $t+1$ to the value of the same function in the previous period t only. Suppose x_0 is given. Repeatedly applying (11.8.1) gives $x_1 = ax_0$; then $x_2 = ax_1 = a \cdot ax_0 = a^2 x_0$; next, $x_3 = ax_2 = a \cdot a^2 x_0 = a^3 x_0$; and so on. In general,

$$x_t = x_0 a^t \qquad (11.8.2)$$

The function $x_t = x_0 a^t$ satisfies (11.8.1) for all t, as can be verified directly. For the given value of x_0, there is clearly no other function that satisfies the equation.

EXAMPLE 11.8.1 Consider the difference equation $x_{t+1} = 0.2x_t$, for $t = 0, 1, \ldots$, where $x_0 = 100$. From Eq. (11.8.2), we have $x_t = 100(0.2)^t$.

EXAMPLE 11.8.2 Let K_t denote the balance in an account at the beginning of period t when the interest rate is r per period. Then the balance in the account at time $t+1$ is given by the difference equation $K_{t+1} = K_t + rK_t = (1+r)K_t$, for $t = 0, 1, \ldots$. It follows immediately from (11.8.2) that $K_t = K_0(1+r)^t$, as is well known to us already from Section 2.2, and from earlier in this chapter. In general, this difference equation describes growth at the constant proportional rate r each period.

EXAMPLE 11.8.3 (**A Multiplier–Accelerator Model of Economic Growth**). Let Y_t denote GDP, I_t total investment, and S_t total saving, all in period t. Suppose that savings are proportional to GDP, and that investment is proportional to the change in income from period t to $t+1$. Then, for $t = 0, 1, 2, \ldots$,

(i) $S_t = \alpha Y_t$ (ii) $I_{t+1} = \beta(Y_{t+1} - Y_t)$ (iii) $S_t = I_t$

The last equation is the equilibrium condition requiring that saving equals investment in each period. Here α and β are positive constants, and we assume that $\beta > \alpha > 0$. Deduce a difference equation determining the path of Y_t given Y_0, and solve it.

Solution: From equations (i) and (iii) we have $I_t = \alpha Y_t$, and so $I_{t+1} = \alpha Y_{t+1}$. Inserting this into (ii) yields $\alpha Y_{t+1} = \beta(Y_{t+1} - Y_t)$, or $(\alpha - \beta)Y_{t+1} = -\beta Y_t$. Thus,

$$Y_{t+1} = \frac{\beta}{\beta - \alpha} Y_t = \left(1 + \frac{\alpha}{\beta - \alpha}\right) Y_t \qquad (*)$$

Using (11.8.2) gives the solution

$$Y_t = \left(1 + \frac{\alpha}{\beta - \alpha}\right)^t Y_0 \text{ for } t = 1, 2, \ldots$$

Linear First-order Equations with Constant Coefficients

Consider next the first-order linear difference equation

$$x_{t+1} = ax_t + b \qquad (11.8.3)$$

for $t = 0, 1, 2, \ldots$, where a and b are constant coefficients. Equation (11.8.1) is the special case where $b = 0$. Starting with a given x_0, we can calculate x_t algebraically for small t. Indeed,

$$x_1 = ax_0 + b$$
$$x_2 = ax_1 + b = a(ax_0 + b) + b = a^2 x_0 + (a+1)b$$
$$x_3 = ax_2 + b = a(a^2 x_0 + (a+1)b) + b = a^3 x_0 + (a^2 + a + 1)b$$

and so on. This suggests a clear pattern. In general, provided that $a \neq 1$, we have

$$x_t = a^t x_0 + (a^{t-1} + a^{t-2} + \cdots + a + 1)b$$

It is straightforward to check directly that this satisfies (11.8.3). By the summation formula for a geometric series, for $a \neq 1$ we have $1 + a + a^2 + \cdots + a^{t-1} = (1 - a^t)/(1 - a)$. Thus:

Given that $a \neq 1$,

$$x_{t+1} = ax_t + b \Leftrightarrow x_t = a^t \left(x_0 - \frac{b}{1-a} \right) + \frac{b}{1-a} \quad \text{for } t = 0, 1, 2, \ldots \quad (11.8.4)$$

When $a = 1$, we have $1 + a + \cdots + a^{t-1} = t$ and $x_t = x_0 + tb$ for $t = 1, 2, \ldots$.

EXAMPLE 11.8.4 Solve the difference equation $x_{t+1} = \frac{1}{3}x_t - 8$.

Solution: Using Eq. (11.8.4), we obtain the solution $x_t = \left(\frac{1}{3}\right)^t (x_0 + 12) - 12$.

Equilibrium States and Stability

Consider the solution of $x_{t+1} = ax_t + b$ given in (11.8.4). In case $x_0 = b/(1-a)$, the solution reduces to $x_t = b/(1-a)$ for all t. For this reason, the constant $x^* = b/(1-a)$ is called an *equilibrium*, or a *stationary* or *steady* state, for the difference equation $x_{t+1} = ax_t + b$.

Alternatively, note that if x^* is a steady state, there must be a solution of the difference equation that satisfies $x_t = x^*$ for all t. In the case of Eq. (11.8.3), we must have $x_{t+1} = x_t = x^*$ and so $x^* = ax^* + b$. So, provided $a \neq 1$, we get $x^* = b/(1-a)$ as before.

Suppose the constant a in Eq. (11.8.3) satisfies $|a| < 1$, or equivalently, $-1 < a < 1$. Then $a^t \to 0$ as $t \to \infty$, so Eq. (11.8.4) implies that

$$x_t \to x^* = b/(1-a) \quad \text{as } t \to \infty$$

Hence, if $|a| < 1$, the solution converges to the equilibrium state as $t \to \infty$. Then Eq. (11.8.3) is said to be *globally asymptotically stable*. But if $|a| > 1$, then the absolute value of a^t tends to ∞ as $t \to \infty$. Now Eq. (11.8.4) implies that, except when $x_0 = b/(1-a)$, the solution x_t moves farther and farther away from the equilibrium state. Then Eq. (11.8.3) is said to be *unstable*. Illustrations of the different possibilities are given in Section 11.1 of FMEA.

EXAMPLE 11.8.5 The equation in Example 11.8.4 is stable because $a = 1/3$. The equilibrium state is -12. The solution given in that example shows that $x_t \to -12$ as $t \to \infty$.

EXAMPLE 11.8.6 (**Mortgage Repayments**). A particular case of the difference equation in (11.8.3) occurs when a family borrows an amount K at time 0 as a home mortgage. Suppose there is a fixed interest rate r per period (usually a month rather than a year). Suppose too that the mortgage payments are a each period, until the mortgage is paid off after n periods (for example, 360 months, or 30 years). The outstanding balance or *principal* b_t on the loan in period t satisfies the difference equation $b_{t+1} = (1+r)b_t - a$, with $b_0 = K$ and $b_n = 0$. Equation (11.8.4) gives the solution to this difference equation, which is

$$b_t = (1+r)^t (K - a/r) + a/r$$

But $b_t = 0$ when $t = n$, so $0 = (1+r)^n (K - a/r) + a/r$. Solving for K yields

$$K = \frac{a}{r}\left[1 - (1+r)^{-n}\right] = a\sum_{t=1}^{n}(1+r)^{-t} \qquad (*)$$

The original loan, therefore, must be equal to the present discounted value of n equal repayments of amount a each period, starting in period 1. Solving for a instead yields

$$a = \frac{rK}{1 - (1+r)^{-n}} = \frac{rK(1+r)^n}{(1+r)^n - 1} \qquad (**)$$

Formulas $(*)$ and $(**)$ are the same as those in Eqs (11.6.1) and (11.6.2), which were derived by a more direct argument.

EXERCISES FOR SECTION 11.8

1. Find the solutions of the following difference equations:

    (a) $x_{t+1} = -2x_t$ (b) $6x_{t+1} = 5x_t$ (c) $x_{t+1} = -0.3x_t$

2. Find the solutions of the following difference equations with the given values of x_0:

    (a) $x_{t+1} = x_t - 4, \quad x_0 = 0$ (b) $x_{t+1} = \frac{1}{2}x_t + 2, \quad x_0 = 6$
    (c) $2x_{t+1} + 6x_t + 5 = 0, \quad x_0 = 1$ (d) $x_{t+1} + x_t = 8, \quad x_0 = 2$

3. Suppose supply at price P_t is $S(P_t) = \alpha P_t - \beta$ and demand at price P_{t+1} is $D(P_{t+1}) = \gamma - \delta P_{t+1}$. Solve the difference equation $S(P_t) = D(P_{t+1})$, assuming that all constants are positive.

11.9 Essentials of Differential Equations

In economic growth theory, in studies of the extraction of natural resources, in many models in environmental economics, and in several other areas of economics, one encounters equations where the unknowns include not only functions, but also the derivatives of these functions. Such equations are called *differential equations*. Their study is one of the most fascinating fields of mathematics.

Here we shall consider only a few simple types of differential equation. They will involve functions of an independent variable that we denote by t, because most of the differential equations in economics have time as the independent variable.

We have already solved the simplest type of differential equation. Given a particular function $f(t)$, find all functions that have $f(t)$ as their derivative. This requires one to solve

$\dot{x}(t) = f(t)$ for the unknown function $x(t)$, where $\dot{x}$ denotes the derivative of x w.r.t. time t. We already know that the solution is the indefinite integral:

$$\dot{x}(t) = f(t) \iff x(t) = \int f(t)\, dt + C$$

We call $x(t) = \int f(t)\, dt + C$ the *general* solution of the equation $\dot{x}(t) = f(t)$.

We move on to some more challenging types of differential equation.

The Exponential Growth Law

Let $x(t)$ denote an economic quantity such as the GDP of China. The ratio $\dot{x}(t)/x(t)$ has previously been called the *relative rate of change* of this quantity. Several economic models postulate that the relative rate of change is a constant r. Thus, for all t

$$\dot{x}(t) = rx(t) \tag{11.9.1}$$

Which functions have a constant relative rate of change? For $r = 1$ the differential equation is $\dot{x} = x$, and we know that the derivative of $x = e^t$ is $\dot{x} = e^t$, the same function. More generally, the function $x = Ae^t$ satisfies $\dot{x} = x$ for all values of the constant A.

By trial and error you will probably be able to come up with $x(t) = Ae^{rt}$ as a solution of (11.9.1). In any case, this is easy to verify. Indeed, if $x = Ae^{rt}$, then $\dot{x}(t) = Are^{rt} = rx(t)$. Moreover, we can prove that no other function satisfies (11.9.1). To do so, multiply Eq. (11.9.1) by the positive function e^{-rt}, then collect all terms on the left-hand side. This gives

$$\dot{x}(t)e^{-rt} - rx(t)e^{-rt} = 0 \tag{11.9.2}$$

Now Eq. (11.9.2) is entirely equivalent to Eq. (11.9.1). But the left-hand side of Eq. (11.9.2) is the derivative of the product $x(t)e^{-rt}$. So Eq. (11.9.2) can be rewritten as $\frac{d}{dt}[x(t)e^{-rt}] = 0$. It follows that $x(t)e^{-rt}$ must equal a constant A. Hence, any solution of (11.9.1) takes the form $x(t) = Ae^{rt}$. To determine the constant A, note that if the value of $x(t)$ at $t = 0$ is x_0, then $x_0 = Ae^0 = A$. We conclude that:

EXPONENTIAL GROWTH

$$\dot{x}(t) = rx(t) \text{ with } x(0) = x_0 \iff x(t) = x_0 e^{rt} \tag{11.9.3}$$

EXAMPLE 11.9.1   Let $S(t)$ denote the sales volume per unit of time of a particular commodity, evaluated at time t. Suppose that no sales promotion is carried out, leading sales to decelerate at the constant proportional rate $a > 0$, implying that $\dot{S}(t) = -aS(t)$.

(a) Find an expression for $S(t)$ when sales at time 0 are S_0.

(b) Solve the equation $S_0 e^{-at} = \frac{1}{2}S_0$ for t. Interpret the answer.

Solution:

(a) This is an equation like Eq. (11.9.1) with $x = S$ and $r = -a$. According to Eq. (11.9.3), the solution is $S(t) = S_0 e^{-at}$.

(b) From $S_0 e^{-at} = \frac{1}{2} S_0$, we obtain $e^{-at} = \frac{1}{2}$. Taking the natural logarithm of each side yields $-at = \ln(1/2) = -\ln 2$. Hence $t = \ln 2 / a$. This is how much time it takes for sales to halve.

Equation (11.9.1) has often been called the *law of natural growth*. Regardless of its name, it is probably the most important differential equation in economics. So all economists should know how to solve it.

The same equation is also important in biology. Indeed, let $x(t)$ denote the number of individuals in a population at time t. The population could be, for instance, a particular colony of bacteria, or polar bears in the Arctic. In such a setting, the proportional rate of growth $\dot{x}(t)/x(t)$ can be called the *per capita growth rate* of the population. If there is neither immigration nor emigration, then the per capita growth rate will be equal to the difference between the per capita birth and death rates. These rates will depend on many factors such as food supply, age distribution, available living space, predators, disease, and parasites, among other things.

Equation (11.9.1) specifies a simple model of population growth, following what economists often call *Malthus's law*. According to the solution (11.9.3), if the per capita growth rate is constant, then the population must grow exponentially. In reality, of course, exponential growth can go on only for a limited time. It is time to consider some more general models of population growth.

Another way to solve (11.9.1) is to take logarithms. Note that $d(\ln x)/dt = \dot{x}/x = r$, so $\ln x(t) = \int r \, dt = rt + C$. This implies that $x(t) = e^{rt+C} = e^{rt} e^C = A e^{rt}$, where $A = e^C$. In fact, a generalized version of Eq. (11.9.1) allows for the growth rate r to be a function $r(t)$ of time, giving the differential equation:

$$\dot{x}(t) = r(t) x(t) \tag{11.9.4}$$

Provided that $x(t) \neq 0$, this can be rearranged to get

$$\frac{d}{dt} \ln x(t) = \frac{\dot{x}(t)}{x(t)} = r(t)$$

The solution is $\ln x(t) - \ln x(0) = R(t)$, where $R(t) = \int_0^t r(s) \, ds$. Taking exponentials, we get $x(t) = x(0) e^{R(t)}$.

In applications, it is sometimes useful to have an "initial value" for a differential equation at a time t other than $t = 0$. This is easily done, as $t = 0$ is essentially no more than a convention. Indeed, if the evolution of x is given by Eq. (11.9.1), we know from (11.9.3) that, for any other starting time t_0, for all t one has

$$x(t_0) = x_0 e^{rt_0} \quad \text{and} \quad x(t) = x_0 e^{rt}$$

Now, the latter is equivalent to

$$x(t) = x_0 e^{r(t-t_0+t_0)} = x_0 e^{r(t-t_0)} e^{rt_0} = (x_0 e^{rt_0}) e^{r(t-t_0)} = x(t_0) e^{r(t-t_0)}$$

Thus, the initial reference point of the equation has been moved to t_0.

Growth Towards An Upper Limit

Suppose that the population size $x(t)$ cannot exceed some carrying capacity K. Suppose to that the rate of change of population is proportional to its deviation from this carrying capacity. This is expressed by the equation

$$\dot{x}(t) = a[K - x(t)] \qquad (11.9.5)$$

With a little trick, it is easy to find all the solutions to this equation. Define a new function $u(t) = K - x(t)$, which at each time t measures the deviation of the population size from the carrying capacity K. Then $\dot{u}(t) = -\dot{x}(t)$. Inserting this into (∗) gives $-\dot{u}(t) = au(t)$, or $\dot{u}(t) = -au(t)$. This is an equation like (11.9.1). The solution is $u(t) = Ae^{-at}$, so that $K - x(t) = Ae^{-at}$, hence $x(t) = K - Ae^{-at}$. If $x(0) = x_0$, then $x_0 = K - A$, and so $A = K - x_0$. It follows that:

BOUNDED EXPONENTIAL GROWTH

$$\dot{x}(t) = a[K - x(t)] \text{ with } x(0) = x_0 \iff x(t) = K - (K - x_0)e^{-at} \qquad (11.9.6)$$

In Exercise 4 we shall see that the same equation describes the population in countries where the indigenous population has a fixed relative rate of growth, but where there is a fixed numerical quota of immigrants each year. The same equation can also represent several other phenomena, some of which are discussed in other exercises for this section.

EXAMPLE 11.9.2   Let $x(t)$ denote the population in millions of individuals at time t. Suppose that $x(t)$ starts from 50 million at time $t = 0$, and then follows the differential equation (11.9.5) with $a = 0.05$ and a carrying capacity of $K = 200$ million. Find the solution of Eq. (11.9.5) in this case, then sketch its graph.

Solution: Using Eq. (11.9.6) with $a = 0.05$ and $K = 200$, we find the solution

$$x(t) = 200 - (200 - 50)e^{-0.05t} = 200 - 150e^{-0.05t}$$

The graph is drawn in Fig. 11.9.1.

Note that the differential equation (11.9.5) is a special case of the general equation

$$\dot{x} + ax = b \qquad (11.9.7)$$

A trivial case occurs when $a = 0$ and the solution is $x(t) = bt + C$. Ruling this case out, we show how a changing the variable from x to $y = x - b/a$ can transform (11.9.7) into (11.9.1), whose solution is already known.[6] Indeed, inserting $x = y + b/a$ into (11.9.7) gives the new differential equation $\dot{y} + a(y + b/a) = b$, which reduces to $\dot{y} + ay = 0$. This,

---

[6] Section 11.10 provides some motivation for this transformation.

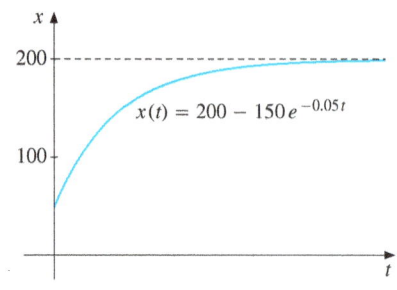

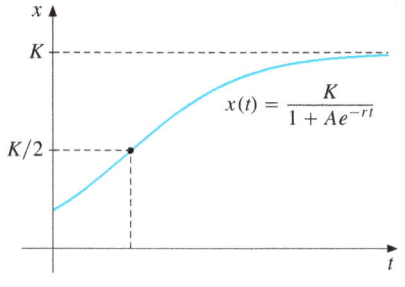

Figure 11.9.1 Growth to level 200

Figure 11.9.2 Logistic growth to level K

of course, is just the differential equation (11.9.1), but with x replaced by y and r replaced by $-a$. The solution therefore takes the form $y = Ae^{-at}$, where A is a constant. Because $x = y + b/a$, the solution to $\dot{x} + ax = b$ is

$$x(t) = Ae^{-at} + b/a \tag{11.9.8}$$

Logistic Growth

Instead of the differential equation (11.9.5), a more realistic assumption is that the relative rate of increase is approximately constant while the population is small, but that it converges to zero as the population approaches its carrying capacity K. A special form of this assumption is expressed by the equation

$$\dot{x}(t) = rx(t)\left[1 - \frac{x(t)}{K}\right] \tag{11.9.9}$$

Indeed, when the population $x(t)$ is small in proportion to K, so that $x(t)/K$ is small, then $\dot{x}(t) \approx rx(t)$, which implies that $x(t)$ increases (approximately) exponentially. As $x(t)$ becomes larger and approaches K, however, the shrinking factor $1 - x(t)/K$ becomes much smaller and so increases in significance. In general, we claim that if $x(t)$ satisfies (11.9.9) and is not identically equal to 0, then $x(t)$ must have the form

$$x(t) = \frac{K}{1 + Ae^{-rt}} \tag{11.9.10}$$

for some constant A. The function x given in (11.9.10) is called a *logistic function*.

Proof: In order to prove that the solution in Eq. (11.9.10) is valid, we use a trick. Suppose that $x = x(t)$ is not 0 and introduce the new variable $u = u(t) = -1 + K/x$. Then differentiating using the chain rule gives $\dot{u} = -K\dot{x}/x^2$. Substituting for $\dot{x}$ from Eq. (11.9.9) gives $\dot{u} = -(Kr/x) + r = r(-K/x + 1) = -ru$. Hence $u = u(t) = Ae^{-rt}$ for some constant A. But then $-1 + K/x(t) = Ae^{-rt}$. Finally, solving this equation for $x(t)$ yields (11.9.10). ∎

Suppose that a population consists of x_0 individuals at time $t = 0$, so that $x(0) = x_0$. Then (11.9.10) gives $x_0 = K/(1 + A)$, implying that $A = (K - x_0)/x_0$. To sum up, we have shown that the unique solution to (11.9.9) with $x(0) = x_0$ is

$$x(t) = \frac{K}{1 + Ae^{-rt}}, \quad \text{where} \quad A = \frac{K - x_0}{x_0} \tag{11.9.11}$$

If $0 < x_0 < K$, it follows from (11.9.11) that $x(t)$ is strictly increasing and that $x(t) \to K$ as $t \to \infty$, assuming $r > 0$. We say in this case that there is *logistic growth* up to the level K. The graph of the solution is shown in Fig. 11.9.2. It has an inflection point at the height $K/2$ above the t-axis. We verify this by differentiating Eq. (11.9.9) with respect to t. This gives $\ddot{x} = r\dot{x}(1 - x/K) + rx(-\dot{x}/K) = r\dot{x}(1 - 2x/K)$. So $\ddot{x} = 0$ when $x = K/2$, with $\ddot{x} > 0$ for $x < K/2$ and $\ddot{x} < 0$ for $x > K/2$.

Equations like (11.9.9), whose solutions are logistic functions of the form (11.9.10), appear in many economic models, some of which are featured in the exercises.

The differential equation (11.9.9) can also be expressed in the simpler form

$$\dot{x} + ax = bx^2$$

where $a = -r$ and $b = -r/K$. Other than the trivial solution $x = 0$, the solution is given by (11.9.10), where $r = -a$ and $K = -r/b = a/b$. It follows that the non-trivial solution to $\dot{x} + ax = bx^2$ is

$$x(t) = \frac{a/b}{1 + Ae^{at}} = \frac{a}{b - A_1 e^{at}} \tag{11.9.12}$$

where the arbitrary constants A and A_1 are related by the equation $A_1 = -bA$.

Recapitulation

The simple differential equations that have appeared in this section are so important that we present them and their general solutions in a form which emphasizes a common structure. As is often done in the theory of differential equations, we compress notation so that $x(t)$ and $\dot{x}(t)$ become simply x and $\dot{x}$.

SOLUTIONS OF SOME SIMPLE DIFFERENTIAL EQUATIONS

$$\dot{x} = ax \text{ for all } t \iff x = Ae^{at} \text{ for some constant } A \tag{11.9.3}$$

$$\dot{x} + ax = b \text{ for all } t \iff x = Ae^{-at} + \frac{b}{a} \text{ for some constant } A \tag{11.9.8}$$

$$\dot{x} + ax = bx^2 \text{ for all } t \iff x = \frac{a}{b - Ae^{at}} \text{ for some constant } A \tag{11.9.12}$$

Note that in (11.9.8) we must assume that $a \neq 0$. Also, in (11.9.12), we have ignored the trivial solution with $x(t) = 0$ for all t.

EXERCISES FOR SECTION 11.9

1. For which of the following functions is the relative rate of increase $\dot{x}/x$ constant?

(a) $x = 5t + 10$ (b) $x = \ln(t + 1)$ (c) $x = 5e^t$

(d) $x = -3 \cdot 2^t$ (e) $x = e^{t^2}$ (f) $x = e^t + e^{-t}$

2. Suppose that a firm's capital stock $K(t)$ satisfies the differential equation $\dot{K}(t) = I - \delta K(t)$, where investment I is constant, and $\delta K(t)$ denotes depreciation, with δ a positive constant.

   (a) Find the solution of the equation if the capital stock at time $t = 0$ is K_0.

   (b) Let $\delta = 0.05$ and $I = 10$. Explain what happens to $K(t)$ as $t \to \infty$ when:

   (a) $K_0 = 150$;   (b) $K_0 = 250$.

3. Let $N(t)$ denote the number of people in a country whose homes have access to broadband internet. Suppose that the rate at which new people gain access is proportional to the number of people who still have no access. If the total population size is P, therefore, the differential equation for $N(t)$ is $\dot{N}(t) = k(P - N(t))$, where k is a positive constant. Find the solution of this equation if $N(0) = 0$. Then find the limit of $N(t)$ as $t \to \infty$.

4. A country's annual natural rate of population growth (births minus deaths) is 2%. In addition there is a net immigration of 40 000 persons per year. Write down a differential equation for the function $N(t)$ which denotes the number of persons in the country at time t (measured in years). Suppose that the population at time $t = 0$ is 2 000 000. Find $N(t)$.

5. As in Examples 4.5.1 and 4.9.1, let $P(t)$ denote Europe's population in millions t years after the year 1960. According to UN estimates, $P(0) = 641$ and $P(10) = 705$. Suppose that $P(t)$ grows exponentially, with $P(t) = 641e^{kt}$. Compute k and then find $P(15)$, $P(40)$ and $P(55)$, which are estimates of the population in the years 1975, 2000, and 2015.

6. When a colony of bacteria is subjected to strong ultraviolet light, they die as their DNA is destroyed. In a laboratory experiment it was found that the number of living bacteria decreased approximately exponentially with the length of time they were exposed to ultraviolet light. Suppose that 70.5% of the bacteria still survive after 7 seconds of exposure. What percentage will be alive after 30 seconds? How long does it take to kill 95% of the bacteria?

7. Solve the following differential equations by using one of (11.9.3), (11.9.8), and (11.9.12), whichever is appropriate:

   (a) $\dot{x} = -0.5x$ (b) $\dot{K} = 0.02K$ (c) $\dot{x} = -0.5x + 5$

   (d) $\dot{K} - 0.2K = 100$ (e) $\dot{x} + 0.1x = 3x^2$ (f) $\dot{K} = K(-1 + 2K)$

8. A study of how fast British agriculture mechanized during the years from 1950 onwards estimated y, the number of tractors in use (measured in thousands), as a function of t (measured in years, with $t = 0$ corresponding to 1950). The estimated function was approximately $y(t) = 250 + x(t)$, where $x = x(t)$ satisfies the logistic differential equation $\dot{x} = 0.34x(1 - x/230)$, with $x(0) = 25$.

   (a) Find an expression for $y(t)$.

   (b) Find the limit of $y(t)$ as $t \to \infty$, and draw the graph of $y(t)$.

9. In a model of how influenza spreads among a quarantined group of one thousand people, let $N(t)$ denote the number of group members who develop influenza t days after all its 1 000 members have been in contact with a carrier of infection. Assume that

$$\dot{N}(t) = 0.39N(t)\left[1 - \frac{N(t)}{1000}\right], \text{ where } N(0) = 1$$

   (a) Find a formula for $N(t)$. How many group members develop influenza after twenty days?

(b) How many days does it take until 800 group members are sick?

(c) Will all one thousand group members eventually get influenza?

SM **10.** The logistic function (11.9.9) has been used for describing the stock of certain fish populations. Suppose such a population is harvested at a rate proportional to the stock, so that

$$\dot{x}(t) = rx(t)\left[1 - \frac{x(t)}{K}\right] - fx(t)$$

(a) Solve this equation, when the population at time $t = 0$ is x_0.

(b) Suppose $f > r$. Examine the limit of $x(t)$ as $t \to \infty$.

11. [HARDER] According to *Newton's law of cooling*, the rate at which a warm object cools is proportional to the difference between the temperature of the object and the "ambient" temperature of its surroundings. If the temperature of the object at time t is $T(t)$ and the (constant) ambient temperature is C, then $\dot{T}(t) = k[C - T(t)]$ for some constant $k > 0$. Note that this equation is like (11.9.6).

At 12 noon, some police enter a room and discover a dead body. Immediately they measure its temperature, which is 35° Celsius. At 1 pm they take its temperature again, which is now down to 32°. The temperature in the room is constant at 20°. When did the person die? (*Hint*: Let the temperature be $T(t)$, where t is measured in hours and 12 noon corresponds to $t = 0$.)

11.10 Separable and Linear Differential Equations

In this final section of the chapter we consider two general types of differential equation that are frequently encountered in economics. The discussion will be brief. For a more extensive treatment, we refer the reader to FMEA.

Separable Equations

A differential equation is called *separable* if it takes the form

$$\dot{x} = f(t)g(x) \qquad (11.10.1)$$

Here the unknown function is $x = x(t)$, and its rate of change $\dot{x}$ is given as the product of a function $f(t)$ only of t and another function $g(x)$ only of x. A simple case is $\dot{x} = tx$, which is obviously separable, whereas $\dot{x} = t + x$ is not. In fact, all the differential equations studied Section 11.9 were separable equations of the especially simple form $\dot{x} = g(x)$, with $f(t) \equiv 1$. The equation $\dot{x} + ax = bx^2$ in (11.9.12), for instance, is separable because it can be rewritten as $\dot{x} = g(x)$ where $g(x) = -ax + bx^2$.

METHOD FOR SOLVING SEPARABLE DIFFERENTIAL EQUATIONS

The following general method for solving separable equations is justified in FMEA.

(i) Write Eq. (11.10.1) as
$$\frac{dx}{dt} = f(t)g(x) \qquad (*)$$

(ii) Separate the variables to get $\dfrac{1}{g(x)}\,dx = f(t)\,dt$.

(iii) Integrate each side to get $\displaystyle\int \frac{1}{g(x)}\,dx = \int f(t)\,dt$.

(iv) Evaluate the two integrals, if possible, thus obtaining a solution of $(*)$, possibly in implicit form. Then, if possible, solve for $x(t)$.

Note that at step (ii) we divided by $g(x)$, implicitly assuming that $g(x) \neq 0$. If in fact there exists a such that $g(a) = 0$, then a particular solution of $(*)$ will be $x(t) = a$ for all t. Given the logistic equation (11.9.9), for instance, both $x(t) = 0$ for all t and $x(t) = K$ for all t are particular solutions.

EXAMPLE 11.10.1 Solve the differential equation $dx/dt = e^t x^2$ and find the solution curve, which is also called the *integral curve*, that passes through the point $(t, x) = (0, 1)$.

Solution: We observe first that $x(t) \equiv 0$ is one (trivial) solution. To find the other solutions we follow the remaining steps (ii)–(iv) of the recipe:

(ii) Separate: $(1/x^2)\,dx = e^t\,dt$;

(iii) Integrate: $\int (1/x^2)\,dx = \int e^t\,dt$;

(iv) Evaluate: $-1/x = e^t + C$.

From the result of (iv), it follows that:
$$x = \frac{-1}{e^t + C} \qquad (*)$$

To find the integral curve through $(0, 1)$, we must determine the correct value of C. Because we require $x = 1$ for $t = 0$, it follows from $(*)$ that $1 = -1/(1 + C)$, so $C = -2$. Thus, the integral curve passing through $(0, 1)$ is $x = -1/(e^t - 2) = 1/(2 - e^t)$.

EXAMPLE 11.10.2 (**Economic Growth**[7]). Let $X = X(t)$ denote the national product, $K = K(t)$ the capital stock, and $L = L(t)$ the number of workers in a country at time t. Suppose that, for all $t \geq 0$, one has

(a) $X = \sqrt{K}\sqrt{L}$ \qquad (b) $\dot{K} = 0.4X$ \qquad (c) $L = e^{0.04t}$

---

[7] This is a special case of the Solow–Swan growth model, developed jointly by American Nobel Prize laureate Robert Solow (born 1924) and Australian economist Trevor Swan (1918–1989). See Example 5.7.3 in FMEA.

Derive from these equations a single differential equation for $K = K(t)$. Then find the solution of that equation that satisfies $K(0) = 10\,000$.[8]

Solution: From equations (a)–(c), we derive the single differential equation

$$\dot{K} = \frac{dK}{dt} = 0.4\sqrt{K}\sqrt{L} = 0.4e^{0.02t}\sqrt{K} \tag{i}$$

This is clearly separable. Using the recipe yields the successive equations:

(ii) $\dfrac{1}{\sqrt{K}}\,dK = 0.4e^{0.02t}\,dt$

(iii) $\displaystyle\int \dfrac{1}{\sqrt{K}}\,dK = \int 0.4e^{0.02t}\,dt$

(iv) $2\sqrt{K} = 20e^{0.02t} + C$.

If $K = 10\,000$ for $t = 0$, then $2\sqrt{10\,000} = 20 + C$, so $C = 180$. Then $\sqrt{K} = 10e^{0.02t} + 90$, and so the required solution is

$$K(t) = (10e^{0.02t} + 90)^2 = 100(e^{0.02t} + 9)^2$$

The capital–labour ratio has a somewhat bizarre limiting value in this model: as $t \to \infty$, so

$$\frac{K(t)}{L(t)} = 100 \times \frac{(e^{0.02t} + 9)^2}{e^{0.04t}} = 100\left[\frac{e^{0.02t} + 9}{e^{0.02t}}\right]^2 = 100(1 + 9e^{-0.02t})^2 \to 100$$

EXAMPLE 11.10.3 Solve the separable differential equation $(\ln x)\dot{x} = e^{1-t}$.

Solution: Following the recipe yields

(i) $\ln x \dfrac{dx}{dt} = e^{1-t}$;

(ii) $\ln x\,dx = e^{1-t}\,dt$;

(iii) $\int \ln x\,dx = \int e^{1-t}\,dt$;

(iv) $x \ln x - x = -e^{1-t} + C$, using the result in Example 10.1.3.

The desired functions $x = x(t)$ are those that satisfy the last equation for all t in some interval.

Why do we say "in some interval"? Note that $x \ln x - x \geq -1$ for all real numbers x, so the equation $x \ln x - x = -e^{1-t} + C$ requires that $C \geq -1 + e^{1-t}$, and so $e^{1-t} \leq C + 1$. This is equivalent to $t \geq 1 - \ln(C + 1)$.

We usually say that we have solved a differential equation even if, as in Example 11.10.3, the solution cannot be expressed as an explicit function of t. The important point is that we have defined the solution implicitly by an equation that does not include the derivative of the unknown function.

---

[8] In (a) we have a Cobb–Douglas production function; (b) says that aggregate investment is proportional to output; (c) implies that the labour force grows exponentially.

First-Order Linear Equations

A *first-order linear differential equation* in the unknown function $x = x(t)$ defined on an interval I is one that can be written in the form

$$\dot{x} + a(t)x = b(t) \tag{11.10.2}$$

where $a(t)$ and $b(t)$ denote known continuous functions of t in I. Equation (11.10.2) is called is called "first-order" because it only involves the first derivative of x, and not higher-order derivatives. It is called "linear" because the left-hand side is a linear function of x and $\dot{x}$.

The special case when $a(t)$ and $b(t)$ are both constants was discussed in Section 11.9. There we introduced the new variable $y = x - b/a$ to find the solution in (11.9.8). This can be written as:

$$\dot{x} + ax = b \Leftrightarrow x = Ce^{-at} + \frac{b}{a} \tag{11.10.3}$$

where C is a constant. In fact, the equation is separable, so the method we set out for solving separable equations will also lead to the same solution.

If we let $C = 0$ we obtain the constant solution $x(t) = b/a$. We say that $x = b/a$ is an *equilibrium state*, *steady state*, or *stationary state* of the equation $\dot{x} + ax = b$ in (11.10.2). Observe how this solution can be obtained from $\dot{x} + ax = b$ by letting $\dot{x} = 0$ and then solving the resulting equation for x.

If the constant a is positive, then the solution $x = Ce^{-at} + b/a$ in (11.10.3) converges to b/a as $t \to \infty$. In this case, because every solution of the equation converges to the steady state as t approaches infinity, we say that the equation is *stable*. Stability like this is an important issue for differential equations appearing in economics.[9]

EXAMPLE 11.10.4   Find the solution of $\dot{x} + 3x = -9$, and determine whether the equation is stable.

Solution: By (11.10.3), the solution is $x = Ce^{-3t} - 3$. Here the equilibrium state is $x = -3$. Moreover the equation is stable because $a = 3 > 0$, so $x \to -3$ as $t \to \infty$.

EXAMPLE 11.10.5   (**A Stable Price Adjustment Mechanism**). Let $D(P) = a - bP$ and $S(P) = \alpha + \beta P$ denote, respectively, the demand and the supply of a certain commodity, as functions of the price P. Here a, b, α, and β are positive constants. Assume that the price $P = P(t)$ varies with time, and that $\dot{P}$ is proportional to excess demand $D(P) - S(P)$. Thus,

$$\dot{P} = \lambda[D(P) - S(P)]$$

where λ is a positive constant. Inserting the expressions for $D(P)$ and $S(P)$ into this equation gives $\dot{P} = \lambda(a - bP - \alpha - \beta P)$. Rearranging, we then obtain

$$\dot{P} + \lambda(b + \beta)P = \lambda(a - \alpha)$$

According to (11.10.3), the solution is

$$P = Ce^{-\lambda(b+\beta)t} + \frac{a - \alpha}{b + \beta}$$

---

[9] For an extensive discussion of stability see, for instance, FMEA.

Because $\lambda(b+\beta)$ is positive, as t tends to infinity, so P converges to the equilibrium price $P^e = (a-\alpha)/(b+\beta)$ at which $D(P^e) = S(P^e)$. Thus, the equilibrium is stable.

Variable Right-Hand Side

Consider next the case where the right-hand side is not constant:

$$\dot{x} + ax = b(t) \tag{11.10.4}$$

In this case the equation is no longer separable. Nevertheless, a clever trick helps find the solution. We multiply each side of (11.10.4) by the positive factor e^{at}, called an *integrating factor*. This gives the equivalent equation

$$\dot{x}e^{at} + axe^{at} = b(t)e^{at} \tag{*}$$

Though it may not be obvious beforehand, this idea it works well because the left-hand side of (*) happens to be the exact derivative of the product xe^{at}. Thus (*) is equivalent to

$$\frac{d}{dt}(xe^{at}) = b(t)e^{at} \tag{**}$$

This can be solved by simple integration. Indeed, by definition of the indefinite integral, equation (**) holds for all t in an interval if and only if $xe^{at} = \int b(t)e^{at}\,dt + C$ for some constant C. Multiplying this equation by e^{-at} gives the solution for x. Briefly formulated:

NON-AUTONOMOUS, FIRST-ORDER LINEAR EQUATION

$$\dot{x} + ax = b(t) \iff x = Ce^{-at} + e^{-at}\int e^{at}b(t)\,dt \tag{11.10.5}$$

EXAMPLE 11.10.6 Find the solution of $\dot{x} + x = t$, and determine the solution curve passing through $(0,0)$.

Solution: According to (11.10.5) with $a = 1$ and $b(t) = t$, the solution is given by

$$x = Ce^{-t} + e^{-t}\int te^t\,dt = Ce^{-t} + e^{-t}(te^t - e^t) = Ce^{-t} + t - 1$$

where the second equality is shown by using integration by parts, as in Example 10.5.1, to evaluate $\int te^t\,dt$. If $x = 0$ when $t = 0$, we get $0 = C - 1$, so $C = 1$. So the required solution is $x = e^{-t} + t - 1$.

EXAMPLE 11.10.7 (**Economic Growth**). Consider the following model of economic growth:

(a) $X(t) = 0.2K(t)$ (b) $\dot{K}(t) = 0.1X(t) + H(t)$ (c) $N(t) = 50e^{0.03t}$

This model is meant to capture the features of a developing country. Here $X(t)$ is annual GDP, $K(t)$ is capital stock, $H(t)$ is the net inflow of foreign investment per year, and $N(t)$

is the size of the population, all measured at time t. In (a) we assume that the volume of production is simply proportional to the capital stock, with the factor of proportionality 0.2 being called the *average productivity of capital*. In (b) we assume that the total growth of capital per year is equal to internal savings plus net foreign investment. We assume that savings are proportional to production, with the factor of proportionality 0.1 being called the *savings rate*. Finally, (c) tells us that population increases at a constant proportional rate of growth 0.03.

Assume that $H(t) = 10e^{0.04t}$ and derive from these equations a differential equation for $K(t)$. Find its solution given that $K(0) = 200$. Find also an expression for $x(t) = X(t)/N(t)$, which is domestic product per capita.

Solution: From (a) and (b), it follows that $K(t)$ must satisfy the linear equation

$$\dot{K}(t) - 0.02K(t) = 10e^{0.04t}$$

Using (11.10.5), we obtain the solution

$$K(t) = Ce^{0.02t} + e^{0.02t} \int e^{-0.02t} 10e^{0.04t}\, dt$$

$$= Ce^{0.02t} + 10e^{0.02t} \int e^{0.02t}\, dt$$

$$= Ce^{0.02t} + \frac{10}{0.02}e^{0.04t} = Ce^{0.02t} + 500e^{0.04t}$$

At $t = 0$, where $K(0) = C + 500$, we must have $K(0) = 200$. So $C = -300$ and then

$$K(t) = 500e^{0.04t} - 300e^{0.02t} \qquad (*)$$

Per capita production is $x(t) = X(t)/N(t) = 0.2K(t)/50e^{0.03t} = 2e^{0.01t} - 1.2e^{-0.01t}$.

Solving the general linear differential equation (11.10.2) is somewhat more complicated. Once again we refer the interested reader to FMEA for a detailed treatment. For the moment, however, let us define $A(t)$ as the indefinite integral $\int a(t)dt$ of the coefficient $a(t)$ of x in Eq. (11.10.2). Then it turns out that the exponential $e^{A(t)}$ is an integrating factor that we can apply as we did in deriving (11.10.5). Indeed, multiplying both sides of (11.10.2) by this exponential gives

$$\dot{x}e^{A(t)} + a(t)xe^{A(t)} = b(t)e^{A(t)}$$

Because we assumed that $A(t) = \int a(t)dt$, the left-hand side of this equation equals the derivative $\frac{d}{dt}(xe^{A(t)})$. So the equation can be rewritten as $\frac{d}{dt}(xe^{A(t)}) = b(t)e^{A(t)}$. Integrating each side of this equation gives $xe^{A(t)} = C + \int b(t)e^{A(t)}dt$, where C is a constant. Finally, multiplying each side by $e^{-A(t)}$ gives the solution

$$x = Ce^{-A(t)} + e^{-A(t)} \int e^{A(t)}b(t)\, dt$$

This generalizes Eq. (11.10.5) to the case when $a(t)$ is not a constant a.

EXERCISES FOR SECTION 11.10

1. Solve the equation $x^4 \dot{x} = 1 - t$. Find the integral curve through $(t, x) = (1, 1)$.

2. Solve the following differential equations:

   (a) $\dot{x} = e^{2t}/x^2$
   (b) $\dot{x} = e^{-t+x}$
   (c) $\dot{x} - 3x = 18$
   (d) $\dot{x} = (1+t)^6/x^6$
   (e) $\dot{x} - 2x = -t$
   (f) $\dot{x} + 3x = te^{t^2 - 3t}$

3. Suppose that $y = \alpha k e^{\beta t}$ denotes output as a function of capital k, where the factor $e^{\beta t}$ is due to technical progress. Suppose that a constant fraction $s \in (0, 1)$ of output is saved, and that capital accumulation is equal to savings. Then we have the separable differential equation $\dot{k} = s\alpha k e^{\beta t}$, with $k(0) = k_0$. The constants α, β, and k_0 are positive. Find the solution.

4. Suppose $Y = Y(t)$ is GDP, $C(t)$ is consumption, and $\bar{I}$ is investment, which is constant. Suppose $\dot{Y} = \alpha(C + \bar{I} - Y)$ and $C = aY + b$, where a, b, and α are positive constants with $a < 1$.

   (a) Derive a differential equation in which Y is the only variable that depends on t.

   (b) Find its solution when $Y(0) = Y_0$ is given. What happens to $Y(t)$ as $t \to \infty$?

5. In a growth model, suppose that production Q is a function of capital K and labour L. Suppose too that: (a) $\dot{K} = \gamma Q$; (b) $Q = K^\alpha L$; and (c) $\dot{L}/L = \beta$. Assuming that $L(0) = L_0$, $\beta \neq 0$ and $\alpha \in (0, 1)$, derive a differential equation for K. Then solve this equation when $K(0) = K_0$.

6. As in Section 7.7, let $\mathrm{El}_t\, x(t)$ denote the elasticity of $x(t)$ w.r.t. t. Assuming that both t and x are positive and that a is a constant, find $x(t)$ when $\mathrm{El}_t\, x(t) = a$ for all $t > 0$.

REVIEW EXERCISES

1. An amount $5 000 earns interest at 3% per year.

   (a) What will this amount have grown to after ten years?

   (b) How long does it take for the $5 000 to double?

2. An amount of €8 000 is invested at 5% per year.

   (a) What is the balance in the account after three years?

   (b) What is the balance after 13 years?

   (c) How long does it take, approximately, for the balance to reach €32 000?

3. Which is preferable for a borrower: (i) to borrow at the annual interest rate of 11% with interest paid yearly; or (ii) to borrow at annual interest rate 10% with interest paid monthly?

4. Suppose the sum of £15 000 is invested in an account earning interest at an annual rate of 7%. What is the balance after 12 years if interest is compounded continuously?

5. (a) How much has $8 000 increased to after three years, if the annual interest rate is 6%, with continuous compounding?

   (b) How long does it take before the $8 000 has doubled?

6. Find the sums of the following infinite series:

   (a) $44 + 44 \cdot 0.56 + 44 \cdot (0.56)^2 + \cdots$

   (b) $\sum_{n=0}^{\infty} 20 \left(\frac{1}{1.2}\right)^n$

   (c) $3 + \dfrac{3 \cdot 2}{5} + \dfrac{3 \cdot 2^2}{5^2} + \cdots + \dfrac{3 \cdot 2^{n-1}}{5^{n-1}} + \cdots$

   (d) $\sum_{j=-2}^{\infty} \dfrac{1}{20^j}$

7. A constant income stream of a dollars per year is expected over the next T years.

   (a) Find its PDV, assuming an interest rate of r annually, compounded continuously.

   (b) What is the limit of the PDV as $T \to \infty$? Compare this result with Eq. (11.5.4).

8. At the beginning of a year $5 000 is deposited in an account earning 4% annual interest. What is the balance after four years?

(SM) 9. At the end of each year for four years, $5 000 is deposited in an account earning 4% annual interest. What is the balance immediately after the fourth deposit?

(SM) 10. Suppose you had $10 000 in your account on 1st January 2006. The annual interest rate is 4%. You agreed to deposit a fixed amount K each year for eight years, the first deposit on 1st January 2009. What choice of the fixed amount K will imply that you have a balance of $70 000 immediately after the last deposit?

11. A business borrows €500 000 from a bank at the beginning of one year. It agrees to pay it off in ten equal instalments at the end of each year, with interest at 7% compounding annually.

    (a) Find the annual payment. What is the total amount paid to the bank?

    (b) What is the total amount if the business has to pay twice a year?

12. Lucy is offered the choice between the following three options:

    (i) She gets $3 200 each year for ten years, with the first payment due after one year.

    (ii) She gets $7 000 today, and thereafter $3 000 each year for five years, with the first payment after one year.

    (iii) She gets $4 000 each year for ten years, with the first payment only due after five years.

    The annual interest rate is 8%. Calculate the present values of the three options. What would you advise Lucy to choose?

(SM) 13. With reference to Example 11.3.2, suppose that the market value of the tree is $P(t) = 100e^{\sqrt{t}/2}$, so that its present value is $f(t) = 100e^{\sqrt{t}/2}e^{-rt}$.

    (a) Find the optimal cutting time t^*. By studying the sign variation of $f'(t)$, show that you have indeed found the maximum. What is t^* if $r = 0.05$?[10]

    (b) Solve the same problem when $P(t) = 200e^{-1/t}$ and $r = 0.04$.

---

[10] Note that t^* decreases as r increases.

14. The revenue produced by a new oil well is $1 million per year initially ($t = 0$), which is expected to rise uniformly to $5 million per year after ten years. If we measure time in years and let $f(t)$ denote the revenue, in millions of dollars, per unit of time at time t, it follows that $f(t) = 1 + 0.4t$. If $F(t)$ denotes the total revenue that accumulates over the time interval $[0, t]$, then $F'(t) = f(t)$.

   (a) Calculate the total revenue earned during the ten year period, $F(10)$.

   (b) Find the present value of the revenue stream over the time interval $[0, 10]$, if we assume continuously compounded interest at the rate $r = 0.05$ per year.

15. Solve the following difference equations with the given values of x_0:

   (a) $x_{t+1} = -0.1x_t$ with $x_0 = 1$ (b) $x_{t+1} = x_t - 2$ with $x_0 = 4$

   (c) $2x_{t+1} - 3x_t = 2$ with $x_0 = 2$

16. Solve the following differential equations:

   (a) $\dot{x} = -3x$ (b) $\dot{x} + 4x = 12$ (c) $\dot{x} - 3x = 12x^2$

   (d) $5\dot{x} = -x$ (e) $3\dot{x} + 6x = 10$ (f) $\dot{x} - \frac{1}{2}x = x^2$

SM 17. Solve the following differential equations:

   (a) $\dot{x} = tx^2$ (b) $2\dot{x} + 3x = -15$ (c) $\dot{x} - 3x = 30$

   (d) $\dot{x} + 5x = 10t$ (e) $\dot{x} + \frac{1}{2}x = e^t$ (f) $\dot{x} + 3x = t^2$

18. Let $V(x)$ denote the number of litres of fuel which is left in an aircraft's fuel tank after it has flown x km since takeoff. Suppose that $V(x)$ satisfies the differential equation $V'(x) = -aV(x) - b$, where a and b are positive constants. (Thus, fuel consumption per km is the constant b plus the extra amount $aV(x)$ due to the weight of the remaining fuel.)

   (a) Find the solution of the equation with $V(0) = V_0$.

   (b) How many km, x^*, can the plane fly if it takes off with V_0 litres in its tank?

   (c) What is the minimum number of litres, V_m, needed at takeoff if the plane is to fly $\hat{x}$ km?

   (d) Suppose that $b = 8$, $a = 0.001$, $V_0 = 12\,000$, and $\hat{x} = 1200$. Find x^* and V_m in this case.

III

MULTIVARIABLE ALGEBRA

12 MATRIX ALGEBRA

Indeed, models basically play the same role in economics as in fashion. They provide an articulated frame on which to show off your material to advantage... a useful role, but fraught with the dangers that the designer may get carried away by his personal inclination for the model, while the customer may forget that the model is more streamlined than reality.
—Jacques H. Drèze (1984)

Most mathematical models used by economists ultimately involve a system of several equations, which usually express how one or more endogenous variables depend on several exogenous parameters. If these equations are all linear, the study of such systems belongs to an area of mathematics called *linear algebra*. Even if the equations are Hyphenate as non-linear, we may still learn much from linear approximations around the solution we are interested in. For example, we may learn how the solution responds to small shocks to the exogenous parameters.

Indeed, linear models of this kind provide the logical basis for the econometric techniques that are routinely used in most modern empirical economic analysis. Linear models become much easier to understand if we use some key mathematical concepts such as matrices, vectors, and determinants. These, as well as their application to economic models, will be introduced in this chapter and in the next.

It is important to note that the usefulness of linear algebra extends far beyond its ability to solve systems of linear equations. Fields of applied mathematics which rely on linear algebra extensively include, for instance, the theory of differential and difference equations, linear and nonlinear optimization theory, as well as statistics and econometrics.

12.1 Matrices and Vectors

A *matrix* is simply a rectangular array of numbers considered as one mathematical object. Suppose the array has m *rows* and n *columns*. Then we have an m-by-n matrix, written as $m \times n$. We usually denote a matrix with a bold capital letter such as **A**, **B**, and so on. A

448 CHAPTER 12 / MATRIX ALGEBRA

general $m \times n$ matrix takes the form

$$\mathbf{A} = \begin{pmatrix} a_{11} & a_{12} & \cdots & a_{1n} \\ a_{21} & a_{22} & \cdots & a_{2n} \\ \vdots & \vdots & \ddots & \vdots \\ a_{m1} & a_{m2} & \cdots & a_{mn} \end{pmatrix} \qquad (12.1.1)$$

The matrix $\mathbf{A}$ in (12.1.1) is said to have *order* (or *dimension*) $m \times n$. The mn numbers that constitute $\mathbf{A}$ are called its *entries* or *elements*. In particular, a_{ij} denotes the entry in the ith row and the jth column. For brevity, the $m \times n$ matrix in (12.1.1) is often expressed as $(a_{ij})_{m \times n}$, or more simply as (a_{ij}), if the order $m \times n$ is clear (or unimportant).

EXAMPLE 12.1.1   The following four rectangular arrays are all matrices:

$$\mathbf{A} = \begin{pmatrix} 3 & -2 \\ 5 & 8 \end{pmatrix}, \quad \mathbf{B} = \begin{pmatrix} -1, & 2, & \sqrt{3}, & 16 \end{pmatrix}, \quad \mathbf{C} = \begin{pmatrix} -1 & 2 \\ 8 & 5 \\ 7 & 6 \\ 1 & 1 \end{pmatrix}, \quad \text{and} \quad \mathbf{D} = \begin{pmatrix} 3 \\ -1 \\ 12 \end{pmatrix}$$

Matrix $\mathbf{A}$ is 2×2, $\mathbf{B}$ is 1×4, $\mathbf{C}$ is 4×2, and $\mathbf{D}$ is 3×1. Also $a_{21} = 5$ and $c_{32} = 6$. Note that a_{23} and c_{23} are both undefined because $\mathbf{A}$ and $\mathbf{C}$ only have two columns.

A matrix with either only one row or only one column is called a *vector*. It is usual to distinguish between a *row vector*, which has only one row, and a *column vector*, which has only one column. In Example 12.1.1, matrix $\mathbf{B}$ is a row vector, whereas $\mathbf{D}$ is a column vector. Also, it is usual to denote vectors by bold lower-case letters such as $\mathbf{x}$ or $\mathbf{y}$, rather than by capital letters.

Thus, in case $\mathbf{a}$ is a $1 \times n$ row vector, we write

$$\mathbf{a} = (a_1, a_2, \ldots, a_n)$$

The n numbers $a_1, a_2, \ldots, a_n$ are called the *coordinates* or *components* of $\mathbf{a}$, with a_i denoting its ith coordinate or component. To emphasize that a vector has n components, we can call it an *n-vector*, and say that it has *dimension n*.

EXAMPLE 12.1.2   Construct the 4×3 matrix $\mathbf{A} = (a_{ij})_{4 \times 3}$ with $a_{ij} = 2i - j$ for all i and J.

Solution: The matrix $\mathbf{A}$ has $4 \cdot 3 = 12$ entries. Because $a_{ij} = 2i - j$, it follows that $a_{11} = 2 \cdot 1 - 1 = 1$, $a_{12} = 2 \cdot 1 - 2 = 0$, $a_{13} = 2 \cdot 1 - 3 = -1$, and so on. The complete matrix is

$$\mathbf{A} = \begin{pmatrix} 2 \cdot 1 - 1 & 2 \cdot 1 - 2 & 2 \cdot 1 - 3 \\ 2 \cdot 2 - 1 & 2 \cdot 2 - 2 & 2 \cdot 2 - 3 \\ 2 \cdot 3 - 1 & 2 \cdot 3 - 2 & 2 \cdot 3 - 3 \\ 2 \cdot 4 - 1 & 2 \cdot 4 - 2 & 2 \cdot 4 - 3 \end{pmatrix} = \begin{pmatrix} 1 & 0 & -1 \\ 3 & 2 & 1 \\ 5 & 4 & 3 \\ 7 & 6 & 5 \end{pmatrix}$$

Suppose an $m \times n$ matrix has $m = n$, so that it has the same number of columns as rows. Then it is called a *square matrix* of order n. In this case, if $\mathbf{A} = (a_{ij})_{n \times n}$, then the n elements $a_{11}, a_{22}, \ldots, a_{nn}$ constitute the *main*, or *principal, diagonal* that runs from the top left element a_{11} to the bottom right element a_{nn}. For instance, the matrix **A** in Example 12.1.1 is a square matrix of order 2, whose main diagonal consists of the numbers 3 and 8. Note that only a square matrix can have a main diagonal.

EXAMPLE 12.1.3   In Section 3.6 we considered the linear system of two equations in the two unknown variables x and y. It took the form:

$$ax + by = c$$
$$dx + ey = f \tag{12.1.2}$$

It is natural to represent the coefficients of these unknowns by the 2×2 matrix

$$\begin{pmatrix} a & b \\ d & e \end{pmatrix}$$

Also, the two constants on the right-hand side of the system constitute the column vector

$$\begin{pmatrix} c \\ f \end{pmatrix}$$

For instance, consider the system

$$3x - 2y = 5$$
$$5x + y = -2$$

Its coefficient matrix and right-hand side column vector are respectively

$$\begin{pmatrix} 3 & -2 \\ 5 & 1 \end{pmatrix} \quad \text{and} \quad \begin{pmatrix} 5 \\ -2 \end{pmatrix}$$

EXAMPLE 12.1.4   Consider a chain of stores with four outlets, each selling eight different commodities. Let a_{ij} denote (the dollar value of) the sales of commodity i at outlet j during a certain month. A suitable way of recording these data is in the 8×4 matrix

$$\mathbf{A} = \begin{pmatrix} a_{11} & a_{12} & a_{13} & a_{14} \\ a_{21} & a_{22} & a_{23} & a_{24} \\ \vdots & \vdots & \vdots & \vdots \\ a_{81} & a_{82} & a_{83} & a_{84} \end{pmatrix}$$

The eight rows refer to the eight commodities, whereas the four columns refer to the four outlets. For instance, if $a_{73} = 225$, this means that the sales of commodity 7 at outlet 3 were worth $225 for the month in question.

Suppose that $\mathbf{A} = (a_{ij})_{m \times n}$ and $\mathbf{B} = (b_{ij})_{m \times n}$ are both $m \times n$ matrices. Provided that $a_{ij} = b_{ij}$ for all $i = 1, 2, \ldots, m$ and for all $j = 1, 2, \ldots, n$, we say that **A** and **B** are *equal*, and write $\mathbf{A} = \mathbf{B}$. Thus, two matrices **A** and **B** are equal if they both have the same order *and* all their corresponding entries are equal. If **A** and **B** are *not* equal, then we write $\mathbf{A} \neq \mathbf{B}$.

EXAMPLE 12.1.5

Determine the conditions under which

$$\begin{pmatrix} 3 & t-1 \\ 2t & u \end{pmatrix} = \begin{pmatrix} t & 2v \\ u+1 & t+w \end{pmatrix}$$

Solution: Both sides of the equation are 2×2 matrices, each with four elements. So equality requires all four equations $3 = t$, $t - 1 = 2v$, $2t = u + 1$, and $u = t + w$ between pairs of corresponding elements to be satisfied. Solving these simultaneous equations shows that the two matrices are equal if and only if $t = 3$, $v = 1$, $u = 5$, and $w = 2$. Then both matrices are equal to each other, and also equal to $\begin{pmatrix} 3 & 2 \\ 6 & 5 \end{pmatrix}$.

EXERCISES FOR SECTION 12.1

1. Determine the order of each of the following matrices:

   (a) $\mathbf{A} = \begin{pmatrix} 3 & 4 \\ 7 & -2 \end{pmatrix}$

   (b) $\mathbf{T} = \begin{pmatrix} 0.85 & 0.10 & 0.10 \\ 0.05 & 0.55 & 0.05 \end{pmatrix}$

   (c) $\mathbf{C} = \begin{pmatrix} c_{11} & \cdots & c_{1j} & \cdots & c_{1n} \\ \vdots & & \vdots & & \vdots \\ c_{i1} & \cdots & c_{ij} & \cdots & c_{in} \\ \vdots & & \vdots & & \vdots \\ c_{m1} & \cdots & c_{mj} & \cdots & c_{mn} \end{pmatrix}$

2. Construct the matrix $\mathbf{A} = (a_{ij})_{3 \times 3}$ where $a_{ii} = 1$ for $i = 1, 2, 3$, and $a_{ij} = 0$ for all pairs $i \neq j$.

3. Determine for what values of u and v the following equality holds:

$$\begin{pmatrix} (1-u)^2 & v^2 & 3 \\ v & 2u & 5 \\ 6 & u & -1 \end{pmatrix} = \begin{pmatrix} 4 & 4 & u \\ v & -3v & u-v \\ 6 & v+5 & -1 \end{pmatrix}$$

12.2 Systems of Linear Equations

Section 3.6 has already introduced systems of two simultaneous linear equations in two variables. Example 12.1.3 showed how matrices can be used to express those systems more succinctly. We now use these ideas to study general systems of linear equations more systematically.

The first key step is to introduce suitable notation for what may be a large linear system of equations. Specifically, we consider m equations in n unknowns, where m may be greater than, equal to, or less than n. If the unknowns are denoted by $x_1, \ldots, x_n$, we usually write such a system in the form

$$a_{11}x_1 + a_{12}x_2 + \cdots + a_{1n}x_n = b_1$$
$$a_{21}x_1 + a_{22}x_2 + \cdots + a_{2n}x_n = b_2$$
$$\cdots\cdots\cdots\cdots\cdots\cdots\cdots\cdots\cdots\cdots\cdots\cdots$$
$$a_{m1}x_1 + a_{m2}x_2 + \cdots + a_{mn}x_n = b_m$$

(12.2.1)

Here $a_{11}, a_{12}, \ldots, a_{mn}$ are called the *coefficients* of the system, and $b_1, \ldots, b_m$ are called the *constant terms*, or *right-hand sides*. All of them are real numbers.

Note carefully the order of the subscripts. In general, a_{ij} denotes the coefficient in the *i*th equation of the *j*th variable, which is x_j. One or more of these coefficients may be 0. Indeed, the system usually becomes easier to analyse and solve if many coefficients are 0.

A *solution* of system (12.2.1) is a list $s_1, s_2, \ldots, s_n$ of n numbers such that all the equations are satisfied simultaneously when we put $x_1 = s_1$, $x_2 = s_2$, $\ldots, x_n = s_n$. Usually, a solution is written as $(s_1, s_2, \ldots, s_n)$. Note that the order in which we write the components is essential in the sense that, even if $(s_1, s_2, \ldots, s_n)$ satisfies (12.2.1), then a rearranged list like $(s_n, s_{n-1}, \ldots, s_1)$ will usually *not* be a solution.

If system (12.2.1) has at least one solution, it is said to be *consistent*. When the system has no solution, it is said to be *inconsistent*.

EXAMPLE 12.2.1

(a) Write down the system of equations (12.2.1) when $n = m = 3$ and $a_{ij} = i + j$ for $i, j = 1, 2, 3$, whereas $b_i = i$ for $i = 1, 2, 3$.

(b) Verify that $(x_1, x_2, x_3) = (2, -1, 0)$ is a solution, but $(x_1, x_2, x_3) = (2, 0, -1)$ is not.

Solution:

(a) The coefficients are $a_{11} = 1 + 1 = 2$, $a_{12} = 1 + 2 = 3$, etc. Set out in full, the system of equations is

$$2x_1 + 3x_2 + 4x_3 = 1$$
$$3x_1 + 4x_2 + 5x_3 = 2$$
$$4x_1 + 5x_2 + 6x_3 = 3$$

(b) Inserting $(x_1, x_2, x_3) = (2, -1, 0)$ in the system, we see that all three equations are satisfied, so this is a solution. On the other hand, suppose we change the order of the numbers 2, -1 and 0 to form the triple $(x_1, x_2, x_3) = (2, 0, -1)$. Then $2x_1 + 3x_2 + 4x_3 = 0$, so the first equation is not satisfied, and so $(2, 0, -1)$ is not a solution to the system.

It is natural to represent the coefficients of the unknowns in system (12.2.1) by the $m \times n$ matrix $\mathbf{A}$ that is arranged as in (12.1.1). Then $\mathbf{A}$ is called the *coefficient matrix* of (12.2.1). The *vector of constants* on the right-hand side of the system is

$$\mathbf{b} = \begin{pmatrix} b_1 \\ b_2 \\ \vdots \\ b_m \end{pmatrix}$$

EXAMPLE 12.2.2

The coefficient matrix of the system

$$3x_1 - 2x_2 + 6x_3 = 5$$
$$5x_1 + x_2 + 2x_3 = -2$$

is

$$\begin{pmatrix} 3 & -2 & 6 \\ 5 & 1 & 2 \end{pmatrix}$$

The vector of constants of the system is the same as in Example 12.1.3.

EXERCISES FOR SECTION 12.2

1. Decide which of the following single equations in the variables x, y, z, and w are linear, and which are not:

   (a) $3x - y - z - w = 50$
   (b) $\sqrt{3}x + 8xy - z + w = 0$
   (c) $3.33x - 4y + \frac{800}{3}z = 3$
   (d) $3(x + y - z) = 4(x - 2y + 3z)$
   (e) $(x - y)^2 + 3z - w = -3$
   (f) $2a^2 x - \sqrt{|b|}\, y + (2 + \sqrt{|a|}\,)z = b^2$

2. Let x_1, y_1, x_2, and y_2 be four constants, and consider the following equations in the four variables a, b, c, and d.[1]

   $$ax_1^2 + bx_1 y_1 + cy_1^2 + d = 0$$
   $$ax_2^2 + bx_2 y_2 + cy_2^2 + d = 0$$

   Is this a linear system of equations in a, b, c, and d?

3. Write down the system of equations (12.2.1) for the case when $n = 4$, $m = 3$, and

   $$a_{ij} = i + 2j + (-1)^i$$

   for $i = 1, 2, 3$ and $j = 1, 2, 3, 4$, whereas $b_i = 2^i$ for $i = 1, 2, 3$.

4. Write down the system of equations (12.2.1) for the case when $n = m = 4$ and $a_{ij} = 1$ for all $i \neq j$, while $a_{ii} = 0$ for $i = 1, 2, 3, 4$. Sum the four equations to derive a simple equation for $\sum_{i=1}^{4} x_i$, then solve the whole system.

5. Consider a collection of n individuals, each of whom owns a quantity of m different commodities. Let a_{ij} be the number of units of commodity i owned by individual j, for $i = 1, 2, \ldots, m$ and $j = 1, 2, \ldots, n$.

   (a) What does the list $(a_{1j}, a_{2j}, \ldots, a_{mj})$ represent?
   (b) Explain in words what the sums $a_{11} + a_{12} + \cdots + a_{1n}$ and $a_{i1} + a_{i2} + \cdots + a_{in}$ represent.
   (c) Let p_i denote the price per unit of commodity i, for $i = 1, 2, \ldots, m$. What is the total value of the commodities owned by individual j?

---

[1] We remark that in *almost* all other cases in this book, the letters a, b, c, and d denote constants!

6. Trygve Haavelmo (1911–1999), a Norwegian Nobel prize-winning economist, devised a model of the US economy for the years 1929–1941 that is based on the following four equations:

(i) $C = 0.712Y + 95.05$ (ii) $Y = C + X - S$ (iii) $S = 0.158(C + X) - 34.30$ (iv) $X = 93.53$

Here X denotes total investment, Y is disposable income, S is the total saving by firms, and C is total consumption. Write the system of equations in the form (12.2.1) when the variables appear in the order X, Y, S, and C. Then find the solution of the system.

12.3 Matrix Addition

Matrices could be regarded as merely rectangular arrays of numbers that can store information. Yet the real motivation for studying them is that there are useful rules for manipulating them. These correspond, to some extent, with the familiar rules of ordinary algebra.

Let us return to Example 12.1.4. There the 8×4 matrix $\mathbf{A}$ represents, for a particular month, the total sales of eight commodities at four outlets. Suppose that the (dollar values of) sales for the next month are given by a corresponding 8×4 matrix $\mathbf{B} = (b_{ij})_{8 \times 4}$. For these two months combined, the total sales revenues from each commodity in each of the outlets would then be given by a new 8×4 matrix $\mathbf{C} = (c_{ij})_{8 \times 4}$, with elements given by $c_{ij} = a_{ij} + b_{ij}$ for $i = 1, \ldots, 8$ and for $j = 1, \ldots, 4$. The matrix $\mathbf{C}$ is called the "sum" of $\mathbf{A}$ and $\mathbf{B}$, and we write $\mathbf{C} = \mathbf{A} + \mathbf{B}$.

MATRIX ADDITION

If $\mathbf{A} = (a_{ij})_{m \times n}$ and $\mathbf{B} = (b_{ij})_{m \times n}$ are two matrices of the same order, we define the *sum* $\mathbf{A} + \mathbf{B}$ of $\mathbf{A}$ and $\mathbf{B}$ as the $m \times n$ matrix $(a_{ij} + b_{ij})_{m \times n}$. Thus,

$$\mathbf{A} + \mathbf{B} = (a_{ij})_{m \times n} + (b_{ij})_{m \times n} = (a_{ij} + b_{ij})_{m \times n} \tag{12.3.1}$$

To summarize, we add two matrices of the same order by adding their corresponding entries. Now we argue that, to multiply a matrix by a *scalar* (which is just another word for a number in matrix and vector algebra), we should multiply *every* entry in the matrix by that scalar.

Returning to the chain of stores considered in Example 12.1.4, suppose that the sales of each commodity from each outlet just happen to be exactly the same for both the two months we are considering. This means that we have $a_{ij} = b_{ij}$ for all $i = 1, \ldots, 8$ and for all $j = 1, \ldots, 4$, so $\mathbf{A} = \mathbf{B}$. Hence, the sum $\mathbf{C} = \mathbf{A} + \mathbf{B}$ has elements given by $c_{ij} = 2a_{ij}$ for all i and all j. In this case, we would like to say that matrix $\mathbf{C}$ is "twice" or "double" the matrix $\mathbf{A}$. This motivates the following definition.

MULTIPLICATION OF A MATRIX BY A SCALAR

If $\mathbf{A} = (a_{ij})_{m \times n}$ and α is any real number, we define the product $\alpha \mathbf{A}$ as the $m \times n$ matrix

$$\alpha \mathbf{A} = \alpha (a_{ij})_{m \times n} = (\alpha a_{ij})_{m \times n} \tag{12.3.2}$$

EXAMPLE 12.3.1

Compute $\mathbf{A} + \mathbf{B}$, $3\mathbf{A}$, and $\left(-\frac{1}{2}\right)\mathbf{B}$ when

$$\mathbf{A} = \begin{pmatrix} 1 & 2 & 0 \\ 4 & -3 & -1 \end{pmatrix} \quad \text{and} \quad \mathbf{B} = \begin{pmatrix} 0 & 1 & 2 \\ 1 & 0 & 2 \end{pmatrix}$$

Solution: Using either Eq. (12.3.1) or (12.3.2), whichever is appropriate, we obtain

$$\mathbf{A} + \mathbf{B} = \begin{pmatrix} 1 & 3 & 2 \\ 5 & -3 & 1 \end{pmatrix}, \quad 3\mathbf{A} = \begin{pmatrix} 3 & 6 & 0 \\ 12 & -9 & -3 \end{pmatrix}, \quad \left(-\frac{1}{2}\right)\mathbf{B} = \begin{pmatrix} 0 & -\frac{1}{2} & -1 \\ -\frac{1}{2} & 0 & -1 \end{pmatrix}$$

The matrix $(-1)\mathbf{A}$ is usually denoted by $-\mathbf{A}$. Then the difference $\mathbf{A} - \mathbf{B}$ between two matrices $\mathbf{A}$ and $\mathbf{B}$ of the same order can be defined as the sum $\mathbf{A} + (-\mathbf{B})$. In our chain store example, the matrix $\mathbf{B} - \mathbf{A}$ denotes the increase in sales from the first month to the second for each commodity from each outlet. Positive entries represent increases and negative entries represent decreases.

Given the above definitions, it is easy to derive the following useful rules.

RULES FOR MATRIX ADDITION AND MULTIPLICATION BY SCALARS

Let $\mathbf{A}$, $\mathbf{B}$, and $\mathbf{C}$ be arbitrary $m \times n$ matrices, and let α and β be real numbers. Also, let $\mathbf{0}$ denote the $m \times n$ matrix whose mn elements are all zero, which is called the *zero matrix*. Then:

(a) $(\mathbf{A} + \mathbf{B}) + \mathbf{C} = \mathbf{A} + (\mathbf{B} + \mathbf{C})$
(b) $\mathbf{A} + \mathbf{B} = \mathbf{B} + \mathbf{A}$
(c) $\mathbf{A} + \mathbf{0} = \mathbf{A}$
(d) $\mathbf{A} + (-\mathbf{A}) = \mathbf{0}$
(e) $(\alpha + \beta)\mathbf{A} = \alpha\mathbf{A} + \beta\mathbf{A}$
(f) $\alpha(\mathbf{A} + \mathbf{B}) = \alpha\mathbf{A} + \alpha\mathbf{B}$

Each of these rules follows directly from the definitions and the corresponding rules for ordinary numbers. Because of rule (a), there is no need to insert any parentheses in sums like $\mathbf{A} + \mathbf{B} + \mathbf{C}$. Note also that definitions (12.3.1) and (12.3.2) imply, for example, that $\mathbf{A} + \mathbf{A} + \mathbf{A}$ is equal to $3\mathbf{A}$.

EXERCISES FOR SECTION 12.3

1. Evaluate $\mathbf{A} + \mathbf{B}$ and $3\mathbf{A}$ when $\mathbf{A} = \begin{pmatrix} 0 & 1 \\ 2 & 3 \end{pmatrix}$ and $\mathbf{B} = \begin{pmatrix} 1 & -1 \\ 5 & 2 \end{pmatrix}$.

2. Evaluate $\mathbf{A} + \mathbf{B}$, $\mathbf{A} - \mathbf{B}$, and $5\mathbf{A} - 3\mathbf{B}$ when $\mathbf{A} = \begin{pmatrix} 0 & 1 & -1 \\ 2 & 3 & 7 \end{pmatrix}$ and $\mathbf{B} = \begin{pmatrix} 1 & -1 & 5 \\ 0 & 1 & 9 \end{pmatrix}$.

12.4 Algebra of Vectors

Recall that a matrix with only one row is called a row vector, whereas a matrix with only one column is called a column vector. We refer to both types as *vectors* and denote them by bold lower-case letters. Clearly both the row vector $(7, 13, 4)$ and the column vector

$$\begin{pmatrix} 7 \\ 13 \\ 4 \end{pmatrix}$$

contain exactly the same information. Indeed, both the numerical elements and their order are the same; only the arrangement of the numbers is different.

Operations on Vectors

Since a vector is just a special type of matrix, the algebraic operations introduced for matrices are equally valid for vectors. So:

(i) Two n-vectors **a** and **b** are *equal* if and only if all their n corresponding components are equal; then we write $\mathbf{a} = \mathbf{b}$.

(ii) If **a** and **b** are two n-vectors, their *sum*, denoted by $\mathbf{a} + \mathbf{b}$, is the n-vector obtained by adding each component of **a** to the corresponding component of **b**.[2]

(iii) If **a** is an n-vector and t is a real number, we define $t\mathbf{a}$ as the n-vector for which each component is t times the corresponding component in **a**.

(iv) The *difference* between two n-vectors **a** and **b** is defined as $\mathbf{a} - \mathbf{b} = \mathbf{a} + (-1)\mathbf{b}$.

Let **a** and **b** be two n-vectors, with t and s as real numbers. Then the n-vector $t\mathbf{a} + s\mathbf{b}$ is said to be a *linear combination* of **a** and **b**. In symbols, using column vectors, we have

$$t \begin{pmatrix} a_1 \\ a_2 \\ \vdots \\ a_n \end{pmatrix} + s \begin{pmatrix} b_1 \\ b_2 \\ \vdots \\ b_n \end{pmatrix} = \begin{pmatrix} ta_1 + sb_1 \\ ta_2 + sb_2 \\ \vdots \\ ta_n + sb_n \end{pmatrix}$$

Linear combinations are frequently found in economics. For example, suppose **a** and **b** are commodity vectors, whose jth components are quantities of commodity number j. Now, if t persons all buy the same commodity vector **a** and s persons all buy commodity vector **b**, then the vector $t\mathbf{a} + s\mathbf{b}$ represents the total amounts bought by all $t + s$ persons combined.

Of course, the rules for matrix addition and multiplication by scalars seen in Section 12.3 apply to vectors also.

---

[2] If two vectors do not have the same dimension, their sum is simply not defined, nor is their difference. Nor should one add a row vector to a column vector, even if they have the same number of elements.

The Inner Product

Let us consider four different commodities such as apples, bananas, cherries, and dates. Suppose you buy the commodity bundle $\mathbf{x} = (5, 3, 6, 7)$. This means, of course, that you buy five units (say, kilos) of apples, three kilos of bananas, etc. Suppose the prices per kilo of these four different fruits are given by the price vector $\mathbf{p} = (4, 5, 3, 8)$, meaning that the price per kilo of the first good is \$4, that of the second is \$5, etc. Then you spend $4 \cdot 5 = 20$ dollars on apples, $5 \cdot 3 = 15$ dollars on bananas, etc. Thus, the total value of the fruit you buy is $4 \cdot 5 + 5 \cdot 3 + 3 \cdot 6 + 8 \cdot 7 = 109$.

Now, we can regard this total amount spent as the result of an operation denoted by $\mathbf{p} \cdot \mathbf{x}$ that we apply to the two vectors $\mathbf{p}$ and $\mathbf{x}$. The operation is called the *inner product*, *scalar product*, or *dot product* of $\mathbf{p}$ and $\mathbf{x}$. In general, we have the following definition, formulated here for row vectors:

INNER PRODUCT

The *inner product* of the two *n*-vectors

$$\mathbf{a} = (a_1, a_2, \ldots, a_n) \quad \text{and} \quad \mathbf{b} = (b_1, b_2, \ldots, b_n)$$

is defined as

$$\mathbf{a} \cdot \mathbf{b} = a_1 b_1 + a_2 b_2 + \cdots + a_n b_n = \sum_{i=1}^{n} a_i b_i \qquad (12.4.1)$$

Note that the inner product of two vectors is not a vector but a *number*. It is obtained by simply multiplying all the pairs (a_j, b_j) (for $j = 1, 2, \ldots, n$) of corresponding components in the two vectors $\mathbf{a}$ and $\mathbf{b}$ to obtain the n products $a_j b_j$, then adding all these products. Note too that $\mathbf{a} \cdot \mathbf{b}$ is *defined only if* $\mathbf{a}$ and $\mathbf{b}$ both have the same dimension.

Previously we considered the case when $\mathbf{p}$ is a price vector whose n components are measured in dollars per kilo, whereas $\mathbf{x}$ is a commodity vector whose n components are measured in kilos. In this case, for each $j = 1, 2, \ldots, n$, the product $p_j x_j$ is the amount of money, measured in dollars, spent on commodity j. Then the inner product $\mathbf{p} \cdot \mathbf{x} = \sum_{j=1}^{n} p_j x_j$ is the total amount spent on the n commodities, also measured in dollars.

EXAMPLE 12.4.1   If $\mathbf{a} = (1, -2, 3)$ and $\mathbf{b} = (-3, 2, 5)$, compute $\mathbf{a} \cdot \mathbf{b}$.

Solution: We get $\mathbf{a} \cdot \mathbf{b} = 1 \cdot (-3) + (-2) \cdot 2 + 3 \cdot 5 = 8$.

SECTION 12.4 / ALGEBRA OF VECTORS

Here are five important properties of the inner product:

RULES FOR THE INNER PRODUCT

If **a**, **b**, and **c** are all n-vectors and α is a scalar, then

(a) $\mathbf{a} \cdot \mathbf{b} = \mathbf{b} \cdot \mathbf{a}$

(b) $(\alpha \mathbf{a}) \cdot \mathbf{b} = \mathbf{a} \cdot (\alpha \mathbf{b}) = \alpha(\mathbf{a} \cdot \mathbf{b})$

(c) $\mathbf{a} \cdot (\mathbf{b} + \mathbf{c}) = \mathbf{a} \cdot \mathbf{b} + \mathbf{a} \cdot \mathbf{c}$

(d) $\mathbf{a} \cdot \mathbf{a} \geq 0$

(e) $\mathbf{a} \cdot \mathbf{a} = 0$ if and only if $\mathbf{a} = \mathbf{0}$

Here, rules (a) and (b) are easy implications of the definitions. Rule (a) says that the inner product is *commutative*, in the sense that reversing the order of the two vectors being multiplied does not change their product. Rule (c) is the *distributive law*, which also follows by definition. Rules (a) and (c) together imply that

$$(\mathbf{a} + \mathbf{b}) \cdot \mathbf{c} = \mathbf{a} \cdot \mathbf{c} + \mathbf{b} \cdot \mathbf{c}$$

Furthermore, rules (d) and (e) together imply that

$$\mathbf{a} \cdot \mathbf{a} > 0 \Leftrightarrow \mathbf{a} \neq \mathbf{0}.$$

To see why this statement is true, note first that $\mathbf{a} \cdot \mathbf{a} = a_1^2 + a_2^2 + \cdots + a_n^2$, which is always nonnegative. Also, as in rule (e), it is zero if and only if all the components a_i of **a** are 0.

EXERCISES FOR SECTION 12.4

1. Compute $\mathbf{a} + \mathbf{b}$, $\mathbf{a} - \mathbf{b}$, $2\mathbf{a} + 3\mathbf{b}$, and $-5\mathbf{a} + 2\mathbf{b}$ when $\mathbf{a} = \begin{pmatrix} 2 \\ -1 \end{pmatrix}$ and $\mathbf{b} = \begin{pmatrix} 3 \\ 4 \end{pmatrix}$.

2. Let $\mathbf{a} = (1, 2, 2)$, $\mathbf{b} = (0, 0, -3)$, and $\mathbf{c} = (-2, 4, -3)$. Compute the three vectors $\mathbf{a} + \mathbf{b} + \mathbf{c}$, $\mathbf{a} - 2\mathbf{b} + 2\mathbf{c}$, and $3\mathbf{a} + 2\mathbf{b} - 3\mathbf{c}$.

3. If $3(x, y, z) + 5(-1, 2, 3) = (4, 1, 3)$, find x, y, and z.

4. If $\mathbf{x} + \mathbf{0} = \mathbf{0}$, what do you know about the components of $\mathbf{x}$?

5. If $0\mathbf{x} = \mathbf{0}$, what do you know about the components of $\mathbf{x}$?

6. Express the vector $(4, -11)$ as a linear combination of $(2, -1)$ and $(1, 4)$.

7. Solve the vector equation $4\mathbf{x} - 7\mathbf{a} = 2\mathbf{x} + 8\mathbf{b} - \mathbf{a}$ for $\mathbf{x}$ in terms of **a** and **b**.

8. Suppose that **a** and **b** are the two vectors specified in Exercise 1. Find the three inner products $\mathbf{a} \cdot \mathbf{a}$, $\mathbf{a} \cdot \mathbf{b}$ and $\mathbf{a} \cdot (\mathbf{a} + \mathbf{b})$. Then verify that $\mathbf{a} \cdot \mathbf{a} + \mathbf{a} \cdot \mathbf{b} = \mathbf{a} \cdot (\mathbf{a} + \mathbf{b})$.

9. For what values of x is the inner product of $(x, x - 1, 3)$ and $(x, x, 3x)$ equal to 0?

10. A residential construction company plans to build several houses of three different types: five of type A, seven of type B, and 12 of type C. Suppose that each house of type A requires 20 units of timber, type B requires 18 units, and type C requires 25 units.

(a) Write down a 3-vector **x** whose components give the number of houses of each type.

(b) Write down a 3-vector **u** whose components give, for each type of house, the quantity of timber required to build one house of that type.

(c) Find the total timber requirement, and show that it is given by the inner product $\mathbf{u} \cdot \mathbf{x}$.

11. A firm produces nonnegative output quantities $z_1, z_2, \ldots, z_n$ of n different goods, using as inputs the nonnegative quantities $x_1, x_2, \ldots, x_n$ of the same n goods. For each good i, define $y_i = z_i - x_i$ as the net output of good i, and let p_i be the price of good i. Let $\mathbf{p} = (p_1, \ldots, p_n)$, $\mathbf{x} = (x_1, \ldots, x_n)$, $\mathbf{y} = (y_1, \ldots, y_n)$, and $\mathbf{z} = (z_1, \ldots, z_n)$.

    (a) Calculate the firm's revenue and its costs.

    (b) Show that the firm's profit is given by the inner product $\mathbf{p} \cdot \mathbf{y}$. What if $\mathbf{p} \cdot \mathbf{y}$ is negative?

12. A firm produces the first of two different goods as its output, using the second good as its input. Its net output vector, as defined in Exercise 11, is $\begin{pmatrix} 2 \\ -1 \end{pmatrix}$. The price vector it faces is $(1, 3)$. Find the firm's input vector, output vector, costs, revenue, value of net output, and its profit or loss.

12.5 Matrix Multiplication

The rules we have given for adding or subtracting matrices, and for multiplying a matrix by a scalar, should all seem entirely natural and intuitive. The rule we are about to give for matrix multiplication, however, is much more subtle.[3] Before stating the rule, however, we motivate it by considering how to manipulate a particular equation system.

Consider first, as a simple example, the following two linear equation systems:

$$y_1 = b_{11}x_1 + b_{12}x_2$$
$$y_2 = b_{21}x_1 + b_{22}x_2 \quad \text{(i)}$$
$$y_3 = b_{31}x_1 + b_{32}x_2$$

and

$$z_1 = a_{11}y_1 + a_{12}y_2 + a_{13}y_3$$
$$z_2 = a_{21}y_1 + a_{22}y_2 + a_{23}y_3 \quad \text{(ii)}$$

The coefficient matrices of these two systems of equations are, respectively,

$$\mathbf{B} = \begin{pmatrix} b_{11} & b_{12} \\ b_{21} & b_{22} \\ b_{31} & b_{32} \end{pmatrix} \quad \text{and} \quad \mathbf{A} = \begin{pmatrix} a_{11} & a_{12} & a_{13} \\ a_{21} & a_{22} & a_{23} \end{pmatrix}$$

---

[3] It may be tempting to define the product of two matrices $\mathbf{A} = (a_{ij})_{m \times n}$ and $\mathbf{B} = (b_{ij})_{m \times n}$ of the same order as simply the matrix $\mathbf{C} = (c_{ij})_{m \times n}$, where each element $c_{ij} = a_{ij}b_{ij}$ is obtained by multiplying the entries of the two matrices term by term. This is a respectable matrix operation that generates the *Hadamard product* of $\mathbf{A}$ and $\mathbf{B}$. However, the definition of matrix multiplication that we give below is by far the most used and most useful in linear algebra.

System (i) expresses the three y variables in terms of the two x variables, whereas in (ii) the two z variables are expressed in terms of the y variables. So the z variables must be related to the x variables. Indeed, take the expressions for y_1, y_2, and y_3 in (i), then insert them into (ii). The result is

$$z_1 = a_{11}(b_{11}x_1 + b_{12}x_2) + a_{12}(b_{21}x_1 + b_{22}x_2) + a_{13}(b_{31}x_1 + b_{32}x_2)$$
$$z_2 = a_{21}(b_{11}x_1 + b_{12}x_2) + a_{22}(b_{21}x_1 + b_{22}x_2) + a_{23}(b_{31}x_1 + b_{32}x_2)$$

Now gather the terms in x_1, followed by those in x_2. This yields

$$z_1 = (a_{11}b_{11} + a_{12}b_{21} + a_{13}b_{31})x_1 + (a_{11}b_{12} + a_{12}b_{22} + a_{13}b_{32})x_2$$
$$z_2 = (a_{21}b_{11} + a_{22}b_{21} + a_{23}b_{31})x_1 + (a_{21}b_{12} + a_{22}b_{22} + a_{23}b_{32})x_2$$

The coefficients of x_1 and x_2 in these expressions can be assembled in the following 2×2 coefficient matrix:

$$\mathbf{C} = \begin{pmatrix} a_{11}b_{11} + a_{12}b_{21} + a_{13}b_{31} & a_{11}b_{12} + a_{12}b_{22} + a_{13}b_{32} \\ a_{21}b_{11} + a_{22}b_{21} + a_{23}b_{31} & a_{21}b_{12} + a_{22}b_{22} + a_{23}b_{32} \end{pmatrix}$$

The matrix $\mathbf{A}$ is 2×3 and $\mathbf{B}$ is 3×2. In particular, $\mathbf{B}$ *has as many rows as* $\mathbf{A}$ *has columns.* Note that if we let $\mathbf{C} = (c_{ik})_{2\times 2}$, then the number

$$c_{11} = a_{11}b_{11} + a_{12}b_{21} + a_{13}b_{31}$$

is the inner product of the first row in $\mathbf{A}$ and the first column in $\mathbf{B}$. Likewise, c_{12} is the inner product of the first row in $\mathbf{A}$ and the second column in $\mathbf{B}$, and so on. Generally, each element c_{ik} in $\mathbf{C}$ is the inner product of the ith row in $\mathbf{A}$ and the kth column in $\mathbf{B}$.

The matrix $\mathbf{C}$ in this example is called the *(matrix) product* of $\mathbf{A}$ and $\mathbf{B}$, and we write $\mathbf{C} = \mathbf{AB}$. Here is a numerical example.

EXAMPLE 12.5.1   By definition, in this example the matrix product $\mathbf{AB}$ is:

$$\begin{pmatrix} 1 & 0 & 3 \\ 2 & 1 & 5 \end{pmatrix} \begin{pmatrix} 1 & 3 \\ 2 & 5 \\ 6 & 2 \end{pmatrix} = \begin{pmatrix} 1 \cdot 1 + 0 \cdot 2 + 3 \cdot 6 & 1 \cdot 3 + 0 \cdot 5 + 3 \cdot 2 \\ 2 \cdot 1 + 1 \cdot 2 + 5 \cdot 6 & 2 \cdot 3 + 1 \cdot 5 + 5 \cdot 2 \end{pmatrix} = \begin{pmatrix} 19 & 9 \\ 34 & 21 \end{pmatrix}$$

In order to extend the argument to general matrices, assume that, as in (i), the variables $z_1, \ldots, z_m$ are expressed linearly in terms of $y_1, \ldots, y_n$, and that, as in (ii), the variables $y_1, \ldots, y_n$ are expressed linearly in terms of $x_1, \ldots, x_p$. Then $z_1, \ldots, z_m$ can be expressed linearly in terms of $x_1, \ldots, x_p$. Provided that the matrix $\mathbf{B}$ does indeed have as many rows as $\mathbf{A}$ has columns, the result we get leads directly to the following definition:

MATRIX MULTIPLICATION

Suppose that $\mathbf{A} = (a_{ij})_{m\times n}$ and that $\mathbf{B} = (b_{jk})_{n\times p}$. Then the matrix product $\mathbf{C} = \mathbf{AB}$ is the $m \times p$ matrix $\mathbf{C} = (c_{ik})_{m\times p}$, whose element in the ith row and the

kth column is the inner product of the ith row of **A** and the kth column of **B**. That is:

$$c_{ik} = \sum_{j=1}^{n} a_{ij}b_{jk} = a_{i1}b_{1k} + a_{i2}b_{2k} + \cdots + a_{ij}b_{jk} + \cdots + a_{in}b_{nk} \tag{12.5.1}$$

Note that, in order to get the entry c_{ik} in row i and column k of **C**, we multiply each component a_{ij} in the ith row of **A** by the corresponding component b_{jk} in the kth column of **B**, then add all the products. One way of visualizing matrix multiplication is this:

$$\begin{pmatrix} a_{11} & \cdots & a_{1j} & \cdots & a_{1n} \\ \vdots & & \vdots & & \vdots \\ a_{i1} & \cdots & a_{ij} & \cdots & a_{in} \\ \vdots & & \vdots & & \vdots \\ a_{m1} & \cdots & a_{mj} & \cdots & a_{mn} \end{pmatrix} \begin{pmatrix} b_{11} & \cdots & b_{1j} & \cdots & b_{1p} \\ \vdots & & \vdots & & \vdots \\ b_{j1} & \cdots & b_{kj} & \cdots & b_{kp} \\ \vdots & & \vdots & & \vdots \\ b_{n1} & \cdots & b_{nj} & \cdots & b_{np} \end{pmatrix} = \begin{pmatrix} c_{11} & \cdots & c_{1j} & \cdots & c_{1p} \\ \vdots & & \vdots & & \vdots \\ c_{i1} & \cdots & c_{ij} & \cdots & c_{ip} \\ \vdots & & \vdots & & \vdots \\ c_{m1} & \cdots & c_{mj} & \cdots & c_{mp} \end{pmatrix}$$

It bears repeating that the matrix product **AB** is defined if and only if the number of columns in **A** is equal to the number of rows in **B**. Also, if it is defined, the product **AB** has as many rows as **A** and as many columns as **B**.

Note too that **AB** might be defined, even if **BA** is not. For instance, if **A** is 6×3 and **B** is 3×5, then **AB** is defined as a 6×5 matrix, whereas **BA** is not defined.

EXAMPLE 12.5.2 Let

$$\mathbf{A} = \begin{pmatrix} 0 & 1 & 2 \\ 2 & 3 & 1 \\ 4 & -1 & 6 \end{pmatrix} \quad \text{and} \quad \mathbf{B} = \begin{pmatrix} 3 & 2 \\ 1 & 0 \\ -1 & 1 \end{pmatrix}$$

Compute the matrix product **AB**. Is the product **BA** defined?

Solution: **A** is 3×3 and **B** is 3×2, so **AB** is the following 3×2 matrix:[4]

$$\mathbf{AB} = \begin{pmatrix} 0 & 1 & 2 \\ 2 & 3 & 1 \\ 4 & -1 & 6 \end{pmatrix} \begin{pmatrix} 3 & 2 \\ 1 & 0 \\ -1 & 1 \end{pmatrix} = \begin{pmatrix} -1 & 2 \\ 8 & 5 \\ 5 & 14 \end{pmatrix}$$

The matrix product **BA** is not defined because the number of columns in **B** is not equal to the number of rows in **A**.

Note that in the Example 12.5.2, the matrix product **AB** was defined but **BA** was not. Exercise 1 and Example 12.6.4 show how, even in cases in which **AB** and **BA** are both

---

[4] We have used colouring to indicate how the element in the second row and first column of **AB** is found. It is the inner product of the second row in **A** and the first column in **B**; this is $2 \cdot 3 + 3 \cdot 1 + 1 \cdot (-1) = 8$.

defined, they are usually not equal. To recognize this important distinction between the two matrix products, when we write **AB**, we say that we *postmultiply* **A** by **B**, whereas in **BA** we *premultiply* **A** by **B**.

EXAMPLE 12.5.3   Three firms share the market for a certain commodity. Initially, firm A has 20% of the market, firm B has 60%, and firm C has 20%. In the course of the next year, the following changes occur:

(a) firm A keeps 85% of its customers, while losing 5% to B and 10% to C;

(b) firm B keeps 55% of its customers, while losing 10% to A and 35% to C;

(c) firm C keeps 85% of its customers, while losing 10% to A and 5% to B.

We can represent market shares of the three firms by means of a *market share vector*, defined as a column vector **s** whose components are all nonnegative and sum to 1. Define the matrix **T** and the initial market share vector **s** by

$$\mathbf{T} = \begin{pmatrix} 0.85 & 0.10 & 0.10 \\ 0.05 & 0.55 & 0.05 \\ 0.10 & 0.35 & 0.85 \end{pmatrix} \quad \text{and} \quad \mathbf{s} = \begin{pmatrix} 0.2 \\ 0.6 \\ 0.2 \end{pmatrix}$$

Notice that we have defined each element t_{ij} as the percentage of j's customers who become i's customers in the next period. So **T** is called the *transition matrix*.

Compute the vector **Ts**. Then show that it is also a market share vector, and give an interpretation. What is the interpretation of the successive products **T(Ts)**, **T(T(Ts))**, ...?

Solution: Computing directly, we obtain

$$\mathbf{Ts} = \begin{pmatrix} 0.85 & 0.10 & 0.10 \\ 0.05 & 0.55 & 0.05 \\ 0.10 & 0.35 & 0.85 \end{pmatrix} \begin{pmatrix} 0.2 \\ 0.6 \\ 0.2 \end{pmatrix} = \begin{pmatrix} 0.25 \\ 0.35 \\ 0.40 \end{pmatrix}$$

Because $0.25 + 0.35 + 0.40 = 1$, the product **Ts** is also a market share vector. The first entry in **Ts** is obtained from the calculation

$$0.85 \cdot 0.2 + 0.10 \cdot 0.6 + 0.10 \cdot 0.2 = 0.25$$

Here $0.85 \cdot 0.2$ is A's share of the market that it retains after one year, whereas $0.10 \cdot 0.6$ is the share A gains from B, and $0.10 \cdot 0.2$ is the share A gains from C. The sum, is therefore, firm A's total share of the market after one year. The other entries in **Ts** can be interpreted similarly. So **Ts** must be the new market share vector after one year, and **T(Ts)** (which Exercise 8 asks you to find) is the market share vector after two years. And so on.

Systems of Equations in Matrix Form

The definition of matrix multiplication allows us to write linear systems of equations very compactly by means of matrix multiplication. For instance, consider the system

$$3x_1 + 4x_2 = 5$$
$$7x_1 - 2x_2 = 2$$

Now define the 2 × 2 coefficient matrix **A**, the 2-vector **x** of unknowns, and the right-hand side 2-vector **b**, respectively, by

$$\mathbf{A} = \begin{pmatrix} 3 & 4 \\ 7 & -2 \end{pmatrix}, \quad \mathbf{x} = \begin{pmatrix} x_1 \\ x_2 \end{pmatrix}, \quad \text{and} \quad \mathbf{b} = \begin{pmatrix} 5 \\ 2 \end{pmatrix}$$

Then we see that

$$\mathbf{Ax} = \begin{pmatrix} 3 & 4 \\ 7 & -2 \end{pmatrix} \begin{pmatrix} x_1 \\ x_2 \end{pmatrix} = \begin{pmatrix} 3x_1 + 4x_2 \\ 7x_1 - 2x_2 \end{pmatrix}$$

So the original system is equivalent to the matrix equation $\mathbf{Ax} = \mathbf{b}$.

In general, consider the linear system (12.2.1) with m equations and n unknowns. Suppose we define

$$\mathbf{A} = \begin{pmatrix} a_{11} & a_{12} & \cdots & a_{1n} \\ a_{21} & a_{22} & \cdots & a_{2n} \\ \vdots & \vdots & & \vdots \\ a_{m1} & a_{m2} & \cdots & a_{mn} \end{pmatrix}, \quad \mathbf{x} = \begin{pmatrix} x_1 \\ x_2 \\ \vdots \\ x_n \end{pmatrix}, \quad \text{and} \quad \mathbf{b} = \begin{pmatrix} b_1 \\ b_2 \\ \vdots \\ b_m \end{pmatrix}$$

So **A** is $m \times n$ and **x** is $n \times 1$. The matrix product **Ax** is therefore defined and is $m \times 1$. Moreover, you can easily check that (12.2.1) can be written as $\mathbf{Ax} = \mathbf{b}$. This very concise notation turns out to be extremely useful.

EXERCISES FOR SECTION 12.5

1. Compute the products **AB** and **BA**, if possible, when **A** and **B** are, respectively:

   (a) $\begin{pmatrix} 0 & -2 \\ 3 & 1 \end{pmatrix}$ and $\begin{pmatrix} -1 & 4 \\ 1 & 5 \end{pmatrix}$

   (b) $\begin{pmatrix} 8 & 3 & -2 \\ 1 & 0 & 4 \end{pmatrix}$ and $\begin{pmatrix} 2 & -2 \\ 4 & 3 \\ 1 & -5 \end{pmatrix}$

   (c) $\begin{pmatrix} -1 & 0 \\ 2 & 4 \end{pmatrix}$ and $\begin{pmatrix} 3 & 1 \\ -1 & 1 \\ 0 & 2 \end{pmatrix}$

   (d) $\begin{pmatrix} 0 \\ -2 \\ 4 \end{pmatrix}$ and $\begin{pmatrix} 0 & -2 & 3 \end{pmatrix}$

2. Calculate the three matrices $3\mathbf{A} + 2\mathbf{B} - 2\mathbf{C} + \mathbf{D}$, **AB**, and **C(AB)**, given the matrices

$$\mathbf{A} = \begin{pmatrix} 2 & 4 \\ 1 & 2 \end{pmatrix}, \quad \mathbf{B} = \begin{pmatrix} -2 & 4 \\ 1 & -2 \end{pmatrix}, \quad \mathbf{C} = \begin{pmatrix} 2 & 3 \\ 6 & 9 \end{pmatrix}, \quad \text{and} \quad \mathbf{D} = \begin{pmatrix} 1 & 1 \\ 1 & 3 \end{pmatrix}$$

3. Find the six matrices $\mathbf{A} + \mathbf{B}$, $\mathbf{A} - \mathbf{B}$, **AB**, **BA**, **A(BC)**, and **(AB)C**, given that

$$\mathbf{A} = \begin{pmatrix} 1 & 2 & -3 \\ 5 & 0 & 2 \\ 1 & -1 & 1 \end{pmatrix}, \quad \mathbf{B} = \begin{pmatrix} 3 & -1 & 2 \\ 4 & 2 & 5 \\ 2 & 0 & 3 \end{pmatrix}, \quad \text{and} \quad \mathbf{C} = \begin{pmatrix} 4 & 1 & 2 \\ 0 & 3 & 2 \\ 1 & -2 & 3 \end{pmatrix}$$

4. Write out the three matrix equations that correspond to the following systems:

   (a) $\begin{aligned} x_1 + x_2 &= 3 \\ 3x_1 + 5x_2 &= 5 \end{aligned}$

   (b) $\begin{aligned} x_1 + 2x_2 + x_3 &= 4 \\ x_1 - x_2 + x_3 &= 5 \\ 2x_1 + 3x_2 - x_3 &= 1 \end{aligned}$

   (c) $\begin{aligned} 2x_1 - 3x_2 + x_3 &= 0 \\ x_1 + x_2 - x_3 &= 0 \end{aligned}$

5. Consider the three matrices

$$\mathbf{A} = \begin{pmatrix} 2 & 2 \\ 1 & 5 \end{pmatrix}, \quad \mathbf{B} = \begin{pmatrix} 2 & 0 \\ 3 & 2 \end{pmatrix}, \quad \text{and} \quad \mathbf{I} = \begin{pmatrix} 1 & 0 \\ 0 & 1 \end{pmatrix}$$

(a) Find a matrix $\mathbf{C}$ satisfying $(\mathbf{A} - 2\mathbf{I})\mathbf{C} = \mathbf{I}$.

(b) Is there a matrix $\mathbf{D}$ satisfying $(\mathbf{B} - 2\mathbf{I})\mathbf{D} = \mathbf{I}$?

(SM) 6. Suppose that $\mathbf{A}$ is an $m \times n$ matrix and that $\mathbf{B}$ is another matrix such that the products $\mathbf{AB}$ and $\mathbf{BA}$ are both defined. What must the order of $\mathbf{B}$ be?

(SM) 7. Find all matrices $\mathbf{B}$ that "commute" with $\mathbf{A} = \begin{pmatrix} 1 & 2 \\ 2 & 3 \end{pmatrix}$ in the sense that $\mathbf{AB} = \mathbf{BA}$.

8. In Example 12.5.3, compute $\mathbf{T}(\mathbf{Ts})$.

12.6 Rules for Matrix Multiplication

In Section 12.5 we saw that matrix multiplication is more complicated than the rather obvious operations of matrix addition and multiplication by a scalar that had been set out in Section 12.3. So we need to examine carefully what rules matrix multiplication does satisfy. We have already noticed that the commutative law $\mathbf{AB} = \mathbf{BA}$ does *not* hold in general. The following important rules *are* generally valid, however.

RULES FOR MATRIX MULTIPLICATION

Let $\mathbf{A}$, $\mathbf{B}$, and $\mathbf{C}$ be matrices and α a scalar. Then, whenever the orders of the specified matrices are such that the matrix operations are defined, one has:

$$(\mathbf{AB})\mathbf{C} = \mathbf{A}(\mathbf{BC}) \tag{12.6.1}$$

$$\mathbf{A}(\mathbf{B} + \mathbf{C}) = \mathbf{AB} + \mathbf{AC} \tag{12.6.2}$$

$$(\mathbf{A} + \mathbf{B})\mathbf{C} = \mathbf{AC} + \mathbf{BC} \tag{12.6.3}$$

$$(\alpha\mathbf{A})\mathbf{B} = \mathbf{A}(\alpha\mathbf{B}) = \alpha(\mathbf{AB}) \tag{12.6.4}$$

Rule (12.6.1) is known as the *associative law*, while rules (12.6.2) and (12.6.3) are, respectively, the *left* and *right distributive laws*. Note that two laws are stated here because, unlike for numbers, matrix multiplication is not *commutative*, and so $\mathbf{A}(\mathbf{B} + \mathbf{C})$ is in general different from $(\mathbf{B} + \mathbf{C})\mathbf{A}$.

EXAMPLE 12.6.1 Verify rules (12.6.1)–(12.6.2) for the following matrices:

$$\mathbf{A} = \begin{pmatrix} 1 & 2 \\ 0 & 1 \end{pmatrix}, \quad \mathbf{B} = \begin{pmatrix} 0 & -1 \\ 3 & 2 \end{pmatrix}, \quad \text{and} \quad \mathbf{C} = \begin{pmatrix} 1 & 1 \\ 2 & 1 \end{pmatrix}$$

Solution: All operations of multiplication and addition are defined, with

$$\mathbf{AB} = \begin{pmatrix} 6 & 3 \\ 3 & 2 \end{pmatrix}, \qquad (\mathbf{AB})\mathbf{C} = \begin{pmatrix} 6 & 3 \\ 3 & 2 \end{pmatrix}\begin{pmatrix} 1 & 1 \\ 2 & 1 \end{pmatrix} = \begin{pmatrix} 12 & 9 \\ 7 & 5 \end{pmatrix}$$

$$\mathbf{BC} = \begin{pmatrix} -2 & -1 \\ 7 & 5 \end{pmatrix}, \qquad \mathbf{A}(\mathbf{BC}) = \begin{pmatrix} 1 & 2 \\ 0 & 1 \end{pmatrix}\begin{pmatrix} -2 & -1 \\ 7 & 5 \end{pmatrix} = \begin{pmatrix} 12 & 9 \\ 7 & 5 \end{pmatrix}$$

Thus, $(\mathbf{AB})\mathbf{C} = \mathbf{A}(\mathbf{BC})$ in this case. Moreover,

$$\mathbf{B} + \mathbf{C} = \begin{pmatrix} 1 & 0 \\ 5 & 3 \end{pmatrix}, \qquad \mathbf{A}(\mathbf{B}+\mathbf{C}) = \begin{pmatrix} 1 & 2 \\ 0 & 1 \end{pmatrix}\begin{pmatrix} 1 & 0 \\ 5 & 3 \end{pmatrix} = \begin{pmatrix} 11 & 6 \\ 5 & 3 \end{pmatrix}$$

and

$$\mathbf{AC} = \begin{pmatrix} 5 & 3 \\ 2 & 1 \end{pmatrix}, \qquad \mathbf{AB} + \mathbf{AC} = \begin{pmatrix} 6 & 3 \\ 3 & 2 \end{pmatrix} + \begin{pmatrix} 5 & 3 \\ 2 & 1 \end{pmatrix} = \begin{pmatrix} 11 & 6 \\ 5 & 3 \end{pmatrix}$$

So $\mathbf{A}(\mathbf{B}+\mathbf{C}) = \mathbf{AB} + \mathbf{AC}$.

Rules (12.6.1)–(12.6.4) for matrix multiplication can be proved simply by carefully applying the definitions of the relevant operations, as well as the rules for the inner product of two vectors. To illustrate, we now prove the associative law:

Proof of rule (12.6.1): Suppose $\mathbf{A} = (a_{ij})_{m\times n}$, $\mathbf{B} = (b_{jk})_{n\times p}$, and $\mathbf{C} = (c_{kl})_{p\times q}$. It is easy to verify that these orders imply that $(\mathbf{AB})\mathbf{C}$ and $\mathbf{A}(\mathbf{BC})$ are both defined as $m \times q$ matrices. We have to prove that their corresponding elements are all equal.

The element in row i and column l of $(\mathbf{AB})\mathbf{C}$, denoted by $[(\mathbf{AB})\mathbf{C}]_{il}$, is the inner product of the ith row in $\mathbf{AB}$ and the lth column in $\mathbf{C}$. Similarly for the element $[\mathbf{A}(\mathbf{BC})]_{il}$ of $\mathbf{A}(\mathbf{BC})$. Using summation notation, we must prove the middle equality in the chain

$$[(\mathbf{AB})\mathbf{C}]_{il} = \sum_{k=1}^{p}\left(\sum_{j=1}^{n} a_{ij}b_{jk}\right)c_{kl} = \sum_{j=1}^{n} a_{ij}\left(\sum_{k=1}^{p} b_{jk}c_{kl}\right) = [\mathbf{A}(\mathbf{BC})]_{il}$$

But this middle equality holds because the double sums on each side are both equal to the overall sum of all the np terms $a_{ij}b_{jk}c_{kl}$, as j runs from 1 to n and k runs from 1 to p.

We emphasize that proving rule (12.6.1) involved checking in detail that each element of $(\mathbf{AB})\mathbf{C}$ equals the corresponding element of $\mathbf{A}(\mathbf{BC})$. The same sort of check is required to prove the other three rules. We leave the details of these proofs to the reader.

Because of (12.6.1), parentheses are not required in a matrix product such as $\mathbf{ABC}$. Of course, a corresponding result is valid for products of more factors.

A useful technique in matrix algebra is to prove new results by using rules (12.6.1)–(12.6.4), repeatedly if necessary, rather than by examining individual elements. For instance, consider the statement that if $\mathbf{A} = (a_{ij})$ and $\mathbf{B} = (b_{ij})$ are both $n \times n$ matrices, then

$$(\mathbf{A}+\mathbf{B})(\mathbf{A}+\mathbf{B}) = \mathbf{AA} + \mathbf{AB} + \mathbf{BA} + \mathbf{BB} \tag{12.6.5}$$

To prove this statement, note first that rules (12.6.2) and (12.6.3) together imply that

$$(\mathbf{A}+\mathbf{B})(\mathbf{A}+\mathbf{B}) = (\mathbf{A}+\mathbf{B})\mathbf{A} + (\mathbf{A}+\mathbf{B})\mathbf{B} = (\mathbf{AA} + \mathbf{BA}) + (\mathbf{AB} + \mathbf{BB})$$

Equation (12.6.5) now follows from rules (a) and (b) for matrix addition that were set out in Section 12.3.

Powers of Matrices

If $\mathbf{A}$ is a square matrix, we write the product $\mathbf{AA}$ as $\mathbf{A}^2$. The associative law (12.6.1) shows that $(\mathbf{A})^2\mathbf{A} = (\mathbf{AA})\mathbf{A} = \mathbf{A}(\mathbf{AA}) = \mathbf{A}(\mathbf{A})^2$, so we can write this product unambiguously as $\mathbf{A}^3$. In general, for any natural number n, we write

$$\mathbf{A}^n = \underbrace{\mathbf{AA}\cdots\mathbf{A}}_{n \text{ factors}}$$

EXAMPLE 12.6.2   Given the matrix $\mathbf{A} = \begin{pmatrix} 1 & -1 \\ 0 & 1 \end{pmatrix}$, compute $\mathbf{A}^2$, $\mathbf{A}^3$, and $\mathbf{A}^4$. Then guess the general form of $\mathbf{A}^n$. Finally, confirm your guess by using the principle of mathematical induction introduced in Section 1.4.

Solution: Routine calculation shows that

$$\mathbf{A}^2 = \mathbf{AA} = \begin{pmatrix} 1 & -2 \\ 0 & 1 \end{pmatrix}, \quad \mathbf{A}^3 = \mathbf{A}^2\mathbf{A} = \begin{pmatrix} 1 & -3 \\ 0 & 1 \end{pmatrix}, \quad \text{and} \quad \mathbf{A}^4 = \mathbf{A}^3\mathbf{A} = \begin{pmatrix} 1 & -4 \\ 0 & 1 \end{pmatrix}$$

A reasonable guess, therefore, is that for all natural numbers n, one has

$$\mathbf{A}^n = \begin{pmatrix} 1 & -n \\ 0 & 1 \end{pmatrix} \qquad (*)$$

We confirm this by induction on n. Obviously, formula $(*)$ is correct for $n = 1$. As the induction hypothesis, suppose that $(*)$ holds for $n = k$, that is,

$$\mathbf{A}^k = \begin{pmatrix} 1 & -k \\ 0 & 1 \end{pmatrix}$$

Then, by definition, one has

$$\mathbf{A}^{k+1} = \mathbf{A}^k\mathbf{A} = \begin{pmatrix} 1 & -k \\ 0 & 1 \end{pmatrix}\begin{pmatrix} 1 & -1 \\ 0 & 1 \end{pmatrix} = \begin{pmatrix} 1 & -k-1 \\ 0 & 1 \end{pmatrix} = \begin{pmatrix} 1 & -(k+1) \\ 0 & 1 \end{pmatrix}$$

This completes the induction step showing that, if $(*)$ holds for $n = k$, then it holds for $n = k + 1$. It follows that $(*)$ holds for all natural numbers n.

EXAMPLE 12.6.3   Suppose $\mathbf{P}$ and $\mathbf{Q}$ are two $n \times n$ matrices that satisfy $\mathbf{PQ} = \mathbf{Q}^2\mathbf{P}$. Prove then that $(\mathbf{PQ})^2 = \mathbf{Q}^6\mathbf{P}^2$.

Solution: The proof is simple if we repeatedly use rule (12.6.1) and also substitute $\mathbf{PQ}$ for $\mathbf{Q}^2\mathbf{P}$ twice in order to derive the following chain of equalities:

$$(\mathbf{PQ})^2 = (\mathbf{PQ})(\mathbf{PQ}) = (\mathbf{Q}^2\mathbf{P})(\mathbf{Q}^2\mathbf{P}) = (\mathbf{Q}^2\mathbf{P})\mathbf{Q}(\mathbf{QP}) = \mathbf{Q}^2(\mathbf{PQ})(\mathbf{QP})$$

Substituting $\mathbf{Q}^2\mathbf{P}$ for $\mathbf{PQ}$ twice while using rule (12.6.1) generates this second chain:

$$\mathbf{Q}^2(\mathbf{PQ})(\mathbf{QP}) = \mathbf{Q}^2(\mathbf{Q}^2\mathbf{P})(\mathbf{QP}) = \mathbf{Q}^2\mathbf{Q}^2(\mathbf{PQ})\mathbf{P} = \mathbf{Q}^4(\mathbf{Q}^2\mathbf{P})\mathbf{P} = \mathbf{Q}^6\mathbf{P}^2$$

Put together, these two chains imply that $(\mathbf{PQ})^2 = \mathbf{Q}^6\mathbf{P}^2$.

Note that it would be virtually impossible to solve this example by looking at individual elements. It is important to note too that, in general $(\mathbf{PQ})^2$ is *not* equal to $\mathbf{P}^2\mathbf{Q}^2$.

The Identity Matrix

The *identity matrix* of order n, denoted by $\mathbf{I}_n$ (or often just $\mathbf{I}$), is defined as the $n \times n$ matrix having as entries 1 along the main diagonal and 0 everywhere else. That is

$$\mathbf{I}_n = \begin{pmatrix} 1 & 0 & \cdots & 0 \\ 0 & 1 & \cdots & 0 \\ \vdots & \vdots & \ddots & \vdots \\ 0 & 0 & \cdots & 1 \end{pmatrix}_{n \times n}$$

If $\mathbf{A}$ is any $m \times n$ matrix, it is routine to use rule (12.5.1) for matrix multiplication in order to verify that $\mathbf{AI}_n = \mathbf{A}$. Likewise, if $\mathbf{B}$ is any $n \times m$ matrix, then $\mathbf{I}_n\mathbf{B} = \mathbf{B}$.

From the previous paragraph, it follows that, for every $n \times n$ matrix $\mathbf{A}$, one has

$$\mathbf{AI}_n = \mathbf{I}_n\mathbf{A} = \mathbf{A} \qquad (12.6.6)$$

Thus, $\mathbf{I}_n$ is the matrix equivalent of 1 in the real number system. In fact, it is the only matrix with this property. To prove this, suppose $\mathbf{E}$ is an arbitrary $n \times n$ matrix such that $\mathbf{AE} = \mathbf{A}$ for all $n \times n$ matrices $\mathbf{A}$. Putting $\mathbf{A} = \mathbf{I}_n$ in particular yields $\mathbf{I}_n\mathbf{E} = \mathbf{I}_n$. But $\mathbf{I}_n\mathbf{E} = \mathbf{E}$ according to Eq. (12.6.6). So $\mathbf{E} = \mathbf{I}_n$.

Errors to Avoid

The rules of matrix algebra make many arguments very easy. But it is essential to avoid inventing new rules that do not work when multiplying general matrices, even if they would work for numbers (or for 1×1 matrices). For example, consider Eq. (12.6.5). It is tempting to simplify the expression $\mathbf{AA} + \mathbf{AB} + \mathbf{BA} + \mathbf{BB}$ on the right-hand side to $\mathbf{AA} + 2\mathbf{AB} + \mathbf{BB}$. This is wrong! Even when $\mathbf{AB}$ and $\mathbf{BA}$ are both defined, $\mathbf{AB}$ is not necessarily equal to $\mathbf{BA}$. As the next example shows, matrix multiplication is *not* commutative.

EXAMPLE 12.6.4 Show that $\mathbf{AB} \neq \mathbf{BA}$ in case $\mathbf{A} = \begin{pmatrix} 2 & 0 \\ 0 & 3 \end{pmatrix}$ and $\mathbf{B} = \begin{pmatrix} 0 & 1 \\ 1 & 0 \end{pmatrix}$.

Solution: Direct computation shows that $\mathbf{AB} = \begin{pmatrix} 0 & 2 \\ 3 & 0 \end{pmatrix} \neq \mathbf{BA} = \begin{pmatrix} 0 & 3 \\ 2 & 0 \end{pmatrix}$.

One more result that does not extend from scalars to matrices is the following: if a and b are real numbers, then $ab = 0$ implies that either a or b is 0. The corresponding result is not true for matrices, as $\mathbf{AB}$ can be the zero matrix even if neither $\mathbf{A}$ nor $\mathbf{B}$ is the zero matrix. The following example illustrates this.

EXAMPLE 12.6.5   Compute **AB**, given that $\mathbf{A} = \begin{pmatrix} 3 & 1 \\ 6 & 2 \end{pmatrix}$ and $\mathbf{B} = \begin{pmatrix} 1 & 2 \\ -3 & -6 \end{pmatrix}$.

Solution: Direct computation gives $\mathbf{AB} = \begin{pmatrix} 3 & 1 \\ 6 & 2 \end{pmatrix} \begin{pmatrix} 1 & 2 \\ -3 & -6 \end{pmatrix} = \begin{pmatrix} 0 & 0 \\ 0 & 0 \end{pmatrix}$.

Another rule for real numbers is that, if $ab = ac$ and $a \neq 0$, then we can multiply each side of the equation by $1/a$ to derive $b = c$. This is the cancellation rule. An immediate implication of Example 12.6.5 is that the corresponding cancellation "rule" for matrices is not valid: there, $\mathbf{AB} = \mathbf{A0}$ and $\mathbf{A} \neq \mathbf{0}$, yet $\mathbf{B} \neq \mathbf{0}$. To summarize, in general:

(i) $\mathbf{AB} \neq \mathbf{BA}$;

(ii) $\mathbf{AB} = \mathbf{0}$ does not imply that either $\mathbf{A} = \mathbf{0}$ or $\mathbf{B} = \mathbf{0}$; and

(iii) $\mathbf{AB} = \mathbf{AC}$ and $\mathbf{A} \neq \mathbf{0}$ do not imply that $\mathbf{B} = \mathbf{C}$.

Here, (i) says that matrix multiplication is not *commutative* in general, whereas (iii) shows us that the cancellation law is generally invalid for matrix multiplication.[5]

The following two examples illustrate natural applications of matrix multiplication.

EXAMPLE 12.6.6   A firm uses m different raw materials $R_1, R_2, \ldots, R_m$ in order to produce the n different commodities $V_1, V_2, \ldots, V_n$. Suppose that for each $j = 1, 2, \ldots, n$, each unit of commodity V_j requires as inputs a_{ij} units of R_i, for all $i = 1, 2, \ldots, m$. These *input coefficients* form the matrix

$$\mathbf{A} = (a_{ij})_{m \times n} = \begin{pmatrix} a_{11} & a_{12} & \cdots & a_{1n} \\ a_{21} & a_{22} & \cdots & a_{2n} \\ \vdots & \vdots & & \vdots \\ a_{m1} & a_{m2} & \cdots & a_{mn} \end{pmatrix}$$

Suppose that the firm plans a monthly production of u_j units of each commodity V_j, $j = 1, 2, \ldots, n$. This plan can be represented by an $n \times 1$ matrix (column vector) $\mathbf{u}$, called the firm's monthly production vector:

$$\mathbf{u} = \begin{pmatrix} u_1 \\ u_2 \\ \vdots \\ u_n \end{pmatrix}$$

Since a_{i1}, in particular, is the amount of raw material R_i which is needed to produce one unit of commodity V_1, it follows that $a_{i1}u_1$ is the amount of raw material R_i which is needed to produce u_1 units of commodity V_1. Similarly $a_{ij}u_j$ is the amount needed for u_j units of V_j ($j = 2, \ldots, n$). The total monthly requirement of raw material R_i is therefore

$$a_{i1}u_1 + a_{i2}u_2 + \cdots + a_{in}u_n = \sum_{j=1}^{n} a_{ij}u_j$$

---

[5] The cancellation law (iii) *is* valid, however, in case **A** has an inverse, as defined in Section 13.6.

This is the inner product of the ith row vector in $\mathbf{A}$ and the column vector $\mathbf{u}$. The firm's monthly requirement vector $\mathbf{r}$ for all raw materials is therefore given by the matrix product $\mathbf{r} = \mathbf{Au}$. Thus $\mathbf{r}$ is an $m \times 1$ matrix, or a column vector.

Suppose that the prices per unit of the m raw materials are respectively $p_1, p_2, \ldots, p_m$. Let us denote by $\mathbf{p}$ by the price vector $(p_1, p_2, \ldots, p_m)$. Then the total monthly cost K of acquiring the required raw materials to produce the vector $\mathbf{u}$ is $\sum_{i=1}^{m} p_i r_i$. This sum can also be written as the matrix product $\mathbf{pr}$. Hence, $K = \mathbf{pr} = \mathbf{p}(\mathbf{Au})$. But Rule (12.6.1) tells us that matrix multiplication is associative, which allows us to write $K = \mathbf{pAu}$ without parentheses.

EXAMPLE 12.6.7 Figure 12.6.1 indicates the number of daily international flights between major airports in three different countries A, B, and C. The number attached to each connecting line shows how many flights there are between the two airports. For instance, from airport b_3 in country B there are 4 flights to airport c_3 in country C each day, but none to airport c_2 in country C.

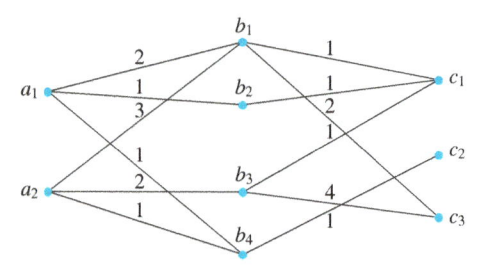

Figure 12.6.1 Example 12.6.7

The relevant data can also be represented by the following two extended matrices, in which we have added to each row and column the label for the corresponding airport:

$$\mathbf{P}: \quad \begin{matrix} & b_1 & b_2 & b_3 & b_4 \\ a_1 & \begin{pmatrix} 2 & 1 & 0 & 1 \\ 3 & 0 & 2 & 1 \end{pmatrix} \\ a_2 & \end{matrix} \qquad \mathbf{Q}: \quad \begin{matrix} & c_1 & c_2 & c_3 \\ b_1 & \begin{pmatrix} 1 & 0 & 2 \\ 1 & 0 & 0 \\ 1 & 0 & 4 \\ 0 & 1 & 0 \end{pmatrix} \\ b_2 & \\ b_3 & \\ b_4 & \end{matrix}$$

Each element p_{ij} of the matrix $\mathbf{P}$ represents the number of daily flights between airports a_i and b_j. Similarly, each element q_{jk} of $\mathbf{Q}$ represents the number of daily flights between airports b_j and c_k. How many ways are there of getting from a_i to c_k using two flights, with one connection in country B? Between a_2 and c_3, for example, there are $3 \cdot 2 + 0 \cdot 0 + 2 \cdot 4 + 1 \cdot 0 = 14$ possibilities. This is the inner product of the second row vector in $\mathbf{P}$ and the third column vector in $\mathbf{Q}$. The same reasoning applies for each a_i and c_k. So the total number of flight connections between the different airports in countries A and C is given by the matrix product

$$\mathbf{R} = \mathbf{PQ} = \begin{pmatrix} 2 & 1 & 0 & 1 \\ 3 & 0 & 2 & 1 \end{pmatrix} \begin{pmatrix} 1 & 0 & 2 \\ 1 & 0 & 0 \\ 1 & 0 & 4 \\ 0 & 1 & 0 \end{pmatrix} = \begin{pmatrix} 3 & 1 & 4 \\ 5 & 1 & 14 \end{pmatrix}$$

EXERCISES FOR SECTION 12.6

1. Verify the distributive law $\mathbf{A}(\mathbf{B} + \mathbf{C}) = \mathbf{AB} + \mathbf{AC}$ when

$$\mathbf{A} = \begin{pmatrix} 1 & 2 \\ 3 & 4 \end{pmatrix}, \quad \mathbf{B} = \begin{pmatrix} 2 & -1 & 1 & 0 \\ 3 & -1 & 2 & 1 \end{pmatrix}, \quad \text{and} \quad \mathbf{C} = \begin{pmatrix} -1 & 1 & 1 & 2 \\ -2 & 2 & 0 & -1 \end{pmatrix}$$

(SM) 2. Compute the matrix product

$$(x \ y \ z) \begin{pmatrix} a & d & e \\ d & b & f \\ e & f & c \end{pmatrix} \begin{pmatrix} x \\ y \\ z \end{pmatrix}$$

3. Use explicit calculation to verify that $(\mathbf{AB})\mathbf{C} = \mathbf{A}(\mathbf{BC})$ in case

$$\mathbf{A} = \begin{pmatrix} a_{11} & a_{12} \\ a_{21} & a_{22} \end{pmatrix}, \quad \mathbf{B} = \begin{pmatrix} b_{11} & b_{12} \\ b_{21} & b_{22} \end{pmatrix}, \quad \text{and} \quad \mathbf{C} = \begin{pmatrix} c_{11} & c_{12} \\ c_{21} & c_{22} \end{pmatrix}$$

4. Compute the following matrix products:

(a) $\begin{pmatrix} 1 & 0 & 0 \\ 0 & 1 & 0 \\ 0 & 0 & 1 \end{pmatrix} \begin{pmatrix} 5 & 3 & 1 \\ 2 & 0 & 9 \\ 1 & 3 & 3 \end{pmatrix}$ (b) $\begin{pmatrix} 1 & 2 & -3 \end{pmatrix} \begin{pmatrix} 1 & 0 & 0 \\ 0 & 1 & 0 \\ 0 & 0 & 1 \end{pmatrix}$

5. Suppose that $\mathbf{A}$ and $\mathbf{B}$ are square matrices of order n. Prove that, in general:

   (a) $(\mathbf{A} + \mathbf{B})(\mathbf{A} - \mathbf{B}) \neq \mathbf{A}^2 - \mathbf{B}^2$;   (b) $(\mathbf{A} - \mathbf{B})(\mathbf{A} - \mathbf{B}) \neq \mathbf{A}^2 - 2\mathbf{AB} + \mathbf{B}^2$.

   Find a necessary and sufficient condition for equality to hold in each case.

6. A square matrix $\mathbf{A}$ is said to be *idempotent* if $\mathbf{A}^2 = \mathbf{A}$.

   (a) Show that the matrix $\begin{pmatrix} 2 & -2 & -4 \\ -1 & 3 & 4 \\ 1 & -2 & -3 \end{pmatrix}$ is idempotent.

   (b) Show that if $\mathbf{AB} = \mathbf{A}$ and $\mathbf{BA} = \mathbf{B}$, then $\mathbf{A}$ and $\mathbf{B}$ are both idempotent.

   (c) Show that if $\mathbf{A}$ is idempotent, then $\mathbf{A}^n = \mathbf{A}$ for all positive integers n.

7. Suppose that $\mathbf{P}$ and $\mathbf{Q}$ are $n \times n$ matrices that satisfy $\mathbf{P}^3\mathbf{Q} = \mathbf{PQ}$. Prove that $\mathbf{P}^5\mathbf{Q} = \mathbf{PQ}$.

(SM) 8. [HARDER] Consider the general 2×2 matrix $\mathbf{A} = \begin{pmatrix} a & b \\ c & d \end{pmatrix}$.

   (a) Prove that $\mathbf{A}^2 = (a+d)\mathbf{A} - (ad - bc)\mathbf{I}_2$.

   (b) Use (a) to find an example of a 2×2 matrix $\mathbf{A}$ such that $\mathbf{A}^2 = \mathbf{0}$, but $\mathbf{A} \neq \mathbf{0}$.

   (c) Use part (a) to show that if any 2×2 matrix $\mathbf{A}$ satisfies $\mathbf{A}^3 = \mathbf{0}$, then $\mathbf{A}^2 = \mathbf{0}$. (*Hint*: Multiply the equality in part (a) by $\mathbf{A}$, then use the equality $\mathbf{A}^3 = \mathbf{0}$ to derive an equation that you should then multiply by $\mathbf{A}$ once again.)

12.7 The Transpose

Consider any $m \times n$ matrix $\mathbf{A}$. The *transpose* of $\mathbf{A}$, denoted by $\mathbf{A}'$ or sometimes by $\mathbf{A}^\top$, is defined as the $n \times m$ matrix whose first row is the first column of $\mathbf{A}$, whose second row is the second column of $\mathbf{A}$, and so on. Thus, the transpose of the $m \times n$ matrix

$$\mathbf{A} = (a_{ij})_{m \times n} = \begin{pmatrix} a_{11} & a_{12} & \cdots & a_{1n} \\ a_{21} & a_{22} & \cdots & a_{2n} \\ \vdots & \vdots & & \vdots \\ a_{m1} & a_{m2} & \cdots & a_{mn} \end{pmatrix}$$

is the $n \times m$ matrix

$$\mathbf{A}' = (a'_{rs})_{n \times m} = \begin{pmatrix} a'_{11} & a'_{12} & \cdots & a'_{1m} \\ a'_{21} & a'_{22} & \cdots & a'_{2m} \\ \vdots & \vdots & & \vdots \\ a'_{n1} & a'_{n2} & \cdots & a'_{nm} \end{pmatrix} = \begin{pmatrix} a_{11} & a_{21} & \cdots & a_{m1} \\ a_{12} & a_{22} & \cdots & a_{m2} \\ \vdots & \vdots & & \vdots \\ a_{1n} & a_{2n} & \cdots & a_{mn} \end{pmatrix} \qquad (12.7.1)$$

Succinctly, we have written $\mathbf{A}' = (a'_{rs})$ where $a'_{rs} = a_{sr}$ for all r and s. The subscripts r and s have had to be interchanged because, for example, the ith row of $\mathbf{A}$ becomes the ith column of $\mathbf{A}'$, whereas the jth column of $\mathbf{A}$ becomes the jth row of $\mathbf{A}'$.

EXAMPLE 12.7.1   Find $\mathbf{A}'$ and $\mathbf{B}'$ for the matrices

$$\mathbf{A} = \begin{pmatrix} -1 & 0 \\ 2 & 3 \\ 5 & -1 \end{pmatrix} \quad \text{and} \quad \mathbf{B} = \begin{pmatrix} 1 & -1 & 0 & 4 \\ 2 & 1 & 1 & 1 \end{pmatrix}$$

Solution: Applying the definition (12.7.1) of transpose gives

$$\mathbf{A}' = \begin{pmatrix} -1 & 2 & 5 \\ 0 & 3 & -1 \end{pmatrix} \quad \text{and} \quad \mathbf{B}' = \begin{pmatrix} 1 & 2 \\ -1 & 1 \\ 0 & 1 \\ 4 & 1 \end{pmatrix}$$

EXAMPLE 12.7.2   Suppose that we treat the two n-vectors

$$\mathbf{a} = \begin{pmatrix} a_1 \\ \vdots \\ a_n \end{pmatrix} \quad \text{and} \quad \mathbf{b} = \begin{pmatrix} b_1 \\ \vdots \\ b_n \end{pmatrix}$$

as $n \times 1$ matrices. Then the transpose $\mathbf{a}'$ is a $1 \times n$ matrix, so the matrix product $\mathbf{a}'\mathbf{b}$ is well defined as a 1×1 matrix. In fact,

$$\mathbf{a}'\mathbf{b} = (a_1 b_1 + a_2 b_2 + \cdots + a_n b_n)$$

We see that the single element of the matrix $\mathbf{a}'\mathbf{b}$ is just the inner product of the two vectors $\mathbf{a}$ and $\mathbf{b}$, and with a slight abuse of notation we often write $\mathbf{a}'\mathbf{b} = \mathbf{a} \cdot \mathbf{b}$.

It is usual in economics to regard a typical vector **x** as a column vector, unless otherwise specified. This is especially true if it is a quantity or commodity vector. Another common convention is to regard a price vector as a row vector, often denoted by **p**'. Then **p**'**x** is the 1×1 matrix whose single element is equal to the inner product $\mathbf{p} \cdot \mathbf{x}$.

The following rules apply to matrix transposition:

RULES FOR TRANSPOSITION

Given any two matrices **A** and **B** as well as any scalar α:

$$(\mathbf{A}')' = \mathbf{A} \tag{12.7.2}$$

$$(\mathbf{A} + \mathbf{B})' = \mathbf{A}' + \mathbf{B}' \text{ provided that } \mathbf{A} + \mathbf{B} \text{ is defined} \tag{12.7.3}$$

$$(\alpha \mathbf{A})' = \alpha \mathbf{A}' \tag{12.7.4}$$

$$(\mathbf{AB})' = \mathbf{B}'\mathbf{A}' \text{ provided that } \mathbf{AB} \text{ is defined} \tag{12.7.5}$$

Verifying the first three rules is very easy, and you should prove them in detail, using the fact that $a'_{ij} = a_{ji}$ for each i, j. Next, we prove the last rule:

Proof of (12.7.5) Suppose that **A** is $m \times n$ and **B** is $n \times p$, so **AB** is defined as an $m \times p$ matrix. Then **A**' is $n \times m$, and **B**' is $p \times n$, so **B**'**A**' is also defined. It follows that both $(\mathbf{AB})'$ and $\mathbf{B}'\mathbf{A}'$ are $p \times m$. It remains to prove that all the corresponding pairs of elements in these two $p \times m$ matrices are equal.

Now the *ki* element of the transpose $(\mathbf{AB})'$ is, by definition, the *ik* element of **AB**, which is

$$a_{i1}b_{1k} + a_{i2}b_{2k} + \cdots + a_{in}b_{nk} \tag{*}$$

On the other hand, the *ki* element in $\mathbf{B}'\mathbf{A}'$ is

$$b'_{k1}a'_{1i} + b'_{k2}a'_{2i} + \cdots + b'_{kn}a'_{ni} \tag{**}$$

By definition of the transpose, one has $b'_{kj} = b_{jk}$ and $a'_{ji} = a_{ij}$ for all $j = 1, \ldots, n$. So the expression (**) becomes

$$b_{1k}a_{i1} + b_{2k}a_{i2} + \cdots + b_{nk}a_{in} \tag{***}$$

Since $a_{ij}b_{jk} = b_{jk}a_{ij}$ for all $j = 1, \ldots, n$, the sums in (*) and (***) are clearly equal, as required.

EXAMPLE 12.7.3   Let **x** be the column vector $(x_1, x_2, \ldots, x_n)'$. Then **x**' is a row vector of n elements. By Example 12.7.2, the product **x**'**x** equals the scalar product $\mathbf{x} \cdot \mathbf{x}$, which also equals $\sum_{i=1}^{n} x_i^2$.

The reverse product **xx**', however, as the product of $n \times 1$ and $1 \times n$ matrices in that order, is an $n \times n$ matrix whose *ij* element is $x_i x_j$.

Symmetric Matrices

Square matrices with the property that they are equal to their own transposes are called *symmetric*. For example,

$$\begin{pmatrix} -3 & 2 \\ 2 & 0 \end{pmatrix}, \quad \begin{pmatrix} 2 & -1 & 5 \\ -1 & -3 & 2 \\ 5 & 2 & 8 \end{pmatrix} \quad \text{and} \quad \begin{pmatrix} a & b & c \\ b & d & e \\ c & e & f \end{pmatrix}$$

are all symmetric. Such matrices deserve this name because they are symmetric about the main diagonal, in the sense that $a_{ij} = a_{ji}$ for all i and j. Formally,

---
SYMMETRIC MATRIX

The matrix $\mathbf{A} = (a_{ij})_{n \times n}$ is symmetric if and only if $a_{ij} = a_{ji}$ for all i, j. More succinctly,

$$\mathbf{A} \text{ is symmetric} \iff \mathbf{A} = \mathbf{A}'$$

EXAMPLE 12.7.4 If $\mathbf{X}$ is an $m \times n$ matrix, show that $\mathbf{XX}'$ and $\mathbf{X}'\mathbf{X}$ are both symmetric.

Solution: First, note that $\mathbf{XX}'$ is $m \times m$, whereas $\mathbf{X}'\mathbf{X}$ is $n \times n$. Using rule (12.7.5) and then (12.7.2), we find that

$$(\mathbf{XX}')' = (\mathbf{X}')'\mathbf{X}' = \mathbf{XX}'$$

This proves that $\mathbf{XX}'$ is symmetric. The proof that $\mathbf{X}'\mathbf{X}$ is symmetric is almost identical.

EXERCISES FOR SECTION 12.7

1. Find the transposes of the three matrices

$$\mathbf{A} = \begin{pmatrix} 3 & 5 & 8 & 3 \\ -1 & 2 & 6 & 2 \end{pmatrix}, \quad \mathbf{B} = \begin{pmatrix} 0 \\ 1 \\ -1 \\ 2 \end{pmatrix}, \quad \text{and} \quad \mathbf{C} = \begin{pmatrix} 1 & 5 & 0 & -1 \end{pmatrix}$$

2. Let $\mathbf{A} = \begin{pmatrix} 3 & 2 \\ -1 & 5 \end{pmatrix}$, $\mathbf{B} = \begin{pmatrix} 0 & 2 \\ 2 & 2 \end{pmatrix}$, and $\alpha = -2$.

   (a) Compute the eight matrices $\mathbf{A}'$, $\mathbf{B}'$, $(\mathbf{A} + \mathbf{B})'$, $(\alpha \mathbf{A})'$, $\mathbf{AB}$, $(\mathbf{AB})'$, $\mathbf{B}'\mathbf{A}'$, and $\mathbf{A}'\mathbf{B}'$.

   (b) For these particular values of $\mathbf{A}$, $\mathbf{B}$, and α, verify all the rules for transposition specified in Eqs (12.7.2)–(12.7.5).

3. Show that the matrices $\mathbf{A} = \begin{pmatrix} 3 & 2 & 3 \\ 2 & -1 & 1 \\ 3 & 1 & 0 \end{pmatrix}$ and $\mathbf{B} = \begin{pmatrix} 0 & 4 & 8 \\ 4 & 0 & 13 \\ 8 & 13 & 0 \end{pmatrix}$ are both symmetric.

4. Determine all the values of a for which the matrix $\begin{pmatrix} a & a^2 - 1 & -3 \\ a+1 & 2 & a^2 + 4 \\ -3 & 4a & -1 \end{pmatrix}$ is symmetric.

5. Is the product of two symmetric matrices necessarily symmetric?

⑤ 6. Provided that $\mathbf{A}_1, \mathbf{A}_2$, and $\mathbf{A}_3$ are three matrices for which all the relevant products are all defined, show that $(\mathbf{A}_1\mathbf{A}_2\mathbf{A}_3)' = \mathbf{A}_3'\mathbf{A}_2'\mathbf{A}_1'$. Generalize to products of n matrices.

7. An $n \times n$ matrix $\mathbf{P}$ is said to be *orthogonal* if $\mathbf{P}'\mathbf{P} = \mathbf{I}_n$.

(a) For $\lambda = \pm 1/\sqrt{2}$, show that the matrix $\mathbf{P} = \begin{pmatrix} \lambda & 0 & \lambda \\ \lambda & 0 & -\lambda \\ 0 & 1 & 0 \end{pmatrix}$ is orthogonal.

(b) Show that the 2×2 matrix $\begin{pmatrix} p & -q \\ q & p \end{pmatrix}$ is orthogonal if and only if $p^2 + q^2 = 1$.

(c) Show that the product of two orthogonal $n \times n$ matrices is orthogonal.

⑤ 8. Define the two matrices $\mathbf{T} = \begin{pmatrix} p & q & 0 \\ \frac{1}{2}p & \frac{1}{2} & \frac{1}{2}q \\ 0 & p & q \end{pmatrix}$ and $\mathbf{S} = \begin{pmatrix} p^2 & 2pq & q^2 \\ p^2 & 2pq & q^2 \\ p^2 & 2pq & q^2 \end{pmatrix}$, where $p + q = 1$.

(a) Prove that $\mathbf{TS} = \mathbf{S}$, that $\mathbf{T}^2 = \frac{1}{2}\mathbf{T} + \frac{1}{2}\mathbf{S}$, and that $\mathbf{T}^3 = \frac{1}{4}\mathbf{T} + \frac{3}{4}\mathbf{S}$.

(b) Introduce the hypothesis that for $n = 2, 3, \ldots$ there exist two constants α_n and β_n such that $\mathbf{T}^n = \alpha_n \mathbf{T} + \beta_n \mathbf{S}$. Under this hypothesis, use the results of part (a) to express α_{n+1} and β_{n+1} as functions of α_n and β_n. Use these relations to conjecture formulas for the constants α_n and β_n. Then prove the formulas by induction.

12.8 Gaussian Elimination

In Example 3.6.1, the procedure of eliminating unknowns was introduced as Method 2 for finding solutions to two simultaneous equations in two unknowns. The same procedure can be extended to larger equation systems. Because of its efficiency, it is the usual starting point for computer algorithms. To see how it works, consider first the following example.

EXAMPLE 12.8.1   Find all possible solutions of the system

$$2x_2 - x_3 = -7$$
$$x_1 + x_2 + 3x_3 = 2 \quad \text{(i)}$$
$$-3x_1 + 2x_2 + 2x_3 = -10$$

Solution: The idea will be to modify the system in such a way that: (a) x_1 appears only in the first equation; (b) x_2 appears only in the first and second equations; (c) finally x_3 remains as the only variable in the third equation. And, of course, we must make sure that the modified system has exactly the same solutions as the original system.

In the example, we begin by interchanging the first two equations, which certainly will not alter the set of solutions. We obtain

$$x_1 + x_2 + 3x_3 = 2$$
$$2x_2 - x_3 = -7 \quad \text{(ii)}$$
$$-3x_1 + 2x_2 + 2x_3 = -10$$

This has removed x_1 from the second equation. The next step is to use the first equation in (ii) to eliminate x_1 from the third equation. This is done by adding three times the first equation to the last equation.[6] This gives

$$x_1 + x_2 + 3x_3 = 2$$
$$2x_2 - x_3 = -7 \quad \text{(iii)}$$
$$5x_2 + 11x_3 = -4$$

Having eliminated x_1, the next step in the systematic procedure is to multiply the second equation in (iii) by 1/2, so that the coefficient of x_2 becomes 1. Thus,

$$x_1 + x_2 + 3x_3 = 2$$
$$x_2 - \tfrac{1}{2}x_3 = -\tfrac{7}{2} \quad \text{(iv)}$$
$$5x_2 + 11x_3 = -4$$

Next, eliminate x_2 from the last equation by multiplying the second equation by -5 and adding the result to the last equation. This gives:

$$x_1 + x_2 + 3x_3 = 2$$
$$x_2 - \tfrac{1}{2}x_3 = -\tfrac{7}{2} \quad \text{(v)}$$
$$\tfrac{27}{2}x_3 = \tfrac{27}{2}$$

Finally, multiply the last equation by 2/27 to obtain $x_3 = 1$. After this the other two unknowns can easily be found by "back substitution". Indeed, inserting $x_3 = 1$ into the second equation in (v) gives $x_2 = -3$. Next, inserting $x_2 = -3$ and $x_3 = 1$ into the first equation in (v) yields $x_1 = 2$. Therefore the only solution of system (i) is $(x_1, x_2, x_3) = (2, -3, 1)$.

Our elimination procedure led to a "staircase" in system (v), with x_1, x_2, and x_3 as *leading entries*. In matrix notation, we have

$$\begin{pmatrix} 1 & 1 & 3 \\ 0 & 1 & -1/2 \\ 0 & 0 & 1 \end{pmatrix} \begin{pmatrix} x_1 \\ x_2 \\ x_3 \end{pmatrix} = \begin{pmatrix} 2 \\ -7/2 \\ 1 \end{pmatrix}$$

The coefficient matrix on the left-hand side is said to be *upper triangular* because its only nonzero entries are on or above the main diagonal. Moreover, in this example the diagonal elements are all 1.

---

[6] The same result is obtained if we solve the first equation for x_1 to obtain $x_1 = -x_2 - 3x_3 + 2$, and then substitute this into the last equation.

The solution method illustrated in Example 12.8.1 is called *Gaussian elimination*, or sometimes the *Gauss–Jordan method*. The operations performed on the given system of equations in order to arrive at system (v) are called *elementary row operations*. These come in three different kinds:

1. Interchange any pair of rows, as in the step from (i) to (ii) in the above solution. This will be indicated by a suitable two-way arrow linking the two rows.

2. Multiply any row by a nonzero scalar, as in the step from (iii) to (iv) in the above solution. This will be indicated by writing the scalar multiplier beside the appropriate row.

3. Add any multiple of one row to a different row, as in the steps from (ii) to (iii) and from (iv) to (v) in the above solution. This will be indicated by writing the scalar multiplier beside the appropriate row, then using an arrow to link that number to the other row.

Sometimes the elementary row operations are continued until we also obtain zeros above the leading entries. In the example above, this takes three more operations of type 3. The first is as indicated in

$$x_1 + x_2 + 3x_3 = 2$$
$$x_2 - \tfrac{1}{2}x_3 = -\tfrac{7}{2} \quad -1$$
$$x_3 = 1$$
(12.8.1)

This results in

$$x_1 \quad + \tfrac{7}{2}x_3 = \tfrac{11}{2}$$
$$x_2 - \tfrac{1}{2}x_3 = -\tfrac{7}{2}$$
$$x_3 = 1 \quad \tfrac{1}{2} \quad -\tfrac{7}{2}$$
(12.8.2)

Display (12.8.2) indicates the next *two* operations, which affect rows 1 and 2 respectively. The final result is the simple equation system $x_1 = 2$, $x_2 = -3$, and $x_3 = 1$.

Let us apply this method to another example.

EXAMPLE 12.8.2   Find all possible solutions of the following system of equations:

$$x_1 + 3x_2 - x_3 = 4$$
$$2x_1 + x_2 + x_3 = 7$$
$$2x_1 - 4x_2 + 4x_3 = 6$$
$$3x_1 + 4x_2 = 11$$

Solution: We begin with three operations to remove x_1 from the second, third, and fourth equations, as indicated below:

$$x_1 + 3x_2 - x_3 = 4 \quad -2 \quad -2 \quad -3$$
$$2x_1 + x_2 + x_3 = 7$$
$$2x_1 - 4x_2 + 4x_3 = 6$$
$$3x_1 + 4x_2 = 11$$

The result is:
$$x_1 + 3x_2 - x_3 = 4$$
$$-5x_2 + 3x_3 = -1 \quad \times(-\tfrac{1}{5})$$
$$-10x_2 + 6x_3 = -2$$
$$-5x_2 + 3x_3 = -1$$

where we have also indicated the next operation of multiplying row 2 by $-\tfrac{1}{5}$. Further operations on the result lead to
$$x_1 + 3x_2 - x_3 = 4$$
$$x_2 - \tfrac{3}{5}x_3 = \tfrac{1}{5} \quad 10 \quad 5$$
$$-10x_2 + 6x_3 = -2$$
$$-5x_2 + 3x_3 = -1$$

and then to
$$x_1 + 3x_2 - x_3 = 4$$
$$x_2 - \tfrac{3}{5}x_3 = \tfrac{1}{5} \quad -3$$
$$0 = 0$$
$$0 = 0$$

We have now constructed the staircase. The last two equations are superfluous, so we drop them, while applying one more row operation to create a zero above the leading entry x_2. The result is:
$$x_1 + \tfrac{4}{5}x_3 = \tfrac{17}{5}$$
$$x_2 - \tfrac{3}{5}x_3 = \tfrac{1}{5}$$

Equivalently, one has
$$x_1 = -\tfrac{4}{5}x_3 + \tfrac{17}{5}$$
$$x_2 = \tfrac{3}{5}x_3 + \tfrac{1}{5} \tag{$*$}$$

Clearly, x_3 can be chosen freely, after which both x_1 and x_2 are uniquely determined by ($*$). Putting $x_3 = t$, we can represent the set of all possible solutions as
$$(x_1, x_2, x_3) = \left(-\tfrac{4}{5}t + \tfrac{17}{5}, \tfrac{3}{5}t + \tfrac{1}{5}, t\right)$$

where t is any real number. This solution will be discussed further in Example 15.10.1.

GAUSSIAN ELIMINATION METHOD

In order to solve a system of linear equations:

(i) Make a staircase with 1 as the coefficient for each nonzero leading entry.

(ii) Produce zeros above each leading entry.

(iii) The general solution is found by expressing the unknowns that occur as leading entries in terms only of those unknowns that do not. The latter unknowns, if there are any, can then be chosen freely.

The number of unknowns that can be chosen freely, which may be none, is the number of *degrees of freedom*.

This description of the recipe assumes that the system has solutions. However, the Gaussian elimination method can also be used to show whether a linear system of equations is inconsistent, in the sense of having no solutions. Before showing you an example of this, let us introduce a device that reduces considerably the amount of notation we need. Looking back at the last two examples, we realize that we only need to know the coefficients of the system of equations and the right-hand side vector, while the variables only serve to indicate the column in which to place the different coefficients. Thus, Example 12.8.2 can be represented as follows by *augmented coefficient matrices* which each have an extra column consisting of the corresponding vector of right-hand sides to the equations.

$$\begin{pmatrix} 1 & 3 & -1 & 4 \\ 2 & 1 & 1 & 7 \\ 2 & -4 & 4 & 6 \\ 3 & 4 & 0 & 11 \end{pmatrix} \sim \begin{pmatrix} 1 & 3 & -1 & 4 \\ 0 & -5 & 3 & -1 \\ 0 & -10 & 6 & -2 \\ 0 & -5 & 3 & -1 \end{pmatrix} \times (-\tfrac{1}{5})$$

$$\sim \begin{pmatrix} 1 & 3 & -1 & 4 \\ 0 & 1 & -3/5 & 1/5 \\ 0 & -10 & 6 & -2 \\ 0 & -5 & 3 & -1 \end{pmatrix} \sim \begin{pmatrix} 1 & 3 & -1 & 4 \\ 0 & 1 & -3/5 & 1/5 \\ 0 & 0 & 0 & 0 \\ 0 & 0 & 0 & 0 \end{pmatrix}$$

$$\sim \begin{pmatrix} 1 & 0 & 4/5 & 17/5 \\ 0 & 1 & -3/5 & 1/5 \\ 0 & 0 & 0 & 0 \\ 0 & 0 & 0 & 0 \end{pmatrix}$$

The above display shows the *elementary row operations* that we have performed on four successive different 4×4 augmented matrices. Also, we have used the equivalence symbol $\sim$ between two matrices to indicate that the latter has been obtained by applying elementary operations to the former. This is justified because such operations do always produce an equivalent system of equations. Note carefully how the system of equations in Example 12.8.2 is represented by the first matrix, and how the last matrix is equivalent to the system consisting of the two equations $x_1 + \tfrac{4}{5}x_3 = \tfrac{17}{5}$ and $x_2 - \tfrac{3}{5}x_3 = \tfrac{1}{5}$.

EXAMPLE 12.8.3   For what values of the numbers a, b, and c does the following system have solutions? Find the solutions when they exist.

$$x_1 - 2x_2 + x_3 + 2x_4 = a$$
$$x_1 + x_2 - x_3 + x_4 = b$$
$$x_1 + 7x_2 - 5x_3 - x_4 = c$$

478 CHAPTER 12 / MATRIX ALGEBRA

Solution: We represent the system by its augmented matrix. Then we perform elementary row operations as required by the Gaussian method:

$$\begin{pmatrix} 1 & -2 & 1 & 2 & a \\ 1 & 1 & -1 & 1 & b \\ 1 & 7 & -5 & -1 & c \end{pmatrix} \begin{matrix} \leftarrow -1 \\ \leftarrow -1 \end{matrix} \sim \begin{pmatrix} 1 & -2 & 1 & 2 & a \\ 0 & 3 & -2 & -1 & b-a \\ 0 & 9 & -6 & -3 & c-a \end{pmatrix} \begin{matrix} \\ -3 \\ \leftarrow \end{matrix}$$

$$\sim \begin{pmatrix} 1 & -2 & 1 & 2 & a \\ 0 & 3 & -2 & -1 & b-a \\ 0 & 0 & 0 & 0 & 2a-3b+c \end{pmatrix}$$

The last row represents the equation $0 \cdot x_1 + 0 \cdot x_2 + 0 \cdot x_3 + 0 \cdot x_4 = 2a - 3b + c$. The system therefore has solutions only if $2a - 3b + c = 0$. In this case the last row has only zeros. We continue using elementary operations till we end up with the following matrix:

$$\begin{pmatrix} 1 & 0 & -\frac{1}{3} & \frac{4}{3} & \frac{1}{3}(a+2b) \\ 0 & 1 & -\frac{2}{3} & -\frac{1}{3} & \frac{1}{3}(b-a) \\ 0 & 0 & 0 & 0 & 0 \end{pmatrix}$$

This represents the equation system

$$x_1 \quad - \tfrac{1}{3}x_3 + \tfrac{4}{3}x_4 = \tfrac{1}{3}(a+2b)$$
$$x_2 - \tfrac{2}{3}x_3 - \tfrac{1}{3}x_4 = \tfrac{1}{3}(b-a)$$

Here x_3 and x_4 can be freely chosen. Once these have been chosen, however, components x_1 and x_2 are uniquely determined linear functions of $s = x_3$ and $t = x_4$. The solution is:

$$x_1 = \tfrac{1}{3}(a+2b) + \tfrac{1}{3}s - \tfrac{4}{3}t$$
$$x_2 = \tfrac{1}{3}(b-a) + \tfrac{2}{3}s + \tfrac{1}{3}t$$

where s and t are arbitrary real numbers.

EXERCISES FOR SECTION 12.8

1. Solve the following systems by Gaussian elimination.

(a) $\begin{aligned} x_1 + x_2 &= 3 \\ 3x_1 + 5x_2 &= 5 \end{aligned}$

(b) $\begin{aligned} x_1 + 2x_2 + x_3 &= 4 \\ x_1 - x_2 + x_3 &= 5 \\ 2x_1 + 3x_2 - x_3 &= 1 \end{aligned}$

(c) $\begin{aligned} 2x_1 - 3x_2 + x_3 &= 0 \\ x_1 + x_2 - x_3 &= 0 \end{aligned}$

2. Use Gaussian elimination to discuss, for different values of a and b, what are the possible solutions of the system

$$x + y - z = 1$$
$$x - y + 2z = 2$$
$$x + 2y + az = b$$

3. Find the values of c for which the following system has a solution, and find the complete solution for these values of c:

$$2w + x + 4y + 3z = 1$$
$$w + 3x + 2y - z = 3c$$
$$w + x + 2y + z = c^2$$

4. Find the values of a for which the following system has a unique solution:

$$ax + y + (a+1)z = b_1$$
$$x + 2y + z = b_2$$
$$3x + 4y + 7z = b_3$$

5. Find all solutions to the following system:

$$\tfrac{3}{4}x + y + \tfrac{7}{4}z = b_1$$
$$x + 2y + z = b_2$$
$$3x + 4y + 7z = b_3$$

12.9 Geometric Interpretation of Vectors

Vectors, unlike general matrices, are easily interpreted geometrically, at least if they have dimension two or perhaps three. Actually, the word "vector" is originally Latin and was used to mean both "carrier" and "passenger". In particular, the word is related to the act of moving a person or object from one place to another. Following this idea, a biologist is likely to think of a "vector" as a carrier of disease, such as mosquitoes are for malaria.

In the xy-plane, any shift can be described by the distance a_1 moved in the x-direction and by the distance a_2 moved in the y-direction. A movement in the plane is therefore uniquely determined by an ordered pair or 2-vector (a_1, a_2). As Fig. 12.9.1 shows, such a movement can be represented by an arrow from the start point P to the end point Q.

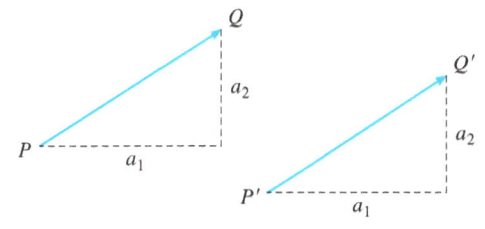

Figure 12.9.1 Vectors as movements in the plane

If we make a parallel displacement of the arrow so that it starts at P' and ends at Q', the resulting arrow will represent exactly the same shift, because the x and y components are still a_1 and a_2, respectively. The vector from P to Q is denoted by $\overrightarrow{PQ}$, and we refer to it as a *geometric vector* or *directed line segment*. Two geometric vectors that have the same direction and the same length are said to be equal (in much the same way as the two fractions 2/6 and 1/3 are equal because they represent the same real number).

Suppose that the geometric vector $\mathbf{a} = (a_1, a_2)$ involves a movement from $P = (p_1, p_2)$ to $Q = (q_1, q_2)$. Then the pair (a_1, a_2) that describes the movement in both the x and y directions is given by $a_1 = q_1 - p_1, a_2 = q_2 - p_2$, or by $(a_1, a_2) = (q_1, q_2) - (p_1, p_2)$. This is illustrated in Fig. 12.9.2.

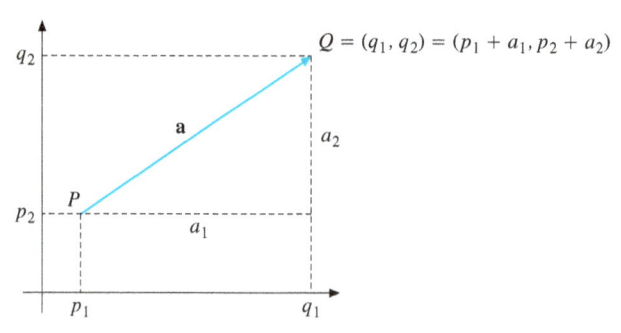

Figure 12.9.2 Vectors as ordered pairs

On the other hand, if the pair (a_1, a_2) is given, the corresponding shift is obtained by moving a_1 units in the direction of the x-axis, as well as a_2 units in the direction of the y-axis. If we start at the point $P = (p_1, p_2)$, therefore, we arrive at the point Q with coordinates $(q_1, q_2) = (p_1 + a_1, p_2 + a_2)$, also shown in Fig. 12.9.2.

This correspondence makes it a matter of convenience whether we think of a vector as an ordered pair of numbers (a_1, a_2), or as a directed line segment such as $\overrightarrow{PQ}$ in Fig. 12.9.2.

Vector Operations

If we represent vectors by directed line segments, the vector operations $\mathbf{a} + \mathbf{b}$, $\mathbf{a} - \mathbf{b}$, and $t\mathbf{a}$ can be given interesting geometric interpretations. Let $\mathbf{a} = (a_1, a_2)$ and $\mathbf{b} = (b_1, b_2)$ both start at the origin $(0, 0)$ of the coordinate system.

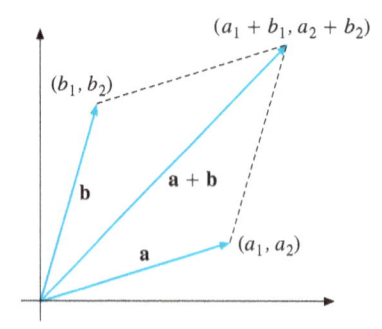

Figure 12.9.3 Vector addition

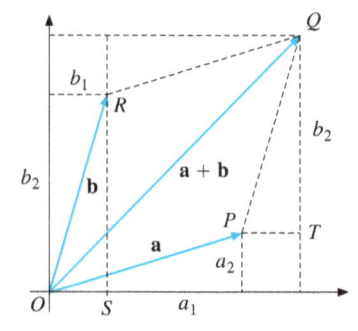

Figure 12.9.4 Geometry of vector addition

The sum $\mathbf{a} + \mathbf{b}$ shown in Fig. 12.9.3 is the diagonal in the parallelogram determined by the two sides $\mathbf{a}$ and $\mathbf{b}$. The geometric reason for this can be seen from Fig. 12.9.4, in which the two right-angled triangles *OSR* and *PTQ* are congruent. Thus, *OR* is parallel to *PQ* and has the same length, so *OPQR* is a parallelogram.[7]

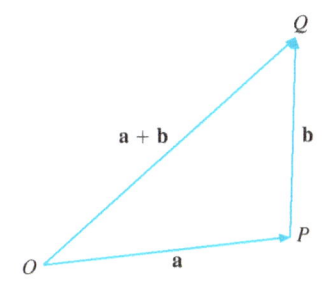

Figure 12.9.5 Vector addition

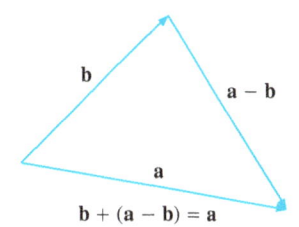

Figure 12.9.6 Vector subtraction

The parallelogram law of addition is also illustrated in Fig. 12.9.5. One way of interpreting this figure is that if **a** takes you from *O* to *P* and **b** takes you on from *P* to *Q*, then the combined movement **a** + **b** takes you from *O* to *Q*. Moreover, looking at Fig. 12.9.4 again, the vector **b** takes you from *O* to *R*, whereas **a** takes you on from *R* to *Q*. So the combined movement **b** + **a** takes you from *O* to *Q*. Of course, this verifies that **a** + **b** = **b** + **a**.

Figure 12.9.6 gives a geometric interpretation to the vector **a** − **b**. Note carefully the direction of the geometric vector **a** − **b**. And note that **b** + (**a** − **b**) = **a** = (**a** − **b**) + **b**.

The geometric interpretation of *t***a**, for any real number *t*, is also straightforward. If $t > 0$, then *t***a** is the vector with the same direction as **a** and whose length is *t* times the length of **a**. If $t < 0$, the direction is reversed and the length is multiplied by the absolute value of *t*. Indeed, multiplication by *t* is like rescaling the vector **a**; that is why the number *t* is often called a *scalar*.

3-Space

Recall how, given any point in a plane, we used a pair of real numbers to represent it with reference to a rectangular coordinate system in the plane that is specified by two mutually orthogonal coordinate lines. This makes the plane a two-dimensional space, which is often called 2-space and denoted by $\mathbb{R}^2$. Similarly, any point or vector in three-dimensional space, also called 3-space and denoted by $\mathbb{R}^3$, can be represented by an ordered triple of real numbers.

The three dimensions of the space $\mathbb{R}^3$ are enough to allow three mutually orthogonal coordinate axes, which are represented graphically in Fig. 12.9.7. The three lines that are orthogonal to each other and intersect at the point *O* in the figure are the *coordinate axes*. They are usually called the *x*-axis, *y*-axis, and *z*-axis respectively. We choose a unit to measure the length along each axis. We also select a positive direction along each axis, indicated by an arrow.

---

[7] This parallelogram law of adding vectors will be familiar to readers who have studied physics. For example, if **a** and **b** represent two forces acting on a particle located at the point *O*, then the single combined force **a** + **b** acting on the particle will produce exactly the same physical effect.

Figure 12.9.7 A coordinate system

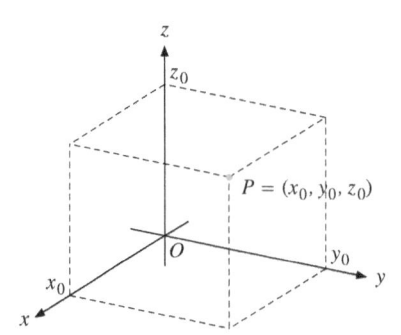

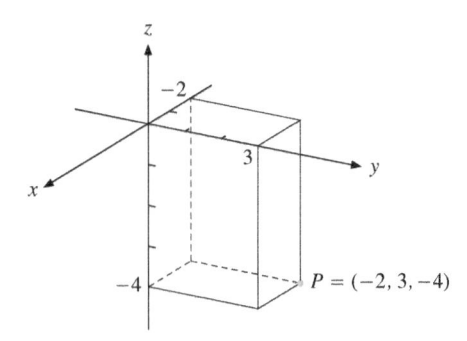

Figure 12.9.8 $P = (-2, 3, -4)$

The equation $x = 0$ is satisfied by all the points in the unique *coordinate plane* that contains both the y-axis and the z-axis. This is called the yz-plane. Two other coordinate planes are the xy-plane in which $z = 0$, and the xz-plane in which $y = 0$. We often think of the xy-plane as horizontal, with the z-axis passing vertically through it.

Each coordinate plane divides the space into two *half-spaces*. For example, the xy-plane whose equation is $z = 0$ separates the space into two regions: (i) above the xy-plane, where $z > 0$; (ii) below the xy-plane, where $z < 0$. The three coordinate planes together divide up the space into eight *octants*. The particular octant in which $x \geq 0$, $y \geq 0$, and $z \geq 0$ is called the *nonnegative octant*.

Every point P in 3-space is now associated with a triple of numbers (x_0, y_0, z_0) which measure its respective distances from each of the closest points in the three planes $x = 0$, $y = 0$, and $z = 0$. Conversely, it is clear that every triple of three real numbers also represents a unique point in 3-space, as suggested in Fig. 12.9.7. Note in particular that when z_0 is negative, the point (x_0, y_0, z_0) lies below the xy-plane in which $z = 0$. Figure 12.9.8 shows how to construct the point P with coordinates $(-2, 3, -4)$. The point P in Fig. 12.9.7 lies in the positive octant where x, y, and z are all positive.

Furthermore, as with ordered pairs in the plane, there is a natural correspondence between: (i) any ordered triple (a_1, a_2, a_3); (ii) a geometric vector or movement in 3-space, regarded as a directed line segment. The parallelogram law of addition remains valid in 3-space, as does the geometric interpretation of the multiplication of a vector by a scalar.

n-Space

The 3-space $\mathbf{R}^3$ of all ordered triples of real numbers can obviously be extended to the n-space $\mathbf{R}^n$ of all n-vectors. These vectors were introduced in Section 12.1 as either row vectors that are $1 \times n$ matrices, or column vectors that are $n \times 1$ matrices. Then it is usual to call the set of all possible n-vectors $\mathbf{x} = (x_1, x_2, \ldots, x_n)$ of real numbers the *Euclidean n-dimensional space*, or *n-space*, denoted by $\mathbb{R}^n$.

For $n = 1$, $n = 2$, and $n = 3$, we have geometric representations of $\mathbb{R}^n$ as a line, a plane, and a 3-space, respectively. When $n \geq 4$, however, neither n-vectors nor the n-space $\mathbb{R}^n$ to which they belong have any natural spatial interpretation. Nevertheless, because many properties of $\mathbb{R}^2$ and $\mathbb{R}^3$ carry over to $\mathbb{R}^n$, geometric language is sometimes still used to

SECTION 12.9 / GEOMETRIC INTERPRETATION OF VECTORS   483

discuss its properties. In particular, the rules for addition, subtraction, and multiplication of vectors by a scalar that were set out in Section 12.4 all remain exactly the same in $\mathbb{R}^n$ as they are in $\mathbb{R}^2$ and $\mathbb{R}^3$.

Distances and Lengths of Vectors

In Section 5.5 we gave the formula for the distance between two points in the plane. Now we want to do the same for points in 3-space.

Consider a rectangular box with edges of length a, b, and c, as shown in Fig. 12.9.9. Applying Pythagoras's theorem once, we conclude that $(PR)^2 = a^2 + b^2$. Applying it a second time shows that $(PQ)^2 = (PR)^2 + (RQ)^2 = a^2 + b^2 + c^2$. It follows that the diagonal that joins the points P and Q that are opposite corners of the box has length $PQ = \sqrt{a^2 + b^2 + c^2}$.

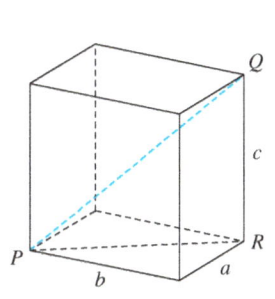

Figure 12.9.9 The distance PQ between the two points P and Q

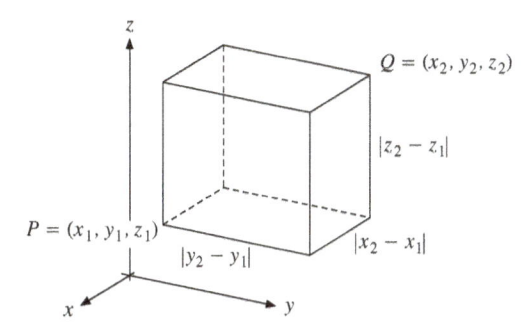

Figure 12.9.10 The distance between two typical points

Next we find the distance between two typical points $P = (x_1, y_1, z_1)$ and $Q = (x_2, y_2, z_2)$ in 3-space, as illustrated in Fig. 12.9.10. These two points lie precisely at the opposite corners of a rectangular box whose edges have lengths $a = |x_2 - x_1|$, $b = |y_2 - y_1|$, and $c = |z_2 - z_1|$ respectively. Inserting these into our result for the box in Fig. 12.9.9 gives

$$(PQ)^2 = |x_2 - x_1|^2 + |y_2 - y_1|^2 + |z_2 - z_1|^2 = (x_2 - x_1)^2 + (y_2 - y_1)^2 + (z_2 - z_1)^2$$

This formula motivates the following definition:

DISTANCE

The *distance* d between two points (x_1, y_1, z_1) and (x_2, y_2, z_2) in 3-space is

$$d = \sqrt{(x_2 - x_1)^2 + (y_2 - y_1)^2 + (z_2 - z_1)^2} \tag{12.9.1}$$

EXAMPLE 12.9.1 Calculate the distance d between the two points $(1, 2, -3)$ and $(-2, 4, 5)$.

Solution: According to formula (12.9.1),

$$d = \sqrt{(-2-1)^2 + (4-2)^2 + (5-(-3))^2} = \sqrt{(-3)^2 + 2^2 + 8^2} = \sqrt{77} \approx 8.77$$

We also define the length or norm of the 3-vector $\mathbf{a} = (a_1, a_2, a_3)$, denoted by $\|\mathbf{a}\|$, as the distance between $\mathbf{a}$ and the zero 3-vector $\mathbf{0} = (0, 0, 0)$. By formula (12.9.1), as well as the definition of inner product in Section 12.4, we have

$$\|\mathbf{a}\| = \sqrt{a_1^2 + a_2^2 + a_3^2} = \sqrt{\mathbf{a} \cdot \mathbf{a}} \qquad (12.9.2)$$

The two definitions (12.9.1) and (12.9.2) evidently imply that the distance $d(\mathbf{u}, \mathbf{v})$ in $\mathbb{R}^3$ between the two 3-vectors $\mathbf{u} = (u_1, u_2, u_3)$ and $\mathbf{v} = (v_1, v_2, v_3)$ is equal to the distance between $\mathbf{u} - \mathbf{v}$ and $\mathbf{0}$, which is the length of $\mathbf{u} - \mathbf{v}$. Hence $d(\mathbf{u}, \mathbf{v}) = d(\mathbf{u} - \mathbf{v}, \mathbf{0}) = \|\mathbf{u} - \mathbf{v}\|$.

Next, we move onto n-space and introduce the following definitions:

LENGTH AND DISTANCE IN n-SPACE

Given any n-vector $\mathbf{a} = (a_1, a_2, \ldots, a_n)$, its *length*, or *norm*, is

$$\|\mathbf{a}\| = \sqrt{a_1^2 + a_2^2 + \cdots + a_n^2} = \sqrt{\mathbf{a} \cdot \mathbf{a}} \qquad (12.9.3)$$

The *distance* between any two n-vectors $\mathbf{u}$ and $\mathbf{v}$ is

$$d(\mathbf{u}, \mathbf{v}) = \|\mathbf{u} - \mathbf{v}\| = \sqrt{(u_1 - v_1)^2 + (u_2 - v_2)^2 + \cdots + (u_n - v_n)^2} \qquad (12.9.4)$$

Note that, for any vector $\mathbf{a}$ in $\mathbb{R}^n$, definition (12.9.3) implies:

$$\|\alpha \mathbf{a}\| = \sqrt{(\alpha \mathbf{a}) \cdot (\alpha \mathbf{a})} = |\alpha| \sqrt{\mathbf{a} \cdot \mathbf{a}} = |\alpha| \, \|\mathbf{a}\| \text{ for all real } \alpha \qquad (12.9.5)$$

$$\|\mathbf{a}\| \geq 0 \text{ for all } n\text{-vectors } \mathbf{a}, \text{ with } \|\mathbf{a}\| = 0 \text{ if and only if } \mathbf{a} = \mathbf{0} \qquad (12.9.6)$$

These accord with rules (b), (d) and (e) for inner products that were introduced in Section 12.4.

The Cauchy–Schwarz Inequality

Definition (12.9.3) specifies $\|\mathbf{a}\|$ as the distance in $\mathbb{R}^n$ of the point $(a_1, a_2, \ldots, a_n)$ from the origin $(0, 0, \ldots, 0)$. Exercise 4.6.9 asked you to prove the famous *Cauchy–Schwarz inequality*. Using the notation we have just introduced, this inequality can be expressed as $(\mathbf{a} \cdot \mathbf{b})^2 \leq \|\mathbf{a}\|^2 \cdot \|\mathbf{b}\|^2$. Because $\|\mathbf{a}\| \cdot \|\mathbf{b}\| \geq 0$ by definition (12.9.3), this is equivalent to

$$|\mathbf{a} \cdot \mathbf{b}| \leq \|\mathbf{a}\| \cdot \|\mathbf{b}\| \qquad (12.9.7)$$

EXAMPLE 12.9.2   Verify the Cauchy–Schwarz inequality (12.9.7) for the two 3-vectors $\mathbf{a} = (1, -2, 3)$ and $\mathbf{b} = (-3, 2, 5)$.

Solution: First, we find that

$$\|\mathbf{a}\| = \sqrt{1^2 + (-2)^2 + 3^2} = \sqrt{14} \quad \text{and} \quad \|\mathbf{b}\| = \sqrt{(-3)^2 + 2^2 + 5^2} = \sqrt{38}$$

In Example 12.4.1, we calculated that $\mathbf{a} \cdot \mathbf{b} = 8$. So inequality (12.9.7) makes the claim that $8 \leq \sqrt{14}\sqrt{38}$. This is certainly true because $\sqrt{14} > 3$ and $\sqrt{38} > 6$.

Orthogonality

Consider any two n-vectors $\mathbf{a}$ and $\mathbf{b}$ in $\mathbb{R}^n$, where $n \geq 2$. Following Fig. 12.9.6, we use Fig. 12.9.11 to represent the three vectors $\mathbf{a}$, $\mathbf{b}$, and $\mathbf{a} - \mathbf{b}$ in the unique two-dimensional plane in $\mathbb{R}^n$ that includes the three points O, A, and B.

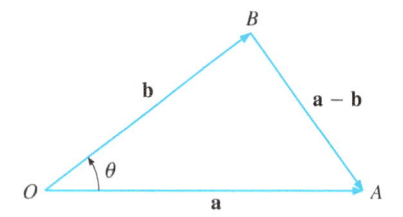

Figure 12.9.11 The angle between $\mathbf{a}$ and $\mathbf{b}$

According to Pythagoras's theorem, the angle θ between the two vectors $\mathbf{a}$ and $\mathbf{b}$ is a right angle if and only if $(OA)^2 + (OB)^2 = (AB)^2$, or $\|\mathbf{a}\|^2 + \|\mathbf{b}\|^2 = \|\mathbf{a} - \mathbf{b}\|^2$. This implies that $\theta = 90°$ if and only if

$$\mathbf{a} \cdot \mathbf{a} + \mathbf{b} \cdot \mathbf{b} = (\mathbf{a} - \mathbf{b}) \cdot (\mathbf{a} - \mathbf{b}) = \mathbf{a} \cdot \mathbf{a} - \mathbf{a} \cdot \mathbf{b} - \mathbf{b} \cdot \mathbf{a} + \mathbf{b} \cdot \mathbf{b} \quad (*)$$

Because $\mathbf{a} \cdot \mathbf{b} = \mathbf{b} \cdot \mathbf{a}$, equality (*) requires that $2\mathbf{a} \cdot \mathbf{b} = 0$, and so $\mathbf{a} \cdot \mathbf{b} = 0$. When the angle between two vectors $\mathbf{a}$ and $\mathbf{b}$ is $90°$, they are said to be *orthogonal*, and we write $\mathbf{a} \perp \mathbf{b}$. Thus, we have proved that two vectors in $\mathbb{R}^n$ are orthogonal if and only if their inner product is 0. In symbols:

$$\mathbf{a} \perp \mathbf{b} \iff \mathbf{a} \cdot \mathbf{b} = 0 \qquad (12.9.8)$$

Let $\mathbf{a}$ and $\mathbf{b}$ be two nonzero vectors in $\mathbb{R}^n$. Applying some elementary trigonometry to Fig. 12.9.11 shows that the *angle* between them is the unique $\theta \in [0, \pi]$ that satisfies

$$\cos \theta = \frac{\mathbf{a} \cdot \mathbf{b}}{\|\mathbf{a}\| \cdot \|\mathbf{b}\|} \qquad (12.9.9)$$

This definition makes sense because the Cauchy–Schwarz inequality implies that the right-hand side has an absolute value ≤ 1. Note also that according to Eq. (12.9.9), $\cos \theta = 0$ if and only if $\mathbf{a} \cdot \mathbf{b} = 0$. This agrees with (12.9.8) because, for $\theta \in [0, \pi]$, we have $\cos \theta = 0$ if and only if $\theta = \pi/2$.

EXAMPLE 12.9.3 Suppose we repeatedly observe a commodity's price and the quantity demanded. After n observations suppose we have the n pairs $\{(p_1, d_1), (p_2, d_2), \ldots, (p_n, d_n)\}$, where p_i represents the price and d_i is the quantity at observation i, for $i = 1, 2, \ldots, n$. Define the statistical means

$$\bar{p} = \frac{1}{n} \sum_{i=1}^{n} p_i \quad \text{and} \quad \bar{d} = \frac{1}{n} \sum_{i=1}^{n} d_i$$

Also, write the n deviations of the observed pairs (p_i, d_i) from these means as the vectors

$$\mathbf{a} = (p_1 - \bar{p}, p_2 - \bar{p}, \ldots, p_n - \bar{p}), \quad \mathbf{b} = (d_1 - \bar{d}, d_2 - \bar{d}, \ldots, d_n - \bar{d})$$

In statistics, the ratio $\mathbf{a} \cdot \mathbf{b} / (\|\mathbf{a}\| \cdot \|\mathbf{b}\|)$ that appears on the right-hand side of Eq. (12.9.9) is called the *correlation coefficient*, often denoted by ρ. It is a measure of the degree of "correlation" between the prices and demand quantities in the data. When $\rho = 1$, there is a positive constant $\alpha > 0$ such that $d_i - \bar{d} = \alpha(p_i - \bar{p})$, implying that demand and price are *perfectly correlated*. It is more plausible, however, that $\rho = -1$ because this relationship holds for some $\alpha < 0$. Generally, if $\rho > 0$ the variables are *positively correlated*, whereas if $\rho < 0$ the variables are *negatively correlated*, and if $\rho = 0$ they are *uncorrelated*.

EXAMPLE 12.9.4 (**Orthogonality in econometrics**). In Example 9.3.1 on linear regression, we assumed that the mean values of the observations of x and y satisfy $\mu_x = \mu_y = 0$. Then the regression coefficient β was chosen to minimize the *mean squared error* loss function defined by

$$L(\beta) = \frac{1}{T} \sum_{t=1}^{T} e_t^2 = \frac{1}{T} \sum_{t=1}^{T} (y_t - \beta x_t)^2$$

This required choosing $\hat{\beta} = \sigma_{xy} / \sigma_{xx}$, where σ_{xx} denotes the variance of x_t, and σ_{xy} denotes the covariance between x_t and y_t. For $t = 1, 2, \ldots, T$, the resulting errors become

$$\hat{e}_t = y_t - \hat{\beta} x_t = y_t - \frac{\sigma_{xy}}{\sigma_{xx}} x_t$$

From our assumption that $\mu_x = \mu_y = 0$, it is immediate that the mean error satisfies

$$\frac{1}{T} \sum_{t=1}^{T} \hat{e}_t = \frac{1}{T} \sum_{t=1}^{T} y_t - \hat{\beta} \sum_{t=1}^{T} x_t = \mu_y - \hat{\beta} \mu_x = 0 \qquad (*)$$

In addition,

$$\frac{1}{T} \sum_{t=1}^{T} x_t \hat{e}_t = \frac{1}{T} \sum_{t=1}^{T} x_t y_t - \frac{1}{T} \frac{\sigma_{xy}}{\sigma_{xx}} \sum_{t=1}^{T} x_t^2 = \sigma_{xy} - \frac{\sigma_{xy}}{\sigma_{xx}} \sigma_{xx} = 0 \qquad (**)$$

Define the three vectors $\mathbf{1} = (1, 1 \ldots, 1)$, $\mathbf{x} = (x_1, \ldots, x_T)$, and $\hat{\mathbf{e}} = (\hat{e}_1, \ldots, \hat{e}_T)$. Then equality $(*)$ shows that $\hat{\mathbf{e}}$ and $\mathbf{1}$ are orthogonal, whereas $(**)$ shows that $\hat{\mathbf{e}}$ and $\mathbf{x}$ are orthogonal.

EXERCISES FOR SECTION 12.9

1. Let $\mathbf{a} = (5, -1)$ and $\mathbf{b} = (-2, 4)$. Compute $\mathbf{a} + \mathbf{b}$ and $-\frac{1}{2}\mathbf{a}$, then illustrate geometrically with vectors starting at the origin.

2. (SM) Given $\mathbf{a} = (3, 1)$ and $\mathbf{b} = (-1, 2)$, define $\mathbf{x} = \lambda \mathbf{a} + (1 - \lambda)\mathbf{b}$ for any scalar λ.

   (a) Compute $\mathbf{x}$ when $\lambda = 0$, 1/4, 1/2, 3/4, and 1, and illustrate the answers.

   (b) If $\lambda \in [0, 1]$, what set of points does $\mathbf{x} = \lambda \mathbf{a} + (1 - \lambda)\mathbf{b}$ trace out?

   (c) Show that if $\lambda \in \mathbb{R}$, then $\mathbf{x}$ traces out the whole straight line through $(3, 1)$ and $(-1, 2)$.

3. Draw a three-dimensional coordinate system, including a box like those shown in Figs 12.9.7 and 12.9.8. Then mark in this coordinate system the four points $P = (3, 0, 0)$, $Q = (0, 2, 0)$, $R = (0, 0, -1)$, and $S = (3, -2, 4)$.

4. Describe geometrically the set of points (x, y, z) in three dimensions, where:

   (a) $y = 2$ and $z = 3$, while x varies freely;   (b) $y = x$, while z varies freely.

5. Let $\mathbf{a} = (1, 2, 2)$, $\mathbf{b} = (0, 0, -3)$, and $\mathbf{c} = (-2, 4, -3)$. Compute $\|\mathbf{a}\|$, $\|\mathbf{b}\|$, and $\|\mathbf{c}\|$. Then verify that $\mathbf{a}$ and $\mathbf{b}$ satisfy the Cauchy–Schwarz inequality (12.9.7).

6. Let $\mathbf{a} = (1, 2, 1)$ and $\mathbf{b} = (-3, 0, -2)$.

   (a) Find numbers x_1 and x_2 such that $x_1 \mathbf{a} + x_2 \mathbf{b} = (5, 4, 4)$.

   (b) Prove that there are no real numbers x_1 and x_2 satisfying $x_1 \mathbf{a} + x_2 \mathbf{b} = (-3, 6, 1)$.

7. Check which of the following three pairs of vectors are orthogonal:

   (a) $(1, 2)$ and $(-2, 1)$ (b) $(1, -1, 1)$ and $(-1, 1, -1)$ (c) $(a, -b, 1)$ and $(b, a, 0)$

8. For what values of x are the 4-vectors $(x, -x - 8, x, x)$ and $(x, 1, -2, 1)$ orthogonal?

9. [HARDER] In Exercise 12.7.7, an $n \times n$ matrix $\mathbf{P}$ was defined as orthogonal if $\mathbf{P}'\mathbf{P} = \mathbf{I}_n$. Show that $\mathbf{P}$ is orthogonal if and only if all pairs of different columns (or all pairs of different rows) are orthogonal vectors.

10. [HARDER] If $\mathbf{a}$ and $\mathbf{b}$ are n-vectors, prove the *triangle inequality* $\|\mathbf{a} + \mathbf{b}\| \leq \|\mathbf{a}\| + \|\mathbf{b}\|$. (*Hint*: Note that $\|\mathbf{a} + \mathbf{b}\|^2 = (\mathbf{a} + \mathbf{b}) \cdot (\mathbf{a} + \mathbf{b})$. Then use the Cauchy–Schwarz inequality (12.9.7).)

12.10 Lines and Planes

Let $\mathbf{a} = (a_1, a_2, a_3)$ and $\mathbf{b} = (b_1, b_2, b_3)$ be two distinct vectors in $\mathbb{R}^3$. We can think of them as arrows from the origin to the points with coordinates (a_1, a_2, a_3) and (b_1, b_2, b_3), respectively. The straight line L passing through these two points is shown in Fig. 12.10.1.

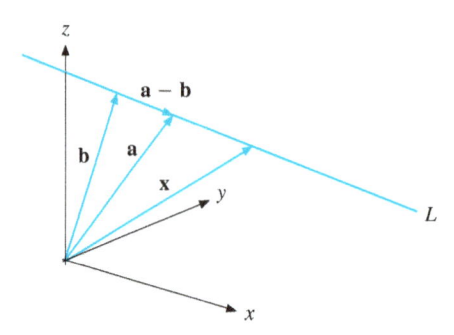

Figure 12.10.1 Line L goes through **a** and **b**

Now define the vector $\mathbf{x}(t) = (x_1(t), x_2(t), x_3(t))$ for each real number t so that

$$\mathbf{x}(t) = \mathbf{b} + t(\mathbf{a} - \mathbf{b}) = t\mathbf{a} + (1 - t)\mathbf{b} \qquad (12.10.1)$$

This makes $\mathbf{x}(t)$ a function of t that satisfies $\mathbf{x}(0) = \mathbf{b}$ and $\mathbf{x}(1) = \mathbf{a}$. In Fig. 12.10.1, the point $\mathbf{x}(t)$ moves to the left as t decreases, but to the right as t increases. By the geometric rules for vectors that were presented in Section 12.9, the particular vector marked $\mathbf{x}$ in Fig. 12.10.1 is approximately $\mathbf{b} + 2.5(\mathbf{a} - \mathbf{b})$. As t runs through all the real numbers, the function $\mathbf{x}(t)$ defined by (12.10.1) has a range consisting of the entire straight line L.

In the space $\mathbb{R}^n$, after removing the three axes marked x, y and z from Fig. 12.10.1, we can regard the resulting diagram as showing the four vectors $\mathbf{a}$, $\mathbf{b}$, $\mathbf{x}$, and $\mathbf{a} - \mathbf{b}$ in the unique two-dimensional plane that contains $\mathbf{a}$, $\mathbf{b}$, and the origin $\mathbf{0}$. There is also the unique line L that passes through $\mathbf{a}$ and $\mathbf{b}$, which also includes $\mathbf{x}$. This line meets the following definition:

LINE IN n-SPACE

The line L in $\mathbb{R}^n$ through the two distinct points $\mathbf{a} = (a_1, \ldots, a_n)$ and $\mathbf{b} = (b_1, \ldots, b_n)$ is the range of the function $\mathbf{x}(t) = (x_1(t), \ldots, x_n(t))$ defined for each real number t by

$$\mathbf{x}(t) = t\mathbf{a} + (1 - t)\mathbf{b} = \mathbf{b} + t(\mathbf{a} - \mathbf{b}) \qquad (12.10.2)$$

In terms of the coordinates of $\mathbf{a}$ and $\mathbf{b}$, Eq. (12.10.2) is equivalent to

$$x_1(t) = ta_1 + (1-t)b_1, \ x_2(t) = ta_2 + (1-t)b_2, \ \ldots, \ x_n(t) = ta_n + (1-t)b_n \qquad (12.10.3)$$

By definition (12.10.2) as well as rule (12.9.5), for all real t one has

$$\|\mathbf{x}(t) - \mathbf{b}\| = \|t(\mathbf{a} - \mathbf{b})\| = |t| \|\mathbf{a} - \mathbf{b}\| \qquad (12.10.4)$$

In case $t > 0$ because $\mathbf{x}(t)$ and $\mathbf{a}$ are on the same side of $\mathbf{b}$, it follows that t equals the ratio $\|\mathbf{x}(t) - \mathbf{b}\|/\|\mathbf{a} - \mathbf{b}\|$ of the distance between $\mathbf{x}(t)$ and $\mathbf{b}$ to the distance between $\mathbf{a}$ and $\mathbf{b}$. But if $t < 0$ because $\mathbf{x}(t)$ and $\mathbf{a}$ are on opposite sides of $\mathbf{b}$, then t is minus this ratio.

SECTION 12.10 / LINES AND PLANES

EXAMPLE 12.10.1 Describe the straight line in $\mathbb{R}^3$ through the two points $(1, 2, 2)$ and $(-1, -1, 4)$. Where does it meet the $x_1 x_2$-plane?

Solution: According to (12.10.3), the straight line is given by the three equations:

$$\begin{aligned} x_1 &= t \cdot 1 + (1-t) \cdot (-1) = 2t - 1 \\ x_2 &= t \cdot 2 + (1-t) \cdot (-1) = 3t - 1 \\ x_3 &= t \cdot 2 + (1-t) \cdot 4 = 4 - 2t \end{aligned}$$

This line meets the $x_1 x_2$-plane when $x_3 = 0$. Then $4 - 2t = 0$, so $t = 2$, implying that $x_1 = 3$ and $x_2 = 5$. It follows that the intersection occurs at $(3, 5, 0)$, as shown in Fig. 12.10.2.

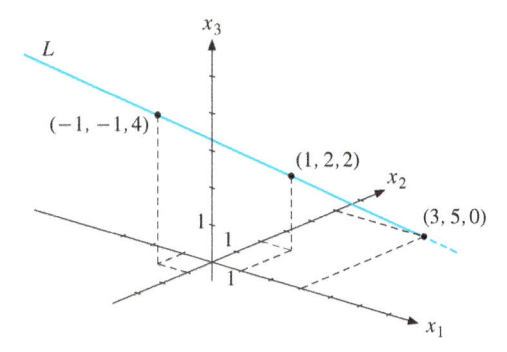

Figure 12.10.2 The line L through $(1, 2, 2)$ and $(-1, -1, 4)$

Suppose that $\mathbf{p} = (p_1, \ldots, p_n) \in \mathbb{R}^n$. The straight line L in $\mathbb{R}^n$ that passes through $\mathbf{p}$ in the same direction as vector $\mathbf{a} = (a_1, \ldots, a_n) \neq \mathbf{0}$ is the set of all $\mathbf{x}$ in $\mathbb{R}^n$ for which there exists a real number t such that

$$\mathbf{x} = \mathbf{p} + t\mathbf{a} \tag{12.10.5}$$

Note that, according to Eq. (12.10.2), the line through $\mathbf{p}$ in the direction $\mathbf{a} \neq \mathbf{0}$ is the line through $\mathbf{p}$ and $\mathbf{p} + \mathbf{a}$. Conversely, provided that $\mathbf{a} \neq \mathbf{b}$, the line through $\mathbf{a}$ and $\mathbf{b}$ is the line through $\mathbf{b}$ in the direction $\mathbf{a} - \mathbf{b}$.

Hyperplanes

As shown in Fig. 12.10.3, a plane $\mathcal{P}$ in $\mathbb{R}^3$ is defined by one point $\mathbf{a} = (a_1, a_2, a_3)$ in the plane, as well as one vector $\mathbf{p} = (p_1, p_2, p_3) \neq (0, 0, 0)$ which is orthogonal or perpendicular to any line in the plane. Then the vector $\mathbf{p}$ is said to be a *normal* to the plane. Thus, if $\mathbf{x} = (x_1, x_2, x_3)$ is any point in $\mathcal{P}$ other than $\mathbf{a}$, then the vector $\mathbf{x} - \mathbf{a}$ is in a direction orthogonal to $\mathbf{p}$. So the inner product of $\mathbf{p}$ and $\mathbf{x} - \mathbf{a}$ must be 0, implying that

$$\mathbf{p} \cdot (\mathbf{x} - \mathbf{a}) = 0 \tag{12.10.6}$$

It follows that Eq. (12.10.6) is the general equation of a plane in $\mathbb{R}^3$ passing through the point $\mathbf{a}$ with normal $\mathbf{p} \neq \mathbf{0}$.

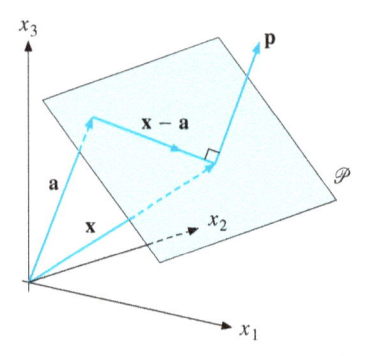

Figure 12.10.3 A hyperplane in $\mathbb{R}^3$

EXAMPLE 12.10.2 Find the equation for the plane in $\mathbb{R}^3$ through $\mathbf{a} = (2, 1, -1)$ with $\mathbf{p} = (-1, 1, 3)$ as a normal. Does the line in Example 12.10.1 intersect this plane?

Solution: Using Eq. (12.10.6), the equation is

$$-1 \cdot (x_1 - 2) + 1 \cdot (x_2 - 1) + 3 \cdot (x_3 - (-1)) = 0$$

or, equivalently, $-x_1 + x_2 + 3x_3 = -4$. The line in Example 12.10.1 is given by the three equations $x_1 = 2t - 1$, $x_2 = 3t - 1$, and $x_3 = 4 - 2t$. It follows that, at any point where this line is to meet the plane, we must have

$$-(2t - 1) + (3t - 1) + 3(4 - 2t) = -4$$

Solving this equation for t yields $t = 16/5$. So the unique point of intersection is given by $x_1 = 32/5 - 1 = 27/5$, $x_2 = 43/5$, and $x_3 = -12/5$.

Motivated by this characterization of a plane in $\mathbb{R}^3$, we introduce the following general definition in $\mathbb{R}^n$.

HYPERPLANE IN n-SPACE

The hyperplane H in $\mathbb{R}^n$ through $\mathbf{a} = (a_1, \ldots, a_n)$ which is orthogonal to the nonzero vector $\mathbf{p} = (p_1, \ldots, p_n)$ is the set of all points $\mathbf{x} = (x_1, \ldots, x_n)$ satisfying

$$\mathbf{p} \cdot (\mathbf{x} - \mathbf{a}) = 0 \tag{12.10.7}$$

Note that if the normal vector $\mathbf{p}$ is replaced by any scalar multiple $s\mathbf{p}$ with $s \neq 0$, then precisely the same set of vectors $\mathbf{x}$ will satisfy the hyperplane equation (12.10.7).

Using the coordinate representation of the vectors, the hyperplane defined by (12.10.7) has the equation

$$p_1(x_1 - a_1) + p_2(x_2 - a_2) + \cdots + p_n(x_n - a_n) = 0 \tag{12.10.8}$$

or equivalently $p_1 x_1 + p_2 x_2 + \cdots + p_n x_n = A$, where $A = p_1 a_1 + p_2 a_2 + \cdots + p_n a_n$.

EXAMPLE 12.10.3   A person has an amount m to spend on n different commodities, whose prices per unit are $p_1, p_2, \ldots, p_n$, respectively. She can therefore afford any commodity vector $\mathbf{x} = (x_1, x_2, \ldots, x_n)$ that satisfies the budget inequality

$$p_1 x_1 + p_2 x_2 + \cdots + p_n x_n \leq m \qquad (12.10.9)$$

When Eq. (12.10.9) is satisfied with equality, it describes the *budget hyperplane*, whose normal is the price vector $(p_1, p_2, \ldots, p_n)$.

Usually, it is implicitly assumed that $x_1 \geq 0, x_2 \geq 0, \ldots, x_n \geq 0$. For the case of two commodities, we already found a graphical representation of the budget set in Fig. 4.4.12.[8] For an example with $n = 3$ see Fig. 12.10.4. In both cases the vector of prices is normal to the budget hyperplane.

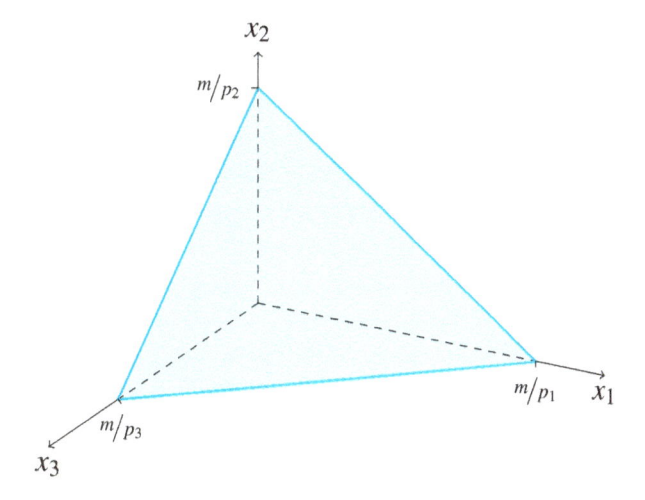

Figure 12.10.4 Budget hyperplane

EXERCISES FOR SECTION 12.10

1. Find the equation for the line:

    (a) that passes through the points $(3, -2, 2)$ and $(10, 2, 1)$;

    (b) that passes through the point $(1, 3, 2)$ and has the same direction as the vector $(0, -1, 1)$.

2. The line L in $\mathbb{R}^3$ is given by the three equations $x_1 = -t + 2$, $x_2 = 2t - 1$, and $x_3 = t + 3$.

    (a) Verify that the point $\mathbf{a} = (2, -1, 3)$ lies on L, but that $(1, 1, 1)$ does not.

    (b) Find the equation for the plane $\mathcal{P}$ through $\mathbf{a}$ that is orthogonal to L.

    (c) Find the point P where L intersects the plane $3x_1 + 5x_2 - x_3 = 6$.

SM 3. Find the equation for the plane through the three points $(1, 0, 2)$, $(5, 2, 1)$, and $(2, -1, 4)$.

---

[8] There, the notation we used was $p_1 = p$ and $p_2 = q$.

492 CHAPTER 12 / MATRIX ALGEBRA

4. In Example 12.10.3, suppose that the price vector is $(2, 3, 5)$, and that you can just afford the commodity vector $(10, 5, 8)$. What inequality describes your budget constraint?

5. Let $\mathbf{a} = (-2, 1, -1)$.

   (a) Show that $\mathbf{a}$ is a point in the plane $-x + 2y + 3z = 1$.

   (b) Find the equation for the normal at $\mathbf{a}$ to the plane in part (a).

REVIEW EXERCISES

1. Construct the two matrices $\mathbf{A} = (a_{ij})_{2\times 3}$, where for each pair (i, j) one has:

   (a) $a_{ij} = i + j$

   (b) $a_{ij} = (-1)^{i+j}$

2. Given the matrices
$$\mathbf{A} = \begin{pmatrix} 2 & 0 \\ -1 & 1 \end{pmatrix}, \quad \mathbf{B} = \begin{pmatrix} -1 & 2 \\ 1 & -1 \end{pmatrix}, \quad \mathbf{C} = \begin{pmatrix} 2 & 3 \\ 1 & 4 \end{pmatrix}, \quad \text{and} \quad \mathbf{D} = \begin{pmatrix} 1 & 1 & 1 \\ 1 & 3 & 4 \end{pmatrix}$$

   calculate (where possible):

   (a) $\mathbf{A} - \mathbf{B}$ (b) $\mathbf{A} + \mathbf{B} - 2\mathbf{C}$ (c) $\mathbf{AB}$ (d) $\mathbf{C}(\mathbf{AB})$

   (e) $\mathbf{AD}$ (f) $\mathbf{DC}$ (g) $2\mathbf{A} - 3\mathbf{B}$ (h) $(\mathbf{A} - \mathbf{B})'$

   (i) $(\mathbf{C}'\mathbf{A}')\mathbf{B}'$ (j) $\mathbf{C}'(\mathbf{A}'\mathbf{B}')$ (k) $\mathbf{D}'\mathbf{D}'$ (l) $\mathbf{D}'\mathbf{D}$

3. Write the following three systems of equations in matrix notation:

   (a) $\begin{aligned} 2x_1 - 5x_2 &= 3 \\ 5x_1 + 8x_2 &= 5 \end{aligned}$

   (b) $\begin{aligned} x + y + z + t &= a \\ x + 3y + 2z + 4t &= b \\ x + 4y + 8z &= c \\ 2x + z - t &= d \end{aligned}$

   (c) $\begin{aligned} (a-1)x + 3y - 2z &= 5 \\ ax + 2y - z &= 2 \\ x - 2y + 3z &= 1 \end{aligned}$

4. Find the matrices $\mathbf{A} + \mathbf{B}$, $\mathbf{A} - \mathbf{B}$, $\mathbf{AB}$, $\mathbf{BA}$, $\mathbf{A}(\mathbf{BC})$, and $(\mathbf{AB})\mathbf{C}$, if
$$\mathbf{A} = \begin{pmatrix} 0 & 1 & -2 \\ 3 & 4 & 5 \\ -6 & 7 & 15 \end{pmatrix}, \quad \mathbf{B} = \begin{pmatrix} 0 & -5 & 3 \\ 5 & 2 & -1 \\ -4 & 2 & 0 \end{pmatrix}, \quad \text{and} \quad \mathbf{C} = \begin{pmatrix} 6 & -2 & -3 \\ 2 & 0 & 1 \\ 0 & 5 & 7 \end{pmatrix}$$

5. Find real numbers a, b, and x such that
$$\begin{pmatrix} a & b \\ x & 0 \end{pmatrix} \begin{pmatrix} 2 & 1 \\ 1 & 1 \end{pmatrix} - \begin{pmatrix} 1 & 0 \\ 2 & 1 \end{pmatrix} \begin{pmatrix} a & b \\ x & 0 \end{pmatrix} = \begin{pmatrix} 2 & 1 \\ 4 & 4 \end{pmatrix}$$

6. Let $\mathbf{A}$ denote the matrix $\begin{pmatrix} a & b & 0 \\ -b & a & b \\ 0 & -b & a \end{pmatrix}$ where a and b are arbitrary constants.

   (a) Find $\mathbf{AA} = \mathbf{A}^2$.

(b) A square matrix $\mathbf{B}$ is called *skew-symmetric* if $\mathbf{B} = -\mathbf{B}'$, where $\mathbf{B}'$ denotes the transpose of $\mathbf{B}$. Show that if $\mathbf{C}$ is an arbitrary matrix such that $\mathbf{C}'\mathbf{BC}$ is defined, then $\mathbf{C}'\mathbf{BC}$ is skew-symmetric if $\mathbf{B}$ is. When is the matrix $\mathbf{A}$ defined above skew-symmetric?

(c) If $\mathbf{A}$ is any square matrix, prove that the matrix $\mathbf{A}_1 = \frac{1}{2}(\mathbf{A} + \mathbf{A}')$ is symmetric, whereas $\mathbf{A}_2 = \frac{1}{2}(\mathbf{A} - \mathbf{A}')$ is skew-symmetric. Verify that $\mathbf{A} = \mathbf{A}_1 + \mathbf{A}_2$, then explain in words what you have proved.

SM 7. Solve each of the following three different equation systems by Gaussian elimination.

(a) $\begin{aligned} x_1 + 4x_2 &= 1 \\ 2x_1 + 2x_2 &= 8 \end{aligned}$

(b) $\begin{aligned} 2x_1 + 2x_2 - x_3 &= 2 \\ x_1 - 3x_2 + x_3 &= 0 \\ 3x_1 + 4x_2 - x_3 &= 1 \end{aligned}$

(c) $\begin{aligned} x_1 + 3x_2 + 4x_3 &= 0 \\ 5x_1 + x_2 + x_3 &= 0 \end{aligned}$

8. Use Gaussian elimination to find for what values of a the following system has solutions. Then find all the possible solutions.

$$\begin{aligned} x + ay + 2z &= 0 \\ -2x - ay + z &= 4 \\ 2ax + 3a^2y + 9z &= 4 \end{aligned}$$

9. Let $\mathbf{a} = (-1, 5, 3)$, $\mathbf{b} = (1, 1, -3)$, and $\mathbf{c} = (-1, 2, 8)$. Compute $\|\mathbf{a}\|$, $\|\mathbf{b}\|$, and $\|\mathbf{c}\|$. Then verify that the Cauchy–Schwarz inequality holds for $\mathbf{a}$ and $\mathbf{b}$.

SM 10. Suppose that $\mathbf{P}$ and $\mathbf{Q}$ are $n \times n$ matrices with $\mathbf{PQ} - \mathbf{QP} = \mathbf{P}$.

(a) Prove that $\mathbf{P}^2\mathbf{Q} - \mathbf{QP}^2 = 2\mathbf{P}^2$ and $\mathbf{P}^3\mathbf{Q} - \mathbf{QP}^3 = 3\mathbf{P}^3$.

(b) Use induction to prove that $\mathbf{P}^k\mathbf{Q} - \mathbf{QP}^k = k\mathbf{P}^k$ for $k = 1, 2, \ldots$.

13 DETERMINANTS, INVERSES, AND QUADRATIC FORMS

You know we all became mathematicians for the same reason: we were lazy.
—Maxwell A. (Max) Rosenlicht (1949)

This chapter continues the study of matrix algebra. The first topic discussed is the determinant of a square matrix. Though it is only one number, it nevertheless determines on its own some key properties of the n^2 elements of an $n \times n$ matrix. Some economists regard determinants as almost obsolete because calculations that rely on them are very inefficient when the matrix is large. Nevertheless, they are important in several areas of mathematics that interest economists.

After introducing determinants in Sections 13.1 to 13.5, we consider in Sections 13.6 and 13.7 the fundamentally important concept of the inverse of a square matrix and its main properties. Inverse matrices play a major role in the study of systems of linear equations. They are also important in econometrics for deriving a linear relationship that fits a data set as well as possible.

Next, Section 13.8 discusses Cramer's rule for the solution of a system of n linear equations and n unknowns. Although it becomes increasingly inefficient for solving systems of equations as the number of unknowns expands beyond 3, Cramer's rule is often used in theoretical studies. An important theorem on homogeneous systems of equations is included. Then Section 13.9 gives a brief introduction to the Leontief input/output model.

The chapter ends with some material that is important when considering the concavity or convexity of functions of several variables, as well as second-order conditions for optimization. Section 13.10 is concerned with eigenvalues and eigenvectors, Section 13.11 with diagonalizing square matrices, and the last Section 13.12 with quadratic forms.

13.1 Determinants of Order 2

Consider the pair of linear equations

$$\begin{aligned} a_{11}x_1 + a_{12}x_2 &= b_1 \\ a_{21}x_1 + a_{22}x_2 &= b_2 \end{aligned} \quad (13.1.1)$$

Its associated coefficient matrix is:

$$\mathbf{A} = \begin{pmatrix} a_{11} & a_{12} \\ a_{21} & a_{22} \end{pmatrix}$$

Following a procedure such as that presented in Section 12.8 allows us to find the solution to the equation system (13.1.1). Let D denote the number $a_{11}a_{22} - a_{21}a_{12}$. Provided that $D \neq 0$, system (13.1.1) has a unique solution given by

$$x_1 = \frac{b_1 a_{22} - b_2 a_{12}}{a_{11}a_{22} - a_{21}a_{12}}, \quad x_2 = \frac{b_2 a_{11} - b_1 a_{21}}{a_{11}a_{22} - a_{21}a_{12}} \tag{13.1.2}$$

In particular, the constant D is the common denominator D in (13.1.2). Thus, the value of D determines whether system (13.1.1) has a unique solution. Partly for this reason, the number $D = a_{11}a_{22} - a_{21}a_{12}$ is called the "determinant" of the matrix $\mathbf{A}$. This determinant is denoted by either $\det(\mathbf{A})$ or more usually, as in this book, simply by $|\mathbf{A}|$. Thus,

DETERMINANT OF A 2 × 2 MATRIX

For any 2×2 matrix $\mathbf{A} = (a_{ij})_{2 \times 2}$, its *determinant* is

$$|\mathbf{A}| = \begin{vmatrix} a_{11} & a_{12} \\ a_{21} & a_{22} \end{vmatrix} = a_{11}a_{22} - a_{21}a_{12} \tag{13.1.3}$$

If a matrix is 2×2, its determinant is said to have *order* 2. For the special case of order 2 determinants, the rule for calculating $|\mathbf{A}|$ is: (a) multiply together the two elements on the main diagonal; (b) multiply together the two off-diagonal elements; (c) subtract the product of the off-diagonal elements from the product of the diagonal elements.

EXAMPLE 13.1.1   By direct computation:

$$\begin{vmatrix} 4 & 1 \\ 3 & 2 \end{vmatrix} = 4 \cdot 2 - 3 \cdot 1 = 5, \quad \begin{vmatrix} b_1 & a_{12} \\ b_2 & a_{22} \end{vmatrix} = b_1 a_{22} - b_2 a_{12}, \text{ and } \begin{vmatrix} a_{11} & b_1 \\ a_{21} & b_2 \end{vmatrix} = b_2 a_{11} - b_1 a_{21}$$

Geometrically, each of the two equations in (13.1.1) represents the graph of a straight line. If $D = |\mathbf{A}| \neq 0$, then the two lines intersect at a unique point (x_1, x_2) given by (13.1.2). But if $D = |\mathbf{A}| = 0$, then the expressions in (13.1.2) for x_1 and x_2 become meaningless. Indeed, in this case, equation system (13.1.1): (i) either has no solution because the two lines are distinct but parallel; (ii) or else has infinitely many solutions because the two lines coincide.

The last two parts of Example 13.1.1 show us how the *numerators* of the expressions for x_1 and x_2 in the solution (13.1.2) can also be written as determinants. Indeed, provided that $|\mathbf{A}| \neq 0$, one has

$$x_1 = \frac{1}{|\mathbf{A}|} \begin{vmatrix} b_1 & a_{12} \\ b_2 & a_{22} \end{vmatrix} \text{ and } x_2 = \frac{1}{|\mathbf{A}|} \begin{vmatrix} a_{11} & b_1 \\ a_{21} & b_2 \end{vmatrix} \tag{13.1.4}$$

This is a special case of a result referred to as *Cramer's rule*.[1] It is quite convenient when there are only two equations in two unknowns. But as Exercise 8 shows, it is often easier to solve macroeconomic equation systems in particular by simple substitution.

EXAMPLE 13.1.2   Use (13.1.4) to find the solutions of

$$2x_1 + 4x_2 = 7$$
$$2x_1 - 2x_2 = -2$$

Solution: Applying (13.1.4) as well as definition (13.1.3) gives

$$x_1 = \frac{\begin{vmatrix} 7 & 4 \\ -2 & -2 \end{vmatrix}}{\begin{vmatrix} 2 & 4 \\ 2 & -2 \end{vmatrix}} = \frac{-6}{-12} = \frac{1}{2} \quad \text{and} \quad x_2 = \frac{\begin{vmatrix} 2 & 7 \\ 2 & -2 \end{vmatrix}}{\begin{vmatrix} 2 & 4 \\ 2 & -2 \end{vmatrix}} = \frac{-18}{-12} = \frac{3}{2}$$

Now you should check by substitution that $x_1 = 1/2$, $x_2 = 3/2$ really is a solution.

EXAMPLE 13.1.3   Use (13.1.4) to find Q_1^D and Q_2^D in terms of the parameters when

$$2(b + \beta_1)Q_1^D + bQ_2^D = a - \alpha_1$$
$$bQ_1^D + 2(b + \beta_2)Q_2^D = a - \alpha_2$$

Solution: The determinant of the coefficient matrix is

$$\Delta = \begin{vmatrix} 2(b + \beta_1) & b \\ b & 2(b + \beta_2) \end{vmatrix} = 4(b + \beta_1)(b + \beta_2) - b^2$$

Provided that $\Delta \neq 0$, Eq. (13.1.4) tells us that the solution for Q_1^D is

$$Q_1^D = \frac{\begin{vmatrix} a - \alpha_1 & b \\ a - \alpha_2 & 2(b + \beta_2) \end{vmatrix}}{\Delta} = \frac{2(b + \beta_2)(a - \alpha_1) - b(a - \alpha_2)}{\Delta}$$

with a similar expression for Q_2^D.

In the next section, Cramer's rule is extended to three equations in three unknowns, and then in Section 13.8 to n equations in n unknowns.

A Geometric Interpretation

Determinants of order 2 have a nice geometric interpretation. Suppose we represent the two rows of the matrix $\mathbf{A} = (a_{ij})_{2 \times 2}$ as the two 2-vectors shown in Fig. 13.1.1. Then its determinant equals the shaded area of the parallelogram. If we interchange the two rows, however, the determinant becomes a negative number equal to minus this shaded area.

Figure 13.1.2 illustrates why the result claimed in Fig. 13.1.1 is true. We want to find area T. Note that the area of the whole rectangle in Fig. 13.1.2 satisfies

---

[1] Named after the Swiss mathematician Gabriel Cramer, 1704–1752.

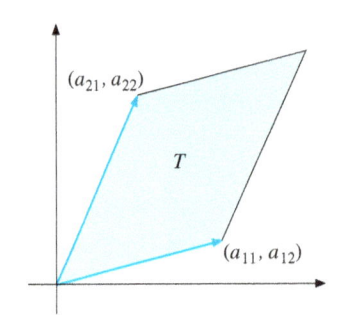

Figure 13.1.1 Area T is the absolute value of the determinant, Eq. (13.1.3)

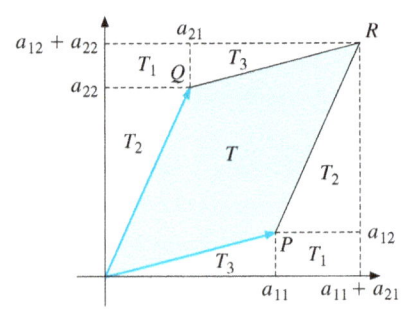

Figure 13.1.2 Illustration of Eq. (13.1.5)

$$2T_1 + 2T_2 + 2T_3 + T = (a_{11} + a_{21})(a_{12} + a_{22}) \quad (13.1.5)$$

where $T_1 = a_{12}a_{21}$, $T_2 = \frac{1}{2}a_{21}a_{22}$, and $T_3 = \frac{1}{2}a_{11}a_{12}$. By elementary algebra, it follows that $T = a_{11}a_{22} - a_{21}a_{12}$.

Note that a particularly simple case occurs when $a_{12} = 0$. Then the area determined by the two rows of the matrix is as shown in Fig. 13.1.3. So the area of T can be computed simply as the product of its base and its height, namely $a_{11}a_{22}$. Indeed, for this case one has $T_1 = T_3 = 0$ as well as $a_{12} = 0$, so Eq. (13.1.5) reduces to $2T_2 + T = (a_{11} + a_{21})a_{22}$. Because $T_2 = \frac{1}{2}a_{21}a_{22}$, it follows that $T = a_{11}a_{22} = |\mathbf{A}|$ in this simple case.

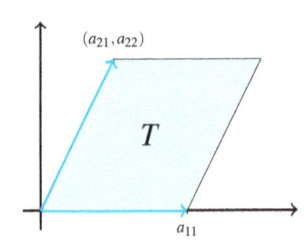

Figure 13.1.3 Area T is the absolute value of the determinant, Eq. (13.1.3), when $a_{12} = 0$

EXERCISES FOR SECTION 13.1

1. Calculate the following determinants:

   (a) $\begin{vmatrix} 3 & 0 \\ 2 & 6 \end{vmatrix}$ (b) $\begin{vmatrix} a & a \\ b & b \end{vmatrix}$ (c) $\begin{vmatrix} 2-x & 1 \\ 8 & -x \end{vmatrix}$ (d) $\begin{vmatrix} a+b & a-b \\ a-b & a+b \end{vmatrix}$ (e) $\begin{vmatrix} 3^t & 2^t \\ 3^{t-1} & 2^{t-1} \end{vmatrix}$

2. Illustrate the geometric interpretation in Fig. 13.1.1 for the determinant in Exercise 1(a).

3. Use Cramer's rule (13.1.4) to solve the following systems of equations for x and y. Test each answer by substitution.

   (a) $\begin{aligned} 3x - y &= 8 \\ x - 2y &= 5 \end{aligned}$ (b) $\begin{aligned} x + 3y &= 1 \\ 3x - 2y &= 14 \end{aligned}$ (c) $\begin{aligned} ax - by &= 1 \\ bx + ay &= 2 \end{aligned}$

4. The *trace* of a square matrix $\mathbf{A}$ is the sum of its diagonal elements, denoted by $\mathrm{tr}(\mathbf{A})$. Given the variable matrix $\mathbf{A} = \begin{pmatrix} a & 3 \\ b & 1 \end{pmatrix}$, find two numbers a and b such that $\mathrm{tr}(\mathbf{A}) = 0$ and $|\mathbf{A}| = -10$.

5. Find all the solutions to the equation $\begin{vmatrix} 2-x & 1 \\ 8 & -x \end{vmatrix} = 0$

6. Show that $|\mathbf{AB}| = |\mathbf{A}| \cdot |\mathbf{B}|$ for the matrices $\mathbf{A} = \begin{pmatrix} a_{11} & a_{12} \\ a_{21} & a_{22} \end{pmatrix}$ and $\mathbf{B} = \begin{pmatrix} b_{11} & b_{12} \\ b_{21} & b_{22} \end{pmatrix}$.[2]

7. Find two 2×2 matrices $\mathbf{A}$ and $\mathbf{B}$ such that $|\mathbf{A} + \mathbf{B}| \neq |\mathbf{A}| + |\mathbf{B}|$.

8. Let Y denote GDP and C private consumption. Suppose that investment I_0 and public expenditure G_0 are exogenous. Use Cramer's rule to solve the system of equations

$$Y = C + I_0 + G_0 \text{ and } C = a + bY$$

where a and b represent constants, with $b < 1$. Then look for an alternative simpler way of solving the equations.

(SM) 9. [HARDER] Consider the following macroeconomic model of two nations, $i = 1, 2$, that trade only with each other:

$$Y_1 = C_1 + A_1 + X_1 - M_1; \qquad C_1 = c_1 Y_1; \qquad M_1 = m_1 Y_1 = X_2$$
$$Y_2 = C_2 + A_2 + X_2 - M_2; \qquad C_2 = c_2 Y_2; \qquad M_2 = m_2 Y_2 = X_1$$

Here, for each nation $i = 1, 2$, the variable Y_i is its GDP, C_i is its consumption, A_i is its exogenous expenditure, X_i denotes its exports, and M_i denotes its imports.

(a) Interpret the two equations $M_1 = X_2$ and $M_2 = X_1$.

(b) Given the system of eight equations in eight unknowns, use substitution to reduce it to a pair of simultaneous equations that determine the two endogenous variables Y_1 and Y_2. Then solve for the values of Y_1, Y_2 as functions of the exogenous variables A_1 and A_2.

(c) How does an increase in A_1 affect Y_2? Interpret your answer.

13.2 Determinants of Order 3

Consider the general system of three linear equations in three unknowns

$$\begin{aligned} a_{11}x_1 + a_{12}x_2 + a_{13}x_3 &= b_1 \\ a_{21}x_1 + a_{22}x_2 + a_{23}x_3 &= b_2 \\ a_{31}x_1 + a_{32}x_2 + a_{33}x_3 &= b_3 \end{aligned} \tag{13.2.1}$$

---

[2] This is a particular case of rule (13.4.1) below.

Here the coefficient matrix $\mathbf{A}$ is 3×3. If we apply the method of elimination along with some rather heavy algebraic computation, the system can be solved eventually for x_1, x_2, and x_3, except in a degenerate case. The resulting expression for x_1 is

$$x_1 = \frac{b_1 a_{22} a_{33} - b_1 a_{23} a_{32} - b_2 a_{12} a_{33} + b_2 a_{13} a_{32} + b_3 a_{12} a_{23} - b_3 a_{22} a_{13}}{a_{11} a_{22} a_{33} - a_{11} a_{23} a_{32} + a_{12} a_{23} a_{31} - a_{12} a_{21} a_{33} + a_{13} a_{21} a_{32} - a_{13} a_{22} a_{31}} \quad (13.2.2)$$

We shall not triple the demands on the reader's patience and eyesight by giving the corresponding expressions for x_2 and x_3. However, we do claim that these expressions share the same denominator as that given for x_1. This common denominator is called the *determinant* of $\mathbf{A}$, denoted by $\det(\mathbf{A})$ or $|\mathbf{A}|$. When it is zero, we have a degenerate case. Thus,

---

DETERMINANT OF A 3 × 3 MATRIX

For any 3×3 matrix $\mathbf{A}$, its *determinant* is

$$|\mathbf{A}| = \begin{vmatrix} a_{11} & a_{12} & a_{13} \\ a_{21} & a_{22} & a_{23} \\ a_{31} & a_{32} & a_{33} \end{vmatrix} = \begin{cases} a_{11} a_{22} a_{33} - a_{11} a_{23} a_{32} + a_{12} a_{23} a_{31} \\ \quad - a_{12} a_{21} a_{33} + a_{13} a_{21} a_{32} - a_{13} a_{22} a_{31} \end{cases} \quad (13.2.3)$$

Expansion by Cofactors

The right-hand side of (13.2.3) is the sum of six terms. At first it looks quite messy, but a method called expansion by cofactors makes it relatively easy to write down all the terms. First, note that each of the three elements a_{11}, a_{12}, and a_{13} in the first row of $\mathbf{A}$ appears in exactly two terms of (13.2.3). In fact, grouping terms allows $|\mathbf{A}|$ to be written as

$$|\mathbf{A}| = a_{11}(a_{22} a_{33} - a_{23} a_{32}) - a_{12}(a_{21} a_{33} - a_{23} a_{31}) + a_{13}(a_{21} a_{32} - a_{22} a_{31})$$

Applying the rule for evaluating determinants of order 2, we see that this is the same as

$$|\mathbf{A}| = a_{11} \begin{vmatrix} a_{22} & a_{23} \\ a_{32} & a_{33} \end{vmatrix} - a_{12} \begin{vmatrix} a_{21} & a_{23} \\ a_{31} & a_{33} \end{vmatrix} + a_{13} \begin{vmatrix} a_{21} & a_{22} \\ a_{31} & a_{32} \end{vmatrix} \quad (13.2.4)$$

In this way, the computation of a determinant of order 3 can be reduced to calculating three determinants of order 2. Note that a_{11} is multiplied by the second-order determinant obtained by deleting row 1 and column 1 of $|\mathbf{A}|$. Likewise a_{12}, with a minus sign attached to it, is multiplied by the determinant obtained by deleting row 1 and column 2 of $|\mathbf{A}|$. Finally, a_{13} is multiplied by the determinant obtained by deleting row 1 and column 3 of $|\mathbf{A}|$.

EXAMPLE 13.2.1 Use formula (13.2.4) to calculate

$$|\mathbf{A}| = \begin{vmatrix} 3 & 0 & 2 \\ -1 & 1 & 0 \\ 5 & 2 & 3 \end{vmatrix}$$

Solution: By direct application of formulas (13.2.4) and (13.1.3), one has

$$|\mathbf{A}| = 3 \cdot \begin{vmatrix} 1 & 0 \\ 2 & 3 \end{vmatrix} - 0 \cdot \begin{vmatrix} -1 & 0 \\ 5 & 3 \end{vmatrix} + 2 \cdot \begin{vmatrix} -1 & 1 \\ 5 & 2 \end{vmatrix} = 3 \cdot 3 - 0 \cdot (-3) + 2 \cdot (-7) = -5$$

EXAMPLE 13.2.2   Use formula (13.2.4) to prove that

$$|\mathbf{A}| = \begin{vmatrix} 1 & a & a^2 \\ 1 & b & b^2 \\ 1 & c & c^2 \end{vmatrix} = (b-a)(c-a)(c-b)$$

Solution: By direct computation,

$$|\mathbf{A}| = 1 \cdot \begin{vmatrix} b & b^2 \\ c & c^2 \end{vmatrix} - a \cdot \begin{vmatrix} 1 & b^2 \\ 1 & c^2 \end{vmatrix} + a^2 \cdot \begin{vmatrix} 1 & b \\ 1 & c \end{vmatrix} = bc^2 - b^2c - a(c^2 - b^2) + a^2(c-b)$$

You are not expected to "see" that these six terms can be written as $(b-a)(c-a)(c-b)$. Rather, you should expand $(b-a)[(c-a)(c-b)]$ and verify the equality that way.

A careful study of the numerator in (13.2.2) reveals that it can also be written as a determinant. The same is true of the corresponding formulas for x_2 and x_3. In fact, provided that $|\mathbf{A}| \neq 0$, one can write the solution to the equation system (13.2.1) as

$$x_1 = \frac{\begin{vmatrix} b_1 & a_{12} & a_{13} \\ b_2 & a_{22} & a_{23} \\ b_3 & a_{32} & a_{33} \end{vmatrix}}{|\mathbf{A}|}, \quad x_2 = \frac{\begin{vmatrix} a_{11} & b_1 & a_{13} \\ a_{21} & b_2 & a_{23} \\ a_{31} & b_3 & a_{33} \end{vmatrix}}{|\mathbf{A}|}, \quad \text{and} \quad x_3 = \frac{\begin{vmatrix} a_{11} & a_{12} & b_1 \\ a_{21} & a_{22} & b_2 \\ a_{31} & a_{32} & b_3 \end{vmatrix}}{|\mathbf{A}|} \quad (13.2.5)$$

This is Cramer's rule for the solution of (13.2.1), in the case when there are three equations in three unknowns. See Section 13.8 for a full proof of the solution (13.2.5) in the general case of n equations in n unknowns.

Each determinant appearing in the numerators of the expressions for x_1, x_2, and x_3 in (13.2.5) includes one column which equals

$$\begin{pmatrix} b_1 \\ b_2 \\ b_3 \end{pmatrix}$$

This, of course, is the right-hand column in (13.2.1). This particular column vector shifts from column 1 when solving for x_1, to column 2 when solving for x_2, and finally to column 3 when solving for x_3. This makes it very easy to remember Cramer's rule.

The method used in (13.2.4) for calculating the value of a 3×3 determinant is called *cofactor expansion along row* 1. If we focus on the elements in row i instead of row 1, we again find that $|\mathbf{A}| = a_{i1}C_{i1} + a_{i2}C_{i2} + a_{i3}C_{i3}$, where for $j = 1, 2, 3$, the factor C_{ij} equals $(-1)^{i+j}$ times the determinant of the 2×2 matrix we get by deleting row i and column j from $\mathbf{A}$. Thus, for $j = 1, 2,$ or 3, we can also find the value of the determinant by cofactor expansion along row i. Moreover, it turns out that $|\mathbf{A}| = a_{1j}C_{1j} + a_{2j}C_{2j} + a_{3j}C_{3j}$. In other words, we can calculate the determinant by cofactor expansion along column j. See Section 13.5 for more about cofactor expansion.

EXAMPLE 13.2.3   Use Cramer's rule to solve the following system of equations:

$$2x_1 + 2x_2 - x_3 = -3$$
$$4x_1 + 2x_3 = 8$$
$$ 6x_2 - 3x_3 = -12$$

Solution: In this case, the determinant $|\mathbf{A}|$ that appears in formula (13.2.5) is seen to be

$$|\mathbf{A}| = \begin{vmatrix} 2 & 2 & -1 \\ 4 & 0 & 2 \\ 0 & 6 & -3 \end{vmatrix} = -24$$

As you should verify, the three numerators in (13.2.5) are

$$\begin{vmatrix} -3 & 2 & -1 \\ 8 & 0 & 2 \\ -12 & 6 & -3 \end{vmatrix} = -12, \quad \begin{vmatrix} 2 & -3 & -1 \\ 4 & 8 & 2 \\ 0 & -12 & -3 \end{vmatrix} = 12, \quad \text{and} \quad \begin{vmatrix} 2 & 2 & -3 \\ 4 & 0 & 8 \\ 0 & 6 & -12 \end{vmatrix} = -72$$

Hence, formula (13.2.5) yields the solution

$$x_1 = (-12)/(-24) = 1/2, \quad x_2 = 12/(-24) = -1/2, \quad \text{and} \quad x_3 = (-72)/(-24) = 3$$

Inserting this into the original system of equations verifies that this is a correct answer. ∎

A Geometric Interpretation

Like determinants of order 2, those of order 3 also have a geometric interpretation. This is shown in Fig. 13.2.1. The rows of the determinant correspond to three different 3-vectors represented in the diagram. Rather than a cuboid whose six faces are all rectangles (with right-angles at each corner), these vectors determine a "parallelepiped" whose six faces are all parallelograms, i.e. quadrilaterals whose opposite edges are parallel. Then the volume of this parallelepiped must equal the absolute value of the determinant $|\mathbf{A}|$, as defined by Eq. (13.2.3).

To help see why this is the case, it is useful to consider the simple case when $a_{12} = a_{13} = a_{23} = 0$, when the parallelepiped looks as in Fig. 13.2.2. The parallelogram that forms the base of the parallelepiped is similar to Fig 13.1.3. As we saw in Section 13.1, its area is the absolute value of the order 2 determinant

$$\begin{vmatrix} a_{11} & 0 \\ a_{21} & a_{22} \end{vmatrix} = a_{11}a_{22}$$

To compute the volume, then, we just need to multiply the area of the base by the height of the parallelogram, which is $|a_{33}|$. We thus obtain that the volume is the absolute value of

$$a_{11}a_{22}a_{33} = a_{33}\begin{vmatrix} a_{11} & 0 \\ a_{21} & a_{22} \end{vmatrix} = \begin{vmatrix} a_{11} & 0 & 0 \\ a_{21} & a_{22} & 0 \\ a_{31} & a_{32} & a_{33} \end{vmatrix}$$

Figure 13.2.1 Parallelepiped spanned by the three row vectors in the matrix

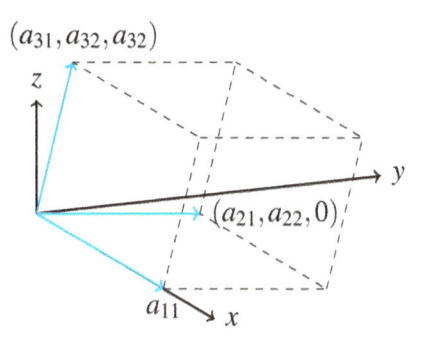

Figure 13.2.2 Parallelepiped in the case when $a_{12} = a_{13} = a_{23} = 0$

Sarrus's Rule for 3 × 3 Determinants

Here is an alternative way of evaluating determinants of order 3 that many people find convenient. First, form a 3 × 5 matrix, as shown below, by putting two copies of the original 3 × 3 matrix next to each other, but then deleting the copy of the last column:

$$\begin{matrix} a_{11} & a_{12} & a_{13} & a_{11} & a_{12} \\ a_{21} & a_{22} & a_{23} & a_{21} & a_{22} \\ a_{31} & a_{32} & a_{33} & a_{31} & a_{32} \end{matrix}$$

Now, first, multiply along the three diagonal lines falling to the right, giving all these products a plus sign, to yield the sum:

$$a_{11}a_{22}a_{33} + a_{12}a_{23}a_{31} + a_{13}a_{21}a_{32}$$

Second, multiply along the three diagonal lines rising to the right, giving all these products a minus sign, to yield the sum:

$$-a_{13}a_{22}a_{31} - a_{11}a_{23}a_{32} - a_{12}a_{21}a_{33}$$

The sum of all the six terms is exactly equal to formula (13.2.3) for the determinant $|\mathbf{A}|$ of order 3. It is very important to note that this method, known as *Sarrus's rule, only applies to determinants of order 3*.

EXERCISES FOR SECTION 13.2

SM 1. Use either (13.2.4) or Sarrus's rule to calculate the following determinants:

(a) $\begin{vmatrix} 1 & -1 & 0 \\ 1 & 3 & 2 \\ 1 & 0 & 0 \end{vmatrix}$
(b) $\begin{vmatrix} 1 & -1 & 0 \\ 1 & 3 & 2 \\ 1 & 2 & 1 \end{vmatrix}$
(c) $\begin{vmatrix} a & b & c \\ 0 & d & e \\ 0 & 0 & f \end{vmatrix}$
(d) $\begin{vmatrix} a & 0 & b \\ 0 & e & 0 \\ c & 0 & d \end{vmatrix}$

2. Let
$$\mathbf{A} = \begin{pmatrix} 1 & -1 & 0 \\ 1 & 3 & 2 \\ 1 & 2 & 1 \end{pmatrix} \quad \text{and} \quad \mathbf{B} = \begin{pmatrix} 1 & 2 & 3 \\ 2 & 3 & 4 \\ 0 & 1 & -1 \end{pmatrix}$$
Calculate $\mathbf{AB}$, $|\mathbf{A}|$, $|\mathbf{B}|$, $|\mathbf{A}| \cdot |\mathbf{B}|$, and $|\mathbf{AB}|$, then verify that $|\mathbf{AB}| = |\mathbf{A}| \cdot |\mathbf{B}|$.

(SM) 3. Use Cramer's rule to solve the following systems of equations. Check your answers.

(a) $\begin{aligned} x_1 - x_2 + x_3 &= 2 \\ x_1 + x_2 - x_3 &= 0 \\ -x_1 - x_2 - x_3 &= -6 \end{aligned}$
(b) $\begin{aligned} x_1 - x_2 &= 0 \\ x_1 + 3x_2 + 2x_3 &= 0 \\ x_1 + 2x_2 + x_3 &= 0 \end{aligned}$
(c) $\begin{aligned} x + 3y - 2z &= 1 \\ 3x - 2y + 5z &= 14 \\ 2x - 5y + 3z &= 1 \end{aligned}$

4. Show that $\begin{vmatrix} 1+a & 1 & 1 \\ 1 & 1+b & 1 \\ 1 & 1 & 1+c \end{vmatrix} = abc + ab + ac + bc$.

5. Given the matrix $\mathbf{A} = \begin{pmatrix} a & 1 & 0 \\ 0 & -1 & a \\ -b & 0 & b \end{pmatrix}$, find two numbers a and b such that $\text{tr}(\mathbf{A}) = 0$ and $|\mathbf{A}| = 12$, where $\text{tr}(\mathbf{A})$ denotes the sum of $\mathbf{A}$'s principal diagonal elements.

6. Solve the equation $\begin{vmatrix} 1-x & 2 & 2 \\ 2 & 1-x & 2 \\ 2 & 2 & 1-x \end{vmatrix} = 0$. (*Hint:* All roots of the equation are integers.)

7. For each value of the real parameter t, define the matrix $\mathbf{A}_t = \begin{pmatrix} 1 & t & 0 \\ -2 & -2 & -1 \\ 0 & 1 & t \end{pmatrix}$.

   (a) Calculate the determinant of $\mathbf{A}_t$, and show that it is never 0.

   (b) Find the matrix product $\mathbf{A}_t^3$, then show that there exists a value of t such that $\mathbf{A}_t^3$ equals the identity matrix $\mathbf{I}_3$.

(SM) 8. Consider the simple macroeconomic model described by the three equations:

$$\text{(i) } Y = C + A_0; \quad \text{(ii) } C = a + b(Y - T); \quad \text{(iii) } T = d + tY.$$

Here Y is GDP, C is consumption, T is tax revenue, A_0 is the constant (exogenous) autonomous expenditure, and a, b, d, and t are all positive parameters. Assuming that $b(1-t) < 1$, find the equilibrium values of the endogenous variables Y, C, and T by:

(a) successive elimination or substitution;

(b) writing the three equations in matrix form and applying Cramer's rule.

13.3 Determinants in General

This section gives a definition of $n \times n$ determinants that is particularly useful when proving general results. If you are not so interested in these proofs, you might skip this section and rely instead on expansion by cofactors, as explained in Section 13.5), for all your work on determinants.

Formula (13.2.3) expressed the determinant of a 3×3 matrix $\mathbf{A} = (a_{ij})_{3 \times 3}$ in the form

$$a_{11}a_{22}a_{33} - a_{11}a_{23}a_{32} + a_{12}a_{23}a_{31} - a_{12}a_{21}a_{33} + a_{13}a_{21}a_{32} - a_{13}a_{22}a_{31} \qquad (13.3.1)$$

Examining this expression more closely reveals a definite pattern. Each term is the product of three different elements of the matrix. Each product contains precisely one element from each row of $\mathbf{A}$, as well as precisely one element from each column.

Now, in a 3×3 matrix, there are precisely six different ways of picking three elements that include one element from each row and one element from each column. All six corresponding products appear in (13.3.1). Now consider the six patterns, each consisting of three circles, which are displayed in Fig. 13.3.1, You should disregard for now the lines and signs below each pattern. The six different patterns of three circles are arranged in the order of the corresponding products of three terms that appear in formula (13.3.1).

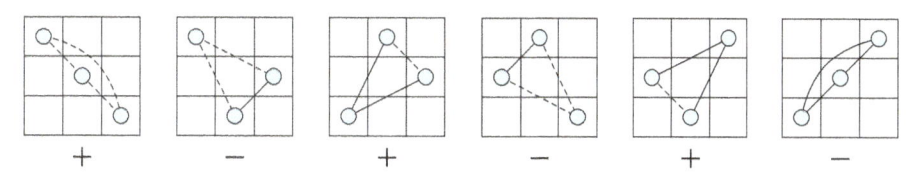

Figure 13.3.1 The terms of a 3×3 determinant

It remains to determine the sign of each term in (13.3.1), which is repeated as the sign of the corresponding pattern in Fig. 13.3.1. How do we do this? In Fig. 13.3.1, we have joined each pair of circles in every box by a line. This line is solid if it rises to the right, but dashed if it falls to the right. Now count the number of solid lines drawn in each of the six boxes, and see if it is odd or even. This procedure leads to the following rule:

THE SIGN RULE

To determine the sign of any term in the sum, mark all the elements that appear within the product in a corresponding pattern. Join each possible pair of elements in the pattern with a line. Each line must either rise or fall as one moves to the right. If the number of the rising lines is even, then the corresponding term in the sum is assigned a plus sign; if it is odd, it is assigned a minus sign.

Let us apply this rule to the six boxes in Fig. 13.3.1. In the first box, for example, no lines rise to the right, so $a_{11}a_{22}a_{33}$ has a plus sign. In the fourth box, exactly one line rises to the right, so $a_{12}a_{21}a_{33}$ has a minus sign. Similarly for the other four boxes.

Suppose $\mathbf{A} = (a_{ij})_{n \times n}$ is an arbitrary $n \times n$ matrix. Suppose we pick n elements from $\mathbf{A}$, including exactly one element from each row and exactly one element from each column. The product of these n elements can be written in the form

$$a_{1r_1} \cdot a_{2r_2} \cdot \ldots \cdot a_{nr_n}$$

Here the order $r_1, r_2, \ldots, r_n$ of the second subscripts that indicate columns represents a shuffling (or permutation) of the successive row numbers $1, 2, \ldots, n$. Now the numbers $1, 2, \ldots, n$ can be permuted in $n! = 1 \cdot 2 \ldots (n-1)n$ different ways: indeed, for the first element r_1, there are n choices; for each of these first choices, there are $n-1$ choices for the second element r_2; and so on. So overall there are $n!$ different products of n factors to consider.

Given any $n \times n$ matrix $\mathbf{A}$, we are now equipped to define its determinant, denoted by $\det(\mathbf{A})$ or $|\mathbf{A}|$, as follows:

DETERMINANT

Let $\mathbf{A}$ be an $n \times n$ matrix. Then $|\mathbf{A}|$ is a sum of $n!$ terms where:

1. Each term is the product of n elements of the matrix, consisting of one element from each row and one element from each column. Moreover, every product of n factors, in which each row and each column is represented exactly once, must appear in this sum.

2. The sign of each term is found by applying the sign rule.

Using $(\pm)$ to denote the appropriate choice of either a plus or minus sign, as determined by the sign rule, one can write

$$|\mathbf{A}| = \begin{vmatrix} a_{11} & a_{12} & \cdots & a_{1n} \\ a_{21} & a_{22} & \cdots & a_{2n} \\ \vdots & \vdots & \ddots & \vdots \\ a_{n1} & a_{n2} & \cdots & a_{nn} \end{vmatrix} = \sum (\pm) a_{1r_1} a_{2r_2} \cdots a_{nr_n} \qquad (13.3.2)$$

You should take the time to see how, in the case of a 2×2 matrix, this definition agrees with (13.1.3).

EXAMPLE 13.3.1 Consider the determinant of an arbitrary 4×4 matrix $\mathbf{A} = (a_{ij})_{4 \times 4}$. There are $4! = 4 \cdot 3 \cdot 2 \cdot 1 = 24$ terms. One of these is $a_{13} a_{21} a_{32} a_{44}$, whose corresponding factors appear as boxed elements in the following array.

$$|\mathbf{A}| = \begin{vmatrix} a_{11} & a_{12} & \boxed{a_{13}} & a_{14} \\ \boxed{a_{21}} & a_{22} & a_{23} & a_{24} \\ a_{31} & \boxed{a_{32}} & a_{33} & a_{34} \\ a_{41} & a_{42} & a_{43} & \boxed{a_{44}} \end{vmatrix}$$

What sign should this term have? According to the sign rule, the term should have the plus sign because there are two rising lines.[3] Use three more similar diagrams to check

---

[3] We have omitted the dashed lines, because these do not count.

that the three other indicated terms in the following sum have all been given the correct sign:

$$|\mathbf{A}| = a_{11}a_{22}a_{33}a_{44} - a_{12}a_{21}a_{33}a_{44} + \cdots + a_{13}a_{21}a_{32}a_{44} - \cdots + a_{14}a_{23}a_{32}a_{41}$$

Note that there are 20 other terms which we have left out.

The determinant of an $n \times n$ matrix is called a *determinant of order n*. In general, it is difficult to evaluate determinants by using definition (13.3.2) directly, even if n is only 4 or 5. If $n > 5$, the work is usually enormous. For example, if $n = 6$, then $n! = 720$, so there are 720 terms in the sum (13.3.2). Fortunately other methods based on the elementary row operations discussed in Section 12.8 can reduce the work considerably. Several standard computer algorithms for evaluating determinants are based on such methods.

There are a few special cases where it is easy to evaluate a determinant, even if the order is high. One prominent example is

$$\begin{vmatrix} a_{11} & a_{12} & \cdots & a_{1n} \\ 0 & a_{22} & \cdots & a_{2n} \\ \vdots & \vdots & \ddots & \vdots \\ 0 & 0 & \cdots & a_{nn} \end{vmatrix} = a_{11}a_{22}\ldots a_{nn} \tag{13.3.3}$$

Here all the elements *below* the main diagonal are 0. The matrix whose determinant is given in (13.3.3) is called *upper triangular* because all the nonzero terms lie in the triangle on or above the main diagonal. For an upper triangular matrix, the sum (13.3.2) has at most one nonzero term, and the determinant can be evaluated by taking the product of all the elements on the main diagonal. To see why, note that in order to have a term in the sum (13.3.2) that is not 0, we have to choose a_{11} from column 1. From column 2, having already picked a_{11} from the first row, we cannot choose a_{12}. So the only way to get a nonzero product is to pick a_{22}. From the third column, a similar argument shows that we have to pick a_{33}, and so on. Thus, only the term $a_{11}a_{22}\ldots a_{nn}$ can be nonzero. Of course, even this term is zero in the case when at least one element a_{ii} on the principal diagonal is zero. The sign of the term $a_{11}a_{22}\ldots a_{nn}$ is plus because no line joining any pair of elements appearing in the product rises to the right.

If a matrix is a transpose of an upper triangular matrix, so that all elements *above* the main diagonal are 0, then the matrix is *lower triangular*. By using essentially the same argument as for (13.3.3), we see that the determinant of a lower triangular matrix is also equal to the product of the elements on its main diagonal:

$$\begin{vmatrix} a_{11} & 0 & \cdots & 0 \\ a_{21} & a_{22} & \cdots & 0 \\ \vdots & \vdots & \ddots & \vdots \\ a_{n1} & a_{n2} & \cdots & a_{nn} \end{vmatrix} = a_{11}a_{22}\ldots a_{nn} \tag{13.3.4}$$

EXERCISES FOR SECTION 13.3

1. Use definition (13.3.2) of a determinant along with the sign rule in order to calculate each of the following:

(a) $\begin{vmatrix} 1 & 0 & 0 & 0 \\ 0 & 2 & 0 & 0 \\ 0 & 0 & 3 & 0 \\ 0 & 0 & 0 & 4 \end{vmatrix}$
(b) $\begin{vmatrix} 1 & 0 & 0 & 1 \\ 0 & 1 & 0 & 0 \\ 0 & 0 & 1 & 0 \\ a & b & c & d \end{vmatrix}$
(c) $\begin{vmatrix} 1 & 0 & 0 & 2 \\ 0 & 1 & 0 & -3 \\ 0 & 0 & 1 & 4 \\ 2 & 3 & 4 & 11 \end{vmatrix}$

2. In case the two $n \times n$ matrices $\mathbf{A}$ and $\mathbf{B}$ are both upper triangular, show that $|\mathbf{AB}| = |\mathbf{A}||\mathbf{B}|$.

3. The determinant of the following 5×5 matrix consists of $5! = 120$ terms. One of them is the product of the boxed elements. Write this term with its correct sign.

$$\begin{vmatrix} a_{11} & \boxed{a_{12}} & a_{13} & a_{14} & a_{15} \\ a_{21} & a_{22} & \boxed{a_{23}} & a_{24} & a_{25} \\ a_{31} & a_{32} & a_{33} & a_{34} & \boxed{a_{35}} \\ \boxed{a_{41}} & a_{42} & a_{43} & a_{44} & a_{45} \\ a_{51} & a_{52} & a_{53} & \boxed{a_{54}} & a_{55} \end{vmatrix}$$

4. Write the term indicated by the marked boxes with its correct sign.

$$\begin{vmatrix} a_{11} & a_{12} & a_{13} & a_{14} & \boxed{a_{15}} \\ a_{21} & a_{22} & a_{23} & \boxed{a_{24}} & a_{25} \\ a_{31} & \boxed{a_{32}} & a_{33} & a_{34} & a_{35} \\ a_{41} & a_{42} & \boxed{a_{43}} & a_{44} & a_{45} \\ \boxed{a_{51}} & a_{52} & a_{53} & a_{54} & a_{55} \end{vmatrix}$$

5. Solve the following equation for x:

$$\begin{vmatrix} 2-x & 0 & 3 & 0 \\ 1 & 2-x & 0 & 3 \\ 0 & 0 & 2-x & 0 \\ 0 & 0 & 1 & 2-x \end{vmatrix} = 0$$

13.4 Basic Rules for Determinants

Definition (13.3.2) of the determinant of an $n \times n$ matrix $\mathbf{A}$ implies a number of important properties. Eight are stated below. All are of theoretical interest, but some also make it simpler to evaluate determinants.

THEOREM 13.4.1 (RULES FOR DETERMINANTS)

Let $\mathbf{A}$ be an $n \times n$ matrix. Then:

(i) If all the elements in a row (or column) of $\mathbf{A}$ are 0, then $|\mathbf{A}| = 0$.

(ii) $|\mathbf{A}'| = |\mathbf{A}|$, where $\mathbf{A}'$ is the transpose of $\mathbf{A}$.

(iii) If all the elements in a single row (or column) of $\mathbf{A}$ are multiplied by any number α, the determinant is multiplied by α.

(iv) If two rows (or two columns) of $\mathbf{A}$ are interchanged, the determinant changes sign but its absolute value remains unchanged.

(v) If two of the rows (or columns) of $\mathbf{A}$ are proportional, then $|\mathbf{A}| = 0$.

(vi) The value of the determinant of $\mathbf{A}$ is unchanged if a multiple of one row (or one column) is added to a different row (or column) of $\mathbf{A}$.

(vii) The determinant of the product of two $n \times n$ matrices $\mathbf{A}$ and $\mathbf{B}$ is the product of the determinants of both matrices:

$$|\mathbf{AB}| = |\mathbf{A}| \cdot |\mathbf{B}| \tag{13.4.1}$$

(viii) If α is any real number, then

$$|\alpha \mathbf{A}| = \alpha^n |\mathbf{A}| \tag{13.4.2}$$

It should be recalled that, in general, the determinant of a sum is *not* the sum of the determinants:

$$|\mathbf{A} + \mathbf{B}| \neq |\mathbf{A}| + |\mathbf{B}| \tag{13.4.3}$$

Exercise 13.1.7 asked for an example of this general inequality.

Our geometric interpretations of determinants of order 2 and 3 support several of these rules. For example, rule (iii) with, say, $\alpha = 2$, reflects the fact that if one of the vectors in Figs 13.1.1 or 13.2.1 is doubled in length, then the area or volume is twice as big. A good exercise is to try to provide geometric interpretations of rules (i), (v), and (viii).

Proofs for most of these properties are given at the end of this section. First, however, let us verify them in the special case when $\mathbf{A}$ and $\mathbf{B}$ are general 2×2 matrices.

(i) $\begin{vmatrix} a_{11} & a_{12} \\ 0 & 0 \end{vmatrix} = a_{11} \cdot 0 - a_{12} \cdot 0 = 0.$

(ii) $|\mathbf{A}| = \begin{vmatrix} a_{11} & a_{12} \\ a_{21} & a_{22} \end{vmatrix} = a_{11}a_{22} - a_{12}a_{21}$, while $|\mathbf{A}'| = \begin{vmatrix} a_{11} & a_{21} \\ a_{12} & a_{22} \end{vmatrix} = a_{11}a_{22} - a_{12}a_{21}.$

(iii) $\begin{vmatrix} a_{11} & \alpha a_{12} \\ a_{21} & \alpha a_{22} \end{vmatrix} = a_{11}(\alpha a_{22}) - a_{12}(\alpha a_{21}) = \alpha(a_{11}a_{22} - a_{12}a_{21}) = \alpha \begin{vmatrix} a_{11} & a_{12} \\ a_{21} & a_{22} \end{vmatrix}.$

(iv) $\begin{vmatrix} a_{21} & a_{22} \\ a_{11} & a_{12} \end{vmatrix} = a_{21}a_{12} - a_{11}a_{22} = -(a_{11}a_{22} - a_{12}a_{21}) = -\begin{vmatrix} a_{11} & a_{12} \\ a_{21} & a_{22} \end{vmatrix}.$

(v) $\begin{vmatrix} a_{11} & a_{12} \\ \beta a_{11} & \beta a_{12} \end{vmatrix} = a_{11}(\beta a_{12}) - a_{12}(\beta a_{11}) = \beta(a_{11}a_{12} - a_{11}a_{12}) = 0.$[4]

(vi) Multiply each entry in the first row of a determinant of order 2 by α and add it to the corresponding entry in the second row. That is,[5]

$$\begin{vmatrix} a_{11} & a_{12} \\ a_{21} & a_{22} \end{vmatrix} \overset{\alpha}{\hookleftarrow} = \begin{vmatrix} a_{11} & a_{12} \\ a_{21} + \alpha a_{11} & a_{22} + \alpha a_{12} \end{vmatrix}$$

$$= a_{11}(a_{22} + \alpha a_{12}) - a_{12}(a_{21} + \alpha a_{11})$$

$$= a_{11}a_{22} + \alpha a_{11}a_{12} - a_{12}a_{21} - \alpha a_{12}a_{11} = a_{11}a_{22} - a_{12}a_{21}$$

$$= \begin{vmatrix} a_{11} & a_{12} \\ a_{21} & a_{22} \end{vmatrix}$$

so the determinant does not change its value.

(vii) Exercise 13.1.6 already asked for a proof of this rule, for general 2×2 matrices.

(viii) $\begin{vmatrix} \alpha a_{11} & \alpha a_{12} \\ \alpha a_{21} & \alpha a_{22} \end{vmatrix} = \alpha a_{11} \alpha a_{22} - \alpha a_{12} \alpha a_{21} = \alpha^2(a_{11}a_{22} - a_{12}a_{21}) = \alpha^2 \begin{vmatrix} a_{11} & a_{12} \\ a_{21} & a_{22} \end{vmatrix}$

Theorem 13.4.1 lists some of the most important rules for determinants. Confidence in applying them comes only from doing many problems.

Rule (vi) is particularly useful for evaluating large or complicated determinants.[6] The idea is to convert the matrix into one that is (upper or lower) triangular. This can be done by adapting the Gaussian elimination method that we described in Section 12.8. We give two examples involving 3×3 matrices.

EXAMPLE 13.4.1

$$\begin{vmatrix} 1 & 5 & -1 \\ -1 & 1 & 3 \\ 3 & 2 & 1 \end{vmatrix} \overset{1}{\hookleftarrow} = \begin{vmatrix} 1 & 5 & -1 \\ -1+1 & 1+5 & 3+(-1) \\ 3 & 2 & 1 \end{vmatrix} = \begin{vmatrix} 1 & 5 & -1 \\ 0 & 6 & 2 \\ 3 & 2 & 1 \end{vmatrix} \overset{-3}{\hookleftarrow}$$

$$= \begin{vmatrix} 1 & 5 & -1 \\ 0 & 6 & 2 \\ 0 & -13 & 4 \end{vmatrix} \overset{\frac{13}{6}}{\hookleftarrow} = \begin{vmatrix} 1 & 5 & -1 \\ 0 & 6 & 2 \\ 0 & 0 & 25/3 \end{vmatrix} = 1 \cdot 6 \cdot \frac{25}{3} = 50$$

Here at step one, 1 times the first row has been added to the second row in order to obtain a zero in the first column. At step two (-3) times the first row has been added to the third, which gives a second zero in the first column. At step three 13/6 times the second row has been added to the third, which creates an extra zero in the second column. Note the way in which we have indicated these operations. In the end, they produce an upper triangular matrix whose determinant is easy to evaluate using formula (13.3.3). ∎

---

[4] This rule helps to confirm, in part, the result in Example 13.2.2. Note that the product $(b-a)(c-a)(c-b)$ is 0 if $b=a$, or if $c=a$, or if $c=b$. Also, in each of these three cases, two rows of the matrix are proportional, in fact equal.

[5] Note carefully the way in which we indicate this operation. See also Section 12.8.

[6] To calculate a general 10×10 determinant using definition (13.3.2) directly requires no fewer than $10! - 1 = 3\,628\,799$ operations of addition or multiplication! Systematic use of rule (vi) can reduce the required number of operations to about 380.

SECTION 13.4 / BASIC RULES FOR DETERMINANTS

EXAMPLE 13.4.2 In this example, the first and third equalities both result from applying more than one operation simultaneously. The second equality makes use of rule (iii). The fourth equality follows from formula (13.3.3).

$$\begin{vmatrix} a+b & a & a \\ a & a+b & a \\ a & a & a+b \end{vmatrix} = \begin{vmatrix} 3a+b & 3a+b & 3a+b \\ a & a+b & a \\ a & a & a+b \end{vmatrix}$$

$$= (3a+b) \begin{vmatrix} 1 & 1 & 1 \\ a & a+b & a \\ a & a & a+b \end{vmatrix} = (3a+b) \begin{vmatrix} 1 & 1 & 1 \\ 0 & b & 0 \\ 0 & 0 & b \end{vmatrix}$$

$$= (3a+b) \cdot 1 \cdot b \cdot b = b^2(3a+b)$$

EXAMPLE 13.4.3 Check that $|\mathbf{AB}| = |\mathbf{A}| \cdot |\mathbf{B}|$ when

$$\mathbf{A} = \begin{pmatrix} 1 & 5 & -1 \\ -1 & 1 & 3 \\ 3 & 2 & 1 \end{pmatrix} \quad \text{and} \quad \mathbf{B} = \begin{pmatrix} 3 & 0 & 2 \\ -1 & 1 & 0 \\ 5 & 2 & 3 \end{pmatrix}$$

Solution: In Example 13.4.1 we showed that $|\mathbf{A}| = 50$. Using Sarrus's rule, or otherwise, you should verify that $|\mathbf{B}| = -5$. Moreover, multiplying the two matrices yields

$$\mathbf{AB} = \begin{pmatrix} -7 & 3 & -1 \\ 11 & 7 & 7 \\ 12 & 4 & 9 \end{pmatrix}$$

Again, by using Sarrus's rule, or otherwise, we find that $|\mathbf{AB}| = -250 = 50 \cdot (-5)$. This confirms that $|\mathbf{AB}| = |\mathbf{A}| \cdot |\mathbf{B}|$.

For general $n \times n$ matrices, we offer an argument for Theorem 13.4.1, one rule at a time:

(i) Each of the $n!$ terms in the determinant must take one element from whichever row (or column) consists of only zeros. So the whole determinant is 0.

(ii) Each term in $|\mathbf{A}|$ is the product of entries chosen from $\mathbf{A}$ to include exactly one element from each row and one element from each column. Exactly the same terms, therefore, must appear also in $|\mathbf{A}'|$ also.

The sign of each term depends on the number of lines joining one pair (i, j) to another pair (k, l) that rise upward to the right, which occurs if and only if $i - k$ and $j - l$ have opposite signs. But each such line linking (i, j) to (k, l) in $\mathbf{A}$ corresponds exactly to one and only one line linking (j, i) to (l, k) in $\mathbf{A}'$. Moreover, the pair $i - k$ and $j - l$ have opposite signs if and only if the matching pair $k - i$ and $l - j$ have opposite signs, since both signs are reversed. Hence each term in $\mathbf{A}$ is matched by a corresponding term in $\mathbf{A}'$ that also has the same sign.

(iii) Let $\mathbf{B}$ be the matrix obtained from $\mathbf{A}$ by multiplying every element in a certain row (or column) of $\mathbf{A}$ by α. Then each term in the sum defining $|\mathbf{B}|$ is the corresponding term in the sum defining $|\mathbf{A}|$ multiplied by α. Hence, $|\mathbf{B}| = \alpha |\mathbf{A}|$.

(iv) If two rows are interchanged, or two columns, the terms involved in definition (13.3.2) of determinant remain the same, except that the sign of each term is reversed. Showing this, however, involves a somewhat intricate argument, so we offer only this brief explanation.[7]

(v) By rule (iii), the factor of proportionality can be put outside the determinant. The resulting determinant then has two equal rows (or columns). Interchanging these two rows (or columns) obviously leaves the determinant unchanged. Yet by rule (iv), the determinant changes its sign. So $|\mathbf{A}| = -|\mathbf{A}|$, implying that $|\mathbf{A}| = 0$.

(vi) For the case when the scalar multiple α of row i is added to row j, one has

$$\sum (\pm) a_{1r_1} \ldots a_{ir_i} \ldots (a_{jr_j} + \alpha a_{ir_j}) \ldots a_{nr_n}$$
$$= \sum (\pm) a_{1r_1} \ldots a_{ir_i} \ldots a_{jr_j} \ldots a_{nr_n} + \alpha \sum (\pm) a_{1r_1} \ldots a_{ir_i} \ldots a_{ir_j} \ldots a_{nr_n}$$

By rule (v) the last sum is zero because it is equal to a determinant with rows i and j equal. So the left-hand side reduces to $|\mathbf{A}| + \alpha \cdot 0 = |\mathbf{A}|$.

(vii) The proof of this rule for the case $n = 2$ is the object of Exercise 13.1.6. The case when $\mathbf{A}$ and $\mathbf{B}$ are both upper triangular is covered in Problem 13.3.2. To prove the general case, one can use elementary row and column operations to convert both matrices $\mathbf{A}$ and $\mathbf{B}$ to upper triangular form. But we omit the proof.

(viii) The matrix $\alpha \mathbf{A}$ is obtained by multiplying *every* row of $\mathbf{A}$ by α. This involves n multiplications, one for each row. By rule (iii) applied n times, $|\alpha \mathbf{A}| = \alpha^n |\mathbf{A}|$.

EXERCISES FOR SECTION 13.4

1. Let $\mathbf{A} = \begin{pmatrix} 1 & 2 \\ 3 & 4 \end{pmatrix}$ and $\mathbf{B} = \begin{pmatrix} 3 & 4 \\ 5 & 6 \end{pmatrix}$.

   (a) Calculate $\mathbf{AB}$, $\mathbf{BA}$, $\mathbf{A'B'}$, and $\mathbf{B'A'}$.

   (b) Show that $|\mathbf{A}| = |\mathbf{A'}|$ and $|\mathbf{AB}| = |\mathbf{A}| \cdot |\mathbf{B}|$.

   (c) Is $|\mathbf{A'B'}| = |\mathbf{A'}| \cdot |\mathbf{B'}|$?

2. Given the matrix $\mathbf{A} = \begin{pmatrix} 2 & 1 & 3 \\ 1 & 0 & 1 \\ 1 & 2 & 5 \end{pmatrix}$, first determine $\mathbf{A'}$, and then show that $|\mathbf{A}| = |\mathbf{A'}|$.

3. Evaluate the following three determinants as simply as possible:

   (a) $\begin{vmatrix} 3 & 0 & 1 \\ 1 & 0 & -1 \\ 2 & 0 & 5 \end{vmatrix}$
   (b) $\begin{vmatrix} 1 & 2 & 3 & 4 \\ 0 & -1 & 2 & 4 \\ 0 & 0 & 3 & -1 \\ -3 & -6 & -9 & -12 \end{vmatrix}$
   (c) $\begin{vmatrix} a_1 - x & a_2 & a_3 & a_4 \\ 0 & -x & 0 & 0 \\ 0 & 1 & -x & 0 \\ 0 & 0 & 1 & -x \end{vmatrix}$

4. Suppose that $\mathbf{A}$ and $\mathbf{B}$ are both 3×3 matrices with $|\mathbf{A}| = 3$ and $|\mathbf{B}| = -4$. Consider the six expressions $|\mathbf{AB}|$, $3|\mathbf{A}|$, $|-2\mathbf{B}|$, $|4\mathbf{A}|$, $|\mathbf{A}| + |\mathbf{B}|$, and $|\mathbf{A} + \mathbf{B}|$. For each expression, specify its numerical value given $|\mathbf{A}|$ and $|\mathbf{B}|$ when this is uniquely determined; otherwise, specify that the value cannot be uniquely determined.

---

[7] Most books on linear algebra offer proofs of this rule and of rule (vii), which we also leave unproved.

SECTION 13.4 / BASIC RULES FOR DETERMINANTS

5. Calculate $\mathbf{A}^2$ and $|\mathbf{A}|$ for the matrix $\mathbf{A} = \begin{pmatrix} a & 1 & 4 \\ 2 & 1 & a^2 \\ 1 & 0 & -3 \end{pmatrix}$.

6. Prove that each of the following determinants is zero:

   (a) $\begin{vmatrix} 1 & 2 & 3 \\ 2 & 4 & 5 \\ 3 & 6 & 8 \end{vmatrix}$
   (b) $\begin{vmatrix} 1 & a & b+c \\ 1 & b & c+a \\ 1 & c & a+b \end{vmatrix}$
   (c) $\begin{vmatrix} x-y & x-y & x^2-y^2 \\ 1 & 1 & x+y \\ y & 1 & x \end{vmatrix}$

7. Calculate $\mathbf{X}'\mathbf{X}$ and $|\mathbf{X}'\mathbf{X}|$ if

$$\mathbf{X} = \begin{pmatrix} 1 & 0 & 0 \\ 1 & 1 & 1 \\ 1 & 2 & 0 \\ 1 & 0 & 1 \end{pmatrix}$$

8. For each a calculate $|\mathbf{A}_a|$ if $\mathbf{A}_a = \begin{pmatrix} a & 2 & 2 \\ 2 & a^2+1 & 1 \\ 2 & 1 & 1 \end{pmatrix}$. Then, in case $a=1$, calculate $|\mathbf{A}_1^6|$.

9. For an orthogonal matrix $\mathbf{P}$, as defined in Exercise 12.7.7, show that $|\mathbf{P}|$ must be 1 or -1.

10. A square matrix $\mathbf{A}$ of order n is called *involutive* if $\mathbf{A}^2 = \mathbf{I}_n$.

    (a) Show that the determinant of an involutive matrix is 1 or -1.

    (b) Show that for all a the two matrices $\begin{pmatrix} -1 & 0 \\ 0 & -1 \end{pmatrix}$ and $\begin{pmatrix} a & 1-a^2 \\ 1 & -a \end{pmatrix}$ are both involutive.

    (c) Show that the square matrix $\mathbf{A}$ is involutive if and only if $(\mathbf{I}_n - \mathbf{A})(\mathbf{I}_n + \mathbf{A}) = \mathbf{0}$.

11. Determine which of the following equalities are (generally) true or false:

    (a) $\begin{vmatrix} a & b \\ c & d \end{vmatrix} = -\begin{vmatrix} a & -b \\ c & -d \end{vmatrix} = 2\begin{vmatrix} a/2 & b/2 \\ c/2 & d/2 \end{vmatrix}$
    (b) $\begin{vmatrix} a & b \\ c & d \end{vmatrix} = \begin{vmatrix} a & b \\ 0 & 0 \end{vmatrix} + \begin{vmatrix} 0 & 0 \\ c & d \end{vmatrix}$

    (c) $\begin{vmatrix} a & b \\ c & d \end{vmatrix} = \begin{vmatrix} 0 & b \\ 0 & d \end{vmatrix} + \begin{vmatrix} a & b \\ c & d \end{vmatrix} = \begin{vmatrix} a & 0 & b \\ -1 & 1 & 0 \\ c & 0 & d \end{vmatrix}$
    (d) $\begin{vmatrix} a & b \\ c & d \end{vmatrix} = \begin{vmatrix} a & b \\ c-2a & d-2b \end{vmatrix}$

12. Let $\mathbf{B}$ be a given $n \times n$ matrix. An $n \times n$ matrix $\mathbf{P}$ is said to *commute* with $\mathbf{B}$ if $\mathbf{BP} = \mathbf{PB}$. Show that if $\mathbf{P}$ and $\mathbf{Q}$ both commute with $\mathbf{B}$, then $\mathbf{PQ}$ will also commute with $\mathbf{B}$.

13. [HARDER] Without computing the determinants, show that

$$\begin{vmatrix} b^2+c^2 & ab & ac \\ ab & a^2+c^2 & bc \\ ac & bc & a^2+b^2 \end{vmatrix} = \begin{vmatrix} 0 & c & b \\ c & 0 & a \\ b & a & 0 \end{vmatrix}^2$$

14. [HARDER] Prove the following useful result (which reduces to Example 13.4.2 in case $n = 3$):

$$D_n = \begin{vmatrix} a+b & a & \cdots & a \\ a & a+b & \cdots & a \\ \vdots & \vdots & \ddots & \vdots \\ a & a & \cdots & a+b \end{vmatrix} = b^{n-1}(na+b)$$

13.5 Expansion by Cofactors

In Section 13.2, which was devoted to determinants of order 3, we introduced the topic of expansion by cofactors. We gave formula (13.2.4) as rule for calculating such determinants. That formula involved cofactors expressed as determinants of order 2. In this section we will consider expansion by cofactors for determinants of order $n \geq 3$, including formulas that involve cofactors expressed as determinants of order $n-1$.

According to definition (13.3.2), the determinant of an $n \times n$ matrix $\mathbf{A} = (a_{ij})$ is a sum of $n!$ terms. Each term contains one element from each row and one element from each column. Consider in particular row i. First pick out all the terms that have a_{i1} as a factor, then all the terms that have a_{i2} as a factor, and so on. Because all these selected terms have precisely one factor from row i, in this way we include all the terms of $|\mathbf{A}|$. So we can write

$$|\mathbf{A}| = a_{i1}C_{i1} + a_{i2}C_{i2} + \cdots + a_{ij}C_{ij} + \cdots + a_{in}C_{in} \qquad (13.5.1)$$

The coefficients $C_{i1}, \ldots, C_{in}$ are the *cofactors* of the elements $a_{i1}, \ldots, a_{in}$. Then Eq. (13.5.1) is called the *cofactor expansion of* $|\mathbf{A}|$ *along* (or by) *row i*.

Similarly, one has the *cofactor expansion of* $|\mathbf{A}|$ *along* (or by) *column j*, which is

$$|\mathbf{A}| = a_{1j}C_{1j} + a_{2j}C_{2j} + \cdots + a_{ij}C_{ij} + \cdots + a_{nj}C_{nj} \qquad (13.5.2)$$

What makes expansions (13.5.1) and (13.5.2) useful is the following procedure for calculating any cofactor C_{ij} of the determinant $|\mathbf{A}|$. First, delete row i and column j to arrive at a determinant of order $n-1$, which is called a *minor*. Second, multiply the minor by the factor $(-1)^{i+j}$. This gives the cofactor C_{ij} which, in symbols, is given by

$$C_{ij} = (-1)^{i+j} \begin{vmatrix} a_{11} & \cdots & a_{1,j-1} & a_{1j} & a_{1,j+1} & \cdots & a_{1n} \\ a_{21} & \cdots & a_{2,j-1} & a_{2j} & a_{2,j+1} & \cdots & a_{2n} \\ \vdots & & \vdots & \vdots & \vdots & & \vdots \\ a_{i1} & \cdots & a_{i,j-1} & a_{ij} & a_{i,j+1} & \cdots & a_{in} \\ \vdots & & \vdots & \vdots & \vdots & & \vdots \\ a_{n1} & \cdots & a_{n,j-1} & a_{nj} & a_{n,j+1} & \cdots & a_{nn} \end{vmatrix} \qquad (13.5.3)$$

Note that we have drawn a box to indicate the particular element c_{ij}, as well as lines to cross out row i and column j, both of which have to be deleted from the determinant $|\mathbf{A}|$.

The claim is that one can find the determinant $|\mathbf{A}|$ by inserting the cofactors that are defined by formula (13.5.3) into either formula (13.5.1) for any row i, or formula (13.5.2) for any column j. We skip the proof. But if we look back at (13.2.4), it does confirm (13.5.3) in the special case when we expand a determinant of order 3 along its first row. Indeed, the three relevant cofactors are

$$C_{11} = (-1)^{1+1}\begin{vmatrix} a_{22} & a_{23} \\ a_{32} & a_{33} \end{vmatrix}, \quad C_{12} = (-1)^{1+2}\begin{vmatrix} a_{21} & a_{23} \\ a_{31} & a_{33} \end{vmatrix}, \quad \text{and } C_{13} = (-1)^{1+3}\begin{vmatrix} a_{21} & a_{22} \\ a_{31} & a_{32} \end{vmatrix}$$

Putting these into formula (13.5.1) for row $i = 1$ gives $|\mathbf{A}| = a_{11}C_{11} + a_{12}C_{12} + a_{13}C_{13}$, which accords precisely with (13.2.4).

For $n > 3$ formula (13.5.3) is rather complicated. Studying the following example should aid your understanding.

EXAMPLE 13.5.1   Check that the cofactor of the element c in the determinant

$$|\mathbf{A}| = \begin{vmatrix} 3 & 0 & 0 & 2 \\ 6 & 1 & \boxed{c} & 2 \\ -1 & 1 & 0 & 0 \\ 5 & 2 & 0 & 3 \end{vmatrix} \quad \text{is} \quad C_{23} = (-1)^{2+3}\begin{vmatrix} 3 & 0 & 2 \\ -1 & 1 & 0 \\ 5 & 2 & 3 \end{vmatrix}$$

Then find the value of $|\mathbf{A}|$ by using (13.5.2) and Example 13.2.1.

Solution: Because the element c is in row 2 and column 3, its cofactor has been written correctly. To find the numerical value of $|\mathbf{A}|$ we use the cofactor expansion along its *third column*, because this has more zeros than any other row or column. Using the answer to Example 13.2.3, this yields

$$|\mathbf{A}| = a_{23}C_{23} = c \cdot (-1)^{2+3}\begin{vmatrix} 3 & 0 & 2 \\ -1 & 1 & 0 \\ 5 & 2 & 3 \end{vmatrix} = c \cdot (-1)(-5) = 5c$$

In Example 13.5.1, column 3 of the matrix $\mathbf{A}$ has only one nonzero term, so expansion by cofactors along this column is particularly simple. Even if not enough zeros are there initially, we can often create more by using elementary row operations while appealing to rule (vi) in Theorem 13.4.1. The following two examples illustrate this approach.

EXAMPLE 13.5.2

$$\begin{vmatrix} 3 & -1 & 2 \\ 0 & -1 & -1 \\ 6 & 1 & 2 \end{vmatrix} \overset{-2}{\underset{\leftarrow}{\rule{0pt}{12pt}}} = \begin{vmatrix} 3 & -1 & 2 \\ 0 & -1 & -1 \\ 0 & 3 & -2 \end{vmatrix} \overset{(*)}{=} 3\begin{vmatrix} -1 & -1 \\ 3 & -2 \end{vmatrix} = 3(2+3) = 15$$

To derive the equality labelled $(*)$, expand by column 1.

EXAMPLE 13.5.3

$$\begin{vmatrix} 2 & 0 & 3 & -1 \\ 0 & 4 & 0 & 0 \\ 0 & 1 & -1 & 2 \\ 3 & 2 & 5 & -3 \end{vmatrix} \stackrel{(*)}{=} (-1)^{2+2} \cdot 4 \begin{vmatrix} 2 & 3 & -1 \\ 0 & -1 & 2 \\ 3 & 5 & -3 \end{vmatrix} \begin{array}{c} -3/2 \\ \\ \longleftarrow \end{array} = 4 \begin{vmatrix} 2 & 3 & -1 \\ 0 & -1 & 2 \\ 0 & 1/2 & -3/2 \end{vmatrix}$$

$$\stackrel{(**)}{=} 4 \cdot 2 \begin{vmatrix} -1 & 2 \\ 1/2 & -3/2 \end{vmatrix} = 8 \left(\tfrac{3}{2} - \tfrac{2}{2} \right) = 4$$

For equality $(*)$, expand by row 2. For equality $(**)$, expand by column 1.

Expansion by Alien Cofactors

According to the cofactor expansions (13.5.1) and (13.5.2), if each element a_{ij} in any row or column of a determinant is multiplied by the corresponding cofactor C_{ij} and then all the products are added, the result is the value of the determinant. What happens if we multiply the elements of a row by the cofactors of a different (alien) row? Or the elements of a column by the cofactors of an alien column? Consider the following example.

EXAMPLE 13.5.4

If $\mathbf{A} = (a_{ij})_{3 \times 3}$, the cofactor expansion of $|\mathbf{A}|$ along the second row is

$$|\mathbf{A}| = a_{21} C_{21} + a_{22} C_{22} + a_{23} C_{23}$$

Suppose we replace the elements a_{21}, a_{22}, and a_{23} of the second row by a, b, and c. Then, the corresponding cofactors C_{21}, C_{22}, and C_{23} remain unchanged. So the cofactor expansion of the new determinant along its second row is

$$\begin{vmatrix} a_{11} & a_{12} & a_{13} \\ a & b & c \\ a_{31} & a_{32} & a_{33} \end{vmatrix} = a C_{21} + b C_{22} + c C_{23} \qquad (*)$$

In particular, suppose we replace a, b, and c in $(*)$ by a_{11}, a_{12}, and a_{13} taken from row 1, or by a_{31}, a_{32}, and a_{33} taken from row 3. In either case two rows of the determinant in $(*)$ become equal, so the right-hand side becomes 0. Hence,

$$a_{11} C_{21} + a_{12} C_{22} + a_{13} C_{23} = 0$$
$$a_{31} C_{21} + a_{32} C_{22} + a_{33} C_{23} = 0$$

That is, the sum of the products of all the elements in either row 1 or row 3 multiplied by the corresponding cofactors of the elements in row 2 is zero.

Obviously, the argument used in this example can be generalized: If we multiply the elements of any row by the cofactors of an alien row, and then add the products, the result is 0. Similarly if we multiply the elements of a column by the cofactors of an alien column, then add.

We summarize all the results in this section in the following theorem:

THEOREM 13.5.1 (COFACTOR EXPANSION OF A DETERMINANT)

Let $\mathbf{A} = (a_{ij})_{n \times n}$. Suppose that the cofactors C_{ij} are defined as in (13.5.3). Then:

(i) $a_{i1}C_{i1} + a_{i2}C_{i2} + \cdots + a_{in}C_{in} = |\mathbf{A}|$;

(ii) if $k \neq i$, then $a_{i1}C_{k1} + a_{i2}C_{k2} + \cdots + a_{in}C_{kn} = 0$;

(iii) $a_{1j}C_{1j} + a_{2j}C_{2j} + \cdots + a_{nj}C_{nj} = |\mathbf{A}|$;

(iv) if $k \neq j$, then $a_{1j}C_{1k} + a_{2j}C_{2k} + \cdots + a_{nj}C_{nk} = 0$.

Theorem 13.5.1 says that an expansion of a determinant by row i in terms of the cofactors of row k vanishes when $k \neq i$, but is equal to $|\mathbf{A}|$ if $k = i$. Likewise, an expansion by column j in terms of the cofactors of column k vanishes when $k \neq j$, but is equal to $|\mathbf{A}|$ if $k = j$.

EXERCISES FOR SECTION 13.5

SM 1. Calculate the following determinants:

(a) $\begin{vmatrix} 1 & 2 & 4 \\ 1 & 3 & 9 \\ 1 & 4 & 16 \end{vmatrix}$
(b) $\begin{vmatrix} 1 & 2 & 3 & 4 \\ 0 & -1 & 0 & 11 \\ 2 & -1 & 0 & 3 \\ -2 & 0 & -1 & 3 \end{vmatrix}$
(c) $\begin{vmatrix} 2 & 1 & 3 & 3 \\ 3 & 2 & 1 & 6 \\ 1 & 3 & 0 & 9 \\ 2 & 4 & 1 & 12 \end{vmatrix}$

2. Calculate the following determinants:

(a) $\begin{vmatrix} 0 & 0 & a \\ 0 & b & 0 \\ c & 0 & 0 \end{vmatrix}$
(b) $\begin{vmatrix} 0 & 0 & 0 & a \\ 0 & 0 & b & 0 \\ 0 & c & 0 & 0 \\ d & 0 & 0 & 0 \end{vmatrix}$
(c) $\begin{vmatrix} 0 & 0 & 0 & 0 & 1 \\ 0 & 0 & 0 & 5 & 1 \\ 0 & 0 & 3 & 1 & 2 \\ 0 & 4 & 0 & 3 & 4 \\ 6 & 2 & 3 & 1 & 2 \end{vmatrix}$

13.6 The Inverse of a Matrix

The number 1 is the "multiplicative identity" in the real number system in the sense that $1 \cdot \alpha = \alpha \cdot 1 = \alpha$ for all real α. Furthermore, in case $\alpha \neq 0$, there is a unique number α^{-1} with the property that $\alpha \alpha^{-1} = \alpha^{-1} \alpha = 1$. We call α^{-1} the (multiplicative) inverse of α. In Section 12.6 we introduced the $n \times n$ identity matrix $\mathbf{I}$, with elements equal to 1 all along the main diagonal and to 0 everywhere else.[8] It is the multiplicative identity among $n \times n$ matrices in the sense that $\mathbf{IX} = \mathbf{XI} = \mathbf{X}$ for all $n \times n$ matrices $\mathbf{X}$. By analogy with the real number system, we look for a (multiplicative) inverse $\mathbf{X}$ of an $n \times n$ matrix $\mathbf{A}$ that satisfies $\mathbf{AX} = \mathbf{XA} = \mathbf{I}$.

Formally, for any given matrix $\mathbf{A}$, we say that $\mathbf{X}$ is an *inverse* of $\mathbf{A}$ if it satisfies

$$\mathbf{AX} = \mathbf{XA} = \mathbf{I} \tag{13.6.1}$$

Provided such an inverse exists, the matrix $\mathbf{A}$ is said to be *invertible*. The equivalent equations $\mathbf{XA} = \mathbf{AX} = \mathbf{I}$ imply that the matrix $\mathbf{A}$ is also an inverse of $\mathbf{X}$. That is, $\mathbf{A}$ and $\mathbf{X}$ are inverses of each other.

Note that the two matrix products $\mathbf{AX}$ and $\mathbf{XA}$ are defined and equal only if $\mathbf{A}$ and $\mathbf{X}$ are square matrices of the same order. *Thus, only square matrices can have inverses.* But not even all square matrices have inverses, as part (b) of the following example shows.

EXAMPLE 13.6.1

(a) Show that the following matrices are inverses of each other:

$$\mathbf{A} = \begin{pmatrix} 5 & 6 \\ 5 & 10 \end{pmatrix} \quad \text{and} \quad \mathbf{X} = \begin{pmatrix} 1/2 & -3/10 \\ -1/4 & 1/4 \end{pmatrix}$$

(b) Show that the matrix $\mathbf{A} = \begin{pmatrix} 1 & 0 \\ 0 & 0 \end{pmatrix}$ has no inverse.

Solution:

(a) We simply multiply directly to show that

$$\begin{pmatrix} 5 & 6 \\ 5 & 10 \end{pmatrix} \begin{pmatrix} 1/2 & -3/10 \\ -1/4 & 1/4 \end{pmatrix} = \begin{pmatrix} 5/2 - 6/4 & -15/10 + 6/4 \\ 5/2 - 10/4 & -15/10 + 10/4 \end{pmatrix} = \begin{pmatrix} 1 & 0 \\ 0 & 1 \end{pmatrix}$$

Likewise, we verify that $\mathbf{XA} = \mathbf{I}$.

(b) Observe that for all real numbers x, y, z, and w, one has

$$\begin{pmatrix} 1 & 0 \\ 0 & 0 \end{pmatrix} \begin{pmatrix} x & y \\ z & w \end{pmatrix} = \begin{pmatrix} x & y \\ 0 & 0 \end{pmatrix}$$

Because the element in row 2 and column 2 of the last matrix is 0 and not 1, there is no way of choosing x, y, z, and w to make the product of these two matrices equal to $\mathbf{I}$.

The following questions arise: (i) *Which matrices have inverses?* (ii) *Can a given matrix have more than one inverse?* (iii) *How do we find the inverse if it exists?*

For question (i), it is easy to find a *necessary* condition for a matrix $\mathbf{A}$ to have an inverse. In fact, from (13.6.1) and rule (vii) in Theorem 13.4.1, it follows that $|\mathbf{AX}| = |\mathbf{A}| \cdot |\mathbf{X}| = |\mathbf{I}|$. Using (13.3.3), we see that the identity matrix of any order has

---

[8] From now on, we often write $\mathbf{I}$ instead of $\mathbf{I}_n$ whenever the order n of the identity matrix seems obvious.

determinant 1. So if **X** is an inverse of **A**, then $|\mathbf{A}| \cdot |\mathbf{X}| = 1$. Because $|\mathbf{A}| = 0$ would contradict this equation, we conclude that $|\mathbf{A}| \neq 0$ is a necessary condition for **A** to have an inverse.

As we shall see in Section 13.7, the condition $|\mathbf{A}| \neq 0$ is also *sufficient* for **A** to have an inverse. Hence, for any square matrix **A**,

$$\mathbf{A} \text{ has an inverse} \iff |\mathbf{A}| \neq 0 \tag{13.6.2}$$

A square matrix **A** is said to be *singular* if $|\mathbf{A}| = 0$, but *nonsingular* if $|\mathbf{A}| \neq 0$. According to (13.6.2), therefore, a matrix is invertible if and only if it is nonsingular.

Concerning question (ii), the answer is that a matrix cannot have more than one inverse. Indeed, suppose that **X** satisfies (13.6.1) and that $\mathbf{AY} = \mathbf{I}$ for any square matrix **Y**. Then

$$\mathbf{Y} = \mathbf{IY} = (\mathbf{XA})\mathbf{Y} = \mathbf{X}(\mathbf{AY}) = \mathbf{XI} = \mathbf{X}$$

A similar argument shows that if $\mathbf{YA} = \mathbf{I}$, then $\mathbf{Y} = \mathbf{X}$. Thus, *the inverse of* **A** *is unique, if it exists.*

If the inverse of **A** exists, it is usually written as $\mathbf{A}^{-1}$. Whereas for numbers we can write $a^{-1} = 1/a$, the symbol $\mathbf{I}/\mathbf{A}$ has *no* meaning. *Dividing matrices makes no sense.* Note also that even if the product $\mathbf{A}^{-1}\mathbf{B}$ is defined, it is usually quite different from $\mathbf{B}\mathbf{A}^{-1}$ because in general matrix multiplication is not commutative.

The full answer to question (iii) is given in the next section. For now we only consider the case of 2×2 matrices.

EXAMPLE 13.6.2   Find the inverse of the matrix $\mathbf{A} = \begin{pmatrix} a & b \\ c & d \end{pmatrix}$, when it exists.

Solution: We look for a 2×2 matrix **X** such that $\mathbf{AX} = \mathbf{I}$, after which it is easy to check that $\mathbf{XA} = \mathbf{I}$. Solving $\mathbf{AX} = \mathbf{I}$ requires finding numbers x, y, z, and w such that

$$\begin{pmatrix} a & b \\ c & d \end{pmatrix} \begin{pmatrix} x & y \\ z & w \end{pmatrix} = \begin{pmatrix} 1 & 0 \\ 0 & 1 \end{pmatrix}$$

Matrix multiplication implies that

$$ax + bz = 1, \quad cx + dz = 0, \quad ay + bw = 0, \quad \text{and} \quad cy + dw = 1 \tag{$*$}$$

Note that here we have two different systems of two equations in two unknowns, one given by the first pair of equations, and the other by the second pair of equations. Both these systems have **A** as a common coefficient matrix. Now recall Cramer's rule for the 2×2 case, as stated in (13.1.4). Provided that $|\mathbf{A}| = ad - bc \neq 0$, we can use it twice to find the unique solution to $(*)$, which is

$$x = \frac{d}{ad - bc}, \quad z = \frac{-c}{ad - bc}, \quad y = \frac{-b}{ad - bc}, \quad \text{and} \quad w = \frac{a}{ad - bc}$$

Hence, we have proved the following result:

INVERSE OF A MATRIX OF ORDER 2

Provided that $|\mathbf{A}| = ad - bc \neq 0$,

$$\mathbf{A} = \begin{pmatrix} a & b \\ c & d \end{pmatrix} \implies \mathbf{A}^{-1} = \frac{1}{ad - bc} \begin{pmatrix} d & -b \\ -c & a \end{pmatrix} \qquad (13.6.3)$$

Note that in the inverse matrix, the elements on the main diagonal of the original 2 × 2 matrix changed places, whereas the off-diagonal elements just changed sign, and then the whole matrix was divided by the determinant of $\mathbf{A}$.

For square matrices of order 3, one can use Cramer's rule (13.2.5) to derive a formula for the inverse. Again, the requirement for the inverse to exist is that the determinant of the coefficient matrix is not 0. Full details will be given in Section 13.7.

Some Useful Implications

If $\mathbf{A}^{-1}$ is the inverse of $\mathbf{A}$, then $\mathbf{A}^{-1}\mathbf{A} = \mathbf{I}$ and $\mathbf{A}\mathbf{A}^{-1} = \mathbf{I}$. Actually, each of these equations characterizes the inverse of $\mathbf{A}$, in the sense that

$$\mathbf{AX} = \mathbf{I} \iff \mathbf{X} = \mathbf{A}^{-1} \qquad (13.6.4)$$

$$\mathbf{YA} = \mathbf{I} \iff \mathbf{Y} = \mathbf{A}^{-1} \qquad (13.6.5)$$

The implications in the direction $\Leftarrow$ follow immediately from the definition of an inverse matrix. To prove $\Rightarrow$ in (13.6.4), suppose $\mathbf{AX} = \mathbf{I}$. Then $|\mathbf{A}| \cdot |\mathbf{X}| = 1$, and so $|\mathbf{A}| \neq 0$. By (13.6.2), it follows that $\mathbf{A}^{-1}$ exists. Multiplying $\mathbf{AX} = \mathbf{I}$ from the left by $\mathbf{A}^{-1}$ yields $\mathbf{X} = \mathbf{A}^{-1}$. The proof of $\Rightarrow$ in (13.6.5) is almost the same.

Implications (13.6.4) and (13.6.5) are used repeatedly in proving properties of the inverse. Here are two examples.

EXAMPLE 13.6.3   Find the inverse of the $n \times n$ matrix $\mathbf{A}$ if $\mathbf{A} - \mathbf{A}^2 = \mathbf{I}$.

Solution: The matrix equation $\mathbf{A} - \mathbf{A}^2 = \mathbf{I}$ is equivalent to $\mathbf{A}(\mathbf{I} - \mathbf{A}) = \mathbf{I}$. Then (13.6.4) implies that $\mathbf{A}$ has the inverse $\mathbf{A}^{-1} = \mathbf{I} - \mathbf{A}$.

EXAMPLE 13.6.4   Let $\mathbf{B}$ be a nonzero $n \times n$ matrix such that $\mathbf{B}^2 = 3\mathbf{B}$. Prove that there exists a unique number s such that $\mathbf{I} + s\mathbf{B}$ is the inverse of $\mathbf{I} + \mathbf{B}$.

Solution: Because of (13.6.5), it suffices to find a number s such that $(\mathbf{I} + s\mathbf{B})(\mathbf{I} + \mathbf{B}) = \mathbf{I}$. Repeatedly applying the rules for matrix multiplication, the definition of $\mathbf{I}$, and the equality $\mathbf{B}^2 = 3\mathbf{B}$ together imply that

$$(\mathbf{I} + s\mathbf{B})(\mathbf{I} + \mathbf{B}) = \mathbf{II} + \mathbf{IB} + s\mathbf{BI} + s\mathbf{B}^2 = \mathbf{I} + \mathbf{B} + s\mathbf{B} + 3s\mathbf{B} = \mathbf{I} + (1 + 4s)\mathbf{B}$$

This equals $\mathbf{I}$ if and only if $(1 + 4s)\mathbf{B} = \mathbf{0}$. Because $\mathbf{B} \neq \mathbf{0}$, this holds if and only if $1 + 4s = 0$, or if and only if $s = -1/4$.

Properties of The Inverse

We shall now prove some useful rules for the inverse.

THEOREM 13.6.1 (PROPERTIES OF THE INVERSE)

Suppose that $\mathbf{A}$ and $\mathbf{B}$ are invertible $n \times n$ matrices. Then:

(a) the matrix $\mathbf{A}^{-1}$ is invertible, and $(\mathbf{A}^{-1})^{-1} = \mathbf{A}$;
(b) the matrix $\mathbf{AB}$ is invertible, and $(\mathbf{AB})^{-1} = \mathbf{B}^{-1}\mathbf{A}^{-1}$;
(c) the transpose matrix $\mathbf{A}'$ is invertible, and $(\mathbf{A}')^{-1} = (\mathbf{A}^{-1})'$;
(d) if c is a nonzero scalar, then $(c\mathbf{A})^{-1} = c^{-1}\mathbf{A}^{-1}$.

In order to prove these properties, we use (13.6.4) or (13.6.5) in each case:

Proof:

(a) By (13.6.1) we have $\mathbf{A}^{-1}\mathbf{A} = \mathbf{I}$. Now apply (13.6.4) with $\mathbf{A}$ replaced by $\mathbf{A}^{-1}$. This shows that $\mathbf{A} = (\mathbf{A}^{-1})^{-1}$.

(b) By rule (12.6.1) as well as the definitions of $\mathbf{I}$ and matrix inverse, we have

$$(\mathbf{AB})(\mathbf{B}^{-1}\mathbf{A}^{-1}) = \mathbf{A}(\mathbf{BB}^{-1})\mathbf{A}^{-1} = \mathbf{AIA}^{-1} = \mathbf{AA}^{-1} = \mathbf{I}$$

From (13.6.4), it follows that $(\mathbf{AB})^{-1} = \mathbf{B}^{-1}\mathbf{A}^{-1}$.

(c) Rule (12.7.5) states that $(\mathbf{AC})' = \mathbf{C}'\mathbf{A}'$ for every $n \times n$ matrix $\mathbf{C}$. Applying this rule with $\mathbf{C} = \mathbf{A}^{-1}$ implies that $(\mathbf{A}^{-1})'\mathbf{A}' = (\mathbf{AA}^{-1})' = \mathbf{I}' = \mathbf{I}$. By (13.6.5), it follows that $(\mathbf{A}')^{-1} = (\mathbf{A}^{-1})'$.

(d) Here rule (12.6.4) implies that $(c\mathbf{A})(c^{-1}\mathbf{A}^{-1}) = cc^{-1}\mathbf{AA}^{-1} = 1 \cdot \mathbf{I} = \mathbf{I}$. From (13.6.4), it follows that $(c\mathbf{A})^{-1} = c^{-1}\mathbf{A}^{-1}$.

Suppose that the invertible matrix $\mathbf{A}$ is symmetric, in the sense that $\mathbf{A}' = \mathbf{A}$. Then property (c) implies that $(\mathbf{A}^{-1})' = (\mathbf{A}')^{-1} = \mathbf{A}^{-1}$, so $\mathbf{A}^{-1}$ is symmetric. In summary, *the inverse of a symmetric matrix is symmetric*.

Also note that property (b) can be extended to products of several matrices. For instance, if $\mathbf{A}$, $\mathbf{B}$, and $\mathbf{C}$ are all invertible $n \times n$ matrices, then using property (b) twice implies that

$$(\mathbf{ABC})^{-1} = [(\mathbf{AB})\mathbf{C}]^{-1} = \mathbf{C}^{-1}(\mathbf{AB})^{-1} = \mathbf{C}^{-1}(\mathbf{B}^{-1}\mathbf{A}^{-1}) = \mathbf{C}^{-1}\mathbf{B}^{-1}\mathbf{A}^{-1}$$

Finally, note the assumption in property (b) that $\mathbf{A}$ and $\mathbf{B}$ are both $n \times n$ matrices. In statistics and econometrics, we often consider products of the form $\mathbf{XX}'$, where $\mathbf{X}$ is $n \times m$, with $n \neq m$. Then $\mathbf{XX}'$ is $n \times n$. If the determinant $|\mathbf{XX}'|$ is not 0, then $(\mathbf{XX}')^{-1}$ exists, but property (b) does not apply because $\mathbf{X}^{-1}$ and $\mathbf{X}'^{-1}$ are only defined if $n = m$.

Solving Equations by Matrix Inversion

Let $\mathbf{A}$ be any $n \times n$ matrix. If $\mathbf{B}$ is an arbitrary matrix, we consider whether there are matrices $\mathbf{X}$ and $\mathbf{Y}$ of suitable order such that $\mathbf{AX} = \mathbf{B}$ and $\mathbf{YA} = \mathbf{B}$. For the first requirement to be possible, the matrix $\mathbf{B}$ must have n rows; for the second, $\mathbf{B}$ must have n columns. These prior considerations should help explain the following result:

THEOREM 13.6.2

Suppose that $\mathbf{A}$ is an $n \times n$ matrix satisfying $|\mathbf{A}| \neq 0$. Then:

$$\text{provided that } \mathbf{B} \text{ has } n \text{ rows}, \quad \mathbf{AX} = \mathbf{B} \iff \mathbf{X} = \mathbf{A}^{-1}\mathbf{B} \tag{13.6.6}$$

$$\text{provided that } \mathbf{B} \text{ has } n \text{ columns}, \quad \mathbf{YA} = \mathbf{B} \iff \mathbf{Y} = \mathbf{B}\mathbf{A}^{-1} \tag{13.6.7}$$

Proof: (This is easy.) Provided that $|\mathbf{A}| \neq 0$ and $\mathbf{B}$ has n rows, we can multiply each side of the equation $\mathbf{AX} = \mathbf{B}$ in (13.6.6) on the left by $\mathbf{A}^{-1}$. This yields $\mathbf{A}^{-1}(\mathbf{AX}) = \mathbf{A}^{-1}\mathbf{B}$. Because $(\mathbf{A}^{-1}\mathbf{A})\mathbf{X} = \mathbf{IX} = \mathbf{X}$, we conclude that $\mathbf{X} = \mathbf{A}^{-1}\mathbf{B}$ is the only possible solution of $\mathbf{AX} = \mathbf{B}$. On the other hand, by substituting $\mathbf{X} = \mathbf{A}^{-1}\mathbf{B}$ into $\mathbf{AX} = \mathbf{B}$, we see that this value of $\mathbf{X}$ really does satisfy the equation.

The proof of (13.6.7) is similar: multiply each side of $\mathbf{YA} = \mathbf{B}$ on the right by $\mathbf{A}^{-1}$. ∎

EXAMPLE 13.6.5 Solve the following system of equations by using Theorem 13.6.2:

$$2x + y = 3$$
$$2x + 2y = 4$$

Solution: Suppose we define the matrices

$$\mathbf{A} = \begin{pmatrix} 2 & 1 \\ 2 & 2 \end{pmatrix}, \quad \mathbf{x} = \begin{pmatrix} x \\ y \end{pmatrix}, \quad \text{and} \quad \mathbf{b} = \begin{pmatrix} 3 \\ 4 \end{pmatrix}$$

Then the system is equivalent to the matrix equation $\mathbf{Ax} = \mathbf{b}$. Because $|\mathbf{A}| = 2 \neq 0$, the matrix $\mathbf{A}$ has an inverse. So according to Eq. (13.6.6) in the case when $\mathbf{B}$ and $\mathbf{X}$ both have only one column, one has $\mathbf{x} = \mathbf{A}^{-1}\mathbf{b}$. After using Eq. (13.6.3) to find $\mathbf{A}^{-1}$, we have

$$\begin{pmatrix} x \\ y \end{pmatrix} = \mathbf{A}^{-1} \begin{pmatrix} 3 \\ 4 \end{pmatrix} = \frac{1}{2} \begin{pmatrix} 2 & -1 \\ -2 & 2 \end{pmatrix} \begin{pmatrix} 3 \\ 4 \end{pmatrix} = \begin{pmatrix} 1 & -1/2 \\ -1 & 1 \end{pmatrix} \begin{pmatrix} 3 \\ 4 \end{pmatrix} = \begin{pmatrix} 1 \\ 1 \end{pmatrix}$$

The solution is therefore $x = 1$, $y = 1$. ∎

You should check by substitution that this really is the correct solution to Example 13.6.5. Note also that it is much easier to solve the system by subtracting the first equation from the second to obtain $y = 1$ immediately, from which it follows that $x = 1$.

EXERCISES FOR SECTION 13.6

1. Prove that:

   (a) $\begin{pmatrix} 3 & 0 \\ 2 & -1 \end{pmatrix}^{-1} = \begin{pmatrix} 1/3 & 0 \\ 2/3 & -1 \end{pmatrix}$

   (b) $\begin{pmatrix} 1 & 1 & -3 \\ 2 & 1 & -3 \\ 2 & 2 & 1 \end{pmatrix}^{-1} = \begin{pmatrix} -1 & 1 & 0 \\ 8/7 & -1 & 3/7 \\ -2/7 & 0 & 1/7 \end{pmatrix}$

2. Find numbers a and b that make $\mathbf{A}$ the inverse of $\mathbf{B}$ when

   $$\mathbf{A} = \begin{pmatrix} 2 & -1 & -1 \\ a & 1/4 & b \\ 1/8 & 1/8 & -1/8 \end{pmatrix} \quad \text{and} \quad \mathbf{B} = \begin{pmatrix} 1 & 2 & 4 \\ 0 & 1 & 6 \\ 1 & 3 & 2 \end{pmatrix}$$

3. Solve the following systems of equations by using Theorem 13.6.2 and then formula (13.6.3):

   (a) $\begin{array}{l} 2x - 3y = 3 \\ 3x - 4y = 5 \end{array}$
   (b) $\begin{array}{l} 2x - 3y = 8 \\ 3x - 4y = 11 \end{array}$
   (c) $\begin{array}{l} 2x - 3y = 0 \\ 3x - 4y = 0 \end{array}$

4. Given the matrix $\mathbf{A} = \dfrac{1}{2}\begin{pmatrix} -1 & -\sqrt{3} \\ \sqrt{3} & -1 \end{pmatrix}$, show that $\mathbf{A}^3 = \mathbf{I}_2$, and then use this to find $\mathbf{A}^{-1}$.

5. Let $\mathbf{A} = \begin{pmatrix} 0 & 1 & 0 \\ 0 & 1 & 1 \\ 1 & 0 & 1 \end{pmatrix}$.

   (a) Calculate $|\mathbf{A}|$, $\mathbf{A}^2$, $\mathbf{A}^3$, and $\mathbf{A}^3 - 2\mathbf{A}^2 + \mathbf{A} - \mathbf{I}_3$.

   (b) Use the last calculation to show that $\mathbf{A}$ has an inverse and that $\mathbf{A}^{-1} = (\mathbf{A} - \mathbf{I}_3)^2$.

   (c) Find a matrix $\mathbf{P}$ such that $\mathbf{P}^2 = \mathbf{A}$. Are there any other matrices with this property?

6. Let $\mathbf{A} = \begin{pmatrix} 2 & 1 & 4 \\ 0 & -1 & 3 \end{pmatrix}$.

   (a) Calculate $\mathbf{AA}'$, $|\mathbf{AA}'|$, and $(\mathbf{AA}')^{-1}$.

   (b) The matrices $\mathbf{AA}'$ and $(\mathbf{AA}')^{-1}$ in part (a) are both symmetric. Is this a coincidence?

SM 7. Given $\mathbf{B} = \begin{pmatrix} -1/2 & 5 \\ 1/4 & -1/2 \end{pmatrix}$, calculate $\mathbf{B}^2 + \mathbf{B}$ and $\mathbf{B}^3 - 2\mathbf{B} + \mathbf{I}$. Then find $\mathbf{B}^{-1}$.

8. Suppose that $\mathbf{X}$ is an $m \times n$ matrix and that $|\mathbf{X}'\mathbf{X}| \neq 0$. Show that the matrix defined by $\mathbf{A} = \mathbf{I}_m - \mathbf{X}(\mathbf{X}'\mathbf{X})^{-1}\mathbf{X}'$ satisfies $\mathbf{A}^2 = \mathbf{A}$ (and so is idempotent, as defined in Exercise 12.6.6).

9. Find a matrix $\mathbf{X}$ that satisfies $\mathbf{AB} + \mathbf{CX} = \mathbf{D}$, where:

$$\mathbf{A} = \begin{pmatrix} -2 & 0 & 1 \\ 1 & -1 & 5 \end{pmatrix}, \quad \mathbf{B} = \begin{pmatrix} 3 & 1 \\ 0 & 1 \\ -1 & 2 \end{pmatrix}, \quad \mathbf{C} = \begin{pmatrix} 1 & 2 \\ 3 & 4 \end{pmatrix}, \quad \text{and} \quad \mathbf{D} = \begin{pmatrix} -9 & 3 \\ -8 & 17 \end{pmatrix}.$$

10. Let $\mathbf{C}$ be an $n \times n$ matrix that satisfies $\mathbf{C}^2 + \mathbf{C} = \mathbf{I}$.
    (a) Show that $\mathbf{C}^{-1} = \mathbf{I} + \mathbf{C}$.   (b) Show that $\mathbf{C}^3 = -\mathbf{I} + 2\mathbf{C}$ and $\mathbf{C}^4 = 2\mathbf{I} - 3\mathbf{C}$.

13.7 A General Formula for the Inverse

The previous section presents the most important facts about the inverse and its properties. As such, it contains "what every economist should know". It is perhaps less important for most economists to know much about how to calculate the inverses of large matrices, because powerful computer programs are available. Nevertheless, this section presents an explicit formula for the inverse of any nonsingular $n \times n$ matrix $\mathbf{A}$. Though this formula is extremely inefficient for computing inverses of large matrices, it does have theoretical interest. The key to this formula are the rules for the cofactor expansion of determinants.

Let $C_{11}, \ldots, C_{nn}$ denote the n^2 cofactors of the elements in $\mathbf{A}$. By Theorem 13.5.1, the n^2 cofactor expansions for $i, k = 1, \ldots, n$ result in the n^2 equations

$$a_{i1}C_{k1} + a_{i2}C_{k2} + \cdots + a_{in}C_{kn} = \begin{cases} |\mathbf{A}| & \text{if } i = k \\ 0 & \text{if } i \neq k \end{cases} \qquad (*)$$

Note that each sum on the left-hand side looks very much like the kind of inner product that appears in the definition of matrix multiplication. In fact, the collection of all the n^2 different equations in $(*)$ can be reduced to the single matrix equation

$$\begin{pmatrix} a_{11} & a_{12} & \cdots & a_{1n} \\ \vdots & \vdots & & \vdots \\ a_{i1} & a_{i2} & \cdots & a_{in} \\ \vdots & \vdots & & \vdots \\ a_{n1} & a_{n2} & \cdots & a_{nn} \end{pmatrix} \begin{pmatrix} C_{11} & \cdots & C_{k1} & \cdots & C_{n1} \\ C_{12} & \cdots & C_{k2} & \cdots & C_{n2} \\ \vdots & & \vdots & & \vdots \\ C_{1n} & \cdots & C_{kn} & \cdots & C_{nn} \end{pmatrix} = \begin{pmatrix} |\mathbf{A}| & 0 & \cdots & 0 \\ 0 & |\mathbf{A}| & \cdots & 0 \\ \vdots & \vdots & \ddots & \vdots \\ 0 & 0 & \cdots & |\mathbf{A}| \end{pmatrix} \qquad (**)$$

The matrix on the right-hand side of $(**)$ equals the product $|\mathbf{A}| \cdot \mathbf{I}_n$ of the scalar $|\mathbf{A}|$ and the identity matrix. As for the left-hand side of $(**)$, let $\mathbf{C}^+ = (C_{ij})_{n \times n}$ denote the matrix of all the cofactors of $\mathbf{A}$. Then the second matrix in the product on the left-hand side is $\mathbf{C}^+$, except that its row and column indices have been interchanged. This makes it the *transpose* $(\mathbf{C}^+)'$ of $\mathbf{C}^+$. This special matrix is called the *adjugate* of $\mathbf{A}$, denoted by adj($\mathbf{A}$). That is

$$\text{adj}(\mathbf{A}) = (\mathbf{C}^+)' = \begin{pmatrix} C_{11} & \cdots & C_{k1} & \cdots & C_{n1} \\ C_{12} & \cdots & C_{k2} & \cdots & C_{n2} \\ \vdots & & \vdots & & \vdots \\ C_{1n} & \cdots & C_{kn} & \cdots & C_{nn} \end{pmatrix} \qquad (13.7.1)$$

SECTION 13.7 / A GENERAL FORMULA FOR THE INVERSE

Now definition (13.7.1) allows equation (∗∗) to be written as $\mathbf{A}\,\mathrm{adj}(\mathbf{A}) = |\mathbf{A}| \cdot \mathbf{I}_n$. In case $|\mathbf{A}| \neq 0$, this evidently implies that $\mathbf{A}^{-1} = (1/|\mathbf{A}|) \cdot \mathrm{adj}(\mathbf{A})$. To summarize:

THEOREM 13.7.1 (GENERAL FORMULA FOR THE INVERSE)

Any square matrix $\mathbf{A} = (a_{ij})_{n \times n}$ with determinant $|\mathbf{A}| \neq 0$ has a unique inverse $\mathbf{A}^{-1}$ satisfying $\mathbf{A}\mathbf{A}^{-1} = \mathbf{A}^{-1}\mathbf{A} = \mathbf{I}$. This inverse matrix is given by

$$\mathbf{A}^{-1} = \frac{1}{|\mathbf{A}|} \cdot \mathrm{adj}(\mathbf{A}) \tag{13.7.2}$$

If $|\mathbf{A}| = 0$, then there is no matrix $\mathbf{X}$ such that $\mathbf{AX} = \mathbf{XA} = \mathbf{I}$.

EXAMPLE 13.7.1 Use Theorem 13.7.1 to show that the matrix

$$\mathbf{A} = \begin{pmatrix} 2 & 3 & 4 \\ 4 & 3 & 1 \\ 1 & 2 & 4 \end{pmatrix}$$

has an inverse. Then find that inverse.

Solution: According to Theorem 13.7.1, the matrix $\mathbf{A}$ has an inverse if and only if $|\mathbf{A}| \neq 0$. Some computation determines that $|\mathbf{A}| = -5$. So the inverse exists. The cofactors of $\mathbf{A}$ are

$$C_{11} = \begin{vmatrix} 3 & 1 \\ 2 & 4 \end{vmatrix} = 10, \quad C_{12} = -\begin{vmatrix} 4 & 1 \\ 1 & 4 \end{vmatrix} = -15, \quad C_{13} = \begin{vmatrix} 4 & 3 \\ 1 & 2 \end{vmatrix} = 5$$

$$C_{21} = -\begin{vmatrix} 3 & 4 \\ 2 & 4 \end{vmatrix} = -4, \quad C_{22} = \begin{vmatrix} 2 & 4 \\ 1 & 4 \end{vmatrix} = 4, \quad C_{23} = -\begin{vmatrix} 2 & 3 \\ 1 & 2 \end{vmatrix} = -1$$

$$C_{31} = \begin{vmatrix} 3 & 4 \\ 3 & 1 \end{vmatrix} = -9, \quad C_{32} = -\begin{vmatrix} 2 & 4 \\ 4 & 1 \end{vmatrix} = 14, \quad C_{33} = \begin{vmatrix} 2 & 3 \\ 4 & 3 \end{vmatrix} = -6$$

By formulas (13.7.2) and (13.7.1), the inverse of $\mathbf{A}$ is

$$\mathbf{A}^{-1} = \frac{1}{|\mathbf{A}|} \begin{pmatrix} C_{11} & C_{21} & C_{31} \\ C_{12} & C_{22} & C_{32} \\ C_{13} & C_{23} & C_{33} \end{pmatrix} = -\frac{1}{5} \begin{pmatrix} 10 & -4 & -9 \\ -15 & 4 & 14 \\ 5 & -1 & -6 \end{pmatrix}$$

One should check the result by showing that $\mathbf{A}\mathbf{A}^{-1} = \mathbf{I}$.

Finding Inverses by Elementary Row Operations

Theorem 13.7.1 presented a general formula for the inverse of a nonsingular matrix. Although this formula is important theoretically, it is computationally useless for matrices much larger than 2×2.

Instead, an efficient way to find the inverse of an invertible $n \times n$ matrix $\mathbf{A}$ starts by first forming the $n \times 2n$ matrix $(\mathbf{A} \mid \mathbf{I})$ consisting of the n columns of $\mathbf{A}$, followed by a vertical bar, and then the n columns of $\mathbf{I}$. Next, we apply a sequence of elementary row operations systematically to successive $n \times 2n$ matrices in order to transform, if possible, the initial matrix $(\mathbf{A} \mid \mathbf{I})$ to a final matrix $(\mathbf{I} \mid \mathbf{B})$ whose first n columns form the identity matrix $\mathbf{I}$. If this transformation succeeds, it will follow that $\mathbf{B} = \mathbf{A}^{-1}$. But if it fails because the systematic procedure cannot be completed successfully, that will be because $\mathbf{A}$ has no inverse. The method is illustrated by the following example.

EXAMPLE 13.7.2   Use elementary row operations to find the inverse of

$$\mathbf{A} = \begin{pmatrix} 1 & 3 & 3 \\ 1 & 3 & 4 \\ 1 & 4 & 3 \end{pmatrix}$$

Solution: First, write down the 3×6 matrix

$$(\mathbf{A} \mid \mathbf{I}) = \begin{pmatrix} 1 & 3 & 3 & | & 1 & 0 & 0 \\ 1 & 3 & 4 & | & 0 & 1 & 0 \\ 1 & 4 & 3 & | & 0 & 0 & 1 \end{pmatrix}$$

whose first three columns are the columns of $\mathbf{A}$, and whose last three columns are those of the 3×3 identity matrix. The idea is now to use elementary operations on this matrix so that, in the end, the first three columns constitute an identity matrix. Then the last three columns will constitute the inverse of $\mathbf{A}$.

For the first step, we multiply the first row by -1 and add the result to the second row. This gives a zero in the second row and the first column. You should be able then to understand the other operations used and why they are chosen. Note that the last operation involves interchanging rows 2 and 3.

$$\begin{pmatrix} 1 & 3 & 3 & | & 1 & 0 & 0 \\ 1 & 3 & 4 & | & 0 & 1 & 0 \\ 1 & 4 & 3 & | & 0 & 0 & 1 \end{pmatrix} \sim \begin{pmatrix} 1 & 3 & 3 & | & 1 & 0 & 0 \\ 0 & 0 & 1 & | & -1 & 1 & 0 \\ 1 & 4 & 3 & | & 0 & 0 & 1 \end{pmatrix}$$

$$\sim \begin{pmatrix} 1 & 3 & 3 & | & 1 & 0 & 0 \\ 0 & 0 & 1 & | & -1 & 1 & 0 \\ 0 & 1 & 0 & | & -1 & 0 & 1 \end{pmatrix} \sim \begin{pmatrix} 1 & 0 & 3 & | & 4 & 0 & -3 \\ 0 & 0 & 1 & | & -1 & 1 & 0 \\ 0 & 1 & 0 & | & -1 & 0 & 1 \end{pmatrix}$$

$$\sim \begin{pmatrix} 1 & 0 & 0 & | & 7 & -3 & -3 \\ 0 & 0 & 1 & | & -1 & 1 & 0 \\ 0 & 1 & 0 & | & -1 & 0 & 1 \end{pmatrix} \sim \begin{pmatrix} 1 & 0 & 0 & | & 7 & -3 & -3 \\ 0 & 1 & 0 & | & -1 & 0 & 1 \\ 0 & 0 & 1 & | & -1 & 1 & 0 \end{pmatrix}$$

Hence $\mathbf{A}^{-1} = \begin{pmatrix} 7 & -3 & -3 \\ -1 & 0 & 1 \\ -1 & 1 & 0 \end{pmatrix}$, as can be checked by verifying that $\mathbf{A}\mathbf{A}^{-1} = \mathbf{I}$.

EXERCISES FOR SECTION 13.7

SM 1. Use Theorem 13.7.1 to calculate the inverses of the following matrices, if they exist:

(a) $\begin{pmatrix} 2 & 3 \\ 4 & 5 \end{pmatrix}$
(b) $\begin{pmatrix} 1 & 0 & 2 \\ 2 & -1 & 0 \\ 0 & 2 & -1 \end{pmatrix}$
(c) $\begin{pmatrix} 1 & 0 & 0 \\ -3 & -2 & 1 \\ 4 & -16 & 8 \end{pmatrix}$

2. Find the inverse of
$$\mathbf{A} = \begin{pmatrix} -2 & 3 & 2 \\ 6 & 0 & 3 \\ 4 & 1 & -1 \end{pmatrix}$$

SM 3. Find $(\mathbf{I} - \mathbf{A})^{-1}$ when
$$\mathbf{A} = \begin{pmatrix} 0.2 & 0.6 & 0.2 \\ 0 & 0.2 & 0.4 \\ 0.2 & 0.2 & 0 \end{pmatrix}$$

SM 4. Repeated observations of an empirical phenomenon lead to p different systems of equations

$$a_{11}x_1 + \cdots + a_{1n}x_n = b_{1k}$$
$$\cdots\cdots\cdots\cdots\cdots\cdots\cdots\cdots\cdots\cdots \quad (*)$$
$$a_{n1}x_1 + \cdots + a_{nn}x_n = b_{nk}$$

for $k = 1, \ldots, p$, which all share the same $n \times n$ coefficient matrix (a_{ij}). Explain how to find all p solutions $(x_{k1}, \ldots, x_{kn})$ $(k = 1, \ldots, p)$ of the system simultaneously by using elementary row operations to get

$$\begin{pmatrix} a_{11} & \cdots & a_{1n} & b_{11} & \cdots & b_{1p} \\ \vdots & \ddots & \vdots & \vdots & & \vdots \\ a_{n1} & \cdots & a_{nn} & b_{n1} & \cdots & b_{np} \end{pmatrix} \sim \begin{pmatrix} 1 & \cdots & 0 & b_{11}^* & \cdots & b_{1p}^* \\ \vdots & \ddots & \vdots & \vdots & & \vdots \\ 0 & \cdots & 1 & b_{n1}^* & \cdots & b_{np}^* \end{pmatrix}$$

What is the solution of the system of equations $(*)$ when there is an r such that the vector of right-hand sides has components b_{jr} for $j = 1, 2, \ldots, n$?

SM 5. Use the method of elementary row operations described in Example 13.7.2 in order to calculate the inverse, provided it exists, for each of the three matrices:

(a) $\mathbf{A} = \begin{pmatrix} 1 & 2 \\ 3 & 4 \end{pmatrix}$
(b) $\mathbf{B} = \begin{pmatrix} 1 & 2 & 3 \\ 2 & 4 & 5 \\ 3 & 5 & 6 \end{pmatrix}$
(b) $\mathbf{C} = \begin{pmatrix} 3 & 2 & -1 \\ -1 & 5 & 8 \\ -9 & -6 & 3 \end{pmatrix}$

13.8 Cramer's Rule

Cramer's rule for solving n linear equations in n unknowns is a direct generalization of the same rule for systems of equations with two or three unknowns, as set out in formulas

(13.1.4) and (13.2.5). Indeed, consider the system

$$\begin{aligned} a_{11}x_1 + a_{12}x_2 + \cdots + a_{1n}x_n &= b_1 \\ a_{21}x_1 + a_{22}x_2 + \cdots + a_{2n}x_n &= b_2 \\ &\vdots \\ a_{n1}x_1 + a_{n2}x_2 + \cdots + a_{nn}x_n &= b_n \end{aligned} \quad (13.8.1)$$

For $j = 1, \ldots, n$, let D_j denote the determinant obtained from $|\mathbf{A}|$ by replacing the original jth column with the alternative column whose elements are $b_1, b_2, \ldots, b_n$. Thus,

$$D_j = \begin{vmatrix} a_{11} & \cdots & a_{1,j-1} & b_1 & a_{1,j+1} & \cdots & a_{1n} \\ a_{21} & \cdots & a_{2,j-1} & b_2 & a_{2,j+1} & \cdots & a_{2n} \\ \vdots & & \vdots & \vdots & \vdots & & \vdots \\ a_{n1} & \cdots & a_{n,j-1} & b_n & a_{n,j+1} & \cdots & a_{nn} \end{vmatrix} \quad (13.8.2)$$

The cofactor expansion of D_j along its jth column is

$$D_j = C_{1j}b_1 + C_{2j}b_2 + \cdots + C_{nj}b_n \quad (13.8.3)$$

where the cofactors C_{ij} ($i = 1, 2, \ldots, n$) are given by (13.5.3). Now we have:

THEOREM 13.8.1 (CRAMER'S RULE)

The general linear system of equations (13.8.1) with n equations and n unknowns has a unique solution if and only if the coefficient matrix $\mathbf{A}$ is nonsingular ($|\mathbf{A}| \neq 0$). In this case the solution is

$$x_1 = \frac{D_1}{|\mathbf{A}|}, \quad x_2 = \frac{D_2}{|\mathbf{A}|}, \quad \ldots, \quad x_n = \frac{D_n}{|\mathbf{A}|} \quad (13.8.4)$$

where $D_1, D_2, \ldots, D_n$ are the determinants defined by (13.8.2).

A proof of the "if" part is as follows:

Proof of $\Leftarrow$: System (13.8.1) can be written in matrix form as $\mathbf{Ax} = \mathbf{b}$. Suppose that $|\mathbf{A}| \neq 0$. Then the inverse $\mathbf{A}^{-1}$ exists, and Eq. (13.6.6) implies that there is a unique solution $\mathbf{x} = \mathbf{A}^{-1}\mathbf{b}$. Using formulas (13.7.2) and (13.7.1), this solution can be expressed as

$$\begin{pmatrix} x_1 \\ x_2 \\ \vdots \\ x_n \end{pmatrix} = \frac{1}{|\mathbf{A}|} \begin{pmatrix} C_{11} & C_{21} & \cdots & C_{n1} \\ C_{12} & C_{22} & \cdots & C_{n2} \\ \vdots & \vdots & \ddots & \vdots \\ C_{1n} & C_{2n} & \cdots & C_{nn} \end{pmatrix} \begin{pmatrix} b_1 \\ b_2 \\ \vdots \\ b_n \end{pmatrix} \quad (*)$$

where the cofactors C_{ij} are given by (13.5.3). For each $j = 1, 2, \ldots, n$, the jth row of Eq. (∗) is

$$x_j = \frac{1}{|\mathbf{A}|}(C_{1j}b_1 + C_{2j}b_2 + \cdots + C_{nj}b_n) = \frac{D_j}{|\mathbf{A}|}$$

where the last equality follows from formula (13.8.3). This proves (13.8.4). ∎

The "only if" part is proved in detail in FMEA. Here, in the next subsection, we will merely give some intuition behind the argument.

EXAMPLE 13.8.1   For all values of p, find the solutions of the system

$$\begin{aligned} px + y &= 1 \\ x - y + z &= 0 \\ 2y - z &= 3 \end{aligned}$$

Solution: A cofactor expansion along its first row or column shows that the coefficient matrix has determinant

$$|\mathbf{A}| = \begin{vmatrix} p & 1 & 0 \\ 1 & -1 & 1 \\ 0 & 2 & -1 \end{vmatrix} = 1 - p$$

According to Theorem 13.8.1, the system has a unique solution if and only if $1 - p \neq 0$, or equivalently, if and only if $p \neq 1$. In this case, the determinants in (13.8.2) are

$$D_1 = \begin{vmatrix} 1 & 1 & 0 \\ 0 & -1 & 1 \\ 3 & 2 & -1 \end{vmatrix}, \quad D_2 = \begin{vmatrix} p & 1 & 0 \\ 1 & 0 & 1 \\ 0 & 3 & -1 \end{vmatrix} \quad \text{and} \quad D_3 = \begin{vmatrix} p & 1 & 1 \\ 1 & -1 & 0 \\ 0 & 2 & 3 \end{vmatrix}$$

Their values are respectively $D_1 = 2$, $D_2 = 1 - 3p$, and $D_3 = -1 - 3p$. Then, provided that $p \neq 1$, Eq. (13.8.4) yields the solution

$$x = \frac{D_1}{|\mathbf{A}|} = \frac{2}{1-p}, \quad y = \frac{D_2}{|\mathbf{A}|} = \frac{1-3p}{1-p}, \quad \text{and} \quad z = \frac{D_3}{|\mathbf{A}|} = \frac{-1-3p}{1-p}$$

On the other hand, in case $p = 1$, the first equation becomes $x + y = 1$. Yet adding the last two of the original three equations implies that $x + y = 3$. There is no solution to these two contradictory equations in case $p = 1$.[9] ∎

Homogeneous Systems of Equations

Consider the special case in which the right-hand side of the equation system (13.8.1) consists only of zeros. Then the system of n equations and n unknowns, whose matrix form is $\mathbf{Ax} = \mathbf{0}$, is called *homogeneous*. A homogeneous system always has the so-called *trivial solution* $x_1 = x_2 = \cdots = x_n = 0$. Often it is important to know when a homogeneous system has *nontrivial* solutions.

---

[9] It should be instructive to solve this problem by using Gaussian elimination, starting by interchanging the first two equations.

THEOREM 13.8.2 (NONTRIVIAL SOLUTIONS OF HOMOGENEOUS SYSTEMS)

Let $\mathbf{A}$ denote the coefficient matrix $(a_{ij})_{n \times n}$, and $\mathbf{0}$ denote the zero column n-vector. Then the homogeneous linear system takes the form

$$\mathbf{A}\mathbf{x} = \mathbf{0} \tag{13.8.5}$$

It has nontrivial solutions if and only if $|\mathbf{A}| = 0$.

As with Theorem 13.8.1, we prove one part of this result, the "only if" part in this case:

Proof of $\Rightarrow$: Suppose that $|\mathbf{A}| \neq 0$. Then the inverse $\mathbf{A}^{-1}$ exists, and Eq. (13.6.6) implies that there is a unique solution $\mathbf{x} = \mathbf{A}^{-1}\mathbf{0}$. Because $\mathbf{A}^{-1}\mathbf{0} = \mathbf{0}$, the system only has the trivial solution. In other words, *system (13.8.5) has nontrivial solutions only if the determinant $|\mathbf{A}|$ vanishes*.

As for the "if" part, concepts from FMEA can be used to show that in case $|\mathbf{A}| = 0$, the rank of $\mathbf{A}$ is less than n, so system (13.8.5) has at least one degree of freedom. That is, apart from the trivial solution, there are infinitely many nontrivial solutions which take the form $\alpha\mathbf{x}$ where $\mathbf{x} \neq \mathbf{0}$, and α is an arbitrary nonzero scalar.

Theorem 13.8.2 allows us to provide the following:

Proof: of $\Rightarrow$ *in Theorem 13.8.1:* In case $|\mathbf{A}| = 0$, there are two possibilities. First, the equation system (13.8.1), which we write in matrix form $\mathbf{A}\mathbf{x} = \mathbf{b}$, may have no solutions. Second, it may have at least one particular solution $\mathbf{x}^P$. But by Theorem 13.8.2 the corresponding homogeneous system $\mathbf{A}\mathbf{x} = \mathbf{0}$ certainly has solutions of the form $\alpha\mathbf{x}^H$, where $\mathbf{x}^H$ is a nonzero vector with $\mathbf{A}\mathbf{x}^H = \mathbf{0}$, and α is an arbitrary real number. Then all vectors of the form $\mathbf{x}^P + \alpha\mathbf{x}^H$ are also solutions of the equation system $\mathbf{A}\mathbf{x} = \mathbf{b}$. In particular, (13.8.1) has a unique solution only if $|\mathbf{A}| \neq 0$.

Suppose that $\mathbf{x}^P$ is any particular solution of $\mathbf{A}\mathbf{x} = \mathbf{b}$, and that $\hat{\mathbf{x}}$ is any alternative solution. Then $\mathbf{A}\hat{\mathbf{x}} = \mathbf{A}\mathbf{x}^P = \mathbf{b}$, implying that $\mathbf{A}(\hat{\mathbf{x}} - \mathbf{x}^P) = \mathbf{0}$. It follows that the general solution of $\mathbf{A}\mathbf{x} = \mathbf{b}$ is the sum $\mathbf{x} = \mathbf{x}^P + \mathbf{x}^H$ of any particular solution $\mathbf{x}^P$, plus any solution $\mathbf{x}^H$ of the homogeneous system $\mathbf{A}\mathbf{x} = \mathbf{0}$.

EXAMPLE 13.8.2 Find the values of λ for which the following system of equations has nontrivial solutions:

$$\begin{aligned} 5x + 2y + z &= \lambda x \\ 2x + y &= \lambda y \\ x + z &= \lambda z \end{aligned} \tag{$*$}$$

Solution: The variables x, y, and z appear on both sides of the equations, so we start by putting the system into standard form:

$$\begin{aligned} (5-\lambda)x + 2y + z &= 0 \\ 2x + (1-\lambda)y &= 0 \\ x + (1-\lambda)z &= 0 \end{aligned}$$

According to Theorem 13.8.2, this homogeneous system has a nontrivial solution if and only if the coefficient matrix is singular, or if and only if:

$$\begin{vmatrix} 5-\lambda & 2 & 1 \\ 2 & 1-\lambda & 0 \\ 1 & 0 & 1-\lambda \end{vmatrix} = 0$$

Using expansion by cofactors, it is routine to find the value of the determinant, which is $\lambda(1-\lambda)(\lambda-6)$. Hence, the equation system (∗) has nontrivial solutions if and only if $\lambda = 0, 1,$ or 6.[10]

EXERCISES FOR SECTION 13.8

SM 1. Use Cramer's rule to solve the following two systems of equations:

(i) $\begin{aligned} x + 2y - z &= -5 \\ 2x - y + z &= 6 \\ x - y - 3z &= -3 \end{aligned}$

(ii) $\begin{aligned} x + y &= 3 \\ x + z &= 2 \\ y + z + u &= 6 \\ y + u &= 1 \end{aligned}$

2. Use Theorem 13.8.1 to prove that the following system of equations has a unique solution for all values of b_1, b_2, b_3, and then find that solution.

$$\begin{aligned} 3x_1 + x_2 &= b_1 \\ x_1 - x_2 + 2x_3 &= b_2 \\ 2x_1 + 3x_2 - x_3 &= b_3 \end{aligned}$$

SM 3. Prove that the homogeneous system of equations

$$\begin{aligned} ax + by + cz &= 0 \\ bx + cy + az &= 0 \\ cx + ay + bz &= 0 \end{aligned}$$

has a nontrivial solution if and only if $a^3 + b^3 + c^3 - 3abc = 0$.

13.9 The Leontief Model

In order to illustrate why linear systems of equations are important in economics, we briefly discuss a simple example of the Leontief model.

EXAMPLE 13.9.1 Once upon a time, in an ancient land perhaps not too far from Norway, an economy had only three industries. These were fishing, forestry, and boat building.

---

[10] Using terminology explained in Section 13.10 below, this example asks us to find the eigenvalues of the coefficient matrix that appears on the left-hand side of system (∗).

(i) To produce each ton of fish requires the services of α fishing boats.

(ii) To produce each ton of timber requires β tons of fish, as extra food for the energetic foresters.

(iii) To produce each fishing boat requires γ tons of timber.

These are the only inputs needed for each of these three industries. Suppose there is no final (external) demand for fishing boats because their only use is to help catch fish. Find what gross outputs each of the three industries must produce in order to meet the final demands of d_1 tons of fish to feed the general population, plus d_2 tons of timber to build houses.

Solution: Let x_1 denote the total number of tons of fish to be produced, x_2 the total number of tons of timber, and x_3 the total number of fishing boats.

Consider first the demand for fish. Because βx_2 tons of fish are needed to produce x_2 units of timber, and because the final demand for fish is d_1, we must have $x_1 = \beta x_2 + d_1$. Note that producing fishing boats does not require any fish as an input, so there is no term with x_3.

In the case of timber, a similar argument shows that the equation $x_2 = \gamma x_3 + d_2$ must be satisfied. Finally, for boat building, only the fishing industry needs boats; there is no final demand in this case, and so $x_3 = \alpha x_1$. Thus, the following three equations must be satisfied:

$$\text{(i)} \ x_1 = \beta x_2 + d_1 \qquad \text{(ii)} \ x_2 = \gamma x_3 + d_2 \qquad \text{(iii)} \ x_3 = \alpha x_1 \qquad (*)$$

One way to solve these equations begins by using (iii) to insert $x_3 = \alpha x_1$ into (ii). This gives $x_2 = \gamma \alpha x_1 + d_2$, which inserted into (i) yields $x_1 = \alpha\beta\gamma x_1 + \beta d_2 + d_1$. Provided that $\alpha\beta\gamma \neq 1$, we can solve this last equation for x_1 to obtain $x_1 = (d_1 + \beta d_2)/(1 - \alpha\beta\gamma)$. The corresponding expressions for the two other variables are easily found. The results are:

$$x_1 = \frac{d_1 + \beta d_2}{1 - \alpha\beta\gamma}, \qquad x_2 = \frac{\alpha\gamma d_1 + d_2}{1 - \alpha\beta\gamma}, \qquad \text{and} \qquad x_3 = \frac{\alpha d_1 + \alpha\beta d_2}{1 - \alpha\beta\gamma} \qquad (**)$$

Clearly, this solution for (x_1, x_2, x_3) only makes sense when $\alpha\beta\gamma < 1$. Let us now think about the economic significance of this key inequality.

Suppose we fix the final demands (d_1, d_2) for fish and timber, and consider an increase in any one of the three parameters α, β and γ. This increase can be regarded as due to a decrease in the productivity of whichever industry is directly affected. Yet evidently all three output levels (x_1, x_2, x_3) given by $(**)$ must increase. This is because whichever industry has become less efficient requires more input from one other industry. Producing this affects the remaining industry in turn.

In general, consider any increases in the three parameters α, β and γ which together make $\alpha\beta\gamma$ approach 1. Then the economy is becoming so much less productive that all the required outputs levels given by $(**)$ tend to $+\infty$. Even worse, if $\alpha\beta\gamma > 1$, there is no solution to $(**)$ with x_1, x_2 and x_3 all positive unless we allow at least at least one of the pair (d_1, d_2) to become negative. This signifies that the economy has become so unproductive that it needs an outside supply of fish or timber in order to function. Or of boats if we replace equation (iii) of $(*)$ with $x_3 = \alpha x_1 + d_3$ where $d_3 < 0$. Note that as one moves from a productive economy to one that is unproductive, one passes through the critical case when $\alpha\beta\gamma = 1$ and so the solution in $(**)$ becomes undefined.

To summarize, if $\alpha\beta\gamma \geq 1$, then without some outside supplies it is impossible for this economy to meet any positive final demands for fish and timber, because production in the economy is too inefficient.

The General Leontief Model

In Example 13.9.1 we considered a simple example of the Leontief model. More generally, the Leontief model describes an economy with n interlinked industries, each of which produces a single good using only one process of production. To produce its output good, each industry typically uses inputs from at least some other industries. For example, the steel industry needs goods from the iron mining and coal industries, as well as from many other industries. In addition to supplying its own good to other industries that need it, each industry also faces an external demand for its product from consumers, governments, foreigners, and so on. The amount of each good needed to meet this external demand is called the *final demand*.

Given any industry i, let x_i denote the total number of units of good i that it is going to produce in a certain year. Furthermore, let

$$a_{ij} = \text{the number of units of good } i \text{ needed to produce one unit of good } j \qquad (13.9.1)$$

An important feature of the Leontief model is that the input requirements are assumed to be directly proportional to the amount produced. Thus

$$a_{ij}x_j = \text{the number of units of good } i \text{ needed to produce } x_j \text{ units of good } j \qquad (13.9.2)$$

In order that the combination of x_1 units of good 1, x_2 units of good 2, ..., and x_n units of good n can be produced, each industry i needs to supply a total of

$$a_{i1}x_1 + a_{i2}x_2 + \cdots + a_{in}x_n$$

units of good i. If we require industry i also to supply b_i units to meet final demand, then equilibrium between supply and demand requires that

$$x_i = a_{i1}x_1 + a_{i2}x_2 + \cdots + a_{in}x_n + b_i$$

The same goes for all $i = 1, 2, \ldots, n$. So we arrive at the following system of equations:

$$\begin{aligned} x_1 &= a_{11}x_1 + a_{12}x_2 + \cdots + a_{1n}x_n + b_1 \\ x_2 &= a_{21}x_1 + a_{22}x_2 + \cdots + a_{2n}x_n + b_2 \\ &\cdots\cdots\cdots\cdots\cdots\cdots\cdots\cdots\cdots\cdots\cdots \\ x_n &= a_{n1}x_1 + a_{n2}x_2 + \cdots + a_{nn}x_n + b_n \end{aligned} \qquad (13.9.3)$$

Note that in the first equation, x_1 appears on the left-hand side and also in the first term on the right-hand side. In the second equation, x_2 appears on the left-hand side and also in the second term on the right-hand side, and so on. To put system (13.9.3) into standard form, we move all terms involving $x_1, \ldots, x_n$ to the left-hand side, then rearrange. The result is the system of equations

$$\begin{aligned}
(1-a_{11})x_1 - \phantom{a_{21}x_1 +} a_{12}x_2 - \cdots - a_{1n}x_n &= b_1 \\
-a_{21}x_1 + (1-a_{22})x_2 - \cdots - a_{2n}x_n &= b_2 \\
\cdots\cdots\cdots\cdots\cdots\cdots\cdots\cdots\cdots\cdots\cdots\cdots\cdots\cdots \\
-a_{n1}x_1 - a_{n2}x_2 - \cdots + (1-a_{nn})x_n &= b_n
\end{aligned} \qquad (13.9.4)$$

This system of equations is called the *Leontief system*. The numbers $a_{11}, a_{12}, \ldots, a_{nn}$ are called *input* (or *technical*) *coefficients*. Given any collection of final demand quantities $(b_1, b_2, \ldots, b_n)$, a solution $(x_1, x_2, \ldots, x_n)$ of (13.9.4) will give outputs for each industry that are just enough to meet the combination of interindustry and final demands. Of course, since industrial activities are typically irreversible, only nonnegative values for x_i make sense.

It is natural to use matrix algebra to study the Leontief model. Define the matrices:

$$\mathbf{A} = \begin{pmatrix} a_{11} & a_{12} & \cdots & a_{1n} \\ a_{21} & a_{22} & \cdots & a_{2n} \\ \vdots & \vdots & \ddots & \vdots \\ a_{n1} & a_{n2} & \cdots & a_{nn} \end{pmatrix}, \quad \mathbf{x} = \begin{pmatrix} x_1 \\ x_2 \\ \vdots \\ x_n \end{pmatrix} \quad \text{and} \quad \mathbf{b} = \begin{pmatrix} b_1 \\ b_2 \\ \vdots \\ b_n \end{pmatrix} \qquad (13.9.5)$$

The elements of the matrix $\mathbf{A}$ are the input coefficients, so it is called the *input* or *Leontief matrix*. Recall that the element a_{ij} denotes the number of units of commodity i which is needed to produce one unit of commodity j.

With these definitions, system (13.9.3) can expressed as

$$\mathbf{x} = \mathbf{A}\mathbf{x} + \mathbf{b} \qquad (13.9.6)$$

This equation is evidently equivalent to the equation $\mathbf{x} - \mathbf{A}\mathbf{x} = \mathbf{b}$. If $\mathbf{I}_n$ denotes the identity matrix of order n, then $(\mathbf{I}_n - \mathbf{A})\mathbf{x} = \mathbf{I}_n\mathbf{x} - \mathbf{A}\mathbf{x} = \mathbf{x} - \mathbf{A}\mathbf{x}$. So Eq. (13.9.3) is equivalent to the following matrix version of system (13.9.4):[11]

$$(\mathbf{I}_n - \mathbf{A})\mathbf{x} = \mathbf{b} \qquad (13.9.7)$$

Suppose now that we introduce prices into the Leontief model, with p_i denoting the price of one unit of commodity i. Because a_{ij} denotes the number of units of commodity i needed to produce one unit of commodity j, the sum $a_{1j}p_1 + a_{2j}p_2 + \cdots + a_{nj}p_n$ is the total cost of the n commodities needed to produce each unit of commodity j. The expression

$$p_j - a_{1j}p_1 - a_{2j}p_2 - \cdots - a_{nj}p_n$$

is the difference between the price of one unit of commodity j and the cost of producing that unit. This is called *unit value added* in sector j, which we denote by v_j. Then for each sector $j = 1, 2, \ldots, n$, we have:

$$\begin{aligned}
p_1 - a_{11}p_1 - a_{21}p_2 - \cdots - a_{n1}p_n &= v_1 \\
p_2 - a_{12}p_1 - a_{22}p_2 - \cdots - a_{n2}p_n &= v_2 \\
\cdots\cdots\cdots\cdots\cdots\cdots\cdots\cdots\cdots\cdots\cdots\cdots \\
p_n - a_{1n}p_1 - a_{2n}p_2 - \cdots - a_{nn}p_n &= v_n
\end{aligned} \qquad (13.9.8)$$

---

[11] Note in particular that "$\mathbf{x} - \mathbf{A}\mathbf{x} = (1 - \mathbf{A})\mathbf{x}$" is nonsensical: $1 - \mathbf{A}$, with the number 1, is meaningless.

Note that the input–output coefficients a_{ij} appear in transposed order. Suppose we define

$$\mathbf{p} = \begin{pmatrix} p_1 \\ p_2 \\ \vdots \\ p_n \end{pmatrix} \quad \text{and} \quad \mathbf{v} = \begin{pmatrix} v_1 \\ v_2 \\ \vdots \\ v_n \end{pmatrix} \tag{13.9.9}$$

This allows us to write (13.9.8) in the matrix form $\mathbf{p} - \mathbf{A}'\mathbf{p} = \mathbf{v}$, or

$$(\mathbf{I}_n - \mathbf{A}')\mathbf{p} = \mathbf{v} \tag{13.9.10}$$

Now transpose each side of (13.9.10) while using Eq. (12.7.4). Because $\mathbf{I}'_n = \mathbf{I}_n$ and $(\mathbf{A}')' = \mathbf{A}$, the result is

$$\mathbf{p}'(\mathbf{I}_n - \mathbf{A}) = \mathbf{v}' \tag{13.9.11}$$

Evidently this is closely related to the system (13.9.7). See, for example, Exercise 7.

EXERCISES FOR SECTION 13.9

1. In Example 13.9.1, let $\alpha = 1/2$, $\beta = 1/4$, $\gamma = 2$, $d_1 = 100$, and $d_2 = 80$. Write down system (∗) in this case and find the solution of the system. Confirm that this solution is given by the general formulas in (∗∗).

2. Consider an economy which is divided into an agricultural sector labelled A, and an industrial sector labelled I. To produce one unit in sector A requires 1/6 unit from A and 1/4 unit from sector I. To produce one unit in sector I requires 1/4 unit from A and 1/4 unit from I. Suppose that the final demand in each of the two sectors is 60 units.

    (a) Write down the Leontief system for this economy.

    (b) How many units must each sector produce in order to meet the final demands?

3. Consider the Leontief model described by the equation system (13.9.4).

    (a) What is the interpretation of the condition that $a_{ii} = 0$ for all i.

    (b) What is the interpretation of the sum $a_{i1} + a_{i2} + \cdots + a_{in}$?

    (c) What is the interpretation of the row vector $(a_{1j}, a_{2j}, \ldots, a_{nj})$ of input coefficients?

    (d) Can you give any interpretation to the sum $a_{1j} + a_{2j} + \cdots + a_{nj}$?

4. Write down system (13.9.4) when $n = 2$, $a_{11} = 0.2$, $a_{12} = 0.3$, $a_{21} = 0.4$, $a_{22} = 0.1$, $b_1 = 120$, and $b_2 = 90$. What is the solution to this system?

5. Consider an input–output model with three sectors. Sector 1 is heavy industry, sector 2 is light industry, and sector 3 is agriculture. The input requirements per unit of output for each of these three sectors are given by the following table:

	Heavy industry	Light industry	Agriculture
Input of heavy industry goods	$a_{11} = 0.1$	$a_{12} = 0.2$	$a_{13} = 0.1$
Input of light industry goods	$a_{21} = 0.3$	$a_{22} = 0.2$	$a_{23} = 0.2$
Input of agricultural goods	$a_{31} = 0.2$	$a_{32} = 0.2$	$a_{33} = 0.1$

Suppose the final demands for the goods produced by these three industries are 85, 95, and 20 units, respectively. If x_1, x_2, and x_3 denote the number of units that have to be produced in the three sectors, write down the Leontief system for the problem. Verify that $x_1 = 150$, $x_2 = 200$, and $x_3 = 100$ is a solution.

6. Write down the input matrix for the simple Leontief model of Example 13.9.1. Compare the condition for efficient production discussed in that example with the requirement that the sum of the elements of each column in the input matrix be less than 1.

7. Suppose that $\mathbf{x} = \mathbf{x}_0$ is a solution of (13.9.3) and that $\mathbf{p}' = \mathbf{p}'_0$ is a solution of (13.9.11). Prove that $\mathbf{p}'_0 \mathbf{b} = \mathbf{v}' \mathbf{x}_0$.

13.10 Eigenvalues and Eigenvectors

Many applied problems, especially in dynamic economics, involve successive powers $\mathbf{A}^n$ ($n = 1, 2, \ldots$), of a square matrix $\mathbf{A}$. Let $\mathbf{x}$ be a given nonzero vector. If the dimension of $\mathbf{A}$ is very large, then it will usually be a major problem to compute $\mathbf{A}^5 \mathbf{x}$ or, even worse, $\mathbf{A}^{100} \mathbf{x}$. But suppose there is a scalar λ which, together with the given vector $\mathbf{x}$, happens to satisfy the special property that

$$\mathbf{A}\mathbf{x} = \lambda \mathbf{x} \tag{13.10.1}$$

In this case, we would have $\mathbf{A}^2 \mathbf{x} = \mathbf{A}(\mathbf{A}\mathbf{x}) = \mathbf{A}(\lambda \mathbf{x}) = \lambda \mathbf{A} \mathbf{x} = \lambda \lambda \mathbf{x} = \lambda^2 \mathbf{x}$ and, in general, $\mathbf{A}^n \mathbf{x} = \lambda^n \mathbf{x}$. Many of the properties of $\mathbf{A}$ and $\mathbf{A}^n$ can be deduced by finding the pairs $(\lambda, \mathbf{x})$ with $\mathbf{x} \neq \mathbf{0}$ that satisfy (13.10.1). These satisfy the following definition:

EIGENVALUES AND EIGENVECTORS

A nonzero vector $\mathbf{x}$ that solves (13.10.1) is called an *eigenvector* of $\mathbf{A}$, and the associated scalar λ is called an *eigenvalue*.

The eigenvalues and eigenvectors of a matrix are also referred to as its characteristic values and vectors.[12]

It should be noted that if $\mathbf{x}$ is an eigenvector associated with the eigenvalue λ, then so is $\alpha \mathbf{x}$ for every scalar $\alpha \neq 0$. The zero solution $\mathbf{x} = \mathbf{0}$ of (13.10.1) is not very interesting, of course, because $\mathbf{A}\mathbf{0} = \lambda \mathbf{0}$ for every square matrix $\mathbf{A}$ and every scalar λ.

---

[12] The English noun "eigenvalue" is a partial translation of the German noun "Eigenwert", which the mathematical giant David Hilbert (1862–1943) introduced in his 1912 work on integral equations. The German (and Dutch) word *eigen* translates roughly as the adjective "own", chosen to indicate that the linear function $\mathbf{A}\mathbf{x}$ on the left-hand side of Eq. (13.10.1) maps the nonzero vector $\mathbf{x}$ into a scalar multiple of itself. Latinate languages such as French, Italian, Portuguese, and Spanish also use phrases including a word meaning "own" or "self" to describe eigenvalues and eigenvectors.

Matrices of Order 2

In the case when $n = 2$, Eq. (13.10.1) reduces to

$$\begin{pmatrix} a_{11} & a_{12} \\ a_{21} & a_{22} \end{pmatrix} \begin{pmatrix} x_1 \\ x_2 \end{pmatrix} = \lambda \begin{pmatrix} x_1 \\ x_2 \end{pmatrix}$$

This is the matrix representation of the equation system

$$a_{11}x_1 + a_{12}x_2 = \lambda x_1$$
$$a_{21}x_1 + a_{22}x_2 = \lambda x_2$$

This system can be rewritten as

$$(a_{11} - \lambda)x_1 + a_{12}x_2 = 0$$
$$a_{21}x_1 + (a_{22} - \lambda)x_2 = 0$$

In matrix form, this is the system

$$(\mathbf{A} - \lambda \mathbf{I})\mathbf{x} = \mathbf{0} \tag{13.10.2}$$

where $\mathbf{I}$ denotes the identity matrix of order 2. According to Theorem 13.8.1, this homogeneous system has a solution $\mathbf{x} \neq \mathbf{0}$ if and only if its coefficient matrix has determinant $|\mathbf{A} - \lambda \mathbf{I}|$ that is *equal* to 0. Evaluating this 2×2 determinant, we get the equation

$$|\mathbf{A} - \lambda \mathbf{I}| = \begin{vmatrix} a_{11} - \lambda & a_{12} \\ a_{21} & a_{22} - \lambda \end{vmatrix} = \lambda^2 - (a_{11} + a_{22})\lambda + (a_{11}a_{22} - a_{12}a_{21}) = 0 \tag{13.10.3}$$

So the eigenvalues λ are the solutions of this quadratic equation, and the eigenvectors are the nonzero vectors $\mathbf{x}$ that satisfy system (13.10.2).

EXAMPLE 13.10.1 Find the eigenvalues and associated eigenvectors of the 2×2 matrix $\mathbf{A} = \begin{pmatrix} 1 & 2 \\ 3 & 0 \end{pmatrix}$.

Solution: For this matrix, the eigenvalue equation (13.10.3) becomes

$$|\mathbf{A} - \lambda \mathbf{I}| = \begin{vmatrix} 1 - \lambda & 2 \\ 3 & -\lambda \end{vmatrix} = \lambda^2 - \lambda - 6 = 0$$

This quadratic equation has the two solutions $\lambda_1 = -2$ and $\lambda_2 = 3$, which are the eigenvalues of $\mathbf{A}$.

For the eigenvalue $\lambda = \lambda_1 = -2$, the two equations of system (13.10.2) both reduce to $3x_1 + 2x_2 = 0$. Choosing $x_2 = t$, we have $x_1 = -\frac{2}{3}t$. The eigenvectors associated with $\lambda_1 = -2$, therefore, are the nonzero scalar multiples

$$\mathbf{x} = t \begin{pmatrix} -2/3 \\ 1 \end{pmatrix}, \quad t \neq 0$$

of the vector $\begin{pmatrix} -2/3 \\ 1 \end{pmatrix}$. Putting $t = -3s$, we can equivalently represent the eigenvectors as

$$\mathbf{x} = s \begin{pmatrix} 2 \\ -3 \end{pmatrix}, \quad s \neq 0$$

For the other eigenvalue $\lambda = 3$, system (13.10.2) implies that $x_1 = x_2$, so the associated eigenvectors are the nonzero scalar multiples

$$t \begin{pmatrix} 1 \\ 1 \end{pmatrix}, \quad t \neq 0$$

For a general 2×2 matrix $\mathbf{A}$, its eigenvalues λ_1 and λ_2 are the two roots of the quadratic equation (13.10.3). Given these roots, the left-hand side of Eq. (13.10.3) can be written as

$$\begin{aligned} \lambda^2 - (a_{11} + a_{22})\lambda + (a_{11}a_{22} - a_{12}a_{21}) &= (\lambda - \lambda_1)(\lambda - \lambda_2) \\ &= \lambda^2 - (\lambda_1 + \lambda_2)\lambda + \lambda_1\lambda_2 \end{aligned} \quad (13.10.4)$$

We see from Eq. (13.10.4) that the sum $\lambda_1 + \lambda_2$ of the eigenvalues is equal to $a_{11} + a_{22}$, the sum of the diagonal elements. This is also called the *trace* of the matrix, denoted by tr $\mathbf{A}$. The product $\lambda_1 \lambda_2$ of the eigenvalues is equal to $a_{11}a_{22} - a_{12}a_{21} = |\mathbf{A}|$. In symbols,

$$\lambda_1 + \lambda_2 = \operatorname{tr} \mathbf{A} \quad \text{and} \quad \lambda_1 \lambda_2 = |\mathbf{A}| \quad (13.10.5)$$

Many dynamic economic models involve a square matrix. Its eigenvalues determine the model's stability properties. It is important to know when the eigenvalues are real and what signs they have. In the 2×2 case, Eq. (13.10.3) is quadratic with roots

$$\begin{aligned} \lambda_{1,2} &= \tfrac{1}{2}(a_{11} + a_{22}) \pm \sqrt{\tfrac{1}{4}(a_{11} + a_{22})^2 - (a_{11}a_{22} - a_{12}a_{21})} \\ &= \tfrac{1}{2} \operatorname{tr} \mathbf{A} \pm \sqrt{\tfrac{1}{4}(\operatorname{tr} \mathbf{A})^2 - |\mathbf{A}|} \end{aligned} \quad (13.10.6)$$

These two roots are real if and only if $(\operatorname{tr} \mathbf{A})^2 \geq 4|\mathbf{A}|$ or $(a_{11} + a_{22})^2 \geq 4(a_{11}a_{22} - a_{12}a_{21})$, which is equivalent to $(a_{11} - a_{22})^2 + 4a_{12}a_{21} \geq 0$. In particular, if the matrix is symmetric because $a_{12} = a_{21}$, then we have the sum of two squares and so both eigenvalues are real. But Example 13.10.1 shows that a matrix may have real eigenvalues even if it is not symmetric. On the other hand, the following example shows that the 2×2 orthogonal matrix presented in part (b) of Exercise 12.7.7 has no real eigenvalues except in a degenerate case when it is either plus or minus the identity matrix.

EXAMPLE 13.10.2   Prove that any matrix $\mathbf{P} = \begin{pmatrix} p & -q \\ q & p \end{pmatrix}$ with $q \neq 0$ and $p^2 + q^2 = 1$ has no real eigenvalues.

Solution: In this case Eq. (13.10.3) becomes

$$|\mathbf{P} - \lambda \mathbf{I}| = \begin{vmatrix} p - \lambda & -q \\ q & p - \lambda \end{vmatrix} = (p - \lambda)^2 + q^2$$

It follows that $|\mathbf{P} - \lambda \mathbf{I}| > 0$ for all real λ except in the degenerate case when $q = 0$ and so $p = \pm 1$, implying that $\mathbf{P} = \pm \mathbf{I}_2$.

We conclude our treatment of 2×2 matrices with the following useful rules, which are implied by the discussion surrounding (13.10.6):

SECTION 13.10 / EIGENVALUES AND EIGENVECTORS 539

RULES FOR THE EIGENVALUES OF 2 × 2 MATRICES

For a 2 × 2 matrix $\mathbf{A}$, its two eigenvalues are real if and only if $(\operatorname{tr}\mathbf{A})^2 \geq 4|\mathbf{A}|$, which holds if (but *not* only if) the matrix is symmetric. In case the eigenvalues are real:

(a) both are positive if and only if $|\mathbf{A}| > 0$ and $\operatorname{tr}\mathbf{A} > 0$;
(b) both are negative if and only if $|\mathbf{A}| > 0$ and $\operatorname{tr}\mathbf{A} < 0$;
(c) they have opposite signs if and only if $|\mathbf{A}| < 0$;
(d) they coincide if and only if $|\mathbf{A}| = \frac{1}{4}(\operatorname{tr}\mathbf{A})^2$;
(e) there is a 0 eigenvalue if and only if $|\mathbf{A}| = 0$, and then the other eigenvalue is $\operatorname{tr}\mathbf{A}$.

Matrices of Order n

Let us turn briefly to the general case in which $\mathbf{A}$ is an $n \times n$ matrix. As in the 2 × 2 case, if $\mathbf{A}$ is an $n \times n$ matrix, then a scalar λ is an *eigenvalue* of $\mathbf{A}$ if there is a nonzero n-vector $\mathbf{x}$ such that Eq. (13.10.1) holds. In this case $\mathbf{x}$ is an *eigenvector* of $\mathbf{A}$ associated with λ. If the vector $\mathbf{x}$ has components $x_1, \ldots, x_n$, then (13.10.1) can be written as

$$
\begin{aligned}
(a_{11} - \lambda)x_1 + & \quad a_{12}x_2 + \cdots + \quad a_{1n}x_n = 0 \\
a_{21}x_1 + (a_{22} - \lambda)x_2 + \cdots + & \quad a_{2n}x_n = 0 \\
& \cdots \\
a_{n1}x_1 + & \quad a_{n2}x_2 + \cdots + (a_{nn} - \lambda)x_n = 0
\end{aligned}
\qquad (13.10.7)
$$

An eigenvector associated with λ is any non-trivial solution $(x_1, \ldots, x_n)$ of (13.10.7).

Once again, suppose we rewrite the system (13.10.7) in matrix form $(\mathbf{A} - \lambda\mathbf{I})\mathbf{x} = \mathbf{0}$, as in Eq. (13.10.2), where $\mathbf{I}$ now denotes the identity matrix of order n. Notice that this is the homogeneous matrix equation (13.8.5), but with the matrix $\mathbf{A}$ replaced by $\mathbf{A} - \lambda\mathbf{I}$. So according to Theorem 13.8.5, the equation $(\mathbf{A} - \lambda\mathbf{I})\mathbf{x} = \mathbf{0}$ has a non-trivial solution $\mathbf{x} \neq \mathbf{0}$ if and only if the coefficient matrix satisfies the equation $|\mathbf{A} - \lambda\mathbf{I}| = 0$.

To study the solutions to this equation, consider the function $p(\lambda)$ which is defined for all real λ by

$$
p(\lambda) = |\mathbf{A} - \lambda\mathbf{I}| = \begin{vmatrix} a_{11} - \lambda & a_{12} & \cdots & a_{1n} \\ a_{21} & a_{22} - \lambda & \cdots & a_{2n} \\ \vdots & \vdots & \ddots & \vdots \\ a_{n1} & a_{n2} & \cdots & a_{nn} - \lambda \end{vmatrix}
\qquad (13.10.8)
$$

In case $n = 2$, one has $p(\lambda) = (a_{11} - \lambda)(a_{22} - \lambda) - a_{12}a_{21}$, which is the quadratic function $\lambda^2 - \lambda \operatorname{tr}\mathbf{A} + |\mathbf{A}|$. The two roots λ_1 and λ_2, which equal the eigenvalues of $\mathbf{A}$, have a sum $\lambda_1 + \lambda_2$ equal to the trace $\operatorname{tr}\mathbf{A}$, and a product $\lambda_1\lambda_2$ equal to the determinant $|\mathbf{A}|$.

For $n > 2$, we state the following corresponding result for $n \times n$ matrices. It involves the *trace* of $\mathbf{A}$ defined by

$$\operatorname{tr}\mathbf{A} = a_{11} + a_{22} + \cdots + a_{nn}$$

THEOREM 13.10.1 (CHARACTERISTIC POLYNOMIAL)

The function $p(\lambda)$ defined by Eq. (13.10.8) is a polynomial of degree n called the *characteristic polynomial* of $\mathbf{A}$. The equation $p(\lambda) = 0$ has n roots (real or complex, possibly repeated) which are the n eigenvalues $\lambda_1, \lambda_2, \ldots, \lambda_n$. This polynomial takes the form

$$p(\lambda) = (-1)^n (\lambda - \lambda_1)(\lambda - \lambda_2) \ldots (\lambda - \lambda_n) = (-\lambda)^n + \text{tr}\,\mathbf{A}(-\lambda)^{n-1} + \cdots + |\mathbf{A}|$$

Moreover, the n eigenvalues of $\mathbf{A}$ satisfy

$$\text{tr}\,\mathbf{A} = \lambda_1 + \lambda_2 + \cdots + \lambda_n \quad \text{and} \quad |\mathbf{A}| = \lambda_1 \lambda_2 \ldots \lambda_n$$

Proof. Following Eq. (13.3.2), the determinant in Eq. (13.10.8) is the sum of $n!$ terms, each made up of the product of n terms that include exactly one element from each row and exactly one element from each column of the matrix $\mathbf{A} - \lambda \mathbf{I}$. One is the product $(a_{11} - \lambda)(a_{22} - \lambda) \cdots (a_{nn} - \lambda)$ of the n terms on the principal diagonal of $\mathbf{A} - \lambda \mathbf{I}$. This product is evidently a polynomial of degree n in λ whose two leading terms are $(-\lambda)^n$ and $\text{tr}\,\mathbf{A}(-\lambda)^{n-1}$. But the coefficient of λ^{n-1} in the polynomial $p(\lambda)$ is $(-1)^n(-\lambda_1 - \lambda_2 - \cdots - \lambda_n) = (-1)^{n-1}(\lambda_1 + \lambda_2 + \cdots + \lambda_n)$.

Each of the other $n! - 1$ products will be a polynomial of degree k in λ, where k is the number of diagonal elements in the product. This number satisfies $k \leq n - 2$ because, once $n - 1$ diagonal elements have been included, the one remaining diagonal element must also be included. Hence the overall sum of all the other $n! - 1$ products must be a polynomial of degree $n - 2$.

Finally, putting $\lambda = 0$ gives the constant term of the polynomial. Definition (13.10.8) implies that this is $p(0) = |\mathbf{A}|$. But it also equals $(-1)^n(-\lambda_1)(-\lambda_2)\ldots(-\lambda_n)$, so $|\mathbf{A}| = \lambda_1 \lambda_2 \ldots \lambda_n$. ∎

The equation

$$p(\lambda) = |\mathbf{A} - \lambda \mathbf{I}| = 0 \qquad (13.10.9)$$

is called the *characteristic equation* of $\mathbf{A}$. Because $p(\lambda)$ is a polynomial of degree n in λ, the fundamental theorem of algebra that was discussed in Section 4.7 implies that the characteristic Eq. (13.10.9) has *exactly n roots*, provided that we include complex roots and count any multiple roots appropriately. Because these roots may not all be real, a full understanding of eigenvalues and eigenvectors requires knowledge of *complex* numbers. We defer a more detailed study of this topic to FMEA. Here we conclude with an example of a 3×3 matrix.

EXAMPLE 13.10.3 Find the eigenvalues and the associated eigenvectors of the matrix

$$\mathbf{A} = \begin{pmatrix} 5 & -6 & -6 \\ -1 & 4 & 2 \\ 3 & -6 & -4 \end{pmatrix}$$

Solution: After some routine calculation, one can show that the characteristic polynomial satisfies

$$|\mathbf{A} - \lambda \mathbf{I}| = \begin{vmatrix} 5-\lambda & -6 & -6 \\ -1 & 4-\lambda & 2 \\ 3 & -6 & -4-\lambda \end{vmatrix} = -(\lambda - 2)^2(\lambda - 1)$$

Its two distinct roots $\lambda_1 = 1$ and $\lambda_2 = 2$ are the eigenvalues of $\mathbf{A}$.

For $\lambda_1 = 1$, the eigenvectors are the nonzero solutions of the matrix equation

$$(\mathbf{A} - \mathbf{I})\mathbf{x} = \begin{pmatrix} 4 & -6 & -6 \\ -1 & 3 & 2 \\ 3 & -6 & -5 \end{pmatrix} \begin{pmatrix} x_1 \\ x_2 \\ x_3 \end{pmatrix} = \begin{pmatrix} 0 \\ 0 \\ 0 \end{pmatrix}$$

By Gaussian elimination or some similar procedure, it can be shown that these solutions take the form

$$\mathbf{x} = t \begin{pmatrix} 3 \\ -1 \\ 3 \end{pmatrix}, \quad t \neq 0$$

For $\lambda_2 = 2$, the eigenvectors are the nonzero solutions of the equation system

$$3x_1 - 6x_2 - 6x_3 = 0$$
$$-x_1 + 2x_2 + 2x_3 = 0$$
$$3x_1 - 6x_2 - 6x_3 = 0$$

The three equations are all proportional, so only one of them is relevant. From the second equation, the solution is any nonzero (x_1, x_2, x_3) with $x_1 = 2x_2 + 2x_3$. The solution therefore takes the form

$$\mathbf{x} = \begin{pmatrix} 2s + 2t \\ s \\ t \end{pmatrix} = \begin{pmatrix} 2 \\ 1 \\ 0 \end{pmatrix} s + \begin{pmatrix} 2 \\ 0 \\ 1 \end{pmatrix} t$$

with s and t not both equal to 0.

EXAMPLE 13.10.4 Let $\mathbf{D} = \text{diag}[a_1, \ldots, a_n]$ be an $n \times n$ diagonal matrix with diagonal elements $a_1, \ldots, a_n$. The characteristic polynomial is

$$|\mathbf{D} - \lambda \mathbf{I}| = (a_1 - \lambda)(a_2 - \lambda) \cdots (a_n - \lambda)$$

Hence, the eigenvalues of $\mathbf{D}$ are precisely the diagonal elements of $\mathbf{D}$. Let $\mathbf{e}_j$ denote the jth unit vector in $\mathbb{R}^n$, defined so that its jth component is 1, but all the other components equal 0. Then $\mathbf{D}\mathbf{e}_j$ is a vector of the form $\lambda \mathbf{e}_j$, with all components except its jth equal to zero. In fact $\mathbf{D}\mathbf{e}_j = a_j \mathbf{e}_j$. It follows that, for any $j = 1, 2, \ldots, n$, every nonzero multiple of $\mathbf{e}_j$ is an eigenvector associated with the eigenvalue a_j.

EXAMPLE 13.10.5 Let $t = 0, 1, \ldots$ denote different time periods. Suppose we know that the evolution of some n-vector $\mathbf{x}$ of economic variables is governed by the following "difference equation": if the variables take the value $\mathbf{x}_t$ at time t, then in the next period they are given by $\mathbf{x}_{t+1} = \mathbf{A}\mathbf{x}_t$, where $\mathbf{A}$ is a known constant $n \times n$ coefficient matrix.

Suppose further that the evolution of this vector starts from an initial value $\mathbf{x}_0$. Then, by applying the difference equation $\mathbf{x}_{t+1} = \mathbf{A}\mathbf{x}_t$ repeatedly, we obtain

$$\mathbf{x}_1 = \mathbf{A}\mathbf{x}_0$$
$$\mathbf{x}_2 = \mathbf{A}\mathbf{x}_1 = \mathbf{A}\mathbf{A}\mathbf{x}_0 = \mathbf{A}^2\mathbf{x}_0$$
$$\mathbf{x}_3 = \mathbf{A}\mathbf{x}_2 = \mathbf{A}\mathbf{A}^2\mathbf{x}_0 = \mathbf{A}^3\mathbf{x}_0 \qquad (*)$$
$$\vdots$$
$$\mathbf{x}_t = \mathbf{A}\mathbf{x}_{t-1} = \mathbf{A}\mathbf{A}^{t-1}\mathbf{x}_0 = \mathbf{A}^t\mathbf{x}_0$$

Suppose too that $\mathbf{x}_0$ just happens to be an eigenvector for matrix $\mathbf{A}$, with associated eigenvalue λ. Then we will have

$$\mathbf{A}\mathbf{x}_0 = \lambda\mathbf{x}_0$$

In this case, the sequence in $(*)$ becomes, simply

$$\mathbf{x}_1 = \mathbf{A}\mathbf{x}_0 = \lambda\mathbf{x}_0$$
$$\mathbf{x}_2 = \mathbf{A}\mathbf{x}_1 = \mathbf{A}\lambda\mathbf{x}_0 = \lambda\mathbf{A}\mathbf{x}_0 = \lambda\lambda\mathbf{x}_0 = \lambda^2\mathbf{x}_0$$
$$\mathbf{x}_3 = \mathbf{A}\mathbf{x}_2 = \mathbf{A}\lambda^2\mathbf{x}_0 = \lambda^2\mathbf{A}\mathbf{x}_0 = \lambda^2\lambda\mathbf{x}_0 = \lambda^3\mathbf{x}_0 \qquad (**)$$
$$\vdots$$
$$\mathbf{x}_t = \mathbf{A}\mathbf{x}_{t-1} = \mathbf{A}\lambda^{t-1}\mathbf{x}_0 = \lambda^{t-1}\mathbf{A}\mathbf{x}_0 = \lambda^{t-1}\lambda\mathbf{x}_0 = \lambda^t\mathbf{x}_0$$

Now the equation $\mathbf{x}_t = \lambda^t\mathbf{x}_0$ describes the evolution, as time progresses, of the n-vector $\mathbf{x}$ of variables under the assumption that the initial value $\mathbf{x}_0$ is an eigenvector of the coefficient matrix. System $(**)$ also shows that the sign and magnitude of the associated eigenvalue are critical in determining this evolution. For example, if $\lambda = 1$, then the variables remain constant at all times, whereas if $\lambda = -1$, then they oscillate between $\mathbf{x}_0$ in even periods and $-\mathbf{x}_0$ in odd periods. Furthermore, if $|\lambda| < 1$, then all components of $\mathbf{x}_t$ converge to 0 as $t \to \infty$. But if $|\lambda| > 1$, then at least one component of $\mathbf{x}_t$ will diverge to infinity as $t \to \infty$.

EXERCISES FOR SECTION 13.10

(SM) 1. For each of the following matrices, find both the eigenvalues and the eigenvectors that are associated with each eigenvalue:

(a) $\begin{pmatrix} 2 & -7 \\ 3 & -8 \end{pmatrix}$ (b) $\begin{pmatrix} 1 & 4 \\ 6 & -1 \end{pmatrix}$ (c) $\begin{pmatrix} 2 & 0 & 0 \\ 0 & 3 & 0 \\ 0 & 0 & 4 \end{pmatrix}$

2. Suppose that the symmetric matrix $\mathbf{A} = \begin{pmatrix} a & b & c \\ b & d & e \\ c & e & f \end{pmatrix}$ is known to have the three eigenvalues $\lambda_1 = 3$, $\lambda_2 = 1$, and $\lambda_3 = 4$ with corresponding eigenvectors

$$\mathbf{v}_1 = \begin{pmatrix} 1 \\ 0 \\ -1 \end{pmatrix}, \quad \mathbf{v}_2 = \begin{pmatrix} 1 \\ 2 \\ 1 \end{pmatrix}, \quad \text{and} \quad \mathbf{v}_3 = \begin{pmatrix} 1 \\ -1 \\ 1 \end{pmatrix}$$

Determine the numerical values of a, b, c, d, e, f.

13.11 Diagonalization

We begin by noting a simple and useful result. Let $\mathbf{A}$ and $\mathbf{P}$ be $n \times n$ matrices with $\mathbf{P}$ invertible. Then

$$\mathbf{A} \quad \text{and} \quad \mathbf{P}^{-1}\mathbf{A}\mathbf{P} \quad \text{have the same eigenvalues} \tag{13.11.1}$$

This is true because the two matrices have the same characteristic polynomial:

$$|\mathbf{P}^{-1}\mathbf{A}\mathbf{P} - \lambda\mathbf{I}| = |\mathbf{P}^{-1}(\mathbf{A} - \lambda\mathbf{I})\mathbf{P}| = |\mathbf{P}^{-1}||\mathbf{A} - \lambda\mathbf{I}||\mathbf{P}| = |\mathbf{A} - \lambda\mathbf{I}|$$

where we made use of the product rule for determinants, as stated in part (vii) of Theorem 13.4.1, which also implies that $|\mathbf{P}^{-1}| = 1/|\mathbf{P}|$. The following theorem confirms this, as well as showing how the matrix $\mathbf{P}$ transforms each eigenvector of the first matrix into an eigenvector of the second matrix that is associated with the same eigenvalue.

THEOREM 13.11.1

Let $\mathbf{A}$ and $\mathbf{P}$ be $n \times n$ matrices with $\mathbf{P}$ invertible. Then the nonzero vector $\mathbf{x}$ is an eigenvector of $\mathbf{P}^{-1}\mathbf{A}\mathbf{P}$ with eigenvalue λ if and only if $\mathbf{P}\mathbf{x}$ is an eigenvector of $\mathbf{A}$ with the same eigenvalue λ.

Proof: First, note that if any n-vector $\mathbf{x}$ satisfies $\mathbf{P}\mathbf{x} = \mathbf{0}$, then because $\mathbf{P}$ is invertible, it follows that $\mathbf{x} = \mathbf{P}^{-1}\mathbf{P}\mathbf{x} = \mathbf{0}$. Conversely, if $\mathbf{x} \neq \mathbf{0}$, then $\mathbf{P}\mathbf{x} \neq \mathbf{0}$.

Let $\mathbf{B}$ denote $\mathbf{P}^{-1}\mathbf{A}\mathbf{P}$. Suppose that λ and $\mathbf{x} \neq \mathbf{0}$ are an eigenvalue and associated eigenvector of $\mathbf{B}$ because they jointly satisfy $\mathbf{B}\mathbf{x} = \lambda\mathbf{x}$. So $\mathbf{P}^{-1}\mathbf{A}\mathbf{P}\mathbf{x} = \lambda\mathbf{x}$. Multiplying the last equation on the left by the matrix $\mathbf{P}$ implies that

$$\lambda\mathbf{P}\mathbf{x} = \mathbf{P}\mathbf{P}^{-1}\mathbf{A}\mathbf{P}\mathbf{x} = \mathbf{I}\mathbf{A}\mathbf{P}\mathbf{x} = \mathbf{A}\mathbf{P}\mathbf{x}$$

Furthermore, $\mathbf{x} \neq \mathbf{0}$ implies that $\mathbf{P}\mathbf{x} \neq \mathbf{0}$. It follows that $\mathbf{P}\mathbf{x}$ is an eigenvector of $\mathbf{A}$ with eigenvalue λ.

For the converse, note that $\mathbf{B} = \mathbf{P}^{-1}\mathbf{A}\mathbf{P}$ implies $\mathbf{A} = \mathbf{P}\mathbf{B}\mathbf{P}^{-1} = \mathbf{Q}^{-1}\mathbf{B}\mathbf{Q}$ where $\mathbf{Q} = \mathbf{P}^{-1}$ and so $\mathbf{Q}^{-1} = \mathbf{P}$. Now apply the result of the first part of the proof with $\mathbf{A}$ and $\mathbf{P}$ replaced by $\mathbf{B}$ and $\mathbf{Q}$. It follows that if λ and $\mathbf{P}\mathbf{x} = \mathbf{y} \neq \mathbf{0}$ are an eigenvalue and associated eigenvector of $\mathbf{A} = \mathbf{Q}^{-1}\mathbf{BQ}$, then λ and $\mathbf{Qy} = \mathbf{P}^{-1}\mathbf{Px} = \mathbf{x}$ are an eigenvalue and associated eigenvector of $\mathbf{B}$.

Now we introduce the following key definition:

An $n \times n$ matrix $\mathbf{A}$ is *diagonalizable* if there exist an invertible $n \times n$ matrix $\mathbf{P}$ and an $n \times n$ diagonal matrix $\mathbf{D}$ such that

$$\mathbf{P}^{-1}\mathbf{AP} = \mathbf{D} \tag{13.11.2}$$

If $\mathbf{A}$ is diagonalizable, so that (13.11.2) holds, then either Eq. (13.11.1) or Theorem 13.11.1 implies that the matrices $\mathbf{A}$ and $\mathbf{D}$ have the same eigenvalues. But then Example 13.10.4 shows that the eigenvalues of the diagonal matrix $\mathbf{D}$ are its diagonal elements. It follows that $\mathbf{P}^{-1}\mathbf{AP} = \mathrm{diag}(\lambda_1, \ldots, \lambda_n)$ where $\lambda_1, \ldots, \lambda_n$ are the eigenvalues of $\mathbf{A}$. Two questions arise:

(A) Which square matrices are diagonalizable?

(B) If $\mathbf{A}$ is diagonalizable, how do we find the matrix $\mathbf{P}$ in (13.11.2)?

The answers to both of these questions are given in the next theorem:

THEOREM 13.11.2 (DIAGONALIZABLE MATRICES)

An $n \times n$ matrix $\mathbf{A}$ is diagonalizable if and only if there exists an invertible $n \times n$ matrix $\mathbf{P}$ whose columns are n eigenvectors $\mathbf{x}_1, \ldots, \mathbf{x}_n$ of $\mathbf{A}$, with $\lambda_1, \ldots, \lambda_n$ respectively as associated eigenvalues. In that case, one has

$$\mathbf{P}^{-1}\mathbf{AP} = \mathrm{diag}(\lambda_1, \ldots, \lambda_n) \tag{13.11.3}$$

Proof: Suppose that the matrix $\mathbf{P}$ with eigenvectors as columns is invertible. Now $\mathbf{AP}$ is the matrix whose jth column, for each $j = 1, 2, \ldots, n$, equals $\mathbf{Ax}_j$, and so $\lambda_j \mathbf{x}_j$ because of the hypothesis that $\mathbf{x}_j$ is an eigenvector with associated eigenvalue λ_j. But $\lambda_j \mathbf{x}_j$ is evidently the jth column of the matrix $\mathbf{PD}$ where $\mathbf{D} = \mathrm{diag}(\lambda_1, \ldots, \lambda_n)$. Since all n columns of the two matrices $\mathbf{AP}$ and $\mathbf{PD}$ are equal, we have $\mathbf{AP} = \mathbf{PD}$. Because $\mathbf{P}$ is invertible by hypothesis, we can premultiply by $\mathbf{P}^{-1}$ to obtain (13.11.3).

Conversely, if $\mathbf{A}$ is diagonalizable, then by definition (13.11.2) must hold. Premultiplying by $\mathbf{P}$ gives $\mathbf{AP} = \mathbf{PD}$. Then the columns of $\mathbf{P}$ must be eigenvectors of $\mathbf{A}$, and the diagonal elements of $\mathbf{D}$ must be the corresponding eigenvalues.

EXAMPLE 13.11.1   It follows from (13.11.3) that $\mathbf{A} = \mathbf{P}\,\mathrm{diag}(\lambda_1, \ldots, \lambda_n)\,\mathbf{P}^{-1}$. It follows from Exercise 3 that for any natural number m, one has

$$\mathbf{A}^m = \mathbf{P}\,\mathrm{diag}(\lambda_1^m, \ldots, \lambda_n^m)\,\mathbf{P}^{-1} \tag{13.11.4}$$

When $\mathbf{A}$ is diagonalizable, this offers a simple formula for computing $\mathbf{A}^m$ even if m is large.

The Symmetric Case

Many of the matrices encountered in economics are symmetric. One reason for this is the key role of symmetric matrices in the theory of multivariable optimization, the subject of Chapter 17. Though many non-symmetric matrices cannot be diagonalized, it turns out that *every* symmetric matrix is diagonalizable. Moreover, the invertible matrix **P** that appears in the diagonalization (13.11.3) of Theorem 13.11.2 has the special property of *orthogonality* that we have already encountered in Exercise 12.7.7 and in Example 13.10.2. Here is a formal definition:

An $n \times n$ matrix **P** is said to be *orthogonal* if it and its transpose **P**′ together satisfy $\mathbf{P}'\mathbf{P} = \mathbf{I}$, implying that $\mathbf{P}' = \mathbf{P}^{-1}$.

This definition implies that any matrix **P** is orthogonal if and only if its transpose **P**′ is also orthogonal. Furthermore, given any pair of vectors **x** and **y**, consider the dot product defined by (12.4.1) of the transformed vectors **Px** and **Py**. Because of Example 12.7.2, this must satisfy

$$(\mathbf{Px}) \cdot (\mathbf{Py}) = (\mathbf{Px})'(\mathbf{Py}) = \mathbf{x}'\mathbf{P}'\mathbf{P}\mathbf{y} = \mathbf{x}'\mathbf{I}\mathbf{y} = \mathbf{x}'\mathbf{y} = \mathbf{x} \cdot \mathbf{y}$$

From the subsequent respective definitions (12.9.3), (12.9.8), and (12.9.9), it follows that pre-multiplication by any orthogonal matrix **P** preserves the length $\sqrt{\mathbf{x} \cdot \mathbf{x}}$ of any vector **x**, as well as the orthogonality of and the angle between any pair of vectors **x** and **y**.

Let $\mathbf{x}_1, \ldots, \mathbf{x}_n$ denote the list of n column vectors of an orthogonal matrix **P**. Then their respective transposes $\mathbf{x}'_1, \ldots, \mathbf{x}'_n$ are the row vectors of the transposed matrix **P**′. With this notation, the orthogonality condition $\mathbf{P}'\mathbf{P} = \mathbf{I}$ is equivalent to a system of n^2 equations stating that, for all pairs (i,j), the inner product $\mathbf{x}'_i\mathbf{x}_j$ of columns i and j in **P** satisfies $\mathbf{x}'_i\mathbf{x}_j = 1$ if $i = j$, but $\mathbf{x}'_i\mathbf{x}_j = 0$ if $i \neq j$. Thus, following the definitions (12.9.8) and (12.9.3), we have the following result:

THEOREM 13.11.3 (CHARACTERIZATION OF AN ORTHOGONAL MATRIX)

The $n \times n$ matrix **P** is orthogonal if and only if its columns $\mathbf{x}_1, \ldots, \mathbf{x}_n$ are mutually orthogonal vectors, all of which have length 1.

For symmetric matrices, we now have the following important diagonalization result:[13]

---

[13] In 1904 Hilbert gave the name "spectral theory" to the study of the eigenvalues of linear operators, which are more general than square matrices. Only in the late 1920s was the close connection to the quantum mechanics of light spectra recognized.

THEOREM 13.11.4 (SPECTRAL THEOREM FOR SYMMETRIC MATRICES)

Suppose that the $n \times n$ matrix $\mathbf{A}$ is symmetric. Then:

(a) any eigenvalue of $\mathbf{A}$ is real;

(b) any two eigenvectors associated with different eigenvalues are orthogonal;

(c) there exists an $n \times n$ *orthogonal* matrix $\mathbf{P}$ with columns $\mathbf{v}_1, \mathbf{v}_2, \ldots, \mathbf{v}_n$ such that

$$\mathbf{P}^{-1}\mathbf{A}\mathbf{P} = \begin{pmatrix} \lambda_1 & 0 & \cdots & 0 \\ 0 & \lambda_2 & \cdots & 0 \\ \vdots & \vdots & \ddots & \vdots \\ 0 & 0 & \cdots & \lambda_n \end{pmatrix} \tag{13.11.5}$$

where, for $i = 1, 2, \ldots, n$, each diagonal element λ_i is an eigenvalue of $\mathbf{A}$ associated with the corresponding eigenvector $\mathbf{v}_i$ of length 1.

Proof:

(a) Suppose λ is any eigenvalue of $\mathbf{A}$, possibly complex, so that $\mathbf{A}\mathbf{x} = \lambda \mathbf{x}$ for some vector $\mathbf{x} \neq \mathbf{0}$ that may have complex components.[14] Then $(\overline{\mathbf{A}\mathbf{x}})'(\mathbf{A}\mathbf{x})$ is a real number ≥ 0. Also, because $\mathbf{A}$ is a symmetric matrix with real entries, one has $\overline{\mathbf{A}} = \mathbf{A} = \mathbf{A}'$ and $(\overline{\mathbf{A}\mathbf{x}})' = (\overline{\mathbf{A}}\overline{\mathbf{x}})' = \overline{\mathbf{x}}'\mathbf{A}$. So

$$0 \leq (\overline{\mathbf{A}\mathbf{x}})'(\mathbf{A}\mathbf{x}) = (\overline{\mathbf{x}}'\mathbf{A})(\mathbf{A}\mathbf{x}) = (\overline{\mathbf{x}}'\mathbf{A})(\lambda \mathbf{x}) = \lambda \overline{\mathbf{x}}'(\mathbf{A}\mathbf{x}) = \lambda \overline{\mathbf{x}}'(\lambda \mathbf{x}) = \lambda^2 \overline{\mathbf{x}}'\mathbf{x}.$$

Since $\overline{\mathbf{x}}'\mathbf{x}$ is a positive real number, it follows that λ^2 is real and ≥ 0. We conclude that λ is real.

(b) Suppose that $\mathbf{A}\mathbf{x}_i = \lambda_i \mathbf{x}_i$ and $\mathbf{A}\mathbf{x}_j = \lambda_j \mathbf{x}_j$ with $\lambda_i \neq \lambda_j$. Since $\mathbf{A}$ is symmetric, transposing the second equality yields $\mathbf{x}_j'\mathbf{A} = \lambda_j \mathbf{x}_j'$. Multiplying this equality on the right by $\mathbf{x}_i$ yields $\mathbf{x}_j'\mathbf{A}\mathbf{x}_i = \lambda_j \mathbf{x}_j'\mathbf{x}_i$, whereas multiplying the first equality on the left by $\mathbf{x}_j'$ yields $\mathbf{x}_j'\mathbf{A}\mathbf{x}_i = \lambda_i \mathbf{x}_j'\mathbf{x}_i$. But then we have $\lambda_i \mathbf{x}_i'\mathbf{x}_j = \lambda_j \mathbf{x}_i'\mathbf{x}_j$, which implies that $(\lambda_i - \lambda_j)\mathbf{x}_i'\mathbf{x}_j = 0$. Since $\lambda_i \neq \lambda_j$, it follows that $\mathbf{x}_i'\mathbf{x}_j = 0$. So $\mathbf{x}_i$ and $\mathbf{x}_j$ are orthogonal vectors.

(c) Our proof restricts attention to the case when there are n different eigenvalues $\lambda_1, \lambda_2, \ldots, \lambda_n$. By part (a), all the eigenvalues are real, and so therefore are the n associated eigenvectors $\mathbf{x}_1, \mathbf{x}_2, \ldots, \mathbf{x}_n$. According to part (b), because the eigenvalues are different, these eigenvectors are mutually orthogonal. Now replace each eigenvector $\mathbf{x}_j$ by $\mathbf{x}_j/\|\mathbf{x}_j\|$ so that the rescaled eigenvector has length 1. Consider the matrix $\mathbf{P}$ whose respective columns are the n rescaled eigenvectors. By Theorem 13.11.3, the $n \times n$ matrix $\mathbf{P}$ is orthogonal. Moreover, the matrix $\mathbf{P}$ satisfies the sufficiency condition in

---

[14] This proof is the only part of the book that uses *complex* numbers. These take the form $x = a + ib$, where a and b are real and i is the basic *imaginary* number defined to satisfy $i^2 = -1$. The *complex conjugate* of $x = a + ib$ is defined by $\bar{x} = a - ib$. There are similar definitions for the complex conjugate of any vector or matrix with complex components. Two key properties of complex conjugates used in the proof are that, for any complex n-vector $\mathbf{x}$ and any complex $n \times n$ matrix $\mathbf{A}$: (i) $\overline{\mathbf{x}}'\mathbf{x}$ is real and ≥ 0, with $\overline{\mathbf{x}}'\mathbf{x} > 0$ if $\mathbf{x} \neq \mathbf{0}$; (ii) $\overline{\mathbf{A}\mathbf{x}} = \overline{\mathbf{A}}\overline{\mathbf{x}}$.

Theorem 13.11.2 for **A** to be diagonalizable. Finally, Eq. (13.11.3) is satisfied, which implies Eq. (13.11.5).

In the general case when some of the eigenvalues may be coincident real roots of the characteristic equation, it is still possible to construct recursively n eigenvectors which form the columns of an orthogonal matrix. For a proof see, for example, Theorem 8.2.5 of Körner (2013).

EXERCISES FOR SECTION 13.11

SM 1. Verify Eq. (13.11.5) for the following matrices by finding the matrix **P** explicitly:

(a) $\begin{pmatrix} 2 & 1 \\ 1 & 2 \end{pmatrix}$
(b) $\begin{pmatrix} 1 & 1 & 0 \\ 1 & 1 & 0 \\ 0 & 0 & 2 \end{pmatrix}$
(c) $\begin{pmatrix} 1 & 3 & 4 \\ 3 & 1 & 0 \\ 4 & 0 & 1 \end{pmatrix}$

2. Let the matrices $\mathbf{A}_k$ and **P** be given by

$$\mathbf{A}_k = \begin{pmatrix} 1 & k & 0 \\ 3 & -2 & -1 \\ 0 & -1 & 1 \end{pmatrix} \quad \text{and} \quad \mathbf{P} = \begin{pmatrix} 1/\sqrt{10} & -3/\sqrt{35} & 3/\sqrt{14} \\ 0 & 5/\sqrt{35} & 2/\sqrt{14} \\ 3/\sqrt{10} & 1/\sqrt{35} & -1/\sqrt{14} \end{pmatrix}$$

(a) Find the characteristic equation of $\mathbf{A}_k$ and show that it has a root equal to 1.

(b) Determine the values of k that make all the eigenvalues of $\mathbf{A}_k$ real. What are its eigenvalues in case $k = 3$?

(c) Show that the columns of **P** are eigenvectors of $\mathbf{A}_3$, and compute the matrix product $\mathbf{P}'\mathbf{A}_3\mathbf{P}$. What do you see?

3. (a) Prove that if $\mathbf{A} = \mathbf{PDP}^{-1}$, where **P** and **D** are $n \times n$ matrices, then $\mathbf{A}^2 = \mathbf{PD}^2\mathbf{P}^{-1}$.

(b) Show by induction that $\mathbf{A}^m = \mathbf{PD}^m\mathbf{P}^{-1}$ for every positive integer m.

4. Use Eq. (13.11.1) to prove that if **A** and **B** are both invertible $n \times n$ matrices, then **AB** and **BA** have the same eigenvalues.

13.12 Quadratic Forms

Many applications of mathematics to economics, including our discussion of multivariable optimization in Chapter 17, use a special kind of function of n variables called a *quadratic form*. A general quadratic form in two variables is

$$Q(x_1, x_2) = a_{11}x_1^2 + a_{12}x_1x_2 + a_{21}x_2x_1 + a_{22}x_2^2 \tag{13.12.1}$$

It follows from the definition of matrix multiplication that

$$Q(x_1, x_2) = (x_1, x_2) \begin{pmatrix} a_{11} & a_{12} \\ a_{21} & a_{22} \end{pmatrix} \begin{pmatrix} x_1 \\ x_2 \end{pmatrix} \tag{13.12.2}$$

Of course, $x_1x_2 = x_2x_1$, so we can write $a_{12}x_1x_2 + a_{21}x_2x_1 = (a_{12} + a_{21})x_1x_2$. Suppose we replace each of a_{12} and a_{21} by their average $\frac{1}{2}(a_{12} + a_{21})$. Then the new numbers a_{12} and a_{21} become equal without changing $Q(x_1, x_2)$. Thus, in (13.12.1) we can assume that $a_{12} = a_{21}$. This makes the matrix $(a_{ij})_{2 \times 2}$ in (13.12.2) become symmetric, and then

$$Q(x_1, x_2) = a_{11}x_1^2 + 2a_{12}x_1x_2 + a_{22}x_2^2 \qquad (13.12.3)$$

Especially in optimization theory, we are often interested in conditions on the coefficients a_{11}, a_{12}, and a_{22} which ensure that $Q(x_1, x_2)$ in (13.12.3) has the same sign for all (x_1, x_2). Actually there are five cases to consider, depending on what happens to the sign of $Q(x_1, x_2)$ as the pair (x_1, x_2) assumes all possible values except $(0, 0)$ where $Q(x_1, x_2) = 0$ trivially. In fact, according as $Q(x_1, x_2) > 0$, $Q(x_1, x_2) \geq 0$, $Q(x_1, x_2) < 0$, or $Q(x_1, x_2) \leq 0$ for all $(x_1, x_2) \neq (0, 0)$, both the quadratic form $Q(x_1, x_2)$ and its associated symmetric matrix in (13.12.2) are said to be *positive definite, positive semidefinite, negative definite,* or *negative semidefinite*. There is a fifth case when there exist vectors (x_1^*, x_2^*) and (y_1^*, y_2^*) such that $Q(x_1^*, x_2^*) < 0$ and $Q(y_1^*, y_2^*) > 0$; then the quadratic form $Q(x_1, x_2)$ is said to be *indefinite*. Thus, an indefinite quadratic form assumes both negative and positive values. Indefiniteness should be seen as a commonly occurring case.

Sometimes we can see the sign of a quadratic form immediately, as in the next example.

EXAMPLE 13.12.1   Determine the definiteness of the following five quadratic forms:

$$Q_1 = x_1^2 + x_2^2, \quad Q_2 = -x_1^2 - x_2^2, \quad Q_3 = (x_1 - x_2)^2 = x_1^2 - 2x_1x_2 + x_2^2$$
$$Q_4 = -(x_1 - x_2)^2 = -x_1^2 + 2x_1x_2 - x_2^2, \quad Q_5 = x_1^2 - x_2^2$$

Solution: Q_1 is positive definite because it is always ≥ 0 and it is 0 only if both x_1 and x_2 are 0. Q_3 is positive semidefinite because it is always ≥ 0, but it is not positive definite because it is 0 if, say, $x_1 = x_2 = 1$. Q_5 is indefinite, because it is 1 for $x_1 = 1$, $x_2 = 0$, but it is -1 for $x_1 = 0$, $x_2 = 1$. Evidently, $Q_2 = -Q_1$ is negative definite and $Q_4 = -Q_3$ is negative semidefinite.

In Example 13.12.1 it was very easy to determine the sign of all five quadratic forms. In general, this task is harder. Nevertheless, in the case we have been considering of two variables and an associated 2×2 symmetric matrix, the old trick of completing the square is useful. Indeed, provided that $a_{11} > 0$, Eq. (13.12.3) implies that

$$Q(x_1, x_2) = a_{11}\left(x_1 + \frac{a_{12}}{a_{11}}x_2\right)^2 + \left(a_{22} - \frac{a_{12}^2}{a_{11}}\right)x_2^2 \qquad (13.12.4)$$

Now we have:

The quadratic form $Q(x_1, x_2)$ and its associated symmetric matrix $(a_{ij})_{2 \times 2}$ are:

(a)   positive definite $\iff a_{11} > 0$ and $a_{11}a_{22} - a_{12}^2 > 0$ (13.12.5)

(b)   positive semidefinite $\iff a_{11} \geq 0$, $a_{22} \geq 0$, and $a_{11}a_{22} - a_{12}^2 \geq 0$ (13.12.6)

(c)   negative definite $\iff a_{11} < 0$ and $a_{11}a_{22} - a_{12}^2 > 0$ (13.12.7)

(d)   negative semidefinite $\iff a_{11} \leq 0$, $a_{22} \leq 0$, and $a_{11}a_{22} - a_{12}^2 \geq 0$ (13.12.8)

Proof: To prove $\Leftarrow$ in part (a), suppose that $a_{11} > 0$ and $a_{11}a_{22} - a_{12}^2 > 0$. By (13.12.4), one has $Q(x_1, x_2) \geq 0$ for all (x_1, x_2). If $Q(x_1, x_2) = 0$, then $x_1 + a_{12}x_2/a_{11} = 0$ and $x_2^2 = 0$, so $x_1 = x_2 = 0$.

To prove $\Rightarrow$ in part (a), suppose $Q(x_1, x_2) > 0$ for all $(x_1, x_2) \neq (0, 0)$. In particular $Q(1, 0) = a_{11} > 0$. Hence (13.12.4) is valid, and so $Q(-a_{12}/a_{11}, 1) = (a_{11}a_{22} - a_{12}^2)/a_{11}$. Because $a_{11} > 0$ and $Q(-a_{12}/a_{11}, 1) > 0$, it follows that $a_{11}a_{22} - a_{12}^2 > 0$.

To prove $\Leftarrow$ in part (b), suppose first that $a_{11} \geq 0$, $a_{22} \geq 0$, and $a_{11}a_{22} - a_{12}^2 \geq 0$. In case $a_{11} = 0$, then $a_{11}a_{22} - a_{12}^2 \geq 0$ implies $a_{12} = 0$, and so $Q(x_1, x_2) = a_{22}x_2^2 \geq 0$ for all (x_1, x_2). But in case $a_{11} > 0$ and $a_{11}a_{22} - a_{12}^2 \geq 0$, Eq. (13.12.4) evidently implies that $Q(x_1, x_2) \geq 0$ for all (x_1, x_2).

To prove $\Rightarrow$ in part (b), suppose that $Q(x_1, x_2)$ is positive semidefinite. Then in particular one has $Q(1, 0) = a_{11} \geq 0$ and $Q(0, 1) = a_{22} \geq 0$. To find the sign of $a_{11}a_{22} - a_{12}^2$, consider first the case when $a_{11} > 0$ and so (13.12.4) is valid. Because Q is assumed to be positive semidefinite, one has $Q(-a_{12}/a_{11}, 1) = a_{22} - a_{12}^2/a_{11} \geq 0$, so $a_{11}a_{22} - a_{12}^2 \geq 0$. In the other case when $a_{11} = 0$ one has $Q(x_1, 1) = 2a_{12}x_1 + a_{22}$. Now $a_{12} \leq 0$ because otherwise choosing $x_1 < -\frac{1}{2}a_{22}/a_{12}$ would make $Q(x_1, 1) < 0$. Similarly $a_{12} \geq 0$ because otherwise choosing $x_1 > -\frac{1}{2}a_{22}/a_{12}$ would make $Q(x_1, 1) < 0$. It follows that $a_{12} = 0$ as well, and so $a_{11}a_{22} - a_{12}^2 = 0$.

Finally, parts (c) and (d) follow easily from parts (a) and (b) because $Q(x_1, x_2)$ is evidently negative definite or semidefinite if and only if $-Q(x_1, x_2) = -a_{11}x_1^2 - 2a_{12}x_1x_2 - a_{22}x_2^2$ is, respectively, positive definite or semidefinite. ∎

EXAMPLE 13.12.2   Use whichever of conditions (13.12.5)–(13.12.8) is appropriate in order to investigate the definiteness or semi definiteness of

(i) $Q(x_1, x_2) = 5x_1^2 - 2x_1x_2 + x_2^2$ (ii) $Q(x_1, x_2) = -4x_1^2 + 12x_1x_2 - 9x_2^2$

Solution: (a) Note that $a_{11} = 5$, $a_{12} = -1$ (not -2!), and $a_{22} = 1$. Thus $a_{11} > 0$ and $a_{11}a_{22} - a_{12}^2 = 5 - 1 = 4 > 0$. So (13.12.5) implies that $Q(x_1, x_2)$ is positive definite.

(b) Here $a_{11} = -4$, $a_{12} = 6$ (not 12), and $a_{22} = -9$. It follows that $a_{11} \leq 0$, $a_{22} \leq 0$, and $a_{11}a_{22} - a_{12}^2 = 36 - 36 = 0 \geq 0$. By (13.12.8), $Q(x_1, x_2)$ is negative semidefinite. ∎

Note: Conditions (13.12.5) and (13.12.7) say nothing about the sign of a_{22}. To explain why, note how $a_{11}a_{22} - a_{12}^2 > 0$ implies that $a_{11}a_{22} > a_{12}^2 \geq 0$, so $a_{11}a_{22} > 0$. It follows that either both a_{11} and a_{22} are positive, or both are negative. So it would be superfluous to add any condition on the sign of a_{22}.

In conditions (13.12.6) and (13.12.8), however, one cannot drop the condition on the sign of a_{22}. Consider for example $Q(x_1, x_2) = -x_2^2$, which is Eq. (13.12.1) with $a_{11} = 0$, $a_{12} = 0$, and $a_{22} = -1$. Even though $a_{11} \geq 0$ and $a_{11}a_{22} - a_{12}^2 = 1 \geq 0$, the quadratic form is evidently not positive semidefinite because $Q(0, 1) = -1 < 0$.

Quadratic Forms in n Variables

A *quadratic form* in n variables is a function Q that can be expressed as

$$Q(x_1, \ldots, x_n) = \sum_{i=1}^{n} \sum_{j=1}^{n} a_{ij} x_i x_j = a_{11} x_1^2 + a_{12} x_1 x_2 + \cdots + a_{ij} x_i x_j + \cdots + a_{nn} x_n^2$$
(13.12.9)

with constant coefficients a_{ij}. Each term in the double sum contains either the square x_i^2 of one variable, or the product $x_i x_j$ of exactly two distinct variables. To see the structure of the quadratic form better, we write it as:

$$\begin{aligned} Q(x_1, \ldots, x_n) = \;& a_{11} x_1^2 + a_{12} x_1 x_2 + \cdots + a_{1n} x_1 x_n \\ & + a_{21} x_2 x_1 + a_{22} x_2^2 + \cdots + a_{2n} x_2 x_n \\ & \quad \cdots\cdots\cdots\cdots\cdots\cdots\cdots\cdots\cdots \\ & + a_{n1} x_n x_1 + a_{n2} x_n x_2 + \cdots + a_{nn} x_n^2 \end{aligned}$$
(13.12.10)

Suppose we put $\mathbf{x} = (x_1, x_2, \ldots, x_n)'$ and $\mathbf{A} = (a_{ij})_{n \times n}$. By definition of matrix multiplication, it follows that

$$Q(x_1, \ldots, x_n) = Q(\mathbf{x}) = \mathbf{x}' \mathbf{A} \mathbf{x}$$
(13.12.11)

Following the argument we used to derive the symmetric expression (13.12.3) when $n = 2$, in (13.12.10) we can assume that $a_{ij} = a_{ji}$ for all i and j. Then $\mathbf{A}$ in (13.12.11) is the *symmetric matrix associated with Q*, and Q is a *symmetric quadratic form*.

EXAMPLE 13.12.3 Write $Q(x_1, x_2, x_3) = 3x_1^2 + 6x_1 x_3 + x_2^2 - 4x_2 x_3 + 8x_3^2$ in the matrix form (13.12.11) with $\mathbf{A}$ symmetric.

Solution: We first write Q as follows:

$$Q = 3x_1^2 + 0 \cdot x_1 x_2 + 3 x_1 x_3 + 0 \cdot x_2 x_1 + x_2^2 - 2 x_2 x_3 + 3 x_3 x_1 - 2 x_3 x_2 + 8 x_3^2$$

Then $Q = \mathbf{x}' \mathbf{A} \mathbf{x}$, where $\mathbf{A} = \begin{pmatrix} 3 & 0 & 3 \\ 0 & 1 & -2 \\ 3 & -2 & 8 \end{pmatrix}$ and $\mathbf{x} = \begin{pmatrix} x_1 \\ x_2 \\ x_3 \end{pmatrix}$.

Next, we want to generalize to general quadratic forms the definitions after (13.12.3) and associated characterization results like (13.12.5) to (13.12.8).

DEFINITENESS OF A QUADRATIC FORM

A quadratic form $Q(\mathbf{x}) = \mathbf{x}' \mathbf{A} \mathbf{x}$, as well as its associated symmetric matrix $\mathbf{A}$, are said to be *positive definite*, *positive semidefinite*, *negative definite*, or *negative semidefinite* according as, for all $\mathbf{x} \neq \mathbf{0}$, one has

$$Q(\mathbf{x}) > 0, \quad Q(\mathbf{x}) \geq 0, \quad Q(\mathbf{x}) < 0, \quad Q(\mathbf{x}) \leq 0$$

The quadratic form $Q(\mathbf{x})$ is said to be *indefinite* if there exist vectors $\mathbf{x}^*$ and $\mathbf{y}^*$ such that $Q(\mathbf{x}^*) < 0$ and $Q(\mathbf{y}^*) > 0$. Thus an indefinite quadratic form assumes both negative and positive values.

The easiest way to determine the definiteness of a quadratic form is often just to consider the signs of the eigenvalues of the associated matrix. Recall that, by Theorem 13.11.4, these eigenvalues are all real. Here is the elegant result:

THEOREM 13.12.1

Let $Q = \mathbf{x}'\mathbf{A}\mathbf{x}$ be a quadratic form, where the matrix $\mathbf{A}$ is symmetric. Let $\lambda_1, \lambda_2, \ldots, \lambda_n$ denote the (real) eigenvalues of $\mathbf{A}$. Then:

(a) Q is positive definite $\iff$ $\lambda_1 > 0, \lambda_2 > 0, \ldots, \lambda_n > 0$

(b) Q is positive semidefinite $\iff$ $\lambda_1 \geq 0, \lambda_2 \geq 0, \ldots, \lambda_n \geq 0$

(c) Q is negative definite $\iff$ $\lambda_1 < 0, \lambda_2 < 0, \ldots, \lambda_n < 0$

(d) Q is negative semidefinite $\iff$ $\lambda_1 \leq 0, \lambda_2 \leq 0, \ldots, \lambda_n \leq 0$

(e) Q is indefinite $\iff$ $\mathbf{A}$ has both positive and negative eigenvalues

Proof: By Theorem 13.11.4, there exists an orthogonal matrix $\mathbf{P}$ such that $\mathbf{P}'\mathbf{A}\mathbf{P} = \mathbf{P}^{-1}\mathbf{A}\mathbf{P}$ is the matrix $\operatorname{diag}(\lambda_1, \lambda_2, \ldots, \lambda_n)$. Given any column n-vector $\mathbf{x}$, let $\mathbf{y} = (y_1, y_2, \ldots, y_n)'$ be the column n-vector defined by $\mathbf{y} = \mathbf{P}^{-1}\mathbf{x}$. Then $\mathbf{x} = \mathbf{P}\mathbf{y}$, and also $\mathbf{x} = \mathbf{0}$ if and only if $\mathbf{y} = \mathbf{0}$. It follows that

$$\mathbf{x}'\mathbf{A}\mathbf{x} = \mathbf{y}'\mathbf{P}'\mathbf{A}\mathbf{P}\mathbf{y} = \mathbf{y}'\operatorname{diag}(\lambda_1, \lambda_2, \ldots, \lambda_n)\mathbf{y} = \lambda_1 y_1^2 + \lambda_2 y_2^2 + \cdots + \lambda_n y_n^2 \quad (13.12.12)$$

So $\mathbf{x}'\mathbf{A}\mathbf{x} \geq 0$ (resp. ≤ 0) for all $\mathbf{x} \neq \mathbf{0}$ if and only if $\mathbf{y}'\mathbf{P}'\mathbf{A}\mathbf{P}\mathbf{y} \geq 0$ (resp. ≤ 0) for all $\mathbf{y} \neq \mathbf{0}$. Also $\mathbf{x}'\mathbf{A}\mathbf{x} > 0$ (resp. < 0) for all $\mathbf{x} \neq \mathbf{0}$ if and only if $\mathbf{y}'\mathbf{P}'\mathbf{A}\mathbf{P}\mathbf{y} > 0$ (resp. < 0) for all $\mathbf{y} \neq \mathbf{0}$. Because $\mathbf{y}'\mathbf{P}'\mathbf{A}\mathbf{P}\mathbf{y} = \lambda_1 y_1^2 + \lambda_2 y_2^2 + \cdots + \lambda_n y_n^2$, parts (a)–(d) all follow immediately. Furthermore, case (e) occurs if and only if none of cases (a)–(d) are true. ∎

EXAMPLE 13.12.4

Use Theorem 13.12.1 to determine the definiteness of the quadratic form $Q = -x_1^2 + 6x_1 x_2 - 9x_2^2 - 2x_3^2$.

Solution: The symmetric matrix and corresponding characteristic polynomial associated with Q are

$$\mathbf{A} = \begin{pmatrix} -1 & 3 & 0 \\ 3 & -9 & 0 \\ 0 & 0 & -2 \end{pmatrix} \quad \text{and} \quad \begin{vmatrix} -1-\lambda & 3 & 0 \\ 3 & -9-\lambda & 0 \\ 0 & 0 & -2-\lambda \end{vmatrix}$$

The characteristic equation is

$$|\mathbf{A} - \lambda\mathbf{I}| = (-2 - \lambda)[(1 + \lambda)(9 + \lambda) - 9] = -(\lambda + 2)(\lambda^2 + 10\lambda)$$
$$= -\lambda(\lambda + 2)(\lambda + 10) = 0$$

So the eigenvalues are 0, -2, and -10. Because all are non positive, Theorem 13.12.1 tells us that the quadratic form is negative semidefinite (but not negative definite).

It should be noted that the definiteness of the quadratic form in Example 13.12.4 is most easily checked by noting that for all $(x_1, x_2, x_3) \neq (0, 0, 0)$ one has

$$Q = -x_1^2 + 6x_1x_2 - 9x_2^2 - 2x_3^2 = -(x_1 - 3x_2)^2 - 2x_3^2 \leq 0$$

with $Q < 0$ unless $x_1 = 3x_2$.

Characterization by Principal Minors

In order to generalize to $n \times n$ symmetric matrices the characterization results (13.12.5) to (13.12.8), we need a few new concepts. In Section 13.5 we defined the minors of a matrix. We need some particular minors in order to determine the definiteness of quadratic forms.

An arbitrary *principal minor* of order r in an $n \times n$ matrix $\mathbf{A} = (a_{ij})$ is the determinant of an $r \times r$ matrix obtained by deleting $n - r$ matching rows and columns of $\mathbf{A}$. That is, the ith row is deleted if and only if the ith column is also deleted. This implies that a principal minor of order r always includes exactly r elements of the main (principal) diagonal. The determinant $|\mathbf{A}|$ itself is also the particular principal minor in which no rows or columns are deleted.

A principal minor is called a *leading principal minor* of order r ($1 \leq r \leq n$) if it consists of the first ("leading") r rows and columns of $|\mathbf{A}|$. Thus, for each r, there are $\binom{n}{r}$ principal minors of order r, but only one leading principal minor of order r.

Note that if the matrix $\mathbf{A}$ is symmetric, then so is each matrix whose determinant is a principal minor.

EXAMPLE 13.12.5 Write down the principal and the leading principal minors of

$$\mathbf{A} = \begin{pmatrix} a_{11} & a_{12} \\ a_{21} & a_{22} \end{pmatrix} \quad \text{and} \quad \mathbf{B} = \begin{pmatrix} b_{11} & b_{12} & b_{13} \\ b_{21} & b_{22} & b_{23} \\ b_{31} & b_{32} & b_{33} \end{pmatrix}$$

Solution: By deleting row 2 and column 2 in $\mathbf{A}$ we get (a_{11}), which has determinant a_{11}. Deleting row 1 and column 1 in $\mathbf{A}$ we get (a_{22}), which has determinant a_{22}. The principal minors of $\mathbf{A}$ are therefore a_{11}, a_{22}, and $|\mathbf{A}|$. The *leading* principal minors are a_{11} and $|\mathbf{A}|$.

The principal minors of $\mathbf{B}$ are $|\mathbf{B}|$ itself, and

$$b_{11}, \quad b_{22}, \quad b_{33}, \quad \begin{vmatrix} b_{11} & b_{12} \\ b_{21} & b_{22} \end{vmatrix}, \quad \begin{vmatrix} b_{11} & b_{13} \\ b_{31} & b_{33} \end{vmatrix}, \quad \text{and} \quad \begin{vmatrix} b_{22} & b_{23} \\ b_{32} & b_{33} \end{vmatrix}$$

while the leading principal minors are b_{11}, $\begin{vmatrix} b_{11} & b_{12} \\ b_{21} & b_{22} \end{vmatrix}$, and $|\mathbf{B}|$ itself.

Suppose $\mathbf{A} = (a_{ij})_{n \times n}$ is an arbitrary $n \times n$ matrix. Its leading principal minors are

$$D_k = \begin{vmatrix} a_{11} & a_{12} & \cdots & a_{1k} \\ a_{21} & a_{22} & \cdots & a_{2k} \\ \vdots & \vdots & \ddots & \vdots \\ a_{k1} & a_{k2} & \cdots & a_{kk} \end{vmatrix}, \quad k = 1, 2, \ldots, n \tag{13.12.13}$$

For successive values of k, these are obtained from $\mathbf{A}$ according to the following pattern:

$$\begin{vmatrix} a_{11} & a_{12} & a_{13} & \cdots & a_{1n} \\ a_{21} & a_{22} & a_{23} & \cdots & a_{2n} \\ a_{31} & a_{32} & a_{33} & \cdots & a_{3n} \\ \vdots & \vdots & \vdots & \ddots & \vdots \\ a_{n1} & a_{n2} & a_{n3} & \cdots & a_{nn} \end{vmatrix} \tag{13.12.14}$$

Given any $k = 1, 2, \ldots, n$ and any subset K consisting of k elements chosen from the set $\{1, 2, \ldots, n\}$, let Δ_k^K denote the principal minor of order k. This is the determinant of the $k \times k$ submatrix of $\mathbf{A}$ whose diagonal elements form the set $\{a_{ii} : i \in K\}$. Evidently this definition implies that for each $k = 1, 2, \ldots, n$, the principal minor $\Delta_k^{\{1,2,\ldots,k\}}$ equals the leading principal minor D_k.

These definitions allow us to formulate the following theorem:

THEOREM 13.12.2 (SYLVESTER'S CRITERION)

Given the symmetric matrix $\mathbf{A}$, consider the quadratic form

$$Q(\mathbf{x}) = \sum_{i=1}^{n} \sum_{j=1}^{n} a_{ij} x_i x_j = \mathbf{x}' \mathbf{A} \mathbf{x}$$

For each $k = 1, \ldots, n$, let D_k denote the leading principal minor of order k defined by (13.12.13), and let Δ_k^K denote an arbitrary principal minor of $\mathbf{A}$ of order k. Then Q is:

(a)   positive definite $\iff D_k > 0$ for all $k = 1, \ldots, n$

(b)   positive semidefinite $\iff \Delta_k^K \geq 0$ for all Δ_k^K of any order k

(c)   negative definite $\iff (-1)^k D_k > 0$ for all $k = 1, \ldots, n$

(d)   negative semidefinite $\iff (-1)^k \Delta_k^K \geq 0$ for all Δ_k^K of any order k

For the case when $n = 2$ the conclusions of Theorem 13.12.2 are set out in (13.12.5)–(13.12.8), which have already been proved. For the case when $n > 2$, first note that if $\mathbf{B}$ is any $k \times k$ matrix, then rule (viii) of Theorem 13.4.1 implies that

$|-\mathbf{B}| = |(-1)\mathbf{B}| = (-1)^k|\mathbf{B}|$. But the quadratic form $Q = \sum\sum a_{ij}x_ix_j$ is negative definite (or semidefinite) if and only if $-Q = \sum\sum(-a_{ij})x_ix_j$ is positive definite (or semidefinite). It follows that parts (c) and (d) in Theorem 13.12.2 follow from parts (a) and (b) respectively.

For the important special case when $\mathbf{A}$ is a diagonal matrix, each principal minor Δ_k^K, or leading principal minor D_k, is the product of a subset of diagonal elements, which are also the eigenvalues of $\mathbf{A}$. Now Theorem 13.12.1 tells us how the definiteness of $\mathbf{A}$ is related to the signs of these eigenvalues, so Theorem 13.12.2 is easy to prove in this special case. For a proof that applies to a general symmetric matrix $\mathbf{A}$, see for example Section 7.6 of Meyer (2000).

WARNING: A rather common misconception is that to obtain a sufficient condition for a symmetric matrix $\mathbf{A}$ to be positive semidefinite, one can weaken each inequality $D_k > 0$ in part (a) of Theorem 13.12.2 to $D_k \geq 0$. Yet part (b) tells us that the condition for positive semidefiniteness involves the sign of *every* principal minor, not just every leading principal minor. For a counterexample see the note that follows Example 13.12.2.

EXAMPLE 13.12.6   Use Theorem 13.12.2 to determine the definiteness of the quadratic forms

(a) $Q = 3x_1^2 + 6x_1x_3 + x_2^2 - 4x_2x_3 + 8x_3^2;$ (b) $Q = -x_1^2 + 6x_1x_2 - 9x_2^2 - 2x_3^2.$

Solution: It makes sense to check the leading principal minors first, in case the matrix turns out to be definite rather than merely semidefinite.

(a) The associated symmetric matrix $\mathbf{A}$ was set out in Example 13.12.3. Its leading principal minors are

$$D_1 = 3, \quad D_2 = \begin{vmatrix} 3 & 0 \\ 0 & 1 \end{vmatrix} = 3, \quad \text{and} \quad D_3 = \begin{vmatrix} 3 & 0 & 3 \\ 0 & 1 & -2 \\ 3 & -2 & 8 \end{vmatrix} = 3$$

All are positive, so we conclude that Q is positive definite.

(b) We encountered this quadratic form already in Example 13.12.4. The associated symmetric matrix is

$$\mathbf{A} = \begin{pmatrix} -1 & 3 & 0 \\ 3 & -9 & 0 \\ 0 & 0 & -2 \end{pmatrix}$$

Note that the second row of $\mathbf{A}$ is -3 times its first row. Thus, the leading principal minors are $D_1 = -1$, $D_2 = 0$, and $D_3 = 0$. It follows that none of the conditions in parts (a), (b), or (c) of Theorem 13.12.2 are satisfied.

To check the conditions in part (d) of Theorem 13.12.2, we examine all the principal minors of $\mathbf{A}$, including those that are not leading. As in Example 13.12.5, the 3×3 matrix $\mathbf{A}$ has three principal minors of order 1 whose values are the three diagonal elements. So these principal minors satisfy

$(-1)^1\Delta_1^{\{1\}} = (-1)(-1) = 1, \quad (-1)^1\Delta_1^{\{2\}} = (-1)(-9) = 9, \quad (-1)^1\Delta_1^{\{3\}} = (-1)(-2) = 2$

There are also three second-order principal minors, which satisfy

$$\Delta_2^{\{1,2\}} = \begin{vmatrix} -1 & 3 \\ 3 & -9 \end{vmatrix} = 0, \quad \Delta_2^{\{1,3\}} = \begin{vmatrix} -1 & 0 \\ 0 & -2 \end{vmatrix} = 2, \quad \Delta_2^{\{2,3\}} = \begin{vmatrix} -9 & 0 \\ 0 & -2 \end{vmatrix} = 18$$

Hence $(-1)^2 \Delta_2^{\{1,2\}} = 0$, $(-1)^2 \Delta_2^{\{1,3\}} = 2$, and $(-1)^2 \Delta_2^{\{2,3\}} = 18$. Finally, the only third-order principal minor satisfies $(-1)^3 \Delta_3^{\{1,2,3\}} = (-1)^3 D_3 = 0$. It follows that for $k = 1, 2, 3$, one has $(-1)^k \Delta_k^K \geq 0$ for each principal minor Δ_k^K of order k in the matrix **A**. This verifies the sufficient condition in part (d) of Theorem 13.12.2. It follows that Q is negative semidefinite.

Our observation after Example 13.12.4 bears repeating: analysing the second quadratic form in Example 13.12.6 is much easier if one recognizes that $Q = -(x_1 - 3x_2)^2 - 2x_3^2$.

EXERCISES FOR SECTION 13.12

1. Use whichever of conditions (13.12.5)–(13.12.8) is appropriate in order to investigate the definiteness or semi definiteness of

   (a) $Q(x_1, x_2) = -x_1^2 + 2x_1 x_2 - 6x_2^2$ (b) $Q(x_1, x_2) = 4x_1^2 + 2x_1 x_2 + 25x_2^2$

2. Write out the double sum in Eq. (13.12.9) when $n = 3$ and $a_{ij} = a_{ji}$ for $i, j = 1, 2, 3$.

3. Find the symmetric matrix **A** that is associated with each of the following quadratic forms:

   (a) $x^2 + 2xy + y^2$ (b) $ax^2 + bxy + cy^2$ (c) $3x_1^2 - 2x_1 x_2 + 3x_1 x_3 + x_2^2 + 3x_3^2$

4. Find the symmetric matrix **A** that is associated with the quadratic form

   $$3x_1^2 - 2x_1 x_2 + 4x_1 x_3 + 8x_1 x_4 + x_2^2 + 3x_2 x_3 + x_3^2 - 2x_3 x_4 + x_4^2$$

SM 5. Using Theorem 13.12.1, or Theorem 13.12.2, or otherwise, determine the definiteness of

   (a) $Q = x_1^2 + 8x_2^2$ (b) $Q = 5x_1^2 + 2x_1 x_3 + 2x_2^2 + 2x_2 x_3 + 4x_3^2$

   (c) $Q = -(x_1 - x_2)^2$ (d) $Q = -3x_1^2 + 2x_1 x_2 - x_2^2 + 4x_2 x_3 - 8x_3^2$

6. Let $\mathbf{A} = (a_{ij})_{n \times n}$ be symmetric and positive semidefinite. Prove that

   $$\mathbf{A} \text{ is positive definite} \iff |\mathbf{A}| \neq 0$$

SM 7. For what values of c is the quadratic form $Q(x, y) = 3x^2 - (5 + c)xy + 2cy^2$: (i) positive definite; (ii) positive semidefinite; (iii) indefinite?

SM 8. Let **B** be an $n \times n$ matrix. Show that the matrix $\mathbf{A} = \mathbf{B}'\mathbf{B}$ is positive semidefinite. Can you find a necessary and sufficient condition on **B** for **A** to be positive definite rather than just positive semidefinite?

9. Use Theorem 13.12.2 to show that if the quadratic form $Q = \mathbf{x}'\mathbf{A}\mathbf{x}$ in (13.12.11) is positive definite, then: (a) $a_{ii} > 0$ for $i = 1, \ldots, n$; (b) $\begin{vmatrix} a_{ii} & a_{ij} \\ a_{ji} & a_{jj} \end{vmatrix} > 0$ for all $i, j = 1, \ldots, n$ with $i < j$.

10. [HARDER] Let **A** be a symmetric matrix. Write its characteristic polynomial (13.10.8) as

$$\varphi(\lambda) = (-1)^n(\lambda^n + a_{n-1}\lambda^{n-1} + \cdots + a_1\lambda + a_0)$$

Prove that **A** is negative definite if and only if $a_i > 0$ for $i = 0, 1, \ldots, n-1$.

REVIEW EXERCISES

1. Calculate the following determinants:

   (a) $\begin{vmatrix} 5 & -2 \\ 3 & -2 \end{vmatrix}$
   (b) $\begin{vmatrix} 1 & a \\ a & 1 \end{vmatrix}$
   (c) $\begin{vmatrix} (a+b)^2 & a-b \\ (a-b)^2 & a+b \end{vmatrix}$
   (d) $\begin{vmatrix} 1-\lambda & 2 \\ 2 & 4-\lambda \end{vmatrix}$

2. Calculate the following determinants, using suitable elementary row operations for (b) and (c):

   (a) $\begin{vmatrix} 2 & 2 & 3 \\ 0 & 3 & 5 \\ 0 & 4 & 6 \end{vmatrix}$
   (b) $\begin{vmatrix} 4 & 5 & 6 \\ 5 & 6 & 8 \\ 6 & 7 & 9 \end{vmatrix}$
   (c) $\begin{vmatrix} 31 & 32 & 33 \\ 32 & 33 & 35 \\ 33 & 34 & 36 \end{vmatrix}$

3. Find **A** when $\mathbf{A}^{-1} - 2\mathbf{I}_2 = -2\begin{pmatrix} 1 & 1 \\ 1 & 0 \end{pmatrix}$.

4. For each real t, let $\mathbf{A}_t = \begin{pmatrix} 1 & 0 & t \\ 2 & 1 & t \\ 0 & 1 & 1 \end{pmatrix}$ and $\mathbf{B} = \begin{pmatrix} 1 & 0 & 0 \\ 0 & 0 & 1 \\ 0 & 1 & 0 \end{pmatrix}$.

   (a) For what values of t does $\mathbf{A}_t$ have an inverse?

   (b) When $t = 1$, find a matrix **X** such that $\mathbf{B} + \mathbf{X}\mathbf{A}_1^{-1} = \mathbf{A}_1^{-1}$.

SM 5. Define the two 3×3 matrices $\mathbf{A} = \begin{pmatrix} q & -1 & q-2 \\ 1 & -p & 2-p \\ 2 & -1 & 0 \end{pmatrix}$ and $\mathbf{E} = \begin{pmatrix} 1 & 1 & 1 \\ 1 & 1 & 1 \\ 1 & 1 & 1 \end{pmatrix}$.

   (a) Calculate $|\mathbf{A}|$ and $|\mathbf{A} + \mathbf{E}|$.

   (b) For what values of p and q does $\mathbf{A} + \mathbf{E}$ have an inverse?

   (c) Why does the product matrix **BE** never have an inverse for any 3×3 matrix **B**?

6. Use Cramer's rule to find the values of t for which the system of equations

$$-2x + 4y - tz = t - 4$$
$$-3x + y + tz = 3 - 4t$$
$$(t-2)x - 7y + 4z = 23$$

has a unique solution for the three variables x, y, and z.

7. Prove that if **A** is any $n \times n$ matrix such that $\mathbf{A}^4 = \mathbf{0}$, then $(\mathbf{I} - \mathbf{A})^{-1} = \mathbf{I} + \mathbf{A} + \mathbf{A}^2 + \mathbf{A}^3$.

CHAPTER 13 / REVIEW EXERCISES **557**

SM **8.** Let $\mathbf{U}$ denote the $n \times n$ matrix where all n^2 elements are equal to 1.

(a) Show that $(\mathbf{I}_n + a\mathbf{U})(\mathbf{I}_n + b\mathbf{U}) = \mathbf{I}_n + (a + b + nab)\mathbf{U}$ for all real numbers a and b.

(b) Use the result in (a) to find the inverse of $\mathbf{A} = \begin{pmatrix} 4 & 3 & 3 \\ 3 & 4 & 3 \\ 3 & 3 & 4 \end{pmatrix}$.

9. Let $\mathbf{A}, \mathbf{B}, \mathbf{C}, \mathbf{X}$, and $\mathbf{Y}$ be $n \times n$ matrices, with $|\mathbf{A}| \neq 0$, which satisfy the two matrix equations $\mathbf{AX} + \mathbf{Y} = \mathbf{B}$ and $\mathbf{X} + 2\mathbf{A}^{-1}\mathbf{Y} = \mathbf{C}$. Find $\mathbf{X}$ and $\mathbf{Y}$ expressed in terms of $\mathbf{A}, \mathbf{B}$, and $\mathbf{C}$.

SM **10.** Consider the system of equations $\begin{cases} ax + y + 4z = 2 \\ 2x + y + a^2z = 2 \\ x \quad\;\; - 3z = a \end{cases}$ in the unknowns x, y, z.

(a) For what values of a does the system have one, none, or infinitely many solutions?

(b) Replace the right-hand sides of the system by b_1, b_2, and b_3, respectively. Find a necessary and sufficient condition for the new system of equations to have infinitely many solutions.

11. Let $\mathbf{A} = \begin{pmatrix} 11 & -6 \\ 18 & -10 \end{pmatrix}$.

(a) Compute $|\mathbf{A}|$. Show that there exists a real number c such that $\mathbf{A}^2 + c\mathbf{A} = 2\mathbf{I}_2$, and then find the inverse of $\mathbf{A}$.

(b) Show that there is no 2×2 matrix $\mathbf{B}$ such that $\mathbf{B}^2 = \mathbf{A}$.

12. Suppose $\mathbf{A}$ and $\mathbf{B}$ are invertible $n \times n$ matrices with $\mathbf{A}'\mathbf{A} = \mathbf{I}_n$. Show that $(\mathbf{A}'\mathbf{BA})^{-1} = \mathbf{A}'\mathbf{B}^{-1}\mathbf{A}$.

13. Examine for what values of the constants a and b the system of equations

$$ax + y = 3$$
$$x + z = 2$$
$$y + az + bu = 6$$
$$y + u = 1$$

has a unique solution in the unknowns x, y, z, and u. When it exists, find this unique solution, expressed in terms of a and b.

14. Prove that $\begin{vmatrix} a+x & b+y \\ c & d \end{vmatrix} = \begin{vmatrix} a & b \\ c & d \end{vmatrix} + \begin{vmatrix} x & y \\ c & d \end{vmatrix}$.

15. [HARDER] Suppose that the 3×3 matrix $\mathbf{B}$ satisfies the equation $\mathbf{B}^3 = -\mathbf{B}$. Show that $\mathbf{B}$ cannot have an inverse. (*Hint:* Use part (vii) of Theorem 13.4.1.)

SM **16.** [HARDER] Suppose that $\mathbf{A}, \mathbf{B}$, and $\mathbf{C}$ are $n \times n$ matrices that differ only in their rth rows, with the rth row in $\mathbf{C}$ equal to the sum of the rth rows of $\mathbf{A}$ and $\mathbf{B}$ respectively. Prove that then $|\mathbf{A}| + |\mathbf{B}| = |\mathbf{C}|$. (*Hint:* Consider the cofactor expansions of the determinants along the rth row.)

SM 17. [HARDER] Solve for x the equation
$$\begin{vmatrix} x & a & x & b \\ b & x & a & x \\ x & b & x & a \\ a & x & b & x \end{vmatrix} = 0$$

(*Hint:* Use elementary row or column operations to evaluate the determinant.)

18. Prove that λ is an eigenvalue of the matrix $\mathbf{A}$ if and only if λ is an eigenvalue of $\mathbf{A}'$.

19. Suppose $\mathbf{A}$ is a square matrix and let λ be an eigenvalue of $\mathbf{A}$. Prove that if $|\mathbf{A}| \neq 0$, then $\lambda \neq 0$. In this case, show that $1/\lambda$ is an eigenvalue of the inverse $\mathbf{A}^{-1}$.

20. Let $\mathbf{A} = (a_{ij})_{n \times n}$ be a matrix in which, for each $j = 1, 2, \ldots, n$, the jth column sum satisfies $\sum_{i=1}^{n} a_{ij} = 1$. Prove that $\lambda = 1$ is an eigenvalue of $\mathbf{A}$.

SM 21. For each of the following matrices, find both the eigenvalues and the eigenvectors associated with each of those eigenvalues:

(a) $\begin{pmatrix} 2 & 1 & -1 \\ 0 & 1 & 1 \\ 2 & 0 & -2 \end{pmatrix}$ (b) $\begin{pmatrix} 1 & -1 & 0 \\ -1 & 2 & -1 \\ 0 & -1 & 1 \end{pmatrix}$

(*Hint:* The eigenvalues are all integers.)

IV

MULTIVARIABLE CALCULUS

14 FUNCTIONS OF MANY VARIABLES

Mathematics is not a careful march down a well-cleared highway, but a journey into a strange wilderness, where the explorers often get lost.
—William S. Anglin (1992)

The first two parts of this book were concerned almost exclusively with functions of one variable. Yet a realistic description of economic phenomena often requires considering a large number of variables. For example, one consumer's demand for a good like orange juice depends not only on its price, but also on the consumer's income, as well as on the prices of substitutes like other soft drinks, or complements like some kinds of food.

So we now move on to functions of several variables. Most of what economists need to know about them consists of relatively simple extensions of properties presented in the previous chapters for functions of one variable. Moreover, most of the difficulties already arise in the transition from one variable to two variables. To help readers see how to overcome these difficulties, Sections 14.1 to 14.3 deal exclusively with functions of two variables. These have graphs in three dimensions which can be represented even in two-dimensional figures, though with some difficulty. However, as the previous example of the demand for orange juice suggests, there are many interesting economic problems that can only be represented mathematically by functions of many variables. These are discussed in Sections 14.4 to 14.9. We devote the final Section 14.10 to the economically important topic of elasticity.

14.1 Functions of Two Variables

We begin with the following definition, where D is a subset of the xy-plane.

FUNCTIONS OF TWO VARIABLES

> A *function f of two real variables x and y with domain D* is a rule that assigns a specified number
>
> $$f(x,y) \text{ to each point } (x,y) \text{ in } D. \qquad (14.1.1)$$

If f is a function of two variables, we often let a letter like z denote the value of f at a point (x, y), so $z = f(x, y)$. Then we call x and y the *independent variables*, or the *arguments* of f, whereas z is called the *dependent variable*. This is because the value z, in general, depends on the values of x and y. The *domain* of the function f is then the set of all pairs (x, y) of the independent variables where $f(x, y)$ is defined, whereas its *range* is the set of corresponding values of the dependent variable. In economics, x and y are often called the *exogenous* variables, whereas z is the *endogenous* variable.[1]

EXAMPLE 14.1.1 Consider the function f that, to every pair of real numbers (x, y), assigns the number $2x + x^2y^3$. The function f is thus defined by

$$f(x,y) = 2x + x^2y^3$$

What are $f(1, 0), f(0, 1), f(-2, 3)$, and $f(a+1, b)$?

Solution: First, $f(1, 0)$ is the value when $x = 1$ and $y = 0$. So $f(1, 0) = 2 \cdot 1 + 1^2 \cdot 0^3 = 2$. Similarly, we have $f(0, 1) = 2 \cdot 0 + 0^2 \cdot 1^3 = 0$, and then $f(-2, 3) = 2(-2) + (-2)^2 \cdot 3^3 = -4 + 4 \cdot 27 = 104$. Finally, we find $f(a+1, b)$ by replacing x with $a+1$ and y with b in the formula for $f(x, y)$, which gives $f(a+1, b) = 2(a+1) + (a+1)^2 b^3$.

EXAMPLE 14.1.2 A study of the demand for milk found the relationship

$$x = A \frac{m^{2.08}}{p^{1.5}}$$

where x is milk consumption, p is the relative price of milk, m is income per family, and A is a positive constant. This equation defines x as a function of p and m whenever both are positive. Note that, as seems reasonable, milk consumption goes up when income increases, and down when the price of milk increases.

EXAMPLE 14.1.3 A function of two variables appearing in many economic models is

$$F(x,y) = Ax^a y^b \qquad (14.1.2)$$

where A, a, and b are constants. Economists usually assume that F is defined only for $x > 0$ and $y > 0$.

---

[1] In economic models with several simultaneous equations, the distinction between exogenous and endogenous variables is much more nuanced.

A function F of the form (14.1.2) is generally called a *Cobb–Douglas function*.[2] It is most often used to describe certain production processes. Then x and y are called *input factors*, while $F(x, y)$ is the number of units produced, or the *output*. In this case, F is called a *production function*.

Note that the function defined in Example 14.1.2 is a Cobb–Douglas function, because we have $x = Ap^{-1.5}m^{2.08}$.

It is important to become thoroughly familiar with standard functional notation.

EXAMPLE 14.1.4   For the function F specified in Example 14.1.3, find expressions for $F(2x, 2y)$ and for $F(tx, ty)$, where t is an arbitrary positive number. Find also an expression for $F(x + h, y) - F(x, y)$. Give economic interpretations.

Solution: We find that

$$F(2x, 2y) = A(2x)^a(2y)^b = A2^a x^a 2^b y^b = 2^a 2^b A x^a y^b = 2^{a+b} F(x, y)$$

When F is a production function, this shows that if each of the input factors is doubled, then the output is 2^{a+b} times as large. For example, if $a + b = 1$, then doubling both inputs will double the output. In the general case,

$$F(tx, ty) = A(tx)^a(ty)^b = A t^a x^a t^b y^b = t^a t^b A x^a y^b = t^{a+b} F(x, y) \qquad (*)$$

(How do you formulate this result in your own words?)[3]

Finally, we see that

$$F(x + h, y) - F(x, y) = A(x + h)^a y^b - A x^a y^b = A y^b [(x + h)^a - x^a] \qquad (**)$$

This shows the change in output when the first input factor is changed by h units while the other input factor is unchanged. For example, suppose $A = 100$, $a = 1/2$, and $b = 1/4$, in which case $F(x, y) = 100 x^{1/2} y^{1/4}$. If we now choose $x = 16$, $y = 16$, and $h = 1$, then $(**)$ implies that the change of output is

$$F(16 + 1, 16) - F(16, 16) = 100 \cdot 16^{1/4}[17^{1/2} - 16^{1/2}] = 100 \cdot 2[\sqrt{17} - 4] \approx 24.6$$

Hence, if we increase the input of the first factor from 16 to 17, while keeping the input of the second factor constant at 16 units, then we increase production by about 24.6 units.

Domains

For functions studied in economics, there are usually explicit or implicit restrictions on the domain where the function is defined. For instance, if $f(x, y)$ is a production function, we usually assume that the input quantities are nonnegative, so $x \geq 0$ and $y \geq 0$. In economics, it is often crucially important to be clear what are the domains of the functions being used.

---

[2] The function in (14.1.2) is named after American researchers C.W. Cobb and P.H. Douglas, who applied it, with $a + b = 1$, in a paper that appeared in 1927 on the estimation of production functions. The function, however, should properly be called a "Wicksell function", because the Swedish economist K. Wicksell (1851–1926) introduced such production functions before 1900.

[3] Because of property $(*)$, we call function F *homogeneous of degree* $a + b$. Homogeneous functions are discussed in Sections 15.6 and 15.7.

In the same way as for functions of one variable, we assume, unless otherwise stated, that the domain of a function defined by a formula is the largest domain in which that formula gives a meaningful and unique value.

Sometimes it is helpful to draw a graph of the domain D in the xy-plane.

EXAMPLE 14.1.5   For each of the two functions specified by the following formulas, determine its domain, then draw the graph of that domain in the xy-plane.

(a) $f(x, y) = \sqrt{x-1} + \sqrt{y}$ (b) $g(x, y) = \dfrac{2}{(x^2 + y^2 - 4)^{1/2}} + \sqrt{9 - (x^2 + y^2)}$

Solution: (a) The two square roots $\sqrt{x-1}$ and $\sqrt{y}$ only have meaning in case $x \geq 1$ and $y \geq 0$. The (unbounded) domain where both these inequalities are satisfied is indicated in Fig. 14.1.1.

(b) The square root $(x^2 + y^2 - 4)^{1/2} = \sqrt{x^2 + y^2 - 4}$ is only defined if $x^2 + y^2 \geq 4$. We must also have $x^2 + y^2 \neq 4$, otherwise the denominator would be 0. Moreover we require that $9 - (x^2 + y^2) \geq 0$, or $x^2 + y^2 \leq 9$. All in all, therefore, we must have $4 < x^2 + y^2 \leq 9$. Now the graph of $x^2 + y^2 = r^2$ consists of all the points on the circle with centre at the origin and radius r. So the domain of g is the set of points (x, y) that lie both: (i) outside, but not on, the circle $x^2 + y^2 = 4$; and (ii) inside or on the circle $x^2 + y^2 = 9$. This set is shown in Fig. 14.1.2, where the solid circle is in the domain, but the dashed circle is excluded from it.

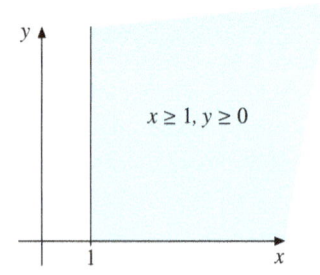

Figure 14.1.1 Domain of $f(x, y)$

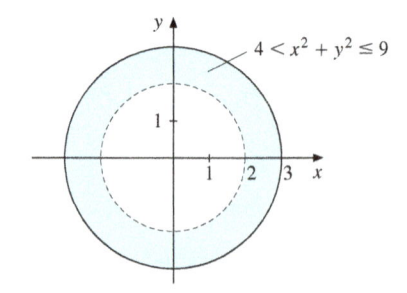

Figure 14.1.2 Domain of $g(x, y)$

EXERCISES FOR SECTION 14.1

1. Let $f(x, y) = x + 2y$. Find the values of $f(0, 1), f(2, -1), f(a, a)$, and $f(a + h, b) - f(a, b)$.

2. Let $f(x, y) = xy^2$. Find the values of $f(0, 1)$, $f(-1, 2)$, $f(10^4, 10^{-2})$, $f(a, a)$, $f(a + h, b)$, and $f(a, b + k) - f(a, b)$.

3. Let $f(x, y) = 3x^2 - 2xy + y^3$. Find the values of $f(1, 1), f(-2, 3), f(1/x, 1/y)$, as well as of $p = [f(x + h, y) - f(x, y)]/h$ and $q = [f(x, y + k) - f(x, y)]/k$.

4. Let $f(x, y) = x^2 + 2xy + y^2$.

    (a) Find the values of $f(-1, 2), f(a, a)$, and $f(a + h, b) - f(a, b)$.

    (b) Prove that $f(2x, 2y) = 2^2 f(x, y)$ and that $f(tx, ty) = t^2 f(x, y)$ for all t.

5. Let $F(K, L) = 10K^{1/2}L^{1/3}$, for $K \geq 0$ and $L \geq 0$. Find the values of $F(1, 1)$, $F(4, 27)$, $F(9, 1/27)$, $F(3, \sqrt{2})$, $F(100, 1000)$, and $F(2K, 2L)$.

6. Examine the domains of the functions given by the following formulas. Then for (b) and (c) draw in the xy-plane the graphs of the domains:

   (a) $\dfrac{x^2 + y^3}{y - x + 2}$

   (b) $\sqrt{2 - (x^2 + y^2)}$

   (c) $\sqrt{(4 - x^2 - y^2)(x^2 + y^2 - 1)}$

7. Find the domains of the functions defined by the following formulas:

   (a) $1/(e^{x+y} - 3)$

   (b) $\ln(x - a)^2 + \ln(y - b)^2$

   (c) $2\ln(x - a) + 2\ln(y - b)$

14.2 Partial Derivatives with Two Variables

For a function $y = f(x)$ of one variable, the derivative $f'(x)$ is a number which measures the function's rate of change as x changes. For a function of two variables such as $z = f(x, y)$, we also want to examine how quickly the value of the function changes w.r.t. a change in the value of either one of the two independent variables. For instance, if $f(x, y)$ is a firm's profit when it uses quantities x and y of two different inputs, we want to know whether and by how much profit can increase as either x or y is varied.

As an example, consider the function

$$z = x^3 + 2y^2 \qquad (*)$$

Suppose first that y is held constant. Then the term $2y^2$ is constant, which implies that z has been reduced to a function of the single variable x. Of course, because x^3 is differentiable, the rate of change of z w.r.t. x is given by

$$\frac{dz}{dx} = 3x^2$$

On the other hand, we can keep x fixed in $(*)$ and examine how z varies as y varies. This involves taking the derivative of z w.r.t. y while keeping x constant. The result is

$$\frac{dz}{dy} = 4y$$

Obviously, there are many other variations we could study. For example, x and y could vary simultaneously. But in this section, we restrict our attention to variations in *either* x or y.

For functions of two variables, mathematicians (and economists) usually write $\partial z/\partial x$ instead of dz/dx for the derivative of z w.r.t. x when y is held fixed. This slight but important change of notation, replacing d by ∂, is intended to remind the reader that only one independent variable is changing, with the other(s) held fixed. In the same way, we write $\partial z/\partial y$ instead of dz/dy when y varies with x held fixed. With this notation, we have

$$z = x^3 + 2y^2 \implies \frac{\partial z}{\partial x} = 3x^2 \text{ and } \frac{\partial z}{\partial y} = 4y$$

In general, we introduce the following definitions:

PARTIAL DERIVATIVES

If $z = f(x, y)$, then

$\partial z/\partial x$ is the derivative of $f(x, y)$ w.r.t. x, when y is held constant (14.2.1)

$\partial z/\partial y$ is the derivative of $f(x, y)$ w.r.t. y, when x is held constant (14.2.2)

When $z = f(x, y)$, we also denote the derivative $\partial z/\partial x$ by $\partial f/\partial x$, and this is called the *partial derivative of z (or f) w.r.t. x*. Similarly $\partial z/\partial y = \partial f/\partial y$ denotes the *partial derivative of z (or f) w.r.t. y*. Note that $\partial f/\partial x$ indicates the rate of change of $f(x, y)$ w.r.t. x when y is constant, and correspondingly for $\partial f/\partial y$. Of course, because there are two variables, there can be two different partial derivatives.

It is usually easy to find the partial derivatives of a function $z = f(x, y)$. To find $\partial f/\partial x$, just think of y as a constant and differentiate $f(x, y)$ w.r.t. x as if f were a function only of x. The rules for finding derivatives of functions of one variable can all be used when we want to compute $\partial f/\partial x$. The same is true for $\partial f/\partial y$. Let us look at some further examples.

EXAMPLE 14.2.1   Find the partial derivatives of the following functions:

(a) $f(x, y) = x^3 y + x^2 y^2 + x + y^2$ (b) $f(x, y) = \dfrac{xy}{x^2 + y^2}$

Solution: (a) Holding y constant, we find $\dfrac{\partial f}{\partial x} = 3x^2 y + 2xy^2 + 1$.

Similarly, holding x constant, we find $\dfrac{\partial f}{\partial y} = x^3 + 2x^2 y + 2y$.

(b) For this function, applying the quotient rule to find each partial derivative gives

$$\frac{\partial f}{\partial x} = \frac{y(x^2 + y^2) - xy \cdot 2x}{(x^2 + y^2)^2} = \frac{y^3 - x^2 y}{(x^2 + y^2)^2}, \qquad \frac{\partial f}{\partial y} = \frac{x^3 - y^2 x}{(x^2 + y^2)^2}$$

Observe that the function is symmetric in x and y, in the sense that its value is unchanged if we interchange x and y. By interchanging x and y in the formula for $\partial f/\partial x$, therefore, we will find the correct formula for $\partial f/\partial y$.

It is a good exercise for you to find $\partial f/\partial y$ in the usual way and check that the foregoing answer is correct.

Several other forms of notation are often used to indicate the partial derivatives of the function $z = f(x, y)$. Some of the most common are

$$\frac{\partial f}{\partial x} = \frac{\partial z}{\partial x} = z'_x = f'_x(x,y) = f'_1(x,y) = \frac{\partial}{\partial x}f(x,y) = \frac{\partial f(x,y)}{\partial x} = \frac{\partial f}{\partial x}(x,y)$$

$$\frac{\partial f}{\partial y} = \frac{\partial z}{\partial y} = z'_y = f'_y(x,y) = f'_2(x,y) = \frac{\partial}{\partial y}f(x,y) = \frac{\partial f(x,y)}{\partial y} = \frac{\partial f}{\partial y}(x,y)$$

Among these, we find $f'_1(x,y)$ and $f'_2(x,y)$ to be the most satisfactory. Here the numerical subscript refers to the position of the argument in the function. Thus, f'_1 indicates the partial derivative w.r.t. the first variable, and f'_2 w.r.t. the second variable. This notation also reminds us that the partial derivatives themselves are functions of x and y. Finally, the notation $f'_1(a,b)$ and $f'_2(a,b)$ is suitable to indicate the values of the partial derivatives at a specific point (a,b) rather than at the general point (x,y). For example, given the function $f(x,y) = x^3y + x^2y^2 + x + y^2$ in part (a) of Example 14.2.1, one has

$$f'_1(x,y) = 3x^2y + 2xy^2 + 1, \quad f'_1(a,b) = 3a^2b + 2ab^2 + 1$$

In particular, $f'_1(0,0) = 1$ and $f'_1(-1,2) = 3(-1)^22 + 2(-1)2^2 + 1 = -1$.

We note that the alternative notation $f'_x(x,y)$ and $f'_y(x,y)$ is often used, but it is sometimes too ambiguous when applied to composite functions. For instance, what is meant by the expression $f'_x(x^2y, x - y)$?

Remember that the two expressions $f'_1(x,y)$ and $f'_2(x,y)$ represent numbers that measure the rate of change of f w.r.t. x and y, respectively. For example, if $f'_1(x,y) > 0$, then a small increase in x will lead to an increase in $f(x,y)$.

EXAMPLE 14.2.2   In Example 14.1.2 we studied the function $x = Ap^{-1.5}m^{2.08}$. Find the partial derivatives of x w.r.t. p and m, and discuss their signs.

Solution: By the usual rules for differentiating a function of one variable, we find that $\partial x/\partial p = -1.5Ap^{-2.5}m^{2.08}$ and $\partial x/\partial m = 2.08Ap^{-1.5}m^{1.08}$. Because we assumed that A, p, and m are all positive, it follows that $\partial x/\partial p < 0$ and $\partial x/\partial m > 0$. These signs accord with the remarks at the end of Example 14.1.2.

Formal Definitions of Partial Derivatives

So far all the functions considered in this Chapter have been given by explicit formulas for which we could find the partial derivatives by using the ordinary rules for differentiation. When these rules cannot be used, however, we must resort to the formal definition of partial derivative. This is derived from the definition of derivative for functions of one variable in the following rather obvious way.

Given the function $z = f(x,y)$ of two variables, for each fixed y we can define the function $g(x) = f(x,y)$ of one variable. Then the partial derivative of $f(x,y)$ w.r.t. x is simply $g'(x)$. By definition of derivative, one has

$$g'(x) = \lim_{h \to 0} \frac{g(x+h) - g(x)}{h} \qquad (14.2.3)$$

But $f_1'(x, y) = g'(x)$, so it follows that:

PARTIAL DERIVATIVES

Let $f(x, y)$ be a function of two variables. Then, provided that the relevant limit exists, one has

$$f_1'(x, y) = \lim_{h \to 0} \frac{f(x + h, y) - f(x, y)}{h} \tag{14.2.4}$$

$$f_2'(x, y) = \lim_{k \to 0} \frac{f(x, y + k) - f(x, y)}{k} \tag{14.2.5}$$

If the limit in (14.2.4) does not exist, we say that $f_1'(x, y)$ *does not exist*, or that f is *not differentiable* w.r.t. x at the point. Similarly, if the limit in (14.2.5) does not exist, then $f_2'(x, y)$ does not exist and f is not differentiable w.r.t. y at that point. For instance, the function $f(x, y) = |x| + |y|$ is not differentiable, w.r.t. either x or y, at the point $(x, y) = (0, 0)$.

If h is small in absolute value, then Eq. (14.2.4) implies the approximation

$$f_1'(x, y) \approx \frac{f(x + h, y) - f(x, y)}{h} \tag{14.2.6}$$

Similarly, if k is small in absolute value, then Eq. (14.2.5) implies

$$f_2'(x, y) \approx \frac{f(x, y + k) - f(x, y)}{k} \tag{14.2.7}$$

These two approximations can be interpreted as follows:

APPROXIMATIONS TO PARTIAL DERIVATIVES

Given $f(x, y)$:

(i) The partial derivative $f_1'(x, y)$ is approximately equal to the change in $f(x, y)$ per unit increase in x, holding y constant.

(ii) The partial derivative $f_2'(x, y)$ is approximately equal to the change in $f(x, y)$ per unit increase in y, holding x constant.

These approximations must be used with caution. Roughly speaking, each will not be too inaccurate provided that the partial derivative does not vary too much over the relevant interval. Of course, this warning was also true in the one-variable case we first saw in Section 6.4, and then in Section 7.4. But it applies more forcefully here, as even a seemingly small variation in either x or y can change $f_1'(x, y)$, say, in a significant manner. Section 15.8 and FMEA discuss such approximations in more detail.

SECTION 14.2 / PARTIAL DERIVATIVES WITH TWO VARIABLES

EXAMPLE 14.2.3 Let $Y = F(K, L)$ be the number of units produced when K units of capital and L units of labour are used as inputs in a production process. What is the economic interpretation of $F'_K(100, 50) = 5$?

Solution: The statement $F'_K(100, 50) = 5$ means that, starting from $K = 100$ and holding labour input fixed at 50, any small enough increase in K increases output by five units per unit increase in K.

Higher-Order Partial Derivatives

If $z = f(x, y)$, then $\partial f/\partial x$ and $\partial f/\partial y$ are called *first-order partial derivatives*. These partial derivatives are, in general, again functions of the two variables. From $\partial f/\partial x$, provided this derivative is itself differentiable, we can generate two new functions by taking the partial derivatives of $\partial f/\partial x$ w.r.t. x and y. In the same way, we can take the partial derivatives of $\partial f/\partial y$ w.r.t. x and y. The four functions we obtain by differentiating twice in this way are called *second-order partial derivatives* of $f(x, y)$. They can be expressed as

$$\frac{\partial}{\partial x}\left(\frac{\partial f}{\partial x}\right) = \frac{\partial^2 f}{\partial x^2}, \quad \frac{\partial}{\partial x}\left(\frac{\partial f}{\partial y}\right) = \frac{\partial^2 f}{\partial x \partial y}, \quad \frac{\partial}{\partial y}\left(\frac{\partial f}{\partial x}\right) = \frac{\partial^2 f}{\partial y \partial x}, \quad \text{and} \quad \frac{\partial}{\partial y}\left(\frac{\partial f}{\partial y}\right) = \frac{\partial^2 f}{\partial y^2}$$

For brevity, we sometimes refer to the first- and second-order "partials", suppressing the word "derivatives".

EXAMPLE 14.2.4 For the function in part (a) of Example 14.2.1, differentiating their two first-order partials gives

$$\frac{\partial^2 f}{\partial x^2} = 6xy + 2y^2, \quad \frac{\partial^2 f}{\partial y \partial x} = 3x^2 + 4xy, \quad \frac{\partial^2 f}{\partial x \partial y} = 3x^2 + 4xy, \quad \text{and} \quad \frac{\partial^2 f}{\partial y^2} = 2x^2 + 2$$

As with first-order partial derivatives, several other kinds of notation for second-order partial derivatives are also in frequent use. For example, $\partial^2 f/\partial x^2$ may also be denoted by $f''_{11}(x, y)$ or $f''_{xx}(x, y)$. In the same way, $\partial^2 f/\partial y \partial x$ may also be written as $f''_{12}(x, y)$ or $f''_{xy}(x, y)$. Note that $f''_{12}(x, y)$ means that we differentiate $f(x, y)$ first w.r.t. the first argument x and then second w.r.t. the second argument y. To find $f''_{21}(x, y)$, we must differentiate in the reverse order. It is important to recognize how these conventions imply that

$$f''_{xy}(x, y) = \frac{\partial}{\partial y}\frac{\partial f}{\partial x} = \frac{\partial^2 f}{\partial y \partial x} \quad \text{and} \quad f''_{yx}(x, y) = \frac{\partial}{\partial x}\frac{\partial f}{\partial y} = \frac{\partial^2 f}{\partial x \partial y} \tag{14.2.8}$$

with the order of x and y interchanged in each case.

In Example 14.2.4, these two second-order "cross" partial derivatives (otherwise called "mixed-partials") are equal. For most functions $z = f(x, y)$, it will actually be the case that

$$\frac{\partial^2 f}{\partial x \partial y} = \frac{\partial^2 f}{\partial y \partial x} \tag{14.2.9}$$

Sufficient conditions for this equality are given in Theorem 14.6.1.

It is very important to note the exact meaning of the different symbols for partial differentiation that have been introduced. For example, it would be a serious mistake to believe that the two expressions in (14.2.9) are equal because $\partial x \partial y$ is the same as $\partial y \partial x$. As (14.2.8) should make clear, the left-hand side of (14.2.9) is in fact the partial derivative of $\partial f/\partial y$ w.r.t. x, whereas the right-hand side is the partial derivative of $\partial f/\partial x$ w.r.t. y. It is a remarkable fact, and not a triviality, that these two are usually equal.

It is also very important to observe that $\partial^2 z/\partial x^2$ is quite different from $(\partial z/\partial x)^2$. For example, if $z = x^2 + y^2$, then $\partial z/\partial x = 2x$. So $\partial^2 z/\partial x^2 = 2$, whereas $(\partial z/\partial x)^2 = 4x^2$.

We can define partial derivatives of the third, fourth, and higher orders analogously. For example, we write $\partial^4 z/\partial x \partial y^3 = z^{(4)}_{yyyx}$ to indicate that we first differentiate z three times w.r.t. y, and then differentiate the result once more w.r.t. x. Here is an additional example.

EXAMPLE 14.2.5   If $f(x, y) = x^3 e^{y^2}$, find the first- and second-order partial derivatives at the point $(x, y) = (1, 0)$.

Solution: To find $f_1'(x, y)$, we differentiate $x^3 e^{y^2}$ w.r.t. x while treating y as a constant. When y is a constant, so is e^{y^2}. Hence, $f_1'(x, y) = 3x^2 e^{y^2}$. At $(x, y) = (1, 0)$ we have

$$f_1'(1, 0) = 3 \cdot 1^2 e^{0^2} = 3$$

To find $f_2'(x, y)$, we differentiate $f(x, y)$ w.r.t. y while treating x as a constant:

$$f_2'(x, y) = x^3 2y e^{y^2} = 2x^3 y e^{y^2}$$

At $(x, y) = (1, 0)$ we have $f_2'(1, 0) = 0$.

To find the second-order partial $f_{11}''(x, y)$, we must differentiate $f_1'(x, y)$ w.r.t. x once more, while treating y as a constant. Hence, $f_{11}''(x, y) = 6x e^{y^2}$ and so

$$f_{11}''(1, 0) = 6 \cdot 1 e^{0^2} = 6$$

To find $f_{22}''(x, y)$, we must differentiate $f_2'(x, y) = 2x^3 y e^{y^2}$ w.r.t. y once more, while treating x as a constant. Because $y e^{y^2}$ is a product of two functions, each involving y, we use the product rule to obtain

$$f_{22}''(x, y) = (2x^3)(1 \cdot e^{y^2} + y \cdot 2y e^{y^2}) = 2x^3 e^{y^2} + 4x^3 y^2 e^{y^2}$$

Evaluating this at $(1, 0)$ gives $f_{22}''(1, 0) = 2$. Moreover,

$$f_{12}''(x, y) = \frac{\partial}{\partial y}[f_1'(x, y)] = \frac{\partial}{\partial y}(3x^2 e^{y^2}) = 3x^2 \cdot 2y e^{y^2} = 6x^2 y e^{y^2}$$

and $\quad f_{21}''(x, y) = \dfrac{\partial}{\partial x}[f_2'(x, y)] = \dfrac{\partial}{\partial x}(2x^3 y e^{y^2}) = 6x^2 y e^{y^2}$

Hence, $f_{12}''(x, y) = f_{21}''(x, y)$ for all x and y, with $f_{12}''(1, 0) = f_{21}''(1, 0) = 0$.

EXERCISES FOR SECTION 14.2

1. Find $\partial z/\partial x$ and $\partial z/\partial y$ for each of the following functions:

   (a) $z = 2x + 3y$ (b) $z = x^2 + y^3$ (c) $z = x^3 y^4$ (d) $z = (x + y)^2$

2. Find $\partial z/\partial x$ and $\partial z/\partial y$ for each of the following functions:
   (a) $z = x^2 + 3y^2$
   (b) $z = xy$
   (c) $z = 5x^4y^2 - 2xy^5$
   (d) $z = e^{x+y}$
   (e) $z = e^{xy}$
   (f) $z = e^x/y$
   (g) $z = \ln(x+y)$
   (h) $z = \ln(xy)$

3. Find $f_1'(x, y)$, $f_2'(x, y)$, and $f_{12}''(x, y)$ for each of the following functions:
   (a) $f(x, y) = x^7 - y^7$
   (b) $f(x, y) = x^5 \ln y$
   (c) $f(x, y) = (x^2 - 2y^2)^5$

4. Find all the first- and second-order partial derivatives for each of the following functions:
   (a) $z = 3x + 4y$
   (b) $z = x^3y^2$
   (c) $z = x^5 - 3x^2y + y^6$
   (d) $z = x/y$
   (e) $z = (x-y)/(x+y)$
   (f) $z = \sqrt{x^2 + y^2}$

SM 5. Find all the first- and second-order partial derivatives for each of the following functions:
   (a) $z = x^2 + e^{2y}$
   (b) $z = y \ln x$
   (c) $z = xy^2 - e^{xy}$
   (d) $z = x^y$

6. The estimated production function for a certain fishery is $F(S, E) = 2.26 S^{0.44} E^{0.48}$, where S denotes the stock of lobsters, E the harvesting effort, and $F(S, E)$ the catch.
   (a) Find $F_S'(S, E)$ and $F_E'(S, E)$.
   (b) Show that $SF_S' + EF_E' = kF$ for a suitable constant k.

7. Prove that if $z = (ax + by)^2$, then $xz_x' + yz_y' = 2z$.

8. Let $z = \frac{1}{2} \ln(x^2 + y^2)$. Show that $\partial^2 z/\partial x^2 + \partial^2 z/\partial y^2 = 0$.

9. Suppose that if a household consumes x units of one good and y units of a second good, its satisfaction is measured by the function $s(x, y) = 2 \ln x + 4 \ln y$. Suppose that the household presently consumes 20 units of the first good and 30 units of the second. What is the approximate increase in satisfaction from consuming one extra unit of: (a) the first good? (b) the second good?

14.3 Geometric Representation

When studying functions of one variable, we saw how useful it was to represent the function by its graph in a coordinate system in the plane. This section considers how to visualize functions of two variables as having graphs which form surfaces in a three-dimensional space, or 3-space.

The Graph of a Function of Two Variables

Suppose $z = f(x, y)$ is a function of two variables defined over a domain D in the xy-plane. The *graph* of the function f is the set of all points $(x, y, f(x, y))$ in 3-space that are obtained by letting (x, y) "run through" the whole of D. Provided that f is a sufficiently "nice" function, the graph of f will be a connected smooth surface in 3-space, like that shown in Fig. 14.3.1. In particular, if (x_0, y_0) is a point in the domain D, we see how the point $P = (x_0, y_0, f(x_0, y_0))$ on the surface is obtained by letting $f(x_0, y_0)$ be the "height" of f at (x_0, y_0).

Figure 14.3.1 Graph of $z = f(x, y)$

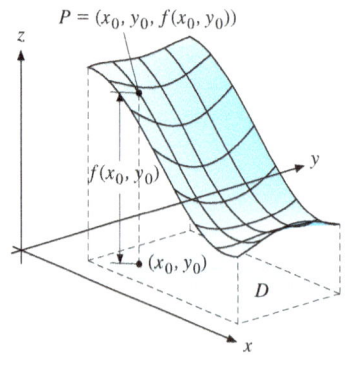

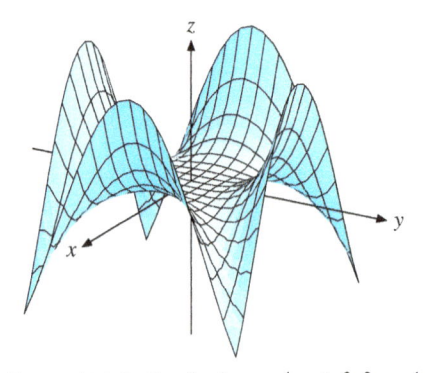

Figure 14.3.2 Graph of $z = x^4 - 3x^2y^2 + y^4$

A 3D printer (or a talented sculptor with plenty of time and resources) could in principle construct a three-dimensional graph of the function $z = f(x, y)$, or as another example, of the graph that appears in Fig. 14.3.2 of the function $z = x^4 - 3x^2y^2 + y^4$. Even drawing figures like 14.3.1 and 14.3.2, which represent the functions in two dimensions, requires some artistic ability.[4]

We now describe a second kind of geometric representation that often does better when we are confined to two dimensions, as we are in the pages of this book.

Level Curves

Skilled map makers can describe some topographical features of the earth's surface such as hills and valleys even within the confines of a plane surface. The usual way involves a set of *level curves* or *contours* that connect points on the map which represent places on the earth's surface having the same altitude above sea level. For instance, one contour may correspond to 100 metres above sea level, others to 200, 300, and 400 metres above sea level, and so on. Off the coast, or in places like the valley of the River Jordan, which drains into the Dead Sea, there may be contours for 100 metres below sea level, etc. Where the contours are closer together, that indicates a hill with a steeper slope. Thus, studying a contour map carefully can give a good idea how the altitude varies on the ground.

The same idea can be used to give a geometric representation of an arbitrary function $z = f(x, y)$. The graph of the function in 3-space is visualized as being cut by horizontal planes parallel to the xy-plane. The resulting intersection between each plane and the graph

---

[4] Computer graphics can produce fairly easily graphs of quite complicated functions of two variables. These can even be rotated, coloured, or otherwise transformed in order to display the shape of the graph better.

is then projected onto the xy-plane. If the intersecting plane is $z = c$, then the projection of the intersection onto the xy-plane is called the *level curve* at height c for f. This level curve will consist of all the points that satisfy the equation $f(x, y) = c$. Figure 14.3.3 illustrates how to construct one such level curve.

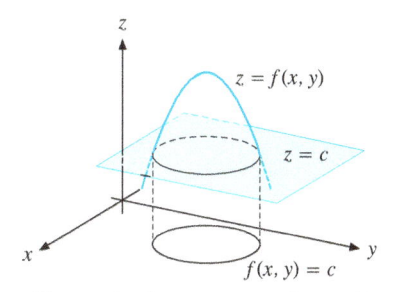

Figure 14.3.3 The graph of $z = f(x, y)$ and one of its level curves

EXAMPLE 14.3.1 Consider the function of two variables defined by the equation

$$z = x^2 + y^2 \qquad (*)$$

What are its level curves? Draw both a set of level curves and the graph of the function.

Solution: The variable z can only assume values ≥ 0. Each level curve has the equation

$$x^2 + y^2 = c$$

for some $c \geq 0$. We see that these are circles in the xy-plane centred at the origin and with radius $\sqrt{c}$, as in Fig. 14.3.4, which also shows the level curves for $c = 1, 2, 3, 4, 5$.

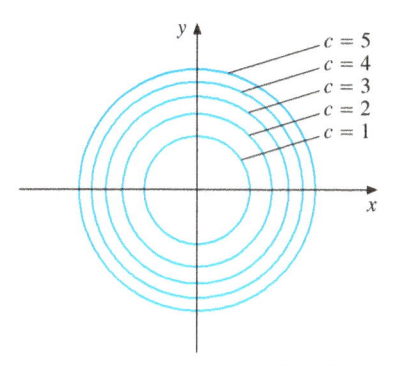

Figure 14.3.4 Solutions of $x^2 + y^2 = c$ 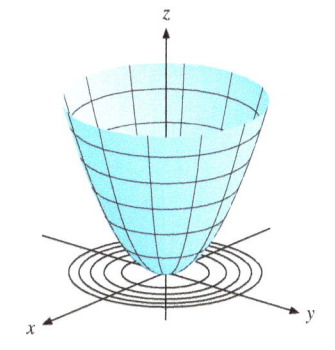   **Figure 14.3.5** The graph of $z = x^2 + y^2$

Now we turn to the three-dimensional graph of the function defined by $(*)$. For $y = 0$, we have $z = x^2$, implying that the graph of $(*)$ cuts the xz-plane (where $y = 0$) in a parabola. Similarly, for $x = 0$, we have $z = y^2$, which is the graph of a parabola in the yz-plane. In fact, the graph of $(*)$ is obtained by rotating the parabola $z = x^2$ around the z-axis. This surface of revolution is called a *paraboloid*, with its lowest part shown in Fig. 14.3.5. This

EXAMPLE 14.3.2 Suppose $F(K, L)$ denotes a firm's output when its inputs of capital and labour are, respectively, K and L. A level curve for this production function is a curve in the KL-plane given by $F(K, L) = Y_0$, where Y_0 is a constant. This curve is called an *isoquant*, signifying "equal quantity". Consider the Cobb–Douglas function $F(K, L) = AK^a L^b$, with $a + b < 1$ and $A > 0$. Figures 14.3.6 and 14.3.7, respectively, show a part of the graph near the origin, and three of the isoquants.

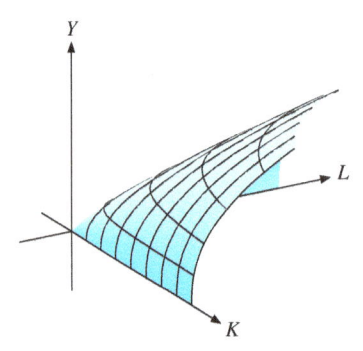

Figure 14.3.6 Graph of a Cobb–Douglas production function

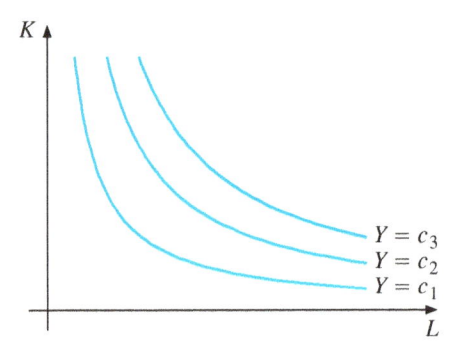

Figure 14.3.7 Isoquants of a Cobb–Douglas production function

EXAMPLE 14.3.3 Show that all points (x, y) satisfying $xy = 3$ lie on the same level curve of the function
$$g(x, y) = \frac{3(xy + 1)^2}{x^4 y^4 - 1}$$

Solution: By substituting $xy = 3$ in the expression for g, we find
$$g(x, y) = \frac{3(xy + 1)^2}{(xy)^4 - 1} = \frac{3(3 + 1)^2}{3^4 - 1} = \frac{48}{80} = \frac{3}{5}$$

This shows that, for all (x, y) where $xy = 3$, the value of $g(x, y)$ is a constant $3/5$. Hence, any point (x, y) satisfying $xy = 3$ is on a level curve (at height $3/5$) for g.[5]

Geometric Interpretations of Partial Derivatives

Partial derivatives of the first order have an interesting geometric interpretation. Let $z = f(x, y)$ be a function of two variables, with its graph as shown in Fig. 14.3.8. Let us keep the value of y fixed at b. The points $(x, y, f(x, y))$ on the graph of f that have $y = b$ are

---
[5] In fact, $g(x, y) = 3(c + 1)^2/(c^4 - 1)$ whenever $xy = c \neq \pm 1$, so this equation represents a level curve for g for every $c \neq \pm 1$.

those that lie on the curve K_y indicated in the figure. The partial derivative $f'_x(a, b)$ is the derivative of $z = f(x, b)$ w.r.t. x at the point $x = a$, and is therefore the slope of the tangent line ℓ_y to the curve K_y at $x = a$. In the same way, $f'_y(a, b)$ is the slope of the tangent line ℓ_x to the curve K_x at $y = b$.

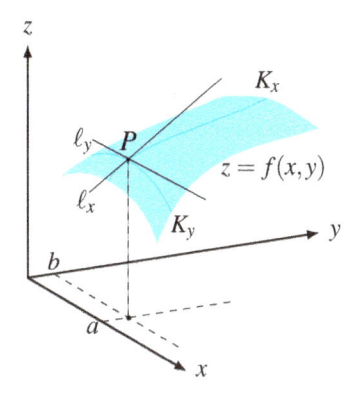

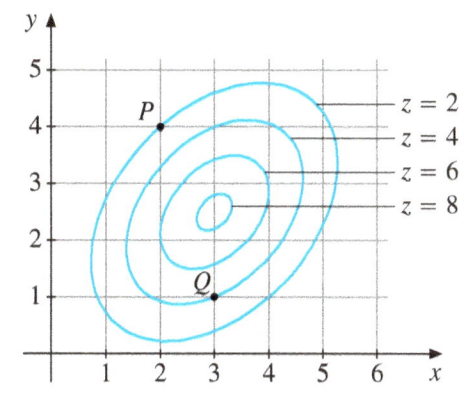

Figure 14.3.8 Partial derivatives

Figure 14.3.9 Level curves

This geometric interpretation of the two partial derivatives can be explained in another way. Imagine that the graph of f looks like the surface of a mountain, as in Fig. 14.3.8, and suppose that we are standing at point P with coordinates $(a, b, f(a, b))$ in three dimensions, where the height is $f(a, b)$ units above the xy-plane. The slope of the ground at P varies as we look in different directions. In particular, suppose we look in the direction parallel to the positive x-axis. Then $f'_x(a, b)$ is a measure of the "steepness" in this direction, which in Fig. 14.3.8 is negative. This is because moving away from P along the tangent line ℓ_x in the direction of increasing x will take us downwards. Similarly, we see that $f'_y(x_0, y_0)$ measures the "steepness" along ℓ_y in the direction of increasing y. In Fig. 14.3.8 we see that $f'_y(x_0, y_0)$ is positive, meaning that the slope is upward in this direction.

Let us now briefly consider the geometric interpretation of the "direct" second-order derivatives f''_{xx} and f''_{yy}. Consider the curve K_y on the graph of f, as shown in Fig. 14.3.8. It seems that $f''_{xx}(x, b)$ is negative, because $f'_x(x, b)$ decreases as x increases along this curve. In particular, $f''_{xx}(a, b) < 0$. In the same way, we see that moving along K_x makes $f'_y(a, y)$ decrease as y increases, so $f''_{yy}(a, y) < 0$. In particular, $f''_{yy}(a, b) < 0$.

The cross-partials f''_{xy} and f''_{yx} are not so easy to interpret geometrically. Indeed, consider again the curve K_y in Fig. 14.3.8. Recall that its position is determined by the value of y, namely b, which is kept fixed when computing the partial w.r.t. x. The first partial is $f'_x(x, b)$, which is the slope of the line l_y in the direction of the x-axis. Suppose now you increase b slightly, so that the curve K_y gets pushed in the direction of the y-axis. Of course, the line l_y gets pushed too, and its slope may change. The cross-partial f''_{xy} measures the magnitude of that change.

EXAMPLE 14.3.4   Consider Fig. 14.3.9 which shows some level curves of a function $z = f(x, y)$. On the basis of this figure, answer the following questions:

576 CHAPTER 14 / FUNCTIONS OF MANY VARIABLES

(a) What are the signs of $f'_x(x, y)$ and $f'_y(x, y)$ at the points P and Q? Estimate also the *value* of $f'_x(3, 1)$.

(b) What are the solutions of the equations: (i) $f(3, y) = 4$; and (ii) $f(x, 4) = 6$?

(c) What is the largest value that $f(x, y)$ can attain when $x = 2$, and for which y value does this maximum occur?

Solution: (a) If you stand at P, you are on the level curve $f(x, y) = 2$. If you look in the direction of the positive x-axis, along the line $y = 4$, then you will see the terrain sloping upwards, because the nearest level curves correspond to larger z values. Hence, $f'_x > 0$. But if you look from P in the direction of the positive y-axis, along $x = 2$, the terrain will slope downwards. Thus, at P, we must have $f'_y < 0$. At Q, we find similarly that $f'_x < 0$ and $f'_y > 0$. To estimate $f'_x(3, 1)$, we use $f'_x(3, 1) \approx f(4, 1) - f(3, 1) = 2 - 4 = -2$.[6]

(b) Equation (i) has the solutions $y = 1$ and $y = 4$, because the line $x = 3$ cuts the level curve $f(x, y) = 4$ at $(3, 1)$ and at $(3, 4)$. Equation (ii) has no solutions, because the line $y = 4$ does not meet the level curve $f(x, y) = 6$ at all.

(c) The highest value of c for which the level curve $f(x, y) = c$ has a point in common with the line $x = 2$ is $c = 6$. The largest value of $f(x, y)$ when $x = 2$ is therefore 6, and we see from Fig. 14.3.9 that this maximum value is attained when $y \approx 2.2$.

Gradients

To conclude this section, we give a geometric interpretation in the xy-plane of the two partial derivatives. At any point $(x, y) = (a, b)$, these can be written together as the ordered pair

$$(f'_1(a, b), f'_2(a, b)) \qquad (14.3.1)$$

This pair represents a point in the plane, which in Fig. 14.3.10 is denoted by $\nabla f(a, b)$.[7]

As in Fig. 12.9.1, we have also drawn with an arrow the two-dimensional vector that corresponds to a movement that starts at the origin and ends at the point $\nabla f(a, b)$. Suppose that, as in Fig. 12.9.2, we shift this vector so that its starting point is the point (a, b) rather than the origin. Then the point in Fig. 14.3.10 where the shifted vector ends has co-ordinates that can be found by adding (a, b) to the pair $(*)$, which yields

$$(a, b) + \nabla f(a, b) = (a + f'_1(a, b), b + f'_2(a, b))$$

This property leads us to define the ordered pair $\nabla f(a, b)$ given by (14.3.1) as *the gradient vector of the function f at the point (a, b)*.

---

[6] This approximation is actually far from exact. If we keep $y = 1$ and *decrease* x by one unit, then $f(2, 1) \approx 4$, which should give the estimate $f'_x(3, 1) \approx 4 - 4 = 0$. The "map" has too few contours near the point Q.

[7] The symbol ∇, which looks somewhat like an upside down Δ, is often pronounced as "nabla", or sometimes as "del". The ancient Greeks applied the word "nabla" to a harp, whose foreign origins are disputed.

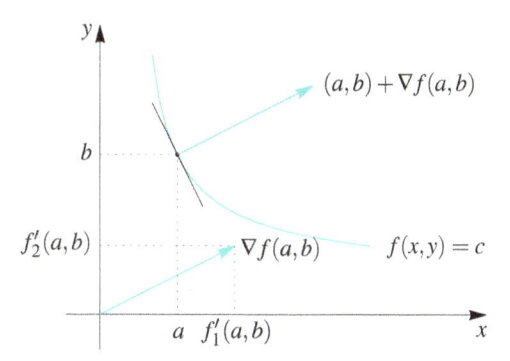

Figure 14.3.10 The gradient vector

In Fig. 14.3.10 we have also drawn a line through the point (a,b) that is perpendicular to the shifted vector that goes from (a,b) to $(a,b) + \nabla f(a,b)$. As the figure suggests, this line happens to be the tangent to the level curve through (a,b) at that point. Indeed, as we explain in FMEA, there are three important ideas to remember:

1. The line that is perpendicular to the arrow is also tangent to the level curve; this implies that a small change to (x,y) in the direction of that line leaves the value of the function unchanged.

2. A small change to (x,y) in the direction of the arrow, on the other hand, induces the fastest possible increase in the value of the function. A step in the direction opposite to the arrow would induce the fastest possible decrease in the value of the function.

3. The length of the arrow indicates the rate of change by which the function would increase after a perturbation to (x,y) in that direction. The longer the arrow, the faster the increase.

The gradient vector defined by (14.3.1) is a very useful object. In more advanced differential calculus, it allows our analysis to be generalized to changes in (x,y) in any direction on the plane, and not just parallel to one of the two axes. Furthermore, given a function $z = f(x_1, \ldots, x_n) = f(\mathbf{x})$ of n variables that is differentiable at the n-vector $\mathbf{x}^0 = (x_1^0, \ldots, x_n^0)$, in FMEA we present similar results concerning the tangent to a level surface, as well as the rate at which f increases in different directions. These results involve the gradient n-vector of f at $\mathbf{x}^0$, which is defined by

$$\nabla f(\mathbf{x}^0) = (f_1'(\mathbf{x}^0), f_2'(\mathbf{x}^0), \ldots, f_n'(\mathbf{x}^0)) \tag{14.3.2}$$

EXERCISES FOR SECTION 14.3

1. Show that $x^2 + y^2 = 6$ is a level curve of $f(x,y) = \sqrt{x^2 + y^2} - x^2 - y^2 + 2$.

2. Show that $x^2 - y^2 = c$ is a level curve of $f(x,y) = e^{x^2} e^{-y^2} + x^4 - 2x^2 y^2 + y^4$ for all values of the constant c.

3. Explain why two level curves of the function $z = f(x,y)$ corresponding to different values of z cannot intersect.

4. Let $f(x)$ represent a function of one variable. The equation $g(x, y) = f(x)$ defines a function of two variables, without y in its formula. Explain how the graph of g is obtained from the graph of f. Illustrate with the two functions $f(x) = x$ and $f(x) = -x^3$.

5. Draw the graphs of the following functions in 3-space, as well as a few level curves for each:

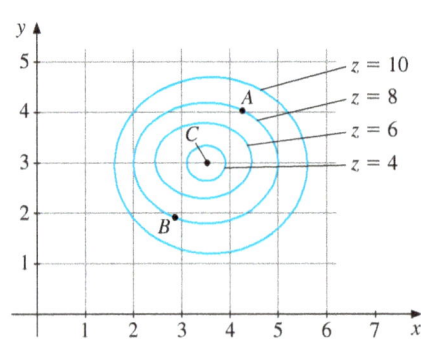

   (a) $z = 3 - x - y$

   (b) $z = \sqrt{3 - x^2 - y^2}$

Figure 14.3.11 Exercise 6.

Figure 14.3.12 Exercise 7.

6. Suppose that Fig. 14.3.11 shows some level curves for the function $z = f(x, y)$.

   (a) What is $f(2, 3)$? Solve the equation $f(x, 3) = 8$ for x.

   (b) Find the smallest value of $z = f(x, y)$ if $x = 2$. What is the corresponding value of y?

   (c) What are the signs of $f_1'(x, y)$ and $f_2'(x, y)$ at the points A, B, and C? Estimate the values of these two partial derivatives at A.

(SM) 7. Figure 14.3.12 shows some level curves for $z = f(x, y)$, as well as the line $2x + 3y = 12$.

   (a) What are the signs of f_x' and f_y' at the points P and Q?

   (b) Find possible solutions of the equations: (i) $f(1, y) = 2$; (ii) $f(x, 2) = 2$.

   (c) Among those (x, y) that satisfy $2x + 3y = 12$, which gives the largest value of $f(x, y)$?

(SM) 8. [HARDER] Suppose $F(x, y)$ is a function about which all we know is that: (i) $F(0, 0) = 0$; (ii) $F_1'(x, y) \geq 2$ for all (x, y); (iii) $F_2'(x, y) \leq 1$ for all (x, y). What can be said about the relative values of $F(0, 0)$, $F(1, 0)$, $F(2, 0)$, $F(0, 1)$, and $F(1, 1)$? Write down all the inequalities that must hold between these five numbers.

14.4 Surfaces and Distance

In Section 5.4 we saw how an equation in *two* variables, such as $f(x, y) = c$, can be represented by a set of points in the co-ordinate plane, called the graph of the equation. Similarly, an equation in the *three* variables x, y, and z, such as $g(x, y, z) = c$, can be represented by a set of points in 3-space, also called the *graph* of the equation. This graph consists of all triples (x, y, z) that satisfy the equation. It will often form what we call a *surface* in 3-space.

One of the simplest types of equation in three variables is

$$ax + by + cz = d \tag{14.4.1}$$

with a, b, and c not all 0. This particular case of Eq. (12.10.7) is the general equation for a plane in the three-dimensional Euclidean space. Assuming that a and b are not both 0, the graph of this equation intersects the xy-plane when $z = 0$. Then $ax + by = d$, which is a straight line in the xy-plane, unless $a = b = 0$. In the same way we see that, provided at most one of a, b, and c is equal to zero, the graph intersects the two other coordinate planes in straight lines.

Let us rename the coefficients and consider the equation

$$p_1 x_1 + p_2 x_2 + p_3 x_3 = m \tag{14.4.2}$$

where p_1, p_2, p_3, and m are all positive. This is the budget equation considered in Example 12.10.3 for a person who has an amount m to spend on three different commodities, whose prices per unit are p_1, p_2, and p_3. If the person buys x_1 units of the first, x_2 units of the second, and x_3 units of the third commodity, then the total expense is the left-hand side of Eq. (14.4.2). Only bundles (x_1, x_2, x_2) that satisfy (14.4.2) can be bought if expenditure must equal m. Assuming that the individual cannot consume negative amounts of any of the three commodities but can underspend, the *budget set* is defined as

$$B = \{(x_1, x_2, x_3) : p_1 x_1 + p_2 x_2 + p_3 x_3 \leq m, \; x_1 \geq 0, \; x_2 \geq 0, \; x_3 \geq 0\}$$

This represents the three-dimensional body bounded by the three coordinate planes and the budget plane, as in Fig. 12.10.4.

Another rather interesting surface, called an *ellipsoid*, appears in Fig. 14.4.1. It intersects the three axes at the points $(\pm a, 0, 0)$, $(0, \pm b, 0)$, and $(0, 0, \pm c)$, where $a > b = c$. Some readers may recognize it as having the shape of a rugby ball.

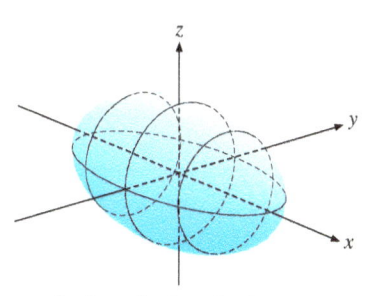

Figure 14.4.1 $x^2/a^2 + y^2/b^2 + z^2/c^2 = 1$ where $a > b = c$

Spheres in 3-Space

Let (a, b, c) be a point in 3-space. The sphere with radius r and centre at (a, b, c) is the set of all points (x, y, z) whose distance from (a, b, c) is equal to r. Using the distance formula (12.9.1), we obtain

$$\sqrt{(x-a)^2 + (y-b)^2 + (z-c)^2} = r$$

Squaring each side yields:

EQUATION FOR A SPHERE

The equation for the *sphere* in 3-space with centre at (a, b, c) and radius r is

$$(x-a)^2 + (y-b)^2 + (z-c)^2 = r^2 \tag{14.4.3}$$

EXAMPLE 14.4.1 Find the equation for the sphere with centre at $(-2, -2, -2)$ and radius 4.

Solution: According to formula (14.4.3), the equation is

$$(x-(-2))^2 + (y-(-2))^2 + (z-(-2))^2 = 4^2$$

This can be simplified to

$$(x+2)^2 + (y+2)^2 + (z+2)^2 = 16$$

EXAMPLE 14.4.2 How do you interpret the expression $(x+4)^2 + (y-3)^2 + (z+5)^2$? Is it: (a) the sphere with centre at the point $(-4, 3, -5)$; (b) the distance between the points (x, y, z) and $(-4, 3, -5)$; or (c) the square of the distance between the points (x, y, z) and $(-4, 3, -5)$?

Solution: Only (iii) is correct.

EXERCISES FOR SECTION 14.4

1. Sketch graphs of the surfaces in 3-space described by each of the following equations:

    (a) $x = a$ (b) $y = b$ (c) $z = c$

2. Find the distance between each of the following pairs of points:

    (a) $(-1, 2, 3)$ and $(4, -2, 0)$ (b) (a, b, c) and $(a+1, b+1, c+1)$

3. Find the equation for the sphere with centre at $(2, 1, 1)$ and radius 5.

4. What is the geometric interpretation of the equation $(x+3)^2 + (y-3)^2 + (z-4)^2 = 25$?

5. Suppose that the graph of $z = x^2 + y^2$ is a paraboloid, as shown in Fig. 14.3.5. If the point (x, y, z) lies on this paraboloid, interpret the expression $(x-4)^2 + (y-4)^2 + (z-1/2)^2$.

14.5 Functions of *n* Variables

Many of the most important functions we study in economics, such as the GDP of a country, depend on a very large number of variables. Mathematicians and economists express this dependence by saying that GDP is a *function* of the different variables.

Following the terminology and notation introduced in Section 12.1, any ordered collection $(x_1, x_1, \ldots, x_n)$ of n numbers will be called an *n-vector*, denoted by **x**.

FUNCTIONS OF *n* VARIABLES

Given a domain D of *n*-vectors, *a function f of n variables* $x_1, \ldots, x_n$ with domain D is a rule that for each *n*-vector $\mathbf{x} = (x_1, \ldots, x_n)$ in D specifies a unique number

$$f(\mathbf{x}) = f(x_1, \ldots, x_n) \tag{14.5.1}$$

EXAMPLE 14.5.1

(a) The demand for sugar in the United States during the period 1929–1935 was estimated to be given, approximately, by the formula

$$x = 108.83 - 6.0294p + 0.164w - 0.4217t$$

Here x is the demand for sugar, p is its price, w is a production index, and t is the date (where $t = 0$ corresponds to 1929).

(b) The following formula is an estimate for the demand for beer in the UK:

$$x = 1.058 x_1^{0.136} x_2^{-0.727} x_3^{0.914} x_4^{0.816}$$

Here the quantity demanded x is a function of four variables: x_1, the income of the individual; x_2, the price of beer; x_3, a general price index for all other commodities; and x_4, the strength of the beer.

The simpler of the two functions in Example 14.5.1 is the one in part (a). This is because the variables p, w, and t occur here only to the first power. Moreover, they are only multiplied by constants, not by each other. Such functions are called *linear*.[8] In general, a *linear function* in n variables takes the form

$$f(x_1, x_2, \ldots, x_n) = a_1 x_1 + a_2 x_2 + \cdots + a_n x_n + b \tag{14.5.2}$$

where $a_1, a_2, \ldots, a_n$, and b are constants.

---

[8] This is rather common terminology, although many mathematicians would insist that f should really be called *affine* if $b \neq 0$, and *linear* only if $b = 0$.

The function in part (b) of Example 14.5.1 is a special case of the general Cobb–Douglas function

$$F(x_1, x_2, \ldots, x_n) = A x_1^{a_1} x_2^{a_2} \cdots x_n^{a_n} \tag{14.5.3}$$

with $A > 0$, $a_1, \ldots, a_n$ as constants. The function is defined for all $x_1 > 0, x_2 > 0, \ldots, x_n > 0$. It is used very often in this book.

Note that taking the natural logarithm of each side of Eq. (14.5.3) gives

$$\ln F = \ln A + a_1 \ln x_1 + a_2 \ln x_2 + \cdots + a_n \ln x_n \tag{14.5.4}$$

This shows that the Cobb–Douglas function is *log-linear* (or ln-linear), because $\ln F$ is a linear function of $\ln x_1, \ln x_2, \ldots, \ln x_n$.

EXAMPLE 14.5.2 Suppose that an economist records the price of apples in n different stores, and observes the n positive numbers $x_1, x_2, \ldots, x_n$. In statistics, several different measures for the average price are used. Three of the most common are the following, which appeared in Exercise 2.6.8 for the case $n = 2$:

(a) the *arithmetic mean*: $\bar{x}_A = \frac{1}{n}(x_1 + x_2 + \cdots + x_n)$

(b) the *geometric mean*: $\bar{x}_G = \sqrt[n]{x_1 x_2 \cdots x_n}$

(c) the *harmonic mean*: $\bar{x}_H = \dfrac{1}{\frac{1}{n}\left(\frac{1}{x_1} + \frac{1}{x_2} + \cdots + \frac{1}{x_n}\right)}$

Note that $\bar{x}_A$ is a linear function of $x_1, \ldots, x_n$, whereas $\bar{x}_G$ and $\bar{x}_H$ are nonlinear functions, though $\bar{x}_G$ is log-linear.

As an example, if four observations are $x_1 = 1$, $x_2 = 2$, $x_3 = 3$, and $x_4 = 4$, then

$$\bar{x}_A = (1 + 2 + 3 + 4)/4 = 2.5, \quad \bar{x}_G = \sqrt[4]{1 \cdot 2 \cdot 3 \cdot 4} = \sqrt[4]{24} \approx 2.21,$$

and $\quad \bar{x}_H = [(1/1 + 1/2 + 1/3 + 1/4)/4]^{-1} = 48/25 = 1.92$

In this case $\bar{x}_H < \bar{x}_G < \bar{x}_A$. As Exercise 2.6.8 asked you to show for the case $n = 2$, it turns out that for general n one has the corresponding weak inequalities

$$\bar{x}_H \leq \bar{x}_G \leq \bar{x}_A \tag{14.5.5}$$

EXAMPLE 14.5.3 A household must decide what quantities of n different commodities to buy during a given time period. Consumer demand theory often assumes that the household's preferences can be represented by a utility function $U(x_1, x_2, \ldots, x_n)$ which measures the household's satisfaction from acquiring x_1 units of good 1, x_2 units of good 2, and so on. This is an important economic example of a function of n variables, to which we return several times.

One model of consumer demand is the *linear expenditure system*, which is based on the particular utility function

$$U(x_1, x_2, \ldots, x_n) = a_1 \ln(x_1 - c_1) + a_2 \ln(x_2 - c_2) + \cdots + a_n \ln(x_n - c_n)$$

This depends on the $2n$ nonnegative parameters $a_1, a_2, \ldots, a_n$ and $c_1, c_2, \ldots, c_n$. Here, each c_i represents the quantity of the commodity numbered i that the household needs to survive. Some, or even all, of the constants c_i could be 0.

Because $\ln z$ is only defined when $z > 0$, we see that all n inequalities $x_1 > c_1, x_2 > c_2$, $\ldots, x_n > c_n$ must be satisfied if $U(x_1, x_2, \ldots, x_n)$ is to be defined. Of course, the condition $a_i > 0$ implies that the consumer prefers more of the particular good i.

Limits and Continuity with *n* Variables

In Sections 7.8 and 7.9, we introduced the concept of continuity for functions of one variable that we provided in (7.8.1). Here we extend this concept to functions of several variables. Roughly speaking, a function $z = f(x_1, x_2, \ldots, x_n) = f(\mathbf{x})$ of n variables is *continuous* if any small enough change in the n-vector $\mathbf{x}$ of independent variables induces a small change in the function value $f(\mathbf{x})$.

To make this more precise requires first specifying what we mean by a "small change" in the n-vector $\mathbf{x}$. In one dimension, the change from a to x is said to be small if $|x - a|$ is small. We note, of course, that $|x - a| = \sqrt{(x-a)^2}$. Then, in n dimensions, we consider the norm $\|\mathbf{x} - \mathbf{a}\|$ of their difference $\mathbf{x} - \mathbf{a}$, which was defined in (12.9.3) as

$$\|\mathbf{x} - \mathbf{a}\| = \sqrt{(x_1 - a_1)^2 + (x_2 - a_2)^2 + \ldots + (x_n - a_n)^2}$$

Specifically, the change from $\mathbf{a}$ to $\mathbf{x}$ is said to be small if the norm $\|\mathbf{x} - \mathbf{a}\|$ is small.

This definition permits the following obvious extension to a function $z = f(\mathbf{x})$ of n variables of the informal definition of limit that was set out in Section 6.5, as well as of the subsequent more formal definition in Section 7.9.

LIMIT OF A FUNCTION OF *n* VARIABLES

$\lim_{\mathbf{x} \to \mathbf{a}} f(\mathbf{x}) = A$ means that $|f(\mathbf{x}) - A|$ can be made as small as we want for all $\mathbf{x} \neq \mathbf{a}$ with $\|\mathbf{x} - \mathbf{a}\|$ sufficiently small.

More formally, say that $f(\mathbf{x})$ has limit A as $\mathbf{x}$ tends to $\mathbf{a}$ if, for each number $\varepsilon > 0$, there exists an associated number $\delta > 0$ such that $|f(\mathbf{x}) - A| < \varepsilon$ for every $\mathbf{x}$ with $0 < \|\mathbf{x} - \mathbf{a}\| < \delta$.

Here is the promised extension to functions of n variables of the definition in (7.8.1).

CONTINUITY

The function $f(\mathbf{x}$ is *continuous at* $\mathbf{x} = \mathbf{a}$ if $\lim_{\mathbf{x} \to \mathbf{a}} f(\mathbf{x}) = f(\mathbf{a})$ (14.5.6)

Just as in the one-variable case, we have the following useful rule:

PRESERVATION OF CONTINUITY

Any function of n variables that can be constructed from continuous functions by combining the operations of addition, subtraction, multiplication, division and functional composition is continuous wherever it is defined.

If a function of one variable is continuous, it will also be continuous when considered as a function of several variables. For example, $f(x, y, z) = x^2$ is a continuous function of x, y, and z because small changes in x, y, and z give at most small changes in x^2.

EXAMPLE 14.5.4 Where are the functions given by the following formulas continuous?

(a) $f(x, y, z) = x^2y + 8x^2y^5z - xy + 8z$ (b) $g(x, y) = \dfrac{xy - 3}{x^2 + y^2 - 4}$

Solution: (a) As the sum of products of positive powers, the function f is defined and continuous for all x, y, and z.

(b) The function g is defined and continuous for all pairs (x, y) except those that lie on the circle $x^2 + y^2 = 4$. There the denominator is zero, so $g(x, y)$ is not defined.

Representing Functions of n Variables

In Section 12.9, we introduced the n-space $\mathbb{R}^n$ as the set of all possible n-vectors $\mathbf{x} = (x_1, x_2, \ldots, x_n)$, each of which is an ordered set of n real numbers. Suppose that the equation $z = f(x_1, x_2, \ldots, x_n) = f(\mathbf{x})$ represents a function of n variables. When $n = 1$, its graph is defined as the set in the plane $\mathbb{R}^2$ that consists of all pairs $(x_1, f(x_1))$ with x_1 in the domain of f. It often forms a curve in the plane. When $n = 2$, its graph is defined as the set in the 3-space $\mathbb{R}^3$ that consists of all triples $(x_1, x_2, f(x_1, x_2))$ with (x_1, x_2) in the domain of f. It often forms a surface in 3-space. For general n, including when $n \geq 3$, a corresponding definition of the graph of f would be as a subset of $\mathbb{R}^{n+1}$. Even though points in the space $\mathbb{R}^{n+1}$ lack the obvious interpretation of points in $\mathbb{R}^2$ of $\mathbb{R}^3$ when $n \geq 3$, we still use this definition of the graph of a function of three or more variables.

Specifically, if $z = f(x_1, x_2, \ldots, x_n) = f(\mathbf{x})$ represents a function of n variables, we define the *graph* of f as the set of all points $(\mathbf{x}, f(\mathbf{x}))$ in $\mathbb{R}^{n+1}$ for which $\mathbf{x}$ belongs to the domain of f. We also call this graph a *surface* (or sometimes a *hypersurface*) in $\mathbb{R}^{n+1}$.

For $z = z_0$ (constant), the set of points in $\mathbb{R}^n$ satisfying $f(\mathbf{x}) = z_0$ is called a *level surface* of f. Notice that when $n = 3$, in principle these level curves can be represented in $\mathbb{R}^3$, even though the graph of the function in $\mathbf{R}^4$ has no direct graphical representation. When $f(\mathbf{x})$ is a linear function such as $a_1x_1 + a_2x_2 + \cdots + a_nx_n + b$, then any level surface, which would be a line if $n = 2$ or a plane if $n = 3$, is called a *hyperplane* when $n > 3$.

In both producer and consumer theory, it is usual to give level surfaces a different name. If $x = f(\mathbf{v}) = f(v_1, v_2, \ldots, v_n)$ is the amount produced when the input quantities of n different factors of production are respectively $v_1, v_2, \ldots, v_n$, the level surfaces where

SECTION 14.5 / FUNCTIONS OF N VARIABLES 585

$f(v_1, v_2, \ldots, v_n) = x_0$ (constant) are called *isoquants*, as in Example 14.3.2. On the other hand, if $u = U(\mathbf{x})$ is a utility function that represents the consumer's preferences, the level surface where $U(\mathbf{x}) = u_0$ is called an *indifference surface*.

EXERCISES FOR SECTION 14.5

1. Let $f(x, y, z) = xy + xz + yz$.

    (a) Find $f(-1, 2, 3)$ and $f(a+1, b+1, c+1) - f(a, b, c)$.

    (b) Show that $f(tx, ty, tz) = t^2 f(x, y, z)$ for all t.

2. A study of milk production found that
$$y = 2.90 \, x_1^{0.015} \, x_2^{0.250} \, x_3^{0.350} \, x_4^{0.408} \, x_5^{0.030}$$
    where y is the output of milk, and $x_1, \ldots, x_5$ are the quantities of five different input factors.

    (a) If all the factors of production were doubled, what would happen to y?

    (b) Write the relation in log-linear form.

SM 3. A pension fund decides to invest \$720 million in the shares of XYZ Inc., a company with a volatile share price. Rather than invest everything all at once and so risk paying an unduly high price, the fund practises "dollar cost averaging" by investing \$120 million per week in each of six consecutive weeks. The prices it pays are \$50 per share in the first week, followed by \$60, \$45, \$40, \$75, and then \$80 in the subsequent five weeks.

    (a) How many shares in total does it buy?

    (b) Which is the most accurate representation of the average price: the arithmetic mean, the geometric mean, or the harmonic mean?

4. An American bank A and a European bank E agree a currency swap. In n successive weeks $w = 1, 2, \ldots, n$, bank A will buy \$100 million worth of euros from bank E, at a price of $\$p_w$ per euro determined by the spot exchange rate at the end of week w. After n weeks:

    (a) How many euros will bank A have bought?

    (b) What is the dollar price per euro it will have paid, on average?

5. [HARDER] It is observed that three machines A, B, and C produce, respectively, 60, 80, and 40 units of a product during one workday lasting 8 hours. The average output is then 60 units per day. We see that A, B, and C use, respectively, 8, 6, and 12 minutes to make one unit.

    (a) If all machines were equally efficient and jointly produced $60 + 80 + 40 = 180$ units during a day, then how much time would be required to produce each unit? (Note that the answer is not $(8 + 6 + 12)/3$.)

    (b) Suppose that n machines $A_1, A_2, \ldots, A_n$ produce the same product simultaneously during a time interval of length T. Given that the production times per unit are respectively $t_1, t_2, \ldots, t_n$, find the total output Q. Show that if all the machines were equally efficient and together had produced exactly the same total amount Q in the time span T, then the time needed for each machine to produce one unit would be precisely the harmonic mean $\bar{t}_H$ of $t_1, t_2, \ldots, t_n$.

14.6 Partial Derivatives with Many Variables

The last section gave several economic examples of functions involving many variables. Accordingly, we need to extend the concept of partial derivative to functions of more than two variables.

PARTIAL DERIVATIVES IN n VARIABLES

Suppose that $z = f(\mathbf{x}) = f(x_1, x_2, \ldots, x_n)$. Then $\partial f / \partial x_i$, for $i = 1, 2, \ldots, n$, denotes the partial derivative of $f(x_1, x_2, \ldots, x_n)$ w.r.t. x_i, when all the other variables x_j, for $j \neq i$, are held constant.

So, provided that they all exist, there are n partial derivatives of first order, one for each variable x_i, for $i = 1, \ldots, n$. Other notation used for the first-order partials of $z = f(x_1, x_2, \ldots, x_n)$ includes

$$\frac{\partial f}{\partial x_i} = \frac{\partial z}{\partial x_i} = \partial z / \partial x_i = z'_i = f'_i(x_1, x_2, \ldots, x_n)$$

EXAMPLE 14.6.1 Find the three first-order partials of $f(x_1, x_2, x_3) = 5x_1^2 + x_1 x_2^3 - x_2^2 x_3^2 + x_3^3$.

Solution: We find that

$$f'_1 = 10x_1 + x_2^3, \quad f'_2 = 3x_1 x_2^2 - 2x_2 x_3^2, \quad \text{and } f'_3 = -2x_2^2 x_3 + 3x_3^2$$

As in (14.2.6), we have the following rough approximation:

APPROXIMATE PARTIAL DERIVATIVES

The partial derivative $\partial z / \partial x_i$ is approximately equal to the per-unit change in $z = f(x_1, x_2, \ldots, x_n)$ caused by an increase in x_i, while holding constant all the other x_j for $j \neq i$.

In symbols, for small h one has

$$f'_i(x_1, \ldots, x_n) \approx \frac{f(x_1, \ldots, x_{i-1}, x_i + h, x_{i+1}, \ldots, x_n) - f(x_1, \ldots, x_{i-1}, x_i, x_{i+1}, \ldots, x_n)}{h} \quad (14.6.1)$$

For each of the n first-order partials $\partial z / \partial x_i$ of f, we have the n second-order partials:

$$\frac{\partial}{\partial x_j}\left(\frac{\partial f}{\partial x_i}\right) = \frac{\partial^2 f}{\partial x_j \partial x_i} = z''_{ij}$$

provided that all the derivatives exist. Here both i and j may take any value 1, 2, ..., n, so altogether there are n^2 second-order partials.

It is usual to display these second-order partials in an $n \times n$ square array

$$\mathbf{f}''(\mathbf{x}) = \begin{pmatrix} f''_{11}(\mathbf{x}) & f''_{12}(\mathbf{x}) & \cdots & f''_{1n}(\mathbf{x}) \\ f''_{21}(\mathbf{x}) & f''_{22}(\mathbf{x}) & \cdots & f''_{2n}(\mathbf{x}) \\ \vdots & \vdots & \ddots & \vdots \\ f''_{n1}(\mathbf{x}) & f''_{n2}(\mathbf{x}) & \cdots & f''_{nn}(\mathbf{x}) \end{pmatrix} \qquad (14.6.2)$$

Following the terminology of Chapter 12, the RHS of (14.6.2) is an $n \times n$ matrix that we call the *Hessian matrix* (or simply *Hessian*) of f at the point $\mathbf{x} = (x_1, x_2, \ldots, x_n)$.

The n second-order partial derivatives f''_{ii} found by differentiating twice w.r.t. the same variable are called *direct second-order partials*. The other $n(n-1)$ second-order partial derivatives f''_{ij}, where $i \neq j$, are called *mixed* or *cross* partials.

EXAMPLE 14.6.2 Find the Hessian matrix of the function f defined in Example 14.6.1.

Solution: We differentiate partially the first-order partial derivatives that were found in Example 14.6.1. The resulting Hessian matrix is

$$\begin{pmatrix} f''_{11} & f''_{12} & f''_{13} \\ f''_{21} & f''_{22} & f''_{23} \\ f''_{31} & f''_{32} & f''_{33} \end{pmatrix} = \begin{pmatrix} 10 & 3x_2^2 & 0 \\ 3x_2^2 & 6x_1 x_2 - 2x_3^2 & -4x_2 x_3 \\ 0 & -4x_2 x_3 & -2x_2^2 + 6x_3 \end{pmatrix}$$

EXAMPLE 14.6.3 For any square matrix $\mathbf{A}$, consider the quadratic function $q(\mathbf{x})$ of n variables which, for each n-vector $\mathbf{x} = (x_1, x_2, \ldots, x_n)$, is defined by the double sum

$$q(\mathbf{x}) = \mathbf{x}'\mathbf{A}\mathbf{x} = \sum_{i=1}^{n} \sum_{j=1}^{n} a_{ij} x_i x_j \qquad (14.6.3)$$

Show that at any n-vector $\mathbf{x}$, the Hessian matrix $\mathbf{q}''(\mathbf{x})$ of $q(\mathbf{x})$ is the sum $\mathbf{A} + \mathbf{A}'$ of $\mathbf{A}$ and its transpose, which is symmetric.

Solution: First, in order to make partial differentiation easier, we separate out the square terms in the double sum (14.6.3) and rewrite it as

$$q(\mathbf{x}) = \sum_{i=1}^{n} a_{ii} x_i^2 + \sum_{i \neq j} a_{ij} x_i x_j \qquad (*)$$

Now, for each $k = 1, 2, \ldots, n$, the terms in $(*)$ that involve the variable x_k are $a_{kk} x_k^2$, as well as $a_{kj} x_k x_j$ for each $j \neq k$ when $i = k$, and also $a_{ik} x_i x_k$ for each $i \neq k$ when $j = k$. It follows that differentiating the sum $(*)$ term by term partially w.r.t. x_k gives

$$q'_k(\mathbf{x}) = \frac{\partial}{\partial x_k} q(\mathbf{x}) = 2 a_{kk} x_k + \sum_{j \neq k} a_{kj} x_j + \sum_{i \neq k} a_{ik} x_i \qquad (**)$$

So evidently $q''_{kk}(\mathbf{x}) = 2 a_{kk}$. Furthermore, for each $\ell = 1, 2, \ldots, n$ with $\ell \neq k$, the terms in $(**)$ that involve x_ℓ are $a_{k\ell} x_\ell$ when $j = \ell$, and $a_{\ell k} x_\ell$ when $i = \ell$. Differentiating $(**)$ partially once again, therefore, it follows that $q''_{k\ell}(\mathbf{x}) = a_{k\ell} + a_{\ell k}$ whenever $\ell \neq k$.

To summarize, after replacing k by i and ℓ by j, we see that all the elements $q''_{ij}(\mathbf{x})$ of the Hessian matrix $q''(\mathbf{x})$ satisfy

$$q''_{ii} = 2a_{ii} \ (i = 1, \ldots, n) \quad \text{and} \quad q''_{ij} = q''_{ji} = a_{ij} + a_{ji} \ (i,j = 1, \ldots, n)$$

By definition of the transpose matrix $\mathbf{A}'$, it follows that $q''(\mathbf{x}) = \mathbf{A} + \mathbf{A}'$.

In the important special case when $\mathbf{A}' = \mathbf{A}$ because $\mathbf{A}$ is symmetric, then Eq. (14.6.3) defines the quadratic form in Eq. (13.12.9) that is associated with $\mathbf{A}$, and Example 14.6.3 shows that its Hessian matrix satisfies $q''(\mathbf{x}) = 2\mathbf{A}$.

Young's Theorem

If $z = f(x_1, x_2, \ldots, x_n)$, then the two second-order cross-partial derivatives z''_{ij} and z''_{ji} are usually equal, as they were in Examples 14.6.2 and 14.6.3. That is,

$$\frac{\partial}{\partial x_j}\left(\frac{\partial f}{\partial x_i}\right) = \frac{\partial}{\partial x_i}\left(\frac{\partial f}{\partial x_j}\right)$$

This means that the order of differentiation does not matter, and so the Hessian matrix is symmetric. The next theorem makes precise a more general result.

THEOREM 14.6.1 (YOUNG'S THEOREM)

Suppose that all the mth order partial derivatives of the function $f(x_1, x_2, \ldots, x_n)$ are continuous. If any two of them involve differentiating w.r.t. each of the variables the same number of times, then they are necessarily equal.

To explain this result, suppose that $m = m_1 + \cdots + m_n$, and that $f(x_1, x_2, \ldots, x_n)$ is differentiated partially m_1 times w.r.t. x_1, m_2 times w.r.t. x_2, …, and m_n times w.r.t. x_n. Of course, some of the integers $m_1, \ldots, m_n$ can be zero. Suppose too that all these mth order partial derivatives are themselves continuous functions. Then we end up with exactly the same result no matter what is the order of differentiation, because each of the final partial derivatives is equal to

$$\frac{\partial^m f}{\partial x_1^{m_1} \partial x_2^{m_2} \ldots \partial x_n^{m_n}}$$

In the particular case when $m = 2$, for $i = 1, \ldots, n$ and $j = 1, \ldots, n$, one has

$$\frac{\partial^2 f}{\partial x_j \partial x_i} = \frac{\partial^2 f}{\partial x_i \partial x_j}$$

provided that both these partial derivatives are continuous. A proof of Young's theorem is given in most advanced calculus books. Exercise 11 shows that the cross partial derivatives are not always equal.

Formal Definitions of Partial Derivatives

In Section 14.2, we gave a formal definition of partial derivatives for functions of two variables. This was done by modifying the definition of the derivative for a function of one variable. The same modification works for a function of n variables.

Indeed, if $z = f(x_1, \ldots, x_n)$, then for each $i = 1, 2, \ldots, n$ we can define the function

$$g(x_i) = f(x_1, \ldots, x_{i-1}, x_i, x_{i+1}, \ldots, x_n)$$

of the single variable x_i, where we think of all the variables x_j other than x_i as constants. Following the justification of (14.2.4) and (14.2.5) for the case of two variables, the definition of partial derivative evidently implies that $\partial z / \partial x_i = g'(x_i)$. Now we can use the definition (6.2.2) of $g'(x_i)$, provided the limit exists, to obtain

$$\frac{\partial z}{\partial x_i} = \lim_{h \to 0} \frac{f(x_1, \ldots, x_i + h, \ldots, x_n) - f(x_1, \ldots, x_i, \ldots, x_n)}{h} \qquad (14.6.4)$$

As in Section 14.2, if the limit in (14.6.4) does not exist, then we say that $\partial z / \partial x_i$ does *not exist*, or that z is not differentiable w.r.t. x_i at the point. Similarly, the approximation in (14.6.1) holds because the fraction on the right-hand side of Eq. (14.6.4) is close to the limit if $h \neq 0$ is small enough.

Virtually all the functions we consider have continuous partial derivatives everywhere in their domains. If $z = f(x_1, x_2, \ldots, x_n)$ has continuous partial derivatives of first order in a domain D, we call f *continuously differentiable* in D. In this case, f is also called a C^1 *function* on D. If all partial derivatives up to order k exist and are continuous, then f is called a C^k *function*.

EXERCISES FOR SECTION 14.6

1. For the function $F(x, y, z) = x^2 e^{xz} + y^3 e^{xy}$ of three variables, calculate the three first-order partial derivatives $F_1'(1, 1, 1)$, $F_2'(1, 1, 1)$, and $F_3'(1, 1, 1)$.

2. Calculate all the first-order partial derivatives of the following six functions:

    (a) $f(x, y, z) = x^2 + y^3 + z^4$ 　　(b) $f(x, y, z) = 5x^2 - 3y^3 + 3z^4$ 　　(c) $f(x, y, z) = xyz$

    (d) $f(x, y, z) = x^4 / yz$ 　　(e) $f(x, y, z) = (x^2 + y^3 + z^4)^6$ 　　(f) $f(x, y, z) = e^{xyz}$

3. Let x and y be the populations of two cities and d the distance between them. Suppose that the number of travellers T between the two cities is given by $T = kxy/d^n$, where k and n are positive constants.[9] Find $\partial T / \partial x$, $\partial T / \partial y$, and $\partial T / \partial d$, then discuss their signs.

4. Let g be defined for all (x, y, z) by

$$g(x, y, z) = 2x^2 - 4xy + 10y^2 + z^2 - 4x - 28y - z + 24$$

    (a) Calculate $g(2, 1, 1)$, $g(3, -4, 2)$, and $g(1, 1, a+h) - g(1, 1, a)$.

---

[9] Especially when $n = 2$, economists often refer to this as a "gravity model", following Newton's "inverse square law" of gravitational attraction between two point masses.

(b) Find all partial derivatives of the first and second order.

5. Suppose that $\pi(p, r, w) = \frac{1}{4}p^2(1/r + 1/w)$. Find the partial derivatives of π w.r.t. p, r, and w.

6. Find all first- and second-order partials of $w(x, y, z) = 3xyz + x^2y - xz^3$.

7. If $f(x, y, z) = p(x) + q(y) + r(z)$, what are f_1', f_2', and f_3'?

8. Find the Hessian matrices of: (a) $f(x, y, z) = ax^2 + by^2 + cz^2$; (b) $g(x, y, z) = Ax^a y^b z^c$.

9. Prove that if $w = \left(\dfrac{x - y + z}{x + y - z}\right)^h$, then $x\dfrac{\partial w}{\partial x} + y\dfrac{\partial w}{\partial y} + z\dfrac{\partial w}{\partial z} = 0$.

SM 10. Define the function $f(x, y, z) = x^{y^z}$ for $x > 0$, $y > 0$, and $z > 0$. Find its first-order partial derivatives by differentiating $\ln f$.

SM 11. [HARDER] Consider the function which is defined by $f(x, y) = xy(x^2 - y^2)/(x^2 + y^2)$ for all $(x, y) \neq (0, 0)$, with $f(0, 0) = 0$. Find expressions for $f_1'(0, y)$ and $f_2'(x, 0)$. Then show that $f_{12}''(0, 0) = -1$ and $f_{21}''(0, 0) = 1$. Check that nevertheless Young's theorem is not contradicted because f_{12}'' and f_{21}'' are both discontinuous at the point $(0, 0)$.

14.7 Convex Sets

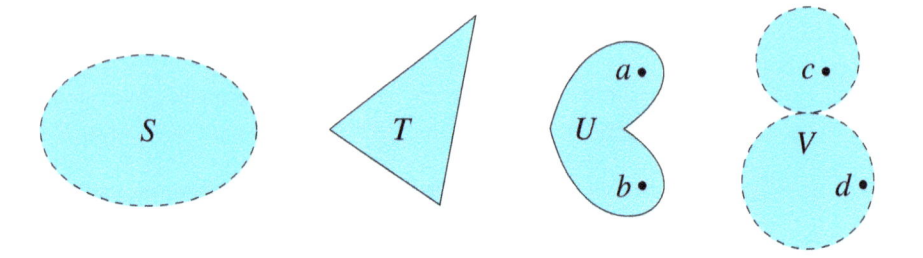

Figure 14.7.1 Two convex and two non-convex sets

A set in the plane is said to be *convex* if each pair of points in the set can be joined by a line segment lying entirely within it. Examples include the sets S and T shown in Fig. 14.7.1. In both of these sets, if you take *any* pair of points and then draw the line segment that connects them, this does not leave the set. This is not true for the other two sets U and V. The segment that connects points a and b in U, for instance, passes outside the set. The same is true of points c and d in V. These two sets, therefore, are not convex.

To be sure, there are non-convex sets where one can find *some* pairs of points that are connected by segments contained entirely within the sets. This is true of sets U and V in Fig. 14.7.1. But the property of convexity requires that the segment connecting *any* two points be contained within the set. Thus, for a set to be non-convex, it suffices that there are two points for which the segment that joins them leaves the set somewhere.

EXAMPLE 14.7.1 (**Budget set**). Consider Example 4.4.7 once again. A consumer can buy any nonnegative amounts x and y of two commodities, subject to the constraint that total expenditure is at most m when the prices of the two commodities are $p > 0$ and $q > 0$, respectively. The consumer's budget set, which was shown in Fig. 4.4.12, is

$$B = \{(x, y) : px + qy \leq m, \ x \geq 0, \ y \geq 0\}$$

From that earlier figure, it is easy to see that any two points in the set B are connected by a straight line segment that lies entirely within B. So B is convex.

EXAMPLE 14.7.2 (**An indivisible commodity**). In the consumer situation of the previous example, suppose that commodity y is *indivisible* in the sense that it is available only in integer amounts. This is true, for instance, of cars or cell phones. If we let $\mathbb{Z}_+$ denote the set of nonnegative integers, then the requirement is that $y \in \mathbb{Z}_+$. Assuming that commodity x is not subject to a similar indivisibility, the budget set now is

$$\{(x, y) : px + qy \leq m, \ x \geq 0, \ y = 0, 1, 2, \ldots\} = \{(x, y) : px + qy \leq m, \ x \geq 0, \ y \in \mathbb{Z}_+\}$$

This set consists of the horizontal lines illustrated in Fig. 14.7.2. Each horizontal line corresponds to a different integer level of y, and it consists of all the values of $x \geq 0$ which satisfy $px \leq m - qy$ for that value of y.

To show that the budget set is not convex in this case, take any two bundles on different horizontal lines. Because y is restricted to the set $\mathbb{Z}_+$, it is then obvious that the line segment which connects these two will not lie entirely within the budget set.

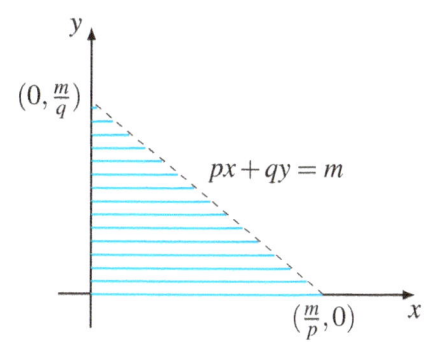

Figure 14.7.2 The budget set in Example 14.7.2

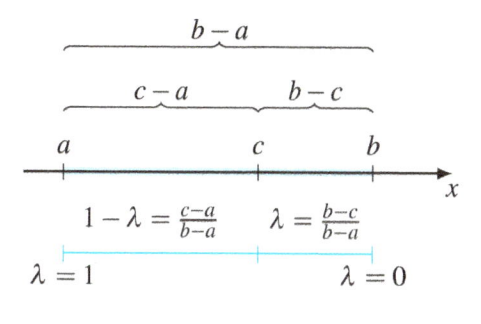

Figure 14.7.3 c as a weighted average of a and b

For a more formal definition of convexity, we must characterize the concept of a "line segment that connects two points". In the case of the real line, given any two numbers a and b with $a < b$, the line segment joining them is simply the closed interval $[a, b]$. Also, note that $a \leq c \leq b$ if and only if c belongs to the interval $[a, b]$, in which case we have

$$c = \frac{b-c}{b-a}a + \frac{c-a}{b-a}b$$

Now let $\lambda = (b-c)/(b-a)$. Then $1 - \lambda = (c-a)/(b-a)$, whereas $0 \leq \lambda \leq 1$ and

$$c = \lambda a + (1 - \lambda)b \qquad (14.7.1)$$

In this way the number c has been expressed as a *weighted average* of a and b, with respective weights λ and $1 - \lambda$. Figure 14.7.3 illustrates this construction. The length $b - a$ of the interval $[a, b]$ is divided in proportion to the differences $b - c$ and $c - a$. Then the resulting weights are assigned to the two points a and b, taking care that $\lambda = 0$ corresponds to the case $c = b$, while $\lambda = 1$ gives $c = a$. This procedure allows any point c in $[a, b]$ to be written as in Eq. (14.7.1) for a unique appropriately chosen λ in $[0, 1]$. So we can write

$$[a, b] = \{c \in \mathbb{R} : c = \lambda a + (1 - \lambda)b \text{ for some } \lambda \text{ in } [0, 1]\}$$

or, more concisely

$$[a, b] = \{\lambda a + (1 - \lambda)b : \lambda \in [0, 1]\}$$

Once we go beyond the one-dimensional real line, recall that according to definition (12.10.2), the unique straight line in $\mathbb{R}^n$ that joins any two distinct n-vectors $\mathbf{a}$ and $\mathbf{b}$ is the entire range of the function defined by

$$\mathbf{x}(\lambda) = \lambda \mathbf{a} + (1 - \lambda)\mathbf{b} = \mathbf{b} + \lambda(\mathbf{a} - \mathbf{b}) \qquad (14.7.2)$$

as λ ranges over the whole of the real line $\mathbb{R}$. Figure 12.10.1 illustrates this line in the three-dimensional case, and Fig. 14.7.4 in the two-dimensional case.

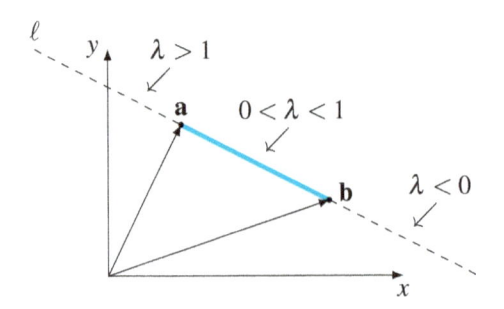

Figure 14.7.4 The line segment connecting $\mathbf{a}$ and $\mathbf{b}$.

Note that for any n, even $n = 1$, as λ increases from large negative to large positive numbers, so the point $\mathbf{x}(\lambda)$ defined by Eq. (14.7.2): (i) starts out when $\lambda < 0$ on the other side of $\mathbf{b}$ from $\mathbf{a}$; (ii) passes through $\mathbf{b}$ when $\lambda = 0$; (iii) moves along the line away from $\mathbf{b}$ and toward $\mathbf{a}$ as λ increases from 0 toward 1; (iv) passes through $\mathbf{a}$ when $\lambda = 1$; (v) is on the side of $\mathbf{a}$ away from $\mathbf{b}$ when $\lambda > 1$, and moves further away from $\mathbf{a}$ as λ increases away from 1. In particular, by applying Eq. (14.7.2) with λ ranging from 0 to 1, we obtain any point in the "interval" $[\mathbf{a}, \mathbf{b}]$ as we did in Eq. (14.7.1), though now in n dimensions.

With this in mind, it is now easy to formulate the definitions of a line segment and of a convex set in $\mathbb{R}^n$:

DEFINITIONS OF A LINE SEGMENT AND CONVEX SET IN n-SPACE

1. Given any two distinct vectors **a** and **b** in $\mathbb{R}^n$, the *line segment* [**a**, **b**] joining **a** to **b** is the subset of $\mathbb{R}^n$ defined by

$$[\mathbf{a}, \mathbf{b}] = \{\lambda \mathbf{a} + (1 - \lambda)\mathbf{b} : \lambda \in [0, 1]\} \tag{14.7.3}$$

2. A set S in $\mathbb{R}^n$ is said to be *convex* if the line segment [**a**, **b**] joining **a** to **b** is a subset of S for all distinct vectors **a** and **b** in S, or equivalently, if:

$$\lambda \mathbf{a} + (1 - \lambda)\mathbf{b} \in S \text{ for all } \mathbf{a}, \mathbf{b} \text{ in } S \text{ and all } \lambda \text{ in } [0, 1] \tag{14.7.4}$$

Another way to help remember this definition is to define a *convex combination* of two points **a** and **b** in $\mathbb{R}^n$ as any point that can be written as $\lambda \mathbf{a} + (1 - \lambda)\mathbf{b}$, with λ in $[0, 1]$. Thus, the line segment [**a**, **b**] joining **a** and **b** is the set of all convex combinations of those two points. And a set is convex if and only if it contains all the convex combinations of any pair of points within it.

EXAMPLE 14.7.3   We can now verify, formally, the conclusion from Example 14.7.1 that, with two goods, the standard budget set B defined in Example 4.4.7 is convex. To do this, fix any two bundles $\mathbf{a} = (a_1, a_2)$ and $\mathbf{b} = (b_1, b_2)$ in B, as well as *any* $\lambda \in [0, 1]$. By definition of B, we have $a_1 \geq 0$, $a_2 \geq 0$, $b_1 \geq 0$, $b_2 \geq 0$, as well as the budget inequalities $pa_1 + qa_2 \leq m$ and $pb_1 + qb_2 \leq m$.

Let (x, y) be the convex combination $\lambda \mathbf{a} + (1 - \lambda)\mathbf{b}$, meaning that

$$x = \lambda a_1 + (1 - \lambda)b_1 \quad \text{and} \quad y = \lambda a_2 + (1 - \lambda)b_2$$

Since $\lambda \in [0, 1]$, we have $\lambda \geq 0$ and $1 - \lambda \geq 0$. Moreover, because $a_1 \geq 0$ and $b_1 \geq 0$, we can conclude that $\lambda a_1 \geq 0$ and $(1 - \lambda)b_1 \geq 0$. These imply in turn that

$$x = \lambda a_1 + (1 - \lambda)b_1 \geq 0 \tag{i}$$

Similarly we have

$$y = \lambda a_2 + (1 - \lambda)b_2 \geq 0 \tag{ii}$$

After recalling the definition of the inner product from Section 12.4, it follows from (i) and (ii) that

$$\begin{aligned}(p, q) \cdot (x, y) = px + qy &= p[\lambda a_1 + (1 - \lambda)b_1] + q[\lambda a_2 + (1 - \lambda)b_2] \\ &= \lambda(pa_1 + qa_2) + (1 - \lambda)(pb_1 + qb_2)\end{aligned} \tag{iii}$$

Now, using once again the inequalities $\lambda \geq 0$ and $1 - \lambda \geq 0$, but this time in combination with the budget inequalities, we have

$$\lambda(pa_1 + qa_2) \leq \lambda m \quad \text{and} \quad (1-\lambda)(pb_1 + qb_2) \leq (1-\lambda)m \qquad \text{(iv)}$$

Incorporating (iii) with the sum of these two inequalities yields

$$(p, q) \cdot (x, y) \leq \lambda m + (1-\lambda)m = m \qquad \text{(v)}$$

Conditions (i), (ii) and (v) together imply that the bundle (x, y) is in the budget set. Since the two points $\mathbf{a} = (a_1, a_2)$ and $\mathbf{b} = (b_1, b_2)$ in B along with the scalar $\lambda \in [0, 1]$ were arbitrary, this argument proves that the set B is convex.

EXAMPLE 14.7.4   Suppose that one of the commodities in indivisible, as in Example 14.7.2. Then the budget set is no longer convex. To see this, suppose that $m > q$, implying that the bundles $(0, 0)$ and $(0, 1)$ are both in the budget set of that example. Then the bundle $(0, 1/2)$ is a convex combination of $(0, 0)$ and $(0, 1)$ with $\lambda = 1/2$. Yet it is not in the budget set since the quantity of the indivisible commodity y is not an integer.

Note in particular that the empty set and also any set consisting of one single point are convex. Intuitively speaking, a convex set must be "connected" without any "holes", and its boundary must not "bend inwards" at any point.

INTERSECTION AND UNION OF CONVEX SETS

If S and T are two convex sets, then their intersection $S \cap T$ is also convex. The union of convex sets, however, is usually not convex.

The reason why this result is true can be seen in Fig. 14.7.5. Since the two sets S and T are both convex, their intersection is also convex, but their union is not. The formal proof of the first statement is, in fact, almost as easy as the graphical argument:

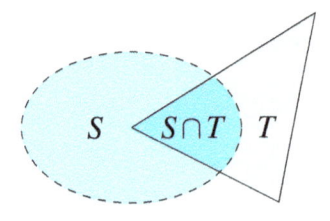

Figure 14.7.5 Sets S, T, and $S \cap T$ are all convex; set $S \cup T$ is not

Proof: Suppose that $\mathbf{a}$ and $\mathbf{b}$ both lie in $S \cap T$. Then $\mathbf{a}$ and $\mathbf{b}$ both lie both in S and in T. Because S is convex, any convex combination of $\mathbf{x}$ and $\mathbf{y}$ must lie in S. The same is true for T. It follows that the convex combination lies in the intersection $S \cap T$. This means that $S \cap T$ is convex.

EXERCISES FOR SECTION 14.7

1. Determine which of the following sets are convex by drawing each of them in the xy-plane.

   (a) $\{(x, y) : x^2 + y^2 < 2\}$
   (b) $\{(x, y) : x \geq 0, \ y \geq 0\}$
   (c) $\{(x, y) : x^2 + y^2 > 8\}$
   (d) $\{(x, y) : x \geq 0, \ y \geq 0, \ xy \geq 1\}$
   (e) $\{(x, y) : xy \geq 1\}$
   (f) $\{(x, y) : \sqrt{x} + \sqrt{y} \leq 2\}$

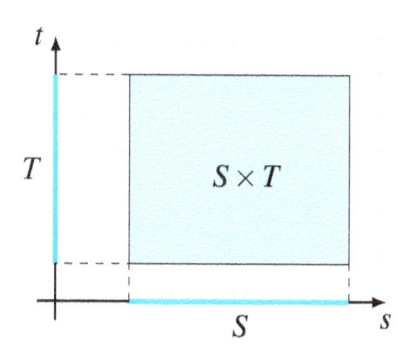

Figure 14.7.6 Exercise 2

2. If S and T are any two sets, the *Cartesian product* $S \times T$ of S and T is defined as the set
$$S \times T = \{(s, t) : s \in S, \ t \in T\}$$
of all ordered pairs (s, t) with $s \in S$ and $t \in T$ (see Section 4.3).

   (a) For the case illustrated in Fig 14.7.6 when S and T are both intervals of the real line, so convex, prove that $S \times T$ is a convex subset of the plane.

   (b) The Cartesian product of $\mathbb{R}^m$ and $\mathbb{R}^n$ can be identified with $\mathbb{R}^{m+n}$ via the correspondence between the pair $((x_1, \ldots, x_m), (y_1, \ldots, y_n))$ in $\mathbb{R}^m \times \mathbb{R}^n$ and $(x_1, \ldots, x_m, y_1, \ldots, y_n)$ in $\mathbb{R}^{m+n}$. Given two arbitrary convex sets S and T in $\mathbb{R}^m$ and $\mathbb{R}^n$, respectively, is the Cartesian product $S \times T$ convex in $\mathbb{R}^{m+n}$?

14.8 Concave and Convex Functions

Two Variables

Recall from Chapter 8 that a function of one variable $y = f(x)$ defined on interval I is called concave if its graph looks like ∩, with its hollow side turned downwards, like a cave roof. On the other hand, the function $y = f(x)$ is convex on I if its graph looks like ∪, with its hollow side turned upwards, like a ditch.

We now look for a definition that is valid for functions of more than one variable. Intuition based on the geometry in the case of one variable suggests this: *A function f is concave (convex) if it is defined on a convex set and the line segment joining any two points on its graph is never above (below) the graph.*

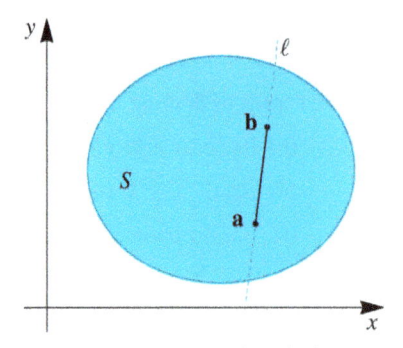

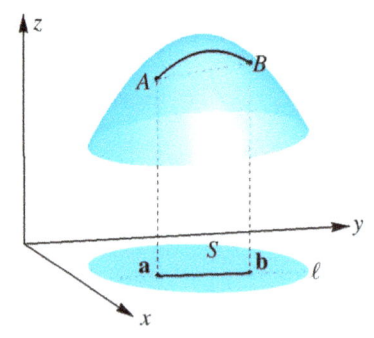

Figure 14.8.1 A convex domain for $f(x, y)$

Figure 14.8.2 A concave function defined on S

In order to allow the graph of a function to be drawn in three dimensions, we consider the special case when $z = f(x, y)$, a function of two variables. Suppose that f is defined on the convex set S illustrated in Fig. 14.8.1, which has the particular points $\mathbf{a} = (a_1, a_2)$ and $\mathbf{b} = (b_1, b_2)$ as two of its members. Figure 14.8.1 also shows the unique line ℓ in the xy-plane that includes these two points. From the discussion surrounding Eqs (14.7.3) and (14.7.4), convexity of S implies that every point of ℓ which belongs to the line segment $[\mathbf{a}, \mathbf{b}]$ connecting these two points also lies within S.

Figure 8.2.1 showed the graph in two dimensions of a concave function of one variable. The analogue for a function of two variables is a graph in three dimensions, part of which is represented in Fig. 14.8.2. The figure also includes the shaded set marked S which represents all points whose coordinates (x, y, z) satisfy (x, y) in S and $z = 0$; this is effectively a copy of the set S shown in Fig. 14.8.1.

The graph of f consists of all points (x, y, z) in 3-space that satisfy (x, y) in S and $z = f(x, y)$. It includes the two particular points A and B shown in Fig. 14.8.2, whose coordinates in three dimensions are respectively

$$(\mathbf{a}, f(\mathbf{a})) = (a_1, a_2, f(a_1, a_2)) \quad \text{and} \quad (\mathbf{b}, f(\mathbf{b})) = (b_1, b_2, f(b_1, b_2))$$

Because f is defined on the whole of the convex set S, it is defined in particular for each point (x, y) in the line segment $[\mathbf{a}, \mathbf{b}]$. Figure 14.8.2 includes a curve joining the two points A and B that appears highlighted. It is the part of the graph of f defined on S that, in Fig. 14.8.2, lies above the line segment $[\mathbf{a}, \mathbf{b}]$ in the plane $z = 0$. This curve consists of all the triples (x, y, z) in $\mathbb{R}^3$ where (x, y) is a convex combination of $\mathbf{a}$ and $\mathbf{b}$, and $z = f(x, y)$. The solid straight line connecting the two end points A and B of this curve is never above the highlighted curve joining A to B that forms the relevant part of the graph of the function. This is precisely what is required for the function f to be concave, as in the following:

CONCAVE AND CONVEX FUNCTIONS

Let $z = f(\mathbf{x})$ be a function defined on a convex set S in the plane. Then f is *concave* if, for all $\mathbf{a}$ and $\mathbf{b}$ in S and for all λ in $[0, 1]$, one has

$$f(\lambda \mathbf{a} + (1 - \lambda)\mathbf{b}) \geq \lambda f(\mathbf{a}) + (1 - \lambda) f(\mathbf{b}) \tag{14.8.1}$$

Similarly, f is *convex* on S if, for all **a** and **b** in S and for all λ in $[0, 1]$, one has

$$f(\lambda \mathbf{a} + (1 - \lambda)\mathbf{b}) \leq \lambda f(\mathbf{a}) + (1 - \lambda)f(\mathbf{b}) \tag{14.8.2}$$

Clearly, these definitions imply that f is concave if and only $-f$ is convex.

The arguments of f in these two definitions are written in vector form. For the function $z = f(x, y)$ of two variables, an equivalent version of (14.8.1) is

$$f(\lambda x_1 + (1 - \lambda)x_2, \lambda y_1 + (1 - \lambda)y_2) \geq \lambda f(x_1, y_1) + (1 - \lambda)f(x_2, y_2)$$

Similarly for Eq. (14.8.2). It is useful to note, also, that the inequalities (14.8.1) and (14.8.2) are identical to (8.2.1) and (8.2.2), respectively, except that f now has two arguments. This shows that the definitions of concavity and convexity we just gave are rather simple extensions of those we saw in Chapter 8.

As in that chapter, if the inequality (14.8.1) is *always* strict when $\mathbf{a} \neq \mathbf{b}$ and $0 < \lambda < 1$, then f is *strictly concave*, whereas if the inequality (14.8.2) is *always* strict when $\mathbf{a} \neq \mathbf{b}$ and $0 < \lambda < 1$, then the function is *strictly convex*. Unsurprisingly, f is strictly convex if and only if $-f$ is strictly concave.

It is usually impractical to apply the definition directly to show that a function is concave or convex in a certain set. We shall later develop a number of theorems that often help us to decide with ease whether a function is concave or convex. Even so, here is one example where we use the definition directly.

EXAMPLE 14.8.1   Consider the function $f(x, y)$ of two variables defined by $f(x, y) = 1 - x^2$ (so y does not appear in the formula for f). Show that f is concave. Is it strictly concave?

Solution: Let (x_1, y_1) and (x_2, y_2) be two arbitrary points in the plane. For f to be concave, we must show that for all λ in $[0, 1]$, one has

$$f(\lambda x_1 + (1 - \lambda)x_2, \lambda y_1 + (1 - \lambda)y_2) \geq \lambda f(x_1, y_1) + (1 - \lambda)f(x_2, y_2) \tag{$*$}$$

Using the definition of f, we see that inequality ($*$) is equivalent to

$$1 - [\lambda x_1 + (1 - \lambda)x_2]^2 \geq \lambda(1 - x_1^2) + (1 - \lambda)(1 - x_2^2)$$

or to

$$1 - [\lambda x_1 + (1 - \lambda)x_2]^2 - \lambda(1 - x_1^2) - (1 - \lambda)(1 - x_2^2) \geq 0 \tag{$**$}$$

Expanding and collecting all terms on the LHS of the inequality ($**$) yields the expression

$$\lambda(1 - \lambda)[x_1^2 - 2x_1 x_2 + x_2^2] = \lambda(1 - \lambda)(x_1 - x_2)^2 \tag{$***$}$$

This expression is obviously nonnegative for all λ in $[0, 1]$. So ($**$) is satisfied, confirming that $f(x, y)$ is concave.

When $x_1 = x_2$, the expression ($***$) is zero, implying equality in ($**$), and so in ($*$), for all values of y_1 and y_2, even when $y_1 \neq y_2$. It follows that f cannot be strictly concave.

The one-variable function $g(x) = 1 - x^2$ is concave. The previous example showed that it is also concave considered as a function of the two variables x and y.

Figure 14.8.3 shows a portion of the graph of a particular function that takes the form $f(x, y) = g(x)$. Here g is concave, and therefore so is f. Through each point on the graph there is a straight line parallel to the y-axis that lies *in* the graph. This shows that f cannot be strictly concave, even though g is.

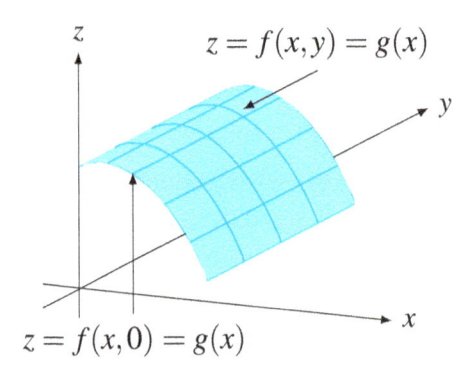

Figure 14.8.3 Function $g(x)$ is strictly concave, but $f(x, y)$ is only concave

EXAMPLE 14.8.2 Consider the linear (affine) function $f(x, y) = ax + by + c$, where a, b and c are constants. It follows immediately from the definition that f is both concave and convex. The graph of f is a plane in $\mathbb{R}^3$. All points on the line segment between any two points in the plane lie within the same plane.

Sums and Composite Functions

In Section 8.3 we presented some useful results for sums and composites of functions that are concave or convex. With only some obvious formal modifications, the same results hold for functions of two variables as well. Since the way to demonstrate them is actually just the same, we simply state them here without further discussion.

THEOREM 14.8.1 (PROPERTIES OF CONCAVE FUNCTIONS)

Let S be a convex subset in the plane, and $f(x, y)$ a function defined on S.

(i) Let h be the function defined on S by $h(x, y) = -f(x, y)$. Then f is (strictly) concave if and only if h is (strictly) convex.

(ii) Suppose now that $g(x, y)$ is another function defined on S. If f and g are both concave, then so is the function $f(x, y) + g(x, y)$. If either f or g is also strictly concave, then so is the function $f(x, y) + g(x, y)$.

(iii) Let $F(z)$ be an increasing and concave function defined over an interval that includes the range of f. If f is concave, then so is the composite function $F(f(x, y))$. If f is strictly concave, and F is strictly increasing as well as concave, then $F(f(x, y))$ is strictly concave.

Concavity and Convexity Using Second Derivatives

For functions of one variable, the four characterizations (8.5.3) to (8.5.6) often provide a quick way to decide where a function is (strictly) concave or (strictly) convex by checking the sign of the second derivative. For functions of two variables there is a corresponding test which is very often used.

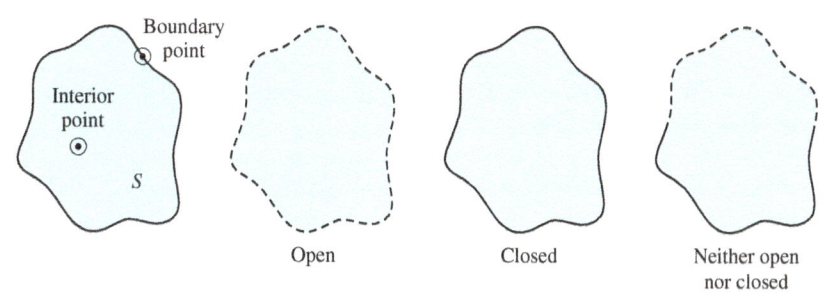

Figure 14.8.4 Open and closed sets

Our test of concavity or convexity requires us to extend the concept of an open interval in the line $\mathbb{R}^1$ to that of an open set in the plane $\mathbb{R}^2$. First, a point **a** is called an *interior point* of a set S in $\mathbb{R}^2$ if there exists a circle centred at **a** such that all points inside the circle lie in S. This is illustrated by the point marked "interior point" in Fig. 14.8.4. On the other hand, if every circle around **a** contains at least one point from S and at least one that does not belong to S, then **a** is called a *boundary point* of S. Finally, **a** is an *exterior point* of S if there is a circle centred at **a** that does not contain any points of S. Note that, since any circle contains its centre, no exterior point of S can belong to S.

A set S in $\mathbb{R}^2$ is *open* if all its points are interior points. This is true for the second set illustrated in Fig. 14.8.4, where we indicate boundary points that belong to the set by a solid curve, and those that do not by a dashed curve. Some other examples include: the open first quadrant $\{(x, y) : x > 0, \ y > 0\}$; the set $\{(x, y) : x^2 + y^2 < 1\}$ of all points strictly inside the unit circle; the open rectangle $\{(x, y) : 0 < x < 5, \ 2 < y < 4\}$; the entire plane $\mathbb{R}^2$; and the empty set $\varnothing$.

In all but the last of these examples it will be obvious from a picture that for any point in the set we can find a small circle around that point such that anything inside that circle belongs to the set. But what about the empty set? Well, there is no point at all in $\varnothing$, so every point in $\varnothing$ is trivially an interior point.

The set of all interior points of a set S is called the *interior* of S. It is not hard to show that the interior of S is an open set.

A boundary point of S does not necessarily belong to S. If S contains all its boundary points, like the third set in Fig. 14.8.4, then S is called *closed*. Note that a set that contains some but not all of its boundary points, like the last of those illustrated in Fig. 14.8.4, is neither open nor closed. In fact, a set is closed if and only if its complement is open.[10]

Given any subset S of the plane, its interior, exterior, and boundary together form a "partition" of the entire plane into three pairwise disjoint sets. Of these three sets, the interior and exterior of S are both open, whereas the boundary that "separates" the interior of S from its exterior is closed.

These illustrations give only very loose indications of what it means for a set to be either open or closed. Of course, if a set is not even precisely defined, it is impossible to decide conclusively whether it is open or closed.

Having explained the concept of an open set, we can formulate the following result:

CONCAVITY AND CONVEXITY CONDITIONS USING SECOND DERIVATIVES

Suppose that the function $z = f(x, y)$ is defined and C^2 on a set S that is open and convex. Then,

$$f \text{ is concave} \iff f_{11}'' \leq 0, f_{22}'' \leq 0, \text{ and } f_{11}''f_{22}'' - (f_{12}'')^2 \geq 0 \qquad (14.8.3)$$

$$f \text{ is convex} \iff f_{11}'' \geq 0, f_{22}'' \geq 0, \text{ and } f_{11}''f_{22}'' - (f_{12}'')^2 \geq 0 \qquad (14.8.4)$$

For strict concavity or convexity, here are sufficient but not necessary conditions:

$$f_{11}'' < 0 \text{ and } f_{11}''f_{22}'' - (f_{12}'')^2 > 0 \implies f \text{ is strictly concave} \qquad (14.8.5)$$

$$f_{11}'' > 0 \text{ and } f_{11}''f_{22}'' - (f_{12}'')^2 > 0 \implies f \text{ is strictly convex} \qquad (14.8.6)$$

The inequalities in all four statements are understood to hold at all points (x, y) in S.

The implications in (14.8.5) and (14.8.6) cannot be reversed. For example, the function $f(x, y) = x^4 + y^4$ is strictly convex in the whole plane, even though $f_{11}''(0, 0) = 0$.

Note too that the two inequalities specified in (14.8.5) together imply that $f_{22}''(x, y) < 0$ as well.[11] Similarly, the two inequalities in (14.8.6) together imply that $f_{22}'' > 0$.

EXAMPLE 14.8.3 Let $f(x, y) = 2x - y - x^2 + 2xy - y^2$ for all (x, y). Is f concave/convex?

Solution: Here $f_{11}'' = -2$, $f_{12}'' = f_{21}'' = 2$, and $f_{22}'' = -2$. Hence $f_{11}''f_{22}'' - (f_{12}'')^2 = 0$. So all three conditions in (14.8.3) are satisfied, implying that f is concave for all (x, y).

EXAMPLE 14.8.4 Find the largest set S on which $f(x, y) = x^2 - y^2 - xy - x^3$ is concave.

---

[10] In everyday usage the words "open" and "closed" are antonyms: a shop is either open or closed. In topology, however, a set that contains some but not all its boundary points is neither open nor closed. To make matters even stranger, in topology there always exist "clopen" sets that are *both* open *and* closed. In $\mathbb{R}^2$ these include $\varnothing$ and $\mathbb{R}^2$ itself. This is explained in FMEA.

[11] In fact, the second inequality implies that $f_{11}''f_{22}'' > (f_{12}'')^2 \geq 0$. So f_{11}'' and f_{22}'' must have the same sign.

Solution: Here $f''_{11} = 2 - 6x$, $f''_{12} = f''_{21} = -1$, and $f''_{22} = -2$. Hence $f''_{11} \leq 0$ iff $x \geq 1/3$. Moreover, $f''_{11}f''_{22} - (f''_{12})^2 = 12x - 5 \geq 0$ iff $x \geq 5/12$. Since $5/12 > 1/3$, we conclude from (14.8.3) that the set S consists of all (x, y) where $x \geq 5/12$.

EXAMPLE 14.8.5 Check the (strict) concavity or convexity of the Cobb–Douglas function defined on the set $S = \{(x, y) : x > 0, y > 0\}$ by $f(x, y) = x^a y^b$, where the parameters a and b together satisfy $a \geq 0$, $b \geq 0$, and $a + b \leq 1$.

Solution: Here $f''_{11} = a(a-1)x^{a-2}y^b$, $f''_{12} = abx^{a-1}y^{b-1}$, and $f''_{22} = b(b-1)x^a y^{b-2}$. Since a and b belong to the interval $[0, 1]$, one has $f''_{11} \leq 0$ and $f''_{22} \leq 0$. Moreover, throughout S one has $f''_{11}f''_{22} - (f''_{12})^2 = abx^{2a-2}y^{2b-2}(1 - a - b) \geq 0$. So the conditions in Eq. (14.8.3) are satisfied, implying that $f(x, y)$ is concave in S. In case $a > 0$, $b > 0$, and $a + b < 1$, one has $f''_{11} < 0$ and $f''_{11}f''_{22} - (f''_{12})^2 > 0$. Then (14.8.5) implies that f is strictly concave.

Finally, in (14.6.2) we introduced the notation that, in the case of a function of two variables reduces to

$$\mathbf{f}''(x, y) = \begin{pmatrix} f''_{11}(x, y) & f''_{12}(x, y) \\ f''_{21}(x, y) & f''_{22}(x, y) \end{pmatrix}$$

for the symmetric Hessian matrix. Students who are already familiar with determinants will know that, following (13.1.3), one has $|\mathbf{f}''| = f''_{11}f''_{22} - (f''_{12})^2$. With this notation, conditions (14.8.3)–(14.8.6) may become easier to remember when restated as follows:

CONCAVITY AND CONVEXITY USING SECOND DERIVATIVES

Let the function $z = f(x, y)$ be defined and C^2 on an open and convex set S in the plane. Then

$$f \text{ is concave} \iff f''_{11} \leq 0, \ f''_{22} \leq 0, \text{ and } |\mathbf{f}''| \geq 0 \quad (14.8.7)$$

$$f \text{ is convex} \iff f''_{11} \geq 0, \ f''_{22} \geq 0, \text{ and } |\mathbf{f}''| \geq 0 \quad (14.8.8)$$

$$f''_{11} < 0 \text{ and } |\mathbf{f}''| > 0 \implies f \text{ is strictly concave} \quad (14.8.9)$$

$$f''_{11} > 0 \text{ and } |\mathbf{f}''| > 0 \implies f \text{ is strictly convex} \quad (14.8.10)$$

where the inequalities in the four statements are understood to hold throughout S.

Many Variables

We now consider conditions for the concavity or convexity of a function $z = f(\mathbf{x})$ of $n > 2$ variables which is defined on a subset S of $\mathbb{R}^n$. Of course, we can no longer draw the graph of f, since that is a set in $n + 1$-space and $n + 1 > 3$. Nevertheless, it is fairly easy to extend the concepts and definitions of convex set and of (strictly) concave (or convex) function from the case of two variables (x, y) that we have been considering so far to the case of n variables specified by the n-vector $\mathbf{x}$.

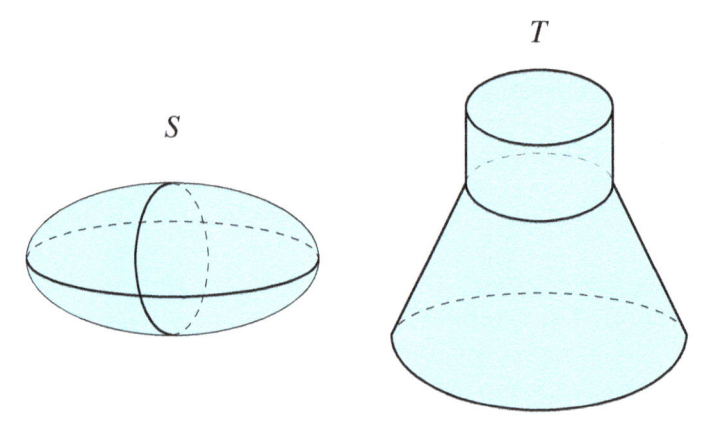

Figure 14.8.5 One convex and one non-convex set in $\mathbb{R}^3$

First, note that definitions (14.8.1) and (14.8.2) of concave and convex function have already been expressed in a way that allows the domain S of the function $z = f(\mathbf{x})$ to be a subset of $\mathbb{R}^n$. To use the definitions, however, we must check whether the domain S of $z = f(\mathbf{x})$ is a convex set. Following definitions (14.7.3) and (14.7.4), a set S in $\mathbf{R}^n$ is convex if and only if, for every pair of points $\mathbf{a}, \mathbf{b}$ in S, it contains the line segment $[\mathbf{a}, \mathbf{b}]$ consisting of all convex combinations of $\mathbf{a}$ and $\mathbf{b}$. For three-dimensional sets such as those in Fig. 14.8.5, a graphical representation is still possible, and allows us to see that the set S, which is shaped like a solid rugby ball, is convex, unlike the set T, which is a solid whose boundary is shaped like a conical flask or coffee pot with a neck and a tight-fitting cover on top. For $n > 3$, however, we must rely on definition (14.7.4) to determine whether a set S in $\mathbf{R}^n$ is convex or non-convex.

Second, we need to extend from the plane $\mathbb{R}^2$ to $\mathbb{R}^n$ our previous definitions of an interior point and open set. Indeed, the modification is rather obvious: for a point $\mathbf{a}$ in $\mathbb{R}^n$ to be an interior point of the set S, there must be an sphere rather than a circle centred at $\mathbf{a}$ such that all points in the sphere lie in S. To understand this clearly, you may need to review the definition (14.4.3) of a sphere with centre $\mathbf{a}$ and radius r in $\mathbb{R}^3$, which in $\mathbb{R}^n$ becomes the set $\{\mathbf{x} : \|\mathbf{x} - \mathbf{a}\| = r\}$. With this definition, that of an open set does not change: a set S in $\mathbb{R}^n$ is open if every point of S is in the interior of S.

Third, even though we cannot draw the graph of $z = f(\mathbf{x})$ when $\mathbf{x}$ is an n-vector with $n \geq 3$, a two-dimensional graphical representation of the inequalities in definitions (14.8.1) and (14.8.2) is still possible. Indeed, given any two distinct points $\mathbf{a}$ and $\mathbf{b}$ of the convex set S, consider the function $\varphi(t)$ of one variable defined for all t in the interval $[0, 1]$ by

$$\varphi(t) = f(t\mathbf{a} + (1-t)\mathbf{b})$$

As a function of only one variable, this has a graph in two dimensions. That graph will be a curve in the plane joining the two end points where $(t, z) = (0, f(\mathbf{b}))$ and $(t, z) = (1, f(\mathbf{a}))$. Then definition (14.8.1), for instance, states that if f is concave, then every point on the curve that is the graph of $z = \varphi(t)$ for $0 \leq t \leq 1$ must be on or above the line segment that joins its two end points. That line segment is the set $\{(t, z) : 0 \leq t \leq 1 \text{ and } z = t\mathbf{a} + (1-t)\mathbf{b}\}$. Another implication of $z = f(\mathbf{x})$ being concave is that the function $z = \varphi(t)$ is concave over the whole of [0, 1]. In other words, f is concave over the line segment $[\mathbf{a}, \mathbf{b}]$. Conversely, if f is concave over every line segment in S, then f is concave over S.

Fourth, it is easy to see that the results of Theorem 14.8.1 extend from functions of two variables to functions of n variables.

Much less straightforward is the characterization of a concave or convex function using its second derivatives. Already the conditions in (14.8.3) to (14.8.6) for functions of two variables are certainly more complicated than their counterparts (8.5.3) to (8.5.6) for functions of one variable. They also require that the function f have continuous first- and second-order partial derivatives. There are even more complications when considering a function of $n \geq 3$ variables. The conditions given below involve the definiteness of the Hessian matrix, relying on the definitions we introduced in Section 13.12. See FMEA for further discussion of the result.

THEOREM 14.8.2 (CONCAVITY AND CONVEXITY USING SECOND DERIVATIVES)

Suppose that the function $f(\mathbf{x})$ is defined and C^2 on a set S in the space $\mathbb{R}^n$ that is open and convex. Let $\mathbf{f}''(\mathbf{x})$ denote the Hessian matrix defined in (14.6.2). Then:

(i) f is concave if and only if for all $\mathbf{x}$ in S the matrix $\mathbf{f}''(\mathbf{x})$ is negative semidefinite;

(ii) f is convex if and only if for all $\mathbf{x}$ in S the matrix $\mathbf{f}''(\mathbf{x})$ is positive semidefinite;

(iii) f is strictly concave if for all $\mathbf{x}$ in S the matrix $\mathbf{f}''(\mathbf{x})$ is negative definite;

(iv) f is strictly convex if for all $\mathbf{x}$ in S the matrix $\mathbf{f}''(\mathbf{x})$ is positive definite.

Note that, like the corresponding results for functions of one or two variables, although the conditions specified in parts (i) and (ii) are both necessary and sufficient for f to be concave or convex, those specified in parts (iii) and (iv) are sufficient but not necessary for f to be strictly concave or strictly convex.

EXAMPLE 14.8.6   Prove that the function defined for all real x_1, x_2, and x_3 by

$$f(x_1, x_2, x_3) = 100 - 2x_1^2 - x_2^2 - 3x_3 - x_1 x_2 - e^{x_1 + x_2 + x_3}$$

is strictly concave.

Solution: We have to show that the Hessian matrix of f is negative definite. Routine calculation of the first-order and then the second-order partial derivatives of f shows that

$$\mathbf{f}''(x_1, x_2, x_3) = \begin{pmatrix} -4 - e^u & -1 - e^u & -e^u \\ -1 - e^u & -2 - e^u & -e^u \\ -e^u & -e^u & -e^u \end{pmatrix}$$

where $u = x_1 + x_2 + x_3$. By Theorem 13.12.2, it is enough to show that the three principal minors of $\mathbf{f}''$ satisfy: (i) $f''_{11} < 0$; (ii) $\begin{vmatrix} f''_{11} & f''_{12} \\ f''_{21} & f''_{22} \end{vmatrix} > 0$; (iii) $|\mathbf{f}''| < 0$.

Note first that $f''_{11} = -4 - e^u < 0$. To check (ii), we subtract the first row of the second-order principal minor from its second row to obtain

$$\begin{vmatrix} f''_{11} & f''_{12} \\ f''_{21} & f''_{22} \end{vmatrix} = \begin{vmatrix} -4 - e^u & -1 - e^u \\ -1 - e^u & -2 - e^u \end{vmatrix} = \begin{vmatrix} -4 - e^u & -1 - e^u \\ 3 & -1 \end{vmatrix} = 7 + 4e^u > 0$$

As for (iii), to evaluate the determinant of $\mathbf{f}''(x_1, x_2, x_3)$ we first subtract its third row from both its first and second rows, then use cofactor expansion along the third column. The result is

$$|\mathbf{f}''| = \begin{vmatrix} -4 - e^u & -1 - e^u & -e^u \\ -1 - e^u & -2 - e^u & -e^u \\ -e^u & -e^u & -e^u \end{vmatrix} = \begin{vmatrix} -4 & -1 & 0 \\ -1 & -2 & 0 \\ -e^u & -e^u & -e^u \end{vmatrix} = (-e^u) \begin{vmatrix} -4 & -1 \\ -1 & -2 \end{vmatrix} = -7e^u < 0$$

By Theorem 13.12.2, this sign pattern confirms that the Hessian matrix $\mathbf{f}''$ is negative definite, so f is strictly concave. ∎

Rather than a proof of the characterization we introduced in Theorem 14.8.2, instead we offer an informative example.

EXAMPLE 14.8.7   Given any symmetric matrix $\mathbf{A} = (a_{ij})_{n \times n}$, show that the function defined on $\mathbb{R}^n$ by $f(\mathbf{x}) = \mathbf{x}'\mathbf{A}\mathbf{x}$ is concave, strictly concave, convex, or strictly convex according as the matrix $\mathbf{A}$ is negative semidefinite, negative definite, positive semidefinite, or positive definite. Consider first the special case when $\mathbf{A}$ is a diagonal matrix, then treat the general case by considering the diagonalization $\mathbf{P}'\mathbf{A}\mathbf{P}$ of $\mathbf{A}$ whose existence is ensured by the Spectral Theorem 13.11.4.

Solution: In the special case when $\mathbf{A}$ is the $n \times n$ diagonal matrix $\mathbf{D} = \text{diag}(\lambda_1, \lambda_2, \ldots, \lambda_n)$, the quadratic form is $f(\mathbf{x}) = \mathbf{x}'\mathbf{D}\mathbf{x} = \sum_{i=1}^n \lambda_i x_i^2$. Now each term $\lambda_i x_i^2$ of the sum is respectively strictly concave, both concave and convex, or strictly convex according as λ_i is negative, zero, or positive. It follows from Theorem 14.8.1 extended to functions of n variables that the sum of all n terms is respectively concave, or strictly concave, or convex, or strictly convex according as the coefficients λ_i, which are the eigenvalues of the diagonal matrix $\mathbf{D}$, are all simultaneously nonpositive, or negative, or nonnegative, or positive. By Theorem 13.12.1, this is equivalent to $\mathbf{D}$ being respectively negative semidefinite, or negative definite, or positive semidefinite, or positive definite.

For the general case, because $\mathbf{A}$ is symmetric, the Spectral Theorem 13.11.4 implies that $\mathbf{A}$ has a diagonalization $\mathbf{D} = \mathbf{P}'\mathbf{A}\mathbf{P}$, where $\mathbf{P}$ is orthogonal in the sense that $\mathbf{P}^{-1} = \mathbf{P}'$. Then, arguing as in the proof of Theorem 13.12.1, the diagonal elements of $\mathbf{D}$ are the eigenvalues of both $\mathbf{D}$ and $\mathbf{A}$. Moreover, following Eq. (13.12.12), one has $\mathbf{x}'\mathbf{A}\mathbf{x} = \mathbf{y}'\mathbf{D}\mathbf{y} = \sum_{i=1}^n \lambda_i y_i^2$ where $\mathbf{y} = \mathbf{P}'\mathbf{x}$. As in the previous special case when $\mathbf{A}$ is diagonal, the result follows from Theorem 13.12.1. ∎

Recall from Example 14.6.3 that, given any symmetric $n \times n$ matrix $\mathbf{A}$, the Hessian matrix of the quadratic form $\mathbf{x}'\mathbf{A}\mathbf{x}$ satisfies $\mathbf{f}'' = 2\mathbf{A}$.

This result and its proof should help reinforce in your mind the importance and usefulness of the Spectral Theorem 13.11.4, as well as of Theorem 13.12.1 which characterizes the definiteness of the quadratic form by the signs of the eigenvalues of its associated symmetric matrix. A very closely related result will appear in Chapter 17 when we consider second-order conditions for optimization.

EXERCISES FOR SECTION 14.8

1. Which of the functions whose graphs are shown in Fig. 14.8.6 below are (presumably) convex/concave, strictly concave/strictly convex?

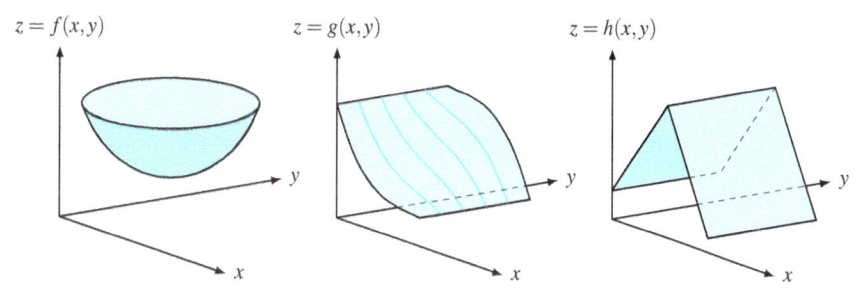

Figure 14.8.6 Exercise 14.8.1

2. For what values of the constant a is the following function concave/convex?

$$f(x, y) = -6x^2 + (2a + 4)xy - y^2 + 4ay$$

(SM) 3. Examine the convexity/concavity of the following functions:

(a) $z = x + y - e^x - e^{x+y}$ (b) $z = e^{x+y} + e^{x-y} - \frac{1}{2}y$ (c) $w = (x + 2y + 3z)^2$

(*Hint:* For part (c), recognize that w is a quadratic form, and determine its sign. Then use the result of Example 14.8.7.)

4. [HARDER] Suppose that $z = f(x, y)$ is a production function which determines output z as a function of the pair (x, y) of nonnegative factor inputs Assume that $f(0, 0) = 0$. Also, for each fixed (x, y) with $x \geq 0$, and $y \geq 0$, for all $\lambda > 0$, define $g(\lambda; x, y) = f(\lambda x, \lambda y)/\lambda$. Show that:

(a) If f is twice continuously differentiable and concave, then for all x, y one has $f''_{11}(x, y) \leq 0$ and $f''_{22}(x, y) \leq 0$ (so each marginal product is decreasing).

(b) If f is concave, then $g(\lambda; x, y)$ is decreasing as a function of λ, for each $x \geq 0$ and $y \geq 0$.

(c) In case there exists a fixed (x, y) with $x \geq 0$ and $y \geq 0$ such that f displays "constant returns" in the sense that $g(\lambda; x, y)$ is independent of λ, then f is not strictly concave.

(*Hint:* For parts (b) and (c), given any fixed $x \geq 0$ and $y \geq 0$ with $(x, y) \neq (0, 0)$, show that $g(\lambda; x, y)$ is the slope $s(0, \lambda)$ of $f(\lambda x, \lambda y)$, viewed as a function of the one variable λ defined for all $\lambda \geq 0$. Then use Theorem 8.2.1.)

14.9 Economic Applications

This section considers several economic applications of partial derivatives.

EXAMPLE 14.9.1 Consider an agricultural production function $Y = F(K, L, T)$, where Y is the output produced, K is capital invested, L is labour input, and T is the area of agricultural land that is used. Then $\partial Y/\partial K = F'_K$ is called the *marginal product of capital*. It is the rate of change of output Y w.r.t. K when L and T are held fixed. Similarly, $\partial Y/\partial L = F'_L$ and $\partial Y/\partial T = F'_T$ are the *marginal products of labour and of land*, respectively. For example, if K is the value of capital equipment measured in dollars, and $\partial Y/\partial K = 5$, then increasing capital input by h units would increase output by approximately $5h$ units.

Suppose, in particular, that F is the Cobb–Douglas function $F(K, L, T) = AK^a L^b T^c$, where A, a, b, and c are positive constants. Find the marginal products, and the second-order partials. Discuss their signs.

Solution: The three marginal products are

$$F'_K = AaK^{a-1}L^b T^c, \quad F'_L = AbK^a L^{b-1} T^c, \quad \text{and} \quad F'_T = AcK^a L^b T^{c-1}$$

When K, L, and T are all positive, the marginal products are all positive. Thus, an increase in capital, labour, or land will increase output.

The cross second-order partials, also called mixed partials, are:[12]

$$F''_{KL} = AabK^{a-1}L^{b-1}T^c, \quad F''_{KT} = AacK^{a-1}L^b T^{c-1}, \quad \text{and} \quad F''_{LT} = AbcK^a L^{b-1} T^{c-1}$$

Note that all these cross partials are positive. For any two inputs, we say they any are *complementary* because more of one increases the marginal product of the other.

The direct second-order partials are

$$F''_{KK} = Aa(a-1)K^{a-2}L^b T^c, \quad F''_{LL} = Ab(b-1)K^a L^{b-2}T^c, \quad F''_{TT} = Ac(c-1)K^a L^b T^{c-2}$$

For instance, F''_{KK} is the partial derivative of the marginal product F'_K of capital w.r.t. K. If $a < 1$, then $F''_{KK} < 0$, indicating that there is a diminishing marginal product of capital. That is, a small increase in the capital invested will lead to a decrease in the marginal product of capital. We can interpret this as saying that, although small increases in capital cause output to rise, so that $F'_K > 0$, this rise occurs at a decreasing rate, since $F''_{KK} < 0$. Similarly for labour if $b < 1$, and for land if $c < 1$.

EXAMPLE 14.9.2 Let x be the GDP of a country, and let y be a measure of its level of pollution. Suppose that the function $u(x, y)$ purports to measure the total well-being of the society. What signs do you expect $u'_x(x, y)$ and $u'_y(x, y)$ to have? Can you guess what economists usually assume about the sign of $u''_{xy}(x, y)$?

Solution: It is reasonable to believe that social well-being increases as GDP x increases, but decreases as pollution y increases. So we expect that $u'_x(x, y) > 0$ and $u'_z(x, y) < 0$.

---

[12] Check for yourself that Young's Theorem 14.6.1 holds by differentiating in the reverse order to obtain F'''_{LK}, F'''_{TK}, and F'''_{TL}, respectively.

According to Eq. (14.6.1) applied to the function $u'_x(x, y)$, its partial derivative $u''_{xy} = (\partial/\partial y)(u'_x)$ is the approximate change in u'_x per unit increase in y, the level of pollution. Moreover, u'_x is the approximate increase in well-being per unit increase in x.

It is often assumed that $u''_{xy} < 0$. This implies that the increase in well-being obtained from a fixed small increase h in GDP x is likely to decrease when the level of pollution increases.[13] Economists usually assume, often without any thought, that the function u is C^2. By Young's Theorem 14.6.1, the inequality $u''_{xy} < 0$ then implies that $u''_{yx} < 0$. Thus the increase in welfare obtained from being exposed to a little less pollution, which is approximately $-u'_y$ per unit, increases with consumption x. This accords with the highly controversial view that poor people may tolerate pollution more easily.[14]

EXERCISES FOR SECTION 14.9

1. One estimate of the demand for money M in the United States during the period 1929–1952 involves the equation
$$M = 0.14Y + 76.03(r - 2)^{-0.84}$$
Here Y denotes annual national income, and r denotes the interest rate in percent per year, with $r > 2$. Find the partial derivatives $\partial M/\partial Y$ and $\partial M/\partial r$, then discuss their signs.

(SM) 2. If a and b are positive constants, compute the expression $KY'_K + LY'_L$ for the following:

   (a) $Y = AK^a + BL^a$ (b) $Y = AK^a L^b$ (c) $Y = \dfrac{K^2 L^2}{aL^3 + bK^3}$

3. The demand D for a firm's product depends on the price p that it charges, as well as on the price q charged by a competing firm. It is given by $D(p,q) = a - bpq^{-\alpha}$, where a, b, and α are positive constants with $\alpha < 1$. Find the partial derivatives $D'_p(p,q)$ and $D'_q(p,q)$, then comment on their signs.

4. Let $F(K, L, M) = AK^a L^b M^c$. Show that $KF'_K + LF'_L + MF'_M = (a + b + c)F$.

5. Let $D(p,q)$ and $E(p,q)$ be the demands for two commodities when the prices per unit are p and q, respectively. Suppose the commodities are *substitutes* in consumption, such as butter and margarine. What are the normal signs of the partial derivatives of D and E w.r.t. p and q?

6. Find $\partial U/\partial x_i$ when $U(x_1, x_2, \ldots, x_n) = 100 - e^{-x_1} - e^{-x_2} - \cdots - e^{-x_n}$.

(SM) 7. [HARDER] Calculate the expression $KY'_K + LY'_L$ for the CES production function specified by
$$Y = Ae^{\lambda t}\left[aK^{-\rho} + bL^{-\rho}\right]^{-\mu/\rho}$$

---

[13] Here is an example. When a nonsmoker sits in a room filled with tobacco smoke, the extra satisfaction from eating a slightly larger piece of cake might well decrease if the concentration of smoke increases too much.

[14] A particular controversy arose from the claim that dumping polluting activities on poor countries, where they might be better tolerated, could be better for the world as a whole. The sorry history of a "doctored" World Bank "toxic memo" suggesting this is set out in the May 2001 issue of the *Harvard Magazine*, available at https://www.harvardmagazine.com/2001/05/toxic-memo.html.

14.10 Partial Elasticities

Section 7.7 introduced the concept of elasticity for functions of one variable. Here we extend that concept to functions of several variables. This enables us to consider, for instance, the price and income elasticities of demand, as well as different price elasticities.

Two Variables

Suppose that $z = f(x, y)$. We use the partial derivatives of z, when they exist, to define its partial elasticities w.r.t. x and y as

$$\text{El}_x z = \frac{x}{z}\frac{\partial z}{\partial x}, \qquad \text{El}_y z = \frac{y}{z}\frac{\partial z}{\partial y} \tag{14.10.1}$$

Often economists just refer to the elasticity rather than the partial elasticity. Thus, $\text{El}_x z$ is the elasticity of z w.r.t. x when y is held constant, and $\text{El}_y z$ is the elasticity of z w.r.t. y when x is held constant. The number $\text{El}_x z$ is, very roughly, the percentage change in z caused by a 1% increase in x when y is held constant; $\text{El}_y z$ has a corresponding interpretation.

As in Section 7.7, when all the variables are positive, elasticities can be expressed as logarithmic derivatives. Accordingly,

$$\text{El}_x z = \frac{\partial \ln z}{\partial \ln x} \quad \text{and} \quad \text{El}_y z = \frac{\partial \ln z}{\partial \ln y} \tag{14.10.2}$$

EXAMPLE 14.10.1 Find the partial elasticity $\text{El}_x z$ when: (a) $z = Ax^a y^b$; (b) $z = xye^{x+y}$.

Solution: (a) When finding the elasticity of $Ax^a y^b$ w.r.t. x, the variable y, and thus Ay^b, is held constant. From Example 7.7.1 we obtain $\text{El}_x z = a$. In the same way, $\text{El}_y z = b$.

(b) It is convenient here to use Eq. (14.10.2). Assuming all variables are positive, taking appropriate natural logarithms gives $\ln z = \ln x + \ln y + x + y = \ln x + \ln y + e^{\ln x} + y$. Hence $\text{El}_x z = \partial \ln z / \partial \ln x = 1 + e^{\ln x} = 1 + x$.

EXAMPLE 14.10.2 One estimate of the demand D_1 for potatoes in the United States during the period 1927 to 1941 is given by $D_1 = Ap^{-0.28}m^{0.34}$, where p is the price of potatoes and m is mean income. The demand for apples was estimated to be $D_2 = Bq^{-1.27}m^{1.32}$, where q is the price of apples.

Find the price elasticities of demand, $\text{El}_p D_1$ and $\text{El}_q D_2$, as well as the income elasticities of demand, $\text{El}_m D_1$ and $\text{El}_m D_2$. Then comment on their respective signs.

Solution: According to part (a) in Example 14.10.1, we have $\text{El}_p D_1 = -0.28$. So if the price of potatoes increases by the small proportion $h\%$, their demand decreases by approximately $0.28h\%$. Furthermore, $\text{El}_q D_2 = -1.27$, $\text{El}_m D_1 = 0.34$, and $\text{El}_m D_2 = 1.32$.

Both price elasticities $\text{El}_p D_1$ and $\text{El}_q D_2$ are negative. So demand decreases when the own price increases, as seems reasonable. Both income elasticities $\text{El}_m D_1$ and $\text{El}_m D_2$ are positive. So demand for both potatoes and apples increases when mean income increases, as seems reasonable once again. Note that the demand for apples is more sensitive to both price and income changes than the demand for potatoes. This also seems reasonable, since at that time potatoes were more indispensable than apples for most consumers.

More Variables

For the function $z = f(x_1, x_2, \ldots, x_n) = f(\mathbf{x})$ of n variables, we define the *(partial) elasticity* of z, or of f, w.r.t. x_i as the elasticity of z w.r.t. x_i when the other $n-1$ variables are all held constant. Thus, assuming all the variables are positive, we can write

$$\text{El}_i\, z = \frac{x_i}{f(\mathbf{x})} \frac{\partial f(\mathbf{x})}{\partial x_i} = \frac{x_i}{z} \frac{\partial z}{\partial x_i} = \frac{\partial \ln z}{\partial \ln x_i} \qquad (14.10.3)$$

So, for small changes, the number $\text{El}_i\, z$ is approximately equal to the percentage change in z per 1% increase in the ith variable x_i, keeping all the other variables x_j constant. Apart from $\text{El}_i\, z$, other commonly used forms of notation include $\text{El}_i f(\mathbf{x})$, $\text{El}_{x_i} z$, ε_i, e_i, and $\hat{z}_i$. The latter, of course, is pronounced "z hat i".

EXAMPLE 14.10.3 Suppose $D = A x_1^{a_1} x_2^{a_2} \cdots x_n^{a_n}$ is defined for all $x_1 > 0, x_2 > 0, \ldots, x_n > 0$, where $A > 0$ and $a_1, a_2, \ldots, a_n$ are constants. For $i = 1, \ldots, n$, find the elasticity of D w.r.t. x_i.

Solution: Calculating the partial elasticity w.r.t. any x_i requires us to keep all the factors except $x_i^{a_i}$ constant. So we can apply Eq. (7.7.3) to obtain the result $\text{El}_i\, D = a_i$.

As a special case of Example 14.10.3, suppose that the demand for good i is given by

$$D_i = A m^\alpha p_i^{-\beta} p_j^\gamma \qquad (14.10.4)$$

where m denotes income, p_i denotes the own price, and p_j denotes the price of a substitute good. Then α is the income elasticity of demand, defined as in Example 14.10.2. On the other hand, $-\beta$ is the elasticity of demand w.r.t. changes in its own price p_i, so it is called the *own-price elasticity* of demand. Because own-price elasticities of demand are usually negative, however, one often describes β rather than $-\beta$ as being the own-price elasticity of demand. Finally, γ is the elasticity of demand w.r.t. the price of the specified substitute. By analogy with the cross-partial derivatives defined in Section 14.6, it is called a *cross-price elasticity* of demand.

Given the demand function specified by Eq. (14.10.4), note that the proportion of income spent on good i is

$$\frac{p_i D_i}{m} = A m^{\alpha - 1} p_i^{1-\beta} p_j^\gamma$$

When the income elasticity $\alpha < 1$, this proportion is a decreasing function of income. Economists describe a good with this property as a *necessity*. When $\alpha > 1$, on the other hand, the proportion of income spent on good i rises with income, in which case economists describe good i as a *luxury*. Referring back to Example 14.10.2, these definitions imply that during the period 1927–1941, which includes the years of the Great Depression, potatoes were a necessity, but apples were a (relative) luxury.

Exercise 4 considers this distinction between necessities and luxuries for more general demand functions.

EXERCISES FOR SECTION 14.10

1. Find the partial elasticities of z w.r.t. x and y in the following cases:

   (a) $z = xy$ (b) $z = x^2 y^5$ (c) $z = x^n e^x y^n e^y$ (d) $z = x + y$

2. Let $z = (ax_1^d + bx_2^d + cx_3^d)^g$, where a, b, c, d, and g are constants. Find $\sum_{i=1}^{3} \text{El}_i z$.

3. Suppose that $z = x_1^p \cdots x_n^p \exp(a_1 x_1 + \cdots + a_n x_n)$, where the common power p and the parameters $a_1, \ldots, a_n$ are all constants. Find the partial elasticities of z w.r.t. $x_1, \ldots, x_n$.

SM 4. Let $D(p, m)$ indicate a typical consumer's demand for a particular commodity, as a function of its price p and the consumer's own income m. Show that the proportion pD/m of income spent on the commodity increases with income if $\text{El}_m D > 1$ (in which case the good is a "luxury", whereas it is a "necessity" if $\text{El}_m D < 1$).

REVIEW EXERCISES

1. Let $f(x, y) = 3x - 5y$. Find the values of $f(0, 1)$, $f(2, -1)$, $f(a, a)$, and $f(a + h, b) - f(a, b)$.

2. Let $f(x, y) = 2x^2 - 3y^2$. Find the values of $f(-1, 2)$, $f(2a, 2a)$, $f(a, b + k) - f(a, b)$, and $f(tx, ty) - t^2 f(x, y)$.

3. Let $f(x, y, z) = \sqrt{x^2 + y^2 + z^2}$. Find the values of $f(3, 4, 0)$, $f(-2, 1, 3)$, and of $f(tx, ty, tz)$ for any $t \geq 0$.

4. Let $Y = F(K, L) = 15K^{1/5} L^{2/5}$ denote the number of units of output that are produced when K units of capital and L units of labour are used as inputs.

   (a) Compute $F(0, 0)$, $F(1, 1)$, and $F(32, 243)$.

   (b) Find an expression for $F(K + 1, L) - F(K, L)$, and give an economic interpretation.

   (c) Compute $F(32 + 1, 243) - F(32, 243)$, and compare the result with what you get by calculating $F'_K(32, 243)$.

   (d) Show that $F(tK, tL) = t^k F(K, L)$ for a constant k.

5. A study of industrial fishing concluded that the annual herring catch Y, as a function of the catching effort K and the herring stock S, is given by $Y(K, S) = 0.06157 K^{1.356} S^{0.562}$.

   (a) Find $\partial Y/\partial K$ and $\partial Y/\partial S$.

   (b) If K and S are both doubled, what happens to the catch?

6. For which pairs of numbers (x, y) are the functions given by the following formulas defined?

   (a) $3xy^3 - 45x^4 - 3y$ (b) $\sqrt{1 - xy}$ (c) $\ln(2 - (x^2 + y^2))$

7. For which pairs of numbers (x, y) are the functions given by the following formulas defined?

   (a) $1/\sqrt{x + y - 1}$ (b) $\sqrt{x^2 - y^2} + \sqrt{x^2 + y^2 - 1}$ (c) $\sqrt{y - x^2} - \sqrt{\sqrt{x} - y}$

8. Complete the following implications:

    (a) $z = (x^2y^4 + 2)^5 \Rightarrow \dfrac{\partial z}{\partial x} =$

    (b) $F(K, L) = (\sqrt{K} + \sqrt{L})^2 \Rightarrow \sqrt{K}\dfrac{\partial F}{\partial K} =$

    (c) $F(K, L) = (K^a + L^a)^{1/a} \Rightarrow KF'_K(K, L) + LF'_L(K, L) =$

    (d) $g(t, w) = \dfrac{3t}{w} + wt^2 \Rightarrow \dfrac{\partial^2 g}{\partial w \partial t} =$

    (e) $g(t_1, t_2, t_3) = (t_1^2 + t_2^2 + t_3^2)^{1/2} \Rightarrow g'_3(t_1, t_2, t_3) =$

    (f) $f(x, y, z) = 2x^2yz - y^3 + x^2z^2 \Rightarrow f'_1(x, y, z) = \qquad$ and $f''_{13}(x, y, z) =$

9. Let f be defined for all (x, y) by $f(x, y) = (x - 2)^2(y + 3)^2$.

    (a) Calculate $f(0, 0)$, $f(-2, -3)$, and $f(a + 2, b - 3)$. (b) Find f'_x and f'_y.

10. Verify that the points $(-1, 5)$ and $(1, 1)$ lie on the same level curve for the function

$$g(x, y) = (2x + y)^3 - 2x + \frac{5}{y}$$

11. For each $c \neq 0$, verify that $x - y = c$ is a level curve for $F(x, y) = \ln(x^2 - 2xy + y^2) + e^{2x-2y}$.

(SM) 12. Let f be defined for all (x, y) by $f(x, y) = x^4 + 2y^2 - 4x^2y + 4y$.

    (a) Find $f'_1(x, y)$ and $f'_2(x, y)$.

    (b) Find all pairs (x, y) which solve both equations $f'_1(x, y) = 0$ and $f'_2(x, y) = 0$.

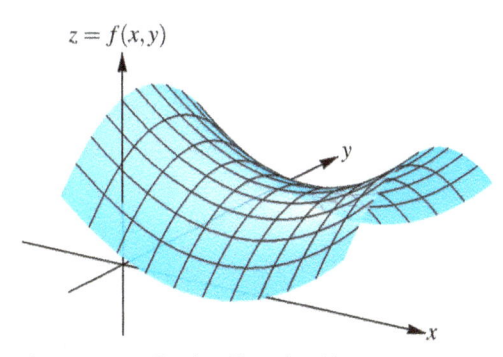

Figure 14.R.1 Review Exercise 13

13. The graph of the function $z = f(x, y) = (x - \frac{1}{2})^2 - (y - \frac{1}{2})^2 + \frac{1}{2}$ appears in Fig. 14.R.1.

    (a) Use this graph in order to determine whether the function is concave, strictly concave, convex, or strictly convex.

    (b) Use Eqs (14.8.7) to (14.8.10) to confirm your conclusion.

14. Let f be defined for all x, y by $f(x, y) = x - y - x^2$.

   (a) Use (14.8.3) to show that f is concave. (b) Show that $-e^{-f(x,y)}$ is concave.

15. Let $f(x, y) = ax^2 + 2bxy + cy^2 + px + qy + r$, where a, b, c, p, q and r are constants.

   (a) Show that f is: (i) strictly concave if $ac - b^2 > 0$ and $a < 0$; (ii) strictly convex if $ac - b^2 > 0$ and $a > 0$.

   (b) Find necessary and sufficient conditions for $f(x, y)$ to be concave/convex.

16. Find the partial elasticities of z w.r.t. x and y in the following cases:

   (a) $z = x^3 y^{-4}$ (b) $z = \ln(x^2 + y^2)$ (c) $z = e^{x+y}$ (d) $z = (x^2 + y^2)^{1/2}$

17. (a) If $F(x, y) = e^{2x}(1 - y)^2$, find $\partial F / \partial y$.

   (b) If $F(K, L, M) = (\ln K)(\ln L)(\ln M)$, find F'_L and F''_{LK}.

   (c) If $w = x^x y^x z^x$, with x, y, and z positive, find w'_x using logarithmic differentiation.

18. [HARDER] Compute $\partial^{p+q} z / \partial y^q \partial x^p$ at $(0, 0)$ for the following:

   (a) $z = e^x \ln(1 + y)$

   (b) $z = e^{x+y}(xy + y - 1)$ (*Hint:* First prove by induction on n that $\dfrac{d^n}{du^n}(e^u u) = e^u(u + n)$.)

19. [HARDER] Show that if $u = Ax^a y^b$, then $u''_{xy} / u'_x u'_y$ can be expressed as a function of u alone. Use this to prove that

$$\frac{1}{u'_x} \frac{\partial}{\partial x} \left(\frac{u''_{xy}}{u'_x u'_y} \right) = \frac{1}{u'_y} \frac{\partial}{\partial y} \left(\frac{u''_{xy}}{u'_x u'_y} \right)$$

15 PARTIAL DERIVATIVES IN USE

Logic merely sanctions the conquests of the intuition.
—Jacques S. Hadamard (1945)

Economists use the phrase "comparative statics" to describe a particular technique that uses partial derivatives. The analysis starts with a mathematical model showing how economic quantities such as demand and supply are determined as endogenous variables that satisfy an equation system. It then addresses the question of how these variables respond to changes in exogenous parameters, like preferences or productivity shocks. More generally, when the parameters of an optimization problem change, what happens to its solution? Or to the solution of an equation system that describes an equilibrium of demand and supply? Some simple examples will be studied in this chapter; more demanding problems are treated in FMEA.

When differentiating functions of one variable, a key tool is the chain rule that was introduced in Section 6.8. Here Sections 15.1 to 15.4 introduce what we need to extend the chain rule to functions of two or more variables. Thereafter Section 15.5 discusses the concept of elasticity of substitution, which economists often use to characterize the "curvature" of a level curve. Another important topic in economics concerns the homogeneous and homothetic functions that are studied in Sections 15.6 and 15.7. Then Sections 15.8 and 15.9 consider linear approximations and then differentials, respectively. The final two Sections 15.10 and 15.11 of the chapter are concerned with systems of equations, along with some properties of their differentials.

15.1 A Simple Chain Rule

Many economic models involve composite functions, which for functions of one variable were introduced in Section 6.8. Here we consider functions of several variables which are themselves functions of other basic variables. For example, many models of economic growth regard output as a function of capital and labour, both of which are functions of time. How then does output vary with time? More generally, what happens to the value of a composite function as its basic variables change? This is the general problem we address in this and the next three sections.

Suppose $z = f(x, y)$ is a function of x and y, where both $x = g(t)$ and $y = h(t)$ are functions of a variable t. Substituting for x and y in $z = f(x, y)$ gives the composite function

$$z = F(t) = f(g(t), h(t))$$

This reduces z to a function of t alone. A change in t will in general lead to changes in both $g(t)$ and $h(t)$, as well as a resulting change in $z = F(t)$. How then does z change when t changes? For example, will a small increase in t lead to an increase or a decrease in z? Answering such questions becomes much easier once we have found an expression for dz/dt, the rate of change of z w.r.t. t. This is provided by the following extension to two variables of the chain rule that was introduced in Section 6.8:

THE CHAIN RULE

Let $z = f(x, y)$ with $x = g(t)$ and $y = h(t)$. If f is C^1 (i.e., if it has continuous first-order partial derivatives), and if g and h are differentiable, then

$$\frac{dz}{dt} = f_1'(x, y)\frac{dx}{dt} + f_2'(x, y)\frac{dy}{dt} \qquad (15.1.1)$$

It is important to understand the precise content of (15.1.1). It gives the derivative of $z = f(x, y)$ w.r.t. t when x and y are both differentiable functions of t. This derivative is called the *total derivative* of z w.r.t. t. According to (15.1.1), one contribution to the total derivative occurs because the first variable x in $f(x, y)$ depends on t. This first contribution is $f_1'(x, y)\,dx/dt$. A second contribution arises because the second variable y in $f(x, y)$ also depends on t. This second contribution is $f_2'(x, y)\,dy/dt$. The total derivative dz/dt is the *sum* of these two contributions.

Note: It is important to realize that if f is not C^1, then formula (15.1.1) may fail, as Exercise 9 shows.

EXAMPLE 15.1.1 Find dz/dt when $z = f(x, y) = x^2 + y^3$ with $x = t^2$ and $y = 2t$.

Solution: In this case $f_1'(x, y) = 2x$, $f_2'(x, y) = 3y^2$, $dx/dt = 2t$, and $dy/dt = 2$. Inserting these four expressions into formula (15.1.1) gives

$$\frac{dz}{dt} = 2x \cdot 2t + 3y^2 \cdot 2 = 4tx + 6y^2 = 4t^3 + 24t^2$$

Here the last equality comes from substituting the appropriate functions of t for x and y respectively. In a simple case like this, we can verify the chain rule by substituting $x = t^2$ and $y = 2t$ in the formula for $f(x, y)$, then differentiating w.r.t. t. The result is

$$z = x^2 + y^3 = (t^2)^2 + (2t)^3 = t^4 + 8t^3 \Rightarrow \frac{dz}{dt} = 4t^3 + 24t^2$$

This is the same answer as before.

EXAMPLE 15.1.2

Find dz/dt when $z = f(x, y) = xe^{2y}$ with $x = \sqrt{t}$ and $y = \ln t$.

Solution: Here $f_1'(x, y) = e^{2y}$, $f_2'(x, y) = 2xe^{2y}$, $dx/dt = 1/2\sqrt{t}$, and $dy/dt = 1/t$. Note that $y = \ln t$ implies $e^{2y} = e^{2\ln t} = (e^{\ln t})^2 = t^2$, so formula (15.1.1) gives

$$\frac{dz}{dt} = e^{2y}\frac{1}{2\sqrt{t}} + 2xe^{2y}\frac{1}{t} = t^2 \frac{1}{2\sqrt{t}} + 2\sqrt{t} t^2 \frac{1}{t} = \frac{5}{2}t^{3/2}$$

As in Example 15.1.1, we can verify the chain rule directly by substituting $x = \sqrt{t}$ and $y = \ln t$ in the formula for $f(x, y)$. Doing so gives $z = xe^{2y} = \sqrt{t} \cdot t^2 = t^{5/2}$, whose derivative is $dz/dt = \frac{5}{2}t^{3/2}$.

Here are some typical examples of how economists use (15.1.1).

EXAMPLE 15.1.3

Let $D = D(p, m)$ denote a consumer's demand for a commodity as a function of both its price p and the consumer's income m. Suppose that $p = p(t)$ and $m = m(t)$ are both differentiable functions of time t. So demand is a function $D = D(p(t), m(t))$ of t alone. Find an expression for $\dot{D}/D$, the relative rate of growth of D.

Solution: Using (15.1.1) with time derivatives denoted by "dots", we obtain

$$\dot{D} = \frac{\partial D(p, m)}{\partial p}\dot{p} + \frac{\partial D(p, m)}{\partial m}\dot{m}$$

The first term on the right-hand side gives the effect on demand that arises because the price p is changing, whereas the second term gives the effect of the change in m. We can write the relative rate of growth of D as

$$\frac{\dot{D}}{D} = \frac{p}{D}\frac{\partial D(p,m)}{\partial p}\frac{\dot{p}}{p} + \frac{m}{D}\frac{\partial D(p,m)}{\partial m}\frac{\dot{m}}{m} = \frac{\dot{p}}{p}\text{El}_p D + \frac{\dot{m}}{m}\text{El}_m D$$

Here the last equality follows from the formula for partial elasticity that was introduced in Section 14.10. So the relative rate of growth is found by multiplying the relative rates of change of price and income by their respective partial elasticities, then adding.

EXAMPLE 15.1.4

As in Example 14.9.2, let $u(x, y)$ denote the total well-being of a society, where x denotes GDP and y denotes a measure of the pollution level. As in that example, assume that $u_x'(x, y) > 0$ and $u_y'(x, y) < 0$.

Suppose now that pollution increases as the economy grows, thus making pollution an increasing function $y = h(x)$ of x, with $h'(x) > 0$. Then total well-being becomes a function $U(x) = u(x, h(x))$ of x alone. Find a necessary condition for $U(x)$ to have a maximum at $x = x^* > 0$, and give this condition an economic interpretation.

Solution: By Theorem 9.1.1, a necessary condition for $U(x)$ to have a maximum at $x^* > 0$ is that $U'(x^*) = 0$. Now we use the chain rule (15.1.1) to obtain:

$$U'(x) = u_x'(x, h(x)) \cdot 1 + u_y'(x, h(x)) \cdot h'(x) \qquad (*)$$

So $U'(x^*) = 0$ requires that

$$u'_x(x^*, h(x^*)) = -u'_y(x^*, h(x^*))h'(x^*) \qquad (**)$$

To interpret this condition, consider increasing x^* by a small amount δ, which can be positive or negative. By Eq. (14.2.6), the gain due to the increase in GDP is approximately $u'_x(x^*, h(x^*))\delta$. On the other hand, the level of pollution increases by about $h'(x^*)\delta$ units. But we lose $-u'_y(x^*, h(x^*))$ in well-being per unit increase in pollution. So all in all we lose about $-u'_y(x^*, h(x^*))h'(x^*)\delta$ from the extra pollution that results from this increase in x^*. Equation $(**)$ just states that the direct gain from increasing x^* by any small amount δ must equal the indirect loss from the increased pollution that results from this increase. Otherwise a slight increase in well-being could be achieved by a small change δ in x whose sign matches the sign of $U'(x^*)$ given by Eq. $(*)$.

Higher-Order Derivatives

Sometimes we use the second derivative of a composite function. A general formula for d^2z/dt^2, based on formula (15.1.1), is suggested in Exercise 8. Here we consider a special case that is relevant to optimization theory, the subject of Chapter 17. It concerns the function F that records what happens to f as one moves away from the point (a, b) to $(a + t\ell, b + tk)$. If $t > 0$, this move is in the direction (ℓ, k), but if $t < 0$ it is in the reverse direction $(-\ell, -k)$. See Fig. 15.1.1.

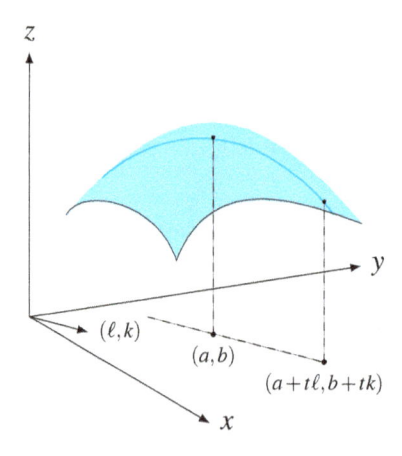

Figure 15.1.1 $F(t) = f(a + t\ell, b + tk)$

EXAMPLE 15.1.5 Suppose that $z = f(x, y)$ where $x = a + t\ell$ and $y = b + tk$. Keeping (a, b) and (ℓ, k) fixed makes z a function $z = F(t)$ of the one variable t. Find expressions for $F'(t)$ and $F''(t)$.

Solution: With $x = a + t\ell$ and $y = b + tk$, we have $F(t) = f(x, y)$. Using (15.1.1) we get

$$F'(t) = f'_1(x, y)\frac{dx}{dt} + f'_2(x, y)\frac{dy}{dt} = f'_1(a + t\ell, b + tk)\ell + f'_2(a + t\ell, b + tk)k$$

To find the second derivative $F''(t)$ requires differentiating again w.r.t. t. This yields

$$F''(t) = \frac{d}{dt} f_1'(x,y)\ell + \frac{d}{dt} f_2'(x,y)k \qquad (*)$$

To evaluate the derivatives on the right-hand side, we use the chain rule (15.1.1) once again. This gives

$$\frac{d}{dt} f_1'(x,y) = f_{11}''(x,y)\frac{dx}{dt} + f_{12}''(x,y)\frac{dy}{dt} = f_{11}''(x,y)\ell + f_{12}''(x,y)k$$

$$\frac{d}{dt} f_2'(x,y) = f_{21}''(x,y)\frac{dx}{dt} + f_{22}''(x,y)\frac{dy}{dt} = f_{21}''(x,y)\ell + f_{22}''(x,y)k$$

After inserting these two expressions into $(*)$, while also using the equality $f_{12}'' = f_{21}''$ due to Young's Theorem in order to simplify, we obtain

$$F''(t) = f_{11}''(x,y)\ell^2 + 2f_{12}''(x,y)\ell k + f_{22}''(x,y)k^2$$

A Proof of the Chain Rule

None of the earlier rules for partial differentiation is enough to show that the chain rule (15.1.1) for a function of two variables is valid. Instead, we extend the argument that was used in Section 6.8 to prove the chain rule for functions of one variable.

Proof of 15.1.1: Suppose that $z = f(x, y)$ is continuously differentiable, where $x = g(t)$ and $y = h(t)$ are both differentiable. Fix any s that lies in the domains of both g and h, as well as $a = g(s)$ and $b = h(s)$. Given the function $F(t) = f(g(t), h(t))$, we need to prove the following version of Eq. (15.1.1):

$$F'(a) = f_1'(a,b)g'(s) + f_2'(a,b)h'(s)$$

To do so, define the following two functions of (x, y):

$$\varphi_1(x,y) = \begin{cases} \dfrac{f(x,y) - f(a,y)}{x - a} & \text{if } x \neq a \\ f_1'(a,y) & \text{if } x = a \end{cases} \quad \text{and} \quad \varphi_2(x,y) = \begin{cases} \dfrac{f(x,y) - f(x,b)}{y - b} & \text{if } y \neq b \\ f_2'(x,b) & \text{if } y = b \end{cases}$$

Define also the following function of t:

$$\gamma(t) = \begin{cases} \dfrac{g(t) - a}{t - s} & \text{if } t \neq s \\ g'(s) & \text{if } t = s \end{cases} \quad \text{and} \quad \eta(t) = \begin{cases} \dfrac{h(t) - b}{t - s} & \text{if } t \neq s \\ h'(s) & \text{if } t = s \end{cases}$$

By construction, the following six properties all hold:

(i) for all y, $\lim_{x \to a} \varphi_1(x,y) = \varphi_1(a,y)$;   (ii) for all x, $\lim_{y \to b} \varphi_2(x,y) = \varphi_2(x,b)$;

(iii) $\gamma(t) \to \gamma(s)$ and $\eta(t) \to \eta(s)$ as $t \to s$;   (iv) $f(x,y) - f(a,y) = \varphi_1(x,y)(x - a)$;

(v) $f(x,y) - f(x,b) = \varphi_2(x,y)(y - b)$;   (vi) $g(t) - a = \gamma(t)(t - s)$ and $h(t) - b = \eta(t)(t - s)$.

Now, for all δ sufficiently close to 0,

$$\begin{aligned}F(s+\delta)-F(s) &= f(g(s+\delta), h(s+\delta)) - f(g(s), h(s)) \\ &= f(g(s+\delta), h(s+\delta)) - f(a, h(s+\delta)) + f(a, h(s+\delta)) - f(a,b) \\ &= \varphi_1(g(s+\delta), h(s+\delta))[g(s+\delta) - a] + \varphi_2(a, h(s+\delta))[h(s+\delta) - b] \\ &= \varphi_1(g(s+\delta), h(s+\delta))\gamma(s+\delta)\delta + \varphi_2(a, h(s+\delta))\eta(s+\delta)\delta\end{aligned}$$

where the first equality follows from the definition of F, the second just adds and subtracts the same number, the third uses properties (iv) and (v), and the last uses property (vi). It follows that the Newton quotient of F at s is:

$$\frac{F(s+\delta) - F(s)}{\delta} = \varphi_1(g(s+\delta), h(s+\delta))\gamma(s+\delta) + \varphi_2(a, h(s+\delta))\eta(s+\delta)$$

By definition of derivative, it follows that

$$F'(s) = \lim_{\delta \to 0}[\varphi_1(g(s+\delta), h(s+\delta))\gamma(s+\delta) + \varphi_2(a, h(s+\delta))\eta(s+\delta)] \quad (*)$$

By property (iii), as $\delta \to 0$, so $\gamma(s+\delta) \to g'(s)$ and $\eta(s+\delta) \to h'(s)$. Since h is differentiable, it is also continuous and so $h(s+\delta) \to b$ By (ii), it follows that

$$\varphi_2(a, h(s+\delta)) \to f'_2(a,b) \quad (**)$$

All that remains to consider is the term $\varphi_1(g(s+\delta), h(s+\delta))$, which is slightly more complicated. Because g is also continuous, we have $g(s+\delta) \to a$. Since f is continuously differentiable, both f'_1 and φ_1 are continuous functions. So property (i) and continuity of $h(t)$ at $t = s$ together imply that

$$\lim_{\delta \to 0} \varphi_1(g(s+\delta), h(s+\delta)) = \varphi_1(a,b) = f'_1(a,b) \quad (***)$$

Substituting (**) and (***) into (*), we get

$$\begin{aligned}F'(s) &= \lim_{\delta \to 0}[\varphi_1(g(s+\delta), h(s+\delta))\gamma(s+\delta)] + \lim_{\delta \to 0}[\varphi_2(a, h(s+\delta))\eta(s+\delta)] \\ &= \varphi_1(a,b)g'(s) + f'_2(a,b)h'(s) = f'_1(a,b)g'(s) + f'_2(a,b)h'(s)\end{aligned}$$

EXERCISES FOR SECTION 15.1

1. In the following cases, find dz/dt by using the chain rule (15.1.1). Check each answer by first substituting the expressions for x and y and then differentiating.

   (a) $z = F(x,y) = x + y^2$, $x = t^2$, $y = t^3$ (b) $z = F(x,y) = x^p y^q$, $x = at$, $y = bt$

2. Find dz/dt when:

   (a) $z = F(x,y) = x\ln y + y\ln x$ with $x = t+1$ and $y = \ln t$.

   (b) $z = F(x,y) = \ln x + \ln y$ with $x = Ae^{at}$ and $y = Be^{bt}$.

3. If $z = F(t,y)$ and $y = g(t)$, find a formula for dz/dt. Consider in particular the case where $z = t^2 + ye^y$ and $y = t^2$.

4. If $Y = F(K, L)$ and $K = g(L)$, find a formula for dY/dL.

5. Let $Y = 10KL - \sqrt{K} - \sqrt{L}$. Suppose too that $K = 0.2t + 5$ and $L = 5e^{0.1t}$. Find dY/dt when $t = 0$.

(SM) 6. Suppose that $x = g(t)$, $y = h(t)$, and $G(x)$ are differentiable functions. What is the result in each case if you apply the chain rule of Eq. (15.1.1) to the following five functions $f(x, y)$?
(a) $f(x, y) = x + y$; (b) $f(x, y) = x - y$; (c) $f(x, y) = x \cdot y$; (d) $f(x, y) = x/y$; (e) $f(x, y) = G(x)$.

(SM) 7. [HARDER] Consider Example 15.1.4, where $u(x, y) = \ln(x^\alpha + y^\alpha) - \alpha \ln y$ and $y = h(x) = \sqrt[3]{ax^4 + b}$ with positive constant parameters α, a, and b. Find the optimal x^* in this case.

(SM) 8. [HARDER] Suppose that $z = F(x, y)$, $x = g(t)$, and $y = h(t)$. Modify the solution to Example 15.1.5 in order to prove that, under appropriate assumptions on F, g, and h, one has

$$\frac{d^2z}{dt^2} = \frac{\partial z}{\partial x}\frac{d^2x}{dt^2} + \frac{\partial z}{\partial y}\frac{d^2y}{dt^2} + \frac{\partial^2 z}{\partial x^2}\left(\frac{dx}{dt}\right)^2 + 2\frac{\partial^2 z}{\partial x \partial y}\left(\frac{dx}{dt}\right)\left(\frac{dy}{dt}\right) + \frac{\partial^2 z}{\partial y^2}\left(\frac{dy}{dt}\right)^2$$

(SM) 9. [HARDER] Consider the function $f : \mathbb{R}^2 \to \mathbb{R}$ given by

$$f(x, y) = \begin{cases} \dfrac{y^3}{x^2 + y^2}, & \text{if } (x, y) \neq (0, 0) \\ 0, & \text{if } (x, y) = (0, 0) \end{cases}$$

Furthermore, suppose that $x(t) = at$ and $y(t) = bt$ where $a \neq 0$ and $b \neq 0$ are constants.

(a) Find $f'_1(0, 0)$ and $f'_2(0, 0)$.

(b) Let $z(t) = f(x(t), y(t))$ and find $z'(0)$.

(c) Show that $z'(0) \neq f'_1(x(0), y(0))\dfrac{dx}{dt} + f'_2(x(0), y(0))\dfrac{dy}{dt}$.

(d) Explain why the inequality in part (c) does not contradict the chain rule in Eq. (15.1.1).

15.2 Chain Rules for Many Variables

Economists often need even more general chain rules than the simple one for two variables presented in the previous section. Exercise 11, for example, considers the example of a railway company whose fares for peak and off-peak fares are set by a regulatory authority. The costs it faces for running enough trains to carry all the passengers depend on demand for both kinds of journey. These demands are obviously affected by both peak and off-peak fares because some passengers will choose when to travel based on the fare difference. The general chain rule we are about to present allows us to work out how these costs change when either fare is increased.

A general problem of this kind involves the function $z = f(x, y)$, with $x = g(t, s)$ and $y = h(t, s)$. In this case z is a function of both t and s, with

$$z = F(t, s) = f(g(t, s), h(t, s))$$

Here it makes sense to look for both partial derivatives $\partial z/\partial t$ and $\partial z/\partial s$. If we keep s fixed, then z is a function of t alone. Provided that f is C^1 and g, h are partially differentiable w.r.t. t, this allows us to use the chain rule (15.1.1). Similarly, keeping t fixed, provided that f is C^1 and g, h are partially differentiable w.r.t. s, we can differentiate z partially w.r.t. s. The result is the following:

THE CHAIN RULE

If $z = f(x, y)$ with $x = g(t, s)$ and $y = h(t, s)$, then

$$\frac{\partial z}{\partial t} = f_1'(x, y)\frac{\partial x}{\partial t} + f_2'(x, y)\frac{\partial y}{\partial t} \quad (15.2.1)$$

and

$$\frac{\partial z}{\partial s} = f_1'(x, y)\frac{\partial x}{\partial s} + f_2'(x, y)\frac{\partial y}{\partial s} \quad (15.2.2)$$

EXAMPLE 15.2.1 Find $\partial z/\partial t$ and $\partial z/\partial s$ when $z = F(x, y) = x^2 + 2y^2$, with $x = t - s^2$ and $y = ts$.

Solution: We obtain

$$F_1'(x, y) = 2x, \; F_2'(x, y) = 4y, \; \frac{\partial x}{\partial t} = 1, \; \frac{\partial x}{\partial s} = -2s, \; \frac{\partial y}{\partial t} = s, \text{ and } \frac{\partial y}{\partial s} = t$$

Equations (15.2.1) and (15.2.2) therefore give:

$$\frac{\partial z}{\partial t} = 2x \cdot 1 + 4y \cdot s = 2(t - s^2) + 4tss = 2t - 2s^2 + 4ts^2$$

$$\frac{\partial z}{\partial s} = 2x \cdot (-2s) + 4y \cdot t = 2(t - s^2)(-2s) + 4tst = -4ts + 4s^3 + 4t^2s$$

It is a good exercise to check these answers by first expressing z as a function of t and s, then finding the partial derivatives directly.

EXAMPLE 15.2.2 Find $z_t'(1, 0)$ if $z = e^{x^2} + y^2 e^{xy}$, with $x = 2t + 3s$ and $y = t^2 s^3$.

Solution: We obtain

$$\frac{\partial z}{\partial x} = 2xe^{x^2} + y^3 e^{xy}, \; \frac{\partial z}{\partial y} = 2ye^{xy} + xy^2 e^{xy}, \; \frac{\partial x}{\partial t} = 2, \text{ and } \frac{\partial y}{\partial t} = 2ts^3$$

Using somewhat more concise notation, the chain rule gives

$$z_t'(t, s) = \frac{\partial z}{\partial x}\frac{\partial x}{\partial t} + \frac{\partial z}{\partial y}\frac{\partial}{\partial t} = (2xe^{x^2} + y^3 e^{xy}) \cdot 2 + (2ye^{xy} + xy^2 e^{xy}) \cdot 2ts^3$$

When $t = 1$ and $s = 0$, then $x = 2$ and $y = 0$, so $z_t'(1, 0) = 4e^4 \cdot 2 = 8e^4$.

The General Case

In consumer demand theory, economists typically assume that a household's utility depends on the number of units of each good it is able to consume. The number of units consumed will depend in turn on the prices of these goods and on the household's income. Thus the household's utility is related, indirectly, to all the prices and to income. By how much, then, does utility respond to an increase in one of the prices, or to an increase in income? The following general chain rule extends to this kind of problem.

Suppose that $z = f(x_1, \ldots, x_n)$, where for each $i = 1, 2, \ldots, n$ the variable x_i is given by the function $x_i = g_i(t_1, \ldots, t_m)$ of the m variables $t_1, \ldots, t_m$. Substituting into the function f for all the variables x_i as functions of the variables t_j allows z to be expressed as the *composite function*

$$z = F(t_1, \ldots, t_m) = f(g_1(t_1, \ldots, t_m), \ldots, g_n(t_1, \ldots, t_m))$$

Using vector notation allows us to write $z = F(\mathbf{t}) = f(\mathbf{x}(\mathbf{t}))$. An obvious generalization of (15.2.1) and (15.2.2) is as follows:

THE GENERAL CHAIN RULE

Suppose that $z = f(x_1, \ldots, x_n)$ is continuously differentiable, and that the function $x_i = g_i(t_1, \ldots, t_m)$ is differentiable, for each $i = 1, 2, \ldots, n$. Then for each $j = 1, 2, \ldots, m$ one has

$$\frac{\partial z}{\partial t_j} = \frac{\partial z}{\partial x_1} \frac{\partial x_1}{\partial t_j} + \frac{\partial z}{\partial x_2} \frac{\partial x_2}{\partial t_j} + \cdots + \frac{\partial z}{\partial x_n} \frac{\partial x_n}{\partial t_j} \qquad (15.2.3)$$

This is an important formula that every economist should understand. A small change in a basic variable t_j sets off a chain reaction. First, every x_i depends on t_j in general, so it changes when t_j is changed. This affects z in turn. The contribution to the total derivative of z w.r.t. t_j that results from the change in x_i is $(\partial z/\partial x_i)(\partial x_i/\partial t_j)$. Formula (15.2.3) shows that $\partial z/\partial t_j$ is the sum of all these contributions. In alternative notation,

$$F_j'(\mathbf{t}) = f_1'(\mathbf{x}(\mathbf{t})) \frac{\partial g_1}{\partial t_j}(\mathbf{t}) + f_2'(\mathbf{x}(\mathbf{t})) \frac{\partial g_2}{\partial t_j}(\mathbf{t}) + \cdots + f_n'(\mathbf{x}(\mathbf{t})) \frac{\partial g_n}{\partial t_j}(\mathbf{t})$$

EXAMPLE 15.2.3 Example 14.9.1 considered an agricultural production function taking the form $Y = F(K, L, T)$, where Y is the size of the harvest, K is capital invested, L is labour, and T is the area of agricultural land used to grow the crop. Suppose that K, L, and T are all functions of time, which is denoted by t. Then, according to (15.2.3),

$$\frac{dY}{dt} = \frac{\partial F}{\partial K} \frac{dK}{dt} + \frac{\partial F}{\partial L} \frac{dL}{dt} + \frac{\partial F}{\partial T} \frac{dT}{dt}$$

In the special case when F is the Cobb–Douglas function $F(K, L, T) = AK^a L^b T^c$, we have

$$\frac{dY}{dt} = aAK^{a-1} L^b T^c \frac{dK}{dt} + bAK^a L^{b-1} T^c \frac{dL}{dt} + cAK^a L^b T^{c-1} \frac{dT}{dt} \qquad (*)$$

Denoting time derivatives by dots, and dividing each term in (∗) by $Y = AK^a L^b T^c$, we get

$$\frac{\dot{Y}}{Y} = a\frac{\dot{K}}{K} + b\frac{\dot{L}}{L} + c\frac{\dot{T}}{T}$$

The relative rate of change of output is, therefore, a weighted sum of the relative rates of change of capital, labour, and land. The weights are the respective powers a, b, and c.

EXERCISES FOR SECTION 15.2

1. Use (15.2.1) and (15.2.2) to find $\partial z/\partial t$ and $\partial z/\partial s$ for the following cases:
   (a) $z = F(x, y) = x + y^2$, where $x = t - s$ and $y = ts$;
   (b) $z = F(x, y) = 2x^2 + 3y^3$, where $x = t^2 - s$ and $y = t + 2s^3$.

SM 2. Using (15.2.1) and (15.2.2), find $\partial z/\partial t$ and $\partial z/\partial s$ for the following cases:
   (a) $z = xy^2$, where $x = t + s^2$ and $y = t^2 s$;
   (b) $z = \dfrac{x-y}{x+y}$, where $x = e^{t+s}$ and $y = e^{ts}$.

3. If $z = F(u, v, w)$ where $u = r^2$, $v = -2s^2$, and $w = \ln r + \ln s$, find $\partial z/\partial r$ and $\partial z/\partial s$.

4. If $z = F(x)$ and $x = g(t_1, t_2)$, find $\partial z/\partial t_1$ and $\partial z/\partial t_2$.

5. If $x = F(s, g(s), h(s, t))$, find $\partial x/\partial s$ and $\partial x/\partial t$.

6. If $z = F(u, v, w)$ where $u = f(x, y)$, $v = x^2 h(y)$ and $w = 1/y$, find $\partial z/\partial x$ and $\partial z/\partial y$.

7. Use the general chain rule in Eq. (15.2.3) to find $\partial w/\partial t$ for the following cases:
   (a) $w = xy^2 z^3$, where $x = t^2$, $y = s$, and $z = t$;
   (b) $w = x^2 + y^2 + z^2$, where $x = \sqrt{t+s}$, $y = e^{ts}$, and $z = s^3$.

8. Find expressions for dz/dt when:
   (a) $z = F(t, t^2, t^3)$
   (b) $z = F(t, f(t), g(t^2))$

9. Suppose $Z = G + Y^2 + r^2$, where Y and r are both differentiable functions of G. Find dZ/dG.

10. Suppose $Z = G + I(Y, r)$, where I is a differentiable function of two variables, and Y, r are both differentiable functions of G. Find dZ/dG.

11. Each week a suburban railway company has a long-run cost $C = aQ_1 + bQ_2 + cQ_1^2$ of providing Q_1 passenger kilometres of service during rush hours and Q_2 passenger kilometres during off-peak hours. As functions of the regulated fares p_1 and p_2 per kilometre for the rush hours and off-peak hours, respectively, the demands for the two kinds of service are $Q_1 = Ap_1^{-\alpha_1} p_2^{\beta_1}$ and $Q_2 = Bp_1^{\alpha_2} p_2^{-\beta_2}$, where the constants $A, B, \alpha_1, \alpha_2, \beta_1, \beta_2$ are all positive. Assuming that the company runs enough trains to meet the demand, find expressions for the partial derivatives of C w.r.t. p_1 and p_2.

SM 12. If $u = \ln(x^3 + y^3 + z^3 - 3xyz)$, show that

(a) $x\dfrac{\partial u}{\partial x} + y\dfrac{\partial u}{\partial y} + z\dfrac{\partial u}{\partial z} = 3$ (b) $(x+y+z)\left(\dfrac{\partial u}{\partial x} + \dfrac{\partial u}{\partial y} + \dfrac{\partial u}{\partial z}\right) = 3$

13. If $z = f(x^2 y)$ where f is a differentiable function of one variable, show that $x\dfrac{\partial z}{\partial x} = 2y\dfrac{\partial z}{\partial y}$.

14. Find a formula for $\partial u/\partial r$ in case $u = f(x, y, z, w)$ where f is C^1 and x, y, z, and w are all differentiable functions of two variables r and s.

15. Suppose that $u = xyzw$, where $x = r + s$, $y = r - s$, $z = rs$, and $w = r/s$. Find $\partial u/\partial r$ at the point $(r, s) = (2, 1)$.

15.3 Implicit Differentiation along a Level Curve

Economists often need to differentiate functions that are defined implicitly by an equation. In Section 9.3 we considered some simple cases; it is a good idea to review those examples now. Here we study the problem from a more general point of view.

Let F be a C^1 function of two variables, and consider the equation $F(x, y) = c$, where c is a constant. The equation represents a level curve for F, as defined in Section 14.3. Suppose this equation defines y implicitly as a function $y = f(x)$ of x in some interval I, as illustrated in Fig. 15.3.1. This means that, for all x in I, one has

$$F(x, f(x)) = c \qquad (15.3.1)$$

If f is differentiable, what is the derivative of $y = f(x)$? If the graph of f looks like that in Fig. 15.3.1, the problem is to find the slope of the graph at each point like P.[1]

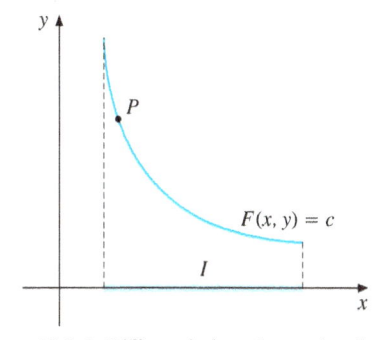

Figure 15.3.1 Differentiation along a level curve

To find an expression for this slope, we introduce the auxiliary function u that is defined for all x in I by $u(x) = F(x, f(x))$. Then, since the function F is C^1, the chain rule gives

$$u'(x) = F_1'(x, f(x)) \cdot 1 + F_2'(x, f(x)) \cdot f'(x)$$

---

[1] A particular case of this problem was Example 7.1.5.

Also, together with the definition of the function u, Eq. (15.3.1) implies that $u(x) = c$ for all x in I. The derivative of a constant is 0, so we have

$$u'(x) = F'_1(x, f(x)) + F'_2(x, f(x)) \cdot f'(x) = 0$$

If we replace $f(x)$ by y and solve for $f'(x) = y'$, we reach the conclusion:

SLOPE OF A LEVEL CURVE

If $F(x, y) = c$, then provided that $F'_2(x, y) \neq 0$, one has

$$y' = -\frac{F'_1(x, y)}{F'_2(x, y)} \qquad (15.3.2)$$

This is an important result. Before applying this formula for y', however, recall that the pair (x, y) must satisfy the equation $F(x, y) = c$. On the other hand, note that there is no need to solve the equation $F(x, y) = c$ explicitly for y before applying (15.3.2) in order to find y'. Example 15.3.3 shows how this can be important.

The same argument with x and y interchanged gives a result analogous to (15.3.2). Thus, if x is a continuously differentiable function of y which satisfies $F(x, y) = c$, then

$$F(x, y) = c \implies \frac{dx}{dy} = -\frac{\partial F/\partial y}{\partial F/\partial x} = -\frac{F'_2(x, y)}{F'_1(x, y)} \qquad (15.3.3)$$

provided that $\partial F/\partial x \neq 0$.

EXAMPLE 15.3.1 Use formula (15.3.2) to find y' when $xy = 5$.

Solution: We put $F(x, y) = xy$. Then $F'_1(x, y) = y$ and $F'_2(x, y) = x$. Hence, (15.3.2) gives

$$y' = -\frac{F'_1(x, y)}{F'_2(x, y)} = -\frac{y}{x}$$

This confirms the result in Example 7.1.1.

EXAMPLE 15.3.2 For the curve given by $x^3 + x^2y - 2y^2 - 10y = 0$, find the slope and then the equation for the tangent at the point $(x, y) = (2, 1)$.

Solution: Let $F(x, y) = x^3 + x^2y - 2y^2 - 10y$, implying that the given equation is equivalent to $F(x, y) = 0$, which is a level curve for F. First, note that $F(2, 1) = 0$, confirming that $(x, y) = (2, 1)$ is a point on the level curve. Also, $F'_1(x, y) = 3x^2 + 2xy$ and $F'_2(x, y) = x^2 - 4y - 10$. So (15.3.2) implies that

$$y' = -\frac{3x^2 + 2xy}{x^2 - 4y - 10}$$

For $x = 2$ and $y = 1$ in particular, one has $y' = 8/5$. Then the point–slope formula for a line implies that the tangent at $(2, 1)$ must have the equation $y - 1 = (8/5)(x - 2)$, or $5y = 8x - 11$. See Fig. 15.3.2, in which the curve has been drawn by a computer program.

Note that, for many values of x, there is more than one corresponding value of y such that (x, y) lies on the curve. For instance, the two points $(2, 1)$ and $(2, -4)$ with $x = 2$ both lie on the curve. Note that $y' = 0.4$ at $(2, -4)$; confirming this would be good practice.

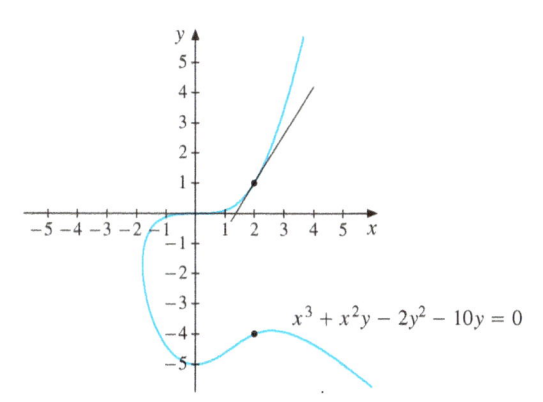

Figure 15.3.2 Example 15.3.2

EXAMPLE 15.3.3 Assume that the equation $e^{xy^2} - 2x - 4y = c$ implicitly defines y as a differentiable function $y = f(x)$ of x. Find a value of the constant c such that $f(0) = 1$. Then find y' at $(x, y) = (0, 1)$.

Solution: When $x = 0$ and $y = 1$, the equation becomes $1 - 4 = c$, so $c = -3$.
To find the derivative y', define $F(x, y) = e^{xy^2} - 2x - 4y$. Then $F'_1(x, y) = y^2 e^{xy^2} - 2$, and $F'_2(x, y) = 2xye^{xy^2} - 4$. Thus, from (15.3.2) we have $y' = -\dfrac{F'_1(x, y)}{F'_2(x, y)} = -\dfrac{y^2 e^{xy^2} - 2}{2xye^{xy^2} - 4}$.
At $(x, y) = (0, 1)$, we find $y' = -1/4$.

Note that in this example it was impossible to solve $e^{xy^2} - 2x - 4y = -3$ explicitly for y. Even so, we managed to find an explicit expression for the derivative of y w.r.t. x.

Here is an important economic example involving a function that is defined implicitly by the equation which says that demand must equal supply.

EXAMPLE 15.3.4 We generalize Example 7.2.2, and assume that $D = f(t, P)$ is the demand for a commodity that depends on the price P before tax, as well as on the sales tax per unit, denoted by t. Suppose that $S = g(P)$ is the supply function. At equilibrium, when supply is equal to demand, the equilibrium price $P = P(t)$ depends on t. Indeed, $P = P(t)$ must satisfy the equation

$$f(t, P) = g(P) \qquad (*)$$

for all t in some relevant interval. Suppose that $(*)$ defines P implicitly as a differentiable function of t. Find an expression for dP/dt, then discuss its sign.

Solution: Let $F(t, P) = f(t, P) - g(P)$. Then $(*)$ becomes $F(t, P) = 0$, so (15.3.2) yields

$$\dfrac{dP}{dt} = -\dfrac{F'_t(t, P)}{F'_P(t, P)} = -\dfrac{f'_t(t, P)}{f'_P(t, P) - g'(P)} = \dfrac{f'_t(t, P)}{g'(P) - f'_P(t, P)} \qquad (**)$$

It is reasonable to assume that $g'(P) > 0$, meaning that supply increases if price increases, as well as that $f'_t(t, P)$ and $f'_P(t, P)$ are both < 0, meaning that demand decreases if either the tax or the price increases. Then (∗∗) tells us that $dP/dt < 0$, implying that the pre-tax price P faced by suppliers decreases as the tax t increases. Thus the suppliers, as well as the consumers, are adversely affected if the tax on their product rises.

We can also derive formula (∗∗) by implicitly differentiating (∗) w.r.t. t. This gives

$$f'_t(t, P) \cdot 1 + f'_P(t, P) \frac{dP}{dt} = g'(P) \frac{dP}{dt}$$

Solving this equation for dP/dt yields (∗∗) once again.

Marginal Rate of Substitution

Economists are often interested in the slope of the tangent to a level curve at a particular point. Often, the level curve is downwards sloping, but economists prefer a positive answer. So, inspired by Example 7.1.5, we change the sign of the slope defined by (15.3.2), and use a special name:

MARGINAL RATE OF SUBSTITUTION

The ratio

$$R_{yx} = \frac{F'_x(x, y)}{F'_y(x, y)} \tag{15.3.4}$$

is known as *the marginal rate of substitution of y for x*, abbreviated as MRS.

Note that $R_{yx} = -y' \approx -\Delta y / \Delta x$ when we move along the level curve $F(x, y) = c$. If $\Delta x = -1$ in particular, then $R_{yx} \approx \Delta y$. Thus, R_{yx} is approximately the quantity of y we must add per unit of x removed, if we are to stay on the same level curve.

EXAMPLE 15.3.5 Let $F(K, L) = 100$ be an isoquant for a production function, where K is capital input, L is labour input, and 100 is the output. Look at Fig. 15.3.3. At all the points P, Q, and R, an output of 100 units is produced. At P a little capital input and a lot of labour input are used. The slope of the isoquant at P is approximately -4, so the MRS at P is approximately 4. This means that for each four units of labour that are taken away, adding only one unit of capital will ensure that output remains at (approximately) 100 units. Provided that units are chosen so that capital and labour have the same price, at P capital is more "valuable" than labour. At Q the MRS is approximately 1, so capital and labour are equally "valuable". Finally, at R, the MRS is approximately 1/5, so here approximately five units of capital are required to compensate for the loss of one unit of labour.

The Second Derivative

As in Eq. (15.3.1), suppose that the equation $F(x, y) = c$ of a level curve defines the function $y = f(x)$ implicitly. Sometimes economists need to know whether this function is concave

SECTION 15.3 / IMPLICIT DIFFERENTIATION ALONG A LEVEL CURVE

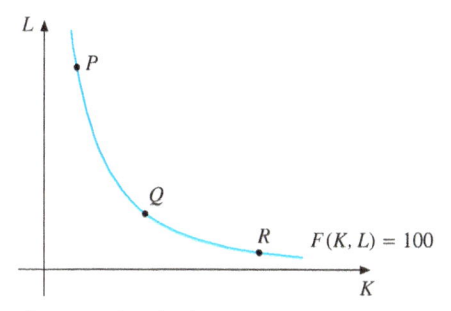

Figure 15.3.3 An isoquant

or convex. One way to find out is to calculate y'', the derivative of $y' = -F_1'(x, y)/F_2'(x, y)$. Write $G(x) = F_1'(x, y)$ and $H(x) = F_2'(x, y)$, where y is a function of x. Now we want to differentiate $y' = -G(x)/H(x)$ w.r.t. x. The rule for differentiating quotients gives us

$$y'' = -\frac{G'(x)H(x) - G(x)H'(x)}{[H(x)]^2} \qquad (*)$$

Keeping in mind that y is a function of x, both $G(x)$ and $H(x)$ are composite functions. So we differentiate them both by using the chain rule, thereby obtaining

$$G'(x) = F_{11}''(x, y) \cdot 1 + F_{12}''(x, y) \cdot y'$$
$$H'(x) = F_{21}''(x, y) \cdot 1 + F_{22}''(x, y) \cdot y'$$

Assume that F is a C^2 function, so Young's Theorem 14.6.1 implies $F_{12}'' = F_{21}''$. Now replace y' in both the preceding equations by the quotient $-F_1'/F_2'$, and then insert the results into $(*)$. After some algebraic simplification, this yields the formula

$$y'' = -\frac{1}{(F_2')^3}[F_{11}''(F_2')^2 - 2F_{12}''F_1'F_2' + F_{22}''(F_1')^2] \qquad (15.3.5)$$

Using formula (13.2.3) for the determinant of a 3×3 matrix allows us to express this result in a more memorable form as

$$\frac{d^2y}{dx^2} = \frac{1}{(F_2')^3} \begin{vmatrix} 0 & F_1' & F_2' \\ F_1' & F_{11}'' & F_{12}'' \\ F_2' & F_{21}'' & F_{22}'' \end{vmatrix}$$

This requires, of course, that $F_2' \neq 0$.

Occasionally, formula (15.3.5) is used in theoretical arguments. Generally, however, it is easier to find y'' by direct differentiation, as in the examples we considered in Section 7.1.

EXAMPLE 15.3.6   Use (15.3.5) to find y'' when $xy = 5$.

Solution: With $F(x, y) = xy$ we have $F_1' = y$, $F_2' = x$, $F_{11}'' = 0$, $F_{12}'' = 1$, and $F_{22}'' = 0$. According to (15.3.5), we obtain

$$y'' = -\frac{1}{x^3}(-2 \cdot 1 \cdot y \cdot x) = \frac{2y}{x^2}$$

This result is the same as the one we found in Example 7.1.6.

EXERCISES FOR SECTION 15.3

1. Use formula (15.3.2) with $F(x, y) = 2x^2 + 6xy + y^2$ and $c = 18$ to find y' when y is defined implicitly by $2x^2 + 6xy + y^2 = 18$. Compare with the result in Exercise 7.1.5.

(SM) 2. Along each of the following level curves, use (15.3.2) to find y', and then (15.3.5) to find y''.

   (a) $x^2 y = 1$ (b) $x - y + 3xy = 2$ (c) $y^5 - x^6 = 0$

(SM) 3. A curve in the xy-plane is given by the equation $2x^2 + xy + y^2 - 8 = 0$.

   (a) Find y', y'', and the equation for the tangent at the point $(2, 0)$.

   (b) At which points on the curve is there a horizontal tangent?

4. The equation $3x^2 - 3xy^2 + y^3 + 3y^2 = 4$ defines y implicitly as a function $h(x)$ of x in a neighbourhood of the point $(1, 1)$. Find $h'(1)$.

5. Suppose that the aggregate demand $D(P, r)$ for a certain commodity (like an electric car) depends on its price P and the interest rate r. What signs should one expect the partial derivatives of D w.r.t. P and r to have? Suppose the supply S is constant, so that $D(P, r) = S$ in equilibrium. Differentiate implicitly to find dP/dr, and comment on its sign.

6. Let $D = f(R, P)$ denote the demand for a commodity when the price is P and R is advertising expenditure. What signs should one expect the partial derivatives f'_R and f'_P to have? If the supply is $S = g(P)$, equilibrium in the market requires that $f(R, P) = g(P)$. What is dP/dR? Discuss its sign.

7. Let f be a differentiable function of one variable, and let a and b be two constants. Suppose that the equation $x - az = f(y - bz)$ defines z as a differentiable function of x and y. Prove that z satisfies $az'_x + bz'_y = 1$.

15.4 Level Surfaces

Consider the function $F(x, y, z)$ of three variables. It has level surfaces in three-dimensional space consisting of all the triples (x, y, z) that, for some value of the constant c, satisfy the equation $F(x, y, z) = c$. Often this level surface will include the graph of a function $z = f(x, y)$ that, for all (x, y) in some domain A that is an open set in the plane, is defined implicitly by the equation $F(x, y, z) = c$. Consider the function g defined by $g(x, y) = F(x, y, f(x, y))$ for all (x, y) in A. Then, for all (x, y) in this domain A, one has

$$g(x, y) = F(x, y, f(x, y)) = c \qquad (15.4.1)$$

Suppose that the functions F and f are both differentiable. Because Eq. (15.4.1) must hold for all (x, y) in A, the partial derivatives g'_x and g'_y must both be 0. But $g(x, y)$ is a composite function of x and y whose partial derivatives can be found by using the general chain rule in Eq. (15.2.3). Therefore,

$$g'_x = F'_x \cdot 1 + F'_z \cdot z'_x = 0, \quad g'_y = F'_y \cdot 1 + F'_z \cdot z'_y = 0$$

Provided that $F'_z \neq 0$, this equation implies the following expressions for the partial derivatives of $z = f(x, y)$:

$$F(x, y, z) = c \implies z'_x = -\frac{F'_x}{F'_z} \quad \text{and} \quad z'_y = -\frac{F'_y}{F'_z} \qquad (15.4.2)$$

We emphasize once again that Eq. (15.4.2) allows z'_x and z'_y to be found even if it is impossible to solve the equation $F(x, y, z) = c$ explicitly for z as a function of x and y.

EXAMPLE 15.4.1 The equation $x - 2y - 3z + z^2 = -2$ implicitly defines z as a twice differentiable function of x and y about the point $(x, y, z) = (0, 0, 2)$. Find z'_x and z'_y, followed by z''_{xx}, z''_{xy}, and z''_{yy}. Find also the values at $(x, y) = (0, 0)$ of all these partial derivatives.

Solution: Let $F(x, y, z) = x - 2y - 3z + z^2$ and $c = -2$. Then one has $F'_x = 1$, $F'_y = -2$, and $F'_z = 2z - 3$. Whenever $z \neq 3/2$, we have $F'_z \neq 0$, so (15.4.2) gives

$$z'_x = -\frac{1}{2z - 3} \quad \text{and} \quad z'_y = -\frac{-2}{2z - 3} = \frac{2}{2z - 3}$$

For $x = 0$, $y = 0$, and $z = 2$ in particular, we obtain $z'_x = -1$ and $z'_y = 2$.

We find z''_{xx} by differentiating the expression for z'_x partially w.r.t. x. Near $(x, y, z) = (0, 0, 2)$, keeping in mind that z is a function of x and y, we get $z''_{xx} = (\partial/\partial x)(-(2z-3)^{-1}) = (2z-3)^{-2} 2z'_x$. At the point $(x, y, z) = (0, 0, 2)$, where $z'_x = -1$, we have

$$z''_{xx} = \frac{\partial}{\partial x} z'_x = \frac{\partial}{\partial x}[-(2z-3)^{-1}] = (2z-3)^{-2} 2z'_x = \frac{-2}{(2z-3)^3} = -2$$

Correspondingly,

$$z''_{xy} = \frac{\partial}{\partial y} z'_x = \frac{\partial}{\partial y}[-(2z-3)^{-1}] = (2z-3)^{-2} 2z'_y = \frac{4}{(2z-3)^3} = 4$$

and

$$z''_{yy} = \frac{\partial}{\partial y} z'_y = \frac{\partial}{\partial y}[2(2z-3)^{-1}] = -2(2z-3)^{-2} 2z'_y = \frac{-8}{(2z-3)^3} = -8$$

EXAMPLE 15.4.2 A firm produces $Q = f(L)$ units of a commodity using L units of labour. We assume that $f'(L) > 0$ and $f''(L) < 0$, so f is strictly increasing and strictly concave.[2]

(a) If the firm is paid P per unit produced and pays w for a unit of labour, write down the profit function, then find the first-order condition for profits to be maximized at $L^* > 0$.

(b) Use implicit differentiation of the first-order condition to examine how changes in P and w influence the optimal choice of L^*.

---

[2] See Exercise 3, where a special case is considered.

Solution:

(a) The profit function is $\pi(L) = Pf(L) - wL$, so $\pi'(L) = Pf'(L) - w$. By Theorem 9.1.1, an optimal L^* must satisfy the first-order condition

$$Pf'(L^*) - w = 0 \qquad (*)$$

(b) Suppose we define $F(P, w, L^*) = Pf'(L^*) - w$. Then $(*)$ is equivalent to $F(P, w, L^*) = 0$. According to (15.4.2), one has

$$\frac{\partial L^*}{\partial P} = -\frac{F'_P}{F'_{L^*}} = -\frac{f'(L^*)}{Pf''(L^*)} \quad \text{and} \quad \frac{\partial L^*}{\partial w} = -\frac{F'_w}{F'_{L^*}} = -\frac{-1}{Pf''(L^*)} = \frac{1}{Pf''(L^*)}$$

The sign assumptions on f' and f'' imply that $\partial L^*/\partial P > 0$ and $\partial L^*/\partial w < 0$. Thus, the optimal labour input goes up if the price P increases, but goes down if labour costs increase. This accords with the usual economic intuition.[3]

EXAMPLE 15.4.3 **(Gains from search).** Suppose a baker intends to buy x^0 units of flour. Right now, it can be bought at a price of p^0 per kilo. But the baker expects that searching among other sellers will uncover a lower price. Let $p(t)$ denote the lowest price per kilo that the baker expects to find after searching the market for t hours. It is reasonable to assume that $p'(t) < 0$. Moreover, since it is usually harder to find lower prices as the search progresses, we assume that $p''(t) > 0$.

Suppose the baker's hourly wage is w. By searching for t hours, the baker's saving is $p^0 - p(t)$ dollars for each kilo bought, so the total savings from buying x^0 units are $[p^0 - p(t)]x^0$. On the other hand, searching for t hours costs wt in forgone wages. So the baker's expected profit from searching for t hours is

$$\pi(t) = [p^0 - p(t)]x^0 - wt$$

A necessary first-order condition for $t = t^* > 0$ to maximize the baker's profit is that

$$\pi'(t^*) = -p'(t^*)x^0 - w = 0 \qquad (*)$$

This condition is also sufficient, because $\pi''(t) = -p''(t)x^0 < 0$ for all t.

To interpret $(*)$, first we rewrite it as $-p'(t^*)x^0 = w$. Suppose now that the baker searches for an extra small fraction τ of an hour. The gain expected from finding a lower price is $[p(t^*) - p(t^* + \tau)]x^0$, which is approximately $-p'(t^*)\tau x^0$. On the other hand, the baker loses $w\tau$ of wage income. So the first-order condition says that the baker should search until the marginal gain per unit of extra search time is just offset by the wage.

The optimal search time t^* depends on x^0 and w. Economists typically want to know how t^* changes as x^0 or w changes. We see that Eq. $(*)$ here is similar to Eq. $(*)$ in Example 15.4.2, but with $x^0 = -P$, $p = f$, and $t^* = L^*$. It follows immediately that

$$\frac{\partial t^*}{\partial x^0} = -\frac{p'(t^*)}{p''(t^*)x^0} > 0, \quad \text{and} \quad \frac{\partial t^*}{\partial w} = -\frac{1}{p''(t^*)x^0} < 0$$

---

[3] Economists often prefer to use implicit differentiation rather than relying on formula (15.4.2).

with the signs as indicated because $p'(t^*) < 0$, $p''(t^*) > 0$, and $x^0 > 0$. Thus, the optimal search time t^* rises as the quantity to be bought increases, and falls as the wage rate rises.

These qualitative results can easily be obtained by a geometric argument. Figure 15.4.1 illustrates how the optimal search time t^* is the value of t at which the tangent to the curve $R = [p^0 − p(t)]x^0$ has slope w, and so is parallel to the line $C = wt$. If x^0 increases, the R curve expands vertically but not horizontally, so t^* moves to the right. But if w increases, the straight line $C = wt$ rotates anti-clockwise about the origin, so the optimal t^* decreases.

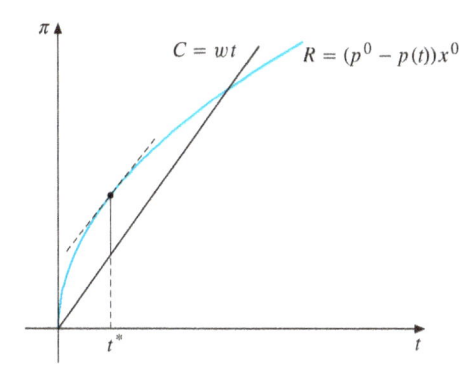

Figure 15.4.1 Optimal search

The General Case

The foregoing analysis can be extended to a function of any number of variables. Assuming that $\partial F/\partial z \neq 0$, we have

$$F(x_1, \ldots, x_n, z) = c \implies \frac{\partial z}{\partial x_i} = -\frac{\partial F/\partial x_i}{\partial F/\partial z} \quad \text{for all } i = 1, 2, \ldots, n \tag{15.4.3}$$

The proof of this is a direct extension of the argument that we gave for Eq. (15.4.2), so is left to the reader.

EXERCISES FOR SECTION 15.4

1. Use (15.4.2) to find $\partial z/\partial x$ for the following equations:

   (a) $3x + y − z = 0$ (b) $xyz + xz^3 − xy^2z^5 = 1$ (c) $e^{xyz} = 3xyz$

2. Find z'_x, z'_y, and z''_{xy} when $x^3 + y^3 + z^3 − 3z = 0$.

3. Consider the problem that was analysed in Example 15.4.2.

   (a) Suppose that $Q = f(L) = \sqrt{L}$. Write down the first-order condition in Eq. (∗) for this case, and then find an explicit expression for L^* as a function of P and w. Find the partial derivatives of L^* w.r.t. P and w. Then verify that their signs are those that were obtained in the example.

(b) Suppose the profit function is replaced by $\pi(L) = Pf(L) - C(L, w)$, where $C(L, w)$ is the "cost function". What is the first-order condition for L^* to be optimal in this case? Find the partial derivatives of L^* w.r.t. P and w.

4. For all $x > 0$ and $y > 0$, the equation $x^y + y^z + z^x = k$, where k is a positive constant, defines z as a positive-valued function of x and y. Find the partial derivatives of z w.r.t. x and y.

5. Consider the model of Exercise 15.3.6, applied to the market for an agricultural crop. Replace $S = g(P)$ by $S = g(w, P)$, where w is an index for how favourable the weather has been. Assume that $g'_w(w, P) > 0$. Equilibrium now requires $f(R, P) = g(w, P)$. Assume that this equation defines P implicitly as a differentiable function of R and w. Find an expression for P'_w, and comment on its sign.

(SM) 6. The function F is defined for all x and y by $F(x, y) = xe^{y-3} + xy^2 - 2y$. Show that the point $(1, 3)$ lies on the level curve $F(x, y) = 4$, and find the equation for the tangent line to the curve at the point $(1, 3)$.

(SM) 7. The Nerlove–Ringstad production function $y = y(K, L)$ is defined implicitly by

$$y^{1+c\ln y} = AK^\alpha L^\beta$$

where A, α, and β are positive constants. Find the marginal productivities of capital and labour, namely $\partial y/\partial K$ and $\partial y/\partial L$. (*Hint*: Take the logarithm of each side and then differentiate implicitly.)

15.5 Elasticity of Substitution

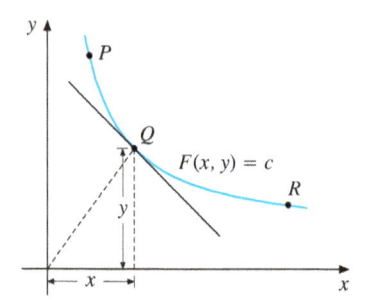

Figure 15.5.1 R_{yx} at Q

Consider a level curve $F(x, y) = c$ for a function F of two variables. The MRS R_{yx}, which was defined in Eq. (15.3.4), is minus the slope of the tangent to this level curve at a point like Q shown in Fig. 15.5.1. At point P, the MRS is a large positive number. At point Q, the number R_{yx} is about 1, and at point R it is about 0.2. As we move along the level curve from left to right, the MRS R_{yx} is strictly decreasing as a function of the ratio x/y, with values that range over some positive interval I. Conversely, for each value of R_{yx} in I, there is a unique corresponding point (x, y) on the level curve $F(x, y) = c$, and thus a corresponding value of y/x. The ratio y/x is therefore a function of R_{yx}, allowing us to define the following:

ELASTICITY OF SUBSTITUTION

Along the level curve $F(x, y) = c$, the *elasticity of substitution between y and x* is

$$\sigma_{yx} = \text{El}_{R_{yx}}(y/x) \tag{15.5.1}$$

This defines σ_{yx} as the elasticity of the fraction y/x w.r.t. the MRS R_{yx}. Thus, for every small δ, the number $\sigma_{yx}\delta$ is the approximate percentage change in the fraction y/x when we move along the level curve $F(x, y) = c$ far enough so that δ is the percentage increase in R_{yx}. Note that σ_{yx} is symmetric in x and y. In fact, $R_{xy} = 1/R_{yx}$, and so the logarithmic formula for elasticities implies that $\sigma_{xy} = \sigma_{yx}$. Also, Exercise 3 asks you to work with a (symmetric) expression for the elasticity of substitution in terms of the first- and second-order partial derivatives of F.

EXAMPLE 15.5.1 Calculate σ_{KL} for the Cobb–Douglas function $F(K, L) = AK^a L^b$.

Solution: The MRS of K for L is

$$R_{KL} = \frac{F'_L}{F'_K} = \frac{bAK^a L^{b-1}}{aAK^{a-1} L^b} = \frac{b}{a}\frac{K}{L}$$

Thus, $K/L = (a/b) R_{KL}$. So the elasticity of K/L w.r.t. R_{KL} is 1. This shows that $\sigma_{KL} = 1$ for the Cobb–Douglas function.

EXAMPLE 15.5.2 Find the elasticity of substitution for the CES function

$$F(K, L) = A(aK^{-\rho} + bL^{-\rho})^{-\mu/\rho}$$

where A, a, b, μ, and ρ are constants, with $A > 0$, $a > 0$, $b > 0$, $\mu \neq 0$, $\rho > -1$, and $\rho \neq 0$.

Solution: Here

$$F'_K = A(-\mu/\rho)(aK^{-\rho} + bL^{-\rho})^{(-\mu/\rho)-1} a(-\rho) K^{-\rho-1}$$

and $F'_L = A(-\mu/\rho)(aK^{-\rho} + bL^{-\rho})^{(-\mu/\rho)-1} b(-\rho) L^{-\rho-1}$

It follows that the MRS between K and L is given by

$$R_{KL} = \frac{F'_L}{F'_K} = \frac{b}{a}\frac{L^{-\rho-1}}{K^{-\rho-1}} = \frac{b}{a}\left(\frac{K}{L}\right)^{\rho+1}$$

Inverting this equation gives

$$\frac{K}{L} = \left(\frac{a}{b}\right)^{1/(\rho+1)} (R_{KL})^{1/(\rho+1)}$$

Recalling that the elasticity of Ax^b w.r.t. x is b, definition (15.5.1) implies that

$$\sigma_{KL} = \text{El}_{R_{KL}}\left(\frac{K}{L}\right) = \frac{1}{\rho+1}$$

So the function F has constant elasticity of substitution $1/(\rho + 1)$. This, of course, explains why the function F is said to be CES, which stands for "constant elasticity of substitution".

Note that the elasticity of substitution for the CES function tends to 1 as $\rho \to 0$, which is precisely the elasticity of substitution for the Cobb–Douglas function in the previous example. This accords with the result in Example 7.12.5.

EXERCISES FOR SECTION 15.5

1. Calculate the elasticity of substitution between y and x for $F(x, y) = 10x^2 + 15y^2$.

2. Let $F(x, y) = x^a + y^a$, where a is a constant with $a \neq 0$ and $a \neq 1$.

    (a) Find the marginal rate of substitution of y for x.

    (b) Calculate the elasticity of substitution between y and x.

SM 3. The elasticity of substitution defined in (15.5.1) can be expressed in terms of the partial derivatives of the function F. Indeed, along the typical isoquant $F(x, y) = c$, one has

$$\sigma_{yx} = \frac{-F_1' F_2' (xF_1' + yF_2')}{xy[(F_2')^2 F_{11}'' - 2F_1' F_2' F_{12}'' + (F_1')^2 F_{22}'']}$$

Use this formula to derive the result in Example 15.5.1.

15.6 Homogeneous Functions of Two Variables

A production function like $Y = F(K, L)$ indicates the amount Y of output that can be produced when K units of capital and L units of labour are used as inputs. For such a production function, economists often ask what happens to output if we double the inputs of both capital and labour? Will production rise by more or less than a factor of two? Example 14.1.4 answered such questions for Cobb–Douglas technologies. To answer them for general functions of two variables, we introduce the concept of *homogeneity*.

HOMOGENEITY

A function $f(x, y)$ of two variables x and y defined in a domain D is said to be *homogeneous of degree k* if, for all (x, y) in D and all $t > 0$, one has

$$f(tx, ty) = t^k f(x, y) \tag{15.6.1}$$

In words, this means that multiplying both variables by a positive factor t will multiply the value of the function by the factor t^k.

The degree of homogeneity of a function can be an arbitrary real number—positive, zero, or negative. Earlier, we determined the degree of homogeneity for several particular

SECTION 15.6 / HOMOGENEOUS FUNCTIONS OF TWO VARIABLES

functions. In Example 14.1.4, for instance, we found that the Cobb–Douglas function F defined by $F(x, y) = Ax^a y^b$ is homogeneous of degree $a + b$. An even simpler example is:

EXAMPLE 15.6.1   Show that $f(x, y) = 3x^2 y - y^3$ is homogeneous of degree 3.

Solution: If we replace x by tx and y by ty in the formula for $f(x, y)$, we obtain

$$f(tx, ty) = 3(tx)^2(ty) - (ty)^3 = 3t^2 x^2 \cdot ty - t^3 y^3 = t^3(3x^2 y - y^3) = t^3 f(x, y)$$

So f is homogeneous of degree 3. If we let $t = 2$, for example, then

$$f(2x, 2y) = 2^3 f(x, y) = 8 f(x, y)$$

After doubling both x and y, the value of this function increases by a factor of 8.

Note that the sum of the exponents in each term of the polynomial in Example 15.6.1 is equal to 3. In general, a polynomial is homogeneous of degree k if and only if the sum of the exponents in every one of its terms is equal to k. Other types of polynomial with different sums of exponents in different terms, such as $f(x, y) = 1 + xy$ or $g(x, y) = x^3 + xy$, are not homogeneous of any degree, as Exercise 6 asks you to show.

Euler's Theorem

Homogeneous functions of two variables have some important properties of interest to economists. The first is:

THEOREM 15.6.1 (EULER'S THEOREM)

The continuously differentiable function $f(x, y)$ is homogeneous of degree k if and only if

$$x f_1'(x, y) + y f_2'(x, y) = k f(x, y) \qquad (15.6.2)$$

Here is an easy demonstration that Eq. (15.6.2) must hold when f is homogeneous of degree k:

Proof: Differentiate each side of Eq. (15.6.1) w.r.t. t, using the chain rule to differentiate the left-hand side. The result is

$$x f_1'(tx, ty) + y f_2'(tx, ty) = k t^{k-1} f(x, y)$$

Putting $t = 1$ gives $x f_1'(x, y) + y f_2'(x, y) = k f(x, y)$ immediately.

Theorem 15.7.1 in the next section proves the converse, and also considers the case of n variables.

We note three other interesting general properties of functions $f(x, y)$ that are homogeneous of degree k:

$$f_1'(x, y) \text{ and } f_2'(x, y) \text{ are both homogeneous of degree } k - 1 \qquad (15.6.3)$$

$$f(x, y) = x^k f(1, y/x) = y^k f(x/y, 1) \quad \text{provided that } x > 0 \text{ and } y > 0 \tag{15.6.4}$$

$$x^2 f_{11}''(x, y) + 2xy f_{12}''(x, y) + y^2 f_{22}''(x, y) = k(k-1) f(x, y) \tag{15.6.5}$$

Again, these results are not difficult to demonstrate:

Proof: To prove (15.6.3), we keep t and y constant while differentiating Eq. (15.6.1) partially w.r.t. x. The result is $t f_1'(tx, ty) = t^k f_1'(x, y)$, implying that $f_1'(tx, ty) = t^{k-1} f_1'(x, y)$. This confirms that $f_1'(x, y)$ is homogeneous of degree $k - 1$. A similar argument shows that $f_2'(x, y)$ is homogeneous of degree $k - 1$.

To prove the two equalities in (15.6.4), we replace t in (15.6.1) first by $1/x$ and then by $1/y$, respectively.

Finally, to show (15.6.5), assuming that $f(x, y)$ is twice continuously differentiable, we note first that because $f_1'(x, y)$ and $f_2'(x, y)$ are both homogeneous of degree $k - 1$, Euler's theorem (15.6.2) can be applied separately first to f_1' and then to f_2'. Doing so gives us

$$x f_{11}''(x, y) + y f_{12}''(x, y) = (k-1) f_1'(x, y) \tag{15.6.6}$$

$$x f_{21}''(x, y) + y f_{22}''(x, y) = (k-1) f_2'(x, y) \tag{15.6.7}$$

Let us now multiply (15.6.6) by x and (15.6.7) by y, before adding the two. Because f is C^2, Young's theorem (Theorem 14.6.1) implies that $f_{12}'' = f_{21}''$, so the resulting equation simplifies to

$$x^2 f_{11}''(x, y) + 2xy f_{12}''(x, y) + y^2 f_{22}''(x, y) = (k-1)[x f_1'(x, y) + y f_2'(x, y)]$$

By Euler's theorem, however, $x f_1'(x, y) + y f_2'(x, y) = k f(x, y)$, so (15.6.5) is verified. ∎

EXAMPLE 15.6.2 Check properties (15.6.2) to (15.6.5) for the function $f(x, y) = 3x^2 y - y^3$.

Solution: We find that $f_1'(x, y) = 6xy$ and $f_2'(x, y) = 3x^2 - 3y^2$. Hence,

$$x f_1'(x, y) + y f_2'(x, y) = 6x^2 y + 3x^2 y - 3y^3 = 3(3x^2 y - y^3) = 3 f(x, y)$$

Example 15.6.1 showed that f is homogeneous of degree 3, so this confirms (15.6.2).

Obviously, f_1' and f_2' are both polynomials that are homogeneous of degree 2, which confirms (15.6.3). As for (15.6.4), in this case it takes the form

$$3x^2 y - y^3 = x^3 [3(y/x) - (y/x)^3] = y^3 [3(x/y)^2 - 1]$$

Finally, to show (15.6.5), we first calculate all the second-order partial derivatives of f, which are $f_{11}''(x, y) = 6y$, $f_{12}''(x, y) = 6x$, and $f_{22}''(x, y) = -6y$. Hence,

$$x^2 f_{11}''(x, y) + 2xy f_{12}''(x, y) + y^2 f_{22}''(x, y) = 6x^2 y + 12x^2 y - 6y^3 = 6(3x^2 y - y^3)$$

$$= 3 \cdot 2 f(x, y)$$

This confirms (15.6.5) as well. ∎

EXAMPLE 15.6.3 Suppose that the production function $Y = F(K, L)$ is homogeneous of degree 1. Show that one can express the output–labour ratio Y/L as a function $Y/L = f(K/L)$ of the capital–labour ratio $k = K/L$, where $f(k) = F(k, 1)$. Find the form of f when F is the Cobb–Douglas function AK^aL^b, with $a + b = 1$.

Solution: Because F is homogeneous of degree 1, as a special case of (15.6.4) one has

$$Y = F(K, L) = F(L(K/L), L \cdot 1) = LF(k, 1) = Lf(k) \text{ where } k = K/L$$

For the function $F(K, L) = AK^aL^{1-a}$, one has $f(k) = F(k, 1) = Ak^a$.

Geometric Aspects of Homogeneous Functions

Homogeneous functions in two variables have some interesting geometric properties. Let $f(x, y)$ be homogeneous of degree k. As shown in Fig 15.6.1, consider a ray in the xy-plane that starts from the origin $(0, 0)$ and passes through the point $(x_0, y_0) \neq (0, 0)$. An arbitrary point on this ray takes the form (tx_0, ty_0) for some positive number t. If we let $f(x_0, y_0) = c$, then $f(tx_0, ty_0) = t^k f(x_0, y_0) = t^k c$. This shows that, above any ray in the xy-plane through a point (x_0, y_0), the relevant portion of the graph of f consists of the curve $z = t^k c$, where t measures the distance along the ray from the origin, and $c = f(x_0, y_0)$. A function that is homogeneous of degree k is therefore completely determined by its value $c = f(x_0, y_0)$ at any one point (x_0, y_0) on each ray through the origin.

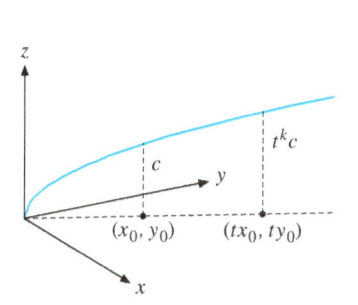

Figure 15.6.1 Function f along a ray

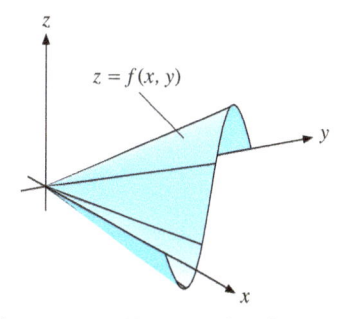

Figure 15.6.2 Homogeneity of degree 1

In particular, let $k = 1$ so that $f(x, y)$ is homogeneous of degree 1. The curve $z = t^k c$ that lies vertically above each relevant ray through the origin is then the straight line $z = tc$. Because of this, it is often said that *the graph of a homogeneous function of degree 1 is generated by straight lines through the origin*. The portion of the graph of $z = f(x, y)$ that is shown in Figure 15.6.2 illustrates this.

For a function $f(x, y)$ of two variables, we have seen how it is often convenient to consider its level curves in the xy-plane instead of its three-dimensional graph. What can we say about the level curves of a homogeneous function? It turns out that *for a homogeneous function, even if only one of its level curves is known, then so are all its other level curves.* To see this, consider a function $f(x, y)$ that is homogeneous of degree k, and let $f(x, y) = c$ be one of its level curves, as illustrated in Fig. 15.6.3.

We now explain how to construct the level curve through an arbitrary point A not lying on $f(x, y) = c$: First, draw the unique ray from the origin that passes through A. This ray

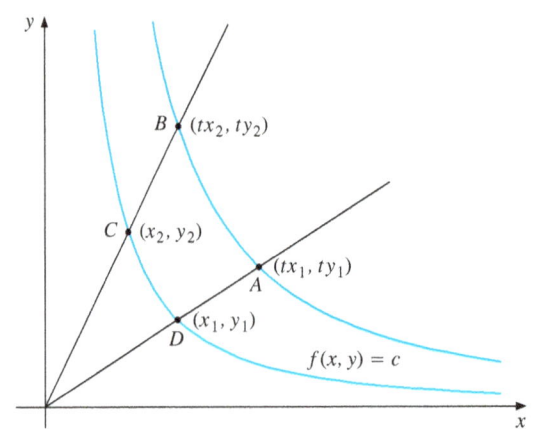

Figure 15.6.3 Level curves for a homogeneous function

must intersect the level curve $f(x, y) = c$ at a unique point D whose coordinates we denote by (x_1, y_1). The coordinates of A will then be (tx_1, ty_1) for some unique value of t, which in the figure is about 1.7.

In order to construct any other point on the same level curve $f(x, y) = f(tx_1, ty_1)$ through A, first draw any new ray through the origin. Again, this must intersect the original level curve $f(x, y) = c$ at a unique point C whose coordinates we denote by (x_2, y_2). Now move along the ray through C to the new point B with coordinates (tx_2, ty_2), where t is the value found earlier when constructing D from A. The new point B must be on the same level curve as A because homogeneity of degree k implies that

$$f(tx_2, ty_2) = t^k f(x_2, y_2) = t^k c = t^k f(x_1, y_1) = f(tx_1, ty_1)$$

By repeating this construction for different rays through the origin that intersect the level curve $f(x, y) = c$, we can find any point we wish on the new level curve $f(x, y) = f(tx_1, ty_1)$. Moreover, the output at each point (x, y) on this new level curve is $f(x, y) = t^k f(x_1, y_1)$.

The preceding argument shows that a homogeneous function $f(x, y)$ is entirely determined by any one of its level curves and by its degree of homogeneity. The shape of each level curve of a homogeneous function is often determined by specifying its elasticity of substitution, as defined in (15.5.1).

Another feature of Fig. 15.6.3 is that, given any two points on a ray through the origin, the tangents to the two level curves at those points are parallel lines. To see why, recall from Eq. (15.3.2) that the slope of the level curve $f(x, y) = c$ at any point (x, y) is $-f_1'(x, y)/f_2'(x, y)$. Now keep the assumption that f is homogeneous of degree k. By Eq. (15.6.3), it follows that the first-order partial derivatives of f are both homogeneous of degree $k - 1$. At the points A and D in Fig. 15.6.3, therefore, there is a common slope of the level curve that satisfies

$$-\frac{f_1'(tx_1, ty_1)}{f_2'(tx_1, ty_1)} = -\frac{t^{k-1} f_1'(x_1, y_1)}{t^{k-1} f_2'(x_1, y_1)} = -\frac{f_1'(x_1, y_1)}{f_2'(x_1, y_1)} \qquad (15.6.8)$$

This shows that, along any ray from the origin, the slope of the corresponding level curve at any point will be constant. Moreover, following the definition in Eq. (15.3.4) of the MRS of

SECTION 15.7 / HOMOGENEOUS AND HOMOTHETIC FUNCTIONS   **639**

y for x, removing the minus signs from Eq. (15.6.8) tells us that this MRS is a homogeneous function of degree 0.

EXERCISES FOR SECTION 15.6

1. Use definition (15.6.1) to show that $f(x, y) = x^4 + x^2y^2$ is homogeneous of degree 4.

2. Find the degree of homogeneity of $x(p, r) = Ap^{-1.5}r^{2.08}$.

(SM) 3. Show that $f(x, y) = xy^2 + x^3$ is homogeneous of degree 3. Verify that the four properties stated in Eqs (15.6.2) to (15.6.5) all hold.

4. Determine whether the function $f(x, y) = xy/(x^2 + y^2)$ is homogeneous, and if it is, check Euler's theorem.

5. Prove that the CES function $F(K, L) = A(aK^{-\rho} + bL^{-\rho})^{-1/\rho}$ is homogeneous of degree one. Then adapt the argument of Example 15.6.3 to express $F(K, L)/L$ as a function of $k = K/L$.

6. Show that $f(x, y) = x^3 + xy$ is not homogeneous of any degree. (*Hint:* Let $x = y = 1$. Apply (15.6.1) with $t = 2$ and $t = 4$ to get a contradiction.)

7. Use Eqs (15.6.6) and (15.6.7) to show that if $f(x, y)$ is homogeneous of degree 1, for all $x > 0$ and $y > 0$, then $f''_{11}(x, y)f''_{22}(x, y) - [f''_{12}(x, y)]^2 = 0$.

8. Suppose that $f(x, y)$ is homogeneous of degree 2, with $f'_1(2, 3) = 4$ and $f'_2(4, 6) = 12$. Find $f(6, 9)$.

(SM) 9. [HARDER] Prove that if $F(x, y)$ is homogeneous of degree 1, then the elasticity of substitution can be expressed as $\sigma_{yx} = F'_1 F'_2/FF''_{12}$. (*Hint:* Use Euler's theorem, together with Eqs (15.6.6) and (15.6.7), as well as the result in Exercise 15.5.3.)

15.7 Homogeneous and Homothetic Functions

Suppose that f is a function of n variables defined in a domain D. The set D is called a *cone* if, whenever $(x_1, x_2, \ldots, x_n) \in D$ and $t > 0$, the point $(tx_1, tx_2, \ldots, tx_n)$ also lies in D. When D is a cone, we say that f is *homogeneous of degree k* on D if

$$f(tx_1, tx_2, \ldots, tx_n) = t^k f(x_1, x_2, \ldots, x_n) \qquad (15.7.1)$$

for all $t > 0$. The constant k can be any real number—positive, zero, or negative.

EXAMPLE 15.7.1   Test the homogeneity of

$$f(x_1, x_2, x_3) = \frac{x_1 + 2x_2 + 3x_3}{x_1^2 + x_2^2 + x_3^2}$$

Solution: Here, f is defined on the set D of all points in three-dimensional space excluding the origin, which is a cone. Also,

$$f(tx_1, tx_2, tx_3) = \frac{tx_1 + 2tx_2 + 3tx_3}{(tx_1)^2 + (tx_2)^2 + (tx_3)^2} = \frac{t(x_1 + 2x_2 + 3x_3)}{t^2(x_1^2 + x_2^2 + x_3^2)} = t^{-1} f(x_1, x_2, x_3)$$

Hence, f is homogeneous of degree -1.

Euler's theorem, which we saw as Theorem 15.6.1 for the case of functions of two variables, can be generalized to functions of n variables:

THEOREM 15.7.1 (EULER'S THEOREM)

Suppose f is a C^1 function of n variables, defined in an open cone D. Then f is homogeneous of degree k if and only if, for all $\mathbf{x}$ in D, one has:

$$\sum_{i=1}^{n} x_i f_i'(\mathbf{x}) = k f(\mathbf{x}) \tag{15.7.2}$$

The following proof of this result is a routine extension of the argument we gave for Theorem 15.6.1:

Proof of Euler's Theorem: Suppose f is homogeneous of degree k, so that Eq. (15.7.1) holds. Differentiating this equation w.r.t. t, with $\mathbf{x}$ fixed, yields

$$\sum_{i=1}^{n} x_i f_i'(t\mathbf{x}) = k t^{k-1} f(\mathbf{x})$$

Setting $t = 1$ gives (15.7.2) immediately.

To prove the converse, assume that Eq. (15.7.2) is valid for all $\mathbf{x}$ in the cone D. Keep $\mathbf{x}$ fixed and define the function g for all $t > 0$ by $g(t) = t^{-k} f(t\mathbf{x}) - f(\mathbf{x})$. Differentiating this w.r.t. t gives

$$g'(t) = -k t^{-k-1} f(t\mathbf{x}) + t^{-k} \sum_{i=1}^{n} x_i f_i'(t\mathbf{x}) \tag{$*$}$$

Because $t\mathbf{x}$ lies in D, Eq. (15.7.2) must also be valid when each x_i is replaced by tx_i, which implies that $\sum_{i=1}^{n} (tx_i) f_i'(t\mathbf{x}) = k f(t\mathbf{x})$. Multiplying each side of this last equation by t^{-k-1} gives

$$t^{-k} \sum_{i=1}^{n} x_i f_i'(t\mathbf{x}) = k t^{-k-1} f(t\mathbf{x}) \tag{$**$}$$

It follows from ($*$) and ($**$) that, for all $t > 0$, one has $g'(t) = 0$, so $g(t)$ must be a constant C. Obviously $g(1) = 0$, so $C = 0$, implying that $g(t) = 0$ for *all* $t > 0$. By definition of g, this proves that $f(t\mathbf{x}) = t^k f(\mathbf{x})$, so f is indeed homogeneous of degree k.

An interesting version of the Euler equation (15.7.2) results from dividing each term of the equation by $f(\mathbf{x})$, provided this is not 0. Using the definition of partial elasticity in (14.10.3), we can write $\text{El}_i f(\mathbf{x}) = (x_i/f(\mathbf{x})) f_i'(\mathbf{x})$. So

$$\text{El}_1 f(\mathbf{x}) + \text{El}_2 f(\mathbf{x}) + \cdots + \text{El}_n f(\mathbf{x}) = k \tag{15.7.3}$$

Thus, given a function of n variables that is homogeneous of degree k, the sum of its partial elasticities must equal k.

The results in Eqs (15.6.3) to (15.6.5) can also be extended to functions of n variables. The proofs are similar, so they can be left to the interested reader. We simply state the extensions of Eqs (15.6.3) and (15.6.5): if $f(\mathbf{x})$ is homogeneous of degree k, then for each $i = 1, 2, \ldots, n$ one has:

$$f_i'(\mathbf{x}) \text{ is homogeneous of degree } k-1 \tag{15.7.4}$$

$$\sum_{i=1}^n \sum_{j=1}^n x_i x_j f_{ij}''(\mathbf{x}) = k(k-1)f(\mathbf{x}) \tag{15.7.5}$$

Economic Applications

Let us consider some typical examples of homogeneous functions in economics.

EXAMPLE 15.7.2 Let $f(\mathbf{v}) = f(v_1, \ldots, v_n)$ denote the output of a production process when the input quantities are $v_1, \ldots, v_n$. It is often assumed that if all the input quantities are scaled by a factor t, then t times as much output as before is produced, so that for all $t > 0$,

$$f(t\mathbf{v}) = tf(\mathbf{v}) \tag{$*$}$$

This implies that f is homogeneous of degree 1. Production functions with this property are said to exhibit *constant returns to scale*.

For any fixed input vector $\mathbf{v}$, consider the function $\varphi(t) = f(t\mathbf{v})/t$. This indicates the average returns to scale, meaning the average output per unit input when all inputs are rescaled by the same factor. When $t = 2$, for example, all inputs are doubled. But when $t = 3/4$, all inputs are reduced proportionally by $1/4$.

Now, when ($*$) holds, then $\varphi(t) = f(\mathbf{v})$, independent of t. Also, a production function that is homogeneous of degree $k < 1$ is said to have *decreasing returns to scale* because $\varphi(t) = t^{k-1}f(\mathbf{v})$ and so $\varphi'(t) < 0$. On the other hand, a production function has *increasing returns to scale* if $k > 1$ because then $\varphi'(t) > 0$.

EXAMPLE 15.7.3 The general Cobb–Douglas function $F(v_1, \ldots, v_n) = Av_1^{a_1} \cdots v_n^{a_n}$ is often used as an example of a production function with n inputs. Prove that it is homogeneous, and examine whether it has constant, decreasing, or increasing returns to scale. Also confirm Eq. (15.7.3) in this case.

Solution: The definition of Cobb–Douglas function implies that

$$F(t\mathbf{v}) = A(tv_1)^{a_1} \cdots (tv_n)^{a_n} = At^{a_1} v_1^{a_1} \cdots t^{a_n} v_n^{a_n} = t^{a_1 + \cdots + a_n} F(\mathbf{v})$$

It follows that F is homogeneous of degree $a_1 + \cdots + a_n$. So F has constant, decreasing, or increasing returns to scale according as the sum $a_1 + \cdots + a_n$ of its powers is equal, smaller, or greater than 1. Also, for each $i = 1, \ldots, n$ the partial elasticity is $\text{El}_i F = a_i$, implying that $\sum_{i=1}^n \text{El}_i F = \sum_{i=1}^n a_i$. This confirms (15.7.3).

EXAMPLE 15.7.4 Consider a market with three commodities whose quantities are denoted by x, y, and z, with prices per unit that are p, q, and r respectively. Suppose that the demand for one of the commodities by a consumer with income m is given by $D(p, q, r, m)$. Suppose too that the three prices and income m are all multiplied by the same factor $t > 0$.[4] Then the consumer's budget constraint $px + qy + rz \leq m$ becomes $tpx + tqy + trz \leq tm$, which is exactly the same constraint. The multiplicative constant t is irrelevant to the consumer. It is therefore natural to assume that the consumer's demand remains unchanged, with

$$D(tp, tq, tr, tm) = D(p, q, r, m)$$

Requiring this equation to be valid for all $t > 0$ means that the demand function D is homogeneous of degree 0. In this case, it is often said that demand is not influenced by "money illusion": a consumer with 10% more money to spend should realize that nothing has really changed if all prices have also risen by 10%.

As a specific example of a function that is common in demand analysis, consider

$$D(p, q, r, m) = \frac{mp^b}{p^{b+1} + q^{b+1} + r^{b+1}}$$

where b is a constant. Here

$$D(tp, tq, tr, tm) = \frac{(tm)(tp)^b}{(tp)^{b+1} + (tq)^{b+1} + (tr)^{b+1}} = D(p, q, r, m)$$

because the factor t^{b+1} in each term can be cancelled.

Sometimes we encounter non-homogeneous functions of several variables that are, however, "partially homogeneous" in the sense that they are homogeneous when regarded as functions of some of the variables only, with the other variables fixed. For instance, the (minimum) cost of producing y units of a single output good is often expressed as a function $C(\mathbf{w}, y)$ of y and of the vector $\mathbf{w} = (w_1, \ldots, w_n)$ whose components are the prices of n different input factors. In this case, if all input prices double, an economist usually expects the production cost to double. So a common assumption is that $C(t\mathbf{w}, y) = t C(\mathbf{w}, y)$ for all $t > 0$, meaning that the cost function is "partially homogeneous" of degree 1 in the input price vector $\mathbf{w}$, for each fixed output level y. See Exercise 7 for a prominent example.

Homothetic Functions

Let f be a function of n variables $\mathbf{x} = (x_1, \ldots, x_n)$ defined in a cone K. Then f is called *homothetic* if

$$\mathbf{x}, \mathbf{y} \in K, \ f(\mathbf{x}) = f(\mathbf{y}), \ t > 0 \implies f(t\mathbf{x}) = f(t\mathbf{y}) \qquad (15.7.6)$$

For instance, if f is some consumer's utility function, Eq. (15.7.6) requires that whenever there is indifference between the two commodity bundles $\mathbf{x}$ and $\mathbf{y}$, then there is also indifference after they have both been magnified or shrunk by the same proportion t. For example,

---

[4] Imagine, for example, that income and the prices of all commodities rise by 10%. Or that all prices and incomes have been converted into euros from, say, German marks.

a consumer who is indifferent between two litres of soda and three litres of juice must also be indifferent between four litres of soda and six litres of juice. Evidently, this property may be true of some consumers, but one should not assume it of all people.

A homogeneous function f of any degree k is homothetic. In fact, it is easy to prove a more general result:

THEOREM 15.7.2

Suppose that function F can be written as the composition of two real-valued functions H and f, so that $F(\mathbf{x}) = H(f(\mathbf{x}))$. If H is strictly increasing and f is homogeneous of any degree, then F is homothetic.

Proof: Suppose that $F(\mathbf{x}) = F(\mathbf{y})$, or equivalently, that $H(f(\mathbf{x})) = H(f(\mathbf{y}))$. Because H is strictly increasing, this implies that $f(\mathbf{x}) = f(\mathbf{y})$. Suppose that f is homogeneous of degree k. Then for any $t > 0$ one has

$$F(t\mathbf{x}) = H(f(t\mathbf{x})) = H(t^k f(\mathbf{x})) = H(t^k f(\mathbf{y})) = H(f(t\mathbf{y})) = F(t\mathbf{y})$$

This proves that $F(\mathbf{x})$ satisfies definition (15.7.6), and so is homothetic.

Hence, any strictly increasing function of a homogeneous function is homothetic. It is actually quite common to take this property as the definition of a homothetic function, usually with $k = 1$.[5]

The next example shows that not all homothetic functions are homogeneous.

EXAMPLE 15.7.5
Show that the function $F(x, y) = xy + 1$, which is obviously not homogeneous, is nevertheless homothetic.

Solution: Define the two functions $H(u) = u + 1$ and $f(x, y) = xy$. Then for all x, y one has $F(x, y) = xy + 1 = H(f(x, y))$, where H is strictly increasing and f is homogeneous of degree 2. So Theorem 15.7.2 implies that F is homothetic. Alternatively, one can use the definition in (15.7.6) to show directly that F is homothetic.

Suppose that $F(\mathbf{x}) = F(x_1, x_2, \ldots, x_n)$ is a differentiable production function, defined for all n-vectors $\mathbf{x} = (x_1, \ldots, x_n)$ satisfying $x_i \geq 0$ for $i = 1, \ldots, n$. Recall that the marginal rate of substitution, or MRS, of factor j for factor i is defined, for $i, j = 1, 2, \ldots, n$, by

$$h_{ji}(\mathbf{x}) = \frac{\partial F(\mathbf{x})}{\partial x_i} \div \frac{\partial F(\mathbf{x})}{\partial x_j} \qquad (15.7.7)$$

---

[5] Suppose that $F(\mathbf{x})$ is any continuous homothetic function defined on the cone K consisting of all n-vectors $\mathbf{x}$ satisfying $x_i \geq 0$ for all $i = 1, \ldots, n$. (In other words, K is the nonnegative orthant of $\mathbb{R}^n$.) Suppose too that $F(t\mathbf{x}_0)$ is a strictly increasing function of t for each fixed $\mathbf{x}_0 \neq \mathbf{0}$ in K. Then one can prove that there exists a strictly increasing function H such that $F(\mathbf{x}) = H(f(\mathbf{x}))$, where the function $f(\mathbf{x})$ is homogeneous of degree 1. Actually, f could be made a homogeneous function of any positive degree k by modifying H so it becomes the power function $\tilde{H}(u) = u^k$.

Suppose that $F(\mathbf{x}) = H(f(\mathbf{x}))$, where H is a differentiable function of one variable with $H'(u) > 0$ for all u in its domain. Suppose too that $f(\mathbf{x})$ is homogeneous of degree k. Then

$$\frac{\partial F(\mathbf{x})}{\partial x_i} = H'(f(\mathbf{x}))\frac{\partial f(\mathbf{x})}{\partial x_i}$$

This implies that wherever $f'_j(\mathbf{x}) > 0$ and so $F'_j(\mathbf{x}) > 0$, one has

$$\frac{\partial F(\mathbf{x})}{\partial x_i} \div \frac{\partial F(\mathbf{x})}{\partial x_j} = \frac{\partial f(\mathbf{x})}{\partial x_i} \div \frac{\partial f(\mathbf{x})}{\partial x_j} \qquad (15.7.8)$$

Replacing $\mathbf{x}$ by $t\mathbf{x}$ in (15.7.7) and (15.7.8) implies that

$$h_{ji}(t\mathbf{x}) = \frac{\partial f(t\mathbf{x})}{\partial x_i} \div \frac{\partial f(t\mathbf{x})}{\partial x_j} \qquad (15.7.9)$$

But f is homogeneous of degree k. So (15.7.4) and (15.7.9) together imply that, for all $t > 0$, one has

$$h_{ji}(t\mathbf{x}) = \frac{\partial f(t\mathbf{x})}{\partial x_i} \div \frac{\partial f(t\mathbf{x})}{\partial x_j} = t^{k-1}\frac{\partial f(\mathbf{x})}{\partial x_i} \div \left[t^{k-1}\frac{\partial f(\mathbf{x})}{\partial x_j}\right] = h_{ji}(\mathbf{x}) \qquad (15.7.10)$$

Formula (15.7.10) shows that the marginal rates of substitution are homogeneous of degree 0. This demonstrates the following general result: *Suppose that the function $F(\mathbf{x}) = H(f(\mathbf{x}))$ is a strictly increasing transformation $H(u)$ of a homogeneous function $u = f(\mathbf{x})$, as in the premises of Theorem 15.7.2, where H is differentiable with $H'(u) > 0$ for all u in its domain. Then the marginal rates of substitution of $F(\mathbf{x})$ are homogeneous of degree 0.*[6] This result generalizes to n variables the observation made for the case of two variables at the end of Section 15.6.

EXERCISES FOR SECTION 15.7

SM **1.** Find the degree of homogeneity, if there is one, for each of the following functions:

(a) $f(x, y, z) = 3x + 4y - 3z$

(b) $g(x, y, z) = 3x + 4y - 2z - 2$

(c) $h(x, y, z) = \dfrac{\sqrt{x} + \sqrt{y} + \sqrt{z}}{x + y + z}$

(d) $G(x, y) = \sqrt{xy} \ln\left(\dfrac{x^2 + y^2}{xy}\right)$

(e) $H(x, y) = \ln x + \ln y$

(f) $p(x_1, \ldots, x_n) = \sum_{i=1}^{n} x_i^n$

SM **2.** Find the degree of homogeneity, if there is one, for each of the following functions:

(a) $f(x_1, x_2, x_3) = \dfrac{(x_1 x_2 x_3)^2}{x_1^4 + x_2^4 + x_3^4}\left(\dfrac{1}{x_1} + \dfrac{1}{x_2} + \dfrac{1}{x_3}\right)$

(b) the CES function: $x(v_1, v_2, \ldots, v_n) = A\left(\delta_1 v_1^{-\rho} + \delta_2 v_2^{-\rho} + \cdots + \delta_n v_n^{-\rho}\right)^{-\mu/\rho}$

3. Examine the homogeneity of the three means $\bar{x}_A$, $\bar{x}_G$, and $\bar{x}_H$, as defined in Example 14.5.2.

---

[6] Because of our previous footnote, the same must be true if F is any homothetic function with the property that $F(t\mathbf{x})$ is an increasing function of the scalar t for each fixed vector $\mathbf{x}$.

4. Consider a utility function $u(\mathbf{x}) = u(x_1, \ldots, x_n)$ whose continuous partial derivatives, for some constant a, satisfy $\sum_{i=1}^{n} x_i \dfrac{\partial u}{\partial x_i} = a$ for all $x_1 > 0, \ldots, x_n > 0$. Show that the function $v(\mathbf{x}) = u(\mathbf{x}) - a \ln(x_1 + \cdots + x_n)$ is homogeneous of degree 0.[7] (*Hint:* Use Euler's theorem.)

(SM) 5. Which of the following functions $f(x, y)$ are homothetic?

(a) $(xy)^2 + 1$ (b) $\dfrac{2(xy)^2}{(xy)^2 + 1}$ (c) $x^2 + y^3$ (d) $e^{x^2 y}$

6. [HARDER] Suppose that $f(\mathbf{x})$ and $g(\mathbf{x})$ are homogeneous of degree r and s, respectively. Determine which of the following functions h are homogeneous. Find the degree of homogeneity in each case, if there is one.

(a) $h(\mathbf{x}) = f(x_1^m, x_2^m, \ldots, x_n^m)$ (b) $h(\mathbf{x}) = g(\mathbf{x})^p$ (c) $h = f + g$

(d) $h = fg$ (e) $h = f/g$

(SM) 7. [HARDER] The *transcendental logarithmic*, or "translog", *cost function* $C(\mathbf{w}, y)$ is defined implicitly, for each n-vector $\mathbf{w} = (w_1, w_2, \ldots,)$ of positive factor prices, and each positive level of output y, by

$$\ln C(\mathbf{w}, y) = a_0 + c_1 \ln y + \sum_{i=1}^{n} a_i \ln w_i + \frac{1}{2} \sum_{i=1}^{n} \sum_{j=1}^{n} b_{ij} \ln w_i \ln w_j + \ln y \sum_{i=1}^{n} c_i \ln w_i$$

Prove that, for each fixed y, this cost function is homogeneous of degree 1 in $\mathbf{w}$ provided that the various parameters satisfy all the following equations: (i) $\sum_{i=1}^{n} a_i = 1$; (ii) $\sum_{i=1}^{n} c_i = 0$; (iii) $\sum_{j=1}^{n} b_{ij} = 0$ for all i; and (iv) $\sum_{i=1}^{n} b_{ij} = 0$ for all j.

15.8 Linear Approximations

In Section 7.4 we discussed the linear approximation $f(a + h) \approx f(a) + f'(a)h$ for a function of one variable, which can be derived by putting $h = x - a$ in (7.4.1). It is important to understand the size of the error or remainder $R(h) = f(a + h) - f(a) - f'(a)h$ in this approximation. It is rather obvious that $R(h) \to 0$ as $h \to 0$. But the definition of the derivative $f'(a)$ implies the stronger property that, as $h \to 0$, so

$$\frac{1}{h} R(h) = \frac{1}{h}[f(a + h) - f(a)] - f'(a) \to f'(a) - f'(a) = 0 \quad (15.8.1)$$

We will now find a similar linear approximation for a C^1 function f of two variables, and later for a function of n variables.

For fixed numbers x_0, y_0, x, and y, define the function $g(t)$ of one variable by

$$g(t) = f(x_0 + t(x - x_0), y_0 + t(y - y_0)) \quad (15.8.2)$$

---

[7] This function was first studied by D.W. Katzner.

We see that $g(0) = f(x_0, y_0)$ and $g(1) = f(x, y)$. For general t, we see that $g(t)$ is the value of f at the point

$$(x(t), y(t)) = (x_0 + t(x - x_0), y_0 + t(y - y_0)) = ((1-t)x_0 + tx, (1-t)y_0 + ty)$$

which lies on the line joining (x_0, y_0) to (x, y). According to the chain rule (15.1.1), because $x'(t) = x - x_0$ and $y'(t) = y - y_0$, the derivative $g'(t)$ equals

$$f_1'(x_0 + t(x - x_0), y_0 + t(y - y_0))(x - x_0) + f_2'(x_0 + t(x - x_0), y_0 + t(y - y_0))(y - y_0)$$

Putting $t = 0$ gives

$$g'(0) = f_1'(x_0, y_0)(x - x_0) + f_2'(x_0, y_0)(y - y_0) \qquad (15.8.3)$$

So, using the approximation $g(1) \approx g(0) + g'(0)$, we obtain the result:

LINEAR APPROXIMATION

The linear approximation to $f(x, y)$ about (x_0, y_0) is

$$f(x, y) \approx f(x_0, y_0) + f_1'(x_0, y_0)(x - x_0) + f_2'(x_0, y_0)(y - y_0) \qquad (15.8.4)$$

Putting $h = x - x_0$ and $k = y - y_0$ in (15.8.4) and including the remainder or error term $R(h, k)$ gives

$$f(x_0 + h, y_0 + k) = f(x_0, y_0) + f_1'(x_0, y_0)h + f_2'(x_0, y_0)k + R(h, k)$$

Let $\|(h, k)\| = \sqrt{h^2 + k^2}$ denote the norm of (h, k). Provided that the function $f(x, y)$ is C^1 near (x_0, y_0), this error term satisfies $R(h, k)/\|(h, k)\| \to 0$ as $\|(h, k)\| \to 0$. This is the extension of (15.8.1) to functions of two variables. Later in this section we will discuss the corresponding general result when f is a function of n variables.

EXAMPLE 15.8.1 Find the linear approximation to $f(x, y) = e^{x+y}(xy - 1)$ about $(0, 0)$.

Solution: Here one has $f(0, 0) = -1$, as well as

$$f_1'(x, y) = e^{x+y}(xy - 1) + e^{x+y}y \quad \text{and} \quad f_2'(x, y) = e^{x+y}(xy - 1) + e^{x+y}x$$

So $f_1'(0, 0) = -1$ and $f_2'(0, 0) = -1$. Hence, Eq. (15.8.4) gives

$$e^{x+y}(xy - 1) \approx -1 - x - y$$

So for x and y close to 0, the complicated function $z = e^{x+y}(xy - 1)$ is approximated by the simple linear function $z = -1 - x - y$.

Formula (15.8.4) can be used to find approximate values of a function near any point where the function and its derivatives are easily evaluated, as in the following example.

EXAMPLE 15.8.2   Let $f(x,y) = xy^3 - 2x^3$. Then $f(2,3) = 38$. Using (15.8.4), find an approximate numerical value for $f(2.01, 2.98)$.

Solution: Here $f_1'(x,y) = y^3 - 6x^2$ and $f_2'(x,y) = 3xy^2$, so $f_1'(2,3) = 3$ and $f_2'(2,3) = 54$. Putting $x_0 = 2$, $y_0 = 3$, $x = 2 + 0.01$, and $y = 3 - 0.02$, we obtain

$$f(2.01, 2.98) \approx f(2,3) + f_1'(2,3) \cdot 0.01 + f_2'(2,3) \cdot (-0.02) = 38 + 3(0.01) + 54(-0.02)$$

which equals 36.95. The exact value is $f(2.01, 2.98) = 36.95061792$. The error in the approximation, therefore, is only a little larger than 0.0006 in absolute value.

Approximation (15.8.4) can be generalized to functions of several variables.

LINEAR APPROXIMATION

Given a C^1 function $f(\mathbf{x}) = f(x_1, \ldots, x_n)$ of n variables, the linear approximation to f about the point $\mathbf{x}^0 = (x_1^0, \ldots, x_n^0)$ is

$$f(\mathbf{x}) \approx f(\mathbf{x}^0) + f_1'(\mathbf{x}^0)(x_1 - x_1^0) + \cdots + f_n'(\mathbf{x}^0)(x_n - x_n^0) \tag{15.8.5}$$

Exercise 8 asks you to provide a proof. Equation (14.3.2) introduced the notation $\nabla f(\mathbf{x}^0) = \bigl(f_1'(\mathbf{x}^0), \ldots, f_n'(\mathbf{x}^0)\bigr)$ for the gradient n-vector evaluated at $\mathbf{x}^0$. Using dot product notation then allows us to rewrite Eq. (15.8.5) more concisely as

$$f(\mathbf{x}) \approx f(\mathbf{x}^0) + \nabla f(\mathbf{x}^0) \cdot (\mathbf{x} - \mathbf{x}^0) \tag{15.8.6}$$

Differentiability and Gradient Vectors

In order to discuss the size of the error in Eq. (15.8.6), we will use the definition in (14.5.6) of continuity for a function of n variables, as well as the following definition:

DIFFERENTIABILITY AND DERIVATIVE

Suppose that the function $f(\mathbf{x}) = f(x_1, \ldots, x_n)$ of n variables is defined on the subset S of $\mathbb{R}^n$. Let $\mathbf{a}$ be an interior point of S. Then f is said to be *differentiable* at $\mathbf{a}$, with the n-vector $\mathbf{p}$ as its *derivative* at $\mathbf{a}$, provided that

$$\frac{1}{\|\mathbf{h}\|}[f(\mathbf{a} + \mathbf{h}) - f(\mathbf{a}) - \mathbf{p} \cdot \mathbf{h}] \to 0 \quad \text{as} \quad \mathbf{h} \to \mathbf{0} \tag{15.8.7}$$

In n-space, a *direction* can be identified with an n-vector $\mathbf{u}$ which lies in the unit sphere because $\|\mathbf{u}\| = \sqrt{\mathbf{u} \cdot \mathbf{u}} = 1$. In the case when $n = 2$ and so the unit sphere is a circle, one can think of a compass whose needle points in a direction $\mathbf{u}$ that is measured around a circle marked with indicators such as SW for south-west. There is a close relationship between the derivative of a function of n variables, which is defined by (15.8.7), and its directional derivatives, which we are about to define.

DIRECTIONAL DERIVATIVE

Suppose that the function $f(\mathbf{x})$ of n variables is defined on the subset S of $\mathbb{R}^n$. Let $\mathbf{a}$ be an interior point of S, and $\mathbf{u}$ any direction vector. Then the *directional derivative* of f at $\mathbf{a}$, in the direction $\mathbf{u}$, is defined by

$$\nabla_\mathbf{u} f(\mathbf{a}) = \lim_{\theta \to 0} \frac{1}{\theta}[f(\mathbf{a} + \theta \mathbf{u}) - f(\mathbf{a})] \tag{15.8.8}$$

Thus $\nabla_\mathbf{u} f(\mathbf{a})$ is the ordinary derivative of the function of one variable defined for all small θ by $g_\mathbf{u}(\mathbf{a}; \theta) = f(\mathbf{a} + \theta \mathbf{u})$. The following result uses both directional derivatives and the gradient vector to characterize the derivative $\mathbf{p}$ that was defined in (15.8.7).

THEOREM 15.8.1 (CHARACTERIZING THE DERIVATIVE)

Suppose that the function $f(\mathbf{x})$ of n variables is defined on the subset S of $\mathbb{R}^n$ and is differentiable at an interior point $\mathbf{a}$ of S, with derivative equal to the n-vector $\mathbf{p}$. Then the derivative $\mathbf{p}$ equals the gradient vector $\nabla f(\mathbf{a})$. Moreover, the directional derivative $\nabla_\mathbf{u} f(\mathbf{a})$ of f at $\mathbf{a}$ in any direction $\mathbf{u}$ with $\|\mathbf{u}\| = 1$ exists and is given by

$$\nabla_\mathbf{u} f(\mathbf{a}) = \mathbf{p} \cdot \mathbf{u} = \nabla f(\mathbf{a}) \cdot \mathbf{u} \tag{15.8.9}$$

Proof: Given any direction $\mathbf{u}$ in the unit sphere of n-space and any small $\theta > 0$, put $\mathbf{h} = \theta \mathbf{u}$. Then one has

$$\frac{1}{\theta}[f(\mathbf{a} + \theta \mathbf{u}) - f(\mathbf{a}) - \mathbf{p} \cdot (\theta \mathbf{u})] = \frac{1}{\|\mathbf{h}\|}[f(\mathbf{a} + \mathbf{h}) - f(\mathbf{a}) - \mathbf{p} \cdot \mathbf{h}]$$

As $\theta \to 0$ and so $\mathbf{h} \to \mathbf{0}$, using (15.8.8) shows that the limit of the left-hand side equals $\nabla_\mathbf{u} f(\mathbf{a}) - \mathbf{p} \cdot \mathbf{u}$, whereas using (15.8.7) shows that the limit of the right-hand side is 0. This proves that $\nabla_\mathbf{u} f(\mathbf{a}) = \mathbf{p} \cdot \mathbf{u}$.

Next, for each $i = 1, 2, \ldots, n$, consider the case when $\mathbf{u} = \mathbf{e}_i$, defined as the direction vector whose ith component is 1, implying that all other components are 0. Then the equality $\nabla_{\mathbf{e}_i} f(\mathbf{a}) = \mathbf{p} \cdot \mathbf{e}_i$ evidently implies that the ith partial derivative satisfies $f_i'(\mathbf{a}) = p_i$, the ith component of $\mathbf{p}$. So the definition of $\nabla f(\mathbf{a})$ as the vector of partial derivatives implies that it must equal the derivative $\mathbf{p}$. ∎

In (7.9.3) we showed that if a function of one variable is differentiable at $x = a$, then it is continuous at $x = a$. The definition in (15.8.7) implies a similar result for a function of n variables.

THEOREM 15.8.2 (DIFFERENTIABILITY IMPLIES CONTINUITY)

If the function $f(\mathbf{x})$ of n variables is defined on the subset S of $\mathbb{R}^n$ and is differentiable at an interior point $\mathbf{a}$ of S, then f is continuous at $\mathbf{a}$.

Proof: Let $\mathbf{p}$ denote the derivative, defined so that Eq. (15.8.7) is satisfied. As discussed in Section 14.5, the linear function $\mathbf{p} \cdot \mathbf{x} = p_1 + \cdots + p_n x_n$ is evidently continuous in $\mathbf{x}$. It follows that $\mathbf{p} \cdot \mathbf{h} \to 0$ as $\mathbf{h} \to \mathbf{0}$. Furthermore

$$f(\mathbf{a} + \mathbf{h}) - f(\mathbf{a}) = \|\mathbf{h}\| \left(\frac{1}{\|\mathbf{h}\|} [f(\mathbf{a} + \mathbf{h}) - f(\mathbf{a}) - \mathbf{p} \cdot \mathbf{h}] \right) + \mathbf{p} \cdot \mathbf{h}$$

Now, as $\mathbf{h} \to \mathbf{0}$, the definition of $\mathbf{p}$ implies that the fraction in parentheses tends to 0, as does $\mathbf{p} \cdot \mathbf{h}$. It follows that $f(\mathbf{a} + \mathbf{h}) \to f(\mathbf{a})$, so f is continuous at $\mathbf{a}$. ∎

Exercise 10 asks you to consider a function of two variables which has both partial derivatives at $(0, 0)$. Using the argument that was used to derive Eq. (15.8.3), it follows that f has a directional derivative $\nabla_{\mathbf{u}} f(\mathbf{a})$ for every direction vector $\mathbf{u}$ in the unit circle of 2-space. Yet f is not even continuous, let alone differentiable, at $(0, 0)$. As the following result shows, this is because its partial derivatives are not continuous.

A C^1 FUNCTION IS DIFFERENTIABLE

If the function $f(\mathbf{x})$ of n variables is defined and C^1 on the subset S of $\mathbb{R}^n$, then f is differentiable at any interior point $\mathbf{a}$ of S.

The following proof considers the two-dimensional case. For a proof that applies for $n > 2$, see FMEA.

Proof: In the two-dimensional case, given any $(h, k) \neq (0, 0)$, we have

$$f(x+h, y+k) - f(x, y) = [f(x+h, y+k) - f(x+h, y)] + [f(x+h, y) - f(x, y)] \quad (*)$$

Because the partial derivatives of $f(x+h, y+k)$ w.r.t. both h and k are continuous for all small h and k, so are the derivatives of the functions $\varphi(\theta) = f(x + \theta h, y)$ of θ and $\psi(\eta) = f(x+h, y + \eta k)$ of η, both defined on $[0, 1]$. It follows from the Mean Value Theorem 9.4.2 that there exist θ^* and η^* in $(0, 1)$ such that

$$f(x+h, y) - f(x, y) = \varphi(1) - \varphi(0) = \varphi'(\theta^*) = f_1'(x + \theta^* h, y) h \quad (**)$$

and $\quad f(x+h, y+k) - f(x+h, y) = \psi(1) - \psi(0) = \psi'(\eta^*) = f_2'(x+h, y + \eta^* k) k$
$$(***)$$

Now, for all (h, k) near but not equal to $(0, 0)$, define

$$R(h, k) = f(x+h, y+k) - f(x, y) - f_1'(x, y) h - f_2'(x, y) k$$

It follows from (∗), (∗∗) and (∗∗∗) that

$$R(h,k) = [f_1'(x+\theta^*h, y) - f_1'(x,y)]h + [f_2'(x+h, y+\eta^*k) - f_2'(x,y)]k$$

Dividing each side of this equation by the norm $\|(h,k)\|$, we see that

$$\frac{1}{\|(h,k)\|}R(h,k) = [f_1'(x+\theta^*h, y) - f_1'(x,y)]\frac{h}{\|(h,k)\|} + [f_2'(x+h, y+\eta^*k) - f_2'(x,y)]\frac{k}{\|(h,k)\|}$$

We have assumed that f_1' and f_2' are both continuous at (x,y), so $R(h,k)/\|(h,k)\| \to 0$ as $(h,k) \to (0,0)$. It follows that the function f is differentiable at (x,y), with derivative equal to the gradient vector $(f_1'(x,y), f_2'(x,y))$.

Tangent Planes

In Eq. (15.8.4), the function $z = f(x,y)$ is approximated by the *linear function*

$$z = f(x_0, y_0) + f_1'(x_0, y_0)(x - x_0) + f_2'(x_0, y_0)(y - y_0)$$

The graph of $z = f(x,y)$ is a plane which passes through the point $P = (x_0, y_0, z_0)$ that is on the graph because $z_0 = f(x_0, y_0)$. This plane is called the *tangent plane* to $z = f(x,y)$ at P:

TANGENT PLANE

At the point (x_0, y_0, z_0) with $z_0 = f(x_0, y_0)$, the tangent plane to the graph of $z = f(x,y)$ has the equation

$$z - z_0 = f_1'(x_0, y_0)(x - x_0) + f_2'(x_0, y_0)(y - y_0) \tag{15.8.10}$$

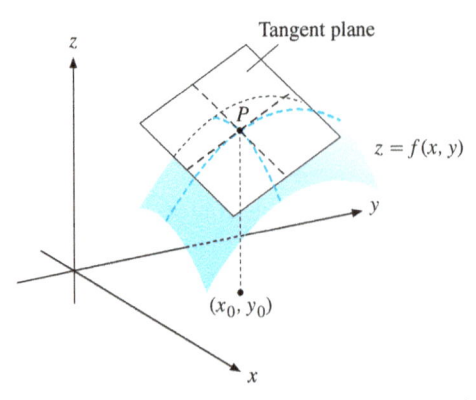

Figure 15.8.1 The graph of $z = f(x,y)$ and the tangent plane at P

This tangent plane is illustrated in Fig. 15.8.1. Does it deserve that name? Look back at Fig. 14.3.8, where l_x and l_y are the tangents at P to the two curves K_x and K_y that lie in the surface. Since the slope of the line l_x is $f_2'(x_0, y_0)$, the points (x, y, z) of l_x are characterized by $x = x_0$ and $z - z_0 = f_2'(x_0, y_0)(y - y_0)$. But Eq. (15.8.10) implies that these points also lie in the tangent plane. Similarly, we see that the line l_y also lies in the tangent plane. Because the graph of Eq. (15.8.10) is the only plane that contains both tangent lines l_x and l_y, it makes good sense to call it the "tangent plane" at (x_0, y_0, z_0).

EXAMPLE 15.8.3   Find the tangent plane at $P = (x_0, y_0, z_0) = (1, 1, 5)$ to the graph of

$$f(x, y) = x^2 + 2xy + 2y^2$$

Solution: Because $f(1, 1) = 5$, the point P is on the graph of f. But $f_1'(x, y) = 2x + 2y$ and $f_2'(x, y) = 2x + 4y$, so $f_1'(1, 1) = 4$ and $f_2'(1, 1) = 6$. Applying Eq. (15.8.10) yields

$$z - 5 = 4(x - 1) + 6(y - 1)$$

This simplifies to $z = 4x + 6y - 5$.

Supergradients and Subgradients

Let $z = f(x, y)$ be any function defined on the domain S in the xy-plane. Recall from definition (14.3.1) that if f is differentiable at the point (x_0, y_0), then its gradient vector $\nabla f(x_0, y_0)$ at that point is the ordered pair $(f_1'(x_0, y_0), f_2'(x_0, y_0))$ of its partial derivatives.

Particularly in the case of a function which is concave or convex, we may be able to specify the sign of the error in the linear approximation (15.8.4). Indeed, following the definitions (8.4.1) and (8.4.2) of supergradient and subgradient for a function of one variable, we introduce the following definitions for functions of two variables:

SUPERGRADIENT AND SUBGRADIENT VECTORS

Suppose that the function $z = f(x, y)$ defined on the domain S in the xy-plane is differentiable at (x_0, y_0). Then its gradient vector $\nabla f(x_0, y_0) = (f_1'(x_0, y_0), f_2'(x_0, y_0))$ at that point is said to be:

(i) a *supergradient vector* if, for all x in S, one has

$$f(x, y) \leq f(x_0, y_0) + f_1'(x_0, y_0)(x - x_0) + f_2'(x_0, y_0)(y - y_0) \tag{15.8.11}$$

(ii) a *subgradient vector* if, for all x in S, one has

$$f(x, y) \geq f(x_0, y_0) + f_1'(x_0, y_0)(x - x_0) + f_2'(x_0, y_0)(y - y_0) \tag{15.8.12}$$

Thus, in the case of a supergradient vector, the error in the linear approximation formula (15.8.4) is nonnegative, so it gives an over-approximation. On the other hand, in the case of a subgradient vector, formula (15.8.4) gives an under-approximation, because the error is nonpositive.

The main reason for introducing the concepts of supergradient and subgradient vectors is that they allow us to state the following important result:

THEOREM 15.8.3 (SUPERGRADIENTS AND SUBGRADIENTS)

Suppose the function $z = f(x, y)$ is defined on the convex domain S in the xy-plane, and is differentiable at the interior point (x_0, y_0) of S. Then the gradient vector $\nabla f(x_0, y_0) = (f_1'(x_0, y_0), f_2'(x_0, y_0))$ at (x_0, y_0) is:

(i) a supergradient vector in case f is concave;

(ii) a subgradient vector in case f is convex.

Proof: Fix any pair (x, y) in S that is different from (x_0, y_0). Then consider once again the function of one variable defined in (15.8.2) by

$$g(t) = f(x_0 + t(x - x_0), y_0 + t(y - y_0))$$

Because S is convex, the function $g(t)$ is defined for all t in $[0, 1]$. Because (x_0, y_0) is an interior point of S, there exists an $\varepsilon > 0$ that is small enough for $g(t)$ to be defined on an interval I that includes $(-\varepsilon, 1]$. Finally, because f is differentiable at (x_0, y_0), it follows from (15.8.3) that g is differentiable at $t = 0$ with

$$g'(0) = f_1'(x_0, y_0)(x - x_0) + f_2'(x_0, y_0)(y - y_0)$$

Consider now the case when the function f is concave on S. Suppose that u and v are any two points in I. Fix any scalar λ in $[0, 1]$, and let $s = \lambda u + (1 - \lambda)v$. Consider the three points $(x(t), y(t)) = (x_0 + t(x - x_0), y_0 + t(y - y_0))$ defined for $t = u, v, s$. The above definitions imply that all three points belong to S, and satisfy $(x(s), y(s)) = \lambda(x(u), y(u)) + (1 - \lambda)(x(v), y(v))$. Now concavity of f on S implies that g is concave on I because

$$g(s) = f(x(s), y(s)) \geq \lambda f(x(u), y(u)) + (1 - \lambda) f(x(v), y(v)) = \lambda g(u) + (1 - \lambda) g(v)$$

Because $g(t)$ is concave on I and differentiable at $t = 0$, which is an interior point of I, it follows from the supergradient property in Theorem 8.4.1 for functions of one variable that, for all t in I, one has $g(t) - g(0) \leq g'(0)(t - 0)$. In particular, when $t = 1$ one has $g(1) \leq g(0) + g'(0)$. By definition of g, it follows that the gradient vector $\nabla f(x_0, y_0)$ at (x_0, y_0) has the supergradient property defined by the inequality (15.8.11).

The case when f is convex follows because then $-f$ is concave, implying that its gradient vector $\nabla(-f) = -\nabla f$ is a supergradient vector of $-f$. This is equivalent to ∇f being a subgradient vector of f. ∎

With n variables, the two inequalities (15.8.11) and (15.8.12) that determine whether the gradient vector $\nabla f(\mathbf{x}^0) = (f_1'(\mathbf{x}^0), \ldots, f_n'(\mathbf{x}^0))$ is a supergradient or subgradient, respectively, can be written using dot product notation as:

$$f(\mathbf{x}) - f(\mathbf{x}^0) \leq f_1'(\mathbf{x}^0)(x_1 - x_1^0) + \cdots + f_n'(\mathbf{x}^0)(x_n - x_n^0) = \nabla f(\mathbf{x}^0) \cdot (\mathbf{x} - \mathbf{x}^0) \quad (15.8.13)$$

$$f(\mathbf{x}) - f(\mathbf{x}^0) \geq f_1'(\mathbf{x}^0)(x_1 - x_1^0) + \cdots + f_n'(\mathbf{x}^0)(x_n - x_n^0) = \nabla f(\mathbf{x}^0) \cdot (\mathbf{x} - \mathbf{x}^0) \quad (15.8.14)$$

Apart from their inherent interest, Theorem 15.8.3 and the two inequalities (15.8.13) and (15.8.14) will be used in Chapter 17 to show that any interior critical point of a concave function is a maximum, whereas any interior critical point of a convex function is a minimum.

We conclude this section by extending Theorem 8.4.2 to functions of n variables, thus deriving a supergradient sufficient condition for concavity, and a subgradient sufficient condition for concavity.

THEOREM 15.8.4 (SUFFICIENT CONDITIONS FOR CONCAVITY AND CONVEXITY)

Suppose that the function f is defined on an open convex domain D in n-space. Then f will be:

(i) concave if it is has a supergradient vector $\mathbf{p}$ at every point of I;

(ii) convex if it is has a subgradient vector $\mathbf{p}$ at every point of I.

Proof: Fix $\mathbf{a}$ and $\mathbf{b}$ in D, as well as λ in $[0, 1]$. Let $\mathbf{c} = \lambda \mathbf{a} + (1-\lambda)\mathbf{b}$, which belongs to D since we assumed that D is a convex set. Suppose f has a supergradient vector $\mathbf{p}$ at $\mathbf{c}$, so

$$\text{both} \quad f(\mathbf{a}) - f(\mathbf{c}) \leq \mathbf{p} \cdot (\mathbf{a} - \mathbf{c}) \quad \text{and} \quad f(\mathbf{b}) - f(\mathbf{c}) \leq \mathbf{p} \cdot (\mathbf{b} - \mathbf{c})$$

Now multiply both sides of the first inequality by λ, and then both sides of the second inequality by $1 - \lambda$, then add. Because both multipliers are nonnegative, we obtain

$$\lambda f(\mathbf{a}) + (1-\lambda)f(\mathbf{b}) - f(\mathbf{c}) \leq \mathbf{p} \cdot [\lambda(\mathbf{a} - \mathbf{c}) + (1-\lambda)(\mathbf{b} - \mathbf{c})] = \mathbf{p} \cdot \mathbf{0} = 0$$

Hence $f(\lambda \mathbf{a} + (1-\lambda)\mathbf{b}) \geq \lambda f(\mathbf{a}) + (1-\lambda)f(\mathbf{b})$, as required for f to be concave.

EXERCISES FOR SECTION 15.8

1. Find the linear approximation about $(0, 0)$ for each of the following:

    (a) $f(x, y) = (x+1)^5(y+1)^6$ (b) $f(x, y) = \sqrt{1+x+y}$ (c) $f(x, y) = e^x \ln(1+y)$

2. Find the linear approximation about (x_0, y_0) for $f(x, y) = Ax^a y^b$.

3. Suppose that $g(\mu, \varepsilon) = [(1+\mu)(1+\varepsilon)^\alpha]^{1/(1-\beta)} - 1$, with α and β as constants. Show that if μ and ε are close to 0, then $g(\mu, \varepsilon) \approx (\mu + \alpha\varepsilon)/(1-\beta)$.

4. Let $f(x, y) = 3x^2y + 2y^3$, implying that $f(1, -1) = -5$. Use the linear approximation (15.8.4) about the point $(x, y) = (1, -1)$ in order to estimate the value of $f(0.98, -1.01)$. How large is the error involved in this approximation?

5. Let $f(x, y) = 3x^2 + xy - y^2$.

    (a) Compute $f(1.02, 1.99)$ exactly.

    (b) Use (15.8.4) to find the linear approximation about $(x, y) = (1, 2)$ to the function value $f(1.02, 1.99) = f(1 + 0.02, 2 - 0.01)$. How large is the error?

6. Suppose you are told that a differentiable function v of two variables satisfies $v(1, 0) = -1$, $v'_1(1, 0) = -4/3$, and $v'_2(1, 0) = 1/3$. Find an approximate value for $v(1.01, 0.02)$.

SM 7. Find the tangent planes to the following two surfaces at the indicated points:

(a) $z = x^2 + y^2$ at $(1, 2, 5)$;

(b) $z = (y - x^2)(y - 2x^2)$ at $(1, 3, 2)$.

SM 8. [HARDER] Define the function

$$g(t) = f(x_1^0 + t(x_1 - x_1^0), \ldots, x_n^0 + t(x_n - x_n^0))$$

Following the argument used to derive Eq. (15.8.4), use the approximation $g(1) \approx g(0) + g'(0)$ in order to derive Eq. (15.8.5).

9. [HARDER] Let $f(x, y)$ be any continuously differentiable function. Prove that f is homogeneous of degree 1 if and only if the tangent plane at every point on its graph passes through the origin.

10. [HARDER] For all $(x, y) \neq (0, 0)$, define $f(x, y) = \dfrac{xy^2}{x^2 + y^4}$, and let $f(0, 0) = 0$.

(a) For each real α, show that in the xy-plane, all points on the curve $x = \alpha y^2$ other than $(0, 0)$ are on the same level curve of f.

(b) Show that f is not continuous at $(0, 0)$.

(c) Show that $f_1'(x, y)$ and $f_2'(x, y)$ both exist for all (x, y).

(d) Show that f has a directional derivative in every direction at every point.

(e) Is f differentiable at $(0, 0)$?

15.9 Differentials

Suppose that $z = f(x, y)$ is a continuously differentiable function of two variables. Let dx and dy be any two real numbers, not necessarily small. Then we define the *differential* of $z = f(x, y)$ at (x, y), denoted by dz or df, so that

$$z = f(x, y) \implies dz = f_1'(x, y)\, dx + f_2'(x, y)\, dy \tag{15.9.1}$$

On the other hand, when x is changed to $x + dx$ and y is changed to $y + dy$, then the actual change in the value of the function is the *increment*

$$\Delta z = f(x + dx, y + dy) - f(x, y)$$

If dx and dy are small in absolute value, then Δz can be approximated by dz:

$$\Delta z \approx dz = f_1'(x, y)\, dx + f_2'(x, y)\, dy, \text{ when } |dx| \text{ and } |dy| \text{ are small} \tag{15.9.2}$$

This approximation follows from (15.8.4). To show this, we first replace $x - x_0$ by dx and $y - y_0$ by dy. Then, in the formula which emerges, replace x_0 by x and y_0 by y.

The approximation in (15.9.2) can be interpreted geometrically, as shown in Fig. 15.9.1. The error that arises from replacing Δz by dz is a result of "following the tangent plane" from P to the point S, instead of "following the graph" from P to the point R.

More formally, the tangent plane at $P = (x, y, f(x, y))$ is defined as the set of points (X, Y, Z) whose co-ordinates satisfy the linear equation

$$Z - f(x, y) = f_1'(x, y)(X - x) + f_2'(x, y)(Y - y)$$

Letting $X = x + dx$ and $Y = y + dy$, we obtain

$$Z = f(x, y) + f_1'(x, y)\, dx + f_2'(x, y)\, dy = f(x, y) + dz$$

The length of the line segment QS in Fig. 15.9.1 is therefore $f(x, y) + dz$.

Figure 15.9.1 Δz and the differential dz

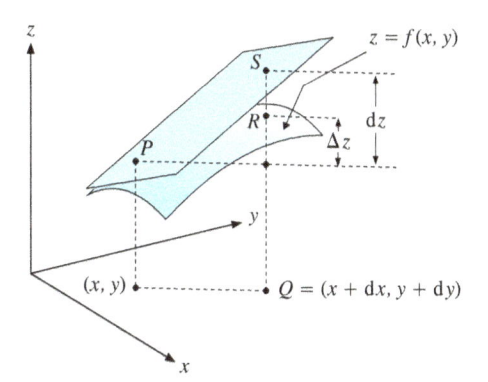

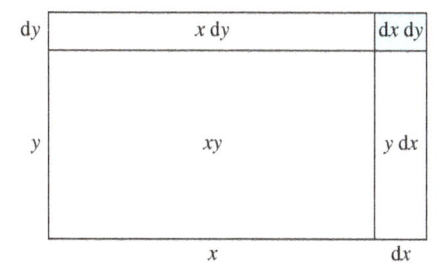

Figure 15.9.2 $\Delta z - dz = dx\, dy$

A word of caution is worthwhile here. In the literature on mathematics for economists, a common definition of the differential dz in Eq. (15.9.1) requires that dx and dy be "infinitesimal", or "infinitely small". In this case, it is often claimed, Δz becomes equal to dz. Imprecise ideas of this sort have caused confusion over the centuries since Leibniz first introduced them, and they have largely been abandoned in mathematics.[8]

EXAMPLE 15.9.1   Let $z = f(x, y) = xy$. Then

$$\Delta z = f(x + dx, y + dy) - f(x, y) = (x + dx)(y + dy) - xy = y\, dx + x\, dy + dx\, dy$$

In this case $dz = f_1'(x, y)dx + f_2'(x, y)dy = y\, dx + x\, dy$, so $\Delta z - dz = dx\, dy$. The error term is $dx\, dy$, and the approximation is illustrated in Fig. 15.9.2. In this example, if dx and dy are both "very small" numbers like 10^{-3}, then the error term $dx\, dy$ will be a "very, very small" number like 10^{-6}.

EXAMPLE 15.9.2   Let $Y = F(K, L)$ be a production function with K and L as capital and labour inputs, respectively. Then F_K' and F_L' are the marginal products of capital and labour. Now, if dK and dL are arbitrary increments in K and L, respectively, then the *differential* of $Y = F(K, L)$ is $dY = F_K'\, dK + F_L'\, dL$. Then the increment $\Delta Y = F(K + dK, L + dL) - F(K, L)$ in Y can

---

[8] However, in nonstandard analysis, a respectable branch of modern mathematics, a modified version of Leibniz's ideas about infinitesimals can be made precise. There have been some interesting applications of nonstandard analysis to theoretical economics.

be approximated by dY provided that dK and dL are small in absolute value. This allows us to write

$$\Delta Y = F(K + dK, L + dL) - F(K, L) \approx F'_K \, dK + F'_L \, dL$$

Note that, provided $z = f(x, y)$ is differentiable, we can always find its differential $dz = df$ by first finding the partial derivatives $f'_1(x, y)$ and $f'_2(x, y)$, and then using the definition (15.9.1) of dz. Conversely, once we know the differential df of a function f of two variables, this allows us to find the partial derivatives. Indeed, suppose that $dz = A \, dx + B \, dy$ for all dx and dy. By definition, $dz = f'_1(x, y) \, dx + f'_2(x, y) \, dy$ for all dx and dy. Putting $dx = 1$ and $dy = 0$ yields $A = f'_1(x, y)$. Similarly, putting $dx = 0$ and $dy = 1$ yields $B = f'_2(x, y)$. So

$$dz = A \, dx + B \, dy \implies \frac{\partial z}{\partial x} = A \text{ and } \frac{\partial z}{\partial y} = B \tag{15.9.3}$$

Rules for Differentials

Section 7.4 developed several rules for working with differentials of functions of one variable. The same rules apply to functions of several variables. Indeed, suppose that $f(x, y)$ and $g(x, y)$ are differentiable, with differentials $df = f'_1 \, dx + f'_2 \, dy$ and $dg = g'_1 \, dx + g'_2 \, dy$, respectively. Using d( ) to denote the differential of the expression inside the parentheses, the following rules are exactly the same as rules (7.4.4) to (7.4.6):

RULES FOR DIFFERENTIALS

Let f and g be differentiable functions of x and y, and let a and b be constants. Then the following rules hold:

$$d(af + bg) = a \, df + b \, dg \tag{15.9.4}$$

$$d(fg) = g \, df + f \, dg \tag{15.9.5}$$

and, if $g \neq 0$,

$$d\left(\frac{f}{g}\right) = \frac{g \, df - f \, dg}{g^2} \tag{15.9.6}$$

These rules are, again, quite easy to prove. The argument for rule (15.9.5) is not very different from the one we gave for rule (7.4.5). Indeed, because $(fg)(x, y) = f(x, y) \cdot g(x, y)$, we have

$$d(fg) = \frac{\partial}{\partial x}[f(x, y) \cdot g(x, y)] \, dx + \frac{\partial}{\partial y}[f(x, y) \cdot g(x, y)] \, dy$$

$$= (f'_x \cdot g + f \cdot g'_x) \, dx + (f'_y \cdot g + f \cdot g'_y) \, dy$$

$$= g(f'_x \, dx + f'_y \, dy) + f(g'_x \, dx + g'_y \, dy)$$

$$= g \, df + f \, dg$$

There is also a chain rule for differentials. Suppose that $z = F(x, y) = g(f(x, y))$, where g is a differentiable function of one variable. Then,

$$dz = F'_x\, dx + F'_y\, dy$$
$$= g'(f(x, y))f'_x\, dx + g'(f(x, y))f'_y\, dy$$
$$= g'(f(x, y))(f'_x\, dx + f'_y\, dy)$$
$$= g'(f(x, y))\, df$$

because $F'_x = g'f'_x$, $F'_y = g'f'_y$, and $df = f'_x\, dx + f'_y\, dy$. Briefly formulated:

THE CHAIN RULE FOR DIFFERENTIALS

$$z = g(f(x, y)) \implies dz = g'(f(x, y))\, df \tag{15.9.7}$$

EXAMPLE 15.9.3 Find an expression for dz in terms of dx and dy for the following:

(a) $z = Ax^a + By^b$;   (b) $z = e^{xu}$ with $u = u(x, y)$;   (c) $z = \ln(x^2 + y)$.

Solution:

(a) $dz = A\, d(x^a) + B\, d(y^b) = Aax^{a-1}\, dx + Bby^{b-1}\, dy$

(b) Arguing directly, using abbreviated notation that drops (x, y) throughout, one has

$$dz = e^{xu}\, d(xu) = e^{xu}(x\, du + u\, dx) = e^{xu}\{x[u'_1\, dx + u'_2\, dy] + u\, dx\}$$
$$= e^{xu}\{[xu'_1 + u]\, dx + xu'_2\, dy\}$$

(c) $dz = d\ln(x^2 + y) = \dfrac{d(x^2 + y)}{x^2 + y} = \dfrac{2x\, dx + dy}{x^2 + y}$

Invariance of the Differential

Suppose that $z = f(x, y)$, $x = g(t, s)$, and $y = h(t, s)$ are all differentiable functions. Then z is a differentiable composite function of t and s together. Suppose that t and s are changed by dt and ds, respectively. The differential of z is then

$$dz = z'_t\, dt + z'_s\, ds$$

Using the expressions for z'_t and z'_s obtained from the chain rule (15.1.1), we find that

$$dz = [f'_1(x, y)x'_t + f'_2(x, y)y'_t]\, dt + [f'_1(x, y)x'_s + f'_2(x, y)y'_s]\, ds$$
$$= f'_1(x, y)(x'_t\, dt + x'_s\, ds) + f'_2(x, y)(y'_t\, dt + y'_s\, ds)$$
$$= f'_1(x, y)\, dx + f'_2(x, y)\, dy$$

Here dx and dy denote the differentials of $x = g(t, s)$ and $y = h(t, s)$, respectively, as functions of t and s.

Note especially that the final expression for dz is precisely the definition of the differential of $z = f(x, y)$ when x and y are changed by dx and dy, respectively. Thus, *the differential of z has the same form whether x and y are free variables, or depend on other variables t and s*. This property is referred to as the *invariance* of the differential.

The Differential of a Function of n Variables

As an obvious extension of (15.9.1), we define the differential of a differentiable function $z = f(x_1, x_2, \ldots, x_n)$ of n variables as

$$dz = df = f'_1\, dx_1 + f'_2\, dx_2 + \cdots + f'_n\, dx_n \tag{15.9.8}$$

If the absolute values of dx_1, ..., dx_n are all small, then as in (15.9.2) one has $\Delta z \approx dz$, where Δz is the actual increment of z when the n-vector $\mathbf{x} = (x_1, \ldots, x_n)$ is changed to $\mathbf{x} + d\mathbf{x} = (x_1 + dx_1, \ldots, x_n + dx_n)$.

The rules for differentials in Eqs (15.9.4) to (15.9.6), as well as the chain rule (15.9.7), are all valid for functions of n variables. There is also a general rule for invariance of the differential: *The differential of $z = F(x_1, \ldots, x_n)$ has the same form whether $x_1, \ldots, x_n$ are free variables, or depend on other basic variables*. Proofs of these results are easy extensions of those for two variables.

EXERCISES FOR SECTION 15.9

1. Determine the differential of $z = xy^2 + x^3$ by:

   (a) computing $\partial z/\partial x$ and $\partial z/\partial y$, then using the definition of dz;

   (b) using the rules in Eqs (15.9.4) to (15.9.6).

2. Calculate the differentials of the following functions:

   (a) $z = x^3 + y^3$ (b) $z = xe^{y^2}$ (c) $z = \ln(x^2 - y^2)$

3. Find dz expressed in terms of dx and dy when $u = u(x, y)$ and

   (a) $z = x^2 u$ (b) $z = u^2$ (c) $z = \ln(xy + yu)$

SM 4. Find an approximate value for $T = [(2.01)^2 + (2.99)^2 + (6.02)^2]^{1/2}$ by using the approximation $\Delta T \approx dT$.

5. Find dU expressed in terms of dx and dy when $U = U(x, y)$ satisfies the equation $Ue^U = x\sqrt{y}$.

6. Find the differential of the function $X = AN^\beta e^{\rho t}$, where A, β, and ρ are constants.

7. Find the differential of the function $X_1 = BX^E N^{1-E}$, where B and E are constants.

8. Calculate the differentials of the following functions, where $a_1, \ldots, a_n, A, \delta_1, \ldots, \delta_n$, and ρ all are positive constants:

   (a) $U = a_1 u_1^2 + \cdots + a_n u_n^2$

   (b) $U = A(\delta_1 u_1^{-\rho} + \cdots + \delta_n u_n^{-\rho})^{-1/\rho}$

9. Find dz when $z = A x_1^{a_1} x_2^{a_2} \ldots x_n^{a_n}$ for $x_1 > 0, x_2 > 0, \ldots, x_n > 0$, where $A, a_1, a_2, \ldots, a_n$ are all constants with A positive. (*Hint*: First, take the natural logarithm of each side.)

10. [HARDER] The differential dz defined in (15.9.1) is called the *differential of first order*. If f has continuous second-order partial derivatives, we define the *differential of second order* $d^2 z$ as the differential $d(dz)$ of $dz = f_1'(x, y)\,dx + f_2'(x, y)\,dy$. This implies that

$$d^2 z = d(dz) = f_{11}''(x, y)\,(dx)^2 + 2 f_{12}''(x, y)\,dx\,dy + f_{22}''(x, y)\,(dy)^2$$

   (a) Calculate $d^2 z$ for $z = xy + y^2$.

   (b) Suppose that $x = t$ and $y = t^2$. For the function in part (a), express dz and $d^2 z$ in terms of dt. Also find $d^2 z / dt^2$, then show that $d^2 z \neq (d^2 z / dt^2)(dt)^2$. (This result shows that there is no invariance property for the second-order differential.)

15.10 Systems of Equations

Many economic models relate a large number of variables to each other through a system of simultaneous equations. To keep track of the structure of the model, the concept of *degrees of freedom* is very useful.

Let $x_1, x_2, \ldots, x_n$ be n variables. Suppose no restrictions are placed on them. Then, by definition, there are n *degrees of freedom*, because all n variables can be freely chosen.[9] If the variables are required to satisfy *one* equation of the form $f_1(x_1, x_2, \ldots, x_n) = 0$, then the number of degrees of freedom is usually reduced by one. Whenever one further "independent" restriction is introduced, the number of degrees of freedom is again reduced by one. In general, introducing $m < n$ independent restrictions on the variables $x_1, x_2, \ldots, x_n$ means that they satisfy a system of m independent equations having the form

$$\begin{aligned} f_1(x_1, x_2, \ldots, x_n) &= 0 \\ f_2(x_1, x_2, \ldots, x_n) &= 0 \\ &\cdots\cdots\cdots \\ f_m(x_1, x_2, \ldots, x_n) &= 0 \end{aligned} \quad (15.10.1)$$

Then, provided that $m < n$, the remaining number of degrees of freedom is $n - m$. The rule that emerges from these considerations is rather vague, especially as it is hard to explain precisely what it means for equations to be "independent". Nevertheless, the following rule is much used in economics and statistics:

---

[9] When the system gives zero degrees of freedom, none of the variables can be freely chosen and so all of them must be solved from the system.

THE COUNTING RULE

The number of degrees of freedom for a system of equations depends on n, the number of variables, and m, the number of "independent" equations. In general:

(i) if $n > m$, then the system has $n - m$ degrees of freedom;

(ii) if $n < m$, then the system has no solution.

This rule of counting variables and equations is used to justify the following economic proposition: "The number of independent targets the government can pursue cannot possibly exceed the number of available policy instruments". For example, suppose that a national government seeks simultaneous low inflation, low unemployment, and stability of its currency's exchange rate against, say, the US dollar. Then to meet these three targets it needs at least three independent policy instruments.[10]

It is obvious that the word "independent" cannot be dropped from the statement of the counting rule. For instance, if we just repeat an equation that has appeared before, the number of degrees of freedom will certainly not be reduced. Furthermore, part (b) of Exercise 4 shows that the counting rule is not generally valid even if there is only one equation.

The concept of degrees of freedom introduced earlier needs to be generalized.

DEGREES OF FREEDOM FOR A SYSTEM OF EQUATIONS

A system of equations in n variables is said to *have k degrees of freedom* if there is a set of k variables that can be freely chosen, while the remaining $n - k$ variables are uniquely determined once the k free variables have been assigned specific values.

In order for a system to have k degrees of freedom, it suffices that *there exist k* of the variables that can be freely chosen. We do not require that *any* set of k variables can be chosen freely. If the n variables are restricted to vary within a subset A of $\mathbb{R}^n$, we say that the system *has k degrees of freedom in A*.

EXAMPLE 15.10.1   In Example 12.8.2 we considered the system of equations

$$x_1 + 3x_2 - x_3 = 4$$
$$2x_1 + x_2 + x_3 = 7$$
$$2x_1 - 4x_2 + 4x_3 = 6$$
$$3x_1 + 4x_2 = 11$$

---

[10] Many economists know this as the "Tinbergen rule". It is named after Jan Tinbergen (1903–1994), who shared the first Nobel Prize in Economics. The rule appeared in his 1956 book *Economic Policy: Principles and Design*.

We showed that the solutions of this system are given by

$$(x_1, x_2, x_3) = \left(-\tfrac{4}{5}t + \tfrac{17}{5}, \tfrac{3}{5}t + \tfrac{1}{5}, t\right)$$

where t is any real number. This leads us to say that the solution set of the system has *one degree of freedom*, since one of the variables can be freely chosen. Once this variable has been given a fixed value, however, the other two variables are uniquely determined.

In Example 15.10.1, there is one degree of freedom even though the system has four equations in only three unknowns. Nevertheless, in general, the counting rule claims that if the number of equations is larger than the number of variables, then the system is *inconsistent* in the sense that it has no solutions. Consider, for example, the system of two variables and the following three equations

$$f(x, y) = 0, \quad g(x, y) = 0, \quad h(x, y) = 0$$

This system is usually inconsistent. Indeed, each of the three equations represents a curve in the plane, and any pair of curves will usually have at least one point in common. But if we add a third equation, the corresponding curve will seldom pass through any point where the first two curves intersect, so the system is usually inconsistent.

So far, we have discussed the two cases $m < n$ and $m > n$. What about the case $m = n$, in which the number of equations is equal to the number of unknowns? Even in the simplest case of one equation $f(x) = 0$ in one variable, there could be any number of solutions. Consider, for instance, the following three different single equations in one variable:

$$x^2 + 1 = 0, \quad x - 1 = 0, \quad (x-1)(x-2)(x-3)(x-4)(x-5) = 0$$

These three equations have zero, one, and five solutions, respectively. Those of you who know something about trigonometric functions will realize that the simple equation $\sin x = 0$ has infinitely many solutions, namely $x = n\pi$ for any integer n.

In general, a system with as many equations as unknowns is usually *consistent* in the sense of having solutions, but it may have several solutions. Economists, however, ideally like their models to have a system of equations that produces a unique, economically meaningful solution, because then the model purports to predict the values of particular economic variables. Based on the earlier discussion, we can at least formulate the following rough rule: *A system of equations does not, in general, have a unique solution unless there are exactly as many equations as unknowns.*

EXAMPLE 15.10.2 Consider the macroeconomic model described by the system of equations:

(i) $Y = C + I + G$; (ii) $C = f(Y - T)$; (iii) $I = h(r)$; (iv) $r = m(M)$.

Here f, h, and m are given functions, whereas Y is GDP, C is consumption, I is investment, G is public expenditure, T is tax revenue, r is the interest rate, and M is the quantity of money in circulation. How many degrees of freedom are there?

Solution: The system has seven variables and four equations, so the counting rule says that there should be $7 - 4 = 3$ degrees of freedom. Usually macroeconomists regard M,

T, and G as the exogenous (free) variables determined by economic policy. Then generally the system will determine the four endogenous variables Y, C, I, and r simultaneously as functions of the three exogenous variables M, T, and G.[11]

EXAMPLE 15.10.3   Consider the alternative macroeconomic model consisting of the equations

(i) $Y = C + I + G$,   (ii) $C = f(Y - T)$,   (iii) $G = \bar{G}$,

whose variables are to be interpreted as they were in Example 15.10.2. Here the level of public expenditure is the constant $\bar{G}$. Determine the number of degrees of freedom in the model.

Solution: There are now three equations in the five variables Y, C, I, G, and T. So the counting rule suggests that there should be two degrees of freedom. Provided that the function f is suitable, two variables can be freely chosen, while allowing the other three variables to be determined once the values of these two are fixed. It is natural to consider I and T as the two free variables. Note that G cannot be chosen as a free variable in this case because it is fixed by equation (iii).

EXERCISES FOR SECTION 15.10

1. Use the counting rule to find the number of degrees of freedom for each of the following equation systems, where in (c) you should assume that f and g are specified functions:

   (a) $\begin{array}{l} xu^3 + v = y^2 \\ 3uv - x = 4 \end{array}$

   (b) $\begin{array}{l} x_2^2 - x_3^3 + 2y_1 - y_2^3 = 1 \\ x_1^3 - x_2 + y_1^5 - y_2 = 0 \end{array}$

   (c) $\begin{array}{l} f(y + z + w) = x^3 \\ x^2 + y^2 + z^2 = w^2 \\ g(x, y) - z^3 = w^3 \end{array}$

2. Consider the macroeconomic model with the equations (i) $Y = C + I + G$; (ii) $C = F(Y, T, r)$; and (iii) $I = f(Y, r)$. Here the variables are to be interpreted as in Example 15.10.2, with F and f as two given functions. Use the counting rule to find the number of degrees of freedom.

3. For each of the following three systems of equations, determine the number of degrees of freedom, if any, and discuss whether the counting rule applies:

   (a) $\begin{array}{l} 3x - y = 2 \\ 6x - 2y = 4 \\ 9x - 3y = 6 \end{array}$

   (b) $\begin{array}{l} x - 2y = 3 \\ x - 2y = 4 \end{array}$

   (c) $\begin{array}{l} x - 2y = 3 \\ 2x - 4y = 6 \end{array}$

4. For each of the following two "systems" consisting of just one equation, determine the number of degrees of freedom, if any, and discuss whether the counting rule applies:

   (a) $x_1^2 + x_2^2 + \cdots + x_{100}^2 = 1$ (b) $x_1^2 + x_2^2 + \cdots + x_{100}^2 = -1$

---

[11] For a further analysis of this model, see Example 15.11.3. For further discussion of exogenous and endogenous variables, see Section 15.11.

15.11 Differentiating Systems of Equations

This section shows how using differentials can be an efficient way to find the partial derivatives of functions defined implicitly by a system of equations. We begin with three examples.

EXAMPLE 15.11.1 Consider the following system of two linear equations in four variables:

$$5u + 5v = 2x - 3y$$
$$2u + 4v = 3x - 2y$$

It has two degrees of freedom, and can be used to define u and v as functions of x and y. Differentiate the system and then find the differentials du and dv expressed in terms of dx and dy. Derive the partial derivatives of u and v w.r.t. x and y. Check the results by solving the system explicitly for u and v.

Solution: For both equations, use the rules in Section 15.9 to take the differential of each side. The result is

$$5\,du + 5\,dv = 2\,dx - 3\,dy$$
$$2\,du + 4\,dv = 3\,dx - 2\,dy$$

Note that in a linear system like this, without any constant terms, the differentials satisfy exactly the same equations as the variables.

Solving simultaneously for du and dv in terms of dx and dy yields the unique solution

$$du = -\frac{7}{10}\,dx - \frac{1}{5}\,dy, \qquad dv = \frac{11}{10}\,dx - \frac{2}{5}\,dy$$

Now we can simply read off the partial derivatives, which are $u'_x = -\frac{7}{10}$, $u'_y = -\frac{1}{5}$, $v'_x = \frac{11}{10}$, and $v'_y = -\frac{2}{5}$.

Suppose that instead of finding the differential, we solve the given equation system directly for u and v as functions of x and y. The result is $u = -\frac{7}{10}x - \frac{1}{5}y$ and $v = \frac{11}{10}x - \frac{2}{5}y$. From these expressions we easily confirm the above values for the partial derivatives.

EXAMPLE 15.11.2 Consider the following system of two nonlinear equations:

$$u^2 + v = xy \quad \text{and} \quad uv = -x^2 + y^2$$

(a) What has the counting rule to say about this system?

(b) Find the differentials of u and v expressed in terms of dx and dy. What are the partial derivatives of u and v w.r.t. x and y?

(c) The point $P = (x, y, u, v) = (1, 0, 1, -1)$ satisfies the system. If $x = 1$ is increased by 0.01 and $y = 0$ is increased by 0.02, what is an approximate new value of u?

(d) Calculate u''_{12} at the point P.

Solution:

(a) There are four variables and two equations, so there should be two degrees of freedom. Suppose we choose fixed values for x and y. Then there are two equations for determining the two remaining variables, u and v. For example, if $x = 1$ and $y = 0$, then the system reduces to $u^2 = -v$ and $uv = -1$, from which we find that $u^3 = 1$, so $u = 1$ and $v = -1$. For other values of x and y, it is more difficult to find solutions for u and v. However, it seems reasonable to assume that the system defines $u = u(x, y)$ and $v = v(x, y)$ as differentiable functions of x and y, at least if the domain of the pair (x, y) is suitably restricted.

(b) The two sides of each equation in the system must be equal functions of x and y. So we can equate the differentials of each side to obtain the two equations $d(u^2 + v) = d(xy)$ and $d(uv) = d(-x^2 + y^2)$. Using the rules for differentials, we obtain

$$2u\,du + dv = y\,dx + x\,dy$$
$$v\,du + u\,dv = -2x\,dx + 2y\,dy$$

Using matrix notation, this can be written as the equation

$$\begin{pmatrix} 2u & 1 \\ v & u \end{pmatrix} \begin{pmatrix} du \\ dv \end{pmatrix} = \begin{pmatrix} y & x \\ -2x & 2y \end{pmatrix} \begin{pmatrix} dx \\ dy \end{pmatrix} \quad (15.11.1)$$

Note that by the invariance property of the differential stated in Section 15.9, this system is valid no matter which pair of variables we treat as independent.

Provided that $v \neq 2u^2$, we can use one of the methods set out in Section 3.6 or Chapter 13 to find the unique solution of the 2×2 matrix equation (15.11.1), which is

$$du = \frac{2x + yu}{2u^2 - v}\,dx + \frac{xu - 2y}{2u^2 - v}\,dy, \qquad dv = \frac{-4xu - yv}{2u^2 - v}\,dx + \frac{4uy - xv}{2u^2 - v}\,dy$$

From these two equations, we obtain immediately that

$$u'_1 = \frac{2x + yu}{2u^2 - v}, \quad u'_2 = \frac{xu - 2y}{2u^2 - v}, \quad v'_1 = \frac{-4xu - yv}{2u^2 - v}, \quad v'_2 = \frac{4uy - xv}{2u^2 - v} \quad (*)$$

(c) We use the approximation $u(x + dx, y + dy) \approx u(x, y) + du$ near the point P, where $(x, y, u, v) = (1, 0, 1, -1)$. By $(*)$ one has $u'_1 = \frac{2}{3}$ and $u'_2 = \frac{1}{3}$ at P, so

$$u(1 + 0.01, 0 + 0.02) \approx u(1, 0) + u'_1(1, 0) \cdot 0.01 + u'_2(1, 0) \cdot 0.02$$
$$= 1 + \tfrac{2}{3} \cdot 0.01 + \tfrac{1}{3} \cdot 0.02$$
$$= 1 + \tfrac{4}{3} \cdot 0.01$$
$$\approx 1.0133$$

Note that, in this case, it is not easy to find the exact value of $u(1.01, 0.02)$.

(d) To find u''_{12} we use the chain rule as follows:

$$u''_{12} = \frac{\partial}{\partial y}(u'_1) = \frac{\partial}{\partial y}\left(\frac{2x+yu}{2u^2-v}\right) = \frac{(yu'_2+u)(2u^2-v)-(2x+yu)(4uu'_2-v'_2)}{(2u^2-v)^2}$$

At the point P where $(x, y, u, v) = (1, 0, 1, -1)$, it follows from part (c) that $u'_2 = 1/3$ and from (∗) that $v'_2 = 1/3$, so $u''_{12} = 1/9$.

EXAMPLE 15.11.3

Consider again the macroeconomic model of Example 15.10.2. Assume that f, h, and m are differentiable functions with $0 < f' < 1$, $h' < 0$, and $m' < 0$. Then the four equations of the model will determine the endogenous variables Y, C, I, and r as differentiable functions of the exogenous variables M, T, and G.

(a) Differentiate the system and express the differentials of Y, C, I, and r in terms of the differentials of M, T, and G. Find $\partial Y/\partial T$ and $\partial C/\partial T$, and comment on their signs.

(b) Suppose moreover that $P_0 = (M_0, T_0, G_0, Y_0, C_0, I_0, r_0)$ is an initial equilibrium point for the system. If the money supply M, tax revenue T, and public expenditure G are all slightly changed as a result of government policy or central bank intervention, find the approximate changes ΔY and ΔC in national income Y and consumption C.

Solution:

(a) Taking differentials of Eqs (i)–(iv) in Example 15.10.2 yields the system of four equations

$$dY = dC + dI + dG \tag{v}$$

$$dC = f'(Y-T)(dY - dT) \tag{vi}$$

$$dI = h'(r)\,dr \tag{vii}$$

$$dr = m'(M)\,dM \tag{viii}$$

We wish to solve this linear system in order to express the differential changes dY, dC, dI, and dr in the four endogenous variables in terms of the differentials dM, dT, and dG of the three exogenous policy variables. To do so, start by substituting (viii) into (vii) to obtain $dI = h'(r)m'(M)\,dM$. Then insert into (v) this expression for dI and the right-hand side of (vi) for dC in order to obtain the single equation

$$dY = f'(Y-T)(dY - dT) + h'(r)m'(M)\,dM + dG$$

Because we assumed that $f' < 1$, we can solve this equation for dY. In simplified notation, the result is

$$dY = \frac{h'm'}{1-f'}\,dM - \frac{f'}{1-f'}\,dT + \frac{1}{1-f'}\,dG \tag{ix}$$

Next, after inserting (ix) into (vi) and simplifying the result, one obtains

$$dC = \frac{f'h'm'}{1-f'}\,dM - \frac{f'}{1-f'}\,dT + \frac{f'}{1-f'}\,dG \tag{x}$$

Equations (ix) and (x) express the differentials dY and dC as linear functions of the differentials dM, dT, and dG.

From the four equations (vii)–(x), it is easy to find the partial derivatives of Y, C, I, and r w.r.t. M, T, and G. For example, $\partial Y/\partial T = \partial C/\partial T = -f'/(1-f')$ and $\partial r/\partial T = 0$. Note that because $0 < f' < 1$, we have $\partial Y/\partial T = \partial C/\partial T < 0$. Thus, a small increase in the tax level, keeping M and G constant, decreases GDP. But if the extra tax revenue is all spent by the government, one will have $dT = dG = dx$ (and $dM = 0$). In this case the changes will be $dY = dx$ and $dC = dI = dr = 0$.

(b) If $|dM|$, $|dT|$, and $|dG|$ are all small, then the approximate changes will satisfy

$$\Delta Y = Y(M_0 + dM, T_0 + dT, G_0 + dG) - Y(M_0, T_0, G_0) \approx dY$$
$$\text{and} \quad \Delta C = C(M_0 + dM, T_0 + dT, G_0 + dG) - C(M_0, T_0, G_0) \approx dC$$

When computing dY and dC, all the partial derivatives must be evaluated at the initial equilibrium point P_0.

Some textbooks recommend that students should first use a matrix equation to represent macro models like the one we analysed in Examples 15.10.2 and 15.11.3, before going on to use either Cramer's rule or matrix inversion to find the solution. When it works, the elimination method we used to solve Example 15.11.3 is much simpler, which drastically reduces the risk of making errors.

EXAMPLE 15.11.4   Suppose that the two equations

$$(z + 2w)^5 + xy^2 = 2z - yw$$
$$(1 + z^2)^3 - z^2 w = 8x + y^5 w^2$$

define z and w as differentiable functions $z = \varphi(x, y)$ and $w = \psi(x, y)$ of x and y in a neighbourhood around the point $(x, y, z, w) = (1, 1, 1, 0)$.

(a) Compute $\partial z/\partial x$, $\partial z/\partial y$, $\partial w/\partial x$, and $\partial w/\partial y$ at $(1, 1, 1, 0)$.

(b) Use the above results to find an approximate value of $\varphi(1 + 0.1, 1 + 0.2)$.

Solution:

(a) Equating the differentials of each side of the two equations, treated as functions of (x, y), we obtain

$$5(z + 2w)^4(dz + 2\,dw) + y^2\,dx + 2xy\,dy = 2\,dz - w\,dy - y\,dw$$
$$3(1 + z^2)^2 2z\,dz - 2zw\,dz - z^2\,dw = 8\,dx + 5y^4 w^2\,dy + 2y^5 w\,dw$$

At the particular point $(x, y, z, w) = (1, 1, 1, 0)$, this system reduces to:

$$3\,dz + 11\,dw = -dx - 2\,dy; \quad 24\,dz - dw = 8\,dx$$

Solving these two equations simultaneously for dz and dw in terms of dx and dy yields

$$dz = \frac{29}{89} dx - \frac{2}{267} dy \quad \text{and} \quad dw = -\frac{16}{89} dx - \frac{16}{89} dy$$

So $\partial z/\partial x = 29/89$, $\partial z/\partial y = -2/267$, $\partial w/\partial x = -16/89$, and $\partial w/\partial y = -16/89$.

(b) If $x = 1$ is increased by $dx = 0.1$ and $y = 1$ is increased by $dy = 0.2$, the associated change in $z = \varphi(x, y)$ is approximately $dz = (29/89) \cdot 0.1 - (2/267) \cdot 0.2 \approx 0.03$. Hence $\varphi(1 + 0.1, 1 + 0.2) \approx \varphi(1, 1) + dz \approx 1 + 0.03 = 1.03$.

General Systems

When economists deal with systems of equations, notably in comparative static analysis, the variables are usually divided a priori into two types: *endogenous* variables, which the model is intended to determine; and *exogenous* variables, which are supposed to be determined by "forces" outside the economic model such as government policy, consumers' tastes, or technical progress. This classification depends on the model in question. Public expenditure, for example, is often treated as exogenous in public finance theory, which seeks to understand how tax changes affect the economy. But it is often endogenous in a "political economy" model which tries to explain how political variables like public expenditure emerge from the political system.

Economic models often give rise to a general system of *structural equations* having the form

$$\begin{aligned} f_1(x_1, x_2, \ldots, x_n, y_1, y_2, \ldots, y_m) &= 0 \\ f_2(x_1, x_2, \ldots, x_n, y_1, y_2, \ldots, y_m) &= 0 \\ &\cdots \\ f_m(x_1, x_2, \ldots, x_n, y_1, y_2, \ldots, y_m) &= 0 \end{aligned} \tag{15.11.2}$$

Here we distinguish between the n-vector $\mathbf{x} = (x_1, \ldots, x_n)$ of exogenous variables and the m-vector $\mathbf{y} = (y_1, \ldots, y_m)$ of endogenous variables. We assume that there is an "initial equilibrium" or "status quo" solution $(\mathbf{x}^0, \mathbf{y}^0) = (x_1^0, \ldots, x_n^0, y_1^0, \ldots, y_m^0)$. This *equilibrium* might, for instance, represent a state in which the m endogenous variables are determined so that they equate the current supply and demand for each of m different goods.

Note that system (15.11.2) has m equations in $n + m$ unknowns. So if the counting rule applies, there are $n + m - m = n$ degrees of freedom. Suppose the system defines all the endogenous variables $y_1, \ldots, y_m$ as C^1 functions of $x_1, \ldots, x_n$ in a neighbourhood of points near $(\mathbf{x}^0, \mathbf{y}^0)$. "In principle" one can solve for $y_1, \ldots, y_m$ in terms of $x_1, \ldots, x_n$ to give

$$y_1 = \varphi_1(x_1, \ldots, x_n), \quad \ldots, \quad y_m = \varphi_m(x_1, \ldots, x_n) \tag{15.11.3}$$

In this case, system (15.11.3) is said to be the *reduced form* of the structural equation system (15.11.2). The endogenous variables have all been expressed as functions of the exogenous variables. The form of the functions $\varphi_1, \varphi_2, \ldots, \varphi_m$ is not necessarily known.

The previous examples show how we can often find an explicit expression for the partial derivative of any endogenous variable w.r.t. any exogenous variable. The same type of argument can be used more generally, but a detailed discussion is left for FMEA.

EXERCISES FOR SECTION 15.11

1. Suppose that a, b, c, d, e, f, g, and h are constants satisfying $af \neq be$. Differentiate the system

$$au + bv = cx + dy$$
$$eu + fv = gx + hy$$

   Then find the partial derivatives of u and v w.r.t. x and y.

2. Consider the equation system defined by $xu^3 + v = y^2$ and $3uv - x = 4$.

   (a) Differentiate the system and then solve for du and dv in terms of dx and dy.

   (b) Find u'_x and v'_x by using the results in part (a).

   (c) Verify that the point $(x, y, u, v) = (0, 1, 4/3, 1)$ satisfies the system. Then find u'_x and v'_x at this point.

SM 3. Suppose that y_1 and y_2 are implicitly defined as differentiable functions of x_1 and x_2 by the system: $3x_1 + x_2^2 - y_1 - 3y_2^3 = 0$; $x_1^3 - 2x_2 + 2y_1^3 - y_2 = 0$. Find $\partial y_1 / \partial x_1$ and $\partial y_2 / \partial x_1$.

SM 4. A version of the "IS-LM" macroeconomic model leads to the system of equations $I(r) = S(Y)$ and $aY + L(r) = M$, where a is a positive parameter, whereas I, S, and L are three given continuously differentiable functions.[12] Suppose that the system defines Y and r implicitly as differentiable functions of a and M. Find expressions for $\partial Y / \partial M$ and $\partial r / \partial M$.

5. Find the second derivative u''_{xx} when u and v are defined as functions of x and y by the two equations $xy + uv = 1$ and $xu + yv = 0$.

6. Consider the macroeconomic model

   (i) $Y = C + I + G$ (ii) $C = F(Y, T, r)$ (iii) $I = f(Y, r)$

   where F and f are continuously differentiable functions, with $F'_Y > 0$, $F'_T < 0$, $F'_r < 0$, $f'_Y > 0$, $f'_r < 0$, and $F'_Y + f'_Y < 1$.

   (a) Differentiate the system, and express dY in terms of dT, dG, and dr.

   (b) What happens to Y if T increases? What if T and G undergo equal increases?

7. Suppose that Y is GDP, r is the interest rate, I is total investment, α is public consumption, β is public investment, and M is the money supply. Consider the macroeconomic model

   (i) $Y = C(Y, r) + I + \alpha$ (ii) $I = F(Y, r) + \beta$ (iii) $M = L(Y, r)$

   where C, F, and L are given differentiable functions.

   (a) Determine the number of degrees of freedom in the model.

---

[12] The first "IS" equation involves the investment function I and savings function S. The second "LM" equation involves the liquidity preference function L (the demand for money) and the money supply M. The variable Y denotes GDP and r denotes the interest rate. The IS-LM model was originally devised by J.R. Hicks.

(b) Differentiate the system. Put $d\beta = dM = 0$, and then find dY, dr, and dI expressed in terms of $d\alpha$.

8. A standard macroeconomic model consists of the two equations:

   (i) $M = \alpha Py + L(r)$ and   (ii) $S(y, r, g) = I(y, r)$

   where M, α, and P are positive constants, whereas L, S, and I are differentiable functions.

   (a) By using the counting rule, explain why it is reasonable to assume that the system, in general, defines y and r as differentiable functions of g.

   (b) Differentiate the system and find expressions for dy/dg and dr/dg.

9. The two equations $u^2v - u = x^3 + 2y^3$ and $e^{ux} = vy$ together define u and v as differentiable functions of x and y around the point $P = (x, y, u, v) = (0, 1, 2, 1)$.

   (a) Find the differentials of u and v expressed in terms of the differentials of x and y. Then find $\partial u/\partial y$ and $\partial v/\partial x$ at P.

   (b) If x increases by 0.1 and y decreases by 0.2 from their values at P, what are the approximate changes in u and v?

10. [HARDER] When there are two goods, consumer demand theory involves the equation system

    (i) $U_1'(x_1, x_2) = \lambda p_1$ (ii) $U_2'(x_1, x_2) = \lambda p_2$ (iii) $p_1 x_1 + p_2 x_2 = m$

    Here $U(x_1, x_2)$ is a given utility function. Suppose that the system defines x_1, x_2, and λ as differentiable functions of p_1, p_2, and m. Find an expression for $\partial x_1/\partial p_1$.

REVIEW EXERCISES

1. In each of the following two cases, first find dz/dt by using the chain rule. Second, check the answers by inserting the expressions for x and y into F, then differentiating:

   (a) $z = F(x, y) = 6x + y^3$, with $x = 2t^2$ and $y = 3t^3$

   (b) $z = F(x, y) = x^p + y^p$, with $x = at$ and $y = bt$

2. Let $z = G(u, v)$, with $u = \varphi(t, s)$ and $v = \psi(s)$. Find expressions for $\partial z/\partial t$ and $\partial z/\partial s$.

3. Find expressions for $\partial w/\partial t$ and $\partial w/\partial s$ when $w = x^2 + y^3 + z^4$ with $x = t + s$, $y = t - s$, and $z = st$.

4. Suppose production X depends on the number of workers N according to the formula $X = Ng(\varphi(N)/N)$, where g and φ are given differentiable functions. Find expressions for dX/dN and d^2X/dN^2.

5. Suppose that a household's demand for a commodity is a function $E(p, m) = Ap^{-a}m^b$ of the price p and income m, where A, a, and b are positive constants.

(a) Suppose that p and m are both differentiable functions of time t. Then demand E is a function only of t. Find an expression for $\dot{E}/E$ in terms of $\dot{p}/p$ and $\dot{m}/m$.

(b) Put $p = p_0(1.06)^t$ and $m = m_0(1.08)^t$, where p_0 is the price and m_0 is the income at time $t = 0$. Show that in this case $\dot{E}/E = \ln Q$, where $Q = (1.08)^b/(1.06)^a$.

6. The equation $x^3 \ln x + y^3 \ln y = 2z^3 \ln z$ defines z as a differentiable function of x and y in a neighbourhood of the point $(x, y, z) = (e, e, e)$. Calculate $z_1'(e, e)$ and $z_{11}''(e, e)$.

7. What is the elasticity of substitution between y and x when $F(x, y) = x^2 - 10y^2$?

8. Find the MRS between y and x when:

   (a) $U(x, y) = 2x^{0.4}y^{0.6}$ (b) $U(x, y) = xy + y$ (c) $U(x, y) = 10(x^{-2} + y^{-2})^{-4}$

9. Find the degree of homogeneity, if there is one, for each of the following functions:

   (a) $f(x, y) = 3x^3y^{-4} + 2xy^{-2}$ (b) $Y(K, L) = (K^a + L^a)^{2c} e^{K^2/L^2}$

   (c) $f(x_1, x_2) = 5x_1^4 + 6x_1 x_2^3$ (d) $F(x_1, x_2, x_3) = e^{x_1 + x_2 + x_3}$

10. What is the elasticity of substitution between y and x when $U(x, y) = 10(x^{-2} + y^{-2})^{-4}$?

SM 11. Find the elasticity of y w.r.t. x when $y^2 e^{x+1/y} = 3$. (*Hint:* Put $u = \ln x$ and $v = \ln y$, and recall that then $\text{El}_x y = v_u'$.)

12. Find the degree of homogeneity, if there is one, for each of the following functions:

   (a) $f(x, y) = xg(y/x)$, where g is an arbitrary function of one variable.

   (b) $F(x, y, z) = z^k f(x/z, y/z)$, where f is an arbitrary function of two variables.

   (c) $G(K, L, M, N) = K^{a-b} L^{b-c} M^{c-d} N^{d-a}$, where a, b, c, and d are constants.

13. Suppose that the production function $F(K, L)$, which is defined for all $K > 0$ and $L > 0$, is homogeneous of degree 1. If $F_{KK}'' < 0$, so that the marginal productivity of capital is strictly decreasing as K increases, prove that $F_{KL}'' > 0$, so that the marginal productivity of capital is strictly increasing as labour input increases.[13] (*Hint:* Use Eq. (15.6.6) or (15.6.7).)

14. Show that no generalization of the concept of a homogeneous function emerges if one replaces t^k in definitions (15.6.1) or (15.7.1) by an arbitrary function $g(t)$. (*Hint:* Differentiate the new definition w.r.t. t, and let $t = 1$. Then use Euler's theorem.)

15. The following pair of equations defines $u = u(x, y)$ and $v = v(x, y)$ as differentiable functions of x and y around the point $P = (x, y, u, v) = (1, 1, -1, 0)$:

$$u + xe^y + v = e - 1; \quad x + e^{u+v^2} - y = e^{-1}$$

Differentiate the system and find the values of u_x', u_y', v_x', and v_y' at the point P.

SM 16. An equilibrium model of labour demand and output pricing leads to the pair of equations:

$$pF'(L) - w = 0; \quad pF(L) - wL - B = 0$$

---
[13] This is called *Wicksell's law*.

Here, assume that all the variables are positive and that the function $F(L)$ is defined and twice differentiable for all $L > 0$, with $F'(L) > 0$ and $F''(L) < 0$. Treat w, B as exogenous variables, and p, L as endogenous variables which are functions of w and B.

(a) Use implicit differentiation to find expressions for $\partial p/\partial w$, $\partial p/\partial B$, $\partial L/\partial w$, and $\partial L/\partial B$.

(b) What can be said about the signs of these partial derivatives? Show, in particular, that $\partial L/\partial w < 0$.

17. Given the positive constant powers α and β, the following pair of equations defines $u = u(x, y)$ and $v = v(x, y)$ as differentiable functions of x and y around the point $P = (x, y, u, v) = (1, 1, 1, 2)$:

$$u^\alpha + v^\beta = 2^\beta x + y^3; \quad u^\alpha v^\beta - v^\beta = x - y$$

(a) Differentiate the system, then find $\partial u/\partial x$, $\partial u/\partial y$, $\partial v/\partial x$, and $\partial v/\partial y$ at the point P.

(b) Find an approximation to $u(0.99, 1.01)$.

18. A study of a commodity market involves, for positive constants T, r, and g, the integral

$$S = \int_0^T e^{-rx}(e^{g(T-x)} - 1)\,dx$$

(a) Show that

$$r(r+g)S = re^{gT} + ge^{-rT} - (r+g) \qquad (*)$$

(b) Equation $(*)$ defines T as a differentiable function of g, r, and S. Use the equation to find an expression for $\partial T/\partial g$.

SM 19. Suppose that a vintage car has an appreciating market value given by the function $V(t)$ of time t. Suppose that maintaining the car requires a continuous expenditure at the constant rate m per year, until the time it is sold. So, allowing for continuous time discounting at the constant rate of r per year, the present discounted value from selling the car at time t would be $P(t) = V(t)e^{-rt} - \int_0^t me^{-r\tau}\,d\tau$.

(a) Show that the optimal choice t^* of t that maximizes $P(t)$ must satisfy the equation $V'(t^*) = rV(t^*) + m$, and give this condition an economic interpretation.

(b) Show that the standard second-order condition $P''(t^*)$ for $P(t)$ to have a strict local maximum at $t^*(r, m)$ reduces to the condition that $D = V''(t^*) - rV'(t^*) < 0$.

(c) Find the partial derivatives $\partial t^*/\partial r$ and $\partial t^*/\partial m$. Then use the condition $D < 0$ derived in the answer to (b) in order to discuss how an economist would interpret their signs.

16 MULTIPLE INTEGRALS

A mathematical theory is not to be considered complete until you have made it so clear that you can explain it to the first man whom you meet on the street.[1]
—David Hilbert (1900)

This chapter is a brief introduction to the topic of multiple integrals. These arise in statistics when considering multidimensional continuous (probability) distributions. Double integrals also play a role in some interesting continuous time dynamic optimization problems. We study only the simplest case where the domain of integration is essentially a rectangle. We leave more general cases for FMEA.

16.1 Double Integrals Over Finite Rectangles

The first topic is integration of functions of two variables defined over rectangles in the xy-plane. In Section 10.2 we related the definite integral of a function of one variable that has nonnegative values to the area under its two-dimensional graph. Here we relate the integral of a function of two variables that has nonnegative values to the volume under its three-dimensional graph.

By definition, the Cartesian product of the two intervals $[a, b]$ and $[c, d]$ is the rectangular set $R = [a, b] \times [c, d]$ of points (x, y) in the plane that satisfy the four inequalities $a \leq x \leq b$ and $c \leq y \leq d$. Let f be a continuous function defined on R that happens to satisfy $f(x, y) \geq 0$ for all (x, y) in R. Now consider Fig. 16.1.1, which shows a solid block of a material like wood. The base of this block is the perfectly flat rectangle R in the horizontal plane $z = 0$, whereas its curved top surface is the graph of f. The block consists of all points (x, y, z) in 3-space satisfying $(x, y) \in R$ and $0 \leq z \leq f(x, y)$. This is also called the *ordinate set* of f over R.

---

[1] Part of the famous address by Hilbert (Germany, 1862–1943) to the Second International Congress of Mathematicians held in Paris 1900, where he presented what he then considered to be the greatest open problems in mathematics. The ultimate source seems to be a much earlier letter written in French by J.-D. Gergonne to W.H. Fox Talbot, dated 16 December 1826.

674 CHAPTER 16 / MULTIPLE INTEGRALS

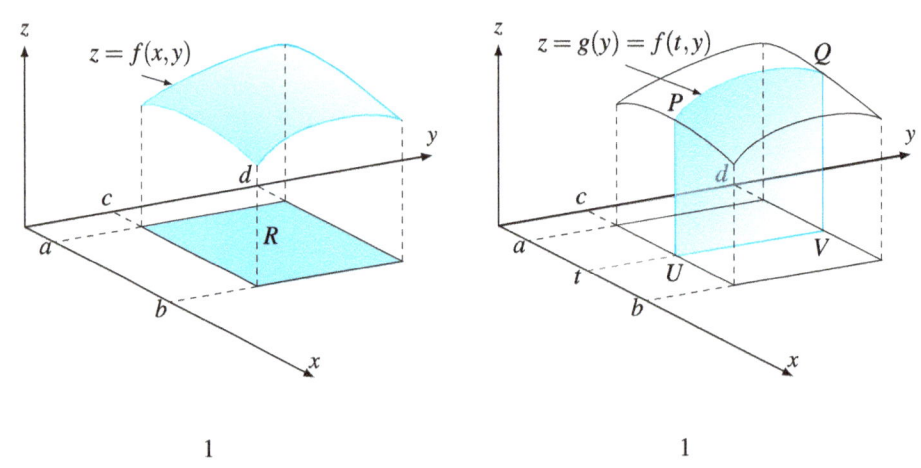

Figure 16.1.1 Volume under the graph

Figure 16.1.2 Limiting the domain to $x \leq t$

We will define the double integral of f over R so that it equals the volume V of this block. Figure 10.2.1 illustrated the relationship between the definite integral of a nonnegative valued function of one variable and the area beneath its graph. The analogue for a function f defined on the rectangular domain R is shown in Fig. 16.1.1.

Let t be an arbitrary point in the interval $[a, b]$. In Fig. 10.2.2, we illustrated the truncated area that results from the restricting the domain of integration to the interval $[a, t]$, whose upper limit occurs at $x = t$. Similarly, in Fig. 16.1.2 we have constructed the unique vertical plane that is parallel to the yz-plane and intersects the x-axis at $x = t$. This plane cuts the ordinate set of f into two parts. Indeed, using a very thin saw to cut a block of wood along this plane would produce two smaller blocks separated by the shaded plane surface in Fig. 16.1.2 that is labelled as $UPQV$. The area of this surface depends on t, so we denote it by the function $\alpha(t)$. It is the area under the curve PQ shown in Fig. 16.1.2 that connects P to Q as y varies over the interval $[c, d]$. This curve is the intersection between the graph of $z = f(x, y)$ and the plane $x = t$, so we can write its equation as $z = g(y) = f(t, y)$, with t fixed and $y \in [c, d]$. So the area under the curve PQ is

$$\alpha(t) = \int_c^d g(y)\, dy = \int_c^d f(t, y)\, dy \tag{16.1.1}$$

Consider next the volume of the truncated ordinate set of f whose base has become the variable rectangle $[a, t] \times [c, d]$, after sawing off the part of the ordinate set that lies above $(t, b] \times [c, d]$. Let $V(t)$ denote this truncated volume, which is analogous to the truncated area $A(t)$ defined in Fig. 10.2.2. Evidently $V(t)$ is an increasing function of t. In particular, at the lower end of the interval $[a, b]$ one has $V(a) = 0$, and at the upper end $V(b) = V$, which is the total volume to be evaluated.

If we add $\delta > 0$ to t, the incremental volume is $\Delta = V(t + \delta) - V(t)$. In Fig. 16.1.3 this is the volume of the slice that lies between the two parallel surfaces $UPQV$ and $U'P'Q'V'$. If δ were the thickness of the saw used to cut the wood block into two pieces, this could be regarded as the slice that the sawing process has converted into sawdust. Provided that

SECTION 16.1 / DOUBLE INTEGRALS OVER FINITE RECTANGLES

δ is small, the volume of the sawdust that had constituted this slice is approximately equal to $\alpha(t)\delta$. It follows that $V(t+\delta) - V(t) \approx \alpha(t)\delta$, implying that after dividing each side by $\delta > 0$, one has

$$\frac{V(t+\delta) - V(t)}{\delta} \approx \alpha(t)$$

In general this approximation improves as the slice gets thinner because the area function varies less over $[t, t+\delta]$ as δ gets smaller. Think of a slice of bread: the thinner it is, the less variation is there in the thickness of the crust. The left-hand side of the approximation is a Newton quotient of the function $V(t)$, so we can reasonably expect that, for each t in $[a, b]$, one has $V'(t) = \alpha(t)$ in the limit as $\delta \to 0$. Then the definition of definite integral implies that $V(b) - V(a) = \int_a^b \alpha(t)\, dt$. Because $V(a) = 0$ and $V(b) = V$, we can use Eq. (16.1.1) to derive the double integral

$$V = \int_a^b \left[\int_c^d f(t, y)\, dy \right] dt \tag{16.1.2}$$

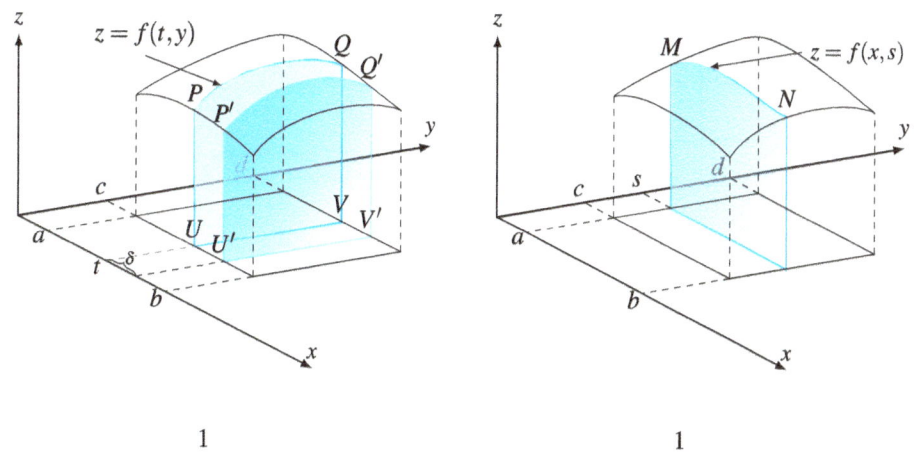

Figure 16.1.3 Cross sections of f over x

Figure 16.1.4 A cross section of f over y

EXAMPLE 16.1.1 Suppose that $f(x, y) = k$ for all (x, y) in the rectangle $R = [a, b] \times [c, d]$ shown in Fig. 16.1.1, where k is a positive constant. Then the block that makes up the ordinate set of f over R is a solid rectangular box or prism, also called a cuboid. Its base area is $(b-a)(d-c)$ and its height is k, so its volume is $k(b-a)(d-c)$. Show that (16.1.2) gives the same result.

Solution: We insert $f(x, y) = k$ into (16.1.2), then evaluate the integrals, to obtain

$$\int_a^b \left[\int_c^d k\, dy \right] dt = \int_a^b \left(\Big|_c^d ky \right) dt = \int_a^b k(d-c)\, dt = \Big|_a^b k(d-c)t = k(d-c)(b-a)$$

This example suggests that formula (16.1.2) does indeed give a correct measure of the volume under the graph of a function f. Before confirming this, we should understand what happens if we change the order in which we integrate w.r.t. the two variables x and y.

Suppose we try to find the volume V of the ordinate set of f over $R = [a, b] \times [c, d]$ by using the same argument above, except for one important change. Specifically suppose that, as illustrated in Fig. 16.1.4, we first choose s in $[c, d]$, and then construct the intersecting plane as the only one that is parallel to the xz-plane while passing through the point $y = s$ on the y-axis. The intersection between the ordinate set and the plane $y = s$ is the area of the plane surface below the curve labelled MN in Fig. 16.1.4. This curve has the equation $z = f(x, s)$, where s is fixed. So the area below the curve is $\int_a^b f(x, s)\, dx$. The formula for the volume becomes the integral of this area, as s varies from c to d, which is

$$V = \int_c^d \left[\int_a^b f(x, s)\, dx \right] ds \tag{16.1.3}$$

Because we are computing the same volume V in both cases, then provided our intuitive argument above is correct, we should get the same answer. The next theorem guarantees that the two numbers obtained in Eqs (16.1.2) and (16.1.3) are indeed equal, provided that f is continuous on R. Replacing the dummy variables t and s of integration by x and y respectively, we obtain the following result.[2]

THEOREM 16.1.1 (INVARIANCE TO ORDER OF INTEGRATION)

Let f be a continuous function defined over the rectangle $R = [a, b] \times [c, d]$. Then

$$\int_a^b \left[\int_c^d f(x, y)\, dy \right] dx = \int_c^d \left[\int_a^b f(x, y)\, dx \right] dy$$

Let f be an arbitrary continuous function over the rectangle $R = [a, b] \times [c, d]$. We define the *double integral of f over R*, denoted by $\iint_R f(x, y)\, dx\, dy$, as

$$\iint_R f(x, y)\, dx\, dy = \int_a^b \left[\int_c^d f(x, y)\, dy \right] dx = \int_c^d \left[\int_a^b f(x, y)\, dx \right] dy \tag{16.1.4}$$

We can use either of the two last expressions to define the double integral because Theorem 16.1.1 tells us that both are equal. Together Theorem 16.1.1 and formula (16.1.4) allow us to calculate $\int_a^b [\int_c^d f(x, y)\, dy]\, dx$ in two stages as follows:

(a) First, keep x fixed and integrate $f(x, y)$ w.r.t. y from $y = c$ to $y = d$. This gives $\alpha(x) = \int_c^d f(x, y)\, dy$, a function of x.

(b) Then integrate $\alpha(x)$ from $x = a$ to $x = b$ to obtain $\int_a^b [\int_c^d f(x, y)\, dy]\, dx$.

---

[2] See Protter and Morrey (1991), Chapter 8, for one of many possible proofs.

SECTION 16.1 / DOUBLE INTEGRALS OVER FINITE RECTANGLES 677

Notice that definition (16.1.4) does not require that the integrand $f(x, y)$ should be nonnegative. Just as a single integral need not always be interpreted as an area, so a double integral need not always be interpreted as a volume.

Here are some applications of formula (16.1.4).

EXAMPLE 16.1.2   Compute $\iint_R (x^2 y + xy^2 + 2x)\, dx\, dy$ where $R = [0, 1] \times [-1, 3]$.

Solution: The integrand is continuous everywhere. Consider first

$$\int_0^1 \left[\int_{-1}^3 (x^2 y + xy^2 + 2x)\, dy \right] dx$$

Treating x as a constant, first evaluate the inner integral to obtain:

$$\int_{-1}^3 (x^2 y + xy^2 + 2x)\, dy = \Big|_{y=-1}^{y=3} \left(\tfrac{1}{2} x^2 y^2 + \tfrac{1}{3} xy^3 + 2xy\right)$$

$$= \left(\tfrac{9}{2} x^2 + 9x + 6x\right) - \left(\tfrac{1}{2} x^2 - \tfrac{1}{3} x - 2x\right) = 4x^2 + \tfrac{52}{3} x$$

Integrating a second time gives

$$\int_0^1 \left[\int_{-1}^3 (x^2 y + xy^2 + 2x)\, dy \right] dx = \int_0^1 \left(4x^2 + \tfrac{52}{3} x\right) dx = \Big|_0^1 \left(\tfrac{4}{3} x^3 + \tfrac{26}{3} x^2\right) = 10$$

Let us now perform the integration in the reverse order. First, holding y constant, we get

$$\int_0^1 (x^2 y + xy^2 + 2x)\, dx = \Big|_{x=0}^{x=1} \left(\tfrac{1}{3} x^3 y + \tfrac{1}{2} x^2 y^2 + x^2\right) = \tfrac{1}{3} y + \tfrac{1}{2} y^2 + 1$$

Therefore, integrating a second time gives

$$\int_{-1}^3 \left[\int_0^1 (x^2 y + xy^2 + 2x)\, dx \right] dy = \int_{-1}^3 \left(\tfrac{1}{3} y + \tfrac{1}{2} y^2 + 1\right) dy = \Big|_{y=-1}^{y=3} \left(\tfrac{1}{6} y^2 + \tfrac{1}{6} y^3 + y\right)$$

$$= \left(\tfrac{3}{2} + \tfrac{9}{2} + 3\right) - \left(\tfrac{1}{6} - \tfrac{1}{6} - 1\right) = 10$$

Both procedures gave the same answer, which confirms Theorem 16.1.1 in this case. So there is no ambiguity in writing

$$\iint_R (x^2 y + xy^2 + 2x)\, dx\, dy = 10$$

when $R = [0, 1] \times [-1, 3]$

EXAMPLE 16.1.3   Compute $\int_1^b \left[\int_1^d \dfrac{y - x}{(y + x)^3}\, dy \right] dx$ where b and d are both constants greater than 1.

678 CHAPTER 16 / MULTIPLE INTEGRALS

Solution: First, to make it somewhat easier to integrate w.r.t. y, note that

$$\frac{y-x}{(y+x)^3} = \frac{1}{(y+x)^2} - \frac{2x}{(y+x)^3}$$

Now the inner integral becomes

$$\int_1^d \frac{y-x}{(y+x)^3}\,dy = \int_1^d \frac{1}{(y+x)^2}\,dy - 2x\int_1^d \frac{1}{(y+x)^3}\,dy$$

$$= \Big|_{y=1}^{y=d}\left(-\frac{1}{y+x}\right) - 2x \Big|_{y=1}^{y=d}\left(-\frac{1}{2}\frac{1}{(y+x)^2}\right)$$

$$= -\frac{1}{d+x} + \frac{1}{1+x} + \frac{x}{(x+d)^2} - \frac{x}{(1+x)^2} = -\frac{d}{(x+d)^2} + \frac{1}{(x+1)^2}$$

Next, integrating this w.r.t. x gives

$$\int_1^b \left[\int_1^d \frac{y-x}{(y+x)^3}\,dy\right] dx = \int_1^b \left[-\frac{d}{(x+d)^2} + \frac{1}{(x+1)^2}\right] dx = \Big|_{x=1}^{x=b}\left(\frac{d}{x+d} - \frac{1}{x+1}\right)$$

$$= \frac{d}{b+d} - \frac{1}{b+1} - \frac{d}{d+1} + \frac{1}{2} \qquad (*)$$

Choosing instead to integrate w.r.t. x first, a similar trick leads to

$$\frac{y-x}{(y+x)^3} = -\frac{1}{(y+x)^2} + \frac{2y}{(y+x)^3}$$

Now the inner integral w.r.t. x becomes

$$\int_1^b \frac{y-x}{(y+x)^3}\,dx = \Big|_{x=1}^{x=b}\left[\frac{1}{y+x} - \frac{y}{(y+x)^2}\right]$$

$$= \left[\frac{1}{y+b} - \frac{y}{(y+b)^2}\right] - \left[\frac{1}{y+1} - \frac{y}{(y+1)^2}\right] = \frac{b}{(y+b)^2} - \frac{1}{(y+1)^2}$$

Then

$$\int_1^d \left[\int_1^b \frac{y-x}{(y+x)^3}\,dx\right] dy = \Big|_{y=1}^{y=d}\left(-\frac{b}{y+b} + \frac{1}{y+1}\right) = -\frac{b}{b+d} + \frac{b}{b+1} + \frac{1}{d+1} - \frac{1}{2} \qquad (**)$$

One way to show that the two results are equal is to subtract $(**)$ from $(*)$, which gives

$$\left(\frac{d}{b+d} - \frac{1}{b+1} - \frac{d}{d+1} + \frac{1}{2}\right) - \left(-\frac{b}{b+d} + \frac{b}{b+1} + \frac{1}{d+1} - \frac{1}{2}\right)$$

By simple algebra, this can be reduced to $1 - 1 - 1 + 1 = 0$. ∎

It is important to note that the equality in Theorem 16.1.1 does not always hold if the limits of integration are infinite.

SECTION 16.1 / DOUBLE INTEGRALS OVER FINITE RECTANGLES

EXAMPLE 16.1.4 In statistics, two random variables X and Y are said to have the *bivariate uniform distribution* over the set $[a, b] \times [c, d]$ with $a < b$ and $c < d$ if, for any pair of numbers x in $[a, b]$ and y in $[c, d]$, the probability $F(x, y)$ that both $X \leq x$ and $Y \leq y$ is given by

$$F(x, y) = \frac{x-a}{b-a} \cdot \frac{y-c}{d-c}$$

The function $F(x, y)$ and is called the *joint probability distribution* of X and Y. The corresponding *joint density function* is defined for all x in $[a, b]$ and y in $[c, d]$ by

$$f(x, y) = k = \frac{1}{(b-a)(d-c)} \qquad (*)$$

independent of x and y. It is easy to check that these definitions of F and f imply that, for all x in $[a, b]$ and y in $[c, d]$, one has $F(x, y) = \int_a^x \int_c^y f(s, t) \, dt \, ds$.

Now, given the random variable $Z = X + Y$, compute its *expected value*, which is defined as

$$E(Z) = \int_a^b \int_c^d (x+y) f(x, y) \, dy \, dx$$

Solution: Because of $(*)$, one has

$$E(Z) = k \int_a^b \left[\int_c^d (x+y) \, dy \right] dx = k \int_a^b \left[\left. \left(xy + \tfrac{1}{2} y^2 \right) \right|_c^d \right] dx$$

$$= k \int_a^b \left(xd + \tfrac{1}{2} d^2 - xc - \tfrac{1}{2} c^2 \right) dx = k \int_a^b \left[(d-c)x + \tfrac{1}{2}(d^2 - c^2) \right] dx$$

$$= k \left. \left[(d-c) \tfrac{1}{2} x^2 + \tfrac{1}{2}(d^2 - c^2) x \right] \right|_a^b = \tfrac{1}{2} k \left[(d-c)(b^2 - a^2) + (d^2 - c^2)(b-a) \right]$$

$$= \tfrac{1}{2} k \left[(d-c)(b+a)(b-a) + (d-c)(d+c)(b-a) \right]$$

$$= \tfrac{1}{2} k (b-a)(d-c)(a+b+c+d) = \tfrac{1}{2}(a+b+c+d)$$

EXERCISES FOR SECTION 16.1

(SM) 1. Evaluate the following double integrals:

(a) $\displaystyle\int_0^2 \int_0^1 (2x + 3y + 4) \, dx \, dy$ (b) $\displaystyle\int_0^a \int_0^b (x-a)(x-b) \, dx \, dy$ (c) $\displaystyle\int_1^3 \int_1^2 \frac{x-y}{x+y} \, dx \, dy$

(SM) 2. Assuming that $a > 1$ and $b > 0$, find

$$I = \int_1^a \left(\int_0^b \frac{1}{x^3} e^{y/x} \, dy \right) dx$$

680 CHAPTER 16 / MULTIPLE INTEGRALS

SM **3.** Consider the function
$$f(x, y) = \frac{2k}{(x + y + 1)^3}$$
where k is a constant. Let R be the rectangle $R = [0, a] \times [0, 1]$, where $a > 0$ is a constant. Determine the value k_a of k such that $\iint_R f(x, y) \, dx \, dy = 1$. Show that $k_a > 2$ for all $a > 0$.

4. Compute the double integral $I = \int_0^2 \left[\int_{-2}^1 (x^2 y^3 - (y+1)^2) \, dy \right] dx$.

16.2 Infinite Rectangles of Integration

In Section 10.7 we extended the definition of the integral of a one-variable function to the case of an infinite interval of integration. In Eq. (10.7.3) this interval was the whole real line. Let us now consider the analogous bi-variate problem of extending our definition (16.1.4) of a double integral so that

$$\iint_R f(x, y) \, dy \, dx \qquad (16.2.1)$$

makes sense even when the rectangle R becomes the whole xy-plane $(-\infty, \infty) \times (-\infty, \infty)$. We postpone a deeper analysis to FMEA. Here we merely try rewriting the integral in Eq. (16.2.1) as the double integral

$$\int_{-\infty}^{\infty} \left[\int_{-\infty}^{\infty} f(x, y) \, dy \right] dx$$

Note first that the inner integral $\int_{-\infty}^{\infty} f(x, y) \, dy$ is an improper integral of the kind that was considered in (10.7.3). Suppose that this inner integral converges for *all* values of x to a value we denote by $I(x) = \int_{-\infty}^{\infty} f(x, y) \, dy$. Then we can further re-write

$$\iint_R f(x, y) \, dy \, dx = \int_{-\infty}^{\infty} I(x) \, dx \qquad (16.2.2)$$

Now, the right-hand side of (16.2.2) is once again an improper integral of one variable. So, provided that it also converges so that Eq. (10.7.3) applies, then we can define the improper double integral (16.2.1) as $\int_{-\infty}^{\infty} I(x) \, dx$.

EXAMPLE 16.2.1 In Example 10.7.5 and then Exercise 10.7.12, we considered the *normal distribution*, with density function[3]
$$f(x) = \frac{1}{\sqrt{2\pi}} e^{-\frac{1}{2}x^2}$$

---
[3] This is actually the *standard normal* density function. It is the function considered in Exercise 10.7.12, in the special case when $\mu = 0$ and $\sigma^2 = 1$.

SECTION 16.2 / INFINITE RECTANGLES OF INTEGRATION

We observed that there that the distribution is well defined in the sense that the improper integral $\int_{-\infty}^{+\infty} f(x)\,dx$ converges, and satisfies

$$\int_{-\infty}^{+\infty} f(x)\,dx = \frac{1}{\sqrt{2\pi}} \int_{-\infty}^{+\infty} e^{-\frac{1}{2}x^2}\,dx = 1 \tag{16.2.3}$$

The bi-variate normal distribution is a natural extension of this distribution to $\mathbb{R}^2$. It is defined by the joint density

$$f(x, y) = \frac{1}{2\pi} \frac{1}{\sqrt{1-\rho^2}} \exp\left\{-\left[\frac{x^2 - 2\rho xy + y^2}{2(1-\rho^2)}\right]\right\}$$

Here ρ is a constant in the interval $[-1, 1]$, known as the *correlation coefficient* between X and Y. Show that the improper integral

$$\int_{-\infty}^{+\infty} \int_{-\infty}^{+\infty} f(x, y)\,dy\,dx$$

converges to 1.

Solution: The integral in question can be written as

$$\frac{1}{2\pi} \frac{1}{\sqrt{1-\rho^2}} \int_{-\infty}^{+\infty} \int_{-\infty}^{+\infty} \exp\left\{-\left[\frac{x^2 - 2\rho xy + y^2}{2(1-\rho^2)}\right]\right\} dy\,dx \tag{16.2.4}$$

Ignoring for the moment the constant terms and the outer integral, we first need to compute, for any value of the constant x, the inner integral

$$I(x) = \int_{-\infty}^{+\infty} \exp\left\{-\left[\frac{x^2 - 2\rho xy + y^2}{2(1-\rho^2)}\right]\right\} dy \tag{$*$}$$

Now use integration by substitution with the new variable $u = (y - \rho x)/\sqrt{2(1-\rho^2)}$. Note that, with x fixed, one has

$$du = \frac{1}{\sqrt{2(1-\rho^2)}}\,dy \quad \text{and} \quad u^2 = \frac{y^2 - 2\rho xy + \rho^2 x^2}{2(1-\rho^2)}$$

Then the fraction in square brackets in $(*)$ becomes

$$\frac{x^2 - 2\rho xy + y^2}{2(1-\rho^2)} = \frac{x^2 - \rho^2 x^2 + \rho^2 x^2 - 2\rho xy + y^2}{2(1-\rho^2)} = \frac{x^2}{2} + u^2$$

Because $dy = \sqrt{2(1-\rho^2)}\,du$ and x is a constant, the integral $(*)$ can be rewritten as

$$I(x) = \int_{-\infty}^{+\infty} e^{-\left(\frac{1}{2}x^2 + u^2\right)} \sqrt{2(1-\rho^2)}\,du = e^{-\frac{1}{2}x^2} \sqrt{2(1-\rho^2)} \int_{-\infty}^{+\infty} e^{-u^2}\,du$$

As discussed in Eq. (10.7.9), however, the last integral is $\sqrt{\pi}$. So, substituting the result for $I(x)$ into Eq. (16.2.4) and then using Eq. (16.2.3) for the last step, we get

$$\int_{-\infty}^{+\infty} \int_{-\infty}^{+\infty} f(x,y) \, dy \, dx = \frac{1}{2\pi} \frac{1}{\sqrt{1-\rho^2}} \int_{-\infty}^{+\infty} I(x) \, dx$$

$$= \frac{1}{2\pi} \frac{1}{\sqrt{1-\rho^2}} \int_{-\infty}^{+\infty} e^{-x^2/2} \sqrt{2(1-\rho^2)} \sqrt{\pi} \, dx$$

$$= \frac{1}{\sqrt{2\pi}} \int_{-\infty}^{+\infty} e^{-x^2/2} \, dx = 1$$

16.3 Discontinuous Integrands and Other Extensions

So far we have only considered double integrals where the integrand is continuous. Consider now two random variables X and Y whose joint density is the discontinuous function

$$f(x,y) = \begin{cases} e^{-y}, & \text{if } 0 < x < y; \\ 0, & \text{otherwise} \end{cases} \quad (16.3.1)$$

In order to verify that this is a well-defined density, we need to check that the volume under its graph is exactly 1 because

$$\int_{-\infty}^{\infty} \int_{-\infty}^{\infty} f(x,y) \, dy \, dx = 1 \quad (16.3.2)$$

But since function f is defined piecewise, it is convenient for us to divide the domain of integration as in Fig. 16.3.1. This is drawn so that the density $f(x,y)$ is positive if and only if (x,y) belongs to the shaded area where $0 < x < y$. This infinite wedge-shaped area allows any $x > 0$, but for any given value of x, permits only y in the interval (x, ∞). So we can calculate the volume as the double integral

$$\int_0^{\infty} \left[\int_x^{\infty} e^{-y} \, dy \right] dx$$

Here x is both the lower bound of the inner integral and the variable of integration of the outer integral.

In FMEA we discuss general integrals that display this feature. In this chapter, however, we just verify that the density function in (16.3.1) does satisfy (16.3.2). To do so, first note that, since the inner integral treats x as a constant, it is simply

$$\int_x^{\infty} e^{-y} \, dy = \lim_{b \to \infty} \int_x^b e^{-y} \, dy = -\lim_{b \to \infty} \left. e^{-y} \right|_x^b = -\lim_{b \to \infty} e^{-b} + e^{-x} = e^{-x}$$

SECTION 16.3 / DISCONTINUOUS INTEGRANDS AND OTHER EXTENSIONS

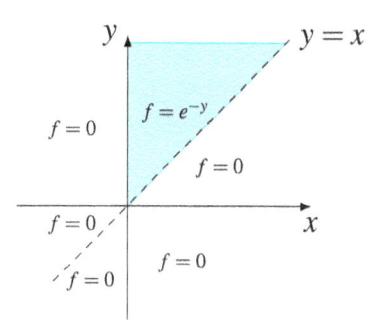

Figure 16.3.1 Domain of $f(x, y)$ in Eq. (16.3.1)

It follows that

$$\int_0^\infty \left[\int_x^\infty e^{-y}\, dy \right] dx = \int_0^\infty e^{-x}\, dx = \lim_{b \to \infty} \int_0^b e^{-x}\, dx = -\lim_{b \to \infty} \Big|_0^b e^{-x} = -\lim_{b \to \infty} e^{-b} + 1 = 1$$

This confirms Eq. (16.3.2).

EXAMPLE 16.3.1 Consider the two random variables X and Y of Example 16.1.4, for the special case when $a = c = 0$ and $b = d = 1$. Compute the density function of variable Z, and use it to confirm that the value of $E(Z)$ is 1 in this special case.

Solution: First define the distribution function $G(z)$ of Z for all real z so that $G(z)$ is the probability that $Z = X + Y \leq z$. Note that both X and Y take values in the interval $[0, 1]$. It follows that if $z < 0$ then $X + Y \leq z$ is impossible and so $G(z) = 0$, whereas if $z > 2$ then $X + Y \leq z$ is certain and so $G(z) = 1$.

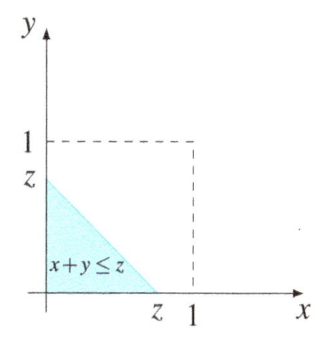

Figure 16.3.2 $x + y \leq z$ when $z \leq 1$ in Example 16.1.4

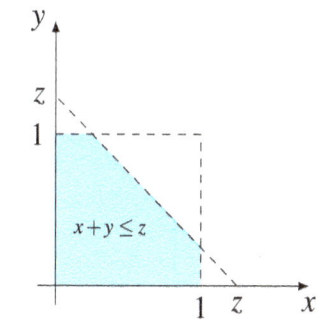

Figure 16.3.3 $x + y \leq z$ when $1 < z \leq 2$ in Example 16.1.4

Now, in case $0 \leq z \leq 1$, the probability that $X + Y \leq z$ equals the area of the shaded region in Fig. 16.3.2. This is the probability that $X \leq z$ and $Y \leq z - X$, which is

$$G(z) = \int_0^z \left[\int_0^{z-x} f(x,y) \, dy \right] dx = \int_0^z \left(\int_0^{z-x} 1 \, dy \right) dx = \int_0^z \left(\Big|_0^{z-x} y \right) dx$$

$$= \int_0^z (z - x) \, dx = \Big|_0^z \left(zx - \tfrac{1}{2}x^2 \right) = \tfrac{1}{2}z^2$$

In this case when $0 < z < 1$, the associated density of Z is $g(z) = G'(z) = z$.

On the other hand, in case $1 < z \leq 2$, the probability that $X + Y \leq z$ equals the area of the shaded region in Fig. 16.3.3. Exercise 1 asks you to show that

$$G(z) = 1 - \tfrac{1}{2}(2 - z)^2$$

In this case when $1 < z < 2$, the associated density of Z is $g(z) = G'(z) = 2 - z$.

It follows that the expectation of Z is given by

$$E(Z) = \int_0^2 z g(z) \, dx = \int_0^1 z^2 \, dx + \int_1^2 (2z - z^2) \, dx$$

$$= \Big|_0^1 \tfrac{1}{3}z^3 + \Big|_1^2 \left(z^2 - \tfrac{1}{3}z^3 \right) = \tfrac{1}{3} - 0 + \left(4 - \tfrac{8}{3} - 1 + \tfrac{1}{3} \right) = 1$$

EXERCISES FOR SECTION 16.3

1. Show that the area of the shaded region in Fig. 16.3.3 equals $1 - (2 - z)^2/2$.

16.4 Integration Over Many Variables

In this brief section we discuss how to go beyond integrals of functions that have only two variables. Instead of a two-dimensional rectangle, let $\mathcal{R}$ denote the n-fold Cartesian product $[a_1, b_1] \times \cdots \times [a_n, b_n]$ of the closed intervals $[a_1, b_1]$, ..., $[a_n, b_n]$. It is the set of all n-vectors $\mathbf{x} = (x_1, x_2, \ldots, x_n)$ in $\mathbb{R}^n$ such that $a_i \leq x_i \leq b_i$ for $i = 1, 2, \ldots, n$. We call the set $\mathcal{R}$ an *n-dimensional rectangle* or *n-dimensional cuboid*.

Suppose that f is a continuous function defined on $\mathcal{R}$. Then we define the *multiple integral* of f over $\mathcal{R}$ as

$$\int \cdots \int_\mathcal{R} f(x_1, \ldots, x_{n-1}, x_n) \, dx_1 \ldots dx_{n-1} dx_n$$

$$= \int_{a_n}^{b_n} \left\{ \int_{a_{n-1}}^{b_{n-1}} \cdots \left[\int_{a_1}^{b_1} f(x_1, \ldots, x_{n-1}, x_n) dx_1 \right] \ldots dx_{n-1} \right\} dx_n \quad (16.4.1)$$

The meaning of the notation on the right-hand side of Eq. (16.4.1) is that integration is to be performed n times. We start by integrating w.r.t. x_1, all other variables being treated as constants. Next we integrate w.r.t. x_2, treating the remaining variables $(x_3, \ldots, x_n)$ as constants. And so on, for n steps in all.

Definition (16.4.1) is a simple generalization of (16.1.4). In this general case with n variables of integration, one can still prove that the order of integration on the right-hand side is immaterial, provided that f is continuous in $\mathcal{R}$.

EXERCISE FOR SECTION 16.4

(SM) 1. [HARDER] Find
$$I = \iiint_C (x_1^2 + x_2^2 + x_3^2)\, dx_1\, dx_2\, dx_3$$
where C is the *unit cube* in $\mathbb{R}^3$ that is determined by the inequalities $0 \le x_i \le 1$ for $i = 1, 2, 3$.

V

MULTIVARIABLE OPTIMIZATION

17
UNCONSTRAINED OPTIMIZATION

At first sight it is curious that a subject as pure and passionless as mathematics can have anything useful to say about that messy, ill-structured, chancy world in which we live.
Fortunately we find that whenever we comprehend what was previously mysterious, there is at the centre of everything order, pattern and common sense.
—Patrick (B.H.P.) Rivett (1978)

Chapter 9 was concerned with optimization problems involving functions of one variable. Most interesting economic optimization problems, however, require the simultaneous choice of several variables. For example, a profit-maximizing producer of a single commodity chooses not only its output level, but also the quantities of many different inputs. A consumer chooses quantities of the many different goods that are available to buy in a market.

Most of the mathematical difficulties arise already in the transition from one to two variables. Furthermore, textbooks in economics often illustrate economic problems by using functions of only two variables, for which one can at least draw level curves in the plane. We therefore begin this chapter by studying the two-variable case. Section 17.1 presents the basic results, illustrated by relatively simple examples and problems. In Sections 17.2, 17.3, and 17.5 we give a more systematic presentation of the theory with two variables. The intermediate Section 17.4 treats the relatively simple special case when the objective is to maximize or minimize a quadratic function. Subsequently, in Section 17.6, we consider how the theory can be extended to functions of several variables.

Much of economic analysis involves seeing how the solution to an optimization problem responds when the situation changes. Often, this changing situation is described by alterations in some relevant parameters. Thus, the theory of the firm considers how a change in the price of a good that is either an input or an output can affect the optimal quantities of all the inputs and outputs, as well as the maximum profit. Some simple results of this kind are briefly introduced at the end of the chapter.

This chapter treats unconstrained optimization problems. Different kinds of constrained optimization problem are the subject of our last three chapters.

17.1 Two Choice Variables: Necessary Conditions

Consider a differentiable function $z = f(x, y)$ defined on a set S in the xy-plane. Recall from Section 14.8 the definition of an interior point. Suppose that f attains its largest value (its maximum) at an interior point (x_0, y_0) of S, as indicated in Fig. 17.1.1 by the point P in three-dimensional space, whose coordinates are $(x, y, z) = (x_0, y_0, f(x_0, y_0))$.[1]

Suppose we now we keep y fixed at y_0, and let D denote the set of all x such that (x, y_0) is in S. Consider now the function of one variable defined by $g(x) = f(x, y_0)$ for all x in the domain D. Because f is differentiable, so is g, with derivative $g'(x)$ exactly the same as the partial derivative $f_1'(x, y_0)$ for all x in D. Furthermore, the hypothesis that $f(x, y) \leq f(x_0, y_0)$ for all (x, y) in S implies that $g(x) \leq g(x_0) = f(x_0, y_0)$ for all $x \in D$, so x_0 is a maximum point of g over D. Finally, because we assumed that (x_0, y_0) is an interior point of S, and so can be surrounded by a small circle of points in S, it follows that x_0 can be surrounded by a small interval of points in D, implying that x_0 is an interior point in D.

The argument in the paragraph above implies that all the conditions of Theorem 9.1.1 hold. By that theorem, it follows that at x_0 one has $g'(x_0) = 0$. But $g'(x) = f_1'(x, y_0)$ for all x in D, so $f_1'(x_0, y_0) = 0$.

Suppose next that we keep x fixed at x_0 rather than y at y_0, and then consider the function h of the single variable y that is defined for all y near y_0 by $h(y) = f(x_0, y)$. Using a similar argument, one can show that h is differentiable with derivative $h'(y) = f_2'(x_0, y)$, and that it achieves a maximum at the interior point $y = y_0$. Once again, therefore, we can invoke Theorem 9.1.1, which implies that $h'(y_0) = f_2'(x_0, y) = 0$.

A point (x_0, y_0) where both first-order partial derivatives are 0 is called a *critical* (or *stationary*) *point* of f.

If f attains its smallest value (its minimum) at an interior point (x_0, y_0) of S, a similar argument shows that in this case too (x_0, y_0) must be a critical point. So we have the following important result:

THEOREM 17.1.1 (NECESSARY FIRST-ORDER CONDITIONS)

A differentiable function $z = f(x, y)$ can have a maximum or minimum at an interior point (x_0, y_0) of its domain only if it is a *critical point* in the sense that the pair $(x, y) = (x_0, y_0)$ satisfies the following two first-order conditions, or FOCs:

$$f_1'(x, y) = 0 \text{ and } f_2'(x, y) = 0 \qquad (17.1.1)$$

In Fig. 17.1.2, the three points P, Q, and R of the graph all correspond to critical points in the domain S of f, but only P is a maximum.[2] In the examples and exercises of this

---

[1] The concept of interior point was introduced in Section 14.8, before the statements of the second-order conditions (14.8.3)–(14.8.6) for a function to be concave or convex.

[2] Later, we shall say that Q corresponds to a *local maximum*, whereas R corresponds to a *saddle point*.

SECTION 17.1 / TWO CHOICE VARIABLES: NECESSARY CONDITIONS

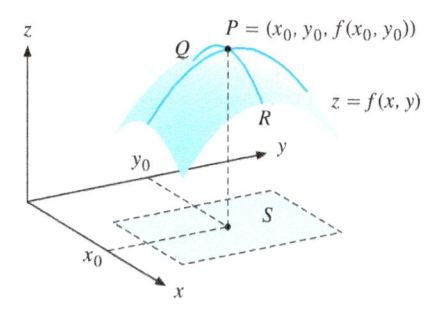

Figure 17.1.1 At the maximum point P, (x_0, y_0) is critical.

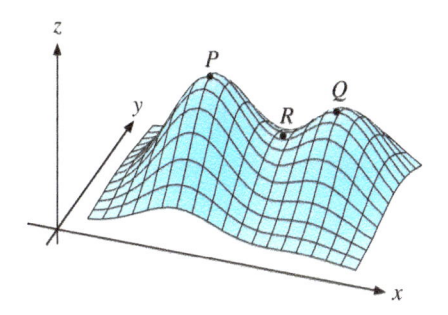

Figure 17.1.2 Only point P is a maximum.

Section, only the first-order conditions are considered. Section 17.2 explains how to use second-order conditions in order to verify that we have found a maximum or minimum.

EXAMPLE 17.1.1 The function f is defined for all (x, y) by

$$f(x, y) = -2x^2 - 2xy - 2y^2 + 36x + 42y - 158$$

Assume that f has a maximum point. Find it.

Solution: Theorem 17.1.1 applies, so a maximum point (x, y) must be a critical point that satisfies the two first-order conditions:

$$f'_1(x, y) = -4x - 2y + 36 = 0 \quad \text{and} \quad f'_2(x, y) = -2x - 4y + 42 = 0$$

These are two linear simultaneous equations which together determine both x and y. They can be solved to show that $(x, y) = (5, 8)$ is the only pair of numbers which satisfies both equations. Assuming there is a maximum point, these must be its coordinates. Inserting $(x, y) = (5, 8)$ into the definition of f determines the maximum value, which is $f(5, 8) = 100$. (In Example 17.2.2 we will prove that $(5, 8)$ really is a maximum point.)

EXAMPLE 17.1.2 A firm produces two different kinds of a commodity, which are labelled A and B. The daily cost in dollars of producing x units of A and y units of B is

$$C(x, y) = 0.04x^2 + 0.01xy + 0.01y^2 + 4x + 2y + 500$$

Suppose that the firm sells all its output at a price per unit of \$15 for A and \$9 for B. Find the daily production levels x and y that maximize profit per day.

Solution: Profit per day in dollars is $\pi(x, y) = 15x + 9y - C(x, y)$, implying that

$$\pi(x, y) = 15x + 9y - 0.04x^2 - 0.01xy - 0.01y^2 - 4x - 2y - 500$$
$$= -0.04x^2 - 0.01xy - 0.01y^2 + 11x + 7y - 500$$

If the two quantities $x > 0$ and $y > 0$ jointly maximize profit, then the pair (x, y) must satisfy the following two FOCs:

$$\frac{\partial \pi}{\partial x} = -0.08x - 0.01y + 11 = 0 \quad \text{and} \quad \frac{\partial \pi}{\partial y} = -0.01x - 0.02y + 7 = 0$$

These two linear equations in x and y have the unique solution $x = 100$, $y = 300$. The corresponding maximum dollar profit is $\pi(100, 300) = 1100$. (We have not proved that this actually is a maximum. For that, see Exercise 17.2.1.)

EXAMPLE 17.1.3 (**Profit Maximization**). Suppose that $Q = F(K, L)$ is a production function, with $K \geq 0$ as the capital input, and $L \geq 0$ as the labour input. Denote the price per unit of output by p, the cost (or rental) per unit of capital by r, and the wage rate by w, where p, r, and w are all positive constants. The profit π from producing and selling $F(K, L)$ units is then given by the function

$$\pi(K, L) = pF(K, L) - rK - wL$$

If F is differentiable and π has a maximum with $K > 0$, $L > 0$, then the two FOCs are

$$\pi'_K(K, L) = pF'_K(K, L) - r = 0 \quad \text{and} \quad \pi'_L(K, L) = pF'_L(K, L) - w = 0$$

So the necessary conditions for profit to be a maximum when $K = K^*$ and $L = L^*$ are

$$pF'_K(K^*, L^*) = r \quad \text{and} \quad pF'_L(K^*, L^*) = w \tag{$*$}$$

The first equation in ($*$) says that r, the cost of capital, must equal the value, at the price p per unit, of the marginal product of capital. Suppose we think of increasing capital input from the level K^* by k units, where k is small. How much would profit increase? Production would increase by approximately $F'_K(K^*, L^*)k$ units. Because each extra unit is priced at p, the revenue gain is approximately $pF'_K(K^*, L^*)k$. But how much is lost? The answer is rk, because r is the cost of each unit of capital. At a profit maximum, these two must be equal.

The second equation in ($*$) has a similar interpretation. Provided that ℓ is small, increasing labour input by ℓ units from level L^* will lead to the approximate gain $pF'_L(K^*, L^*)\ell$ in revenue, whereas the extra labour cost is approximately $w\ell$. The profit-maximizing pair (K^*, L^*) thus has the property that the extra revenue from increasing either input is just offset by the extra cost.

Economists often divide the first-order conditions ($*$) by the positive price p to reach the alternative form $F'_K(K, L) = r/p$ and $F'_L(K, L) = w/p$. So, to obtain maximum profit, the firm must choose K and L to equate the marginal productivity of capital to its "relative" price r/p, and also to equate the marginal productivity of labour to its relative price w/p.

Note that the conditions in ($*$) are necessary, but generally not sufficient for an interior maximum. Conditions that are sufficient for an optimum are explored in Example 17.3.3.

EXAMPLE 17.1.4 Find the only possible solution to the following special case of Example 17.1.3:

$$\max \pi(K, L) = 12K^{1/2}L^{1/4} - 1.2K - 0.6L$$

Solution: The first-order conditions are

$$\pi'_K(K, L) = 6K^{-1/2}L^{1/4} - 1.2 = 0 \quad \text{and} \quad \pi'_L(K, L) = 3K^{1/2}L^{-3/4} - 0.6 = 0$$

These equations imply that $K^{-1/2}L^{1/4} = K^{1/2}L^{-3/4} = 0.2 = 1/5$. Multiplying each side of the first equation here by $K^{1/2}L^{3/4}$ reduces it to $L = K$. So $K^{-1/4} = L^{-1/4} = 1/5$. It follows that $K = L = 5^4 = 625$ is the only possible solution. (See Example 17.2.3 for a proof that this is indeed a maximum point.)

EXAMPLE 17.1.5   Consider a firm that is a monopolist in its domestic market, but takes as given the price p_w of its product in the world market. Denote the quantities it sells in the two markets by x_d and x_w, respectively. Suppose that the price obtained in the domestic market, as a function of its sales, is given by the inverse demand function $p_d = P(x_d)$. Suppose too that the cost of producing x units in total is $C(x)$, regardless of how this output is distributed between the domestic and world markets.

(a) Find the profit function $\pi(x_d, x_w)$, then write down the FOCs for profit to be maximized at $x_d > 0$, $x_w > 0$. Give economic interpretations of these conditions.

(b) Suppose that in the domestic market the firm is faced with a demand curve whose constant price elasticity is equal to -2. What is the relationship between the prices in the domestic and world markets?

Solution:

(a) The revenue from selling x_d units in the domestic market at the price $p_d = P(x_d)$ is $P(x_d) \cdot x_d$. In the world market the revenue is $p_w x_w$. The profit function is $\pi = \pi(x_d, x_w) = P(x_d)x_d + p_w x_w - C(x_d + x_w)$. So the two first-order conditions are

$$\pi_1' = p_d + P'(x_d)x_d - C'(x_d + x_w) = 0 \qquad (*)$$

$$\pi_2' = p_w - C'(x_d + x_w) = 0 \qquad (**)$$

According to (∗∗), in the world market the marginal cost must equal the price p_w, which is the marginal revenue in this case. In the domestic market the marginal cost must also equal the marginal revenue, which is $p_d + P'(x_d)x_d$.

Suppose the firm contemplates producing and selling a little extra in its domestic market. The extra revenue per unit increase in output equals p_d minus the loss that arises because of the induced price reduction for all domestic sales. The latter loss is approximately $P'(x_d) \cdot x_d$. Since the cost of an extra unit of output is approximately the marginal cost $C'(x_d + x_w)$, condition (∗) expresses the requirement that, per unit of extra output, the domestic revenue gain is just offset by the cost increase.

(b) The price elasticity of demand is -2, meaning that $\text{El}_{p_d} x_d = (p_d/x_d)(dx_d/dp_d) = -2$. From the rule for differentiating inverse functions, it follows that

$$P'(x_d) = \frac{dp_d}{dx_d} = 1/(dx_d/dp_d) = -\frac{1}{2}\frac{p_d}{x_d} \qquad (***)$$

Then Eqs (∗), (∗∗), and (∗∗∗) together imply that $\frac{1}{2}p_d = C'(x_d + x_w) = p_w$. So in the domestic market where the firm is a monopolist, the price it receives is twice that in the world market, where it must take the price as given.

EXERCISES FOR SECTION 17.1

1. The function f defined for all (x, y) by $f(x, y) = -2x^2 - y^2 + 4x + 4y - 3$ has a maximum. Find the corresponding values of x and y.

2. Consider the function f defined for all (x, y) by $f(x, y) = x^2 + y^2 - 6x + 8y + 35$.

   (a) The function has a minimum point. Find it.

   (b) Show that $f(x, y)$ can be written in the form $f(x, y) = (x - 3)^2 + (y + 4)^2 + 10$. Explain why this shows that you have really found the minimum in part (a).

3. In the profit-maximizing problem of Example 17.1.3, let $p = 1$, $r = 0.65$, $w = 1.2$, and

   $$F(K, L) = 80 - (K - 3)^2 - 2(L - 6)^2 - (K - 3)(L - 6)$$

   Find the only possible values of K and L that maximize profits.

4. Suppose that a firm's annual profit is given by $P(x, y) = -x^2 - y^2 + 22x + 18y - 102$, where x and y denote the amounts spent per year on, respectively, product development and advertising.

   (a) Find the firm's annual profit when $x = 10$, $y = 8$ and when $x = 12$, $y = 10$.

   (b) Find the only possible values of x and y that can maximize profit, along with the corresponding profit.

17.2 Two Choice Variables: Sufficient Conditions

Concavity or Convexity as a Sufficient Condition

We start by recalling some relevant results from Chapters 8 and 9. Indeed, suppose that f is a concave function of one variable defined in an interval I of the real line. Recall the supergradient property set out in Theorem 8.4.1, stating that the gradient of the function at any interior point where it is differentiable is a supergradient, in the sense that the tangent line lies above the graph of the function. This led to Theorem 9.2.2, stating a very simple sufficient condition for an interior critical point of I to be a maximum point, which is that the function f is concave. The reason is that the gradient of f at a critical point is zero, by definition. So, by the supergradient property of concave functions, at a critical point zero is a supergradient, implying immediately that the critical point is a maximum point.

This result for one variable is valid even if the function f is not differentiable at many points of I. Indeed, all that matters is that it should be differentiable at an interior critical point, since that is sufficient for a concave function to have a maximum point there. Similarly, a sufficient condition for an interior critical point in I to be a minimum point is that f is convex.

For a function of two variables, similar results hold. First, recall from Section 14.7 that a set S in the xy-plane is convex if for each pair of points P and Q in S, the whole line segment between P and Q lies in S. Recall too from Section 14.8 the definition of a concave or convex function. Now let $z = f(x, y)$ be a concave function of two variables defined on a convex set S. At any interior point (x^0, y^0) where f is differentiable, consider its gradient vector $\nabla f(x^0, y^0) = (f_1'(x^0, y^0), f_2'(x^0, y^0))$ and associated tangent plane given by Eq. (15.8.10), which can be rewritten as

$$z - f(x^0, y^0) = f_1'(x^0, y^0)(x - x^0) + f_2'(x^0, y^0)(y - y^0) \qquad (17.2.1)$$

Then the supergradient property set out in Theorem 15.8.3 states that the gradient vector $\nabla f(x^0, y^0)$ of the concave function f is a supergradient vector, in the sense that the tangent plane given by Eq. (17.2.1) lies above the graph of the function. That is, for all (x, y) in S, one has

$$f(x, y) - f(x^0, y^0) \leq f_1'(x^0, y^0)(x - x^0) + f_2'(x^0, y^0)(y - y^0) \qquad (17.2.2)$$

Now, by the definition in Theorem 17.1.1, the gradient vector $\nabla f(x^0, y^0)$ of the function f at an interior critical point (x^0, y^0) is the zero vector $(0, 0)$. Putting $f_1'(x^0, y^0) = f_2'(x^0, y^0) = 0$ in (17.2.2) evidently implies that, for all (x, y) in S, one has

$$f(x, y) - f(x^0, y^0) \leq 0 \qquad (17.2.3)$$

This, of course, states that the interior critical point (x^0, y^0) is a maximum point of the concave function f. Also, using a standard argument, in case the function f is convex and so $-f$ is concave, the interior critical point (x^0, y^0) is a maximum point of the concave function $-f$ and so a minimum point of the convex function f. So we have proved the following key result:

THEOREM 17.2.1 (CONCAVITY OR CONVEXITY AS A SUFFICIENT CONDITION)

Suppose that the function $z = f(x, y)$ of two variables is defined on a convex domain S, and that (x^0, y^0) is an interior critical point in S. Then:

(a) in case the function f is concave, the point (x^0, y^0) is a maximum point;

(b) in case the function f is convex, the point (x^0, y^0) is a minimum point.

Second-order Conditions for Concavity or Convexity

Now we look for conditions on the second-order partial derivatives of a function f which ensure that it is concave or convex, thus allowing Theorem 17.2.1 to be applied. First, suppose that f is a twice differentiable function of only one variable defined in an interval I of the real line. In this case Eq. (8.5.3) provides a necessary and sufficient condition for f to be concave on I, which is that $f''(x) \leq 0$ for all x in the interior of I. Similarly, Eq. (8.5.4) provides a necessary and sufficient condition for f to be convex on I, which is that $f''(x) \geq 0$ for all x in the interior of I.

For a function of two variables, in (14.8.3)–(14.8.6) we provided corresponding tests for concavity or convexity, as well as sufficient conditions for strict concavity or convexity, based on second-order *partial* derivatives. Provided the function has an interior critical point, this test implies that its graph is a surface shaped like the one in Fig. 17.1.1.

Consider any curve which, like QPR in Fig. 17.1.1, lies in the surface and is parallel to the xz-plane. Any such curve is the graph of a concave function of one variable, implying that $f''_{11}(x, y) \leq 0$. A similar argument holds for any curve in the surface that is parallel to the yz-plane, implying that $f''_{22}(x, y) \leq 0$. In general, however, having these two second-order partial derivatives be nonpositive is *not* sufficient on its own to ensure that the function is concave, with a graph whose shape is like that in Fig. 17.1.1. This is clear from the next example.

EXAMPLE 17.2.1   The function $f(x, y) = 3xy - x^2 - y^2$ has $f''_{11}(x, y) = f''_{22}(x, y) = -2$. Each curve parallel to the xz-plane that lies in the surface defined by the graph has the equation $z = 3xy_0 - x^2 - y_0^2$ for some fixed y_0. It is therefore a concave parabola. So is each curve parallel to the yz-plane that lies in the surface. But along the line $y = x$ the function reduces to $f(x, x) = x^2$, whose graph is a convex rather than a concave parabola. It follows that f has no maximum (or minimum) at $(0, 0)$, which is its only critical point.

What Example 17.2.1 shows is that conditions ensuring that the graph of f looks like the one in Fig. 17.1.1 cannot ignore the second-order cross partial derivative $f''_{12}(x, y)$.

Let $z = f(x, y)$ be a twice differentiable function of two variables defined on a convex domain S. Recall the second-order conditions in (14.8.3) for f to be concave, and those in (14.8.4) for f to be convex. The following result builds on Theorem 17.2.1 by using those second-order conditions for concavity or convexity in order to derive sufficient conditions for an interior critical point of f to be a maximum or minimum.

THEOREM 17.2.2 (SUFFICIENT CONDITIONS FOR A MAXIMUM OR MINIMUM)

Suppose that (x^0, y^0) is an interior critical point for a C^2 function $f(x, y)$ defined in a convex set S in $\mathbb{R}^2$.

(a) If for all (x, y) in S, one has

$$f''_{11}(x, y) \leq 0, \quad f''_{22}(x, y) \leq 0, \quad \text{and} \quad f''_{11}(x, y)f''_{22}(x, y) - [f''_{12}(x, y)]^2 \geq 0$$

then f is concave, and (x^0, y^0) is a maximum point for $f(x, y)$ in S.

(b) If for all (x, y) in S, one has

$$f''_{11}(x, y) \geq 0, \quad f''_{22}(x, y) \geq 0, \quad \text{and} \quad f''_{11}(x, y)f''_{22}(x, y) - [f''_{12}(x, y)]^2 \geq 0$$

then f is convex, and (x^0, y^0) is a minimum point for $f(x, y)$ in S.

The conditions in part (a) of Theorem 17.2.2 are sufficient for an interior critical point to be a maximum point. They are far from being necessary. This is clear from the function whose graph is shown in Fig. 17.1.2, which *has* a maximum at P, but where the conditions in (a) are certainly not satisfied in the whole of its domain.

EXAMPLE 17.2.2
Show that the critical point we found in Example 17.1.1 is a maximum.

Solution: We found that $f_1'(x, y) = -4x - 2y + 36$ and $f_2'(x, y) = -2x - 4y + 42$. Furthermore, $f_{11}'' = -4$, $f_{12}'' = -2$, and $f_{22}'' = -4$. Thus, $f_{11}''(x,y) \leq 0$, $f_{22}''(x,y) \leq 0$, and

$$f_{11}''(x,y)f_{22}''(x,y) - [f_{12}''(x,y)]^2 = 16 - 4 = 12 \geq 0$$

According to part (a) in Theorem 17.2.2, these inequalities guarantee that the critical point $(5, 8)$ is a maximum point.

EXAMPLE 17.2.3
Show that the critical point we found in Example 17.1.4 is a maximum.

Solution: For all $K > 0$ and $L > 0$, the second-order partial derivatives are

$$\pi_{KK}'' = -3K^{-3/2}L^{1/4}, \quad \pi_{KL}'' = \tfrac{3}{2}K^{-1/2}L^{-3/4}, \text{ and } \pi_{LL}'' = -\tfrac{9}{4}K^{1/2}L^{-7/4}$$

Clearly we have $\pi_{KK}'' < 0$ and $\pi_{LL}'' < 0$. Moreover

$$\pi_{KK}''\pi_{LL}'' - (\pi_{KL}'')^2 = \tfrac{27}{4}K^{-1}L^{-3/2} - \tfrac{9}{4}K^{-1}L^{-3/2} = \tfrac{9}{2}K^{-1}L^{-3/2} > 0$$

These three signs tell us that the critical point $(K, L) = (625, 625)$ maximizes profit.

This section concludes with two examples of optimization problems where the choice of variables is subject to constraints. Nevertheless, a simple transformation can be used to convert the problem into the form we have been discussing, without any constraints.

EXAMPLE 17.2.4
Suppose that any production by the firm in Example 17.1.2 creates pollution, so it is legally restricted to produce a total of 320 units of the two kinds of output. The firm's problem has become

$$\max -0.04x^2 - 0.01xy - 0.01y^2 + 11x + 7y - 500 \quad \text{subject to} \quad x + y = 320$$

What are the optimal quantities of the two kinds of output now?

Solution: The firm still wants to maximize its profits. Because of the restriction $y = 320 - x$, however, its profit can be expressed as a function only of x. Indeed, the new profit function is

$$\hat{\pi}(x) = -0.04x^2 - 0.01x(320 - x) - 0.01(320 - x)^2 + 11x + 7(320 - x) - 500$$

We find that $\hat{\pi}'(x) = -0.08x + 7.2$, so $\hat{\pi}'(x) = 0$ for $x = 7.2/0.08 = 90$. But we have $\hat{\pi}''(x) = -0.08 < 0$ for all x, so the critical point $x = 90$ does maximize $\hat{\pi}$. The corresponding value of y is $y = 320 - 90 = 230$. The maximum profit is 1040.

EXAMPLE 17.2.5
A firm has three factories that all produce the same output good. Let x, y, and z denote the respective output quantities that the three factories produce in order to fulfil an order for 2 000 units in total. Hence, $x + y + z = 2000$. Suppose that the respective cost functions for the three factories are

$$C_1(x) = 200 + \frac{1}{100}x^2, \quad C_2(y) = 200 + y + \frac{1}{300}y^3, \quad \text{and} \quad C_3(z) = 200 + 10z$$

Find the values of x, y, and z that minimize the total cost $C(x,y,z) = C_1(x) + C_2(y) + C_3(z)$ of fulfilling the order.

Solution: Solving the equation $x + y + z = 2000$ for z in terms of x and Y gives $z = 2000 - x - y$. Inserting this expression for z into the expression for C, then simplifying, yields

$$\widehat{C}(x,y) = C_1(x) + C_2(y) + C_3(2000 - x - y) = \frac{1}{100}x^2 - 10x + \frac{1}{300}y^3 - 9y + 20\,600$$

Any critical points of $\widehat{C}$ must satisfy the two equations

$$\widehat{C}'_1(x,y) = \frac{1}{50}x - 10 = 0 \quad \text{and} \quad \widehat{C}'_2(x,y) = \frac{1}{100}y^2 - 9 = 0$$

We rule out the solution with $y < 0$, leaving $x = 500$ and $y = 30$ as the only economically sensible solution. It follows that $z = 1470$. The corresponding value of C is $17\,920$.
The second-order partials of $\widehat{C}$ are

$$\widehat{C}''_{11}(x,y) = \frac{1}{50}, \quad \widehat{C}''_{12}(x,y) = 0, \quad \text{and} \quad \widehat{C}''_{22}(x,y) = \frac{1}{50}y$$

It follows that for all $x \geq 0$, $y \geq 0$, one has $\widehat{C}''_{11}(x,y) \geq 0$, $\widehat{C}''_{22}(x,y) \geq 0$, and

$$\widehat{C}''_{11}(x,y)\widehat{C}''_{22}(x,y) - \widehat{C}''_{12}(x,y)^2 = \frac{y}{2500} \geq 0$$

Now we can apply part (b) of Theorem 17.2.2 to show that $(500, 30)$ is a minimum point of $\widehat{C}$ within the convex domain of points (x,y) satisfying $x \geq 0$, $y \geq 0$, and $x + y \leq 2000$. It follows that $(500, 30, 1470)$ is a minimum point of C within the domain of (x, y, z) satisfying $x \geq 0$, $y \geq 0$, $z \geq 0$, and $x + y + z = 2000$.

EXERCISES FOR SECTION 17.2

1. Prove that the true maximum has been found in each of the following:

   (a) Example 17.1.2; (b) Exercise 17.1.1; (c) Exercise 17.1.3.

2. A firm produces two different kinds of a commodity, labelled A and B. The total daily cost of producing x units of A and y units of B is

   $$C(x,y) = 2x^2 - 4xy + 4y^2 - 40x - 20y + 514$$

   Suppose that the firm sells all its output of each kind of good at a price per unit of $24 for A and $12 for B.

   (a) Find the daily production levels x and y that maximize profit.

   (b) The firm is required to produce exactly 54 units per day of the two kinds combined. What is the optimal production plan now?

3. Maximize the utility function $U(x,y,z) = xyz$ subject to $x + 3y + 4z = 108$ and $x, y, z > 0$, by eliminating the variable x and defining an appropriate function of only y and z.

4. The prices p and q per unit that a monopolist receives for each of its two products are determined by the inverse demand functions $p = 25 - x$ and $q = 24 - 2y$, where x and y are the corresponding output quantities, which the monopolist chooses. The total cost of producing x units of the first good and y units of the second is $C(x, y) = 3x^2 + 3xy + y^2$.

   (a) Find the monopolist's profit $\pi(x, y)$ from producing and selling x units of the first good and y units of the other.

   (b) Find the values of x and y that maximize $\pi(x, y)$. Verify that you have found the maximum profit.

5. A firm produces two goods. The cost of producing x units of good 1 and y units of good 2 is
$$C(x, y) = x^2 + xy + y^2 + x + y + 14$$
Suppose the firm sells all its output of each good at positive prices per unit of p and q respectively. Assuming $\frac{1}{2}p + \frac{1}{2} < q < 2p - 1$, find the values of x and y that maximize profit.

6. The profit function of a firm is $\pi(x, y) = px + qy - \alpha x^2 - \beta y^2$, where p and q are the prices per unit, and $\alpha x^2 + \beta y^2$ is the total cost of producing and selling x units of the first good and y units of the other. The constants are all positive.

   (a) Find the values of x and y that maximize profits. Denote them by x^* and y^*. Verify that the second-order conditions are satisfied.

   (b) Define the function π^* so that $\pi^*(p, q) = \pi(x^*, y^*)$ is the firm's maximum profit at prices p and q. Verify that $\partial \pi^*(p, q)/\partial p = x^*$ and $\partial \pi^*(p, q)/\partial q = y^*$. Give these two equations economic interpretations.

7. Find the smallest value of $x^2 + y^2 + z^2$ when we require that $4x + 2y - z = 5$.[3]

8. Let A, a, and b be positive constants, and p, q, and r arbitrary constants. Show that the function $f(x, y) = Ax^a y^b - px - qy - r$ is concave for $x > 0$, $y > 0$ provided that $a + b \leq 1$.

17.3 Local Extreme Points

Quite often economists need to consider *local* extreme points of a function of two variables. Here we extend the definitions and results for functions of one variable that we gave in Section 9.6. Thus, the point (x^0, y^0) is said to be a *local maximum point* of f in S if $f(x, y) \leq f(x^0, y^0)$ for all pairs (x, y) in S that lie sufficiently close to (x^0, y^0). More precisely, the definition is that there exists a positive number r such that $f(x, y) \leq f(x^0, y^0)$ for all (x, y) in S that lie inside the circle with centre (x^0, y^0) and radius r. If the inequality is strict for $(x, y) \neq (x^0, y^0)$, then (x^0, y^0) is a *strict* local maximum point.

A *(strict) local minimum* point is defined in the obvious way. It should also be clear what we mean by *local maximum and minimum values*, *local extreme points*, and *local extreme*

---

[3] Geometrically, the problem is to find the point in the plane $4x + 2y - z = 5$ which is closest to the origin.

values. Note how these definitions imply that a global extreme point is also a local extreme point; the converse is not true, of course.

In searching for maximum and minimum points, the first-order conditions we presented in Theorem 17.1.1 were very useful. The same conditions also apply to local extreme points: *Any local extreme point in the interior of the domain of a differentiable function must be critical.* This follows because, in the argument for Theorem 17.1.1, it was enough to consider how the function behaves in a small neighbourhood of the optimal point.

These first-order conditions are necessary in the sense that, given any differentiable function $z = f(x, y)$ defined on a set S in the plane, only a critical point can be a local extreme point. However, a critical point may not be a local extreme point. Indeed, consider a critical point (x^0, y^0) of f which, like the point $(0, 0)$ in Fig. 17.3.1, is neither a local maximum nor a local minimum point. Because the graph shown in that figure is shaped rather like the saddle that one usually finds on the back of a horse which a rider is about to mount, that critical point is called a *saddle point* of f. More precisely: A *saddle point* (x^0, y^0) is a critical point with the property that there exist points (x, y) and (x', y'), both arbitrarily close to (x^0, y^0), such that $f(x, y) < f(x^0, y^0)$ and $f(x', y') > f(x^0, y^0)$.

EXAMPLE 17.3.1 Show that $(0, 0)$ is a saddle point of $f(x, y) = x^2 - y^2$, and draw its graph.

Solution: It is easy to check that $(0, 0)$ is a critical point at which $f(0, 0) = 0$. Moreover, one has $f(x, 0) = x^2$ and $f(0, y) = -y^2$. So $f(x, y)$ takes both positive and negative values arbitrarily close to the origin. This shows that $(0, 0)$ is a saddle point. See the graph in Fig. 17.3.1.

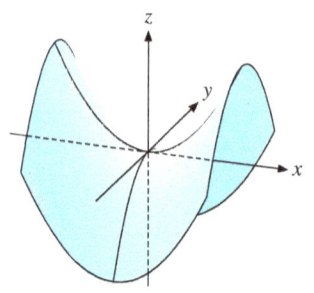

Figure 17.3.1 $z = x^2 - y^2$, with saddle point at $(0, 0)$

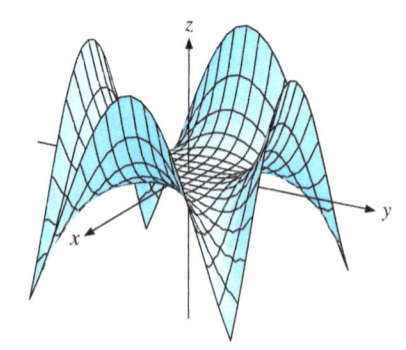

Figure 17.3.2 $z = x^4 - 3x^2y^2 + y^4$, with saddle point at $(0, 0)$

Local extreme points and saddle points can be illustrated by thinking of the mountains in the Himalayas. Every summit is a local maximum, but only the highest (Mount Everest) is the (global) maximum. The deepest points of the lakes or glaciers are local minima. At every mountain pass there will be a saddle point that is the highest point in one compass direction but the lowest in another. That said, the surface in Fig. 17.3.2 shows that not all saddle points have graphs that look as neat as the one shown in Fig. 17.3.1.

Our definitions imply that the critical points of a function thus fall into one of three categories: local maximum points, local minimum points, and saddle points. How do we distinguish between these three?

Consider first the case when $z = f(x, y)$ has a local maximum at (x^0, y^0). The two functions $g(x) = f(x, y^0)$ and $h(y) = f(x^0, y)$ describe the behaviour of f along the respective straight lines $y = y^0$ and $x = x^0$, as shown in Fig. 17.1.1. The functions g and h must achieve local maxima at x^0 and y^0, respectively. It follows that the two second-order conditions $g''(x^0) = f''_{11}(x^0, y^0) \leq 0$ and $h''(y^0) = f''_{22}(x^0, y^0) \leq 0$ must both be satisfied.

On the other hand, if $g''(x^0) < 0$ and $h''(y^0) < 0$, then we know that g and h really do achieve local maxima at x^0 and y^0, respectively. Stated differently, the conditions $f''_{11}(x^0, y^0) < 0$ and $f''_{22}(x^0, y^0) < 0$ will ensure that $f(x, y)$ has a local maximum in the two particular directions through (x^0, y^0) that happen to be parallel to the x-axis and the y-axis. Note, however, that the signs of $f''_{11}(x^0, y^0)$ and $f''_{22}(x^0, y^0)$ on their own do not reveal much about the behaviour of the graph of $z = f(x, y)$ when we move away from (x^0, y^0) in directions other than these two particular directions. Example 17.3.1 illustrates the difficulty. Thus, in order to have a correct second-derivative test for functions f of two variables, it turns out that the mixed second-order partial $f''_{12}(x^0, y^0)$ must also be considered, just as it had to be in Section 17.2.

For a function $f(x)$ of one variable defined on an interval I, let x^0 be a critical point in the interior of I. Now Theorem 9.2.2 implies that if the weak inequality $f''(x) \leq 0$ holds throughout I, then f is concave and so x^0 is a maximum point. On the other hand, Theorem 9.6.2 implies that if f is twice continuously differentiable near x^0 and the strict inequality $f''(x^0) < 0$ holds at the critical point, then x^0 is a strict local maximum point. There are obvious corresponding tests for x^0 to be a minimum point, or local minimum point.

Next, consider a function $f(x, y)$ of two variables defined on a set S in the plane, and let (x^0, y^0) be a critical point in the interior of S. Now, provided the domain S is convex, Theorem 17.2.2 implies that if the three weak inequalities $f''_{11}(x, y) \leq 0, f''_{22}(x, y) \leq 0$, and $f''_{11}(x, y)f''_{22}(x, y) - [f''_{12}(x, y)]^2 \geq 0$ all hold throughout S, then f is concave and so (x^0, y^0), is a maximum point. As ever, there is an obvious corresponding test for a minimum point. Now, as for functions of one variable, by making the inequalities strict but requiring them to hold only at the critical point, we arrive at conditions which are sufficient for that point to be a strict local maximum or minimum point. This is implied by the following theorem:

THEOREM 17.3.1 (SECOND-DERIVATIVE TEST FOR LOCAL EXTREMA)

Suppose that the function $f(x, y)$ is C^2 in its domain S. Let (x^0, y^0) be an interior critical point of S, and define

$$A = f''_{11}(x^0, y^0), \; B = f''_{12}(x^0, y^0), \; \text{and} \; C = f''_{22}(x^0, y^0)$$

Now:

(a) if $A < 0$ and $AC - B^2 > 0$, then (x^0, y^0) is a strict local maximum point.

(b) if $A > 0$ and $AC - B^2 > 0$, then (x^0, y^0) is a strict local minimum point.

(c) if $AC - B^2 < 0$, then (x^0, y^0) is a saddle point.

(d) if $AC - B^2 = 0$, then (x^0, y^0) could be a local maximum, a local minimum, or a saddle point.

Note that the condition $AC - B^2 > 0$ in parts (a) and (b) implies that $AC > B^2 \geq 0$, and so $AC > 0$. It follows that either A and C are both positive, or both negative. So the inequality $C < 0$ in part (a) or $C > 0$ in part (b) is included indirectly in the other assumptions.

The conditions in parts (a), (b), and (c) are usually called local *second-order conditions*. Note that these are sufficient conditions for a critical point to be, respectively, a *strict local* maximum point, a *strict local* minimum point, or a saddle point. None of these conditions is necessary. The results in Exercise 4 will confirm part (d), because they show that a critical point where $AC - B^2 = 0$ can fall into any of the other three categories. The second-derivative test is inconclusive in this case.

The proof of Theorem 17.3.1 is discussed at the end of this section.

EXAMPLE 17.3.2   Find the critical points and classify them when $f(x, y) = x^3 - x^2 - y^2 + 8$.

Solution: The critical points must satisfy the two equations $f_1'(x, y) = 3x^2 - 2x = 0$ and $f_2'(x, y) = -2y = 0$. Because $3x^2 - 2x = x(3x - 2)$, we see that the first equation has the solutions $x = 0$ and $x = 2/3$. The second equation has the solution $y = 0$. We conclude that $(0, 0)$ and $(2/3, 0)$ are the only critical points.

Furthermore, $f_{11}''(x, y) = 6x - 2$, $f_{12}''(x, y) = 0$, and $f_{22}''(x, y) = -2$. Using the notation A, B, and C as defined in Theorem 17.3.1, it is convenient to classify the critical points in a table like the following:

(x, y)	A	B	C	$AC - B^2$	Type of point
$(0, 0)$	-2	0	-2	4	Local maximum point
$(2/3, 0)$	2	0	-2	-4	Saddle point

EXAMPLE 17.3.3   Consider Example 17.1.3 and suppose that the production function F is twice differentiable. Define

$$\Delta(K, L) = F_{KK}''(K, L)F_{LL}''(K, L) - \left[F_{KL}''(K, L)\right]^2$$

Then let (K^*, L^*) be an input pair satisfying the first-order conditions $(*)$ in the example.

(a) Prove that if

$$F_{KK}''(K, L) \leq 0, \ F_{LL}''(K, L) \leq 0 \ \text{and} \ \Delta(K, L) \geq 0 \ \text{for all} \ K \geq 0 \ \text{and} \ L \geq 0 \quad (*)$$

so that the production function F is concave, then (K^*, L^*) maximizes profit.

(b) Prove also that if

$$F_{KK}''(K^*, L^*) < 0 \ \text{and} \ \Delta(K^*, L^*) > 0 \quad (17.3.1)$$

then (K^*, L^*) is a strict local maximum for the profit function.

Solution:

(a) The second-order partials of the profit function are:

$$\pi_{KK}''(K, L) = pF_{KK}''(K, L); \quad \pi_{KL}''(K, L) = pF_{KL}''(K, L); \quad \pi_{LL}''(K, L) = pF_{LL}''(K, L)$$

Since $p > 0$, the conclusion follows from part (a) in Theorem 17.2.2.

(b) In this case the conclusion follows from part (a) in Theorem 17.3.1.

On Proving the Second-Derivative Test

We now want to discuss how one might prove the sufficiency Theorem 17.3.1. The discussion will build on the corresponding Theorem 9.6.2, which applies when f is a function of only one variable. Before doing so, however, it is instructive to develop some intuition by determining some *necessary conditions* for a critical point to be a local extremum.

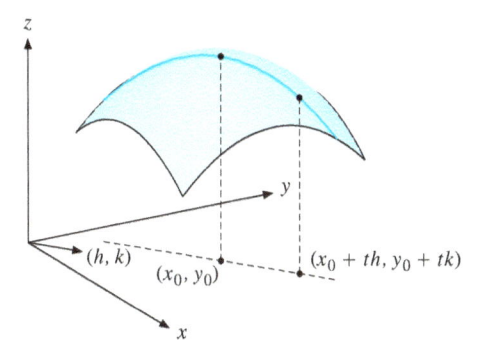

Figure 17.3.3 The second-derivative test

Let $z = f(x, y)$ be the C^2 function graphed in Fig. 17.3.3, with (x^0, y^0) as a local maximum point in the interior of the domain of f. Take any fixed real numbers h and k satisfying $(h, k) \neq (0, 0)$. Then whenever $|t|$ is sufficiently small, the function f will be defined at $(x^0 + th, y^0 + tk)$. So for all small $|t|$, we can define the function g of one variable by

$$g(t) = f(x^0 + th, y^0 + tk)$$

This function tells us the value of f as one moves away from (x^0, y^0) a small distance in the direction (h, k) when $t > 0$, or in the reverse direction $(-h, -k)$ when $t < 0$.

Following the application of the chain rule that was used to derive Eq. (15.8.3) from the definition (15.8.2), it follows that the first and second derivatives of $g(t)$ both exist for all small $|t|$. Moreover, they can be calculated as

$$g'(t) = f_1'(x^0 + th, y^0 + tk)\, h + f_2'(x^0 + th, y^0 + tk)\, k$$
$$g''(t) = f_{11}''(x^0 + th, y^0 + tk)\, h^2 + 2 f_{12}''(x^0 + th, y^0 + tk)\, hk + f_{22}''(x^0 + th, y^0 + tk)\, k^2$$

In particular, the second derivative of g at $t = 0$ is

$$g''(0) = f_{11}''(x^0, y^0)\, h^2 + 2 f_{12}''(x^0, y^0)\, hk + f_{22}''(x^0, y^0)\, k^2 \qquad (17.3.2)$$

Now, if f has a local maximum at (x^0, y^0), then $g(t)$ must certainly have a local maximum at $t = 0$. Because $g(t)$ is a C^2 function for small $|t|$, it follows from Theorem 9.1.1 and Eq. (9.6.3) that the necessary conditions $g'(0) = 0$ and $g''(0) \leq 0$ must hold. So if f is to have a local maximum at (x^0, y^0), then the expression in Eq. (17.3.2) must be nonpositive for all choices of the pair (h, k).

Having obtained a *necessary* condition for f to have a local maximum at (x^0, y^0), we now look for *sufficient* conditions. For the one-variable case, we know from part (i) in

Theorem 9.6.2 that the conditions $g'(0) = 0$ and $g''(0) < 0$ are sufficient for g to have a strict local maximum at $t = 0$. So the following conjecture seems plausible:

If $f_1'(x^0, y^0) = f_2'(x^0, y^0) = 0$ and the expression for $g''(0)$ in (17.3.2) is negative for all directions $(h, k) \neq (0, 0)$, then (x^0, y^0) is a (strict) local maximum point for f.

This turns out to be correct, as will be proved in FMEA. Exercise 6, however, shows that the expression in (17.3.2) really must be negative for *all* directions (h, k), without exception. Relying on this conjecture, we can prove part (a) of Theorem 17.3.1 by considering the quadratic form $Ah^2 + 2Bhk + Ck^2$ and invoking condition (13.12.7) for it to be negative definite. It follows straight away that $A < 0$ and $AC - B^2 > 0$ together imply

$$Ah^2 + 2Bhk + Ck^2 < 0 \quad \text{for all} \quad (h, k) \neq (0, 0) \tag{17.3.3}$$

This is what we needed to prove.

EXERCISES FOR SECTION 17.3

1. Consider the function f defined for all (x, y) by $f(x, y) = 5 - x^2 + 6x - 2y^2 + 8y$.

   (a) Find all its partial derivatives of the first and second order.

   (b) Find the only critical point and classify it by using the second-derivative test. What does Theorem 17.2.2 tell us?

2. Consider the function f defined for all (x, y) by $f(x, y) = x^2 + 2xy^2 + 2y^2$.

   (a) Find all its partial derivatives of the first and second order.

   (b) Show that its critical points are $(0, 0)$, $(-1, 1)$ and $(-1, -1)$, and classify them.

SM 3. Let f be the function of two variables which, for each pair (x, y) in the plane, is given by $f(x, y; a) = (x^2 - axy)e^y$, where $a \neq 0$ is a parameter.

   (a) For each $a \neq 0$, find the critical points of f and decide for each of them if it is a local maximum point, a local minimum point, or a saddle point.

   (b) For each $a \neq 0$, let $(x^*(a), y^*(a))$ denote the critical point that satisfies $x^*(a) \neq 0$, and then define the function f^* so that $f^*(a) = f(x^*(a), y^*(a); a)$. Show that f^* is differentiable, then find $df^*(a)/da$. Show too that, if we regard f as a function of (x, y, a), then

   $$f_3'(x^*(a), y^*(a); a) = \frac{df^*(a)}{da}$$

4. Consider the three functions: (i) $z = -x^4 - y^4$; (ii) $z = x^4 + y^4$; and (iii) $z = x^3 + y^3$.

   (a) Prove that the origin is a critical point for each one of these functions, and that using the notation of Theorem 17.3.1, in each case one has $AC - B^2 = 0$ at the origin.

(b) By studying each of the three functions directly, prove that the origin is respectively a maximum point for (i), a minimum point for (ii), and a saddle point for (iii).

(SM) 5. [HARDER] Consider the function $f(x, y) = \ln(1 + x^2 y)$.

   (a) Find the domain on which it is defined.

   (b) Prove that its critical points are all the points on the y-axis.

   (c) Show that the second-derivative test fails to identify any local maxima or minima.

   (d) Classify the critical points by looking directly at the sign of $f(x, y)$.

6. [HARDER] Consider the function $f(x, y) = (y - x^2)(y - 2x^2)$ defined on the whole xy-plane.

   (a) Show that the graph of f intersects the xy-plane $z = 0$ in two parabolas.

   (b) In the xy-plane, draw the regions where f is negative, and where f is positive.

   (c) Show that $(0, 0)$ is the only critical point, and that it is a saddle point.

   (d) For any fixed direction vector $(h, k) \neq (0, 0)$, define $g(t) = f(th, tk)$ for all real t. Show that the function g has a local minimum at $t = 0$, whatever the direction (h, k) may be.[4]

17.4 Linear Models with Quadratic Objectives

In this section we consider some other interesting economic applications of optimization theory when there are two variables. Versions of the first example have already appeared in Example 17.1.5 and Exercise 17.2.4.

EXAMPLE 17.4.1 (**Discriminating Monopolist**). Consider a firm that sells the same product in two isolated geographical areas. Unless prohibited from doing so, it may want to charge different prices in the two different areas because what is sold in one area cannot easily be resold in the other.[5] Suppose that such a firm also has some monopoly power to influence the different prices it faces in the two separate markets by adjusting the quantity it sells in each. Economists generally use the term "discriminating monopolist" to describe a firm having this power.

Faced with two such isolated markets, the discriminating monopolist faces two independent demand curves. Suppose that, in inverse form, these are

$$P_1 = a_1 - b_1 Q_1 \quad \text{and} \quad P_2 = a_2 - b_2 Q_2 \qquad (17.4.1)$$

---

[4] Thus, although $(0, 0)$ is a saddle point, the function has a local minimum at the origin in every direction.

[5] As an example, it seems that express mail or courier services find it possible to charge much higher prices in Europe than they can in North America. An even more prominent example is that pharmaceutical firms often charge much more for the same medication in the USA than they do in Europe or Canada.

for market areas 1 and 2, respectively. Suppose too that the total cost is proportional to total production, so $C(Q) = \alpha Q$ for some positive constant α.[6] We assume that the other four parameters a_1, a_2, b_1, b_2 are also positive, with a_1 and a_2 both greater than α.

As a function of Q_1 and Q_2, total profits are

$$\pi(Q_1, Q_2) = P_1 Q_1 + P_2 Q_2 - C(Q_1 + Q_2)$$
$$= (a_1 - b_1 Q_1) Q_1 + (a_2 - b_2 Q_2) Q_2 - \alpha(Q_1 + Q_2)$$
$$= (a_1 - \alpha) Q_1 + (a_2 - \alpha) Q_2 - b_1 Q_1^2 - b_2 Q_2^2$$

The firm wants to find the values of $Q_1 \geq 0$ and $Q_2 \geq 0$ that maximize its profits. The first-order conditions are

$$\pi_1'(Q_1, Q_2) = (a_1 - \alpha) - 2b_1 Q_1 = 0 \quad \text{and} \quad \pi_2'(Q_1, Q_2) = (a_2 - \alpha) - 2b_2 Q_2 = 0$$

The solutions of these two equations are obviously

$$Q_1^* = (a_1 - \alpha)/2b_1 \quad \text{and} \quad Q_2^* = (a_2 - \alpha)/2b_2 \tag{17.4.2}$$

Our assumptions on parameter values imply that Q_1^* and Q_2^* are both positive.

Furthermore, one has $\pi_{11}''(Q_1, Q_2) = -2b_1$, $\pi_{12}''(Q_1, Q_2) = 0$, and $\pi_{22}''(Q_1, Q_2) = -2b_2$. Hence, for all (Q_1, Q_2), it follows that

$$\pi_{11}'' \leq 0, \ \pi_{22}'' \leq 0, \quad \text{and} \quad \pi_{11}'' \pi_{22}'' - (\pi_{12}'')^2 = 4 b_1 b_2 \geq 0$$

At the critical point both Q_1^* and Q_2^* are positive, so (Q_1^*, Q_2^*) is an interior point in the domain of π. Hence, by Theorem 17.2.2, the pair (Q_1^*, Q_2^*) really does maximize profits.

The corresponding prices can be found by inserting these values into (17.4.1) to get

$$P_1^* = a_1 - b_1 Q_1^* = \tfrac{1}{2}(a_1 + \alpha) \quad \text{and} \quad P_2^* = a_2 - b_2 Q_2^* = \tfrac{1}{2}(a_2 + \alpha) \tag{17.4.3}$$

The maximum profit is

$$\pi^* = \frac{(a_1 - \alpha)^2}{4 b_1} + \frac{(a_2 - \alpha)^2}{4 b_2}$$

Given our assumptions that $a_1 > \alpha$ and $a_2 > \alpha$, both P_1^* and P_2^* exceed α. This implies that there is no "dumping", with the price in one market less than the cost α. Nor is there any "cross-subsidy", with the losses due to dumping in one market being subsidized out of profits in the other market. It is notable that the optimal prices are independent of b_1 and b_2. More important, note that the prices are *not* the same in the two markets, except in the special case when $a_1 = a_2$. Indeed, $P_1^* > P_2^*$ if and only if $a_1 > a_2$. This says that the price is higher in the market where consumers are willing to pay a higher price for each unit when the quantity is close to zero.

---

[6] It is true that this cost function neglects transport costs. But the point to be made is that, even though supplies to the two areas are perfect substitutes in production, the monopolist will generally be able to earn higher profits by charging different prices, if this is allowed.

EXAMPLE 17.4.2

Suppose that the monopolist in Example 17.4.1 faces the demand functions $P_1 = 100 - Q_1$ and $P_2 = 80 - Q_2$, and that its cost function is $C(Q) = 6Q$.

(a) How much should be sold in the two markets to maximize profits? What are the corresponding prices?

(b) How much profit is lost if it becomes illegal to discriminate?

(c) The authorities impose a tax of τ per unit sold in the first market. Discuss the consequences.

Solution:

(a) This is Example 17.4.1 with specific numerical parameter values $a_1 = 100$, $a_2 = 80$, $b_1 = b_2 = 1$, and $\alpha = 6$. Inserting these values into Eqs (17.4.2) and (17.4.3) gives the numerical answers

$$Q_1^* = (100-6)/2 = 47, \quad Q_2^* = 37, \quad P_1^* = \tfrac{1}{2}(100+6) = 53, \quad \text{and} \quad P_2^* = 43$$

The corresponding profit is $P_1^* Q_1^* + P_2^* Q_2^* - 6(Q_1^* + Q_2^*) = 3578$.

(b) If price discrimination is not permitted, so $P_1 = P_2 = P$, then the demand equations (17.4.1) imply that $Q_1 = 100 - P$ and $Q_2 = 80 - P$. Then total demand is given by $Q = Q_1 + Q_2 = 180 - 2P$, implying that $P = 90 - \tfrac{1}{2}Q$. So profits become

$$\pi = \left(90 - \tfrac{1}{2}Q\right)Q - 6Q = 84Q - \tfrac{1}{2}Q^2$$

This has a maximum at $Q = 84$. Then $P = 48$. The corresponding profit has become $\pi = 3528$, so the loss in profit is $3578 - 3528 = 50$.

(c) With the introduction of the tax on sales in the first market, the new profit function is

$$\hat{\pi} = (100 - Q_1)Q_1 + (80 - Q_2)Q_2 - 6(Q_1 + Q_2) - \tau Q_1$$

It is easy to see that this has a maximum at $\hat{Q}_1 = 47 - \tfrac{1}{2}\tau$ and $\hat{Q}_2 = 37$, with corresponding prices $\hat{P}_1 = 53 + \tfrac{1}{2}\tau$ and $\hat{P}_2 = 43$. The tax therefore has no influence on sales in market 2. In market 1, however, the amount sold falls while the price rises. The optimal profit π^* is easily worked out: it equals

$$(53 + \tfrac{1}{2}\tau)(47 - \tfrac{1}{2}\tau) + 43 \cdot 37 - 6(84 - \tfrac{1}{2}\tau) - \tau(47 - \tfrac{1}{2}\tau) = 3578 - 47\tau + \tfrac{1}{4}\tau^2$$

So, compared to (a), introducing the tax makes the profit fall by $47\tau - \tfrac{1}{4}\tau^2$. The authorities who control market 1 receive an amount of tax revenue given by

$$T = \tau \hat{Q}_1 = \tau(47 - \tfrac{1}{2}\tau) = 47\tau - \tfrac{1}{2}\tau^2$$

This shows that profits fall by $\tfrac{1}{4}\tau^2$ more than the tax revenue. The amount $\tfrac{1}{4}\tau^2$ represents the so-called *deadweight loss* from the tax.

A monopolistic firm faces a downward-sloping demand curve. A *discriminating monopolist* such as in Example 17.4.1 faces separate downward-sloping demand curves in two or more isolated markets. A *monopsonistic firm*, on the other hand, faces an upward-sloping supply curve for one or more of its factors of production. Then, by definition, a *discriminating monopsonist* faces two or more upward-sloping supply curves for different kinds of the same input, such as workers of different race or gender. With good reason, discrimination by race or gender has been made illegal in many countries. Economists, however, should understand the possible implications for wages and jobs of failing to institute and enforce regulations that prohibit such discrimination.

EXAMPLE 17.4.3 (**Discriminating Monopsonist**). Consider a firm that uses quantities L_1 and L_2 of two kinds of labour as its only inputs in order to produce output Q according to the simple production function $Q = L_1 + L_2$. Thus, both output and labour supply are measured so that each unit of labour produces one unit of output. Note especially how the two kinds of labour are essentially indistinguishable, because each unit of each type makes an equal contribution to the firm's output. Suppose, however, that there are two segmented labour markets, with different inverse supply functions specifying the wage that must be paid to attract a given labour supply. Specifically, suppose that

$$w_1 = \alpha_1 + \beta_1 L_1 \quad \text{and} \quad w_2 = \alpha_2 + \beta_2 L_2$$

where the parameters α_1, β_1, α_2, and β_2 are all positive. Assume moreover that the firm is competitive in its output market, taking price P as fixed. Then the firm's profits are

$$\begin{aligned}\pi(L_1, L_2) &= PQ - w_1 L_1 - w_2 L_2 \\ &= P(L_1 + L_2) - (\alpha_1 + \beta_1 L_1)L_1 - (\alpha_2 + \beta_2 L_2)L_2 \\ &= (P - \alpha_1)L_1 - \beta_1 L_1^2 + (P - \alpha_2)L_2 - \beta_2 L_2^2\end{aligned}$$

The firm wants to maximize profits. The first-order conditions for it to do so are

$$\pi_1'(L_1, L_2) = (P - \alpha_1) - 2\beta_1 L_1 = 0 \quad \text{and} \quad \pi_2'(L_1, L_2) = (P - \alpha_2) - 2\beta_2 L_2 = 0$$

These have the solutions

$$L_1^* = \frac{P - \alpha_1}{2\beta_1} \quad \text{and} \quad L_2^* = \frac{P - \alpha_2}{2\beta_2}$$

Provided that $P > \alpha_1$ and $P > \alpha_2$, it is easy to see that the sufficient conditions in Theorem 13.2.1 are satisfied, so that L_1^*, L_2^* really do maximize profits. The maximum profit is

$$\pi^* = \frac{(P - \alpha_1)^2}{4\beta_1} + \frac{(P - \alpha_2)^2}{4\beta_2}$$

The corresponding wages are

$$w_1^* = \alpha_1 + \beta_1 L_1^* = \tfrac{1}{2}(P + \alpha_1) \quad \text{and} \quad w_2^* = \alpha_2 + \beta_2 L_2^* = \tfrac{1}{2}(P + \alpha_2)$$

Hence, $w_1^* = w_2^*$ only if $\alpha_1 = \alpha_2$. Generally, the wage is higher for the type of labour that demands a higher wage for very low levels of labour supply. Perhaps this is the type of labour that can find better job prospects elsewhere.

EXAMPLE 17.4.4

(Econometrics: Linear Regression II). Suppose it is thought that one economic variable y depends upon another economic variable x. Suppose moreover that we have observations (x_t, y_t) of both variables at times $t = 1, 2, \ldots, T$. Under the assumption that both variables have zero arithmetical mean, in Example 9.3.1 we introduced the technique of *linear regression* that allows economists to estimate a function of the form $y_t = \beta x_t$. If the variables in question have a nonzero mean, however, the technique of linear regression seeks to fit to the data a linear function

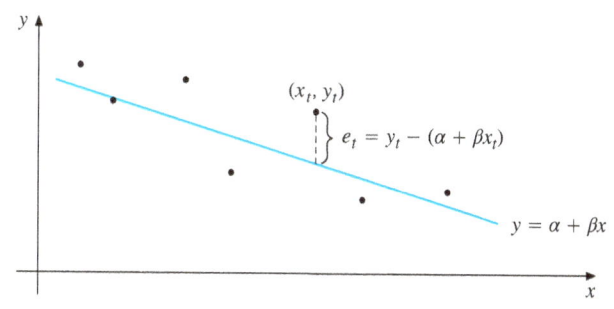

$$y = \alpha + \beta x \qquad (*)$$

Figure 17.4.1 Linear regression

Figure 17.4.1 shows seven data points, as well as a line that fits them as closely as possible, in some sense. Indeed, as the figure suggests, regardless of how α and β are chosen in Eq. $(*)$, one has to allow an error term. This leads us to consider instead the equation

$$y_t = \alpha + \beta x_t + e_t, \quad \text{for} \quad t = 1, 2, \ldots, T$$

In Example 9.3.1 we considered the quadratic loss function that equals the mean (or average) square error. In this example the corresponding loss becomes

$$L(\alpha, \beta) = \frac{1}{T}\sum_{t=1}^{T} e_t^2 = \frac{1}{T}\sum_{t=1}^{T}(y_t - \alpha - \beta x_t)^2 \qquad (**)$$

Expanding the square now gives the following quadratic function of α and β:

$$L(\alpha, \beta) = \frac{1}{T}\sum_{t=1}^{T}\left(y_t^2 + \alpha^2 + \beta^2 x_t^2 - 2\alpha y_t - 2\beta x_t y_t + 2\alpha\beta x_t\right)$$

Let us denote by $\mu_x = \frac{1}{T}\sum_{t=1}^{T} x_t$ and $\mu_y = \frac{1}{T}\sum_{t=1}^{T} y_t$ the arithmetic means of the two variables, as defined in Example 2.10.2. Let us also extend the definition of their *statistical variances* and *covariance*, respectively, so that they become

$$\sigma_{xx} = \frac{1}{T}\sum_{t=1}^{T}(x_t - \mu_x)^2, \quad \sigma_{yy} = \frac{1}{T}\sum_{t=1}^{T}(y_t - \mu_y)^2, \quad \text{and} \quad \sigma_{xy} = \frac{1}{T}\sum_{t=1}^{T}(x_t - \mu_x)(y_t - \mu_y)$$

Assume once again that $\sigma_{xx} > 0$. Using the result in Example 2.10.2, we have

$$\sigma_{xx} = \frac{1}{T}\sum_{t=1}^{T} x_t^2 - \mu_x^2 \quad \text{and} \quad \sigma_{yy} = \frac{1}{T}\sum_{t=1}^{T} y_t^2 - \mu_y^2$$

You should then verify that, similarly,

$$\sigma_{xy} = \frac{1}{T}\sum_{t=1}^{T} x_t y_t - \mu_x \mu_y$$

With this notation, the expression for $L(\alpha, \beta)$ becomes

$$L(\alpha, \beta) = (\sigma_{yy} + \mu_y^2) + \alpha^2 + \beta^2(\sigma_{xx} + \mu_x^2) - 2\alpha\mu_y - 2\beta(\sigma_{xy} + \mu_x\mu_y) + 2\alpha\beta\mu_x$$
$$= \alpha^2 + \mu_y^2 + \beta^2\mu_x^2 - 2\alpha\mu_y - 2\beta\mu_x\mu_y + 2\alpha\beta\mu_x + \beta^2\sigma_{xx} - 2\beta\sigma_{xy} + \sigma_{yy}$$

The first-order conditions for a minimum of $L(\alpha, \beta)$ take the form

$$L_1'(\alpha, \beta) = 2\alpha - 2\mu_y + 2\beta\mu_x = 0$$
$$L_2'(\alpha, \beta) = 2\beta\mu_x^2 - 2\mu_x\mu_y + 2\alpha\mu_x + 2\beta\sigma_{xx} - 2\sigma_{xy} = 0$$

Note that $L_2'(\alpha, \beta) = \mu_x L_1'(\alpha, \beta) + 2\beta\sigma_{xx} - 2\sigma_{xy}$. So the unique critical point of $L(\alpha, \beta)$ occurs at $(\hat{\alpha}, \hat{\beta})$, where

$$\hat{\beta} = \frac{\sigma_{xy}}{\sigma_{xx}} \quad \text{and} \quad \hat{\alpha} = \mu_y - \hat{\beta}\mu_x = \mu_y - \frac{\sigma_{xy}}{\sigma_{xx}}\mu_x \qquad (***)$$

Furthermore, $L_{11}'' = 2$, $L_{12}'' = 2\mu_x$, $L_{22}'' = 2\mu_x^2 + 2\sigma_{xx}$. Thus $L_{11}'' \geq 0$, $L_{22}'' \geq 0$, and

$$L_{11}'' L_{22}'' - (L_{12}'')^2 = 2(2\mu_x^2 + 2\sigma_{xx}) - (2\mu_x)^2 = 4\sigma_{xx} = \frac{4}{T}\sum_{t=1}^{T}(x_t - \mu_x)^2 \geq 0$$

We conclude that the conditions in part (b) of Theorem 17.2.2 are satisfied, and therefore the pair $(\hat{\alpha}, \hat{\beta})$ given by $(***)$ minimizes $L(\alpha, \beta)$. The problem is then completely solved:

The straight line that best fits the observations $(x_1, y_1), (x_2, y_2), \ldots, (x_T, y_T)$, in the sense of minimizing the mean square error in $(**)$, is $y = \hat{\alpha} + \hat{\beta}x$, where the estimated coefficients $\hat{\alpha}$ and $\hat{\beta}$ are given by $(***)$.

Note in particular that this estimated straight line passes through the mean (μ_x, μ_y) of the observed pairs (x_t, y_t), $t = 1, \ldots, T$. Also, with a little bit of tedious algebra we obtain

$$L(\alpha, \beta) = (\alpha + \beta\mu_x - \mu_y)^2 + \sigma_{xx}\left(\beta - \frac{\sigma_{xy}}{\sigma_{xx}}\right)^2 + \frac{\sigma_{xx}\sigma_{yy} - \sigma_{xy}^2}{\sigma_{xx}}$$

The first two terms on the right are always nonnegative. Moreover, with $\alpha = \hat{\alpha}$ and $\beta = \hat{\beta}$ both these terms are zero. This confirms that the pair $(\hat{\alpha}, \hat{\beta})$ really does minimize $L(\alpha, \beta)$.

EXERCISES FOR SECTION 17.4

1. Suppose that the monopolist in Example 17.4.1 faces the two inverse demand functions $P_1 = 200 - 2Q_1$ and $P_2 = 180 - 4Q_2$, and that the cost function is $C = 20(Q_1 + Q_2)$.

    (a) How much should be sold in the two markets to maximize total profit? What are the corresponding prices?

SECTION 17.4 / LINEAR MODELS WITH QUADRATIC OBJECTIVES 711

(b) How much profit is lost if it becomes illegal to discriminate?

(c) Discuss the consequences of imposing a tax of $\tau = 5$ per unit on the product sold in market 1.

(SM) 2. A firm produces and sells a product in two separate markets. When the price in market 1 is P_1 per ton, and the price in market 2 is P_2 per ton, the demand in tons per week in the two markets are, respectively, $Q_1 = \alpha_1 - \beta_1 P_1$ and $Q_2 = \alpha_2 - \beta_2 P_2$. The cost function is $C(Q_1, Q_2) = \gamma + \delta(Q_1 + Q_2)$. All constants are positive.

(a) Find the firm's profit as a function of the prices P_1 and P_2, and then find the pair (P_1^*, P_2^*) that maximizes profit.

(b) Suppose it becomes unlawful to discriminate by price, so that the firm must charge the same price in the two markets. What price $\hat{P}$ will now maximize profit?

(c) In the case $\delta = 0$, find the firm's loss of profit if it has to charge the same price in both markets. Comment.

3. In Example 17.4.1, discuss the effects of a tax of τ per unit imposed on the output Q_1 in market 1.

(SM) 4. The following table shows the Norwegian gross national product (GNP) and spending on foreign aid (FA) for the period 1970–1973, measured in millions of Norwegian crowns:

Year	1970	1971	1972	1973
GNP	79 835	89 112	97 339	110 156
FA	274	307	436	524

The growth of both GNP and FA was almost exponential during the period. Specifically, one has the approximation $\text{GNP} = Ae^{a(t-t_0)}$, with $t_0 = 1970$. Define $x = t - t_0$ and $b = \ln A$. Then taking natural logs gives $\ln(\text{GNP}) = ax + b$. On the basis of the table above, one gets the following

Year	1970	1971	1972	1973
$y = \ln(\text{GNP})$	11.29	11.40	11.49	11.61

(a) Using the method of least squares, determine the straight line $y = ax + b$ which best fits the data in the last table.

(b) Repeat the method above to estimate c and d, where $\ln(\text{FA}) = cx + d$.

(c) The Norwegian government had a stated goal of eventually giving 1% of its GNP as foreign aid. If the time trends of the two variables had continued as they did during the years 1970–1973, when would this goal have been reached?

(SM) 5. *(Duopoly)* Each of two firms A and B produces its own brand of a commodity such as mineral water in amounts denoted by x and y, which are sold at prices p and q per unit, respectively. Each firm determines its own price and produces exactly as much as is demanded. The demands for the two brands are given by

$$x = 29 - 5p + 4q \text{ and } y = 16 + 4p - 6q$$

Firm A has total costs $5 + x$, whereas firm B has total costs $3 + 2y$. (In the following, you may assume that the functions to be maximized achieve maxima at positive prices.)

(a) Initially, the two firms collude in order to maximize their combined profit, as one monopolist would. Find the prices (p, q), the production levels (x, y), and the total profit of the two firms A and B.

(b) Then an anti-trust authority prohibits collusion, leading each producer to maximize its own profit, taking the other's price as given. If q is fixed, how will A choose p as a function $p = p_A(q)$ of q? If p is fixed, how will B choose q as a function $q = q_B(p)$ of p?

(c) Under the assumptions in part (b), what pairs of prices (p, q) are possible? What are the production levels and profits in this case?

(d) Draw a diagram with p along the horizontal axis and q along the vertical axis, and draw the "reaction" curves $p_A(q)$ and $q_B(p)$. Show on the diagram how the two firms' prices change over time if A breaks the cooperation first by maximizing its profit, taking B's initial price as fixed, then B answers by maximizing its profit with A's price fixed, then A responds, and so on.

17.5 The Extreme Value Theorem

As with functions of one variable, it is easy to find examples of functions of several variables that do not have any maximum or minimum points. But the extreme value Theorem 9.4.1 provides very useful sufficient conditions which ensure that extreme points do exist for functions of one variable. The theorem can be directly generalized to functions of several variables. Before formulating the extreme value theorem for many variables, however, we should recall the key concepts of open and closed sets, as well as of interior and boundary points. These were introduced in Section 14.8 and illustrated in Fig. 14.8.4 which, for convenience, is reproduced below as Fig. 17.5.1.

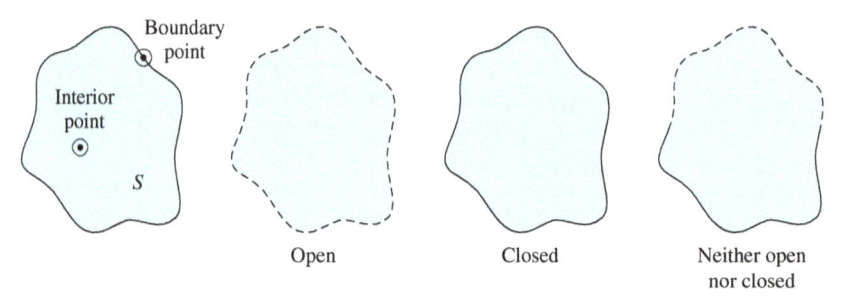

Figure 17.5.1 Open and closed sets

In many of the optimization problems considered in economics, sets are defined by one or more inequalities. Then boundary points occur where one or more of these inequalities are satisfied with equality. For instance, provided that p, q, and m are positive parameters, there is a closed "budget" set of points (x, y) that satisfy the inequalities

$$px + qy \leq m, \quad x \geq 0, \quad y \geq 0 \qquad (*)$$

This set is a triangle, as was shown in Fig. 4.4.12. Its boundary consists of the three sides of the triangle. Each of the three sides corresponds to having one of the inequalities in $(*)$ be satisfied with equality. On the other hand, the set that results from replacing $\leq$ by $<$ and each $\geq$ by $>$ in $(*)$ is open.

In general, suppose that $g(x, y)$ is a continuous function and c is a real number. Then the three sets

$$\{(x, y) : g(x, y) \geq c\}, \quad \{(x, y) : g(x, y) \leq c\}, \quad \{(x, y) : g(x, y) = c\}$$

with weak inequality signs are all closed. But the corresponding three sets

$$\{(x, y) : g(x, y) > c\}, \quad \{(x, y) : g(x, y) < c\}, \quad \{(x, y) : g(x, y) \neq c\}$$

with strict inequality signs are all open.

A set S in the plane is said to be *bounded* if the whole set S can be enclosed within a sufficiently large circle of finite radius. The four sets in Fig. 17.5.1 and the budget triangle in Fig. 4.4.12 are all bounded. On the other hand, the set of all (x, y) satisfying $x \geq 1$ and $y \geq 0$, which appears in Fig. 14.1.1, is a closed but unbounded set. It is closed because it contains all its boundary points, but it is unbounded because no circle of finite radius can enclose all of it. This example shows that closed sets need not be bounded. The opposite implication does not hold either: for example, the fourth set depicted in Fig. 17.5.1 is neither open nor closed, but it is bounded. Importantly, a set in the plane that is both closed and bounded is often called *compact*.

We are now ready to formulate the main result in this section.

THEOREM 17.5.1 (THE EXTREME VALUE THEOREM)

Suppose that the function $f(x, y)$ is continuous throughout a nonempty, closed and bounded set S in the plane. Then there exist both a point (a, b) in S where f has a minimum and a point (c, d) in S where it has a maximum. That is, there exist points (a, b) and (c, d) in S such that, for all (x, y) in S, one has

$$f(a, b) \leq f(x, y) \leq f(c, d)$$

Theorem 17.5.1 is a pure existence theorem. It tells us nothing about *how to find* the extreme points. Its proof is found in most advanced calculus books and in FMEA. Also, even though the conditions of the theorem are *sufficient* to ensure the existence of extreme points, they are far from necessary. This is true even for functions of one variable, as was discussed in Section 9.4.

Finding Maxima and Minima

Sections 17.1 and 17.2 presented some simple cases where we could find the maximum and minimum points of a function of two variables by finding its critical points. The procedure set out in the following frame covers many additional optimization problems. Its parts (i) and (ii) usually find only a small finite set of interior and boundary points, respectively. Thus, the comparisons required in part (iii) should not be too onerous.

FINDING MAXIMA AND MINIMA

In order to find the maximum and minimum values of a differentiable function $f(x, y)$ defined on a closed, bounded set S in the plane:

(i) Find all critical points of f in the interior of S.

(ii) Find the largest value and the smallest value of f on the boundary of S, along with the associated points. If it is convenient, subdivide the boundary into several pieces and find the largest and smallest value on each piece.

(iii) Compute the values of the function at all the different points found in parts (i) and (ii). The largest function value is the maximum value of f in S; the smallest one is the minimum value of f in S.

We try out this procedure on the function whose graph is depicted in Fig. 17.5.2. Because the function is not specified analytically, we can give only a rough geometric argument. Note first that the function has a rectangular domain S of points (x, y) in the xy-plane.

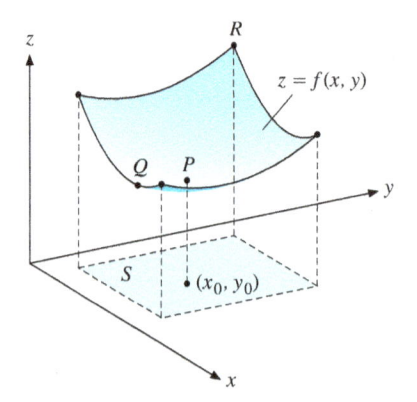

Figure 17.5.2 Finding maxima and minima

Part (i) of the procedure yields the only critical point of f, which is (x^0, y^0), corresponding to the point P of the graph. Moving onto part (ii) of the procedure, the boundary of S consists of four straight-line segments. The point R vertically above one corner point of S represents the maximum value of f along the boundary; similarly, Q represents the minimum value of f along the boundary. The only candidates for a maximum or minimum are, therefore, the three points P, Q, and R. Moving on to part (iii) of the procedure, we compare the values of f at these three points. The result that emerges is that P represents the minimum value of f in S, whereas R represents the maximum value.

As an aspiring economist, doubtless you will be glad to hear that most optimization problems in economics, especially those appearing in textbooks, rarely create enough difficulties to call for the full recipe. Usually, there is an interior optimum that can be found by equating all the first-order partial derivatives to zero. Conditions that are sufficient for this easier approach to work were already discussed in Section 17.2. Nevertheless, we consider an example of a harder problem which illustrates how the whole recipe is sometimes needed. This recipe is also needed in several of the examples and exercises in this section. In particular, Exercise 3 provides a practical economic application.

EXAMPLE 17.5.1   Find the extreme values for $f(x, y)$ defined over S, where

$$f(x, y) = x^2 + y^2 + y - 1 \quad \text{and} \quad S = \{(x, y) : x^2 + y^2 \leq 1\}$$

Solution: As shown in Fig. 17.5.3, the set S consists of all the points on or inside the circle of radius 1 centred at the origin. Because the function f is continuous and the domain S is closed and bounded, the extreme value theorem 17.5.1 implies that f attains both a maximum and a minimum over S.

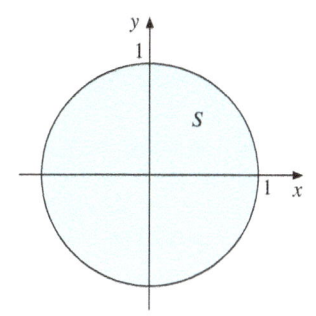

Figure 17.5.3 The domain in Example 17.5.1

Following part (i) of the preceding recipe, we start by finding all the critical points in the interior of S. These critical points satisfy the two equations

$$f_1'(x, y) = 2x = 0 \quad \text{and} \quad f_2'(x, y) = 2y + 1 = 0$$

It follows that $(x, y) = (0, -1/2)$ is the only critical point. Moreover, it is in the interior of S, with $f(0, -1/2) = -5/4$.

Moving on to part (ii) of the recipe, the boundary of S consists of the circle $x^2 + y^2 = 1$. Note that if (x, y) lies on this circle, then in particular both x and y lie in the interval $[-1, 1]$. Inserting $x^2 + y^2 = 1$ into the expression for $f(x, y)$ shows that, *along the boundary of S*, the value of f is given by the following function of one variable:

$$g(y) = 1 + y - 1 = y, \quad \text{defined for } y \in [-1, 1]$$

The maximum value of g is 1 at $y = 1$, where $x = 0$. The minimum value is -1 at $y = -1$, where again $x = 0$.

We have now found the only three possible candidates for extreme points, which are

$$(0, -\frac{1}{2}), \quad (0, 1), \quad \text{and} \quad (0, -1)$$

But $f(0, -\frac{1}{2}) = -5/4$, $f(0, 1) = 1$, and $f(0, -1) = -1$. We conclude that the *maximum value* of f in S is 1, which is attained at $(0, 1)$, whereas the *minimum value* is $-5/4$, which is attained at $(0, -\frac{1}{2})$.

EXERCISES FOR SECTION 17.5

1. Suppose $f(x, y) = 4x - 2x^2 - 2y^2$ is defined on the domain $S = \{(x, y) : x^2 + y^2 \leq 25\}$.

   (a) Compute $f_1'(x, y)$ and $f_2'(x, y)$, then find the only critical point for f.

   (b) Find the extreme points for f over S.

SM 2. Find the maximum and minimum points for the following two functions:

   (a) $f(x, y) = x^3 + y^3 - 9xy + 27$ defined on $S = \{(x, y) : 0 \leq x \leq 4 \text{ and } 0 \leq y \leq 4\}$.

   (b) $f(x, y) = x^2 + 2y^2 - x$ defined on $S = \{(x, y) : x^2 + y^2 \leq 1\}$.

SM 3. In one study of the quantities x and y of natural gas that Western Europe should import from Norway and Siberia, respectively, it was assumed that the benefits were given by the function

$$f(x, y) = 9x + 8y - 6(x + y)^2$$

Because of capacity constraints, the quantities x and y had to satisfy $0 \leq x \leq 5$ and $0 \leq y \leq 3$. Finally, for political reasons, it was felt that imports from Norway should not provide too small a fraction of total imports at the margin, so that $x \geq 2(y - 1)$. In the xy-plane, draw the set S of all points satisfying all the constraints. Then find the quantities that maximize the benefits, subject to these constraints.

4. Consider the function $f(x, y) = ax^2y + bxy + 2xy^2 + c$.

   (a) Determine values of the constants a, b, and c such that f has a local minimum at the point $(2/3, 1/3)$, with local minimum value $-1/9$.

   (b) With the values of a, b, and c found in part (a), find the maximum and minimum values of f over the set $S = \{(x, y) : x \geq 0, \ y \geq 0, \ 2x + y \leq 4\}$.

SM 5. Consider the function defined for all real x and y by $f(x, y) = xe^{-x}(y^2 - 4y)$.

   (a) Find all the critical points of f, then classify them by using the second-derivative test.

   (b) Show that f has neither a global maximum nor a global minimum.

   (c) Let $S = \{(x, y) : 0 \leq x \leq 5, \ 0 \leq y \leq 4\}$. Prove that f has global maximum and minimum points in S, then find them.

   (d) Find the slope of the tangent to the level curve $xe^{-x}(y^2 - 4y) = e - 4$ at the point where $x = 1$ and $y = 4 - e$.

6. Determine whether each of the following sets is open, closed, bounded, or compact:

   (a) $\{(x, y) : 5x^2 + 5y^2 \leq 9\}$ (b) $\{(x, y) : x^2 + y^2 > 9\}$ (c) $\{(x, y) : x^2 + y^2 \leq 9\}$

   (d) $\{(x, y) : 2x + 5y \geq 6\}$ (e) $\{(x, y) : 5x + 8y = 8\}$ (f) $\{(x, y) : 5x + 8y > 8\}$

7. [HARDER] Give an example of a discontinuous function g of one variable such that the set $\{x : g(x) \leq 1\}$ is not closed.

17.6 Functions of More Variables

So far, this chapter has considered optimization problems for functions of two variables. In order to be prepared to understand modern economic theory we need to extend the analysis to an arbitrary number of variables.

There are almost obvious extensions of the definitions of maximum and minimum points, extreme points, etc. Let $f(\mathbf{x}) = f(x_1, \ldots, x_n)$ be a function of n variables defined on set S in $\mathbb{R}^n$. Then $\mathbf{c} = (c_1, \ldots, c_n)$ is a (global) *maximum point* for f in S if

$$f(\mathbf{x}) \leq f(\mathbf{c}) \quad \text{for all } \mathbf{x} \text{ in } S \tag{17.6.1}$$

If this is the case, then $-f(\mathbf{x}) \geq -f(\mathbf{c})$ for all $\mathbf{x}$ in S. Thus, $\mathbf{c}$ maximizes f over S if and only if $\mathbf{c}$ minimizes $-f$ over S. We can use this simple observation to convert maximization problems into minimization problems and vice versa.[7]

The concepts of interior and boundary points, and of open, closed, and bounded sets, are also easy to generalize. First, define the *distance* between any two points $\mathbf{x} = (x_1, \ldots, x_n)$ and $\mathbf{y} = (y_1, \ldots, y_n)$ in $\mathbb{R}^n$ by

$$\|\mathbf{x} - \mathbf{y}\| = \sqrt{(x_1 - y_1)^2 + (x_2 - y_2)^2 + \cdots + (x_n - y_n)^2} \tag{17.6.2}$$

For $n = 1$, 2, and 3 this reduces to the concept of Euclidean distance that we discussed earlier. In particular, if $\mathbf{y} = \mathbf{0}$, then Eq. (17.6.2) reduces to

$$\|\mathbf{x}\| = \sqrt{x_1^2 + x_2^2 + \cdots + x_n^2}$$

This, of course, is the distance between $\mathbf{x}$ and the origin. The number $\|\mathbf{x}\|$ is also called the *norm* or *length* of the vector $\mathbf{x}$.

The *open ball* with centre at $\mathbf{a} = (a_1, \ldots, a_n)$ and radius r is the set of all points $\mathbf{x} = (x_1, \ldots, x_n)$ in $\mathbb{R}^n$ such that $\|\mathbf{x} - \mathbf{a}\| < r$. The definitions in Section 17.5 of interior point, open set, boundary point, closed set, bounded set, and compact set all become valid for sets in $\mathbb{R}^n$, provided that we replace the word "circle" by "ball". If A is an arbitrary set in $\mathbb{R}^n$, we define the *interior* of A as the set of interior points in A. If A is open, the interior of A is equal to the set itself.[8]

If $g(\mathbf{x}) = g(x_1, \ldots, x_n)$ is a continuous function, and c is a real number, then each of the three sets $\{\mathbf{x} : g(\mathbf{x}) \geq c\}$, $\{\mathbf{x} : g(\mathbf{x}) \leq c\}$, and $\{\mathbf{x} : g(\mathbf{x}) = c\}$ is closed. As in the case when $n = 1$ or 2, if $\geq$ is replaced by $>$, $\leq$ by $<$, or $=$ by $\neq$, then the corresponding set is open.

A *critical* (or *stationary*) *point* for a function of n variables is a point where all the first-order partial derivatives exist and equal 0. We have the following important generalization of Theorem 17.1.1:

THEOREM 17.6.1 (NECESSARY FIRST-ORDER CONDITIONS FOR AN INTERIOR EXTREMUM)

Suppose that the function f is defined in a set S in $\mathbb{R}^n$. Let $\mathbf{c} = (c_1, \ldots, c_n)$ be an interior point in the domain S where f is differentiable. A necessary condition

---

[7] Recall Fig. 9.1.1, which illustrates this for the case of functions of one variable.
[8] These topological definitions and results are dealt with in some detail in FMEA.

for **c** to be a maximum or minimum point for f is that **c** is a critical point for f. That is, the point $\mathbf{x} = \mathbf{c}$ must satisfy the n first-order conditions stating that, for each $i = 1, \ldots, n$,

$$f'_i(\mathbf{x}) = 0 \tag{17.6.3}$$

We already have everything we need to prove this theorem.

Proof: Let the point **c** be a maximum point for f in the interior of S at which f is differentiable. Given any fixed $i = 1, \ldots, n$, let $S_i(\mathbf{c})$ denote the set of all those real x such that $(c_1, \ldots, c_{i-1}, x, c_{i+1}, \ldots, c_n)$ belongs to S. On the domain $S_i(\mathbf{c})$, we can define the function

$$g(x) = f(c_1, \ldots, c_{i-1}, x, c_{i+1}, \ldots, c_n)$$

If $\mathbf{c} = (c_1, \ldots, c_n)$ is a maximum point for f, then the function g of one variable must attain a maximum at $x = c_i$. Because **c** is an interior point of S, it follows that c_i is also an interior point in $S_i(\mathbf{c})$. Hence, according to Theorem 9.1.1, we must have $g'(c_i) = 0$. But $g'(c_i) = f'_i(c_1, \ldots, c_n)$, so the conclusion follows. The argument when **c** is a minimum is identical.

In the space $\mathbb{R}^n$, a set S is said to be *bounded* if there exists a point $\mathbf{x}^0$ in $\mathbb{R}^n$ and a finite $r \geq 0$ such that S is a subset of the ball $\{\mathbf{x} \in \mathbb{R}^n : \|\mathbf{x} - \mathbf{x}^0\| \leq r\}$ with centre $\mathbf{x}^0$ and radius r. With this definition, the extreme value theorem is valid also for functions of n variables:

THEOREM 17.6.2 (THE EXTREME VALUE THEOREM)

Suppose that function f is continuous throughout a nonempty, closed and bounded set S in $\mathbb{R}^n$. Then there exist both a point **a** in S where f has a minimum and a point **c** in S where f has a maximum. That is, there exist **a** and **c** in S such that, for all **x** in S, one has

$$f(\mathbf{a}) \leq f(\mathbf{x}) \leq f(\mathbf{c})$$

If $f(\mathbf{x})$ is defined over a set S in $\mathbb{R}^n$, then the maximum and minimum points, if there are any, must lie either in the interior of S or on the boundary of S. According to Theorem 17.6.1, if f is differentiable, then any maximum or minimum point in the interior must satisfy the first-order conditions. Consequently, the recipe in Section 17.5 is also valid for any function of n variables defined on a closed and bounded set in $\mathbb{R}^n$.

Sufficient Conditions with Concavity or Convexity

In the first part of Section 17.2 we discussed how, for a function of two variables, concavity or convexity would serve as a sufficient condition for an interior critical point to be a maximum or minimum. We also presented second-order conditions for concavity or convexity. Here we present extensions of these results for functions of n variables, making free use of vector notation. The second-order conditions for functions of n variables do become considerably more complicated than they were for two variables.

Indeed, let $z = f(\mathbf{x})$ be a function of n variables defined on a convex set S in $\mathbb{R}^n$. At any interior point $\mathbf{x}^0$ of S where f is differentiable, consider its gradient vector

$$\nabla f(\mathbf{x}^0) = \big(f_1'(\mathbf{x}^0), f_2'(\mathbf{x}^0), \ldots, f_n'(\mathbf{x}^0)\big)$$

of first-order partial derivatives. Now, if f is concave, then $\nabla f(\mathbf{x}^0)$ is a supergradient vector, as specified in (15.8.13), in the sense that

$$f(\mathbf{x}) - f(\mathbf{x}^0) \leq \nabla f(\mathbf{x}^0) \cdot (\mathbf{x} - \mathbf{x}^0) \text{ for all } \mathbf{x} \text{ in } S \qquad (17.6.4)$$

On the other hand, if f is convex, then $\nabla f(\mathbf{x}^0)$ is a subgradient vector, as specified in (15.8.14), in the sense that (17.6.4) holds with $\leq$ replaced by $\geq$. These results lead immediately to the following extension of Theorem 17.2.1 when $\mathbf{x}^0$ is a critical point at which $\nabla f(\mathbf{x}^0) = \mathbf{0}$.

THEOREM 17.6.3 (CONCAVITY OR CONVEXITY AS A SUFFICIENT CONDITION)

Suppose that the function $z = f(\mathbf{x})$ of n variables is defined on a convex domain S in $\mathbb{R}^n$, and that $\mathbf{x}^0$ is an interior critical point in S. Then:

(a) in case the function f is concave, the point $\mathbf{x}^0$ is a maximum point;

(b) in case the function f is convex, the point $\mathbf{x}^0$ is a minimum point.

Second-Order Conditions for Concavity or Convexity

Following what we did in Section 17.2 for functions of two variables, here we look for conditions on the second-order partial derivatives of a function f of n variables which ensure that it is concave or convex, thus allowing Theorem 17.6.3 to be applied. Indeed, let $z = f(\mathbf{x})$ be any C^2 function of n variables defined on a convex domain S. In this case, Theorem 14.8.2 provided conditions on the Hessian matrix $\mathbf{f}''(\mathbf{x})$ of second-order partial derivatives at each interior point of S which ensure that f is concave or convex, possibly strictly. This result allows us to apply Theorem 17.6.3 in order to derive sufficient conditions for an interior critical point of f to be a maximum or minimum.

THEOREM 17.6.4 (SUFFICIENT CONDITIONS FOR A MAXIMUM OR MINIMUM)

Suppose that $z = f(\mathbf{x})$ is a C^2 function of n variables which is defined on a convex set S in $\mathbb{R}^n$, with Hessian matrix $\mathbf{f}''(\mathbf{x})$ at each point $\mathbf{x}$ in the interior of S. Let $\mathbf{x}^0$ be an interior critical point.

(a) If $\mathbf{f}''(\mathbf{x})$ is negative semi definite for all (x, y) in S, then f is concave, and $\mathbf{x}^0$ is a maximum point for $f(x, y)$ in S.

(b) If $\mathbf{f}''(\mathbf{x})$ is positive semi definite for all (x, y) in S, then f is convex, and $\mathbf{x}^0$ is a minimum point for $f(x, y)$ in S.

(c) If $\mathbf{f}''(\mathbf{x})$ is negative definite for all (x, y) in S, then f is strictly concave, and $\mathbf{x}^0$ is the unique maximum point for $f(x, y)$ in S.

(d) If $\mathbf{f}''(\mathbf{x})$ is positive definite for all (x, y) in S, then f is strictly convex, and $\mathbf{x}^0$ is the unique minimum point for $f(x, y)$ in S.

We note that Theorem 17.2.2 is a special case of this result because the conditions it uses for a function of two variables ensure that the 2×2 Hessian matrix is negative or positive semi definite. Another special case considered in Example 14.8.7 occurs when the function $z = f(\mathbf{x})$ is itself a quadratic form $\mathbf{x}'\mathbf{A}\mathbf{x}$ where $\mathbf{A}$ is a symmetric $n \times n$ matrix.

Conditions for Local Extreme Points

We began Section 17.3 with definitions for functions of two variables of local maximum, local minimum, strict local maximum, and strict local minimum points. We refrain from stating the obvious extensions of these definitions for functions of n variables. Instead we merely state extensions for functions of n variables of the results regarding local extreme points that were set out for functions of one variable in Section 9.6, and for functions of two variables in Theorem 17.3.1. These extensions rely on the definiteness properties of the Hessian matrix of second-order partial derivatives evaluated at the relevant critical point. Recall that these definiteness properties were defined and characterized in Section 13.12.

THEOREM 17.6.5 (SECOND-DERIVATIVE TESTS FOR LOCAL EXTREMA)

Suppose that the function $z = f(\mathbf{x})$ of n variables is C^2 in its domain S. Let $\mathbf{x}^0$ be an interior critical point of S, where the $n \times n$ Hessian matrix is $\mathbf{f}''(\mathbf{x}^0)$. Now:

(a) If $\mathbf{f}''(\mathbf{x}^0)$ is negative definite, then $\mathbf{x}^0$ is a strict local maximum point.

(b) If $\mathbf{f}''(\mathbf{x}^0)$ is positive definite, then $\mathbf{x}^0$ is a strict local minimum point.

(c) If $\mathbf{f}''(\mathbf{x}^0)$ is either negative semi definite or positive semi definite, then $\mathbf{x}^0$ could be a local maximum, a local minimum, or a saddle point.

(d) If $\mathbf{f}''(\mathbf{x}^0)$ is indefinite, then $\mathbf{x}^0$ is a saddle point.

(e) If $\mathbf{x}^0$ is a local maximum point, then $\mathbf{f}''(\mathbf{x}^0)$ is negative semi definite.

(f) If $\mathbf{x}^0$ is a local minimum point, then $\mathbf{f}''(\mathbf{x}^0)$ is positive semi definite.

Of the six statements in Theorem 17.6.5, the first two are sufficient conditions for a strict local maximum or minimum, whereas the last two are necessary conditions for a local maximum or minimum, even if it is not strict. Condition (d) is a sufficient condition for a saddle point. Finally, condition (c) emphasizes that negative or positive semidefiniteness is insufficient to establish that the interior critical point $\mathbf{x}^0$ is even a weak local maximum or minimum. The results of Exercise 17.3.4 can be used to justify this claim.

Increasing Transformations

We conclude this section with one simple result of considerable interest in theoretical economics. It is this: *maximizing a function is equivalent to maximizing a strictly increasing transformation of that function*. For instance, suppose we want to find all pairs (x, y) that maximize $f(x, y)$ over a set S in the xy-plane. Instead we can find those (x, y) that maximize over S any one of the following objective functions:

1. $af(x, y) + b$ (provided that the constant $a > 0$);
2. $e^{f(x,y)}$; and
3. $\ln f(x, y)$ (provided that $f(x, y) > 0$ throughout S).

The maximum *points* are exactly the same. But the maximum *values* are, of course, quite different. As a concrete example, because the transformation $u \mapsto \ln u$ is strictly increasing when $u > 0$, the following two problems have exactly the same solutions: for $(x, y) \in S$,

$$\max\ e^{x^2 + 2xy^2 - y^3} \quad \text{and} \quad \max\ x^2 + 2xy^2 - y^3$$

THEOREM 17.6.6

Suppose $f(\mathbf{x}) = f(x_1, \ldots, x_n)$ is defined over a set S in $\mathbb{R}^n$. Let F be a function of one variable defined over the range of f, and let $\mathbf{c}$ be a point in S. Define the function g over S by $g(\mathbf{x}) = F(f(\mathbf{x}))$.

(a) If F is increasing and $\mathbf{c}$ maximizes (minimizes) f over S, then the same point $\mathbf{c}$ also maximizes (resp. minimizes) g over S.

(b) If F is strictly increasing, then $\mathbf{c}$ maximizes (minimizes) f over S if and only if $\mathbf{c}$ maximizes (resp. minimizes) g over S.

We give a proof only for the maximization case, since the minimization case is similar.

Proof:

(a) Because the point $\mathbf{c}$ maximizes f over S, we have $f(\mathbf{x}) \leq f(\mathbf{c})$ for all $\mathbf{x}$ in S. Then, because F is increasing, we have $g(\mathbf{x}) = F(f(\mathbf{x})) \leq F(f(\mathbf{c})) = g(\mathbf{c})$ for all $\mathbf{x}$ in S. It follows that $\mathbf{c}$ maximizes g over S.

(b) Suppose that F is also strictly increasing and $f(\mathbf{x}) > f(\mathbf{c})$. Then one has $g(\mathbf{x}) = F(f(\mathbf{x})) > F(f(\mathbf{c})) = g(\mathbf{c})$. So $g(\mathbf{x}) \leq g(\mathbf{c})$ for all $\mathbf{x}$ in S implies that $f(\mathbf{x}) \leq f(\mathbf{c})$ for all $\mathbf{x}$ in S.

Note how extremely simple the argument was. No continuity or differentiability assumptions were required; instead, the proof is based only on the concepts of maximum, and of increasing/strictly increasing functions. Some people appear to distrust such simple, direct arguments and replace them by inefficient or even insufficient arguments based on "differentiating everything in sight" in order to use first- or second-order conditions. Such distrust merely makes matters unnecessarily complicated and risks introducing errors.

EXERCISES FOR SECTION 17.6

1. Each of the following functions has a maximum point. Find it.
   (a) $f(x, y, z) = 2x - x^2 + 10y - y^2 + 3 - z^2$
   (b) $f(x, y, z) = 3 - x^2 - 2y^2 - 3z^2 - 2xy - 2xz$

2. Define $f(x) = e^{-x^2}$.
   (a) Let $F(u) = \ln u$. Verify that the two functions $f(x)$ and $F(f(x))$ both have maxima at the same values of x.
   (b) Let $F(u) = 5$. Then $g(x) = F(f(x)) = 5$. Explain why this example shows that the implication in part (a) of Theorem 17.6.6 cannot be reversed. (Recall that our definition of an increasing function is satisfied by a constant function.)

3. Suppose $g(\mathbf{x}) = F(f(\mathbf{x}))$ where $f : \mathbb{R}^n \to \mathbb{R}$ and $F : \mathbb{R} \to \mathbb{R}$ are differentiable functions, with $F' \neq 0$ everywhere. Prove that $\mathbf{x}$ is a critical point for f if and only if it is a critical point for g.

SM 4. Find the first-order partial derivatives of the function of three variables given by

$$f(x, y, z) = -2x^3 + 15x^2 - 36x + 2y - 3z + \int_y^z e^{t^2} dt$$

Then determine its eight critical points.

5. Suggest how to simplify each of the following two maximization problems:
   (a) $\max \frac{1}{2}[e^{x^2+y^2-2x} - e^{-(x^2+y^2-2x)}]$, subject to $(x, y) \in S$;
   (b) $\max Ax_1^{a_1} \cdots x_n^{a_n}$, subject to $x_1 + x_2 + \cdots + x_n = 1$, where $A > 0$ and $x_1 > 0, \ldots, x_n > 0$.

17.7 Comparative Statics and the Envelope Theorem

Optimization problems in economics typically involve either maximizing or minimizing an objective function which depends on endogenous variables that can be chosen. But very often the function also depends on one or more exogenous parameters like prices, tax rates, or income levels that cannot be chosen. Although these parameters must be held constant during the optimization, they vary according to exogenous circumstances affecting the economic situation. For example, according to the standard definition of a perfectly competitive or "price-taking" firm, we should calculate its profit-maximizing input and output quantities while treating the prices it faces as parameters. But then we may ask how these optimal quantities respond to changes in those prices, or to changes in any other exogenous parameters which affect the maximization problem we are considering.

Consider first the following simple problem, which we treat as a maximization problem while noting the theory is essentially identical for the case of minimization. Suppose a

SECTION 17.7 / COMPARATIVE STATICS AND THE ENVELOPE THEOREM

function f depends on a single variable x as well as on a single parameter r. We wish to maximize $f(x, r)$ w.r.t. x while keeping r constant, which we write as:

$$\max_x f(x, r)$$

The value of x that maximizes f will usually depend on r, so we denote it by $x^*(r)$. Inserting $x^*(r)$ into $f(x, r)$, we obtain the *value function*:

$$f^*(r) = f(x^*(r), r)$$

What happens to the value function as r changes? Assuming that $f^*(r)$ is differentiable, applying the chain rule yields

$$\frac{df^*(r)}{dr} = f_1'(x^*(r), r) \frac{dx^*(r)}{dr} + f_2'(x^*(r), r) \tag{17.7.1}$$

Now, if f achieves a maximum at an interior point $x^*(r)$ in the domain where $f(x)$ is defined, then the FOC $f_1'(x^*(r), r) = 0$ must be satisfied. It follows that the first term on the right-hand side of Eq. (17.7.1) is zero, so the equation reduces to

$$\frac{df^*(r)}{dr} = f_2'(x^*(r), r) \tag{17.7.2}$$

Note that when the parameter r is changed, then $f^*(r)$ changes for two reasons. First, a change in r changes the value of f^* directly because r is the second variable in $f(x, r)$. Second, a change in r changes the value of the function $x^*(r)$, and hence $f(x^*(r), r)$ is changed indirectly. Equation (17.7.2) shows that the total effect is simply found by computing the partial derivative of $f(x^*(r), r)$ w.r.t. r, ignoring entirely the indirect effect of the dependence of x^* on r. At first sight, this seems very surprising. On further reflection, however, you may realize that the first-order condition $f_1'(x^*(r), r) = 0$ for $x^*(r)$ to maximize $f(x, r)$ w.r.t. x implies that any small change in x, whether or not it is induced by a small change in r, must have a zero marginal effect on the value $f^*(r)$ of $f(x^*, r)$.

EXAMPLE 17.7.1   Suppose that when a firm produces and sells x units of a commodity, it has revenue $R(x) = rx$, where the price r is a positive parameter. Suppose too that the firm's cost is $C(x) = x^2$, so the firm's profit is

$$\pi(x, r) = R(x) - C(x) = rx - x^2$$

Find the optimal choice x^* of x, and verify (17.7.2) in this case.

Solution: The quadratic profit function has a maximum when $\pi_1' = r - 2x = 0$, which occurs when $x^* = r/2$. So the maximum profit as a function of r is given by

$$\pi^*(r) = rx^* - (x^*)^2 = r(r/2) - (r/2)^2 = r^2/4$$

Its derivative is $d\pi^*/dr = r/2$. Using (17.7.2) is much more direct, however. Indeed, because $\pi_2'(x, r) = x$, the formula implies that $d\pi^*/dr = \pi_2'(x^*(r), r) = x^*(r) = \frac{1}{2}r$.

EXAMPLE 17.7.2

In Example 9.6.5 we studied a firm with the profit function $\hat{\pi}(Q, \tau) = R(Q) - C(Q) - \tau Q$, where τ denoted a tax per unit produced. Let $Q^* = Q^*(\tau)$ denote the optimal choice of Q as a function of the tax rate τ, and let $\pi^*(\tau)$ denote the corresponding value function. Because $\hat{\pi}'_2 = -Q$, formula (17.7.2) yields

$$\frac{d}{d\tau}\pi^*(\tau) = \hat{\pi}'_2(Q^*(\tau), \tau) = -Q^*(\tau)$$

This is the result we found earlier.

Consider the case when there is an n-vector $\mathbf{x} = (x_1, \ldots, x_n)$ of choice variables and an m-vector $\mathbf{r} = (r_1, \ldots, r_m)$ of parameters. Then, assuming that the function $f(\mathbf{x}, \mathbf{r})$ and the *value function* $f^*(\mathbf{r})$ are suitably differentiable, here is an obvious generalization of formula (17.7.2) that holds for all the m first-order partial derivatives $(\partial/\partial r_j) f^*(\mathbf{r})$:

THEOREM 17.7.1 (ENVELOPE THEOREM)

For all parameter vectors $\mathbf{r}$ near $\mathbf{r}^0$, suppose that the value function $f^*(\mathbf{r}) = \max_{\mathbf{x}} f(\mathbf{x}, \mathbf{r})$ exists, and let $\mathbf{x}^*(\mathbf{r})$ denote a value of $\mathbf{x}$ that maximizes $f(\mathbf{x}, \mathbf{r})$ w.r.t. $\mathbf{x}$. Also, let $\mathbf{x}^0$ denote $\mathbf{x}^*(\mathbf{r}^0)$. Assuming that the two functions $f(\mathbf{x}^0, \mathbf{r})$ and $f^*(\mathbf{r})$ of $\mathbf{r}$ are both differentiable at $\mathbf{r}^0$, for each $j = 1, \ldots, m$, their respective jth partial derivatives at $\mathbf{r}^0$ satisfy

$$\left.\frac{\partial f^*(\mathbf{r})}{\partial r_j}\right|_{\mathbf{r}=\mathbf{r}^0} = \left.\frac{\partial f(\mathbf{x}^*(\mathbf{r}), \mathbf{r})}{\partial r_j}\right|_{\mathbf{r}=\mathbf{r}^0} \tag{17.7.3}$$

Note that the equalities (17.7.3) hold if we minimize $f(\mathbf{x}, \mathbf{r})$ w.r.t. $\mathbf{x}$ instead of maximizing it, or even if $\mathbf{x}^*(\mathbf{r})$ for each $\mathbf{r}$ near $\mathbf{r}^0$ is any critical point.

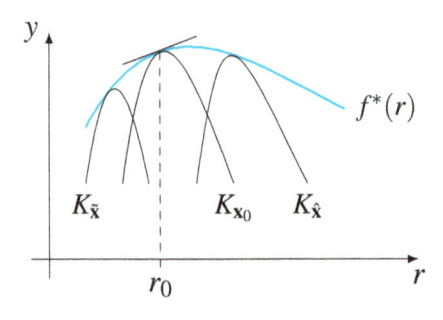

Figure 17.7.1 The curve $y = f^*(r)$ is the envelope of all the curves $y = f(\mathbf{x}, r)$

Figure 17.7.1 illustrates Eq. (17.7.3) in the case where only one parameter r is allowed to vary. For each fixed value of $\mathbf{x}$ there is a curve $K_{\mathbf{x}}$ in the ry-plane, given by the equation

$y = f(\mathbf{x}, r)$. Figure 17.7.1 shows three of these curves together with the graph of $f^*(r)$. For all $\tilde{\mathbf{x}}$ and all r we have

$$f(\tilde{\mathbf{x}}, r) \leq \max_{\mathbf{x}} f(\mathbf{x}, r) = f^*(r)$$

It follows that none of the $K_\mathbf{x}$-curves can ever lie above the curve $y = f^*(r)$. On the other hand, for each value of r there is at least one value $\mathbf{x}^*(r)$ such that $f(\mathbf{x}^*(r), r) = f^*(r)$, namely a choice of $\mathbf{x}$ that solves the maximization problem for the given value of r. For instance, if we fix $r = r_0$ and let $\mathbf{x}_0$ denote $\mathbf{x}^*(r_0)$, then the curve $K_{\mathbf{x}_0}$ will touch the curve $y = f^*(r)$ at the point $(r_0, f^*(r_0))$, as in the figure. Moreover, because $K_{\mathbf{x}_0}$ can never go above this graph, it must have exactly the same tangent as the graph of f^* at the point where the curves touch. The slope of this common tangent, therefore, must be equal to not only df^*/dr, the slope of the tangent to the graph of f^* at $(r_0, f^*(r_0))$, but also to $\partial f(\mathbf{x}_0, r)/\partial r$, the slope of the tangent to the curve $K_{\mathbf{x}_0}$ at the point $(r_0, f(\mathbf{x}_0, r_0))$. Equation (17.7.3) follows because $K_{\mathbf{x}_0}$ is the graph of $f(\mathbf{x}_0, r)$ when $\mathbf{x}_0$ is fixed.

As Fig. 17.7.1 suggests, the graph of $y = f^*(r)$ is the lowest curve with the property that it lies on or above all the curves $K_\mathbf{x}$. So its graph is like an envelope or some "cling film" that is used to enclose or wrap up all these curves. Indeed, a point is on or below the graph if and only if it lies on or below one of the curves $K_\mathbf{x}$. For this reason we call the graph of f^* the *envelope* of the family of $K_\mathbf{x}$-curves.

EXAMPLE 17.7.3

In Example 17.1.3, we let $Q = F(K, L)$ denote a production function with K as the capital input and L as the labour input. The price per unit of the product was p, the price per unit of capital was r, and the price per unit of labour was w. The profit obtained by using K and L units of the inputs, then producing and selling $F(K, L)$ units of the product, is given by

$$\hat{\pi}(K, L, p, r, w) = pF(K, L) - rK - wL$$

Here profit has been expressed as a new function $\hat{\pi}$ of the parameters p, r, and w, as well as of the choice variables K and L. We keep p, r, and w fixed and maximize $\hat{\pi}$ w.r.t. K and L. The optimal values of K and L are functions of p, r, and w, which we denote by $K^* = K^*(p, r, w)$ and $L^* = L^*(p, r, w)$. The value function for the problem is $\hat{\pi}^*(p, r, w) = \hat{\pi}(K^*, L^*, p, r, w)$. Most economists call $\hat{\pi}^*$ the firm's *profit function*, though it would be more accurately described as the "maximum profit function". It is found by taking prices as given and choosing the optimal quantities of all inputs and outputs.

According to Theorem 17.7.1, one has

$$\frac{\partial \hat{\pi}^*}{\partial p} = F(K^*, L^*) = Q^*, \quad \frac{\partial \hat{\pi}^*}{\partial r} = -K^*, \quad \frac{\partial \hat{\pi}^*}{\partial w} = -L^* \qquad (*)$$

These three equalities are instances of what is known in production theory as *Hotelling's lemma*. An economic interpretation of the middle equality is this: How much profit is lost if the price of capital increases by a small amount? At the optimum the firm uses K^* units of capital, so the answer is K^* per unit increase in the price. See Exercise 4 for further interesting relationships.

Proving the Envelope Theorem

One way to prove Theorem 17.7.1 is to use the first-order conditions to eliminate other terms, as in the argument we gave for Eq. (17.7.2). The following alternative proof that we offer may be simpler. We construct a suitable "trick" function which, by design, must have a local maximum at $\mathbf{r}^0$. Then we argue that the equations (17.7.3) are first-order necessary conditions for $\mathbf{r}^0$ to be a local maximum point of this function.

Proof: To prove Theorem 17.7.1, fix the parameter m-vector $\mathbf{r}^0$ and the associated n-vector $\mathbf{x}^0 = \mathbf{x}^*(\mathbf{r}^0)$ of choice variables that maximizes $f(\mathbf{x}, \mathbf{r}^0)$ w.r.t. $\mathbf{x}$. Then, for all parameter vectors $\mathbf{r}$ near $\mathbf{r}^0$, define the "trick" function

$$\varphi(\mathbf{r}) = f(\mathbf{x}^0, \mathbf{r}) - f^*(\mathbf{r}) \tag{*}$$

By definition of the value function $f^*(\mathbf{r})$ and of the maximum point $\mathbf{x}^*(\mathbf{r})$, for all $\mathbf{r}$ near $\mathbf{r}^0$ one has

$$f(\mathbf{x}^0, \mathbf{r}) \leq f(\mathbf{x}^*(\mathbf{r}), \mathbf{r}) = f^*(\mathbf{r})$$

This inequality implies that $\varphi(\mathbf{r}) \leq 0$. But at $\mathbf{r} = \mathbf{r}^0$ one has

$$f(\mathbf{x}^0, \mathbf{r}^0) = f(\mathbf{x}^*(\mathbf{r}^0), \mathbf{r}^0) = f^*(\mathbf{r}^0)$$

This equality implies that $\varphi(\mathbf{r}^0) = 0$. We have therefore proved that, for all $\mathbf{r}$ near $\mathbf{r}^0$, one has $\varphi(\mathbf{r}) \leq \varphi(\mathbf{r}^0) = 0$. So $\varphi(\mathbf{r})$ has a local maximum point at $\mathbf{r}^0$.

Finally, the stated differentiability assumptions imply that the function $\varphi(\mathbf{r})$ defined by $(*)$ is differentiable at $\mathbf{r}^0$, with partial derivatives given by

$$\varphi_j'(\mathbf{r}^0) = \left.\frac{\partial f^*(\mathbf{r})}{\partial r_j}\right|_{\mathbf{r}=\mathbf{r}^0} - \left.\frac{\partial f(\mathbf{x}^*(\mathbf{r}), \mathbf{r})}{\partial r_j}\right|_{\mathbf{r}=\mathbf{r}^0}$$

Since $\mathbf{r}^0$ is a local maximum of $\varphi(\mathbf{r})$, it must be a critical point. Then for each $j = 1, 2, \ldots, m$, Eq. (17.7.3) is implied immediately by the necessary first-order condition $\varphi_j'(\mathbf{r}^0) = 0$. ∎

EXERCISES FOR SECTION 17.7

1. A firm produces a single commodity and gets paid the price p for each unit sold. The cost of producing x units is $ax + bx^2$ and the tax per unit is t. Assume that the parameters are positive with $p > a + t$. The firm wants to maximize its profit.

   (a) Find the optimal production x^* and the optimal profit π^*.

   (b) Prove that $\partial \pi^*/\partial p = x^*$, and give an economic interpretation.

2. A firm produces $Q = \sqrt{L}$ units of a commodity when labour input is L units. The price obtained per unit of output is P, and the price per unit of labour is w, both positive.

   (a) Write down the profit function π. What choice of labour input $L = L^*$ maximizes profits?

SECTION 17.7 / COMPARATIVE STATICS AND THE ENVELOPE THEOREM   727

(b) Consider L^* as a function $L^*(P, w)$ of the two prices, and define the value function

$$\pi^*(P, w) = \pi(L^*(P, w), P, w)$$

Verify that $\partial \pi^*/\partial P = \pi'_P(L^*, P, w)$ and $\partial \pi^*/\partial w = \pi'_w(L^*, P, w)$, thus confirming the envelope theorem.

SM 3. A firm uses capital K, labour L, and land T to produce Q units of a commodity, where

$$Q = K^{2/3} + L^{1/2} + T^{1/3}$$

Suppose that the firm is paid a positive price p for each unit it produces, and that the positive prices it pays per unit of capital, labour, and land are r, w, and q, respectively.

(a) Express the firm's profits as a function π of (K, L, T). Then find the values of K, L, and T, as functions of the four prices, that maximize the firm's profit. (You may assume that a maximum exists.)

(b) Let Q^* denote the optimal number of units produced and K^* the optimal capital stock. Show that $\partial Q^*/\partial r = -\partial K^*/\partial p$.

4. With reference to Example 17.7.3, assuming that F is a C^2 function, prove the symmetry relations:

$$\frac{\partial Q^*}{\partial r} = -\frac{\partial K^*}{\partial p}, \quad \frac{\partial Q^*}{\partial w} = -\frac{\partial L^*}{\partial p}, \quad \text{and} \quad \frac{\partial L^*}{\partial r} = \frac{\partial K^*}{\partial w}$$

(Hint: First establish that $\dfrac{\partial Q^*}{\partial r} = \dfrac{\partial}{\partial r}\left(\dfrac{\partial \hat{\pi}^*}{\partial p}\right) = \dfrac{\partial}{\partial p}\left(\dfrac{\partial \hat{\pi}^*}{\partial r}\right)$ by combining the first result in Example 17.7.3 with Young's Theorem 14.6.1. Then use the other results in Example 17.7.3.)

SM 5. With reference to Example 17.1.3, let us consider how the optimal demands for capital and labour, the two input factors, respond to changes in any price.

(a) Take the differentials of the first-order conditions $(*)$ in Example 17.1.3 to verify that

$$F'_K(K^*, L^*)\,dp + pF''_{KK}(K^*, L^*)\,dK + pF''_{KL}(K^*, L^*)\,dL = dr$$

$$F'_L(K^*, L^*)\,dp + pF''_{LK}(K^*, L^*)\,dK + pF''_{LL}(K^*, L^*)\,dL = dw$$

(b) Use equations derived in part (a) to find the partials of K^* and L^* w.r.t. p, r, and w. (Hint: It may be easier first to find $\partial K^*/\partial p$ and $\partial L^*/\partial p$ by putting $dr = dw = 0$, etc. in (a).)

(c) Assume that the local second-order conditions in Theorem 17.3.1 for a strict local maximum are satisfied. What does this assumption let you say about the signs of the six partial derivatives you found in part (a)? In particular, show that the demand for each factor is decreasing as a function of its own price. Finally, verify that $\partial K^*/\partial w = \partial L^*/\partial r$.

SM 6. A profit-maximizing monopolist produces two commodities whose respective quantities are denoted by x_1 and x_2. Good 1 is subsidized at the rate of σ per unit, whereas good 2 is taxed at τ per unit. The monopolist's profit function is therefore given by

$$\pi(x_1, x_2) = R(x_1, x_2) - C(x_1, x_2) + \sigma x_1 - \tau x_2$$

where R and C are the firm's revenue and cost functions, respectively. Assume that these functions are both C^2 for all positive x_1 and x_2, with partial derivatives that satisfy

$$R'_1 > 0, \quad R'_2 > 0, \quad R''_{11} < 0, \quad R''_{12} = R''_{21} < 0, \quad R''_{22} < 0$$

$$C'_1 > 0, \quad C'_2 > 0, \quad C''_{11} > 0, \quad C''_{12} = C''_{21} > 0, \quad C''_{22} > 0$$

(a) Find the first-order conditions for maximum profit.

(b) Write down the local second-order conditions for maximum profit.

(c) Suppose that $x_1^* = x_1^*(\sigma, \tau)$ and $x_2^* = x_2^*(\sigma, \tau)$ solve the problem. Assuming that the local second-order conditions are satisfied, find the signs of $\partial x_1^*/\partial \sigma$, $\partial x_1^*/\partial \tau$, $\partial x_2^*/\partial \sigma$, and $\partial x_2^*/\partial \tau$.

(d) Show that $\partial x_1^*/\partial \tau = -\partial x_2^*/\partial \sigma$.

REVIEW EXERCISES

1. The function f defined for all (x, y) by $f(x, y) = -2x^2 + 2xy - y^2 + 18x - 14y + 4$ has a maximum. Find the corresponding values of x and y. Use Theorem 17.2.2 to prove that it is a maximum point.

SM 2. A firm produces two different kinds of a commodity, which are labelled A and B. The daily cost of producing Q_1 units of A and Q_2 units of B is $C(Q_1, Q_2) = 0.1(Q_1^2 + Q_1Q_2 + Q_2^2)$. Suppose that the firm sells all its output at a price per unit of $P_1 = 120$ for commodity A and $P_2 = 90$ for commodity B.

(a) Find the daily production levels that maximize profit.

(b) If P_2 remains unchanged at 90, what new price P_1 per unit of A would imply that the optimal daily production level for A is 400 units?

3. Assume that a firm's profit from producing and selling x and y units of two brands of a commodity is given by $P(x, y) = -0.1x^2 - 0.2xy - 0.2y^2 + 47x + 48y - 600$.

(a) Find the production levels that maximize profit.

(b) A key raw material is rationed so that total production must be restricted to 200 units. Find the production levels that now maximize profit.

SM 4. Find the critical points for each of the following functions of (x, y):

(a) $x^3 - x^2y + y^2$ (b) $xye^{4x^2 - 5xy + y^2}$ (c) $4y^3 + 12x^2y - 24x^2 - 24y^2$

5. Define $f(x, y, a) = ax^2 - 2x + y^2 - 4ay$, where a is a parameter. For each fixed $a \neq 0$, find the unique critical point $(x^*(a), y^*(a))$ of the function f w.r.t. (x, y). Find also the value function $f^*(a) = f(x^*(a), y^*(a), a)$, and verify the envelope theorem in this case.

SM 6. Suppose the production function in Exercise 17.7.3 is replaced by $Q = K^a + L^b + T^c$, for parameters $a, b, c \in (0, 1)$.

(a) Assuming that a maximum exists, find the values of K, L, and T that maximize the firm's profit.

(b) Let π^* denote the optimal profit as a function of the four prices p, q, r, and w. Compute the partial derivative $\partial \pi^*/\partial r$.

(c) Verify the envelope theorem in this case.

7. Define $f(x, y)$ for all (x, y) by $f(x, y) = e^{x+y} + e^{x-y} - \frac{3}{2}x - \frac{1}{2}y$.

   (a) Find the first- and second-order partial derivatives of f, then show that $f(x, y)$ is convex.

   (b) Find the minimum point of $f(x, y)$.

SM 8. Consider the function $f(x, y) = x^2 - y^2 - xy - x^3$.

   (a) Find and classify its critical points.

   (b) Find the domain S where f is concave, and find the largest value of f in S.

SM 9. Given the parameter a, consider the function f defined for all (x, y) by

$$f(x, y) = \tfrac{1}{2}x^2 - x + ay(x - 1) - \tfrac{1}{3}y^3 + a^2 y^2$$

   (a) Prove that $(x^*, y^*) = (1 - a^3, a^2)$ is a critical point of f.

   (b) Verify the envelope theorem in this case.

   (c) Where in the xy-plane is f convex?

10. In this problem we will generalize several of the economic examples and problems considered so far. Consider a firm that produces output quantities x and y of two different goods that are labelled A and B, whose prices are p and q respectively. Assuming that the total cost function is $C(x, y)$, the firm's profit is

$$\pi(x, y) = px + qy - C(x, y) \qquad (i)$$

   (a) Suppose first that the firm has a small share in the markets for both these goods, and so takes p and q as given. Write down and interpret the first-order conditions for $x^* > 0$ and $y^* > 0$ to maximize profit.

   (b) Suppose next that the firm has a monopoly in the sale of both goods. The prices are no longer fixed, but are given as functions of x and y by the inverse demand functions

$$p = F(x, y) \quad \text{and} \quad q = G(x, y) \qquad (ii)$$

   So profit as a function of x and y is

$$\pi(x, y) = xF(x, y) + yG(x, y) - C(x, y) \qquad (iii)$$

   Write down and interpret the first-order conditions for $x^* > 0$ and $y^* > 0$ to maximize profit.

   (c) Suppose $p = a - bx - cy$ and $q = \alpha - \beta x - \gamma y$, where b and γ are positive.[9] If the cost function is $C(x, y) = Px + Qy + R$, write down the first-order conditions for maximum profit.

   (d) Prove that the (global) second-order conditions are satisfied provided $4\gamma b \geq (\beta + c)^2$.

---

[9] An increase in the price of either good decreases the demand for that good, but may increase or decrease the demand for the other good.

18 EQUALITY CONSTRAINTS

Mathematics is removed from this turmoil of human life, but its methods and the relations are a mirror, an incredibly pure mirror, of the relations that link facts of our existence.
—Konrad Knopp (1928)

The previous chapter introduced unconstrained optimization problems with several variables. In economics, however, the variables to be chosen must often satisfy one or more constraints. Accordingly, this chapter is the first of three that considers constrained optimization problems. Specifically, here we consider equality constraints, whereas the following Chapters 19 and 20 consider inequality constraints.

The main topic of this chapter is the method of Lagrange multipliers. This method is introduced in Section 18.1, for the case of two choice variables subject to one equality constraint. An important issue discussed in Section 18.2 is how to interpret the Lagrange multiplier associated with the equality constraint. The brief topic of Section 18.3 is how to treat multiple solution candidates that emerge from the method of Lagrange multipliers because they all satisfy the relevant first-order conditions. Section 18.4 offers an explanation of why the Lagrange multiplier method works. Sufficient conditions for a vector of choice variables to be a constrained optimum are treated in Section 18.5. Thereafter, Section 18.6 extends our analysis beyond the special case of two choice variables and one constraint. The final Section 18.7 presents some comparative static results and an envelope theorem.

More general constrained optimization problems allowing inequality constraints are introduced in Chapters 19 and 20. A much fuller treatment of constrained optimization generally can be found in FMEA.

18.1 The Lagrange Multiplier Method

A typical economic example of a constrained optimization problem concerns a consumer who must choose how much of the available income m to spend on the quantity x of a good whose price is p, and how much income y to leave over for expenditure on other goods. Note that with this notation the consumer then faces the budget constraint $px + y = m$. Suppose that preferences are represented by the utility function $u(x, y)$. In mathematical terms the consumer's problem can be expressed as

$$\max \ u(x, y) \ \text{s.t.} \ px + y = m$$

where "s.t." stands for "subject to". This is a typical *constrained maximization problem*. In this case, because $y = m - px$, the same problem can be expressed as the *unconstrained maximization* of the function $h(x) = u(x, m - px)$ w.r.t. the single variable x. Indeed, in Section 17.2 we used this method of converting a constrained optimization problem involving two variables and one constraint into an unconstrained one-variable problem.

When the constraint involves a complicated function, or when there are several equality constraints to consider, this substitution method might be difficult or even impossible to carry out in practice. In such cases, economists make much use of the *Lagrange multiplier method* that we will now present.[1]

We start with the problem of maximizing a function $f(x, y)$ of two variables x and y when these are restricted to satisfy a single equality constraint $g(x, y) = c$. This problem can be written as

$$\max \ f(x, y) \ \text{s.t.} \ g(x, y) = c \tag{18.1.1}$$

The first step of the method is to introduce a *Lagrange multiplier*, often denoted by λ, which is "associated" with the constraint $g(x, y) = c$. To do this, we define the following *Lagrangian* function

$$\mathcal{L}(x, y) = f(x, y) - \lambda[g(x, y) - c] \tag{18.1.2}$$

Here the expression $g(x, y) - c$, which the constraint says must be 0, has been multiplied by λ. Then the product has been subtracted from the maximand $f(x, y)$. For future reference, note that $\mathcal{L}(x, y) = f(x, y)$ for all (x, y) satisfying the constraint $g(x, y) = c$.

We now derive appropriate first-order conditions for solving problem (18.1.1). To do so, we treat the Lagrange multiplier λ as a constant, and consider the two partial derivatives of $\mathcal{L}(x, y)$ w.r.t. x and y. These are

$$\mathcal{L}'_1(x, y) = f'_1(x, y) - \lambda g'_1(x, y) \ \text{and} \ \mathcal{L}'_2(x, y) = f'_2(x, y) - \lambda g'_2(x, y) \tag{18.1.3}$$

As we will explain in Section 18.4, except in rare cases, a solution of problem (18.1.1) can only be a pair (x, y) which, for a suitable value of the multiplier λ, is not only a critical point of the Lagrangian $\mathcal{L}$, but also satisfies the equality constraint $g(x, y) = c$. As in Chapters 9 and 17, we refer to a combination of the two Eqs (18.1.3) with the constraint as "first-order" conditions.

---

[1] Named after its discoverer, the Italian-born French mathematician J.-L. Lagrange (1736–1813). The Danish economist Harald Westergaard seems to have been the first to use it in economics, in 1876. As a matter of practice, this method is often used even for problems that are quite easy to express as unconstrained problems. One reason is that Lagrange multipliers have an important economic interpretation. In addition, a similar method works for many more complicated optimization problems, such as those where the constraints are expressed in terms of inequalities, as we will see later in Chapters 19 and 20.

Here is a simple economic application.

EXAMPLE 18.1.1   A consumer has the utility function $u(x, y) = xy$ defined for all positive x, y, and faces the budget constraint $2x + y = 100$. Use the Lagrange multiplier method to find the only solution candidate to the constrained utility maximization problem. Then confirm that this solves the problem by considering the unconstrained maximization problem that results from using the budget constraint to eliminate one of the variables.

Solution: The constrained maximization problem is

$$\max\ xy \text{ s.t. } 2x + y = 100$$

Following the recipe that led to (18.1.2), the associated Lagrangian is

$$\mathcal{L}(x, y) = xy - \lambda(2x + y - 100)$$

Including the constraint, the first-order conditions for solving the problem are the three simultaneous equations

$$\mathcal{L}'_1(x, y) = y - 2\lambda = 0, \quad \mathcal{L}'_2(x, y) = x - \lambda = 0, \quad \text{and} \quad 2x + y = 100$$

The first two equations imply that $y = 2\lambda$ and $x = \lambda$. So $y = 2x$. Inserting this into the constraint yields $2x + 2x = 100$. Hence $x = 25$ and $y = 50$, implying that $\lambda = x = 25$.

This solution can be confirmed by the substitution method. From $2x + y = 100$ we get $y = 100 - 2x$. Replacing y by $100 - 2x$ in the utility function reduces the original problem to that of maximizing the function $h(x) = x(100 - 2x) = -2x^2 + 100x$ defined on the open interval $(0, 50)$, without any constraint. The first-order condition for this unconstrained maximization problem is $h'(x) = -4x + 100 = 0$. The unique critical point occurs at $x = 25$. Because $h''(x) = -4 < 0$ for all x, the function h is concave on $(0, 50)$, so the critical point $x = 25$ *is* a maximum point. Inserting this into the budget constraint gives $y = 50$, which is the unique solution of the original constrained maximization problem.

Perhaps surprisingly, for the alternative minimization problem

$$\min\ f(x, y) \text{ s.t. } g(x, y) = c \tag{18.1.4}$$

the Lagrangian function $\mathcal{L}$ is defined in exactly the same way, by Eq. (18.1.2). Moreover, the relevant first-order conditions are the same. Because of this, we often write

$$\max\ (\min) f(x, y) \text{ s.t. } g(x, y) = c$$

when referring to both the maximization and minimization problems.[2]

Example 18.1.1 illustrates the following general method:

---

[2] The reader may have seen expressions like max min $f(x, y)$ in, for instance, game theory courses. Those expressions mean something entirely different.

THE LAGRANGE MULTIPLIER METHOD

To find the only possible solutions of problems (18.1.1) and (18.1.4), proceed as follows:

(i) Write down the Lagrangian function, as in Eq. (18.1.2), where λ is a constant.

(ii) Differentiate $\mathcal{L}$ w.r.t. x and y, and equate the partial derivatives to 0.

(iii) The two equations in (ii), together with the constraint, yield the following three *first-order conditions*:

$$\mathcal{L}'_1(x, y) = f'_1(x, y) - \lambda g'_1(x, y) = 0$$
$$\mathcal{L}'_2(x, y) = f'_2(x, y) - \lambda g'_2(x, y) = 0$$
$$g(x, y) = c$$

(iv) Solve the three equations in (iii) simultaneously for the three unknowns x, y, and λ. Any triple (x, y, λ) that solves these equations is a *candidate* for solving the constrained maximization/minimization problem. At least one of those candidates must solve that problem, if it has a solution.

Importantly, if $g'_1(x, y)$ and $g'_2(x, y)$ both vanish at the true solution, the method might fail to give the right answer.

Some economists prefer to consider the Lagrangian as a function $\tilde{\mathcal{L}}(x, y, \lambda)$ of three variables. Then the third first-order condition $\tilde{\mathcal{L}}'_3(x, y, \lambda) = 0$ immediately yields the constraint $g(x, y) = c$ of the problem. The advantage of this alternative view is that, written this way, all three necessary conditions are obtained by equating the three partial derivatives of $\tilde{\mathcal{L}}$ to 0. This allows the first-order conditions to be summarized as requiring us to find a critical point (x, y, λ) of the Lagrangian $\tilde{\mathcal{L}}(x, y, \lambda)$.

It seems unnatural, however, to rely on differentiation in order to derive such an obvious necessary condition as the equation that specifies the constraint. Moreover, this procedure can easily lead to trouble when treating problems with inequality constraints. A third reason for considering the Lagrangian as a function $\mathcal{L}(x, y)$ of only two variables is that this allows us to derive some important results later in this chapter concerning the maximum/minimum points of $\mathcal{L}$ w.r.t. (x, y). These are particularly useful because, as discussed in Section 18.5, the function $\mathcal{L}(x, y)$ of two variables may well be concave or convex, whereas the function $\tilde{\mathcal{L}}(x, y, \lambda)$ of three variables is very unlikely to be concave or convex. For these three reasons, we prefer to consider the function $\mathcal{L}(x, y)$ of only two variables.

EXAMPLE 18.1.2 A single-product firm plans to produce 30 units of output as cheaply as possible. By using K units of capital and L units of labour, both nonnegative, it can produce $\sqrt{K} + L$ units. Suppose the prices per unit of capital and labour are, respectively, $1 and $20. So the firm's problem is:

$$\min K + 20L \quad \text{s.t.} \quad \sqrt{K} + L = 30$$

(a) Find the optimal choices of K and L.

(b) What is the additional cost of producing 31 rather than 30 units?

Solution:

(a) The Lagrangian is
$$\mathcal{L} = K + 20L - \lambda(\sqrt{K} + L - 30)$$

So the first-order conditions are:
$$\mathcal{L}'_K = 1 - \lambda/2\sqrt{K} = 0, \quad \mathcal{L}'_L = 20 - \lambda = 0, \quad \text{and} \quad \sqrt{K} + L = 30$$

The second equation gives $\lambda = 20$. Now, inserting this into the first equation yields $1 = 20/2\sqrt{K}$. It follows that $\sqrt{K} = 10$, and hence $K = 100$. Finally, inserting this into the constraint gives $\sqrt{100} + L = 30$, and so $L = 20$.

The cheapest way to produce 30 units of output is therefore to use 100 units of capital and 20 units of labour. The associated cost is $K + 20L = 500$.[3]

(b) Solving the problem with the revised constraint $\sqrt{K} + L = 31$, we see that still one has $\lambda = 20$ and $K = 100$, while $L = 31 - 10 = 21$. The associated minimum cost becomes $100 + 20 \cdot 21 = 520$, so the extra cost is $520 - 500 = 20$, which precisely equals the Lagrange multiplier! Thus, in this case the Lagrange multiplier tells us by how much costs rise if the output requirement increases by one unit from 30 to 31.[4]

EXAMPLE 18.1.3 A consumer has the Cobb–Douglas utility function $u(x, y) = Ax^a y^b$, defined for all nonnegative x, y, and faces the budget constraint $px + qy = m$, where A, a, b, p, q, and m are all positive constants. Find the only solution candidate to the consumer demand problem

$$\max Ax^a y^b \text{ s.t. } px + qy = m \qquad (*)$$

Solution: The Lagrangian is $\mathcal{L}(x, y) = Ax^a y^b - \lambda(px + qy - m)$, so the three first-order conditions are

$$\mathcal{L}'_1(x, y) = aAx^{a-1}y^b - \lambda p = 0, \quad \mathcal{L}'_2(x, y) = bAx^a y^{b-1} - \lambda q = 0, \quad \text{and} \quad px + qy = m$$

We begin by solving both the first two equations for λ in terms of x, y and the parameters. This yields the two equalities

$$\lambda = \frac{aAx^{a-1}y^b}{p} = \frac{bAx^a y^{b-1}}{q}$$

Cancelling the common factor $Ax^{a-1}y^{b-1}$ from the last equality gives $ay/p = bx/q$. Solving this equation for qy yields $qy = (b/a)px$. Then, inserting this into the budget constraint gives $px + (b/a)px = m$. From this last equation we can find first x and then y. The results are the following *demand functions*:

$$x = x(p, q, m) = \frac{a}{a+b}\frac{m}{p} \quad \text{and} \quad y = y(p, q, m) = \frac{b}{a+b}\frac{m}{q} \qquad (**)$$

---

[3] Theorem 18.5.1 will tell us that, because $\mathcal{L}$ is convex in (K, L), this is the constrained minimum.
[4] Section 18.2 will tell us why this is not entirely coincidental.

The solution we have found makes good economic sense. Indeed, it follows from (∗∗) that for all $t > 0$ one has $x(tp, tq, tm) = x(p, q, m)$ and $y(tp, tq, tm) = y(p, q, m)$, implying that both demand functions are homogeneous of degree 0. According to Example 15.7.4, this as one should expect because, if the triple (p, q, m) is changed to (tp, tq, tm), then the constraint in (∗) is unchanged, and so the optimal choices of x and y are unchanged.

Note that the relative sizes of the coefficients a and b in the utility function $Ax^a y^b$ indicate the relative importance of x and y in the individual's preferences. For instance, in case a is larger than b, the consumer values a 1% increase in x more than a 1% increase in y. Now, the product px is the amount spent on the first good, so (∗∗) implies that the consumer should spend the fraction $a/(a+b)$ of income on this first good and the fraction $b/(a+b)$ on the second good.

Formula (∗∗) can be applied immediately to find the correct answer to thousands of exam problems in mathematical economics courses given each year all over the world! But note that, unless the utility function happens to be exactly of the Cobb–Douglas type $Ax^a y^b$, or something equivalent, the demands given by (∗∗) are certain to be wrong.[5]

Another warning is in order here: we assumed in problem (∗) that $x \geq 0$ and $y \geq 0$. Thus, we maximize a continuous function $Ax^a y^b$ over the closed bounded set $S = \{(x, y) : px + qy = m, x \geq 0, y \geq 0\}$. According to the extreme value Theorem 17.5.1, therefore, a maximum must exist. Since utility is 0 when $x = 0$ or when $y = 0$, and positive at the point given by (∗∗), this point indeed solves the problem. Without the nonnegativity conditions on x and y, however, the problem might fail to have a maximum. Indeed, consider the problem max $x^2 y$ s.t. $x + y = 1$, which is a special case of problem (∗). For all real t, the pair $(x, y) = (-t, 1 + t)$ satisfies the constraint. Yet $x^2 y = t^2(1 + t) \to \infty$ as $t \to \infty$, so there is no maximum point.

EXAMPLE 18.1.4 Under the assumption that whenever $x > 0$ and $y > 0$, the utility function $u(x, y)$ is defined and has positive first-order partial derivatives u'_x and u'_y, analyse the following general *utility maximization problem* with two goods:

$$\max u(x, y) \text{ s.t. } px + qy = m \qquad (18.1.5)$$

Solution: The Lagrangian is $\mathcal{L}(x, y) = u(x, y) - \lambda(px + qy - m)$. So the three first-order conditions are

$$\mathcal{L}'_x(x, y) = u'_x(x, y) - \lambda p = 0 \qquad \text{(i)}$$

$$\mathcal{L}'_y(x, y) = u'_y(x, y) - \lambda q = 0 \qquad \text{(ii)}$$

$$px + qy = m \qquad \text{(iii)}$$

From equation (i) we get $\lambda = u'_x(x, y)/p$, and from (ii) we get $\lambda = u'_y(x, y)/q$. It follows that $u'_x(x, y)/p = u'_y(x, y)/q$, which can be rewritten as

$$\frac{u'_x(x, y)}{u'_y(x, y)} = \frac{p}{q} \qquad (18.1.6)$$

---

[5] When $u(x, y) = x^a + y^b$, for instance, the solution is *not* given by (∗∗). To check this, assuming that $0 < a < 1$, see: (i) Exercise 9, for the case when $b = 1$; and (ii) Exercise 18.5.4, for the case when $a = b$.

The left-hand side of Eq. (18.1.6) is the *marginal rate of substitution*, or MRS, which was studied in Section 15.5. Utility maximization therefore requires equating the MRS to the price ratio p/q.

A geometric interpretation of Eq. (18.1.6) is that the consumer should choose the point on the budget line $px + qy = m$ at which the slope of the level curve of the utility function, which is $-u'_x(x, y)/u'_y(x, y)$, equals the slope of the budget line, which is $-p/q$.[6] Thus, at the optimal point the budget line is tangent to a level curve of the utility function, as illustrated by point P in Fig. 18.1.1. The level curves of the utility function are the *indifference curves*, along which the utility level is constant by definition. It follows that utility is maximized at a point where the budget line is tangent to an indifference curve. The fact that $\lambda = u'_x(x, y)/p = u'_y(x, y)/q$ at point P means that the marginal utility per dollar is the same for both goods. At any other point (x, y) where $u'_x(x, y)/p > u'_y(x, y)/q$, for example, the consumer can increase utility by shifting expenditure away from y toward x. Indeed, then the increase in utility per extra dollar spent on x would equal $u'_x(x, y)/p$; this exceeds the decrease in utility per dollar reduction in the amount spent on y, which equals $u'_y(x, y)/q$.

As in Example 18.1.3, the optimal choices of x and y can be expressed as *demand functions* of (p, q, m), which must be homogeneous of degree zero in the three variables (p, q, m) together.

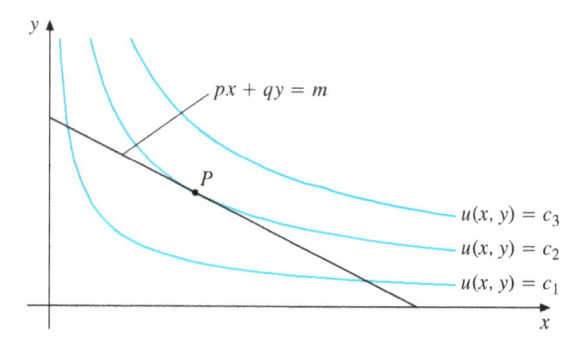

Figure 18.1.1 The solution to Example 18.1.4 is at point P.

Each exercise at the end of this section has only one solution candidate, which is the optimum.

EXERCISES FOR SECTION 18.1

1. Consider the problem: max xy s.t. $x + 3y = 24$.

   (a) Use the Lagrange multiplier method to find the only possible solution.

   (b) Check the solution by using the results in Example 18.1.3.

2. Use the Lagrange multiplier method to solve the problem

$$\min -40Q_1 + Q_1^2 - 2Q_1Q_2 - 20Q_2 + Q_2^2 \quad \text{s.t.} \quad Q_1 + Q_2 = 15$$

---

[6] You may want to recall Section 15.3 where it shows how to compute these slopes.

3. Use the results in Example 18.1.3 to solve the following problems:

   (a) max $10x^{1/2}y^{1/3}$ s.t. $2x + 4y = m$

   (b) max $x^{1/2}y^{1/2}$ s.t. $50\,000x + 0.08y = 1\,000\,000$

   (c) max $12x\sqrt{y}$ s.t. $3x + 4y = 12$

(SM) 4. Solve the following problems:

   (a) min $f(x, y) = x^2 + y^2$ s.t. $g(x, y) = x + 2y = 4$

   (b) min $f(x, y) = x^2 + 2y^2$ s.t. $g(x, y) = x + y = 12$

   (c) max $f(x, y) = x^2 + 3xy + y^2$ s.t. $g(x, y) = x + y = 100$

5. A person has the utility function $u(x, y) = 100xy + x + 2y$. Suppose that the price per unit of x is \$2, and that the price per unit of y is \$4. The person receives \$1 000 that all has to be spent on the two commodities x and y. Solve the utility maximization problem.

6. An individual has a Cobb–Douglas utility function $U(m, l) = Am^a l^b$, where m is income and l is leisure, and A, a, and b are positive constants, with $a + b \leq 1$. A total of T_0 hours are to be allocated between work W and leisure l, so that $W + l = T_0$. If the hourly wage is w, then $m = wW$, and the individual's problem is

$$\max Am^a l^b \text{ s.t. } \frac{m}{w} + l = T_0$$

Solve the problem by using (∗∗) in Example 18.1.3.

7. Use the Lagrange multiplier method to solve part (b) of Review Exercise 17.3.

8. A firm produces and sells two commodities. By selling x tons of the first commodity the firm gets a price per ton given by $p = 96 - 4x$. By selling y tons of the other commodity the price per ton is given by $q = 84 - 2y$. The total cost of producing and selling x tons of the first commodity and y tons of the second is given by $C(x, y) = 2x^2 + 2xy + y^2$.

   (a) Show that the firm's profit function is $P(x, y) = -6x^2 - 3y^2 - 2xy + 96x + 84y$.

   (b) Compute the first-order partial derivatives of P, and find its only critical point.

   (c) Suppose that the firm's production activity causes so much pollution that the authorities limit its output to 11 tons in total. Solve the firm's maximization problem in this case. Verify that the limit on total output does reduce the maximum possible value of $P(x, y)$.

(SM) 9. Consider the utility maximization problem max $x^a + y$ s.t. $px + y = m$, where the three parameters p, q, and m are positive, and the constant a satisfies $0 < a < 1$.

   (a) Find the demand functions, $x^*(p, m)$ and $y^*(p, m)$.

   (b) Find the first-order partial derivatives of the demand functions w.r.t. p and m, and check their signs.

   (c) How does the optimal expenditure on the x good vary with p? Then check the elasticity of $px^*(p, m)$ w.r.t. p.

(d) Put $a = 1/2$. What are the demand functions in this case? Denote the maximal utility as a function of p and m by $U^*(p, m)$, the value function, also called the indirect utility function. Verify that $\partial U^*/\partial p = -x^*(p, m)$.

SM 10. [HARDER] Consider the problem max $U(x, y) = 100 - e^{-x} - e^{-y}$ s.t. $px + qy = m$.

(a) Write down the first-order conditions for the problem and then solve them for x, y, and λ as functions of the positive parameters p, q, and m.

(b) What assumptions are needed for x and y to be nonnegative?

(c) Verify that x and y are homogeneous of degree 0 as functions of p, q, and m.

18.2 Interpreting the Lagrange Multiplier

Consider again the problem

$$\max(\min) f(x, y) \text{ s.t. } g(x, y) = c$$

Let x^* and y^* denote values of x and y that solve this problem. In general x^* and y^* both depend on c, so we write $x^* = x^*(c)$ and $y^* = y^*(c)$. Now *assume* that these solutions are differentiable functions of c. The associated maximum value of $f(x, y)$ is then also a function of c, which we call the (optimal) *value function* and denote by

$$f^*(c) = f(x^*(c), y^*(c)) \qquad (18.2.1)$$

Of course, the associated value of the Lagrange multiplier λ also depends on c, in general, so we write $\lambda(c)$. Now, provided that certain regularity conditions are satisfied, we have the remarkable result that

$$\frac{df^*(c)}{dc} = \lambda(c) \qquad (18.2.2)$$

Thus, *the Lagrange multiplier $\lambda = \lambda(c)$ is the rate at which the optimal value of the objective function changes with respect to changes in the constraint constant c.*

In particular, if dc is a small change in c, then

$$f^*(c + dc) - f^*(c) \approx \lambda(c) \, dc \qquad (18.2.3)$$

In economic applications, we often use c to denote the available stock of some resource, whereas $f(x, y)$ denotes utility or profit. Then $\lambda(c) \, dc$ measures the approximate change in utility or profit that can be obtained from being allowed to use dc units more, or $-dc$ units less in case $dc < 0$. Economists call λ a *shadow price* of the resource. Given our definition of $f^*(c)$ as the maximum profit when the resource input is c, Eq. (18.2.3) says that λ indicates the approximate increase in profit per unit increase in the resource.

Assuming that $f^*(c)$ is differentiable, we can prove Eq. (18.2.2) as follows:

Conditional proof: Taking the differential of the value function defined by Eq. (18.2.1) gives

$$df^*(c) = df(x^*, y^*) = f_1'(x^*, y^*)\,dx^* + f_2'(x^*, y^*)\,dy^* \qquad (*)$$

But the first-order conditions imply that $f_1'(x^*, y^*) = \lambda g_1'(x^*, y^*)$ and $f_2'(x^*, y^*) = \lambda g_2'(x^*, y^*)$. So $(*)$ can be written as

$$df^*(c) = \lambda g_1'(x^*, y^*)\,dx^* + \lambda g_2'(x^*, y^*)\,dy^*$$
$$= \lambda[g_1'(x^*, y^*)\,dx^* + g_2'(x^*, y^*)\,dy^*] \qquad (**)$$

Moreover, the equality constraint implies the identity $g(x^*(c), y^*(c)) = c$. Taking the differential of each side yields the equality

$$dg(x^*, y^*) = g_1'(x^*, y^*)\,dx^* + g_2'(x^*, y^*)\,dy^* = dc$$

Substituting this equality into $(**)$ implies that $df^*(c) = \lambda\,dc$.

EXAMPLE 18.2.1 Consider the following generalization of Example 18.1.1:

$$\max\ xy \text{ s.t. } 2x + y = m$$

Once again, the first-order conditions imply that $y = 2x$ with $\lambda = x$. Inserting $y = 2x$ into the constraint now gives $2x + 2x = m$, so $x = \tfrac{1}{4}m$. In the notation introduced at the beginning of this section, we can write the solution as $x^*(m) = \tfrac{1}{4}m$ and $y^*(m) = \tfrac{1}{2}m$, with $\lambda(m) = \tfrac{1}{4}m$. So the value function is $f^*(m) = (\tfrac{1}{4}m)(\tfrac{1}{2}m) = \tfrac{1}{8}m^2$. It follows that $df^*(m)/dm = \tfrac{1}{4}m = \lambda(m)$, which confirms (18.2.2).

Suppose in particular that $m = 100$, so that $f^*(100) = 100^2/8$. If m increases by 1 from 100, the new value is $f^*(101) = 101^2/8$. It follows that

$$f^*(101) - f^*(100) = 101^2/8 - 100^2/8 = 201/8 = 25.125$$

Note that Eq. (18.2.3) with $dc = 1$ gives $f^*(101) - f^*(100) \approx \lambda(100) \cdot 1 = 25 \cdot 1 = 25$, which is quite close to the exact value of 25.125.

EXAMPLE 18.2.2 Suppose that $Q = F(K, L)$ denotes the output of a state-owned firm when its input of capital is K and its input of labour is L. Suppose that the prices of capital and labour it faces are r and w dollars per unit, respectively. Suppose too that the firm is given a total budget of m dollars to spend on the two input factors. The firm wishes to find the choice of inputs it can afford that maximizes output. So it faces the problem

$$\max\ F(K, L) \text{ s.t. } rK + wL = m$$

After solving this problem by using Lagrange's method, the value of the Lagrange multiplier will tell us the approximate increase in output if the budget m is increased by 1 dollar.

Consider, for example, the specific problem max $120KL$ s.t. $2K + 5L = m$. Note that this is, mathematically, a special case of the problem in Example 18.1.3. Indeed, only the notation is different, along with the fact that the consumer who wants to maximize utility has been replaced with a firm that wants to maximize output.

From (∗∗) in Example 18.1.3, we find the solution $K^* = m/4$ and $L^* = m/10$, with $\lambda = 6m$. The optimal output is

$$Q^*(m) = 120 K^* L^* = 120 \cdot \frac{1}{4}m \cdot \frac{1}{10}m = 3m^2$$

It follows that $dQ^*/dm = 6m = \lambda$, so Eq. (18.2.2) is confirmed.

EXERCISES FOR SECTION 18.2

1. Verify that Eq. (18.2.2) holds for the problem max $x^3 y$ s.t. $2x + 3y = m$.

2. With reference to Example 18.1.2:

   (a) Solve the problem min $rK + wL$ s.t. $\sqrt{K} + L = Q$, assuming that $Q > w/2r$, where r, w, and Q are positive constants.

   (b) Verify Eq. (18.2.2).

3. Consider the problem min $x^2 + y^2$ s.t. $x + 2y = a$, where a is a constant.

   (a) Solve the problem by transforming it into an unconstrained optimization problem with one variable.

   (b) Show that the Lagrange method leads to the same solution, and verify Eq. (18.2.2).

   (c) Explain the solution by studying the level curves of $f(x, y) = x^2 + y^2$ and the graph of the straight line $x + 2y = a$. Can you give a geometric interpretation of the problem? Does the corresponding maximization problem have a solution?

(SM) 4. Consider the utility maximization problem max $U(x, y) = \sqrt{x} + y$ s.t. $x + 4y = 100$.

   (a) Using the Lagrange method, find the quantities demanded of the two goods.

   (b) Suppose income increases from 100 to 101. What is the exact increase in the optimal value of $U(x, y)$? Compare with the value found in (a) for the Lagrange multiplier.

   (c) Suppose we change the budget constraint to $px + qy = m$, but keep the same utility function. Derive the quantities demanded of the two goods in case $m > q^2/4p$.

(SM) 5. Consider the consumer demand problem

$$\max\ U(x, y) = \alpha \ln(x - a) + \beta \ln(y - b) \quad \text{s.t.} \quad px + qy = m \qquad (*)$$

where α, β, a, b, p, q, and m are positive constants, with $\alpha + \beta = 1$ and $m > ap + bq$.

   (a) Show that if the pair (x^*, y^*) solves problem $(*)$, then expenditure on the two goods is given by the two linear functions

$$px^* = \alpha m + pa - \alpha(pa + qb) \quad \text{and} \quad qy^* = \beta m + qb - \beta(pa + qb) \qquad (**)$$

of the three variables (m, p, q).[7]

---

[7] This is a special case of the *linear expenditure system* that the Nobel prize-winning British economist Richard (J.R.N.) Stone fitted to UK data, as described in the *Economic Journal*, 1954.

(b) Let $U^*(p, q, m) = U(x^*, y^*)$ denote the indirect utility function. Show that $\partial U^*/\partial m > 0$, then verify the so-called Roy's identities:

$$\frac{\partial U^*}{\partial p} = -\frac{\partial U^*}{\partial m} x^* \quad \text{and} \quad \frac{\partial U^*}{\partial q} = -\frac{\partial U^*}{\partial m} y^*$$

(SM) **6.** [HARDER] An oil producer starts extracting oil from a well at time $t = 0$, and ends extraction at a time $t = T$ that the producer chooses. Suppose that the output flow at any time t in the interval $[0, T]$ is $xt(T-t)$ barrels per unit of time, where the extraction intensity x can also be chosen. It follows that the total amount of oil extracted during the given time span is given by the function $g(x, T) = \int_0^T xt(T-t)\,dt$ of x and T.

Assume further that the sales price per barrel at time t is $p = 1 + t$, and that the cost per barrel extracted is equal to αT^2, where α is a positive constant. The profit per unit of time is then $(1 + t - \alpha T^2)xt(T-t)$, so that the total profit earned during the time interval $[0, T]$ is a function of x and T given by

$$f(x, T) = \int_0^T (1 + t - \alpha T^2) xt(T-t)\,dt$$

If the total amount of extractable oil in the field is M barrels, the producer can choose values of x and T subject to $g(x, T) = M$. The producer's problem is thus

$$\max f(x, T) \quad \text{s.t.} \quad g(x, T) = M \qquad (*)$$

Find explicit expressions for $f(x, T)$ and $g(x, T)$ by calculating the given integrals. Then solve problem $(*)$ and verify Eq. (18.2.2).

18.3 Multiple Solution Candidates

In all the examples and exercises considered so far in this chapter, the recipe for solving constrained optimization problems produced only one solution candidate. In this section we consider a problem where there are several candidates. In such cases, we have to decide which candidate actually solves the problem, assuming it has any solution at all.

EXAMPLE 18.3.1 Solve the problems

$$\max(\min) f(x, y) = x^2 + y^2 \quad \text{s.t.} \quad g(x, y) = x^2 + xy + y^2 = 3$$

Solution: For both the maximization and the minimization problems, the Lagrangian is

$$\mathcal{L}(x, y) = x^2 + y^2 - \lambda(x^2 + xy + y^2 - 3)$$

So the three FOCs we need to consider are

$$\mathcal{L}'_1(x, y) = 2x - \lambda(2x + y) = 0 \qquad \text{(i)}$$

$$\mathcal{L}'_2(x, y) = 2y - \lambda(x + 2y) = 0 \qquad \text{(ii)}$$

$$x^2 + xy + y^2 - 3 = 0 \qquad \text{(iii)}$$

To solve these, let us first eliminate λ from (i) and (ii). From (i) we get $\lambda = 2x/(2x+y)$ provided that $y \neq -2x$. Inserting this value of λ into (ii) gives

$$2y = \frac{2x}{2x+y}(x+2y)$$

Multiplying each side of this equation by $2x+y$ and then simplifying reduces it to $y^2 = x^2$. It follows that $y = \pm x$. This leaves us with the following three possibilities:

1. *Suppose, first, that $y = x$.* Then (iii) yields $x^2 = 1$, so $x = 1$ or $x = -1$. This gives the two solution candidates $(x, y) = (1, 1)$ and $(-1, -1)$, with $\lambda = 2/3$.
2. *Alternatively, suppose $y = -x$.* Then (iii) yields $x^2 = 3$, so $x = \sqrt{3}$ or $x = -\sqrt{3}$. This gives the two solution candidates $(x, y) = (\sqrt{3}, -\sqrt{3})$ and $(-\sqrt{3}, \sqrt{3})$, with $\lambda = 2$.
3. It only remains to consider the case $y = -2x$. Then from (i) we would have $x = 0$ and so $y = 0$. But this would contradict (iii), so this case cannot occur.

So we have found the only four points (x, y) that can solve the problem. Furthermore,

$$f(1, 1) = f(-1, -1) = 2 \text{ and } f(\sqrt{3}, -\sqrt{3}) = f(-\sqrt{3}, \sqrt{3}) = 6$$

We conclude that if the problem has solutions, then $(1, 1)$ and $(-1, -1)$ solve the minimization problem, whereas $(\sqrt{3}, -\sqrt{3})$ and $(-\sqrt{3}, \sqrt{3})$ solve the maximization problem.

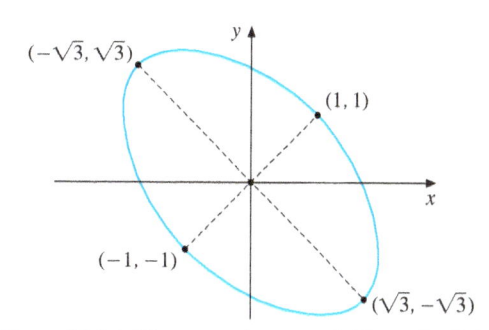

Figure 18.3.1 The constraint curve in Example 18.3.1

Geometrically, the equality constraint determines an ellipse. The problem is therefore to find what points on the ellipse are either nearest to or furthest from the origin, as shown in Fig. 18.3.1. It is "geometrically obvious" that the ellipse is a closed and bounded set. Because distance is a continuous function of (x, y), the extreme value theorem ensures that these nearest and furthest points must both exist.

EXERCISES FOR SECTION 18.3

SM 1. Solve the problems:

(a) max(min) $3xy$ s.t. $x^2 + y^2 = 8$ (b) max(min) $x + y$ s.t. $x^2 + 3xy + 3y^2 = 3$

2. Solve the problems:[8]
   (a) max $x^2 + y^2 - 2x + 1$ s.t. $x^2 + 4y^2 = 16$ (b) min $\ln(2 + x^2) + y^2$ s.t. $x^2 + 2y = 2$

3. Consider the problem max (min) $f(x, y) = x + y$ s.t. $g(x, y) = x^2 + y = 1$.
   (a) Find the solutions to the necessary conditions for these problems.
   (b) Explain the solution geometrically by drawing appropriate level curves for $f(x, y)$ together with the graph of the parabola $x^2 + y = 1$. Does the associated minimization problem have a solution?
   (c) Replace the constraint by $x^2 + y = 1.1$, and solve the revised problem in this new case. Find the corresponding change in the optimal value of $f(x, y) = x + y$. Then check whether this change is approximately equal to $\lambda \cdot 0.1$, as Eq. (18.2.3) suggests it should be.

4. Consider the problem max $f(x, y) = 24x - x^2 + 16y - 2y^2$ s.t. $g(x, y) = x^2 + 2y^2 = 44$.
   (a) Solve the problem.
   (b) What is the approximate change in the optimal value of $f(x, y)$ if 44 is changed to 45?

5. [HARDER] Consider the problem
$$\max(\min) Q = 2x_1^2 + 14x_1 x_2 + 2x_2^2 \quad \text{subject to} \quad x_1^2 + x_2^2 = 1$$
   (a) Show that Q can be written as the quadratic form $Q = \mathbf{x}'\mathbf{A}\mathbf{x}$, where $\mathbf{x}$ is a column 2-vector and $\mathbf{A}$ is a symmetric 2×2 matrix.
   (b) Use the Lagrange multiplier method to show that the first-order condition for the vector $\mathbf{x}$ to solve either problem is that $\mathbf{x}$ is an eigenvector of $\mathbf{A}$, with the eigenvalue as the associated Lagrange multiplier.
   (c) Prove that the largest (smallest) eigenvalue of $\mathbf{A}$ is the maximum (minimum) value of Q subject to the constraint. (*Hint:* Multiply each side of $\mathbf{Ax} = \lambda \mathbf{x}$ from the left by the row vector $\mathbf{x}'$.)
   (d) Find the solutions to the constrained maximization and minimization problems.

18.4 Why Does the Lagrange Multiplier Method Work?

So far we have merely offered the Lagrange multiplier method as a procedure for solving a maximization problem with two variables subject to an equality constraint that can be set out in the following standard form:

$$\max f(x, y) \quad \text{s.t.} \quad g(x, y) = c \tag{18.4.1}$$

Now it is time in this section to provide both a geometric and an analytical explanation of why the Lagrange multiplier method works.

---
[8] In (b) you should take it for granted that the minimum value exists.

A Geometric Argument

Figure 18.4.1 represents geometrically in three dimensions the maximization problem in (18.4.1). It shows the graph of f as something that looks like the surface of an inverted bowl. On the other hand, the equation $g(x, y) = c$ is represented by a dashed curve in the xy-plane. Then the shaded curve K in Fig. 18.4.1 consists of those points in the surface of the bowl that lie directly above the curve $g(x, y) = c$.

If we were to ignore the constraint, the maximum of $f(x, y)$ would occur at the peak A in Fig. 18.4.1. Imposing the constraint $g(x, y) = c$, however, allows us to choose only points along the curve K. So the solution to problem (18.4.1) occurs at B, the highest point on K. If we think of the graph of f as representing a mountain, and K as a mountain path, then we must ascend to the highest point on the path, which is at B. Analytically, the problem is to find the coordinates of B.

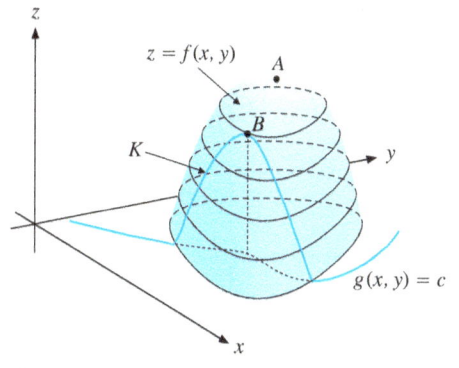

Figure 18.4.1 Constrained optimization

Figure 18.4.2 Geometry of the Lagrange multiplier method

Figure 18.4.2 "projects" the information in the three-dimensional Fig. 18.4.1 onto the two-dimensional xy-plane. Given the inverted bowl that is the graph of f, Figs. 18.4.1 and 18.4.2 both show some of its corresponding level curves. The curve $g(x, y) = c$, which also appears in both figures, is merely copied from Fig. 18.4.1 to Fig. 18.4.2. Figure 18.4.2 includes, but also extends, the projection onto the xy-plane of the three-dimensional curve K, which is the shaded part of the curve $g(x, y) = c$.

In ascending to the point A on the surface shown in Fig. 18.4.1, one is moving up to higher and higher level curves until one runs out of curves that are higher. The corresponding movement in Fig. 18.4.2 is to smaller and smaller level curves, until at point A' the level curve has shrunk to a single point at which $f(x, y)$ reaches its unconstrained maximum. The closer a level curve of f is to the summit at point A', the higher is the constant value of f along that level curve.

The maximization problem in (18.4.1) asks us to find that point on the constraint curve $g(x, y) = c$ where f attains its highest value. In Fig. 18.4.2, if we start at point P on the constraint curve and move along that curve toward A', then we ascend to points on level curves with higher and higher values of f. Notice that any level curve of f separates points in the plane where f is higher from points where f is lower. Now, at the point marked Q in Fig. 18.4.2, our path along the constraint curve *crosses* the level curve of f which passes through Q. So walking in one direction away from Q will take us back down toward P, whereas walking in the reverse direction away from Q will take us further up. For this reason, the point marked Q in Fig. 18.4.2 is definitely not the point on $g(x,y) = c$ at which f has its highest value.

Once we have got as far as point B in Fig. 18.4.1, however, we cannot go any higher along the curve K. Indeed, continuing along K beyond B starts taking us down to lower and lower level curves of f. Together Figs. 18.4.1 and 18.4.2 should make it intuitively clear that the highest point B along the path K corresponds to the point B' in the plane. Moreover, that point occurs precisely where the constraint curve $g(x,y) = c$ just *touches* a level curve for f, *without crossing it*. This key observation implies that, in Fig. 18.4.2, the slope of the tangent to the curve $g(x,y) = c$ at the optimal point B' *must equal* the slope of the tangent to the level curve of f at that same point.

Given any level curve $F(x,y) = c$ of a function F, recall from Section 15.3 that at any point (x,y) where F is differentiable, the slope of the level curve is given by $dy/dx = -F_1'(x,y)/F_2'(x,y)$. Disregard for now any point where any first-order partial derivative is zero. Then the condition that the slopes of the respective tangents to the constraint curve $g(x,y) = c$ and to the level curve for $f(x,y)$ should be equal where they meet can be expressed analytically as:

$$-\frac{g_1'(x,y)}{g_2'(x,y)} = -\frac{f_1'(x,y)}{f_2'(x,y)}$$

Because we are assuming that none of the partial derivatives are zero, this is evidently equivalent to

$$\frac{f_1'(x,y)}{g_1'(x,y)} = \frac{f_2'(x,y)}{g_2'(x,y)} \qquad (18.4.2)$$

It follows that a necessary condition for (x,y) to solve problem (18.4.1) is that the left- and right-hand sides of Eq. (18.4.2) be equal at (x,y). Let λ denote the common value of these two fractions. This is the Lagrange multiplier we introduced in Section 18.1. With this definition, one has

$$f_1'(x,y) - \lambda g_1'(x,y) = 0 \quad \text{and} \quad f_2'(x,y) - \lambda g_2'(x,y) = 0 \qquad (18.4.3)$$

Indeed, we see that (18.4.3) just tells us that the Lagrangian defined in Eq. (18.1.2) must have a critical point at (x,y). An analogous argument for the problem of minimizing $f(x,y)$ subject to $g(x,y) = c$ gives the same condition.

The geometric argument we have just given should be sufficiently convincing. Nevertheless, the analytic argument that follows is easier to extend to more than two variables.

An Analytical Argument

So far in this chapter we have studied the problem of finding the largest or smallest value of $f(x,y)$ subject only to the constraint $g(x,y) = c$. Sometimes economists need to consider points that are a local maximum or minimum, in the same sense as in Section 17.3. That is, we look for points (x^0, y^0) with $g(x^0, y^0) = c$ where, for all pairs (x,y) satisfying $g(x,y) = c$

SECTION 18.4 / WHY DOES THE LAGRANGE MULTIPLIER METHOD WORK?

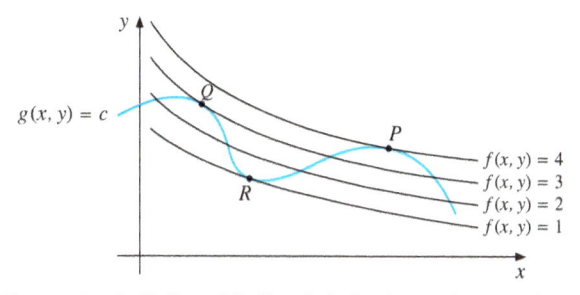

Figure 18.4.3 Q, R, and P all satisfy the first-order conditions

that lie sufficiently close to (x^0, y^0), one has: (i) either $f(x, y) \leq f(x^0, y^0)$ in case (x^0, y^0) is a local maximum; (ii) or $f(x, y) \geq f(x^0, y^0)$ in case (x^0, y^0) is a local minimum.

Graphically, possible local extrema are illustrated in Fig. 18.4.3. Here R is a local minimum point for $f(x, y)$ subject to $g(x, y) = c$, whereas both Q and P are local maximum points. The global maximum of $f(x, y)$ subject to $g(x, y) = c$ is attained only at P. At each of the three points P, Q, and R in Fig. 18.4.3 the constraint curve $g(x, y) = c$ and the level curve share a common tangent, so condition (18.4.2) is satisfied. That is, the first-order conditions are exactly as before. Let us now derive these conditions in a way that does not rely on geometric intuition.

As discussed in Section 15.3, except in some special cases, the equation $g(x, y) = c$ with c fixed defines y implicitly as a differentiable function $y = h(x)$ of x near any point (x, y) which satisfies the equation as well as the condition $g_2'(x, y) \neq 0$. Furthermore, provided this condition is satisfied, according to formula (15.3.2) one has

$$y' = h'(x) = -\frac{g_1'(x, y)}{g_2'(x, y)} \tag{18.4.4}$$

Now, inserting $y = h(x)$ into $f(x, y)$ yields $z = f(x, y) = f(x, h(x))$, thus making the objective function depend on x alone. Then a necessary condition for a local extreme point is that $dz/dx = 0$. But combining the chain rule with Eq. (18.4.4) gives

$$\frac{dz}{dx} = f_1'(x, y) + f_2'(x, y)y' = f_1'(x, y) + f_2'(x, y)h'(x) = f_1'(x, y) - f_2'(x, y)\frac{g_1'(x, y)}{g_2'(x, y)}$$

So we have the following necessary condition for (x, y) to solve problem (18.4.1):

$$\frac{dz}{dx} = f_1'(x, y) - f_2'(x, y)\frac{g_1'(x, y)}{g_2'(x, y)} = 0 \tag{18.4.5}$$

Assuming that $g_2'(x, y) \neq 0$, we can define $\lambda = f_2'(x, y)/g_2'(x, y)$, implying that the two equations $f_1'(x, y) - \lambda g_1'(x, y) = 0$ and $f_2'(x, y) - \lambda g_2'(x, y) = 0$ must both be satisfied, as they were in (18.4.3). Once again, therefore, the Lagrangian defined in Eq. (18.1.2) must have a critical point at (x, y). The same result holds, by an analogous argument, provided $g_1'(x, y) \neq 0$. To summarize, one can prove the following precise result:

THEOREM 18.4.1 (LAGRANGE'S THEOREM)

Suppose that $f(x, y)$ and $g(x, y)$ have continuous partial derivatives in a domain A of the xy-plane, and that (x^0, y^0) is both an interior point of A and a local extreme point for $f(x, y)$ subject to the constraint $g(x, y) = c$. Suppose further that $g'_1(x^0, y^0)$ and $g'_2(x^0, y^0)$ are not both 0. Then there exists a unique number λ such that the Lagrangian has a critical point at (x^0, y^0).

Exercise 3 asks you to show how trouble can result from uncritical use of the Lagrange multiplier method that disregards the assumptions in Theorem 18.4.1. Exercise 4 asks you to show what can go wrong if $g'_1(x^0, y^0)$ and $g'_2(x^0, y^0)$ are both 0.

In constrained optimization problems in economics, it is often implicitly assumed that the variables are nonnegative. This was certainly the case for the specific utility maximization problem in Example 18.1.3. Because the optimal solutions were positive, nothing was lost by disregarding the nonnegativity constraints. Here is an example showing that sometimes we must take greater care.

EXAMPLE 18.4.1   Consider the utility maximization problem

$$\max\ xy + x + 2y \text{ s.t. } 2x + y = m,\ x \geq 0 \text{ and } y \geq 0$$

Here we require explicitly that the amount of each good is nonnegative. The Lagrangian is $\mathcal{L} = xy + x + 2y - \lambda(2x + y - m)$. So the first-order conditions, disregarding the nonnegativity constraints for now, are

$$\mathcal{L}'_1 = y + 1 - 2\lambda = 0 \text{ and } \mathcal{L}'_2(x, y) = x + 2 - \lambda = 0$$

To eliminate λ, we find that $y = 2\lambda - 1 = 2(x + 2) - 1 = 2x + 3$. Inserting this into the budget constraint gives $2x + 2x + 3 = m$, so $x = \frac{1}{4}(m - 3)$. It is easy to find the corresponding value of y. The suggested solution that emerges is $x^* = \frac{1}{4}(m - 3)$, $y^* = \frac{1}{2}(m + 3)$.

Note that in case $m < 3$ we have $x^* < 0$, implying that the suggested solution is not the actual one. As we show below, the solution in this case is actually $x^* = 0$, $y^* = m$. So when income is low, the consumer spends everything on just the second commodity.

Let us analyse the problem further by converting it into an unconstrained maximization problem. To do this, note how the constraint implies that $y = m - 2x$. In order for both x and y to be nonnegative, one must have $0 \leq x \leq m/2$ and $0 \leq y \leq m$. Substituting $y = m - 2x$ into the utility function gives utility as the following function $U(x)$ of x alone:

$$U(x) = x(m - 2x) + x + 2(m - 2x) = -2x^2 + (m - 3)x + 2m, \text{ for all } x \in [0, m/2]$$

In the interval $[0, \frac{1}{2}m]$ this is a quadratic function with $x = \frac{1}{4}(m - 3)$ as its only critical point. In case $m > 3$, this is an interior critical point of the concave function U, so it is a maximum point. But in case $m \leq 3$, one has $U'(x) = -4x + (m - 3) < 0$ for all $x > 0$. Because x must belong to $[0, \frac{1}{2}m]$, in this case $x = 0$ is the unique maximum point of $U(x)$.

When motivating the Lagrange multiplier method, a frequently occurring error in the economics literature (including some leading textbooks) is the claim that it transforms a constrained optimization problem into that of finding an unconstrained optimum of the

Lagrangian. Exercise 1 shows that this is wrong. What the method does instead is to transform a constrained optimization problem into that of finding the appropriate *critical points* of the Lagrangian. Sometimes these happen to be maximum points, but often they are not.

To test your understanding of when the Lagrange procedure can be used, it is a good exercise to explain why it certainly works, for instance, in Exercise 1, but not in either Exercise 3 or Exercise 4.

EXERCISES FOR SECTION 18.4

1. Consider the problem max xy s.t. $x + y = 2$. Reduce it to the one-variable problem of maximizing $x(2 - x)$, and show that $(x, y) = (1, 1)$ is the only possible solution. Check that this satisfies the first-order conditions for the constrained maximization problem, with Lagrange multiplier $\lambda = 1$. Show that $(1, 1)$ does not maximize the Lagrangian $\mathcal{L}(x, y) = xy - 1 \cdot (x + y - 2)$. Does this matter?

2. The following text, which attempts to justify the Lagrange method, is taken from a book on mathematics for management. It contains *grave* errors. Sort them out.

    "Consider the general problem of finding the extreme points of $z = f(x, y)$ subject to the constraint $g(x, y) = 0$. Clearly the extreme points must satisfy the pair of equations $f'_x(x, y) = 0, f'_y(x, y) = 0$ in addition to the constraint $g(x, y) = 0$. Thus, there are three equations that must be satisfied by the pair of unknowns x, y. Because there are more equations than unknowns, the system is said to be overdetermined and, in general, is difficult to solve. In order to facilitate computation ..."

3. [HARDER] Consider the problem max $f(x, y) = 2x + 3y$ s.t. $g(x, y) = \sqrt{x} + \sqrt{y} = 5$.

    (a) Show that the Lagrange multiplier method suggests the solution $(x, y) = (9, 4)$. Show that this does not solve the constrained maximization problem because $f(9, 4) = 30$, yet $f(25, 0) = 50$.

    (b) Find the true solution to the problem by studying the level curves of $f(x, y) = 2x + 3y$, along with the graph of the constraint equation. (*Hint:* See Exercise 5.4.2.)

    (c) Which assumption of Theorem 18.4.1 is violated?

SM 4. [HARDER] Solve the problem

$$\min f(x, y) = (x + 2)^2 + y^2 \text{ s.t. } g(x, y) = y^2 - x(x + 1)^2 = 0$$

Show that the Lagrange multiplier method cannot locate this minimum. (*Hint*: Draw a graph of $g(x, y) = 0$. Note in particular that $g(-1, 0) = 0$.)

18.5 Sufficient Conditions

Theorem 18.4.1 gives *necessary* conditions for the local solution of constrained optimization problems. In order to confirm that we have really found the solution, however, a more careful check is needed. The examples and exercises of Section 18.3 have geometric interpretations which strongly suggest we have found the solution. Indeed, if the constraint set is closed and bounded, then the Extreme Value Theorem 17.5.1 guarantees that a continuous function *will* attain both maximum and minimum values over this set.

Consider, for example, Example 18.3.1. Here the constraint set, which was graphed in Fig. 18.3.1, *is* closed and bounded. The continuous function $f(x, y) = x^2 + y^2$ will therefore attain both a maximum value and a minimum value over the constraint set. Since there are four points satisfying the first-order conditions, it remains only to check which of them gives f its highest and lowest values.

Concave/Convex Lagrangian

Consider the problem

$$\max (\min) f(x, y) \text{ s.t. } g(x, y) = c \qquad (18.5.1)$$

with the Lagrangian

$$\mathcal{L}(x, y) = f(x, y) - \lambda[g(x, y) - c] \qquad (18.5.2)$$

We already know that if (x^0, y^0) solves (18.5.1), then the Lagrangian (18.5.2) usually has a critical point at (x^0, y^0). But Exercise 18.4.1 shows how $\mathcal{L}$ may not have a maximum (minimum) at (x^0, y^0). Suppose, however, that $\mathcal{L}$ happens to reach an *unconstrained global maximum* at (x^0, y^0), in the sense that $\mathcal{L}(x^0, y^0) \geq \mathcal{L}(x, y)$ for *all* (x, y) in the plane. Then, for all (x, y), one has

$$\mathcal{L}(x^0, y^0) = f(x^0, y^0) - \lambda[g(x^0, y^0) - c] \geq \mathcal{L}(x, y) = f(x, y) - \lambda[g(x, y) - c] \quad (*)$$

Now, provided that (x^0, y^0) also satisfies the constraint $g(x^0, y^0) = c$, then for all (x, y) such that $g(x, y) = c$, both terms in $(*)$ that are within brackets become zero, so it reduces to

$$\mathcal{L}(x^0, y^0) = f(x^0, y^0) \geq \mathcal{L}(x, y) = f(x, y)$$

It follows that $f(x^0, y^0) \geq f(x, y)$ for all (x, y) that satisfy the constraint $g(x, y) = c$. So (x^0, y^0) really does solve the maximization problem in (18.5.1). A corresponding result is obtained for the minimization problem in (18.5.1), provided that $\mathcal{L}$ reaches an unconstrained global minimum at (x^0, y^0).

Next, recall from Theorem 17.2.1 that a critical point (x^0, y^0) for a concave (convex) function really does maximize (minimize) the function. To summarize, we have the following key result:

THEOREM 18.5.1 (CONCAVE/CONVEX LAGRANGIAN)

Consider the problems in (18.5.1). Let (x^0, y^0) be any critical point for the Lagrangian $\mathcal{L}$ defined in (18.5.2) that satisfies the equality constraint $g(x^0, y^0) = c$. Now:

(a) if $\mathcal{L}$ is concave, or if (x^0, y^0) happens to maximize $\mathcal{L}$ anyway, then (x^0, y^0) solves the constrained maximization problem;

(b) if $\mathcal{L}$ is convex, or if (x^0, y^0) happens to minimize $\mathcal{L}$ anyway, then (x^0, y^0) solves the constrained minimization problem.

Warning: When applying Theorem 18.5.1 to a specific problem, it is important to remember that the concavity or convexity of $\mathcal{L}$ often depends upon the sign of λ. Suppose, for example, that f is concave and g is convex. Then the Lagrangian $\mathcal{L} = f - \lambda g$ will be concave if $\lambda \geq 0$, but generally will not be concave if $\lambda < 0$. An interesting exception where it is concave even when $\lambda < 0$ occurs if g is not only convex, but also concave because it happens to be linear.

EXAMPLE 18.5.1

Consider a firm that uses positive inputs K and L of capital and labour, respectively, to produce a single output Q according to the Cobb–Douglas production function $Q = F(K, L) = AK^a L^b$, where A, a, and b are positive parameters satisfying $a + b \leq 1$. Suppose that the prices per unit of capital and labour are $r > 0$ and $w > 0$, respectively. The cost-minimizing inputs of K and L must solve the problem

$$\min rK + wL \text{ s.t. } AK^a L^b = Q$$

Explain why the Lagrange multiplier λ is positive at any critical point of the Lagrangian. Expain too why this implies that a critical point does minimize costs. (*Hint*: See Exercise 17.2.8.)

Solution: The Lagrangian is $\mathcal{L} = rK + wL - \lambda(AK^a L^b - Q)$. The first-order conditions for a critical point are $r = \lambda A a K^{a-1} L^b$ and $w = \lambda A b K^a L^{b-1}$, implying that $\lambda > 0$. From Exercise 17.2.8, we see that $-\mathcal{L}$ is concave, so $\mathcal{L}$ is convex.

Local Second-Order Conditions

Sometimes economists are interested in conditions that are sufficient for (x^0, y^0) to be a local extreme point of $f(x, y)$ subject to $g(x, y) = c$. We start by looking at the expression (18.4.5) for dz/dx. The condition $dz/dx = 0$ is necessary for local optimality. If $d^2z/dx^2 < 0$ in addition at the critical point of the Lagrangian, then that point must solve the local maximization problem.

The second derivative d^2z/dx^2 is just the total derivative of dz/dx w.r.t. x. Assuming that both f and g are C^2 functions, and that $g'_2(x^0, y^0) \neq 0$, we differentiate (18.4.5) once again, while recalling that y is a function of x. The result is

$$\frac{d^2 z}{dx^2} = f''_{11} + f''_{12} y' - (f''_{21} + f''_{22} y') \frac{g'_1}{g'_2} - f'_2 \frac{(g''_{11} + g''_{12} y') g'_2 - (g''_{21} + g''_{22} y') g'_1}{(g'_2)^2}$$

But f and g are both C^2 functions, so $f''_{12} = f''_{21}$ and $g''_{12} = g''_{21}$. Moreover $y' = -g'_1/g'_2$. Also at any critical point of the Lagrangian, the first-order conditions imply that $f'_1 = \lambda g'_1$ and $f'_2 = \lambda g'_2$. After using these relationships to eliminate y' and f'_2, followed by some elementary algebra, we finally obtain

$$\frac{d^2 z}{dx^2} = \frac{1}{(g'_2)^2} \left[(f''_{11} - \lambda g''_{11})(g'_2)^2 - 2(f''_{12} - \lambda g''_{12}) g'_1 g'_2 + (f''_{22} - \lambda g''_{22})(g'_1)^2 \right]$$

Next, let us define

$$D(x, y, \lambda) = (f''_{11} - \lambda g''_{11})(g'_2)^2 - 2(f''_{12} - \lambda g''_{12}) g'_1 g'_2 + (f''_{22} - \lambda g''_{22})(g'_1)^2 \quad (18.5.3)$$

Evidently $d^2z/dx^2 < 0$ provided $D(x, y, \lambda) < 0$. Also $d^2z/dx^2 > 0$ provided $D(x, y, \lambda) > 0$. So we have the following result, in which the condition on the sign of $D(x^0, y^0, \lambda)$ is called the *local second-order condition*:

THEOREM 18.5.2 (LOCAL SECOND-ORDER CONDITION)

For the problems in Eq. (18.5.1), suppose the triple (x^0, y^0, λ) satisfies the three first-order conditions

$$f_1'(x^0, y^0) = \lambda g_1'(x^0, y^0), \quad f_2'(x^0, y^0) = \lambda g_2'(x^0, y^0), \quad \text{and} \quad g(x^0, y^0) = c$$

Then, given the definition of $D(x^0, y^0, \lambda)$ in (18.5.3):

(a) if $D(x^0, y^0, \lambda) < 0$, then (x^0, y^0) solves the maximization problem locally;

(b) if $D(x^0, y^0, \lambda) > 0$, then (x^0, y^0) solves the minimization problem locally.

EXAMPLE 18.5.2   Consider the problem

$$\max(\min) f(x, y) = x^2 + y^2 \text{ s.t. } g(x, y) = x^2 + xy + y^2 = 3$$

In Example 18.3.1 we saw that the first-order conditions give as solution candidates the two points $(1, 1)$ and $(-1, -1)$ with $\lambda = 2/3$, as well as both $(\sqrt{3}, -\sqrt{3})$ and $(-\sqrt{3}, \sqrt{3})$ with $\lambda = 2$. Check the local second-order condition of Theorem 18.5.2 in this case.

Solution: We find that $f_{11}'' = 2, f_{12}'' = 0, f_{22}'' = 2, g_{11}'' = 2, g_{12}'' = 1$, and $g_{22}'' = 2$. So definition (18.5.3) implies that

$$D(x, y, \lambda) = (2 - 2\lambda)(x + 2y)^2 + 2\lambda(2x + y)(x + 2y) + (2 - 2\lambda)(2x + y)^2$$

With some routine calculations, one can show that

$$D(1, 1, \tfrac{2}{3}) = D(-1, -1, \tfrac{2}{3}) = 24 \quad \text{and} \quad D(\sqrt{3}, -\sqrt{3}, 2) = D(-\sqrt{3}, \sqrt{3}, 2) = -24$$

The respective signs of D at these four solution candidates imply that $(1, 1)$ and $(-1, -1)$ are local constrained minimum points, whereas $(\sqrt{3}, -\sqrt{3})$ and $(-\sqrt{3}, \sqrt{3})$ are local constrained maximum points.[9]

As with Eq. (15.3.5), the concept of 3×3 determinants that we saw in Section 13.2 allows formula (18.5.3) to be written in a symmetric form that is easier to remember, namely

$$D(x, y, \lambda) = - \begin{vmatrix} 0 & g_1'(x, y) & g_2'(x, y) \\ g_1'(x, y) & \mathcal{L}_{11}''(x, y) & \mathcal{L}_{12}''(x, y) \\ g_2'(x, y) & \mathcal{L}_{21}''(x, y) & \mathcal{L}_{22}''(x, y) \end{vmatrix} \qquad (18.5.4)$$

Note that according to definition (14.6.2), the 2×2 matrix at the bottom right of the determinant is the Hessian of the Lagrangian. So the determinant in Eq. (18.5.4) is naturally

---

[9] In Example 18.3.1 we proved that these points were actually *global* extrema.

called a *bordered Hessian*; its borders in the first row and first column, apart from 0 at the top left, are 2-vectors whose components are the two first-order partial derivatives of g.

EXERCISES FOR SECTION 18.5

1. Use Theorem 18.5.1 to check that the solution found in part (a) of Exercise 18.1.3 is optimal.

2. Consider the problem max $\ln x + \ln y$ s.t. $px + qy = m$. Compute $D(x, y, \lambda)$, as defined in (18.5.3), then verify that the appropriate second-order condition in Theorem 18.5.2 is satisfied.[10]

3. Compute $D(x, y, \lambda)$ in Theorem 18.5.1 for part (a) of Exercise 18.2.2. What can you conclude?

(SM) 4. Prove that $U(x, y) = x^a + y^a$, where $a \in (0, 1)$, is concave for all $x > 0$ and $y > 0$. Then, solve the problem max $U(x, y)$ s.t. $px + qy = m$, where p, q, and m are positive constants.

18.6 Additional Variables and Constraints

Many constrained optimization problems in economics involve more than just two variables. The typical problem with n variables and one constraint can be written in the form

$$\max(\min) f(x_1, \ldots, x_n) \text{ s.t. } g(x_1, \ldots, x_n) = c \qquad (18.6.1)$$

The Lagrange multiplier method presented in the previous sections can be easily generalized. As before, associate a Lagrange multiplier λ with the constraint and form the Lagrangian function

$$\mathcal{L}(x_1, \ldots, x_n) = f(x_1, \ldots, x_n) - \lambda[g(x_1, \ldots, x_n) - c] \qquad (18.6.2)$$

Next, find all the first-order partial derivatives of $\mathcal{L}$ and equate them to zero, so that

$$\mathcal{L}'_1 = f'_1(x_1, \ldots, x_n) - \lambda g'_1(x_1, \ldots, x_n) = 0$$
$$\vdots \qquad (18.6.3)$$
$$\mathcal{L}'_n = f'_n(x_1, \ldots, x_n) - \lambda g'_n(x_1, \ldots, x_n) = 0$$

These n equations, together with the constraint, form $n + 1$ equations that should be solved simultaneously to determine the $n + 1$ unknowns, which are $x_1, \ldots, x_n$, and λ.

This method will fail, in general, to give correct necessary conditions if all the first-order partial derivatives of $g(x_1, \ldots, x_n)$ happen to vanish at the critical point of the Lagrangian. Otherwise, an easy generalization of the analytic argument in Section 18.4 can be used to prove the obvious extension to n variables of the first-order conditions

---

[10] Note that for this problem the Lagrangian is concave as a function of (x, y), for all real λ, as is easily checked. So the unique solution $(x, y) = (m/2p, m/2q)$ to the first-order conditions is actually a global constrained maximum.

in Theorem 18.4.1. Indeed, suppose $\partial g/\partial x_n \neq 0$, say. Then near the critical point we can "solve" $g(x_1, \ldots, x_n) = c$ for x_n, and thus reduce the problem to an unconstrained extremum problem in the remaining $n - 1$ variables $x_1, \ldots, x_{n-1}$.

EXAMPLE 18.6.1 Solve the consumer's demand problem

$$\max\ U(x, y, z) = x^2 y^3 z \quad \text{s.t.} \quad x + y + z = 12$$

Solution: Define the Lagrangian $\mathcal{L}(x, y, z) = x^2 y^3 z - \lambda(x + y + z - 12)$. Then, in addition to the constraint $x + y + z = 12$, the three first-order conditions are

$$\mathcal{L}_1' = 2xy^3 z - \lambda = 0, \quad \mathcal{L}_2' = 3x^2 y^2 z - \lambda = 0, \quad \text{and} \quad \mathcal{L}_3' = x^2 y^3 - \lambda = 0 \qquad (*)$$

Now, if *any* of the variables x, y, and z is 0, then $x^2 y^3 z = 0$. This is definitely not the maximum value because choosing $(x, y, z) = (4, 4, 4)$, for instance, makes $U(x, y, z)$ positive. So suppose that x, y, and z are all positive.

From the first two equations in $(*)$, we have $\lambda = 2xy^3 z = 3x^2 y^2 z$, so $y = 3x/2$. The first and third equations in $(*)$ likewise imply that $\lambda = 2xy^3 z = x^2 y^3$, so $z = x/2$. Inserting $y = 3x/2$ and $z = x/2$ into the constraint yields $x + 3x/2 + x/2 = 12$, so $x = 4$. Then $y = 3x/2 = 6$ and $z = x/2 = 2$. Thus, the only possible solution is $(x, y, z) = (4, 6, 2)$.

EXAMPLE 18.6.2 Solve the problem

$$\min\ f(x, y, z) = (x - 4)^2 + (y - 4)^2 + \left(z - \tfrac{1}{2}\right)^2 \quad \text{s.t.} \quad x^2 + y^2 = z$$

Can you give a geometric interpretation of the problem?

Solution: The Lagrangian is

$$\mathcal{L}(x, y, z) = (x - 4)^2 + (y - 4)^2 + \left(z - \tfrac{1}{2}\right)^2 - \lambda(x^2 + y^2 - z)$$

Including the constraint, the four first-order conditions are:

$$\mathcal{L}_1'(x, y, z) = 2(x - 4) - 2\lambda x = 0 \qquad (i)$$

$$\mathcal{L}_2'(x, y, z) = 2(y - 4) - 2\lambda y = 0 \qquad (ii)$$

$$\mathcal{L}_3'(x, y, z) = 2\left(z - \tfrac{1}{2}\right) + \lambda = 0 \qquad (iii)$$

$$x^2 + y^2 = z \qquad (iv)$$

From (i) we see that $x = 0$ is impossible. Equation (i) thus gives $\lambda = 1 - 4/x$. Inserting this into (ii) and (iii) gives $y = x$ and $z = 2/x$. Using these results, Eq. (iv) reduces to $2x^2 = 2/x$, that is, $x^3 = 1$, so $x = 1$. It follows that $(x, y, z) = (1, 1, 2)$, with $\lambda = -3$, is the only solution candidate for the problem.

The expression $(x - 4)^2 + (y - 4)^2 + (z - 1/2)^2$ measures the square of the distance from the point $(4, 4, 1/2)$ to the point (x, y, z). The set of points (x, y, z) that satisfy $z = x^2 + y^2$ is a surface known as a paraboloid, part of which is shown in Fig. 18.6.1. The minimization problem is therefore to find that point on the paraboloid which has the smallest (square) distance from $(4, 4, 1/2)$. It is "geometrically obvious" that this problem has a solution. On the other hand, the problem of finding the largest distance from $(4, 4, 1/2)$ to a point on the paraboloid does not have a solution, as the distance can be made as large as we like.

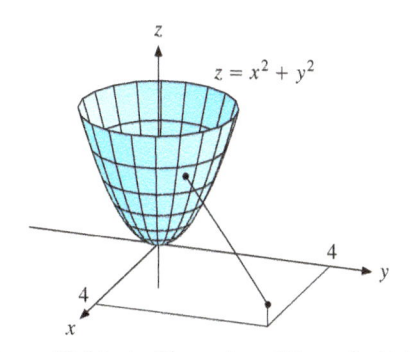

Figure 18.6.1 An illustration of Example 18.6.2

EXAMPLE 18.6.3   The general consumer optimization problem with n goods is

$$\max \ U(x_1, \ldots, x_n) \ \text{s.t.} \ p_1 x_1 + \cdots + p_n x_n = m \tag{18.6.4}$$

Here we assume that the utility function U is defined for all $x_1 \geq 0, \ldots, x_n \geq 0$, and that the prices $p_1, p_2, \cdots, p_n$ are all positive parameters. Let $\mathbf{x}$ denote the n-vector $(x_1, \ldots, x_n)$. Then the Lagrangian is

$$\mathcal{L}(\mathbf{x}) = U(\mathbf{x}) - \lambda(p_1 x_1 + \cdots + p_n x_n - m)$$

In addition to the budget constraint, the other n first-order conditions are

$$\mathcal{L}_i'(\mathbf{x}) = U_i'(\mathbf{x}) - \lambda p_i = 0 \ (i = 1, \ldots, n)$$

These n equations imply that

$$\frac{U_1'(\mathbf{x})}{p_1} = \frac{U_2'(\mathbf{x})}{p_2} = \cdots = \frac{U_n'(\mathbf{x})}{p_n} = \lambda \tag{18.6.5}$$

We can use the last equation to determine the Lagrange multiplier λ. After removing it, we are left with $n - 1$ equations.[11] In addition, the constraint must hold. This gives us a total of n equations to determine the values of the n variables $x_1, \ldots, x_n$.

From Eq. (18.6.5) it also follows that for every pair of goods j and k one has

$$\frac{U_j'(\mathbf{x})}{U_k'(\mathbf{x})} = \frac{p_j}{p_k} \tag{18.6.6}$$

The left-hand side is the MRS of good k for good j, whereas the right-hand side is their price ratio, or rate of exchange of good k for good j. So condition (18.6.6) requires that the MRS for each pair of goods be equal to the corresponding price ratio.

---

[11] For $n = 2$, there is one equation; for $n = 3$, there are two equations; and so on.

Consider the n equations in (18.6.5), together with the budget constraint. Assume that this system of $n+1$ equations is solved for the n-vector $\mathbf{x} = (x_1, \ldots, x_n)$ of demand quantities and for λ, all as functions of the price vector $\mathbf{p} = (p_1, \ldots, p_n)$ and m. The first n variables in this solution can be written as $x_i = D_i(\mathbf{p}, m)$, for $i = 1, \ldots, n$, where $D_i(\mathbf{p}, m)$ denotes the amount of the ith commodity that the consumer demands when faced with prices $\mathbf{p}$ and income m. For this reason the n functions $x_i = D_i(\mathbf{p}, m)$ are called the consumer's *demand functions*. By the same argument as in Examples 15.7.4 and 18.1.3, all these demand functions are homogeneous of degree 0 as functions of $\mathbf{p}$ and m together. As one check that you have correctly derived the demand functions, it is a good idea to verify that all the functions you find are indeed homogeneous of degree 0, as well as satisfying the budget constraint.

In the special case when the consumer has a Cobb–Douglas utility function, the constrained maximization problem in (18.6.4) takes the form

$$\max Ax_1^{a_1} \cdots x_n^{a_n} \quad \text{s.t.} \quad p_1 x_1 + \cdots + p_n x_n = m \tag{18.6.7}$$

where we assume that each "taste" parameter $a_i > 0$. As in part (a) of Exercise 8, the demand functions can be found explicitly. Indeed, they are

$$D_i(\mathbf{p}, m) = \frac{a_i}{a_1 + \cdots + a_n} \frac{m}{p_i} \tag{18.6.8}$$

We see how the pattern of the two-good case in Example 18.1.3 is repeated, with a constant fraction of income m spent on each good, independent of all prices. Note also that the demand for any good i is completely unaffected by changes in the price of any other good. This is an argument against using Cobb–Douglas utility functions, because we expect realistic consumer demand functions to depend on prices of other goods that are either complements or substitutes.

More Constraints

Occasionally economists need to consider optimization problems with more than one equality constraint, although it is much more common to have many inequality constraints. The obvious extension to m equality constraints of the problem set out in (18.6.1) is

$$\max(\min) f(x_1, \ldots, x_n) \quad \text{s.t.} \quad \begin{cases} g_1(x_1, \ldots, x_n) = c_1 \\ \cdots\cdots\cdots \\ g_m(x_1, \ldots, x_n) = c_m \end{cases} \tag{18.6.9}$$

That is, after letting $\mathbf{x} = (x_1, \ldots, x_n)$ denote the n-vector of choice variables, the single constraint $g(\mathbf{x}) = c$ becomes extended into the system of m constraints $g_j(\mathbf{x}) = c_j$ (for $j = 1, 2, \ldots, m$). The Lagrange multiplier method can be extended to treat problem (18.6.9). To do so, first we need to associate a separate Lagrange multiplier λ_j with each constraint $g_j(\mathbf{x}) = c_j$. Thereafter, we replace the single term $\lambda[g(\mathbf{x}) - c]$ in (18.6.1) by a sum of m terms, one for each constraint, resulting in an expanded Lagrangian function of the form

$$\mathcal{L}(\mathbf{x}) = f(\mathbf{x}) - \sum_{j=1}^{m} \lambda_j [g_j(\mathbf{x}) - c_j] \tag{18.6.10}$$

SECTION 18.6 / ADDITIONAL VARIABLES AND CONSTRAINTS

Except in special cases, any optimal point, either local or global, must be a critical point of this Lagrangian. That is, its partial derivative w.r.t. each variable x_i must vanish. Hence, for each $i = 1, 2, \ldots, n$, one has

$$\frac{\partial \mathcal{L}}{\partial x_i} = \frac{\partial f(\mathbf{x})}{\partial x_i} - \sum_{j=1}^{m} \lambda_j \frac{\partial g_j(\mathbf{x})}{\partial x_i} = 0 \tag{18.6.11}$$

Together with the m equality constraints is (18.6.9), these n equations form a total of $n + m$ equations in the combined list $(x_1, \ldots, x_n, \lambda_1, \ldots, \lambda_m)$ of $n + m$ unknowns.

We now present a relatively simple example with three choice variables and two equality constraints.

EXAMPLE 18.6.4 Solve the problem

$$\min x^2 + y^2 + z^2 \text{ s.t.} \begin{cases} x + 2y + z = 30 \\ 2x - y - 3z = 10 \end{cases}$$

Solution: The Lagrangian with two constraints and two corresponding Lagrange multipliers is

$$\mathcal{L}(x, y, z) = x^2 + y^2 + z^2 - \lambda_1(x + 2y + z - 30) - \lambda_2(2x - y - 3z - 10)$$

The FOCs in (18.6.11) require that

$$\frac{\partial \mathcal{L}}{\partial x} = 2x - \lambda_1 - 2\lambda_2 = 0 \tag{i}$$

$$\frac{\partial \mathcal{L}}{\partial y} = 2y - 2\lambda_1 + \lambda_2 = 0 \tag{ii}$$

$$\frac{\partial \mathcal{L}}{\partial z} = 2z - \lambda_1 + 3\lambda_2 = 0 \tag{iii}$$

in addition to the two constraints,

$$x + 2y + z = 30 \tag{iv}$$

$$2x - y - 3z = 10 \tag{v}$$

So there are five equations, labelled (i)–(v), which we should solve in order to determine the five unknowns x, y, z, λ_1, and λ_2.

One way to solve these five equations starts by solving the pair of linear equations (i) and (ii) simultaneously to find λ_1 and λ_2 in terms of x and y. This gives

$$\lambda_1 = \tfrac{2}{5}x + \tfrac{4}{5}y \text{ and } \lambda_2 = \tfrac{4}{5}x - \tfrac{2}{5}y \tag{vi}$$

Inserting these expressions for λ_1 and λ_2 into (iii), then simplifying, we obtain

$$x - y + z = 0 \tag{vii}$$

This equation, together with (iv) and (v), constitutes a system of three linear equations in the unknowns x, y, and z. Solving this system by elimination gives $(x, y, z) = (10, 10, 0)$

758   CHAPTER 18 / EQUALITY CONSTRAINTS

as the only solution. By (vi), the corresponding values of the two Lagrange multipliers are $\lambda_1 = 12$ and $\lambda_2 = 4$.

A geometric argument allows us to confirm that we have solved the minimization problem. Each of the two constraints represents a plane in $\mathbb{R}^3$, and the points satisfying both constraints consequently lie on the straight line where the two planes intersect. Now $x^2 + y^2 + z^2$ measures (the square of) the distance from the origin to a point on this straight line. The problem we face is to make this distance as small as possible by choosing the point on the line that is nearest to the origin. No maximum distance can possibly exist, but it is geometrically obvious that there is a minimum distance, which must be attained at this nearest point.

There is an alternative method to solve this particular problem, which we admit is much simpler. It is to reduce it to a one-variable optimization problem by using the two constraints (iv) and (v) to solve simultaneously for y and z in terms of x, thus obtaining $y = 20 - x$ and $z = x - 10$. Indeed, these are the two equations of the straight line in 3-space where the two planes intersect. Then the square of the distance from the origin is

$$x^2 + y^2 + z^2 = x^2 + (20 - x)^2 + (x - 10)^2 = 3(x - 10)^2 + 200$$

This function is easily seen to have a minimum when $x = 10$, implying that $y = 10$ and $z = 0$. See also Exercise 5.

EXERCISES FOR SECTION 18.6

1. Consider the problem min $x^2 + y^2 + z^2$ s.t. $x + y + z = 1$.

   (a) Write down the Lagrangian for this problem, and find the only point (x, y, z) that satisfies the necessary conditions.

   (b) Give a geometric argument for the existence of a solution. Does the corresponding maximization problem have any solution?

2. Use Eq. (18.6.8) to solve the utility maximization problem

   $$\max 10 x^{1/2} y^{1/3} z^{1/4} \quad \text{s.t.} \quad 4x + 3y + 6z = 390$$

3. A consumer's demands x, y, z for three goods are chosen to maximize the utility function

   $$U(x, y, z) = x + \sqrt{y} - 1/z$$

   which is defined for all $x \geq 0$, $y > 0$ and $z > 0$. The budget constraint is $px + qy + rz = m$, where $p, q, r > 0$ and $m \geq \sqrt{pr} + p^2/4q$.

   (a) Write out the first-order conditions for a constrained maximum.

   (b) Find the utility-maximizing demands for all three goods as functions of the four parameters (p, q, r, m).

   (c) Show that the maximized utility is given by the indirect utility function

   $$U^*(p, q, r, m) = \frac{m}{p} + \frac{p}{4q} - 2\sqrt{\frac{r}{p}}$$

   (d) Find $\partial U^* / \partial m$ and comment on your answer.

4. Each week an individual consumes quantities x and y of two goods, and works for l hours. These three quantities are chosen to maximize the utility function

$$U(x, y, l) = \alpha \ln x + \beta \ln y + (1 - \alpha - \beta) \ln(L - l)$$

which is defined for $0 \leq l < L$ and for $x, y > 0$. Here α and β are positive parameters satisfying $\alpha + \beta < 1$. The individual faces the budget constraint $px + qy = wl$, where w is the wage per hour. Define $\gamma = (\alpha + \beta)/(1 - \alpha - \beta)$. Find the individual's demands x^*, y^*, and labour supply l^* as functions of p, q, and w.

5. Consider the problem in Example 18.6.4, and let $(x, y, z) = (10 + h, 10 + k, l)$. Show that if (x, y, z) satisfies both constraints, then $k = -h$ and $l = h$. Then show that $x^2 + y^2 + z^2 = 200 + 3h^2$. What do you conclude?

6. An important problem in statistics requires solving

$$\min\ a_1^2 x_1^2 + a_2^2 x_2^2 + \cdots + a_n^2 x_n^2 \quad \text{s.t.} \quad x_1 + x_2 + \cdots + x_n = 1$$

where the constants a_i are all nonzero. Solve the problem, taking it for granted that the minimum value exists. What is the solution in case there is at least one i for which $a_i = 0$?

⑤ 7. Solve the problem:

$$\max(\min)\ x + y \quad \text{s.t.} \quad \begin{cases} x^2 + 2y^2 + z^2 = 1 \\ x + y + z = 1 \end{cases}$$

⑤ 8. [HARDER] Consider the consumer optimization problem in Example 18.6.3. Find the demand functions when:

(a) $U(x_1, \ldots, x_n) = A x_1^{a_1} \cdots x_n^{a_n}$, where $A > 0$, $a_1 > 0, \ldots, a_n > 0$.

(b) $U(x_1, \ldots, x_n) = x_1^a + \cdots + x_n^a$, where $0 < a < 1$.

18.7 Comparative Statics

Equation (18.2.2) offers an economic interpretation of the Lagrange multiplier for the case of two variables and one constraint. This can be extended to the problem with n variables and m constraints. Using vector notation, let us write that problem in the form

$$\max(\min) f(\mathbf{x}) \quad \text{s.t.} \quad g_j(\mathbf{x}) = c_j, \quad \text{for } j = 1, \ldots, m \tag{18.7.1}$$

Let $\mathbf{x}^* = (x_1^*, \ldots, x_n^*)$ be the values of $\mathbf{x}$ that satisfy the necessary conditions for the solution to (18.7.1). In general, $\mathbf{x}^*$ depends on the values of the m-vector $\mathbf{c} = (c_1, \ldots, c_m)$ of the parameters that appear on the right-hand sides of the m equality constraints in (18.7.1). We assume that, as the parameter vector $\mathbf{c}$ varies, each $x_i^* = x_i^*(\mathbf{c})$ is a differentiable function. We define the associated value function f^* of $\mathbf{c}$ so that:

$$f^*(\mathbf{c}) = f(\mathbf{x}^*(\mathbf{c})) \tag{18.7.2}$$

The m Lagrange multipliers associated with $\mathbf{x}^*$, namely $\lambda_1, \ldots, \lambda_m$, also depend on $\mathbf{c}$. Provided that certain regularity conditions are satisfied, for each $j = 1, \ldots, m$ we have

$$\frac{\partial f^*(\mathbf{c})}{\partial c_j} = \lambda_j(\mathbf{c}) \tag{18.7.3}$$

Hence, *the Lagrange multiplier $\lambda_j = \lambda_j(\mathbf{c})$ for the jth constraint is the rate at which the optimal value of the objective function changes w.r.t. changes in the parameter c_j*. For this reason λ_j is generally referred to as the imputed *shadow price* (or *marginal value*) per unit of resource j.

Suppose that we change the components of the vector $\mathbf{c} = (c_1, \ldots, c_m)$ by the respective amounts $d\mathbf{c} = (dc_1, \ldots, dc_m)$. According to the linear approximation (15.8.5), provided that the changes $dc_1, \ldots, dc_m$ are all small in absolute value, Eq. (18.7.3) implies that

$$f^*(\mathbf{c} + d\mathbf{c}) - f^*(\mathbf{c}) \approx \lambda_1(\mathbf{c})\, dc_1 + \cdots + \lambda_m(\mathbf{c})\, dc_m \tag{18.7.4}$$

EXAMPLE 18.7.1 Consider Example 18.6.4, and suppose we change the first constraint to $x + 2y + z = 31$ and the second constraint to $2x - y - 3z = 9$. Estimate the corresponding change in the value function by using (18.7.4). Find also the new exact value of the value function.

Solution: Using the notation introduced above and the results in Example 18.6.4, we have

$$c_1 = 30,\ c_2 = 10,\ dc_1 = 1,\ dc_2 = -1,\ \lambda_1(30, 10) = 12,\ \lambda_2(30, 10) = 4$$

Also, the solution we found was $(x^*, y^*, z^*) = (10, 10, 0)$, implying that

$$f^*(c_1, c_2) = f^*(30, 10) = 10^2 + 10^2 + 0^2 = 200$$

Now, approximation (18.7.4) yields

$$f^*(30 + 1, 10 - 1) - f^*(30, 10) \approx \lambda_1(30, 10)\, dc_1 + \lambda_2(30, 10)\, dc_2 = 12 \cdot 1 + 4 \cdot (-1) = 8$$

Thus, $f^*(31, 9) \approx 200 + 8 = 208$.

To find the exact value of $f^*(31, 9)$, observe that equations (i)–(iii), (vi) and (vii) in the solution to Example 18.6.4 are all still valid. Thus, we have the three simultaneous equations $x + 2y + z = 31$, $2x - y - 3z = 9$, $x - y + z = 0$, whose solutions for x, y, and z are $151/15$, $31/3$, and $4/15$, respectively. After some computations with fractions, we find that $f^*(31, 9) = 15\,614/75 \approx 208.19$. The error in the approximation is $14/75 \approx 0.19$.

The Envelope Theorem

Examples 18.7.2 and 18.7.3 below are just two illustrations of how economists make extensive use of results that emerge from introducing a vector $\mathbf{r} = (r_1, \ldots, r_k)$ of k parameters into problem (18.7.1). Specifically, we allow both the objective function f and all the constraint functions g_j to depend not only on the n-vector $\mathbf{x}$ of variables to be chosen, but also on the parameter vector $\mathbf{r}$. With this notation the problem becomes

$$\max(\min)_{\mathbf{x}}\ f(\mathbf{x}, \mathbf{r})\ \text{s.t.}\ g_j(\mathbf{x}, \mathbf{r}) = 0,\ \text{for } j = 1, \ldots, m \tag{18.7.5}$$

Note that the right-hand side of each constraint $g_j(\mathbf{x}) = c_j$ in problem (18.7.1) has become zero. This is because we could always introduce c_j as an extra parameter in the function $g_j(\mathbf{x}, \mathbf{r})$ so that the it becomes $\tilde{g}_j(\mathbf{x}, \mathbf{r}, c_j) = g_j(\mathbf{x}, \mathbf{r}) - c_j$, thus transforming the constraint $g_j(\mathbf{x}, \mathbf{r}) = c_j$ into $\tilde{g}_j(\mathbf{x}, \mathbf{r}, c_j) = 0$.

As usual, for each $j = 1, \ldots, m$, let us associate a Lagrange multiplier λ_j with the jth constraint in problem (18.7.5). Then the Lagrangian can be written as

$$\mathcal{L}(\mathbf{x}, \mathbf{r}) = f(\mathbf{x}, \mathbf{r}) - \sum_{j=1}^{m} \lambda_j g_j(\mathbf{x}, \mathbf{r}) \tag{18.7.6}$$

In addition to the m equality constraints in problem (18.7.5), the other n first-order conditions for a solution take the form

$$0 = \frac{\partial}{\partial x_i} \mathcal{L}(\mathbf{x}, \mathbf{r}) = \frac{\partial}{\partial x_i} f(\mathbf{x}, \mathbf{r}) - \sum_{j=1}^{m} \lambda_j \frac{\partial}{\partial x_i} g_j(\mathbf{x}, \mathbf{r}) \quad \text{(for } i = 1, 2, \ldots, n\text{)}$$

By analogy with Eq. (18.7.2), let $\mathbf{x}^*(\mathbf{r})$ denote the optimal choice of $\mathbf{x}$ when the parameter vector is $\mathbf{r}$. Under suitable regularity assumptions, for each $\mathbf{r}$ and each $j = 1, \ldots, m$ there must exist a Lagrange multiplier function $\lambda_j(\mathbf{r})$ of $\mathbf{r}$ such that $\mathbf{x}^*(\mathbf{r})$ satisfies the $n + m$ first-order conditions

$$\frac{\partial f(\mathbf{x}^*(\mathbf{r}), \mathbf{r})}{\partial x_i} - \sum_{j=1}^{m} \lambda_j \frac{\partial g_j(\mathbf{x}^*(\mathbf{r}), \mathbf{r})}{\partial x_i} = 0 \text{ (all } i\text{)}; \quad g_j(\mathbf{x}^*(\mathbf{r}), \mathbf{r}) = 0 \text{ (all } j\text{)} \tag{18.7.7}$$

Now define the value function

$$f^*(\mathbf{r}) = f(\mathbf{x}^*(\mathbf{r}), \mathbf{r}) \tag{18.7.8}$$

Given the definitions in (18.7.6) and (18.7.8), the following result holds:

THEOREM 18.7.1 (THE ENVELOPE THEOREM)

Let $\mathbf{r}^0$ be any parameter vector and $\mathbf{x}^0$ any vector of choice variables such that:
(a) for all n-vectors $\mathbf{x}$ near $\mathbf{x}^0$ and all parameter vectors $\mathbf{r}$ near $\mathbf{r}^0$, the functions $f(\mathbf{x}, \mathbf{r})$ and $g_j(\mathbf{x}, \mathbf{r})$ ($j = 1, 2, \ldots, m$) are all differentiable as functions of $(\mathbf{x}, \mathbf{r})$;
(b) for all parameter vectors $\mathbf{r}$ near $\mathbf{r}^0$, there exist an n-vector $\mathbf{x}^*(\mathbf{r})$ which is differentiable as a function of $\mathbf{r}$ and satisfies $\mathbf{x}^*(\mathbf{r}^0) = \mathbf{x}^0$, as well as Lagrange multipliers $\lambda_j(\mathbf{r})$ ($j = 1, 2, \ldots, m$), which together satisfy the $n + m$ first-order conditions in (18.7.7).

Then both the value function $f^*(\mathbf{r})$ and the Lagrangian $\mathcal{L}(\mathbf{x}^*(\mathbf{r}), \mathbf{r})$ are differentiable as functions of $\mathbf{r}$ at $\mathbf{r} = \mathbf{r}^0$. Moreover, for each $h = 1, \ldots, k$, one has

$$\left. \frac{\partial f^*(\mathbf{r})}{\partial r_h} \right|_{\mathbf{r} = \mathbf{r}^0} = \left. \frac{\partial \mathcal{L}(\mathbf{x}^0, \mathbf{r})}{\partial r_h} \right|_{\mathbf{r} = \mathbf{r}^0} \tag{18.7.9}$$

This is a very useful general result that should be studied carefully. When any parameter is changed, then $f^*(\mathbf{r})$ changes for two reasons: first, a change in r_h changes the vector $\mathbf{r}$ and thus changes $f(\mathbf{x}^*(\mathbf{r}), \mathbf{r})$ directly; and, second, a change in r_h changes, in general, all the functions $x_1^*(\mathbf{r}), \ldots, x_n^*(\mathbf{r})$, which changes $f(\mathbf{x}^*(\mathbf{r}), \mathbf{r})$ indirectly. Theorem 18.7.1 shows that the total effect on the value function of a small change in any parameter r_h at $\mathbf{r} = \mathbf{r}^0$ is found by computing the *partial* derivative of $\mathcal{L}(\mathbf{x}, \mathbf{r})$ w.r.t. r_h, and evaluating it at $\mathbf{x}^0 = \mathbf{x}^*(\mathbf{r}^0)$, ignoring altogether the indirect effect of the dependence of $\mathbf{x}^*$ on $\mathbf{r}$. The reason is that, because of the FOCs (18.7.7), any small change in $\mathbf{x}$ that preserves the equality constraints of problem (18.7.5) will have a negligible effect on the value of $f(\mathbf{x}^*, \mathbf{r})$, so Eq. (18.7.9) holds.

EXAMPLE 18.7.2   In Example 18.6.3, let $U^*(\mathbf{p}, m)$ denote the *indirect utility function* whose value is the maximum utility obtainable by the consumer when prices are $\mathbf{p} = (p_1, \ldots, p_n)$ and income is m. Let λ denote the Lagrange multiplier associated with the budget constraint. Using Eq. (18.7.3), we see that

$$\lambda = \frac{\partial U^*}{\partial m} \qquad (18.7.10)$$

Thus, λ is the rate of increase in maximum utility as income increases. For this reason, λ is generally called the *marginal utility of income*.

Including the vector $(\mathbf{p}, m)$ of all $n+1$ parameters, the Lagrangian takes the form

$$\mathcal{L}(\mathbf{x}, \mathbf{p}, m) = U(\mathbf{x}) - \lambda(p_1 x_1 + \cdots + p_n x_n - m)$$

Obviously, $\partial \mathcal{L} / \partial m = \lambda$ and $\partial \mathcal{L} / \partial p_i = -\lambda x_i$. Hence, from (18.7.9) we get

$$\frac{\partial U^*(\mathbf{p}, m)}{\partial m} = \frac{\partial \mathcal{L}(\mathbf{x}, \mathbf{p}, m)}{\partial m} = \lambda$$

which repeats (18.7.10). Moreover,

$$\frac{\partial U^*(\mathbf{p}, m)}{\partial p_i} = \frac{\partial \mathcal{L}(\mathbf{x}, \mathbf{p}, m)}{\partial p_i} = -\lambda x_i^*$$

which is called *Roy's identity*.[12] This formula has a nice interpretation: the marginal disutility of a price increase is the marginal utility of income, λ, multiplied by the quantity demanded, x_i^*. Intuitively, this is because, for a small price change, the loss of real income is approximately equal to the change in price multiplied by the quantity demanded.

As an illustration of Roy's identity, consider the consumer optimization problem with a Cobb–Douglas utility function, as in Eq. (18.6.7). Substituting the demands given by Eq. (18.6.8) into the utility function, we obtain the indirect utility function

$$U^*(\mathbf{p}, m) = A \left(\frac{a_1 m}{a p_1} \right)^{a_1} \cdots \left(\frac{a_n m}{a p_n} \right)^{a_n} = \frac{B m^a}{P(p_1, \ldots, p_n)} \qquad (18.7.11)$$

Here we have used the notation $a = a_1 + a_2 + \cdots + a_n$, whereas B denotes the constant $A a_1^{a_1} \cdots a_n^{a_n} / a^a$, and $P = P(p_1, \ldots, p_n)$ denotes the function $p_1^{a_1} \cdots p_n^{a_n}$. Indeed, P is also a Cobb–Douglas function whose powers match those of the original utility function. Also,

---

[12] Named after the French economist René Roy (1894–1977).

because P is homogeneous of degree a, the function defined by $\tilde{P} = P^{1/a}$ is homogeneous of degree 1, and has the property that $U^*(\mathbf{p}, m) = B(m/\tilde{P})^a$, which is an increasing function of $m/\tilde{P}$. Indeed, $m/\tilde{P}$ is homogeneous of degree 0, and is the measure of *real income* one gets after dividing income by a *price index* $\tilde{P}$ that is homogeneous of degree 1 as a function of the price vector $\mathbf{p} = (p_1, \ldots, p_n)$.

Formula (18.7.11) for the indirect utility function implies that $\partial U^*/\partial m = Bam^{a-1}/P$, and also that

$$\frac{\partial U^*}{\partial p_i} = -\frac{Bm^a}{P^2}\frac{\partial P}{\partial p_i} = -\frac{Bm^a}{P^2}\frac{a_i P}{p_i} = -\frac{Bam^{a-1}}{P}\frac{a_i m}{ap_i} = -\frac{\partial U^*}{\partial m} D_i(\mathbf{p}, m)$$

This confirms Roy's identity for the case of a Cobb–Douglas utility function.

EXAMPLE 18.7.3   A firm uses K units of capital and L units of labour to produce an output quantity of $Q = F(K, L)$ units of a commodity. The prices of capital and labour are r and w, respectively. Given the output requirement Q, let $C^*(r, w, Q)$ be the value function for the following problem of finding K and L to minimize the cost of producing Q units of output:

$$\min\ C(K, L) = rK + wL \ \text{ s.t. } \ F(K, L) = Q$$

Find expressions for $\partial C^*/\partial r$, $\partial C^*/\partial w$, and $\partial C^*/\partial Q$.

Solution: Including the output requirement Q and the price parameters r and w, the Lagrangian can be written as

$$\mathcal{L}(K, L, r, w, Q) = rK + wL - \lambda[F(K, L) - Q]$$

Its partial derivatives w.r.t. r, w and Q are

$$\partial \mathcal{L}/\partial r = K, \ \partial \mathcal{L}/\partial w = L, \text{ and } \partial \mathcal{L}/\partial Q = \lambda$$

According to Theorem 18.7.1, we therefore have

$$\frac{\partial C^*}{\partial r} = K^*, \quad \frac{\partial C^*}{\partial w} = L^*, \quad \text{and} \quad \frac{\partial C^*}{\partial Q} = \lambda \qquad (*)$$

The first two equalities are instances of *Shephard's lemma*.[13] The last equation shows that the Lagrange multiplier λ must equal *marginal cost*, the rate at which minimum cost increases w.r.t. changes in output.

To conclude, we present a proof of Theorem 18.7.1:

Proof: In the ensuing argument, all the relevant partial derivatives should be evaluated where $\mathbf{r} = \mathbf{r}^0$ and $\mathbf{x} = \mathbf{x}^0 = \mathbf{x}^*(\mathbf{r}^0)$, at which point the functions $f(\mathbf{x}, \mathbf{r})$, $g_j(\mathbf{x}, \mathbf{r})$ $(j = 1, \ldots, k)$, and $\mathbf{x}^*(\mathbf{r})$ are all assumed to be differentiable. It follows that the composite function $\mathbf{f}^*(\mathbf{r}) = f(\mathbf{x}^*(\mathbf{r}), \mathbf{r})$ defined by (18.7.8) is differentiable at $\mathbf{r} = \mathbf{r}^0$. Moreover, one

---

[13] Named after American mathematical economist Ronald Shephard (1912–1982).

can differentiate the right-hand side of (18.7.8) partially w.r.t. r_h, for each $h = 1, 2, \ldots, k$, using the chain rule to do so. The result is

$$\frac{\partial f^*(\mathbf{r})}{\partial r_h} = \sum_{i=1}^n \frac{\partial f(\mathbf{x}^*(\mathbf{r}), \mathbf{r})}{\partial x_i} \frac{\partial x_i^*(\mathbf{r})}{\partial r_h} + \frac{\partial f(\mathbf{x}^*(\mathbf{r}), \mathbf{r})}{\partial r_h} \quad \text{(i)}$$

But given the Lagrangian defined by (18.7.6), its corresponding partial derivative w.r.t. r_h is

$$\frac{\partial \mathcal{L}(\mathbf{x}^*(\mathbf{r}), \mathbf{r})}{\partial r_h} = \frac{\partial f(\mathbf{x}^*(\mathbf{r}), \mathbf{r})}{\partial r_h} - \sum_{j=1}^m \lambda_j \frac{\partial g_j(\mathbf{x}^*(\mathbf{r}), \mathbf{r})}{\partial r_h} \quad \text{(ii)}$$

Subtracting each side of (ii) from the corresponding side of (i), we obtain

$$\frac{\partial f^*(\mathbf{r})}{\partial r_h} - \frac{\partial \mathcal{L}(\mathbf{x}^*(\mathbf{r}), \mathbf{r})}{\partial r_h} = \sum_{i=1}^n \frac{\partial f(\mathbf{x}^*(\mathbf{r}), \mathbf{r})}{\partial x_i} \frac{\partial x_i^*(\mathbf{r})}{\partial r_h} + \sum_{j=1}^m \lambda_j \frac{\partial g_j(\mathbf{x}^*(\mathbf{r}), \mathbf{r})}{\partial r_h} \quad \text{(iii)}$$

Differentiating each constraint $g_j(\mathbf{x}^*(\mathbf{r}), \mathbf{r}) = 0$ partially w.r.t. r_h, however, yields

$$\sum_{i=1}^n \frac{\partial g_j(\mathbf{x}^*(\mathbf{r}), \mathbf{r})}{\partial x_i} \frac{\partial x_i^*(\mathbf{r})}{\partial r_h} + \frac{\partial g_j(\mathbf{x}^*(\mathbf{r}), \mathbf{r})}{\partial r_h} = 0 \quad \text{(iv)}$$

Using (iv) to substitute for each term $\partial g_j(\mathbf{x}^*(\mathbf{r}), \mathbf{r})/\partial r_h$ in (iii) gives

$$\frac{\partial f^*(\mathbf{r})}{\partial r_h} - \frac{\partial \mathcal{L}(\mathbf{x}^*(\mathbf{r}), \mathbf{r})}{\partial r_h} = \sum_{i=1}^n \left\{ \left[\frac{\partial f(\mathbf{x}^*(\mathbf{r}), \mathbf{r})}{\partial x_i} - \sum_{j=1}^m \lambda_j \frac{\partial g_j(\mathbf{x}^*(\mathbf{r}), \mathbf{r})}{\partial x_i} \right] \frac{\partial x_i^*(\mathbf{r})}{\partial r_h} \right\} \quad \text{(v)}$$

For each $i = 1, 2, \ldots, n$, however, the corresponding term in square brackets is equal to the partial derivative $\partial \mathcal{L}/\partial x_i$. But then the FOCs (18.6.11) require all these to be zero at the optimum $(\mathbf{x}^*(\mathbf{r}), \mathbf{r})$. Hence Eq. (v) reduces to

$$\frac{\partial f^*(\mathbf{r})}{\partial r_h} - \frac{\partial \mathcal{L}(\mathbf{x}^*(\mathbf{r}), \mathbf{r})}{\partial r_h} = 0$$

This proves Eq. (18.7.9). ∎

Note that this proof used only the first-order conditions (18.6.11) for the problem set out in (18.7.5). Therefore, the results in Theorem 18.7.1 are equally valid if we minimize rather than maximize $f(\mathbf{x}, \mathbf{r})$. Note also that we did *not* prove that f^* is differentiable. Sufficient conditions for this are discussed in FMEA.

EXERCISES FOR SECTION 18.7

1. Consider the utility maximization problem max $x + a \ln y$ s.t. $px + qy = m$, assuming that $0 \leq a < m/p$.

   (a) Find the solution (x^*, y^*).

   (b) Find the indirect utility function $U^*(p, q, m, a)$, and then compute its partial derivatives w.r.t. p, q, m, and a.

   (c) Verify the envelope theorem.

SM 2. Consider the problem min $x + 4y + 3z$ s.t. $x^2 + 2y^2 + \frac{1}{3}z^2 = b$, where $b > 0$. Suppose that the problem has a solution, and find it. Then verify Eq. (18.7.3).

3. A firm has L units of labour available to produce three different output commodities. If its outputs of these commodities are x, y, and z units, its labour requirements are αx^2, βy^2, and γz^2 units, respectively.

   (a) Solve the problem max $ax + by + cz$ s.t. $\alpha x^2 + \beta y^2 + \gamma z^2 = L$, where a, b, c, α, β, and γ are positive constants.

   (b) Put $a = 4$, $b = c = 1$, $\alpha = 1$, $\beta = \frac{1}{4}$, and $\gamma = \frac{1}{5}$. Show that in this case the problem in part (a) has the solution $x = \frac{4}{5}\sqrt{L}$, $y = \frac{4}{5}\sqrt{L}$, and $z = \sqrt{L}$.

   (c) What happens to the maximum value of $4x + y + z$ when L increases from 100 to 101? Find the exact increase or decrease, as well as the appropriate linear approximation based on the interpretation of the Lagrange multiplier.

SM 4. Consider the two problems:[14]

$$\max(\min) f(x, y, z) = x^2 + y^2 + z \quad \text{s.t.} \quad g(x, y, z) = x^2 + 2y^2 + 4z^2 = 1$$

   (a) Solve them both for the specified constraint.

   (b) Suppose the constraint is changed to $x^2 + 2y^2 + 4z^2 = 1.02$. What is the approximate change in the maximum value of $f(x, y, z)$?

SM 5. Solve the problem in Example 18.7.3 for the special case when $F(K, L) = K^{1/2}L^{1/4}$, finding explicit expressions for K^*, L^*, C^*, and λ. Verify the equalities (∗) in this special case.

6. Assuming that the cost function C^* in Example 18.7.3 is twice continuously differentiable, prove the symmetry relation $\partial K^*/\partial w = \partial L^*/\partial r$.

7. Given the four positive parameters a, m, p, q that satisfy $m > q^2/4a^2p$, consider the utility maximization problem max $\sqrt{x} + ay$ s.t. $px + qy = m$.

   (a) Find the demand functions $x^*(p, q, m, a)$ and $y^*(p, q, m, a)$, as well as the indirect utility function $U^*(p, q, m, a)$.

   (b) Find all four first-order partial derivatives of $U^*(p, q, m, a) = x^* + a\sqrt{y^*}$, then verify the envelope theorem.

REVIEW EXERCISES

1. Consider the problem max $f(x, y) = 3x + 4y$ s.t. $g(x, y) = x^2 + y^2 = 225$.

   (a) Solve both it, and the corresponding minimization problem, using the Lagrange multiplier method.

   (b) Suppose the right-hand side of the constraint is changed from 225 to 224. What is the approximate change in the maximum value of f?

---

[14] Note that the graph of the constraint is the surface of an ellipsoid in $\mathbb{R}^3$, which is a closed and bounded set.

766 CHAPTER 18 / EQUALITY CONSTRAINTS

2. Use the demand functions $x(p, q, m)$ and $y(p, q, m)$ specified in Eq. (∗∗) of Example 18.1.3 in order to write down, for each of the following three functions $f(x, y)$ defined for all $x \geq 0$ and $y \geq 0$, the solution to the problem of maximizing $f(x, y)$ subject to $px + qy = m$:

   (a) $f(x, y) = 25x^2 y^3$ (b) $f(x, y) = x^{1/5} y^{2/5}$ (c) $f(x, y) = 10\sqrt{x}\sqrt[3]{y}$

SM 3. By selling x tons of one commodity, the firm gets a price per ton given by $p(x)$. By selling y tons of another commodity, the price per ton is $q(y)$. The cost of producing and selling x tons of the first commodity and y tons of the second is given by the differentiable function $C(x, y)$, defined for all $x \geq 0$ and $y \geq 0$.

   (a) Write down the firm's profit function and find necessary conditions for $x^* > 0$ and $y^* > 0$ to solve the problem. Give economic interpretations of the necessary conditions.

   (b) Suppose that the firm's production activity causes so much pollution that the authorities limit its output to no more than m tons of total output. Write down the necessary conditions for $\hat{x} > 0$ and $\hat{y} > 0$ to solve the new problem.

4. Suppose that $U(x, y)$ denotes the utility experienced by a person who enjoys x hours of leisure per day (of 24 hours) and consumes y units per day of other goods. Suppose that the person earns an hourly wage of w and pays an average price of p per unit of the other goods so that, assuming that the person spends all that is earned, x and y must satisfy the constraint

$$py = w(24 - x) \qquad (*)$$

   (a) Show that maximizing $U(x, y)$ subject to the constraint (∗) leads to the equation

$$pU_1'(x, y) = wU_2'(x, y) \qquad (**)$$

   (b) Suppose that the two equations (∗) and (∗∗) determine x and y as differentiable functions $x(p, w), y(p, w)$ of p and w. Show that, under appropriate assumptions on $U(x, y)$, one has

$$\frac{\partial x}{\partial w} = \frac{(24 - x)(wU_{22}'' - pU_{12}'') + pU_2'}{p^2 U_{11}'' - 2pwU_{12}'' + w^2 U_{22}''}$$

SM 5. Consider the problems

$$\max(\min) \; x^2 + y^2 - 2x + 1 \;\; \text{s.t.} \;\; \tfrac{1}{4}x^2 + y^2 = b$$

where b is a constant satisfying $b > \tfrac{4}{9}$.[15]

   (a) Solve both the maximization and minimization problems.

   (b) If $f^*(b)$ denotes the value function for the maximization problem, verify that $df^*(b)/db$ equals the corresponding Lagrange multiplier λ.

6. Consider the utility maximization problem in (18.1.5) in case the utility function $u(x, y)$ takes the "separable" form $v(x) + w(y)$, where $v'(x) > 0$, $w'(y) > 0$, $v''(x) \leq 0$, and $w''(y) \leq 0$.

   (a) State the first-order conditions for utility maximization.

   (b) Why are these conditions sufficient for optimality?

---

[15] The constraint has a graph that is an ellipse in the xy-plane, so it defines a closed and bounded set.

7. Consider the problem

$$\min x^2 - 2x + 1 + y^2 - 2y \text{ s.t. } (x+y)\sqrt{x+y+b} = 2\sqrt{a}$$

where a and b are positive constants and x and y are positive.

(a) Suppose that (x, y) solves the problem. Show that x and y must then satisfy the equations

$$x = y \quad \text{and} \quad 2x^3 + bx^2 = a \qquad (*)$$

(b) The equations in $(*)$ define the solution (x^*, y^*) as a function of (a, b). Find expressions for $\partial x/\partial a$, $\partial^2 x/\partial a^2$, and $\partial x/\partial b$, assuming that each partial derivative exists.

19 LINEAR PROGRAMMING

If one would take statistics about which mathematical problem is using up most of the computer time in the world, then (not counting database handling problems like sorting and searching) the answer would probably be linear programming.
—László Lovász (1980)

Linear programming is the name used to describe constrained optimization problems in which the objective is to maximize or minimize a linear function subject to linear inequality constraints. Because of its extensive use in economic decision problems, all economists should know something about the basic theory of linear programming.

In principle, *any* linear programming problem, often called an LP problem, can be solved numerically, provided that a solution exists. This is because the *simplex method*, introduced by American mathematician George B. Dantzig (1914–2005) in 1947, provides a very efficient numerical algorithm that finds the solution in a finite number of steps. As the above quotation from Lovász indicates, the simplex method has made linear programming a mathematical technique of immense practical importance.[1] That said, the simplex method will not be discussed in this book. After all, faced with a nontrivial LP problem, it is natural to use one of the great number of available LP computer programs to find the solution. In any case, it is probably more important for economists to understand the basic theory of linear programming rather than the details of the simplex method.

Indeed, the importance of LP extends even beyond its practical applications. In particular, the duality theory of linear programming is a basis for understanding key theoretical properties of even nonlinear optimization problems of the kind we shall discuss in Chapter 20. These, of course, have a significantly larger range of interesting economic applications.

This chapter begins, in Section 19.1, with some examples involving only two choice variables, which can be solved graphically. Thereafter Section 19.2 introduces the dual of a linear program, followed by Section 19.3 which focuses on the duality theorem. Section 19.4 focuses on how the variables in a dual LP can be given an economic interpretation as shadow prices. The final

---

[1] It is reported that when the Mobil Oil Company's multimillion-dollar computer system was installed in 1958, its use to solve LP problems allowed the huge investment to pay for itself within just two weeks. See Joel Franklin (1983) "Mathematical methods of economics", *The American Mathematical Monthly* Vol. 90, no. 4.

19.1 A Graphical Approach

A general LP problem with only two decision variables involves maximizing or minimizing a linear *objective function*

$$z = c_1 x_1 + c_2 x_2$$

subject to m linear *inequality constraints*

$$a_{11} x_1 + a_{12} x_2 \leq b_1$$
$$a_{21} x_1 + a_{22} x_2 \leq b_2$$
$$\dots\dots\dots\dots\dots\dots$$
$$a_{m1} x_1 + a_{m2} x_2 \leq b_m$$

Usually, we also impose explicit *nonnegativity constraints* on x_1 and x_2:

$$x_1 \geq 0, \ x_2 \geq 0$$

Note that having a $\leq$ rather than a $\geq$ sign in each of the m inequality constraints is merely a convention. This is because any inequality of the alternative form $ax_1 + bx_2 \geq c$ is equivalent to the inequality $-ax_1 - bx_2 \leq -c$.

Luckily, LP problems with only two decision variables can be solved by a simple graphical method.

EXAMPLE 19.1.1 A commercial baker has supplies consisting of 150 kilograms of flour, 22 kilos of sugar, and 27.5 kilos of butter with which to make biscuits and cakes. Suppose that making one dozen biscuits requires three kilos of flour, one kilo of sugar, and one kilo of butter, whereas making one dozen cakes requires six kilos of flour, half a kilo of sugar, and one kilo of butter.[2] Suppose that the profit from one dozen biscuits is 20, whereas from one dozen cakes it is 30. How many dozen biscuits (x_1) and how many dozen cakes (x_2) should the baker produce in order to maximize profit?

Solution: Producing an output of x_1 dozen biscuits plus x_2 dozen cakes needs a total of $3x_1 + 6x_2$ kilos of flour. Because only 150 kilos of flour are available, the two quantities x_1 and x_2 must satisfy the inequality

$$3x_1 + 6x_2 \leq 150 \qquad \text{(flour constraint)}$$

Similarly, for sugar, one must have

$$x_1 + 0.5 x_2 \leq 22 \qquad \text{(sugar constraint)}$$

---
[2] These quantities are intended only to be illustrative. Anybody intending to bake real biscuits or real cakes intended for real people to eat is urged to consult real recipes intended for real bakers.

Finally, for butter, one must have

$$x_1 + x_2 \leq 27.5 \qquad \text{(butter constraint)}$$

Of course, because biscuits and cakes cannot be "unbaked" back to their original ingredients, one must have $x_1 \geq 0$ and $x_2 \geq 0$. The profit obtained from producing x_1 dozen biscuits and x_2 dozen cakes is $z = 20x_1 + 30x_2$. So the baker's LP problem is

$$\max z = 20x_1 + 30x_2 \text{ s.t.} \begin{cases} 3x_1 + 6x_2 \leq 150 \\ x_1 + 0.5x_2 \leq 22 \\ x_1 + x_2 \leq 27.5 \end{cases} \text{ and } x_1 \geq 0, x_2 \geq 0 \qquad (*)$$

This problem can be solved graphically. The output pair (x_1, x_2) is called *feasible* (or *admissible*) for problem $(*)$ if all five inequality constraints are satisfied. Now look at the flour constraint, $3x_1 + 6x_2 \leq 150$. If we use all the flour, then $3x_1 + 6x_2 = 150$, so we call the corresponding straight line the *flour border*.

We can find two more similar "borders" for the other two inputs. Figure 19.1.1 shows the three straight lines that represent the flour border, the sugar border, and the butter border. In order for (x_1, x_2) to be feasible, it has to be on or below (to the "south-west" of) *each* of the three borders simultaneously. Because constraints $x_1 \geq 0$ and $x_2 \geq 0$ restrict (x_1, x_2) to the nonnegative quadrant, the set of admissible pairs for problem $(*)$ is the shaded set S shown in Fig. 19.1.2.[3]

Figure 19.1.1 Borders for the baker's problem

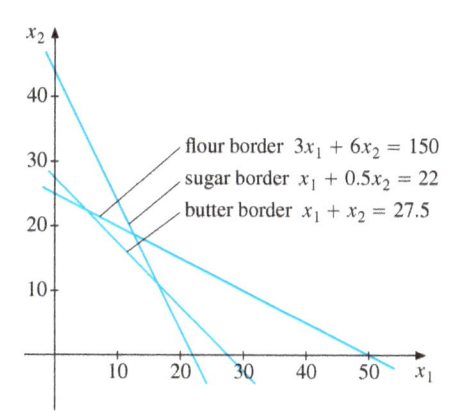

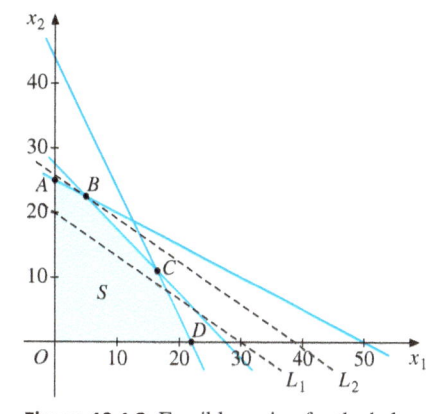

Figure 19.1.2 Feasible region for the baker

To find the point in the feasible region that maximizes profit, a mathematically unsophisticated baker might think of calculating $20x_1 + 30x_2$ at each point of S, and then picking the highest value. In practice, this is impossible because there are infinitely many feasible points.

---

[3] This set S is a so-called *convex polyhedron*. Its five corner points O, A, B, C, and D are called the *extreme points* of S.

Instead, let us begin by asking whether the baker can obtain a profit of, say, 600. If so, the straight line $20x_1 + 30x_2 = 600$ must have points in common with S. This line is represented in Fig. 19.1.2 by the dashed line that is labelled L_1. The line does have points in common with S. One of them, for instance, occurs at $(x_1, x_2) = (0, 20)$, where L_1 intersects the x_2-axis. The two numbers tells us that no biscuits at all are produced, whereas 20 dozen cakes are. At $(0, 20)$ the baker's profit is $20 \cdot 0 + 30 \cdot 20 = 600$.

Can the baker do better? Yes because, for instance, the straight line $20x_1 + 30x_2 = 601$ along which the profit is 601 also has points in common with S. In fact, for each value of the constant c, the straight line

$$20x_1 + 30x_2 = c$$

is parallel to L_1, which has the equation $20x_1 + 30x_2 = 600$. As c increases, the line shifts out farther and farther toward the north-east. But if c becomes too large, the line will pass entirely above and to the right of the feasible set S. In order to maximize profit, the baker should find the straight line $20x_1 + 30x_2 = c$ with the highest value of c that allows the line to have at least one point in common with S. Inspecting Fig. 19.1.2 shows that this is the dashed line labelled L_2, which touches the feasible set S at the single point labelled B.

Note that the point B occurs at the intersection of the flour border, which includes the line segment AB, with the butter border, which includes the line segment BC. Its coordinates, therefore, must satisfy the two equations $3x_1 + 6x_2 = 150$ and $x_1 + x_2 = 27.5$, since these represent the flour border and butter border, respectively. Solving these two simultaneous linear equations yields $x_1 = 5$ and $x_2 = 22.5$. These two numbers tell us that the baker maximizes profit by baking 5 dozen biscuits and 22.5 dozen cakes. These two quantities use all the available flour and butter, by definition. But the amount of sugar used when $x_1 = 5$ and $x_2 = 22.5$ is $x_1 + 0.5x_2 = 5 + 0.5 \cdot 22.5 = 16.25$ kilos, so $22 - 16.25 = 5.75$ kilos of sugar are left over. The profit earned is $20x_1 + 30x_2 = 775$.

EXAMPLE 19.1.2 An electronics firm that produces phones and tablets has two factories that jointly produce the two goods in the following quantities per hour:

	Factory 1	Factory 2
Phones	10	20
Tablets	25	25

The firm receives an order for 300 phones and 500 tablets. The costs of operating the two factories are $10 000 and $8 000 per hour, respectively. Formulate the linear programming problem of minimizing the total cost of meeting this order.

Solution: Let u_1 and u_2 denote the number of hours for which the two factories operate in order to produce the order. Then the above table tells us that a total of $10u_1 + 20u_2$ phones is produced, as well as $25u_1 + 25u_2$ tablets. Because 300 phones and 500 tablets are required, the pair (u_1, u_2) must satisfy

$$10u_1 + 20u_2 \geq 300$$
$$25u_1 + 25u_2 \geq 500$$
(i)

In addition, of course, $u_1 \geq 0$ and $u_2 \geq 0$. The total cost of operating the two factories for u_1 and u_2 hours, respectively, is $10\,000\,u_1 + 8000\,u_2$. The problem is, therefore,

$$\min\ 10\,000\,u_1 + 8000\,u_2 \ \text{s.t.} \ \begin{cases} 10u_1 + 20u_2 \geq 300 \\ 25u_1 + 25u_2 \geq 500 \end{cases} \ \text{and} \ u_1 \geq 0,\ u_2 \geq 0$$

The feasible set S is shown in Fig. 19.1.3. Because the constraints in (i) are $\geq$ inequalities whereas all the coefficients of u_1 and u_2 are positive, the feasible set extends outwards toward the north-east, as shown by the shaded area of Fig. 19.1.3.

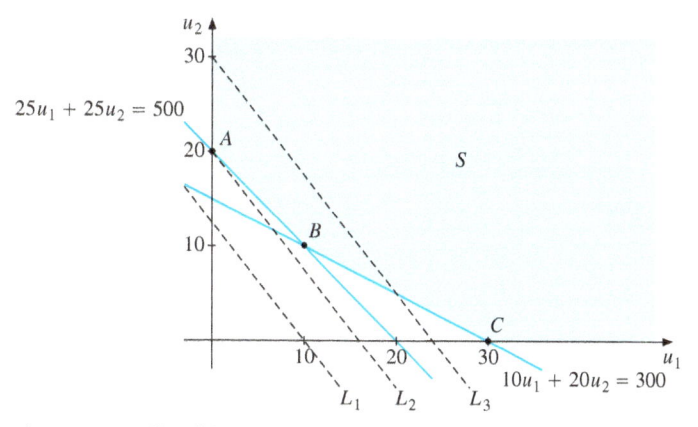

Figure 19.1.3 Feasible set in Example 19.1.2

The firm's cost is given by the linear function $c = 10\,000\,u_1 + 8000\,u_2$. Figure 19.1.3 includes three parallel dashed lines, marked L_1, L_2, and L_3, which correspond to the level curves $10\,000\,u_1 + 8000\,u_2 = c$ for the respective values $100\,000$, $160\,000$, and $240\,000$ of the cost c. As c increases, the level curve moves farther and farther out to the north-east.

In order to minimize cost, the firm needs to choose a point on the lowest level curve $10\,000\,u_1 + 8000\,u_2 = c$ that just touches the feasible set S. So the solution to the cost minimization problem occurs at point A, with coordinates $(0, 20)$. Hence, the optimal solution is to operate factory 2 for 20 hours and not to use factory 1 at all. The resulting minimum cost is $160\,000$.

This graphical method of solving linear programming problems works well when there are only two decision variables. In principle one could extend the method to the case with three decision variables. Then the feasible set is a convex polyhedron in 3-space, and the level surfaces of the objective function are planes in 3-space. Then, however, it is not easy to visualize the solution in three dimensions. For more than three decision variables, no graphical method is available.[4]

Both the previous examples had optimal solutions. If the feasible region is unbounded, however, a finite optimal solution may not exist, as the example in Exercise 4 shows.

---

[4] By using duality theory, however, in Section 19.5 we discuss how to solve LP problems graphically when *either* the number of unknowns *or* the number of constraints does not exceed 2.

The General LP Problem

The general LP problem is that of maximizing (or minimizing) the *objective function*

$$z = c_1 x_1 + \cdots + c_n x_n \tag{19.1.1}$$

Here the n coefficients $c_1, \ldots, c_n$ are all given constants. The objective is to maximize or minimize z subject to m *inequality constraints* of the form

$$\begin{aligned} a_{11} x_1 + \cdots + a_{1n} x_n &\leq b_1 \\ a_{21} x_1 + \cdots + a_{2n} x_n &\leq b_2 \\ &\vdots \\ a_{m1} x_1 + \cdots + a_{mn} x_n &\leq b_m \end{aligned} \tag{19.1.2}$$

Once again, all the elements a_{ij} and b_k are given constants. Usually, we require explicitly that

$$x_1 \geq 0, \ldots, x_n \geq 0 \tag{19.1.3}$$

These are referred to as *nonnegativity constraints*.[5] Any n-vector $(x_1, \ldots, x_n)$ that satisfies all the constraints in both (19.1.2) and (19.1.3) is called *feasible* or *admissible*.

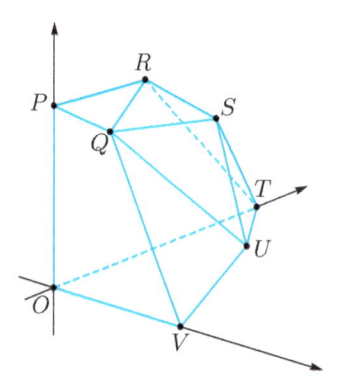

Figure 19.1.4 A convex polyhedron

The set of feasible points is a so-called *convex polyhedron* in the *nonnegative orthant* of n-space. A typical example in 3-space is shown in Fig. 19.1.4. Here the eight points O, P, Q, R, S, T, U, and V are called *extreme points*. The line segments OP, OT, OV, etc. joining two extreme points that are marked in Fig. 19.1.4 are called *edges*. These include OT and RT, which are indicated with dashed lines because they are hidden behind the solid polyhedron. The flat portions of the boundary which are triangles or quadrilaterals lying within three or four of these edges are called *faces*. In n-space, any convex polyhedron has extreme points, edges, and faces.

---

[5] Recall that there is no essential difference between a minimization problem and a maximization problem. This is because an optimal solution $(x_1^*, \ldots, x_n^*)$ that minimizes z (19.1.1) subject to (19.1.2) and (19.1.3) also maximizes $-z$ subject to the same constraints.

SECTION 19.1 / A GRAPHICAL APPROACH

If n and m are large, the number of extreme points of the convex polyhedron defined by the $m + n$ inequalities in (19.1.2) and (19.1.3) can be astronomical, like the number of stars in the universe. In n-dimensional space, the typical extreme point has n of the $m + n$ inequality constraints holding with equality. Thus, there can be as many as $(m + n)!/m!n!$ extreme points. For example, if $n = 50$ and $m = 60$ (which are quite small by the standards of the problems that can be solved numerically), then there can be as many as $110!/50!60!$ or more than $6 \cdot 10^{31}$ extreme points.

Nevertheless, the simplex method can solve such problems. It relies on the fact that if an LP problem has any solution, there must be a solution at an extreme point. Accordingly the method provides a procedure for moving repeatedly between adjacent extreme points of the polyhedron, along its edges, in such a way that the value of the objective function never decreases, and usually increases. The procedure terminates when it reaches an extreme point where no move to an adjacent extreme point will increase the value of the objective function. We have then reached the optimal solution.

EXERCISES FOR SECTION 19.1

1. Use the graphical method to solve both the following LP problems:

   (a) max $3x_1 + 4x_2$ s.t. $\begin{cases} 3x_1 + 2x_2 \leq 6 \\ x_1 + 4x_2 \leq 4 \end{cases}$ $x_1 \geq 0, x_2 \geq 0$

   (b) min $10u_1 + 27u_2$ s.t. $\begin{cases} u_1 + 3u_2 \geq 11 \\ 2u_1 + 5u_2 \geq 20 \end{cases}$ $u_1 \geq 0, u_2 \geq 0$

2. Use the graphical method to solve both the following LP problems:

   (a) max $2x_1 + 5x_2$ s.t. $\begin{cases} -2x_1 + 3x_2 \leq 6 \\ 7x_1 - 2x_2 \leq 14 \\ x_1 + x_2 \leq 5 \end{cases}$ $x_1 \geq 0, x_2 \geq 0$

   (b) max $8x_1 + 9x_2$ s.t. $\begin{cases} x_1 + 2x_2 \leq 8 \\ 2x_1 + 3x_2 \leq 13 \\ x_1 + x_2 \leq 6 \end{cases}$ $x_1 \geq 0, x_2 \geq 0$

   (c) max $-2x_1 + x_2$ s.t. $0 \leq x_1 - 3x_2 \leq 3$, $x_1 \geq 2$, $x_2 \geq 0$

SM 3. The set A consists of all (x_1, x_2) satisfying

$$-2x_1 + x_2 \leq 2, \quad x_1 + 2x_2 \leq 8, \quad x_1 \geq 0, \quad x_2 \geq 0$$

Solve each of the following six problems with A as the common feasible set:

(a) max x_2 (b) max x_1 (c) max $3x_1 + 2x_2$

(d) min $2x_1 - 2x_2$ (e) max $2x_1 + 4x_2$ (f) min $-3x_1 - 2x_2$

4. Consider the following problem:

$$\max x_1 + x_2 \text{ s.t.} \begin{cases} -x_1 + x_2 \leq -1 \\ -x_1 + 3x_2 \leq 3 \end{cases} \quad x_1 \geq 0, \, x_2 \geq 0$$

(a) Is there a solution to this problem?

(b) Is there a solution if the objective function is $z = -x_1 - x_2$ instead?

5. Replace the objective function in Example 19.1.1 by $20x_1 + tx_2$. For what values of t will the maximum profit still be at $x_1 = 5$ and $x_2 = 22.5$?

6. A firm produces two types of television set: an inexpensive type A, and an expensive type B. The firm earns a profit of $700 from each TV of type A, and $1 000 for each TV of type B. There are three stages of the production process, each requiring its own specialized kind of labour. Stage I requires three units of labour on each set of type A and five units of labour on each set of type B. The total available quantity of labour for this stage is 3 900. Stage II requires one unit of labour on each set of type A and three units on each set of type B. The total labour available for this stage is 2 100 units. At stage III, two units of labour are needed for each type, and 2 200 units of labour are available. How many TV sets of each type should the firm produce in order to maximize its profit?

19.2 Introduction to Duality Theory

Confronted with an optimization problem involving scarce resources, an economist will often ask: What happens to the optimal solution if the availability of the resources changes? For linear programming problems, answers to questions like this are intimately related to the so-called duality theory of LP. As a point of departure, let us again consider the baker's problem in Example 19.1.1.

EXAMPLE 19.2.1 Suppose the baker were to stumble across an extra kilo of flour that had been hidden away in storage. How much would this extra kilo add to his maximum profit? How much would an extra kilo of sugar contribute to profit? Or an extra kilo of butter?

Solution: If the baker finds an extra kilo of flour, the flour border becomes $3x_1 + 6x_2 = 151$. It is clear from Fig. 19.1.2 that the feasible set S will expand slightly and point B will move slightly up along the butter border. The new optimal point B' will be at the intersection of the lines $3x_1 + 6x_2 = 151$ and $x_1 + x_2 = 27.5$. Solving these equations gives $x_1 = 14/3$ and $x_2 = 137/6$. The objective function attains the value $20(14/3) + 30(137/6) = 2335/3 = 775 + 10/3$. So profit rises by $10/3$.

If the baker finds an extra kilo of sugar, the feasible set will expand, but the optimal point is still at B. Recall that at the optimum in the original problem, the baker had 5.75 kilos of unused sugar. There is no extra profit.

An extra kilo of butter would give a new optimal point at the intersection of the lines $3x_1 + 6x_2 = 150$ and $x_1 + x_2 = 28.5$. Solving these equations gives $x_1 = 7$ and $x_2 = 21.5$ with $20x_1 + 30x_2 = 775 + 10$. Profit rises by 10.

We introduce the notation u_1^*, u_2^*, and u_3^* for these three amounts of extra profit. Then the three results above can be summarized as follows:

(a) an extra kilo of flour would allow the maximum profit to increase by $u_1^* = 10/3$;
(b) an extra kilo of sugar would allow the maximum profit to increase by $u_2^* = 0$;
(c) an extra kilo of butter would allow the maximum profit to increase by $u_3^* = 10$.

The three numbers $(u_1^*, u_2^*, u_3^*) = (10/3, 0, 10)$ are the *marginal profits* from an extra kilo of flour, sugar, and butter, respectively. These numbers have many interesting properties that we shall now explore.

Suppose (x_1, x_2) is a feasible pair in the problem, so that the three constraints in Example 19.1.1 are satisfied. Suppose we now multiply:

(a) the flour constraint by 10/3, the marginal profit of flour;
(b) the sugar constraint by 0, the marginal profit of sugar;
(c) the butter constraint by 10, the marginal profit of butter.

Because the multipliers are all ≥ 0, the inequalities are preserved. So we have

$$(10/3)(3x_1 + 6x_2) \leq \tfrac{10}{3} \cdot 150$$

$$0(x_1 + 0.5x_2) \leq 0 \cdot 22$$

$$10(x_1 + x_2) \leq 10 \cdot 27.5$$

Now we add all these inequalities, using the fact that if $A \leq B$, $C \leq D$, and $E \leq F$, then $A + C + E \leq B + D + F$. The result is

$$10x_1 + 20x_2 + 10x_1 + 10x_2 \leq \tfrac{10}{3} \cdot 150 + 10 \cdot 27.5$$

This reduces to $20x_1 + 30x_2 \leq 775$. Thus, by using the "magic" numbers u_1^*, u_2^*, and u_3^* defined above, we have managed to prove that if (x_1, x_2) is any feasible pair, then the objective function cannot exceed 775. But $x_1 = 5$ and $x_2 = 22.5$ make z equal 775. This gives an *algebraic proof* that (5, 22.5) *is* a maximum point!

The Dual Problem

The pattern revealed in Example 19.2.1 arises in all linear programming problems. In fact, the numbers u_1^*, u_2^*, and u_3^* we found are solutions to a new LP problem called the *dual*.

Recall the baker's problem in Example 19.1.1. We will now call it the *primal* and denote it by (P). It can be written as

$$\max 20x_1 + 30x_2 \text{ s.t.} \begin{cases} 3x_1 + 6x_2 \leq 150 \\ x_1 + 0.5x_2 \leq 22 \\ x_1 + x_2 \leq 27.5 \end{cases} \quad x_1 \geq 0, \quad x_2 \geq 0 \quad \text{(P)}$$

Suppose that the baker gets tired of running the business. An entrant agrees to take it over and buy all the remaining ingredients. The incumbent baker intends to charge the entrant a price of u_1 for each kilo of flour, of u_2 for each kilo of sugar, and of u_3 for each kilo of butter.

Because one dozen biscuits requires three kilos of flour and one kilo each of sugar and butter, the incumbent baker will charge a total of $3u_1 + u_2 + u_3$ for all the ingredients needed to produce a dozen biscuits. There was originally a profit of 20 for each dozen biscuits, so it seems reasonable for the incumbent baker to expect to earn at least this much from selling these ingredients. This leads the incumbent baker to insist that the price triple (u_1, u_2, u_3) must satisfy

$$3u_1 + u_2 + u_3 \geq 20$$

Otherwise, rather than selling these ingredients needed to produce a dozen biscuits, before turning over the business to the entrant, the incumbent would find it more profitable to use up those ingredients in order to produce a dozen biscuits for sale.

If in addition the baker also wants to earn at least as much as before for the ingredients needed to produce a dozen cakes, the triple of prices (u_1, u_2, u_3) must also satisfy

$$6u_1 + 0.5u_2 + u_3 \geq 30$$

Now the entrant presumably wants to buy the incumbent baker's stocks of ingredients as inexpensively as possible. The total cost of 150 kilos of flour, 22 kilos of sugar, and 27.5 kilos of butter is $150u_1 + 22u_2 + 27.5u_3$. In order to pay as little as possible while having the baker accept the offer, the entrant should suggest a price triple (u_1, u_2, u_3) that solves the LP problem

$$\min\ 150u_1 + 22u_2 + 27.5u_3 \quad \text{s.t.} \quad \begin{cases} 3u_1 + u_2 + u_3 \geq 20 \\ 6u_1 + 0.5u_2 + u_3 \geq 30 \end{cases} \quad u_1 \geq 0,\ u_2 \geq 0,\ u_3 \geq 0 \tag{D}$$

This is called the *dual* of the primal problem, and so we have given it the label (D).

Suppose the baker lets the entrant take over the business and buy the stocks of ingredients at prices that solve (D). Will the baker earn as much as before? It turns out that the answer is yes. The solution to problem (D) consists of the three prices $u_1^* = 10/3$, $u_2^* = 0$, and $u_3^* = 10$ that we found in Example 19.2.1. At these prices the total amount the baker gets for selling the resources is $150u_1^* + 22u_2^* + 27.5u_3^* = 775$, which is precisely the maximum value of the objective function in problem (P). The price per unit that the entrant pays for each ingredient is exactly the marginal profit for that ingredient which was calculated in Example 19.2.1. In particular, the price of sugar is zero, because the baker has more than can be used optimally.

The primal problem (P) and dual problem (D) turn out to be closely related. Let us now explain how to construct the dual of a general LP problem.

The General Case

Consider the general LP problem

$$\max\ c_1 x_1 + \cdots + c_n x_n \quad \text{s.t.} \quad \begin{cases} a_{11} x_1 + \cdots + a_{1n} x_n \leq b_1 \\ \ldots\ldots\ldots\ldots\ldots\ldots\ldots\ldots \\ a_{m1} x_1 + \cdots + a_{mn} x_n \leq b_m \end{cases} \tag{19.2.1}$$

with nonnegativity constraints $x_1 \geq 0, \ldots, x_n \geq 0$. We define its *dual* as the LP problem

$$\min b_1 u_1 + \cdots + b_m u_m \quad \text{s.t.} \quad \begin{cases} a_{11} u_1 + \cdots + a_{m1} u_m \geq c_1 \\ \ldots\ldots\ldots\ldots\ldots\ldots\ldots \\ a_{1n} u_1 + \cdots + a_{mn} u_m \geq c_n \end{cases} \quad (19.2.2)$$

with nonnegativity constraints $u_1 \geq 0, \ldots, u_m \geq 0$. Note that problem (19.2.2) involves exactly the same coefficients $c_1, \ldots, c_n, a_{11}, \ldots, a_{mn}$, and $b_1, \ldots, b_m$ as occur in (19.2.1).

In the *primal* problem (19.2.1), there are n variables $x_1, \ldots, x_n$ and m constraints, disregarding the nonnegativity constraints. In the dual (19.2.2), there are m variables $u_1, \ldots, u_m$ and n constraints. Whereas the primal is a maximization problem, the dual is a minimization problem. In both problems, all variables are nonnegative. There are m "less than or equal to" constraints in the primal problem (19.2.1), but n "greater than or equal to" constraints in the dual problem (19.2.2). The coefficients of the objective function in either problem are the right-hand side elements of the constraints in the other problem. Finally, the two matrices formed by the coefficients of the variables in the constraints in the primal and dual problems are transposes of each other, because they take the form

$$\mathbf{A} = \begin{pmatrix} a_{11} & a_{12} & \cdots & a_{1n} \\ a_{21} & a_{22} & \cdots & a_{2n} \\ \vdots & \vdots & & \vdots \\ a_{m1} & a_{m2} & \cdots & a_{mn} \end{pmatrix} \quad \text{and} \quad \mathbf{A}' = \begin{pmatrix} a_{11} & a_{21} & \cdots & a_{m1} \\ a_{12} & a_{22} & \cdots & a_{m2} \\ \vdots & \vdots & & \vdots \\ a_{1n} & a_{2n} & \cdots & a_{mn} \end{pmatrix} \quad (19.2.3)$$

You should now check carefully that problem (D) really is the dual of problem (P) in the sense just explained. Moreover, one can apply the process of constructing the dual (19.2.2) of the linear program (19.2.1) to the resulting dual. Because of the symmetry between the two problems, this process takes us from (19.2.2) back to the original primal (19.2.1). For this reason, each problem is the dual of the other, as will be shown formally in Theorem 19.2.1 below.

Matrix Formulation

We will now express the primal and dual problems in matrix notation. In order to do so, in addition to the matrices $\mathbf{A}$ and $\mathbf{A}'$ set out in (19.2.3), we introduce the following four column vectors:

$$\mathbf{x} = \begin{pmatrix} x_1 \\ \vdots \\ x_n \end{pmatrix}, \quad \mathbf{c} = \begin{pmatrix} c_1 \\ \vdots \\ c_n \end{pmatrix}, \quad \mathbf{b} = \begin{pmatrix} b_1 \\ \vdots \\ b_m \end{pmatrix}, \quad \text{and} \quad \mathbf{u} = \begin{pmatrix} u_1 \\ \vdots \\ u_m \end{pmatrix} \quad (19.2.4)$$

Also, given any pair of vectors $\mathbf{y}$ and $\mathbf{z}$ of the same dimension, we introduce the notation $\mathbf{y} \leqq \mathbf{z}$ to mean that each component of $\mathbf{y}$ is less than or equal to the corresponding component of $\mathbf{z}$, with $\mathbf{y} \geqq \mathbf{z}$ as the reverse inequality.

With this notation, the primal in (19.2.1) can be written as follows:

$$\max \mathbf{c}'\mathbf{x} \quad \text{s.t.} \quad \mathbf{A}\mathbf{x} \leq \mathbf{b}, \; \mathbf{x} \geq \mathbf{0} \tag{19.2.5}$$

On the other hand, the dual in (19.2.2) can be written as

$$\min \mathbf{b}'\mathbf{u} \quad \text{s.t.} \quad \mathbf{A}'\mathbf{u} \geq \mathbf{c}, \; \mathbf{u} \geq \mathbf{0} \tag{19.2.6}$$

Sometimes it is more convenient, however, to write the dual in a slightly different way. Transposing the vector inequality $\mathbf{A}'\mathbf{u} \geq \mathbf{c}$ by using the transposition rules in Eqs (12.7.2) to (12.7.5), we obtain $\mathbf{u}'\mathbf{A} \geq \mathbf{c}'$. Moreover $\mathbf{b}'\mathbf{u} = \mathbf{u}'\mathbf{b}$. So the dual can also be written as

$$\min \mathbf{u}'\mathbf{b} \quad \text{s.t.} \quad \mathbf{u}'\mathbf{A} \geq \mathbf{c}', \mathbf{u}' \geq \mathbf{0} \tag{19.2.7}$$

One advantage of matrix notation is that it allows a relatively simple proof of the following result:

THEOREM 19.2.1 (THE DUAL OF THE DUAL IS THE PRIMAL)

Given the primal LP in (19.2.5) and the dual LP in (19.2.6), the dual of the dual is the primal.

Proof. By changing the signs of $\mathbf{A}'$, $\mathbf{b}$ and $\mathbf{c}$, the dual LP in (19.2.6) can be rewritten as the following primal LP with a $\leq$ vector constraint:

$$\max (-\mathbf{b}')\mathbf{u} \quad \text{s.t.} \quad (-\mathbf{A}')\mathbf{u} \leq -\mathbf{c}, \; \mathbf{u} \geq \mathbf{0} \tag{$*$}$$

Now, let us follow the rules needed to pass from the primal in (19.2.5) to the dual in (19.2.6), but apply them to the dual of the LP in (∗), regarded as a primal. Because the transpose of $-\mathbf{A}'$ is $-\mathbf{A}$, we obtain

$$\min (-\mathbf{c})'\mathbf{x} \quad \text{s.t.} \quad (-\mathbf{A})\mathbf{x} \geq -\mathbf{b}, \; \mathbf{x} \geq \mathbf{0}$$

After reversing the signs, this is evidently equivalent to the primal LP in (19.2.5). ∎

EXERCISES FOR SECTION 19.2

(SM) **1.** Consider Exercise 19.1.1(a).

(a) Replace the constraint $3x_1 + 2x_2 \leq 6$ by $3x_1 + 2x_2 \leq 7$. Find the new optimal solution and compute the increase u_1^* in the objective function.

(b) Replace the constraint $x_1 + 4x_2 \leq 4$ by $x_1 + 4x_2 \leq 5$. Find the new optimal solution and compute the increase u_2^* in the objective function.

(c) By the same argument as in Example 19.2.1, prove that if (x_1, x_2) is feasible in the original problem, then the objective function can never be larger than 36/5.

2. Write down the dual to part (b) of Exercise 19.1.2.

3. Write down the dual to each LP in parts (a) and (b) of Exercise 19.1.1.

4. Consider the LP problem $\quad \max x_1 + x_2 \quad$ s.t. $\quad \begin{cases} x_1 + 2x_2 \leq 14 \\ 2x_1 + x_2 \leq 13 \end{cases} \quad x_1 \geq 0, \, x_2 \geq 0$

   (a) Use the graphical method to find its solution.

   (b) Write down the dual and find its solution.

19.3 The Duality Theorem

This section presents the main results that relate the solution of an LP problem to that of its dual. We begin by considering yet again the baker's problem that appeared initially as Example 19.1.1.

EXAMPLE 19.3.1 Consider the primal and dual problems that were labelled as (P) and (D) respectively in Section 19.2. Suppose that (x_1, x_2) is an arbitrary feasible pair in (P), in the sense that all five inequalities in (P) are all satisfied. Let (u_1, u_2, u_3) be an arbitrary feasible triple that satisfies all five inequalities in (D). Ignoring the two nonnegativity constraints, let us multiply the other three inequalities in (P) by the nonnegative numbers u_1, u_2, and u_3, respectively. Adding the resulting three inequalities leads to the following

$$(3x_1 + 6x_2)u_1 + (x_1 + 0.5x_2)u_2 + (x_1 + x_2)u_3 \leq 150u_1 + 22u_2 + 27.5u_3$$

Rearranging the terms on the left-hand side yields

$$(3u_1 + u_2 + u_3)x_1 + (6u_1 + 0.5u_2 + u_3)x_2 \leq 150u_1 + 22u_2 + 27.5u_3 \qquad \text{(i)}$$

Similarly, ignoring the three nonnegativity constraints, we multiply the other two inequalities in (D) by the nonnegative numbers x_1 and x_2, respectively, before adding the results. After some rearrangement, this gives

$$(3u_1 + u_2 + u_3)x_1 + (6u_1 + 0.5u_2 + u_3)x_2 \geq 20x_1 + 30x_2 \qquad \text{(ii)}$$

From (i) and (ii) together, we infer that for all feasible (x_1, x_2) in problem (P) and for all feasible (u_1, u_2, u_3) in problem (D), one has

$$150u_1 + 22u_2 + 27.5u_3 \geq 20x_1 + 30x_2 \qquad \text{(iii)}$$

It follows that, however we choose a pair (x_1, x_2) that is feasible in the primal problem (P) together with a triple (u_1, u_2, u_3) that is feasible in the dual problem (D), the value of the objective function in the dual is always greater than or equal to the value of the objective function in the primal.

Inequality (iii) is valid for the feasible pair $(x_1, x_2) = (5, 22.5)$ in particular. For each feasible triple (u_1, u_2, u_3), we therefore obtain

$$150u_1 + 22u_2 + 27.5u_3 \geq 20 \cdot 5 + 30 \cdot 22.5 = 775$$

Suppose that we can find a feasible triple (u_1^*, u_2^*, u_3^*) for problem (D) such that

$$150u_1^* + 22u_2^* + 27.5u_3^* = 775$$

Because no lower value of the objective function in problem (D) is obtainable, it follows that (u_1^*, u_2^*, u_3^*) must solve (D). In our discussion of problem (D) in Section 19.2, we saw that for $(u_1^*, u_2^*, u_3^*) = (10/3, 0, 10)$ the objective function in the dual does have the value 775. So the triple $(10/3, 0, 10)$ does solve the dual problem.

Our analysis of this example illustrates two significant general results in LP theory. Here is the first:

THEOREM 19.3.1

If $(x_1, \ldots, x_n)$ is feasible in the primal problem (19.2.1) and $(u_1, \ldots, u_m)$ is feasible in the dual problem (19.2.2), then

$$b_1 u_1 + \cdots + b_m u_m \geq c_1 x_1 + \cdots + c_n x_n \qquad (19.3.1)$$

So the dual objective function has a value that is always at least as large as that of the primal objective function.

The argument for this result is not difficult:

Proof: Multiply the m inequalities in (19.2.1) by the nonnegative numbers $u_1, \ldots, u_m$, then add all the inequalities together. Also, multiply the n inequalities in (19.2.2) by the nonnegative numbers $x_1, \ldots, x_n$, then add all of these. These two operations yield the two respective inequalities

$$(a_{11} x_1 + \cdots + a_{1n} x_n) u_1 + \cdots + (a_{m1} x_1 + \cdots + a_{mn} x_n) u_m \leq b_1 u_1 + \cdots + b_m u_m$$

$$(a_{11} u_1 + \cdots + a_{m1} u_m) x_1 + \cdots + (a_{1n} u_1 + \cdots + a_{mn} u_m) x_n \geq c_1 x_1 + \cdots + c_n x_n$$

By rearranging the terms on the left-hand side of each inequality, we see that each is equal to the double sum $\sum_{i=1}^{m} \sum_{j=1}^{n} a_{ij} u_i x_j$. So (19.3.1) follows immediately.

From Theorem 19.3.1 we can derive a second significant result:

THEOREM 19.3.2

Suppose that $(x_1^*, \ldots, x_n^*)$ is feasible in the primal problem (19.2.1) and $(u_1^*, \ldots, u_m^*)$ is feasible in the dual problem (19.2.2), with

$$c_1 x_1^* + \cdots + c_n x_n^* = b_1 u_1^* + \cdots + b_m u_m^* \qquad (19.3.2)$$

Then $(x_1^*, \ldots, x_n^*)$ solves the primal problem (19.2.1) and $(u_1^*, \ldots, u_m^*)$ solves the dual problem (19.2.2).

Again, we have all the necessary ingredients we need to prove this important result:

Proof: Let $(x_1, \ldots, x_n)$ be an arbitrary n-vector that is feasible for problem (19.2.1). Using (19.3.1) with $u_1 = u_1^*, \ldots, u_m = u_m^*$, as well as (19.3.2), we obtain

$$c_1 x_1 + \cdots + c_n x_n \leq b_1 u_1^* + \cdots + b_m u_m^* = c_1 x_1^* + \cdots + c_n x_n^*$$

This proves that $(x_1^*, \ldots, x_n^*)$ solves (19.2.1).

On the other hand, suppose that $(u_1, \ldots, u_m)$ is feasible for problem (19.2.2). Then (19.3.1) and (19.3.2) together imply that

$$b_1 u_1 + \cdots + b_m u_m \geq c_1 x_1^* + \cdots + c_n x_n^* = b_1 u_1^* + \cdots + b_m u_m^*$$

This proves that $(u_1^*, \ldots, u_m^*)$ solves (19.2.2).

Theorem 19.3.2 shows that if we are able to find respective *feasible* solutions for the two problems (19.2.1) and (19.2.2) that give the same value to the relevant objective functions, then these feasible solutions are, in fact, *optimal* solutions.

Infeasible and Unbounded LPs

So far all the LPs we have studied have had optimal solutions, which are maximum or minimum points subject to all the inequality constraints. The most important result in duality theory is the duality theorem we shall present at the end of this section. In order to make it more readily comprehensible, however, we should first explain why an LP such as that in (19.2.1) may have no solution.

One obvious reason for (19.2.1) not to have any solution is that its $m + n$ inequality constraints, including nonnegativity constraints, determine an empty feasible set of n-vectors $(x_1, \ldots, x_n)$ that satisfy all of them. In this case the LP is said to be *infeasible*.

It is obvious that the $m + n$ inequality constraints determine a closed set. Suppose this feasible set is non-empty and also bounded. Because a linear function is evidently continuous, then the extreme value theorem applies and tells us that a maximum point exists. This must solve the LP.

Yet the feasible set need not be bounded. In this case the LP could have no solution because there are n-vectors $(x_1, \ldots, x_n)$ in the feasible set which make the objective function $c_1 x_1 + \cdots + c_n x_n$ arbitrarily large. If this happens, the LP is said to be *unbounded*. Note that, as shown by Example 19.1.2, an LP may be bounded even though its feasible set is unbounded.

The various possibilities are explored in the following minimal example involving only one choice variable x and one constraint $ax \leq b$, in addition to $x \geq 0$:

EXAMPLE 19.3.2   For any three real constants a, b, c, all nonzero, consider the following dual pair of LPs:

Primal: max cx s.t. $ax \leq b$, $x \geq 0$ Dual: min bu s.t. $au \geq c$, $u \geq 0$

For each of the following four values of the parameter triple (a, b, c), find the solution to both the primal and the dual, if these exist. Otherwise, explain why there are no solutions.
(a) $(1, 1, 1)$;   (b) $(1, 1, -1)$;   (c) $(1, -1, 1)$;   (d) $(-1, 1, 1)$.

Solution:

(a) With $(a, b, c) = (1, 1, 1)$, the primal is max x s.t. $x \leq 1$, $x \geq 0$, whose solution is evidently $x = 1$, with maximum value 1.
The dual is min u s.t. $u \geq 1$, $u \geq 0$, whose solution is $u = 1$, with minimum value 1.

(b) Here the primal is max $-x$ s.t. $x \leq 1$, $x \geq 0$, whose solution is evidently $x = 0$, with maximum value 0.
The dual is min u s.t. $u \geq -1$, $u \geq 0$, whose solution is $u = 0$, with minimum value 0.

(c) The primal is max x s.t. $x \leq -1$, $x \geq 0$, which is infeasible.
The dual is min $-u$ s.t. $u \geq 1$, $u \geq 0$, which is unbounded.

(d) The primal is max x s.t. $-x \leq -1$, $x \geq 0$, which is unbounded.
The dual is min u s.t. $-u \geq 1$, $u \geq 0$, which is infeasible.

The next example shows that it is also possible for both the primal and dual LPs to be infeasible.

EXAMPLE 19.3.3 Consider the following primal LP:

$$\max\ x_1 + x_2 \ \text{s.t.}\ -x_1 \leq -1,\ x_2 \leq -1,\quad x_1 \geq 0,\ x_2 \geq 0$$

The two constraints $x_2 \leq -1$ and $x_2 \geq 0$ are evidently inconsistent, so the primal LP is infeasible. Its dual is:

$$\min\ -u_1 - u_2\ \text{s.t.}\ -u_1 \geq 1,\ u_2 \geq 1,\quad u_1 \geq 0,\ u_2 \geq 0$$

Here the constraint $-u_1 \geq 1$ implies that $u_1 \leq -1$, which is inconsistent with $u_1 \geq 0$. Thus, the dual LP is also infeasible.

The results presented in Examples 19.3.2 and 19.3.3 accord with the following promised main result:

THEOREM 19.3.3 (THE DUALITY THEOREM)

Consider the primal problem (19.2.1) along with the dual problem (19.2.2).

(a) If the primal is both feasible and bounded, then so is the dual. Also, each LP then has a solution, with the maximum value of the primal equal to the minimum value of the dual.

(b) If the primal is unbounded, then the dual is infeasible.

(c) If the dual is unbounded, then the primal is infeasible.

The proofs of Theorems 19.3.1 and 19.3.2 were very simple. It is much more difficult to prove part (a) of Theorem 19.3.3, and we shall not attempt to do so here.

Part (b) of Theorem 19.3.3, however, follows readily from inequality (19.3.1). For if $(u_1, \ldots, u_m)$ is any feasible solution to the dual problem, then $b_1 u_1 + \cdots + b_m u_m$ is a finite number greater than or equal to *any* number $c_1 x_1 + \cdots + c_n x_n$ when $(x_1, \ldots, x_n)$ is feasible in the primal. This puts an upper bound on the possible values of $c_1 x_1 + \cdots + c_n x_n$.

Finally, part (c) of Theorem 19.3.3 follows from treating the dual LP as a primal. Indeed, part (b) implies that, if the dual is unbounded, then the dual of the dual is infeasible. But by Theorem 19.2.1, the dual of the dual is the primal, so part (c) follows.

An instructive exercise is to formulate and prove Theorems 19.3.1 and 19.3.2 using matrix algebra. Let us do so for Theorem 19.3.1. Suppose the *n*-vector **x** is feasible in (19.2.5), and the *m*-vector **u** is feasible in (19.2.7). Then $\mathbf{x} \geq \mathbf{0}$ and $\mathbf{Ax} \leq \mathbf{b}$ in the primal, whereas $\mathbf{u} \geq \mathbf{0}$ and $\mathbf{u'A} \geq \mathbf{c'}$ in the dual. From these four inequalities, we infer that

$$\mathbf{u'b} \geq \mathbf{u'(Ax)} = \mathbf{(u'A)x} \geq \mathbf{c'x}$$

Note carefully how these inequalities correspond to those we established in the earlier proof of Theorem 19.3.1.

EXERCISES FOR SECTION 19.3

SM **1.** Consider the LP problem $\quad \max 2x + 7y \text{ s.t.} \quad \begin{cases} 4x + 5y \leq 20 \\ 3x + 7y \leq 21 \end{cases} \quad x \geq 0, y \geq 0.$

(a) Solve it by a graphical argument.

(b) Write down the dual and solve it by a graphical argument.

(c) Are the values of the objective functions equal?[6]

2. Write down the dual to the problem in Example 19.1.2 and solve it. Check that the optimal values of the primal and dual objective functions are equal.

SM **3.** A firm produces both small and medium television sets. The profit is 400 for each small TV and 500 for each medium TV. Each TV set has to be processed on three different assembly lines. Each small TV requires respectively two, one, and one hour on lines 1, 2, and 3. The corresponding numbers for medium TVs are one, four, and two. Suppose lines 1 and 2 both have a capacity of at most 16 hours per day, whereas line 3 has a capacity of at most 11 hours per day. Let x_1 and x_2 denote the number of small and medium television sets that are produced per day.

(a) Show that to maximize profits per day, the firm must solve the following problem:

$$\max 400 x_1 + 500 x_2 \text{ s.t.} \quad \begin{cases} 2x_1 + x_2 \leq 16 \\ x_1 + 4x_2 \leq 16 \\ x_1 + 2x_2 \leq 11 \end{cases} \quad x_1 \geq 0, x_2 \geq 0$$

(b) Solve this problem graphically.

(c) Suppose the firm could increase its capacity by one hour a day on just one of its assembly lines. Which line should have its capacity increased?

---

[6] If not, then, according to Theorem 19.3.3, you have made a mistake.

19.4 A General Economic Interpretation

This section gives an economic interpretation of the general LP problem (19.2.1) and its dual (19.2.2). Think of a firm that, like the commercial baker in Example 19.1.1, produces one or more different kinds of output using m different *resources* as inputs. Suppose there are n different *activities* (or processes) involved in the production process. A typical activity needs a certain amount of each resource to run it at unit level. Let a_{ij} denote the number of units of resource i that are needed to run activity j at unit level. Then the m-vector with components $a_{1j}, a_{2j}, \ldots, a_{mj}$ expresses the amounts of the m different resources required to run activity j at unit level. If we run the n different activities at levels $x_1, \ldots, x_n$, then the total requirements for the m different resources can be expressed as the column m-vector

$$x_1 \begin{pmatrix} a_{11} \\ \vdots \\ a_{m1} \end{pmatrix} + \cdots + x_n \begin{pmatrix} a_{1n} \\ \vdots \\ a_{mn} \end{pmatrix}$$

If the available amounts of the m resources are $b_1, \ldots, b_m$, then the feasible activity levels are those that satisfy the m constraints in (19.2.1). The nonnegativity constraints reflect the fact that we cannot run the activities at negative levels.

For each $j = 1, 2, \ldots, n$, running activity j at unit level earns a certain reward (or value) that we denote by c_j. The total reward from running the n activities at levels $x_1, \ldots, x_n$ is then $c_1 x_1 + \cdots + c_n x_n$. So the firm faces the problem of solving the following LP problem:

Find those levels for the n different activities that maximize the total reward, subject to the m given resource constraints.

In the baker's problem of Example 19.1.1, the two activities were baking the two different types of pastry (biscuits and cakes), using as ingredients appropriate amounts of the three different resources (flour, sugar and butter).

Let us turn next to the dual problem (19.2.2). In order to remain in business, the firm has to use some resources. Each resource, therefore, has some value that a typical economist will regard as a price. Let u_j denote the price associated with each unit of resource j. Rather than think of u_j as a market price for resource j, we should think of it as measuring the relative contribution that one unit of resource j makes to the total economic reward. Because these are not real market prices, they are often called *shadow prices*.

Given the quantities $a_{1j}, a_{2j}, \ldots, a_{mj}$ of each of the m resources that are needed to run activity j at unit level, the total shadow cost of running activity j at unit level equals the sum $a_{1j} u_1 + a_{2j} u_2 + \cdots + a_{mj} u_m$. Given that c_j is the reward earned by running activity j at unit level, we can regard the difference

$$c_j - (a_{1j} u_1 + a_{2j} u_2 + \cdots + a_{mj} u_m)$$

as the shadow *profit* from running activity j at unit level. Note that, for each $j = 1, 2, \ldots, m$, the jth constraint in the dual problem (19.2.2) says that the shadow profit from running activity j at unit level cannot be positive.

Equivalently, the part of the reward c_j from running activity j that can be imputed to each resource i is $a_{ij} u_i$. Then the jth constraint in the dual problem (19.2.2) says that the total which can be imputed to all the resources used by running activity j at unit level cannot be less than the corresponding reward c_j.

The objective function $Z = b_1 u_1 + \cdots + b_m u_m$ in the dual LP problem (19.2.2) measures the shadow value of the initial stock of all the resources. The dual problem is, therefore:

Among all choices of nonnegative shadow prices $u_1, \ldots, u_m$ such that the profit from running each activity at unit level is nonpositive, find those prices which together minimize the shadow value of the initial resources.

The Optimal Dual Variables as Shadow Prices

Consider again the primal problem (19.2.1). What happens to the optimal value of the objective function if the numbers $b_1, \ldots, b_m$ change? If the changes $\Delta b_1, \ldots, \Delta b_m$ are positive, then the feasible set increases and the new optimal value of the objective function cannot be smaller; usually it increases. The following analysis also applies when some or all the changes $\Delta b_1, \ldots, \Delta b_m$ are negative.

Suppose the two n-vectors $\mathbf{x}^* = (x_1^*, \ldots, x_n^*)$ and $\mathbf{x}^* + \Delta \mathbf{x} = (x_1^* + \Delta x_1, \ldots, x_n^* + \Delta x_n)$ are optimal solutions to the primal problem when the right-hand sides of the constraints in (19.2.1) are respectively the two m-vectors $(b_1, \ldots, b_m)$ and $(b_1 + \Delta b_1, \ldots, b_m + \Delta b_m)$. Note that the components of these two vectors $\mathbf{b}$ and $\mathbf{b} + \Delta \mathbf{b}$ are the coefficients b_j and $b_j + \Delta b_j$ of the choice variables u_j in the corresponding dual problem given by (19.2.2). Now, the inequality and nonnegativity constraints appearing in each of these dual problems are exactly the same; only the coefficients in the objective functions are slightly different. It follows that the set of all feasible points for both these dual problems will be exactly the same convex polyhedron in m-dimensional space, as illustrated by Fig. 19.1.4. Finally, an optimal solution of each dual problem will occur at a vertex of this polyhedron. Typically, therefore, provided that $|\Delta b_1|, \ldots, |\Delta b_m|$ are all sufficiently small, the solution of both dual problems will occur at exactly the same vertex of this common polyhedron. This implies that both dual problems will have exactly the same optimal solution $u_1^*, \ldots, u_m^*$. In this case, according to Theorem 19.3.3, one has

$$c_1 x_1^* + \cdots + c_n x_n^* = b_1 u_1^* + \cdots + b_m u_m^*$$

and $\quad c_1(x_1^* + \Delta x_1) + \cdots + c_n(x_n^* + \Delta x_n) = (b_1 + \Delta b_1) u_1^* + \cdots + (b_m + \Delta b_m) u_m^*$

Hence, subtracting each side of the first equation from the second, one has

$$c_1 \Delta x_1 + \cdots + c_n \Delta x_n = u_1^* \Delta b_1 + \cdots + u_m^* \Delta b_m$$

Here the left-hand side is the change we obtain in the maximum value of the objective function in (19.2.1) when $b_1, \ldots, b_m$ are increased by $\Delta b_1, \ldots, \Delta b_m$, respectively. Denoting this change in z by Δz^*, we obtain

$$\Delta z^* = u_1^* \Delta b_1 + \cdots + u_m^* \Delta b_m \tag{19.4.1}$$

It is important to note that the assumption used to justify (19.4.1) is that the numbers b_j do not change enough to cause the optimal dual variables to change. In case (19.4.1) does hold, and if $\Delta b_j = 1$, while $\Delta b_i = 0$ for all $i \neq j$, then one will have $\Delta z^* = u_j^*$, which accords with the results in Example 19.2.1. For this reason, the real number u_j^* is also known as the *shadow price* of the jth inequality constraint

$$a_{j1}x_1 + \cdots + a_{jn}x_n \leq b_j$$

EXERCISES FOR SECTION 19.4

1. For the problem in Exercise 19.3.1, we found that its optimal solution was $x^* = 0$ and $y^* = 3$, with $z^* = 2x^* + 7y^* = 21$. The optimal solution of the dual was $u_1^* = 0$ and $u_2^* = 1$. Suppose we change 20 to 20.1 and 21 to 20.8. What is the corresponding change in the maximized value of the objective function?

(SM) 2. A firm produces two goods labelled A and B. The firm earns a profit of 300 from each unit of good A, and 200 from each unit of B. There are three stages of the production process. Good A requires six hours in a machine shop, then four hours on an assembly line, and finally five hours of packing. The corresponding numbers for B are three, six, and five, respectively. The total number of hours available for the three stages are 54, 48, and 50, respectively.

(a) Formulate and solve the LP problem of maximizing profits subject to the given constraints.

(b) Write down and solve the dual problem.

(c) By how much would the optimal profit increase if the firm were allowed two hours more preparation time and one hour more packing time?

19.5 Complementary Slackness

Consider again the baker's problem (P) in Section 19.2, along with its dual (D). The solution to (P) was $x_1^* = 5$ and $x_2^* = 22.5$, at which the first and the third inequalities both hold with equality. The solution to the dual was $u_1^* = 10/3$, $u_2^* = 0$, and $u_3^* = 10$, at which both inequalities in the dual hold with equality. Thus, in this example

$x_1^* > 0$, $x_2^* > 0$ $\Rightarrow$ the first and second inequalities in the dual hold with equality

$u_1^* > 0$, $u_3^* > 0$ $\Rightarrow$ the first and third inequalities in the primal hold with equality

We interpret the second implication as telling us that, because the shadow prices of flour and butter are both positive, the optimal solution requires all the available flour and butter to be used. But because the optimal solution does not use all the available sugar, its shadow price is zero; it is not a scarce resource.

Implications like this hold more generally. Indeed, consider the problem

$$\max c_1 x_1 + c_2 x_2 \text{ s.t.} \begin{cases} a_{11}x_1 + a_{12}x_2 \leq b_1 \\ a_{21}x_1 + a_{22}x_2 \leq b_2 \quad x_1 \geq 0,\ x_2 \geq 0 \\ a_{31}x_1 + a_{32}x_2 \leq b_3 \end{cases} \quad \text{(i)}$$

SECTION 19.5 / COMPLEMENTARY SLACKNESS

Its dual is

$$\min b_1u_1 + b_2u_2 + b_3u_3 \text{ s.t.} \begin{cases} a_{11}u_1 + a_{21}u_2 + a_{31}u_3 \geq c_1 \\ a_{12}u_1 + a_{22}u_2 + a_{32}u_3 \geq c_2 \end{cases} \quad u_1 \geq 0, u_2 \geq 0, u_3 \geq 0 \quad \text{(ii)}$$

Suppose that (x_1^*, x_2^*) solves (i) and (u_1^*, u_2^*, u_3^*) solves (ii). Then

(iii) $\begin{cases} a_{11}x_1^* + a_{12}x_2^* \leq b_1 \\ a_{21}x_1^* + a_{22}x_2^* \leq b_2 \\ a_{31}x_1^* + a_{32}x_2^* \leq b_3 \end{cases}$ and (iv) $\begin{cases} a_{11}u_1^* + a_{21}u_2^* + a_{31}u_3^* \geq c_1 \\ a_{12}u_1^* + a_{22}u_2^* + a_{32}u_3^* \geq c_2 \end{cases}$

Now multiply the three inequalities in (iii) by the nonnegative numbers u_1^*, u_2^*, and u_3^*, respectively. Then add the results. This yields the inequality

$$(a_{11}x_1^* + a_{12}x_2^*)u_1^* + (a_{21}x_1^* + a_{22}x_2^*)u_2^* + (a_{31}x_1^* + a_{32}x_2^*)u_3^* \leq b_1u_1^* + b_2u_2^* + b_3u_3^* \quad \text{(v)}$$

Next, multiply the two inequalities in (iv) by x_1^* and x_2^*, respectively, then add. Because x_1^* and x_2^* are also nonnegative, this gives

$$(a_{11}u_1^* + a_{21}u_2^* + a_{31}u_3^*)x_1^* + (a_{12}u_1^* + a_{22}u_2^* + a_{32}u_3^*)x_2^* \geq c_1x_1^* + c_2x_2^* \quad \text{(vi)}$$

But the left-hand sides of the inequalities (v) and (vi) are both expansions of the common double sum $\sum_{i=1}^{3} \sum_{j=1}^{2} u_i^* a_{ij} x_j^*$, so must be rearrangements of each other. Moreover, by the Duality Theorem 19.3.3, their right-hand sides are equal as the common value of both primal and dual. It follows that

$$c_1 x_1^* + c_2 x_2^* = \sum_{i=1}^{3} \sum_{j=1}^{2} u_i^* a_{ij} x_j^* = b_1 u_1^* + b_2 u_2^* + b_3 u_3^* \quad \text{(vii)}$$

In particular, both the inequalities in (v) and (vi) can be replaced by *equalities*. So we can rearrange the equality version of (v) to obtain

$$(a_{11}x_1^* + a_{12}x_2^* - b_1)u_1^* + (a_{21}x_1^* + a_{22}x_2^* - b_2)u_2^* + (a_{31}x_1^* + a_{32}x_2^* - b_3)u_3^* = 0$$

Because (x_1^*, x_2^*) is feasible, the inequalities in (iii) imply that each of the three terms in parentheses is ≤ 0. But each $u_i^* \geq 0$, so the left-hand side is the sum of three ≤ 0 terms. If any term is negative, so is their sum. Yet the whole sum is 0, so each term is 0. Hence

$$(a_{i1}x_1^* + a_{i2}x_2^* - b_i)u_i^* = 0 \quad (i = 1, 2, 3)$$

We conclude that

$$a_{i1}x_1^* + a_{i2}x_2^* \leq b_i, \text{ with } a_{i1}x_1^* + a_{i2}x_2^* = b_i \text{ if } u_i^* > 0 \quad (i = 1, 2, 3) \quad (*)$$

Next, using (vii) once again, or equivalently, the fact that the inequality sign $\geq$ in (vi) can be replaced by =, we have

$$(a_{11}u_1^* + a_{21}u_2^* + a_{31}u_3^* - c_1)x_1^* + (a_{12}u_1^* + a_{22}u_2^* + a_{32}u_3^* - c_2)x_2^* = 0$$

Then, reasoning in exactly the same way as we did in deriving (∗), this gives

$$a_{1j}u_1^* + a_{2j}u_2^* + a_{3j}u_3^* \geq c_j, \text{ with } a_{1j}u_1^* + a_{2j}u_2^* + a_{3j}u_3^* = c_j \text{ if } x_j^* > 0, \quad (i = 1, 2)$$
(∗∗)

The two sets of inequalities (or equalities) in (∗) and (∗∗) are called *complementary slackness conditions*. The arguments used to show their necessity extend in a straightforward way to general LPs. Furthermore, the same complementary slackness conditions in (∗) and (∗∗) are also sufficient for optimality. Here is a general statement and proof:

THEOREM 19.5.1 (COMPLEMENTARY SLACKNESS)

Suppose that the primal maximization problem (19.2.1) has an optimal solution $\mathbf{x}^* = (x_1^*, \ldots, x_n^*)$, whereas the dual minimization problem (19.2.2) has an optimal solution $\mathbf{u}^* = (u_1^*, \ldots, u_m^*)$. Then for $i = 1, \ldots, m$, and $j = 1, \ldots, n$, one has the complementary slackness conditions

$$a_{1j}u_1^* + \cdots + a_{mj}u_m^* \geq c_j, \text{ with } a_{1j}u_1^* + \cdots + a_{mj}u_m^* = c_j \text{ if } x_j^* > 0 \quad (19.5.1)$$

and

$$a_{i1}x_1^* + \cdots + a_{in}x_n^* \leq b_i, \text{ with } a_{i1}x_1^* + \cdots + a_{in}x_n^* = b_i \text{ if } u_i^* > 0 \quad (19.5.2)$$

Conversely, suppose that $\mathbf{x}^*$ and $\mathbf{u}^*$ have all their components nonnegative while satisfying both (19.5.1) and (19.5.2). Then $\mathbf{x}^*$ solves the primal problem (19.2.1) and $\mathbf{u}^*$ solves the dual problem (19.2.2).

While longer than previous arguments, the following proof of this theorem should be well within your grasp:

Proof: Suppose that the n-vector $\mathbf{x}^* \geqq \mathbf{0}$ solves (19.2.1) and that the m-vector $\mathbf{u}^* \geqq \mathbf{0}$ solves (19.2.2). Using the matrix notation of (19.2.5) and (19.2.7), it follows that

$$\mathbf{A}\mathbf{x}^* \leqq \mathbf{b} \quad \text{and} \quad (\mathbf{u}^*)'\mathbf{A} \geqq \mathbf{c}' \quad \text{(i)}$$

Multiplying each side of the first inequality in (i) on the left by the row vector $(\mathbf{u}^*)' \geqq \mathbf{0}$, and each side of the second inequality on the right by the column vector $\mathbf{x}^* \geqq \mathbf{0}$, we obtain

$$(\mathbf{u}^*)'\mathbf{A}\mathbf{x}^* \leq (\mathbf{u}^*)'\mathbf{b} \quad \text{and} \quad (\mathbf{u}^*)'\mathbf{A}\mathbf{x}^* \geq \mathbf{c}'\mathbf{x}^* \quad \text{(ii)}$$

According to Theorem 19.3.3, one has $(\mathbf{u}^*)'\mathbf{b} = \mathbf{c}'\mathbf{x}^*$. So both inequalities in (ii) must be equalities. They can be written as

$$(\mathbf{u}^*)'(\mathbf{A}\mathbf{x}^* - \mathbf{b}) = 0 \quad \text{and} \quad [(\mathbf{u}^*)'\mathbf{A} - \mathbf{c}']\mathbf{x}^* = 0 \quad \text{(iii)}$$

But these two equations are equivalent to the two equalities

$$\sum_{i=1}^{m} u_i^*(a_{i1}x_1^* + \cdots + a_{in}x_n^* - b_i) = 0 \qquad (\text{iv})$$

$$\sum_{j=1}^{n} (a_{1j}u_1^* + \cdots + a_{mj}u_m^* - c_j)x_j^* = 0 \qquad (\text{v})$$

For $i = 1, \ldots, m$ one has both $u_i^* \geq 0$ and $a_{i1}x_1^* + \cdots + a_{in}x_n^* - b_i \leq 0$. So each term in the sum (iv) is ≤ 0. If any term is negative, so is their sum; but the sum of all m terms is 0, so each term in (iv) must be 0 as well. Therefore,

$$u_i^*(a_{i1}x_1^* + \cdots + a_{in}x_n^* - b_i) = 0, \qquad i = 1, \ldots, m \qquad (\text{vi})$$

Now (19.5.2) follows immediately. Property (19.5.1) is proved in the same way by noting how (v) implies that

$$(a_{1j}u_1^* + \cdots + a_{mj}u_m^* - c_j)x_j^* = 0, \qquad j = 1, \ldots, n \qquad (\text{vii})$$

Suppose conversely that $\mathbf{x}^*$ and $\mathbf{u}^*$ have all their components nonnegative and satisfy (19.5.1) and (19.5.2) respectively. It follows immediately that (vi) and (vii) are satisfied. So summing over i and j, respectively, we obtain (iv) and (v). These equations imply that

$$\sum_{i=1}^{m} b_i u_i^* = \sum_{i=1}^{m}\sum_{j=1}^{n} u_i^* a_{ij} x_j^* \quad \text{and also} \quad \sum_{j=1}^{n} c_j x_j^* = \sum_{j=1}^{n}\sum_{i=1}^{m} u_i^* a_{ij} x_j^*$$

Because the two double sums on the right-hand sides are equal, it follows that $\sum_{i=1}^{m} b_i u_i^* = \sum_{j=1}^{n} c_j x_j^*$. So according to Theorem 19.3.2, $\mathbf{x}^*$ solves problem (19.2.1) and $\mathbf{u}^*$ solves the dual. ∎

Using the economic interpretations we gave in Section 19.4, conditions (19.5.1) and (19.5.2) can be interpreted as follows:

INTERPRETATION OF THE COMPLEMENTARY SLACKNESS CONDITIONS

(i) If the optimal solution of the primal problem implies that activity j is in operation ($x_j^* > 0$), then the (shadow) profit from running that activity at unit level is 0.

(ii) If the shadow price of resource i is positive ($u_i^* > 0$), then all the available stock of resource i must be used in any optimum.

How Complementary Slackness Can Help Solve LP Problems

If the solution to either the primal or the dual problem is known, then the complementary slackness conditions can help find the solution to the other problem. They do so by determining which constraints are slack, and so which hold with equality. Let us look at an example.

EXAMPLE 19.5.1 Write down the dual of the following LP problem, and use a graphical argument to solve that dual.

$$\max 3x_1 + 4x_2 + 6x_3 \text{ s.t.} \begin{cases} 3x_1 + x_2 + x_3 \leq 2 \\ x_1 + 2x_2 + 6x_3 \leq 1 \end{cases}, \quad x_1 \geq 0, x_2 \geq 0, x_3 \geq 0 \quad \text{(i)}$$

Then use complementary slackness to solve problem (i).

Solution: The dual problem is

$$\min 2u_1 + u_2 \text{ s.t.} \begin{cases} 3u_1 + u_2 \geq 3 \\ u_1 + 2u_2 \geq 4 \\ u_1 + 6u_2 \geq 6 \end{cases}, \quad u_1 \geq 0, u_2 \geq 0 \quad \text{(ii)}$$

Using the same graphical technique as we used to solve Example 19.1.2, we find the solution $u_1^* = 2/5$ and $u_2^* = 9/5$. Inserting these values into the three constraints, we have $3u_1^* + u_2^* = 3$, $u_1^* + 2u_2^* = 4$, and $u_1^* + 6u_2^* = 56/5 > 6$.

What does this solution to (ii) tell us about the solution (x_1^*, x_2^*, x_3^*) to (i)? According to (19.5.2), because $u_1^* > 0$ and $u_2^* > 0$, both inequalities in (i) are satisfied with equality. So

$$3x_1^* + x_2^* + x_3^* = 2 \text{ and } x_1^* + 2x_2^* + 6x_3^* = 1 \quad \text{(iii)}$$

Next, because $u_1^* + 6u_2^* > 6$, the complementary slackness condition (19.5.1) implies that $x_3^* = 0$. Putting $x_3^* = 0$ in (iii) and then solving for x_1^* and x_2^*, we obtain

$$x_1^* = 3/5, \qquad x_2^* = 1/5, \qquad x_3^* = 0$$

This is the solution to problem (i). Note that the optimal values of the objective functions in the two problems are indeed equal because $2u_1^* + u_2^* = 13/5$ and $3x_1^* + 4x_2^* + 6x_3^* = 13/5$. This is just what the duality theorem says should happen.

Duality When Some Constraints are Equalities

Suppose that for the ith of the m constraints in the primal problem set out in (19.2.1), instead of inequality we have the equality

$$a_{i1}x_1 + \cdots + a_{in}x_n = b_i \quad (*)$$

In order to put the problem into the standard form in (19.2.1), we can replace the single equality $(*)$ by the double inequality

$$a_{i1}x_1 + \cdots + a_{in}x_n \leq b_i \text{ and } -a_{i1}x_1 - \cdots - a_{in}x_n \leq -b_i \quad (**)$$

Constraint (∗) thus gives rise to two dual variables u'_i and u''_i associated with the two constraints in (∗∗). For each $j = 1, \ldots, n$, the term $a_{ij}u_i$ in the sum on the left-hand side of the dual constraint $\sum_{k=1}^{m} a_{kj}u_k \geq c_j$ in (19.2.2) gets replaced by $a_{ij}u'_i - a_{ij}u''_i$. This allows us to replace the two variables u'_i and u''_i by the single variable $u_i = u'_i - u''_i$, but then there is no restriction on the sign of u_i. We see that *if the ith constraint in the primal is an equality, then the ith dual variable has an unrestricted sign.*

This is consistent with the economic interpretation we have given. If we are forced to use all of resource i, then it is not surprising that the resource may have a negative shadow price; it may be something that is harmful in excess. For instance, if the baker of Example 19.1.1 was forced to include all the stock of sugar in the cakes, the best point in Fig. 19.1.2 would be C, not B. Some profit would be lost.

From the symmetry between the primal and the dual, we realize now that *if one of the variables in the primal has an unrestricted sign, then the corresponding constraint in the dual is an equality.*

EXERCISES FOR SECTION 19.5

1. Consider Exercise 19.3.1. The solution of the primal was $x^* = 0$ and $y^* = 3$, with $u_1^* = 0$ and $u_2^* = 1$ as the solution of the dual. Verify that all the complementary slackness conditions in (19.5.1) and (19.5.2) are satisfied in this case.

2. Consider the following problem:

$$\min y_1 + 2y_2 \text{ s.t.} \begin{cases} y_1 + 6y_2 \geq 15 \\ y_1 + y_2 \geq 5 \\ -y_1 + y_2 \geq -5 \\ y_1 - 2y_2 \geq -20 \end{cases} \quad y_1 \geq 0, y_2 \geq 0$$

   (a) Solve this LP graphically.

   (b) Write down the dual problem and solve it.

   (c) If the first constraint $y_1 + 6y_2 \geq 15$ is changed to $y_1 + 6y_2 \geq 15.1$, what happens to the optimal values of the dual variables?

SM 3. A firm produces two commodities A and B. The firm has three factories that jointly produce both commodities in the amounts per hour given in the following table:

	Factory 1	Factory 2	Factory 3
Commodity A	10	20	20
Commodity B	20	10	20

The firm receives an order for 300 units of A and 500 units of B. The costs per hour of running factories 1, 2, and 3 are respectively €10 000, €8 000, and €11 000.

   (a) Let y_1, y_2, and y_3, respectively, denote the number of hours for which the three factories are used. Write down the linear programming problem of minimizing the costs of fulfilling the order.

(b) Write down the dual LP and solve it graphically. Then find the solution of the problem in part (a).

(c) By how much will the minimum cost of production increase if the cost per hour in factory 1 increases by 100?

4. [HARDER] Consider the LP problem

$$\max 3x_1 + 2x_2 \text{ s.t. } \begin{cases} x_1 + x_2 \leq 3 \\ 2x_1 + x_2 - x_3 \leq 1 \\ x_1 + 2x_2 - 2x_3 \leq 1 \end{cases} \quad x_1 \geq 0, x_2 \geq 0, x_3 \geq 0$$

(a) Suppose x_3 is a fixed number. Solve the problem in each of the two alternative cases when $x_3 = 0$ and $x_3 = 3$.

(b) Formulate and solve the problem for any fixed value of x_3 in $[0, \infty)$. The maximal value of $3x_1 + 2x_2$ becomes a function of x_3. Find this function and maximize it.

(c) Do the results in part (b) say anything about the solution to the original problem, in which the variable x_3 can also be chosen?

REVIEW EXERCISES

1. Consider the LP problem $\max x + 2y$ s.t. $\begin{cases} x + y \leq 4 \\ -x + y \leq 1 \\ 2x - y \leq 3 \end{cases} \quad x \geq 0, y \geq 0$

(a) Find the solution.   (b) Formulate and solve the dual problem.

(SM) 2. Consider the LP problem

$$\min 16y_1 + 6y_2 - 8y_3 - 15y_4 \text{ s.t. } \begin{cases} -y_1 + y_2 - 2y_3 - 4y_4 \geq -1 \\ 2y_1 - 2y_2 - y_3 - 5y_4 \geq 1 \end{cases}$$

where $y_i \geq 0$ for $i = 1, 2, 3, 4$.

(a) Write down the dual problem and solve it.

(b) Find the solution to the primal problem.

(c) If the first constraint in the primal is changed to $-y_1 + y_2 - 2y_3 - 4y_4 \geq k$, for what values of k will the solution of the dual occur at the same point as for $k = -1$?

3. Consider the LP problem

$$\min 5x + y \text{ s.t. } \begin{cases} 4x + y \geq 4 \\ 2x + y \geq 3 \\ 3x + 2y \geq 2 \\ -x + 2y \geq -2 \end{cases} \quad x \geq 0, y \geq 0$$

(a) Solve it.   (b) Formulate the dual problem and solve it.

4. A firm has two plants each of which jointly produces outputs of three different goods. Its total labour force is fixed. When a fraction λ of its labour force is allocated to its first plant and a fraction $1 - \lambda$ to its second plant, with $0 \leq \lambda \leq 1$, the total outputs of the three different goods are given by the components of the vector

$$\lambda(8, 4, 4) + (1 - \lambda)(2, 6, 10) = (6\lambda + 2, -2\lambda + 6, -6\lambda + 10)$$

(a) Is it possible for the firm to produce either of the two output vectors $\mathbf{a} = (5, 5, 7)$ and $\mathbf{b} = (7, 5, 5)$ if output cannot be thrown away?

(b) How do your answers to part (a) change if output can be thrown away?

(c) Let (p_1, p_2, p_3) denote the vector of prices at which the firm can sell the three goods. How will the revenue-maximizing choice of the fraction λ depend upon this price vector? What condition must the vector satisfy if both plants are to remain in use?

5. The production of three goods requires using two machines. Machine 1 can be utilized for b_1 hours, while machine 2 can be utilized for b_2 hours. The time spent for the production of one unit of each good is given by the following table:

	Machine 1	Machine 2
Good 1	3	2
Good 2	1	2
Good 3	4	1

The profits per unit produced of the three goods are £6, £3, and £4, respectively.

(a) Write down the linear programming problem this leads to.

(b) Show that the dual is $\min b_1 y_1 + b_2 y_2$ s.t. $\begin{cases} 3y_1 + 2y_2 \geq 6 \\ y_1 + 2y_2 \geq 3 \\ 4y_1 + y_2 \geq 4 \end{cases}$ $y_1 \geq 0, y_2 \geq 0$.

Solve this problem graphically for $b_1 = b_2 = 100$.

(c) Solve the problem in (a) when $b_1 = b_2 = 100$.

(d) Suppose that the time for which machine 1 can be used increases to 101, while $b_2 = 100$. What is the new maximal profit?

(e) The maximum value of the profit in problem (a) is a function of b_1 and b_2, which we denote by $F(b_1, b_2)$. What is the degree of homogeneity of the function F?

20 NONLINEAR PROGRAMMING

Chapter 18 considered how to maximize or minimize a function subject to equality constraints. Chapter 19 then allowed for inequality constraints, but concentrated on the special case where both the objective function and all the functions defining those constraints are linear. In this last chapter of the book we study "nonlinear programming" problems in which both the objective function and all the functions defining the *inequality constraints* may be nonlinear. Some particularly simple inequality constraints are those requiring certain variables to be nonnegative. These often have to be imposed for the solution to make economic sense. In addition, bounds on resource availability are often expressed as inequalities rather than equalities.

Section 20.1 discusses the simple case of two choice variables and one inequality constraint. Next, Section 20.2 advances our discussion to problems with many choice variables and inequality constraints. The last Section 20.3 concludes by considering an important special case when some of the inequality constraints require one or more choice variables to be nonnegative.

20.1 Two Variables and One Constraint

In this section we consider the simple *nonlinear programming problems* with just two variables and one inequality constraint. In the case of maximization problems, these take the form

$$\max f(x, y) \text{ s.t. } g(x, y) \leq c \tag{20.1.1}$$

Thus, we seek the largest value attained by $f(x, y)$ in the *admissible* or *feasible* set S of all pairs (x, y) satisfying $g(x, y) \leq c$. Problems where one wants to minimize $f(x, y)$ subject to $(x, y) \in S$ can be handled by studying instead the problem of maximizing $-f(x, y)$ subject to $(x, y) \in S$.

Problem (20.1.1) can be solved using the methods for unconstrained optimization that were explained in Chapter 17. This involves examining not only the critical points of f in the interior of the admissible set S, but also the behaviour of f on the boundary of S. Since the 1950s, however, economists have generally tackled such problems by using an extension of the Lagrange multiplier method. This we will call the *Karush–Kuhn–Tucker method*, or *KKT method* for short.[1]

To apply the KKT method, we begin by following a recipe that gives all the points (x, y) in the xy-plane which, except in some bizarre special cases, can possibly solve problem (20.1.1). Since the only difference from problem (18.1.1) is that the equality constraint back there has become an inequality constraint here, it should be no surprise that the recipe closely resembles the Lagrange multiplier method that we put forward in Section 18.1.

THE KKT METHOD, SIMPLE CASE

To find the only possible solutions to problem (20.1.1), proceed as follows:

(i) Associate a constant Lagrange multiplier λ with the constraint $g(x, y) \leq c$, and define the Lagrangian

$$\mathcal{L}(x, y) = f(x, y) - \lambda[g(x, y) - c]$$

(ii) Find the critical points of $\mathcal{L}(x, y)$, by equating its partial derivatives to zero:

$$\begin{aligned} \mathcal{L}'_1(x, y) &= f'_1(x, y) - \lambda g'_1(x, y) = 0 \\ \text{and} \quad \mathcal{L}'_2(x, y) &= f'_2(x, y) - \lambda g'_2(x, y) = 0 \end{aligned} \quad (20.1.2)$$

(iii) Introduce the *complementary slackness condition*:

$$\lambda \geq 0, \text{ with } \lambda = 0 \text{ if } g(x, y) < c \quad (20.1.3)$$

(iv) Require (x, y) to satisfy the constraint

$$g(x, y) \leq c \quad (20.1.4)$$

(v) Find all the points (x, y) that, together with associated values of λ, satisfy all the conditions (20.1.2) to (20.1.4). These are the solution candidates, at least one of which solves the problem, if it has a solution.

If $g = c$ and $g'_1 = g'_2 = 0$ at the maximum of the problem, this method may fail.

---

[1] Most economists continue to call this the Kuhn–Tucker method, after the American H.W. Kuhn (1925–2014) and Canadian A.W. Tucker (1905–1975). Mathematicians, however, including Kuhn in particular, long ago recognized the relevance and even priority of W. Karush's (1939) Master's thesis.

Note that the conditions (20.1.2) are exactly two of the same first-order conditions as those used in the Lagrange multiplier method of Section 18.1. Furthermore, the constraint in condition (20.1.4) obviously has to be satisfied.

So the only new feature is condition (20.1.3), which can be rather tricky. It may be helpful to recall the corresponding complementary slackness condition (19.5.2) for the typical linear programming problem. For the nonlinear programming problem we are considering here, condition (20.1.3) requires that λ be nonnegative, and moreover that $\lambda = 0$ if $g(x, y) < c$. Thus, if $\lambda > 0$, we must have $g(x, y) = c$. An alternative formulation of condition (20.1.3), then, is that

$$\lambda \geq 0, \quad \text{with} \quad \lambda \cdot [g(x, y) - c] = 0 \tag{20.1.5}$$

Later we shall see that the Lagrange multiplier associated with an inequality constraint can be interpreted as a "shadow price", just as it was in Chapter 18 for an equality constraint, and in the latter part of Section 19.4 for linear programming problems. That is, for small changes in the right-hand side c of the "resource constraint" $g(x, y) \leq c$, the multiplier λ is approximately the gain in the maximized objective function per unit increase in c. With this interpretation, the shadow price is nonnegative. When $g(x, y) < c$ at the optimum, so the resource constraint does not bind, then (20.1.3) implies that $\lambda = 0$, signifying that the extra value associated with a small increase in c is 0.

The two inequalities $\lambda \geq 0$ and $g(x, y) \leq c$ are *complementary* in the sense that at most one can be "slack", meaning that at most one can hold with strict inequality. Equivalently, at least one must be an equality. Failing to observe that it *is possible* to have *both* $\lambda = 0$ *and* $g(x, y) = c$ in the complementary slackness condition is probably the most common error when solving nonlinear programming problems.

Parts (ii)–(iv) of the KKT method set out above are together called the *KKT conditions*. Note that these are (essentially) *necessary* conditions for the solution of Problem (20.1.1). In general, though, they are far from sufficient: indeed, suppose that one can find a point (x^0, y^0) where f is critical and $g(x^0, y^0) < c$; then the KKT conditions will automatically be satisfied by (x^0, y^0) together with the Lagrange multiplier $\lambda = 0$, yet then (x^0, y^0) could be a local or global minimum or maximum, or even a saddle point.

We say that these KKT conditions are only *essentially* necessary because there may not always be a Lagrange multiplier for which the KKT conditions hold. The exceptions are some rather rare constrained optimization problems that fail to satisfy a special technical condition called the "constraint qualification". For details, see FMEA.

With equality constraints, setting the partial derivative $\partial \mathcal{L}/\partial \lambda$ equal to zero just recovers the constraint $g(x, y) = c$. Yet with an inequality constraint, one can have $\partial \mathcal{L}/\partial \lambda = -g(x, y) + c > 0$ if the constraint is slack or inactive at an optimum. This was one reason why in Chapter 18 we advised against differentiating the Lagrangian w.r.t. the multiplier λ, even though many other books advocate this procedure.

For the case of an equality constraint, we proved in Theorem 18.5.1 that if the Lagrangian is concave, or if for some other reason a critical point of the Lagrangian happens to be an unconstrained global maximum point of that function, then the first-order conditions in problem (18.5.1) are sufficient for optimality. A very similar result is also valid for the corresponding problem with an inequality constraint:

THEOREM 20.1.1 (SUFFICIENT CONDITIONS)

For the problem set out in (20.1.1), suppose (x^0, y^0) satisfies all the conditions (20.1.2) to (20.1.4) for the Lagrangian function

$$\mathcal{L}(x, y) = f(x, y) - \lambda[g(x, y) - c]$$

If the Lagrangian is concave, or if (x^0, y^0) happens to maximize $\mathcal{L}$ anyway, then (x^0, y^0) solves the constrained maximization problem.

The proof of this result is actually quite instructive:

Proof: Any pair (x^0, y^0) that satisfies conditions (20.1.2) must be a critical point of the Lagrangian. By Theorem 17.2.2, if the Lagrangian is concave, this (x^0, y^0) will give a global maximum. So all pairs (x, y) must satisfy

$$\mathcal{L}(x^0, y^0) = f(x^0, y^0) - \lambda[g(x^0, y^0) - c] \geq \mathcal{L}(x, y) = f(x, y) - \lambda[g(x, y) - c] \quad (*)$$

Now, whether or not $\mathcal{L}$ is not concave, suppose that $(*)$ holds anyway. Then rearranging the terms of $(*)$ gives us

$$f(x^0, y^0) - f(x, y) \geq \lambda[g(x^0, y^0) - g(x, y)] \quad (**)$$

By the complementary slackness condition in its alternative form (20.1.5), one has both $\lambda \geq 0$ and $\lambda[g(x^0, y^0) - c] = 0$. It follows that whenever the pair (x, y) satisfies the inequality constraint $g(x, y) \leq c$, then the right-hand side of $(**)$ satisfies

$$\lambda[g(x^0, y^0) - g(x, y)] = \lambda[c - g(x, y)] \geq 0$$

The inequality $(**)$ therefore implies that $f(x^0, y^0) \geq f(x, y)$. It follows that (x^0, y^0) solves the constrained maximization problem (20.1.1). ∎

EXAMPLE 20.1.1 A firm has a total of L units of labour to allocate to the production of two different goods, which can be sold at fixed positive prices a and b respectively. Producing x units of the first good requires αx^2 units of labour, whereas producing y units of the second good requires βy^2 units of labour, where α and β are positive constants. Find what output levels of the two goods maximize the total revenue that the firm can earn by using this fixed amount of labour.

Solution: The firm's problem is max $ax + by$ s.t. $\alpha x^2 + \beta y^2 \leq L$. The Lagrangian is

$$\mathcal{L}(x, y) = ax + by - \lambda(\alpha x^2 + \beta y^2 - L) \quad (*)$$

According to the recipe in (20.1.2)–(20.1.4), necessary conditions for (x^*, y^*) to solve the problem are

$$\mathcal{L}'_x = a - 2\lambda\alpha x^* = 0 \quad \text{(i)}$$

$$\mathcal{L}'_y = b - 2\lambda\beta y^* = 0 \quad \text{(ii)}$$

together with the complementary slackness condition

$$\lambda \geq 0, \text{ with } \lambda = 0 \text{ if } \alpha(x^*)^2 + \beta(y^*)^2 < L \quad \text{(iii)}$$

and the resource constraint $\alpha x^2 + \beta y^2 \leq L$. Because a and b are positive, equations (i) and (ii) together imply that λ, x^*, and y^* are all positive, with

$$x^* = \frac{a}{2\alpha\lambda} \text{ and } y^* = \frac{b}{2\beta\lambda} \quad (**)$$

Because $\lambda > 0$, condition (iii) implies that $\alpha(x^*)^2 + \beta(y^*)^2 = L$. Inserting the expressions for x^* and y^* into this equality yields

$$\frac{a^2}{4\alpha\lambda^2} + \frac{b^2}{4\beta\lambda^2} = L$$

This equation allows us to find λ, which is

$$\lambda = \tfrac{1}{2}L^{-1/2}\sqrt{\tfrac{a^2}{\alpha} + \tfrac{b^2}{\beta}} \quad (***)$$

Our recipe has produced a unique solution candidate. It has x^* and y^* given by $(**)$ and λ given by $(***)$. Because $\lambda > 0$, the Lagrangian $\mathcal{L}$ given by $(*)$ is obviously concave. By Theorem 20.1.1, therefore, we have solved the constrained maximization problem.

EXAMPLE 20.1.2 Solve the problem

$$\max f(x,y) = x^2 + y^2 + y - 1 \text{ s.t. } g(x,y) = x^2 + y^2 \leq 1$$

Solution: The Lagrangian is

$$\mathcal{L}(x,y) = x^2 + y^2 + y - 1 - \lambda(x^2 + y^2 - 1)$$

Necessary first-order conditions for (x, y) to be a critical point of $\mathcal{L}$ are:

$$\mathcal{L}'_1(x,y) = 2x - 2\lambda x = 0 \quad \text{(i)}$$
$$\mathcal{L}'_2(x,y) = 2y + 1 - 2\lambda y = 0 \quad \text{(ii)}$$

The complementary slackness condition is

$$\lambda \geq 0, \text{ with } \lambda = 0 \text{ if } x^2 + y^2 < 1 \quad \text{(iii)}$$

We now set out to find all solution candidates in the form of triples (x, y, λ) that satisfy conditions (i)–(iii).

Equations (i) and (ii) can be written as $2x(1 - \lambda) = 0$ and $2y(1 - \lambda) = -1$, respectively. The second of these implies that $\lambda \neq 1$, so the first implies that $x = 0$.

Consider the first case when $x^2 + y^2 = 1$. Because $x = 0$, we have $y = \pm 1$. Try $y = 1$ first. Then, (ii) implies $\lambda = 3/2$. Because $\lambda > 0$, condition (iii) is satisfied. It follows that the triple $(x, y, \lambda) = (0, 1, 3/2)$ *is a first candidate for optimality* that satisfies all three conditions (i)–(iii). Next, try $y = -1$ instead. Then condition (ii) yields $\lambda = 1/2 > 0$, so once again (iii) is satisfied. So $(x, y, \lambda) = (0, -1, 1/2)$ *is a second candidate for optimality.*

Consider, finally, the second case when $x^2 + y^2 = y^2 < 1$. With $x = 0$ this implies that $y^2 < 1$ and so $-1 < y < 1$. In this case (iii) implies that $\lambda = 0$, and so equation (ii) yields $y = -1/2$. It follows that the triple $(0, -1/2, 0)$ *is a third candidate for optimality.*

We conclude that there are three candidates for optimality. The associated function values are
$$f(0, 1) = 1, \quad f(0, -1) = -1, \quad \text{and} \quad f(0, -1/2) = -\tfrac{5}{4}$$

Now, we are trying to maximize the continuous function $x^2 + y^2 + y - 1$ over the unit disk of points (x, y) in the plane that satisfy $x^2 + y^2 \leq 1$. Since that set is closed and bounded, the extreme value theorem implies that there is a solution to the problem. Because the only possible solutions are the three points already found, we conclude that $(x, y) = (0, 1)$ solves the maximization problem.[2]

Why Does the KKT Method Work?

Suppose that the point (x^*, y^*) in the xy-plane solves problem (20.1.1). Two cases are possible. Either $g(x^*, y^*) < c$, in which case the constraint $g(x^*, y^*) \leq c$ is said to be *inactive* or *slack* at (x^*, y^*). Alternatively $g(x^*, y^*) = c$, in which case the same inequality constraint is said to *bind* or be *active* or *tight* at (x^*, y^*).

The two different cases are illustrated in Figs 20.1.1 and 20.1.2 for two different values of the parameter c. In addition, both figures display the same four level curves of the same objective function f. This function is assumed to increase as the level curves shrink.

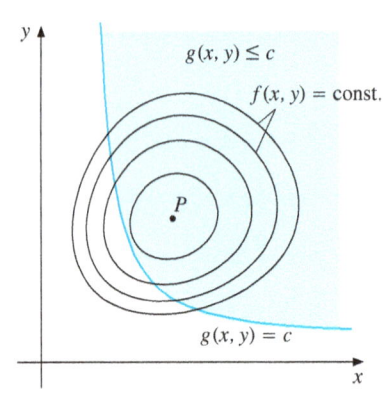

Figure 20.1.1 $P = (x^*, y^*)$ is an interior point of the feasible set.

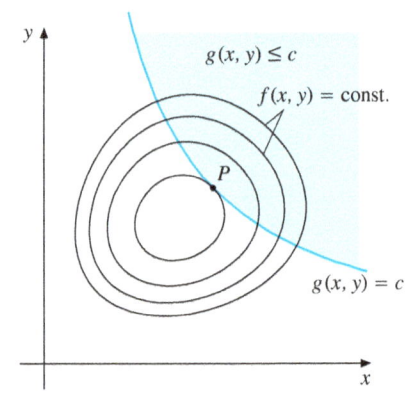

Figure 20.1.2 Constraint $g(x, y) \leq c$ binds at $P = (x^*, y^*)$.

The case shown in Fig. 20.1.1 occurs when the solution (x^*, y^*) to problem (20.1.1) is at an interior point P of the shaded feasible set because it satisfies $g(x^*, y^*) < c$. Then (x^*, y^*) must be a local maximum point of the function f, so it must be a critical point at which $f_1'(x^*, y^*) = f_2'(x^*, y^*) = 0$. In this case, if we set $\lambda = 0$, then the triple $(x^*, y^*, 0)$ satisfies all the conditions (20.1.2) to (20.1.4).

---

[2] The point $(0, -1/2)$ solves the corresponding minimization problem. In Example 17.5.1 we solved both these problems using a different technique.

The other case is shown in Fig. 20.1.2. This occurs when the solution (x^*, y^*) to problem (20.1.1) is on the boundary of the shaded feasible set because it satisfies $g(x^*, y^*) = c$. Then the constraint $g(x, y) \leq c$ binds, and in fact the point (x^*, y^*) must solve the problem

$$\max f(x, y) \text{ s.t. } g(x, y) = c$$

with an equality constraint. Provided that the conditions of Theorem 18.4.1 are all satisfied, there will exist a unique Lagrange multiplier λ such that the Lagrangian satisfies the first-order conditions (20.1.2) at (x^*, y^*). It remains to show that this Lagrange multiplier λ satisfies $\lambda \geq 0$, thus ensuring that (20.1.3) is also satisfied at (x^*, y^*).

To prove that $\lambda \geq 0$, replace the constant c on the right-hand side of the constraint by the variable parameter b, and then consider the following two problems

$$\max f(x, y) \text{ s.t. } g(x, y) \leq b \quad \text{and} \quad \max f(x, y) \text{ s.t. } g(x, y) = b$$

Let $v(b)$ denote the maximum value function for the first problem with the inequality constraint, and $f^*(b)$ the corresponding maximum value function for the second problem with the equality constraint. Recall from (18.2.2) that in case the function $f^*(b)$ is differentiable at $b = c$, the multiplier λ must equal the derivative $df^*(b)/db|_{b=c}$ at that point. We will show that $f^*(b) \leq f^*(c)$ whenever $b < c$. This implies that, at least when f^* is differentiable at $b = c$, one has $\lambda = df^*(b)/db|_{b=c} \geq 0$.

Now, an obvious general property of any constrained maximization problem is that imposing a more stringent constraint never allows a higher maximum value. So, because the equality constraint $g(x, y) = b$ is more stringent than $g(x, y) \leq b$, our definitions of the functions v and f^* imply that $f^*(b) \leq v(b)$ for all b. But also, in case $b < c$, the constraint $g(x, y) \leq b$ is more stringent than $g(x, y) \leq c$, implying that $v(b) \leq v(c)$. Finally, because we are discussing the case when the solution (x^*, y^*) to problem (20.1.1) satisfies $g(x^*, y^*) = c$, we must have $v(c) = f^*(c)$. Thus, whenever $b < c$, one has the inequalities

$$f^*(b) \leq v(b) \leq v(c) = f^*(c)$$

In particular $f^*(b) \leq f^*(c)$, as required.

EXERCISES FOR SECTION 20.1

1. Consider the problem max $-x^2 - y^2$ s.t. $x - 3y \leq -10$.

   (a) Find the pair (x^*, y^*) that solves the problem.

   (b) The same pair (x^*, y^*) also solves the problem of minimizing $x^2 + y^2$ subject to the same constraint $x - 3y \leq -10$. Sketch the feasible set S and explain the solution geometrically.

2. Consider the consumer demand problem max $\sqrt{x} + \sqrt{y}$ s.t. $px + qy \leq m$.

   (a) Find the demand functions that determine the optimal demands x^* and y^* as functions of the parameter triple (p, q, m).

   (b) Are these demand functions homogeneous of degree 0?

3. Consider the problem max $4 - \frac{1}{2}x^2 - 4y$ s.t. $6x - 4y \leq a$.

   (a) Write down the KKT conditions.

   (b) Solve the problem.

   (c) With $V(a)$ denoting the maximum value function, verify that $V'(a) = \lambda$, where λ is the Lagrange multiplier in (b).

4. Consider the problem max $x^2 + 2y^2 - x$ s.t. $x^2 + y^2 \leq 1$.

   (a) Write down the Lagrangian and the two first-order conditions (20.1.2).

   (b) Find the five triples (x, y, λ) that satisfy all the necessary conditions.

   (c) Find the solution to the problem.

(SM) 5. Consider the problem max $f(x, y) = 2 - (x - 1)^2 - e^{y^2}$ s.t. $x^2 + y^2 \leq a$, where a is a positive constant.

   (a) Write down the KKT conditions for the solution of the problem, distinguishing between the cases $a \in (0, 1)$ and $a \geq 1$. Then find the only solution candidate (x, y, λ).

   (b) Use Theorem 20.1.1 to prove that this solution candidate is optimal.

   (c) Let $f^*(a)$ be the value function for the problem. Verify that $df^*(a)/da = \lambda$.

6. Suppose that, as functions of its output $Q \geq 0$, a firm earns revenue $R(Q) = aQ - bQ^2$ and incurs cost $C(Q) = \alpha Q + \beta Q^2$, where a, b, α, and β are all positive parameters. The firm maximizes profit $\pi(Q) = R(Q) - C(Q)$ subject to the constraint $Q \geq 0$. Solve this one-variable problem by the KKT method, and find conditions for the constraint to bind at the optimum.

20.2 Many Variables and Inequality Constraints

A fairly general nonlinear programming problem with n variables and m inequality constraints can be stated as follows:

$$\max f(x_1, \ldots, x_n) \text{ s.t. } \begin{cases} g_1(x_1, \ldots, x_n) \leq c_1 \\ \ldots\ldots\ldots\ldots\ldots \\ g_m(x_1, \ldots, x_n) \leq c_m \end{cases} \quad (20.2.1)$$

The set of n-vectors $\mathbf{x} = (x_1, \ldots, x_n)$ that satisfy all the constraints is called the *admissible set* or the *feasible set*.

Recall that minimizing $f(\mathbf{x})$ is equivalent to maximizing $-f(\mathbf{x})$. Also an inequality constraint of the form $g_j(\mathbf{x}) \geq c_j$ can be rewritten as $-g_j(\mathbf{x}) \leq -c_j$, whereas an equality constraint $g_j(\mathbf{x}) = c_j$ is equivalent to the double inequality constraint $g_j(\mathbf{x}) \leq c_j$ and $-g_j(\mathbf{x}) \leq -c_j$. In this way, most constrained optimization problems can be expressed in the form (20.2.1).

In Section 18.6 the two equations (18.6.10) and (18.6.11) outlined how the Lagrange multiplier method could be applied to the corresponding problem with m equality constraints. Here is a similar recipe for solving the problem set out in (20.2.1):

THE KKT METHOD

To find the only possible solutions to problem (20.2.1), we proceed as follows:

(i) For each $j = 1, \ldots, m$, associate a Lagrange multiplier λ_j with the jth constraint, and then write down the Lagrangian

$$\mathcal{L}(\mathbf{x}) = f(\mathbf{x}) - \sum_{j=1}^{m} \lambda_j [g_j(\mathbf{x}) - c_j] \qquad (20.2.2)$$

(ii) Given the m Lagrange multipliers $\lambda_1, \ldots, \lambda_m$, find the critical points of $\mathcal{L}(\mathbf{x})$ by finding, for each $i = 1, \ldots, n$, its partial derivative w.r.t. x_i, and then solving the n simultaneous equations

$$\frac{\partial \mathcal{L}(\mathbf{x})}{\partial x_i} = \frac{\partial f(\mathbf{x})}{\partial x_i} - \sum_{j=1}^{m} \lambda_j \frac{\partial g_j(\mathbf{x})}{\partial x_i} = 0$$

(iii) For each $j = 1, \ldots, m$, impose the complementary slackness condition:

$$\lambda_j \geq 0, \ \text{ with } \lambda_j = 0 \text{ if } g_j(\mathbf{x}) < c_j$$

(iv) Require $\mathbf{x}$ to satisfy all the constraints $g_j(\mathbf{x}) \leq c_j$.

(v) Find all the vectors $\mathbf{x}$ that, together with associated values of $\lambda_1, \ldots, \lambda_m$, satisfy conditions (ii), (iii), and (v). These combinations $(\mathbf{x}, \lambda_1, \ldots, \lambda_m)$ are the solution candidates. At least one of these solves the problem, if it has a solution.

In order for the conditions to be truly necessary, one needs a constraint qualification of the kind discussed in FMEA.

Note that, as with Eq. (20.1.5), for each $j = 1, \ldots, m$ the conditions in parts (iii) and (iv) of the KKT method regarding the jth constraint can be combined into the triple requirement that

$$\lambda_j \geq 0, \quad g_j(\mathbf{x}) \leq c_j, \quad \text{and} \quad \lambda_j [g_j(\mathbf{x}) - c_j] = 0 \qquad (20.2.3)$$

Actually, some further amalgamation is possible. Evidently, if (20.2.3) does hold for each $j = 1, \ldots, m$, then summing the last equality over j gives

$$\sum_{j=1}^{m} \lambda_j [g_j(\mathbf{x}) - c_j] = 0 \qquad (20.2.4)$$

But a converse result is also true. Indeed, for each $j = 1, \ldots, m$, the first two inequalities in (20.2.3) evidently imply that $\lambda_j [g_j(\mathbf{x}) - c_j] \leq 0$, so each term of the sum on the left-hand side of (20.2.4) is nonpositive. Then, however, for that whole sum to be zero, it is necessary for each term to be zero. It follows that all the m conditions (20.2.3) hold simultaneously if and only if we have the single combined condition

$$\lambda_j \geq 0, \quad g_j(\mathbf{x}) \leq c_j \quad (j=1,\ldots,m) \quad \text{and} \quad \sum_{j=1}^{m} \lambda_j[g_j(\mathbf{x}) - c_j] = 0 \qquad (20.2.5)$$

Both the equivalent conditions (20.2.3) and (20.2.5) may be easier to remember and also make some subsequent derivations rather easier.

Concave Programming

For the case of a maximization problem with one equality constraint, Theorem 18.5.1 showed the importance of the special case when the Lagrangian function $\mathcal{L}(\mathbf{x})$ is concave in $\mathbf{x}$. This is because any critical point of $\mathcal{L}(\mathbf{x})$ that satisfies the equality constraint must solve the maximization problem. Indeed, even if the Lagrangian is not concave, a critical point that maximizes it anyway while satisfying the constraint must solve the maximization problem. With inequality constraints, we have not only similar results, but some useful sufficient conditions for the Lagrangian function to be concave. The following result provides those sufficient conditions:

CONCAVE PROGRAMME

Consider the problem in (20.2.1) of maximizing the function $f(\mathbf{x})$ of n variables subject to the m inequality constraints $g_j(\mathbf{x}) \leq c_j$ $(j=1,2,\ldots,m)$. The problem is said to be a *concave programme* in case the objective function f is concave, and each constraint function g_j $(j=1,2,\ldots,m)$ is convex.

For the problem in (20.2.1), as in (20.2.2) the Lagrangian is

$$\mathcal{L}(\mathbf{x}) = f(\mathbf{x}) - \sum_{j=1}^{m} \lambda_j[g_j(\mathbf{x}) - c_j]$$

Recall from Theorem 14.8.1 that the sum of any finite collection of concave functions is concave, as is minus any nonnegative multiple of a convex function. When the problem in (20.2.1) is a concave programme, therefore, and all the m Lagrange multipliers λ_j $(j=1,2,\ldots,m)$ are nonnegative, then each of the $m+1$ terms of the Lagrangian sum is concave, and so therefore is the Lagrangian $\mathcal{L}(\mathbf{x})$ itself.

THEOREM 20.2.1 (SUFFICIENT CONDITIONS FOR A CONCAVE PROGRAMME)

Given the constrained maximization problem in (20.2.1), let $\mathbf{x}^0$ be any critical point of the Lagrangian function $\mathcal{L}(\mathbf{x})$ defined in (20.2.2) that satisfies the combined complementary slackness condition (20.2.5). If $\mathcal{L}$ is concave, or if $\mathbf{x}^0$ happens to maximize $\mathcal{L}$ anyway, then $\mathbf{x}^0$ solves the constrained maximization problem.

Proof: Suppose that for all $\mathbf{x}$ one has $\mathcal{L}(\mathbf{x}^0) \geq \mathcal{L}(\mathbf{x})$, and so

$$\mathcal{L}(\mathbf{x}^0) = f(\mathbf{x}^0) - \sum_{j=1}^{m} \lambda_j [g_j(\mathbf{x}^0) - c_j] \geq \mathcal{L}(\mathbf{x}) = f(\mathbf{x}) - \sum_{j=1}^{m} \lambda_j [g_j(\mathbf{x}) - c_j] \quad (*)$$

Suppose too that the combined complementary slackness condition (20.2.5) is satisfied, implying that $\sum_{j=1}^{m} \lambda_j [g_j(\mathbf{x}^0) - c_j] = 0$. Then for all $\mathbf{x}$ that satisfy all the m constraints $g_j(\mathbf{x}) \leq c_j$ $(j = 1, \ldots, m)$, because each Lagrange multiplier satisfies $\lambda_j \geq 0$, one has $\sum_{j=1}^{m} \lambda_j [g_j(\mathbf{x}^0) - c_j] \leq 0$. So for any $\mathbf{x}$ satisfying all the m inequality constraints, it follows from $(*)$ that

$$f(\mathbf{x}^0) - \sum_{j=1}^{m} \lambda_j [g_j(\mathbf{x}^0) - c_j] = f(\mathbf{x}^0) \geq f(\mathbf{x}) - \sum_{j=1}^{m} \lambda_j [g_j(\mathbf{x}) - c_j] \geq f(\mathbf{x})$$

This proves that $\mathbf{x}^0$ is a maximum point subject to the constraints.

A minimization problem that corresponds to that in (20.2.1) takes the form

$$\min f(\mathbf{x}) \quad \text{s.t.} \quad g_j(\mathbf{x}) \geq c_j \quad (j = 1, 2, \ldots, m) \quad (20.2.6)$$

Its Lagrangian function, of course, is still

$$\mathcal{L}(\mathbf{x}) = f(\mathbf{x}) - \sum_{j=1}^{m} \lambda_j [g_j(\mathbf{x}) - c_j]$$

The minimization problem in (20.2.6) is said to be a *convex programme* in case the objective function f is convex, and each constraint function g_j $(j = 1, 2, \ldots, m)$ is concave. These conditions ensure that the Lagrangian function is convex. Then there is an obvious counterpart of Theorem 20.2.1 for the convex programme, with "concave" replaced by "convex", and "maximize" replaced by "minimize". Indeed, changing all the signs converts the problem in (20.2.6) to the following concave programming problem:

$$\max -f(\mathbf{x}) \quad \text{s.t.} \quad -g_j(\mathbf{x}) \leq -c_j \quad (j = 1, 2, \ldots, m)$$

Then one can apply Theorem 20.2.1 to this problem.

Examples of Concave Programmes

EXAMPLE 20.2.1   Consider the nonlinear programming problem

$$\max x + 3y - 4e^{-x-y} \quad \text{s.t.} \quad \begin{cases} 2 - x \geq 2y \\ x - 1 \leq -y \end{cases}$$

808 CHAPTER 20 / NONLINEAR PROGRAMMING

(a) Verify that this is a concave programming problem.

(b) Write down the necessary KKT conditions for a point (x^*, y^*) to solve the problem. Are these conditions sufficient for optimality?

(c) Solve the problem.

Solution:

(a) The first step is to write the problem in the same form as (20.2.1):

$$\max x + 3y - 4e^{-x-y} \quad \text{s.t.} \quad \begin{cases} x + 2y \leq 2 \\ x + y \leq 1 \end{cases} \quad (*)$$

The left-hand side of each constraint is a function which is linear, so convex. The objective function $f(x, y) = x + 3y - 4e^{-x-y}$ has second-order partial derivatives satisfying $f''_{11} = f''_{22} = f''_{12} = -4e^{-x-y}$. It follows that the Hessian matrix of f satisfies $f''_{11} = f''_{22} < 0$ and $f''_{11} f''_{22} - (f''_{12})^2 = 0$, implying that the objective function f is concave. So all the conditions for $(*)$ to be a concave programming problem are met.

(b) The Lagrangian is

$$\mathcal{L}(x, y) = x + 3y - 4e^{-x-y} - \lambda_1(x + 2y - 2) - \lambda_2(x + y - 1)$$

Hence, the KKT conditions for (x^*, y^*) to solve the problem are:

$$\mathcal{L}'_1 = 1 + 4e^{-x^*-y^*} - \lambda_1 - \lambda_2 = 0 \qquad \text{(i)}$$

$$\mathcal{L}'_2 = 3 + 4e^{-x^*-y^*} - 2\lambda_1 - \lambda_2 = 0 \qquad \text{(ii)}$$

$$\lambda_1 \geq 0, \quad \text{with } \lambda_1 = 0 \text{ if } x^* + 2y^* < 2 \qquad \text{(iii)}$$

$$\lambda_2 \geq 0, \quad \text{with } \lambda_2 = 0 \text{ if } x^* + y^* < 1 \qquad \text{(iv)}$$

In part (a) we showed that $(*)$ is a concave programming problem, so these KKT conditions are sufficient for optimality.

(c) Subtracting (ii) from (i) we get $-2 + \lambda_1 = 0$ and so $\lambda_1 = 2$. But then (iii) together with $x^* + 2y^* \leq 2$ yields $x^* + 2y^* = 2$.
Suppose we have $\lambda_2 = 0$. Then (i) would imply that $4e^{-x^*-y^*} = 1$, so $-x^* - y^* = \ln(1/4)$. It follows that $x^* + y^* = \ln 4 > 1$, which violates the constraint $x + y \leq 1$.
So we must have $\lambda_2 > 0$. Then from (iv) and $x^* + y^* \leq 1$ we deduce $x^* + y^* = 1$. But we showed that $x^* + 2y^* = 2$, so $x^* = 0$ and $y^* = 1$. Inserting $\lambda_1 = 2$ and these values for x^* and y^* into (i), we find that $\lambda_2 = 4e^{-1} - 1$, which is positive because $e < 4$. We conclude that the solution is $x^* = 0$ and $y^* = 1$, with $\lambda_1 = 2$ and $\lambda_2 = 4e^{-1} - 1$.

EXAMPLE 20.2.2 A worker chooses both consumption c and labour supply l in order to maximize the utility function $\alpha \ln c + (1 - \alpha) \ln(1 - l)$ over consumption $c > 0$ and leisure $1 - l > 0$, where $0 < \alpha < 1$. The worker's budget constraint is $c \leq wl + m$, where $w > 0$ is the wage per unit of labour, and $m \geq 0$ is unearned income. In addition, the worker must choose $l \geq 0$. Solve the worker's constrained maximization problem.

SECTION 20.2 / MANY VARIABLES AND INEQUALITY CONSTRAINTS

Solution: The worker's problem is

$$\max \alpha \ln c + (1-\alpha)\ln(1-l) \text{ s.t. } c \leq wl + m \text{ and } l \geq 0$$

Because $\ln x$ is concave in x when $x > 0$ while $c > 0$, $l < 1$, and $0 < \alpha < 1$, this is evidently a concave programme. The Lagrangian is

$$\mathcal{L}(c,l) = \alpha \ln c + (1-\alpha)\ln(1-l) - \lambda(c - wl - m) + \mu l$$

So the KKT conditions for (c^*, l^*) to solve the problem are

$$\mathcal{L}'_c = \frac{\alpha}{c^*} - \lambda = 0 \tag{i}$$

$$\mathcal{L}'_l = \frac{-(1-\alpha)}{1-l^*} + \lambda w + \mu = 0 \tag{ii}$$

$$\lambda \geq 0, \text{ with } \lambda = 0 \text{ if } c^* < wl^* + m \tag{iii}$$

$$\mu \geq 0, \text{ with } \mu = 0 \text{ if } l^* > 0 \tag{iv}$$

From (i) we have $\lambda = \alpha/c^* > 0$. Then combining (iii) with the first constraint yields

$$c^* = wl^* + m \tag{v}$$

Our assumptions guarantee that $c^* > 0$. Now we have two cases:

Case I: $\mu = 0$. From (i) and (ii) we get $c^* = \alpha/\lambda$ and $l^* = 1 - (1-\alpha)/\lambda w$. Inserting these values into (v) implies that $\alpha/\lambda = w - (1-\alpha)/\lambda + m$. It follows that $\lambda = 1/(w+m)$, so $c^* = \alpha(w+m)$ and $l^* = 1 - (1-\alpha)(w+m)/w = \alpha - (1-\alpha)m/w$. The KKT conditions are all satisfied provided that $l^* \geq 0$, which holds if and only if $m \leq \alpha w/(1-\alpha)$.

Case II: $\mu > 0$. Then (iv) implies that $l^* = 0$, so (v) implies that $c^* = m$, and then (i) implies that $\lambda = \alpha/c^* = \alpha/m$. From (ii) it follows that $\mu = 1 - \alpha - \alpha w/m$. This case holds if and only if $\mu > 0$, or if and only if $m > \alpha w/(1-\alpha)$.

In the last two examples it was not too hard to find which constraints bind (that is, hold with equality) at the optimum. But with more complicated nonlinear programming problems, including the concave programming problems we are considering here, this can be harder. A general method for finding all candidates for optimality in a nonlinear programming problem with two constraints can be formulated as follows: First, examine the case where both constraints bind. Next, examine the two cases where only one constraint binds. Finally, examine the fourth case where neither constraint binds. In each case, find all vectors **x**, with associated nonnegative values of both Lagrange multipliers, that satisfy all the relevant conditions (if any do). Then calculate the value of $f(\mathbf{x})$ for these values of **x**, and select those **x** for which $f(\mathbf{x})$ is largest. Except for perverse problems, this procedure will find the optimum. The next example illustrates how it works in practice.

EXAMPLE 20.2.3 Suppose your utility from consuming x_1 units of good A and x_2 units of good B is $U(x_1, x_2) = \ln x_1 + \ln x_2$. Suppose too that the prices per unit of A and B are \$10 and \$5, respectively, and that you have \$350 to spend on the two goods together. Finally, suppose that it takes 0.1 hours to consume one unit of A and 0.2 hours to consume one unit of B, and that you have eight hours in total to spend on consuming the two goods. How much of each good should you buy in order to maximize your utility?

Solution: The problem is

$$\max U(x_1, x_2) = \ln x_1 + \ln x_2 \text{ s.t. } \begin{cases} 10x_1 + 5x_2 \leq 350 \\ 0.1x_1 + 0.2x_2 \leq 8 \end{cases}$$

The Lagrangian is

$$\mathcal{L} = \ln x_1 + \ln x_2 - \lambda_1(10x_1 + 5x_2 - 350) - \lambda_2(0.1x_1 + 0.2x_2 - 8)$$

The necessary KKT conditions are that there exist numbers λ_1 and λ_2 such that

$$\mathcal{L}_1' = 1/x_1^* - 10\lambda_1 - 0.1\lambda_2 = 0 \tag{i}$$

$$\mathcal{L}_2' = 1/x_2^* - 5\lambda_1 - 0.2\lambda_2 = 0 \tag{ii}$$

$$\lambda_1 \geq 0, \text{ with } \lambda_1 = 0 \text{ if } 10x_1^* + 5x_2^* < 350 \tag{iii}$$

$$\lambda_2 \geq 0, \text{ with } \lambda_2 = 0 \text{ if } 0.1x_1^* + 0.2x_2^* < 8 \tag{iv}$$

We start the systematic procedure:

Case 1: Both constraints bind. Here

$$10x_1^* + 5x_2^* = 350 \tag{v}$$

and $0.1x_1^* + 0.2x_2^* = 8$. The only solution to these two linear equations is $(x_1^*, x_2^*) = (20, 30)$. Inserting these values into (i) and (ii) yields $10\lambda_1 + 0.1\lambda_2 = 1/20$ and $5\lambda_1 + 0.2\lambda_2 = 1/30$, whose unique solution is $(\lambda_1, \lambda_2) = (1/225, 1/18)$. In particular, both λ_1 and λ_2 are nonnegative. So we have found one candidate for optimality that satisfies all the KKT conditions.

Case 2: The first constraint binds, but the second does not. Here (v) holds and $0.1x_1^* + 0.2x_2^* < 8$. From (iv) we obtain $\lambda_2 = 0$. Now (i) and (ii) imply that $x_2^* = 2x_1^*$. Inserting this into (v), we get $x_1^* = 17.5$ and then $x_2^* = 2x_1^* = 35$. But then $0.1x_1^* + 0.2x_2^* = 8.75$, which violates the second constraint. So there is no candidate for optimality in this case.

Case 3: The second constraint binds, but the first does not. Here $10x_1^* + 5x_2^* < 350$ and $0.1x_1^* + 0.2x_2^* = 8$. From (iii), $\lambda_1 = 0$, and (i) and (ii) yield $0.1x_1^* = 0.2x_2^*$. Inserted into $0.1x_1^* + 0.2x_2^* = 8$ this yields $x_2^* = 20$ and so $x_1^* = 40$. But then $10x_1^* + 5x_2^* = 500$, violating the first constraint. So there is no candidate for optimality in this case either.

Case 4: Neither constraint binds. Here $\lambda_1 = \lambda_2 = 0$, in which case (i) and (ii) make no sense.

So there is only one candidate for optimality, which is $(x_1^*, x_2^*) = (20, 30)$. Since it is easily seen that we have a concave programme, this must be the solution to the constrained maximization problem.

Properties of The Value Function

As in previous constrained maximization problems, the *value function* of problem (20.2.1) is defined for each m-vector $\mathbf{c} = (c_1, \ldots, c_m)$ by $f^*(\mathbf{c}) = f(\mathbf{x}^*(\mathbf{c}))$, where $\mathbf{x}^*(\mathbf{c})$ is a solution to the problem. The following properties of f^* are very useful:

$$f^*(\mathbf{c}) \text{ is nondecreasing in each variable } c_1, \ldots, c_m \quad (20.2.7)$$

$$\text{for } j = 1, \ldots, m, \text{ if } \partial f^*(\mathbf{c})/\partial c_j \text{ exists, then it is equal to } \lambda_j(\mathbf{c}) \quad (20.2.8)$$

Property (20.2.7) is immediate because if c_j increases while all the other c_k are fixed, then the feasible set becomes no smaller, so $f^*(\mathbf{c})$ cannot decrease.

As for property (20.2.8), each $\lambda_j(\mathbf{c})$ is a Lagrange multiplier coming from the KKT conditions. However, there is a catch: the value function f^* need not be differentiable. Even if f and $g_1, \ldots, g_m$ are all differentiable, the value function can have sudden changes of slope. Such cases are studied in FMEA.

EXERCISES FOR SECTION 20.2

1. Consider the problem max $\frac{1}{2}x - y$ s.t. $x + e^{-x} \le y$ and $x \ge 0$.

    (a) Write down the Lagrangian and the necessary KKT conditions.

    (b) Find the solution to the problem.

SM 2. Let p, q and m be positive parameters, and suppose that $0 < \alpha < 1$. Solve the following consumer demand problem where, in addition to the budget constraint, there is an upper limit $\bar{x}$ which rations how much of the first good can be bought:

$$\max \alpha \ln x + (1 - \alpha) \ln y \text{ s.t. } px + qy \le m \text{ and } x \le \bar{x}$$

SM 3. Consider the problem max $x + y - e^x - e^{x+y}$ s.t. $x + y \ge 4$, $x \ge -1$ and $y \ge 1$.

    (a) Sketch the feasible set S.

    (b) Find all pairs (x, y) that satisfy all the necessary conditions.

    (c) Find the solution to the problem.

SM 4. Consider the problem max $x + ay$ s.t. $x^2 + y^2 \le 1$ and $x + y \ge 0$, where a is a constant.

    (a) Sketch the feasible set and write down the necessary conditions.

    (b) Find the solution for all values of the constant a.

SM 5. Solve the following problem, assuming it has a solution:

$$\max y - x^2 \text{ s.t. } y \ge 0,\ y - x \ge -2 \text{ and } y^2 \le x$$

SM 6. Consider the problem max $-\left(x + \frac{1}{2}\right)^2 - \frac{1}{2}y^2$ s.t. $e^{-x} - y \le 0$ and $y \le \frac{2}{3}$.

    (a) Sketch the feasible set.

    (b) Write down the KKT conditions, and find the solution of the problem.

7. Consider the problem max $xz + yz$ s.t. $x^2 + y^2 + z^2 \leq 1$.

   (a) Write down the KKT conditions.

   (b) Solve the problem.

20.3 Nonnegativity Constraints

Consider once again the general nonlinear programming problem (20.2.1). Often, variables involved in economic optimization problems must be nonnegative by their very nature. It is not difficult to incorporate such constraints in the formulation of (20.2.1). If $x_1 \geq 0$, for example, this can be represented by the extra constraint $h_1(x_1, \ldots, x_n) = -x_1 \leq 0$. Of course, we must introduce an additional Lagrange multiplier to go with it. In order not to have too many Lagrange multipliers, however, the necessary conditions for a solution to a nonlinear programming problems with nonnegativity constraints are sometimes formulated in a slightly different way.

Consider first the problem

$$\max f(x, y) \text{ s.t. } g(x, y) \leq c, \ x \geq 0, \text{ and } y \geq 0 \tag{20.3.1}$$

Here we introduce the functions $h_1(x, y) = -x$ and $h_2(x, y) = -y$, so that the three constraints in problem (20.3.1) can be expressed $g(x, y) \leq c$, $h_1(x, y) \leq 0$, and $h_2(x, y) \leq 0$. Applying the recipe for solving (20.2.1), we introduce two extra Lagrange multipliers denoted by μ_1 and μ_2, and then form the Lagrangian

$$\mathcal{L}(x, y) = f(x, y) - \lambda[g(x, y) - c] - \mu_1(-x) - \mu_2(-y)$$

The KKT conditions are

$$\mathcal{L}'_1 = f'_1(x, y) - \lambda g'_1(x, y) + \mu_1 = 0 \tag{i}$$

$$\mathcal{L}'_2 = f'_2(x, y) - \lambda g'_2(x, y) + \mu_2 = 0 \tag{ii}$$

$$\lambda \geq 0, \text{ with } \lambda = 0 \text{ if } g(x, y) < c \tag{iii}$$

$$\mu_1 \geq 0, \text{ with } \mu_1 = 0 \text{ if } x > 0 \tag{iv}$$

$$\mu_2 \geq 0, \text{ with } \mu_2 = 0 \text{ if } y > 0 \tag{v}$$

From (i), we have $f'_1(x, y) - \lambda g'_1(x, y) = -\mu_1$. From (iv), we have $-\mu_1 \leq 0$ with $-\mu_1 = 0$ if $x > 0$. This shows that (i) and (iv) are together equivalent to

$$f'_1(x, y) - \lambda g'_1(x, y) \leq 0, \text{ with equality if } x > 0 \tag{vi}$$

In the same way, (ii) and (v) are together equivalent to

$$f'_2(x, y) - \lambda g'_2(x, y) \leq 0, \text{ with equality if } y > 0 \tag{vii}$$

So along with (iii), we have the two modified KKT conditions (vi) and (vii). Note that after replacing (i) and (iv) by (vi), as well as (ii) and (v) by (vii), only the one multiplier λ associated with the inequality constraint $g(x, y) \leq c$ remains.

The same idea can obviously be extended to the following general problem with n nonnegative variables and m inequality constraints:

$$\max f(\mathbf{x}) \text{ s.t. } \begin{cases} g_1(\mathbf{x}) \leq c_1 \\ \dots\dots\dots \\ g_m(\mathbf{x}) \leq c_m \end{cases} \quad x_1 \geq 0, \dots, x_n \geq 0 \quad (20.3.2)$$

Briefly formulated, the necessary conditions for the solution of problem (20.3.2) are that, for each $i = 1, \dots, n$, one has

$$\frac{\partial f(\mathbf{x})}{\partial x_i} - \sum_{j=1}^{m} \lambda_j \frac{\partial g_j(\mathbf{x})}{\partial x_i} \leq 0, \text{ with equality if } x_i > 0 \quad (20.3.3)$$

In addition, for each $j = 1, \dots, m$, one has the complementary slackness condition

$$\lambda_j \geq 0, \text{ with } \lambda_j = 0 \text{ if } g_j(\mathbf{x}) < c_j \quad (20.3.4)$$

As in Theorem 20.2.1, in the case of a concave programme where f is concave and each function g_j is convex, the conditions in (20.3.3) and (20.3.4) are sufficient in the following sense: given any $(\mathbf{x}, \lambda_1, \dots, \lambda_m)$ which satisfies them, the n-vector $\mathbf{x}$ is a solution of maximization problem (20.3.2).

The KKT Theorem Applied to LP Problems

The general LP problem specified in (19.2.1) is a special case of the general nonlinear optimization problem with inequality constraints specified in (20.3.2). Indeed, the objective function is $f(\mathbf{x}) = \sum_{j=1}^{n} c_j x_j$, and for each $i = 1, 2, \dots, m$, the ith constraint is $g_i(\mathbf{x}) = \sum_{j=1}^{n} a_{ij} x_j \leq b_i$. Let us see what form the KKT conditions (20.3.3) and (20.3.4) take in this special case. In fact, an LP problem is actually a concave programme, so the KKT conditions are sufficient to determine a maximum point.

Using the notation of Chapter 19, for each $i = 1, \dots, m$, let u_i^* instead of λ_i denote the nonnegative Lagrange multiplier associated with the ith constraint of the LP problem set out in (19.2.1). Then for each $j = 1, \dots, n$, condition (20.3.3) takes the form

$$c_j - \sum_{i=1}^{m} u_i^* a_{ij} \leq 0, \text{ with equality if } x_j^* > 0 \quad (20.3.5)$$

On the other hand, for $i = 1, \dots, m$, the complementary slackness condition (20.3.4) takes the form

$$u_i^* \geq 0, \text{ with } u_i^* = 0 \text{ if } \sum_{j=1}^{n} a_{ij} x_j^* < b_i \quad (20.3.6)$$

When combined with the requirement that the n-vector $\mathbf{x}^*$ satisfy the inequality and nonnegativity constraints in the LP problem (19.2.1), these conditions are precisely the complementary slackness conditions set out in Theorem 19.5.1.

Three Examples

We conclude the main text of this chapter, as well as of the book, with three economic examples. Together they illustrate the power and wide applicability of the KKT method, especially when applied to concave programmes.

EXAMPLE 20.3.1 (**Importing Norwegian or Siberian natural gas**). As in Exercise 17.5.3, let x and y denote the quantities of natural gas that Western Europe imports from Norway and Siberia respectively. The optimal choice of these import quantities was represented in that Exercise by the following concave programme:

$$\max f(x,y) = 9x + 8y - 6(x+y)^2 \quad \text{s.t.} \quad 0 \leq x \leq 5, \; 0 \leq y \leq 3, \; x \geq 2(y-1)$$

Use conditions (20.3.3) and (20.3.4) to verify that $(x,y) = (\tfrac{3}{4}, 0)$ is the solution.

Solution: We write the last constraint as $-x + 2y \leq 2$. The constrained maximization problem is evidently a concave programme, with Lagrangian

$$\mathcal{L}(x,y) = 9x + 8y - 6(x+y)^2 - \lambda_1(x-5) - \lambda_2(y-3) - \lambda_3(-x+2y-2)$$

Conditions (20.3.3) take the form:

$$9 - 12(x+y) - \lambda_1 + \lambda_3 \leq 0, \quad \text{and} = 0 \text{ if } x > 0;$$

$$8 - 12(x+y) - \lambda_2 - 2\lambda_3 \leq 0, \quad \text{and} = 0 \text{ if } y > 0.$$

It is easy see that $(x,y) = (\tfrac{3}{4}, 0)$ with $(\lambda_1, \lambda_2, \lambda_3) = (0,0,0)$ satisfies these conditions, as well as the complementary slackness conditions in Eq. (20.3.4). So $(\tfrac{3}{4}, 0)$ is a solution.

EXAMPLE 20.3.2 Consider the utility maximization problem

$$\max x + \ln(1+y) \quad \text{s.t.} \quad px + y \leq m, \; x \geq 0 \text{ and } y \geq 0$$

where consumption of both commodities is explicitly required to be nonnegative.

(a) Write down the necessary KKT conditions for a point (x^*, y^*) to be a solution.

(b) Find the solution to the problem, for all positive values of p and m.

Solution:

(a) The Lagrangian is

$$\mathcal{L}(x,y) = x + \ln(1+y) - \lambda(px + y - m)$$

The KKT conditions for (x^*, y^*) to be a solution are that there exists a λ such that

$$\mathcal{L}'_1(x^*, y^*) = 1 - p\lambda \leq 0, \quad \text{with } 1 - p\lambda = 0 \text{ if } x^* > 0 \qquad \text{(i)}$$

$$\mathcal{L}'_2(x^*, y^*) = \frac{1}{1+y^*} - \lambda \leq 0, \quad \text{with } \frac{1}{1+y^*} - \lambda = 0 \text{ if } y^* > 0 \qquad \text{(ii)}$$

$$\lambda \geq 0, \quad \text{with } \lambda = 0 \text{ if } px^* + y^* < m \qquad \text{(iii)}$$

Also, $x^* \geq 0$, $y^* \geq 0$, and the budget constraint has to be satisfied, so $px^* + y^* \leq m$.

(b) Note that we have a concave programme, so any triple (x^*, y^*, λ) that satisfies the KKT conditions will give a maximum point (x^*, y^*). It is clear from (i) that $\lambda \neq 0$ and so $\lambda > 0$. Then (iii) and $px^* + y^* \leq m$ imply that

$$px^* + y^* = m \tag{iv}$$

Depending on which constraints $x \geq 0$ and $y \geq 0$ bind, there are four cases to consider:

Case 1: Suppose $x^* = 0$, $y^* = 0$. Since $m > 0$, this is impossible because of (iv).

Case 2: Suppose $x^* > 0$, $y^* = 0$. From (ii) and $y^* = 0$ we get $\lambda \geq 1$. Then (i) implies that $p = 1/\lambda \leq 1$. Equation (iv) gives $x^* = m/p$, so we get one candidate for a maximum point:

$$(x^*, y^*) = (m/p, 0) \text{ and } \lambda = 1/p, \text{ in case } 0 < p \leq 1$$

Case 3: Suppose $x^* = 0$, $y^* > 0$. By (iv) we have $y^* = m$. Then (ii) yields $\lambda = 1/(1+y^*) = 1/(1+m)$. From (i) we get $p \geq 1/\lambda = m+1$. This gives one more candidate:

$$(x^*, y^*) = (0, m) \text{ and } \lambda = 1/(1+m), \text{ in case } p \geq m+1$$

Case 4: Suppose $x^* > 0$, $y^* > 0$. Here there must be equality in both (i) and (ii), so $\lambda = 1/p = 1/(1+y^*)$. It follows that $y^* = p - 1$, and then $p > 1$ because $y^* > 0$. Equation (iv) implies that $px^* = m - y^* = m - p + 1$, so $x^* = (m+1-p)/p$. Since $x^* > 0$, we must have $p < m+1$. Thus we get one last candidate:

$$(x^*, y^*) = \left(\frac{m+1-p}{p}, p-1\right) \text{ and } \lambda = 1/p, \text{ in case } 1 < p < m+1$$

Putting all these cases together, we see that the solution of the problem is:

For $0 < p \leq 1$, Case 2 applies, and $(x^*, y^*) = (m/p, 0)$ with $\lambda = 1/p$.

For $1 < p < m+1$, Case 4 applies, and $(x^*, y^*) = ((m+1-p)/p, p-1)$ with $\lambda = 1/p$.

For $p \geq m+1$, Case 3 applies, and $(x^*, y^*) = (0, m)$ with $\lambda = 1/(m+1)$.

Note that, except in the intermediate case when $1 < p < m+1$, it is optimal to spend everything on only the cheaper of the two goods, which is either x in case $0 < p \leq 1$, or y in case $p \geq m+1$.

EXAMPLE 20.3.3 (Peak load pricing). Consider a large power producer which generates electricity at a large number of different power plants that obtain power from various sources such as sun, wind, water, natural gas, coal, or nuclear fission. The demand for electricity varies between peak periods, during which most of the generating capacity is used, and off-peak periods when there is considerable spare capacity. We consider a certain time interval (say, a year) which is divided into n periods of equal length. Suppose that the total amounts of electrical power sold in these n periods are $x_1, x_2, \ldots, x_n$. Assume that a regulatory authority fixes the n corresponding prices at levels equal to $p_1, p_2, \ldots, p_n$. Assume too that the total operating cost over all n periods is given by the cost function $C(\mathbf{x})$, where $\mathbf{x} = (x_1, \ldots, x_n)$, and that the constant output capacity in each period is k. Let $D(k)$ denote the cost of maintaining output capacity at level k. The producer's total profit is then

$$\pi(\mathbf{x}, k) = \sum_{i=1}^{n} p_i x_i - C(\mathbf{x}) - D(k)$$

Because the producer cannot exceed capacity k in any period, it faces the constraints

$$x_1 \leq k, \ldots, x_n \leq k$$

We consider the problem of finding $x_1 \geq 0, \ldots, x_n \geq 0$ and $k \geq 0$ such that profit is maximized subject to the above capacity constraints.

This is a nonlinear programming problem with $n + 1$ variables and n constraints, as well as n nonnegativity constraints. The Lagrangian is

$$\mathcal{L}(\mathbf{x}, k) = \sum_{i=1}^{n} p_i x_i - C(\mathbf{x}) - D(k) - \sum_{i=1}^{n} \lambda_i (x_i - k)$$

Following (20.3.3) and (20.3.4), the choice $(\mathbf{x}^0, k^0) \geq 0$ can solve the problem only if there exist nonnegative Lagrange multipliers $\lambda_1, \ldots, \lambda_n$ such that

$$\frac{\partial \mathcal{L}}{\partial x_i} = p_i - C_i'(\mathbf{x}^0) - \lambda_i \leq 0, \text{ with equality if } x_i^0 > 0, \text{ for } i = 1, \ldots, n \quad \text{(i)}$$

$$\frac{\partial \mathcal{L}}{\partial k} = -D'(k^0) + \sum_{i=1}^{n} \lambda_i \leq 0, \text{ with equality if } k^0 > 0 \quad \text{(ii)}$$

$$\lambda_i \geq 0, \text{ with } \lambda_i = 0 \text{ if } x_i^0 < k^0, \text{ for } i = 1, \ldots, n \quad \text{(iii)}$$

Suppose that period i is such that $x_i^0 > 0$. Then (i) implies that

$$p_i = C_i'(\mathbf{x}^0) + \lambda_i \quad \text{(iv)}$$

If period i is an off-peak period, then $x_i^0 < k^0$ and so $\lambda_i = 0$ by (iii). From (iv) it follows that $p_i = C_i'(x_1^0, \ldots, x_n^0)$. Thus, we see that *the profit-maximizing pattern of output $\mathbf{x}^0$ will bring about equality between the regulator's price in any off-peak period and the corresponding marginal operating cost.*

On the other hand, λ_i might be positive in a peak period when $x_i^0 = k^0$. If $k^0 > 0$, it follows from (ii) that $\sum_{i=1}^{n} \lambda_i = D'(k^0)$. We conclude that the optimal output pattern $\mathbf{x}^0$ will be such that *in peak periods the price set by the regulator will exceed the marginal operating cost by an additional amount λ_i, which is really the "shadow price" of the capacity constraint $x_i^0 \leq k^0$. The sum of these shadow prices over all peak periods is equal to the marginal capacity cost $D'(k^0)$.*

EXERCISES FOR SECTION 20.3

1. Consider the utility maximization problem

$$\max x + \ln(1 + y) \quad \text{s.t.} \quad 16x + y \leq 495, \quad x \geq 0, y \geq 0$$

(a) Write down the necessary KKT conditions, including nonnegativity constraints, for a point to be a solution.

(b) Find the solution to the problem.

(c) Estimate by how much utility will increase if income goes up from 495 to 500.

SM 2. Solve the following problem, assuming it has a solution:
$$\max xe^{y-x} - 2ey \quad \text{s.t.} \quad y \leq 1 + x/2, \ x \geq 0, \text{ and } y \geq 0$$

SM 3. Suppose that optimal capacity utilization by a firm requires that its output quantities x_1 and x_2, along with its capacity level k, should be chosen to solve the problem
$$\max x_1 + 3x_2 - x_1^2 - x_2^2 - k^2 \quad \text{s.t.} \quad x_1 \leq k, \ x_2 \leq k, \ x_1 \geq 0, \ x_2 \geq 0, \ k \geq 0$$
Show that $k = 0$ cannot be optimal, and then find the solution.

REVIEW EXERCISES

SM 1. For all $a > 0$, solve the problem $\max 10 - (x-2)^2 - (y-1)^2$ s.t. $x^2 + y^2 \leq a$.

SM 2. Consider the nonlinear programming problem
$$\max xy \quad \text{s.t.} \quad x^2 + ry^2 \leq m \text{ and } x \geq 1$$
Here r and m are positive constants, with $m > 1$.

(a) Write down the necessary KKT conditions for a point (x, y) to solve the problem.

(b) Solve the problem.

(c) Let $V(r, m)$ denote the value function. Find $\partial V(r, m)/\partial m$, and comment on its sign.

(d) Verify that $\partial V(r, m)/\partial r = \partial \mathcal{L}/\partial r$, where $\mathcal{L}$ is the Lagrangian.

SM 3. A firm produces x_1 cars and x_2 trucks per month, where $x_1 \geq 0$ and $x_2 \geq 0$. Suppose each car requires 0.04% of the capacity per month in the body division, 0.025% of the capacity per month in the motor division, and 0.05% of the capacity per month on the specialized car assembly line. The corresponding numbers for trucks are 0.03% in the body division, 0.05% in the motor division, and 0.08% on the specialized truck assembly line. The firm can therefore deliver x_1 cars and x_2 trucks per month provided the following inequalities are satisfied:

$$0.04x_1 + 0.03x_2 \leq 100$$
$$0.025x_1 + 0.05x_2 \leq 100$$
$$0.05x_1 \qquad\qquad \leq 100 \quad (*)$$
$$\qquad\quad 0.08x_2 \leq 100$$

with $x_1 \geq 0$, $x_2 \geq 0$. Suppose the profit per car is $500 - ax_1$, where a is a nonnegative constant, while the profit per truck is 250. The firm thus seeks to solve the problem
$$\max (500 - ax_1)x_1 + 250x_2$$
subject to (*), as well as $x_1 \geq 0$ and $x_2 \geq 0$.

(a) For the case when $a = 0$, and so the maximization problem reduces to a linear programme, solve it graphically.

(b) Write down conditions (20.3.3) and (20.3.4) for the problem when $a \geq 0$.

(c) Use the conditions obtained in (b) to examine for which values of $a \geq 0$ the solution is the same as for $a = 0$.

4. Suppose the firm of Example 9.5.1 earns revenue $R(Q)$ and incurs cost $C(Q)$ as functions of output $Q \geq 0$, where $R'(Q) > 0$, $C'(Q) > 0$, $R''(Q) < 0$, and $C''(Q) > 0$ for all $Q \geq 0$. The firm maximizes profit $\pi(Q) = R(Q) - C(Q)$ subject to $Q \geq 0$. Write down the first-order conditions for the solution to this problem, and find sufficient conditions for the constraint $Q \geq 0$ to bind at the optimum.

5. A firm uses K and L units of two inputs to produce $\sqrt{KL}$ units of a product, where $K > 0$, $L > 0$. The input factor costs are r and w per unit, respectively. The firm wants to minimize the cost of producing at least Q units.

(a) Formulate the nonlinear programming problem that emerges. Reformulate it as a maximization problem, then write down the KKT conditions for the optimum. Solve these conditions to determine K^* and L^* as functions of (r, w, Q).

(b) Define the minimum cost function as $c^*(r, w, Q) = rK^* + wL^*$. Verify that $\partial c^*/\partial r = K^*$ and $\partial c^*/\partial w = L^*$, then give these results economic interpretations.

APPENDIX

Let no one ignorant of geometry enter this door.
—Entrance to Plato's Academy

This appendix is to remind the reader about some simple formulas and results from geometry that are occasionally useful for economists, and sometimes used in this book. At the end there is also a listing of the Greek alphabet, followed by a list of references cited in the text.

Geometry

Triangles

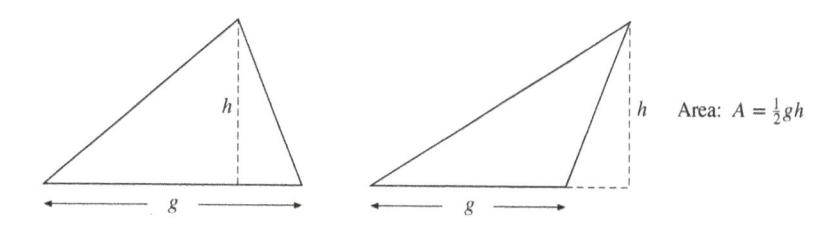

Area: $A = \frac{1}{2}gh$

Circles

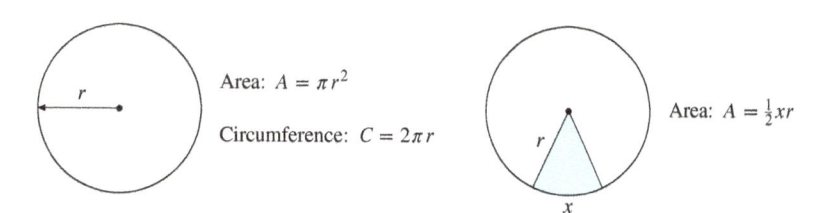

Area: $A = \pi r^2$

Circumference: $C = 2\pi r$

Area: $A = \frac{1}{2}xr$

Rectangular Box

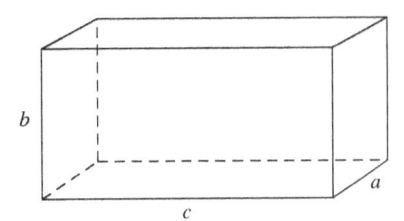

Volume: $V = abc$

Surface Area: $S = 2ab + 2ac + 2bc$

Sphere (Ball)

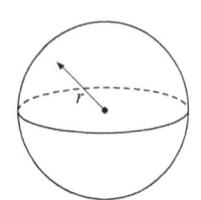

Volume: $V = \frac{4}{3}\pi r^3$

Surface Area: $S = 4\pi r^2$

Cone

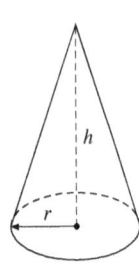

Volume: $V = \frac{1}{3}\pi r^2 h$

Surface Area: $S = \pi r^2 + \pi r\sqrt{h^2 + r^2}$

Pyramid

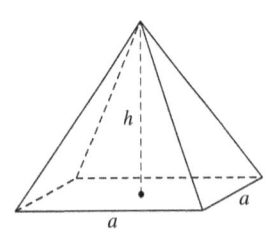

Volume: $V = \frac{1}{3}a^2 h$

Surface Area: $S = a^2 + a\sqrt{a^2 + 4h^2}$

Angles

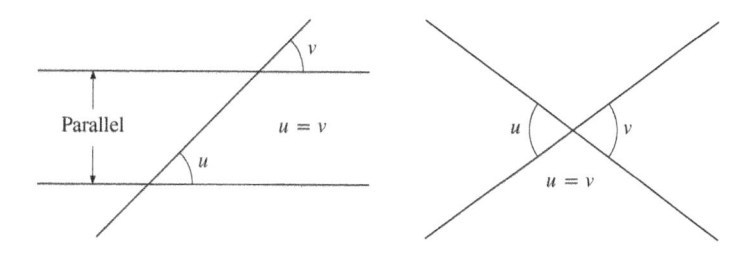

$u = v$

$u = v$

Proportions

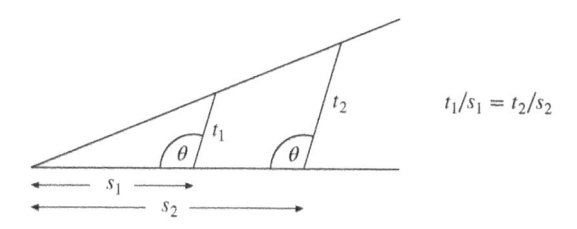

$t_1/s_1 = t_2/s_2$

Sum of Angles in a Triangle

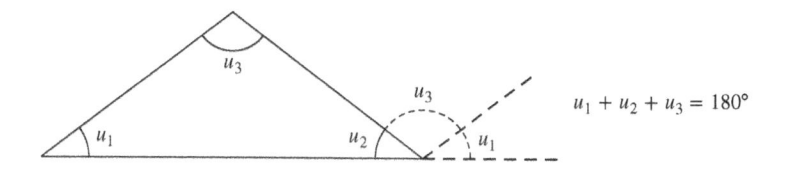

$u_1 + u_2 + u_3 = 180°$

Pythagoras's Theorem

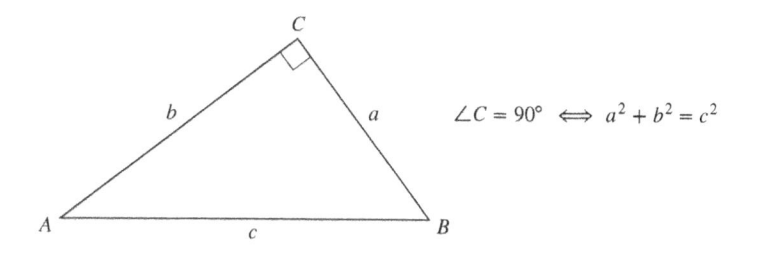

$\angle C = 90° \iff a^2 + b^2 = c^2$

The Greek Alphabet

A α	alpha	H η	eta	N ν	nu	T τ	tau
B β	beta	Θ θ ϑ	theta	Ξ ξ	xi	Υ υ	upsilon
Γ γ	gamma	I ι	iota	O o	omicron	Φ ϕ φ	phi
Δ δ	delta	K κ $\varkappa$	kappa	Π π	pi	X χ	chi
E ϵ ε	epsilon	Λ λ	lambda	P ρ ϱ	rho	Ψ ψ	psi
Z ζ	zeta	M μ	mu	Σ σ	sigma	Ω ω	omega

Bibliography

Körner, T.W. (2013) *Vectors, Pure and Applied* (Cambridge University Press: Cambridge).

Meyer, C.D. (2000) *Matrix Analysis and Applied Linear Algebra* (SIAM: Philadelphia).

Sydsæter, K., Hammond, P., Seierstad, A. and Strøm, A. (2008) *Further Mathematics for Economic Analysis* (2nd ed.) (FT/Prentice Hall: Harlow and London).

Varian, H.L. (2009) *Intermediate Microeconomics: A Modern Approach* (8th ed.) (W.W. Norton: New York and London).

SOLUTIONS TO THE EXERCISES

Chapter 1

1.1

1. (a) $5 \in C$, $D \subseteq C$, and $B = C$ are true. The three others are false. (b) $A \cap B = \{2\}$, $A \cup B = \{2, 3, 4, 5, 6\}$, $A \setminus B = \{3, 4\}$, $B \setminus A = \{5, 6\}$, $(A \cup B) \setminus (A \cap B) = \{3, 4, 5, 6\}$, $A \cup B \cup C \cup D = \{2, 3, 4, 5, 6\}$, $A \cap B \cap C = \{2\}$, and $A \cap B \cap C \cap D = \emptyset$.

2. (a) The set $F \cap B \cap C$ consists of all female biology students in $\mathcal{U}$ who belong to the university choir; $M \cap F$ of all female mathematics students in $\mathcal{U}$; $((M \cap B) \setminus C) \setminus T$ of all students in $\mathcal{U}$ who study both mathematics and biology but neither play tennis nor belong to the university choir.

   (b) (i) $B \subseteq M$ (ii) $F \cap B \cap C \neq \emptyset$ (iii) $T \cap B = \emptyset$ (iv) $(F \setminus T) \setminus C \subseteq B$.

3. Note that $50 - 35 = 15$ liked coffee but not tea, and $40 - 35 = 5$ liked tea but not coffee.

   Because 35 liked both and 10 liked neither, there were $15 + 5 + 35 + 10 = 65$ who responded.

4. The $2^3 = 8$ subsets of $\{a, b, c\}$ are the set itself, and the empty set, together with the six subsets $\{a\}$, $\{b\}$, $\{c\}$, $\{a, b\}$, $\{a, c\}$, and $\{b, c\}$. The $2^4 = 16$ subsets of $\{a, b, c, d\}$ are the 8 preceding sets together with 8 more sets that include d — namely $\{d\}$, $\{a, d\}$, $\{b, d\}$, $\{c, d\}$, $\{a, b, d\}$, $\{a, c, d\}$, $\{b, c, d\}$, and $\{a, b, c, d\}$. Apart from $\{a, b, c, d\}$ and the empty set, there are 14 other subsets.

5. (b) is true because $A \cap (B \cup C) = (A \cap B) \cup (A \cap C) \subseteq (A \cap B) \cup C$; the other three are generally false. Indeed, $A \setminus B \neq B \setminus A$ whenever $B \subseteq A$ with $\emptyset \neq B \neq A$; (c) holds if and only if $A \subseteq C$; (d) is violated when $A = \{1, 2\}$, $B = \{1\}$, and $C = \{1, 3\}$.

6. For $i = 1, 2, 3$, let S_i denote the set marked (i) in Fig. A1.1.6. Also, let S_4 denote the set of all points outside the regions marked (1), (2) or (3). Then:

   (a) $(A \cup B)^c = S_4$ whereas $A^c = S_3 \cup S_4$ and $B^c = S_1 \cup S_4$, so $A^c \cap B^c = S_4$.

   (b) $A \cap B = S_2$ so $(A \cap B)^c = S_1 \cup S_3 \cup S_4$, whereas $A^c \cup B^c = (S_3 \cup S_4) \cup (S_1 \cup S_4) = S_1 \cup S_3 \cup S_4$.

7. (a) Look again at Fig. A1.1.6. Now, $n(A \cup B)$ is the sum of the numbers of elements in the pairwise disjoint sets labelled (1), (2), and (3) respectively—that is, $n(A \setminus B) + n(A \cap B) + n(B \setminus A)$. But $n(A) + n(B)$ is the number of elements in (1) and (2) together, plus the number of elements in (2) and (3) together. Thus, the elements in (2) are counted twice. Hence, you must subtract $n(A \cap B)$, the number of elements in (2), to have equality. (b) Look yet again at Fig. A1.1.6. Now, $n(A \setminus B)$ is the number of elements in set (1), whereas $n(A) - n(A \cap B)$ is the number of elements in (1) and (2) together, minus the number of elements in (2) alone. Hence, it is the number of elements in (1).

8. (a) Consider Fig. A1.1.8, where the circles represent the readership of the three papers. Let n_k denote the number of people in the set marked S_k, for $k = 1, 2, \ldots, 8$. Obviously $n_1 + n_2 + \cdots + n_8 = 1000$. The responses imply that: $n_1 + n_3 + n_4 + n_7 = 420$; $n_1 + n_2 + n_5 + n_7 = 316$; $n_2 + n_3 + n_6 + n_7 = 160$; $n_1 + n_7 = 116$; $n_3 + n_7 = 100$; $n_2 + n_7 = 30$; and $n_7 = 16$.

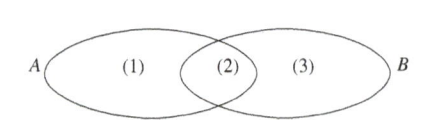

Figure A1.1.6

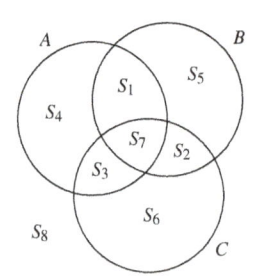

Figure A1.1.8

From these equations we easily find $n_1 = 100$, $n_2 = 14$, $n_3 = 84$, $n_4 = 220$, $n_5 = 186$, $n_6 = 46$, $n_7 = 16$, and $n_8 = 334$. So $n_3 + n_4 = 304$ had read A but not B. (b) $n_6 = 46$. (c) $n_8 = 334$.

(d) We find $n(A \setminus B) = n_3 + n_4 = 304$, $n(C \setminus (A \cup B)) = n_6 = 46$, and $n(\mathcal{U} \setminus (A \cup B \cup C)) = n_8 = 334$. The last equality is a special case of $n(\mathcal{U} \setminus D) = n(\mathcal{U}) - n(D)$. (The number of persons who are in $\mathcal{U}$, but not in D, is the number of persons in all of $\mathcal{U}$ minus the number of those who are in D.)

9. (Note: For the concept of set complement to make sense, it must be assumed that all the sets we consider are subsets of some "universal" set $\mathcal{U}$. Unfortunately, the collection of everything is not a set!)
Let $\{A_i : i \in I\}$ denote the family of sets, with union $A^\cup = \bigcup_{i \in I} A_i$ and intersection $A^\cap = \bigcap_{i \in I} A_i$. Then the two statements in the problem are: (a) $(A^\cup)^c = \bigcap_{i \in I} A_i^c$, (b) $(A^\cap)^c = \bigcup_{i \in I} A_i^c$.

Proofs: (a) $a \in (A^\cup)^c$ if and only if $a \notin A^\cup$, that is, if and only if a does not belong to any of the sets A_i, which holds if and only if $a \in A_i^c$ for all $i \in I$, and so if and only if $a \in \bigcap_{i \in I} A_i^c$.

(b) $a \in (A^\cap)^c$ if and only if $a \notin A^\cap$, that is, if and only if there exists $i \in I$ such that $a \notin A_i$, which holds if and only if there exists $i \in I$ such that $a \in A_i^c$, and so if and only if $a \in \bigcup_{i \in I} A_i^c$. See SM.

1.2

1. (a) $2x - 4 = 2 \Rightarrow x = 3$ (b) $x = 3 \Rightarrow 2x - 4 = 2$ (c) $x = 1 \Rightarrow x^2 - 2x + 1 = 0$ (d) $x^2 > 4 \Leftrightarrow |x| > 2$

2. (a), (b) and (e) are all true; indeed, (e) is a common definition of what it means for two sets to be equal. For (c), suppose for example that $A = \{x\}$, $B = \{y\}$, and $C = \{z\}$, where x, y, z are all different. Then $A \cap B = A \cap C = \emptyset$, yet $B \neq C$. For (d), suppose for example that $A = \{x, y, z\}$, $B = \{y\}$, and $C = \{z\}$, where x, y, z are all different. Then $A \cup B = A \cup C = A$, yet $B \neq C$.

3. (a): $\Rightarrow$ true, $\Leftarrow$ true (b): $\Rightarrow$ true, $\Leftarrow$ false (c): $\Rightarrow$ false, $\Leftarrow$ true
   (d): $\Rightarrow$ true (actually both x and y are 0), $\Leftarrow$ false (e): $\Rightarrow$ true, $\Leftarrow$ true
   (f): $\Rightarrow$ false ($0 \cdot 5 = 0 \cdot 4$, but $5 \neq 4$), $\Leftarrow$ true

4. One has $2x + 5 \geq 13 \Longleftrightarrow 2x \geq 8 \Longleftrightarrow x \geq 4$, so: (a) $x \geq 0$ is necessary, but not sufficient.
   (b) $x \geq 50$ is sufficient, but not necessary. (c) $x \geq 4$ is both necessary and sufficient.

5. (a) $x < 0$ or $y < 0$ (b) There exists x such that $x < a$. (c) $x < 5$ or $y < 5$, or both.
   (d) There exists an $\varepsilon > 0$ such that B is not satisfied for any $\delta > 0$.
   (e) There is someone who is able to resist liking cats. (f) There is someone who never loves anyone.

1.3

1. (b), (d), and (e) all express the same condition. (a) and (c) are different.

2. Logically the two statements are equivalent. The second statement may still be useful as an expressive poetic reinforcement.

3. If x and y are *not* both odd, at least one of them must be even. If, for example, $x = 2n$, where n is an integer, then $xy = 2ny$ is also even. Similarly if $y = 2m$, where m is an integer.

1.4

1. For $n = 1$, both sides are 1. Suppose (∗) is true for $n = k$. Then $1 + 2 + 3 + \cdots + k + (k + 1) = \frac{1}{2}k(k + 1) + (k + 1) = \frac{1}{2}(k + 1)(k + 2)$, which is (∗) for $n = k + 1$. Thus, by induction, (∗) is true for all natural numbers n.

2. For $n = 1$, both sides are $\frac{1}{2}$. Suppose (∗) is true for $n = k$. Then

$$\frac{1}{1 \cdot 2} + \cdots + \frac{1}{k(k+1)} + \frac{1}{(k+1)(k+2)} = \frac{k}{k+1} + \frac{1}{(k+1)(k+2)} = \frac{k(k+2)+1}{(k+1)(k+2)}$$

But $k(k + 2) + 1 = k^2 + 2k + 1 = (k + 1)^2$, so the last fraction simplifies to $(k + 1)/(k + 2)$. Hence (∗) is also true for $n = k + 1$, and it follows by induction that (∗) is true for all natural numbers n.

3. For $n = 1$, the sum $n^3 + (n + 1)^3 + (n + 2)^3 = 36$, which is divisible by 9. As the induction hypothesis for $n = k$, suppose that $k^3 + (k + 1)^3 + (k + 2)^3 = 9m_k$ for some natural number m_k. Then

$$(k+1)^3 + (k+2)^3 + (k+3)^3 = -k^3 + 9m_k + (k+3)^3 = 9m_k + 9k^2 + 27k + 27 = 9(m_k + k^2 + 3k + 3)$$

Obviously, this is also divisible by 9, which confirms the induction hypothesis for $n = k + 1$.

4. The induction step breaks down for $k = 1$: Take two people A and B. Send A outside. B has the same income as himself. Bring A back, and send B outside. A has the same income as himself. But this does *not* imply that the two people have the same income! (The induction step is correct for all $k > 1$, because then the two people sent out have the same income as the others.)

Review exercises for Chapter 1

1. $A \cap B = \{1, 4\}$; $A \cup B = \{1, 3, 4, 6\}$; $A \setminus B = \{3\}$; $B \setminus A = \{6\}$; $(A \cup B) \setminus (A \cap B) = \{3, 6\}$; $A \cup B \cup C \cup D = \{1, 2, 3, 4, 5, 6\}$; $A \cap B \cap C = \{4\}$; and $A \cap B \cap C \cap D = \emptyset$.

2. $A \cap B = \emptyset$; $A \cup B = \{1, 2, 4, 6, 11\}$; $\mathcal{U} \setminus B = \{1, 3, 4, 5, 6, 7, 8, 9, 10\}$; $A^c = \mathcal{U} \setminus A = \{2, 3, 5, 7, 8, 9, 10, 11\}$.

3. Let $n_E = 780$, $n_F = 220$, and $n_S = 52$ denote the numbers studying respectively English, French and Spanish; then let $n_{EF} = 110$, $n_{ES} = 32$, and $n_{FS} = 15$ denote the numbers studying two of the languages, and $n_{EFS} = 10$ the number studying all three.

(a) $n_{EF} - n_{EFS} = 110 - 10 = 100$ study English and French, but not Spanish.

(b) $n_E - n_{EF} = 780 - 110 = 670$ study English but not French.

(c) The number studying at least one language can be calculated as

$$n_E + (n_F - n_{EF}) + (n_S - n_{ES} - n_{FS} + n_{EFS}) = 780 + (220 - 110) + (52 - 32 - 15 + 10) = 780 + 110 + 15 = 905$$

so there are 95 of the 1000 students who study no language.

4. (a) $\Rightarrow$ true, $\Leftarrow$ false. (b) $\Rightarrow$ false because $(-4)^2 = 16$, $\Leftarrow$ true. (c) $\Rightarrow$ true, $\Leftarrow$ false when $x = 3$.

(d) $\Rightarrow$ and $\Leftarrow$ both true.

5. (a) $(1 + x)^2 = 1 + 2x + x^2 \geq 1 + 2x$ for all x since $x^2 \geq 0$.

(b) One has $(1 + x)^3 = 1 + 3x + 3x^2 + x^3 = 1 + 3x + x^2(3 + x)$. If $x \geq -3$ then $x^2(3 + x) \geq 0$, implying that $(1 + x)^3 \geq 1 + 3x$.

(c) We prove the result by induction on n with a fixed $x \geq -1$. Evidently $(1 + x)^n \geq 1 + nx$ holds with equality when $n = 1$. As the induction hypothesis, suppose that $(1 + x)^k \geq 1 + kx$ for some natural

826 SOLUTIONS TO THE EXERCISES

number k. Then, because $1 + x \geq 0$, we find that $(1+x)^{k+1} = (1+x)^k(1+x) \geq (1+kx)(1+x)$. But $(1+kx)(1+x) = 1 + (k+1)x + kx^2 \geq 1 + (k+1)x$, implying that $(1+x)^{k+1} \geq 1 + (k+1)x$. This completes the proof by induction.

Chapter 2

2.1

1. (a) True. (b) False. -5 is less than -3, so on the number line it is to the left of -3.

   (c) False because all natural numbers are positive.

   (d) True. Every natural number is rational. For example $5 = 5/1$. (e) False, since $3.1415 = 31415/10000$, the quotient of two integers. (Note that 3.1415 is only an approximation to the irrational number π.)

   (f) False. Counterexample: $\sqrt{2} + (-\sqrt{2}) = 0$. (g) True. (h) True.

2. In the number $1.01001000100001000001\ldots$, one extra zero is added between each successive pair of ones. So there is obviously no finite sequence of digits that repeats itself indefinitely.

2.2

1. (a) $10^3 = 10 \cdot 10 \cdot 10 = 1000$ (b) $(-0.3)^2 = 0.09$ (c) $4^{-2} = 1/16$ (d) $(0.1)^{-1} = 1/0.1 = 10$

2. (a) $4 = 2^2$ (b) $1 = 2^0$ (c) $64 = 2^6$ (d) $1/16 = 2^{-4}$

3. (a) 15^3 (b) $\left(-\frac{1}{3}\right)^3$ (c) 10^{-1} (d) 10^{-7} (e) t^6 (f) $(a-b)^3$ (g) $a^2 b^4$ (h) $(-a)^3$

4. (a) $2^5 \cdot 2^5 = 2^{5+5} = 2^{10}$ (b) $3^8 \cdot 3^{-2} \cdot 3^{-3} = 3^{8-2-3} = 3^3$ (c) $(2x)^3 = 2^3 x^3 = 8x^3$

   (d) $(-3xy^2)^3 = (-3)^3 x^3 (y^2)^3 = -27 x^3 y^6$ (e) $\dfrac{p^{24} p^3}{p^4 p} = p^{24+3-4-1} = p^{22}$

   (f) $\dfrac{a^4 b^{-3}}{(a^2 b^{-3})^2} = \dfrac{a^4 b^{-3}}{a^4 b^{-6}} = a^{4-4} b^{-3-(-6)} = b^3$ (g) $\dfrac{3^4 (3^2)^6}{(-3)^{15} 3^7} = \dfrac{3^4 3^{12}}{-3^{15} 3^7} = -3^{-6}$ (h) $\dfrac{p^\gamma (pq)^\sigma}{p^{2\gamma+\sigma} q^{\sigma-2}} = p^{-\gamma} q^2$

5. (a) $2^6 = 64$ (b) $64/27$ (c) $8/3$ (d) x^9 (e) y^{12} (f) $8x^3 y^3$ (g) $10^{-2} = 1/100$ (h) k^4 (i) $(x+1)^2$

6. (a) Because $4\pi(3r)^2 = 4\pi 3^2 r^2 = 9(4\pi r^2)$, the surface area increases by the factor 9.

   (b) When r increases by 16%, it increases by a factor of 1.16, and r^2 increases by the factor $(1.16)^2 = 1.3456$, so the surface area increases by 34.56%.

7. (a) False. $a^0 = 1$. (b) True. $c^{-n} = 1/c^n$ for all $c \neq 0$. (c) True. $a^m \cdot a^m = a^{m+m} = a^{2m}$.

   (d) False (unless $m = 0$ or $ab = 1$). $a^m b^m = (ab)^m$.

   (e) False (unless $m = 1$ or $ab = 0$). For example, $(a+b)^2 = a^2 + 2ab + b^2$, which is not $a^2 + b^2$ unless $ab = 0$.

   (f) False (unless $a^m b^n = 1$). For example, $a^2 b^3$ is not equal to $(ab)^{2+3} = (ab)^5 = a^5 b^5$.

8. (a) $x^3 y^3 = (xy)^3 = 3^3 = 27$ (b) $(ab)^4 = (-2)^4 = 16$ (c) $(a^8)^0 = 1$ for all $a \neq 0$. (d) $(-1)^{2n} = [(-1)^2]^n = 1^n = 1$

9. (a) $150 \cdot 0.13 = 19.5$ (b) $2400 \cdot 0.06 = 144$ (c) $200 \cdot 0.055 = 11$

10. (a) With an interest rate of 11% per year, then in 8 years, an initial investment of 50 dollars will be worth $50 \cdot (1.11)^8 \approx 115.23$ dollars. (b) Given a constant interest rate of 12% per year, then in 20 years, an initial investment of 10 000 euros will be worth $10\,000 \cdot (1.12)^{20} \approx 96\,462.93$ euros. (c) $5000 \cdot (1.07)^{-10} \approx 2541.75$ pounds

CHAPTER 2

is what you should have invested 10 years ago in order to have 5000 pounds today, given the constant interest rate of 7%.

11. $1.50 cheaper, which is 15% of $10.

12. (a) $12\,000 \cdot (1.04)^{15} \approx 21611.32$ (b) $50\,000 \cdot (1.06)^{-5} \approx 37362.91$

13. $p \approx 95.3\%$, since $(1.25)^3 \approx 1.953$.

14. (a) The profit was higher in 2010. $((1+0.2)(1-0.17) = 1.2 \cdot 0.83 = 0.996.)$

    (b) If the decrease in profits from 2011 to 2012 were $p\%$, then profits in 2010 and 2012 would be equal provided $1.2 \cdot (1 - p/100) = 1$, or $p = 100(1 - 1/1.2) = 100/6 \approx 16.67$.

2.3

1. (a) 1   (b) 6   (c) -18 (d) -18 (e) $3x + 12$ (f) $45x - 27y$ (g) 3   (h) 0   (i) -1

2. (a) $3a^2 - 5b$ (b) $-2x^2 + 3x + 4y$ (c) t (d) $2r^3 - 6r^2s + 2s^3$

3. (a) $-3n^2 + 6n - 9$ (b) $x^5 + x^2$ (c) $4n^2 - 11n + 6$ (d) $-18a^3b^3 + 30a^3b^2$ (e) $a^3b - ab^3$
   (f) $x^3 - 6x^2y + 11xy^2 - 6y^3$ (g) $acx^2 + (ad + bc)x + bd$ (h) $4 - t^4$
   (i) $[(u-v)(u+v)]^2 = (u^2 - v^2)^2 = u^4 - 2u^2v^2 + v^4$

4. (a) $2t^3 - 5t^2 + 4t - 1$ (b) 4   (c) $x^2 + y^2 + z^2 + 2xy + 2xz + 2yz$ (d) $4xy + 4xz$

5. (a) $x^2 + 4xy + 4y^2$ (b) $1/x^2 - 2 + x^2$ (c) $9u^2 - 30uv + 25v^2$ (d) $4z^2 - 25w^2$

6. (a) $201^2 - 199^2 = (201 + 199)(201 - 199) = 400 \cdot 2 = 800$

   (b) If $u^2 - 4u + 4 = (u - 2)^2 = 1$ then $u - 2 = \pm 1$, so $u = 1$ or $u = 3$.

   (c) $\dfrac{(a+1)^2 - (a-1)^2}{(b+1)^2 - (b-1)^2} = \dfrac{a^2 + 2a + 1 - (a^2 - 2a + 1)}{b^2 + 2b + 1 - (b^2 - 2b + 1)} = \dfrac{4a}{4b} = \dfrac{a}{b}$

7. $1000^2/(252^2 - 248^2) = 1000^2/(252 + 248)(252 - 248) = 1000^2/(500 \cdot 4) = 500$

8. (a) $(a+b)^3 = (a+b)^2(a+b) = (a^2 + 2ab + b^2)(a+b) = a^3 + 3a^2b + 3ab^2 + b^3$
   (b) $(a-b)^3 = (a-b)^2(a-b) = (a^2 - 2ab + b^2)(a-b) = a^3 - 3a^2b + 3ab^2 - b^3$
   (c) and (d): Expand the right-hand sides.

9. (a) $3 \cdot 7 \cdot xxyyy$ (b) $3(x - 3y + 9z)$ (c) $aa(a - b)$ (d) $2 \cdot 2 \cdot 2xy(xy - 2)$ (e) $2 \cdot 2 \cdot 7aabbb$ (f) $2 \cdot 2(x + 2y - 6z)$
   (g) $2x(x - 3y)$ (h) $2aabb(3a + 2b)$ (i) $7x(x - 7y)$ (j) $5xyy(1 - 3x)(1 + 3x)$ (k) $(4 + b)(4 - b)$
   (l) $3(x + 2)(x - 2)$

10. (a) $(a + 2b)(a + 2b)$ (b) $KL(K - L)$ (c) $K^{-5}(K - L)$ (d) $(3z - 4w)(3z + 4w)$ (e) $-\tfrac{1}{5}(x - 5y)(x - 5y)$
    (f) $(a^2 - b^2)(a^2 + b^2) = (a + b)(a - b)(a^2 + b^2)$

11. (a) $(x - 2)(x - 2)$ (b) $2 \cdot 2ts(t - 2s)$ (c) $2 \cdot 2(2a + b)(2a + b)$ (d) $5x(x + \sqrt{2}y)(x - \sqrt{2}y)$ (e) $(5 + a)(x + y)$
    (f) $u^2 - v^2 + 3(u + v) = (u + v)(u - v) + 3(u + v) = (u + v)(u - v + 3)$ (g) $(P + Q)(P^2 + Q^2)$ (h) $KK(K - L)$
    (i) $KL(L^2 + 1)$ (j) $(L + K)(L - K)$ (k) $(K - L)(K - L)$ (l) $KL(K - 2L)(K - 2L)$

2.4

1. (a) 2/7 (b) 13/12 (c) 5/24 (d) 2/25 (e) 9/5 (Recall that the mixed numbers $3\frac{3}{5}$ and $1\frac{4}{5}$ are equal to $3 + \frac{3}{5}$ and $1 + \frac{4}{5}$, respectively.) (f) 1/2 (g) 1/2 (h) 11/27

2. (a) $3x/2$ (b) $3a/5$ (c) $1/5$ (d) $\frac{1}{12}(-5x + 11)$ (e) $-1/(6b)$ (f) $1/b$

3. (a) $\dfrac{5 \cdot 5 \cdot 13}{5 \cdot 5 \cdot 5 \cdot 5} = \dfrac{13}{25}$ (b) $\dfrac{ab^2}{8c^2}$ (c) $\dfrac{2}{3}(a-b)$ (d) $\dfrac{P(P+Q)(P-Q)}{(P+Q)^2} = \dfrac{P(P-Q)}{P+Q}$

4. (a) 1/2 (b) 6 (c) 5/7 (d) 9/2

5. (a) $\dfrac{4}{x^2 - 4}$ (b) $\dfrac{21}{2(2x+1)}$ (c) $\dfrac{a}{a-3b}$ (d) $\dfrac{1}{4ab(a+2)}$ (e) $\dfrac{-3t^2}{t+2}$ (f) $4(1-a)$

6. (a) $\dfrac{2 - 3x^2}{x(x+1)}$ (b) $\dfrac{-2t}{4t^2 - 1}$ (c) $\dfrac{7x^2 + 1}{x^2 - 4}$ (d) $x + y$ (e) $\dfrac{y^2 - x^2}{y^2 + x^2}$ (f) $\dfrac{y - x}{y + x}$

7. $\dfrac{-8x}{x^2 + 2xy - 3y^2}$

8. (a) 400 (b) $\dfrac{-n}{n-1}$ (c) 1 (d) $\dfrac{1}{(x-1)^2}$ (e) $\dfrac{-2x - h}{x^2(x+h)^2}$ (f) $\dfrac{2x}{x-1}$

2.5

1. (a) 3 (b) 40 (c) 10 (d) 5 (e) 1/6 (f) 0.7 (g) 0.1 (h) 1/5

2. (a) =. (Both expressions are equal to 20.) (b) $\neq$. In fact, $\sqrt{25 + 16} = \sqrt{41} \neq 9 = \sqrt{25} + \sqrt{16}$.
   (c) $\neq$. (Put $a = b = 1$.) (d) =. In fact, $(\sqrt{a+b})^{-1} = [(a+b)^{1/2}]^{-1} = (a+b)^{-1/2}$.

3. (a) 81 (b) 4 (c) 623 (d) 15 (e) -1 (f) $2^x - 2^{x-1} = 2^{x-1}(2-1) = 2^{x-1} = 4$ for $x = 3$.

4. (a) $\frac{6}{7}\sqrt{7}$ (b) 4 (c) $\frac{1}{8}\sqrt{6}$ (d) 1 (e) $\frac{1}{6}\sqrt{6}$ (f) $\dfrac{2\sqrt{2y}}{y}$ (g) $\dfrac{\sqrt{2x}}{2}$ (h) $x + \sqrt{x}$

5. (a) $\frac{1}{2}(\sqrt{7} - \sqrt{5})$ (b) $4 - \sqrt{15}$ (c) $-x(\sqrt{3} + 2)$ (d) $\dfrac{(\sqrt{x} - \sqrt{y})^2}{x - y}$ (e) $\sqrt{x+h} + \sqrt{x}$ (f) $\dfrac{1}{x}(2\sqrt{x+1} - x - 2)$

6. (a) $\sqrt[3]{125} = 5$ because $5^3 = 125$. (b) $(243)^{1/5} = 3$ because $3^5 = 243$. (c) -2
   (d) $\sqrt[3]{0.008} = 0.2$ because $(0.2)^3 = 0.008$. (e) 9 (f) $(64)^{-1/3} = (4^3)^{-1/3} = 4^{-1} = 1/4$
   (g) $(16)^{-2.25} = (2^4)^{-9/4} = 2^{-9} = 1/512$ (h) $\left(\dfrac{1}{3^{-2}}\right)^{-2} = (3^2)^{-2} = 3^{-4} = 1/81$

7. (a) $\sqrt[3]{55} \approx 3.80295$ (b) $(160)^{1/4} \approx 3.55656$ (c) $(2.71828)^{1/5} \approx 1.22140$ (d) $(1.0001)^{10000} \approx 2.718146$

8. $40(1 + p/100)^{12} = 60$ gives $(1 + p/100)^{12} = 1.5$, and therefore $1 + p/100 = (1.5)^{1/12}$.
   Solving this for p yields $p = 100[(1.5)^{1/12} - 1] \approx 3.44$.

9. (a) $3x^p y^{2q} z^{4r}$ (b) $(x + 15)^{4/3 - 5/6} = (x + 15)^{1/2} = \sqrt{x + 15}$ (c) $\dfrac{8x^{2/3} y^{1/4} z^{-1/2}}{-2x^{1/3} y^{5/2} z^{1/2}} = -4x^{1/3} y^{-9/4} z^{-1}$

10. (a) $a^{\frac{1}{2} + \frac{2}{3} + \frac{3}{4} + \frac{4}{5}} = a^{1/5}$ (b) $a^{\frac{1}{2} + \frac{2}{3} + \frac{3}{4} + \frac{4}{5}} = a^{163/60}$ (c) $9a^7/2$ (d) $a^{1/4}$

11. $V = (4/3)\pi r^3$ implies $r^3 = 3V/4\pi$ and so $r = (3V/4\pi)^{1/3}$. Hence, $S = 4\pi r^2 = 4\pi(3V/4\pi)^{2/3} = \sqrt[3]{36\pi}\, V^{2/3}$.

12. (a) $(2^x)^2 = 2^{2x}$, so $(2^x)^2 = 2^{x^2}$ iff $2x = x^2$ iff $x = 0$ or $x = 2$. (b) is valid (c) is valid

(d) If $x \neq 0$, then $\dfrac{1}{5^x} = 5^{-x} = 5^{1/x}$ iff $-x^2 = 1$, which is false for all real x.

(e) If $a > 0$ then $a^{x+y} = a^x \cdot a^y \neq a^x + a^y$ when, for example, $a = 1$.

(f) If $x > 0$ and $y > 0$ then $2^{\sqrt{x}} \cdot 2^{\sqrt{y}} = 2^{\sqrt{xy}}$ iff $\sqrt{x} + \sqrt{y} = \sqrt{xy}$. This is false when, for example, $x = y = 1$.

13. $x < 4$. (If $x > 0$, then $32x^{3/2} > 4x^3$ if and only if $8x^{3/2} > x^3$, which is equivalent to $8 > x^{3/2}$, and so $x < 8^{2/3} = 4$.)

2.6

1. (a), (b), (d), (f), and (h) are all true; (c), (e), and (g) are all false.

2. (a) $x \geq -8$ (b) $x < -9$ (c) All x. (d) $x \leq 25/2$ (e) $x \leq 19/7$ (f) $x > -17/12$

3. (a) $-41/6 < x \leq 2/3$ (b) $x < -1/5$

4. (a) $x(x+3) < 0$ for x in $(-3, 0)$, so $\Rightarrow$ (b) $x^2 < 9$ for x in $(-3, 3)$, so $\Rightarrow$ (c) $\Leftarrow$ (d) $y^2 \geq 0$, so $\Rightarrow$

5. (a) Yes (b) No, put $x = \frac{1}{2}$, for example. (c) No, not for $x \leq 0$.

(d) Yes, because the inequality is equivalent to $x^2 - 2xy + y^2 \geq 0$, or $(x-y)^2 \geq 0$, which *is* satisfied for all x and y.

6. (a) $4 \leq C \leq 6$ implies that $\frac{9}{5}4 + 32 \leq F \leq \frac{9}{5}6 + 32$ or $39.2 \leq F \leq 42.8$, in degrees Fahrenheit.

(b) $F = \frac{9}{5}C + 32$ implies that $C = \frac{5}{9}(F - 32)$, so $36 \leq F \leq 40$ implies that $2.2 \leq C \leq 4.4$, approximately.

7. For each $k = 1, 2, \ldots$, let s_k denote the sum $a_1 + a_2 + \cdots + a_k$, and p_k the product $a_1 \cdot a_2 \cdot \ldots \cdot a_k$. The result that both s_2 and p_2 are positive follows directly from (2.6.1). As the induction hypothesis, suppose that s_k and p_k are both positive. Because $s_{k+1} = s_k + a_{k+1}$ and $p_{k+1} = p_k \cdot a_{k+1}$, it follows from (2.6.1) that s_{k+1} and p_{k+1} are both positive. The result follows by induction.

8. $\left(\sqrt{a} - \sqrt{b}\right)^2 = a - 2\sqrt{ab} + b \geq 0$ yields $a + b \geq 2\sqrt{ab}$; dividing by 2 gives $m_A \geq m_G$. Because $\left(\sqrt{a} - \sqrt{b}\right)^2 = 0$ is equivalent to $a = b$, one also has $m_A > m_G$ unless $a = b$. The inequality $m_G \geq m_H$ follows easily from the hint.

2.7

1. (a) $|2 \cdot 0 - 3| = 3$, $|2 \cdot \frac{1}{2} - 3| = 2$, $|2 \cdot \frac{7}{2} - 3| = 4$ (b) $|2x - 3| = 0 \Leftrightarrow 2x - 3 = 0$, so $x = 3/2$.

(c) $|2x - 3| = 2x - 3$ for $x \geq 3/2$, and $3 - 2x$ for $x < 3/2$.

2. (a) $|5 - 3(-1)| = 8$, $|5 - 3 \cdot 2| = 1$, $|5 - 3 \cdot 4| = 7$ (b) $|5 - 3x| = 5 \Leftrightarrow 5 - 3x = \pm 5$, so $x = 0$ or $10/3$.

(c) $|5 - 3x| = 5 - 3x$ for $x \leq 5/3$, and $3x - 5$ for $x > 5/3$

3. (a) $x = -1$ and $x = 4$ (b) $-2 \leq x \leq 2$ (c) $1 \leq x \leq 3$ (d) $-1/4 \leq x \leq 1$ (e) $x > \sqrt{2}$ or $x < -\sqrt{2}$

(f) $-1 \leq x^2 - 2 \leq 1$, so $1 \leq x^2 \leq 3$, implying that $-\sqrt{3} \leq x \leq -1$ or $1 \leq x \leq \sqrt{3}$

4. (a) $4.999 < x < 5.001$ (b) $|x - 5| < 0.001$

2.8

1. (a) $-7 < x < -2$ (b) $n \geq 160$ or $n < 0$ (c) $0 \leq g \leq 2$ (d) $p \geq -1$ and $p \neq 2$

(e) $-4 < n < -10/3$ (f) $-1 < x < 0$ or $0 < x < 1$. (Hint: $x^4 - x^2 = x^2(x+1)(x-1)$.)

2. (a) $-2 < x < 1$ (b) $x < -4$ or $x > 3$ (c) $-5 \leq a \leq 5$ (d) $x < -4$ or $x > 1$ (e) $x > -4$ and $x \neq 1$ (f) $1 \leq x \leq 2$

(g) $x < 1$ and $x \neq 1/5$ (h) $1/5 < x < 1$ (i) $x < 0$ (j) $-3 < x < -2$ or $x > 0$ (k) $x \neq 2$ (l) $x \leq 0$

3. $-1 < x < 0$

2.9

1. (a) $1 + 2 + 3 + \cdots + 10 = 55$ (b) $(5 \cdot 3^0 - 2) + (5 \cdot 3^1 - 3) + (5 \cdot 3^2 - 4) + (5 \cdot 3^3 - 5) + (5 \cdot 3^4 - 6) = 585$
   (c) $1 + 3 + 5 + 7 + 9 + 11 = 36$ (d) $2^{2^0} + 2^{2^1} + 2^{2^2} = 2^1 + 2^2 + 2^4 = 22$ (e) $10 \cdot 2 = 20$
   (f) $2/1 + 3/2 + 4/3 + 5/4 = 73/12$

2. (a) $2\sqrt{0} + 2\sqrt{1} + 2\sqrt{2} + 2\sqrt{3} + 2\sqrt{4} = 2(3 + \sqrt{2} + \sqrt{3})$
   (b) $(x+0)^2 + (x+2)^2 + (x+4)^2 + (x+6)^2 = 4(x^2 + 6x + 14)$
   (c) $a_{1i}b^2 + a_{2i}b^3 + a_{3i}b^4 + \cdots + a_{ni}b^{n+1}$ (d) $f(x_0)\Delta x_0 + f(x_1)\Delta x_1 + f(x_2)\Delta x_2 + \cdots + f(x_m)\Delta x_m$

3. (a) $\sum_{k=1}^{n} 4k$ (b) $\sum_{k=1}^{n} k^3$ (c) $\sum_{k=0}^{n} (-1)^k \frac{1}{2k+1}$ (d) $\sum_{k=1}^{n} a_{ik}b_{kj}$ (e) $\sum_{n=1}^{5} 3^n x^n$ (f) $\sum_{j=3}^{p} d_j b_{i+j}$ (g) $\sum_{k=0}^{p} a_{i+k}^{k+3} b_{i+k+3}$
   (h) $\sum_{k=0}^{3} (81\,297 + 198k)$

4. $\dfrac{2 \cdot 3 + 3 \cdot 5 + 4 \cdot 7}{1 \cdot 3 + 2 \cdot 5 + 3 \cdot 7} \cdot 100 = \dfrac{6 + 15 + 28}{3 + 10 + 21} \cdot 100 = \dfrac{49}{34} \cdot 100 \approx 144.12$

5. (a) $\sum_{k=1}^{10}(k-2)t^k = \sum_{m=-1}^{8} m t^{m+2}$ (b) $\sum_{n=0}^{N} 2^{n+5} = \sum_{j=1}^{N+1} 32 \cdot 2^{j-1}$ (because $32 = 2^5$)

6. (a) The total number of people moving from nation i within the EEA.
   (b) The total number of people moving to nation j within the EEA.

7. (a), (c), (d), and (e) are always true; (b) and (f) are generally not true.

2.10

1. We prove only (2.10.6); the proof of (2.10.5) is very similar, but slightly easier. Note that the last equality in (2.10.6) follows immediately from (2.10.4), so we will concentrate on proving the equality

$$1^3 + 2^3 + 3^3 + \cdots + n^3 = \left[\tfrac{1}{2}n(n+1)\right]^2 \qquad (*)$$

For $n = 1$ the LHS and the RHS of $(*)$ are both equal to 1. As the induction hypothesis, suppose $(*)$ is true for $n = k$. Then $\sum_{i=1}^{k+1} i^3 = \sum_{i=1}^{k} i^3 + (k+1)^3 = [\tfrac{1}{2}k(k+1)]^2 + (k+1)^3 = (k+1)^2(\tfrac{1}{4}k^2 + k + 1)$. But this last expression is equal to $\tfrac{1}{4}(k+1)^2(k^2 + 4k + 4) = [\tfrac{1}{2}(k+1)(k+2)]^2$, which proves that $(*)$ is true for $n = k + 1$. By induction, we have proved $(*)$.

2. $\sum_{k=1}^{n}(k^2 + 3k + 2) = \sum_{k=1}^{n} k^2 + 3\sum_{k=1}^{n} k + \sum_{k=1}^{n} 2 = \tfrac{1}{6}n(n+1)(2n+1) + 3[\tfrac{1}{2}n(n+1)] + 2n$
   $= \tfrac{1}{3}n(n^2 + 6n + 11)$.

3. $\sum_{i=0}^{n-1}(a + id) = \sum_{i=0}^{n-1} a + d\sum_{i=0}^{n-1} i = na + d\tfrac{1}{2}[1 + (n-1)](n-1) = na + \tfrac{1}{2}n(n-1)d$. Using this formula, the sum that Gauss is alleged to have computed is: $100 \cdot 81\,297 + \tfrac{1}{2} 100 \cdot 99 \cdot 198 = 9\,109\,800$. (One does not have to use summation signs. The sum is $a + (a + d) + (a + 2d) + \cdots + (a + (n-1)d)$. There are n terms. The sum of all the a's is na. The rest is $d(1 + 2 + \cdots + (n-1))$. Then use formula (2.10.4).)

4. (a) Writing the sum as $(a_2 - a_1) + (a_3 - a_2) + (a_4 - a_3) + \cdots + (a_n - a_{n-1}) + (a_{n+1} - a_n)$ we see that all the a_i cancel pairwise, except $-a_1$ and a_{n+1}. Actually, this is more striking if we write the sum starting with the last term and

CHAPTER 2   831

working backwards to the first: $(a_{n+1} - a_n) + (a_n - a_{n-1}) + \cdots + (a_4 - a_3) + (a_3 - a_2) + (a_2 - a_1) = a_{n+1} - a_1$.
(b) (i) $1 - (1/51) = 50/51$ (ii) $3^{13} - 3 = 1\,594\,320$ (iii) $ar(r^n - 1)$

2.11

1. $(a+b)^6 = a^6 + 6a^5b + 15a^4b^2 + 20a^3b^3 + 15a^2b^4 + 6ab^5 + b^6$. (The coefficients are those in the row number 6 of Pascal's triangle in the text, counting from the top row as number 0.)

2. (a) $\binom{8}{3} = 56$. Also, $\binom{8}{8-3} = \binom{8}{5} = 56$; $\binom{8}{3} + \binom{8}{3+1} = 56 + 70 = 126$ and $\binom{8+1}{3+1} = \binom{9}{4} = 126$.

   (b) $\binom{m}{k} = \dfrac{m!}{(m-k)!\,k!} = \binom{m}{m-k}$ and $\binom{m}{k} + \binom{m}{k+1} = \dfrac{m!}{(m-k)!\,k!} + \dfrac{m!}{(m-k-1)!\,(k+1)!}$

   The last expression reduces to $\dfrac{m!\,(k+1+m-k)}{(m-k)!\,(k+1)!} = \dfrac{(m+1)!}{(m-k)!\,(k+1)!} = \binom{m+1}{k+1}$.

3. $\sum_{k=0}^{m} \binom{m}{k} = \sum_{k=0}^{m} \binom{m}{k} 1^k 1^{m-k} = (1+1)^m = 2^m$.

2.12

1. (a) $\sum_{i=1}^{3} \sum_{j=1}^{4} i \cdot 3^j = \sum_{i=1}^{3} (i \cdot 3 + i \cdot 9 + i \cdot 27 + i \cdot 81) = \sum_{i=1}^{3} 120i = 720$ (b) $5 + \dfrac{3113}{3600}$ (c) $\tfrac{1}{6} mn(2n^2 + 3n + 3m + 4)$

   (d) $\tfrac{1}{3} m(m+1)(m+2)$

2. (a) The total number of units of good i.   (b) The total number of units of all goods owned by person j.

   (c) The total number of units of goods owned by the group as a whole.

3. First, $\sum_{j=1}^{i} a_{ij}$ is the sum of all the i numbers in the ith row, so in the first double sum we sum all these m row sums. Second, $\sum_{i=j}^{m} a_{ij}$ is the sum of all the $m - j + 1$ numbers in the jth column, so in the second double sum we sum all these m column sums.

4. The mean of the n column means is $\dfrac{1}{n} \sum_{j=1}^{n} \bar{a}_j = \dfrac{1}{n} \sum_{j=1}^{n} \dfrac{1}{m} \sum_{i=1}^{m} a_{ij} = \bar{a}$. Also

$$\sum_{r=1}^{m} \sum_{s=1}^{m} (a_{rj} - \bar{a})(a_{sj} - \bar{a}) = \sum_{r=1}^{m} (a_{rj} - \bar{a}) \sum_{s=1}^{m} (a_{sj} - \bar{a}) = [m(\bar{a}_j - \bar{a})][m(\bar{a}_j - \bar{a})] = m^2(\bar{a}_j - \bar{a})^2$$

See SM.

Review exercises for Chapter 2

1. (a) If the price is p before VAT, then after VAT it is $p + 20p/100 = p(1 + 0.2) = 1.2p$. Thus $a = 1.2p$, so $p = \dfrac{a}{1.2}$.

   (b) $p_1 x_1 + p_2 x_2 + p_3 x_3$ (c) $F + bx$ (d) $(F + cx)/x = F/x + c$

   (e) After the $p\%$ raise, the employee's salary is $L + pL/100 = L(1 + p/100)$. A $q\%$ raise of this new salary gives the final answer: $L(1 + p/100)(1 + q/100)$.

2. (a) $5^3 = 5 \cdot 5 \cdot 5 = 125$ (b) $10^{-3} = 1/10^3 = 1/1000 = 0.0001$ (c) $1/3^{-3} = 3^3 = 27$ (d) -1000 (e) 3

   (f) $(3^{-2})^{-3} = 3^6 = 729$ (g) -1 (h) $\left(-\tfrac{1}{2}\right)^{-3} = \dfrac{1}{(-\tfrac{1}{2})^3} = \dfrac{1}{-\tfrac{1}{8}} = -8$

3. (a) 1   (b) Undefined.   (c) 1   (d) 1

4. (a) $2^{-6} = 1/64$ (b) $\tfrac{3}{2} - \tfrac{3}{4} = \tfrac{3}{4}$ (c) $-45/4$ (d) 1

SOLUTIONS TO THE EXERCISES

5. (a) $16x^4$ (b) 4 (c) $6xyz$ (d) $a^{27}b^9$ (e) a^3 (f) x^{-15}

6. (a) $x^3y^3 = (x^{-1}y^{-1})^{-3} = 3^{-3} = 1/27$ (b) $(x^{-3})^6(x^2)^2 = x^{-18}x^4 = x^{-14} = (x^7)^{-2} = 2^{-2} = 1/4$
(c) $(z/xy)^6 = (xy/z)^{-6} = [(xy/z)^{-2}]^3 = 3^3 = 27$ (d) $(abc)^4 = (a^{-1}b^{-1}c^{-1})^{-4} = (1/4)^{-4} = 4^4 = 256$

7. (a) Given an interest rate of 1% per year, then in 8 years, an investment of 100 million euros will grow to $100 \cdot (1.01)^8 \approx 108.3$ million euros. (b) Given an interest rate of 15% per year, then in 10 years, an initial investment of 50 000 pounds will be worth $50\,000 \cdot (1.15)^{10} \approx 202\,278$ pounds. (c) $6000 \cdot (1.03)^{-8} \approx 4736$ dollars is what you should have deposited 8 years ago in order to have 6000 dollars today, given the constant interest rate of 3%.

8. (a) $100\,000(1.08)^{10} \approx 215\,892$ (b) $25\,000(1.08)^{-6} \approx 15\,754$

9. (a) $a^2 - a$ (b) $x^2 + 4x - 21$ (c) $-3 + 3\sqrt{2}$ (d) $3 - 2\sqrt{2}$ (e) $x^3 - 3x^2 + 3x - 1$ (f) $1 - b^4$ (g) $1 - x^4$
(h) $x^4 + 4x^3 + 6x^2 + 4x + 1$

10. (a) $5(5x - 1)$ (b) $xx(3 - xy)$ (c) $(\sqrt{50} - x)(\sqrt{50} + x)$ (d) $a(a - 2b)^2$

11. (a) $(5 + a)(x + 2y)$ (b) $(a + b)(c - d)$ (c) $(a + 2)(x + y)$ (d) $(2x - y)(x + 5z)$ (e) $(p - q)(p + q + 1)$
(f) $(u - v)(u - v)(u + v)$

12. (a) $16^{1/4} = \sqrt[4]{16} = 2$ (b) $243^{-1/5} = (3^5)^{-1/5} = 3^{-1} = 1/3$ (c) $5^{1/7} \cdot 5^{6/7} = 5^{1/7+6/7} = 5^1 = 5$ (d) $4^{-3/2} = 1/8$
(e) $64^{1/3} + \sqrt[3]{125} = 4 + 5 = 9$ (f) $(-8/27)^{2/3} = (\sqrt[3]{-8/27})^2 = (-2/3)^2 = 4/9$
(g) $(-1/8)^{-2/3} + (1/27)^{-2/3} = (\sqrt[3]{-1/8})^{-2} + (\sqrt[3]{1/27})^{-2} = (-1/2)^{-2} + (1/3)^{-2} = 4 + 9 = 13$
(h) $\dfrac{1000^{-2/3}}{\sqrt[3]{5^{-3}}} = \dfrac{(\sqrt[3]{1000})^{-2}}{5^{-1}} = \dfrac{10^{-2}}{5^{-1}} = \dfrac{1}{20}$

13. (a) $8 = 2^3$, so $x = 3/2$ (b) $1/81 = 3^{-4}$, so $3x + 1 = -4$ or $x = -5/3$ (c) $x^2 - 2x + 2 = 2$, so $x = 0$ or $x = 2$.

14. (a) $5 + x = 3$, so $x = -2$. (b) $3^x - 3^{x-2} = 3^{x-2}(3^2 - 1) = 3^{x-2} \cdot 8$, so $3^{x-2} = 3$, and thus $x = 3$.
(c) $3^x \cdot 3^{x-1} = 3^{2x-1} = 81 = 3^4$ provided $x = 5/2$. (d) $3^5 + 3^5 + 3^5 = 3 \cdot 3^5 = 3^6$, so $x = 6$.
(e) $4^{-6} + 4^{-6} + 4^{-6} + 4^{-6} = 4 \cdot 4^{-6} = 4^{-5}$, so $x = -5$. (f) $\dfrac{2^{26} - 2^{23}}{2^{26} + 2^{23}} = \dfrac{2^{23}(2^3 - 1)}{2^{23}(2^3 + 1)} = \dfrac{7}{9}$, so $x = 7$.

15. (a) $\dfrac{2s}{4s^2 - 1}$ (b) $\dfrac{7}{3 - x}$ (c) $\dfrac{1}{x + y}$

16. (a) $\tfrac{1}{5}a^2b$ (b) $x - y$ (c) $\dfrac{2a - 3b}{2a + 3b}$ (d) $\dfrac{x(x + 2)}{2 - x}$

17. (a) $x < 13/2$ (b) $y \geq -3$ (c) Valid for all x. (d) $x < 29/14$ (e) $-1 \leq x \leq 13/3$
(f) $-\sqrt{6} \leq x \leq -\sqrt{2}$ or $\sqrt{2} \leq x \leq \sqrt{6}$

18. (a) $30 + 0.16x$ (b) Smallest number of hours: 7.5. Largest number of hours: 10.

19. $2\pi(r + 1) - 2\pi r = 2\pi$, where r is the radius of the Earth (as an approximate sphere). So the extended rope is only about 6.28 m longer!

20. (a) Put $p/100 = r$. Then the given expression becomes $a + ar - (a + ar)r = a(1 - r^2)$, as required.
(b) $\$2000 \cdot 1.05 \cdot 0.95 = \$1995$. (c) The result is precisely the formula in (a).
(d) With the notation used in the answer to (a), we have $a - ar + (a - ar)r = a(1 - r^2)$, which is the same expression as in (a).

21. (a) No, for example, $-1 > -2$, but $(-1)^2 < (-2)^2$.

(b) Suppose $a > b$ so that $a - b > 0$. If also $a + b > 0$, then $a^2 - b^2 = (a+b)(a-b) > 0$, so $a^2 > b^2$.

22. (a) $2 > 1$ and $1/2 < 1/1$. Also, $-1 > -2$ and $1/(-1) < -1/2$. On the other hand, $2 > -1$ and $1/2 > 1/(-1)$.

(b) If $ab > 0$ and $a > b$, then $1/b - 1/a = (a-b)/ab > 0$, so $1/b > 1/a$.

(Also, if $ab < 0$ and $a > b$, then $1/b - 1/a = (a-b)/ab < 0$, so $1/b < 1/a$.)

23. (i) For any number c, $|c| = \sqrt{c^2}$. Then $|ab| = \sqrt{(ab)^2} = \sqrt{a^2b^2} = \sqrt{a^2}\sqrt{b^2} = |a| \cdot |b|$.

(ii) Either $a = |a|$ or $a = -|a|$, so $-|a| \le a \le |a|$. Likewise, $-|b| \le b \le |b|$. Adding these inequalities yields $-|a| - |b| \le a + b \le |a| + |b|$, and thus $|a+b| \le |a| + |b|$.

24. Let s denote the length of each side of the equilateral triangle. Then the total area A of the triangle is the sum of the areas of three triangles with base s and heights h_1, h_2 and h_3 respectively. Therefore $A = \frac{1}{2}sh_1 + \frac{1}{2}sh_2 + \frac{1}{2}sh_3$. It follows that $h_1 + h_2 + h_3 = 2A/s$, independent of P. See SM for a figure. (For the curious: $A = \frac{1}{4}\sqrt{3}s^2$, so $h_1 + h_2 + h_3 = \frac{1}{2}\sqrt{3}s$.)

25. (a) $\sum_{i=1}^{4} \frac{1}{i(i+2)} = \frac{1}{1 \cdot 3} + \frac{1}{2 \cdot 4} + \frac{1}{3 \cdot 5} + \frac{1}{4 \cdot 6} = \frac{1}{3} + \frac{1}{8} + \frac{1}{15} + \frac{1}{24} = \frac{40 + 15 + 8 + 5}{120} = \frac{68}{120} = \frac{17}{30}$

(b) $\sum_{j=5}^{9}(2j-8)^2 = 2^2 + 4^2 + 6^2 + 8^2 + 10^2 = 4 + 16 + 36 + 64 + 100 = 220$

(c) $\sum_{k=1}^{5} \frac{k-1}{k+1} = \sum_{k=1}^{5}\left(1 - \frac{2}{k+1}\right) = 5 - \frac{2}{2} - \frac{2}{3} - \frac{2}{4} - \frac{2}{5} - \frac{2}{6} = \frac{21}{10}$

(d) $\sum_{n=2}^{5}(n-1)^2(n+2) = 1^2 \cdot 4 + 2^2 \cdot 5 + 3^2 \cdot 6 + 4^2 \cdot 7 = 4 + 20 + 54 + 112 = 190$

(e) $\sum_{k=1}^{5}\left(\frac{1}{k} - \frac{1}{k+1}\right) = \frac{1}{1} - \frac{1}{6} = \frac{5}{6}$

(f) $\sum_{i=-2}^{3}(i+3)^i = 1^{-2} + 2^{-1} + 3^0 + 4^1 + 5^2 + 6^3 = 1 + \frac{1}{2} + 1 + 4 + 25 + 216 = 247\frac{1}{2}$

26. (a) $3 + 5 + 7 + \cdots + 199 + 201 = \sum_{i=1}^{100}(1 + 2i)$ (b) $\frac{2}{1} + \frac{3}{2} + \frac{4}{3} + \cdots + \frac{97}{96} = \sum_{i=1}^{96} \frac{1+i}{i}$

(c) $4 \cdot 6 + 5 \cdot 7 + 6 \cdot 8 + \cdots + 38 \cdot 40 = \sum_{i=4}^{38} i(i+2)$ (d) $\frac{1}{x} + \frac{1}{x^2} + \cdots + \frac{1}{x^n} = \sum_{i=1}^{n} x^{-i}$

(e) $1 + \frac{x^2}{3} + \frac{x^4}{5} + \frac{x^6}{7} + \cdots + \frac{x^{32}}{33} = \sum_{i=0}^{16} \frac{x^{2i}}{1+2i}$ (f) $1 - \frac{1}{2} + \frac{1}{3} - \frac{1}{4} + \cdots - \frac{1}{80} + \frac{1}{81} = \sum_{i=1}^{81}(-1)^{i-1}\frac{1}{i}$

27. (a) and (c) are right. (b) is wrong unless the difference between the left and right hand sides, which is $2\sum_{i=1}^{n} a_i b_i$, happens to be zero. (d) is also wrong.

28. $3 + 5 + 7 + \cdots + 197 + 199 + 201 = \sum_{i=1}^{100}(1+2i) = 100 + 2\sum_{i=1}^{100} i = 100 + 100 \cdot 101 = 10\,200$;

$1\,001 + 2\,002 + 3\,003 + \cdots + 8\,008 + 9\,009 + 10\,010 = 1\,001 \sum_{i=1}^{10} i = 1\,001 \cdot \frac{1}{2} \cdot 10 \cdot 11 = 55\,055$.

Chapter 3

3.1

1. (a) $x = 3$ (b) $x = 6$ (c) Any x is a solution. (d) $x = 1$ (e) $x = -5$. (*Hint:* $x^2 + 10x + 25 = (x+5)^2$.)

(f) $x = -1$

2. (a) $x = -28/11$ (b) $x = 5/11$ (c) $x = 1$ (d) $x = 121$

3. (a) $x = 0$ (b) $x = -6$ (c) $x = 5$

834 SOLUTIONS TO THE EXERCISES

4. (a) With x as the smallest number, one has $x + (x + 1) + (x + 2) = 10 + 2x$, so $x = 7$. The numbers are 7, 8, and 9.

(b) If x is Jane's regular hourly wage, then $38x + (48 - 38)2x = 812$. Solution: $x = 812/58 = 14$.

(c) $1500 + 12x/100 = 2100$, so $12x = 60000$, implying that $x = 5000$.

(d) $\frac{2}{3}x + \frac{1}{4}x + 100\,000 = x$. Solution: $x = 1\,200\,000$.

5. (a) $y = 17/23$ (b) $x = -4$ (c) $z = 4$ (d) $p = 15/16$

6. She spends $y/3$ euros on each kind of fruit, for $y/9$ kilos of apples, $y/6$ kilos of bananas, and $y/18$ kilos of cherries. So the total weight in kilos is $\left(\frac{1}{9} + \frac{1}{6} + \frac{1}{18}\right)y = \left(\frac{2+3+1}{18}\right)y = \frac{6}{18}y = \frac{1}{3}y$. She pays 3 euros per kilo of fruit.

3.2

1. Inserting the second equation into the first gives $Y = 750 + 0.9Y$, whose solution is $Y = 7500$. Alternatively, formula (**) gives $Y = \dfrac{a}{1-b} + \dfrac{1}{1-b}\bar{I} = \dfrac{600}{1-0.9} + \dfrac{150}{1-0.9} = \dfrac{750}{1-0.9} = 7500$.

2. (a) $x = \frac{1}{2}\left(\dfrac{1}{a} + \dfrac{1}{b}\right)$ (b) $x = \dfrac{dA - b}{a - cA}$ (c) $x = \dfrac{p^2}{4w^2}$ (d) $x = -\dfrac{1}{1+a}$ (e) $x = \pm\dfrac{b}{a}$ (f) $x = 0$

3. (a) $p = 20q/3 - 14/15$ (b) $P = (S - \alpha)/\beta$ (c) $g = 2A/h$ (d) $r = (3V/4\pi)^{1/3}$ (e) $L = (Y_0 A^{-1} K^{-\alpha})^{1/\beta}$

4. (a) $x = (a - b)/(\alpha - \beta)$ (b) $p = (3q + 5)^2/q$ (c) $Y = 100$ (d) $K = (2wQ^4/r)^{1/3}$ (e) $L = rK/2w$

(f) $K = \dfrac{1}{32}p^4 r^{-3} w^{-1} = p^4/(32r^3 w)$

5. (a) $s = \dfrac{tT}{T-t}$ (b) $M = \dfrac{(B + \alpha L)^2}{KL}$ (c) $z = \dfrac{4xy - x + 2y}{x + 4y}$ (d) $T = N\left(1 - \dfrac{V}{C}\right)$

3.3

1. (a) $x(15 - x) = 0$, so the solutions are $x = 0$ and $x = 15$ (b) $p = \pm 4$ (c) $q = 3$ and $q = -4$ (d) No solution.
(e) $x = 0$ and $x = 3$ (f) $x = 2$. (Note that $x^2 - 4x + 4 = (x - 2)^2$.)

2. (a) $x^2 - 5x + 6 = (x - 2)(x - 3) = 0$ for $x = 2$ and for $x = 3$. (With $x^2 - 5x = -6$, completing the square gives $x^2 - 5x + (5/2)^2 = (5/2)^2 - 6 = 25/4 - 6 = 1/4$, or $(x - 5/2)^2 = 1/4$. Hence, $x - 5/2 = \pm 1/2$.)

(b) $y^2 - y - 12 = (y - 4)(y + 3) = 0$ for $y = 4$ and for $y = -3$. (c) No solutions and no factorization.

(d) $-\frac{1}{4}x^2 + \frac{1}{2}x + \frac{1}{2} = -\frac{1}{4}[x - (1 + \sqrt{3})][x - (1 - \sqrt{3})] = 0$ for $x = 1 \pm \sqrt{3}$

(e) $m^2 - 5m - 3 = \left[m - \frac{1}{2}(5 + \sqrt{37})\right]\left[m - \frac{1}{2}(5 - \sqrt{37})\right] = 0$ for $m = \frac{1}{2}(5 \pm \sqrt{37})$

(f) $0.1p^2 + p - 2.4 = 0.1(p - 2)(p + 12) = 0$ for $p = 2$ and for $p = -12$.

3. (a) $r = -13, r = 2$ (b) $p = -16, p = 1$ (c) $K = 100, K = 200$ (d) $r = -\sqrt{3}, r = \sqrt{2}$
(e) $x = -0.5, x = 0.8$ (f) $p = -1/6, p = 1/4$

4. (a) $x = 1, x = 2$ (b) $t = \frac{1}{10}(1 \pm \sqrt{61})$ (c) $x = \frac{1}{4}(3 \pm \sqrt{13})$ (d) $x = \frac{1}{3}(-7 \pm \sqrt{5})$
(e) $x = -300, x = 100$ (f) $x = \frac{1}{6}(5 \pm \sqrt{13})$

5. (a) If the sides have length x and y, then the perimeter has length $2x + 2y = 40$ and the area is $xy = 75$. From the Rules for Quadratic Functions, it follows that x and y are the roots of the quadratic equation $z^2 - 20z + 75 = 0$, so the sides have lengths 5 and 15.

(b) If the two numbers are n and $n + 1$, then $n^2 + (n + 1)^2 = 13$, so $2n^2 + 2n - 12 = 0$. The roots of this equation are $n_1 = 2$, and $n_2 = -3$. But n has to be positive, so the only possibility is $n = 2$, so the two numbers are 2 and 3.

(Of course, with numbers this small it is even easier to use trial and error, starting with the smallest numbers. $1^2+2^2=5$, which is too little, but $2^2 + 3^2 = 13$, which is just right, and further along the numbers get too big, so the answer is 2 and 3.)

(c) The length x of the shortest side satisfies $x^2 + (x + 14)^2 = 34^2$, or $2x^2 + 28x = 1156 - 196 = 960$, or $x^2 + 14x - 480 = 0$. The lengths are 16 cm and 30 cm.

(d) If his usual speed is s, the usual time is $80/s$ hours, or $4800/s$ minutes. Driving at a speed $s + 10$, the time is $\frac{4800}{s+10} = \frac{4800}{s} - 16$. Clearing fractions gives $4800s = (4800 - 16s)(s + 10)$ or $16s^2 + 160s - 48000 = 0$, implying that $s^2 + 10s - 3000 = 0$. The only positive root of this equation is $s = 50$. Hence the usual speed is 50 km/h.

6. (a) $x = -2$, $x = 0$, $x = 2$. ($x(x^2 - 4) = 0$ or $x(x + 2)(x - 2) = 0$)

   (b) $x = -2$, $x = -1$, $x = 1$, $x = 2$. (Let $x^2 = u$.) (c) $z = -1/3$, $z = 1/5$. (Let $z^{-1} = u$.)

3.4

1. (a) $x = 0$ and $x = -3$ (b) $x = 0$ and $x = 1/2$ (c) $x = 1$ and $x = 3$ (d) $x = -5/2$ (e) No solutions.

   (f) $x = 0$ and $x = -1$

2. (a) No solutions. (b) $x = -1$ (c) $x = -3/2$ (d) $x = 0$ and $x = 1/2$

3. (a) $z = 0$ or $z = a/(1 - a - b)$ for $a + b \neq 1$. For $a + b = 1$ the only solution is $z = 0$.

   (b) $\lambda = -1$ or $\mu = 0$ or $x = y$ (c) $\lambda = 0$ and $\mu \neq \pm 1$, or $\mu = 2$ (d) $a = 2$ or $b = 0$ or $\lambda = -1$

3.5

1. $x = -1, 0,$ and 1 make the equation meaningless. Multiplying each term by the common denominator $x(x - 1)(x + 1)$, we derive the only solution from the equivalences

$$\frac{(x+1)^2}{x(x-1)} + \frac{(x-1)^2}{x(x+1)} - 2\frac{3x+1}{x^2-1} = 0 \iff 2x(x^2 - 3x + 2) = 0 \text{ with } x \notin \{-1, 0, 1\}$$

$$\iff 2x(x-1)(x-2) = 0 \text{ with } x \notin \{-1, 0, 1\} \iff x = 2$$

2. (a) Squaring both sides and rearranging yields $x + 2 = \sqrt{4x + 13} \Rightarrow (x + 2)^2 = 4x + 13 \Rightarrow x^2 = 9 \Rightarrow x = \pm 3$. But $x + 2 = \sqrt{4x + 13} \Rightarrow x + 2 \geq 0$. So only $x = 3$ is a solution.

   (b) Squaring both sides and rearranging yields $x(x + 5) = 0$. Both $x = 0$ and $x = -5$ are solutions.

   (c) The equivalent equation $|x|^2 - 2|x| - 3 = 0$ gives $|x| = 3$ or $|x| = -1$. Because $|x| \geq 0$, only $x = \pm 3$ are solutions.

3. (a) No solutions. (b) $x = 20$

4. (a) $x + \sqrt{x + 4} = 2 \Longrightarrow \sqrt{x + 4} = 2 - x \Longrightarrow x + 4 = 4 - 4x + x^2 \Longrightarrow x^2 - 5x = 0 \stackrel{(i)}{\Longrightarrow} x - 5 = 0 \stackrel{(ii)}{\Longleftrightarrow} x = 5$.
   Here implication (i) is incorrect ($x^2 - 5x = 0 \Longrightarrow x - 5 = 0$ or $x = 0$.)
   Implication (ii) is correct, but it breaks the chain of implications.

   (b) $x = 0$. (After correcting implication (i), we see that the given equation implies $x = 5$ or $x = 0$. But only $x = 0$ is a solution; $x = 5$ solves the different equation $x - \sqrt{x + 4} = 2$.)

3.6

1. (a) $x = 8$, $y = 3$ (b) $x = 1/2$, $y = 1/3$ (c) $x = 1.1$, $y = -0.3$

2. (a) $x = 1$, $y = -1$ (b) $x = -4$, $y = 7$ (c) $x = -7/2$, $y = 10/3$

3. (a) $p = 2$, $q = 3$ (b) $r = 2.1$, $s = 0.1$

4. (a) 39 and 13 (b) $120 for a table and $60 for a chair. (c) 450 of quality B and 300 of quality P.
(d) $2000 at 5% and $8000 at 7.2% interest.

Review exercises for Chapter 3

1. (a) $x = 12$ (b) $x = 3$ (c) $x = -3/2$ (d) $x = -19$ (e) $x = 11/7$ (f) $x = 39$

2. (a) $x = 0$ (b) $x = -6$ (c) $x = 5$ (d) $x = -1$

3. (a) $x = \frac{2}{3}(y - 3) + y = \frac{2}{3}y - 2 + y = \frac{5}{3}y - 2$, or $\frac{5}{3}y = x + 2$, so $y = \frac{3}{5}(x + 2)$.
(b) $ax - cx = b + d$, or $(a - c)x = b + d$, so $x = (b + d)/(a - c)$.
(c) $\sqrt{L} = Y_0/AK$, so squaring each side yields $L = (Y_0/AK)^2$. (d) $qy = m - px$, so $y = (m - px)/q$.
(e) Put $s = 1/(1 + r)$. Then $s = (a + bc)/(1 - c)$, so $r = (1/s) - 1 = [(1 - a) - c(1 + b)]/(a + bc)$.
(f) Multiplying by $(Px + Q)^{1/3}$ yields $Px + Px + Q = 0$, and so $x = -Q/2P$.

4. (a) $K = 225L^{2/3}$ (b) $r = 100(2^{1/t} - 1)$ (c) $x_0 = (p/ab)^{1/(b-1)}$ (d) $b = \lambda^{1/\rho}\left(c^{-\rho} - (1 - \lambda)a^{-\rho}\right)^{-1/\rho}$

5. (a) $z = 0$ or $z = 8$ (b) $x = -7$ or $x = 5$ (c) $p = -7$ or $p = 2$ (d) $p = 1/4$ or $p = 1/3$ (e) $y = 4 \pm \sqrt{31}$
(f) $x = -7$ or $x = 6$

6. (a) $x = \pm 2$ or $x = 5$ (b) $x = -4$. ($x^4 + 1$ is never 0.) (c) $\lambda = 1$ or $x = y$

7. If he invested $x at 15% interest and $y at 20%, then $0.15x + 0.20y = 275$. Also, $x + y = 1500$. Solving this system yields $x = 500$, $y = 1000$.

8. (a) From the second and third equations of the model, one has $C = b(Y - tY) = b(1 - t)Y$. Inserting this into the first equation and solving for Y yields $Y = \dfrac{\bar{I} + G}{1 - b(1 - t)}$ and then $C = \dfrac{b(1 - t)(\bar{I} + G)}{1 - b(1 - t)}$.
(b) Note that $0 < b(1 - t) < 1$. When t increases, both Y and $1 - t$ decrease, and so therefore does $C = b(1 - t)Y$.

9. $5^{3x} = 25^{y+2} = 5^{2(y+2)}$ so that $3x = 2(y + 2)$. With $x - 2y = 8$ this gives $x = -2$ and $y = -5$, so $x - y = 3$.

10. (a) Let $u = 1/x$ and $v = 1/y$. Then the system reduces to $2u + 3v = 4$, $3u - 2v = 19$, with solution $u = 5$, $v = -2$, and so $x = 1/u = 1/5$, $y = 1/v = -1/2$.
(b) Let $u = \sqrt{x}$ and $v = \sqrt{y}$. Then $3u + 2v = 2$, $2u - 3v = 1/4$, with solution $u = 1/2$, $v = 1/4$, so $x = 1/4$, $y = 1/16$.
(c) With $u = x^2$ and $v = y^2$, we get $u + v = 13$, $4u - 3v = 24$, with solution $u = 9$, $v = 4$, and so $x = \pm 3$ and $y = \pm 2$.

Chapter 4

4.2

1. (a) $f(0) = 1$, $f(-1) = 2$, $f(1/2) = 5/4$, and $f(\sqrt{2}) = 3$
(b) (i) For all x. (ii) When $x = 1/2$. (iii) When $x = \pm\sqrt{1/2} = \pm\frac{1}{2}\sqrt{2}$.

2. $F(0) = F(-3) = 10$, $F(a + h) - F(a) = 10 - 10 = 0$

3. (a) $f(0) = 0$, $f(a) = a^2$, $f(-a) = a^2 - (-a - a)^2 = -3a^2$, and $f(2a) = 0$
(b) $3f(a) + f(-2a) = 3a^2 + [a^2 - (-2a - a)^2] = 3a^2 + a^2 - 9a^2 = -5a^2$

4. (a) $f(-1/10) = -10/101, f(0) = 0, f(1/\sqrt{2}) = \sqrt{2}/3, f(\sqrt{\pi}) = \sqrt{\pi}/(1+\pi), f(2) = 2/5$
   (b) $f(-x) = -x/(1+(-x)^2) = -x/(1+x^2) = -f(x)$
   and $f(1/x) = (1/x)/[1+(1/x)^2] = (1/x) \cdot x^2/[1+(1/x)^2] \cdot x^2 = x/(1+x^2) = f(x)$.

5. $F(0) = 2$, $F(-3) = \sqrt{19}$, $F(t+1) = \sqrt{t^2+3}$

6. (a) $C(0) = 1000$, $C(100) = 41\,000$, and $C(101) - C(100) = 501$.
   (b) $C(x+1) - C(x) = 2x + 301$ is the incremental cost of increasing production from x to $x+1$.

7. (a) $D(8) = 4$, $D(10) = 3.4$, and $D(10.22) = 3.334$. (b) $P = 10.9$

8. (a) $f(tx) = 100(tx)^2 = 100t^2x^2 = t^2 f(x)$ (b) $P(tx) = (tx)^{1/2} = t^{1/2}x^{1/2} = t^{1/2}P(x)$

9. (a) $b(0) = 0$, $b(50) = 100/11$, $b(100) = 200$
   (b) $b(50+h) - b(50)$ is the additional cost of removing $h\%$ more than 50% of the impurities.

10. (a) No: $f(2+1) = f(3) = 18$, whereas $f(2) + f(1) = 8 + 2 = 10$. (b) Yes: $f(2+1) = f(2) + f(1) = -9$.
    (c) No: $f(2+1) = f(3) = \sqrt{3} \approx 1.73$, whereas $f(2) + f(1) = \sqrt{2} + 1 \approx 2.41$.

11. (a) $f(a+b) = A(a+b) = Aa + Ab = f(a) + f(b)$ (b) $f(a+b) = 10^{a+b} = 10^a \cdot 10^b = f(a) \cdot f(b)$

12. See Figs A4.2.12a and A4.2.12b.

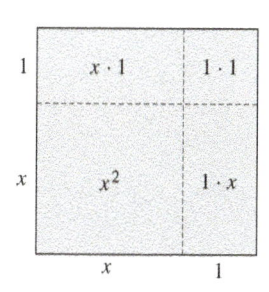

Figure A4.2.12a Area $(x+1)^2 = x^2 + 2x + 1$

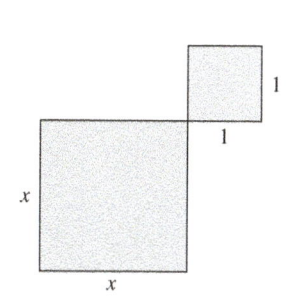

Figure A4.2.12b Area $x^2 + 1$

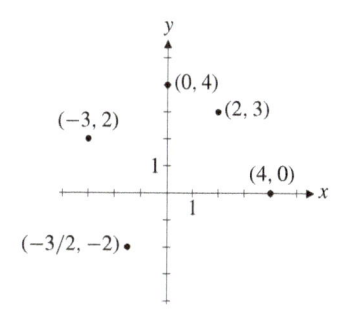

Figure A4.3.1

13. (a) $x \leq 5$ (b) $x \neq 0$ and $x \neq 1$ (c) $-3 < x \leq 1$ or $x > 2$

14. (a) Defined for $x \neq 2$, i.e. $D_f = (-\infty, 2) \cup (2, \infty)$ (b) $f(8) = 5$
    (c) $f(x) = \dfrac{3x+6}{x-2} = 3 \iff 3x + 6 = 3(x-2) \iff 6 = -6$, which is impossible.

15. Since g obviously is defined for $x \geq -2$, $D_g = [-2, \infty)$. Note that $g(-2) = 1$, and $g(x) \leq 1$ for all $x \in D_f$.
    As x increases from -2 to ∞, so $g(x)$ decreases from 1 to $-\infty$, implying that $R_g = (-\infty, 1]$.

4.3

1. See Fig. A4.3.1.

2. (a) $f(-5) = 0$, $f(-3) = -3$, $f(-2) = 0$, $f(0) = 2$, $f(3) = 4$, $f(4) = 0$ (b) $D_f = [-5, 4]$, $R_f = [-3, 4]$

838 SOLUTIONS TO THE EXERCISES

3. (a)

x	0	1	2	3	4
$g(x) = -2x + 5$	5	3	1	-1	-3

See Fig. A4.3.3.

(b)

x	-2	-1	0	1	2	3	4
$h(x) = x^2 - 2x - 3$	5	0	-3	-4	-3	0	5

See Fig. A4.3.4.

(c)

x	-2	-1	0	1	2
$F(x) = 3^x$	$\frac{1}{9}$	$\frac{1}{3}$	1	3	9

See Fig. A4.3.5.

(d)

x	-2	-1	0	1	2	3
$G(x) = 1 - 2^{-x}$	-3	-1	0	1/2	3/4	7/8

See Fig. A4.3.6.

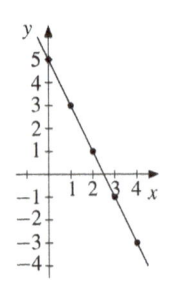

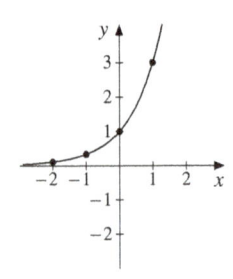

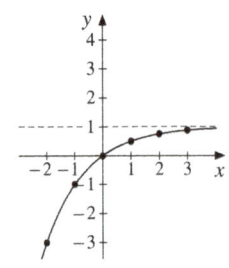

Figure A4.3.3

Figure A4.3.4

Figure A4.3.5

Figure A4.3.6

4.4

1. (a) Slope $= (8 - 3)/(5 - 2) = 5/3$ (b) $-2/3$ (c) $51/5$

2. See Figs A4.4.2a, A4.4.2b, and A4.4.2c.

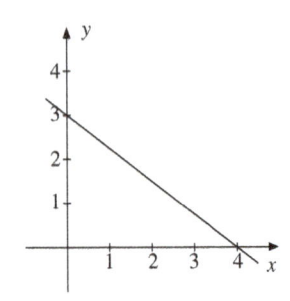

Figure 4.4.2a

Figure 4.4.2b

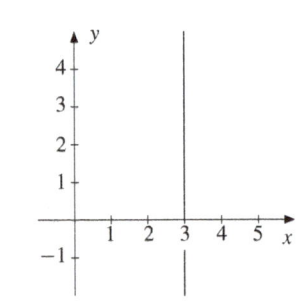

Figure 4.4.2c

3. If $D = a + bP$, then $a + 10b = 200$, and $a + 15b = 150$. Solving for a and b yields $a = 300$ and $b = -10$, so $D = 300 - 10P$.

4. (a), (b), and (d) are all linear; (c) is not, because it is quadratic.

5. If P is the price of Q copies, then $P - 1400 = \dfrac{3000 - 1400}{500 - 100}(Q - 100)$ by the point–point formula, so $P = 1000 + 4Q$.

The price of printing 300 copies is therefore $P = 1000 + 4 \cdot 300 = 2200$.

CHAPTER 4　839

6. ℓ_1: The slope is 1, and the point–slope formula with $(x_1, y_1) = (0, 2)$ and $a = 1$ gives $y = x + 2$.

   ℓ_2: By the point–point formula with $(x_1, y_1) = (0, 3)$ and $(x_2, y_2) = (5, 0)$, we have $y - 3 = \dfrac{0-3}{5-0}x$, or $y = -\tfrac{3}{5}x + 3$.

   ℓ_3 is $y = 1$, with slope 0. ℓ_4 is $y = 3x - 14$, with slope 3. ℓ_5 is $y = \tfrac{1}{9}x + 2$, with slope 1/9.

7. (a) $\ell_1: y - 3 = 2(x - 1)$ or $y = 2x + 1$ (b) $\ell_2: y - 2 = \dfrac{3-2}{3-(-2)}[x - (-2)]$ or $y = x/5 + 12/5$

   (c) $\ell_3: y = -x/2$ (d) $\ell_4: x/a + y/b = 1$, or $y = -bx/a + b$.

8. For (a), shown in Fig. A4.4.8a, the solution is $x = 3$, $y = -2$. For (b), shown in Fig. A4.4.8b, the solution is $x = 2$, $y = 0$. For (c), shown in Fig. A4.4.8c, there are no solutions, because the two lines are parallel.

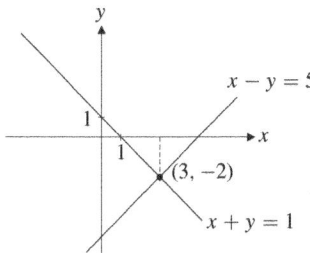

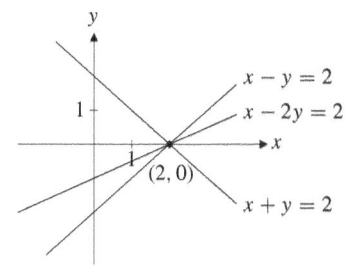

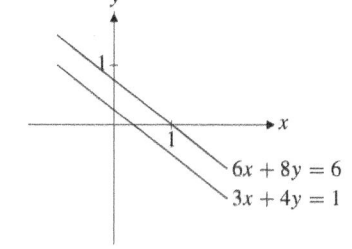

Figure A4.4.8a

Figure A4.4.8b

Figure A4.4.8c

9. (a) See Figs A4.4.9a, A4.4.9b, and A4.4.9c.

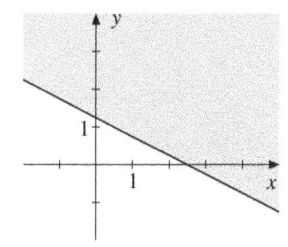

Figure A4.4.9a

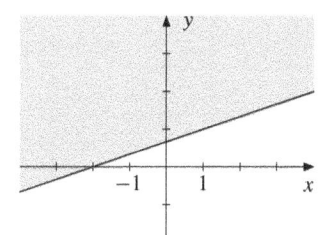

Figure A4.4.9b

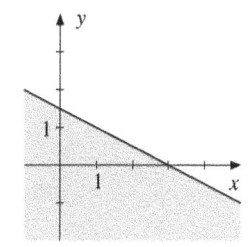

Figure A4.4.9c

10. See Fig. A4.4.10. Each small arrow points toward the side of the line where the relevant inequality is satisfied. The shaded triangle is the required set.

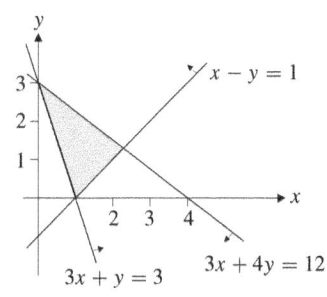

Figure A4.4.10

4.5

1. 0.78

2. (a) $75 - 3P^e = 2P^e$, and hence $P^e = 15$. (b) $P^e = 90$

3. The point–point formula gives $C - 200 = \dfrac{275 - 200}{150 - 100}(x - 100)$, or $C = \frac{3}{2}x + 50$.

4. $C = 0.8y + 100$. (With $C = ay + b$, we are told that $900 = 1000a + b$ and $a = 80/100 = 0.8$, so $b = 100$.)

5. (a) $P(t) = 20\,000 - 2000t$ (b) $W(t) = 500 - 50t$

4.6

1. (a)

x	-1	0	1	2	3	4	5
$f(x) = x^2 - 4x$	5	0	-3	-4	-3	0	5

See Fig. A4.6.1.

(b) Minimum at $x = 2$, with $f(2) = -4$. (c) $x = 0$ and $x = 4$.

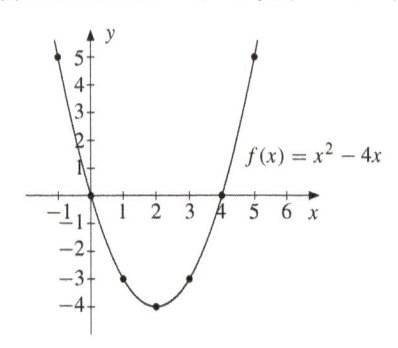

Figure A4.6.1

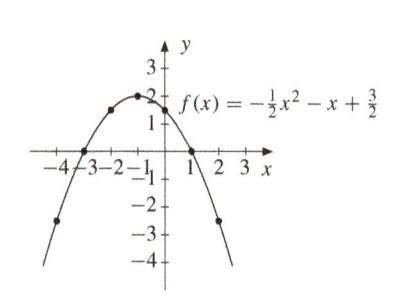

Figure A4.6.2

2. (a)

x	-4	-3	-2	-1	0	1	2
$f(x) = -\frac{1}{2}x^2 - x + \frac{3}{2}$	-2.5	0	1.5	2	1.5	0	-2.5

See Fig. A4.6.2.

(b) Maximum at $x = -1$ with $f(-1) = 2$. (c) $x = -3$ and $x = 1$.

(d) $f(x) > 0$ in $(-3, 1)$, $f(x) < 0$ for $x < -3$ and for $x > 1$.

3. (a) Minimum -4 for $x = -2$. (b) Minimum 9 for $x = -3$. (c) Maximum 45 for $x = 5$.

(d) Minimum -45 for $x = 1/3$. (e) Maximum 40 000 for $x = -100$. (f) Minimum $-22\,500$ for $x = -50$.

4. (a) $x(x + 4)$. Zeros 0 and -4. (b) No factoring is possible. No zeros.

(c) $-3(x - x_1)(x - x_2)$, where the zeros are $x_1 = 5 + \sqrt{15}$ and $x_2 = 5 - \sqrt{15}$.

(d) $9(x - x_1)(x - x_2)$, where the zeros are $x_1 = 1/3 + \sqrt{5}$ and $x_2 = 1/3 - \sqrt{5}$.

(e) $-(x + 300)(x - 100)$. Zeros -300 and 100. (f) $(x + 200)(x - 100)$. Zeros -200 and 100.

5. (a) $x = 2p$ and $x = p$ (b) $x = p$ and $x = q$ (c) $x = \frac{1}{2}p$ and $x = -2q$

6. Expanding gives $U(x) = -(1 + r^2)x^2 + 8(r - 1)x + 40$. By (4.6.4), $U(x)$ has a maximum for $x = 4(r - 1)/(1 + r^2)$.

7. (a) The areas when $x = 100, 250$, and 350 are $100 \cdot 400 = 40\,000$, $250 \cdot 250 = 62\,500$, and $350 \cdot 150 = 52\,500$, respectively. (b) The area is $A = (250 + x)(250 - x) = 62\,500 - x^2$, which obviously has its maximum for $x = 0$. Then the rectangle is a square.

8. (a) $\pi(Q) = (P_E - P_G - \gamma)Q = -\frac{1}{2}Q^2 + (\alpha_1 - \alpha_2 - \gamma)Q$.

(b) Using (4.6.4), we see that $Q^* = \alpha_1 - \alpha_2 - \gamma$ maximizes profit if $\alpha_1 - \alpha_2 - \gamma > 0$. If $\alpha_1 - \alpha_2 - \gamma \le 0$, then $Q^* = 0$.

(c) $\pi(Q) = -\frac{1}{2}Q^2 + (\alpha_1 - \alpha_2 - \gamma - t)Q$ and $Q^* = \alpha_1 - \alpha_2 - \gamma - t$ if $\alpha_1 - \alpha_2 - \gamma - t > 0$.

(d) $T = tQ^* = t(\alpha_1 - \alpha_2 - \gamma - t)$. T is a quadratic function of t; it is 0 when $t = 0$ and when $t = t_1 = \alpha_1 - \alpha_2 - \gamma$, and it is positive for t between 0 and t_1. (e) Export tax revenue is maximized when $t = \frac{1}{2}(\alpha_1 - \alpha_2 - \gamma)$.

9. (a) $361 \le 377$ (b) If $B^2 - 4AC > 0$, then according to formula (2.3.4), the equation $f(x) = Ax^2 + Bx + C = 0$ would have two distinct solutions, contradicting $f(x) \ge 0$ for all x. Hence $B^2 - 4AC \le 0$. (c) (4.6.8) is equivalent to $\frac{1}{4}B^2 \le AC$.

4.7

1. (a) $-2, -1, 1, 3$ (b) $1, -6$ (c) None. (d) $1, 2, -2$

2. (a) 1 and -2 (b) 1, 5, and -5 (c) -1

3. (a) $2x^2 + 2x + 4 + 3/(x-1)$ (b) $x^2 + 1$ (c) $x^3 - 4x^2 + 3x + 1 - 4x/(x^2 + x + 1)$
(d) $3x^5 + 6x^3 - 3x^2 + 12x - 12 + (28x^2 - 36x + 13)/(x^3 - 2x + 1)$

4. (a) $y = \frac{1}{2}(x+1)(x-3)$ (b) $y = -2(x+3)(x-1)(x-2)$ (c) $y = \frac{1}{2}(x+3)(x-2)^2$

5. (a) $x + 4$ (b) $x^2 + x + 1$ (c) $-3x^2 - 12x$

6. $c^4 + 3c^2 + 5 \ge 5 \ne 0$ for every choice of c, so the division has to leave a remainder.

7. Expand the right-hand side. (Note that $R(x) \to a/c$ as $x \to \infty$.)

8. $E = \alpha(x - (\beta + \gamma)) + \dfrac{\alpha\beta(\beta+\gamma)}{x+\beta}$

4.8

1. See Fig. A4.8.1.

2. (a) 1.632 526 9 (b) 36.462 159 6

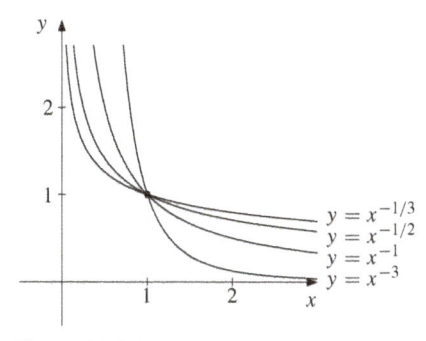

Figure A4.8.1

3. (a) $2^3 = 8$, so $x = 3/2$ (b) $1/81 = 3^{-4}$, so $3x + 1 = -4$, and therefore $x = -5/3$
(c) $x^2 - 2x + 2 = 2$, so $x^2 - 2x = 0$, implying that $x = 0$ or $x = 2$.

842 SOLUTIONS TO THE EXERCISES

4. (a) $3^{5t}9^t = 3^{5t}(3^2)^t = 3^{5t+2t} = 3^{7t}$ and $27 = 3^3$, so $7t = 3$, and then $t = 3/7$.

  (b) $9^t = (3^2)^t = 3^{2t}$ and $(27)^{1/5}/3 = (3^3)^{1/5}/3 = 3^{3/5}/3 = 3^{-2/5}$, and then $2t = -2/5$, so $t = -1/5$.

4.9

1. The amount of savings after t years is $100(1 + 12/100)^t = 100 \cdot (1.12)^t$. We have the following table:

t	1	2	5	10	20	30	50
$100 \cdot (1.12)^t$	112	125.44	176.23	310.58	964.63	2995.99	28 900.21

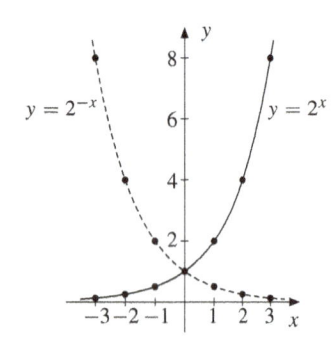

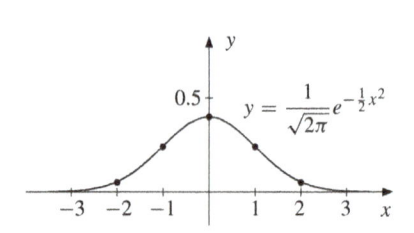

Figure A4.9.2

Figure A4.9.3

2. The graphs are drawn in Fig. A4.9.2. We have the following table:

x	-3	-2	-1	0	1	2	3
2^x	1/8	1/4	1/2	1	2	4	8
2^{-x}	8	4	2	1	1/2	1/4	1/8

3. The graph is drawn in Fig. A4.9.3. Here is a table:

x	-2	-1	0	1	2
$y = \frac{1}{\sqrt{2\pi}}e^{-\frac{1}{2}x^2}$	0.05	0.24	0.40	0.24	0.05

4. (b) and (d) do not define exponential functions. (In (f): $y = (1/2)^x$.)

5. (a) $16(1.19)^5 \approx 38.18$ (b) $4.40(1.19)^{10} \approx 25.06$ (c) $250\,000(1.19)^4 \approx 501\,335$

6. Consider $y = Ab^x$, where $b > 0$. For Graph A, since it passes through the points $(x, y) = (0, 2)$ and $(x, y) = (2, 8)$, we get $2 = Ab^0$, so $A = 2$, and $8 = 2b^2$, so $b = 2$. Hence, $y = 2 \cdot 2^x$.

  For Graph B, we have $\frac{2}{3} = Ab^{-1}$ and $6 = Ab$. It follows that $A = 2$ and $b = 3$, and so $y = 2 \cdot 3^x$.

  For Graph C, we have $4 = Ab^0$ and $1/4 = Ab^4$. It follows that $A = 4$ and $b^4 = 1/16$, so $b = 1/2$. Thus, $y = 4(1/2)^x$.

4.10

1. (a) $\ln 9 = \ln 3^2 = 2\ln 3$ (b) $\frac{1}{2}\ln 3$ (c) $\ln \sqrt[5]{3^2} = \ln 3^{2/5} = \frac{2}{5}\ln 3$ (d) $\ln(1/81) = \ln 3^{-4} = -4\ln 3$

2. (a) $\ln 3^x = x\ln 3 = \ln 8$, so $x = \ln 8/\ln 3$. (b) $x = e^3$ (c) $x^2 - 4x + 5 = 1$ so $(x-2)^2 = 0$. Hence, $x = 2$.
  (d) $x(x-2) = 1$ or $x^2 - 2x - 1 = 0$, so $x = 1 \pm \sqrt{2}$. (e) $x = 0$ or $\ln(x+3) = 0$, so $x = 0$ or $x = -2$.
  (f) $\sqrt{x} - 5 = 1$ so $x = 36$.

3. (a) $x = -\ln 2/\ln 12$ (b) $x = e^{6/7}$ (c) $x = \ln(8/3)/\ln(4/3)$ (d) $x = 4$ (e) $x = e$ (f) $x = 1/27$

4. $t = \dfrac{1}{r-s} \ln \dfrac{B}{A}$

5. The answer to exercise 4 implies that $t \approx 22$, so the date should have been 2012.

6. (a) False. (Let $A = e$.) (b) $2\ln\sqrt{B} = 2\ln B^{1/2} = 2(1/2)\ln B = \ln B$.
   (c) $\ln A^{10} - \ln A^4 = 10\ln A - 4\ln A = 6\ln A = 3 \cdot 2\ln A = 3\ln A^2$. (d) Wrong. (Put $A = B = C = 1$.)
   (e) Correct by rule (2)(b). (f) Correct. (Use (2)(b) twice.)
   (g) Wrong. (If $A = e$ and $p = 2$, then the equality becomes $0 = \ln 2$.) (h) Correct by (2)(c).
   (i) Wrong. (Put $A = 2, B = C = 1$.)

7. (a) $\exp[\ln(x)] - \ln[\exp(x)] = e^{\ln x} - \ln e^x = x - x = 0$ (b) $\ln[x^4 \exp(-x)] = 4\ln x - x$ (c) x^2/y^2

8. The doubling time t^* is determined by $(1.0072)^{t^*} = 2$. Using a calculator, we find $t^* = \ln 2/\ln 1.0072 \approx 96.6$.

9. $P(t) = 1.22 \cdot 1.034^t$. The doubling time t^* is given by the equation $(1.034)^{t^*} = 2$, with solution $t^* \approx 20.7$ (years).

10. We find $(1.035)^t = 3.91 \cdot 10^5/5.1 \approx 76\,666.67$, and using a calculator we find $t \approx 327$. So the year is $1969 + 327 = 2296$. This is when every Zimbabwean would have only 1 m² of land on average.

11. If the initial time is t, the doubling time t^* is given by the equation $Aa^{t+t^*} = 2Aa^t$, which implies $Aa^t a^{t^*} = 2Aa^t$, so $a^{t^*} = 2$, independent of t.

Review exercises for Chapter 4

1. (a) $f(0) = 3, f(-1) = 30, f(1/3) = 2, f(\sqrt[3]{2}) = 3 - 27(2^{1/3})^3 = 3 - 27 \cdot 2 = -51$
   (b) $f(x) + f(-x) = 3 - 27x^3 + 3 - 27(-x)^3 = 3 - 27x^3 + 3 + 27x^3 = 6$

2. (a) $F(0) = 1, F(-2) = 0, F(2) = 2$, and $F(3) = 25/13$
   (b) $F(x) = 1 + \dfrac{4}{x + 4/x}$ tends to 1 as x becomes large positive or negative. (c) See Fig. A4.R.2.

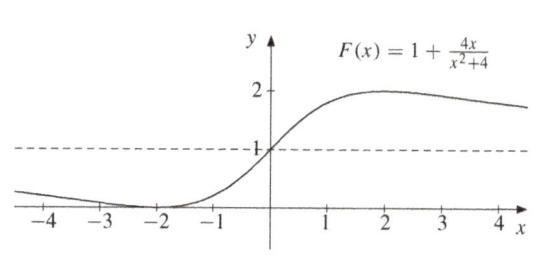

Figure A4.R.2

Figure A4.R.9

3. (i) $f(x) \le g(x)$ when $-2 \le x \le 3$. (ii) $f(x) \le 0$ when $-1 \le x \le 3$. (iii) $g(x) \ge 0$ when $x \le 3$.

4. (a) $x^2 \ge 1$, i.e. $x \ge 1$ or $x \le -1$.
   (b) The square root is defined if $x \ge 4$, but $x = 4$ makes the denominator 0, so we must require $x > 4$.
   (c) We must have $(x - 3)(5 - x) \ge 0$, i.e. $3 \le x \le 5$ (use a sign diagram).

5. (a) $C(0) = 100$, $C(100) = 24\,100$, and $C(101) - C(100) = 24\,542 - 24\,100 = 442$.

(b) $C(x+1) - C(x) = 4x + 42$ is the additional cost of producing one more than x units.

6. (a) Slope -4 (b) Slope $-3/4$ (c) Solving for y gives $y = b[1 - (x/a)] = b - (b/a)x$, so the slope is $-b/a$.

7. (a) The point–slope formula gives $y - 3 = -3(x+2)$, or $y = -3x - 3$.

(b) The point–point formula gives $y - 5 = \dfrac{7-5}{2-(-3)}(x-(-3))$, or $y = 2x/5 + 31/5$.

(c) The point–point formula gives $y - b = \dfrac{3b-b}{2a-a}(x-a)$, or $y = (2b/a)x - b$.

8. $f(2) = 3$ and $f(-1) = -3$ give $2a + b = 3$ and $-a + b = -3$, so $a = 2$, $b = -1$. Hence $f(x) = 2x - 1$ and $f(-3) = -7$. (Or use the point–point formula.)

9.
x	-5	-4	-3	-2	-1	0	1
$y = x^2 e^x$	0.17	0.29	0.45	0.54	0.37	0	2.7

The graph is drawn in Fig. A4.R.9.

10. $(1, -3)$ belongs to the graph if $a + b + c = -3$, $(0, -6)$ belongs to the graph if $c = -6$, and $(3, 15)$ belongs to the graph if $9a + 3b + c = 15$. It follows that $a = 2$, $b = 1$, and $c = -6$.

11. (a) $\pi = (1000 - \frac{1}{3}Q)Q - (800 + \frac{1}{5}Q)Q - 100Q = 100Q - \frac{8}{15}Q^2$. Hence $Q = 1500/16 = 93.75$ maximizes π.

(b) $\hat{\pi} = 100Q - \frac{8}{15}Q^2 - 10Q = 90Q - \frac{8}{15}Q^2$. So $\hat{Q} = 1350/16 = 84.375$ maximizes $\hat{\pi}$.

12. The new profit is $\pi_t = 100Q - \frac{5}{2}Q^2 - tQ$, which is maximized at $Q_t = \frac{1}{5}(100 - t)$.

13. (a) The profit function is $\pi(x) = 100x - 20x - 0.25x^2 = 80x - 0.25x^2$, which has a maximum at $x^* = 160$.

(b) The profit function is $\pi_t(x) = 80x - 0.25x^2 - 10x$, which has a maximum at $x^* = 140$.

(c) The profit function is $\pi_t(x) = (p - \tau - \alpha)x - \beta x^2$, which has a maximum at $x^* = (p - \alpha - \tau)/2\beta$.

14. (a) $p(x) = x(x-3)(x+4)$ (b) $q(x) = 2(x-2)(x+4)(x-1/2)$

15. (a) $x^3 - x - 1$ is not 0 for $x = 1$, so the division leaves a remainder.

(b) $2x^3 - x - 1$ is 0 for $x = 1$, so the division leaves no remainder.

(c) $x^3 - ax^2 + bx - ab$ is 0 for $x = a$, so the division leaves no remainder.

(d) $x^{2n} - 1$ is 0 for $x = -1$, so the division leaves no remainder.

16. We use (4.7.5). (a) $p(2) = 8 - 2k = 0$ for $k = 4$. (b) $p(-2) = 4k^2 + 2k - 6 = 0$ for $k = -3/2$ and $k = 1$.

(c) $p(-2) = -26 + k = 0$ for $k = 26$. (d) $p(1) = k^2 - 3k - 4 = 0$ for $k = -1$ and $k = 4$.

17. $p(x) = \frac{1}{4}(x-2)(x+3)(x-5)$, so the other two roots are $x = -3$ and $x = 5$.

18. $(1 + p/100)^{15} = 2$ gives $p = 100(2^{1/15} - 1) \approx 4.7$ as the percentage rate.

19. (a) Assume $F = aC + b$. Then $32 = a \cdot 0 + b$ and $212 = a \cdot 100 + b$. Therefore $a = 180/100 = 9/5$ and $b = 32$, so $F = 9C/5 + 32$. (b) If $X = 9X/5 + 32$, then $X = -40$.

20. (a) $\ln x = \ln e^{at+b} = at + b$, so $t = (\ln x - b)/a$. (b) $-at = \ln(1/2) = \ln 1 - \ln 2 = -\ln 2$, so $t = (\ln 2)/a$.

(c) $e^{-\frac{1}{2}t^2} = 2^{1/2}\pi^{1/2}2^{-3}$, so $-\frac{1}{2}t^2 = \frac{1}{2}\ln 2 + \frac{1}{2}\ln \pi - 3\ln 2 = -\frac{5}{2}\ln 2 + \frac{1}{2}\ln \pi$, implying that $t^2 = 5\ln 2 - \ln \pi = \ln(32/\pi)$, and finally, $t = \pm\sqrt{\ln(32/\pi)}$.

21. The vertical dashed line is $x = -c$, so $c < 0$. The graph shows that $f(0) = b/c$ is positive, so b is also negative. Because $f(x) = (a + b/x)/(1 + c/x)$ gets closer and closer to a as x becomes very large, the horizontal dashed line is $y = a$, showing that $a > 0$.

CHAPTER 5 845

22. Because $f(x) > 0$ when $|x|$ is large, one has $p > 0$. Because $f(0) < 0$, one has $r < 0$. Because the sum of the two roots of $f(x) = 0$ is evidently positive, one has $q < 0$.

23. (a): C   (b): D   (c): E   (d): B   (e): A   (f): F: the function $y = 2 - (1/2)^x$ is suitable.

24. (a), (b) and (c) are all obviously implied by the Rules for the Natural Logarithmic Function provided that x, y and z are all positive.

    (d) When $x > 0$, note that

    $$\tfrac{1}{2}\ln x - \tfrac{3}{2}\ln(1/x) - \ln(x+1) = \tfrac{1}{2}\ln x + \tfrac{3}{2}\ln x - \ln(x+1) = 2\ln x - \ln(x+1) = \ln x^2 - \ln(x+1)$$
    $$= \ln[x^2/(x+1)]$$

Chapter 5

5.1

1. (a) $y = x^2 + 1$ has the graph of $y = x^2$ shifted up by 1. See Fig. A5.1.1a.

   (b) $y = (x+3)^2$ has the graph of $y = x^2$ moved 3 units to the left. See Fig. Fig: A5.1.1b.

   (c) $y = 3 - (x+1)^2$ has the graph of $y = x^2$ first turned upside down, then with $(0,0)$ shifted to $(-1,3)$. See Fig. A5.1.1c.

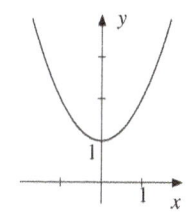

Figure A5.1.1a 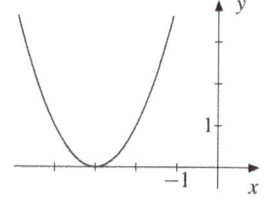   **Figure A5.1.1b** 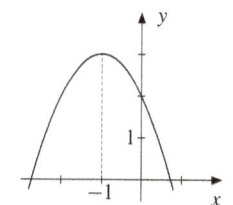   **Figure A5.1.1c**

2. (a) The graph of $y = f(x)$ is moved 2 units to the right. See Fig. A5.1.2a.

   (b) The graph of $y = f(x)$ is moved downwards by 2 units. See Fig. A5.1.2b.

   (c) The graph of $y = f(x)$ is reflected about the y-axis. See Fig. A5.1.2c.

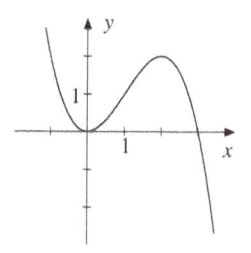

Figure A5.1.2a 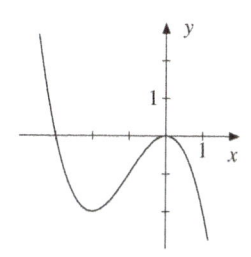   **Figure A5.1.2b** 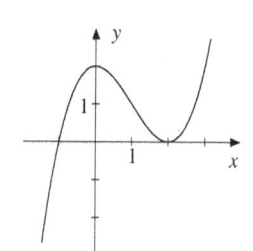   **Figure A5.1.2c**

3. The equilibrium condition is $106 - P = 10 + 2P$, and thus $P = 32$. The corresponding quantity is $Q = 106 - 32 = 74$. See Fig. A5.1.3.

4. Move $y = |x|$ two units to the left. Then reflect the graph about the x-axis, and then move the graph up 2 units. See Fig. A5.1.4.

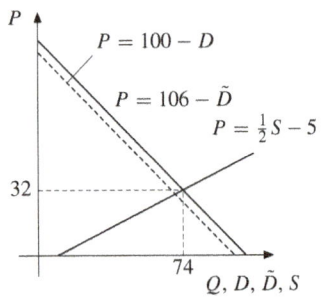

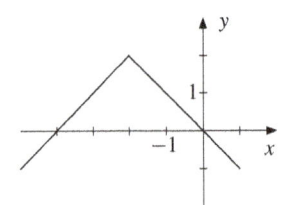

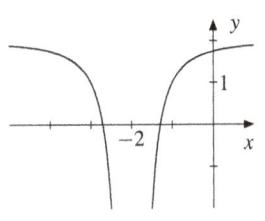

Figure A5.1.3

Figure A5.1.4

Figure A5.1.5

5. Draw the graph of $y = 1/x^2$. Move it two units to the left. Then reflect the graph about the x-axis, and finally move the graph up 2 units to get Fig. A5.1.5.

6. $f(y^* - d) = f(y^*) - c$ gives $A(y^* - d) + B(y^* - d)^2 = Ay^* + B(y^*)^2 - c$, which expands to $Ay^* - Ad + B(y^*)^2 - 2Bdy^* + Bd^2 = Ay^* + B(y^*)^2 - c$. It follows that $y^* = [Bd^2 - Ad + c]/2Bd$.

5.2

1. See Fig. A5.2.1.

2. See Figs A5.2.2a to A5.2.2c.

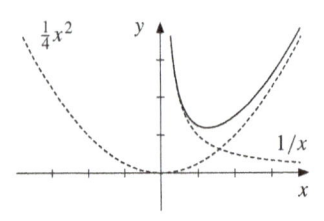

Figure A5.2.1

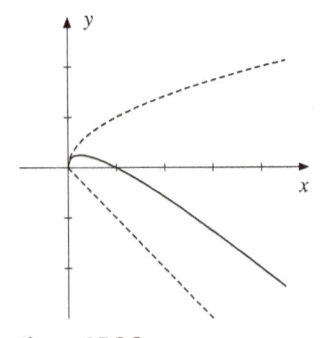

Figure A5.2.2a

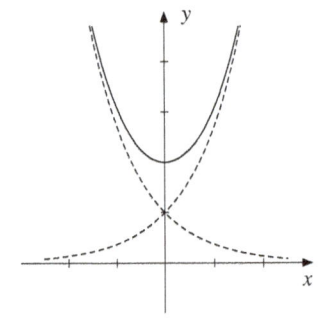

Figure A5.2.2.b

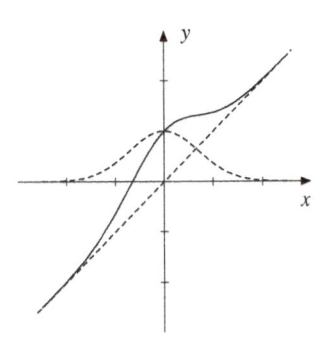

Figure A5.2.2.c

3. $(f+g)(x) = 3x$, $(f-g)(x) = 3x - 2x^3$, $(fg)(x) = 3x^4 - x^6$, $(f/g)(x) = 3/x^2 - 1$, $f(g(1)) = f(1) = 2$, and $g(f(1)) = g(2) = 8$.

4. If $f(x) = 3x + 7$, then $f(f(x)) = f(3x + 7) = 3(3x + 7) + 7 = 9x + 28$. The equality $f(f(x^*)) = 100$ requires $9x^* + 28 = 100$, and so $x^* = 8$.

5. $\ln(\ln e) = \ln 1 = 0$, while $(\ln e)^2 = 1^2 = 1$.

5.3

1. $P = \frac{1}{3}(64 - 10D)$

2. $P = (157.8/D)^{10/3}$

3. (a) Domain and range are both $\mathbb{R}$; inverse is $x = -y/3$. (b) Domain and range are both $\mathbb{R} \setminus \{0\}$; inverse is $x = 1/y$. (c) Domain and range are both $\mathbb{R}$; inverse is $x = y^{1/3}$. (d) Domain is $[4, \infty)$; range is $[0, \infty)$; inverse is $x = (y^2 + 2)^2$.

4. (a) The domain of f^{-1} is $\{-4, -2, 0, 2, 4, 6, 8\}$, and $f^{-1}(2) = -1$. (b) $f(x) = 2x + 4$, with inverse $f^{-1}(x) = \frac{1}{2}x - 2$.

5. $f(x) = x^2$ is not one-to-one over $(-\infty, \infty)$, and therefore has no inverse. Over $[0, \infty)$, the function f is strictly increasing and therefore has the inverse $f^{-1}(x) = \sqrt{x}$.

6. (a) $f(x) = x/2$ and $g(x) = 2x$ are inverse functions. (b) $f(x) = 3x - 2$ and $g(x) = \frac{1}{3}(x + 2)$ are inverse functions. (c) $C = \frac{5}{9}(F - 32)$ and $F = \frac{9}{5}C + 32$ are inverse functions.

7. $f^{-1}(Q)$ determines the cost of Q kilograms of carrots.

8. (a) See Fig. A5.3.8a. (b) See Fig. A5.3.8b. Triangles OBA and OBC are congruent. The point half-way between the two points A and C is $B = (\frac{1}{2}(a + b), \frac{1}{2}(a + b))$.

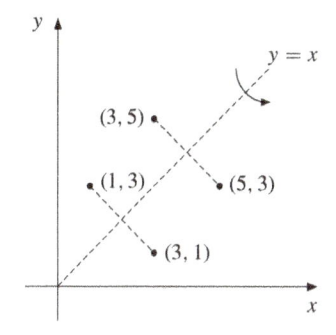

Figure A5.3.8a

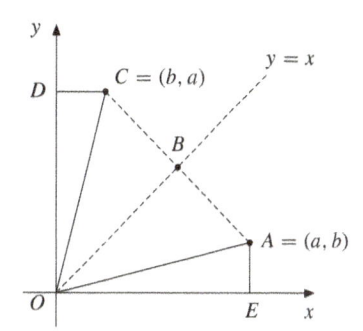

Figure A5.3.8b

9. (a) $f^{-1}(x) = (x^3 + 1)^{1/3}$ (b) $f^{-1}(x) = \dfrac{2x + 1}{x - 1}$ (c) $f^{-1}(x) = \left(1 - (x - 2)^5\right)^{1/3}$

10. (a) $x = \ln y - 4$, defined for $y > 0$. (b) $x = e^{y+4}$, defined for $y \in (-\infty, \infty)$. (c) $x = 3 + \ln(e^y - 2)$, defined for $y > \ln 2$.

11. We must solve $x = \frac{1}{2}(e^y - e^{-y})$ for y. Multiply the equation by e^y to get $\frac{1}{2}e^{2y} - \frac{1}{2} = xe^y$ or $e^{2y} - 2xe^y - 1 = 0$. Letting $e^y = z$ yields $z^2 - 2xz - 1 = 0$, with solution $z = x \pm \sqrt{x^2 + 1}$. Choosing the minus sign would make z negative, contradicting $z = e^y$, so $z = e^y = x + \sqrt{x^2 + 1}$. This gives $y = \ln(x + \sqrt{x^2 + 1})$ as the inverse function.

5.4

1. (a) Some solutions include $(0, \pm\sqrt{3})$, $(\pm\sqrt{6}, 0)$, and $(\pm\sqrt{2}, \pm\sqrt{2})$. See Fig. A5.4.1a.

   (b) Some solutions include $(0, \pm 1)$, $(\pm 1, \pm\sqrt{2})$, and $(\pm 3, \pm\sqrt{10})$. See Fig. A5.4.1b.

2. We see that we must have $x \geq 0$ and $y \geq 0$. If (a, b) lies on the graph, so does (b, a), so the graph is symmetric about the line $y = x$. It also includes the particular points $(25, 0)$, $(0, 25)$, and $(25/4, 25/4)$. An easy way to find points on the graph is the following: Choose nonnegative numbers u and v such that $u + v = 5$, and let $x = u^2$, $y = v^2$. See Fig. A5.4.2.

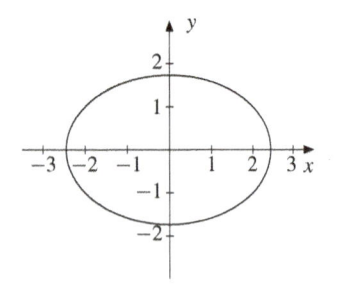

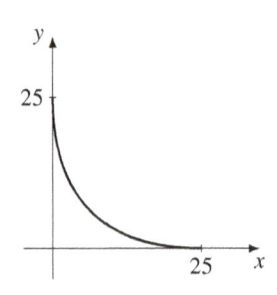

Figure A5.4.1a

Figure A5.4.1b

Figure A5.4.2

3. $F(100\,000) = 4070$. The graph is the thick line sketched in Fig. A5.4.3.

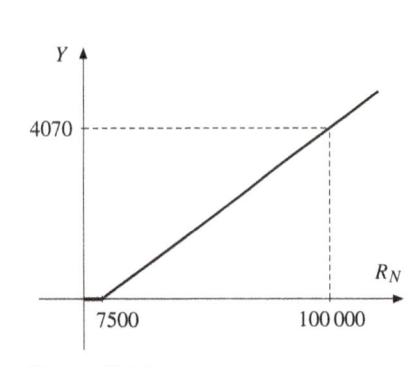

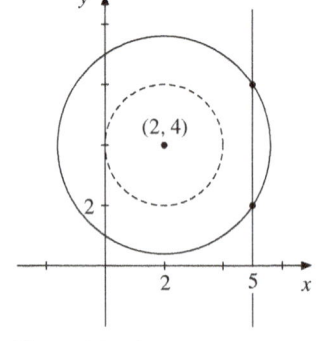

Figure A5.4.3

Figure A5.5.2

5.5

1. (a) $\sqrt{(2-1)^2 + (4-3)^2} = \sqrt{2}$ (b) $\sqrt{5}$ (c) $\frac{1}{2}\sqrt{205}$ (d) $\sqrt{x^2 + 9}$ (e) $2|a|$ (f) $2\sqrt{2}$

2. $(5-2)^2 + (y-4)^2 = 13$, or $y^2 - 8y + 12 = 0$, with solutions $y = 2$ and $y = 6$. A geometric explanation is that the circle with centre at $(2, 4)$ and radius $\sqrt{13}$ intersects the line $x = 5$ at two points. See Fig. A5.5.2.

3. (a) 5.362   (b) $\sqrt{(2\pi)^2 + (2\pi - 1)^2} = \sqrt{8\pi^2 - 4\pi + 1} \approx 8.209$

4. (a) $(x-2)^2 + (y-3)^2 = 16$ (b) Since the circle has centre at $(2, 5)$, its equation is $(x-2)^2 + (y-5)^2 = r^2$. Since $(-1, 3)$ lies on the circle, $(-1-2)^2 + (3-5)^2 = r^2$, so $r^2 = 13$.

5. (a) Completing squares yields $(x+5)^2 + (y-3)^2 = 4$, so the circle has centre at $(-5, 3)$ and radius 2.

   (b) $(x+3)^2 + (y-4)^2 = 12$, which has centre at $(-3, 4)$ and radius $\sqrt{12} = 2\sqrt{3}$.

6. The condition is that $\sqrt{(x+2)^2 + y^2} = 2\sqrt{(x-4)^2 + y^2}$, which reduces to $(x-6)^2 + y^2 = 4^2$.

7. We can write the formula as $cxy - ax + dy - b = 0$. Comparing this with (5), $A = C = 0$ and $B = c$, so $4AC < B^2$ reduces to $0 < c^2$, that is $c \neq 0$, precisely the condition assumed in Example 4.7.7.

8. If $A^2 + B^2 > 4C$, then the graph of the equation is the circle with a centre at $(-\frac{1}{2}A, -\frac{1}{2}B)$ and radius $\sqrt{C - \frac{1}{4}A^2 - \frac{1}{4}B^2}$. If $A^2 + B^2 = 4C$, then the graph is the single point set $\{(-\frac{1}{2}A, -\frac{1}{2}B)\}$. If $A^2 + B^2 < 4C$, it is the empty set.

9. After completing the square when $D = E = 0$, Eq. (5.5.5) is $A\left(x + \dfrac{By}{2A}\right)^2 + \dfrac{1}{4A}(4AC - B^2)y^2 + F = 0$ with $A > 0$.

(i) If $4AC - B^2 > 0$, then the graph is: an ellipse iff $F < 0$ (or a circle in case $4AC - B^2 = 4A^2$); the single point $(-B/2A, 0)$ iff $F = 0$; the empty set iff $F > 0$. (ii) If $4AC - B^2 = 0$, then the graph is: the two parallel lines $x = -By/2A \pm \sqrt{-F/A}$ iff $F < 0$; the single line $x = -By/2A$ iff $F = 0$; the empty set iff $F > 0$. (A parabola cannot occur when $D = E = 0$ in (5.5.5).) (iii) If $4AC - B^2 < 0$, then the graph is: a hyperbola iff $F \neq 0$; the two intersecting lines $x = (-B \pm \sqrt{B^2 - 4AC})y/2A$ iff $F = 0$.

5.6

1. Only (c) does not define a function. (Rectangles with equal areas can have different perimeters.)

2. The function in (b) is one-to-one and has an inverse: the rule mapping each youngest child alive today to his/her mother. (Though the youngest child of a mother with several children will have been different at different dates.)

The function in (d) is one-to-one and has an inverse: the rule mapping the surface area to the volume.

The function in (e) is one-to-one and has an inverse: the rule that maps (u, v) to $(u - 3, v)$.

The function in (a) is many-to-one, in general, and so has no inverse.

Review exercises for Chapter 5

1. The shifts of $y = |x|$ are the same as those of $y = x^2$ in Exercise 5.1.1. See Figs A5.R.1a, A5.R.1b, and A5.R.1c.

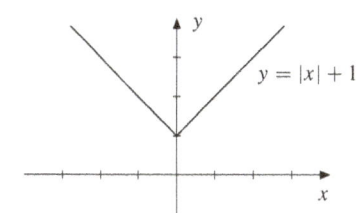

Figure A5.R.1a $y = |x| + 1$

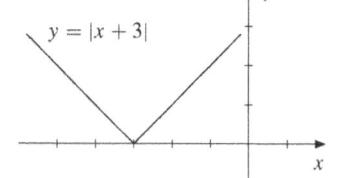

Figure A5.R.1b $y = |x + 3|$

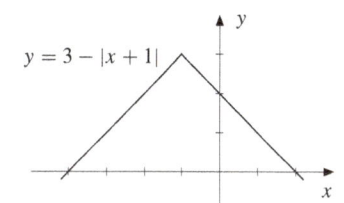

Figure A5.R.1c $y = 3 - |x + 1|$

2. $(f + g)(x) = x^2 - 2$, $(f - g)(x) = 2x^3 - x^2 - 2$, $(fg)(x) = x^2(1 - x)(x^3 - 2)$, $(f/g)(x) = (x^3 - 2)/x^2(1 - x)$, $f(g(1)) = f(0) = -2$, and $g(f(1)) = g(-1) = 2$.

3. (a) The equilibrium condition is $150 - \frac{1}{2}P^* = 20 + 2P^*$, which implies that $P^* = 52$ and $Q^* = 20 + 2P^* = 124$.
   (b) $S = 20 + 2(\widehat{P} - 2) = 16 + 2\widehat{P}$, so $S = D$ when $5\widehat{P}/2 = 134$. Hence $\widehat{P} = 53.6$, $\widehat{Q} = 123.2$.
   (c) Before the tax, $R^* = P^*Q^* = 6448$. After the tax, $\widehat{R} = (\widehat{P} - 2)\widehat{Q} = 51.6 \cdot 123.2 = 6357.12$.

4. $P = (64 - 10D)/3$

5. $P = 24 - \frac{1}{5}D$

6. (a) $x = 50 - \frac{1}{2}y$ (b) $x = \sqrt[5]{y/2}$ (c) $x = \frac{1}{3}[2 + \ln(y/5)]$, defined for $y > 0$

7. (a) $y = \ln(2 + e^{x-3})$, defined for $x \in \mathbb{R}$ (b) $y = -\frac{1}{\lambda}\ln a - \frac{1}{\lambda}\ln\left(\frac{1}{x} - 1\right)$, defined for $x \in (0, 1)$

8. (a) $\sqrt{13}$ (b) $\sqrt{17}$ (c) $\sqrt{(2-3a)^2} = |2-3a|$. (Note that $2 - 3a$ is the correct answer only if $2 - 3a \geq 0$, i.e. $a \leq 2/3$. Check this by putting $a = 3$.)

9. $(x - 2)^2 + (y + 3)^2 = 25$ (b) $(x + 2)^2 + (y - 2)^2 = 65$

10. $(x - 3)^2 + (y - 2)^2 = (x - 5)^2 + (y + 4)^2$, which reduces to $x - 3y = 7$. See Fig. A5.R.10.

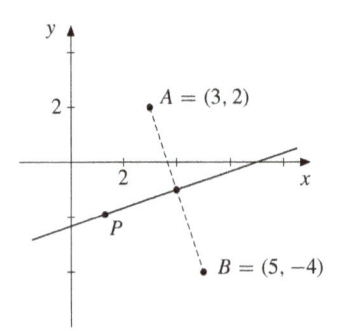

Figure A5.R.10

11. The function cannot be one-to-one, because at least two persons out of any five must have the same blood group.

Chapter 6

6.1

1. $f(3) = 2$. The tangent passes through $(0, 3)$, so has slope $-1/3$. Thus, $f'(3) = -1/3$.

2. $g(5) = 1, g'(5) = 1$.

6.2

1. $f(5 + h) - f(5) = 4(5 + h)^2 - 4 \cdot 5^2 = 4(25 + 10h + h^2) - 100 = 40h + 4h^2$. So $[f(5+h) - f(5)]/h = 40 + 4h \to 40$ as $h \to 0$. Hence, $f'(5) = 40$. This accords with (6) when $a = 4$ and $b = c = 0$.

2. (a) $f'(x) = 6x + 2$ (b) $f'(0) = 2, f'(-2) = -10, f'(3) = 20$. The tangent equation is $y = 2x - 1$.

3. $dD(P)/dP = -b$

4. $C'(x) = 2qx$

5. $\dfrac{f(x+h) - f(x)}{h} = \dfrac{1/(x+h) - 1/x}{h} = \dfrac{x - (x+h)}{hx(x+h)} = \dfrac{-h}{hx(x+h)} = -\dfrac{1}{x(x+h)} \xrightarrow[h \to 0]{} -\dfrac{1}{x^2}$

6. (a) $f'(0) = 3$ (b) $f'(1) = 2$ (c) $f'(3) = -1/3$ (d) $f'(0) = -2$ (e) $f'(-1) = 0$ (f) $f'(1) = 4$

7. (a) $f(x+h) - f(x) = a(x+h)^2 + b(x+h) + c - (ax^2 + bx + c) = 2ahx + bh + ah^2$, so $[f(x+h) - f(x)]/h = 2ax + b + ah \to 2ax + b$ as $h \to 0$. Thus $f'(x) = 2ax + b$.

   (b) $f'(x) = 0$ for $x = -b/2a$. The tangent is parallel to the x-axis at the minimum/maximum point.

8. $f'(a) < 0$, $f'(b) = 0$, $f'(c) > 0$, $f'(d) < 0$

9. (a) Expand the left-hand side.   (b) Rearrange the identity in (a).
(c) Letting $h \to 0$, the formula follows. (Recall that $\sqrt{x} = x^{1/2}$ and $1/\sqrt{x} = x^{-1/2}$.)

10. (a) $f'(x) = 3ax^2 + 2bx + c$.   (b) Put $a = 1$ and $b = c = d = 0$ to get the result in Example 6.2.2. Then put $a = 0$ to get a quadratic expression as in Exercise 7(a).

11. $\dfrac{(x+h)^{1/3} - x^{1/3}}{h} = \dfrac{1}{(x+h)^{2/3} + (x+h)^{1/3}x^{1/3} + x^{2/3}} \to \dfrac{1}{3x^{2/3}}$ as $h \to 0$, and $\dfrac{1}{3x^{2/3}} = \dfrac{1}{3}x^{-2/3}$.

6.3

1. $f'(x) = 2x - 4$, so $f(x)$ is decreasing in $(-\infty, 2]$, increasing in $[2, \infty)$.

2. $f'(x) = -3x^2 + 8x - 1 = -3(x - x_0)(x - x_1)$, where $x_0 = \frac{1}{3}(4 - \sqrt{13}) \approx 0.13$ and $x_1 = \frac{1}{3}(4 + \sqrt{13}) \approx 2.54$.
Then $f(x)$ is decreasing in $(-\infty, x_0]$, increasing in $[x_0, x_1]$, and decreasing in $[x_1, \infty)$.

3. The expression in the bracket is a sum of two squares, so it is never negative and it is 0 only if both $x_1 + \frac{1}{2}x_2$ and x_2 are equal to 0. This happens only when $x_1 = x_2 = 0$. Thus the bracket is always positive if $x_1 \neq x_2$, and then $x_2^3 - x_1^3$ will have the same sign as $x_2 - x_1$. It follows that f is strictly increasing.

6.4

1. $C'(100) = 203$ and $C'(x) = 2x + 3$.

2. Here c is the marginal cost, and also the (constant) incremental cost of producing each additional unit, whereas $\bar{C}$ is the fixed cost.

3. (a) $S'(Y) = s$ (b) $S'(Y) = 0.1 + 0.0004Y$

4. $T'(y) = t$, so the marginal tax rate is constant.

5. The interpretation of $x'(0) = -3$ is that at time $t = 0$, the rate of extraction is 3 barrels per minute.

6. (a) $C'(x) = 3x^2 - 180x + 7500$ (b) By (4.6.3), the quadratic function $C'(x)$ has a minimum at $x = 180/6 = 30$.

7. (a) $\pi'(Q) = 24 - 2Q$, and $Q^* = 12$.   (b) $R'(Q) = 500 - Q^2$ (c) $C'(Q) = -3Q^2 + 428.4Q - 7900$

8. (a) $C'(x) = 2a_1 x + b_1$ (b) $C'(x) = 3a_1 x^2$

6.5

1. (a) 3   (b) $-1/2$ (c) $13^3 = 2197$ (d) 40   (e) 1   (f) $-3/4$

2. (a) 0.6931   (b) 1.0986   (c) 0.4055 (Actually, using the result in Example 7.12.2, the precise values of these three limits are $\ln 2$, $\ln 3$, and $\ln(3/2)$, respectively.)

3. (a) We have the following table (where $*$ denotes undefined):

x	0.9	0.99	0.999	1	1.001	1.01	1.1
$\dfrac{x^2 + 7x - 8}{x - 1}$	8.9	8.99	8.999	*	9.001	9.01	9.1

(b) $x^2 + 7x - 8 = (x - 1)(x + 8)$, so $(x^2 + 7x - 8)/(x - 1) = x + 8 \to 9$ as $x \to 1$.

4. (a) 5   (b) 1/5   (c) 1   (d) -2 (e) $3x^2$ (f) h^2

5. (a) $1/6$ (b) $-\infty$ (the limit does not exist). (c) 2 (d) $\sqrt{3}/6$ (e) $-2/3$ (f) $1/4$

6. (a) 4 (b) 5 (c) 6 (d) $2a + 2$ (e) $2a + 2$ (f) $4a + 4$

7. (a) $x^3 - 8 = (x - 2)(x^2 + 2x + 4)$, so the limit is $1/6$. (b) $\lim_{h \to 0}[\sqrt[3]{27 + h} - 3]/h = \lim_{u \to 3}(u - 3)/(u^3 - 27)$, and $u^3 - 27 = (u - 3)(u^2 + 3u + 9)$, so the limit is $\lim_{u \to 3} 1/(u^2 + 3u + 9) = 1/27$.
(c) $x^n - 1 = (x - 1)(x^{n-1} + x^{n-2} + \cdots + x + 1)$, so the limit is n.

6.6

1. (a) 0 (b) $4x^3$ (c) $90x^9$ (d) 0 (Remember that π is a constant!)

2. (a) $2g'(x)$ (b) $-\frac{1}{6}g'(x)$ (c) $\frac{1}{3}g'(x)$

3. (a) $6x^5$ (b) $33x^{10}$ (c) $50x^{49}$ (d) $28x^{-8}$ (e) x^{11} (f) $4x^{-3}$ (g) $-x^{-4/3}$ (h) $3x^{-5/2}$

4. (a) $8\pi r$ (b) $A(b+1)y^b$ (c) $(-5/2)A^{-7/2}$

5. In (6.2.1) (the definition of the derivative), choose $h = x - a$ so that $a + h$ is replaced by x, and $h \to 0$ implies $x \to a$. For $f(x) = x^2$ we get $f'(a) = 2a$.

6. (a) $F(x) = \frac{1}{3}x^3 + C$ (b) $F(x) = x^2 + 3x + C$ (c) $F(x) = x^{a+1}/(a+1) + C$. (In all cases C is an arbitrary constant.)

7. (a) With $f(x) = x^2$ and $a = 5$, one has $\lim_{h \to 0} \dfrac{(5+h)^2 - 5^2}{h} = \lim_{h \to 0} \dfrac{f(a+h) - f(a)}{h} = f'(a) = f'(5)$.
On the other hand, $f'(x) = 2x$, so $f'(5) = 10$, and the limit is 10.
(b) Let $f(x) = x^5$. Then $f'(x) = 5x^4$, and the limit is equal to $f'(1) = 5 \cdot 1^4 = 5$.
(c) Let $f(x) = 5x^2 + 10$. Then $f'(x) = 10x$, and this is the value of the limit.

6.7

1. (a) 1 (b) $1 + 2x$ (c) $15x^4 + 8x^3$ (d) $32x^3 + x^{-1/2}$ (e) $\frac{1}{2} - 3x + 15x^2$ (f) $-21x^6$

2. (a) $\frac{6}{5}x - 14x^6 - \frac{1}{2}x^{-1/2}$ (b) $4x(3x^4 - x^2 - 1)$ (c) $10x^9 + 5x^4 + 4x^3 - x^{-2}$. (In (b) and (c), first expand and then differentiate.)

3. (a) $-6x^{-7}$ (b) $\frac{3}{2}x^{1/2} - \frac{1}{2}x^{-3/2}$ (c) $-\frac{3}{2}x^{-5/2}$ (d) $-2/(x-1)^2$ (e) $-4x^{-5} - 5x^{-6}$ (f) $34/(2x+8)^2$
(g) $-33x^{-12}$ (h) $(-3x^2 + 2x + 4)/(x^2 + x + 1)^2$

4. (a) $\dfrac{3}{2\sqrt{x}(\sqrt{x}+1)^2}$ (b) $\dfrac{4x}{(x^2+1)^2}$ (c) $\dfrac{-2x^2+2}{(x^2-x+1)^2}$

5. (a) $f'(L^*) < f(L^*)/L^*$. See Fig. A6.7.5. The tangent at P has the slope $f'(L^*)$. We "see" that the tangent at P is less steep than the straight line from the origin to P, which has the slope $f(L^*)/L^* = g(L^*)$. (The inequality follows directly from the characterization of differentiable concave functions in Eq. (8.4.3).)
(b) $\dfrac{d}{dL}\left(\dfrac{f(L)}{L}\right) = \dfrac{1}{L}\left[f'(L) - \dfrac{f(L)}{L}\right]$, as in Example 6.7.7.

6. (a) $[2, \infty)$ (b) $[-\sqrt{3}, 0]$ and $[\sqrt{3}, \infty)$ (c) $[-\sqrt{2}, \sqrt{2}]$ (d) $(-\infty, \frac{1}{2}(-1 - \sqrt{5})]$ and $[0, \frac{1}{2}(-1 + \sqrt{5})]$.

7. (a) $y = -3x + 4$ (b) $y = x - 1$ (c) $y = (17x - 19)/4$ (d) $y = -(x - 3)/9$

8. $\dot{R}(t) = \dot{p}(t)x(t) + p(t)\dot{x}(t)$. Here, $R(t)$ increases for two reasons. First, $R(t)$ increases because of the price increase. This increase is proportional to the amount of extraction $x(t)$ and is equal to $\dot{p}(t)x(t)$. But $R(t)$ also rises because

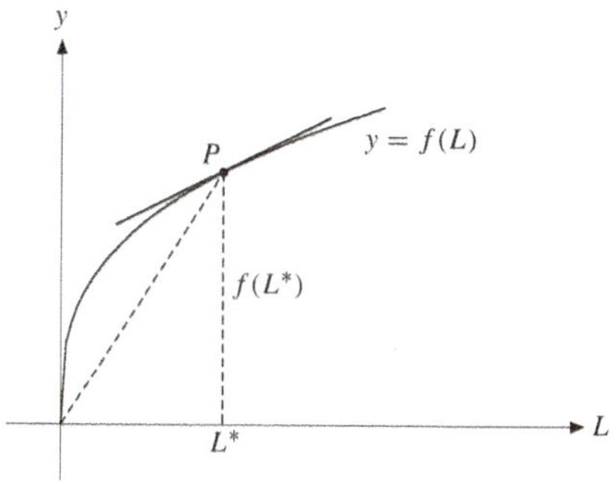

Figure A6.7.5

extraction increases. Its contribution to the rate of change of $R(t)$ must be proportional to the price, and is equal to $p(t)\dot{x}(t)$. In the end $\dot{R}(t)$, the total rate of change of $R(t)$, is the sum of these two parts.

9. (a) $(ad-bc)/(ct+d)^2$ (b) $a(n+\tfrac{1}{2})t^{n-1/2}+nbt^{n-1}$ (c) $-(2at+b)/(at^2+bt+c)^2$

10. The product rule yields $f'(x)\cdot f(x)+f(x)\cdot f'(x)=1$, so $2f'(x)\cdot f(x)=1$. Hence, $f'(x)=1/2f(x)=1/2\sqrt{x}$.

11. If $f(x)=1/x^n$, the quotient rule yields $f'(x)=(0\cdot x^n-1\cdot nx^{n-1})/(x^n)^2=-nx^{-n-1}$, which is the power rule.

6.8

1. (a) $dy/dx=(dy/du)(du/dx)=20u^{4-1}\,du/dx=20(1+x^2)^3 2x=40x(1+x^2)^3$
   (b) $dy/dx=(1-6u^5)\,(du/dx)=(-1/x^2)(1-6(1+1/x)^5)$

2. (a) $dY/dt=(dY/dV)(dV/dt)=(-3)5(V+1)^4 t^2=-15t^2(t^3/3+1)^4$
   (b) $dK/dt=(dK/dL)(dL/dt)=AaL^{a-1}b=Aab(bt+c)^{a-1}$

3. (a) $y'=-5(x^2+x+1)^{-6}(2x+1)$ (b) $y'=\tfrac{1}{2}\bigl[x+(x+x^{1/2})^{1/2}\bigr]^{-1/2}\bigl(1+\tfrac{1}{2}(x+x^{1/2})^{-1/2}(1+\tfrac{1}{2}x^{-1/2})\bigr)$
   (c) $y'=ax^{a-1}(px+q)^b+x^a bp(px+q)^{b-1}=x^{a-1}(px+q)^{b-1}[(a+b)px+aq]$

4. $(dY/dt)_{t=t_0}=(dY/dK)_{t=t_0}\cdot(dK/dt)_{t=t_0}=Y'(K(t_0))K'(t_0)$

5. $dY/dt=F'\bigl(h(t)\bigr)\cdot h'(t)$

6. $x=b-\sqrt{ap-c}=b-\sqrt{u}$, with $u=ap-c$. Then $\dfrac{dx}{dp}=-\dfrac{1}{2\sqrt{u}}u'=-\dfrac{a}{2\sqrt{ap-c}}$.

7. (i) $h'(x)=f'(x^2)2x$ (ii) $h'(x)=f'(x^n g(x))(nx^{n-1}g(x)+x^n g'(x))$

8. $b(t)$ is the total fuel consumption after t hours. Then $b'(t)=B'(s(t))s'(t)$, so the rate of fuel consumption per hour is equal to the rate per kilometre multiplied by the speed in kph.

9. $dC/dx=q(25-\tfrac{1}{2}x)^{-1/2}$

10. (a) $y'=5(x^4)^4\cdot 4x^3=20x^{19}$ (b) $y'=3(1-x)^2(-1)=-3+6x-3x^2$

11. (a) (i) $g(5)$ is the amount accumulated if the interest rate is 5% per year, which is approximately €1629.
    (ii) $g'(5)$ is the increase in this value per unit increase in the interest rate, which is approximately €155.
    (b) $g(p)=1000(1+p/100)^{10}$, so $g(5)=1000\cdot 1.05^{10}=1\,628.89$ to the nearest eurocent.
    Moreover, $g'(p)=1000\cdot 10(1+p/100)^9\cdot 1/100$, so $g'(5)=100\cdot 1.05^9=155.13$ to the nearest eurocent.

854 SOLUTIONS TO THE EXERCISES

12. (a) $1+f'(x)$ (b) $2f(x)f'(x)-1$ (c) $4[f(x)]^3 f'(x)$ (d) $2xf(x)+x^2 f'(x)+3[f(x)]^2 f'(x)$ (e) $f(x)+xf'(x)$
    (f) $f'(x)/[2\sqrt{f(x)}]$ (g) $[2xf(x)-x^2 f'(x)]/[f(x)]^2$ (h) $[2xf(x)f'(x)-3(f(x))^2]/x^4$

13. (a) Provided that $x \neq 0$ and $0 < |h| < |x|$, one has $\dfrac{1}{h}[\varphi(x+h)-\varphi(x)] = \dfrac{1}{h}\left(\dfrac{1}{x+h}-\dfrac{1}{x}\right) = \dfrac{-h}{h(x+h)x} = \dfrac{-1}{(x+h)x}$, which tends to $-1/x^2$ as $h \to 0$. In particular, $\varphi(x) = 1/x$ is differentiable if $x \neq 0$.
    (b) For any x with $g(x) \neq 0$, if f and g are differentiable at x, then:
    (i) combining (a) with the chain rule implies that $1/g(x) = \varphi(g(x))$ is differentiable at x;
    (ii) the product rule implies that $f(x)/g(x) = f(x) \cdot [1/g(x)]$ is differentiable at x.

6.9

1. (a) $y'' = 20x^3 - 36x^2$ (b) $y'' = (-1/4)x^{-3/2}$
   (c) $y' = 20x(1+x^2)^9$, and then $y'' = 20(1+x^2)^9 + 20x \cdot 9 \cdot 2x(1+x^2)^8 = 20(1+x^2)^8(1+19x^2)$

2. $d^2 y/dx^2 = (1+x^2)^{-1/2} - x^2(1+x^2)^{-3/2} = (1+x^2)^{-3/2}$

3. (a) $y'' = 18x$ (b) $Y''' = 36$ (c) $d^3 z/dt^3 = -2$ (d) $f^{(4)}(1) = 84\,000$

4. $g'(t) = \dfrac{2t(t-1)-t^2}{(t-1)^2} = \dfrac{t^2-2t}{(t-1)^2}$, and $g''(t) = \dfrac{2}{(t-1)^3}$, so $g''(2) = 2$.

5. With simplified notation: $y' = f'g + fg'$, $y'' = f''g + f'g' + f'g' + fg'' = f''g + 2f'g' + fg''$,
   and $y''' = f'''g + f''g' + 2f''g' + 2f'g'' + f'g'' + fg''' = f'''g + 3f''g' + 3f'g'' + fg'''$.

6. $L = (2t-1)^{-1/2}$, so $dL/dt = -\tfrac{1}{2} \cdot 2(2t-1)^{-3/2} = -(2t-1)^{-3/2}$, and $d^2 L/dt^2 = 3(2t-1)^{-5/2}$.

7. (a) $R = 0$ (b) $R = 1/2$ (c) $R = 3$ (d) $R = \rho$

8. Because $g(u)$ is not concave.

9. The Secretary of Defense: $P' < 0$. Representative Gray: $P' \geq 0$ and $P'' < 0$.

10. $d^3 L/dt^3 > 0$

6.10

1. (a) $y' = e^x + 2x$ (b) $y' = 5e^x - 9x^2$ (c) $y' = (1 \cdot e^x - xe^x)/e^{2x} = (1-x)e^{-x}$
   (d) $y' = [(1+2x)(e^x+1) - (x+x^2)e^x]/(e^x+1)^2 = [1+2x+e^x(1+x-x^2)]/(e^x+1)^2$
   (e) $y' = -1 - e^x$ (f) $y' = x^2 e^x(3+x)$ (g) $y' = e^x(x-2)/x^3$ (h) $y' = 2(x+e^x)(1+e^x)$

2. (a) $dx/dt = (b+2ct)e^t + (a+bt+ct^2)e^t = (a+b+(b+2c)t+ct^2)e^t$
   (b) $\dfrac{dx}{dt} = \dfrac{3qt^2 te^t - (p+qt^3)(1+t)e^t}{t^2 e^{2t}} = \dfrac{-qt^4 + 2qt^3 - pt - p}{t^2 e^t}$
   (c) $\dfrac{dx}{dt} = [2(at+bt^2)(a+2bt)e^t - (at+bt^2)^2 e^t]/(e^t)^2 = [t(a+bt)(-bt^2 + (4b-a)t + 2a)]e^{-t}$

3. (a) $y' = -3e^{-3x}$ and $y'' = 9e^{-3x}$ (b) $y' = 6x^2 e^{x^3}$ and $y'' = 6xe^{x^3}(3x^3+2)$
   (c) $y' = -x^{-2}e^{1/x}$ and $y'' = x^{-4}e^{1/x}(2x+1)$ (d) $y' = 5(4x-3)e^{2x^2-3x+1}$ and $y'' = 5e^{2x^2-3x+1}(16x^2 - 24x + 13)$

4. (a) $(-\infty, \infty)$ (b) $[0, 1/2]$ (c) $(-\infty, -1]$ and $[0, 1]$

5. (a) $y' = 2xe^{-2x}(1-x)$, so y is increasing in $[0, 1]$. (b) $y' = e^x(1 - 3e^{2x})$, so y is increasing in $(-\infty, -\frac{1}{2}\ln 3]$.
   (c) $y' = (2x+3)e^{2x}/(x+2)^2$, so y is increasing in $[-3/2, \infty)$.

6. (a) $e^{e^x}e^x = e^{e^x + x}$ (b) $\frac{1}{2}(e^{t/2} - e^{-t/2})$ (c) $-\dfrac{e^t - e^{-t}}{(e^t + e^{-t})^2}$ (d) $z^2 e^{z^3}(e^{z^3} - 1)^{-2/3}$

7. (a) $y' = 5^x \ln 5$ (b) $y' = 2^x + x2^x \ln 2 = 2^x(1 + x\ln 2)$ (c) $y' = 2x 2^{x^2}(1 + x^2 \ln 2)$
   (d) $y' = e^x 10^x + e^x 10^x \ln 10 = e^x 10^x (1 + \ln 10)$

6.11

1. (a) $y' = 1/x + 3$ and $y'' = -1/x^2$ (b) $y' = 2x - 2/x$ and $y'' = 2 + 2/x^2$
   (c) $y' = 3x^2 \ln x + x^2$ and $y'' = x(6\ln x + 5)$ (d) $y' = (1 - \ln x)/x^2$ and $y'' = (2\ln x - 3)/x^3$

2. (a) $x^2 \ln x (3 \ln x + 2)$ (b) $x(2 \ln x - 1)/(\ln x)^2$ (c) $10(\ln x)^9/x$ (d) $2\ln x/x + 6\ln x + 18x + 6$

3. (a) $1/(x \ln x)$ (b) $-x/(1-x^2)$ (c) $e^x (\ln x + 1/x)$ (d) $e^{x^3}(3x^2 \ln x^2 + 2/x)$ (e) $e^x/(e^x + 1)$
   (f) $(2x+3)/(x^2 + 3x - 1)$ (g) $-2e^x(e^x - 1)^{-2}$ (h) $(4x - 1)e^{2x^2 - x}$

4. (a) $x > -1$ (b) $1/3 < x < 1$ (c) $x \neq 0$

5. (a) $|x| > 1$ (b) $x > 1$ (c) $x \neq e^e$ and $x > 1$

6. (a) y is defined only in $(-2, 2)$, where $y' = -8x/(4 - x^2) > 0$ iff $x < 0$. Thus, y is increasing in $(-2, 0]$.
   (b) y is defined for $x > 0$, where $y' = x^2(3 \ln x + 1) > 0$ iff $\ln x > -1/3$. Thus, y is increasing in $[e^{-1/3}, \infty)$.
   (c) y is defined for $x > 0$, where $y' = (1 - \ln x)(\ln x - 3)/2x^2 > 0$ iff $1 < \ln x < 3$. Thus, y is increasing in $[e, e^3]$.

7. (a) (i) $y = x - 1$ (ii) $y = 2x - 1 - \ln 2$ (iii) $y = x/e$ (b) (i) $y = x$ (ii) $y = 2ex - e$ (iii) $y = -e^{-2}x - 4e^{-2}$

8. (a) $f'(x)/f(x) = 2\ln x + 2$ (b) $f'(x)/f(x) = 1/(2x - 4) + 2x/(x^2 + 1) + 4x^3/(x^4 + 6)$
   (c) $f'(x)/f(x) = -2/[3(x^2 - 1)]$

9. (a) $(2x)^x (1 + \ln 2 + \ln x)$ (b) $x^{\sqrt{x} - \frac{1}{2}} \left(\frac{1}{2}\ln x + 1\right)$ (c) $\frac{1}{2}(\sqrt{x})^x (\ln x + 1)$

10. $\ln y = v \ln u$, so $y'/y = v' \ln u + vu'/u$ and therefore $y' = u^v (v' \ln u + vu'/u)$.
    (Alternatively, note that $y = (e^{\ln u})^v = e^{v \ln u}$, and then use the chain rule.)

11. (a) Let $f(x) = e^x - (1 + x + \frac{1}{2}x^2)$. Then $f(0) = 0$ and $f'(x) = e^x - (1 + x) > 0$ for all $x > 0$, as shown in the exercise. Hence $f(x) > 0$ for all $x > 0$, and the inequality follows.
    (b) Consider the two functions $f_1(x) = \ln(1 + x) - \frac{1}{2}x$ and $f_2(x) = x - \ln(1 + x)$. For more details, see SM.
    (c) Consider the function $g(x) = 2(\sqrt{x} - 1) - \ln x$. For more details, see SM.

Review exercises for Chapter 6

1. $[f(x+h) - f(x)]/h = [(x+h)^2 - (x+h) + 2 - x^2 + x - 2]/h = [2xh + h^2 - h]/h = 2x + h - 1$.
   Therefore $[f(x+h) - f(x)]/h \to 2x - 1$ as $h \to 0$, so $f'(x) = 2x - 1$.

2. $[f(x+h) - f(x)]/h = -6x^2 + 2x - 6xh - 2h^2 + h \to -6x^2 + 2x$ as $h \to 0$, so $f'(x) = -6x^2 + 2x$.

3. (a) $y' = 2$, $y'' = 0$ (b) $y' = 3x^8$, $y'' = 24x^7$ (c) $y' = -x^9$, $y'' = -9x^8$ (d) $y' = 21x^6$, $y'' = 126x^5$
   (e) $y' = 1/10$, $y'' = 0$ (f) $y' = 5x^4 + 5x^{-6}$, $y'' = 20x^3 - 30x^{-7}$ (g) $y' = x^3 + x^2$, $y'' = 3x^2 + 2x$
   (h) $y' = -x^{-2} - 3x^{-4}$, $y'' = 2x^{-3} + 12x^{-5}$

4. Because $C'(1000) \approx C(1001) - C(1000)$, if $C'(1000) = 25$, the additional cost of producing slightly more than 1000 units is approximately 25 per unit. If the price per unit is fixed at 30, the extra profit from increasing output slightly above 1000 units is approximately $30 - 25 = 5$ per unit.

5. (a) $y = -3$ and $y' = -6x = -6$ at $x = 1$, so $y - (-3) = (-6)(x - 1)$, or $y = -6x + 3$.
   (b) $y = -14$ and $y' = 1/2\sqrt{x} - 2x = -31/4$ at $x = 4$, so $y = -(31/4)x + 17$.
   (c) $y = 0$ and $y' = (-2x^3 - 8x^2 + 6x)/(x + 3)^2 = -1/4$ at $x = 1$, so $y = (-1/4)(x - 1)$.

6. The additional cost of increasing the area by a small amount from 100 m² is approximately \$250 per m².

7. (a) $f(x) = x^3 + x$, so $f'(x) = 3x^2 + 1$. (b) $g'(w) = -5w^{-6}$ (c) $h(y) = y(y^2 - 1) = y^3 - y$, so $h'(y) = 3y^2 - 1$.
   (d) $G'(t) = (-2t^2 - 2t + 6)/(t^2 + 3)^2$ (e) $\varphi'(\xi) = (4 - 2\xi^2)/(\xi^2 + 2)^2$ (f) $F'(s) = -(s^2 + 2)/(s^2 + s - 2)^2$

8. (a) $2at$ (b) $a^2 - 2t$ (c) $2x\varphi - 1/2\sqrt{\varphi}$

9. (a) $y' = 20uu' = 20(5 - x^2)(-2x) = 40x^3 - 200x$ (b) $y' = \dfrac{1}{2\sqrt{u}} \cdot u' = \dfrac{-1}{2x^2\sqrt{1/x - 1}}$

10. (a) $dZ/dt = (dZ/du)(du/dt) = 3(u^2 - 1)^2 2u 3t^2 = 18t^5(t^6 - 1)^2$
    (b) $dK/dt = (dK/dL)(dL/dt) = (1/[2\sqrt{L}])(-1/t^2) = -1/[2t^2\sqrt{1 + 1/t}]$

11. (a) $\dot{x}/x = 2\dot{a}/a + \dot{b}/b$ (b) $\dot{x}/x = \alpha\dot{a}/a + \beta\dot{b}/b$ (c) $\dot{x}/x = (\alpha + \beta)(\alpha a^{\alpha-1}\dot{a} + \beta b^{\beta-1}\dot{b})/(a^\alpha + b^\beta)$

12. $dR/dt = (dR/dS)(dS/dK)(dK/dt) = \alpha S^{\alpha-1}\beta\gamma K^{\gamma-1}Apt^{p-1} = A\alpha\beta\gamma pt^{p-1}S^{\alpha-1}K^{\gamma-1}$

13. (a) $h'(L) = apL^{a-1}(L^a + b)^{p-1}$ (b) $C'(Q) = a + 2bQ$ (c) $P'(x) = ax^{1/q-1}(ax^{1/q} + b)^{q-1}$

14. (a) $y' = -7e^x$ (b) $y' = -6xe^{-3x^2}$ (c) $y' = xe^{-x}(2 - x)$ (d) $y' = e^x[\ln(x^2 + 2) + 2x/(x^2 + 2)]$
    (e) $y' = 15x^2 e^{5x^3}$ (f) $y' = x^3 e^{-x}(x - 4)$ (g) $y' = 10(e^x + 2x)(e^x + x^2)^9$ (h) $y' = 1/2\sqrt{x}(\sqrt{x} + 1)$

15. (a) $[1, \infty)$ (b) $[0, \infty)$ (c) $(-\infty, 1]$ and $[2, \infty)$

16. (a) $\dfrac{d\pi}{dQ} = P(Q) + QP'(Q) - c$ (b) $\dfrac{d\pi}{dL} = PF'(L) - w$

Chapter 7

7.1

1. Differentiating w.r.t. x yields $6x + 2y' = 0$, so $y' = -3x$. Solving the given equation for y yields $y = 5/2 - 3x^2/2$, implying that $y' = -3x$.

2. Implicit differentiation yields (∗) $2xy + x^2(dy/dx) = 0$, and so $dy/dx = -2y/x$. Differentiating (∗) implicitly w.r.t. x gives $2y + 2x(dy/dx) + 2x(dy/dx) + x^2(d^2y/dx^2) = 0$. Inserting the result for dy/dx, and simplifying yields $d^2y/dx^2 = 6y/x^2$. These results follows more easily by differentiating $y = x^{-2}$ twice.

3. (a) $y' = (1 + 3y)/(1 - 3x) = -5/(1 - 3x)^2$ and $y'' = 6y'/(1 - 3x) = -30/(1 - 3x)^3$.
   (b) $y' = 6x^5/5y^4 = (6/5)x^{1/5}$ and $y'' = 6x^4 y^{-4} - (144/25)x^{10}y^{-9} = (6/25)x^{-4/5}$.

4. $2u + v + u(dv/du) - 3v^2(dv/du) = 0$, so $dv/du = (2u+v)/(3v^2-u)$. Hence $dv/du = 0$ when $v = -2u$ (provided $3v^2 - u \neq 0$). Substituting for v in the original equation yields $8u^3 - u^2 = 0$. So the only point on the curve where $dv/du = 0$ and $u \neq 0$ is $(u, v) = (1/8, -1/4)$.

5. Differentiating w.r.t. x yields (∗) $4x + 6y + 6xy' + 2yy' = 0$, so $y' = -(2x+3y)/(3x+y) = -8/5$ at $(1, 2)$. Differentiating (∗) w.r.t. x yields $4 + 6y' + 6y' + 6xy'' + 2(y')^2 + 2yy'' = 0$. Substituting $x = 1$, $y = 2$, and $y' = -8/5$ yields $y'' = 126/125$.

6. (a) $2x + 2yy' = 0$, and solve for y' to get $y' = -x/y$. (b) $1/2\sqrt{x} + y'/2\sqrt{y} = 0$, and solve for y' to get $y' = -\sqrt{y/x}$. (c) $4x^3 - 4y^3 y' = 2xy^3 + x^2 3y^2 y'$, and solve for y' to get $y' = 2x(2x^2 - y^3)/y^2(3x^2 + 4y)$. (d) $e^{xy}(y + xy') - 2xy - x^2 y' = 0$, and solve for y' to get $y' = y(2x - e^{xy})/x(e^{xy} - x)$.

7. (a) Differentiating the equation w.r.t. x yields (∗) $2y + 2xy' - 6yy' = 0$. Inserting $x = 6$ and $y = 1$ into (∗) yields $2 + 12y' - 6y' = 0$, so $y' = -1/3$. (b) Differentiating (∗) w.r.t. x yields (∗∗) $2y' + 2y' + 2xy'' - 6y'y' - 6yy'' = 0$. Inserting $x = 6$, $y = 1$, and $y' = -1/3$ into (∗∗) gives $y'' = 1/3$.

8. (a) $y' = \dfrac{g'(x) - y}{x - 3y^2}$ (b) $y' = \dfrac{2x - g'(x+y)}{g'(x+y) - 2y}$ (c) $y' = \dfrac{2y[xg'(x^2 y) - xy - 1]}{x[2xy + 2 - xg'(x^2 y)]}$

9. Differentiating w.r.t. x yields $3x^2 F(xy) + x^3 F'(xy)(y + xy') + e^{xy}(y + xy') = 1$. Putting $x = 1$ and $y = 0$ in this equation yields $3F(0) + F'(0)y' + y' = 1$. Because $F(0) = 0$, this implies that $y' = 1/[F'(0) + 1]$. (Note that F is a function of only one variable, with argument xy.)

10. (a) $y' = \dfrac{x[a^2 - 2(x^2 + y^2)]}{y[2(x^2+y^2) + a^2]}$ (b) $(\pm\tfrac{1}{4}a\sqrt{6}, \pm\tfrac{1}{4}a\sqrt{2})$, with four possible sign combinations.

7.2

1. Implicit differentiation w.r.t. P, recognizing that Q is a function of P, yields $(dQ/dP) \cdot P^{1/2} + Q \cdot \tfrac{1}{2}P^{-1/2} = 0$. Thus $dQ/dP = -\tfrac{1}{2}QP^{-1} = -19/P^{3/2}$.

2. (a) $1 = C''(Q^*)(dQ^*/dP)$, so $dQ^*/dP = 1/C''(Q^*)$ (b) $dQ^*/dP > 0$, which is reasonable because if the price received by the producer increases, the optimal production should increase.

3. Taking the natural logarithm on both sides yields $\ln A - \alpha \ln P - \beta \ln r = \ln S$. Differentiating with respect to r we have $-(\alpha/P)(dP/dr) - \beta/r = 0$. It follows that $dP/dr = -(\beta/\alpha)(P/r) < 0$. So a rise in the interest rate depresses demand, and the equilibrium price falls to compensate.

4. (a) $Y = f(Y) + I + \bar{X} - g(Y)$ (b) $dY/dI = 1/\bigl[1 - f'(Y) + g'(Y)\bigr] > 0$ because $f'(Y) < 1$ and $g'(Y) > 0$. (c) $d^2 Y/dI^2 = (f'' - g'')/(1 - f' + g')^3$

5. Differentiating (7.2.6) w.r.t. τ yields $f''(P + \tau)\left(\dfrac{dP}{d\tau} + 1\right)^2 + f'(P+\tau)\dfrac{d^2 P}{d\tau^2} = g''(P)\left(\dfrac{dP}{d\tau}\right)^2 + g'(P)\dfrac{d^2 P}{d\tau^2}$.

With simplified notation, this equation becomes $f''(P'+1)^2 + f'P'' = g''(P')^2 + g'P''$. Substituting $P' = f'/(g'-f')$ and then solving for P'', we get $P'' = [f''(g')^2 - g''(f')^2]/(g'-f')^3$.

6. (a) Differentiating (∗) w.r.t. τ yields $f'(P)(dP/d\tau) = g'((1-\tau)P)[-P + (1-\tau)(dP/d\tau)]$, and so

$$\frac{dP}{d\tau} = \frac{-Pg'((1-\tau)P)}{f'(P) - (1-\tau)g'((1-\tau)P)}$$

(b) Both the numerator and denominator are negative, so $dP/d\tau$ is positive. Increasing the tax on producers increases the equilibrium price.

7.3

1. $f(1) = 1$ and $f'(x) = 2e^{2x-2} = 2$ for $x = 1$. So according to (7.3.2), $g'(1) = 1/f'(1) = 1/2$.
The inverse function is $g(x) = 1 + \frac{1}{2}\ln x$, so $g'(x) = 1/2x = 1/2$ for $x = 1$.

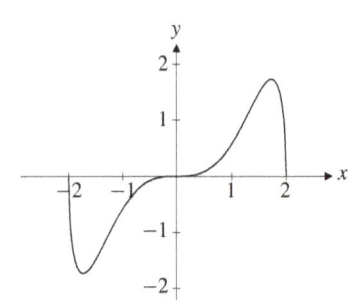

Figure A7.3.2

2. (a) $f'(x) = x^2\sqrt{4-x^2} + \frac{1}{3}x^3 \frac{-2x}{2\sqrt{4-x^2}} = \frac{4x^2(3-x^2)}{3\sqrt{4-x^2}}$. So f increases in $[-\sqrt{3}, \sqrt{3}]$, and decreases in $[-2, -\sqrt{3}]$ and in $[\sqrt{3}, 2]$. See Fig. A7.3.2.
(b) f has an inverse in the interval $[0, \sqrt{3}]$ because f is strictly increasing there. $g'(\frac{1}{3}\sqrt{3}) = 1/f'(1) = 3\sqrt{3}/8$.

3. (a) $f'(x) = e^{x-3}/(e^{x-3} + 2) > 0$ for all x, so f is strictly increasing. Also $f(x) \to \ln 2$ as $x \to -\infty$ and $f(x) \to \infty$ as $x \to \infty$, so the range of f is $(\ln 2, \infty)$. (b) $g(x) = 3 + \ln(e^x - 2)$, defined on $(\ln 2, \infty)$ (c) $f'(3) = 1/g'(f(3)) = 1/3$

4. $dD/dP = -0.3 \cdot 157.8 P^{-1.3} = -47.34 P^{-1.3}$, so $dP/dD = 1/(dD/dP) \approx -0.021 P^{1.3}$.

5. (a) $dx/dy = -e^{x+5} = -1/y$ (b) $dx/dy = -1 - 3e^x$ (c) $dx/dy = x(3y^2 - x^2)/(2 + 3x^2y - y^3)$

7.4

1. If $f(x) = \sqrt{1+x}$, then $f'(x) = 1/(2\sqrt{1+x})$, so $f(0) = 1$ and $f'(0) = 1/2$. By (7.4.1), $\sqrt{1+x} \approx 1 + \frac{1}{2}(x-0) = 1 + \frac{1}{2}x$. See Fig. A7.4.1.

2. Here $f(0) = 1/9$ and $f'(x) = -10(5x+3)^{-3}$, so $f'(0) = -10/27$. Hence $(5x+3)^{-2} \approx 1/9 - 10x/27$.

3. (a) $(1+x)^{-1} \approx 1 - x$ (b) $(1+x)^5 \approx 1 + 5x$ (c) $(1-x)^{1/4} \approx 1 - \frac{1}{4}x$

4. $F(1) = A$ and $F'(K) = \alpha A K^{\alpha-1}$, so $F'(1) = \alpha A$.
Then $F(K) \approx F(1) + F'(1)(K-1) = A + \alpha A(K-1) = A(1 + \alpha(K-1))$.

5. (a) $30x^2\,dx$ (b) $15x^2\,dx - 10x\,dx + 5\,dx$ (c) $-3x^{-4}\,dx$ (d) $(1/x)\,dx$ (e) $(px^{p-1} + qx^{q-1})\,dx$ (f) $(p+q)x^{p+q-1}\,dx$
(g) $rp(px+q)^{r-1}\,dx$ (h) $(pe^{px} + qe^{qx})dx$

6. (a) If $f(x) = (1+x)^m$, then $f(0) = 1$ and $f'(0) = m$, so $1 + mx$ is the linear approximation to $f(x)$ about $x = 0$.
(b) (i) $\sqrt[3]{1.1} = (1 + 1/10)^{1/3} \approx 1 + (1/3)(1/10) \approx 1.033$ (ii) $\sqrt[5]{33} = 2(1 + 1/32)^{1/5} \approx 2(1 + 1/160) = 2.0125$
(iii) $\sqrt[3]{9} = 2(1 + 1/8)^{1/3} \approx 2(1 + 1/24) \approx 2.083$ (iv) $(0.98)^{25} = (1 - 0.02)^{25} = (1 - 1/50)^{25} \approx 1 - 1/2 = 1/2$

7. (a) (i) $\Delta y = 0.61$, $dy = 0.6$ (ii) $\Delta y = 0.0601$, $dy = 0.06$
(b) (i) $\Delta y = 0.011\,494$, $dy = 0.011\,111$ (ii) $\Delta y = 0.001\,115$, $dy = 0.001\,111$
(c) (i) $\Delta y = 0.012\,461$, $dy = 0.0125$ (ii) $\Delta y = 0.002\,498$, $dy = 0.0025$

8. (a) $y' = -3/2$ (b) $y(x) \approx -\frac{3}{2}x + \frac{3}{2}$

9. (a) $A(r + dr) - A(r)$ is the shaded area in Fig. A7.4.9. It is approximately the circumference of the inner circle $2\pi r$ times dr. (b) $V(r + dr) - V(r)$ is the volume of the shell between the sphere with radius $r + dr$ and the sphere with radius r. It is approximately the surface area $4\pi r^2$ of the inner sphere times the thickness dr of the shell.

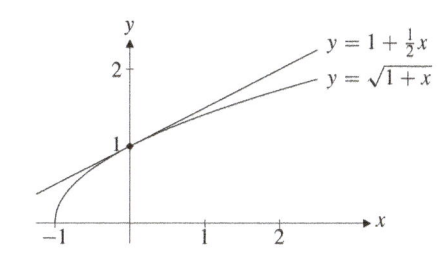

Figure A7.4.1

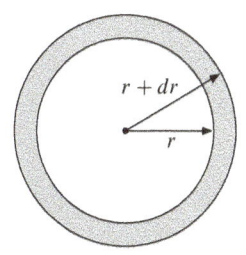

Figure A7.4.9

10. Taking logarithms, we get $\ln K_t = \ln K + t\ln(1 + p/100) \approx \ln K + tp/100$. If $K_t = 2K$, then $\ln K_t = \ln 2 + \ln K$, and with t^* as the doubling time, p must satisfy $\ln 2 \approx t^* p/100$, so $p \approx 100 \ln 2/t^*$. (Using the approximation $\ln 2 \approx 0.7$, this result accords with the "Rule of 70" in Example 7.4.3.) The exact percentage p^* satisfies $\ln 2 = t^* \ln(1 + p^*/100)$, or $p^* = 100\left(2^{1/t^*} - 1\right)$.

11. $g(0) = A - 1$ and $g'(\mu) = \left(Aa/(1+b)\right)(1+\mu)^{[a/(1+b)]-1}$, so $g'(0) = Aa/(1+b)$.
Hence, $g(\mu) \approx g(0) + g'(0)\mu = A - 1 + aA\mu/(1+b)$.

12. Because the derivative exists, $\lim_{h \to 0} \frac{1}{h}[f(a+h) - f(a)] = f'(a)$. But evidently $\lim_{h \to 0} \frac{1}{h}[f'(a)h] = f'(a)$. So, by the rules for limits in Section 6.5, we have $\lim_{h \to 0} \frac{1}{h}[f(a+h) - (f(a) + f'(a)h)] = f'(a) - f'(a) = 0$.

7.5

1. (a) Here $f'(x) = 5(1+x)^4$ and $f''(x) = 20(1+x)^3$. Hence $f(0) = 1, f'(0) = 5$, and $f''(0) = 20$, implying the quadratic approximation $f(x) = (1+x)^5 \approx 1 + 5x + \frac{1}{2}20x^2 = 1 + 5x + 10x^2$.
(b) $AK^\alpha \approx A + \alpha A(K-1) + \frac{1}{2}\alpha(\alpha-1)A(K-1)^2$ (c) $(1 + \frac{3}{2}\varepsilon + \frac{1}{2}\varepsilon^2)^{1/2} \approx 1 + \frac{3}{4}\varepsilon - \frac{1}{32}\varepsilon^2$
(d) Here $H'(x) = (-1)(1-x)^{-2}(-1) = (1-x)^{-2} = 1$ at $x = 0$, and $H''(x) = 2(1-x)^{-3} = 2$ at $x = 0$. It follows that $(1-x)^{-1} \approx 1 + x + x^2$.

2. $x - \frac{1}{2}x^2 + \frac{1}{3}x^3 - \frac{1}{4}x^4 + \frac{1}{5}x^5$

3. $-5 + \frac{5}{2}x - \frac{15}{8}x^2$

4. Use (7.5.2) with $f = U$, $a = y$, and $x = y + M - s$.

5. Implicit differentiation yields (∗) $3x^2y + x^3y' + 1 = \frac{1}{2}y^{-1/2}y'$. Inserting $x = 0$ and $y = 1$ gives $1 = (\frac{1}{2})1^{-1/2}y'$, so $y' = 2$. Differentiating (∗) once more w.r.t. x yields $6xy + 3x^2y' + 3x^2y' + x^3y'' = -\frac{1}{4}y^{-3/2}(y')^2 + \frac{1}{2}y^{-1/2}y''$. Inserting $x = 0, y = 1$, and $y' = 2$ gives $y'' = 2$. Hence, $y(x) \approx 1 + 2x + x^2$.

6. We find $\dot{x}(0) = 2[x(0)]^2 = 2$. Differentiating the expression for $\dot{x}(t)$ yields $\ddot{x}(t) = x(t) + t\dot{x}(t) + 4[x(t)]\dot{x}(t)$, and so $\ddot{x}(0) = x(0) + 4[x(0)]\dot{x}(0) = 1 + 4 \cdot 1 \cdot 2 = 9$. Hence, $x(t) \approx x(0) + \dot{x}(0)t + \frac{1}{2}\ddot{x}(0)t^2 = 1 + 2t + \frac{9}{2}t^2$.

7. Use (7.6.5) with $x = \sigma\sqrt{t/n}$, keeping only three terms on the right-hand side.

8. Use (7.6.2) with $f(x) = (1+x)^n$ and $x = p/100$. Then $f'(x) = n(1+x)^{n-1}$ and $f''(x) = n(n-1)(1+x)^{n-2}$. The approximation follows.

9. $h'(x) = \dfrac{(px^{p-1} - qx^{q-1})(x^p + x^q) - (x^p - x^q)(px^{p-1} + qx^{q-1})}{(x^p + x^q)^2} = \dfrac{2(p-q)x^{p+q-1}}{(x^p + x^q)^2}$, so $h'(1) = \tfrac{1}{2}(p-q)$. This gives the approximation $h(x) \approx h(1) + h'(1)(x-1) = \tfrac{1}{2}(p-q)(x-1)$ because $h(1) = 0$.

7.6

1. Using the answer to Exercise 7.5.2, one has $f(0) = 0$, $f'(0) = 1$, $f''(0) = -1$, and $f'''(z) = 2(1+z)^{-3}$. Then (7.6.3) gives
$$f(x) = f(0) + \frac{1}{1!}f'(0)x + \frac{1}{2!}f''(0)x + \frac{1}{3!}f'''(z)x^3 = x - \frac{1}{2}x^2 + \frac{1}{3}(1+z)^{-3}x^3$$

2. (a) $\sqrt[3]{25} = 3(1 - 2/27)^{1/3} \approx 3\left(1 - \dfrac{1}{3}\dfrac{2}{27} - \dfrac{1}{9}\dfrac{4}{27^2}\right) \approx 2.924$

   (b) $\sqrt[5]{33} = 2(1 + 1/32)^{1/5} \approx 2\left(1 + \dfrac{1}{5 \cdot 32} - \dfrac{2}{25}\dfrac{1}{32^2}\right) \approx 2.0125$

3. $(1 + 1/8)^{1/3} = 1 + 1/24 - 1/576 + R_3(1/8)$, where $0 < R_3(1/8) < 5/(81 \cdot 8^3)$. Thus, $\sqrt[3]{9} = 2(1 + 1/8)^{1/3} \approx 2.080$, correct to three decimal places.

4. (a) $1 + \tfrac{1}{3}x - \tfrac{1}{9}x^2$ (b) $g'''(z) = \dfrac{10}{27}(1+z)^{-8/3}$, so (7.6.2) implies that $R_3(x) = \dfrac{1}{6}\dfrac{10}{27}(1+z)^{-8/3}x^3$ for some $z \in (0, x)$. Hence $|R_3(x)| \leq \dfrac{5}{81}x^3$. For more details, see SM.

   (c) First note that $\sqrt[3]{1003} = 10(1 + 3 \cdot 10^{-3})^{1/3}$. Using the approximation in part (a) gives $(1 + 3 \cdot 10^{-3})^{1/3} \approx 1.000\,999$, and so $\sqrt[3]{1003} \approx 10.009\,99$. By part (b), the error in this approximation is $10R_3(3 \cdot 10^{-3})$, whose absolute value satisfies $10|R_3(3 \cdot 10^{-3})| \leq \dfrac{50}{81} \cdot 27 \cdot 10^{-9} = \dfrac{50}{3}10^{-9} < 2 \cdot 10^{-8}$, implying that the answer is correct to 7 decimal places. For more details, see SM.

7.7

1. In each case we use the elasticity formula (7.7.3):
   (a) -3 (b) 100 (c) $1/2$, since $\sqrt{x} = x^{1/2}$. (d) $-3/2$, since $A/x\sqrt{x} = Ax^{-3/2}$.

2. $\text{El}_K T = 1.06$. A 1% increase in expenditure on road building leads to an increase in the traffic volume of approximately 1.06 %.

3. (a) A 10% increase in fares leads to a decrease in passenger demand of approximately 4%.

   (b) One reason could be that for long-distance travel, more people fly when rail fares go up. Another reason could be that many people may commute 60 km daily, whereas almost nobody commutes 300 km daily, and commuters' demand is likely to be less elastic.

4. (a) $\text{El}_x e^{ax} = (x/e^{ax})ae^{ax} = ax$ (b) $\text{El}_x \ln x = (x/\ln x)(1/x) = 1/\ln x$

   (c) $\text{El}_x(x^p e^{ax}) = \dfrac{x}{x^p e^{ax}}(px^{p-1}e^{ax} + x^p a e^{ax}) = p + ax$ (d) $\text{El}_x(x^p \ln x) = \dfrac{x}{x^p \ln x}\left(px^{p-1}\ln x + \dfrac{x^p}{x}\right) = p + \dfrac{1}{\ln x}$

5. $\text{El}_x(f(x))^p = \dfrac{x}{(f(x))^p}p(f(x))^{p-1}f'(x) = p\dfrac{x}{f(x)}f'(x) = p\,\text{El}_x f(x)$

6. Using (7.7.3) gives $\text{El}_r D = 1.23$. A 1% increase in income leads to an increase in demand of approximately 1.23%.

7. $\ln m = -0.02 + 0.19 \ln N$. When $N = 480\,000$, then $m \approx 11.77$.

CHAPTER 7 861

8. (a) $\text{El}_x (Af(x)) = \dfrac{x}{Af(x)} Af'(x) = \dfrac{x}{f(x)} f'(x) = \text{El}_x f(x)$

   (b) $\text{El}_x (A + f(x)) = \dfrac{x}{A + f(x)} f'(x) = \dfrac{f(x) x f'(x)/f(x)}{A + f(x)} = \dfrac{f(x) \text{El}_x f(x)}{A + f(x)}$

9. Here we prove only (d): $\text{El}_x (f + g) = \dfrac{x(f' + g')}{f + g} = \dfrac{f(xf'/f) + g(xg'/g)}{f + g} = \dfrac{f \text{El}_x f + g \text{El}_x g}{f + g}$.

   For proofs of the other parts, see SM.

10. (a) -5 (b) $\dfrac{1 + 2x}{1 + x}$ (c) $\dfrac{30x^3}{x^3 + 1}$ (d) $\text{El}_x 5x^2 = 2$, so $\text{El}_x (\text{El}_x 5x^2) = 0$ (e) $\dfrac{2x^2}{1 + x^2}$

    (f) $\text{El}_x \left(\dfrac{x - 1}{x^5 + 1} \right) = \text{El}_x (x - 1) - \text{El}_x (x^5 + 1) = \dfrac{x \text{El}_x x}{x - 1} - \dfrac{x^5 \text{El}_x x^5}{x^5 + 1} = \dfrac{x}{x - 1} - \dfrac{5x^5}{x^5 + 1}$

7.8

1. Only the function in (a) is not continuous.

2. f is discontinuous at $x = 0$. g is continuous at $x = 2$. The graphs of f and g are shown in Figs A7.8.2a and A7.8.2b.

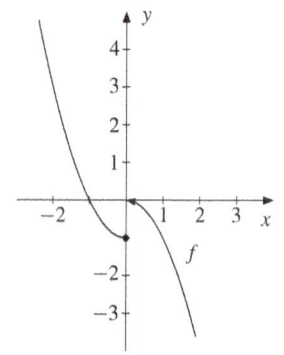

   Figure A7.8.2a

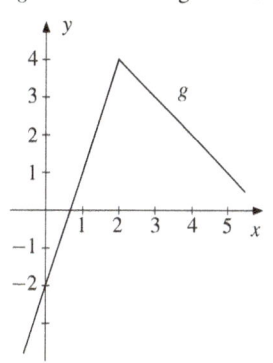

   Figure A7.8.2b

3. (a) Continuous for all x. (b) Continuous for all $x \neq 1$. (c) Continuous for all $x < 2$. (d) Continuous for all x.
   (e) Continuous for all x where $x \neq \sqrt{3} - 1$ and $x \neq -\sqrt{3} - 1$. (f) Continuous for all $x > 0$.

4. See Fig. A7.8.4; y is discontinuous at $x = a$, where the plane is vertically above the top of the overhanging cliff.

5. $a = 5$. (The line $y = ax - 1$ and parabola $y = 3x^2 + 1$ must meet when $x = 1$, which is true if and only if $a = 5$.)

6. See Fig. A7.8.6. (This example shows that the commonly seen statement: "if the inverse function exists, the original and the inverse function must both be monotonic" is wrong. This claim is correct, however, for a function which is continuous on an interval.)

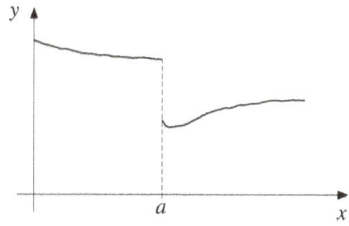

   Figure A7.8.4

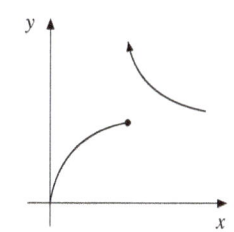

   Figure A7.8.6

7.9

1. (a) A (b) A (c) B (d) 0

2. (a) -4 (b) 0 (c) 2 (d) $-\infty$ (e) ∞ (f) $-\infty$

3. (a) $\dfrac{x-3}{x^2+1} = \dfrac{1/x - 3/x^2}{1 + 1/x^2} \to 0$ as $x \to \infty$. (b) $\sqrt{\dfrac{2+3x}{x-1}} = \sqrt{\dfrac{3+2/x}{1-1/x}} \to \sqrt{3}$ as $x \to \infty$. (c) a^2

4. $\lim_{x \to \infty} f_i(x) = \infty$ for $i = 1, 2, 3$; $\lim_{x \to \infty} f_4(x) = 0$. Then: (a) ∞ (b) 0 (c) $-\infty$ (d) 1 (e) 0 (f) ∞ (g) 1 (h) ∞

5. (a) $y = x - 1$ (with $x = -1$ as a vertical asymptote). (b) $y = 2x - 3$

   (c) $y = 3x + 5$ (with $x = 1$ as a vertical asymptote). (d) $y = 5x$ (with $x = 1$ as a vertical asymptote).

6. $y = Ax + A(b - c) + d$ is an asymptote as $x \to \infty$. ($x = -c$ is not an asymptote because $x \geq 0$.)

7. (a) Neither continuous nor differentiable at $x = 1$. (b) Continuous but not differentiable at $x = 2$.

   (c) Neither continuous nor differentiable at $x = 3$. (d) Continuous but not differentiable at $x = 4$.

8. $f'(0^+) = 1$ and $f'(0^-) = 0$. See Fig. A7.9.8.

9. $f'(x) = \dfrac{3(x-1)(x+1)}{(-x^2+4x-1)^2}$. The denominator is 0 at $x_1 = 2 - \sqrt{3}$ and $x_2 = 2 + \sqrt{3}$. A sign diagram shows that $f(x)$ is increasing in $(-\infty, -1]$, in $[1, x_2)$, and in (x_2, ∞). See Fig. A7.9.9, in which the dashed vertical lines are $x = 2 \pm \sqrt{3}$.

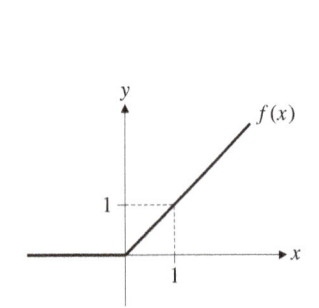

Figure A7.9.8

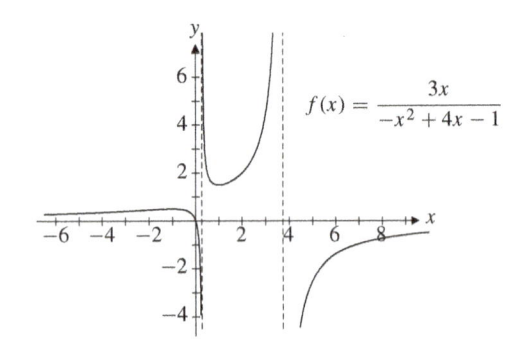

Figure A7.9.9

7.10

1. (a) Let $f(x) = x^7 - 5x^5 + x^3 - 1$. Then f is continuous, $f(-1) = 2$, and $f(1) = -4$, so according to Theorem 7.10.1, the equation $f(x) = 0$ has a solution in $(-1, 1)$.

   (b) Here $f(x) = x^3 + 3x - 8$ is continuous, with $f(1) < 0 < f(3)$.

   (c) Here $f(x) = \sqrt{x^2+1} - 3x$ is continuous, with $f(0) > 0 > f(1)$.

   (d) Here $f(x) = e^{x-1} - 2x$ is continuous, with $f(0) > 0 > f(1)$.

2. A person's height is a continuous function of time (even if growth occurs in intermittent spurts, often overnight). The intermediate value theorem (and common sense) give the conclusion.

3. Let $f(x) = x^3 - 17$. Then $f(x) = 0$ for $x = \sqrt[3]{17}$. Moreover, $f'(x) = 3x^2$. Put $x_0 = 2.5$. Then $f(x_0) = -1.375$ and $f'(x_0) = 18.75$. Formula (7.10.1) with $n = 0$ yields $x_1 = x_0 - f(x_0)/f'(x_0) = 2.5 - (-1.375)/18.75 \approx 2.573$.

4. An integer root is $x = -3$. Applying Newton's method once to each of the three suggested starting values gives the approximations $-1.879, 0.347$, and 1.534 to the three other roots.

5. An integer which is close to a solution is $x = 2$. Put $f(x) = (2x)^x - 15$. Then $f'(x) = (2x)^x[\ln(2x) + 1]$. Formula (7.10.1) with $x_0 = 2$ and $n = 0$ yields $x_1 = x_0 - f(x_0)/f'(x_0) = 2 - f(2)/f'(2) = 2 - 1/[16(\ln 4 + 1)] \approx 1.9738$.

6. If $f(x_0)$ and $f'(x_0)$ have opposite signs, as they do in Fig. 7.10.1, then formula (7.10.1) evidently implies that $x_1 > x_0$. But if they have the same sign, as they do in Fig. 7.10.2, then formula (7.10.1) implies that $x_1 < x_0$.

7.11

1. (a) $\alpha_n = \dfrac{(3/n) - 1}{2 - (1/n)} \to -\dfrac{1}{2}$ as $n \to \infty$ (b) $\beta_n = \dfrac{1 + (2/n) - (1/n^2)}{3 - (2/n^2)} \to \dfrac{1}{3}$ as $n \to \infty$
(c) $3(-1/2) + 4(1/3) = -1/6$ (d) $(-1/2) \cdot (1/3) = -1/6$ (e) $(-1/2) \div (1/3) = -3/2$
(f) $\sqrt{(1/3) - (-1/2)} = \sqrt{5/6} = \sqrt{30}/6$

2. (a) As $n \to \infty$, so $2/n \to 0$ implying that $5 - 2/n \to 5$. (b) As $n \to \infty$, so $\dfrac{n^2 - 1}{n} = n - 1/n \to \infty$.
(c) As $n \to \infty$, so $\dfrac{3n}{\sqrt{2n^2 - 1}} = \dfrac{3n}{n\sqrt{2 - 1/n^2}} = \dfrac{3}{\sqrt{2 - 1/n^2}} \to \dfrac{3}{\sqrt{2}} = \dfrac{3\sqrt{2}}{2}$.

3. For a fixed number x, put $x/n = 1/m$. Then $n = mx$, and as $n \to \infty$, so $m \to \infty$.
Hence $(1 + x/n)^n = (1 + 1/m)^{mx} = [(1 + 1/m)^m]^x \to e^x$ as $m \to \infty$.

7.12

1. (a) $\lim\limits_{x \to 3} \dfrac{3x^2 - 27}{x - 3} = $ "$0/0$" $= \lim\limits_{x \to 3} \dfrac{6x}{1} = 18$ (or use $3x^2 - 27 = 3(x - 3)(x + 3)$).
(b) $\lim\limits_{x \to 0} \dfrac{e^x - 1 - x - \frac{1}{2}x^2}{3x^3} = $ "$0/0$" $= \lim\limits_{x \to 0} \dfrac{e^x - 1 - x}{9x^2} = $ "$0/0$" $= \lim\limits_{x \to 0} \dfrac{e^x - 1}{18x} = $ "$0/0$" $= \lim\limits_{x \to 0} \dfrac{e^x}{18} = \dfrac{1}{18}$
(c) $\lim\limits_{x \to 0} \dfrac{e^{-3x} - e^{-2x} + x}{x^2} = $ "$0/0$" $= \lim\limits_{x \to 0} \dfrac{-3e^{-3x} + 2e^{-2x} + 1}{2x} = $ "$0/0$" $= \lim\limits_{x \to 0} \dfrac{9e^{-3x} - 4e^{-2x}}{2} = \dfrac{5}{2}$

2. (a) $\lim\limits_{x \to a} \dfrac{x^2 - a^2}{x - a} = $ "$0/0$" $= \lim\limits_{x \to a} \dfrac{2x}{1} = 2a$ (or use $x^2 - a^2 = (x + a)(x - a)$).
(b) $\lim\limits_{x \to 0} \dfrac{2(1 + x)^{1/2} - 2 - x}{2(1 + x + x^2)^{1/2} - 2 - x} = $ "$0/0$" $= \lim\limits_{x \to 0} \dfrac{(1 + x)^{-1/2} - 1}{(1 + 2x)(1 + x + x^2)^{-1/2} - 1} = $ "$0/0$"
$= \lim\limits_{x \to 0} \dfrac{-\frac{1}{2}(1 + x)^{-3/2}}{2(1 + x + x^2)^{-1/2} + (1 + 2x)^2(-\frac{1}{2})(1 + x + x^2)^{-3/2}} = \dfrac{-\frac{1}{2}}{2 - \frac{1}{2}} = -\dfrac{1}{3}$

3. (a) $\frac{1}{2}$ (b) 3 (c) 2 (d) $-\frac{1}{2}$ (e) $\frac{3}{8}$ (f) -2

4. (a) $\lim\limits_{x \to \infty} \dfrac{\ln x}{x^{1/2}} = $ "∞/∞" $= \lim\limits_{x \to \infty} \dfrac{1/x}{(1/2)x^{-1/2}} = \lim\limits_{x \to \infty} \dfrac{2}{x^{1/2}} = 0$
(b) 0. (Write $x \ln x = \dfrac{\ln x}{1/x}$, and then use l'Hôpital's rule.)
(c) $+\infty$. (Write $xe^{1/x} - x = x(e^{1/x} - 1) = (e^{1/x} - 1)/(1/x)$, and then use l'Hôpital's rule.)

5. The second fraction is not "$0/0$". The correct limit is $5/2$.

6. $L = \lim_{v \to 0^+} \dfrac{1 - (1 + v^\beta)^{-\gamma}}{v} =$ "0/0" $= \lim_{v \to 0^+} \dfrac{\gamma(1 + v^\beta)^{-\gamma-1}\beta v^{\beta-1}}{1}$. If $\beta = 1$, then $L = \gamma$. If $\beta > 1$, then $L = 0$, and if $\beta < 1$, then $L = \infty$.

7. Because $\dfrac{d}{d\rho}c^{1-\rho} = -c^{1-\rho}\ln c$, one has $\lim_{\rho \to 1}\dfrac{c^{1-\rho} - 1}{1 - \rho} =$ "0/0" $= \lim_{\rho \to 1}\dfrac{-c^{1-\rho}\ln c}{-1} = \ln c$.

8. $\lim_{x \to \infty}\dfrac{f(x)}{g(x)} = \lim_{t \to 0^+}\dfrac{f(1/t)}{g(1/t)} =$ "0/0" $= \lim_{t \to 0^+}\dfrac{f'(1/t)(-1/t^2)}{g'(1/t)(-1/t^2)} = \lim_{t \to 0^+}\dfrac{f'(1/t)}{g'(1/t)} = \lim_{x \to \infty}\dfrac{f'(x)}{g'(x)}$

9. Note that $L = \lim_{x \to a}\dfrac{1/g(x)}{1/f(x)} =$ "0/0" $= \lim_{x \to a}\dfrac{-1/(g(x))^2}{-1/(f(x))^2} \cdot \dfrac{g'(x)}{f'(x)} = L^2 \cdot \lim_{x \to a}\dfrac{g'(x)}{f'(x)}$. See SM for more details.

Review exercises for Chapter 7

1. (a) $y' = -5$, $y'' = 0$ (b) Differentiating w.r.t. x yields $y^3 + 3xy^2 y' = 0$, so $y' = -y/3x$. Then differentiating $y' = -y/3x$ w.r.t. x yields $y'' = -[y'3x - 3y]/9x^2 = -[(-y/3x)3x - 3y]/9x^2 = 4y/9x^2$. Because $y = 5x^{-1/3}$, we get $y' = -(5/3)x^{-4/3}$ and $y'' = (20/9)x^{-7/3}$. The answers from differentiating $y = 5x^{-1/3}$ are the same.

(c) $2y'e^{2y} = 3x^2$, so $y' = (3x^2/2)e^{-2y}$. Then $y'' = 3xe^{-2y} + \tfrac{1}{2}3x^2 e^{-2y}(-2y') = 3xe^{-2y} - \tfrac{1}{2}9x^4 e^{-4y}$. From the given equation we get $2y = \ln x^3 = 3\ln x$, so $y = \tfrac{3}{2}\ln x$, and then $y' = \tfrac{3}{2}x^{-1}$, $y'' = -\tfrac{3}{2}x^{-2}$. By noting that $e^{-2y} = e^{-3\ln x} = (e^{\ln x})^{-3} = x^{-3}$ and $e^{-4y} = (e^{-2y})^2 = x^{-6}$, verify that the answers are the same.

2. $5y^4 y' - y^2 - 2xyy' = 0$, so $y' = \dfrac{y^2}{5y^4 - 2xy} = \dfrac{y}{5y^3 - 2x}$. Because $y = 0$ makes the given equation meaningless, y' is never 0.

3. Differentiating w.r.t. x yields $3x^2 + 3y^2 y' = 3y + 3xy'$. When $x = y = 3/2$, then $y' = -1$. See Fig. 7.R.1.

4. (a) Implicit differentiation yields (*) $2xy + x^2 y' + 9y^2 y' = 0$. Inserting $x = 2$ and $y = 1$ yields $y' = -4/13$.

(b) Differentiating (*) w.r.t. x yields $2y + 2xy' + 2xy' + x^2 y'' + 18yy'y' + 9y^2 y'' = 0$. Inserting $x = 2$, $y = 1$, and $y' = -4/13$ gives the answer.

5. $\tfrac{1}{3}K^{-2/3}L^{1/3} + \tfrac{1}{3}K^{1/3}L^{-2/3}(dL/dK) = 0$, so $dL/dK = -L/K$.

6. Differentiating w.r.t. x gives $y'/y + y' = -2/x - 0.4(\ln x)/x$. Solving for y' gives $y' = \dfrac{-(2/x)(1 + \tfrac{1}{5}\ln x)}{1 + 1/y}$ which is 0 when $1 + \tfrac{1}{5}\ln x = 0$, implying that $\ln x = -5$ and so $x = e^{-5}$.

7. (a) Use (c) to substitute for T in (b), then use the resulting expression to substitute for C in (a).

(b) $dY/dI = f'((1 - \beta)Y - \alpha)(1 - \beta)(dY/dI) + 1$. Solving for dY/dI yields $\dfrac{dY}{dI} = \dfrac{1}{1 - (1 - \beta)f'((1 - \beta)Y - \alpha)}$.

(c) Since $f' \in (0, 1)$ and $\beta \in (0, 1)$, we get $(1 - \beta)f'((1 - \beta)Y - \alpha) \in (0, 1)$, so $dY/dI > 0$.

8. (a) Differentiating w.r.t. x yields $2x - y - xy' + 4yy' = 0$, so $y' = (y - 2x)/(4y - x)$.

(b) Horizontal tangent at $(1, 2)$ and $(-1, -2)$. ($y' = 0$ when $y = 2x$. Insert this into the given equation.) Vertical tangents at $(2\sqrt{2}, \sqrt{2}/2) \approx (2.8, 0.7)$ and at $(-2\sqrt{2}, -\sqrt{2}/2) \approx (-2.8, -0.7)$. (There is a vertical tangent when the denominator in the expression for y' is 0, i.e. when $x = 4y$.) See Fig. 7.R.2.

9. (a) $y' = \dfrac{2 - 2xy}{x^2 - 9y^2} = -\dfrac{1}{2}$ at $(-1, 1)$. (b) Vertical tangent at $(0, 0)$, $(-3, -1)$, and $(3, 1)$. (Vertical tangent requires the denominator of y' to be 0, i.e. $x = \pm 3y$. Inserting $x = 3y$ into the given equation yields $y^3 = y$, so $y = 0$, $y = 1$, or $y = -1$. The corresponding values for x are 0, 3, and -3. Inserting $y = -3x$ gives no new points.)

Horizontal tangent requires $y' = 0$, i.e. $xy = 1$. But inserting $y = 1/x$ into the given equation yields $x^4 = -3$, which has no solution. All these findings accord with Fig. 7.R.3.

10. (a) $D_f = (-1, 1)$, $R_f = (-\infty, \infty)$. (b) The inverse is $g(y) = (e^{2y} - 1)/(e^{2y} + 1)$, and then $g'(\frac{1}{2} \ln 3) = 3/4$.

11. (a) $f(e^2) = 2$ and $f(x) = \ln x (\ln x - 1)^2 = 0$ for $\ln x = 0$ and for $\ln x = 1$, so $x = 1$ or $x = e$.

    (b) $f'(x) = (3/x)(\ln x - 1)(\ln x - 1/3) > 0$ for $x > e$, and so f is strictly increasing in $[e, \infty)$. It therefore has an inverse h. According to (7.3.2), because $f(e^2) = 2$, we have $h'(2) = 1/f'(e^2) = e^2/5$.

12. (a) $f(x) \approx \ln 4 + \frac{1}{2}x - \frac{1}{8}x^2$ (b) $g(x) \approx 1 - \frac{1}{2}x + \frac{3}{8}x^2$ (c) $h(x) \approx x + 2x^2$

13. (a) $x\,dx/\sqrt{1+x^2}$ (b) $8\pi r\,dr$ (c) $400K^3\,dK$ (d) $-3x^2\,dx/(1-x^3)$

14. $df(x) = f'(x)\,dx = 3x^2\,dx/2\sqrt{1+x^3}$. Moreover, $\Delta f(2) \approx df(2) = 3 \cdot 2^2 (0.2)/2\sqrt{1+2^3} = 0.4$.

15. Let $x = \frac{1}{2}$ and $n = 5$ and use formula (7.6.6). $\sqrt{e} \approx 1.649$, correct to 3 decimals.

16. $y' + (1/y)y' = 1$, or (∗) $yy' + y' = y$. Then $y' = 1/2$ at $y = 1$. Differentiating (∗) w.r.t. x gives $(y')^2 + yy'' + y'' = y'$. With $y = 1$ and $y' = 1/2$, we find $y'' = 1/8$, so $y(x) \approx 1 + \frac{1}{2}x + \frac{1}{16}x^2$.

17. (a) Continuous for all $x \neq 0$. (b) Continuous for all $x > 0$. (Note that $x^2 + 2x + 2$ is never 0.)
    (c) Continuous for all x in $(-2, 2)$.

18. (a) $1 = f'(y^2)2yy'$, so $y' = \dfrac{1}{2yf'(y^2)}$ (b) $y^2 + x2yy' = f'(x) - 3y^2 y'$, and so $y' = \dfrac{f'(x) - y^2}{y(2x + 3y)}$

    (c) $f'(2x + y)(2 + y') = 1 + 2yy'$, so $y' = \dfrac{1 - 2f'(2x + y)}{f'(2x + y) - 2y}$

19. $\mathrm{El}_r(D_{\mathrm{marg}}) = -0.165$ and $\mathrm{El}_r(D_{\mathrm{mah}}) = 2.39$. For each 1% increase in income, the demand for margarine decreased by approximately 0.165%, while the demand for meals away from home increased by approximately 2.39%.

20. (a) 5 (using formula (7.7.3)). (b) 1/3 (using $\sqrt[3]{x} = x^{1/3}$ and (7.7.3)).
    (c) $\mathrm{El}_x(x^3 + x^5) = \dfrac{x}{x^3 + x^5}(3x^2 + 5x^4) = (5x^2 + 3)/(x^2 + 1)$, or alternatively use part (d) of Exercise 7.7.9.
    (d) $2x/(x^2 - 1)$, using parts (c) and (d) of Exercise 7.7.9.

21. Put $f(x) = x^3 - x - 5$. Then $f'(x) = 3x^2 - 1$. Taking $x_0 = 2$, formula (7.10.1) with $n = 1$ gives $x_1 = 2 - f(2)/f'(2) = 2 - 1/11 \approx 1.909$.

22. f is continuous, with $f(1) = e - 3 < 0$ and $f(4) = e^2 - 3 > 0$. By Theorem 7.10.1(i), there is a zero for f in $(1, 4)$. Because $f'(x) > 0$, the solution is unique. Formula (7.10.1) yields $x_1 = 1 - f(1)/f'(1) = -1 + 6/e \approx 1.21$.

23. (a) 2 (b) Tends to $+\infty$. (c) No limit exists. (d) $-1/6$ (e) 1/5 (f) 1/16 (g) 1 (h) $-1/16$ (i) 0

24. Does not exist if $b \neq d$. If $b = d$, the limit is $(a - c)/2\sqrt{b}$.

25. $\lim_{x \to 0} \dfrac{a^x - b^x}{e^{ax} - e^{bx}} = $ "0/0" $= \lim_{x \to 0} \dfrac{a^x \ln a - b^x \ln b}{ae^{ax} - be^{bx}} = \dfrac{\ln a - \ln b}{a - b}$

26. $x_1 = 0.9 - f(0.9)/f'(0.9) \approx 0.924\,792\,4$, $x_2 = x_1 - f(x_1)/f'(x_1) \approx 0.927\,956\,5$, $x_3 = x_2 - f(x_2)/f'(x_2) \approx 0.928\,033\,8$, and $x_4 = x_3 - f(x_3)/f'(x_3) \approx 0.928\,033\,9$. This suggests that the answer correct to 3 decimal places is 0.928.

Chapter 8

8.2

1. The graph of f shown in Fig. 8.2.9 consists of two line segments joined at the peak. If the two points a and b belong to the same line segment, including the peak, then the two inequalities (8.2.1) and (8.2.2) are both satisfied with equality.

866   SOLUTIONS TO THE EXERCISES

If a and b belong to different line segments, however, then only (8.2.1) is satisfied. The function is concave, but not strictly concave.

2. (a) When the function f is strictly concave, then the inequality (8.2.1) is satisfied strictly for all distinct a and b in I, and all $0 < \lambda < 1$. It is therefore satisfied weakly. It is also trivially satisfied as an equality if $a = b$ or if $\lambda = 0$ or if $\lambda = 1$.

(b) In case the graph of the function f is a line segment, then the inequalities (8.2.1) and (8.2.2) are both satisfied with equality for all a and b in I, and all $\lambda \in [0, 1]$. So f is both concave and convex.

(c) The function defined by $f(x) = 0$ for all real x is an example of a function which is concave, but not strictly concave. So is any linear function, or the function in Exercise 1.

(d) When a function is strictly concave, the inequality (8.2.1) is satisfied strictly for all distinct a and b in I, and all $0 < \lambda < 1$. This strict inequality contradicts the inequality (8.2.2), so the function cannot be convex.

3. The function with the graph shown in Fig. 8.2.7 is strictly concave, whereas that with the graph shown in Fig. 8.2.8 is strictly convex.

4. Given any output level $Q > 0$, suppose that the firm compares the total costs: (i) $c(Q)$ of producing Q in the original plant, with no new plant; (ii) $2c(\frac{1}{2}Q)$ of using two plants and splitting the output equally between the two. Because of the assumption that c is strictly convex, we have $c\left(\frac{1}{2}Q\right) = c\left(\frac{1}{2}Q + \frac{1}{2}0\right) < \frac{1}{2}c(Q) + \frac{1}{2}c(0) = \frac{1}{2}c(Q)$, which implies that $2c(\frac{1}{2}Q) < c(Q)$. So option (ii) is cheaper, and the firm should split its output.

5. Consider any two income levels y and z with $z > y$. We know from Example 5.4.4 and the graph of the tax function in Fig. 5.4.9 that, as taxable income rises from y to z, not only does the tax payable increase from $T(y)$ to $T(z)$, but the average rate $[T(z) - T(y)]/(z - y)$ on the $z - y$ dollars of extra income is increasing. But this average rate is the slope $s(y, z)$ of the tax function T. From part (iii) of Theorem 8.2.1 it follows that T is convex. But because the graph of T has linear segments, it connot be strictly convex.

6. Suppose that f is increasing but not strictly increasing. Then there exist a, b in I such that $a < b$ and $f(a) = f(b) = f(x)$ for all x in (a, b). It follows that $f(a) = f(b) = f\left(\frac{1}{2}(a+b)\right) \not> \frac{1}{2}[f(a) + f(b)]$, which violates strict concavity. So if f is increasing and strictly concave, it must be strictly increasing.

7. (a) For all a and all x in $(-\infty, \infty)$ with $x \neq a$, the slope of x^2 satisfies $s(a, x) = (x^2 - a^2)/(x - a) = x + a$. This is obviously strictly increasing in x. So x^2 is strictly convex over $(-\infty, \infty)$.

(b) For all a and all x in $[0, \infty)$ with $x \neq a$, the slope of x^n satisfies $s(a, x) = (x^n - a^n)/(x - a) = \sum_{k=1}^{n} x^{n-k}a^{k-1}$. Now, as x varies over the interval $[0, \infty)$, each term of the sum is strictly increasing in x, and each except the constant last term a^{n-1} is strictly increasing in x. It follows that the whole sum $s(a, x)$ is strictly increasing in x, so the power function x^n is strictly convex over $[0, \infty)$.

(c) If n is even, then the slope of the function $y = (-x)^n$ satisfies $s(-a, -x) = \dfrac{(-x)^n - (-a)^n}{(-x) - (-a)} = \dfrac{x^n - a^n}{a - x} = -s(a, x)$. We have proved that when $a \geq 0$ and $x \geq 0$, then $s(a, x)$ is strictly increasing in x. It follows that $s(-a, -x)$ is strictly decreasing in x, so strictly increasing in $-x$. This shows that x^n is strictly convex on $(-\infty, 0]$.

(d) If n is odd, then $s(-a, -x) = \dfrac{(-x)^n - (-a)^n}{(-x) - (-a)} = \dfrac{-x^n + a^n}{a - x} = s(a, x)$. In this case, if $a \geq 0$ and $x \geq 0$, then $s(-a, -x)$ is strictly increasing in x, so strictly decreasing in $-x$. This shows that x^n is strictly concave on $(-\infty, 0]$.

8. (i) The function $f(x) = \ln x$ is increasing in x. Now the inequality of Exercise 2.6.8 implies that $\frac{1}{2}a + \frac{1}{2}b \geq \sqrt{ab}$, so

$$\ln\left(\tfrac{1}{2}a + \tfrac{1}{2}b\right) \geq \ln\left(\sqrt{ab}\right) = \ln\left(\sqrt{a}\right) + \ln\left(\sqrt{b}\right) = \tfrac{1}{2}\ln a + \tfrac{1}{2}\ln b$$

This proves that $\ln x$ is mid-point concave, so concave.

(ii) By the inequality of Exercise 2.6.8, the two numbers e^a and e^b satisfy $\frac{1}{2}e^a + \frac{1}{2}e^b \geq \sqrt{e^a e^b} = e^{\frac{1}{2}a + \frac{1}{2}b}$. It follows immediately that the function $f(x) = e^x$ is mid-point convex, so convex.

9. The definition of concavity implies that the inequality holds when $n = 2$. As the induction hypothesis, suppose it also holds when $n = k$, for $k = 2, 3, \ldots$. Now, suppose that $n = k + 1$ and the $k + 1$ positive constants λ_i ($i = 1, \ldots, k + 1$) satisfy $\sum_{i=1}^{k+1} \lambda_i = 1$. Now define, for each $i = 1, \ldots, k$, the new positive constant $\theta_i = \lambda_i/(1 - \lambda_{k+1})$. Evidently, the hypothesis that $\sum_{i=1}^{k+1} \lambda_i = 1$ implies that $\sum_{i=1}^{k} \theta_i = 1$. Furthermore, let x^k denote $\sum_{i=1}^{k} \theta_i x_i$. Then $\sum_{i=1}^{k+1} \lambda_i x_i = (1 - \lambda_{k+1}) x^k + \lambda_{k+1} x_{k+1}$. Because f is concave and $0 < \lambda_{k+1} = 1 - \sum_{i=1}^{k} \lambda_i < 1$, it follows that

$$f\left(\sum_{i=1}^{k+1} \lambda_i x_i\right) \geq (1 - \lambda_{k+1}) f(x^k) + \lambda_{k+1} f(x_{k+1})$$

But the induction hypothesis implies that $f(x^k) \geq \sum_{i=1}^{k} \theta_i f(x_i)$. Because $\lambda_{k+1} < 1$, the above definitions imply that

$$f\left(\sum_{i=1}^{k+1} \lambda_i x_i\right) \geq (1 - \lambda_{k+1}) \sum_{i=1}^{k} \theta_i f(x_i) + \lambda_{k+1} f(x_{k+1}) = \sum_{i=1}^{k+1} \lambda_i f(x_i)$$

This completes the proof by induction.

8.3

1. The definitions imply that for all distinct a and b in I, and all $0 < \lambda < 1$, we have

$$f(\lambda a + (1 - \lambda) b) > \lambda f(a) + (1 - \lambda) f(b) \quad \text{and} \quad g(\lambda a + (1 - \lambda) b) \geq \lambda g(a) + (1 - \lambda) g(b)$$

Adding these two inequalities shows that the function $h(x) = f(x) + g(x)$ satisfies

$$h(\lambda a + (1 - \lambda) b) > \lambda h(a) + (1 - \lambda) h(b)$$

Therefore, $f + g$ is strictly concave.

2. The inverse of the increasing concave function $g(x) = \sqrt{x}$, defined for all $x \geq 0$, is the increasing convex function $h(x) = x^2$, defined for all $x \geq 0$. Then, provided that $a \geq 0$, the function $f(x) = ax^2 + b = ah(x) + b$, defined for all $x \geq 0$, is an increasing function of the convex function $h(x)$, so convex.

3. Use the function $f(x) = c$, where c is a constant, as an example of a concave function that is not strictly concave. And use the function $g(y) = c'$, where c' is a constant, as an example of a increasing concave function that is not strictly increasing. In either case, the compound function $h(x) = g(f(x))$ will be a constant, so not strictly concave.

4. As the induction hypothesis, suppose that the function defined on the interval I by $f_*^k(x) = \min\{f_i(x) : i = 1, 2, \ldots, k\}$ is concave whenever the k functions $f_i(x)$ ($i = 1, 2, \ldots, k$) are all concave. This was shown in Section 8.3 for the case when $k = 2$. Suppose it is true for some $k \geq 2$. Then $f_*^{k+1}(x) = \min\{f_*^k(x), f_{k+1}(x)\}$, where $f_*^k(x)$ is concave by the induction hypothesis. Assuming that $f_{k+1}(x)$ is also concave, it follows then that $f_*^{k+1}(x)$ is the minimum of two concave functions, so concave. This completes the induction step.

5. (a) Arguing as in Example 8.3.2, the function $f(x) = -|x - 1| = -\max\{x - 1, 1 - x\}$ is concave, whereas the function $g(x) = |x + 1| = \max\{x + 1, -x - 1\}$ must be convex.

(b) Note that $f(x) + g(x) = |x + 1| - |x - 1|$ equals: $-(x + 1) - (1 - x) = -2$ on $(-\infty, -1)$; $(x + 1) - (1 - x) = 2x$ on $(-1, 1)$; $(x + 1) - (x - 1) = 2$ on $(1, \infty)$. So on the interval (a, b) the function $f + g$ is:

(i) convex unless (a, b) includes $x = 1$ where there is one kink;

(ii) concave unless (a, b) includes -1 where there is a second kink;

(iii) both concave and convex if (a, b) excludes both -1 and 1;

(iv) neither concave nor convex if (a, b) includes both -1 and 1.

See Fig. A8.3.5 for the graph of $f + g$.

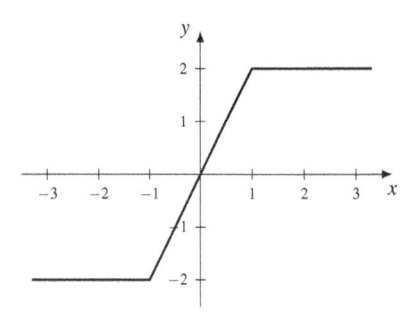

Figure A8.3.5 $y = -|x-1| + |x+1|$

6. By part (a) of Exercise 8.2.7, the function $f(x) = x^2$ is strictly convex on $(-\infty, \infty)$, with range $[0, \infty)$. Furthermore, the function $g(y) = y^m$ is both strictly convex and strictly increasing on $[0, \infty)$. It follows that the composite function $g(f(x)) = (x^2)^m = x^n$ is strictly convex over $(-\infty, \infty)$.

8.5

1. Given $f(x) = \ln x$ defined for all $x > 0$, one has $f''(x) = -x^{-2} < 0$, so $\ln x$ is stictly concave on $(0, \infty)$. Given $g(x) = e^x$ defined for all real x, one has $g''(x) = e^x > 0$, so e^x is strictly convex over the whole real line.

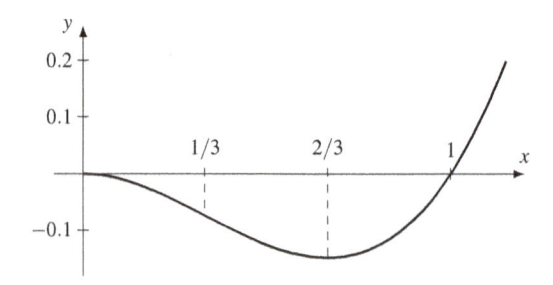

Figure A8.5.2 $y = x^3 - x^2$

2. The first two derivatives of $h(x) = -x^2 + x^3$ are $h'(x) = -2x + 3x^2$ and $h''(x) = -2 + 6x$. So $h''(x) < 0 \Leftrightarrow x < \frac{1}{3}$ and $h''(x) > 0 \Leftrightarrow x > \frac{1}{3}$. Hence h is: (a) concave on (a, b) iff $0 \le a < b \le \frac{1}{3}$; (b) convex on (a, b) iff $\frac{1}{3} \le a < b$; (c) neither concave nor convex on (a, b) iff $a < \frac{1}{3} < b$. See Fig. A8.5.2 for the graph of $h(x)$.

3. Differentiating $h(x) = f(g(x))$ twice using the chain rule gives $h'(x) = g'(f(x))f'(x)$ and then, using the product rule as well, $h''(x) = g''(f(x))(f'(x))^2 + g'(f(x))f''(x)$. Because of the assumptions that $f'' \le 0$, $g' \ge 0$, and $g'' \le 0$, it follows that $h''(x) \le 0$. So $h(x)$ is concave.

4. Consider the function $f(x) = -x^4$, defined for all real x. By Exercise 8.3.6, the even power function x^4 is strictly convex, so f is strictly concave. Yet $f''(x) = -12x^2 \not< 0$ at $x = 0$.

5. (a) Because $f'(x) \ne 0$ for all x in I, the inverse function Theorem 7.3.1 implies that the inverse $g(y) = f^{-1}(y)$ is well defined and differentiable for all y in the range $f(I)$, with $g'(f(x)) = 1/f'(x)$. Moreover, because $f'(x) \ne 0$, the function g is twice differentiable with $g''(f(x)) = -f''(x)/[f'(x)]^3$, as in Eq. (7.3.3).

(b) If $f' < 0$, then f'' and g'' have the same sign. But if $f' > 0$, they have opposite signs.

(c) When $f'(x) \neq 0$ and $f''(x) \neq 0$ for all x in I, we have the following strengthenings of the results in Section 8.3:

(i) if $f' > 0$ throughout I and f is strictly concave, its inverse g satisfies $g' > 0$ and is strictly convex;

(ii) if $f' > 0$ throughout I and f is strictly convex, its inverse g satisfies $g' > 0$ and is strictly concave;

(iii) if $f' < 0$ throughout I and f is strictly concave, its inverse g satisfies $g' < 0$ and is strictly concave;

(iv) if $f' < 0$ throughout I and f is strictly convex, its inverse g satisfies $g' < 0$ and is strictly convex.

8.6

1. (a) $f'(x) = 3x^2 + 3x - 6 = 3(x-1)(x+2)$, so $f'(x) = 0$ at $x = -2$ and $x = 1$.
   A sign diagram reveals that f increases in $(-\infty, -2]$ and in $[1, \infty)$.
   (b) $f''(x) = 6x + 3 = 0$ for $x = -1/2$. Because $f''(x)$ changes sign at $x = -1/2$, this is an inflection point.

2. (a) $f''(x) = 2x(x^2 - 3)/(1 + x^2)^3$. A sign diagram reveals that f is convex in $[-\sqrt{3}, 0]$ and in $[\sqrt{3}, \infty)$. The inflection points where f'' change sign are at $x = -\sqrt{3}, 0, \sqrt{3}$.
   (b) $g''(x) = 4(1+x)^{-3} > 0$ when $x > -1$, so g is (strictly) convex in $(-1, \infty)$. No inflection point.
   (c) $h''(x) = (2+x)e^x$, so h is convex in $[-2, \infty)$. An inflection point occurs at $x = -2$.

3. (a) $x = 0$ is an inflection point; the function is concave in $(-\infty, 0]$, convex in $[0, \infty)$.
   (b) $x = 2$ is an inflection point; the function is convex in $(0, 2]$, concave in $[2, \infty)$.
   (c) Three inflection points: $x_1 = 0$, $x_2 = 3 - \sqrt{3}$, and $x_3 = 3 + \sqrt{3}$. Concave in $(-\infty, x_1]$, convex in $[x_1, x_2]$, concave in $[x_2, x_3]$, convex in $[x_3, \infty)$.
   (d) Inflection point $x_0 = e^{5/6} \approx 2.30$. Concave in $(0, x_0]$, convex in $[x_0, \infty)$.
   (e) Inflection point $x_0 = -\ln 2$. Concave in $(-\infty, -\ln 2]$, convex in $[-\ln 2, \infty)$.
   (f) Inflection points: $x_1 = 1 - \sqrt{3}$ and $x_2 = 1 + \sqrt{3}$. Convex in $(-\infty, x_1]$, concave in $[x_1, x_2]$, convex in $[x_2, \infty)$.

4. Four inflection points: $x = 0$, $x = 1$, $x = 3$, and $x = 5$.

5. $f(-1) = 1$ implies that $-a + b = 1$. Moreover, $f'(x) = 3ax^2 + 2bx$ and $f''(x) = 6ax + 2b$, so $f''(1/2) = 0$ yields $3a + 2b = 0$. Solving the two simultaneous equations for a and b yields $a = -2/5$ and $b = 3/5$.

Review exercises for Chapter 8

1. The function $f(x) = \sqrt{x}$ is concave, whereas $g(y) = y^3$ is convex. The composite function is $h(x) = g(f(x)) = (\sqrt{x})^3 = x^{3/2}$, with $h'(x) = \frac{3}{2}x^{1/2}$ and $h''(x) = \frac{3}{4}x^{-1/2} > 0$. So h is strictly convex for $x > 0$. No contradiction is possible because the results in Section 8.3 say nothing about a convex function of a concave function.

2. (a) Here $g'(x) = 9x^2 - x^4$ and $g''(x) = 18x - 4x^3$. (b) g is increasing in the interval $(-3, 3)$ and concave on each of the intervals $(-\frac{3}{2}\sqrt{2}, 0)$ and $(\frac{3}{2}\sqrt{2}, \infty)$. (c) Figure A8.R.2 shows the graph of g and the inflection points corresponding to $x = 0$ and $x = \pm\frac{3}{2}\sqrt{2} \approx \pm 2.1213$.

3. Here $f'(a) = f'(c) = 0$, $f'(b) < 0$, $f''(a) < 0$, $f''(b) = 0$, and $f''(c) > 0$. So only combination (b) is correct.

4. (a) Here $f''(x) = 12x - 24$. So f is concave on $(-\infty, 2]$, and convex on $[2, \infty)$.
   (b) Here $f''(x) = 8x^{-3}$ for $x \neq 0$. So f is concave on $(-\infty, 0)$, and convex on $(0, \infty)$.
   (c) Here $f''(x) = \dfrac{2x^3 - 96x}{(x^2 + 16)^3}$. So f is concave on $(-\infty, -4\sqrt{3}]$ and $[0, 4\sqrt{3}]$, but convex on $[-4\sqrt{3}, 0]$ and $[4\sqrt{3}, \infty)$.

870 SOLUTIONS TO THE EXERCISES

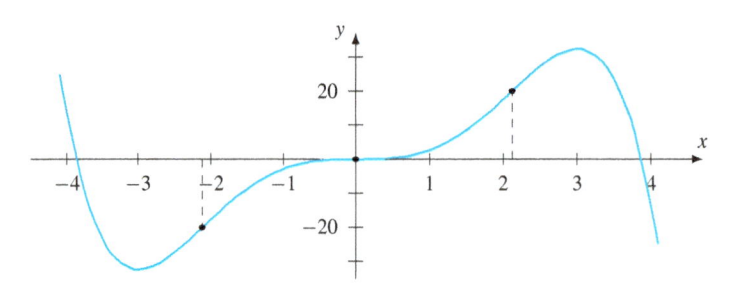

Figure A8.R.2

5. Here $f'(x) = -x^{-2}e^{1/x}$ and so $f''(x) = 2x^{-3}e^{1/x} + x^{-4}e^{1/x} = x^{-4}e^{1/x}(2x+1)$. It follows that f is concave on $(-\infty, -\frac{1}{2}]$, but convex on $[-\frac{1}{2}, 0)$ and on $(0, \infty)$. (It is undefined at $x = 0$. Moreover $e^{1/x} \to 0$ as $x \to 0^-$, but $e^{1/x} \to \infty$ as $x \to 0^+$. But the function tends to 1 as $x \to \infty$ and as $x \to -\infty$.) See Fig. A8.R.5.

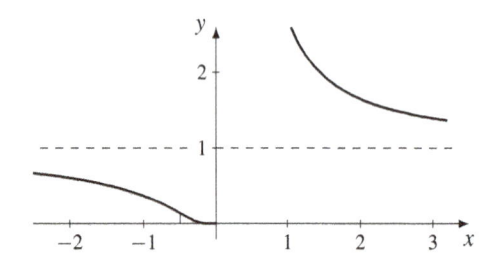

Figure A8.R.5 $y = e^{1/x}$

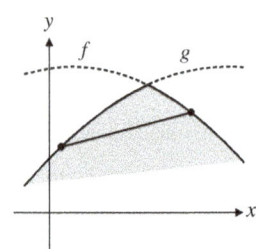

Figure A8.R.7

6. The second derivative is $C''(x) = 6ax + 2b$. So $C(x)$ is concave in $[0, -b/3a]$, convex in $[-b/3a, \infty)$. The unique inflection point occurs at $x = -b/3a$.

7. See Fig. A8.R.7. In Section 8.3 it was shown that the minimum of any two concave functions is concave.

Chapter 9

9.1

1. (a) Because the denominator is never less than 4, we have $f(x) \leq 2$ for all x. But $f(0) = 2$, so $x = 0$ maximizes $f(x)$.

(b) $g(x) \geq -3$ for all x and $g(-2) = -3$. So $x = -2$ minimizes $g(x)$. Also $g(x) \to \infty$ as $x \to \infty$, so there is no maximum.

(c) Because $1 + x^4 \geq 1$, we have $h(x) \leq 1$ for all x. But $h(0) = 2$, so $x = 0$ maximizes h. When $x \in [-1, 1]$ we have $1 + x^4 \leq 2$ so $h(x) \geq \frac{1}{2}$. It follows that the points $x = \pm 1$ minimize h.

(d) For all x one has $2 + x^2 \geq 2$ and so $2/(2 + x^2) \leq 1$, implying that $-2/(2 + x^2) \geq -1 = F(0)$. Hence there is a minimum -1 at $x = 0$, but no maximum.

(e) Maximum 2 at $x = 1$. No minimum.   (f) Minimum 99 at $x = 0$. No maximum. (As $x \to \pm\infty$, so $H(x) \to 100$.)

9.2

1. Here $y' = 1.06 - 0.08x$. Hence $y' \geq 0$ for $x \leq 13.25$ and $y' \leq 0$ for $x \geq 13.25$. So y has a maximum at $x = 13.25$.

2. Here $h'(x) = \dfrac{8(2 - \sqrt{3}x)(2 + \sqrt{3}x)}{(3x^2 + 4)^2}$. The function h has a maximum at $x = \tfrac{2}{3}\sqrt{3}$ and a minimum at $x = -\tfrac{2}{3}\sqrt{3}$.

3. $h'(t) = 1/2\sqrt{t} - \tfrac{1}{2} = (1 - \sqrt{t})/2\sqrt{t}$. We see that $h'(t) \geq 0$ in $(0, 1]$ and $h'(t) \leq 0$ in $[1, \infty)$. According to Theorem 8.2.1(a), the point $t = 1$ maximizes $h(t)$.

4. Here $f'(x) = \dfrac{4x(x^4 + 1) - 2x^2 \cdot 4x^3}{(x^4 + 1)^2} = \dfrac{4x - 4x^5}{(x^4 + 1)^2} = \dfrac{4x(1 + x^2)(1 + x)(1 - x)}{(x^4 + 1)^2}$. For x restricted to $[0, \infty)$, it follows that $f(x)$ increases in $[0, 1]$, but decreases in $[1, \infty)$. So f has a maximum $f(1) = 1$ at $x = 1$.

5. $g'(x) = 3x^2 \ln x + x^3/x = x^2(3 \ln x + 1)$. So $g'(x) = 0$ when $\ln x = -\tfrac{1}{3}$, or $x = e^{-1/3}$. We see that $g'(x) \leq 0$ in $(0, e^{-1/3}]$ and $g'(x) \geq 0$ in $[e^{-1/3}, \infty)$, so $x = e^{-1/3}$ minimizes $g(x)$. Since $g(x) \to \infty$ as $x \to \infty$, there is no maximum.

6. Here $f'(x) = 3e^x(e^{2x} - 2)$. Thus $f'(x) = 0$ when $e^{2x} = 2$, so $x = \tfrac{1}{2} \ln 2$. If $x < \tfrac{1}{2} \ln 2$ then $f'(x) < 0$, and if $x > \tfrac{1}{2} \ln 2$ then $f'(x) > 0$, so $x = \tfrac{1}{2} \ln 2$ is a minimum point. Evidently $f(x)$ tends to $+\infty$ as $x \to \infty$, so f has no maximum.

7. $y' = xe^{-x}(2 - x)$, so $y' > 0$ in $(0, 2)$ and $y' < 0$ in $(2, 4)$. Hence y has a maximum value of $4e^{-2} \approx 0.54$ at $x = 2$.

8. (a) $x = \tfrac{1}{3} \ln 2$ is a minimum point.   (b) $x = \tfrac{1}{3}(a + 2b)$ is a maximum point.   (c) $x = \tfrac{1}{5}$ is a maximum point.

9. $d'(x) = 2(x - a_1) + 2(x - a_2) + \cdots + 2(x - a_n) = 2[nx - (a_1 + a_2 + \cdots + a_n)]$. So $d'(x) = 0$ for $x = \bar{x}$, where $\bar{x} = \tfrac{1}{n}(a_1 + a_2 + \cdots + a_n)$, the *arithmetic mean* of $a_1, a_2, \ldots, a_n$. Since $d''(x) = 2n > 0$, the point $\bar{x}$ minimizes $d(x)$.

10. (a) $x_0 = (1/\alpha) \ln(A\alpha/k)$.   (b) Substituting for A in the expression for x_0 gives the optimal height of the dykes as a function of p_0, V, δ and k. See SM.

9.3

1. (a) $\pi(L) = 320\sqrt{L} - 40L$, so $\pi'(L) = \dfrac{160}{\sqrt{L}} - 40 = \dfrac{40(4 - \sqrt{L})}{\sqrt{L}}$. We see that $\pi'(L) \geq 0$ for $0 \leq L \leq 16$, $\pi'(16) = 0$, and $\pi'(L) \leq 0$ for $L \geq 16$, so $L = 16$ maximizes profits.

(b) The profit function is $\pi(L) = f(L) - wL$, so the first-order condition is $\pi'(L^*) = f'(L^*) - w = 0$.

(c) The first-order condition in (b) defines L^* as a function of w. Differentiating w.r.t. w gives $f''(L^*)(dL^*/dw) - 1 = 0$, or $dL^*/dw = 1/f''(L^*) < 0$. (If the price of labour increases, the optimal labour input decreases.)

2. (a) $Q^* = \tfrac{1}{2}(a - k)$, $\pi(Q^*) = \tfrac{1}{4}(a - k)^2$ (b) $d\pi(Q^*)/dk = -\tfrac{1}{2}(a - k) = -Q^*$ (c) $s = a - k$

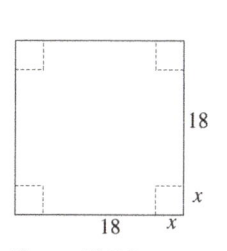

Figure A9.3.3a 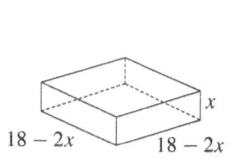   **Figure A9.3.3b** 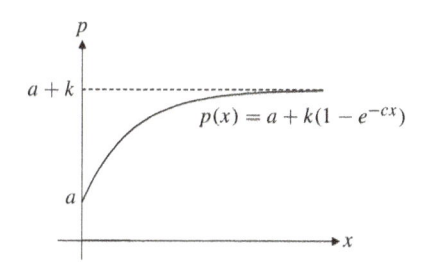   **Figure A9.3.4**

3. See Figs A9.3.3a and A9.3.3b. If $x = 9$, everything will be cut away, so one must have $x \leq 9$. Differentiating the formula for the volume V gives $V'(x) = 12x^2 - 144x + 324 = 12(x - 3)(x - 9)$. So $V'(x) > 0$ if $x < 3$, but $V'(x) < 0$ if $3 < x < 9$. Theorem 8.2.1 implies that the box has maximum volume when the square cut out from each corner has sides of length 3 cm. Then the volume is $12 \times 12 \times 3 = 432$ cm^3.

872 SOLUTIONS TO THE EXERCISES

4. $p'(x) = kce^{-cx} > 0$ and $p''(x) = -kc^2e^{-cx} < 0$ for all x. There is no maximum, but $p(x) \to a+k$ as $x \to \infty$. See Fig. A9.3.4.

5. $\bar{T}'(W) = a\dfrac{pb(bW+c)^{p-1}W - (bW+c)^p}{W^2} = a(bW+c)^{p-1}\dfrac{bW(p-1)-c}{W^2}$, which is 0 for $W^* = c/b(p-1)$.
This must be the minimum point because $\bar{T}'(W)$ is negative for $W < W^*$ and positive for $W > W^*$.

9.4

1. $f'(x) = 8x - 40 = 0$ for $x = 5$. $f(0) = 80$, $f(5) = -20$, and $f(8) = 16$. Maximum 80 for $x = 0$. Minimum -20 for $x = 5$. See Fig. A9.4.1.

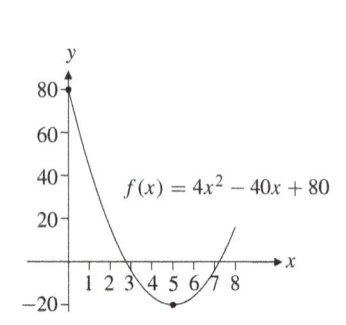

Figure A9.4.1

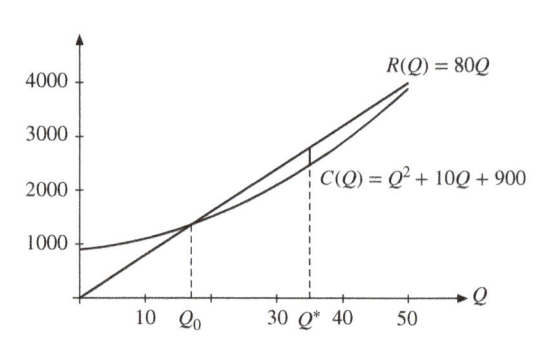

Figure A9.5.2

2. (a) Maximum -1 at $x = 0$; minimum -7 at $x = 3$. (b) Maximum 10 at $x = -1$ and $x = 2$; minimum 6 at $x = 1$.
   (c) Maximum 5/2 at $x = 1/2$ and $x = 2$; minimum 2 at $x = 1$.
   (d) Maximum 4 at $x = -1$; minimum $-6\sqrt{3}$ at $x = \sqrt{3}$. (e) Maximum $4.5 \cdot 10^9$ at $x = 3000$; minimum 0 at $x = 0$.

3. $g'(x) = \frac{2}{3}xe^{x^2}(1 - e^{2-2x^2})$. Critical points: $x = 0$ and $x = \pm 1$. Here $x = 2$ is a maximum point, $x = 1$ and $x = -1$ are minimum points. (Note that $g(2) = \frac{1}{5}(e^4 + e^{-2}) > g(0) = \frac{1}{5}(1 + e^2)$.)

4. (a) Total commission is, respectively, \$4819, \$4900, \$4800, and $C = \frac{1}{10}(60+x)(800-10x) = 4800 + 20x - x^2$, for $x \in [0, 20]$. (When there are $60 + x$ passengers, the charter company earns $800 - 10x$ from each, so they earn $\$(60+x)(800-10x)$. The sports club earns $1/10$ of that amount.)
   (b) The quadratic function C has its maximum for $x = 10$, so the maximum commission is with 70 travellers.

5. (a) $f(x) = \ln x(\ln x - 1)^2$. $f(e^{1/3}) = 4/27$, $f(e^2) = 2$, $f(e^3) = 12$. Zeros: $x = 1$ and $x = e$.
   (b) $f'(x) = (3/x)(\ln x - 1)(\ln x - 1/3)$. Minimum 0 at $x = 1$ and at $x = e$. Maximum 12 at $x = e^3$.
   (c) $f'(x) > 0$ in $[e, e^3]$, so $f(x)$ has an inverse. $g'(2) = 1/f'(e^2) = e^2/5$.

6. (a) $x^* = 3/2$ (b) $x^* = \sqrt{2}/2$ (c) $x^* = \sqrt{12}$ (d) $x^* = \sqrt{3}$

7. There is at least one point where you must be heading in the direction of the straight line joining A to B (even if that straight line hits the shore).

8. f is not continuous at $x = -1$ and $x = 1$. It has no maximum because $f(x)$ is arbitrarily close to 1 for x sufficiently close to 1. But there is no value of x for which $f(x) = 1$. Similarly, there is no minimum.

9. f has a maximum at $x = 1$ and a minimum at all $x > 1$. (Draw your own graph.) Yet the function is discontinuous at $x = 1$, and its domain of definition is neither closed nor bounded.

9.5

1. $\pi(Q) = 10Q - \dfrac{1}{1000}Q^2 - (5000 + 2Q) = 8Q - \dfrac{1}{1000}Q^2 - 5000$.

   Since $\pi'(Q) = 8 - \dfrac{1}{500}Q = 0$ for $Q = 4000$, and $\pi''(Q) = -\dfrac{1}{500} < 0$, output $Q = 4000$ maximizes profits.

2. (a) See Fig. A9.5.2. (b) (i) The requirement is $\pi(Q) \geq 0$ and $Q \in [0, 50]$, that is $-Q^2 + 70Q - 900 \geq 0$ and $Q \in [0, 50]$. The firm must produce at least $Q_0 = 35 - 5\sqrt{13} \approx 17$ units. (ii) Profits are maximized at $Q^* = 35$.

3. Profits are given by $\pi(x) = -0.003x^2 + 120x - 500\,000$, which is maximized at $x = 20\,000$.

4. (i) $Q^* = 450$ (ii) $Q^* = 550$ (iii) $Q^* = 0$

5. (a) $\pi(Q) = QP(Q) - C(Q) = -0.01Q^2 + 14Q - 4500$, which is maximized at $Q = 700$.

   (b) $\mathrm{El}_Q P(Q) = (Q/P(Q))P'(Q) = Q/(Q - 3000) = -1$ for $Q^* = 1500$.

   (c) $R(Q) = QP(Q) = 18Q - 0.006Q^2$, so $R'(Q) = 18 - 0.012Q = 0$ for $Q^* = 1500$.

6. $\pi'(Q) = P - abQ^{b-1} = 0$ when $Q^{b-1} = P/ab$, i.e. $Q = (P/ab)^{1/(b-1)}$. Moreover, $\pi''(Q) = -ab(b-1)Q^{b-2} < 0$ for all $Q > 0$, so this is a maximum point.

9.6

1. $f'(x) = 3x^2 - 12 = 0$ at $x = \pm 2$. A sign diagram shows that $x = 2$ is a local minimum point and $x = -2$ is a local maximum point. Since $f''(x) = 6x$, this is confirmed by Theorem 9.6.2.

2. (a) No local extreme points. (b) Local maximum 10 at $x = -1$. Local minimum 6 at $x = 1$.

   (c) Local maximum -2 at $x = -1$. Local minimum 2 at $x = 1$.

   (d) Local maximum $6\sqrt{3}$ at $x = -\sqrt{3}$. Local minimum $-6\sqrt{3}$ at $x = \sqrt{3}$.

   (e) No local maximum point. Local minimum $1/2$ at $x = 3$.

   (f) Local maximum 2 at $x = -2$. Local minimum -2 at $x = 0$.

3. (a) $D_f = [-6, 0) \cup (0, \infty)$; $f(x) > 0$ in $(-6, -2) \cup (0, \infty)$.

   (b) Local maximum $\tfrac{1}{2}\sqrt{2}$ at $x = -4$. Local minima $(8/3)\sqrt{3}$ at $x = 6$, and 0 at $x = -6$ (where $f'(x)$ is undefined).

   (c) $f(x) \to -\infty$ as $x \to 0^-$, $f(x) \to \infty$ as $x \to 0^+$, $f(x) \to \infty$ as $x \to \infty$, and $f'(x) \to 0$ as $x \to \infty$. So f attains neither a maximum nor a minimum.

4. Look at the point a. Since the graph shows $f'(x)$, one has $f'(x) < 0$ to the left of a, then $f'(a) = 0$, and $f'(x) > 0$ to the right of a, so a is a local minimum point. At the points b and e, one has $f'(x) > 0$ on both sides of each point, so they cannot be extreme points. At c, f has a local maximum, and at d it has a local minimum point.

5. (a) $f'(x) = 3x^2 + 2ax + b$, $f''(x) = 6x + 2a$. $f'(0) = 0$ requires $b = 0$. $f''(0) \geq 0$ requires $a \geq 0$. If $a = 0$ and $b = 0$, then $f(x) = x^3 + c$, which does not have a local minimum at $x = 0$. Hence, f has a local minimum at 0 if and only if $a > 0$ and $b = 0$.

   (b) $f'(1) = 0$ and $f'(3) = 0$ require $3 + 2a + b = 0$ and $27 + 6a + b = 0$, which means that $a = -6$ and $b = 9$.

6. (a) $f'(x) = x^2 e^x(3 + x)$. Use a sign diagram to show that $x = -3$ is a local (and global) minimum point. No local maximum points. ($x = 0$ is an inflection point).

   (b) $g'(x) = x2^x(2 + x \ln 2)$. $x = 0$ is a local minimum point and $x = -2/\ln 2$ is a local maximum point.

7. It is easy to see that $f(x) \to \infty$ as $x \to \infty$ and $f(x) \to -\infty$ if $x \to -\infty$, so by the intermediate value theorem $f(x) = 0$ for at least one x. If $a \geq 0$, then $f'(x) > 0$ for all $x \neq 0$, so f is strictly increasing in all of its domain, and the equation

874 SOLUTIONS TO THE EXERCISES

$f(x) = 0$ cannot have more than one solution. If $a < 0$, then $f'(0) < 0$ and the graph of f has roughly the same shape as the graph in Fig. 4.7.4. Then f has one local maximum point and one local minimum point and it is easy to see that the graph intersects the x-axis at three different points if and only if the local maximum is greater than zero and the local minimum is less that zero. Find expressions for these two local extreme values, then find a criterion for them to have different signs. See SM.

Review exercises for Chapter 9

1. (a) $f'(x) = \dfrac{4x}{(x^2+2)^2}$. Thus $f(x)$ decreases for $x \leq 0$, and increases for $x \geq 0$.

    (b) $f''(x) = 4(2 - 3x^2)/(x^2+2)^3$. There are inflection points at $x = \pm\frac{1}{3}\sqrt{6}$.

    (c) $f(x) \to 1$ as $x \to \pm\infty$. See Fig. A9.R.1.

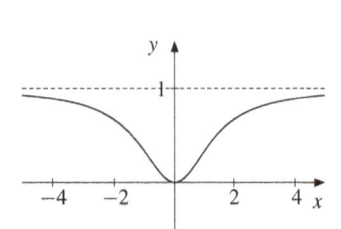

Figure A9.R.1

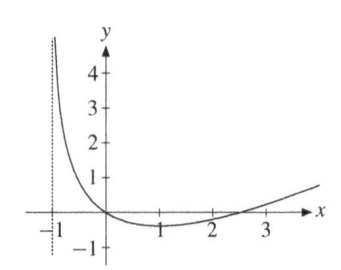

Figure A9.R.7

2. (a) $Q'(L) = 3L(8 - \frac{1}{20}L) = 0$ for $L = 160$, and $Q(L)$ is increasing in $[0, 160]$, decreasing in $[160, 200]$, so $Q^* = 160$ is the maximum value of $Q(L)$. (b) Output per worker is $Q(L)/L = 12L - \frac{1}{20}L^2$, and this quadratic function has a maximum at $L^* = 120$. $Q'(120) = Q(120)/120 = 720$. In general (see Example 6.7.6) one has $(d/dL)(Q(L)/L) = (1/L)(Q'(L) - Q(L)/L)$. If $L > 0$ maximizes output per worker, one must have $Q'(L) = Q(L)/L$.

3. If the side parallel to the river is y and the other side is x, then $2x + y = 1000$, so $y = 1000 - 2x$. The area of the enclosure is $xy = 1000x - 2x^2$. This quadratic function has a maximum at $x = 250$, when $y = 500$.

4. (a) $\pi = -0.0016Q^2 + 44Q - 0.0004Q^2 - 8Q - 64\,000 = -0.002Q^2 + 36Q - 64\,000$, and $Q = 9000$ maximizes π.

    (b) $\mathrm{El}_Q\, C(Q) = \dfrac{Q}{C(Q)} C'(Q) = \dfrac{0.0008Q^2 + 8Q}{0.0004Q^2 + 8Q + 64\,000} \approx 0.12$ when $Q = 1000$.

    This means that if Q increases from 1000 by 1%, then costs will increase by about 0.12%.

5. Profit as a function of Q is $\pi(Q) = PQ - C = (a - bQ^2)Q - \alpha + \beta Q = -bQ^3 + (a+\beta)Q - \alpha$.

    Then $\pi'(Q) = -3bQ^2 + a + \beta$, which is 0 for $Q^2 = (a+\beta)/3b$, and so $Q = \sqrt{(a+\beta)/3b}$.

    This value of Q maximizes profit because $\pi''(Q) = -6bQ \leq 0$ for all $Q \geq 0$.

6. (a) For $x > 0$ one has $R = p\sqrt{x}$, $C = wx + F$, and $\pi(x) = p\sqrt{x} - wx - F$.

    (b) $\pi'(x) = 0$ when $w = p/2\sqrt{x}$. (Marginal cost = price times marginal product.) Then $x = p^2/4w^2$. Moreover, $\pi''(x) = -\frac{1}{4}px^{-3/2} < 0$ for all $x > 0$, so profit is maximized over $(0, \infty)$. When $x = p^2/4w^2$, then $\pi = p^2/2w - p^2/4w - F = p^2/4w - F$. So this is a profit maximum if $F \leq p^2/4w$; otherwise, the firm does better not to start up and to choose $x = 0$.

7. (a) g is defined for $x > -1$. (b) $g'(x) = 1 - 2/(x+1) = (x-1)/(x+1)$, $g''(x) = 2/(x+1)^2$.

    (c) Since $g'(x) < 0$ in $(-1, 1)$, $g'(1) = 0$ and $g'(x) > 0$ in $(1, \infty)$, $x = 1$ is a (global) minimum point.

Since $g''(x) > 0$ for all $x > -1$, the function g is convex and there are no inflection points.

When $x \to (-1)^-$, so $g(x) \to \infty$ and when $x \to \infty$, so $g(x) \to \infty$. See Fig. A9.R.7.

8. (a) $D_f = (-1, \infty)$. (b) A sign diagram shows that $f'(x) \geq 0$ in $(-1, 1]$ and $f'(x) \leq 0$ in $[1, \infty)$. Hence $x = 1$ is a maximum point. f has no minimum. $f''(x) = \dfrac{-x(x^2 + x - 1)}{(x+1)^2} = 0$ for $x = 0$ and for $x = \frac{1}{2}(\sqrt{5} - 1)$. (The point $x = \frac{1}{2}(-\sqrt{5} - 1)$ is outside the domain.) Since $f''(x)$ changes sign around $x = 0$, this an inflection point. (c) $f(x) \to -\infty$ as $x \to (-1)^+$. See Fig. A9.R.8.

9. (a) h is increasing in $(-\infty, \frac{1}{2} \ln 2]$ and decreasing in $[\frac{1}{2} \ln 2, \infty)$, so h has a maximum at $x = \frac{1}{2} \ln 2$. It has no minimum.

(b) h is strictly increasing in $(-\infty, 0]$ (with range $(0, 1/3]$), and therefore has an inverse. This inverse is $h^{-1}(y) = \ln(1 - \sqrt{1 - 8y^2}) - \ln(2y)$. See Fig. A9.R.9.

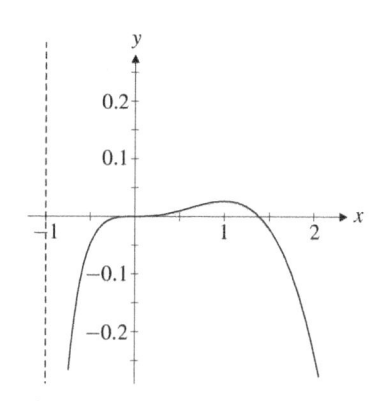

Figure A9.R.8

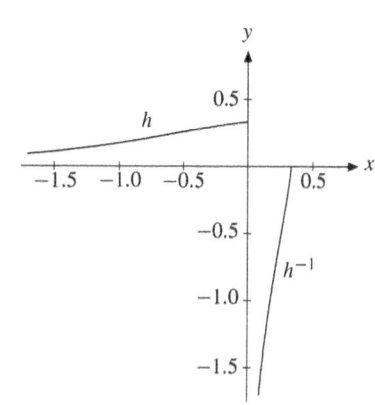

Figure A9.R.9

10. (a) $f'(x) = 4e^{4x} + 8e^x - 32e^{-2x}$, $f''(x) = 16e^{4x} + 8e^x + 64e^{-2x}$ (b) $f'(x) = 4e^{-2x}(e^{3x} + 4)(e^{3x} - 2)$, so $f(x)$ is decreasing in $(-\infty, \frac{1}{3} \ln 2]$, increasing in $[\frac{1}{3} \ln 2, \infty)$. $f''(x) > 0$ for all x so f is strictly convex.

(c) $\frac{1}{3} \ln 2$ is a (global) minimum. No maximum exists because $f(x) \to \infty$ as $x \to \infty$.

11. (a) D_f is the set of all $x \neq \pm\sqrt{a}$. $f(x)$ is positive in $(-\sqrt{a}, 0)$ and in $(\sqrt{a}, \infty)$. The graph is symmetric about the origin because $f(-x) = -f(x)$. See the end of Section 5.2.

(b) $f(x)$ is increasing in $(-\infty, -\sqrt{3a}]$ and in $[\sqrt{3a}, \infty)$, but decreasing in $[-\sqrt{3a}, -\sqrt{a})$, in $(-\sqrt{a}, \sqrt{a})$, and in $(\sqrt{a}, \sqrt{3a}]$. Hence $x = -\sqrt{3a}$ is a local maximum point and $x = \sqrt{3a}$ is a local minimum point.

(c) There are inflection points at $-3\sqrt{a}$, 0, and $3\sqrt{a}$.

12. $x = \sqrt{3}$ is a maximum point, whereas $x = -\sqrt{3}$ is a minimum point, and $x = 0$ is an inflection point. See Fig. A9.R.12.

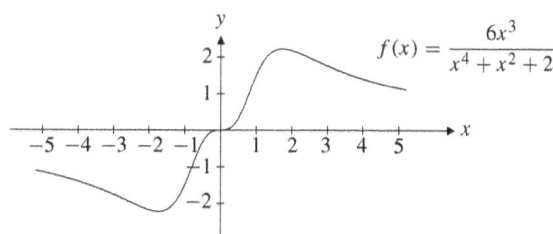

Figure A9.R.12

& SOLUTIONS TO THE EXERCISES

Chapter 10

10.1

1. (a) $\frac{1}{14}x^{14} + C$ (b) $\frac{2}{5}x^2\sqrt{x} + C$. (Note: $x\sqrt{x} = x \cdot x^{1/2} = x^{3/2}$.) (c) $2\sqrt{x} + C$. (Note: $1/\sqrt{x} = x^{-1/2}$.)
   (d) $\frac{8}{15}x^{15/8} + C$. (Note: $\sqrt{x\sqrt{x\sqrt{x}}} = \sqrt{x\sqrt{x^{3/2}}} = \sqrt{x \cdot x^{3/4}} = \sqrt{x^{7/4}} = x^{7/8}$.) (e) $-e^{-x} + C$ (f) $4e^{\frac{1}{4}x} + C$
   (g) $-\frac{3}{2}e^{-2x} + C$ (h) $(1/\ln 2)2^x + C$

2. (a) $C(x) = \frac{3}{2}x^2 + 4x + 40$. (Note: $C(x) = \int (3x + 4)\,dx = \frac{3}{2}x^2 + 4x + C$. Then $C(0) = 40$ implies $C = 40$.)
   (b) $C(x) = \frac{1}{2}ax^2 + bx + C_0$

3. (a) $\frac{1}{4}x^4 + x^2 - 3x + C$ (b) $\frac{1}{3}(x-1)^3 + C$ (c) $\frac{1}{3}x^3 + \frac{1}{2}x^2 - 2x + C$
   (d) $\frac{1}{4}(x+2)^4 + C$ (e) $\frac{1}{3}e^{3x} - \frac{1}{2}e^{2x} + e^x + C$ (f) $\frac{1}{3}x^3 - 3x + 4\ln|x| + C$

4. (a) $\frac{2}{5}y^2\sqrt{y} - \frac{8}{3}y\sqrt{y} + 8\sqrt{y} + C$
   (b) $\frac{1}{3}x^3 - \frac{1}{2}x^2 + x - \ln|x+1| + C$ (Note: $x^3/(x+1) = x^2 - x + 1 - 1/(x+1)$.)
   (c) $\frac{1}{32}(1+x^2)^{16} + C$

5. (a) and (b): Differentiate each right-hand side and check that you get the corresponding integrand.
   (For part (a) see also Problem 10.5.5.)

6. (a) Figure 10.1.1 shows that the quadratic equation $f'(x) = 0$ has roots at $x = -1$ and at $x = 3$. So one must have $f'(x) = A(x+1)(x-3)$.
   (b) Figure 10.1.1 also shows that $f'(1) = -1$, implying that $A = 1/4$, so $f'(x) = \frac{1}{4}(x+1)(x-3) = \frac{1}{4}x^2 - \frac{1}{2}x - \frac{3}{4}$. Integrating yields $f(x) = \frac{1}{12}x^3 - \frac{1}{4}x^2 - \frac{3}{4}x + C$. Since $f(0) = 2$, one has $C = 2$. (c) See Fig. A10.1.6.

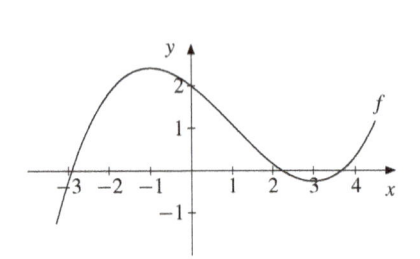

Figure A10.1.6

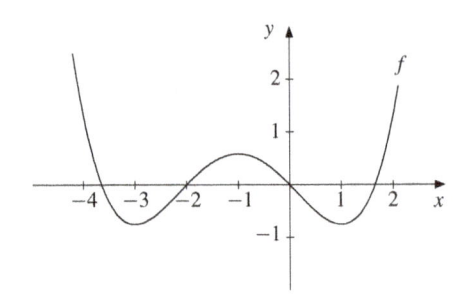

Figure A10.1.7

7. The graph of $f'(x)$ in the problem can be that of a cubic function, with roots at $-3, -1$, and 1, and with $f'(0) = -1$. So $f'(x) = \frac{1}{3}(x+3)(x+1)(x-1) = \frac{1}{3}x^3 + x^2 - \frac{1}{3}x - 1$. If $f(0) = 0$, integrating gives $f(x) = \frac{1}{12}x^4 + \frac{1}{3}x^3 - \frac{1}{6}x^2 - x$. Figure A10.1.7 is the graph of this f.

8. Differentiate the right-hand side and check that you get the integrand.

9. Differentiate the right-hand side. (Once we have learned integration by substitution in Section 10.6, this integral will become easy.)

10. (a) $\frac{1}{10}(2x+1)^5 + C$ (b) $\frac{2}{3}(x+2)^{3/2} + C$ (c) $-2\sqrt{4-x} + C$

11. (a) $F(x) = \int \left(\frac{1}{2}e^x - 2x\right) dx = \frac{1}{2}e^x - x^2 + C$. Then $F(0) = \frac{1}{2}$ implies $C = 0$.

(b) $F(x) = \int (x - x^3) dx = \frac{1}{2}x^2 - \frac{1}{4}x^4 + C$. Then $F(1) = \frac{5}{12}$ implies $C = \frac{1}{6}$.

12. The general form for f' is $f'(x) = \frac{1}{3}x^3 + A$, so that for f is $f(x) = \frac{1}{12}x^4 + Ax + B$. If we require that $f(0) = 1$ and $f'(0) = -1$, then $B = 1$ and $A = -1$, so $f(x) = \frac{1}{12}x^4 - x + 1$.

13. $f(x) = -\ln x + \frac{1}{20}x^5 + x^2 - x - \frac{1}{20}$

10.2

1. (a) $A = \int_0^1 x^3 \, dx = \left|\frac{1}{4}x^4\right|_0^1 = \frac{1}{4}1^4 - \frac{1}{4}0^4 = \frac{1}{4}$. (b) $A = \int_0^1 x^{10} \, dx = \left|\frac{1}{11}x^{11}\right|_0^1 = \frac{1}{11}$

2. (a) $\int_0^2 3x^2 \, dx = \left|x^3\right|_0^2 = 8$ (b) $1/7$ (c) $e - 1/e$. (See the shaded area in Fig. A10.2.2.) (d) $9/10$

3. See Fig. A10.2.3. $A = -\int_{-2}^{-1} x^{-3} \, dx = -\left|_{-2}^{-1}\left(-\frac{1}{2}\right)x^{-2}\right| = -\left[-\frac{1}{2} - \left(-\frac{1}{8}\right)\right] = \frac{3}{8}$

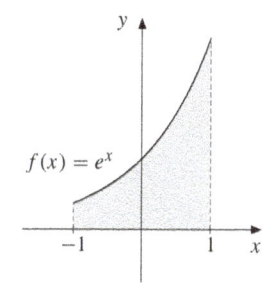

Figure A10.2.2

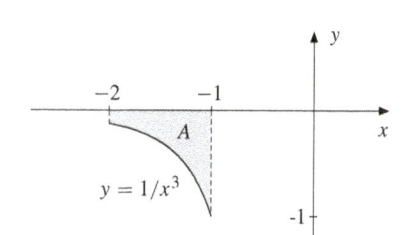

Figure A10.2.3

4. $A = \frac{1}{2}\int_{-1}^{1}(e^x + e^{-x}) \, dx = \frac{1}{2}\left|(e^x - e^{-x})\right|_{-1}^{1} = e - e^{-1}$

5. (a) $\int_0^1 x \, dx = \left|\frac{1}{2}x^2\right|_0^1 = \frac{1}{2}$ (b) $16/3$ (c) $5/12$ (d) $-12/5$ (e) $41/2$ (f) $\ln 2 + 5/2$

6. (a) $f'(x) = 3x^2 - 6x + 2 = 0$ when $x_0 = 1 - \frac{1}{3}\sqrt{3}$ and $x_1 = 1 + \frac{1}{3}\sqrt{3}$. So $f(x)$ increases in $(-\infty, x_0)$ and in (x_1, ∞).

(b) See Fig. A10.2.6. The shaded area is $\frac{1}{4}$.

7. (a) $f'(x) = -1 + 3\,000\,000/x^2 = 0$ for $x = \sqrt{3\,000\,000} = 1000\sqrt{3}$. (Recall $x > 0$.)

Profits are maximized at $x = 1000\sqrt{3}$. See Fig. A10.2.7.

(b) $I = \frac{1}{2000}\left|_{1000}^{3000}\left(4000x - \frac{1}{2}x^2 - 3\,000\,000 \ln x\right)\right| = 2000 - 1500 \ln 3 \approx 352$

8. (a) $6/5$ (b) $26/3$ (c) $\alpha(e^\beta - 1)/\beta$ (d) $-\ln 2$

878 SOLUTIONS TO THE EXERCISES

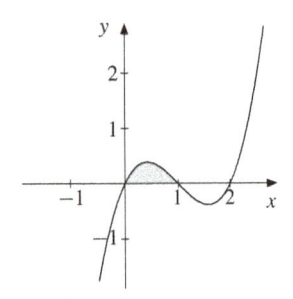

Figure A10.2.6

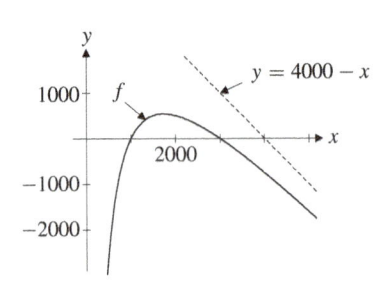

Figure A10.2.7

10.3

1. (a) $\left|_0^5 (\frac{1}{2}x^2 + \frac{1}{3}x^3)\right| = 325/6$ (b) 0 (c) $\ln 9$ (d) $e - 1$ (e) -136 (f) $687/64$

(g) $\int_0^4 \frac{1}{2}x^{1/2}\,dx = \left|_0^4 \frac{1}{2} \cdot \frac{2}{3}x^{3/2}\right| = \frac{8}{3}$ (h) $\int_1^2 \frac{1+x^3}{x^2}\,dx = \int_1^2 \left(\frac{1}{x^2} + x\right) dx = \left|_1^2 \left(-\frac{1}{x} + \frac{1}{2}x^2\right)\right| = 2$

2. $\int_c^b f(x)\,dx = \int_a^b f(x)\,dx - \int_a^c f(x)\,dx = 8 - 4 = 4$

3. Let $A = \int_0^1 f(x)\,dx$ and $B = \int_0^1 g(x)\,dx$. Then the two equations imply that $A - 2B = 6$ and $2A + 2B = 9$. Solving these gives $A = 5$ and $B = -1/2$, so $I = A - B = 11/2$.

4. $1/(p + q + 1) + 1/(p + r + 1)$

5. $f(x) = 4x^3 - 3x^2 + 5$

6. (a) $\left|_0^3 \left[\frac{1}{9}e^{3t-2} + \ln(t + 2)\right]\right| = \frac{1}{9}(e^7 - e^{-2}) + \ln(5/2)$ (b) $83/15$ (c) $2\sqrt{2} - 3/2$

(d) $A\{b - 1 + (b - c)\ln[(b + c)/(1 + c)]\} + d \ln b$

7. Formula (10.3.6) implies that $F'(x) = x^2 + 2$. Combined with the chain rule, it implies that $G'(x) = 2x[(x^2)^2 + 2] = 2x^5 + 4x$.

8. Formula (10.3.6), when combined with the chain rule, implies that $H'(t) = 2tK(t^2)e^{-\rho t^2}$.

9. We use formula (10.3.8) to find the derivatives: (a) t^2 (b) $-e^{-t^2}$ (c) $2/\sqrt{t^4 + 1}$

(d) $[f(2) - g(2)] \cdot 0 - [f(-\lambda) - g(-\lambda)] \cdot (-1) = f(-\lambda) - g(-\lambda)$

10. From $y^2 = 3x$ we get $x = \frac{1}{3}y^2$. Inserting this into the other equation gives $y + 1 = (\frac{1}{3}y^2 - 1)^2$, or $y(y^3 - 6y - 9) = 0$. Here $y^3 - 6y - 9 = (y - 3)(y^2 + 3y + 3)$, where $y^2 + 3y + 3$ is never 0. So $(0, 0)$ and $(3, 3)$ are the only points of intersection. The area between the parabolas is $A = \int_0^3 (\sqrt{3x} - x^2 + 2x)\,dx = 6$. See Fig. A10.3.10.

11. $W(T) = (K/T)\left|_0^T (-1/\rho)e^{-\rho t}\right| = K(1 - e^{-\rho T})/\rho T$

12. (a) The inverse is found by solving $x = 4\ln(\sqrt{y + 4} - 2)$ for y, to obtain $e^{x/4} = \sqrt{y + 4} - 2$ and so $y = (e^{x/4} + 2)^2 - 4$. Thus, $y = g(x) = e^{x/2} + 4e^{x/4}$ defined on $(-\infty, \infty)$. (b) See Fig. A10.3.12.

(c) Because f and g are inverses, the shaded areas marked A and B in Fig. A10.3.12 are equal.

So $\int_5^{10} 4\ln(\sqrt{x + 4} - 2)\,dx = A = B = 10a - \int_0^a \left[e^{x/2} + 4e^{x/4}\right] dx = 10a - 2e^{a/2} - 16e^{a/4} + 18$. See SM.

CHAPTER 10   879

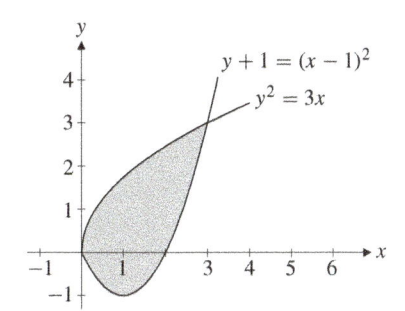

Figure A10.3.10

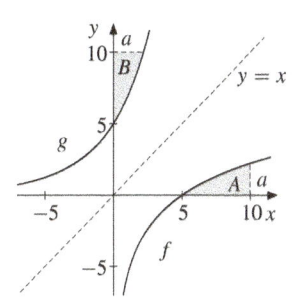

Figure A10.3.12

10.4

1. $x(t) = K - \int_0^t \bar{u}e^{-as}\,ds = K - \bar{u}(1 - e^{-at})/a$. Note that $x(t) \to K - \bar{u}/a$ as $t \to \infty$. If $K \geq \bar{u}/a$, the well will never be exhausted.

2. (a) $m = 2b \ln 2$ (b) $x(p) = nABp^\gamma b^{\delta-1}(2^{\delta-1} - 1)/(\delta - 1)$

3. We have $S = \int_0^T (1/r)e^{rt} = (e^{rT} - 1)/r$, implying that $e^{rT} - 1 = rS$. Solving for T gives $T = \dfrac{1}{r}\ln(1 + rS)$.

4. (a) $K(5) - K(0) = \int_0^5 (3t^2 + 2t + 5)\,dt = 175$ (b) $K(T) - K_0 = (T^3 - t_0^3) + (T^2 - t_0^2) + 5(T - t_0)$

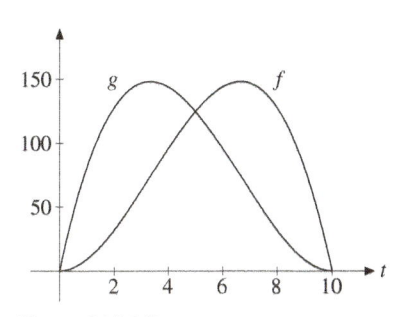

Figure A10.4.5

5. (a) See Fig. A10.4.5. (b) $\int_0^t (g(\tau) - f(\tau))\,d\tau = \int_0^t (2\tau^3 - 30\tau^2 + 100\tau)\,d\tau = \tfrac{1}{2}t^2(t - 10)^2 \geq 0$ for all t.

   (c) $\int_0^{10} p(t)f(t)\,dt = \int_0^{10}(-t^3 + 9t^2 + 11t - 11 + 11/(t+1))\,dt = 940 + 11\ln 11 \approx 966.38$, whereas $\int_0^{10} p(t)g(t)\,dt = \int_0^{10}(t^3 - 19t^2 + 79t + 121 - 121/(t+1))\,dt = 3980/3 - 121\ln 11 \approx 1036.52$. Profile g should be chosen.

6. The equilibrium quantity is $Q^* = 600$, where $P^* = 80$. Then $\text{CS} = \int_0^{600}(120 - 0.2Q)\,dQ = 36\,000$, and $\text{PS} = \int_0^{600}(60 - 0.1Q)\,dQ = 18\,000$.

7. Equilibrium occurs when $6000/(Q^* + 50) = Q^* + 10$. The only positive solution is $Q^* = 50$, and then $P^* = 60$. Then $\text{CS} = \int_0^{50}\left[\dfrac{6000}{Q+50} - 60\right]dQ = \Big|_0^{50}[6000\ln(Q+50) - 60Q] = 6000\ln 2 - 3000$, and $\text{PS} = \int_0^{50}(50 - Q)\,dQ = 1250$.

10.5

1. (a) Use (10.5.1) with $f(x) = x$ and $g'(x) = e^{-x}$: $\int xe^{-x}\,dx = x(-e^{-x}) - \int 1 \cdot (-e^{-x})\,dx = -xe^{-x} - e^{-x} + C$.
   (b) $\frac{3}{4}xe^{4x} - \frac{3}{16}e^{4x} + C$ (c) $-x^2 e^{-x} - 2xe^{-x} - 3e^{-x} + C$ (d) $\frac{1}{2}x^2 \ln x - \frac{1}{4}x^2 + C$

2. (a) $\int_{-1}^{1} x\ln(x+2)\,dx = \left|\frac{1}{2}x^2 \ln(x+2)\right|_{-1}^{1} - \int_{-1}^{1} \frac{1}{2}x^2 \frac{1}{x+2}\,dx = \frac{1}{2}\ln 3 - \frac{1}{2}\int_{-1}^{1}\left(x - 2 + \frac{4}{x+2}\right)dx = 2 - \frac{3}{2}\ln 3$
   (b) $8/(\ln 2) - 3/(\ln 2)^2$ (c) $e - 2$ (d) $7\frac{11}{15} = \frac{116}{15}$

3. (a) $\int_1^4 \sqrt{t}\ln t\,dt = \int_1^4 t^{1/2}\ln t\,dt = \left|\frac{2}{3}t^{3/2}\ln t\right|_1^4 - \frac{2}{3}\int_1^4 t^{3/2}(1/t)\,dt = \frac{16}{3}\ln 4 - \frac{2}{3}\left|\frac{2}{3}t^{3/2}\right|_1^4 = \frac{16}{3}\ln 4 - \frac{28}{9}$
   (b) $\int_0^2 (x-2)e^{-x/2}\,dx = \left|(x-2)(-2)e^{-x/2}\right|_0^2 - \int_0^2 (-2)e^{-x/2}\,dt = -4 - 4\left|e^{-x/2}\right|_0^2 = -4 - 4(e^{-1} - 1) = -4e^{-1}$
   (c) $\int_0^3 (3-x)3^x\,dx = \left|(3-x)(3^x/\ln 3)\right|_0^3 - \int_0^3 (-1)(3^x/\ln 3)\,dx = 26/(\ln 3)^2 - 3/\ln 3$

4. The general formula follows from (10.5.1), and yields $\int \ln x\,dx = x\ln x - x + C$.

5. Use (10.5.1) with $f(x) = \ln x$ and $g'(x) = x^p$. (Alternatively, simply differentiate the right-hand side.)

6. (a) $br^{-2}\left[1 - (1 + rT)e^{-rT}\right]$ (b) $ar^{-1}(1 - e^{-rT}) + br^{-2}\left[1 - (1 + rT)e^{-rT}\right]$
   (c) $ar^{-1}(1 - e^{-rT}) - br^{-2}\left[1 - (1 + rT)e^{-rT}\right] + cr^{-3}\left[2(1 - e^{-rT}) - 2rTe^{-rT} - r^2T^2 e^{-rT}\right]$

10.6

1. (a) $\frac{1}{9}(x^2 + 1)^9 + C$. (Substitute $u = x^2 + 1$, so $du = 2x\,dx$.)   (b) $\frac{1}{11}(x+2)^{11} + C$. (Substitute $u = x + 2$.)
   (c) $\ln|x^2 - x + 8| + C$. (Substitute $u = x^2 - x + 8$.)

2. (a) $\frac{1}{24}(2x^2 + 3)^6 + C$. (Substitute $u = 2x^2 + 3$, so $du = 4x\,dx$.)   (b) $\frac{1}{3}e^{x^3 + 2} + C$. (Substitute $u = e^{x^3 + 2}$.)
   (c) $\frac{1}{4}(\ln(x+2))^2 + C$. (Substitute $u = \ln(x+2)$.)   (d) $\frac{2}{5}(1+x)^{5/2} - \frac{2}{3}(1+x)^{3/2} + C$. (Substitute $u = \sqrt{1+x}$.)
   (e) $\frac{-1}{2(1+x^2)} + \frac{1}{4(1+x^2)^2} + C$ (f) $\frac{2}{15}(4 - x^3)^{5/2} - \frac{8}{9}(4 - x^3)^{3/2} + C$

3. (a) With $u = \sqrt{1+x^2}$, $u^2 = 1 + x^2$, so $u\,du = x\,dx$. If $x = 0$, then $u = 1$; if $x = 1$, then $u = \sqrt{2}$.
   Hence, $\int_0^1 x\sqrt{1+x^2}\,dx = \int_1^{\sqrt{2}} u^2\,du = \left|\frac{1}{3}u^3\right|_1^{\sqrt{2}} = \frac{1}{3}(2\sqrt{2} - 1)$.
   (b) $1/2$. (Let $u = \ln y$.)   (c) $\frac{1}{2}(e^2 - e^{2/3})$. (Let $u = 2/x$.)
   (d) Method 1: $\int_5^8 \frac{x}{x-4}\,dx = \int_5^8 \frac{x - 4 + 4}{x-4}\,dx = \int_5^8 \left(1 + \frac{4}{x-4}\right)dx = \left|[x + 4\ln(x-4)]\right|_5^8 = 3 + 4\ln 4$.
   Method 2: Introduce the new variable $u = x - 4$. Then $du = dx$ and $x = u + 4$. When $x = 5$, $u = 1$, and when $x = 8$, $u = 4$, so $\int_5^8 \frac{x}{x-4}\,dx = \int_1^4 \frac{u+4}{u}\,du = \int_1^4 \left(1 + \frac{4}{u}\right)du = \left|(u + 4\ln u)\right|_1^4 = 3 + 4\ln 4$.

CHAPTER 10 881

4. $\int_3^x \frac{2t-2}{t^2-2t} \, dt = \Big|_3^x \ln(t^2 - 2t) = \ln(x^2 - 2x) - \ln 3 = \ln \frac{1}{3}(x^2 - 2x)$. The equation to be solved becomes $\ln \frac{1}{3}(x^2 - 2x) = \ln(\frac{2}{3}x - 1) = \ln \frac{1}{3}(2x - 3)$, which implies $x^2 - 2x = 2x - 3$. Hence, $x^2 - 4x + 3 = 0$, with solutions $x = 1$ and $x = 3$. But only $x = 3$ is in the specified domain $x > 2$. So the solution is $x = 3$.

5. Substitute $z = x(t)$. Then $dz = \dot{x}(t) \, dt$, and the result follows using (10.6.2).

6. (a) $1/70$. $((x^4 - x^9)(x^5 - 1)^{12} = -x^4(x^5 - 1)^{13}$.) (b) $2\sqrt{x} \ln x - 4\sqrt{x} + C$. (Let $u = \sqrt{x}$.) (c) $8/3$

7. (a) $2\ln(1 + e^2) - 2\ln(1 + e)$ (b) $\ln 2 - \ln(e^{-1/3} + 1)$ (c) $7 + 2\ln 2$

8. Substitute $u = x^{1/6}$. Then $I = 6 \int \frac{u^8}{1 - u^2} \, du$. Here $u^8 \div (-u^2 + 1) = -u^6 - u^4 - u^2 - 1 + 1/(-u^2 + 1)$. It follows that $I = -\frac{6}{7}x^{7/6} - \frac{6}{5}x^{5/6} - 2x^{1/2} - 6x^{1/6} - 3\ln|1 - x^{1/6}| + 3\ln|1 + x^{1/6}| + C$.

9. We find $f(x) = \frac{1}{a - b}\left[\frac{ac + d}{x - a} - \frac{bc + d}{x - b}\right]$.

(a) $\int \frac{x \, dx}{(x+1)(x+2)} = \int \frac{-1 \, dx}{x+1} + \int \frac{2 \, dx}{x+2} = -\ln|x+1| + 2\ln|x+2| + C$

(b) $\int \frac{(1-2x) \, dx}{(x+3)(x-5)} = \int \left[-\frac{7}{8}\frac{1}{x+3} - \frac{9}{8}\frac{1}{x-5}\right] dx = -\frac{7}{8}\ln|x+3| - \frac{9}{8}\ln|x-5| + C$

10.7

1. (a) $\int_1^b x^{-3} \, dx = \Big|_1^b \left(-\frac{1}{2}x^{-2}\right) = \frac{1}{2} - \frac{1}{2}b^{-2} \to \frac{1}{2}$ as $b \to \infty$. So $\int_1^\infty \frac{1}{x^3} \, dx = \frac{1}{2}$.

(b) $\int_1^b x^{-1/2} \, dx = \Big|_1^b 2x^{1/2} = 2b^{1/2} - 2 \to \infty$ as $b \to \infty$, so the integral diverges.

(c) 1 (d) $\int_0^a (x/\sqrt{a^2 - x^2}) \, dx = -\Big|_0^a \sqrt{a^2 - x^2} = a$

2. (a) $\int_{-\infty}^{+\infty} f(x) \, dx = \int_a^b \frac{1}{b-a} \, dx = \frac{1}{b-a}\Big|_a^b x = \frac{1}{b-a}(b-a) = 1$

(b) $\int_{-\infty}^{+\infty} xf(x) \, dx = \frac{1}{b-a}\int_a^b x \, dx = \frac{1}{2(b-a)}\Big|_a^b x^2 = \frac{1}{2(b-a)}(b^2 - a^2) = \frac{1}{2}(a + b)$

(c) $\frac{1}{3(b-a)}\Big|_a^b x^3 = \frac{1}{3}\frac{b^3 - a^3}{b - a} = \frac{1}{3}(a^2 + ab + b^2)$

3. Using a simplified notation and the result in Example 10.7.1, we have:

(a) $\int_0^\infty x\lambda e^{-\lambda x} \, dx = -\Big|_0^\infty xe^{-\lambda x} + \int_0^\infty e^{-\lambda x} \, dx = 1/\lambda$ (b) $1/\lambda^2$ (c) $2/\lambda^3$

4. The first integral diverges because $\int_0^b [x/(1 + x^2)] \, dx = \Big|_0^b \frac{1}{2}\ln(1 + x^2) = \frac{1}{2}\ln(1 + b^2) \to \infty$ as $b \to \infty$.

On the other hand, $\int_{-b}^b [x/(1 + x^2)] \, dx = \Big|_{-b}^b \frac{1}{2}\ln(1 + x^2) = 0$ for all b, so the limit as $b \to \infty$ is 0.

5. (a) f has a maximum at $(e^{1/3}, 1/3e)$, but no minimum. (b) $\int_0^1 x^{-3} \ln x \, dx$ diverges. $\int_1^\infty x^{-3} \ln x \, dx = 1/4$.

6. $\frac{1}{1 + x^2} \leq \frac{1}{x^2}$ for $x \geq 1$, and $\int_1^b \frac{dx}{x^2} = \Big|_1^b -\frac{1}{x} = 1 - \frac{1}{b} \xrightarrow{b \to \infty} 1$, so by Theorem 10.7.1 the integral converges.

7. Put $u = x + 2$ and $v = 3 - x$. Then the integral becomes

$$\int_0^5 u^{-1/2}\,du - \int_5^0 v^{-1/2}\,dv = 2\lim_{\varepsilon \to 0}\int_\varepsilon^5 u^{-1/2}\,du = 4\lim_{\varepsilon \to 0}\Big|_\varepsilon^5 u^{1/2} = 4\lim_{\varepsilon \to 0}\left(\sqrt{5} - \sqrt{\varepsilon}\right) = 4\sqrt{5}.$$

8. (a) $z = \int_0^\tau (1/\tau)e^{-rs}\,ds = (1 - e^{-r\tau})/r\tau$ (b) $z = \int_0^\tau 2(\tau - s)\tau^{-2}e^{-rs}\,ds = (2/r\tau)\left[1 - (1/r\tau)(1 - e^{-r\tau})\right]$

9. $\int x^{-2}\,dx = -x^{-1} + C$. So evaluating $\int_{-1}^1 x^{-2}\,dx$ as $\Big|_{-1}^1 -x^{-1}$ gives the nonsensical answer -2.

The error arises because x^{-2} diverges to $+\infty$ as $x \to 0$. (In fact, $\int_{-1}^1 x^{-2}\,dx$ diverges to $+\infty$.)

10. Using the answer to Exercise 10.6.6(b), one has $\int_h^1 (\ln x/\sqrt{x})\,dx = \Big|_h^1 (2\sqrt{x}\ln x - 4\sqrt{x}) = -4 - (2\sqrt{h}\ln h - 4\sqrt{h})$.
As $h \to 0^+$, l'Hôpital's rule implies that $\sqrt{h}\ln h = \ln h/h^{-1/2} = \text{``}\infty/\infty\text{''} \to 0$, so the given integral converges to -4.

11. $\int_1^A [k/x - k^2/(1 + kx)]\,dx = k\ln[1/(1/A + k)] - k\ln[1/(1 + k)] \to k\ln(1/k) - k\ln[1/(1 + k)] = \ln(1 + 1/k)^k$ as $A \to \infty$. So $I_k = \ln(1 + 1/k)^k$, which tends to $\ln e = 1$ as $k \to \infty$.

12. The suggested substitution $u = (x - \mu)/\sqrt{2}\sigma$ gives $du = dx/\sigma\sqrt{2}$, and so $dx = \sigma\sqrt{2}\,du$. Hence:

(a) $\int_{-\infty}^{+\infty} f(x)\,dx = \dfrac{1}{\sqrt{\pi}}\int_{-\infty}^{+\infty} e^{-u^2}\,du = 1$, by (10.7.9).

(b) $\int_{-\infty}^{+\infty} xf(x)\,dx = \dfrac{1}{\sqrt{\pi}}\int_{-\infty}^{+\infty} (\mu + \sqrt{2}\sigma u)e^{-u^2}\,du = \mu$, using part (a) and (10.7.5).

(c) $\int_{-\infty}^{+\infty} (x - \mu)^2 f(x)\,dx = \int_{-\infty}^{+\infty} 2\sigma^2 u^2 \dfrac{1}{\sigma\sqrt{2\pi}} e^{-u^2}\sigma\sqrt{2}\,du = \sigma^2 \dfrac{2}{\sqrt{\pi}}\int_{-\infty}^{+\infty} u^2 e^{-u^2}\,du$. Now integration by parts

yields $\int u^2 e^{-u^2}\,du = -\tfrac{1}{2}ue^{-u^2} + \int \tfrac{1}{2} e^{-u^2}\,du$, so $\int_{-\infty}^{+\infty} u^2 e^{-u^2}\,du = \tfrac{1}{2}\sqrt{\pi}$. Hence the integral equals σ^2.

Review exercises for Chapter 10

1. (a) $-16x + C$ (b) $5^5 x + C$ (c) $3y - \tfrac{1}{2}y^2 + C$ (d) $\tfrac{1}{2}r^2 - \tfrac{16}{5}r^{5/4} + C$ (e) $\tfrac{1}{9}x^9 + C$
(f) $\tfrac{2}{7}x^{7/2} + C$. $(x^2\sqrt{x} = x^2 \cdot x^{1/2} = x^{5/2}$.) (g) $-\tfrac{1}{4}p^{-4} + C$ (h) $\tfrac{1}{4}x^4 + \tfrac{1}{2}x^2 + C$

2. (a) $e^{2x} + C$ (b) $\tfrac{1}{2}x^2 - \tfrac{25}{2}e^{2x/5} + C$ (c) $-\tfrac{1}{3}e^{-3x} + \tfrac{1}{3}e^{3x} + C$ (d) $2\ln|x + 5| + C$

3. (a) $\int_0^{12} 50\,dx = \Big|_0^{12} 50x = 600$ (b) $\int_0^2 (x - \tfrac{1}{2}x^2)\,dx = \Big|_0^2 (\tfrac{1}{2}x^2 - \tfrac{1}{6}x^3) = \tfrac{2}{3}$

(c) $\int_{-3}^3 (u + 1)^2\,du = \Big|_{-3}^3 \tfrac{1}{3}(u + 1)^3 = 24$ (d) $\int_1^5 \dfrac{2}{z}\,dz = \Big|_1^5 2\ln z = 2\ln 5$

(e) $\int_2^{12} \dfrac{3}{t + 4}\,dt = \Big|_2^{12} 3\ln(t + 4) = 3(\ln 16 - \ln 6) = 3\ln(8/3)$

(f) $I = \int_0^4 v\sqrt{v^2 + 9}\,dv = \Big|_0^4 \tfrac{1}{3}(v^2 + 9)^{3/2} = 98/3$. $\Big($Or let $z = \sqrt{v^2 + 9}$, when $z^2 = v^2 + 9$, so $2z\,dz = 2v\,dv$, or $v\,dv = z\,dz$. When $v = 0$, $z = 3$, and when $v = 4$, $z = 5$, so $I = \int_3^5 z^2\,dz = \Big|_3^5 \tfrac{1}{3}z^3 = 98/3.\Big)$

4. (a) $5/4$ (b) $31/20$ (c) -5 (d) $e - 2$ (e) $52/9$ (f) $\tfrac{1}{3}\ln(6/5)$ (g) $(1/256)(3e^4 + 1)$ (h) $2e^{-1}$.

5. (a) $10 - 18\ln(14/9)$. (Substitute $z = 9 + \sqrt{x}$.) (b) $886/15$. (Substitute $z = \sqrt{t+2}$.)
(c) $195/4$. (Substitute $z = \sqrt[3]{19x^3 + 8}$.)

6. (a) $F'(x) = 4(\sqrt{x} - 1)$. (Note that $\int_4^x (u^{1/2} + xu^{-1/2})\,du = |_4^x (\frac{2}{3}u^{3/2} + 2xu^{1/2}) = \frac{8}{3}x^{3/2} - \frac{16}{3} - 4x$.)
(b) Using (10.3.8), $F'(x) = \ln x - (\ln \sqrt{x})(1/2\sqrt{x}) = \ln x - \ln x/4\sqrt{x}$.

7. $C(Y) = 0.69Y + 1000$

8. Integrating the marginal cost function gives $C(x) = C_0 + \int_0^x (\alpha e^{\beta u} + \gamma)\,du = C_0 + |_0^x \frac{\alpha}{\beta}e^{\beta u} = \frac{\alpha}{\beta}(e^{\beta x} - 1) + \gamma x + C_0$.

9. Let $\int_{-1}^3 f(x)\,dx = A$ and $\int_{-1}^3 g(x)\,dx = B$. Then $A + B = 6$ and $3A + 4B = 9$, from which we find $A = 15$ and $B = -9$. Then $I = A + B = 6$.

10. (a) $P^* = 70$, $Q^* = 600$. $CS = 9000$, $PS = 18\,000$. See Fig. A10.R.10a.
(b) $P^* = Q^* = 5$, $CS = 50\ln 2 - 25$, $PS = 1.25$. See Fig. A10.R.10b.

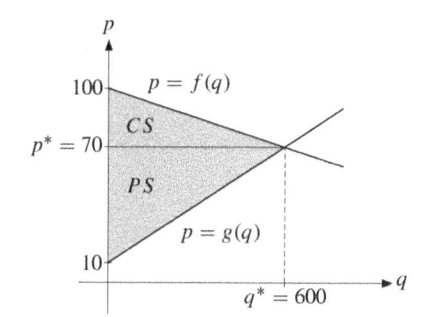

Figure A10.R.10a

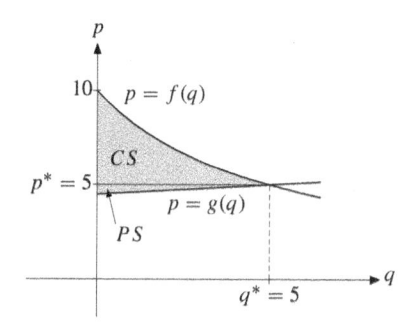

Figure A10.R.10b

11. (a) $f'(t) = 4\ln t(2 - \ln t)/t^2$, $f''(t) = 8[(\ln t)^2 - 3\ln t + 1]/t^3$.
(b) $(e^2, 16/e^2)$ is a local maximum point, $(1, 0)$ is a local (and global) minimum point. See Fig. A10.R.11.
(c) Area $= 32/3$. (*Hint:* $\int f(t)\,dt = \frac{4}{3}(\ln t)^3 + C$.)

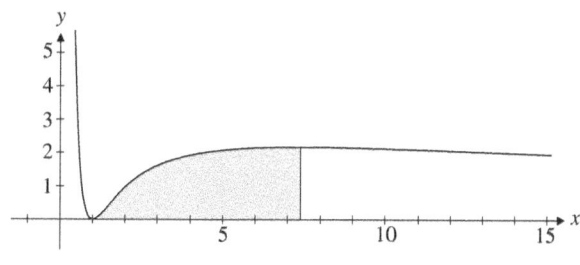

Figure A10.R.11

12. (a) $\int_0^\infty f(r)\,dr = \int_0^\infty (1/m)e^{-r/m}\,dr = 1$, as in Example 10.7.1, and $\int_0^\infty rf(r)\,dr = \int_0^\infty r(1/m)e^{-r/m}\,dr = m$, as in Exercise 10.7.3(a). So mean income is m.
(b) $x(p) = n\int_0^\infty (ar - bp)f(r)\,dr = n\left(a\int_0^\infty rf(r)\,dr - bp\int_0^\infty f(r)\,dr\right) = n(am - bp)$, by the results in part (a).

Chapter 11

11.1

1. (a) (i) $8000(1 + 0.05/12)^{5 \cdot 12} \approx 10\,266.87$ (ii) $8000(1 + 0.05/365)^{5 \cdot 365} \approx 10\,272.03$
   (b) $t = \ln 2/\ln(1 + 0.05/12) \approx 166.7$. It takes approximately $166.7/12 \approx 13.9$ years.

2. (a) $5000(1 + 0.03)^{10} \approx 6719.58$ (b) 37.17 years. $(5000(1.03)^t = 3 \cdot 5000$, so $t = \ln 3/\ln 1.03 \approx 37.17$.)

3. We solve $(1 + p/100)^{100} = 100$ for p. Raising each side to the power $1/100$, we get $1 + p/100 = \sqrt[100]{100}$, so $p = 100(\sqrt[100]{100} - 1) \approx 100(1.047 - 1) = 4.7$.

4. (a) (i) After 2 years: $2000(1.07)^2 = 2289.80$ (ii) After 10 years: $2000(1.07)^{10} \approx 3934.30$
   (b) $2000(1.07)^t = 6000$ gives $(1.07)^t = 3$, so $t = \ln 3/\ln 1.07 \approx 16.2$ years.

5. Use formula (11.1.2). (i) $R = (1 + 0.17/2)^2 - 1 = (1 + 0.085)^2 - 1 = 0.177\,225$ or about 17.72%
   (ii) $100[(1.0425)^4 - 1] \approx 18.11\%$ (iii) $100[(1 + 0.17/12)^{12} - 1] \approx 18.39\%$

6. The effective yearly rate for alternative (ii) is $(1 + 0.2/4)^4 - 1 = 1.05^4 - 1 \approx 0.2155 > 0.215$, so (i) is (slightly) cheaper.

7. (a) $12\,000 \cdot (1.04)^{15} \approx 21\,611.32$ (b) $50\,000 \cdot (1.05)^{-5} \approx 39\,176.31$

8. $100[(1.02)^{12} - 1] \approx 26.82\%$

9. Let the nominal yearly rate be r. By formula (11.1.2), $0.28 = (1 + r/4)^4 - 1$, so $r = 4(\sqrt[4]{1.28} - 1) \approx 0.25$, or 25%.

11.2

1. (a) $8000 e^{0.05 \cdot 5} = 8000 e^{0.25} \approx 10\,272.20$
   (b) $8000 e^{0.05t} = 16\,000$, which gives $e^{0.05t} = 2$. Hence $t = \ln 2/0.05 \approx 13.86$ years.

2. (a) (i) $1000(1 + 0.05/12)^{120} \approx 1647$ (ii) $1000 e^{0.05 \cdot 10} \approx 1649$
   (b) (i) $1000(1 + 0.05/12)^{600} \approx 12\,119$ (ii) $1000 e^{0.05 \cdot 50} \approx 12\,182$

3. (a) $e^{0.1} - 1 \approx 0.105$, so the effective percentage rate is approximately 10.5. (b) Same answer.

4. If it loses 90% of its value, then $e^{-0.1 t^*} = 1/10$, so $-0.1 t^* = -\ln 10$, hence $t^* = (\ln 10)/0.1 \approx 23$ years.

5. $e^{-0.06 t^*} = 1/2$, so $t^* = \ln 2/0.06 \approx 11.55$ years.

11.3

1. (a) The present value is $350\,000 \cdot 1.08^{-10} \approx 162\,117.72$. (b) $350\,000 \cdot e^{-0.08 \cdot 10} \approx 157\,265.14$

2. (a) The present value is $50\,000 \cdot 1.0575^{-5} \approx 37\,806.64$. (b) $50\,000 \cdot e^{-0.0575 \cdot 5} \approx 37\,506.83$

3. (a) We find $f'(t) = 0.05(t + 5)(35 - t)e^{-t}$. Obviously, $f'(t) > 0$ for $t < 35$ and $f'(t) < 0$ for $t > 35$, so $t = 35$ maximizes f (with $f(35) \approx 278$). (b) $f(t) \to 0$ as $t \to \infty$. See the graph in Fig. A11.3.3.

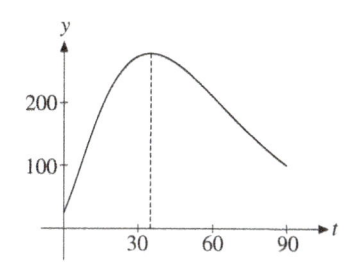

Figure A11.3.3

11.4

1. (a) $s_n = \frac{3}{2}\left[1 - \left(\frac{1}{3}\right)^n\right]$ (b) $s_n \to \frac{3}{2}$ as $n \to \infty$ (c) $\sum_{n=1}^{\infty} \frac{1}{3^{n-1}} = \frac{3}{2}$

2. We use formula (11.4.5). (a) $\dfrac{1/5}{1 - 1/5} = 1/4$ (b) $\dfrac{0.1}{1 - 0.1} = \dfrac{0.1}{0.9} = \dfrac{1}{9}$ (c) $\dfrac{517}{1 - 1/1.1} = 5687$

   (d) $\dfrac{a}{1 - 1/(1+a)} = 1 + a$ (e) $\dfrac{5}{1 - 3/7} = \dfrac{35}{4}$

3. (a) This is a geometric series with quotient $1/8$. Its sum is $8/(1 - \frac{1}{8}) = 64/7$.
   (b) Geometric series with quotient -3. It diverges. (c) Geometric series with sum $2^{1/3}/(1 - 2^{-1/3})$.
   (d) Not geometric. (In fact, one can show that the series converges with sum $\ln 2$.)

4. (a) The quotient is $k = 1/p$. It converges to $1/(p-1)$ if $|p| > 1$, but diverges if $|p| \le 1$.
   (b) Quotient $k = 1/\sqrt{x}$. Converges to $x\sqrt{x}/(\sqrt{x} - 1)$ for $\sqrt{x} > 1$, that is for $x > 1$, but diverges if $0 < x \le 1$.
   (c) Quotient $k = x^2$. Converges to $x^2/(1 - x^2)$ for $|x| < 1$, but diverges if $x \ge 1$.

5. Geometric series with quotient $(1 + p/100)^{-1}$. Its sum is $b/[1 - (1 + p/100)^{-1}] = b(1 + 100/p)$.

6. The resources will be exhausted partway through the year 2028.

7. $1824 \cdot 1.02 + 1824 \cdot 1.02^2 + \cdots + 1824 \cdot 1.02^n = (1824/0.02)(1.02^{n+1} - 1.02)$ must equal $128\,300$. So $n \approx 43.77$. The resources will last until year 2037.

8. (a) $f(t) = \dfrac{P(t)}{e^{rt} - 1}$ (b) Use $f'(t^*) = 0$. (c) $P'(t^*)/P(t^*) \to 1/t^*$ as $r \to 0$.

9. The general term does not approach 0 as $n \to \infty$ in any of these three series, so they all diverge.

10. (a) This is a geometric series with quotient $100/101$ that converges to 100. (b) Diverges according to (10.4.10).
    (c) Converges according to (10.4.10). (d) Diverges because the nth term $a_n = (1+n)/(4n-3) \to 1/4$ as $n \to \infty$.
    (e) Geometric series with quotient $-1/2$ that converges to $-1/3$.
    (f) Geometric series with quotient $1/\sqrt{3}$ converging to $\sqrt{3}/(\sqrt{3} - 1)$.

11. Using the hint, if $p \ge 0$ then $\int_n^{n+1} x^{-p}dx \in [(n+1)^{-p}, n^{-p}]$. So for $m = 2, 3, \ldots$:
    (i) if $p > 1$, then $\sum_{n=2}^m n^{-p} \le \int_1^m x^{-p}dx \le \dfrac{1}{p-1}$; (ii) if $p \le 1$, then $\sum_{n=1}^{m-1} n^{-p} \ge \int_1^m x^{-p}dx \ge \int_1^m x^{-1}dx = \ln m$.

    Also, for $p < 0$, each term $n^{-p} \to \infty$ as $p \to \infty$. Hence $\sum_{n=1}^{\infty} n^{-p}$ converges iff $p > 1$. See SM for more details.

11.5

1. Use formula (11.5.2) with $n = 15$, $r = 0.12$, and $a = 3500$. This gives $P_{15} = \frac{3500}{0.12}\left(1 - \frac{1}{(1.12)^{15}}\right) \approx 23\,838$.

2. 10 years ago the amount was: $100\,000(1.04)^{-10} \approx 67\,556.42$

3. $10\,000(1.06^3 + 1.06^2 + 1.06 + 1) = 10\,000(1.06^4 - 1)/(1.06 - 1)) \approx 43\,746.16$

4. The future value after 10 years of (i) is obviously $13\,000$, whereas according to formula (11.5.3), the corresponding value of (ii) is $F_{10} = (1000/0.06)(1.06^{10} - 1) \approx 13\,180.80$. So (ii) is worth more.

5. Offer (i) is better, because the present value of (ii) is $4600\dfrac{1 - (1.06)^{-5}}{1 - (1.06)^{-1}} \approx 20\,539$.

6. Using formula (11.5.4) gives $\dfrac{1500}{0.08} = 18\,750$.

7. If the largest amount is a, then by formula (11.5.4) one has $a/r = K$, so $a = rK$.

8. This is a geometric series with first term $a = D/(1+r)$ and quotient $k = (1+g)/(1+r)$. It converges if and only if $k < 1$, i.e. if and only if $g < r$. The sum is $\dfrac{a}{1-k} = \dfrac{D/(1+r)}{1 - (1+g)/(1+r)} = \dfrac{D}{r-g}$.

9. $\mathrm{PDV} = \int_0^{15} 500 e^{-0.06t}\, dt = 500 \Big|_0^{15} (-1/0.06)e^{-0.06t} = (500/0.06)\left[1 - e^{-0.9}\right] \approx 4945.25$.

$\mathrm{FDV} = e^{0.06 \cdot 15}\mathrm{PDV} = e^{0.9}\mathrm{PDV} \approx 2.4596 \cdot 4945.25 \approx 12\,163.3$.

11.6

1. (a) Using formula (11.6.2), we find that the annual payment is $a = 0.07 \cdot 80\,000/(1 - (1.07)^{-10}) \approx 11\,390.20$.

   (b) Using (11.6.2), we get $a = (0.07/12) \cdot 80\,000/[1 - (1 + 0.07/12)^{-120}] \approx 928.87$.

2. Using formula (11.5.3) gives $(8000/0.07)[1.07^6 - 1] \approx 57\,226.33$.

   Four years after the last deposit you have $57\,226.33 \cdot 1.07^4 \approx 75\,012.05$.

3. With annual compounding, one has $r = 3^{1/20} - 1 \approx 0.0565$, so the rate of interest is about 5.65 %.

   With continuous compounding, one has $e^{20r} = 3$, so $r = \ln 3/20 \approx 0.0549$. The rate of interest is about 5.49 %.

4. Schedule (ii) has present value $\dfrac{120\,000 \cdot 1.115}{0.115}[1 - (1.115)^{-8}] \approx 676\,444$.

   Schedule (iii) has present value $220\,000 + \dfrac{70\,000}{0.115}[1 - (1.115)^{-12}] \approx 663\,841$. Thus schedule (iii) is cheapest.

   When the interest rate becomes 12.5 %, schedules (ii) and (iii) have present values equal to $659\,076$ and $643\,743$, respectively, so (iii) is cheapest in this case too.

11.7

1. r must satisfy $-50\,000 + 30\,000/(1+r) + 30\,000/(1+r)^2 = 0$. With $s = 1/(1+r)$, this yields $s^2 + s - 5/3 = 0$, with positive solution $s = -1/2 + \sqrt{23/12} \approx 0.884$, so that $r \approx 0.13$.

2. Equation (11.7.1) is here $a/(1+r) + a/(1+r)^2 + \cdots = -a_0$. This reduces to $a/r = -a_0$, so $r = -a/a_0$.

3. By hypothesis, $f(0) = a_0 + a_1 + \cdots + a_n > 0$. Also, $f(r) \to a_0 < 0$ as $r \to \infty$.

   Moreover, $f'(r) = -a_1(1+r)^{-2} - 2a_2(1+r)^{-3} - \cdots - na_n(1+r)^{-n-1} < 0$, so $f(r)$ is strictly decreasing.

   This guarantees that there is a unique internal rate of return, with $r > 0$.

4. The maximum price is $400\,000\left(1/1.175 + (1/1.175)^2 + \cdots + (1/1.175)^7\right) \approx 1\,546\,522.94$, or about \$1.546 million.

5. With $s = (1+r)^{-1}$, Eq. (11.7.1) reduces to $s^{21} - 11s + 10 = 0$. See SM.

6. Applying Eq. (11.5.2) with $a = 1000$ and $n = 5$ gives the equation $P_5 = (1000/r)\left[1 - 1/(1+r)^5\right] = 4340$, which is to be solved for r. For $r = 0.05$ or $p = 5\%$, the present value is \$4329.48; for $r = 0.045$ or $p = 4.5\%$, the present value is \$4389.98. Because $dP_5/dr < 0$, it follows that p is a little less than 5%.

11.8

1. (a) $x_t = x_0(-2)^t$ (b) $x_t = x_0(5/6)^t$ (c) $x_t = x_0(-0.3)^t$

2. (a) $x_t = -4t$. (b) $x_t = 2(1/2)^t + 4$ (c) $x_t = (13/8)(-3)^t - 5/8$ (d) $x_t = -2(-1)^t + 4$

3. The difference equation implies that $\alpha P_t - \beta = \gamma - \delta P_{t+1}$, or $P_{t+1} = -(\alpha/\delta)P_t + (\beta + \gamma)/\delta$.
   Using formula (11.8.4) gives $P_t = \left(-\dfrac{\alpha}{\delta}\right)^t \left(P_0 - \dfrac{\beta + \gamma}{\alpha + \delta}\right) + \dfrac{\beta + \gamma}{\alpha + \delta}$.

11.9

1. The functions in (c) and (d) are the only ones that have a constant relative rate of increase. This accords with (11.9.3). (Note that $2^t = e^{(\ln 2)t}$.)

2. (a) $K(t) = (K_0 - I/\delta)e^{-\delta t} + I/\delta$ (b) (i) $K(t) = 200 - 50e^{-0.05t}$ and $K(t)$ tends to 200 from below as $t \to \infty$.
   (ii) $K(t) = 200 + 50e^{-0.05t}$, and $K(t)$ tends to 200 from above as $t \to \infty$.

3. $N(t) = P(1 - e^{-kt})$. Then $N(t) \to P$ as $t \to \infty$.

4. $\dot{N}(t) = 0.02N(t) + 4 \cdot 10^4$. The solution with $N(0) = 2 \cdot 10^6$ is $N(t) = 2 \cdot 10^6(2e^{0.02t} - 1)$.

5. $P(10) = 705$ gives $641e^{10k} = 705$, or $e^{10k} = 705/641$. Taking the natural logarithm of both sides yields $10k = \ln(705/641)$, so $k = 0.1\ln(705/641) \approx 0.0095$. $P(15) \approx 739$ and $P(40) \approx 938$.

6. The percentage surviving after t seconds satisfies $p(t) = 100e^{-\delta t}$, where $p(7) = 70.5$ and so $\delta = -\ln 0.705/7 \approx 0.05$. Thus $p(30) = 100e^{-30\delta} \approx 22.3\%$ are still alive after 30 seconds. Because $100e^{-\delta t} = 5$ when $t \approx \ln 20/0.05 \approx 60$, it takes about 60 seconds to kill 95%.

7. (a) $x = Ae^{-0.5t}$ (b) $K = Ae^{0.02t}$ (c) $x = Ae^{-0.5t} + 10$ (d) $K = Ae^{0.2t} - 500$ (e) $x = 0.1/(3 - Ae^{0.1t})$ and $x \equiv 0$.
   (f) $K = 1/(2 - Ae^t)$ and $K \equiv 0$.

8. (a) $y(t) = 250 + \dfrac{230}{1 + 8.2e^{-0.34t}}$. (b) $y(t) \to 480$ as $t \to \infty$. See Fig. A11.9.8.

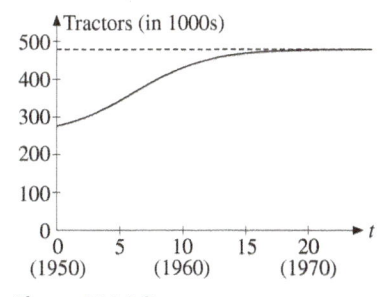

Figure A11.9.8

888 SOLUTIONS TO THE EXERCISES

9. (a) Formula (11.9.11) implies $N(t) = 1000/(1 + 999e^{-0.39t})$. After 20 days, $N(20) \approx 710$ have developed influenza.

   (b) $800 = \dfrac{1000}{1 + 999e^{-0.39t^*}} \iff 999e^{-0.39t^*} = \dfrac{1}{4}$, so $e^{-0.39t^*} = 1/3996$, and so $0.39t^* = \ln 3996$. $t^* \approx 21$ days.

   (c) After about 35 days, 999 will have or have had influenza. $N(t) \to 1000$ as $t \to \infty$.

10. (a) If $f \neq r$, the solution is $x(t) = \dfrac{(1-f/r)K}{1 + \dfrac{(1-f/r)K - x_0}{x_0} e^{-(r-f)t}}$. If $f = r$, then the solution is $x = \dfrac{1}{rt/K + 1/x_0}$.

    (b) If $f > r$, then $x(t) \to 0$ as $t \to \infty$. See SM for details.

11. At about 11:26. (Measuring time in hours, with $t = 0$ being 12 noon, one has $\dot{T} = k(20 - T)$ with $T(0) = 35$ and $T(1) = 32$. So the body temperature at time t is $T(t) = 20 + 15e^{-kt}$ with $k = \ln(5/4)$. Assuming that the temperature was the normal 37 degrees at the time of death t^*, then $t^* = -\ln(17/15)/\ln(5/4) \approx -0.56$ hours, or about 34 minutes before 12:00.)

11.10

1. The equation is separable. The recipe gives $\int x^4 \, dx = \int (1 - t) \, dt$, so $\tfrac{1}{5}x^5 = t - \tfrac{1}{2}t^2 + C_1$, and $x^5 = 5t - \tfrac{5}{2}t^2 + 5C_1$. This implies that $x = \sqrt[5]{5t - \tfrac{5}{2}t^2 + 5C_1} = \sqrt[5]{5t - \tfrac{5}{2}t^2 + C}$, with $C = 5C_1$. Finally, $x(1) = 1$ yields $C = -3/2$.

2. (a) $x = \sqrt[3]{\tfrac{3}{2}e^{2t} + C}$ (b) $x = -\ln(e^{-t} + C)$ (c) $x = Ce^{3t} - 6$ (d) $x = \sqrt[7]{(1 + t)^7 + C}$ (e) $x = Ce^{2t} + \tfrac{1}{2}t + \tfrac{1}{4}$

   (f) $x = Ce^{-3t} + \tfrac{1}{2}e^{t^2 - 3t}$

3. The equation is separable, with $dk/k = s\alpha e^{\beta t} \, dt$, so $\ln k = \dfrac{s\alpha}{\beta} e^{\beta t} + C_1$, or $k = e^{(s\alpha/\beta)e^{\beta t}} e^{C_1} = Ce^{(s\alpha/\beta)e^{\beta t}}$.

   With $k(0) = k_0$, we have $k_0 = Ce^{s\alpha/\beta}$, and thus $k = k_0 e^{(s\alpha/\beta)(e^{\beta t} - 1)}$.

4. (a) $\dot{Y} = \alpha(a - 1)Y + \alpha(b + \bar{I})$ (b) $Y = \left(Y_0 - \dfrac{b + \bar{I}}{1 - a}\right) e^{-\alpha(1-a)t} + \dfrac{b + \bar{I}}{1 - a} \to \dfrac{b + \bar{I}}{1 - a}$ as $t \to \infty$.

5. (a) From (iii), $L = L_0 e^{\beta t}$. Inserting this into (ii), and then inserting the result into (i), one has the separable equation $\dot{K} = \gamma K^\alpha L_0 e^{\beta t}$, or $\int K^{-\alpha} dK = \gamma L_0 \int e^{\beta t} dt$. The solution is $K = \left[\dfrac{(1-\alpha)\gamma}{\beta} L_0(e^{\beta t} - 1) + K_0^{1-\alpha}\right]^{1/(1-\alpha)}$.

6. $\dfrac{t}{x} \dfrac{dx}{dt} = a$ is separable, with $\displaystyle\int \dfrac{dx}{x} = a \int \dfrac{dt}{t}$. Integrating yields $\ln x = a \ln t + C_1$, so $x = e^{a \ln t + C_1} = (e^{\ln t})^a e^{C_1} = Ct^a$, with $C = e^{C_1}$. This shows that the only type of function which has constant elasticity is $x = Ct^a$.

Review exercises for Chapter 11

1. (a) $5000 \cdot 1.03^{10} \approx 6719.58$ (b) $5000(1.03)^{t^*} = 10\,000$, so $(1.03)^{t^*} = 2$, or $t^* = \ln 2/\ln 1.03 \approx 23.45$.

2. (a) $8000 \cdot 1.05^3 = 9261$ (b) $8000 \cdot 1.05^{13} \approx 15\,085.19$ (c) $(1.05)^{t^*} = 4$, so $t^* = \ln 4/1.05 \approx 28.5$

3. If you borrow \$a at the annual interest rate of 11% with interest paid yearly, then the debt after 1 year is equal to $a(1 + 11/100) = a(1.11)$; if you borrow at annual interest rate 10% with interest paid monthly, your debt after 1 year will be $a(1 + 10/(12 \cdot 100))^{12} \approx 1.1047a$, so schedule (ii) is preferable.

4. $15\,000 e^{0.07 \cdot 12} \approx 34\,745.50$

5. (a) $8000 e^{0.06 \cdot 3} \approx 9577.74$ (b) $t^* = \ln 2/0.06 \approx 11.6$

6. We use formula (11.4.5) as follows: (a) The first term is 44 and the quotient is 0.56, so the sum is $\dfrac{44}{1 - 0.56} = 100$.

(b) The first term is 20 and the quotient is 1/1.2, so the sum is $\dfrac{20}{1-1/1.2} = 120$. (c) $\dfrac{3}{1-2/5} = 5$

(d) The first term is $(1/20)^{-2} = 400$ and the quotient is 1/20, so the sum is $\dfrac{400}{1-1/20} = 8000/19$.

7. (a) $\int_0^T ae^{-rt}\, dt = (a/r)(1-e^{-rT})$ (b) a/r, the same as (11.5.4).

8. $5000(1.04)^4 = 5849.29$

9. 21 232.32

10. $K \approx 5990.49$

11. (a) According to formula (11.6.2), the annual payment is: $500\,000 \cdot 0.07(1.07)^{10}/(1.07^{10}-1) \approx 71\,188.80$. The total amount is $10 \cdot 71\,188.80 = 711\,888$. (b) If the person has to pay twice a year, the biannual payment is $500\,000 \cdot 0.035(1.035)^{20}/(1.035^{20}-1) \approx 35\,180.50$. The total amount is then $20 \cdot 35\,180.50 = 703\,610.80$.

12. (a) The present value is $(3200/0.08)[1-(1.08)^{-10}] = 21\,472.26$.

(b) The present value is $7000 + (3000/0.08)[1-1.08^{-5}] = 18\,978.13$.

(c) Four years ahead the present value is $(4000/0.08)[1-(1.08)^{-10}] = 26\,840.33$. The present value when Lucy makes her choice is $26\,840.33 \cdot 1.08^{-4} = 19\,728.44$. So she should choose option (a).

13. (a) $t^* = 1/16r^2 = 25$ for $r = 0.05$. (b) $t^* = 1/\sqrt{r} = 5$ for $r = 0.04$.

14. (a) The total revenue is $F(10) = F(10) - F(0) = \int_0^{10}(1+0.4t)\,dt = \Big|_0^{10}(t+0.2t^2) = 30$. (b) See Example 10.5.3.

15. (a) $x_t = (-0.1)^t$ (b) $x_t = -2t+4$ (c) $x_t = 4\left(\tfrac{3}{2}\right)^t - 2$

16. (a) $x = Ae^{-3t}$ (b) $x = Ae^{-4t} + 3$ (c) $x = 1/(Ae^{-3t}-4)$ and $x \equiv 0$. (d) $x = Ae^{-\frac{1}{3}t}$ (e) $x = Ae^{-2t} + 5/3$

(f) $x = 1/(Ae^{-\frac{1}{2}t} - 2)$ and $x \equiv 0$.

17. (a) $x = 1/(C - \tfrac{1}{2}t^2)$ and $x(t) \equiv 0$. (b) $x = Ce^{-3t/2} - 5$ (c) $x = Ce^{3t} - 10$ (d) $x = Ce^{-5t} + 2t - \tfrac{2}{5}$

(e) $x = Ce^{-t/2} + \tfrac{2}{3}e^t$ (f) $x = Ce^{-3t} + \tfrac{1}{3}t^2 - \tfrac{2}{9}t + \tfrac{2}{27}$

18. (a) $V(x) = (V_0 + b/a)e^{-ax} - b/a$ (b) $V(x^*) = 0$ yields $x^* = (1/a)\ln(1 + aV_0/b)$.

(c) $0 = V(\hat{x}) = (V_m + b/a)e^{-a\hat{x}} - b/a$ yields $V_m = (b/a)(e^{a\hat{x}} - 1)$.

(d) $x^* = (1/0.001)\ln(1 + 0.001 \cdot 12\,000/8) \approx 916$, and $V_m = (8/0.001)(e^{0.001 \cdot 1200} - 1) = 8000(e^{1.2} - 1) \approx 18\,561$.

Chapter 12

12.1

1. (a) 2×2 (b) 2×3 (c) $m \times n$

2. $\mathbf{A} = \begin{pmatrix} 1 & 0 & 0 \\ 0 & 1 & 0 \\ 0 & 0 & 1 \end{pmatrix}$

3. $u = 3$ and $v = -2$. (Equating the elements in row 1 and column 3 gives $u = 3$.

Then, equating those in row 2 and column 3 gives $u - v = 5$ and so $v = -2$.

The other elements then need to be checked, but this is obvious.)

12.2

1. Equations (a), (c), (d), and (f) are linear in x, y, z, and w, whereas (b) and (e) are nonlinear in these variables.

2. Yes: with x_1, y_1, x_2, and y_2 all constants, the system is linear in a, b, c, and d.

3. The three rows are $2x_1 + 4x_2 + 6x_3 + 8x_4 = 2$, $5x_1 + 7x_2 + 9x_3 + 11x_4 = 4$, and $4x_1 + 6x_2 + 8x_3 + 10x_4 = 8$.

4. The system is
$$\begin{cases} x_2 + x_3 + x_4 = b_1 \\ x_1 + x_3 + x_4 = b_2 \\ x_1 + x_2 + x_4 = b_3 \\ x_1 + x_2 + x_3 = b_4 \end{cases}$$
with solution
$$\begin{cases} x_1 = -\tfrac{2}{3}b_1 + \tfrac{1}{3}(b_2 + b_3 + b_4) \\ x_2 = -\tfrac{2}{3}b_2 + \tfrac{1}{3}(b_1 + b_3 + b_4) \\ x_3 = -\tfrac{2}{3}b_3 + \tfrac{1}{3}(b_1 + b_2 + b_4) \\ x_4 = -\tfrac{2}{3}b_4 + \tfrac{1}{3}(b_1 + b_2 + b_3) \end{cases}$$

(Adding the 4 equations, then dividing by 3, gives $x_1 + x_2 + x_3 + x_4 = \tfrac{1}{3}(b_1 + b_2 + b_3 + b_4)$.
Subtracting each of the original equations in turn from this new equation gives the solution for $x_1, \ldots, x_4$.
An alternative solution method is to eliminate the variables systematically, starting with (say) x_4.)

5. (a) The commodity bundle owned by individual j. (b) $a_{i1} + a_{i2} + \cdots + a_{in}$ is the total amount of commodity i owned by all individuals. The first case is when $i = 1$. (c) $p_1 a_{1j} + p_2 a_{2j} + \cdots + p_m a_{mj}$

6. After dropping terms with zero coefficients, the equations are
$$\begin{cases} -0.712Y + C = 95.05 \\ X - Y - S + C = 0.00 \\ 0.158X - S + 0.158C = 34.30 \\ X = 93.53 \end{cases}$$

The solution is $X = 93.53$, $Y \approx 482.11$, $S \approx 49.73$, and $C \approx 438.31$.

12.3

1. $\mathbf{A} + \mathbf{B} = \begin{pmatrix} 1 & 0 \\ 7 & 5 \end{pmatrix}$, $3\mathbf{A} = \begin{pmatrix} 0 & 3 \\ 6 & 9 \end{pmatrix}$

2. $\mathbf{A} + \mathbf{B} = \begin{pmatrix} 1 & 0 & 4 \\ 2 & 4 & 16 \end{pmatrix}$, $\mathbf{A} - \mathbf{B} = \begin{pmatrix} -1 & 2 & -6 \\ 2 & 2 & -2 \end{pmatrix}$, and $5\mathbf{A} - 3\mathbf{B} = \begin{pmatrix} -3 & 8 & -20 \\ 10 & 12 & 8 \end{pmatrix}$

12.4

1. $\mathbf{a} + \mathbf{b} = \begin{pmatrix} 5 \\ 3 \end{pmatrix}$, $\mathbf{a} - \mathbf{b} = \begin{pmatrix} -1 \\ -5 \end{pmatrix}$, $2\mathbf{a} + 3\mathbf{b} = \begin{pmatrix} 13 \\ 10 \end{pmatrix}$, and $-5\mathbf{a} + 2\mathbf{b} = \begin{pmatrix} -4 \\ 13 \end{pmatrix}$

2. $\mathbf{a} + \mathbf{b} + \mathbf{c} = (-1, 6, -4)$, $\mathbf{a} - 2\mathbf{b} + 2\mathbf{c} = (-3, 10, 2)$, $3\mathbf{a} + 2\mathbf{b} - 3\mathbf{c} = (9, -6, 9)$

3. By definition of vector addition and scalar multiplication, the left-hand side of the equation is the vector $3(x, y, z) + 5(-1, 2, 3) = (3x - 5, 3y + 10, 3z + 15)$. For this to equal the vector $(4, 1, 3)$, all three components must be equal. So the vector equation is equivalent to the equation system $3x - 5 = 4$, $3y + 10 = 1$, and $3z + 15 = 3$, with the obvious solution $x = 3$, $y = -3$, $z = -4$.

4. Here $\mathbf{x} = \mathbf{0}$, so for all i, the ith component satisfies $x_i = 0$.

5. Nothing, because $0 \cdot \mathbf{x} = \mathbf{0}$ for all $\mathbf{x}$.

6. We need to find numbers t and s such that $t(2, -1) + s(1, 4) = (4, -11)$. This vector equation is equivalent to $(2t + s, -t + 4s) = (4, -11)$. Equating the two components gives the system (i) $2t + s = 4$; (ii) $-t + 4s = -11$.
This system has the solution $t = 3$, $s = -2$, so $(4, -11) = 3(2, -1) - 2(1, 4)$.

CHAPTER 12   891

7. $4\mathbf{x} - 2\mathbf{x} = 7\mathbf{a} + 8\mathbf{b} - \mathbf{a}$, so $2\mathbf{x} = 6\mathbf{a} + 8\mathbf{b}$, and $\mathbf{x} = 3\mathbf{a} + 4\mathbf{b}$.

8. $\mathbf{a} \cdot \mathbf{a} = 5$, $\mathbf{a} \cdot \mathbf{b} = 2$, and $\mathbf{a} \cdot (\mathbf{a} + \mathbf{b}) = 7$. We see that $\mathbf{a} \cdot \mathbf{a} + \mathbf{a} \cdot \mathbf{b} = \mathbf{a} \cdot (\mathbf{a} + \mathbf{b})$.

9. The inner product of the two vectors is $x^2 + (x-1)x + 3 \cdot 3x = x^2 + x^2 - x + 9x = 2x^2 + 8x = 2x(x+4)$, which is 0 for $x = 0$ and for $x = -4$.

10. (a) $\mathbf{x} = (5, 7, 12)$ (b) $\mathbf{u} = (20, 18, 25)$ (c) $\mathbf{u} \cdot \mathbf{x} = 526$

11. (a) The firm's revenue is $\mathbf{p} \cdot \mathbf{z}$. Its costs are $\mathbf{p} \cdot \mathbf{x}$. (b) Profit = revenue − costs.
    This equals $\mathbf{p} \cdot \mathbf{z} - \mathbf{p} \cdot \mathbf{x} = \mathbf{p} \cdot (\mathbf{z} - \mathbf{x}) = \mathbf{p} \cdot \mathbf{y}$. If $\mathbf{p} \cdot \mathbf{y} < 0$, then the firm makes a loss equal to $-\mathbf{p} \cdot \mathbf{y}$.

12. (a) Input vector = $\begin{pmatrix} 0 \\ 1 \end{pmatrix}$ (b) Output vector = $\begin{pmatrix} 2 \\ 0 \end{pmatrix}$ (c) Cost = $(1, 3) \begin{pmatrix} 0 \\ 1 \end{pmatrix} = 3$ (d) Revenue = $(1, 3) \begin{pmatrix} 2 \\ 0 \end{pmatrix} = 2$

    (e) Value of net output = $(1, 3) \begin{pmatrix} 2 \\ -1 \end{pmatrix} = 2 - 3 = -1$. (f) Loss = cost − revenue = $3 - 2 = 1$, so profit = -1.

12.5

1. (a) $\mathbf{AB} = \begin{pmatrix} 0 & -2 \\ 3 & 1 \end{pmatrix} \begin{pmatrix} -1 & 4 \\ 1 & 5 \end{pmatrix} = \begin{pmatrix} 0 \cdot (-1) + (-2) \cdot 1 & 0 \cdot 4 + (-2) \cdot 5 \\ 3 \cdot (-1) + 1 \cdot 1 & 3 \cdot 4 + 1 \cdot 5 \end{pmatrix} = \begin{pmatrix} -2 & -10 \\ -2 & 17 \end{pmatrix}$ and $\mathbf{BA} = \begin{pmatrix} 12 & 6 \\ 15 & 3 \end{pmatrix}$.

   (b) $\mathbf{AB} = \begin{pmatrix} 26 & 3 \\ 6 & -22 \end{pmatrix}$ and $\mathbf{BA} = \begin{pmatrix} 14 & 6 & -12 \\ 35 & 12 & 4 \\ 3 & 3 & -22 \end{pmatrix}$ (c) $\mathbf{AB}$ is not defined, whereas $\mathbf{BA} = \begin{pmatrix} -1 & 4 \\ 3 & 4 \\ 4 & 8 \end{pmatrix}$

   (d) $\mathbf{AB} = \begin{pmatrix} 0 & 0 & 0 \\ 0 & 4 & -6 \\ 0 & -8 & 12 \end{pmatrix}$ and $\mathbf{BA} = (16)$, a 1×1 matrix.

2. (i) $3\mathbf{A} + 2\mathbf{B} - 2\mathbf{C} + \mathbf{D} = \begin{pmatrix} -1 & 15 \\ -6 & -13 \end{pmatrix}$ (ii) $\mathbf{AB} = \begin{pmatrix} 0 & 0 \\ 0 & 0 \end{pmatrix}$ (iii) From (ii) it follows that $\mathbf{C}(\mathbf{AB}) = \begin{pmatrix} 0 & 0 \\ 0 & 0 \end{pmatrix}$.

3. $\mathbf{A} + \mathbf{B} = \begin{pmatrix} 4 & 1 & -1 \\ 9 & 2 & 7 \\ 3 & -1 & 4 \end{pmatrix}$, $\mathbf{A} - \mathbf{B} = \begin{pmatrix} -2 & 3 & -5 \\ 1 & -2 & -3 \\ -1 & -1 & -2 \end{pmatrix}$, $\mathbf{AB} = \begin{pmatrix} 5 & 3 & 3 \\ 19 & -5 & 16 \\ 1 & -3 & 0 \end{pmatrix}$,

   $\mathbf{BA} = \begin{pmatrix} 0 & 4 & -9 \\ 19 & 3 & -3 \\ 5 & 1 & -3 \end{pmatrix}$, $(\mathbf{AB})\mathbf{C} = \mathbf{A}(\mathbf{BC}) = \begin{pmatrix} 23 & 8 & 25 \\ 92 & -28 & 76 \\ 4 & -8 & -4 \end{pmatrix}$

4. (a) $\begin{pmatrix} 1 & 1 \\ 3 & 5 \end{pmatrix} \begin{pmatrix} x_1 \\ x_2 \end{pmatrix} = \begin{pmatrix} 3 \\ 5 \end{pmatrix}$ (b) $\begin{pmatrix} 1 & 2 & 1 \\ 1 & -1 & 1 \\ 2 & 3 & -1 \end{pmatrix} \begin{pmatrix} x_1 \\ x_2 \\ x_3 \end{pmatrix} = \begin{pmatrix} 4 \\ 5 \\ 1 \end{pmatrix}$ (c) $\begin{pmatrix} 2 & -3 & 1 \\ 1 & 1 & -1 \end{pmatrix} \begin{pmatrix} x_1 \\ x_2 \\ x_3 \end{pmatrix} = \begin{pmatrix} 0 \\ 0 \end{pmatrix}$

5. (a) $\mathbf{A} - 2\mathbf{I} = \begin{pmatrix} 0 & 2 \\ 1 & 3 \end{pmatrix}$. The matrix $\mathbf{C}$ must be 2×2.

   With $\mathbf{C} = \begin{pmatrix} c_{11} & c_{12} \\ c_{21} & c_{22} \end{pmatrix}$, we need $\begin{pmatrix} 0 & 2 \\ 1 & 3 \end{pmatrix} \begin{pmatrix} c_{11} & c_{12} \\ c_{21} & c_{22} \end{pmatrix} = \begin{pmatrix} 1 & 0 \\ 0 & 1 \end{pmatrix}$, or $\begin{pmatrix} 2c_{21} & 2c_{22} \\ c_{11} + 3c_{21} & c_{12} + 3c_{22} \end{pmatrix} = \begin{pmatrix} 1 & 0 \\ 0 & 1 \end{pmatrix}$.

   The last matrix equation has the unique solution $c_{11} = -3/2$, $c_{12} = 1$, $c_{21} = 1/2$, and $c_{22} = 0$.

   (b) $\mathbf{B} - 2\mathbf{I} = \begin{pmatrix} 0 & 0 \\ 3 & 0 \end{pmatrix}$, so the first row of any product matrix $(\mathbf{B} - 2\mathbf{I})\mathbf{D}$ must be $(0, 0)$.
   So no matrix $\mathbf{D}$ can possibly satisfy $(\mathbf{B} - 2\mathbf{I})\mathbf{D} = \mathbf{I}$.

6. The product **AB** is defined only if **B** has n rows. And **BA** is defined only if **B** has m columns. So **B** must be an $n \times m$ matrix.

7. $\mathbf{B} = \begin{pmatrix} w-y & y \\ y & w \end{pmatrix}$, for arbitrary y, w.

8. $\mathbf{T(Ts)} = \begin{pmatrix} 0.85 & 0.10 & 0.10 \\ 0.05 & 0.55 & 0.05 \\ 0.10 & 0.35 & 0.85 \end{pmatrix} \begin{pmatrix} 0.25 \\ 0.35 \\ 0.40 \end{pmatrix} = \begin{pmatrix} 0.2875 \\ 0.2250 \\ 0.4875 \end{pmatrix}$

12.6

1. $\mathbf{A(B+C)} = \mathbf{AB} + \mathbf{AC} = \begin{pmatrix} 3 & 2 & 6 & 2 \\ 7 & 4 & 14 & 6 \end{pmatrix}$

2. The 1×1 matrix $(ax^2 + by^2 + cz^2 + 2dxy + 2exz + 2fyz)$

3. It is straightforward to show that $(\mathbf{AB})\mathbf{C}$ and $\mathbf{A}(\mathbf{BC})$ are both equal to the 2×2 matrix $\mathbf{D} = (d_{ij})_{2\times 2}$, whose four elements are $d_{ij} = a_{i1}b_{11}c_{1j} + a_{i1}b_{12}c_{2j} + a_{i2}b_{21}c_{1j} + a_{i2}b_{22}c_{2j}$ for $i = 1, 2$ and $j = 1, 2$.

4. (a) $\begin{pmatrix} 5 & 3 & 1 \\ 2 & 0 & 9 \\ 1 & 3 & 3 \end{pmatrix}$ (b) $(1, 2, -3)$

5. (a) (i) Note that $(\mathbf{A+B})(\mathbf{A-B}) = \mathbf{A}^2 - \mathbf{AB} + \mathbf{BA} - \mathbf{B}^2 \neq \mathbf{A}^2 - \mathbf{B}^2$ unless $\mathbf{AB} = \mathbf{BA}$.

   (ii) Similarly $(\mathbf{A-B})(\mathbf{A-B}) = \mathbf{A}^2 - \mathbf{AB} - \mathbf{BA} + \mathbf{B}^2 \neq \mathbf{A}^2 - 2\mathbf{AB} + \mathbf{B}^2$ unless $\mathbf{AB} = \mathbf{BA}$.

   (b) Equality occurs in both (i) and (ii) if and only if $\mathbf{AB} = \mathbf{BA}$.

6. (a) Verify directly by matrix multiplication.   (b) $\mathbf{AA} = (\mathbf{AB})\mathbf{A} = \mathbf{A}(\mathbf{BA}) = \mathbf{AB} = \mathbf{A}$, so $\mathbf{A}$ is idempotent. Then just interchange $\mathbf{A}$ and $\mathbf{B}$ to show that $\mathbf{B}$ is idempotent.

   (c) As the induction hypothesis, suppose that $\mathbf{A}^k = \mathbf{A}$, which is true for $k = 1$.
   Then $\mathbf{A}^{k+1} = \mathbf{A}^k \mathbf{A} = \mathbf{AA} = \mathbf{A}$, which completes the proof by induction.

7. If $\mathbf{P}^3 \mathbf{Q} = \mathbf{PQ}$, then $\mathbf{P}^5 \mathbf{Q} = \mathbf{P}^2(\mathbf{P}^3 \mathbf{Q}) = \mathbf{P}^2 (\mathbf{PQ}) = \mathbf{P}^3 \mathbf{Q} = \mathbf{PQ}$.

8. (a) Verify directly by matrix multiplication.   (b) Given $\mathbf{A} = \begin{pmatrix} a & b \\ c & d \end{pmatrix}$, it is enough to have $a + d = ad - bc = 0$ with a, b, c, d not all 0. One example is $\mathbf{A} = \begin{pmatrix} 1 & 1 \\ -1 & -1 \end{pmatrix}$.   (c) See SM.

12.7

1. $\mathbf{A}' = \begin{pmatrix} 3 & -1 \\ 5 & 2 \\ 8 & 6 \\ 3 & 2 \end{pmatrix}$, $\mathbf{B}' = (0, 1, -1, 2)$, $\mathbf{C}' = \begin{pmatrix} 1 \\ 5 \\ 0 \\ -1 \end{pmatrix}$

2. $\mathbf{A}' = \begin{pmatrix} 3 & -1 \\ 2 & 5 \end{pmatrix}$, $\mathbf{B}' = \begin{pmatrix} 0 & 2 \\ 2 & 2 \end{pmatrix}$, $(\mathbf{A+B})' = \begin{pmatrix} 3 & 1 \\ 4 & 7 \end{pmatrix}$, $(\alpha \mathbf{A})' = \begin{pmatrix} -6 & 2 \\ -4 & -10 \end{pmatrix}$, $\mathbf{AB} = \begin{pmatrix} 4 & 10 \\ 10 & 8 \end{pmatrix}$,

   $(\mathbf{AB})' = \begin{pmatrix} 4 & 10 \\ 10 & 8 \end{pmatrix} = \mathbf{B}'\mathbf{A}'$, and $\mathbf{A}'\mathbf{B}' = \begin{pmatrix} -2 & 4 \\ 10 & 14 \end{pmatrix}$.

   Verifying the rules for transposition specified in Eqs (12.7.2)–(12.7.5) is now very easy.

3. Direct verification shows that for each of the two matrices the element in position ij equals the element in position ji, for $i = 1, 2, 3$ and $j = 1, 2, 3$.

4. Symmetry requires $a^2 - 1 = a + 1$ and $a^2 + 4 = 4a$. The second equation has the unique root $a = 2$, which also satisfies the first equation.

5. No! For example: $\begin{pmatrix} 0 & 0 \\ 0 & 1 \end{pmatrix} \begin{pmatrix} 1 & 1 \\ 1 & 1 \end{pmatrix} = \begin{pmatrix} 0 & 0 \\ 1 & 1 \end{pmatrix}$.

6. $(\mathbf{A}_1\mathbf{A}_2\mathbf{A}_3)' = (\mathbf{A}_1(\mathbf{A}_2\mathbf{A}_3))' = (\mathbf{A}_2\mathbf{A}_3)'\mathbf{A}_1' = (\mathbf{A}_3'\mathbf{A}_2')\mathbf{A}_1' = \mathbf{A}_3'\mathbf{A}_2'\mathbf{A}_1'$. To prove the general case, use induction.

7. (a) Verify by direct multiplication. (b) $\begin{pmatrix} p & q \\ -q & p \end{pmatrix} \begin{pmatrix} p & -q \\ q & p \end{pmatrix} = \begin{pmatrix} p^2 + q^2 & 0 \\ 0 & p^2 + q^2 \end{pmatrix} = \begin{pmatrix} 1 & 0 \\ 0 & 1 \end{pmatrix} \Leftrightarrow p^2 + q^2 = 1$.
  (c) If $\mathbf{P}'\mathbf{P} = \mathbf{Q}'\mathbf{Q} = \mathbf{I}_n$, then $(\mathbf{PQ})'(\mathbf{PQ}) = (\mathbf{Q}'\mathbf{P}')(\mathbf{PQ}) = \mathbf{Q}'(\mathbf{P}'\mathbf{P})\mathbf{Q} = \mathbf{Q}'\mathbf{I}_n\mathbf{Q} = \mathbf{Q}'\mathbf{Q} = \mathbf{I}_n$.

8. (a) $\mathbf{TS} = \begin{pmatrix} p^3 + p^2q & 2p^2q + 2pq^2 & pq^2 + q^3 \\ \frac{1}{2}p^3 + \frac{1}{2}p^2 + \frac{1}{2}p^2q & p^2q + pq + pq^2 & \frac{1}{2}pq^2 + \frac{1}{2}q^2 + \frac{1}{2}q^3 \\ p^3 + p^2q & 2p^2q + 2pq^2 & pq^2 + q^3 \end{pmatrix} = \mathbf{S}$ because $p + q = 1$. A similar argument shows that $\mathbf{T}^2 = \frac{1}{2}\mathbf{T} + \frac{1}{2}\mathbf{S}$. To derive the formula for $\mathbf{T}^3$, multiply each side of the last equation on the left by $\mathbf{T}$.
  (b) The appropriate formula is $\mathbf{T}^n = 2^{1-n}\mathbf{T} + (1 - 2^{1-n})\mathbf{S}$.

12.8

1. (a) The solution $x_1 = 5$, $x_2 = -2$ can be found by using Gaussian elimination to obtain

$$\begin{pmatrix} 1 & 1 & 3 \\ 3 & 5 & 5 \end{pmatrix} \begin{matrix} -3 \\ \longleftarrow \end{matrix} \sim \begin{pmatrix} 1 & 1 & 3 \\ 0 & 2 & -4 \end{pmatrix} \begin{matrix} \\ 1/2 \end{matrix} \sim \begin{pmatrix} 1 & 1 & 3 \\ 0 & 1 & -2 \end{pmatrix} \begin{matrix} \longleftarrow \\ -1 \end{matrix} \sim \begin{pmatrix} 1 & 0 & 5 \\ 0 & 1 & -2 \end{pmatrix}$$

(b) Gaussian elimination yields

$$\begin{pmatrix} 1 & 2 & 1 & 4 \\ 1 & -1 & 1 & 5 \\ 2 & 3 & -1 & 1 \end{pmatrix} \begin{matrix} -1 \\ \longleftarrow \\ \longleftarrow \end{matrix} \begin{matrix} -2 \\ \\ \end{matrix} \sim \begin{pmatrix} 1 & 2 & 1 & 4 \\ 0 & -3 & 0 & 1 \\ 0 & -1 & -3 & -7 \end{pmatrix} \begin{matrix} \\ -1/3 \\ \end{matrix} \sim \begin{pmatrix} 1 & 2 & 1 & 4 \\ 0 & 1 & 0 & -1/3 \\ 0 & -1 & -3 & -7 \end{pmatrix} \begin{matrix} \longleftarrow \\ 1 \\ \longleftarrow \end{matrix} \begin{matrix} -2 \\ \\ \end{matrix}$$

$$\sim \begin{pmatrix} 1 & 0 & 1 & 14/3 \\ 0 & 1 & 0 & -1/3 \\ 0 & 0 & -3 & -22/3 \end{pmatrix} \begin{matrix} \\ \\ -1/3 \end{matrix} \sim \begin{pmatrix} 1 & 0 & 1 & 14/3 \\ 0 & 1 & 0 & -1/3 \\ 0 & 0 & 1 & 22/9 \end{pmatrix} \begin{matrix} \longleftarrow \\ \\ -1 \end{matrix} \sim \begin{pmatrix} 1 & 0 & 0 & 20/9 \\ 0 & 1 & 0 & -1/3 \\ 0 & 0 & 1 & 22/9 \end{pmatrix}$$

The solution is therefore: $x_1 = 20/9$, $x_2 = -1/3$, $x_3 = 22/9$.

(c) The general solution is $x_1 = (2/5)s$, $x_2 = (3/5)s$, $x_3 = s$, where s is an arbitrary real number.

2. Using Gaussian elimination to eliminate x from the second and third equations, and then y from the third equation, we arrive at the augmented matrix $\begin{pmatrix} 1 & 1 & -1 & 1 \\ 0 & 1 & -3/2 & -1/2 \\ 0 & 0 & a + 5/2 & b - 1/2 \end{pmatrix}$.

For any z, the first two equations imply that $y = -\frac{1}{2} + \frac{3}{2}z$ and $x = 1 - y + z = \frac{3}{2} - \frac{1}{2}z$.

From the last equation we see that for $a \neq -\frac{5}{2}$, there is a unique solution with $z = (b - \frac{1}{2})/(a + \frac{5}{2})$.

For $a = -\frac{5}{2}$, there are no solutions if $b \neq \frac{1}{2}$, but there is one degree of freedom if $b = \frac{1}{2}$ (with z arbitrary).

3. For $c = 1$ and for $c = -2/5$ the solution is $x = 2c^2 - 1 + t$, $y = s$, $z = t$, $w = 1 - c^2 - 2s - 2t$, for arbitrary s and t.

For other values of c there are no solutions.

4. Move the first row down to row number three and use Gaussian elimination. There is a unique solution if and only if $a \neq 3/4$.

5. If $b_1 \neq \frac{1}{4}b_3$, there is no solution. If $b_1 = \frac{1}{4}b_3$, there is an infinite set of solutions that take the form $x = -2b_2 + b_3 - 5t$, $y = \frac{3}{2}b_2 - \frac{1}{2}b_3 + 2t$, $z = t$, with $t \in \mathbb{R}$.

12.9

1. $\mathbf{a} + \mathbf{b} = (3, 3)$ and $-\frac{1}{2}\mathbf{a} = (-2.5, 0.5)$. See Fig. A12.9.1.

2. (a) (i) $\lambda = 0$ gives $\mathbf{x} = (-1, 2) = \mathbf{b}$; (ii) $\lambda = 1/4$ gives $\mathbf{x} = (0, 7/4)$; (iii) $\lambda = 1/2$ gives $\mathbf{x} = (1, 3/2)$;
   (iv) $\lambda = 3/4$ gives $\mathbf{x} = (2, 5/4)$; (v) $\lambda = 1$ gives $\mathbf{x} = (3, 1) = \mathbf{a}$. See Fig. A12.9.2.
   (b) As λ runs through $[0, 1]$, the vector $\mathbf{x}$ traces out the line segment joining $\mathbf{b}$ to $\mathbf{a}$ in Fig. A12.9.2. (c) See SM.

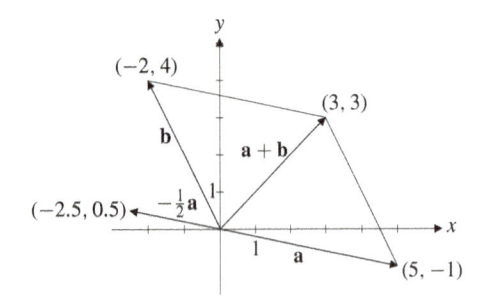

Figure A12.9.1

Figure A12.9.2

3. See Fig. A12.9.3.

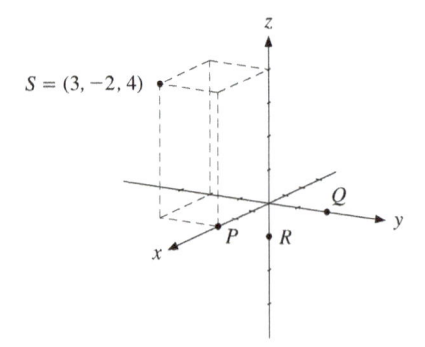

Figure A12.9.3

4. (a) A straight line through $(0, 2, 3)$ parallel to the x-axis.
   (b) A plane parallel to the z-axis whose intersection with the xy-plane is the line $y = x$.

5. $\|\mathbf{a}\| = 3$, $\|\mathbf{b}\| = 3$, $\|\mathbf{c}\| = \sqrt{29}$. Also, $|\mathbf{a} \cdot \mathbf{b}| = 6 \leq \|\mathbf{a}\| \cdot \|\mathbf{b}\| = 9$.

6. (a) $x_1(1, 2, 1) + x_2(-3, 0, -2) = (x_1 - 3x_2, 2x_1, x_1 - 2x_2) = (5, 4, 4)$ when $x_1 = 2$ and $x_2 = -1$.
   (b) x_1 and x_2 would have to satisfy $x_1(1, 2, 1) + x_2(-3, 0, -2) = (-3, 6, 1)$. Then $x_1 - 3x_2 = -3$, $2x_1 = 6$, and $x_1 - 2x_2 = 1$. The first two equations imply that $x_1 = 3$ and $x_2 = 2$, which violate the last equation.

7. The pairs of vectors in (a) and (c) are orthogonal; the pair in (b) is not.

8. The vectors are orthogonal if and only if their inner product is 0. This is true if and only if
   $x^2 - x - 8 - 2x + x = x^2 - 2x - 8 = 0$, which is the case for $x = -2$ and $x = 4$.

9. If **P** is orthogonal and $\mathbf{c}_i$ and $\mathbf{c}_j$ are two different columns of **P**, then $\mathbf{c}'_i \mathbf{c}_j$ is the element in row i and column j of $\mathbf{P}'\mathbf{P} = \mathbf{I}$, so $\mathbf{c}'_i \mathbf{c}_j = 0$. If $\mathbf{r}_i$ and $\mathbf{r}_j$ are two different rows of **P**, then $\mathbf{r}_i \mathbf{r}'_j$ is the element in row i and column j of $\mathbf{PP}' = \mathbf{I}$, so again $\mathbf{r}_i \mathbf{r}'_j = 0$.

10. $(\|\mathbf{a}\| + \|\mathbf{b}\|)^2 = \|\mathbf{a}\|^2 + 2\|\mathbf{a}\| \cdot \|\mathbf{b}\| + \|\mathbf{b}\|^2$, whereas $\|\mathbf{a} + \mathbf{b}\|^2 = (\mathbf{a} + \mathbf{b}) \cdot (\mathbf{a} + \mathbf{b}) = \|\mathbf{a}\|^2 + 2\mathbf{a} \cdot \mathbf{b} + \|\mathbf{b}\|^2$.
Then $(\|\mathbf{a}\| + \|\mathbf{b}\|)^2 - \|\mathbf{a} + \mathbf{b}\|^2 = 2(\|\mathbf{a}\| \cdot \|\mathbf{b}\| - \mathbf{a} \cdot \mathbf{b}) \geq 0$ by the Cauchy–Schwarz inequality (12.9.7).

12.10

1. (a) $x_1 = 3t + 10(1 - t) = 10 - 7t$, $x_2 = (-2)t + 2(1 - t) = 2 - 4t$, and $x_3 = 2t + (1 - t) = 1 + t$
   (b) $x_1 = 1$, $x_2 = 3 - t$, and $x_3 = 2 + t$

2. (a) To show that **a** lies on L, put $t = 0$. (b) The direction of L is given by $(-1, 2, 1)$, and the equation of $\mathcal{P}$ is $(-1)(x_1 - 2) + 2(x_2 - (-1)) + 1 \cdot (x_3 - 3) = 0$, or $-x_1 + 2x_2 + x_3 = -1$.
   (c) We must have $3(-t + 2) + 5(2t - 1) - (t + 3) = 6$, and so $t = 4/3$. Thus $P = (2/3, 5/3, 13/3)$.

3. $x_1 - 3x_2 - 2x_3 = -3$

4. $2x + 3y + 5z \leq m$, with $m \geq 75$.

5. (a) This can be verified directly. (b) $(x_1, x_2, x_3) = (-2, 1, -1) + t(-1, 2, 3) = (-2 - t, 1 + 2t, -1 + 3t)$

Review exercises for Chapter 12

1. (a) $\mathbf{A} = \begin{pmatrix} 2 & 3 & 4 \\ 3 & 4 & 5 \end{pmatrix}$ (b) $\mathbf{A} = \begin{pmatrix} 1 & -1 & 1 \\ -1 & 1 & -1 \end{pmatrix}$

2. (a) $\mathbf{A} - \mathbf{B} = \begin{pmatrix} 3 & -2 \\ -2 & 2 \end{pmatrix}$ (b) $\mathbf{A} + \mathbf{B} - 2\mathbf{C} = \begin{pmatrix} -3 & -4 \\ -2 & -8 \end{pmatrix}$ (c) $\mathbf{AB} = \begin{pmatrix} -2 & 4 \\ 2 & -3 \end{pmatrix}$ (d) $\mathbf{C}(\mathbf{AB}) = \begin{pmatrix} 2 & -1 \\ 6 & -8 \end{pmatrix}$
   (e) $\mathbf{AD} = \begin{pmatrix} 2 & 2 & 2 \\ 0 & 2 & 3 \end{pmatrix}$ (f) $\mathbf{DC}$ is not defined. (g) $2\mathbf{A} - 3\mathbf{B} = \begin{pmatrix} 7 & -6 \\ -5 & 5 \end{pmatrix}$ (h) $(\mathbf{A} - \mathbf{B})' = \begin{pmatrix} 3 & -2 \\ -2 & 2 \end{pmatrix}$
   (i) and (j): $(\mathbf{C}'\mathbf{A}')\mathbf{B}' = \mathbf{C}'(\mathbf{A}'\mathbf{B}') = \begin{pmatrix} -6 & 5 \\ -4 & 5 \end{pmatrix}$ (k) $\mathbf{D}'\mathbf{D}'$ is not defined. (l) $\mathbf{D}'\mathbf{D} = \begin{pmatrix} 2 & 4 & 5 \\ 4 & 10 & 13 \\ 5 & 13 & 17 \end{pmatrix}$.

3. (a) $\begin{pmatrix} 2 & -5 \\ 5 & 8 \end{pmatrix} \begin{pmatrix} x_1 \\ x_2 \end{pmatrix} = \begin{pmatrix} 3 \\ 5 \end{pmatrix}$ (b) $\begin{pmatrix} 1 & 1 & 1 & 1 \\ 1 & 3 & 2 & 4 \\ 1 & 4 & 8 & 0 \\ 2 & 0 & 1 & -1 \end{pmatrix} \begin{pmatrix} x \\ y \\ z \\ t \end{pmatrix} = \begin{pmatrix} a \\ b \\ c \\ d \end{pmatrix}$ (c) $\begin{pmatrix} a - 1 & 3 & -2 \\ a & 2 & -1 \\ 1 & -2 & 3 \end{pmatrix} \begin{pmatrix} x \\ y \\ z \end{pmatrix} = \begin{pmatrix} 5 \\ 2 \\ 1 \end{pmatrix}$

4. $\mathbf{A} + \mathbf{B} = \begin{pmatrix} 0 & -4 & 1 \\ 8 & 6 & 4 \\ -10 & 9 & 15 \end{pmatrix}$, $\mathbf{A} - \mathbf{B} = \begin{pmatrix} 0 & 6 & -5 \\ -2 & 2 & 6 \\ -2 & 5 & 15 \end{pmatrix}$, $\mathbf{AB} = \begin{pmatrix} 13 & -2 & -1 \\ 0 & 3 & 5 \\ -25 & 74 & -25 \end{pmatrix}$,
   $\mathbf{BA} = \begin{pmatrix} -33 & 1 & 20 \\ 12 & 6 & -15 \\ 6 & 4 & 18 \end{pmatrix}$, $(\mathbf{AB})\mathbf{C} = \mathbf{A}(\mathbf{BC}) = \begin{pmatrix} 74 & -31 & -48 \\ 6 & 25 & 38 \\ -2 & -75 & -26 \end{pmatrix}$

5. The two matrix products on the left-hand side of the equation are $\begin{pmatrix} 2a + b & a + b \\ 2x & x \end{pmatrix}$ and $\begin{pmatrix} a & b \\ 2a + x & 2b \end{pmatrix}$. Equating their difference $\begin{pmatrix} a + b & a \\ x - 2a & x - 2b \end{pmatrix}$ to the matrix $\begin{pmatrix} 2 & 1 \\ 4 & 4 \end{pmatrix}$ on the right-hand side yields the following four equalities: $a + b = 2$, $a = 1$, $x - 2a = 4$, and $x - 2b = 4$. It follows that $a = b = 1$, $x = 6$.

896 SOLUTIONS TO THE EXERCISES

6. (a) $\mathbf{A}^2 = \begin{pmatrix} a^2 - b^2 & 2ab & b^2 \\ -2ab & a^2 - 2b^2 & 2ab \\ b^2 & -2ab & a^2 - b^2 \end{pmatrix}$

(b) $(\mathbf{C'BC})' = \mathbf{C'B'(C')'} = \mathbf{C'(-B)C} = -\mathbf{C'BC}$. So $\mathbf{A}$ is skew-symmetric if and only if $a = 0$.

(c) $\mathbf{A}_1' = \frac{1}{2}(\mathbf{A'} + \mathbf{A''}) = \frac{1}{2}(\mathbf{A'} + \mathbf{A}) = \mathbf{A}_1$, so $\mathbf{A}_1$ is symmetric. It is equally easy to prove that $\mathbf{A}_2$ is skew-symmetric, as well as that any square matrix $\mathbf{A}$ is therefore the sum $\mathbf{A}_1 + \mathbf{A}_2$ of a symmetric matrix $\mathbf{A}_1$ and a skew-symmetric matrix $\mathbf{A}_2$.

7. (a) $\begin{pmatrix} 1 & 4 & 1 \\ 2 & 2 & 8 \end{pmatrix} \underset{\longleftarrow}{-2} \sim \begin{pmatrix} 1 & 4 & 1 \\ 0 & -6 & 6 \end{pmatrix} -1/6 \sim \begin{pmatrix} 1 & 4 & 1 \\ 0 & 1 & -1 \end{pmatrix} \underset{-4}{\longleftarrow} \sim \begin{pmatrix} 1 & 0 & 5 \\ 0 & 1 & -1 \end{pmatrix}$

The solution is $x_1 = 5, x_2 = -1$. (b) The solution is $x_1 = 3/7, x_2 = -5/7, x_3 = -18/7$.

(c) The solution is $x_1 = (1/14)x_3, x_2 = -(19/14)x_3$, where x_3 is arbitrary. (One degree of freedom.)

8. We use the method of Gaussian elimination:

$\begin{pmatrix} 1 & a & 2 & 0 \\ -2 & -a & 1 & 4 \\ 2a & 3a^2 & 9 & 4 \end{pmatrix} \underset{\longleftarrow}{\overset{2}{\longleftarrow}} \begin{matrix} -2a \\ \\ \end{matrix} \sim \begin{pmatrix} 1 & a & 2 & 0 \\ 0 & a & 5 & 4 \\ 0 & a^2 & 9-4a & 4 \end{pmatrix} \underset{\longleftarrow}{-a} \sim \begin{pmatrix} 1 & a & 2 & 0 \\ 0 & a & 5 & 4 \\ 0 & 0 & 9-9a & 4-4a \end{pmatrix}$

For $a = 1$, the last equation is superfluous; the solution is $x = 3t - 4, y = -5t + 4, z = t$, with t arbitrary. If $a \neq 1$, we have $(9 - 9a)z = 4 - 4a$, so $z = 4/9$. The two other equations then become $x + ay = -8/9$ and $ay = 16/9$. If $a = 0$, there is no solution. If $a \neq 0$, the solution is $x = -8/3, y = 16/9a$, and $z = 4/9$.

9. Here $\|\mathbf{a}\| = \sqrt{35}, \|\mathbf{b}\| = \sqrt{11}$, and $\|\mathbf{c}\| = \sqrt{69}$. Moreover $|\mathbf{a} \cdot \mathbf{b}| = |(-1) \cdot 1 + 5 \cdot 1 + 3 \cdot (-3)| = |-5| = 5$. Then $\|\mathbf{a}\| \|\mathbf{b}\| = \sqrt{35}\sqrt{11} = \sqrt{385}$ is obviously greater than $|\mathbf{a} \cdot \mathbf{b}| = 5$, so the Cauchy–Schwarz inequality is satisfied.

10. Because $\mathbf{PQ} = \mathbf{QP} + \mathbf{P}$, multiplying on the left by $\mathbf{P}$ gives $\mathbf{P}^2\mathbf{Q} = (\mathbf{PQ})\mathbf{P} + \mathbf{P}^2 = (\mathbf{QP} + \mathbf{P})\mathbf{P} + \mathbf{P}^2 = \mathbf{QP}^2 + 2\mathbf{P}^2$.

See SM for details of how to repeat this argument in order to prove by induction the result for higher powers of $\mathbf{P}$.

Chapter 13

13.1

1. (a) $3 \cdot 6 - 2 \cdot 0 = 18$ (b) $ab - ba = 0$ (c) $(2 - x)(-x) - 1 \cdot 8 = x^2 - 2x + 8$ (d) $(a + b)^2 - (a - b)^2 = 4ab$

(e) $3^t 2^{t-1} - 3^{t-1} 2^t = 3^{t-1} 2^{t-1}(3 - 2) = 6^{t-1}$

2. See Fig. A13.1.2. The shaded parallelogram has area $3 \cdot 6 = 18 = \begin{vmatrix} 3 & 0 \\ 2 & 6 \end{vmatrix}$.

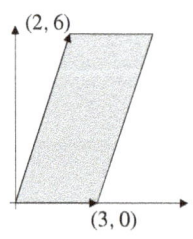

Figure A13.1.2

3. (a) Cramer's rule gives $x = \dfrac{\begin{vmatrix} 8 & -1 \\ 5 & -2 \end{vmatrix}}{\begin{vmatrix} 3 & -1 \\ 1 & -2 \end{vmatrix}} = \dfrac{-16+5}{-6+1} = \dfrac{11}{5}$ and $y = \dfrac{\begin{vmatrix} 3 & 8 \\ 1 & 5 \end{vmatrix}}{\begin{vmatrix} 3 & -1 \\ 1 & -2 \end{vmatrix}} = \dfrac{15-8}{-6+1} = \dfrac{7}{-5} = -\dfrac{7}{5}$.

(b) $x = 4$ and $y = -1$ (c) $x = \dfrac{a + 2b}{a^2 + b^2}$ and $y = \dfrac{2a - b}{a^2 + b^2}$, provided that $a^2 + b^2 \neq 0$.

4. The numbers a and b must satisfy $a + 1 = 0$ and $a - 3b = -10$, so $a = -1$ and $b = 3$.

5. Expanding the determinant gives $(2 - x)(-x) - 8 = 0$ or $x^2 - 2x - 8 = 0$, so $x = -2$ or $x = 4$.

6. The matrix product is $\mathbf{AB} = \begin{pmatrix} a_{11}b_{11} + a_{12}b_{21} & a_{11}b_{12} + a_{12}b_{22} \\ a_{21}b_{11} + a_{22}b_{21} & a_{21}b_{12} + a_{22}b_{22} \end{pmatrix}$, implying that $|\mathbf{AB}| = (a_{11}b_{11} + a_{12}b_{21})(a_{21}b_{12} + a_{22}b_{22}) - (a_{11}b_{12} + a_{12}b_{22})(a_{21}b_{11} + a_{22}b_{21})$. On the other hand, $|\mathbf{A}||\mathbf{B}| = (a_{11}a_{22} - a_{12}a_{21})(b_{11}b_{22} - b_{12}b_{21})$. A tedious process of expanding each expression, then cancelling four terms in the expression for $|\mathbf{AB}|$, reveals that the two expressions are equal.

7. If $\mathbf{A} = \mathbf{B} = \begin{pmatrix} 1 & 0 \\ 0 & 1 \end{pmatrix}$, then $|\mathbf{A} + \mathbf{B}| = 4$, whereas $|\mathbf{A}| + |\mathbf{B}| = 2$.

(This illustrates how $|\mathbf{A} + \mathbf{B}| \neq |\mathbf{A}| + |\mathbf{B}|$ for almost any choice of the matrices $\mathbf{A}$ and $\mathbf{B}$.)

8. Begin by writing the system as $\begin{cases} Y - C = I_0 + G_0 \\ -bY + C = a \end{cases}$. Then Cramer's rule yields

$$Y = \dfrac{\begin{vmatrix} I_0 + G_0 & -1 \\ a & 1 \end{vmatrix}}{\begin{vmatrix} 1 & -1 \\ -b & 1 \end{vmatrix}} = \dfrac{a + I_0 + G_0}{1 - b}, \qquad C = \dfrac{\begin{vmatrix} 1 & I_0 + G_0 \\ -b & a \end{vmatrix}}{\begin{vmatrix} 1 & -1 \\ -b & 1 \end{vmatrix}} = \dfrac{a + b(I_0 + G_0)}{1 - b}$$

Instead of using Cramer's rule, the expression for Y is most easily found by:

(i) solving the second equation to obtain $C = a + bY$; (ii) substituting this expression for C into the first equation; (iii) solving the resulting equation for Y; (iv) finally, using $C = a + bY$ again to find C.

9. (a) The equation $X_1 = M_2$ says that nation 1's exports equal nation 2's imports. Similarly, $X_2 = M_1$.

(b) Substituting for X_1, X_2, M_1, M_2, C_1, and C_2 gives the two equations:

$$(1 - c_1 + m_1)Y_1 - m_2 Y_2 = A_1 \quad \text{and} \quad (1 - c_2 + m_2)Y_2 - m_1 Y_1 = A_2$$

Using Cramer's rule with $D = (1 - c_1 + m_1)(1 - c_2 + m_2) - m_1 m_2$ yields

$$Y_1 = [A_2 m_2 + A_1(1 - c_2 + m_2)]/D \quad \text{and} \quad Y_2 = [A_1 m_1 + A_2(1 - c_1 + m_1)]/D$$

(c) Y_2 increases when A_1 increases.

13.2

1. (a) -2 (b) -2 (c) adf (d) $e(ad - bc)$

2. $\mathbf{AB} = \begin{pmatrix} -1 & -1 & -1 \\ 7 & 13 & 13 \\ 5 & 9 & 10 \end{pmatrix}$, $|\mathbf{A}| = -2$, $|\mathbf{B}| = 3$, $|\mathbf{AB}| = |\mathbf{A}| \cdot |\mathbf{B}| = -6$

3. (a) $x_1 = 1, x_2 = 2$, and $x_3 = 3$ (b) $x_1 = x_2 = x_3 = 0$ (c) $x = 1, y = 2$, and $z = 3$

898 SOLUTIONS TO THE EXERCISES

4. By Sarrus's rule the determinant is $(1+a)(1+b)(1+c) + 1 + 1 - (1+b) - (1+a) - (1+c)$, which simplifies to the given expression.

5. $\text{tr}(\mathbf{A}) = a + b - 1 = 0$ and thus $b = 1 - a$. Also, $|\mathbf{A}| = -2ab = 12$, and so $-2a(1-a) = 12$, or $a^2 - a - 6 = 0$. The roots of this equation are $a = 3$ and $a = -2$. Thus the solutions are $(a, b) = (3, -2)$ and $(a, b) = (-2, 3)$.

6. By Sarrus's rule, the determinant is $p(x) = (1-x)^3 + 8 + 8 - 4(1-x) - 4(1-x) - 4(1-x) = -x^3 + 3x^2 + 9x + 5$.

   The equation we want to solve is therefore the cubic equation $-x^3 + 3x^2 + 9x + 5 = 0$. We have no simple general formula available for solving such equations, but since this is a polynomial equation with integer coefficients, it follows from Eq. (4.7.7) that every integer root of the equation (if there are any) must divide the constant term 5. The only candidates for integer roots are therefore ± 5 and ± 1. It is easily seen that $p(5) = 0$ and $p(-1) = 0$, and so both $x - 5$ and $x + 1$ must be factors in $p(x)$. Thus $p(x) = (x-5)(x+1)q(x)$, and polynomial division yields $q(x) = x + 1$. So $x = -1$ is a repeated root, and the determinant is 0 if and only if $x = -1$ or $x = 5$.

7. (a) $|\mathbf{A}_t| = 2t^2 - 2t + 1 = t^2 + (t-1)^2 > 0$ for all t. (Or show that the quadratic polynomial has no real zeros.)

   (b) $\mathbf{A}_t^3 = \begin{pmatrix} 1 & 2t - 2t^2 & t - t^2 \\ 4t - 4 & 5t - 4 & -t^2 + 4t - 3 \\ 2 - 2t & t^2 - 4t + 3 & t^3 - 2t + 2 \end{pmatrix}$. We find that $\mathbf{A}_t^3 = \mathbf{I}_3$ for $t = 1$.

8. With $k = 1/[1 - b(1-t)]$, in equilibrium we must have $Y = k(a - bd + A_0)$, $C = k[a - bd + A_0 b(1-t)]$, and $T = k[t(a + A_0) + (1-b)d]$.

13.3

1. (a) $1 \cdot 2 \cdot 3 \cdot 4 = 24$ (b) $d - a$ (Only two terms are nonzero.)

   (c) $1 \cdot 1 \cdot 1 \cdot 11 - 1 \cdot 1 \cdot 4 \cdot 4 - 1 \cdot (-3) \cdot 1 \cdot 3 - 2 \cdot 1 \cdot 1 \cdot 2 = 0$

2. With $\mathbf{A} = \begin{pmatrix} a_{11} & a_{12} & \cdots & a_{1n} \\ 0 & a_{22} & \cdots & a_{2n} \\ \vdots & \vdots & \ddots & \vdots \\ 0 & 0 & \cdots & a_{nn} \end{pmatrix}$ and $\mathbf{B} = \begin{pmatrix} b_{11} & b_{12} & \cdots & b_{1n} \\ 0 & b_{22} & \cdots & b_{2n} \\ \vdots & \vdots & \ddots & \vdots \\ 0 & 0 & \cdots & b_{nn} \end{pmatrix}$, the product $\mathbf{AB}$ is easily seen to be upper triangular, with the elements $a_{11}b_{11}, a_{22}b_{22}, \ldots, a_{nn}b_{nn}$ on the main diagonal. The determinant $|\mathbf{AB}|$ is, according to (3), the product of the n numbers $a_{ii}b_{ii}$. On the other hand, $|\mathbf{A}| = a_{11}a_{22}\cdots a_{nn}$, and $|\mathbf{B}| = b_{11}b_{22}\cdots b_{nn}$, so the equality $|\mathbf{AB}| = |\mathbf{A}||\mathbf{B}|$ follows immediately.

3. $+a_{12}a_{23}a_{35}a_{41}a_{54}$. (Four lines between pairs of boxed elements rise as one goes to the right.)

4. $-a_{15}a_{24}a_{32}a_{43}a_{51}$. (There are nine lines that rise to the right.)

5. Carefully examining how formula (13.3.2) applies to this 4×4 determinant reveals that its only nonzero term is the product of its diagonal elements. So the equation is $(2-x)^4 = 0$, whose only solution is $x = 2$.

13.4

1. (a) $\mathbf{AB} = \begin{pmatrix} 13 & 16 \\ 29 & 36 \end{pmatrix}$, $\mathbf{BA} = \begin{pmatrix} 15 & 22 \\ 23 & 34 \end{pmatrix}$, $\mathbf{A'B'} = \begin{pmatrix} 15 & 23 \\ 22 & 34 \end{pmatrix}$, $\mathbf{B'A'} = \begin{pmatrix} 13 & 29 \\ 16 & 36 \end{pmatrix}$.

   (b) $|\mathbf{A}| = |\mathbf{A'}| = -2$ and $|\mathbf{B}| = |\mathbf{B'}| = -2$. So $|\mathbf{AB}| = 4 = |\mathbf{A}| \cdot |\mathbf{B}|$.

   (c) $|\mathbf{A'B'}| = 4$ and $|\mathbf{A'}| \cdot |\mathbf{B'}| = (-2) \cdot (-2) = 4$.

2. $\mathbf{A'} = \begin{pmatrix} 2 & 1 & 1 \\ 1 & 0 & 2 \\ 3 & 1 & 5 \end{pmatrix}$ and $|\mathbf{A}| = |\mathbf{A'}| = -2$.

3. (a) 0 (one column has only zeros).   (b) 0 (rows 1 and 4 are proportional).

   (c) $(a_1 - x)(-x)^3 = x^4 - a_1 x^3$. (Use the definition of a determinant and observe that at most one term is nonzero.)

4. $|\mathbf{AB}| = |\mathbf{A}||\mathbf{B}| = -12$, $3|\mathbf{A}| = 9$, $|-2\mathbf{B}| = (-2)^3(-4) = 32$, $|4\mathbf{A}| = 4^3|\mathbf{A}| = 4^3 \cdot 3 = 192$, and $|\mathbf{A}| + |\mathbf{B}| = -1$, whereas $|\mathbf{A} + \mathbf{B}|$ is not determined.

5. $\mathbf{A}^2 = \begin{pmatrix} a^2 + 6 & a + 1 & a^2 + 4a - 12 \\ a^2 + 2a + 2 & 3 & 8 - 2a^2 \\ a - 3 & 1 & 13 \end{pmatrix}$ and $|\mathbf{A}| = a^2 - 3a + 2$.

6. (a) The first and the second columns are proportional, so by part (v) of Theorem 13.4.1, the determinant is 0.

   (b) Add the second column to the third. This makes the first and third columns of the new determinant proportional.

   (c) The first row is $x - y$ times the second row, so the first two rows are proportional.

7. $\mathbf{X}'\mathbf{X} = \begin{pmatrix} 4 & 3 & 2 \\ 3 & 5 & 1 \\ 2 & 1 & 2 \end{pmatrix}$ and $|\mathbf{X}'\mathbf{X}| = 10$.

8. By Sarrus's rule, for example, $|\mathbf{A}_a| = a(a^2 + 1) + 4 + 4 - 4(a^2 + 1) - a - 4 = a^2(a - 4)$. Putting $a = 1$ gives $|\mathbf{A}_1| = -3$ and so $|\mathbf{A}_1^6| = |\mathbf{A}_1|^6 = (-3)^6 = 729$. (Now how much easier this is than first finding $\mathbf{A}_1^6$ and only then evaluating its determinant.)

9. Because $\mathbf{P}'\mathbf{P} = \mathbf{I}_n$, it follows from rule (13.4.1) that $|\mathbf{P}'||\mathbf{P}| = |\mathbf{I}_n| = 1$. But $|\mathbf{P}'| = |\mathbf{P}|$ by part (ii) of Theorem 13.4.1, so $|\mathbf{P}|^2 = 1$. Hence, $|\mathbf{P}| = \pm 1$.

10. (a) Because $\mathbf{A}^2 = \mathbf{I}_n$, it follows from rule (13.4.1) that $|\mathbf{A}|^2 = |\mathbf{A}^2| = |\mathbf{I}_n| = 1$, and so $|\mathbf{A}| = \pm 1$.

    (b) Direct verification by matrix multiplication.

    (c) We have $(\mathbf{I}_n - \mathbf{A})(\mathbf{I}_n + \mathbf{A}) = \mathbf{I}_n \cdot \mathbf{I}_n - \mathbf{A}\mathbf{I}_n + \mathbf{I}_n\mathbf{A} - \mathbf{A}\mathbf{A} = \mathbf{I}_n - \mathbf{A} + \mathbf{A} - \mathbf{A}^2 = \mathbf{I}_n - \mathbf{A}^2$, which equals $\mathbf{0}$ iff $\mathbf{A}^2 = \mathbf{I}_n$.

11. (a) The first equality is true, the second is false. (The second becomes true if the outside factor 2 is replaced by 4.)

    (b) Generally false. (Both determinants on the right are 0, even if $ad - bc \neq 0$.)   (c) Both equalities are true.

    (d) True. (The second determinant is the result of subtracting 2 times row 1 of the first determinant from its row 2.)

12. We must show that $\mathbf{B}(\mathbf{PQ}) = (\mathbf{PQ})\mathbf{B}$. Repeatedly using the associative law for matrix multiplication, as well as the equalities $\mathbf{BP} = \mathbf{PB}$ and $\mathbf{BQ} = \mathbf{QB}$, we get

$$\mathbf{B}(\mathbf{PQ}) = (\mathbf{BP})\mathbf{Q} = (\mathbf{PB})\mathbf{Q} = \mathbf{P}(\mathbf{BQ}) = \mathbf{P}(\mathbf{QB}) = (\mathbf{PQ})\mathbf{B}$$

13. Let $\mathbf{A} = \begin{pmatrix} 0 & c & b \\ c & 0 & a \\ b & a & 0 \end{pmatrix}$. Then compute $\mathbf{A}^2$ and recall rule (13.4.1).

14. First add each of the last $n - 1$ rows to the first row. Each element in the first row then becomes $na + b$. Factor this out of the determinant. Next, add the first row multiplied by $-a$ to all the other $n - 1$ rows. The result is an upper triangular matrix whose diagonal elements are $1, b, b, \ldots, b$, with product equal to b^{n-1}. The conclusion follows.

13.5

1. (a) 2. (Subtract row 1 from both row 2 and row 3 to get a determinant whose first column has elements $1, 0, 0$. Then expand by the first column.)   (b) 30. (One can apply two elementary row operations so that all elements of the first column below the first are zero. Then again for the reduced 3×3 determinant. See SM for details.)

   (c) 0. (Columns 2 and 4 are proportional.)

2. In each of these cases we keep expanding by the last (remaining) column. With appropriate signs, the answers are:
(a) $a(-bc) = -abc$; (b) $(-a)b(-cd) = abcd$; (c) $1 \cdot (-5) \cdot 3 \cdot -(4 \cdot 6) = 360$.

13.6

1. (a) Using (13.6.4) one has $\begin{pmatrix} 3 & 0 \\ 2 & -1 \end{pmatrix} \cdot \begin{pmatrix} 1/3 & 0 \\ 2/3 & -1 \end{pmatrix} = \begin{pmatrix} 1 & 0 \\ 0 & 1 \end{pmatrix}$. (b) Use (13.6.4).

2. By direct calculation, one has $\mathbf{AB} = \begin{pmatrix} 1 & 0 & 0 \\ a+b & 2a+1/4+3b & 4a+3/2+2b \\ 0 & 0 & 1 \end{pmatrix}$. So one has $\mathbf{AB} = \mathbf{I}$ if and only if $a+b = 4a+3/2+2b = 0$ and $2a+1/4+3b = 1$, which is true if and only if $a = -3/4$ and $b = 3/4$.

3. (a) $\begin{pmatrix} x \\ y \end{pmatrix} = \begin{pmatrix} 2 & -3 \\ 3 & -4 \end{pmatrix}^{-1} \begin{pmatrix} 3 \\ 5 \end{pmatrix} = \begin{pmatrix} -4 & 3 \\ -3 & 2 \end{pmatrix} \begin{pmatrix} 3 \\ 5 \end{pmatrix} = \begin{pmatrix} 3 \\ 1 \end{pmatrix}$

(b) $\begin{pmatrix} x \\ y \end{pmatrix} = \begin{pmatrix} -4 & 3 \\ -3 & 2 \end{pmatrix} \begin{pmatrix} 8 \\ 11 \end{pmatrix} = \begin{pmatrix} 1 \\ -2 \end{pmatrix}$ (c) $\begin{pmatrix} x \\ y \end{pmatrix} = \begin{pmatrix} -4 & 3 \\ -3 & 2 \end{pmatrix} \begin{pmatrix} 0 \\ 0 \end{pmatrix} = \begin{pmatrix} 0 \\ 0 \end{pmatrix}$

4. From $\mathbf{A}^3 = \mathbf{I}$, it follows that $\mathbf{A}^2 \mathbf{A} = \mathbf{I}$, so $\mathbf{A}^{-1} = \mathbf{A}^2 = \frac{1}{2}\begin{pmatrix} -1 & \sqrt{3} \\ -\sqrt{3} & -1 \end{pmatrix}$.

5. (a) $|\mathbf{A}| = 1$, $\mathbf{A}^2 = \begin{pmatrix} 0 & 1 & 1 \\ 1 & 1 & 2 \\ 1 & 1 & 1 \end{pmatrix}$, $\mathbf{A}^3 = \begin{pmatrix} 1 & 1 & 2 \\ 2 & 2 & 3 \\ 1 & 2 & 2 \end{pmatrix}$, and so $\mathbf{A}^3 - 2\mathbf{A}^2 + \mathbf{A} - \mathbf{I}_3 = \mathbf{0}$.

(b) The last equality in (a) is equivalent to $\mathbf{A}(\mathbf{A}^2 - 2\mathbf{A} + \mathbf{I}_3) = \mathbf{A}(\mathbf{A} - \mathbf{I}_3)^2 = \mathbf{I}_3$, so $\mathbf{A}^{-1} = (\mathbf{A} - \mathbf{I}_3)^2$.

(c) Part (b) suggests the choice $\mathbf{P} = (\mathbf{A} - \mathbf{I}_3)^{-1}$ so that $\mathbf{A} = [(\mathbf{A} - \mathbf{I}_3)^2]^{-1} = \mathbf{P}^2$. The matrix $-\mathbf{P}$ also works.

Hence $\mathbf{P} = \pm(\mathbf{A} - \mathbf{I}_3)^{-1} = \pm\begin{pmatrix} -1 & 1 & 0 \\ 0 & 0 & 1 \\ 1 & 0 & 0 \end{pmatrix}^{-1} = \pm\begin{pmatrix} 0 & 0 & 1 \\ 1 & 0 & 1 \\ 0 & 1 & 0 \end{pmatrix}$.

6. (a) $\mathbf{AA}' = \begin{pmatrix} 21 & 11 \\ 11 & 10 \end{pmatrix}$, $|\mathbf{AA}'| = 89$, and $(\mathbf{AA}')^{-1} = \frac{1}{89}\begin{pmatrix} 10 & -11 \\ -11 & 21 \end{pmatrix}$.

(b) No, because by Example 12.7.4, the matrix $\mathbf{AA}'$ must be symmetric. Then its inverse $(\mathbf{AA}')^{-1}$ must also be symmetric, because of the note that follows Theorem 13.6.1.

7. $\mathbf{B}^2 + \mathbf{B} = \mathbf{I}$, $\mathbf{B}^3 - 2\mathbf{B} + \mathbf{I} = \mathbf{0}$, and $\mathbf{B}^{-1} = \mathbf{B} + \mathbf{I} = \begin{pmatrix} 1/2 & 5 \\ 1/4 & 1/2 \end{pmatrix}$.

8. Let $\mathbf{B} = \mathbf{X}(\mathbf{X}'\mathbf{X})^{-1}\mathbf{X}'$. Then $\mathbf{A}^2 = (\mathbf{I}_m - \mathbf{B})(\mathbf{I}_m - \mathbf{B}) = \mathbf{I}_m - \mathbf{B} - \mathbf{B} + \mathbf{B}^2$. Here

$$\mathbf{B}^2 = [\mathbf{X}(\mathbf{X}'\mathbf{X})^{-1}\mathbf{X}'][\mathbf{X}(\mathbf{X}'\mathbf{X})^{-1}\mathbf{X}'] = \mathbf{X}(\mathbf{X}'\mathbf{X})^{-1}(\mathbf{X}'\mathbf{X})(\mathbf{X}'\mathbf{X})^{-1}\mathbf{X}' = \mathbf{X}(\mathbf{X}'\mathbf{X})^{-1}\mathbf{X}' = \mathbf{B}$$

Thus, $\mathbf{A}^2 = \mathbf{I}_m - \mathbf{B} - \mathbf{B} + \mathbf{B} = \mathbf{I}_m - \mathbf{B} = \mathbf{A}$.

9. $\mathbf{AB} = \begin{pmatrix} -7 & 0 \\ -2 & 10 \end{pmatrix}$, so $\mathbf{CX} = \mathbf{D} - \mathbf{AB} = \begin{pmatrix} -2 & 3 \\ -6 & 7 \end{pmatrix}$. But $\mathbf{C}^{-1} = \begin{pmatrix} -2 & 1 \\ 3/2 & -1/2 \end{pmatrix}$, so $\mathbf{X} = \begin{pmatrix} -2 & 1 \\ 0 & 1 \end{pmatrix}$.

10. (a) If $C^2 + C = I$, then $C(C + I) = I$, and so $C^{-1} = C + I = I + C$.

(b) Because $C^2 = I - C$, it follows that $C^3 = C^2 C = (I - C)C = C - C^2 = C - (I - C) = -I + 2C$.
Moreover, $C^4 = C^3 C = (-I + 2C)C = -C + 2C^2 = -C + 2(I - C) = 2I - 3C$.

13.7

1. (a) $\begin{pmatrix} -5/2 & 3/2 \\ 2 & -1 \end{pmatrix}$ (b) $\dfrac{1}{9}\begin{pmatrix} 1 & 4 & 2 \\ 2 & -1 & 4 \\ 4 & -2 & -1 \end{pmatrix}$ (c) The matrix has a zero determinant, so no inverse.

2. The inverse is $\dfrac{1}{|A|}\begin{pmatrix} C_{11} & C_{21} & C_{31} \\ C_{12} & C_{22} & C_{32} \\ C_{13} & C_{23} & C_{33} \end{pmatrix} = \dfrac{1}{72}\begin{pmatrix} -3 & 5 & 9 \\ 18 & -6 & 18 \\ 6 & 14 & -18 \end{pmatrix}$.

3. $(I - A)^{-1} = \dfrac{5}{62}\begin{pmatrix} 18 & 16 & 10 \\ 2 & 19 & 8 \\ 4 & 7 & 16 \end{pmatrix}$

4. When $k = r$, the solution to the system is $x_1 = b_{1r}^*, x_2 = b_{2r}^*, \ldots, x_n = b_{nr}^*$.

5. (a) $A^{-1} = \begin{pmatrix} -2 & 1 \\ 3/2 & -1/2 \end{pmatrix}$ (b) $B^{-1} = \begin{pmatrix} 1 & -3 & 2 \\ -3 & 3 & -1 \\ 2 & -1 & 0 \end{pmatrix}$ (c) $|C| = 0$, so there is no inverse.

13.8

1. (a) $x = 1, y = -2$, and $z = 2$ (b) $x = -3, y = 6, z = 5$, and $u = -5$

2. The determinant of the system is equal to -10, so the solution is unique. The determinants in (13.8.2) are

$$D_1 = \begin{vmatrix} b_1 & 1 & 0 \\ b_2 & -1 & 2 \\ b_3 & 3 & -1 \end{vmatrix}, \quad D_2 = \begin{vmatrix} 3 & b_1 & 0 \\ 1 & b_2 & 2 \\ 2 & b_3 & -1 \end{vmatrix}, \quad D_3 = \begin{vmatrix} 3 & 1 & b_1 \\ 1 & -1 & b_2 \\ 2 & 3 & b_3 \end{vmatrix}$$

Expanding each of these determinants by the column (b_1, b_2, b_3), we find that:

$$D_1 = -5b_1 + b_2 + 2b_3, \quad D_2 = 5b_1 - 3b_2 - 6b_3, \quad D_3 = 5b_1 - 7b_2 - 4b_3$$

Dividing these by -10 gives $x_1 = \tfrac{1}{2}b_1 - \tfrac{1}{10}b_2 - \tfrac{1}{5}b_3$, $x_2 = -\tfrac{1}{2}b_1 + \tfrac{3}{10}b_2 + \tfrac{3}{5}b_3$, and $x_3 = -\tfrac{1}{2}b_1 + \tfrac{7}{10}b_2 + \tfrac{2}{5}b_3$.

3. Show that the coefficient matrix has determinant equal to $-(a^3 + b^3 + c^3 - 3abc)$, then use Theorem 13.8.2.

13.9

1. $x_1 = \tfrac{1}{4}x_2 + 100, x_2 = 2x_3 + 80, x_3 = \tfrac{1}{2}x_1$. The solution is $x_1 = 160, x_2 = 240, x_3 = 80$, as (**) implies.

2. (a) Let x and y denote total production in industries A and I, respectively. These must satisfy $x = \tfrac{1}{6}x + \tfrac{1}{4}y + 60$ and $y = \tfrac{1}{4}x + \tfrac{1}{4}y + 60$. So $\tfrac{5}{6}x - \tfrac{1}{4}y = 60$ and $-\tfrac{1}{4}x + \tfrac{3}{4}y = 60$. (b) The solution is $x = 320/3$ and $y = 1040/9$.

3. (a) No sector delivers to itself. (b) The total amount of good i needed to produce one unit of each good.

(c) This column vector gives the number of units of each good needed to produce one unit of good j.

(d) No meaningful economic interpretation. (The goods are usually measured in different units, so it is meaningless to add them together. As the saying goes: "You can't add apples and oranges!")

4. $0.8x_1 - 0.3x_2 = 120$ and $-0.4x_1 + 0.9x_2 = 90$, with solution $x_1 = 225$ and $x_2 = 200$.

5. The Leontief system for this three-sector model is $\begin{cases} 0.9x_1 - 0.2x_2 - 0.1x_3 = 85 \\ -0.3x_1 + 0.8x_2 - 0.2x_3 = 95 \\ -0.2x_1 - 0.2x_2 + 0.9x_3 = 20 \end{cases}$, which has the claimed solution.

6. The input matrix is $\mathbf{A} = \begin{pmatrix} 0 & \beta & 0 \\ 0 & 0 & \gamma \\ \alpha & 0 & 0 \end{pmatrix}$. The sums of the elements in each column are less than 1 provided that $\alpha < 1$, $\beta < 1$, and $\gamma < 1$, respectively. Then, in particular, the product $\alpha\beta\gamma < 1$.

7. The quantity vector $\mathbf{x}_0$ must satisfy $(*)$ $(\mathbf{I}_n - \mathbf{A})\mathbf{x}_0 = \mathbf{b}$, and the price vector $\mathbf{p}'_0$ must satisfy $(**)$ $\mathbf{p}'_0(\mathbf{I}_n - \mathbf{A}) = \mathbf{v}'$. Multiplying $(**)$ from the right by $\mathbf{x}_0$ and using $(*)$ yields $\mathbf{v}'\mathbf{x}_0 = [\mathbf{p}'_0(\mathbf{I}_n - \mathbf{A})]\mathbf{x}_0 = \mathbf{p}'_0[(\mathbf{I}_n - \mathbf{A})\mathbf{x}_0] = \mathbf{p}'_0\mathbf{b}$.

13.10

1. (a) $-1, -5;$ $\begin{pmatrix} 7 \\ 3 \end{pmatrix}, \begin{pmatrix} 1 \\ 1 \end{pmatrix}$ (b) $5, -5;$ $\begin{pmatrix} 1 \\ 1 \end{pmatrix}, \begin{pmatrix} -2 \\ 3 \end{pmatrix}$ (c) $2, 3, 4;$ $\begin{pmatrix} 1 \\ 0 \\ 0 \end{pmatrix}, \begin{pmatrix} 0 \\ 1 \\ 0 \end{pmatrix}, \begin{pmatrix} 0 \\ 0 \\ 1 \end{pmatrix}$

2. First, $\mathbf{Av}_1 = 3\mathbf{v}_1$ yields $a - c = 3$, $b - e = 0$, and $c - f = -3$. Second, $\mathbf{Av}_2 = \mathbf{v}_2$ yields $a + 2b + c = 1$, $b + 2d + e = 2$, and $c + 2e + f = 1$. Finally, $\mathbf{Av}_3 = 4\mathbf{v}_3$ yields $a - b + c = 4$, $b - d + e = -4$, and $c - e + f = 4$.

Subtracting the equation $a - b + c = 4$ from $a + 2b + c = 1$ yields $b = -1$ and $a + c = 3$. Subtracting $a + c = 3$ from $a - c = 3$ yields $c = 0$ and so $a = 3$. Using a similar approach for the other rows of $\mathbf{A}$ yields the solution

$$\mathbf{A} = \begin{pmatrix} 3 & -1 & 0 \\ -1 & 2 & -1 \\ 0 & -1 & 3 \end{pmatrix}$$

13.11

1. (a) The eigenvalues are 1 and 3, with corresponding eigenvectors $\begin{pmatrix} 1 \\ -1 \end{pmatrix}$ and $\begin{pmatrix} 1 \\ 1 \end{pmatrix}$. The matrix whose columns are the normalized eigenvectors is $\mathbf{P} = \begin{pmatrix} 1/\sqrt{2} & 1/\sqrt{2} \\ -1/\sqrt{2} & 1/\sqrt{2} \end{pmatrix}$. Then $\mathbf{P}^{-1}\mathbf{AP} = \text{diag}(1, 3)$.

(b) $\mathbf{P} = \begin{pmatrix} 1/\sqrt{2} & 1/\sqrt{2} & 0 \\ -1/\sqrt{2} & 1/\sqrt{2} & 0 \\ 0 & 0 & 1 \end{pmatrix}$ (c) $\mathbf{P} = \begin{pmatrix} 0 & \sqrt{2}/2 & -\sqrt{2}/2 \\ -4/5 & 3\sqrt{2}/10 & 3\sqrt{2}/10 \\ 3/5 & 2\sqrt{2}/5 & 2\sqrt{2}/5 \end{pmatrix}$

2. (a) The characteristic equation can be reduced to $(1 - \lambda)[\lambda^2 + \lambda - 3(1 + k)] = 0$.

Because the polynomial $\lambda^2 + \lambda - 3(1 + k)$ is not a multiple of $(1 - \lambda)^2$, at least one root must be $\neq 1$.

(b) All roots are real iff $\lambda^2 + \lambda - 3(1 + k) = 0$ has two real roots, which is true iff $k \geq -13/12$.

If $k = 3$, the eigenvalues are -4, 1, and 3. (c) $\mathbf{P}'\mathbf{A}_3\mathbf{P} = \begin{pmatrix} 1 & 0 & 0 \\ 0 & -4 & 0 \\ 0 & 0 & 3 \end{pmatrix}$, as promised by Theorem 13.11.2.

3. (a) $\mathbf{A}^2 = (\mathbf{PDP}^{-1})(\mathbf{PDP}^{-1}) = \mathbf{PD}(\mathbf{P}^{-1}\mathbf{P})\mathbf{DP}^{-1} = \mathbf{PDIDP}^{-1} = \mathbf{PD}^2\mathbf{P}^{-1}$

(b) The formula is valid for $m = 1$. Suppose it is also valid for $m = k$. Then

$$\mathbf{A}^{k+1} = \mathbf{AA}^k = \mathbf{PDP}^{-1}(\mathbf{PD}^k\mathbf{P}^{-1}) = \mathbf{PD}(\mathbf{P}^{-1}\mathbf{P})\mathbf{D}^k\mathbf{P}^{-1} = \mathbf{PDID}^k\mathbf{P}^{-1} = \mathbf{PDD}^k\mathbf{P}^{-1} = \mathbf{PD}^{k+1}\mathbf{P}^{-1}$$

So the formula holds for $m = k + 1$ as well. By induction, it holds for all positive integers m.

4. According to (13.11.1), the two matrices $\mathbf{AB}$ and $\mathbf{A}^{-1}(\mathbf{AB})\mathbf{A} = \mathbf{BA}$ have the same eigenvalues.

13.12

1. (a) Here $a_{11} = -1$, $a_{12} = 1$ (not 2!), and $a_{22} = -6$. Hence $a_{11} < 0$ and $a_{11}a_{22} - a_{12}^2 = 6 - 1 = 5 > 0$, so according to (13.12.7), $Q(x_1, x_2)$ is negative definite.

   (b) Here $a_{11} = 4$, $a_{12} = 1$, and $a_{22} = 25$. Hence $a_{11} > 0$ and $a_{11}a_{22} - a_{12}^2 = 100 - 1 = 99 > 0$, so according to (13.12.5), $Q(x_1, x_2)$ is positive definite.

2. $a_{11}x_1^2 + 2a_{12}x_1x_2 + 2a_{13}x_1x_3 + a_{22}x_2^2 + 2a_{23}x_2x_3 + a_{33}x_3^2$

3. (a) $\begin{pmatrix} 1 & 1 \\ 1 & 1 \end{pmatrix}$ (b) $\begin{pmatrix} a & \frac{1}{2}b \\ \frac{1}{2}b & c \end{pmatrix}$ (c) $\begin{pmatrix} 3 & -1 & 3/2 \\ -1 & 1 & 0 \\ 3/2 & 0 & 3 \end{pmatrix}$

4. $\mathbf{A} = \begin{pmatrix} 3 & -1 & 2 & 4 \\ -1 & 1 & 3/2 & 0 \\ 2 & 3/2 & 1 & -1 \\ 4 & 0 & -1 & 1 \end{pmatrix}$

5. (a) Positive definite (b) Positive definite (c) Negative semidefinite (d) Negative definite.

6. Since $\mathbf{A}$ is symmetric, by part (a) of Theorem 13.11.4, all the eigenvalues are real. By part (b) of Theorem 13.12.1 they are all nonnegative iff $\mathbf{A}$ is positive semidefinite. Since $|\mathbf{A}| = 0$ iff 0 is an eigenvalue, all the eigenvalues must be positive. The conclusion follows from part (a) of Theorem 13.12.1.

7. The associated symmetric matrix $\mathbf{A}$ is $\begin{pmatrix} 3 & -\frac{1}{2}(5+c) \\ -\frac{1}{2}(5+c) & 2c \end{pmatrix}$ whose determinant is $|\mathbf{A}| = 6c - \frac{1}{4}(5+c)^2$. This can be factored as $|\mathbf{A}| = -\frac{1}{4}(c - c_1)(c - c_2)$ where $c_1 = 7 - 2\sqrt{6} \approx 2.1$ and $c_2 = 7 + 2\sqrt{6} \approx 11.9$. Applying the tests in (13.12.5)–(13.12.8) shows that Q is positive definite iff $c_1 < c < c_2$, positive semidefinite iff $c_1 \leq c \leq c_2$, and indefinite iff $c < c_1$ or $c > c_2$.

8. For any n-vector $\mathbf{x}$ one has $\mathbf{x}'\mathbf{A}\mathbf{x} = \mathbf{x}'(\mathbf{B}'\mathbf{B})\mathbf{x} = (\mathbf{B}\mathbf{x})'(\mathbf{B}\mathbf{x}) = \|\mathbf{B}\mathbf{x}\|^2 \geq 0$, so $\mathbf{A}$ is positive semidefinite. It is positive definite iff $\mathbf{B}\mathbf{x} \neq \mathbf{0}$ for all $\mathbf{x} \neq \mathbf{0}$, which is true iff $|\mathbf{B}| \neq 0$.

9. (a) Because Q is positive definite, one has $Q(0, \ldots, x_i, \ldots, 0) = a_{ii}x_i^2 > 0$ for all $x_i \neq 0$. It follows that $a_{ii} > 0$.

   (b) Again, because Q is positive definite, for all i, j with $i < j$ one has $R(x_i, x_j) = Q(0, \ldots, x_i, \ldots, x_j, \ldots, 0) > 0$ unless $x_i = x_j = 0$. But $R(x_i, x_j)$ is a quadratic form in the two variables x_i and x_j with associated symmetric matrix $\mathbf{B} = \begin{pmatrix} a_{ii} & a_{ij} \\ a_{ji} & a_{jj} \end{pmatrix}$. Since Q is positive definite, so is R. By part (a) of Theorem 13.12.2, it follows that $|\mathbf{B}| > 0$.

10. By part (a) of Theorem 13.11.4, all eigenvalues are real. If $\mathbf{A}$ is negative definite, then by (c) of Theorem 13.12.1, all the n eigenvalues $\lambda_1, \ldots, \lambda_n$ are negative. But then the function defined by $\psi(\lambda) = (-1)^n \varphi(\lambda)$ must satisfy

$$\psi(\lambda) = (\lambda - \lambda_1)(\lambda - \lambda_2) \cdots (\lambda - \lambda_n) = (\lambda + r_1)(\lambda + r_2) \cdots (\lambda + r_n)$$

where each $r_i = -\lambda_i$ is positive. Expanding this product obviously produces a polynomial whose coefficients are all positive. On the other hand, if every coefficient a_i in $\psi(\lambda)$ is positive, then $\psi(\lambda) \geq a_0 > 0$ for all $\lambda \geq 0$. So only a negative number can be an eigenvalue.

Review exercises for Chapter 13

1. (a) $5(-2) - (-2)3 = -4$ (b) $1 - a^2$ (c) $6a^2b + 2b^3$ (d) $\lambda^2 - 5\lambda$

2. (a) -4 (b) 1. (Subtract row 1 from rows 2 and 3. Then subtract twice row 2 from row 3. The resulting determinant has only one nonzero term in its third row.) (c) 1. (Use exactly the same row operations as in (b).)

3. Here $\mathbf{A}^{-1} = 2\mathbf{I}_2 - 2\begin{pmatrix} 1 & 1 \\ 1 & 0 \end{pmatrix} = \begin{pmatrix} 2 & 0 \\ 0 & 2 \end{pmatrix} - \begin{pmatrix} 2 & 2 \\ 2 & 0 \end{pmatrix} = \begin{pmatrix} 0 & -2 \\ -2 & 2 \end{pmatrix}$.

Using formula (13.6.3), it follows that $\mathbf{A} = \begin{pmatrix} 0 & -2 \\ -2 & 2 \end{pmatrix}^{-1} = -\frac{1}{4}\begin{pmatrix} 2 & 2 \\ 2 & 0 \end{pmatrix} = \begin{pmatrix} -1/2 & -1/2 \\ -1/2 & 0 \end{pmatrix}$.

4. (a) Expanding by cofactors along any row or column containing a zero yields $|\mathbf{A}_t| = t + 1$. So $\mathbf{A}_t$ has an inverse if and only if $t \neq -1$. (b) Multiplying the given equation from the right by $\mathbf{A}_1$ yields $\mathbf{BA}_1 + \mathbf{X} = \mathbf{I}_3$.

Hence $\mathbf{X} = \mathbf{I}_3 - \mathbf{BA}_1 = \begin{pmatrix} 0 & 0 & -1 \\ 0 & 0 & -1 \\ -2 & -1 & 0 \end{pmatrix}$.

5. (a) Routine calculation shows that $|\mathbf{A}| = (p+1)(q-2)$. Also $\mathbf{A} + \mathbf{E} = \begin{pmatrix} q+1 & 0 & q-1 \\ 2 & 1-p & 3-p \\ 3 & 0 & 1 \end{pmatrix}$, whose determinant is $|\mathbf{A} + \mathbf{E}| = (1-p)[q+1-3(q-1)] = 2(p-1)(q-2)$. (b) $\mathbf{A} + \mathbf{E}$ has an inverse for $p \neq 1$ and $q \neq 2$.
(c) Obviously, $|\mathbf{E}| = 0$. Then $|\mathbf{BE}| = |\mathbf{B}||\mathbf{E}| = 0$, so $\mathbf{BE}$ has no inverse.

6. The determinant of the coefficient matrix is $\begin{vmatrix} -2 & 4 & -t \\ -3 & 1 & t \\ t-2 & -7 & 4 \end{vmatrix} = 5t^2 - 45t + 40 = 5(t-1)(t-8)$.

So by Cramer's rule, there is a unique solution if and only if $t \neq 1$ and $t \neq 8$.

7. $(\mathbf{I} - \mathbf{A})(\mathbf{I} + \mathbf{A} + \mathbf{A}^2 + \mathbf{A}^3) = \mathbf{I} + \mathbf{A} + \mathbf{A}^2 + \mathbf{A}^3 - \mathbf{A} - \mathbf{A}^2 - \mathbf{A}^3 - \mathbf{A}^4 = \mathbf{I} - \mathbf{A}^4 = \mathbf{I}$. Then use (13.6.4).

8. (a) $(\mathbf{I}_n + a\mathbf{U})(\mathbf{I}_n + b\mathbf{U}) = \mathbf{I}_n^2 + b\mathbf{U} + a\mathbf{U} + ab\mathbf{U}^2$.

Because $\mathbf{U}^2 = n\mathbf{U}$, as is easily verified, the last expression simplifies to $\mathbf{I}_n + (a + b + nab)\mathbf{U}$.

(b) $\mathbf{A} = \mathbf{I}_3 + 3\mathbf{U}$, so a and b in part (a) must satisfy $a = 3$ and $a + b + 3ab = 0$, so that $(\mathbf{I}_n + a\mathbf{U})(\mathbf{I}_n + b\mathbf{U}) = \mathbf{I}_n$.

It follows that $b = -3/(1 + 3a) = -3/10$, and so $\mathbf{A}^{-1} = \frac{1}{10}\begin{pmatrix} 7 & -3 & -3 \\ -3 & 7 & -3 \\ -3 & -3 & 7 \end{pmatrix}$.

9. From the first equation, $\mathbf{Y} = \mathbf{B} - \mathbf{AX}$. Inserting this into the second equation gives $\mathbf{X} + 2\mathbf{A}^{-1}(\mathbf{B} - \mathbf{AX}) = \mathbf{C}$.
Solving for $\mathbf{X}$, one obtains $\mathbf{X} = 2\mathbf{A}^{-1}\mathbf{B} - \mathbf{C}$ and then $\mathbf{Y} = \mathbf{AC} - \mathbf{B}$.

10. (a) For $a \neq 1$ and $a \neq 2$, there is a unique solution. If $a = 1$, there is no solution.
If $a = 2$, there are infinitely many solutions.

(b) When $a = 1$ and $b_1 - b_2 + b_3 = 0$, or when $a = 2$ and $b_1 = b_2$, there are infinitely many solutions.

11. (a) $|\mathbf{A}| = -2$. Also $\mathbf{A}^2 - 2\mathbf{I}_2 = \begin{pmatrix} 11 & -6 \\ 18 & -10 \end{pmatrix} = \mathbf{A}$, so $\mathbf{A}^2 + c\mathbf{A} = 2\mathbf{I}_2$ if $c = -1$. It follows that $\mathbf{A}(\frac{1}{2}\mathbf{A} - \frac{1}{2}\mathbf{I}_2) = \mathbf{I}_2$,
so $\mathbf{A}^{-1} = \frac{1}{2}(\mathbf{A} - \mathbf{I}_2) = \begin{pmatrix} 5 & -3 \\ 9 & -11/2 \end{pmatrix}$. (b) If $\mathbf{B}^2 = \mathbf{A}$, then $|\mathbf{B}|^2 = |\mathbf{A}| = -2$, which is impossible.

12. Note first that if $\mathbf{A}'\mathbf{A} = \mathbf{I}_n$, then rule (13.6.5) implies that $\mathbf{A}^{-1} = \mathbf{A}'$, so $\mathbf{AA}' = \mathbf{I}_n$.
But then $(\mathbf{A}'\mathbf{B}^{-1}\mathbf{A})(\mathbf{A}'\mathbf{BA}) = \mathbf{A}'\mathbf{B}^{-1}(\mathbf{AA}')\mathbf{BA} = \mathbf{A}'\mathbf{B}^{-1}\mathbf{I}_n\mathbf{BA} = \mathbf{A}'(\mathbf{B}^{-1}\mathbf{B})\mathbf{A} = \mathbf{A}'\mathbf{I}_n\mathbf{A} = \mathbf{A}'\mathbf{A} = \mathbf{I}_n$.
By rule (13.6.5) again, it follows that $(\mathbf{A}'\mathbf{BA})^{-1} = \mathbf{A}'\mathbf{B}^{-1}\mathbf{A}$.

13. For once we use "unsystematic elimination". Solve the first equation to get $y = 3 - ax$, the second to get $z = 2 - x$, and the fourth to get $u = 1 - y$. Inserting all these in the third equation gives $3 - ax + a(2 - x) +$

$b(1 - 3 + ax) = 6$ or $a(b - 2)x = -2a + 2b + 3$. There is a unique solution provided that $a(b - 2) \neq 0$. This unique solution is:

$$x = \frac{2b - 2a + 3}{a(b - 2)}, \quad y = \frac{2a + b - 9}{b - 2}, \quad z = \frac{2ab - 2a - 2b - 3}{a(b - 2)}, \quad u = \frac{7 - 2a}{b - 2}$$

14. The determinant on the left is $(a + x)d - c(b + y) = (ad - bc) + (dx - cy)$, which equals the sum of the determinants on the right.

15. $|\mathbf{B}^3| = |\mathbf{B}|^3$. Because $\mathbf{B}$ is a 3×3-matrix, we have $|-\mathbf{B}| = (-1)^3|\mathbf{B}| = -|\mathbf{B}|$. Since $\mathbf{B}^3 = -\mathbf{B}$, it follows that $|\mathbf{B}|^3 = -|\mathbf{B}|$, and so $|\mathbf{B}|(|\mathbf{B}|^2 + 1) = 0$. The last equation implies $|\mathbf{B}| = 0$, and thus $\mathbf{B}$ can have no inverse.

16. For simplicity look at the case $r = 1$. See SM.

17. After elementary row and column operations discussed in the SM, it can be shown that the determinant on the left-hand side equals $(a - b)^2[4x^2 - (a + b)^2]$. So for $a \neq b$ the solutions are $x = \pm\frac{1}{2}(a + b)$. But if $a = b$, the determinant is 0 for all values of x.

18. By rule (12.7.3) and part (ii) of Theorem 13.4.1, for any λ we have $|\mathbf{A} - \lambda \mathbf{I}| = |(\mathbf{A} - \lambda \mathbf{I})'| = |\mathbf{A}' - \lambda \mathbf{I}|$. It follows that $|\mathbf{A} - \lambda \mathbf{I}| = 0 \Leftrightarrow |\mathbf{A}' - \lambda \mathbf{I}| = 0$, so $\mathbf{A}$ and $\mathbf{A}'$ do have the same eigenvalues.

19. The definition of eigenvalue implies that $\lambda = 0 \Leftrightarrow \mathbf{A}$ is singular $\Leftrightarrow |\mathbf{A}| = 0$. So if $\lambda \neq 0$, then $\mathbf{A}$ has an inverse. Then, given this $\lambda \neq 0$ and any $\mathbf{x} \neq \mathbf{0}$ satisfying $\mathbf{Ax} = \lambda \mathbf{x}$, one has $\mathbf{x} = \lambda \mathbf{A}^{-1}\mathbf{x}$, or $\mathbf{A}^{-1}\mathbf{x} = (1/\lambda)\mathbf{x}$. It follows that $1/\lambda$ is an eigenvalue of $\mathbf{A}^{-1}$.

20. $|\mathbf{A} - \mathbf{I}| = \begin{vmatrix} a_{11} - 1 & a_{12} & \cdots & a_{1n} \\ a_{21} & a_{22} - 1 & \cdots & a_{2n} \\ \vdots & \vdots & \ddots & \vdots \\ a_{n1} & a_{n2} & \cdots & a_{nn} - 1 \end{vmatrix}$. Now we can add all the other $n - 1$ rows to the first row without changing the determinant. For each j, the jth entry in the first row of this new determinant will be $\sum_{i=1}^{n} a_{ij} - 1$. By hypothesis, all the column sums in $\mathbf{A}$ are 1, so this first row must be $\mathbf{0}$. It follows that $|\mathbf{A} - \mathbf{I}| = 0$, so 1 is an eigenvalue of $\mathbf{A}$.

21. (a) -1 with $\begin{pmatrix} 1 \\ -1 \\ 2 \end{pmatrix}$; 0 with $\begin{pmatrix} 1 \\ -1 \\ 1 \end{pmatrix}$; 2 with $\begin{pmatrix} 2 \\ 1 \\ 1 \end{pmatrix}$ (b) 0 with $\begin{pmatrix} 1 \\ 1 \\ 1 \end{pmatrix}$; 1 with $\begin{pmatrix} -1 \\ 0 \\ 1 \end{pmatrix}$; 3 with $\begin{pmatrix} 1 \\ -2 \\ 1 \end{pmatrix}$.

Chapter 14

14.1

1. $f(0, 1) = 1 \cdot 0 + 2 \cdot 1 = 2, f(2, -1) = 0, f(a, a) = 3a$, and $f(a + h, b) - f(a, b) = h$

2. $f(0, 1) = 0, f(-1, 2) = -4, f(10^4, 10^{-2}) = 1, f(a, a) = a^3, f(a + h, b) = (a + h)b^2 = ab^2 + hb^2$, and $f(a, b + k) - f(a, b) = 2abk + ak^2$.

3. $f(1, 1) = 2, f(-2, 3) = 51, f(1/x, 1/y) = 3/x^2 - 2/xy + 1/y^3, p = 6x + 3h - 2y, q = -2x + 3y^2 + 3yk + k^2$

4. (a) $f(-1, 2) = 1, f(a, a) = 4a^2, f(a + h, b) - f(a, b) = 2(a + b)h + h^2$
   (b) $f(tx, ty) = (tx)^2 + 2(tx)(ty) + (ty)^2 = t^2(x^2 + 2xy + y^2) = t^2 f(x, y)$ for all t, including $t = 2$.

5. $F(1, 1) = 10, F(4, 27) = 60, F(9, 1/27) = 10, F(3, \sqrt{2}) = 10\sqrt{3} \cdot \sqrt[6]{2}, F(100, 1000) = 1000$, and $F(2K, 2L) = 10 \cdot 2^{5/6} K^{1/2} L^{1/3} = 2^{5/6} F(K, L)$

6. (a) The denominator must be different from 0, so the function is defined for those (x, y) where $y \neq x - 2$.
   (b) Only nonnegative numbers have a square root, so we must require $2 - (x^2 + y^2) \geq 0$, i.e. $x^2 + y^2 \leq 2$.

906 SOLUTIONS TO THE EXERCISES

(c) Put $a = x^2 + y^2$. We must have $(4 - a)(a - 1) \geq 0$, i.e. $1 \leq a \leq 4$. (Use a sign diagram.)

The domains in (b) and (c) are the shaded sets shown in Figs A14.1.6b and A14.1.6c.

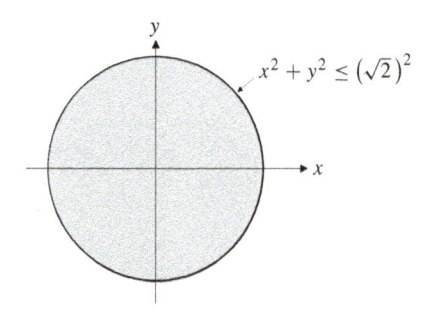

Figure A14.1.6b

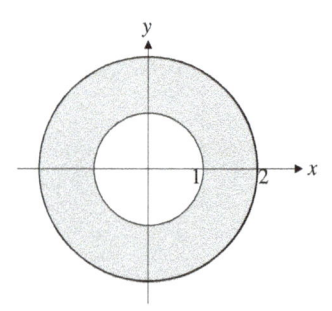

Figure A14.1.6c

7. (a) $e^{x+y} \neq 3$, that is $x + y \neq \ln 3$

(b) In order to take the ln of positive numbers, it suffices to have $x \neq a$ and $y \neq b$ so that $(x - a)^2 > 0$ and $(y - b)^2 > 0$.

(c) $x > a$ and $y > b$.

14.2

1. (a) $\partial z/\partial x = 2$, $\partial z/\partial y = 3$ (b) $\partial z/\partial x = 2x$, $\partial z/\partial y = 3y^2$ (c) $\partial z/\partial x = 3x^2y^4$, $\partial z/\partial y = 4x^3y^3$

(d) $\partial z/\partial x = \partial z/\partial y = 2(x + y)$

2. (a) $\partial z/\partial x = 2x$, $\partial z/\partial y = 6y$ (b) $\partial z/\partial x = y$, $\partial z/\partial y = x$ (c) $\partial z/\partial x = 20x^3y^2 - 2y^5$, $\partial z/\partial y = 10x^4y - 10xy^4$

(d) $\partial z/\partial x = \partial z/\partial y = e^{x+y}$ (e) $\partial z/\partial x = ye^{xy}$, $\partial z/\partial y = xe^{xy}$ (f) $\partial z/\partial x = e^x/y$, $\partial z/\partial y = -e^x/y^2$

(g) $\partial z/\partial x = \partial z/\partial y = 1/(x+y)$ (h) $\partial z/\partial x = 1/x$, $\partial z/\partial y = 1/y$

3. (a) $f_1'(x, y) = 7x^6$, $f_2'(x, y) = -7y^6$, $f_{12}''(x, y) = 0$ (b) $f_1'(x, y) = 5x^4 \ln y$, $f_2'(x, y) = x^5/y$, $f_{12}''(x, y) = 5x^4/y$

(c) $f(x, y) = (x^2 - 2y^2)^5 = u^5$, where $u = x^2 - 2y^2$. Then $f_1'(x, y) = 5u^4u_1' = 5(x^2 - 2y^2)^4 2x = 10x(x^2 - 2y^2)^4$.

In the same way, $f_2'(x, y) = 5u^4u_2' = 5(x^2 - 2y^2)^4(-4y) = -20y(x^2 - 2y^2)^4$.

Finally, $f_{12}''(x, y) = (\partial/\partial y)(10x(x^2 - 2y^2)^4) = 10x4(x^2 - 2y^2)^3(-4y) = -160xy(x^2 - 2y^2)^3$.

4. (a) $z_x' = 3$, $z_y' = 4$, and $z_{xx}'' = z_{xy}'' = z_{yx}'' = z_{yy}'' = 0$

(b) $z_x' = 3x^2y^2$, $z_y' = 2x^3y$, $z_{xx}'' = 6xy^2$, $z_{yy}'' = 2x^3$, and $z_{xy}'' = 6x^2y$

(c) $z_x' = 5x^4 - 6xy$, $z_y' = -3x^2 + 6y^5$, $z_{xx}'' = 20x^3 - 6y$, $z_{yy}'' = 30y^4$, and $z_{xy}'' = -6x$

(d) $z_x' = 1/y$, $z_y' = -x/y^2$, $z_{xx}'' = 0$, $z_{yy}'' = 2x/y^3$, and $z_{xy}'' = -1/y^2$

(e) $z_x' = 2y(x + y)^{-2}$, $z_y' = -2x(x + y)^{-2}$, $z_{xx}'' = -4y(x + y)^{-3}$, $z_{yy}'' = 4x(x + y)^{-3}$, and $z_{xy}'' = 2(x - y)(x + y)^{-3}$

(f) $z_x' = x(x^2 + y^2)^{-1/2}$, $z_y' = y(x^2 + y^2)^{-1/2}$,

then $z_{xx}'' = y^2(x^2 + y^2)^{-3/2}$, $z_{yy}'' = x^2(x^2 + y^2)^{-3/2}$, and $z_{xy}'' = -xy(x^2 + y^2)^{-3/2}$

5. (a) $z_x' = 2x$, $z_y' = 2e^{2y}$, $z_{xx}'' = 2$, $z_{yy}'' = 4e^{2y}$, $z_{xy}'' = 0$ (b) $z_x' = y/x$, $z_y' = \ln x$, $z_{xx}'' = -y/x^2$, $z_{yy}'' = 0$, $z_{xy}'' = 1/x$

(c) $z_x' = y^2 - ye^{xy}$, $z_y' = 2xy - xe^{xy}$, $z_{xx}'' = -y^2e^{xy}$, $z_{yy}'' = 2x - x^2e^{xy}$, $z_{xy}'' = 2y - e^{xy} - xye^{xy}$

(d) $z_x' = yx^{y-1}$, $z_y' = x^y \ln x$, $z_{xx}'' = y(y - 1)x^{y-2}$, $z_{yy}'' = x^y(\ln x)^2$, $z_{xy}'' = x^{y-1} + yx^{y-1} \ln x$

6. (a) $F'_S = 2.26 \cdot 0.44 S^{-0.56} E^{0.48} = 0.9944 S^{-0.56} E^{0.48}$, $F'_E = 2.26 \cdot 0.48 S^{0.44} E^{-0.52} = 1.0848 S^{0.44} E^{-0.52}$
   (b) $SF'_S + EF'_E = S \cdot 2.26 \cdot 0.44 S^{-0.56} E^{0.48} + E \cdot 2.26 \cdot 0.48 S^{0.44} E^{-0.52} = 0.44 F + 0.48 F = 0.92 F$, so $k = 0.92$.

7. $xz'_x + yz'_y = x[2a(ax+by)] + y[2b(ax+by)] = (ax+by)2(ax+by) = 2(ax+by)^2 = 2z$

8. $\partial z/\partial x = x/(x^2+y^2)$, $\partial z/\partial y = y/(x^2+y^2)$, $\partial^2 z/\partial x^2 = (y^2-x^2)/(x^2+y^2)^2$, and $\partial^2 z/\partial y^2 = (x^2-y^2)/(x^2+y^2)^2$. Thus, $\partial^2 z/\partial x^2 + \partial^2 z/\partial y^2 = 0$.

9. (a) $s'_x(x,y) = 2/x$, so $s'_x(20,30) = 2/20 = 1/10$. (b) $s'_y(x,y) = 4/y$, so $s'_y(20,30) = 4/30 = 2/15$.

14.3

1. If $x^2 + y^2 = 6$, then $f(x,y) = \sqrt{6} - 4$, so $x^2 + y^2 = 6$ is a level curve of f at height $c = \sqrt{6} - 4$.

2. $f(x,y) = e^{x^2-y^2} + (x^2-y^2)^2 = e^c + c^2$ when $x^2 - y^2 = c$, so the last equation represents a level curve of f having height $e^c + c^2$.

3. At the point of intersection f would have two different values, which is impossible when f is a function.

4. Generally, the graph of $g(x,y) = f(x)$ in 3-space consists of a surface traced out by moving the graph of $z = f(x)$ parallel to the y-axis in both directions. The graph of $g(x,y) = x$ is the plane through the y-axis at a 45° angle with the xy-plane. The graph of $g(x,y) = -x^3$ is shown in Fig. A14.3.4. (Only a portion of the unbounded graph is indicated, of course.)

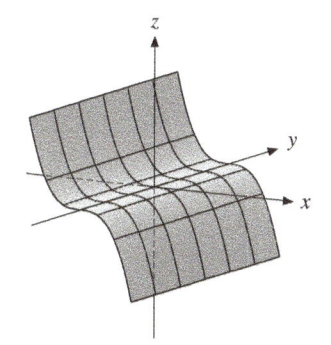

Figure A14.3.4

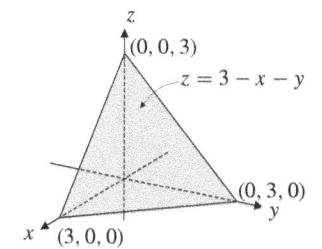

Figure A14.3.5a1

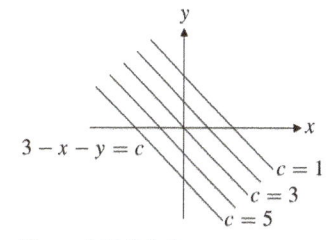

Figure A14.3.5a2

5. See Figs A14.3.5a and A14.3.5b, which are both in two parts. (Note that only a portion of the graph is shown in part (a).)

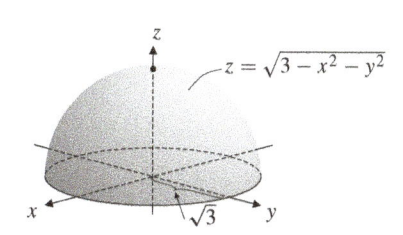

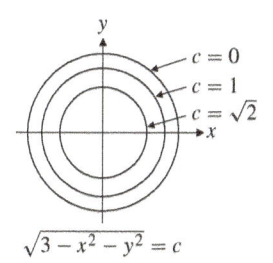

Figure A14.3.5b1

Figure A14.3.5b2

6. (a) The point $(2, 3)$ lies on the level curve $z = 8$, so $f(2, 3) = 8$. The points $(x, 3)$ are those on the line $y = 3$ parallel to the x-axis. This line intersects the level curve $z = 8$ when $x = 2$ and $x = 5$.

(b) As y varies with $x = 2$ fixed, the minimum of $f(2, y)$ is 8 when $y = 3$.

(c) At A, any move in the direction of increasing x with y held fixed reaches higher level curves, so $f_1'(x, y) > 0$. Similarly, any move in the direction of increasing y with x held fixed reaches higher level curves, so $f_2'(x, y) > 0$. At B: $f_1'(x, y) < 0, f_2'(x, y) < 0$. At C: $f_1'(x, y) = 0, f_2'(x, y) = 0$. Finally, to increase z by 2 units when moving away from A, the required increases in x and y are approximately 1 and 0.6 respectively. Hence, $f_1' \approx 2/1 = 2$ and $f_2' \approx 2/0.6 = 10/3$.

7. (a) $f_x' > 0$ and $f_y' < 0$ at P, whereas $f_x' < 0$ and $f_y' > 0$ at Q.

(b) (i) No solutions among points shown in the figure. (ii) $x \approx 2$ and $x \approx 6$

(c) The highest level curve that meets the line is $z = 3$, so 3 is the largest value.

8. $F(1, 0) - F(0, 0), F(2, 0) - F(1, 0)$, and $F(1, 1) - F(0, 1)$ are all ≥ 2; $F(0, 1) - F(0, 0)$ and $F(1, 1) - F(1, 0)$ are both ≤ 1. See SM for more details.

14.4

1. See Figs A14.4.1a–A14.4.1c.

Figure A14.4.1a

Figure A14.4.1b

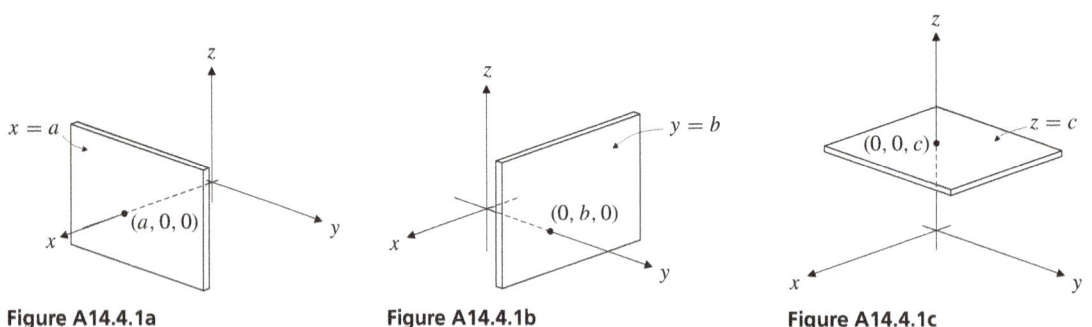

Figure A14.4.1c

2. (a) $d = \sqrt{(4 - (-1))^2 + (-2 - 2)^2 + (0 - 3)^2} = \sqrt{25 + 16 + 9} = \sqrt{50} = 5\sqrt{2}$

(b) $d = \sqrt{(a + 1 - a)^2 + (b + 1 - b)^2 + (c + 1 - c)^2} = \sqrt{3}$

3. $(x - 2)^2 + (y - 1)^2 + (z - 1)^2 = 25$

4. The sphere with centre at $(-3, 3, 4)$ and radius 5.

5. $(x - 4)^2 + (y - 4)^2 + (z - \frac{1}{2})^2$ is the square of the distance from the point $(4, 4, \frac{1}{2})$ to (x, y, z) on the paraboloid.

14.5

1. (a) $f(-1, 2, 3) = 1$ and $f(a + 1, b + 1, c + 1) - f(a, b, c) = 2a + 2b + 2c + 3$.

(b) $f(tx, ty, tz) = (tx)(ty) + (tx)(tz) + (ty)(tz) = t^2(xy + xz + yz) = t^2 f(x, y, z)$

2. (a) Because 1.053 is the sum of exponents, y would become $2^{1.053} \approx 2.07$ times as large.

(b) $\ln y = \ln 2.9 + 0.015 \ln x_1 + 0.25 \ln x_2 + 0.35 \ln x_3 + 0.408 \ln x_4 + 0.03 \ln x_5$

3. (a) In successive weeks it buys $120/50 = 2.4$, then $120/60 = 2$, $120/45 \approx 2.667$, $120/40 = 3$, $120/75 = 1.6$, and finally $120/80 = 1.5$ million shares, so about 13.167 million in total.

  (b) The average price per share is about $720/13.167 \approx 54.68$. This is the harmonic mean price, which is almost $4 a share lower than the arithmetic mean $350/6 \approx 58.67$.

4. (a) In each week w bank A will have bought $100/p_w$ million euros, for a total of $e = \sum_{w=1}^{n} 100/p_w$ million euros.

  (b) Bank A will have paid $100n$ million dollars, so the price p per euro that bank A will have paid, on average, is $p = 100n/e$. It follows that $1/p = e/100n = (1/n)\sum_{w=1}^{n} 1/p_w$ dollars per euro, implying that p is the harmonic mean of $p_1, \ldots, p_n$. Since this is lower than the arithmetic mean (except in the case when p_w is the same every week), this is a supposed advantage of dollar cost averaging.

5. (a) Each machine would produce 60 units per day, so $480/60 = 8$ minutes per unit.

  (b) Total output is $\sum_{i=1}^{n}(T/t_i) = T\sum_{i=1}^{n}(1/t_i)$. If all n machines were equally efficient, the time needed for each unit would be $nT/T\sum_{i=1}^{n}(1/t_i) = n/\sum_{i=1}^{n}(1/t_i)$, the harmonic mean of $t_1, \ldots, t_n$.

14.6

1. $F_1'(x, y, z) = 2xe^{xz} + x^2ze^{xz} + y^4e^{xy}$, so $F_1'(1, 1, 1) = 4e$; $F_2'(x, y, z) = 3y^2e^{xy} + xy^3e^{xy}$, so $F_2'(1, 1, 1) = 4e$; $F_3'(x, y, z) = x^3e^{xz}$, so $F_3'(1, 1, 1) = e$.

2. (a) $f_1' = 2x, f_2' = 3y^2$, and $f_3' = 4z^3$ (b) $f_1' = 10x, f_2' = -9y^2$, and $f_3' = 12z^3$
   (c) $f_1' = yz, f_2' = xz$, and $f_3' = xy$ (d) $f_1' = 4x^3/yz, f_2' = -x^4/y^2z$, and $f_3' = -x^4/yz^2$
   (e) $f_1' = 12x(x^2 + y^3 + z^4)^5, f_2' = 18y^2(x^2 + y^3 + z^4)^5$, and $f_3' = 24z^3(x^2 + y^3 + z^4)^5$
   (f) $f_1' = yze^{xyz}, f_2' = xze^{xyz}$, and $f_3' = xye^{xyz}$

3. $\partial T/\partial x = ky/d^n$ and $\partial T/\partial y = kx/d^n$ are both positive, so that the number of travellers increases if the size of either city increases, which is reasonable. $\partial T/\partial d = -nkxy/d^{n+1}$ is negative, so that the number of travellers decreases if the distance between the cities increases, which is also reasonable.

4. (a) $g(2, 1, 1) = -2, g(3, -4, 2) = 352$, and $g(1, 1, a + h) - g(1, 1, a) = 2ah + h^2 - h$.

  (b) $g_1' = 4x - 4y - 4, g_2' = -4x + 20y - 28, g_3' = 2z - 1$. The second-order partials are: $g_{11}'' = 4, g_{12}'' = -4, g_{13}'' = 0, g_{21}'' = -4, g_{22}'' = 20, g_{23}'' = 0, g_{31}'' = 0, g_{32}'' = 0$, and $g_{33}'' = 2$.

5. $\partial \pi/\partial p = \frac{1}{2}p(1/r + 1/w), \partial \pi/\partial r = -\frac{1}{4}p^2/r^2, \partial \pi/\partial w = -\frac{1}{4}p^2/w^2$

6. First-order partials are: $w_1' = 3yz + 2xy - z^3, w_2' = 3xz + x^2, w_3' = 3xy - 3xz^2$. Second-order partials are: $w_{11}'' = 2y, w_{12}'' = w_{21}'' = 3z + 2x, w_{13}'' = w_{31}'' = 3y - 3z^2, w_{22}'' = 0, w_{23}'' = w_{32}'' = 3x, w_{33}'' = -6xz$.

7. $f_1' = p'(x), f_2' = q'(y), f_3' = r'(z)$

8. (a) $\begin{pmatrix} 2a & 0 & 0 \\ 0 & 2b & 0 \\ 0 & 0 & 2c \end{pmatrix}$ (b) With g denoting $Ax^a y^b z^c$, the Hessian is $\begin{pmatrix} a(a-1)g/x^2 & abg/xy & acg/xz \\ abg/xy & b(b-1)g/y^2 & bcg/yz \\ acg/xz & bcg/yz & c(c-1)g/z^2 \end{pmatrix}$.

9. Put $w = u^h$, where $u = (x - y + z)/(x + y - z)$.

  Then $\partial w/\partial x = hu^{h-1}\partial u/\partial x, \partial w/\partial y = hu^{h-1}\partial u/\partial y$, and $\partial w/\partial z = hu^{h-1}\partial u/\partial z$.

  With $v = x + y - z$, we get $\partial u/\partial x = (2y - 2z)/v^2, \partial u/\partial y = -2x/v^2$, and $\partial u/\partial z = 2x/v^2$.

  Hence $x\,\partial w/\partial x + y\,\partial w/\partial y + z\,\partial w/\partial z = hu^{h-1}v^{-2}[x(2y - 2z) + y(-2x) + z2x] = 0$.

  (In the terminology of Section 15.7, the function w of 3 variables is homogeneous of degree 0. Euler's Theorem 15.7.1 yields the result immediately.)

910 SOLUTIONS TO THE EXERCISES

10. $f'_x = y^z x^{y^z-1}$, $f'_y = z y^{z-1} (\ln x) x^{y^z}$, $f'_z = y^z (\ln x)(\ln y) x^{y^z}$.

11. For all $y \neq 0$, one has $f'_1(0, y) = -y$ and $f''_{12}(0, y) = f''_{21}(0, y) = -1$.
    For all $x \neq 0$, one has $f'_2(x, 0) = x$ and $f''_{21}(x, 0) = f''_{12}(x, 0) = 1$. See SM for more details.

14.7

1. See Figs A14.7.1a–A14.7.1f

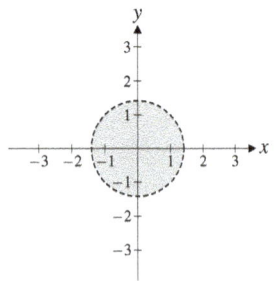

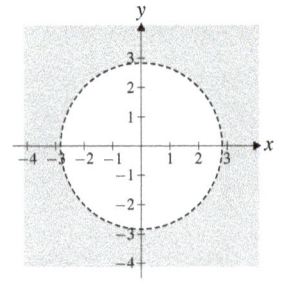

Figure A14.7.1a $x^2 + y^2 < 2$

Figure A14.7.1b $x \geq 0$, $y \geq 0$

Figure A14.7.1c $x^2 + y^2 > 8$

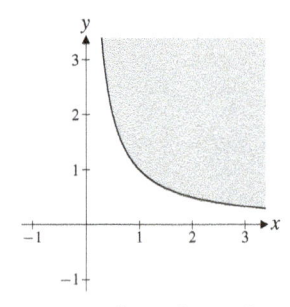

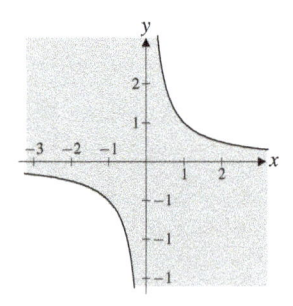

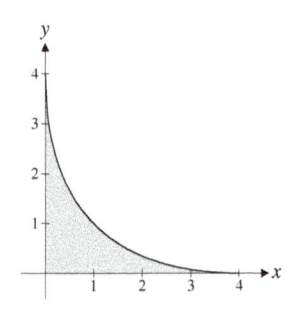

Figure A14.7.1d $x \geq 0$, $y \geq 0$, $xy \geq 1$

Figure A14.7.1e $xy \geq 1$

Figure A14.7.1f $\sqrt{x} + \sqrt{y} \leq 2$

2. (a) Suppose that (s_1, t_1) and (s_2, t_2) both belong to $S \times T$, with $s_1, s_2 \in S$ and $t_1, t_2 \in T$. Given any $\lambda \in [0, 1]$, define $s_0 = \lambda s_1 + (1 - \lambda) s_2$ and $t_0 = \lambda t_1 + (1 - \lambda) t_2$. Then $(s_0, t_0) = \lambda (s_1, t_1) + (1 - \lambda)(s_2, t_2)$. Furthermore, because S and T are both convex, one has $s_0 \in S$ and $t_0 \in T$. It follows that (s_0, t_0) belongs to $S \times T$, so $S \times T$ is a convex set.

    (b) It is. The algebraic argument in part (a) works for general convex sets $S \subseteq \mathbb{R}^m$ and $T \subseteq \mathbb{R}^n$ and points $(\mathbf{s}_1, \mathbf{t}_1)$ and $(\mathbf{s}_2, \mathbf{t}_2)$ in $S \times T$.

14.8

1. The function with the graph on the left is strictly convex. The one in the middle is neither convex nor concave (it seems to be convex on the left, but concave on the right). The one on the right is concave, but *not* strictly concave.

2. $f''_{11} = -12 < 0$, $f''_{12} = 2a + 4$, $f''_{22} = -2 < 0$. Because $f''_{11} < 0$, the function is never convex. It is concave iff $f''_{11} f''_{22} - (f''_{12})^2 = 24 - (2a + 4)^2 \geq 0$, which is true iff $(a + 2)^2 \leq 6$, that is, iff $-2 - \sqrt{6} \leq a \leq -2 + \sqrt{6}$. It is neither concave nor convex if $a < -2 - \sqrt{6}$ or $a > -2 + \sqrt{6}$.

3. For parts (a) and (b), we use the results in Theorem 14.8.1.

    (a) z is strictly concave, as the sum of four concave functions x, y, $-e^x$, and $-e^{x+y}$, of which two are strictly concave.

    (b) z is strictly convex, as the sum of three convex functions e^{x+y}, e^{x-y}, and $-\frac{1}{2} y$, of which two are strictly convex.

    (c) Using the hint, we see that the quadratic form w is positive semi-definite. So w is convex, but not strictly convex.

4. (a) Follows from (14.8.7). (b) Following the hint, note that because $f(0,0) = 0$, the definition of g implies that

$$g(\lambda; x, y) = f(\lambda x, \lambda y)/\lambda = \frac{f(\lambda x, \lambda y) - f(0,0)}{\lambda - 0} = s(0, \lambda) \quad (*)$$

where $s(0, \lambda)$ is the slope of $f(\lambda x, \lambda y)$, viewed as a function of λ defined for all $\lambda \geq 0$. Now, if f is concave, then for all $\mu \in [0, 1]$ and all $\lambda, \lambda' > 0$ one has

$$f\left(\mu(\lambda x, \lambda y) + (1 - \mu)(\lambda' x, \lambda' y)\right) \geq \mu f(\lambda x, \lambda y) + (1 - \mu) f(\lambda' x, \lambda' y) \quad (**)$$

which implies that $f(\lambda x, \lambda y)$ is concave as a function of λ. Then Theorem 8.2.1 implies that $g(\lambda; x, y) = s(0, \lambda)$ is decreasing as a function of λ.

(c) Suppose that f were strictly concave. By an obvious modification of $(**)$, the function $f(\lambda x, \lambda y)$ of λ would be strictly concave. Then Theorem 8.2.1 would imply that $g(\lambda; x, y) = s(0, \lambda)$ is strictly decreasing as a function of λ. This contradicts the hypothesis that $g(\lambda; x, y)$ is independent of λ.

14.9

1. $\partial M/\partial Y = 0.14$ and $\partial M/\partial r = -0.84 \cdot 76.03(r - 2)^{-1.84} = -63.8652(r - 2)^{-1.84}$.

   So $\partial M/\partial Y$ is positive and $\partial M/\partial r$ is negative. Both signs accord with standard economic intuition.

2. (a) $KY'_K + LY'_L = aY$ (b) $KY'_K + LY'_L = (a+b)Y$ (c) $KY'_K + LY'_L = Y$

3. $D'_p(p, q) = -bq^{-\alpha}$ and $D'_q(p, q) = bp\alpha q^{-\alpha-1}$. So $D'_p(p, q) < 0$, showing that demand decreases as price increases. Also $D'_q(p, q) > 0$, showing that demand increases as the price of a competing product increases.

4. $F'_K = aF/K$, $F'_L = bF/L$, and $F'_M = cF/M$, so $KF'_K + LF'_L + MF'_M = (a+b+c)F$.

5. $\partial D/\partial p$ and $\partial E/\partial q$ are normally negative, because the demand for a commodity goes down when its price increases. If the commodities are substitutes, this means that demand increases when the price of the other good increases. So the usual signs are $\partial D/\partial q > 0$ and $\partial E/\partial p > 0$.

6. $\partial U/\partial x_i = e^{-x_i}$, for $i = 1, \ldots, n$

7. $KY'_K + LY'_L = \mu Y$

14.10

1. (a) $\text{El}_x z = 1$ and $\text{El}_y z = 1$ (b) $\text{El}_x z = 2$ and $\text{El}_y z = 5$ (c) $\text{El}_x z = n + x$ and $\text{El}_y z = n + y$
   (d) $\text{El}_x z = x/(x+y)$ and $\text{El}_y z = y/(x+y)$

2. Let $z = u^g$ with $u = ax_1^d + bx_2^d + cx_3^d$. Then $\text{El}_1 z = \text{El}_u u^g \text{El}_1 u = g(x_1/u)adx_1^{d-1} = adgx_1^d/u$.
   Similarly, $\text{El}_2 z = bdgx_2^d/u$ and $\text{El}_3 z = cdgx_3^d/u$, so $\text{El}_1 z + \text{El}_2 z + \text{El}_3 z = dg(ax_1^d + bx_2^d + cx_3^d)/u = dg$.
   (This result follows easily from the fact that z is homogeneous of degree dg and from the elasticity form (15.7.3) of the Euler equation.)

3. $\text{El}_i z = p + a_i x_i$ for $i = 1, \ldots, n$.

4. We differentiate $\ln(pD/m) = \ln p + \ln D - \ln m$ w.r.t. $\ln m$ to obtain $\dfrac{d}{d(\ln m)} \ln(pD/m) = \text{El}_m D - 1$. So evidently pD/m increases with m iff $\text{El}_m D > 1$. See SM for more details.

Review exercises for Chapter 14

1. $f(0, 1) = -5$, $f(2, -1) = 11$, $f(a, a) = -2a$, and $f(a + h, b) - f(a, b) = 3h$

2. $f(-1, 2) = -10$, $f(2a, 2a) = -4a^2$, $f(a, b + k) - f(a, b) = -6bk - 3k^2$, $f(tx, ty) - t^2 f(x, y) = 0$

3. $f(3, 4, 0) = 5$, $f(-2, 1, 3) = \sqrt{14}$, and $f(tx, ty, tz) = \sqrt{t^2 x^2 + t^2 y^2 + t^2 z^2} = tf(x, y, z)$

4. (a) $F(0, 0) = 0$, $F(1, 1) = 15$, and $F(32, 243) = 15 \cdot 2 \cdot 9 = 270$.
   (b) $F(K + 1, L) - F(K, L) = 15(K + 1)^{1/5} L^{2/5} - 15 K^{1/5} L^{2/5} = 15 L^{2/5}[(K + 1)^{1/5} - K^{1/5}]$ is the extra output from one more unit of capital, approximately equal to the marginal productivity of capital.
   (c) $F(32 + 1, 243) - F(32, 243) \approx 1.667$. Moreover, $F'_K(K, L) = 3K^{-4/5} L^{2/5}$, so $F'_K(32, 243) = 3 \cdot 32^{-4/5} 243^{2/5} = 3 \cdot 2^{-4} \cdot 3^2 = 27/16 \approx 1.6875$. As expected, $F(32 + 1, 243) - F(32, 243)$ is close to $F'_K(32, 243)$.
   (d) F is homogeneous of degree $3/5$.

5. (a) $\partial Y / \partial K \approx 0.083 K^{0.356} S^{0.562}$ and $\partial Y / \partial S \approx 0.035 K^{1.356} S^{-0.438}$.
   (b) The catch becomes $2^{1.356 + 0.562} = 2^{1.918} \approx 3.779$ times as large.

6. (a) For all (x, y) (b) For $xy \leq 1$ (c) For $x^2 + y^2 < 2$

7. (a) $x + y > 1$ (b) $x^2 \geq y^2$ and $x^2 + y^2 \geq 1$. So $x^2 + y^2 \geq 1$ and $|x| \geq |y|$.
   (c) $y \geq x^2$, $x \geq 0$, and $\sqrt{x} \geq y$. So $0 \leq x \leq 1$ and $\sqrt{x} \geq y \geq x^2$.

8. (a) $\partial z / \partial x = 10 xy^4 (x^2 y^4 + 2)^4$ (b) $\sqrt{K}(\partial F / \partial K) = 2\sqrt{K}(\sqrt{K} + \sqrt{L})(1/2\sqrt{K}) = \sqrt{K} + \sqrt{L}$
   (c) $KF'_K + LF'_L = K(1/a)aK^{a-1}(K^a + L^a)^{1/a-1} + L(1/a)aL^{a-1}(K^a + L^a)^{1/a-1} = (K^a + L^a)(K^a + L^a)^{1/a-1} = F$
   (d) $\partial g / \partial t = 3/w + 2wt$, so $\partial^2 g / \partial w \partial t = -3/w^2 + 2t$
   (e) $g'_3 = t_3(t_1^2 + t_2^2 + t_3^2)^{-1/2}$ (f) $f'_1 = 4xyz + 2xz^2$, $f''_{13} = 4xy + 4xz$

9. (a) $f(0, 0) = 36$, $f(-2, -3) = 0$, $f(a + 2, b - 3) = a^2 b^2$ (b) $f'_x = 2(x - 2)(y + 3)^2$, $f'_y = 2(x - 2)^2 (y + 3)$

10. Because $g(-1, 5) = g(1, 1) = 30$, the two points are on the same level curve.

11. If $x - y = c \neq 0$, then $F(x, y) = \ln(x - y)^2 + e^{2(x-y)} = \ln c^2 + e^{2c}$, a constant.

12. (a) $f'_1(x, y) = 4x^3 - 8xy$, $f'_2(x, y) = 4y - 4x^2 + 4$ (b) These critical points are $(0, -1)$, $(\sqrt{2}, 1)$, and $(-\sqrt{2}, 1)$.

13. (a) Along the x-axis, the graph in the xz-plane has the shape of a bowl, like that of a strictly convex function. But along the y-axis, the graph in the xz-plane has the shape of a dome, like that of a strictly concave function. The function is therefore neither concave nor convex.
   (b) The Hessian matrix is $\mathbf{f}'' = \begin{pmatrix} 2 & 0 \\ 0 & -2 \end{pmatrix}$, with determinant $|\mathbf{f}''| = -4 < 0$. This inequality implies that all of the four conditions in Eqs (14.8.7) to (14.8.10) are violated. So f is neither concave nor convex.

14. (a) (i) $f''_{11} = -2 \leq 0$, $f''_{22} = 0 \leq 0$, and $f''_{11} f''_{22} - (f''_{12})^2 = 0 \geq 0$. So by (14.8.3) (or (14.8.7)) f is concave.
   (ii) $f(x) = (x - y) + (-x^2)$ is a sum of concave functions, hence concave.
   (b) Note that $-e^{-f(x,y)} = F(f(x, y))$ where $F(u) = -e^{-u}$. But $F'(u) = e^{-u} > 0$ and $F''(u) = -e^{-u} < 0$, where F is (strictly) increasing and concave. By part (iii) of Theorem 14.8.1, it follows that $z = -e^{-f(x,y)}$ is concave.

15. (a) $f''_{11} = 2a$, $f''_{12} = 2b$, $f''_{22} = 2c$, and $f''_{11} f''_{22} - (f''_{12})^2 = 2a2c - (2b)^2 = 4(ac - b^2)$. The result follows from (14.8.5) and (14.8.6). (b) Using (14.8.3), f is concave iff $a \leq 0$, $c \leq 0$, and $ac - b^2 \geq 0$. Using (14.8.4), f is convex iff $a \geq 0$, $c \geq 0$, and $ac - b^2 \geq 0$.

16. (a) $\text{El}_x z = 3$, $\text{El}_y z = -4$ (b) $\text{El}_x z = 2x^2/(x^2 + y^2) \ln(x^2 + y^2)$, $\text{El}_y z = 2y^2/(x^2 + y^2) \ln(x^2 + y^2)$
   (c) $\text{El}_x z = \text{El}_x(e^x e^y) = \text{El}_x e^x = x$, $\text{El}_y z = y$ (d) $\text{El}_x z = x^2/(x^2 + y^2)$, $\text{El}_y z = y^2/(x^2 + y^2)$

17. (a) $\partial F/\partial y = e^{2x}2(1-y)(-1) = -2e^{2x}(1-y)$. (b) $F'_L = (\ln K)(\ln M)/L$, $F'_{LK} = (\ln M)/KL$

(c) Putting $w = x^x y^x z^x$ gives $\ln w = x \ln x + x \ln y + x \ln z$. Differentiating each side w.r.t. x gives $w'_x/w = 1 \cdot \ln x + x(1/x) + \ln y + \ln z$, implying that $w'_x = w(\ln x + 1 + \ln y + \ln z) = x^x y^x z^x [\ln(xyz) + 1]$.

18. (a) Begin by differentiating w.r.t. x to obtain $\partial^p z/\partial x^p = e^x \ln(1+y)$ for any natural number p. Differentiating this repeatedly w.r.t. y yields first $\partial^{p+1}/\partial y \partial x^p = e^x(1+y)^{-1}$, then $\partial^{p+2}/\partial y^2 \partial x^p = e^x(-1)(1+y)^{-2}$, and so on. By induction on q, one has $\partial^{p+q}/\partial y^q \partial x^p = e^x(-1)^{q-1}(q-1)!(1+y)^{-q}$, which is $(-1)^{q-1}(q-1)!$ at $(x,y)=(0,0)$.

(b) Write $z = z_1 + z_2 - z_3$ where $z_1 = xe^x \cdot ye^y$, $z_2 = e^x \cdot ye^y$, and $z_3 = e^x \cdot e^y$. For $n = 1, 2, \ldots,$, one can easily prove by induction that $(d/du)^n u e^u = e^u(u+n)$. Then $\partial^{p+q} z_1/\partial x^p \partial y^q = (d/dx)^p e^x x \cdot (d/dy)^q e^y y = e^x(x+p) \cdot e^y(y+q)$, whereas $\partial^{p+q} z_2/\partial x^p \partial y^q = (d/dx)^p e^x \cdot (d/dy)^q e^y y = e^x \cdot e^y(y+q)$, and $\partial^{p+q} z_3/\partial x^p \partial y^q = e^x \cdot e^y$. Gathering terms, it follows that $\partial^{p+q} z/\partial x^p \partial y^q = e^{x+y}[(x+p+1)(y+q)-1]$. At $(x,y)=(0,0)$ this reduces to $(p+1)q-1$.

19. $u'_x = au/x$ and $u'_y = bu/y$, so $u''_{xy} = au'_y/x = abu/xy$. Hence, $u''_{xy}/u'_x u'_y = 1/u$ (provided $u \neq 0$). Then

$$\frac{1}{u'_x}\frac{\partial}{\partial x}\left(\frac{u''_{xy}}{u'_x u'_y}\right) = \frac{1}{u'_x} \cdot \frac{-u'_x}{u^2} = -\frac{1}{u^2} = \frac{1}{u'_y}\frac{\partial}{\partial y}\left(\frac{u''_{xy}}{u'_x u'_y}\right)$$

Chapter 15

15.1

1. (a) $dz/dt = F'_1(x,y)\,dx/dt + F'_2(x,y)\,dy/dt = 1 \cdot 2t + 2y \cdot 3t^2 = 2t + 6t^5$, the derivative of $z = t^2 + (t^3)^2 = t^2 + t^6$.

(b) $dz/dt = px^{p-1}y^q a + qx^p y^{q-1}b = x^{p-1}y^{q-1}(apy+bqx) = a^p b^q(p+q)t^{p+q-1}$, the derivative of $z = (at)^p \cdot (bt)^q$.

2. (a) $dz/dt = (\ln y + y/x) \cdot 1 + (x/y + \ln x)(1/t) = \ln(\ln t) + \ln t/(t+1) + (t+1)/t \ln t + \ln(t+1)/t$

(b) $dz/dt = Aae^{at}/x + Bbe^{bt}/y = a + b$

3. $dz/dt = F'_1(t,y) + F'_2(t,y)g'(t)$. If $F(t,y) = t^2 + ye^y$ and $g(t) = t^2$, then $F'_1(t,y) = 2t$, $F'_2(t,y) = e^y + ye^y$, and $g'(t) = 2t$. Hence $dz/dt = 2t(1 + e^{t^2} + t^2 e^{t^2})$.

4. $dY/dL = F'_K(K,L)g'(L) + F'_L(K,L)$

5. $dY/dt = \left(10L - \tfrac{1}{2}K^{-1/2}\right)0.2 + \left(10K - \tfrac{1}{2}L^{-1/2}\right)0.5e^{0.1t} = 35 - 7\sqrt{5}/100$ when $t = 0$ and so $K = L = 5$.

6. You should get the usual rules in Sections 6.7 and 6.8 for differentiating:

(a) a sum; (b) a difference; (c) a product; (d) a quotient; (e) a composite function of one variable.

7. $x^* = \sqrt[4]{3b/a}$

8. Differentiating Eq. (15.1.1) w.r.t. t yields $d^2z/dt^2 = (d/dt)[F'_1(x,y)dx/dt] + (d/dt)[F'_2(x,y)dy/dt]$. Next, apply the chain rule (15.1.1) again to evaluate the two derivatives on the right-hand side. The conclusion follows from summing while assuming that $F''_{12} = F''_{21}$. See SM for more details.

9. (a) Using the Newton quotients, we have

$$f'_1(0,0) = \lim_{h \to 0} \frac{1}{h}[f(h,0)-f(0,0)] = \lim_{h \to 0} \frac{1}{h}0 = 0 \quad \text{and} \quad f'_2(0,0) = \lim_{k \to 0} \frac{1}{k}[f(0,k)-f(0,0)] = \lim_{k \to 0} \frac{1}{k} \cdot \frac{k^3}{k^2} = 1$$

(b) For $t \neq 0$ we have $z(t) = \dfrac{b^3 t^3}{a^2 t^2 + b^2 t^2}$. So $z(t) = \dfrac{b^3 t}{a^2 + b^2}$ for all t, implying that $z'(0) = \dfrac{b^3}{a^2+b^2}$.

(c) From part (a), we have $f'_1(x(0), y(0))\dfrac{dx}{dt} + f'_2(x(0), y(0))\dfrac{dy}{dt} = b$. From part (b), because $a \neq 0$ and $b \neq 0$, this differs from $z'(0)$.

(d) There is no contradiction because f is not C^1 at $(0,0)$. Indeed, one has $f'_2(x, y) = \dfrac{3y^2(x^2 + y^2) - y^3(2y)}{(x^2 + y^2)^2}$ for all $(x, y) \neq (0, 0)$. So for all $x \neq 0$ one has $f'_2(x, 0) = 0$, whereas $f'_2(0, 0) = 1$.

15.2

1. (a) $\partial z/\partial t = F'_1(x, y) \partial x/\partial t + F'_2(x, y) \partial y/\partial t = 1 \cdot 1 + 2ys = 1 + 2ts^2$,

   and $\partial z/\partial s = (\partial z/\partial x)(\partial x/\partial s) + (\partial z/\partial y)(\partial y/\partial s) = 1 \cdot (-1) + 2yt = -1 + 2t^2s$

   (b) $\partial z/\partial t = 4x2t + 9y^2 = 8tx + 9y^2 = 8t^3 - 8ts + 9t^2 + 36ts^3 + 36s^6$

   and $\partial z/\partial s = 4x(-1) + 9y^26s^2 = -4x + 54s^2y^2 = -4t^2 + 4s + 54t^2s^2 + 216ts^5 + 216s^8$

2. (a) $\partial z/\partial t = y^2 + 2xy2ts = 5t^4s^2 + 4t^3s^4$ and $\partial z/\partial s = y^22s + 2xyt^2 = 2t^5s + 4t^4s^3$

   (b) $\dfrac{\partial z}{\partial t} = \dfrac{2(1 - s)e^{ts+t+s}}{(e^{t+s} + e^{ts})^2}$ and $\dfrac{\partial z}{\partial s} = \dfrac{2(1 - t)e^{ts+t+s}}{(e^{t+s} + e^{ts})^2}$

3. $\partial z/\partial r = 2r \, \partial F/\partial u + (1/r) \, \partial F/\partial w$, and $\partial z/\partial s = -4s \, \partial F/\partial v + (1/s) \, \partial F/\partial w$

4. $\partial z/\partial t_1 = F'(x)f'_1(t_1, t_2)$, and $\partial z/\partial t_2 = F'(x)f'_2(t_1, t_2)$

5. $\partial x/\partial s = F'_1 + F'_2 f'(s) + F'_3 g'_1(s, t)$, and $\partial x/\partial t = F'_3 g'_2(s, t)$

6. $\partial z/\partial x = F'_1 f'_1(x, y) + F'_2 2xh(y)$ and $\partial z/\partial y = F'_1 f'_2(x, y) + F'_2 x^2 h'(y) + F'_3(-1/y^2)$

7. (a) $\dfrac{\partial w}{\partial t} = \dfrac{\partial w}{\partial x}\dfrac{\partial x}{\partial t} + \dfrac{\partial w}{\partial y}\dfrac{\partial y}{\partial t} + \dfrac{\partial w}{\partial z}\dfrac{\partial z}{\partial t} = y^2 z^3 \cdot 2t + 2xyz^3 \cdot 0 + 3xy^2z^2 \cdot 1 = 5s^2 t^4$

   (b) $\dfrac{\partial w}{\partial t} = 2x\dfrac{\partial x}{\partial t} + 2y\dfrac{\partial y}{\partial t} + 2z\dfrac{\partial z}{\partial t} = \dfrac{x}{\sqrt{t+s}} + 2sye^{ts} = 1 + 2se^{2ts}$

8. (a) We can write $z = F(u_1, u_2, u_3)$, with $u_1 = t$, $u_2 = t^2$ and $u_3 = t^3$.

   Then $\dfrac{dz}{dt} = F'_1 \dfrac{du_1}{dt} + F'_2 \dfrac{du_2}{dt} + F'_3 \dfrac{du_3}{dt} = F'_1(t, t^2, t^3) + F'_2(t, t^2, t^3)2t + F'_3(t, t^2, t^3)3t^2$.

   (b) $z = F(t, f(t), g(t^2)) \implies \dfrac{dz}{dt} = F'_1(t, f(t), g(t^2)) + F'_2(t, f(t), g(t^2))f'(t) + F'_3(t, t^2, t^3)g'(t^2)2t$

9. $\partial Z/\partial G = 1 + 2Y \partial Y/\partial G + 2r \partial r/\partial G$

10. $\partial Z/\partial G = 1 + I'_1(Y, r) \partial Y/\partial G + I'_2(Y, r) \partial r/\partial G$

11. $\dfrac{\partial C}{\partial p_1} = a\dfrac{\partial Q_1}{\partial p_1} + b\dfrac{\partial Q_2}{\partial p_1} + 2cQ_1 \dfrac{\partial Q_1}{\partial p_1} = -\alpha_1 A(a + 2cAp_1^{-\alpha_1} p_2^{\beta_1}) p_1^{-\alpha_1 - 1} p_2^{\beta_1} + \alpha_2 bBp_1^{\alpha_2 - 1} p_2^{-\beta_2}$

    $\dfrac{\partial C}{\partial p_2} = \beta_1 A(a + 2cAp_1^{-\alpha_1} p_2^{\beta_1}) p_1^{-\alpha_1} p_2^{\beta_1 - 1} - \beta_2 bBp_1^{\alpha_2} p_2^{-\beta_2 - 1}$

12. $\partial u/\partial x = 3(x^2 - yz)/(x^3 + y^3 + z^3 - 3xyz)$, etc. See SM.

13. Here $\dfrac{\partial z}{\partial x} = f'(x^2 y)\dfrac{\partial}{\partial x}(x^2 y) = f'(x^2 y)2xy$ and similarly $\dfrac{\partial z}{\partial y} = f'(x^2 y)x^2$. The rest follows from elementary algebra.

14. $\dfrac{\partial u}{\partial r} = \dfrac{\partial f}{\partial x}\dfrac{\partial x}{\partial r} + \dfrac{\partial f}{\partial y}\dfrac{\partial y}{\partial r} + \dfrac{\partial f}{\partial z}\dfrac{\partial z}{\partial r} + \dfrac{\partial f}{\partial w}\dfrac{\partial w}{\partial r}$

15. $\dfrac{\partial u}{\partial r} = yzw + xzw + xyws + xyz(1/s) = 28$

15.3

1. Formula (15.3.2) gives $y' = -F_1'/F_2' = -(4x+6y)/(6x+2y) = -(2x+3y)/(3x+y)$.

2. (a) Put $F(x,y) = x^2 y$. Then $F_1' = 2xy$, $F_2' = x^2$, $F_{11}'' = 2y$, $F_{12}'' = 2x$, $F_{22}'' = 0$,
   so $y' = -F_1'/F_2' = -2xy/x^2 = -2y/x$. Moreover, using equation (15.3.5),
   one has $y'' = -(1/(F_2')^3)\left[F_{11}''(F_2')^2 - 2F_{12}''F_1'F_2' + F_{22}''(F_1')^2\right] = -(1/x^6)[2yx^4 - 2(2x)(2xy)x^2] = 6y/x^2$.
   (See also Exercise 7.1.2.) For (b) and (c), see the answers to Exercise 7.1.3.

3. (a) $y' = -4$ and $y'' = -14$ at $(2, 0)$. The tangent has the equation $y = -4x + 8$.
   (b) There is a horizontal tangent at $(a, -4a)$ and $(-a, 4a)$, where $a = 2\sqrt{7}/7$.

4. With $F(x,y) = 3x^2 - 3xy^2 + y^3 + 3y^2$, we have $F_1'(x,y) = 6x - 3y^2$ and $F_2'(x,y) = -6xy + 3y^2 + 6y$.
   Then formula (15.3.2) implies that $h'(x) = y' = -(6x - 3y^2)/(-6xy + 3y^2 + 6y)$.
   For x near 1 and so (x, y) near $(1, 1)$, we have $h'(1) = -(6-3)/(-6+3+6) = -1$.

5. $D_P' < 0$ and $D_r' < 0$. Differentiating the equation w.r.t. r yields $D_P'(dP/dr) + D_r' = 0$, and so $dP/dr = -D_r'/D_P' < 0$. So a rise in the interest rate depresses demand, and the price falls to compensate.

6. $dP/dR = f_R'(R,P)/(g'(P) - f_P'(R,P))$. It is plausible that $f_R'(R,P) > 0$ (demand increases as advesrtising expenditure increases), and $g'(P) > 0$, $f_P'(R,P) < 0$, so $dP/dR > 0$.

7. Differentiating the equation w.r.t. x and y gives: (i) $1 - az_x' = f'(y - bz)(-bz_x')$; (ii) $-az_y' = f'(y - bz)(1 - bz_y')$.
   If $bz_x' \neq 0$, then solving (i) for f' and inserting it into (ii) yields $az_x' + bz_y' = 1$.
   If $bz_x' = 0$, then (i) implies $az_x' = 1$. But then $z_x' \neq 0$, so $b = 0$ and then again $az_x' + bz_y' = 1$.

15.4

1. (a) With $F(x,y) = 3x + y - z$, the given equation is $F(x,y,z) = 0$, and $\partial z/\partial x = -F_1'/F_3' = -3/(-1) = 3$.
   (b) $\partial z/\partial x = -(yz + z^3 - y^2 z^5)/(xy + 3xz^2 - 5xy^2 z^4)$
   (c) With $F(x,y,z) = e^{xyz} - 3xyz$, the given equation is $F(x,y,z) = 0$.
   Now, $F_x'(x,y,z) = yze^{xyz} - 3yz$ and $F_z'(x,y,z) = xye^{xyz} - 3xy$, so (15.4.2) gives
   $$z_x' = -F_x'/F_z' = -(yze^{xyz} - 3yz)/(xye^{xyz} - 3xy) = -yz(e^{xyz} - 3)/xy(e^{xyz} - 3) = -z/x$$
   (Actually, the equation $e^c = 3c$ has two solutions. From $xyz = c$ (c a constant) we find z_x' much more easily.)

2. Differentiating partially w.r.t. x yields (*) $3x^2 + 3z^2 z_x' - 3z_x' = 0$, so $z_x' = x^2/(1-z^2)$. By symmetry, $z_y' = y^2/(1-z^2)$.
   To find z_{xy}'', differentiate (*) w.r.t. y to obtain $6zz_y' z_x' + 3z^2 z_{xy}'' - 3z_{xy}'' = 0$, so $z_{xy}'' = 2zx^2 y^2/(1-z^2)^3$.
   (Alternatively, differentiate $z_x' = x^2/(1-z^2)$ w.r.t. y, treating z as a function of y and using the expression for z_y'.)

3. (a) $L^* = P^2/4w^2$, $\partial L^*/\partial P = P/2w^2 > 0$ and $\partial L^*/\partial w = -P^2/2w^3 < 0$.
   (b) The first-order condition is $Pf'(L^*) - C_L'(L^*, w) = 0$.
   Then $\partial L^*/\partial P = -f'(L^*)/[Pf''(L^*) - C_{LL}''(L^*, w)]$ and $\partial L^*/\partial w = C_{Lw}''(L^*, w)/[Pf''(L^*) - C_{LL}''(L^*, w)]$.

4. Use formula (15.4.2) to obtain $z_x' = -\dfrac{yx^{y-1} + z^x \ln z}{y^z \ln y + xz^{x-1}}$ and $z_y' = -\dfrac{x^y \ln x + zy^{z-1}}{y^z \ln y + xz^{x-1}}$.

5. Implicit differentiation gives $f_P'(R,P)P_w' = g_w'(w,P) + g_P'(w,P)P_w'$.
   It follows that $P_w' = -g_w'(w,P)/[g_P'(w,P) - f_P'(R,P)]$, which is < 0 because $g_w' > 0$, $g_P' > 0$, and $f_P' < 0$.

6. (a) $F(1, 3) = 4$. The equation for the tangent is $y - 3 = -(F'_x(1, 3)/F'_y(1, 3))(x - 1)$.
Because $F'_x(1, 3) = 10$ and $F'_y(1, 3) = 5$, this reduces to $y = -2x + 5$.

7. $\partial y/\partial K = \alpha y/K(1 + 2c \ln y)$, $\partial y/\partial L = \beta y/L(1 + 2c \ln y)$

15.5

1. The marginal rate of substitution is $R_{yx} = 20x/30y$, so $y/x = (2/3)(R_{yx})^{-1}$, whose elasticity is $\sigma_{yx} = -1$.

2. (a) $R_{yx} = (x/y)^{a-1} = (y/x)^{1-a}$ (b) $\sigma_{yx} = \text{El}_{R_{yx}}(y/x) = \text{El}_{R_{yx}}(R_{yx})^{1/(1-a)} = 1/(1-a)$

3. Find the relevant partial derivatives, insert them into (15.5.1), then simplify. See SM for details.

15.6

1. $f(tx, ty) = (tx)^4 + (tx)^2(ty)^2 = t^4 x^4 + t^2 x^2 t^2 y^2 = t^4(x^4 + x^2 y^2) = t^4 f(x, y)$, so f is homogeneous of degree 4.

2. Here $x(tp, tr) = A(tp)^{-1.5}(tr)^{2.08} = At^{-1.5}p^{-1.5}t^{2.08}r^{2.08} = t^{-1.5}t^{2.08}Ap^{-1.5}r^{2.08} = t^{0.58}x(p, r)$, so the function is homogeneous of degree 0.58. (Alternatively, use the result in Example 14.1.4.)

3. $f(tx, ty) = (tx)(ty)^2 + (tx)^3 = t^3(xy^2 + x^3) = t^3 f(x, y)$. So f is homogeneous of degree 3. For the rest, see SM.

4. $f(tx, ty) = (tx)(ty)/[(tx)^2 + (ty)^2] = t^2 xy/t^2[x^2 + y^2] = f(x, y) = t^0 f(x, y)$, so f is homogeneous of degree 0.

Using the formulas for the partial derivatives of this function in part (b) of Example 14.2.1,

we get $x\dfrac{\partial f}{\partial x} + y\dfrac{\partial f}{\partial y} = \dfrac{xy^3 - x^3 y + x^3 y - xy^3}{(x^2 + y^2)^2} = 0 = 0 \cdot f$, as claimed by Euler's theorem.

5. $F(tK, tL) = A(a(tK)^{-\rho} + b(tL)^{-\rho})^{-1/\rho} = A(t^{-\rho}aK^{-\rho} + t^{-\rho}bL^{-\rho})^{-1/\rho} = (t^{-\rho})^{-1/\rho}A(aK^{-\rho} + bL^{-\rho})^{-1/\rho}$, which reduces to $tF(K, L)$. Using the idea of Example 15.6.3, we get $F(K, L)/L = F(K/L, 1) = A[a(K/L)^{-\rho} + b]^{-1/\rho}$.

6. Equation (15.6.1) requires that for some number k one has $t^3 x^3 + t^2 xy = t^k(x^3 + xy)$ for all $t > 0$ and all (x, y). In particular, for $x = y = 1$, we must have $t^3 + t^2 = 2t^k$ for all $t > 0$. For $t = 2$, we get $12 = 2 \cdot 2^k$, or $2^k = 6$. For $t = 4$, we get $80 = 2 \cdot 4^k$, or $4^k = 40$. But $2^k = 6$ implies $4^k = 36$. So the two values of k must actually be different, implying that f is not homogeneous of any degree.

7. From (15.6.6) and (15.6.7) with $k = 1$, we get $f''_{11} = (-y/x)f''_{12}$ and $f''_{22} = (-x/y)f''_{21}$.
It follows that $f''_{11}f''_{22} - (f''_{12})^2 = (-y/x)f''_{12} \cdot (-x/y)f''_{21} - (f''_{12})^2 = 0$ because $f''_{12} = f''_{21}$.

8. By (15.6.3), $f'_2(x, y)$ is homogeneous of degree 1, so $12 = f'_2(4, 6) = f'_2(2 \cdot 2, 2 \cdot 3) = 2f'_2(2, 3)$, implying that $f'_2(2, 3) = 6$. By Euler's Theorem (15.6.2), one has $2f(2, 3) = 2f'_1(2, 3) + 3f'_2(2, 3) = 2 \cdot 4 + 3 \cdot 6 = 26$, and so $f(2, 3) = 13$. Finally using definition (15.6.1) yields $f(6, 9) = f(3 \cdot 2, 3 \cdot 3) = 3^2 f(2, 3) = 9 \cdot 13 = 117$.

9. Follow the hint. See SM for details.

15.7

1. (a) Homogeneous of degree 1. (b) Not homogeneous. (c) Homogeneous of degree $-1/2$.
(d) Homogeneous of degree 1. (e) Not homogeneous. (f) Homogeneous of degree n.

2. (a) Homogeneous of degree 1. (b) Homogeneous of degree μ.

3. All are homogeneous of degree 1, as is easily checked by using definition (15.7.1) directly.

4. Let s denote $x_1 + \cdots + x_n$. Then $v_i' = u_i' - a/s$, so $\sum_{i=1}^{n} x_i v_i' = \sum_{i=1}^{n} x_i u_i' - \sum_{i=1}^{n} a x_i/s = a - a = 0$.

By Euler's Theorem (15.7.2), it follows that v is homogeneous of degree 0.

5. (a) Homothetic. (b) Homothetic. (c) Not homothetic. (d) Homothetic. See SM for details.

6. (a) Here $h(t\mathbf{x}) = f((tx_1)^m, \ldots, (tx_n)^m) = f(t^m x_1^m, \ldots, t^m x_n^m) = (t^m)^r f(x_1^m, \ldots, x_n^m) = t^{mr} h(\mathbf{x})$, so h is homogeneous of degree mr. (b) Homogeneous of degree sp. (c) Homogeneous of degree r if $r = s$, not homogeneous if $r \neq s$. (d) Homogeneous of degree $r + s$. (e) Homogeneous of degree $r - s$.

7. Routine application of the definitions. See SM for details.

15.8

1. In each case we use the approximation $f(x, y) \approx f(0, 0) + f_1'(0, 0)x + f_2'(0, 0)y$. (a) $f_1'(x, y) = 5(x + 1)^4 (y + 1)^6$ and $f_2'(x, y) = 6(x + 1)^5 (y + 1)^5$, so $f_1'(0, 0) = 5$ and $f_2'(0, 0) = 6$. But $f(0, 0) = 1$, so $f(x, y) \approx 1 + 5x + 6y$.

(b) $f_1'(x, y) = f_2'(x, y) = \frac{1}{2}(1 + x + y)^{-1/2}$, so $f_1'(0, 0) = f_2'(0, 0) = 1/2$. But $f(0, 0) = 1$, so $f(x, y) \approx 1 + \frac{1}{2}x + \frac{1}{2}y$.

(c) $f_1'(x, y) = e^x \ln(1 + y)$, $f_2'(x, y) = e^x/(1 + y)$, so $f_1'(0, 0) = 0$ and $f_2'(0, 0) = 1$. But $f(0, 0) = 0$, so $f(x, y) \approx y$.

2. $f(x, y) \approx A x_0^a y_0^b + a A x_0^{a-1} y_0^b (x - x_0) + b A x_0^a y_0^{b-1} (y - y_0) = A x_0^a y_0^b [1 + a(x - x_0)/x_0 + b(y - y_0)/y_0]$

3. Write the function in the form $g^*(\mu, \varepsilon) = (1 + \mu)^a (1 + \varepsilon)^{\alpha a} - 1$, where $a = 1/(1 - \beta)$.

Then $\partial g^*(\mu, \varepsilon)/\partial \mu = a(1 + \mu)^{a-1}(1 + \varepsilon)^{\alpha a}$ and $\partial g^*(\mu, \varepsilon)/\partial \varepsilon = (1 + \mu)^a \alpha a (1 + \varepsilon)^{\alpha a - 1}$.

Hence, $g^*(0, 0) = 0$, $\partial g^*(0, 0)/\partial \mu = a$, $\partial g^*(0, 0)/\partial \varepsilon = \alpha a$, and $g^*(\mu, \varepsilon) \approx a\mu + \alpha a \varepsilon = (\mu + \alpha \varepsilon)/(1 - \beta)$.

4. $f(0.98, -1.01) \approx -5 - 6(-0.02) + 9(-0.01) = -4.97$. The exact value is -4.970614, so the error is 0.000614.

5. (a) $f(1.02, 1.99) = 1.1909$ (b) $f(1.02, 1.99) \approx f(1, 2) + 0.02 \cdot 8 - 0.01 \cdot (-3) = 1.19$. The error is 0.0009.

6. $v(1.01, 0.02) \approx v(1, 0) + v_1'(1, 0) \cdot 0.01 + v_2'(1, 0) \cdot 0.02 = -1 - 1/150$

7. (a) $z = 2x + 4y - 5$ (b) $z = -10x + 3y + 3$

8. Extend the argument used to establish (15.8.4) from 2 to n variables. See SM for details.

9. The tangent plane (15.8.10) passes through $(x, y, z) = (0, 0, 0)$ iff $-f(x_0, y_0) = f_1'(x_0, y_0)(-x_0) + f_2'(x_0, y_0)(-y_0)$.

Changing the sign on each side of this equation and replacing (x_0, y_0) by (x, y) gives Euler's characterization (15.6.1) of a function $f(x, y)$ that is homogeneous of degree 1.

10. (a) Along the curve $x = \alpha y^2$, for all $y \neq 0$ the point $(\alpha y^2, y)$ is on the level curve $f(x, y) = \alpha/(1 + \alpha^2)$.

(b) When $\alpha = 1$, for instance, one has $f(y^2, y) = \frac{1}{2}$ for all $y \neq 0$, yet when $y = 0$ one has $f(y^2, y) = f(0, 0) = 0$. So f is discontinuous at $(0, 0)$. (c) For all $(x, y) \neq (0, 0)$, the partial derivatives $f_1'(x, y)$ and $f_2'(x, y)$ obviously both exist and are continuous. Moreover one has $f_1'(0, 0) = \lim_{h \to 0}[f(h, 0) - f(0, 0)]/h = 0$, and similarly $f_2'(0, 0) = 0$.

(d) Because f is continuously differentiable at every point $(x, y) \neq (0, 0)$, for all directions $(h, k) \neq (0, 0)$, the directional derivative is given by $\nabla_{(h,k)} f(x, y) = f_1'(x, y) h + f_2'(x, y) k$. At $(x, y) = (0, 0)$, if $(h, k) \neq (0, 0)$ is a direction with $h \neq 0$, then $\nabla_{(h,k)} f(0, 0) = \lim_{\theta \to 0} \frac{1}{\theta}[f(\theta h, \theta k) - f(0, 0)] = \lim_{\theta \to 0} \frac{1}{\theta} \frac{\theta^3 h k^2}{\theta^2 h^2 + \theta^4 k^4} = \frac{k^2}{h}$.

But if $(0, k)$ is a direction with $k \neq 0$, then $\nabla_{(0,k)} f(0, 0) = \lim_{\theta \to 0} \frac{1}{\theta}[f(0, \theta k) - f(0, 0)] = 0$.

(e) Because f is discontinuous at $(0, 0)$, it cannot be differentiable at $(0, 0)$.

15.9

1. Both (a) and (b) give: $dz = (y^2 + 3x^2)\,dx + 2xy\,dy$.

2. We can either use definition (15.9.1) of the differential or, as we do here, the rules for differentials.
   (a) $dz = d(x^3) + d(y^3) = 3x^2\,dx + 3y^2\,dy$
   (b) $dz = (dx)e^{y^2} + x(de^{y^2})$. Here $d(e^{y^2}) = e^{y^2}\,dy^2 = e^{y^2}2y\,dy$, so $dz = e^{y^2}\,dx + 2xye^{y^2}\,dy = e^{y^2}(dx + 2xy\,dy)$.
   (c) $dz = d\ln u$, where $u = x^2 - y^2$. Then $dz = \dfrac{1}{u}\,du = \dfrac{2x\,dx - 2y\,dy}{x^2 - y^2}$.

3. (a) $dz = 2xu\,dx + x^2(u'_x\,dx + u'_y\,dy)$ (b) $dz = 2u(u'_x\,dx + u'_y\,dy)$ (c) $dz = \dfrac{1}{xy + yu}\left[(y + yu'_x)\,dx + (x + u + yu'_y)\,dy\right]$

4. $T \approx 7.015714$. See SM for details.

5. Taking the differential of each side of the equation gives first $d(Ue^U) = d(x\sqrt{y})$, and then $e^U\,dU + Ue^U\,dU = \sqrt{y}\,dx + (x/2\sqrt{y})\,dy$. Solving for dU yields $dU = \sqrt{y}\,dx/(e^U + Ue^U) + x\,dy/2\sqrt{y}(e^U + Ue^U)$.

6. $dX = A\beta N^{\beta-1}e^{\rho t}\,dN + AN^\beta \rho e^{\rho t}\,dt$

7. $dX_1 = BEX^{E-1}N^{1-E}\,dX + B(1 - E)X^E N^{-E}\,dN$

8. (a) $dU = 2a_1 u_1\,du_1 + \cdots + 2a_n u_n\,du_n$ (b) $dU = A(\delta_1 u_1^{-\rho} + \cdots + \delta_n u_n^{-\rho})^{-1-1/\rho}(\delta_1 u_1^{-\rho-1}\,du_1 + \cdots + \delta_n u_n^{-\rho-1}\,du_n)$

9. $d(\ln z) = a_1\,d(\ln x_1) + \cdots + a_n\,d(\ln x_n)$, so $dz/z = a_1\,dx_1/x_1 + a_2\,dx_2/x_2 + \cdots + a_n\,dx_n/x_n$.

10. (a) $d^2z = 2\,dx\,dy + 2(dy)^2$ (b) $dz/dt = 3t^2 + 4t^3$ and then $(d^2z/dt^2)(dt)^2 = (6t + 12t^2)(dt)^2$.
    On the other hand, the expression for d^2z derived from (a) is equal to $2\,dt \cdot 2t\,dt + 2(2t\,dt)^2 = (4t + 8t^2)(dt)^2$.

15.10

1. (a) Two equations in (u, v, x, y), so degrees of freedom $= 4 - 2 = 2$ (b) $5 - 2 = 3$ (c) $4 - 3 = 1$

2. There are 6 variables Y, C, I, G, T, and r, and 3 equations. So there are $6 - 3 = 3$ degrees of freedom.

3. Let m denote the number of equations and n the number of unknowns. (a) $m = 3$, $n = 2$; infinitely many solutions. (b) $m = n = 2$; no solutions. (c) $m = n = 2$; infinitely many solutions.

4. (a) $m = 1$, $n = 100$; infinitely many solutions. (b) $m = 1$, $n = 100$; no solutions. We see that the counting rule fails dramatically.

15.11

1. Differentiating yields the two equations $a\,du + b\,dv = c\,dx + d\,dy$ and $e\,du + f\,dv = g\,dx + h\,dy$. Solving these for du and dv yields $du = [(cf - bg)\,dx + (df - bh)\,dy]/D$ and $dv = [(ag - ce)\,dx + (ah - de)\,dy]/D$, where $D = af - be$. The required partial derivatives are then easily read off.

2. (a) Differentiating yields $u^3\,dx + x3u^2\,du + dv = 2y\,dy$ and $3v\,du + 3u\,dv - dx = 0$. Solving for du and dv with $D = 9xu^3 - 3v$ yields $du = (-3u^4 - 1)\,dx/D + 6yu\,dy/D$ and $dv = (3xu^2 + 3u^3v)\,dx/D - 6yv\,dy/D$.
   (b) $u'_x = (-3u^4 - 1)/D$, $v'_x = (3xu^2 + 3u^3v)/D$ (c) $u'_x = 283/81$ and $v'_x = -64/27$

3. $\partial y_1/\partial x_1 = (3 - 27x_1^2 y_2^2)/J$ and $\partial y_2/\partial x_1 = (3x_1^2 + 18y_1^2)/J$ with $J = 1 + 54y_1^2 y_2^2$.

4. $\partial Y/\partial M = I'(r)/(aI'(r) + L'(r)S'(Y))$ and $\partial r/\partial M = S'(Y)/(aI'(r) + L'(r)S'(Y))$.

5. Differentiating w.r.t. x yields $y + u'_x v + u v'_x = 0$ and $u + x u'_x + y v'_x = 0$. Solving for u'_x and v'_x, we get

$$u'_x = \frac{u^2 - y^2}{yv - xu} = \frac{u^2 - y^2}{2yv}, \quad v'_x = \frac{xy - uv}{yv - xu} = \frac{2xy - 1}{2yv}$$

where we substituted $xu = -yv$ and $uv = 1 - xy$. Differentiating u'_x w.r.t. x finally yields

$$u''_{xx} = \frac{\partial^2 u}{\partial x^2} = \frac{\partial}{\partial x} u'_x = \frac{2 u u'_x 2 y v - (u^2 - y^2) 2 y v'_x}{4 y^2 v^2} = \frac{(u^2 - y^2)(4uv - 1)}{4 y^2 v^3}$$

(The answer to this problem can be expressed in many different ways.)

6. (a) Differentiating yields the equations: $dY = dC + dI + dG$, $dC = F'_Y dY + F'_T dT + F'_r dr$, and $dI = f'_Y dY + f'_r dr$. Hence, $dY = (F'_T dT + dG + (F'_r + f'_r) dr) / (1 - F'_Y - f'_Y)$.

(b) $\partial Y / \partial T = F'_T / (1 - F'_Y - f'_Y) < 0$, so Y decreases as T increases. But if $dT = dG$ with $dr = 0$, then $dY = (1 + F'_T) dT / (1 - F'_Y - f'_Y)$, which is positive provided that $F'_T > -1$.

7. (a) $6 - 3 = 3$ (b) Differentiating, then gathering all terms in dY, dr, and dI on the left-hand side, we obtain

(i) $(C'_Y - 1) dY + C'_r dr + dI = -d\alpha$ (ii) $F'_Y dY + F'_r dr - dI = -d\beta$ (iii) $L'_Y dY + L'_r dr = dM$.
With $d\beta = dM = 0$ we get $dY = -(L'_r / D) d\alpha$, $dr = (L'_Y / D) d\alpha$, and $dI = [(F'_r L'_Y - F'_Y L'_r) / D] d\alpha$, where $D = L'_r (C'_Y + F'_Y - 1) - L'_Y (C'_r + F'_r)$.

8. (a) There are 3 variables and 2 equations, so there is (in general) one degree of freedom.

(b) Differentiation gives $0 = \alpha P dy + L'(r) dr$ and $S'_y dy + S'_r dr + S'_g dg = I'_y dy + I'_r dr$. We find $dy/dg = -L'(r) S'_g / D$ and $dr/dg = \alpha P S'_g / D$, where $D = L'(r)(S'_y - I'_y) - \alpha P(S'_r - I'_r)$.

9. (a) Differentiating yields $2uv \, du + u^2 \, dv - du = 3x^2 \, dx + 6y^2 \, dy$ and $e^{ux}(u \, dx + x \, du) = v \, dy + y \, dv$. At the point P these equations become $3 \, du + 4 \, dv = 6 \, dy$ and $dv = 2 \, dx - dy$. Hence $du = 2 \, dy - (4/3) \, dv = -(8/3) \, dx + (10/3) \, dy$. So $\partial u / \partial y = 10/3$ and $\partial v / \partial x = 2$.

(b) $\Delta u \approx du = -(8/3) 0.1 + (10/3)(-0.2) = -14/15 \approx -0.93$, $\Delta v \approx dv = 2(0.1) + (-1)(-0.2) = 0.4$

10. Taking differentials and putting $dp_2 = dm = 0$ gives:

(i) $U'''_{11} dx_1 + U'''_{12} dx_2 = p_1 \, d\lambda + \lambda \, dp_1$; (ii) $U'''_{21} dx_1 + U'''_{22} dx_2 = p_2 \, d\lambda$; (iii) $p_1 dx_1 + dp_1 x_1 + p_2 dx_2 = 0$.

After solving these three linear equations in $(dx_1, dx_2, d\lambda)$ for dx_1 in particular, we obtain

$$\partial x_1 / \partial p_1 = [\lambda p_2^2 + x_1 (p_2 U'''_{12} - p_1 U'''_{22})] / (p_1^2 U'''_{22} - 2 p_1 p_2 U'''_{12} + p_2^2 U'''_{11}).$$

Review exercises for Chapter 15

1. (a) $dz/dt = 6 \cdot 4t + 3y^2 9t^2 = 24t + 27t^2 y^2 = 24t + 243 t^8$ (b) $dz/dt = px^{p-1} a + py^{p-1} b = pt^{p-1}(a^p + b^p)$

(c) In part (a), $z = 6(2t^2) + (3t^3)^3 = 12t^2 + 27t^9$, so $dz/dt = 24t + 243 t^8$.
In part (b), $z = (at)^p + (bt)^p = a^p t^p + b^p t^p$, so $dz/dt = (a^p + b^p) p t^{p-1}$.

2. $\partial z / \partial t = G'_1(u, v) \phi'_1(t, s)$ and $\partial z / \partial s = G'_1(u, v) \phi'_2(t, s) + G'_2(u, v) \psi'(s)$

3. $\partial w / \partial t = 2x \cdot 1 + 3y^2 \cdot 1 + 4z^3 s = 2x + 3y^2 + 4sz^3 = 4s^4 t^3 + 3s^2 + 3t^2 - 6ts + 2s + 2t$,
$\partial w / \partial s = 2x - 3y^2 + 4tz^3 = 4s^3 t^4 - 3s^2 - 3t^2 + 6ts + 2s + 2t$

4. $dX/dN = g(u) + g'(u)(\varphi'(N) - u)$, where $u = \varphi(N)/N$, and $d^2 X/dN^2 = (1/N) g''(u)(\varphi'(N) - u)^2 + g'(u) \varphi''(N)$.

5. (a) Take the natural logarithm, $\ln E = \ln A - a \ln p + b \ln m$, and then differentiate to get $\dot{E}/E = -a(\dot{p}/p) + b(\dot{m}/m)$.

(b) $\ln p = \ln p_0 + t \ln(1.06)$, so $\dot{p}/p = \ln 1.06$. Likewise, $\dot{m}/m = \ln 1.08$. Then $\dot{E}/E = -a \ln 1.06 + b \ln 1.08 = \ln(1.08^b / 1.06^a) = \ln Q$.

6. Differentiating each side w.r.t. x while holding y constant gives $3x^2 \ln x + x^2 = (6z^2 \ln z + 2z^2)z'_1$. When $x = y = z = e$, this gives $z'_1 = 1/2$. Differentiating a second time gives $6x \ln x + 5x = (12z \ln z + 10z)(z'_1)^2 + (6z^2 \ln z + 2z^2)z''_{11}$. When $x = y = z = e$ and $z'_1 = 1/2$, this gives $z''_{11} = 11/16e$.

7. $R_{yx} = F'_x/F'_y = -x/10y$. Hence $y/x = -(1/10)R_{yx}^{-1}$, and so $\sigma_{yx} = \mathrm{El}_{R_{yx}}(y/x) = -1$.

8. (a) MRS = $R_{yx} = U'_x/U'_y = 2y/3x$ (b) MRS = $R_{yx} = y/(x+1)$ (c) MRS = $R_{yx} = (y/x)^3$

9. (a) -1 (b) $2ac$ (c) 4. (d) Not homogeneous. (If F were homogeneous, then by Euler's theorem, for some constant k, we would have $x_1 e^{x_1+x_2+x_3} + x_2 e^{x_1+x_2+x_3} + x_3 e^{x_1+x_2+x_3} = ke^{x_1+x_2+x_3}$ for all positive x_1, x_2, x_3, and so $x_1 + x_2 + x_3 = k$. This is evidently impossible for general (x_1, x_2, x_3).)

10. Since $y/x = (R_{yx})^{1/3}$, we have $\sigma_{yx} = \mathrm{El}_{R_{yx}}(y/x) = 1/3$.

11. Using the hint, taking ln of each side gives $2 \ln y + x + (1/y) = \ln 3$ or $2v + e^u + e^{-v} = \ln 3$. Differentiating each side of the last equation w.r.t. u yields $2v'_u + e^u - e^{-v}v'_u = 0$, so $\mathrm{El}_x y = v'_u = e^u/(e^{-v} - 2) = x/((1/y) - 2) = xy/(1 - 2y)$.

12. (a) For all $t > 0$ one has $f(tx, ty) = (tx)g(tx/ty) = txg(x/y) = tf(x, y)$, so f is homogeneous of degree 1.

(b) Using a similar argument to part (a) shows that F is homogeneous of degree k.

(c) Using the answer for the general Cobb–Douglas function in Example 15.7.3 shows that the function G is homogeneous of degree $(a - b) + (b - c) + (c - d) + (d - a) = 0$.

13. Since F is homogeneous of degree 1, according to (15.6.6) or (15.6.7), we have $KF''_{KK} + LF''_{KL} = 0$. Because $F''_{KK} < 0$ and $K > 0$, $L > 0$, this implies that $F''_{KL} = -(K/L)F''_{KK} > 0$.

14. Differentiate $f(tx_1, \ldots, tx_n) = g(t)f(x_1, \ldots, x_n)$ w.r.t. t and put $t = 1$, as in the proof of Euler's Theorem 15.7.1. This yields $\sum_{i=1}^n x_i f'_i(x_1, \ldots, x_n) = g'(1)f(x_1, \ldots, x_n)$. Thus, by Euler's theorem, the function f must actually be homogeneous of degree $k = g'(1)$.

15. $du + e^y dx + xe^y dy + dv = 0$ and $dx + e^{u+v^2} du + e^{u+v^2} 2v \, dv - dy = 0$. At the given point, these equations reduce to $du + dv = -e \, dx - e \, dy$ and $du = -e \, dx + e \, dy$, implying that $u'_x = -e$, $u'_y = e$, $v'_x = 0$, and $v'_y = -2e$.

16. (a) $\partial p/\partial w = L/F(L)$, $\partial p/\partial B = 1/F(L)$, $\partial L/\partial w = (F(L) - LF'(L))/pF(L)F''(L)$, and $\partial L/\partial B = -F'(L)/pF(L)F''(L)$

(b) See SM.

17. (a) $\alpha u^{\alpha-1} du + \beta v^{\beta-1} dv = 2^\beta dx + 3y^2 dy$ and $\alpha u^{\alpha-1} v^\beta du + u^\alpha \beta v^{\beta-1} dv - \beta v^{\beta-1} dv = dx - dy$. At P we find $\partial u/\partial x = 2^{-\beta}/\alpha$, $\partial u/\partial y = -2^{-\beta}/\alpha$, $\partial v/\partial x = (2^\beta - 2^{-\beta})/\beta 2^{\beta-1}$, $\partial v/\partial y = (2^{-\beta} + 3)/\beta 2^{\beta-1}$.

(b) $u(0.99, 1.01) \approx u(1, 1) + \partial u(1, 1)/\partial x \cdot (-0.01) + \partial u(1, 1)/\partial y \cdot 0.01 = 1 - 2^{-\beta}/100\alpha - 2^{-\beta}/100\alpha$, which reduces to $1 - 2^{-\beta}/50\alpha$.

18. (a) $S = \int_0^T e^{-rx}(e^{gT-gx} - 1) dx = e^{gT} \int_0^T e^{-(r+g)x} dx - \int_0^T e^{-rx} dx = \dfrac{e^{gT} - e^{-rT}}{r+g} + \dfrac{e^{-rT} - 1}{r}$,

and therefore $r(r+g)S = re^{gT} + ge^{-rT} - (r+g)$. (b) Implicit differentiation w.r.t. g yields

$rS = re^{gT}(T + g\partial T/\partial g) + e^{-rT} + ge^{-rT}(-r\partial T/\partial g) - 1$, so $\partial T/\partial g = [rS + 1 - rTe^{gT} - e^{-rT}]/rg(e^{gT} - e^{-rT})$.

19. (a) The first-order condition is $P'(t^*) = V'(t^*)e^{-rt^*} - rV(t^*)e^{-rt^*} - me^{-rt^*} = 0$. Multiplying by e^{rt^*} gives $V'(t^*) = rV(t^*) + m$. An economic interpretation is that there must be approximate equality between:

(i) the benefit of waiting a fraction dt of a year longer, which is approximately $V'(t^*) dt$;

(ii) the loss of waiting dt longer, which is forgone interest $rV(t^*) dt$ plus the fraction $m \, dt$ of the yearly cost m.

(b) The second-order condition $P'(t^*) < 0$ for a strict local maximum at t^* holds iff $V'(t^*) - rV(t^*) < 0$. See SM for more details.

(c) Taking the differential of $V'(t^*) = rV(t^*) + m$ gives $V''(t^*)dt^* = V(t^*)dr + rV'(t^*)dt^* + dm$. This equation can be used to find the partial derivatives and, provided that the second-order condition is satisfied, determine their signs. See SM for more details.

Chapter 16

16.1

1. (a) $\int_0^2 \left[\int_0^1 (2x + 3y + 4) \, dx \right] dy = \int_0^2 \left[\Big|_{x=0}^{x=1} (x^2 + 3xy + 4x) \right] dy = \int_0^2 (5 + 3y) \, dy = \Big|_0^2 (5y + \frac{3}{2}y^2) = 16$

   (b) $\int_0^a \left[\int_0^b (x-a)(x-b) dx \right] dy = \int_0^a \left[\Big|_{x=0}^{x=b} (\frac{1}{3}x^3 - \frac{1}{2}(a+b)x^2 + abx) \right] dy$
   $= \int_0^a \left(\frac{1}{3}b^3 - \frac{1}{2}(a+b)b^2 + ab^2 \right) dy = a(\frac{1}{3}b^3 + \frac{1}{2}ab^2 - \frac{1}{2}b^3) = \frac{1}{6}ab^2(3a - b)$

   (c) $16 \ln 2 - 3 \ln 3 - 5 \ln 5$. See SM for details.

2. $\frac{1}{b}(e^b - e^{b/a}) + \frac{1}{a} - 1$. See SM for details.

3. $k_a = 2 + 4/(a^2 + 3a) > 2$ for all $a > 0$. See SM for details.

4. The inner integral is $\int_{-2}^1 [x^2 y^3 - (y+1)^2] dy = \Big|_{y=-2}^{y=1} [\frac{1}{4}x^2 y^4 - \frac{1}{3}(y+1)^3] = \frac{1}{4}x^2 - \frac{8}{3} - 4x^2 - \frac{1}{3} = -\frac{15}{4}x^2 - 3$.

   The double integral is therefore $I = -\int_0^2 (\frac{15}{4}x^2 + 3) dx = -\Big|_{x=0}^{x=2} (\frac{5}{4}x^3 + 3x) = -(10 + 6) = -16$.

16.3

1. The shaded area is the difference between the areas of: (i) the unit square; (ii) the triangle with corners at $(z - 1, 1)$, $(1, z - 1)$, and $(1, 1)$. This difference is $1 - \frac{1}{2}(2 - z)^2$.

16.4

1. For $i = 1, 2, 3$, one has $\iiint_C x_i^2 \, dx_1 \, dx_2 \, dx_3 = \int_0^1 x^2 \, dx = \frac{1}{3}$, so $\iiint_C (x_1^2 + x_2^2 + x_3^2) \, dx_1 \, dx_2 \, dx_3 = 3 \int_0^1 x^2 \, dx = 1$.

Chapter 17

17.1

1. The first-order conditions $f_1'(x, y) = -4x + 4 = 0$ and $f_2'(x, y) = -2y + 4 = 0$ are both satisfied when $x = 1$ and $y = 2$.

2. (a) $f_1'(x, y) = 2x - 6$ and $f_2'(x, y) = 2y + 8$, which are both zero at the only critical point $(x, y) = (3, -4)$.

   (b) $f(x, y) = x^2 - 6x + 3^2 + y^2 + 8y + 4^2 + 35 - 3^2 - 4^2 = (x - 3)^2 + (y + 4)^2 + 10 \geq 10$ for all (x, y), whereas $f(3, -4) = 10$, so $(3, -4)$ minimizes f.

3. $F_K' = -2(K - 3) - (L - 6)$ and $F_L' = -4(L - 6) - (K - 3)$. The first-order conditions are $-2(K - 3) - (L - 6) = 0.65$ and $-4(L - 6) - (K - 3) = 1.2$. The only solution of these two simultaneous equations is $(K, L) = (2.8, 5.75)$.

4. (a) $P(10, 8) = P(12, 10) = 98$ (b) The first-order conditions are $P_x' = -2x + 22 = 0$ and $P_y' = -2y + 18 = 0$.
   It follows that $x = 11$ and $y = 9$, where profit is $P(11, 9) = 100$.

17.2

1. We check that the conditions in part (a) of Theorem 17.2.2 are satisfied in all three cases:

(a) For all (x, y) one has $\dfrac{\partial^2 \pi}{\partial x^2} = -0.08 \leq 0$, $\dfrac{\partial^2 \pi}{\partial y^2} = -0.02 \leq 0$, and $\dfrac{\partial^2 \pi}{\partial x^2}\dfrac{\partial^2 \pi}{\partial y^2} - \left(\dfrac{\partial^2 \pi}{\partial x \partial y}\right)^2 = 0.0015 \geq 0$.

(b) For all (x, y) one has $f_{11}''' = -4 \leq 0$, $f_{12}''' = 0$, and $f_{22}''' = -2 \leq 0$, so $f_{11}''' f_{22}''' - (f_{12}''')^2 = 8 \geq 0$.

(c) With $\pi = F(K, L) - 0.65K - 1.2L$, we have $\pi_{KK}'' = -2$, $\pi_{KL}'' = -1$, and $\pi_{LL}'' = -4$, so $\pi_{KK}'' \pi_{LL}'' - (\pi_{KL}'')^2 = 7$.

2. (a) Profit is $\pi(x, y) = 24x + 12y - C(x, y) = -2x^2 - 4y^2 + 4xy + 64x + 32y - 514$. Critical point at $x = 40$, $y = 24$, with $\pi(40, 24) = 1150$. Since $\pi_{11}'' = -4 \leq 0$, $\pi_{22}'' = -8 \leq 0$, and $\pi_{11}'' \pi_{22}'' - (\pi_{12}'')^2 = 16 \geq 0$, this is the maximum.

(b) With $y = 54 - x$, profit is $\hat{\pi} = -2x^2 - 4(54 - x)^2 + 4x(54 - x) + 64x + 32(54 - x) - 514 = -10x^2 + 680x - 10\,450$. This has a maximum where $\hat{\pi}'(x) = 0$, which is at $x = 34$. Then $y = 54 - 34 = 20$. The maximum point is at $x = 34$, $y = 20$, where the maximum value is 1110.

3. Using $x = 108 - 3y - 4z$ gives the modified utility function $\hat{U}(y, z) = (108 - 3y - 4z)yz$.

Maximizing this w.r.t. y and z gives first-order conditions whose solution is $y = 12$, $z = 9$.

Then $x = 36$ and maximum profit is 3888. See SM for details.

4. (a) $\pi(x, y) = px + qy - C(x, y) = (25 - x)x + (24 - 2y)y - (3x^2 + 3xy + y^2) = -4x^2 - 3xy - 3y^2 + 25x + 24y$.

(b) $\pi_1' = -8x - 3y + 25 = 0$ and $\pi_2' = -3x - 6y + 24 = 0$ when $(x, y) = (2, 3)$. Moreover, then $\pi_{11}'' = -8 \leq 0$, $\pi_{22}'' = -6 \leq 0$, and $\pi_{11}'' \pi_{22}'' - (\pi_{12}'')^2 = (-8)(-6) - (-3)^2 = 39 \geq 0$. So $(x, y) = (2, 3)$ maximizes profits.

5. Profit is $\pi(x, y) = px + qy - x^2 - xy - y^2 - x - y - 14$. It has a critical point (x^*, y^*) where $x^* = \tfrac{1}{3}(2p - q - 1)$ and $y^* = \tfrac{1}{3}(-p + 2q - 1)$. Provided that $q < 2p - 1$ and $q > \tfrac{1}{2}(p + 1)$, the interior point (x^*, y^*) with $x^* > 0$ and $y^* > 0$ satisfies the sufficient conditions in Theorem 17.2.2 for a profit maximum.

6. (a) $x^* = p/2\alpha$, $y^* = q/2\beta$, and the second-order conditions are satisfied.

(b) $\pi^*(p, q) = px^* + qy^* - \alpha(x^*)^2 - \beta(y^*)^2 = p^2/4\alpha + q^2/2\beta$. Hence $\partial \pi^*(p, q)/\partial p = p/2\alpha = x^*$. So increasing the price p by one unit increases the optimal profit by approximately x^*, the output of the first good. Furthermore $\partial \pi^*(p, q)/\partial q = y^*$, which has a similar interpretation.

7. The constraint implies that $z = 4x + 2y - 5$. After using this expression to substitute for z, we choose (x, y) to minimize $P(x, y) = x^2 + y^2 + (4x + 2y - 5)^2$ w.r.t. x and y. The two first-order conditions are $P_1' = 34x + 16y - 40 = 0$ and $P_2' = 16x + 10y - 20 = 0$, with solution $x = 20/21$, $y = 10/21$. Since $P_{11}'' = 34$, $P_{12}'' = 16$, and $P_{22}'' = 10$, the second-order conditions for a minimum are satisfied. The minimum value is $525/441$.

8. To check the sufficient conditions in part (a) of Theorem 17.2.2, we calculate $f_{11}'' = a(a-1)Ax^{a-2}y^b$, then $f_{12}'' = f_{21}'' = abAx^{a-1}y^{b-1}$, and $f_{22}'' = b(b-1)Ax^a y^{b-2}$. Thus, $f_{11}'' f_{22}'' - (f_{12}'')^2 = abA^2 x^{2a-2}y^{2b-2}[1 - (a+b)]$. Suppose that $a + b \leq 1$. Then $a \leq 1$ and $b \leq 1$ as well. If $x > 0$ and $y > 0$, then $f_{11}'' \leq 0$ and $f_{22}'' \leq 0$, and $f_{11}'' f_{22}'' - (f_{12}'')^2 \geq 0$. We conclude that f is concave for $x > 0$, $y > 0$.

17.3

1. (a) $f_1' = -2x + 6$, $f_2' = -4y + 8$, $f_{11}'' = -2$, $f_{12}'' = 0$, and $f_{22}'' = -4$.

(b) By Theorem 17.3.1, because $A = -2 < 0$ and $AC - B^2 = 8 > 0$, the point $(3, 2)$ is a local maximum.

Part (a) of Theorem 17.2.2 implies that $(3, 2)$ is actually a (global) maximum point.

2. (a) $f_1' = 2x + 2y^2$, $f_2' = 4xy + 4y$, $f_{11}'' = 2$, $f_{12}'' = 4y$, $f_{22}'' = 4x + 4$

(b) $f_2' = 0 \iff 4y(x + 1) = 0 \iff x = -1$ or $y = 0$. If $x = -1$, then $f_1' = 0$ for $y = \pm 1$.

If $y = 0$, then $f_1' = 0$ for $x = 0$. Thus we get three critical points that are classified in the following table:

(x, y)	A	B	C	$AC - B^2$	Type of critical point
$(0, 0)$	2	0	4	8	Local minimum point
$(-1, 1)$	2	4	0	-16	Saddle point
$(-1, -1)$	2	-4	0	-16	Saddle point

3. (a) $(0, 0)$ is a saddle point and $(-a, -2)$ is a local minimum point.   (b) $df^*(a)/da = -2ae^{-2}$

4. In all three cases $(0, 0)$ is a critical point where $z = 0$ and $A = B = C = 0$, so $AC - B^2 = 0$.

In case (a), $z \leq 0$ for all (x, y), so the origin is a maximum point.

In case (b), $z \geq 0$ for all (x, y), so the origin is a minimum point.

In case (c), z takes both positive and negative values at points arbitrarily close to $(0, 0)$, so it is a saddle point.

5. (a) f is defined for all (x, y) satisfying $1 + x^2 y > 0$, or equivalently $x^2 y > -1$. So it is defined for all (x, y) satisfying either (i) $x = 0$, or (ii) $x \neq 0$ and $y > -1/x^2$.

(b) $f_1'(x, y) = 2xy/(1 + x^2 y)$ and $f_2'(x, y) = x^2/(1 + x^2 y)$. Here $f_1' = f_2' = 0$ at $(0, b)$ for all $b \in \mathbb{R}$.

(c) Because $AC - B^2 = 0$ when $(x, y) = (0, b)$, the second-derivative test fails.

(d) Note that $f(0, b) = 0$ at any critical point $(0, b)$. By considering the sign of $f(x, y) = \ln(1 + x^2 y)$ in the neighbourhood of any critical point, one sees that f has: a local maximum point if $b < 0$; a saddle point if $b = 0$; and a local minimum point if $b > 0$. See Fig. A17.3.5.

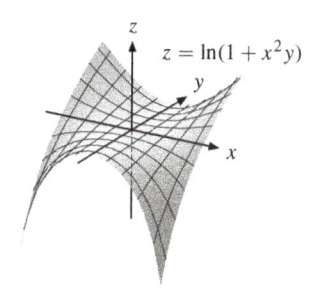

Figure A17.3.5

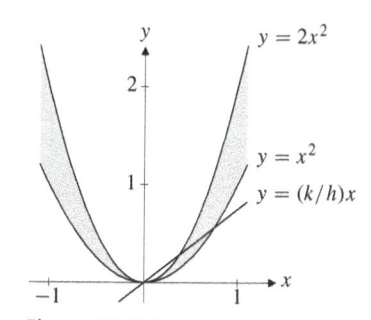

Figure A17.3.6

6. (a) $f(x, y) = 0$ along each of the two parabolas $y = x^2$ and $y = 2x^2$.

(b) See Fig. A17.3.6. The domain $\{(x, y) \in \mathbb{R}^2 : x^2 < y < 2x^2\}$ where $f(x, y)$ is negative is shaded.

(c) $f_1'(x, y) = 8x^3 - 6xy$ and $f_2'(x, y) = 2y - 3x^2$. So the origin is the only critical point, where $f(0, 0) = 0$. As the figure shows, $f(x, y)$ takes positive and negative values for points arbitrary close to $(0, 0)$, so it is a saddle point.

(d) $g(t) = f(th, tk) = (tk - t^2 h^2)(tk - 2t^2 h^2) = 2h^4 t^4 - 3h^2 k t^3 + k^2 t^2$, implying that $g'(t) = 8h^4 t^3 - 9h^2 k t^2 + 2k^2 t$ and $g''(t) = 24h^4 t^2 - 18h^2 k t + 2k^2$. So $g'(0) = 0$ and $g''(0) = 2k^2$. For $k \neq 0$, therefore, the point $t = 0$ is a strict local minimum. It is also when $k = 0$ and so $g(t) = 2t^4 h^4$.

17.4

1. (a) $\pi = P_1 Q_1 + P_2 Q_2 - C(Q_1, Q_2) = -2Q_1^2 - 4Q_2^2 + 180Q_1 + 160Q_2$, which has a maximum at $Q_1^* = 45$, $Q_2^* = 20$, with $P_1^* = 110$, $P_2^* = 100$, and $\pi^* = 5650$.

(b) Let $P = P_1 = P_2$. Then $Q_1 = 100 - \frac{1}{2}P$, $Q_2 = 45 - \frac{1}{4}P$, so profit as a function of P is $\hat{\pi} = (P-20)(Q_1 + Q_2) = (P-20)(145 - \frac{3}{4}P) = -\frac{3}{4}P^2 + 160P - 2900$, which is maximized when $P = 320/3$. The corresponding profit is $16\,900/3$. The loss of profit is $5650 - 16\,900/3 = 50/3$.

(c) The new profit is $\tilde{\pi} = -2Q_1^2 - 4Q_2^2 + 175Q_1 + 160Q_2$, with a maximum at $Q_1 = 43.75$, $Q_2 = 20$, with prices $P_1 = 112.50$ and $P_2 = 100$. The maximized profit is 5428.125. The number of units sold in market 1 goes down, the price goes up and profits are lower. In market 2 the number of units sold and the price are unchanged.

2. (a) $\pi = -bp^2 - dq^2 + (a + \beta b)p + (c + \beta d)q - \alpha - \beta(a + c)$, $p^* = (a + \beta b)/2b$, $q^* = (c + \beta d)/2d$.

The second-order conditions are obviously satisfied because $\pi''_{11} = -2b$, $\pi''_{12} = 0$, and $\pi''_{22} = -2d$.

(b) $\hat{p} = (a + c + \beta(b + d))/2(b + d)$.   (c) The loss of profit is $(ad - bc)^2/4bd(b + d)$. See SM for details.

3. As in part (c) of Example 17.4.2, imposing a tax of t per unit sold in market area 1 implies that the new profit function is $\hat{\pi}(Q_1, Q_2) = \pi(Q_1, Q_2) - tQ_1$. The optimal choice of production in market area 1 is then $\hat{Q}_1 = (a_1 - \alpha - t)/2b_1$, and the tax revenue is $T(t) = t(a_1 - \alpha - t)/2b_1 = [t(a_1 - \alpha) - t^2]/2b_1$. This quadratic function has a maximum when $T'(t) = 0$, so $t = \frac{1}{2}(a_1 - \alpha)$.

4. (a) $\hat{a} = 0.105$ and $\hat{b} = 11.29$.   (b) $\hat{c} = 0.23$ and $\hat{d} = 5.575$.   (c) Late in the year 1978. See SM for details.

5. (a) $p = 9$, $q = 8$, $x = 16$, $y = 4$. Firm A's profit is 123, whereas B's is 21.

(b) Firm A's profit is maximized at $p = p_A(q) = \frac{1}{5}(2q + 17)$. Firm B's profit is maximized at $q = q_B(p) = \frac{1}{3}(p + 7)$.

(c) Equilibrium occurs where the two equations of part (b) hold, which is at $p = 5$, $q = 4$, $x = 20$, $y = 12$. Firm A gets 75, B gets 21.   (d) The two prices p and q change in alternate periods, and (p, q) converges to the equilibrium. See SM for a diagram and further details.

17.5

1. (a) $f'_1(x, y) = 4 - 4x$ and $f'_2(x, y) = -4y$. The only critical point is $(1, 0)$, with $f(1, 0) = 2$.

(b) $f(x, y)$ has a maximum value of 2 at $(1, 0)$ and a minimum value of -70 at $(-5, 0)$. (A maximum and a minimum exist, by the extreme value theorem. Along the circular boundary, the function value is $4x - 50$, with $x \in [-5, 5]$. So its maximum along the boundary is -30 at $x = 5$ and its minimum is -70 at $x = -5$.)

2. (a) Maximum 91 at $(0, 4)$ and at $(4, 0)$. Minimum 0 at $(3, 3)$. See SM for details.

(b) Maximum $9/4$ at $(-1/2, \sqrt{3}/2)$ and at $(-1/2, -\sqrt{3}/2)$. Minimum $-1/4$ at $(1/2, 0)$. See SM for details.

3. See Fig. A17.5.3. There are no critical points in the interior. The maximum value of f is $27/8$ at $(3/4, 0)$. See SM for details.

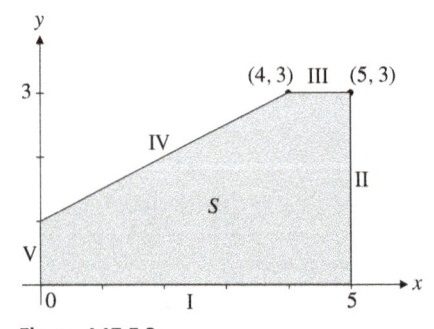

Figure A17.5.3

4. (a) The first-order conditions $2axy + by + 2y^2 = 0$ and $ax^2 + bx + 4xy = 0$ must have $(x, y) = (2/3, 1/3)$ as a solution.

So $a = 1$ and $b = -2$. Also $c = 1/27$, so that $f(2/3, 1/3) = -1/9$. Because $A = f''_{11}(2/3, 1/3) = 2/3$, $B = f''_{12}(2/3, 1/3) = 2/3$, and $C = f''_{22}(2/3, 1/3) = 8/3$, Theorem 13.3.1 shows that this is a local minimum.

(b) Maximum 193/27 at $(2/3, 8/3)$. Minimum $-1/9$ at $(2/3, 1/3)$.

5. (a) $(1, 2)$ is a local minimum; $(0, 0)$ and $(0, 4)$ are saddle points.

(b) Note that $f(x, 1) = -3xe^{-x} \to \infty$ as $x \to -\infty$, and $f(-1, y) = -e(y^2 - 4y) \to -\infty$ as $y \to \infty$.

(c) f has a minimum value of $-4/e$ at $(1, 2)$, and a maximum value of 0 at all $(x, 0)$ and $(x, 4)$ satisfying $x \in [0, 5]$, as well as at all $(0, y)$ satisfying $y \in [0, 4]$. (d) $y' = 0$ when $x = 1$ and $y = 4 - e$.

6. (a) Closed and bounded, so compact. (b) Open and unbounded. (c) Closed and bounded, so compact.

(d) Closed and unbounded. (e) Closed and unbounded. (f) Open and unbounded.

7. Let $g(x) = 1$ in $(-\infty, 1)$, and $g(x) = 2$ in $[1, \infty)$. Then g is discontinuous at $x = 1$, and the set $\{x : g(x) \leq 1\} = (-\infty, 1)$ is not closed. (It is instructive to draw the graph of g, which has a "step" at $x = 1$.)

17.6

1. (a) The three first-order conditions $f'_x(x, y, z) = 2 - 2x = 0$, $f'_y(x, y, z) = 10 - 2y = 0$, and $f'_z(x, y, z) = -2z = 0$ have a unique solution $(x, y, z) = (1, 5, 0)$, which must then be the maximum point.

(b) The three first-order conditions are $f'_x(x, y, z) = -2x - 2y - 2z = 0$, $f'_y(x, y, z) = -4y - 2x = 0$, and $f'_z(x, y, z) = -6z - 2x = 0$. From the last two equations we get $y = -\frac{1}{2}x$ and $z = -\frac{1}{3}x$. Inserting these values into the first equation gives $-2x + x + \frac{2}{3}x = 0$, so $x = 0$, implying that $y = z = 0$. So $(x, y, z) = (0, 0, 0)$ is the maximum point.

2. (a) $f(x) = e^{-x^2}$ and $g(x) = F(f(x)) = \ln(e^{-x^2}) = -x^2$ both have a unique maximum at $x = 0$.

(b) Only $x = 0$ maximizes $f(x)$. But $g(x) = 5$ is maximized at every point x because it is a constant.

3. By the chain rule, $g'_i(\mathbf{x}) = F'(f(\mathbf{x}))f'_i(\mathbf{x})$ for $i = 1, 2, \ldots, n$. Because $F' \neq 0$ everywhere, the assertion follows.

4. $f'_x = -6x^2 + 30x - 36$, $f'_y = 2 - e^{y^2}$, $f'_z = -3 + e^{z^2}$. There are 8 critical points given by $(x, y, z) = (3, \pm\sqrt{\ln 2}, \pm\sqrt{\ln 3})$, and $(x, y, z) = (2, \pm\sqrt{\ln 2}, \pm\sqrt{\ln 3})$, where all possible sign combinations are allowed.

5. (a) $F(u) = \frac{1}{2}(e^u - e^{-u})$ is strictly increasing, so the problem is equivalent to: max $x^2 + y^2 - 2x$ subject to $(x, y) \in S$.

(b) $\ln u$ is strictly increasing for $u > 0$. So the problem is equivalent to: max $\ln A + a_1 \ln x_1 + \cdots + a_n \ln x_n$ subject to $x_1 + \cdots + x_n = 1$.

17.7

1. (a) The profit is $\pi = px - ax - bx^2 - tx$, which has a maximum at $x^* = (p - a - t)/2b$, with $\pi^* = (p - a - t)^2/4b$.

(b) $\partial \pi^*/\partial p = 2(p - a - t)/4b = x^*$. If we increase p by dp dollars, where $|dp|$ is small, then the approximate increase in optimal profit is $x^* dp$ dollars. (For each of the x^* units sold the revenue increases by dp dollars.)

2. (a) The profit function is $\pi = \pi(L, P, w) = P\sqrt{L} - wL$. The value of L that maximizes profit must satisfy $\pi'_L(L, P, w) = P/2\sqrt{L} - w = 0$, which yields $L = (aP/w)^2$. Now $\pi''_{LL} = -P/4L^{3/2} < 0$ for all L. Hence profit is maximized at $L = L^*(P, w) = (P/2w)^2$.

(b) The value function is $\pi^*(P, w) = \pi(L^*, P, w) = P\sqrt{L^*} - wL^* = P(P/2w) - w(P/2w)^2 = P^2/4w$. It follows that $\partial \pi^*/\partial P = P/2w = \sqrt{L^*} = \pi'_P(L^*, P, w, a)$, and also that $\partial \pi^*/\partial w = -P^2/4w^2 = -L^* = \pi'_w(L^*, P, w)$. Thus, the envelope theorem is confirmed for this example.

3. (a) $\pi = p(K^{2/3} + L^{1/2} + T^{1/3}) - rK - wL - q$, and $K^* = \dfrac{8}{27}p^3 r^{-3}$, $L^* = \dfrac{1}{4}p^2 w^{-2}$, $T^* = \dfrac{1}{3\sqrt{3}}p^{3/2}q^{-3/2}$

(b) $Q^* = \dfrac{4}{9}p^2 r^{-2} + \dfrac{1}{2}pw^{-1} + \dfrac{1}{\sqrt{3}}p^{1/2}q^{-1/2}$, so $\dfrac{\partial Q^*}{\partial r} = -\dfrac{8}{9}p^2 r^{-3} = -\dfrac{\partial K^*}{\partial p}$.

4. $\partial Q^*/\partial r = (\partial/\partial r)(\partial \hat{\pi}^*/\partial p) = (\partial/\partial p)(\partial \hat{\pi}^*/\partial r) = (\partial/\partial p)(-K^*) = -\partial K^*/\partial p$.

The other equalities are proved in a similar way.

5. (a) This is a routine application of the rules for differentials in formulas (15.9.4) and (15.9.5).

(b) Suppressing the notation used to indicate that the partials are all evaluated at (K^*, L^*), we get

$$\dfrac{\partial K^*}{\partial p} = \dfrac{-F'_K F''_{LL} + F'_L F''_{KL}}{p[F''_{KK} F''_{LL} - (F''_{KL})^2]} \qquad \dfrac{\partial K^*}{\partial r} = \dfrac{F''_{LL}}{p[F''_{KK} F''_{LL} - (F''_{KL})^2]} \qquad \dfrac{\partial K^*}{\partial w} = \dfrac{-F''_{KL}}{p[F''_{KK} F''_{LL} - (F''_{KL})^2]}$$

$$\dfrac{\partial L^*}{\partial p} = \dfrac{-F'_L F''_{KK} + F'_K F''_{LK}}{p[F''_{KK} F''_{LL} - (F''_{KL})^2]} \qquad \dfrac{\partial L^*}{\partial r} = \dfrac{-F''_{LK}}{p[F''_{KK} F''_{LL} - (F''_{KL})^2]} \qquad \dfrac{\partial L^*}{\partial w} = \dfrac{F''_{KK}}{p[F''_{KK} F''_{LL} - (F''_{KL})^2]}$$

The second-order conditions that are sufficient for a strict local maximum imply that $F''_{KK} < 0$, $F''_{LL} < 0$, and $F''_{KK} F''_{LL} - (F''_{KL})^2 > 0$. It follows that $\partial K^*/\partial r$ and $\partial L^*/\partial w$ are both negative. Lacking information about the sign of F''_{KL}, the signs of the other partials remain undetermined. Because $F''_{KL} = F''_{LK}$, we observe that $\partial K^*/\partial w = \partial L^*/\partial r$.

6. (a) The first-order conditions are: (i) $R'_1 - C'_1 + s = 0$; (ii) $R'_2 - C'_2 - t = 0$.

(b) $\pi''_{11} = R''_{11} - C''_{11} < 0$ and $D = \pi''_{11} \pi''_{22} - (\pi''_{12})^2 = (R''_{11} - C''_{11})(R''_{22} - C''_{22}) - (R''_{12} - C''_{12})^2 > 0$.

(c) As in Exercise 5, take the total differential of the first-order conditions for a maximum. From the signs found in part (b), one can then show that $\partial x_1^*/\partial \sigma$ and $\partial x_1^*/\partial \tau$ are positive, whereas $\partial x_2^*/\partial \sigma$ and $\partial x_2^*/\partial \tau$ are negative. See SM for details. (d) Because $R''_{12} = R''_{21}$ and $C''_{12} = C''_{21}$, this follows from the answers to (c).

Review exercises for Chapter 17

1. The first-order conditions $f'_1(x, y) = -4x + 2y + 18 = 0$ and $f'_2(x, y) = 2x - 2y - 14 = 0$ hold at $(x, y) = (2, -5)$. Moreover $f''_{11} = -4$, $f''_{12} = 2$, and $f''_{22} = -2$, so $f''_{11} f''_{22} - (f''_{12})^2 = 4$. So the conditions in part (a) of Theorem 13.2.1 are satisfied.

2. (a) Looking ahead to part (b) of the exercise, we keep P_1 as a variable, and write profit as $\pi = P_1 Q_1 + 90 Q_2 - 0.1(Q_1^2 + Q_1 Q_2 + Q_2^2)$. When $P_1 = 120$, first-order conditions for a maximum give $(Q_1, Q_2) = (500, 200)$. See SM for details. (b) In order for the first-order conditions derived in part (a) to have a solution with $Q_1 = 400$, one needs $P_1 = 105$. See SM for details.

3. (a) Critical points occur where $P'_1(x, y) = -0.2x - 0.2y + 47 = 0$ and $P'_2(x, y) = -0.2x - 0.4y + 48 = 0$. These imply that $x = 230$ and $y = 5$, where $P''_{11} = -0.2 \leq 0$, $P''_{12} = -0.2$, and $P''_{22} = -0.4 \leq 0$. Since $P''_{11} P''_{22} - (P''_{12})^2 = 0.04 \geq 0$, the pair $(230, 5)$ maximizes profit.

(b) With total production $x + y = 200$, and so $y = 200 - x$, the modified profit function is $\hat{\pi}(x) = f(x, 200 - x) = -0.1x^2 + 39x + 1000$. This function is easily seen to have a maximum at $x = 195$, where $y = 200 - 195 = 5$.

4. (a) The critical points are at $(0, 0)$ and $(3, 9/2)$. (b) $(0, 0)$, $(\tfrac{1}{2}\sqrt{2}, \sqrt{2})$, $(-\tfrac{1}{2}\sqrt{2}, -\sqrt{2})$

(c) $(0, 0)$, $(0, 4)$, $(2, 2)$, and $(-2, 2)$. See SM for details.

5. Critical points are where $f'_x(x, y, a) = 2ax - 2 = 0$ and $f'_y(x, y, a) = 2y - 4a = 0$. These imply that $x = x^*(a) = 1/a$ and $y = y^*(a) = 2a$. The value function is $f^*(a) = a(1/a)^2 - 2(1/a) + (2a)^2 - 4a(2a) = -(1/a) - 4a^2$. Thus $(d/da)f^*(a) = (1/a^2) - 8a$. On the other hand $(\partial/\partial a)f(x, y, a) = x^2 - 4y = (1/a^2) - 8a$ at $(x^*(a), y^*(a)) = (1/a, 2a)$. This verifies the envelope theorem.

6. (a) Profit is $\pi(K, L, T) = p(K^a + L^b + T^c) - rK - wL - qT$, which is concave when K, L and T are all nonnegative. So profits are maximized at its critical point, which occurs when $K^* = (ap/r)^{1/(1-a)}$, $L^* = (bp/w)^{1/(1-b)}$, and $T^* = (cp/q)^{1/(1-c)}$.

(b) Focus on the terms that depend on r to show that $\partial \pi^*/\partial r = -(ap/r)^{1/(1-a)}$. For details see SM.

(c) From part (b) one has $\partial \pi^*/\partial r = -K^*$. A similar technique to part (b) can be used to verify the other three equations of the envelope theorem, which are $\partial \pi^*/\partial p = Q^*$, $\partial \pi^*/\partial w = -L^*$, and $\partial \pi^*/\partial q = -T^*$.

7. (a) $f_1' = e^{x+y} + e^{x-y} - \frac{3}{2}, f_2' = e^{x+y} - e^{x-y} - \frac{1}{2}, f_{11}'' = e^{x+y} + e^{x-y}, f_{12}'' = e^{x+y} - e^{x-y}, f_{22}'' = e^{x+y} + e^{x-y}$.

It follows that $f_{11}'' \geq 0, f_{22}'' \geq 0$, and $f_{11}'' f_{22}'' - (f_{12}'')^2 = (e^{x+y} + e^{x-y})^2 - (e^{x+y} - e^{x-y})^2 = 4e^{x+y}e^{x-y} = 4e^{2x} \geq 0$.

So f is convex.

(b) At any critical point, one has $e^{x+y} = 1$ and $e^{x-y} = \frac{1}{2}$, so $x + y = 0$ and $x - y = -\ln 2$. The only critical point is therefore $(x, y) = (-\frac{1}{2}\ln 2, \frac{1}{2}\ln 2)$, where $f(x, y) = \frac{1}{2}(3 + \ln 2)$. Because f is convex, this is the minimum.

8. (a) The two critical points are $(0, 0)$, which is a saddle point, and $(5/6, -5/12)$, which is a local maximum point.

(b) $f_{11}'' = 2 - 6x \leq 0 \iff x \geq 1/3$, while $f_{22}'' = -2 \leq 0$, and $f_{11}'' f_{22}'' - (f_{12}'')^2 = 12x - 5 \geq 0 \iff x \geq 5/12$. We conclude that f is concave in $S = \{(x, y) : x \geq 5/12\}$. The largest value of f in S occurs at $(5/6, -5/12)$, where the value is $125/432$. See SM for details.

9. (a) $f_1'(x, y) = x - 1 + ay, f_2'(x, y) = a(x - 1) - y^2 + 2a^2 y$, which are both 0 at $(x, y) = (1 - a^3, a^2)$.

(b) At the critical point one has $f^*(a) = -\frac{1}{2} + \frac{1}{6}a^6$, with derivative a^5. The partial derivative of f w.r.t. a is $y(x - 1) + 2ay^2$, which equals a^5 at the critical point $(x, y) = (1 - a^3, a^2)$. See SM for details.

(c) Calculating the second-order partial derivatives of f shows that it is convex where $y \leq \frac{1}{2}a^2$. See SM for details.

10. (a) $p = C_x'(x^*, y^*)$ and $q = C_y'(x^*, y^*)$, which state that the price of each good should equal its marginal cost.

(b) With simplified notation, at the optimum one has $\hat{\pi}_x' = F + xF_x' + yG_x' - C_x' = 0$ and $\hat{\pi}_y' = xF_y' + G + yG_y' - C_y' = 0$. The interpretation is that marginal revenue = marginal cost, as usual, with the twist that a change in output of either good affects marginal revenue in the other market as well.

(c) The profit function is $\pi = x(a - bx - cy) + y(\alpha - \beta x - \gamma y) - Px - Qy - R$, so the first-order conditions are $\partial \pi/\partial x = a - 2bx - cy - \beta y - P = 0$, and $\partial \pi/\partial y = -cx + \alpha - \beta x - 2\gamma y - Q = 0$.

(d) $\partial^2 \pi/\partial x^2 = -2b, \partial^2 \pi/\partial y^2 = -2\gamma, \partial^2 \pi/\partial x \partial y = -(\beta + c)$. The direct partials of order 2 are negative and the cross partials satisfy $\Delta = (\partial^2 \pi/\partial x^2)(\partial^2 \pi/\partial y^2) - (\partial^2 \pi/\partial x \partial y)^2 = 4\gamma b - (\beta + c)^2$, so the conclusion follows.

Chapter 18

18.1

1. (a) $\mathcal{L}(x, y) = xy - \lambda(x + 3y - 24)$. The first-order conditions $\mathcal{L}_1' = y - \lambda = 0, \mathcal{L}_2' = x - 3\lambda = 0$ imply that $x = 3y$. Inserted into the constraint, this yields $3y + 3y = 24$, so $y = 4$, and then $x = 12$.

(b) By ($**$) in Example 18.1.3 with $a = b = p = 1, q = 3, m = 24$, we have $x = \frac{1}{2}(24/1) = 12, y = \frac{1}{2}(24/3) = 4$.

2. With $\mathcal{L} = -40Q_1 + Q_1^2 - 2Q_1 Q_2 - 20Q_2 + Q_2^2 - \lambda(Q_1 + Q_2 - 15)$,

the first-order conditions are $\mathcal{L}_1' = -40 + 2Q_1 - 2Q_2 - \lambda = 0$ and $\mathcal{L}_2' = -2Q_1 - 20 + 2Q_2 - \lambda = 0$.

It follows that $-40 + 2Q_1 - 2Q_2 = -2Q_1 - 20 + 2Q_2$, and so $Q_1 - Q_2 = 5$.

This equation and the constraint together give the solution $Q_1 = 10, Q_2 = 5$, with $\lambda = -30$.

3. (a) By ($**$) in Example 18.1.3, one has $x = \frac{3}{10}m$ and $y = \frac{1}{10}m$. (b) $x = 10, y = 6\,250\,000$ (c) $x = 8/3, y = 1$

4. (a) With $\mathcal{L}(x,y) = x^2 + y^2 - \lambda(x+2y-4)$, the first-order conditions $\mathcal{L}'_1 = 2x - \lambda = 0$, $\mathcal{L}'_2 = 2y - 2\lambda = 0$ imply that $2x = y$. Inserting this into the constraint leads to the solution $(x,y) = (4/5, 8/5)$ with $\lambda = 8/5$.

(b) $(x,y) = (8,4)$ with $\lambda = 16$. See SM.   (c) $(x,y) = (50,50)$ with $\lambda = 250$. See SM.

5. The budget constraint is $2x + 4y = 1000$, so with $\mathcal{L}(x,y) = 100xy + x + 2y - \lambda(2x+4y-1000)$, the first-order conditions are $\mathcal{L}'_1 = 100y + 1 - 2\lambda = 0$ and $\mathcal{L}'_2 = 100x + 2 - 4\lambda = 0$. Eliminating λ from these equations gives $x = 2y$. Inserting this into the constraint gives $2x + 2x = 1000$. So the solution is $x = 250$ and $y = 125$.

6. Formula (**) in Example 18.1.3 with x, y, p, q, m replaced by $m, l, 1/w, 1, T_0$ respectively yields $m = awT_0/(a+b)$ and $l = bT_0/(a+b)$.

7. The problem is max $-0.1x^2 - 0.2xy - 0.2y^2 + 47x + 48y - 600$ subject to $x + y = 200$.

With $\mathcal{L}(x,y) = -0.1x^2 - 0.2xy - 0.2y^2 + 47x + 48y - 600 - \lambda(x+y-200)$,

the first-order conditions are $\mathcal{L}'_1 = -0.2x - 0.2y + 47 - \lambda = 0$ and $\mathcal{L}'_2 = -0.2x - 0.4y + 48 - \lambda = 0$.

Eliminating x and λ yields $y = 5$, and then the budget constraint gives $x = 195$, with $\lambda = 7$.

8. (a) $P(x,y) = (96 - 4x)x + (84 - 2y)y - 2x^2 - 2xy - y^2 = -6x^2 - 3y^2 - 2xy + 96x + 84y$

(b) $P'_x(x,y) = -12x - 2y + 96$, $P'_y(x,y) = -6y - 2x + 84$. The only critical point is $(x,y) = (6,12)$.

(c) The Lagrangian is $\mathcal{L}(x,y) = -6x^2 - 3y^2 - 2xy + 96x + 84y - \lambda(x+y-11)$. The first-order conditions are $\mathcal{L}'_1 = -12x - 2y + 96 - \lambda = 0$, $\mathcal{L}'_2 = -6y - 2x + 84 - \lambda = 0$. Eliminating λ yields $10x - 4y = 12$. The constraint is $x + y = 11$. Solving these two equations simultaneously gives $x = 4$, $y = 7$. Since $P(4,7) = 673 < P(6,12) = 792$, the limit on total output reduces profit by 119.

9. (a) $x^*(p,m) = a^\gamma p^{-\gamma}$ where $\gamma = 1/(1-a)$, and $y^*(p,m) = m - a^\gamma p^{1-\gamma}$.

(b) $\partial x^*/\partial p = -x^*/(1-a)p < 0$, $\partial x^*/\partial m = 0$, $\partial y^*/\partial p = ax^*/(1-a) > 0$, $\partial y^*/\partial m = 1$.

(c) $\text{El}_p\, px^*(p,m) = -a/(1-a) < 0$. See SM.   (d) $U^*(p,m) = m + 1/4p$. See SM for details.

10. (a) $x(p,q,m) = [m + q\ln(q/p)]/(p+q)$ and $y(p,q,m) = [m + p\ln(p/q)]/(p+q)$.

(b) Both are nonnegative if and only if: either (i) $p \geq q$ and $m \geq q\ln(p/q)$; or (ii) $p \leq q$ and $m \geq p\ln(q/p)$.

(c) Direct verification.

18.2

1. According to (**) in Example 18.1.3, the solution is $x^* = 3m/8$, $y^* = m/12$, with $\lambda = 9m^3/512$.

The value function is $f^*(m) = (x^*)^3 y^* = 9m^4/2048$, so we see that $df^*(m)/dm = 9m^3/512 = \lambda$.

2. (a) With $\mathcal{L} = rK + wL - \lambda(\sqrt{K} + L - Q)$, the first-order conditions are $\mathcal{L}'_K = r - \lambda/2\sqrt{K^*} = 0$ and $\mathcal{L}'_L = w - \lambda = 0$. Inserting λ from the last equation into the first yields $\sqrt{K^*} = w/2r$. Then $K^* = w^2/4r^2$ and from the constraint $L^* = Q - w/2r$.   (b) The value function is $C^*(Q) = rK^* + wL^* = wQ - w^2/4r$, and so $dC^*(Q)/dQ = w = \lambda$.

3. (a) $x + 2y = a$ yields $y = \frac{1}{2}a - \frac{1}{2}x$, and then $x^2 + y^2 = x^2 + (\frac{1}{2}a - \frac{1}{2}x)^2 = \frac{5}{4}x^2 - \frac{1}{2}ax + \frac{1}{4}a^2$.

This quadratic function has a minimum at $x = a/5$, and then $y = 2a/5$.

(b) $\mathcal{L}(x,y) = x^2 + y^2 - \lambda(x + 2y - a)$. The necessary conditions are $\mathcal{L}'_1 = 2x - \lambda = 0$, $\mathcal{L}'_2 = 2y - 2\lambda = 0$, implying that $2x = y$. From the constraint one has $x = a/5$, and then $y = 2a/5$, with $\lambda = 2a/5$.

(c) See Fig. A18.2.3. The problem is to find the point on the straight line $x + 2y = a$ that is nearest to the origin. No point on the line is furthest from the origin, so the corresponding maximization problem has no solution.

CHAPTER 18 **929**

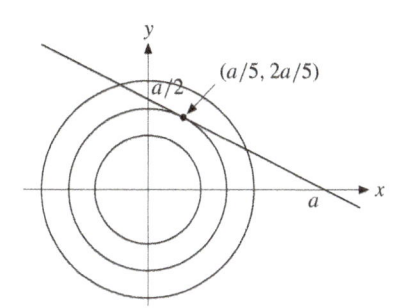

Figure A18.2.3

4. (a) $x^* = 4$, $y^* = 24$, $\lambda = 1/4$. (b) $\hat{y} = 97/4$, $\hat{x} = 4$. The increase is $\Delta U = 105/4 - 104/4 = 1/4$. This equals the value of the Lagrange multiplier in part (a). (The exact equality is because U is linear in one of the variables.)

(c) $x^* = q^2/4p^2$, $y^* = m/q - q/4p$. (Note that $y^* > 0$ if and only if $m > q^2/4p$.)

5. (a) First-order conditions: (i) $\alpha/(x^* - a) = \lambda p$; (ii) $\beta/(y^* - b) = \lambda q$. Hence $px^* = pa + \alpha/\lambda$ and $qy^* = qb + \beta/\lambda$. Use the budget constraint to eliminate λ. The expressions for px^* and qy^* follow.

(b) $U^* = \alpha[\ln\alpha + \ln(m - (ap + bq)) - \ln p] + \beta[\ln\beta + \ln(m - (ap + bq)) - \ln q]$. The results follow.

6. $f(x, T) = -\frac{1}{6}\alpha x T^5 + \frac{1}{12}xT^4 + \frac{1}{6}xT^3$, $g(x, T) = \frac{1}{6}xT^3$. The solution of (∗) is $x = 384\alpha^3 M$, $T = 1/4\alpha$, and $f^*(M) = M + M/16\alpha$, with $\lambda = 1 + 1/16\alpha$. Clearly, $\partial f^*(M)/\partial M = \lambda$, which confirms Eq. (18.2.2).

18.3

1. (a) $(2, 2)$ and $(-2, -2)$ are the only possible solutions of the maximization problem,

whereas $(-2, 2)$ and $(2, -2)$ are the only possible solutions of the minimization problem. See SM for details.

(b) $(3, -1)$ solves the maximization problem, whereas $(-3, 1)$ solves the minimization problem. See SM.

2. (a) Maximum at $(x, y, \lambda) = (-4, 0, 5/4)$, minimum at $(x, y, \lambda) = (4/3, \pm 4\sqrt{2}/3, 1/4)$. See SM for details.

(b) Minimum points: $(\sqrt[4]{2}, 1 - \frac{1}{2}\sqrt{2})$ and $(-\sqrt[4]{2}, 1 - \frac{1}{2}\sqrt{2})$. See SM for details.

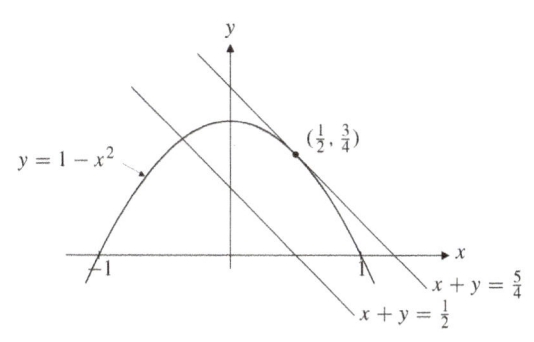

Figure A18.3.3

3. (a) $\mathcal{L} = x + y - \lambda(x^2 + y - 1)$. The equations $\mathcal{L}'_1 = 1 - 2\lambda x = 0$, $\mathcal{L}'_2 = 1 - \lambda = 0$, and $x^2 + y = 1$ have the solution $x = \frac{1}{2}$, $y = \frac{3}{4}$, with $\lambda = 1$.

(b) See Fig. A18.3.3, which shows the maximum at $(x, y) = (\frac{1}{2}, \frac{3}{4})$. The minimization problem has no solution because $f(x, 1 - x^2) = x + 1 - x^2 \to -\infty$ as $x \to \infty$.

(c) The solution to the revised problem is $x = 0.5$ and $y = 0.85$. The change in the value function is $f^*(1.1) - f^*(1) = (0.5 + 0.85) - (0.5 + 0.75) = 0.1$. Because $\lambda = 1$, one has $\lambda \cdot dc = 1 \cdot 0.1 = 0.1$. So, in this case, Eq. (18.2.3) is satisfied with equality. (This is because of the special form of the functions f and g.)

4. (a) $x = 6$, $y = 2$ (b) The approximate change is 1. See SM for details.

5. (a) $Q = \mathbf{x}'\mathbf{A}\mathbf{x}$ where $\mathbf{x}'$ is the row vector (x_1, x_2) and $\mathbf{A}$ is the matrix $\begin{pmatrix} 2 & 7 \\ 7 & 2 \end{pmatrix}$.

(b) With $\mathcal{L} = 2x_1^2 + 14x_1x_2 + 2x_2^2 - \lambda(x_1^2 + x_2^2 - 1)$, the first-order conditions are $\mathcal{L}'_1 = 4x_1 + 14x_2 - 2\lambda x_1 = 0$ and $\mathcal{L}'_2 = 14x_1 + 4x_2 - 2\lambda x_2 = 0$. Dividing each equation by 2, we see that these two equations can be written as $\mathbf{A}\mathbf{x} = \lambda \mathbf{x}$. So any nonzero vector satisfying the first-order conditions is an eigenvector for $\mathbf{A}$, and the Lagrange multiplier is the associated eigenvalue.

(c) Because $Q(\mathbf{x}) = \mathbf{x}'\mathbf{A}\mathbf{x}$ is a continuous function, it achieves both a maximum and minimum over the unit circle $\mathbf{x}'\mathbf{x} = x_1^2 + x_2^2 = 1$, which is a closed and bounded set. So both a maximum point $\mathbf{x}^+$ and a minimum point $\mathbf{x}^-$ must satisfy $\mathbf{x}'\mathbf{x} = 1$ as well as the first-order condition $\mathbf{A}\mathbf{x} = \lambda\mathbf{x}$, which implies that $\mathbf{x}'\mathbf{A}\mathbf{x} = \lambda$. It follows that the larger eigenvalue is the maximum, and the smaller eigenvalue is the minimum.

(d) The characteristic equation is $0 = \begin{vmatrix} 2-\lambda & 7 \\ 7 & 2-\lambda \end{vmatrix} = (2-\lambda)^2 - 49 = \lambda^2 - 4\lambda - 45 = (\lambda - 2)^2 - 49$. Its roots are the two eigenvalues $\lambda^+ = 9$ and $\lambda^- = -5$. Associated with these are the respective eigenvectors $\mathbf{x}^+$ and $\mathbf{x}^-$ that satisfy $\begin{pmatrix} -7 & 7 \\ 7 & -7 \end{pmatrix} \mathbf{x}^+ = 0$ and $\begin{pmatrix} 7 & 7 \\ 7 & 7 \end{pmatrix} \mathbf{x}^- = 0$. Normalizing them to satisfy $\mathbf{x}'\mathbf{x} = 1$, they are the orthogonal vectors $\mathbf{x}^+ = \pm\frac{1}{2}\sqrt{2}\,(1, 1)'$ and $\mathbf{x}^- = \pm\frac{1}{2}\sqrt{2}\,(1, -1)'$, respectively. The vectors $\pm\frac{1}{2}\sqrt{2}\,(1, 1)'$ are the two constrained maximum points of Q, whereas $\pm\frac{1}{2}\sqrt{2}\,(1, -1)'$ are the two constrained minimum points. See SM for details.

18.4

1. Setting $y = 2 - x$ reduces the problem to that of maximizing $x(2 - x) = 2x - x^2$, which has the solution $x = 1$, and so the optimal value of y becomes $2 - x = 1$. Using the Lagrange method, with the Lagrangian $\mathcal{L}(x, y) = xy - \lambda(x + y - 2)$, the first-order conditions for the constrained problem are $y - \lambda = 0$, $x - \lambda = 0$, with the unique solution $x = y = \lambda = 1$ satisfying the constraint $x + y = 2$. Then, when $\lambda = 1$, one has $\mathcal{L}(2, 2) = 2 > \mathcal{L}(1, 1) = 1$, so $(1, 1)$ is not a maximum point for $\mathcal{L}$. (In fact, $\mathcal{L}(x, y)$ has a saddle point at $(1, 1)$.)

2. The problem with systems of three equations and two unknowns is not that they are merely difficult to solve but that they are usually inconsistent, meaning that it is *impossible* to solve them. The equations $f'_x(x, y) = f'_y(x, y) = 0$ are *not* valid at the optimal point.

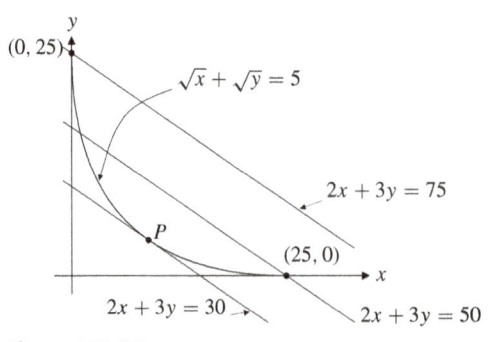

Figure A18.4.3

3. (a) With $\mathcal{L} = 2x + 3y - \lambda(\sqrt{x} + \sqrt{y} - 5)$, the equations $\mathcal{L}'_1(x, y) = 2 - \lambda/2\sqrt{x} = 0$ and $\mathcal{L}'_2(x, y) = 3 - \lambda/2\sqrt{y} = 0$ must be satisfied. They imply that $\lambda = 4\sqrt{x} = 6\sqrt{y}$, so $y = 4x/9$. Hence $x = 9$ and $y = 4$ with $\lambda = 12$.

(b) See Fig. A18.4.3. Move the line $2x + 3y = c$ as far north-east as possible. So the solution is at $(x, y) = (0, 25)$.

(c) $g(x, y)$ is continuously differentiable only on the set A of (x, y) such that $x > 0$ and $y > 0$, so the theorem does not apply at the point $(x, y) = (0, 25)$.

4. The Lagrange multiplier method produces a unique solution candidate $(x, y) = (0, 0)$ with $\lambda = -4$, corresponding to a local minimum. The global minimum is at $(x, y) = (-1, 0)$, however, an isolated point of $g(x, y) = 0$. See SM for details.

18.5

1. The Lagrangian $\mathcal{L} = 10x^{1/2}y^{1/3} - \lambda(2x + 4y - m)$ is concave in (x, y). So Theorem 18.5.1 implies that the solution to part (a) Exercise 18.1.3 is a maximum.

2. With $\mathcal{L} = \ln x + \ln y - \lambda(px + qy - m)$, $\mathcal{L}'_x = 1/x - p\lambda$, $\mathcal{L}'_y = 1/y - q\lambda$, $\mathcal{L}''_{xx} = -1/x^2$, $\mathcal{L}''_{xy} = 0$, and $\mathcal{L}''_{yy} = -1/y^2$. Moreover, $g'_x = p$ and $g'_y = q$. Hence $D(x, y, \lambda) = -q^2/x^2 - p^2/y^2 < 0$. So condition (a) in Theorem 18.5.2 holds.

3. $D(x, y, \lambda) = 10$, so Theorem 18.5.2 implies that $(a/5, 2a/5)$ is a local minimum.

4. $U''_{11}(x, y) = a(a-1)x^{a-2} \leq 0$, $U''_{22}(x, y) = a(a-1)y^{a-2} \leq 0$, and $U''_{12}(x, y) = 0$, so U is concave.
The solution is $x = mp^{1/(a-1)}/R$, and $y = mq^{1/(a-1)}/R$, where $R = p^{a/(a-1)} + q^{a/(a-1)}$.

18.6

1. (a) $\mathcal{L}(x, y, z) = x^2 + y^2 + z^2 - \lambda(x + y + z - 1)$, so $\mathcal{L}'_x = 2x - \lambda = 0$, $\mathcal{L}'_y = 2y - \lambda = 0$, and $\mathcal{L}'_z = 2z - \lambda = 0$.
It follows that $x = y = z = \frac{1}{2}\lambda$. The only solution of the necessary conditions is $(1/3, 1/3, 1/3)$ with $\lambda = 2/3$.

(b) The problem is to find the shortest distance from the origin to a point in the plane $x + y + z = 1$. The corresponding maximization problem has no solution.

2. $x = \dfrac{1/2}{1/2 + 1/3 + 1/4}\dfrac{390}{4} = 45$, $y = \dfrac{1/3}{1/2 + 1/3 + 1/4}\dfrac{390}{3} = 40$, $z = \dfrac{1/4}{1/2 + 1/3 + 1/4}\dfrac{390}{6} = 15$

3. (a) With the Lagrangian $\mathcal{L}(x, y, z) = x + \sqrt{y} - 1/z - \lambda(px + qy + rz - m)$, the first-order conditions (in addition to the constraint) are: (i) $\mathcal{L}'_1 = 1 - \lambda p = 0$; (ii) $\mathcal{L}'_2 = \frac{1}{2}y^{-1/2} - \lambda q = 0$; (iii) $\mathcal{L}'_3 = z^{-2} - \lambda r = 0$.

(b) From the equations in (a) we get $\lambda = 1/p$, then $\frac{1}{2}y^{-1/2} = q/p$, so $y = p^2/4q^2$, and finally $z = \sqrt{p/r}$.
Inserting these values of y and z in the budget constraint and solving for x gives $x = m/p - p/4q - \sqrt{r/p}$.

(c) Straightforward substitution. (d) $\partial U^*/\partial m = 1/p = \lambda$, as expected from Section 18.2.

4. The Lagrangian $\mathcal{L}(x, y, z) = \alpha \ln x + \beta \ln y + (1 - \alpha - \beta) \ln(L - l) - \lambda(px + qy - wl)$ has a critical point at (x^*, y^*, z^*) where: (i) $\mathcal{L}'_1 = \alpha/x^* - \lambda p = 0$; (ii) $\mathcal{L}'_2 = \beta/y^* - \lambda q = 0$; (iii) $\mathcal{L}'_3 = -(1 - \alpha - \beta)/(L - l^*) + \lambda w = 0$.
From (i) and (ii), $qy^* = (\beta/\alpha)px^*$, while (i) and (iii) yield $l^* = L - [(1 - \alpha - \beta)/w\alpha]px^*$.
Using the budget constraint, then solving for x^*, yields $x^* = \alpha w L/p$, $y^* = \beta w L/q$, and $l^* = (\alpha + \beta)L$.

5. The constraints reduce to $h + 2k + l = 0$ and $2h - k - 3l = 0$, so $k = -h$ and $l = h$.
But then $x^2 + y^2 + z^2 = 200 + 3h^2 \geq 200$ for all h, so f is maximized for $h = 0$.
Then $k = l = 0$ also, and we conclude that $(x, y, z) = (10, 10, 0)$ solves the minimization problem.

6. Here $\mathcal{L} = a_1^2 x_1^2 + \cdots + a_n^2 x_n^2 - \lambda(x_1 + \cdots + x_n - 1)$. Necessary conditions are that $\mathcal{L}'_j = 2a_j^2 x_j - \lambda = 0$, and so $x_j = \lambda/2a_j^2$, for each $j = 1, \ldots, n$. Inserting these into the constraint implies that $1 = \frac{1}{2}\lambda(1/a_1^2 + \cdots + 1/a_n^2)$. Thus, for

$j = 1,\ldots,n$, we have $x_j = (1/a_j^2)\big/(1/a_1^2 + \cdots + 1/a_n^2) = (1/a_j^2)\big/\sum_{i=1}^n(1/a_i^2)$. If at least one a_i is 0, the minimum value is 0, which is attained by letting a corresponding x_i be 1, with the other x_j all equal to 0.

7. The point $(x, y, z) = (0, 0, 1)$ with $\lambda = -1/2$ and $\mu = 1$ yields the minimum, whereas $(x, y, z) = (4/5, 2/5, -1/5)$ with $\lambda = 1/2$ and $\mu = 1/5$ yields the maximum.

8. (a) $x_j = a_j m/p_j(a_1 + \cdots + a_n)$ for $k = 1, \ldots, n$. (b) $x_j = m p_j^{-1/(1-a)}\big/\sum_{i=1}^n p_i^{-a/(1-a)}$ for $j = 1, 2, \ldots, n$.

18.7

1. (a) With $\mathcal{L} = x + a\ln y - \lambda(px + qy - m)$, one has $\mathcal{L}_1' = 1 - \lambda p = 0$, $\mathcal{L}_2' = a/y^* - \lambda q = 0$. Thus $\lambda = 1/p$.

   Inserting this into the second equality yields $y^* = ap/q$. From the budget constraint we get $x^* = m/p - a$.

   The Lagrangian is concave, so this is the solution.

   (b) $U^* = x^* + a\ln y^* = m/p - a + a\ln a + a\ln p - a\ln q$. Then $\partial U^*/\partial p = -m/p^2 + a/p$, $\partial U^*/\partial q = -a/q$, $\partial U^*/\partial m = 1/p$, and $\partial U^*/\partial a = \ln a + \ln p - \ln q$.

   (c) $\partial \mathcal{L}/\partial p = -\lambda x$, $\partial \mathcal{L}/\partial q = -\lambda y$, $\partial \mathcal{L}/\partial m = \lambda$, and $\partial \mathcal{L}/\partial a = \ln y$. When we evaluate these four partials at (x^*, y^*), we see that the envelope theorem is confirmed.

2. The minimum point is $(x^*, y^*, z^*) = (a, 2a, 9a)$, where $a = -\sqrt{b}/6$, with $\lambda = -3/\sqrt{b}$.

   The value of the objective function is $f^*(b) = x^* + 4y^* + 3z^* = -6\sqrt{b}$, and $df^*(b)/db = -3/\sqrt{b} = \lambda$.

3. (a) $x = aM/\alpha$, $y = bM/\beta$, $z = cM/\gamma$, $\lambda = 1/2M$, where $M = \sqrt{L}/\sqrt{a^2/\alpha + b^2/\beta + c^2/\gamma}$. (The first-order conditions give $x = a/2\lambda\alpha$, $y = b/2\lambda\beta$, $z = c/2\lambda\gamma$. Substituting in the constraint and solving for λ gives the solution.)

   (b) We find that $M = \sqrt{L}/5$, and the given values of x, y, and z follow.

   (c) For $L = 100$ one has $M = 2$ and $\lambda = 1/4$. As L increases from 100 to 101, the approximate increase in the maximal value is $\lambda \cdot 1 = 0.25$. The exact increase is $5\left(\sqrt{101} - \sqrt{100}\right)$, or about 0.249 378.

4. (a) $(\tfrac{1}{4}\sqrt{15}, 0, \tfrac{1}{8})$ and $(-\tfrac{1}{4}\sqrt{15}, 0, \tfrac{1}{8})$ (with $\lambda = 1$) both solve the maximization problem, while $(0, 0, -\tfrac{1}{2})$ solves the minimization problem. (b) $\Delta f^* \approx \lambda \Delta c = 1 \cdot 0.02 = 0.02$

5. $K^* = 2^{1/3} r^{-1/3} w^{1/3} Q^{4/3}$, $L^* = 2^{-2/3} r^{2/3} w^{-2/3} Q^{4/3}$, $C^* = 3 \cdot 2^{-2/3} r^{2/3} w^{1/3} Q^{4/3}$, $\lambda = 2^{4/3} r^{2/3} w^{1/3} Q^{1/3}$.

   The equalities $(*)$ are easily verified.

6. $\dfrac{\partial K^*}{\partial w} = \dfrac{\partial}{\partial w}\left(\dfrac{\partial C^*}{\partial r}\right) = \dfrac{\partial}{\partial r}\left(\dfrac{\partial C^*}{\partial w}\right) = \dfrac{\partial L^*}{\partial r}$, using the first and second equalities in $(*)$ of Example 18.7.3.

7. (a) With $\mathcal{L} = \sqrt{x} + ay - \lambda(px + qy - m)$, conditions for (x^*, y^*) to solve the problem are $px^* + qy^* = m$ and:
   (i) $\mathcal{L}_1' = 1/2\sqrt{x^*} - \lambda p = 0$; (ii) $\mathcal{L}_2' = a - \lambda q = 0$. Thus $\lambda = a/q$, and $x^* = q^2/4a^2p^2$, $y^* = m/q - q/4a^2p$.

   Because $\mathcal{L}$ is concave in (x, y), this is the solution. Indirect utility is $U^*(p, q, m, a) = \sqrt{x^*} + ay^* = q/4ap + am/q$.

   (b) The partial derivatives of U^* w.r.t. the four parameters p, q, m, a are:

   $\partial U^*/\partial p = -q/4ap^2$, $\partial U^*/\partial q = 1/4ap - am/q^2$, $\partial U^*/\partial m = a/q$, and $\partial U^*/\partial a = -q/4a^2p + m/q$.

   On the other hand, with $\mathcal{L}(x, y, p, q, m, a) = \sqrt{x} + ay - \lambda(px + qy - m)$, when evaluated at (x^*, y^*), the four first-order partial derivatives of $\mathcal{L}$ are: $\partial \mathcal{L}^*/\partial p = -\lambda x^* = -(a/q)(q^2/4a^2p^2) = -q/4ap^2$, then $\partial \mathcal{L}^*/\partial q = -\lambda y^* = -(a/q)(m/q - q/4a^2p) = 1/4ap - am/q^2$, $\partial \mathcal{L}^*/\partial m = \lambda$, and $\partial \mathcal{L}^*/\partial a = y^* = m/q - q/4a^2p$.

   The envelope theorem is confirmed in all cases.

Review exercises for Chapter 18

1. (a) Given the Lagrangian $\mathcal{L}(x, y) = 3x + 4y - \lambda(x^2 + y^2 - 225)$, the first-order conditions imply that $3 - 2\lambda x = 0$ and $4 - 2\lambda y = 0$, so $3y = 4x = 6\lambda$. Inserting these into the constraint yields $x^2 = 81$, so $x = \pm 9$. The two solutions to all the first-order conditions are $(x, y, \lambda) = \pm(9, 12, 1/6)$. Now $\mathcal{L}(x, y)$ is concave or convex according as $\lambda \geq 0$ or $\lambda \leq 0$. So, by Theorem 18.5.1, $(x, y) = (9, 12)$ is a maximum point and $(x, y) = (-9, -12)$ is a minimum point.

   (b) Using (18.2.3), $f^*(225 - 1) - f^*(225) \approx \lambda(-1) = -1/6$.

2. (a) $x = 2m/5p$, $y = 3m/5q$ (b) $x = m/3p$, $y = 2m/3q$ (c) $x = 3m/5p$, $y = 2m/5q$

3. (a) $\pi = xp(x) + yq(y) - C(x, y)$. The first-order conditions imply that marginal revenue equals marginal cost:
   (i) $p(x^*) + x^* p'(x^*) = C_1'(x^*, y^*)$; (ii) $q(y^*) + y^* q'(y^*) = C_2'(x^*, y^*)$. See SM for further discussion.

   (b) With $\mathcal{L} = xp(x) + yq(y) - C(x, y) - \lambda(x + y - m)$, the first-order conditions for $(\hat{x}, \hat{y})$ to solve the problem imply that $\mathcal{L}_1' = p(\hat{x}) + \hat{x} p'(\hat{x}) - C_1'(\hat{x}, \hat{y}) - \lambda = 0$ and $\mathcal{L}_2' = q(\hat{y}) + \hat{y} q'(\hat{y}) - C_2'(\hat{x}, \hat{y}) - \lambda = 0$.

4. (a) The Lagrangian is $\mathcal{L}(x, y) = U(x, y) - \lambda[py - w(24 - x)]$.

   The first-order conditions imply that $pU_1' = wU_2' = \lambda wp$, which immediately yields (∗∗).

   (b) Differentiating (∗) and (∗∗) w.r.t. w gives $py_w' = 24 - x - wx_w'$ and $p(U_{11}'' x_w' + U_{12}'' y_w') = U_2' + w(U_{21}'' x_w' + U_{22}'' y_w')$. Solving these linear equations in the two unknowns x_w' and y_w' yields the given formula for $x_w' = \partial x/\partial w$.

5. (a) $x = -2\sqrt{b}$ and $y = 0$, with $\lambda = 4 + 2/\sqrt{b}$, solve the max problem;

   $x = 4/3$, $y = \pm\sqrt{b - 4/9}$, with $\lambda = 1$, solve the min problem. See SM for details.

   (b) For $(x, y, \lambda) = (-2\sqrt{b}, 0, 4 + 2/\sqrt{b})$, one has $f^*(b) = 4b + 4\sqrt{b} + 1$. So the suggested equality is easily verified.

6. (a) With $\mathcal{L}(x, y) = v(x) + w(y) - \lambda(px + qy - m)$, the first-order conditions imply $v'(x) = \lambda p$ and $w'(y) = \lambda q$. Thus $v'(x)/w'(y) = p/q$. (b) Since $\mathcal{L}_{xx}'' = v''(x)$, $\mathcal{L}_{yy}'' = w''(y)$, and $\mathcal{L}_{xy}'' = 0$, we see that the Lagrangian is concave.

7. (a) The first-order conditions imply that $2x - 2 = 2y - 2$, so $x = y$. Inserting this into the constraint equation and squaring, then simplifying, one obtains the second equation in (∗).

   (b) $\partial x/\partial a = 1/2x(3x + b)$, $\partial^2 x/\partial a^2 = -\frac{1}{4}(6x + b)[x(3x + b)]^{-3}$, and $\partial x/\partial b = -x/2(3x + b)$. See SM.

Chapter 19

19.1

1. (a) From Fig. A19.1.1a we see that the solution is at the intersection of the two lines $3x_1 + 2x_2 = 6$ and $x_1 + 4x_2 = 4$. Solution: max $= 36/5$ for $(x_1, x_2) = (8/5, 3/5)$.

   (b) From Fig. A19.1.1b we see that the solution is at the intersection of the two lines $u_1 + 3u_2 = 11$ and $2u_1 + 5u_2 = 20$. Solution: min $= 104$ for $(u_1, u_2) = (5, 2)$.

2. (a) A graph shows that the solution is at the intersection of the lines $-2x_1 + 3x_2 = 6$ and $x_1 + x_2 = 5$.

   Hence max $= 98/5$ for $(x_1, x_2) = (9/5, 16/5)$.

   (b) The solution satisfies $2x_1 + 3x_2 = 13$ and $x_1 + x_2 = 6$. Hence max $= 49$ for $(x_1, x_2) = (5, 1)$.

   (c) The solution satisfies $x_1 - 3x_2 = 0$ and $x_1 = 2$. Hence max $= -10/3$ for $(x_1, x_2) = (2, 2/3)$.

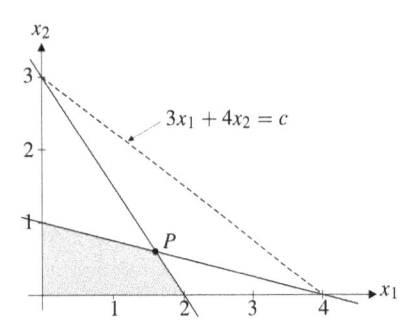

Figure A19.1.1a

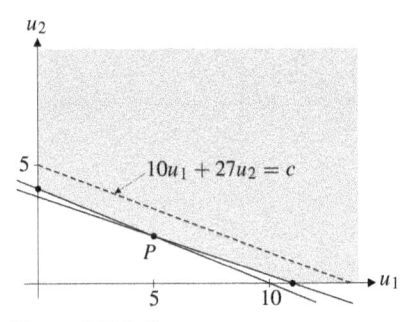

Figure A19.1.1b

3. (a) max $= 18/5$ for $(x_1, x_2) = (4/5, 18/5)$. (b) max $= 8$ for $(x_1, x_2) = (8, 0)$. (c) max $= 24$ for $(x_1, x_2) = (8, 0)$.
(d) min $= -28/5$ for $(x_1, x_2) = (4/5, 18/5)$. (e) max $= 16$ for all $(x_1, x_2) = (\xi, 4 - \frac{1}{2}\xi)$ where $\xi \in [4/5, 8]$.
(f) The answer to (c) implies that min $= -24$ for $(x_1, x_2) = (8, 0)$.

4. (a) No maximum exists. Too see this, consider Fig. A19.1.4. As c becomes arbitrarily large, so the dashed level curve $x_1 + x_2 = c$ moves to the north-east and still has the point $(c, 0)$ in common with the shaded feasible set.
(b) Maximum at $P = (1, 0)$. The level curves are as in (a), but the direction of increase is reversed.

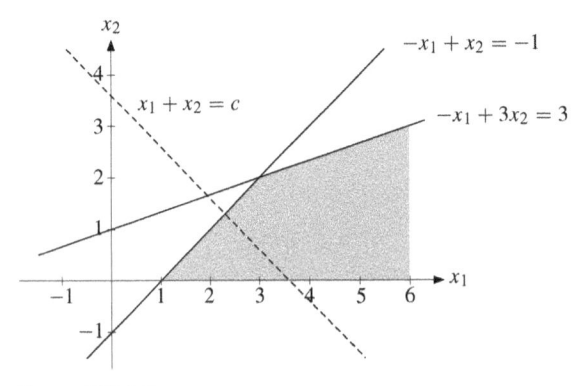

Figure A19.1.4

5. The slope of the line $20x_1 + tx_2 = c$ must lie between $-1/2$ (the slope of the flour border) and -1 (the slope of the butter border). For $t = 0$, the line is vertical and the solution is the point D in Fig. 19.1.2. For $t \neq 0$, the slope of the line is $-20/t$. Thus, $-1 \leq -20/t \leq -1/2$, which implies that $t \in [20, 40]$.

6. The LP problem is: max $700x + 1000y$ subject to $\begin{cases} 3x + 5y \leq 3900 \\ x + 3y \leq 2100 \\ 2x + 2y \leq 2200 \end{cases}$, $x \geq 0$, $y \geq 0$.

A figure showing the admissible set and an appropriate level line for the objective function will demonstrate that the solution is at the intersection of the two lines $3x + 5y = 3900$ and $2x + 2y = 2200$. Solving these two equations yields $x = 800$ and $y = 300$. The firm should produce 800 sets of type A and 300 of type B.

19.2

1. (a) $(x_1, x_2) = (2, 1/2)$ and $u_1^* = 4/5$. (b) $(x_1, x_2) = (7/5, 9/10)$ and $u_2^* = 3/5$.

(c) Multiplying the two $\leq$ constraints by $4/5$ and $3/5$, respectively, then adding,

we obtain $(4/5)(3x_1 + 2x_2) + (3/5)(x_1 + 4x_2) \leq 6 \cdot (4/5) + 4 \cdot (3/5)$, which reduces to $3x_1 + 4x_2 \leq 36/5$.

2. min $8u_1 + 13u_2 + 6u_3$ subject to $\begin{cases} u_1 + 2u_2 + u_3 \geq 8 \\ 2u_1 + 3u_2 + u_3 \geq 9 \end{cases}$, $u_1 \geq 0, u_2 \geq 0, u_3 \geq 0$

3. (a) min $6u_1 + 4u_2$ subject to $\begin{cases} 3u_1 + u_2 \geq 3 \\ 2u_1 + 4u_2 \geq 4 \end{cases}$, $u_1 \geq 0, u_2 \geq 0$

(b) max $11x_1 + 20x_2$ subject to $\begin{cases} x_1 + 2x_2 \leq 10 \\ 3x_1 + 5x_2 \leq 2 \end{cases}$, $u_1 \geq 0, u_2 \geq 0$

4. (a) A graph shows that the solution is at the intersection of the lines $x_1 + 2x_2 = 14$ and $2x_1 + x_2 = 13$.
Hence max $= 9$ for $(x_1^*, x_2^*) = (4, 5)$.

(b) The dual is min $14u_1 + 13u_2$ subject to $\begin{cases} u_1 + 2u_2 \geq 1 \\ 2u_1 + u_2 \geq 1 \end{cases}$, $u_1 \geq 0, u_2 \geq 0$.

A graph shows that the solution is at the intersection of the lines $u_1 + 2u_2 = 1$ and $2u_1 + u_2 = 1$.
Hence min $= 9$ for $(u_1^*, u_2^*) = (1/3, 1/3)$.

19.3

1. (a) $x = 0$ and $y = 3$ gives max $= 21$. See Fig. A19.3.1a, where the optimum is at P.

(b) The dual problem is min $20u_1 + 21u_2$ subject to $\begin{cases} 4u_1 + 3u_2 \geq 2 \\ 5u_1 + 7u_2 \geq 7 \end{cases}$, $u_1 \geq 0, u_2 \geq 0$.

The solution is $u_1 = 0$ and $u_2 = 1$, which gives min $= 21$. See Fig. A19.3.1b. (c) Yes. Both values are 21.

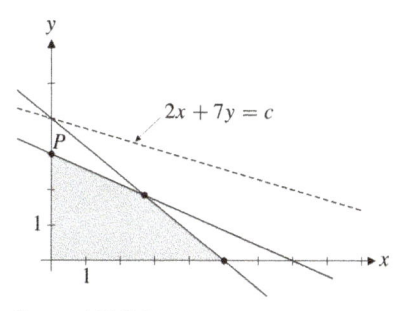

Figure A19.3.1a

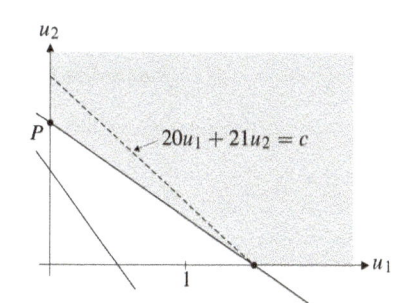

Figure A19.3.1b

2. max $300x_1 + 500x_2$ subject to $\begin{cases} 10x_1 + 25x_2 \leq 10\,000 \\ 20x_1 + 25x_2 \leq 8\,000 \end{cases}$, $x_1 \geq 0, x_2 \geq 0$.

The solution can be found graphically. It is $x_1^* = 0$, $x_2^* = 320$, and the maximum value of the objective function is $160\,000$, which is the same as that found in Example 19.1.2 for the primal problem.

3. (a) The profit from selling x_1 small and x_2 medium television sets is $400x_1 + 500x_2$.

The first constraint, $2x_1 + x_2 \leq 16$, says that we cannot use more hours on assembly line 1 than its capacity allows.

The other constraints have similar interpretations.

(b) max = 3800 for $x_1 = 7$ and $x_2 = 2$. (c) Assembly line 1 should have its capacity increased. See SM for details.

19.4

1. According to formula (19.4.1), one has $\Delta z^* = u_1^* \Delta b_1 + u_2^* \Delta b_2 = 0 \cdot 0.1 + 1 \cdot (-0.2) = -0.2$.

2. (a) max $300x_1 + 200x_2$ subject to $\begin{cases} 6x_1 + 3x_2 \leq 54 \\ 4x_1 + 6x_2 \leq 48 \\ 5x_1 + 5x_2 \leq 50 \end{cases}$, $x_1 \geq 0, x_2 \geq 0$

where x_1 and x_2 are the number of units produced of A and B, respectively. Solution: $(x_1, x_2) = (8, 2)$. See SM.
(b) Dual solution: $(u_1, u_2, u_3) = (100/3, 0, 20)$. (c) Increase in optimal profit: $\Delta \pi^* = u_1^* \cdot 2 + u_3^* \cdot 1 = 260/3$.

19.5

1. $4u_1^* + 3u_2^* = 3 > 2$ and $x^* = 0$; $5u_1^* + 7u_2^* = 7$ and $y^* = 3 > 0$.
Also $4x^* + 5y^* = 15 < 20$ and $u_1^* = 0$; $3x^* + 7y^* = 21$ and $u_2^* = 1 > 0$. So (19.5.1) and (19.5.2) are both satisfied.

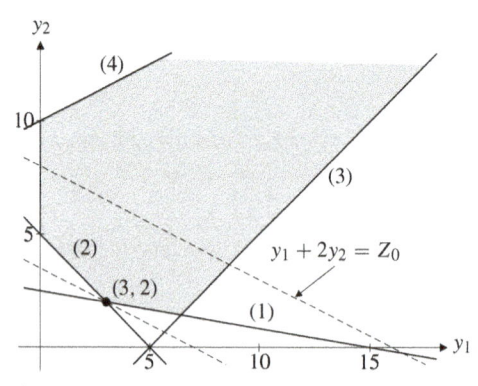

Figure A19.5.2

2. (a) See Fig. A19.5.2. The minimum is attained at $(y_1^*, y_2^*) = (3, 2)$.

(b) The dual is max $15x_1 + 5x_2 - 5x_3 - 20x_4$ s.t. $\begin{cases} x_1 + x_2 - x_3 + x_4 \leq 1 \\ 6x_1 + x_2 + x_3 - 2x_4 \leq 2 \end{cases}$, $x_j \geq 0$ $(j = 1, \ldots, 4)$.

The maximum is at $(x_1^*, x_2^*, x_3^*, x_4^*) = (1/5, 4/5, 0, 0)$.

(c) If the first constraint is changed to $y_1 + 6y_2 \geq 15.1$, then the solution of the primal is still at the intersection of the lines marked (1) and (2) in Fig. A19.5.2, but with line (1) shifted up slightly. The solution of the dual is completely unchanged. In both problems the optimal value increases by $(15.1 - 15) \cdot x_1^* = 0.02$.

3. (a) min $10\,000\, y_1 + 8\,000\, y_2 + 11\,000\, y_3$ s.t. $\begin{cases} 10y_1 + 20y_2 + 20y_3 \geq 300 \\ 20y_1 + 10y_2 + 20y_3 \geq 500 \end{cases}$, $y_1 \geq 0, y_2 \geq 0, y_3 \geq 0$

(b) The dual is: max $300x_1 + 500x_2$ subject to $\begin{cases} 10x_1 + 20x_2 \leq 10\,000 \\ 20x_1 + 10x_2 \leq 8\,000 \\ 20x_1 + 20x_2 \leq 11\,000 \end{cases}$, $x_1 \geq 0, x_2 \geq 0$

Solution: max $= 255\,000$ for $x_1 = 100$ and $x_2 = 450$.
Solution of the primal: min $= 255\,000$ for $(y_1, y_2, y_3) = (20, 0, 5)$. (c) The minimum cost will increase by 2000.

4. (a) For $x_3 = 0$, the solution is $x_1 = x_2 = 1/3$. For $x_3 = 3$, the solution is $x_1 = 1$ and $x_2 = 2$.

(b) Let $z_{\max}$ denote the maximum value of the objective function.

If $0 \leq x_3 \leq 7/3$, then $z_{\max}(x_3) = 2x_3 + 5/3$ for $x_1 = 1/3$ and $x_2 = x_3 + 1/3$.

If $7/3 < x_3 \leq 5$, then $z_{\max}(x_3) = x_3 + 4$ for $x_1 = x_3 - 2$ and $x_2 = 5 - x_3$.

If $x_3 > 5$, then $z_{\max}(x_3) = 9$ for $x_1 = 3$ and $x_2 = 0$. Because $z_{\max}(x_3)$ is increasing, the maximum is 9 for $x_3 \geq 5$.

(c) The solution to the original problem is $x_1 = 3$ and $x_2 = 0$, with x_3 an arbitrary number ≥ 5.

Review exercises for Chapter 19

1. (a) $x^* = 3/2$, $y^* = 5/2$. (A diagram shows that the solution is at the intersection of $x + y = 4$ and $-x + y = 1$.)

(b) The dual is min $4u_1 + u_2 + 3u_3$ subject to
$$\begin{cases} u_1 - u_2 + 2u_3 \geq 1 \\ u_1 + u_2 - u_3 \geq 2 \end{cases}, \quad u_1 \geq 0, u_2 \geq 0, u_3 \geq 0.$$
Using complementary slackness, the solution of the dual is: $u_1^* = 3/2$, $u_2^* = 1/2$, and $u_3^* = 0$.

2. (a) max $-x_1 + x_2$ subject to
$$\begin{cases} -x_1 + 2x_2 \leq 16 \\ x_1 - 2x_2 \leq 6 \\ -2x_1 - x_2 \leq -8 \\ -4x_1 - 5x_2 \leq -15 \end{cases}, \quad x_1 \geq 0, x_2 \geq 0. \text{ Solution: } (x_1, x_2) = (0, 8).$$

(b) $(y_1, y_2, y_3, y_4) = (\tfrac{1}{2}(b+1), 0, b, 0)$ for any b satisfying $0 \leq b \leq 1/5$.

(c) The maximand for the dual becomes $kx_1 + x_2$. The solution is unchanged provided that $k \leq -1/2$.

3. (a) $x^* = 0$, $y^* = 4$. (A diagram shows that the solution is at the intersection of $x = 0$ and $4x + y = 4$.)

(b) The dual problem is

max $4u_1 + 3u_2 + 2u_3 - 2u_4$ subject to
$$\begin{cases} 4u_1 + 2u_2 + 3u_3 - u_4 \leq 5 \\ u_1 + u_2 + 2u_3 + 2u_4 \leq 1 \end{cases}, \quad u_1, u_2, u_3, u_4 \geq 0$$

By complementary slackness, its solution is: $u_1^* = 1$, $u_2^* = u_3^* = u_4^* = 0$.

4. (a) To produce $\mathbf{a} = (5, 5, 7)$, put $\lambda = 1/2$. To produce $\mathbf{b} = (7, 5, 5)$ would require $6\lambda + 2 = 7$, $-2\lambda + 6 = 5$, and $-6\lambda + 10 = 5$, but these equations have no solution.

(b) In part (a) we saw that $\mathbf{a}$ can be produced even without throwing away outputs. For $\mathbf{b}$ to be possible if the firm is allowed to throw away output, there must exist a scalar λ in $[0, 1]$ such that $6\lambda + 2 \geq 7$, $-2\lambda + 6 \geq 5$, and $-6\lambda + 10 \geq 5$. These inequalities reduce to $\lambda \geq 5/6$, $\lambda \leq 1/2$, $\lambda \leq 5/6$, which are incompatible.

(c) Revenue is $R(\lambda) = p_1 x_1 + p_2 x_2 + p_3 x_3 = (6p_1 - 2p_2 - 6p_3)\lambda + 2p_1 + 6p_2 + 10p_3$, with $R'(\lambda)$ equal to the constant $s = 6p_1 - 2p_2 - 6p_3$. If $s > 0$, then $R(\lambda)$ is maximized at $\lambda = 1$; if $s < 0$, then it is maximized at $\lambda = 0$. Only in the special case where $s = 0$ can the two plants both remain in use.

5. (a) If the numbers of units produced of the three goods are x_1, x_2, and x_3, the profit is $6x_1 + 3x_2 + 4x_3$, and the times spent on the two machines are $3x_1 + x_2 + 4x_3$ and $2x_1 + 2x_2 + x_3$, respectively. The LP problem is therefore

max $6x_1 + 3x_2 + 4x_3$ subject to
$$\begin{cases} 3x_1 + x_2 + 4x_3 \leq b_1 \\ 2x_1 + 2x_2 + x_3 \leq b_2 \end{cases}, \quad x_1, x_2, x_3 \geq 0$$

(b) The dual problem is obviously as given. Optimum at $P = (y_1^*, y_2^*) = (3/2, 3/4)$. See SM for details.

(c) Using the solution to part (b) and complementary slackness imply that $x_3^* = 0$ and $x_1^* = x_2^* = 25$. See SM.

(d) The solution to the dual does not change, so its value increases by $y_1^* db_1 = 3/2$ to 226.5, which must equal the increase in the value of the primal. See SM for details.

(e) By Theorem 19.3.3, for all $b_1, b_2 \geq 0$ the value $F(b_1, b_2)$ of the primal in part (a) equals the value of the dual in part (b). So $F(b_1, b_2) = \min_{(y_1, y_2) \in S} b_1 y_1 + b_2 y_2 = b_1 y_1^* + b_2 y_2^*$, the minimum value when (y_1, y_2) are chosen from the set S of pairs that satisfy the five constraints specified in part (b). If b_1 and b_2 are both multiplied by $\alpha > 0$, the transformed objective of the dual is $\alpha(b_1 y_1 + b_2 y_2)$. A simple application of Theorem 17.6.6 implies that this transformation leaves the minimum point (y_1^*, y_2^*) unchanged. Hence $F(\alpha b_1, \alpha b_2) = \alpha(b_1 y_1^* + b_2 y_2^*) = \alpha F(b_1, b_2)$. This proves that F is homogeneous of degree 1.

Chapter 20

20.1

1. (a) With $\mathcal{L} = -x^2 - y^2 - \lambda(x - 3y + 10)$, Eqs (20.1.2) and (20.1.3) yield

(i) $\mathcal{L}_x' = -2x - \lambda = 0$; (ii) $\mathcal{L}_y' = -2y + 3\lambda = 0$; (iii) $\lambda \geq 0$ with $\lambda = 0$ if $x - 3y < -10$.

Suppose $\lambda = 0$. Then (i) and (ii) imply $x = y = 0$, contradicting $x - 3y \leq -10$.

Thus $\lambda > 0$ and from (iii), $x - 3y = -10$. Furthermore, (i) and (ii) imply $\lambda = -2x = \frac{2}{3}y$, so $y = -3x$.

Inserting this into $x - 3y = -10$ yields $x = -1$, and then $y = 3$.

Since the Lagrangian is easily seen to be concave, $(x, y) = (-1, 3)$ is the solution.

(b) See Fig. A20.1.1. The solution is the point on the line $x - 3y = -10$ that is closest to the origin.

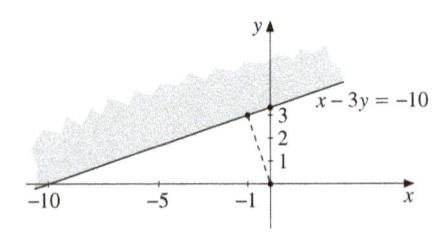

Figure A20.1.1

2. (a) The KKT conditions yield: (i) $1/(2\sqrt{x}) - \lambda p = 0$, (ii) $1/(2\sqrt{y}) - \lambda q = 0$, (iii) $\lambda \geq 0$, and $\lambda = 0$ if $px + qy < m$. Clearing fractions in (i) and (ii) gives $1 = 2\lambda p \sqrt{x} = 2\lambda q \sqrt{y}$, from which we infer that x, y, λ are all positive, and also that $y = p^2 x / q^2$. Because $\lambda > 0$, the budget equation $px + qy = m$ holds, implying that $x = mq/(pq + p^2)$. The corresponding value for y is easily found, and the demand functions are

$$x = x(p, q, m) = \frac{mq}{p(p+q)}, \qquad y = y(p, q, m) = \frac{mp}{q(p+q)}$$

These demand functions solve the problem because $\mathcal{L}(x, y)$ is easily seen to be concave.

(b) It is easy to see that the demand functions are homogeneous of degree 0, as expected.

3. (a) With $\mathcal{L} = 4 - \frac{1}{2}x^2 - 4y - \lambda(6x - 4y - a)$, the KKT conditions are:

(i) $\partial \mathcal{L}/\partial x = -x - 6\lambda = 0$; (ii) $\partial \mathcal{L}/\partial y = -4 + 4\lambda = 0$; (iii) $\lambda \geq 0$ (with $\lambda = 0$ if $6x - 4y < a$).

(b) From (ii), $\lambda = 1$, so (i) gives $x = -6$. From (iii) and the given constraint, $y = -9 - \frac{1}{4}a$.

The Lagrangian is concave, so we have found the solution. (c) $V(a) = a + 22$, so $V'(a) = 1 = \lambda$.

4. (a) $\mathcal{L}(x, y) = x^2 + 2y^2 - x - \lambda(x^2 + y^2 - 1)$. The KKT conditions are:

(i) $2x - 1 - 2\lambda x = 0$; (ii) $4y - 2\lambda y = 0$; (iii) $\lambda \geq 0$, with $\lambda = 0$ if $x^2 + y^2 < 1$.

(b) From (ii), $y(2 - \lambda) = 0$, so either (I) $y = 0$ or (II) $\lambda = 2$.

(I) $y = 0$. First, if $\lambda = 0$, then from (i), $x = 1/2$ and $(x, y) = (1/2, 0)$ is a candidate for an optimum (since it satisfies all the KKT conditions).

Second, if $y = 0$ and $\lambda > 0$ then from (iii) and $x^2 + y^2 \leq 1$, one has $x^2 + y^2 = 1$. But then $x = \pm 1$, so $(x, y) = (\pm 1, 0)$ are candidates, with $\lambda = 1/2$ and $3/2$, respectively.

(II) $\lambda = 2$. Then from (i) $x = -1/2$, and (iii) gives $y^2 = 3/4$, so $y = \pm\sqrt{3}/2$. Hence $(-1/2, \pm\sqrt{3}/2)$ are the two remaining candidates with $\lambda = 2$.

(c) Since f is continuous and the feasible set is closed and bounded, the extreme value theorem guarantees a maximum. The maximum point or points must be among the five points that satisfy the necessary conditions. Evaluating $x^2 + 2y^2 - x$ at each of those points shows that the maximum value is $9/4$, attained at $(-1/2, \pm\sqrt{3}/2)$.

5. (a) For $0 < a < 1$, the solution is $x = \sqrt{a}$, $y = 0$, and $\lambda = a^{-1/2} - 1$; for $a \geq 1$, it is $x = 1$, $y = 0$, and $\lambda = 0$.

(b) Because $\lambda \geq 0$ and so the Lagrangian is concave, these give the respective maxima.

(c) If $a \in (0, 1)$, then $f^*(a) = 2\sqrt{a} - a$, and so $df^*(a)/da = \lambda$. If $a \geq 1$, then $f^*(a) = 1$, so $df^*(a)/da = 0 = \lambda$.

6. With $\mathcal{L} = aQ - bQ^2 - \alpha Q - \beta Q^2 + \lambda Q$, the KKT conditions for Q^* to solve the problem are:

(i) $d\mathcal{L}/dQ = a - \alpha - 2(b + \beta)Q^* + \lambda = 0$; (ii) $\lambda \geq 0$, with $\lambda = 0$ if $Q^* > 0$. By Theorem 20.1.1, because the Lagrangian is concave, these conditions are also sufficient. We find that $Q^* = (a - \alpha)/2(b + \beta)$ and $\lambda = 0$ if $a > \alpha$, whereas $Q^* = 0$ and $\lambda = \alpha - a$ if $a \leq \alpha$. (See also Example 4.6.3.)

20.2

1. (a) Write the constraints as $g_1(x, y) = x + e^{-x} - y \leq 0$ and $g_2(x, y) = -x \leq 0$.

Then the Lagrangian is $\mathcal{L} = \frac{1}{2}x - y - \lambda_1(x + e^{-x} - y) - \lambda_2(-x)$.

So the KKT conditions are: (i) $\frac{1}{2} - \lambda_1(1 - e^{-x}) + \lambda_2 = 0$; (ii) $-1 + \lambda_1 = 0$;

(iii) $\lambda_1 \geq 0$, with $\lambda_1 = 0$ if $x + e^{-x} < y$; (iv) $\lambda_2 \geq 0$, with $\lambda_2 = 0$ if $x > 0$.

(b) From (ii), $\lambda_1 = 1$, so from (iii), $x + e^{-x} = y$. Either $x = 0$ or $x > 0$.

If $x > 0$, then (iv) implies that $\lambda_2 = 0$. Then (i) implies $\frac{1}{2} - (1 - e^{-x}) = 0$, or $e^{-x} = \frac{1}{2}$.

Hence $x = \ln 2$, and so $y = x + e^{-x} = \ln 2 + \frac{1}{2}$.

If $x = 0$, then (i) implies $\lambda_2 = -\frac{1}{2}$, which contradicts $\lambda_2 \geq 0$.

We conclude that $(x, y) = (\ln 2, \ln 2 + \frac{1}{2})$ is the only point satisfying the KKT conditions, with $(\lambda_1, \lambda_2) = (1, 0)$.

(By sketching the feasible set and studying the level curves $\frac{1}{2}x - y = c$, it is easy to see that the point we have found does solve the maximization problem.)

2. If $m \leq p\bar{x}/\alpha$, then $x^* = m\alpha/p$ and $y^* = (1 - \alpha)m/q$, with $\lambda = 1/m$ and $\mu = 0$.

If $m > p\bar{x}/\alpha$, then $x^* = \bar{x}$ and $y^* = (m - p\bar{x})/q$, with $\lambda = (1 - \alpha)/(m - p\bar{x})$ and $\mu = (\alpha m - p\bar{x})/\bar{x}(m - p\bar{x})$.

3. (a) The feasible set is the shaded region in Fig. A20.2.3. (b) The only solution candidate is $(x, y) = (-1, 5)$, with suitable nonnegative values of the three Lagrange multipliers. See SM for details.

(c) Because the Lagrangian is concave when the Lagrange multipliers are nonnegative, the point $(x, y) = (-1, 5)$ must solve the maximation problem. See SM for details.

940 SOLUTIONS TO THE EXERCISES

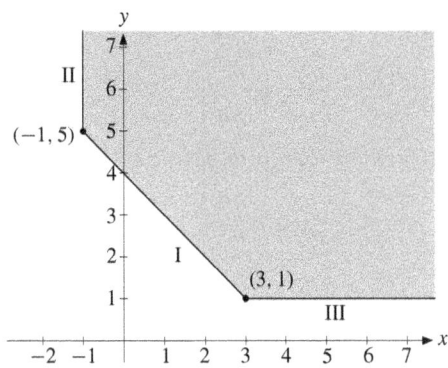

Figure A20.2.3

Figure A20.2.4

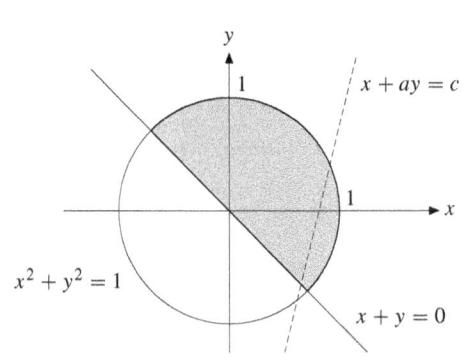

4. (a) The feasible set and one of the level curves for $x + ay$ are shown in Fig. A20.2.4. The requested necessary conditions, with $\mathcal{L} = x + ay - \lambda(x^2 + y^2 - 1) + \mu(x + y)$, are:

(i) $\mathcal{L}'_x = 1 - 2\lambda x + \mu = 0$;   (ii) $\mathcal{L}'_y = a - 2\lambda y + \mu = 0$;   (iii) $\lambda \geq 0$, with $\lambda = 0$ if $x^2 + y^2 < 1$;

(iv) $\mu \geq 0$, with $\mu = 0$ if $x + y > 0$;   (v) $x^2 + y^2 \leq 1$; (vi) $x + y \geq 0$.

(b) The solution is $(x^*, y^*) = (\tfrac{1}{2}\sqrt{2}, -\tfrac{1}{2}\sqrt{2})$ in case $a \leq -1$, but $(x^*, y^*) = (1/\sqrt{1+a^2}, a/\sqrt{1+a^2})$ in case $a > -1$.

5. $(x, y) = (4^{-2/3}, 4^{-1/3})$, with shadow prices $\lambda = 0$, $\mu = 0$, and $\nu = 1/2y = 4^{-1/6}$. See SM.

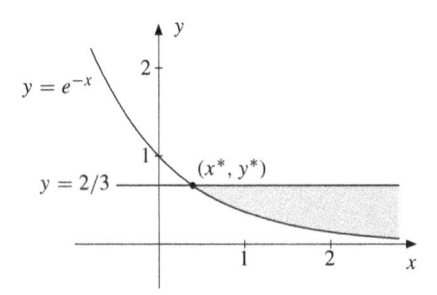

Figure A20.2.6

6. (a) See Fig. A20.2.6.   (b) With $\mathcal{L} = -(x + \tfrac{1}{2})^2 - \tfrac{1}{2}y^2 - \lambda(e^{-x} - y) - \mu(y - \tfrac{2}{3})$, the KKT conditions are:

(i) $\mathcal{L}'_x = -2(x + \tfrac{1}{2}) + \lambda e^{-x} = 0$;   (ii) $\mathcal{L}'_y = -y + \lambda - \mu = 0$;   (iii) $\lambda \geq 0$, with $\lambda = 0$ if $e^{-x} - y < 0$;

(iv) $\mu \geq 0$, with $\mu = 0$ if $y < \tfrac{2}{3}$;   (v) $e^{-x} - y \leq 0$;   (vi) $y \leq \tfrac{2}{3}$.

The solution is $(x^*, y^*) = (\ln(3/2), 2/3)$, with $\lambda = 3[\ln(3/2) + 1/2]$ and $\mu = 3\ln(3/2) + 5/6$. See SM.

7. (a) With $\mathcal{L} = xz + yz - \lambda(x^2 + y^2 + z^2 - 1)$, the KKT conditions are:

(i) $z - 2\lambda x = 0$;   (ii) $z - 2\lambda y = 0$;   (iii) $x + y - 2\lambda z = 0$;   (iv) $\lambda \geq 0$, with $\lambda = 0$ if $x^2 + y^2 + z^2 < 1$.

(b) If $\lambda = 0$, every point $(x, y, 0)$ with $x + y = 0$ satisfies the KKT conditions, but the value of $xz + yz$ at these points is 0, and this is obviously not the maximum value.

Alternatively, in case $\lambda > 0$ and so $x^2 + y^2 + z^2 = 1$, then (i) and (ii) imply that $x = y = z/2\lambda$.

It follows that $(z^2/4\lambda^2) + (z^2/4\lambda^2) + z^2 = 1$, so $z^2 = 4\lambda^2/(4\lambda^2 + 2)$. But then (iii) implies that $z/\lambda = 2\lambda z$ and so, because $z \neq 0$, that $2\lambda^2 = 1$. Therefore $z^2 = \frac{1}{2}$. The points satisfying the KKT conditions are at $\pm(\frac{1}{2}, \frac{1}{2}, \frac{1}{2}\sqrt{2})$, with $\lambda = \frac{1}{2}\sqrt{2}$ and $xz + yz = \frac{1}{2}\sqrt{2}$. The extreme value theorem guarantees the existence of a maximum point, which is either of these two.

20.3

1. (a) With $\mathcal{L}(x, y) = x + \ln(1 + y) - \lambda(16x + y - 495)$, the KKT conditions for (x^*, y^*) to be a solution are:

   (i) $\mathcal{L}_1'(x^*, y^*) = 1 - 16\lambda \leq 0$ ($= 0$ if $x^* > 0$) (ii) $\mathcal{L}_2'(x^*, y^*) = \dfrac{1}{1 + y^*} - \lambda \leq 0$ ($= 0$ if $y^* > 0$)

   (iii) $\lambda \geq 0$, with $\lambda = 0$ if $16x^* + y^* < 495$ (iv) $x^* \geq 0$, $y^* \geq 0$ (v) $16x^* + y^* \leq 495$.

   (b) Note that the Lagrangian is concave, so a point that satisfies the KKT conditions will be a maximum point. From (i), $\lambda \geq 1/16 > 0$, so (iii) and (v) imply (vi) $16x^* + y^* = 495$.

   Suppose $x^* = 0$. Then (v) gives $y^* = 495$, and from (ii), $\lambda = 1/496$, contradicting $\lambda \geq 1/16$. Hence, $x^* > 0$, and so by (i), $\lambda = 1/16$.

   Suppose $y^* = 0$. Then (ii) implies $\lambda \geq 1$, contradicting $\lambda = 1/16$. Thus $y^* > 0$, and so from (ii), $y^* = 15$ and then (v) yields $x^* = 30$.

   So the only solution to the KKT conditions is $(x^*, y^*) = (30, 15)$, with $\lambda = 1/16$.

   (c) Utility will increase by approximately $\lambda \cdot 5 = 5/16$. (Actually, the new solution is $(30\frac{5}{16}, 15)$, and the increase in utility is exactly 5/16. This is because the utility function has a special "quasi-linear" form.)

2. $(x, y) = (1, 0)$ is the only point satisfying all the conditions, with Lagrange multiplier $\lambda = 0$.

3. The only possible solution is $(x_1^*, x_2^*, k^*) = (1/2, 3/4, 3/4)$, with Lagrange multipliers $\lambda = 0$ and $\mu = 3/2$.

Review exercises for Chapter 20

1. For $a \geq 5$, the solution is $(x, y) = (2, 1)$, with $\lambda = 0$. For $a < 5$, it is $(x, y) = (2\sqrt{a/5}, \sqrt{a/5})$, with $\lambda = \sqrt{5/a} - 1$.

2. (a) With $\mathcal{L} = xy - \lambda_1(x^2 + ry^2 - m) - \lambda_2(-x + 1)$, the KKT conditions for (x^*, y^*) to solve the problem are:

   (i) $\mathcal{L}_1' = y^* - 2\lambda_1 x^* + \lambda_2 = 0$; (ii) $\mathcal{L}_2' = x^* - 2r\lambda_1 y^* = 0$; (iii) $\lambda_1 \geq 0$, with $\lambda_1 = 0$ if $(x^*)^2 + r(y^*)^2 < m$;

   (iv) $\lambda_2 \geq 0$, with $\lambda_2 = 0$ if $x^* > 1$; (v) $(x^*)^2 + r(y^*)^2 \leq m$; (vi) $x^* \geq 1$.

   (b) For $m \geq 2$ the solution is $x^* = \sqrt{m/2}$ and $y^* = \sqrt{m/2r}$, with $\lambda_1 = 1/2\sqrt{r}$ and $\lambda_2 = 0$.

   For $1 < m < 2$ it is $x^* = 1$, $y^* = \sqrt{(m-1)/r}$, with $\lambda_1 = 1/2\sqrt{r(m-1)}$ and $\lambda_2 = (2-m)/\sqrt{r(m-1)}$.

   (c) For $m \geq 2$ one has $V(r, m) = m/2\sqrt{r}$, and for $1 < m < 2$ it is $\sqrt{(m-1)/r}$. It is easy to verify that $V_m' = \lambda_1 > 0$, as one expects. See SM for details. (d) Routine verification. See SM for details.

3. (a) See Fig. A20.R.3. The solution is at P, where $(x_1, x_2) = (2000, 2000/3)$.

   (b) There are six pairs of complementarily slack inequalities. See SM for details.

   (c) The challenge is to find Lagrange multipliers λ_i ($i = 1$ to 4) such that the KKT conditions are still satisfied at $(x_1, x_2) = (2000, 2000/3)$. This is possible iff $a \leq 1/24$. See SM for details.

4. With the Lagrangian $\mathcal{L} = R(Q) - C(Q) - \lambda(-Q)$, the KKT conditions for Q^* to be a solution are:

   (i) $R'(Q^*) - C'(Q^*) + \lambda = 0$; (ii) $\lambda \geq 0$, with $\lambda = 0$ if $Q^* > 0$. These conditions are also sufficient for optimality because the Lagrangian is concave in Q. A sufficient (and necessary) condition for $Q^* = 0$ to be optimal is that $\pi'(0) \leq 0$, or equivalently, $R'(0) \leq C'(0)$. (Draw a figure.)

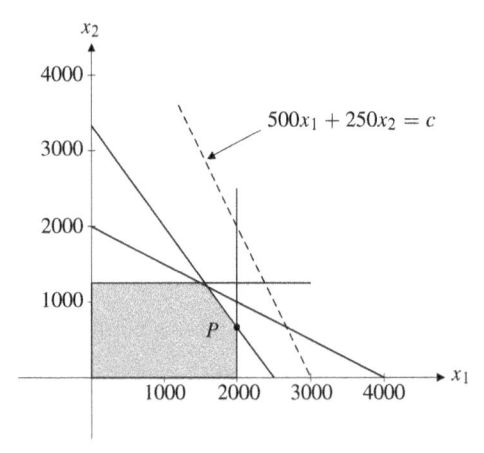

Figure A20.R.3

5. (a) The maximization problem is: $\max(-rK - wL)$ subject to $-\sqrt{KL} \leq -Q$.

With the Lagrangian $\mathcal{L} = -rK - wL - \lambda(-\sqrt{KL} + Q)$, the KKT conditions for (K^*, L^*) to solve the problem are:

(i) $\mathcal{L}'_K = -r + \lambda(\sqrt{L^*}/2\sqrt{K^*}) = 0$; (ii) $\mathcal{L}'_L = -w + \lambda(\sqrt{K^*}/2\sqrt{L^*}) = 0$; (iii) $\lambda \geq 0$ ($\lambda = 0$ if $\sqrt{K^*L^*} > Q$).

Obviously $\lambda = 0$ would contradict (i) and (ii), so $\lambda > 0$ and (iv) $\sqrt{K^*L^*} = Q$. Eliminating λ from (i) and (ii), we find $L^* = rK^*/w$. Then (iv) yields $K^* = Q\sqrt{w/r}$ and $L^* = Q\sqrt{r/w}$.

(b) $c^*(r, w, Q) = rK^* + wL^* = 2Q\sqrt{rw}$, so $\partial c^*/\partial r = Q\sqrt{w/r} = K^*$. If the price of capital r increases by dr, then the minimum cost will increase by about K^*dr, or the optimal choice of capital input per unit increase in r. The equation $\partial c^*/\partial w = Q\sqrt{r/w} = L^*$ has a similar interpretation.

INDEX

∅ – empty set, 4
∈ – element of, 5
∩ – intersection of sets, 5
∪ – union of sets, 5
\ – set difference, 5
⊆ – subset, 5
⇔ – equivalence arrow, 12
⇒, ⇐ – implication arrows, 12
∞ – infinity, 52–53
$f : A \to B$ – function from A to B, 175
→ – "is mapped to," 176
Δx – a (small) change in x, 193
$f'(x)$ – derivative of f at x, 182
$f''(x)$ – second derivative, 218
$f^{(4)}(x)$ – fourth derivative, 219
$f'''(x)$ – third derivative, 219
$\lim_{x \to a} f(x), f(x$, 184, 196, 276
$\lim_{x \to a^-} f(x)$ – limit from below, 271
$\lim_{x \to a^+} f(x)$ – limit from above, 271
d – differential, 654–659
f'_i – partial derivative, 568
∂ – partial differentiation symbol, 569
∫ – integral sign, 356
∫∫ – double integral, 676
∫∫∫ – triple integral, 685
∫ . . . ∫ multiple integral, 684
$\mathbb{R}n$ – Euclidean n-space, 482–483
∇ – "nabla," gradient operator, 576

A

absolute risk aversion, 220
absolute value, 53–55
active constraint, 802
addition of matrices, 453–454
adjugate matrix, 524
admissible point, 771, 774
admissible set, 797, 804
affine function, 581
algebra rules, 33–38
alien cofactor, 516
angle between vectors, 485
angles, 821
annuity
  due, 419
  future value, 416
  ordinary, 421
  present value, 414
antiderivative, 356
approximation
  higher-order, 254–255
  linear, 248–252, 646–654
  polynomial, 253–255
  quadratic, 253–254
  Taylor, 255
area, 361–368
area under a curve, 366–367
argument of a function, 101
  two variables, 562

arithmetic mean, 52, 63, 582
arithmetic series, 66
associative law of matrix
  multiplication, 463
asymptote, 278
  horizontal, 273
  vertical, 271
asymptotes, 172
asymptotic stability (difference
  equations), 427
augmented coefficient matrix, 477
autonomous consumption, 81
average cost, 157
average elasticity, 260
average rate of change, 192
axis of symmetry, 121

B

base (of a power), 26
base 10 system, 24
Bernoulli, J., 21
Bernoulli's inequality, 21
binding constraint, 802
binomial coefficient, 66, 67
binomial formula, 66
bi-variate uniform distribution, 679
bordered Hessian, 753
boundary point, 599, 717
bounded interval, 52, 273

bounded set, 713, 718
budget constraint, 4, 642
budget equation, 579
budget hyperplane, 491
budget set, 4, 591

C

C^1 function, 589
Cantor, G., 8, 9
cardinality of a set, 9
Cartesian coordinate system, 106–107
Cartesian product, 595
Cauchy–Schwarz inequality, 127, 484–485
centre of circle, 171
CES function, 633, 634, 639
chain rule, 212, 213, 613–614, 615–616, 617–618, 657
change of variables in integrals, 385
characteristic equation, 540
characteristic polynomial, 540
characterization of concave/convex functions, 311
circle, 171–172
 area, circumference, 819
 centre, 171
 equation, 172
 radius, 171
C^k function, 589
closed interval, 52
closed set, 599, 717
Cobb–Douglas function, 290, 437, 563, 582, 606, 621, 633, 634, 641, 751, 756
codomain of a function, 175
coefficient, 35
coefficient matrix, 451–452
 augmented, 477
cofactor, 500, 514–517
 alien, 516
cofactor expansion, 516, 517
column (of a matrix), 447
column vector, 448
common factors, 39
commutative inner product, 457
compact set, 713, 717
comparative statics, 759–762
comparison test for convergence of integrals, 393–394
complement of a set, 6
complementary inequalities, 799

complementary inputs, 606
complementary slackness, 770, 788–792, 798, 799, 805, 807
 conditions, interpreting, 791
 interpretation, 791
 theorem, 790
completing the square, 85
components of a vector, 448
composite function, 158–159, 614, 616
compound interest, 29–30
concave function, 595–605
 extrema of, 326, 694, 695–696
 inverse of, 307
 n variables, 603
 one variable, 297, 301
 two variables, 595–597
concave Lagangean, 750–751
concave programme, 806
concave programming, 806
 sufficient conditions, 806–807
concave/convex functions, first-derivative characterization, 311
concavity/convexity
 necessary conditions, 309
 slope characterization, 301–302
 sufficient conditions, 310–311, 653
concavity/convexity conditions for max/min, 694–695
 with equity constraints, 750
 with inequality constraints, 799–800, 807
conclusions, 16
cone, 629, 630, 820
consistent system of equations, 451
constant returns to scale, 641
constant terms of an equation, 451
constraint
 active, 802
 binding, 802
 inactive, 802
 slack, 802
 tight, 802
consumer surplus, 377
consumption function, 117–118
consumption smoothing, 301
continuity, 264–270
continuous compounding, 403–404
continuous depreciation, 138
continuous function, 264, 265, 267, 275, 584

composites, 266
 from the left, 273
 n variables, 583, 584
 properties, 266
 from the right, 273
continuously differentiable, 589, 649
contour, 572
contrapositive (indirect) proof, 16
contrapositive principle, 13
convergence
 general series, 412
 geometric series, 410
 improper integral, 390, 391
comparison test, 394
 sequence, 284
convex combination, 593
convex function, 595–605
 extrema of, 326, 694, 695–696
 inverse of, 307
 n variables, 603
 one variable, 297, 301
 two variables, 595–597
convex Lagangean, 750–751
convex polyhedron, 774, 775
convex programme, 807
convex sets, 590–595
 intersection, 594
coordinate axes, 106, 481
coordinate plane, 482
coordinate system, 481, 482
 Cartesian, 106–107
 rectangular, 106
coordinates of a point, 107
coordinates of a vector, 448
correlation
 negative, 486
 positive, 486
correlation coefficient, 486, 681
counting rule, 660
covariance, 330, 709
Cramer, G., 497
Cramer's rule, 520, 527–531
 three unknowns, 501
 two unknowns, 497
critical point
 n variables, 717
 one variable, 323
 two variables, 690
cross partials, 587, 606
cube root, 44
cubic function, 127–128
cumulative distribution function, 374

D

Dantzig, G., 769
De Morgan's laws, 10
deadweight loss, 707
decimal fraction
   finite, 25
   infinite, 25
   periodic, 25
   recurring, 25
decimal system, 24
decline, exponential, 31
decreasing function, 105, 189–190
decreasing returns to scale, 641
Dedekind, R., 9
deductive reasoning, 17
definite integral, 365, 366
   properties, 368–371
degree of equation, 130
degree of homogeneity, 634
degree of polynomial, 128
degrees of freedom, 477, 607, 659, 660, 661
demand and supply, 118–120, 154, 242, 625–626
demand function, 737, 756
denominator, 38
dependent (endogenous) variable, 101, 562
depreciation
   continuous, 138
   straight line, 119
derivative, 182, 184
   computation, 186
   of a constant, 201
   of a difference, 205
   dot notation, 192
   first, 218
   fourth, 219
   functions of n variables, 648
   left, 276
   partial, 565–566, 568
   of a product, 206–207
   of a quotient, 209, 210
   right, 276
   second, 218, 237
   of a sum, 205
   third, 219
Descartes's folium, 292
determinant
   of 2×2 matrix, 496
   of a 3×3 matrix, 500
   expansion by cofactors, 500
   geometric interpretation, 497–498, 502
   of an $n \times n$ matrix, 504–508
   rules for calculation, 501
deviation from the mean, 63
diagonalizable matrix, 544
difference between functions, 156
difference between vectors, 455
difference equation, 425–428
   globally asymptotically stable, 427
   linear, 426–427
   unstable, 427
difference of sets, 5
difference-of-squares formula, 34
differentiability, n variables, 647
differentiable function, 201
   one variable, 275
   several variables, 647
differentiable implies continuous, 275, 649
differential equation, 428–435
   for bounded exponential growth, 431
   linear, 438
   for logistic growth, 432–433
   for natural growth, 430
   separable, 436, 438
differential notation, 187
differential of a function, 654
   invariance of, 657–658
   n variables, 658
   one variable, 249–251
   rules for, 250–251, 656–657
differentiation
   chain rule, 215
   implicit, 233–234, 245
   logarithmic, 227–228
   power rule, 203
   rules, 201–205
dimension of a matrix, 448
dimension of a vector, 448
direct proof, 16
direct second-order partials, 587
direction, 647–648
directional derivative, 648
discontinuity
   irremovable, 265
   removable, 265
discontinuous function, 265
discount factor, 406
discount rate, 406
discounted value, 406
disjoint sets, 6
distance, 170–174, 483
   between numbers, 54
   in $\mathbb{R}^2$, 170
   in $\mathbb{R}^n$, 717
distribution
   Gaussian, 394–395
   normal, 394
distributive laws
   inner product of vectors, 457
   matrix multiplication, 463
divergence
   general series, 412
   geometric series, 410
   improper integral, 391
divergent sequence, 284
divisible polynomial, 129
dollar cost averaging, 585
domain of a function, 103, 104, 163–164, 175, 562, 563–564
dot product, 456
double integral, 676
doubling time, 145–146
dual problem, 781, 786
duality in linear programming, 726
duality theorem (LP), 781–785
duopoly, 711

E

$e(=2.71828.)$, 139, 220, 223, 228, 285
economic growth, 436–437, 439–440
edges, 774
effective interest rate, 401, 404
eigenvalue, 536, 538, 539
eigenvector, 536, 538
elastic function, 262
elasticity, 259–262
   average, 260
   demand, 260
   Engel, 263
   general definition, 261
   logarithmic derivative, 262, 608
   n variables, 607
   price, 260
   rules for, 262
   of substitution, 632–634
   two variables, 608
element of a matrix, 448
element of a set, 3, 5
elementary row operations, 475, 477

ellipse, 172–173
ellipsoid, 579
endogenous variable, 101, 562, 667
Engel elasticity, 263
entry of a matrix, 448
envelope theorems, 724, 726, 761
equal sets, 5
equal vectors, 455
equality constraints, 731, 792–793
equation
  degree n, 130
  difference, 428
  differential, 438
  equivalent, 78
  integer roots, 130–131
  linear, 80
  nonlinear, 82
  quadratic, 83–88
  solution of, 11, 79
  system of equations, 93–94, 659–662
equilibrium
  demand theory, 118
  difference equations, 428
  differential equations, 438
  equation system, 667
equilibrium point, 154, 377, 665, 666
equilibrium price, 118
equilibrium quantity, 118
equivalence arrow (⇔), 12
equivalent equation, 78
Euclid, 24
Euclidean n-space, 482–483
Euler's number, e, 228
Euler's theorem for homogeneous functions
  n variables, 630
  two variables, 635–636
even function, 159
even number, 23
exhaustion method, 362
exogenous variable, 101, 562, 667
exp – natural exponential function, 221
expansion by cofactors, 516, 517
expectation, 121–122
expected value, 122, 679
exponent, 26
exponential decline, 31
exponential decrease, 136–137
exponential distribution, 390
exponential function, 139
  derivative, 220–221

natural, 220–221
  properties, 139, 222
exponential growth, 30, 429–430
  bounded, 431
exponential increase, 136–137
exterior function, 158, 215
exterior point, 599
extrema
  first-derivative test, 325
  second-order conditions, 325, 348, 695–696, 719, 720, 751–752
extrema of quadratic functions, 121
extreme points (LP), 771, 775
extreme point/value, 322
  local, 346, 699–705
extreme value theorem
  n variables, 718
  one variable, 334
  two variables, 713

F

faces, 774
factor of a polynomial, 129
factorial notation, 68
factoring
  algebraic expressions, 35–36
  polynomial, 129
factorization, 85
  of a quadratic polynomial, 87
family of sets, 6
feasible point, 771, 774
feasible set, 797, 804
first-derivative test
  (global) extrema, 325
  local extrema, 347
first-order conditions, 733, 734
  with equality constraints, 733, 734, 753–754, 758
  with inequality constraints, 799, 805, 812
  n variables, 717–718
  one variable, 323
  two variables, 690
flour border, 771
FOC *see* first-order conditions
fractional powers, 43–48
fractions
  improper, 38
  proper, 38
Franklin, J., 769
function
  affine, 581

argument, 562
from A to B, 175
C^1, 589
C^k, 589
Cobb–Douglas, 563
codomain, 175
composite, 158–159, 215
concave, 297, 301, 595–605
consumption, 118
continuously differentiable, 589
continuous, 265, 584
convex, 297, 301, 595–605
cubic, 127–128
decreasing, 105, 189–190
defined implicitly, 233
differentiable, 201, 275
discontinuous, 265
domain, 103, 104, 163–164, 175, 562
even, 159
exponential, 139
general concept, 174–176
graph, 107, 571–572, 584
homogeneous, 630, 634–636
homothetic, 642–643
increasing, 105, 189–190
inverse, 162–163, 176, 224
linear, 110–116, 582
logarithmic, 141–143, 224–225
logistic, 432
log-linear, 582
many-to-one, 176
n variables, 581
natural exponential, 139–141
non-decreasing, 105
odd, 159–160
one variable, 100
one-to-many, 176
one-to-one, 161, 176, 244–245
piecewise defined, 169–170
polynomial, 127–134
power, 135–136
quadratic, 120–127
range, 101, 176, 562
rational, 133
strictly concave, 301
strictly convex, 301
strictly increasing/decreasing, 105, 189–190
symmetric about a point, 159–160
target, 175
two variables, 561, 562

fundamental theorem of algebra, 130
future discounted value, 418
future value of an annuity, 416

G

Gauss, C., 64
Gaussian distribution, 394–395
Gaussian elimination, 475
Gauss–Jordan method, 475
generalized power rule, 213
geometric mean, 52, 582
geometric series, 408–414
   infinite, 410
   quotient, 408
   sum, 410
geometric vector, 480
Giffen goods, 118
global extreme point/value, 346, 347
globally asymptotically stable
   difference equation, 427
gradient, 576–577
gradient vector, 576, 577
graph
   of an equation, 166–170
   of a function, 107
   n variables, 584–585
   two variables, 571–572
greater than, 48
Greek alphabet, 822
growth factor, 30
growth towards a limit, 431

H

Haavelmo, T., 118
Hadamard, J. S., 613
Hadamard product of matrices, 458
half-open interval, 52
half-space, 482
harmonic mean, 52, 582
Hessian matrix, 587, 719, 720, 808
   bordered, 753
Hilbert, D., 673
homogeneity, degree of, 639
homogeneous function, 634–636, 637–639, 640
homogeneous system of linear
   equations, 529–530
homothetic function, 642–643
horizontal asymptote, 273
horizontal axis, 106
Hotelling's lemma, 725

hyperbola, 133, 172–173
hyperplane, 584
   budget, 491
hypersurface, 584

I

idempotent matrix, 469
identity matrix, 466
if (if and only if), 12
image of an element by a function, 176
implication, 12
implication arrows ($\Rightarrow, \Leftarrow$), 12, 91–92
implicit differentiation, 233–234, 245, 623–628
   second derivative, 237
implicit function, 233–234
improper integral, 390
   convergence, 390, 391, 394
   divergence, 390, 391
improper rational function, 133
In – natural logarithm, 142
inactive constraint, 802
income density function, 374
income distribution, 374–375
inconsistent system of equations, 451
increasing function, 105, 189–190
increasing returns to scale, 641
increment of a function, 654
incremental cost, 193, 194
indefinite integral, 355–361
indefinite quadratic form or matrix, 548, 551
independent (exogenous) variable, 101, 562
indeterminate form, 287
indifference curve, 238, 239, 737
indifference surface, 584
indirect proof, 16
indirect utility function, 762
indivisible commodity, 591
induction hypothesis, 18, 19
induction proof, 18
induction reasoning, 17
induction step, 18, 19
inelastic function, 262
inequality
   double, 49–50
   strict, 48
   weak, 48
inequality constraints, 770, 774

infinite sequence, 281, 282, 283–286
infinity (∞), 52–53, 271
inflection point, 316–317
   test for, 317
inner function, 215
inner product of vectors, 456
   rules, 457
input–output model of Leontief, 535
instantaneous rate of change, 192
integer
   negative, 24
   positive, 23, 24
integer roots of a polynomial
   equation, 130–131
integral
   definite, 365, 366
   double, 676
   improper, 390
   indefinite, 355–361
   infinite limits, 390
   multiple, 684
   Newton–Leibniz (N–L), 371
   Riemann, 371
   unbounded integrand, 392–393
integral curve, 436
integral of an arbitrary exponential, 358
integral of the exponential function, 358
integral sign ($\int$), 356
integrand, 357
integrating factor, 439, 440
integration
   basic rules, 357
   constant of, 356
   by parts, 380–383
   of rational functions, 387–388
   by substitution, 384
   variable, 357
intercept, 110
interest, continuous compounding, 404
interest period, 399
interest rate
   annual, 29, 31, 399
   effective, 401, 404
   nominal, 399
   periodic, 400
interior function, 158
interior of a set, 599, 717
interior of an interval, 53
interior point, 53, 599, 717

intermediate value theorem, 279–282
  proof, 285–286
internal rate of return, 423–424
intersection of sets, 5
interval
  bounded, 52
  closed, 52
  half-open, 52
  open, 52, 53
invariance of the differential, 657–658
inverse function, 160–166, 176, 224
  derivative, 245
inverse function theorem, 244–247
inverse matrix, 517–518, 520
  by elementary operations, 525–526
  general formula, 524–525
  properties, 521, 588
inverse of 2×2 matrix, 519, 520
invertible matrix, 518
investment multiplier, 82
investment projects, 423
involutive matrix, 513
irrational numbers, 24, 25, 286
irremovable discontinuity, 265
IS–LM model, 668
isoquant, 584

J

Jevons, S., 194
joint density function, 679
joint probability distribution, 679

K

Kahn, R.F., 117
Karush, W., 798
Karush–Kuhn–Tucker method, 798
  see also KKT method
Keynes, J.M., 117
kinks, 269
  in a graph, 276
KKT conditions, 799
KKT method, 798
  with multiple inequality constraints, 805
  necessary conditions, 799, 805
  why it works, 802–803
KKT theorem applied to LP, 813–814

Kuhn, H.W., 798
Kuhn–Tucker method see KKT method

L

Laffer curve, 100
Lagrange, J.-L., 256–257, 732
Lagrange multiplier, 731–734, 739–740, 753, 756, 759
Lagrange multiplier method
  economic interpretations, 739, 760
  NLP, 798, 805
  one constraint, 732
  several constraints, 756–757
  sufficient conditions, 749–753
  why it works, 744–749
Lagrange's remainder formula, 256–257
  proof, 339
Lagrange's theorem, 747–748
Lagangean, 750–751, 753, 756, 798, 805, 806
Lagangean function, 732
Laspeyres price index, 61
law for natural growth, 430
LCD, 40
leading entries in systems of equations, 474
leading principal minor, 552
least common denominator (LCD), 40
left continuous, 272–273
left derivative, 276
left distributive law, 463
left limit, 271
Leibniz, G., 181, 187, 218, 655
Leibniz notation, 187
lemniscate, 240
length of a vector, 484, 717
Leontief matrix, 534
Leontief model, 495, 531–535
level curve, 572, 573, 624, 637, 638
  slope of, 624
l'Hôpital's rule, 287
  extension of, 289
limit, 195–196
  from above, 271
  from below, 271
  definition, 274, 276
  equality, 199
  at infinity, 273–274
  left, 271

one-sided, 271–272
right, 271
rules, 197–198
ε–δ definition, 277
limit of a function, 265, 267, 276, 583
  n variables, 583
limit of a sequence, 286
line segment
  directed, 480
  in $\mathbb{R}^n$, 593
linear algebra, 447
linear approximation
  n variables, 647
  one variable, 248–252
  two variables, 646
linear combination, 456
linear difference equation, first-order, with constant coefficient, 426–427
linear differential equation, 438
linear equation, 80
linear expenditure system, 582, 741
linear function
  n variables, 582
  one variable, 110–116
linear inequality, 114–115
  geometric representation, 114
linear models, 116–120
  with quadratic objectives, 705–712
linear programming, 769
  duality theory, 726
  economic interpretation, 786–788
  general problem, 774–776
linear regression, 328, 709
linear system of equations
  in matrix form, 461–462
  n variables, 450
  two variables, 80, 81, 92
local extrema, 346
  first-derivative test, 347
  second-derivative test, 348
  second-order conditions, 350
local maximum/minimum, strict, 347
logarithm
  to base a, 145
  natural, 141
logarithmic differentiation, 227–228
logarithmic function, 141–143, 224–225
logical equivalence, 12
logistic function, 432

INDEX

logistic growth, 432–433
log-linear function, 582
log-linear relation, 262
lower limit of integration, 365
lower triangular matrix, 507
lowest common denominator, 40
LP *see* linear programming

M

main diagonal of a matrix, 448–449
Malthus's law, 430
many-to-one, 176
map/mapping, 176
marginal cost, 188, 693, 763
marginal product, 194
   of capital, 606
   of labour, 606
   of land, 606
marginal productivity, 692
marginal propensity to consume, 81, 117, 194, 240
marginal propensity to save, 195
marginal rate of substitution, 626, 737, 755
marginal revenue, 693
marginal tax rate, 170
marginal utility of income, 762
market share vector, 461
mathematical induction, 18–20
matrix, 447–448
   addition, 453–454
   adjugate, 524
   bordered Hessian, 753
   diagonalizable, 544
   dimension, 448
   element, 448
   entry, 448
   equality, 449
   Hadamard product, 458
   Hessian, 587, 719, 720, 808
   idempotent, 469
   identity, 466
   inverse, 517–518, 520
   invertible, 518
   involutive, 513
   lower triangular, 507
   multiplication, 458–463
   multiplication by a scalar, 454
   nonsingular, 519
   order, 448
   orthogonal, 545
   powers of, 465
   product, 459
   singular, 519
   skew-symmetric, 493
   square, 448
   symmetric, 472
   trace, 538
   transpose, 470
   transposition rules, 471
   upper triangular, 474, 507
   zero, 454
matrix inverse, general formula, 524–525
matrix multiplication, associative law, 463
maximization/minimization, 733
   constrained, 732
   unconstrained, 732
maximizer, 322
maximum point/value, 321–322, 690, 691, 717
   local, 347, 699–700
mean, 63, 582
   arithmetic, 52, 63
   geometric, 52
   harmonic, 52
mean income, 376
mean square deviation, 64
mean square error, 486
mean value theorem, 335
member (element) of a set, 3
Menger, C., 194
minimizer, 322
minimum point/value, 321–322, 690, 691, 717
   local, 346, 699–700
minor, 514
mixed number, 38
mixed partials, 587, 606
monopolist, discriminating, 707
monopoly, 693, 706, 707
monopoly problem, 122
monopsonist, discriminating, 708
monopsony, 708
mortgage repayment, 419–423
MRS, 626, 737, 755
multiple integral, 684
multiplication of matrices, 458–463
multiplier–accelerator model, 426

N

natural exponential function, 139–141, 220–221
natural growth law, 430
natural logarithm, 141
   basic properties, 142
   rules, 142
natural logarithm function, 226–227
   derivative, 224–225
natural numbers, 23
n-dimensional cuboid, 684
n-dimensional rectangle, 684
necessary condition, 13–14
necessity, 13
negative definite/semidefinite quadratic form or matrix, 548, 551
negative integers, 24
Nerlove–Ringstad production function, 632
net investment, 379
net return, 423
Newton, I., 181, 233, 280
Newton quotient, 184, 186, 192
Newton–Leibniz (N–L) integral, 371
Newton's binomial formula, 66
Newton's method for approximating roots, 280–281
   convergence, 282
non-decreasing function, 105
nonlinear equations, 82
nonlinear programming (NLP)
   multiple inequality constraints, 805
   nonnegativity constraints, 812–813
   problem, 797–798
nonnegative octant, 482
nonnegative orthant, 643, 774
nonnegativity constraints
   in LP, 770, 774
   in NLP, 812–813
nonsingular matrix, 519
non-trivial solution, 433, 530
norm, 717
norm of a vector, 484
normal density function, 140, 680
normal distribution, 394, 680–681
normal to a plane, 489
n-space, 482–483, 484
nth power, 26
nth root, 44
number
   even, 23
   irrational, 24, 25, 286
   mixed, 38
   natural, 23

number (*continued*)
    odd, 23
    rational, 24
    real, 23, 25
number line, 24
numerator, 38
n-vector, 448

O

objective function, 721, 770, 774
octant, nonnegative, 482
odd function, 159–160
odd number, 23
one-sided continuity, 272–273
one-sided limit, 271–272
one-to-many, 176
one-to-one, 161, 176, 244–245
open ball, 717
open interval, 52, 53
open set, 599, 717
optimal point/value, 322
order of a matrix, 448
ordered pair, 107
ordinary least squares, 330
ordinate set, 673
origin, 106
orthogonal matrix, 545
orthogonal vectors, 485
orthogonality in econometrics, 486

P

Paasche price index, 61
Pacioli, L., 249
parabola, 120
paraboloid, 573
parallelogram law of addition, 482
parameter, 81
Pareto distribution, 204, 375
partial derivatives, 589
    approximations, 568
    cross, 569, 587
    first-order, 569
    geometric interpretation, 574–576
    higher order, 569
    mixed, 569, 587
    n variables, 586
    second-order, 569
    two variables, 565–566, 568
partial elasticity, 608–609
partial fraction expansion, 387
Pascal, B., 66

Pascal's triangle, 66
PDV, 406
peak load pricing, 815
per capita growth rate, 430
percentage, 29–30
perfect correlation, 486
perfectly competitive firm, 123–124
perfectly elastic/inelastic function, 262
periodic decimal fraction, 25
periodic rate of interest, 400
piecewise functions, 169–170
plane
    in $\mathbb{R}^3$, 489, 490
    in $\mathbb{R}^n$ (hyperplane), 490
point–point formula, 113
point–slope formula, 112
pollution and welfare, 606–607, 615
polynomial
    degree *n*, 128
    divisible, 129
polynomial division, 131–133
polynomial division with remainder, 132–133
polynomial factor, 129
polynomial factoring, 129
polynomial function, 127–134
population growth, 137
positive definite/semidefinite
    quadratic form or matrix, 548, 551
positive integers, 23, 24
postmultiplication, 461
power
    fractional, 43–48
    rational exponent, 46
    rules, 27
power function, 135–136, 229
power rule, 203, 211, 213
powers of matrices, 465
premises, 16
premultiplication, 461
present discounted value, 406
    continuous income stream, 417–418
present value, 406, 416
    annuity, 414
price elasticity of demand, 260
price index, 61
    Laspeyres, 61
    Paasche, 61
primal problem (LP), 781
principal diagonal of a matrix, 448

principal minor, 552
    leading, 552
producer surplus, 378–379
product
    dot, 456
    inner, 456
    scalar, 456
product of functions, 158
production functions, 290, 313, 318, 437, 563, 571, 574, 606, 607, 621, 626, 632, 636–637, 641, 655
productivity, 194
productivity of capital, average, 440
profit function, 158, 725
profit maximization, 320, 350, 692, 702, 725
proof
    by contradiction, 16
    direct, 16
    indirect, 16
    by induction, 18
proper fractions, 38
proper rational function, 133
proportional rates of change, 193
proportions, 821
proposition, 11
pyramid, 820
Pythagoras's theorem, 483, 821

Q

quadrant, 106–107
quadratic approximation, 253–254
quadratic equation, 83–88
    solution, 85
quadratic form, 547–548, 551
    associated symmetric matrix, 551
quadratic formula, 86
quadratic function, 87, 120–127
    extrema, 121
quadratic identities, 34, 36
quartic function, 128
quotient of a geometric series, 408
quotient of functions, 158

R

radius of circle, 171
range of a function, 101, 161, 176, 562
rate of change
    average, 192

INDEX 951

instantaneous, 192
  relative, 193
rate of extraction, 373
rate of interest, 29–30
rate of investment, 192
rational function
  improper, 133
  proper, 133
rational numbers, 24
real line, 25
real numbers, 23, 25
real wage rate, 210
rectangular box, 820
rectangular distribution, 395
recurring decimal fraction, 25
reduced form, 667
reduced form (of a system of equations), 82
reductio ad absurdum, 16
relative rate of change, 193
relative risk aversion, 220
remainder, 132–133
  polynomial division, 129
remainder in Taylor's formula, 256–257
remainder theorem, 129
removable discontinuity, 265
Riemann integral, 371
right continuous, 273
right derivative, 276
right distributive law, 463
right limit, 271
right-hand sides of a system of equations, 451
risk aversion, 220
roots
  of polynomial equations, 130
  of quadratic equations, 86
row (of a matrix), 447
row operations (elementary), 475, 477
row vector, 448
Roy's identity, 762, 763
rule of 70, 249

S

saddle point, 690, 700
  second-order conditions, 701
Sarrus's rule, 503
savings rate, 440
scalar, 481

scalar product, 456
SDLT (UK), 267
search model, 630–631
secant, 183
second-derivative test
  see second-order conditions
second-order conditions
  with equality constraints, 751–752
  global, 325, 695–696, 719
  local, 348, 350, 701, 720, 751–752
  second-derivative test, 312–313
second-order partials
  cross, 587
  direct, 587
  mixed, 587
separable differential equation, 436
series
  general, 411–412
  harmonic, 412
  infinite geometric, 410
sets, 3
  cardinality, 9
  complement, 6
  difference, 5
  disjoint, 6
  element of, 5
  equal, 5
  family of, 6
  intersection, 5
  union, 5
  universal, 6
shadow price, 739, 769, 786, 787, 799
Shephard, R., 763
Shephard's lemma, 763
shifting graphs, 151–156
sign diagram, 56–58
sign rule, 505
simplex method, 769, 775
singular matrix, 519
skew-symmetric matrix, 493
slack constraint, 802
slope
  of a curve, 181–183
  of a level curve, 624
  of a straight line, 110
smaller than, 48
Smith, A., 194
SOC *see* second-order conditions
Solow, R., 436

Solow–Swan growth, 436
solution of a system of equations, 451
solution set, 56, 57, 166
spectral theorem, 546
sphere
  equation, 580
  surface area, volume, 820
square matrix, 448
square root, 10, 11
  properties, 43
stability
  difference equations, 428
  differential equations, 438
stamp duty, 267
stationary point *see* critical point
stationary state
  difference equation, 427
  differential equation, 438
steady state
  difference equation, 427
  differential equation, 438
Stewart, I., 77
Stone, R., 741
straight line
  in $\mathbb{R}^2$
    point–point formula, 113
    point–slope formula, 112
  in $\mathbb{R}^3$, 487
  in $\mathbb{R}^n$, 488
  slope, 110
straight line depreciation, 119
strict maximum/minimum point, 322
  local, 346
strictly concave/convex function, 301, 327, 598–601, 603
  extrema of, 327
strictly greater than, 48
strictly increasing/decreasing function, 105
structural equations, 667
structural form (of a system of equations), 82
subgradient, 309, 311
subgradient vector, 651, 652
subset, 5
subsidies, 124, 125
substitutes in consumption, 607
substitution in integration, 384
sufficiency, 13
sufficient conditions, 13–14
sum of functions, 156

sum of series
   finite geometric, 408, 409
   infinite geometric, 409–410
summation
   additivity, 62
   double, 70
   homogeneity, 62
   rules, 62
summation formulas
   binomial, 66
   finite geometric series, 408, 409
   infinite geometric series, 409–410
   other sums, 63
summation index, 59
summation notation, 59
summation symbol, 59
supergradient, 309, 311
supergradient vector, 651, 652
supply and demand, 118–120, 154, 242, 625–626
supply curve, 124
surface, 584
Sylvester's criterion, 553
symmetric matrix, 472
symmetry of a function, 159–160
system of equations, 93–94
   coefficient matrix, 451–452
   linear, 450–453
   vector of constants, 451–452

T

tangent line, 182, 183, 185
tangent plane, 650–651
target set of a function, 175
Taylor approximation, 255, 257
Taylor polynomial, 255
Taylor's formula, 257
   remainder, 257
Temple, G.F.J., 64, 117
term
   of an algebraic expression, 35
   coefficient of, 35
tight constraint, 802
Tinbergen rule, 660
total derivative, 614
trace of a matrix, 538
transformation, 176

transition matrix, 461
translog cost function, 645
transpose matrix, 470, 521, 588
triangle, 819
   sum of angles, 821
triangle inequality, 74
trivial solution, 433, 436, 529, 530
Tucker, A.W., 798
2×2 linear system, 93–95

U

uncorrelated variables, 486
uniform distribution, 395
union of sets, 5
unit elastic function, 262
universal set, 6
unstable difference equation, 427
upper limit of integration, 365
upper triangular matrix, 474, 507
utility function, 582–583
   indirect, 762
utility maximization, 737

V

value function
   equality constraints, 739, 759
   inequality constraints, 811
   unconstrained, 723
variable, 77
   change of (in integrals), 385
   endogenous, 562
   exogenous, 562
variance, 330, 709
vector
   addition, 455
   component, 448
   coordinate, 448
   geometric, 480
   geometric addition, 481
   length, 484
   norm, 484
   subtraction, 455
vector of constants, 451–452
vectors
   angle between, 485
   column, 448

   difference, 455
   equality, 455
   geometric interpretation, 479–487
   inner product, 456
   linear combination, 455
   market share, 461
   operations, 480–481
   orthogonal, 485
   row, 448
   sum, 455
   3-space, 481–482
Venn, J., 7
Venn diagrams, 7, 8
vertex (of a parabola), 120
vertical asymptote, 271
vertical axis, 106
vertical-line test, 167–168

W

Walras, L., 194
weighted average, 591
Westergaard, H., 732
Whitehead, A.N., 151
Wicksell, K., 563
Wicksell's law, 670
w.r.t. (with respect to), 188

X

x-axis, 106, 481
xy-plane, 106–107

Y

y-axis, 106, 481, 482
y-intercept, 110
Young's theorem, 588, 606

Z

z-axis, 481, 482
zero matrix, 454
zero of a function, 130

PUBLISHER'S ACKNOWLEDGEMENTS

3 Macmillan and Company: William Stanley Jevons The Theory of Political Economy (published 1871); **23 Leopold Kronecker:** Quoted by Leopold Kronecker Attributed; circa 1886; **26 Steven Wright:** Quoted by Steven Wright; **77 Penguin Random House:** From Ian Stewart Concepts of Modern Mathematics (1975), Penguin; **99 George F.J. Temple:** Quoted by George F.J. Temple (1981); **153 Alfred North Whitehead:** Quoted by Alfred North Whitehead (1925); **183 Jacob Bronowski:** Quoted by Jacob Bronowski (1973); **233 Bertrand Russell:** Quoted by Bertrand Russell; **270 The National Archives:** SDLT rates tables, http://webarchive.nationalarchives.gov.uk/20141124143249/; **270 Government Digital Service:** Stamp Duty Land Tax, http:/www.hmrc.gov.uk/sdlt/rates-tables.htm#3; **270 The VATT Institute for Economic Research:** This bar chart is adapted, with the authors' kind permission, from the paper by Teemu Lyytikäinen and Christian Hilber entitled "Housing transfer taxes and household mobility: Distortion on the housing or labour market?" available at http://econpapers.repec.org/paper/ferwpaper/47.htm.; **297 Alan Turing:** Quoted by Alan Turing (1950); **323 Robert Dorfman:** Quoted by Robert Dorfman (1964); **357 Johann Wolfgang von Goethe:** Mephistopheles to Faust, In Johann Wolfgang von Goethe's Faust; **401 Issac Newton:** Isaac Newton Attributed. It is claimed that he said this in 1720 soon after losing a significant part of his financial wealth during the bursting of what was later known as the South Sea bubble; **449 Jacques H. Drèze:** Quoted by Jacques H. Drèze (1984); **497 Maxwell Rosenlicht:** Quoted by Maxwell A. (Max) Rosenlicht (1949); **563 William S. Anglin:** Quoted by William S. Anglin (1992) 615 Jacques S. Hadamard: Quoted by Jacques S. Hadamard (1945); **675 David Hilbert:** David Hilbert (1900). Part of the famous address by Hilbert (Germany, 1862–1943) to the Second International Congress of Mathematicians held in Paris 1900, where he presented what he then considered to be the greatest open problems in mathematics; **691 Patrick Rivett:** Quoted by Patrick (B.H.P.) Rivett (1978); **733 Konrad Knopp:** Quoted by Konrad Knopp (1928); **771 László Lovász:** Quoted by László Lovász (1980); **821 Plato Academy:** Entrance to Plato's Academy.